AMERICA'S FRONTIER STORY

A Documentary History of Westward Expansion

AMERICA'S FRONTIER STORY

A Documentary History of Westward Expansion

Edited by

MARTIN RIDGE
Indiana University

RAY ALLEN BILLINGTON
The Henry E. Huntington Library

HOLT, RINEHART AND WINSTON
New York Chicago San Francisco Atlanta Dallas
Montreal Toronto London Sydney

Credits for photos (in order of their appearance):

PICTURE PORTFOLIO, pages 305–340. Wagon train: The Granger Collection.

PIONEER FARMERS: Denver Public Library Western Collection; Denver Public Library Western Collection; State Historical Society of Wisconsin; Denver Public Library Western Collection; Denver Public Library Western Collection; State Historical Society of Wisconsin; Minnesota Historical Society; State Historical Society of Wisconsin; Minnesota Historical Society.

CATTLEMEN: Courtesy of Charles J. Belden; the next seven, E. E. Smith Collection, Library of Congress.

MINERS: Denver Public Library Western Collection; Library of Congress; Denver Public Library Western Collection; Denver Public Library Western Collection; California State Library; Library of Congress; Library of Congress; Denver Public Library Western Collection; Denver Public Library Western Collection; Weather Bureau; the next three, Library of Congress.

LUMBERMEN: All, Minnesota Historical Society.

SOLDIERS IN INDIAN COUNTRY: Library of Congress; Library of Congress; State Historical Society of Wisconsin; Smithsonian Institution.

OKLAHOMA: THE RUSH FOR LAND: All, Collection of Robert Cunningham.

LIFE IN THE TOWN: Denver Public Library Western Collection; State Historical Society of Wisconsin; State Historical Society of Wisconsin; Minnesota Historical Society; Denver Public Library Western Collection; Denver Public Library Western Collection; University of Oregon Library; State Historical Society of Wisconsin.

Photo essay by Michal Heron

Copyright © 1969 by Holt, Rinehart and Winston, Inc.

All Rights Reserved
Library of Congress Catalog Card Number: 70-81172
SBN: 03-081202-X *College*
SBN: 03-083264-0 *Trade*
Printed in the United States of America
9   8   7   6   5   4   3   2   1

PREFACE

To tell the story of America's three-centuries-long conquest of new frontiers is to chronicle what Lord Bryce has called the most American part of the American past. To tell that story through the words of those who moved westward—the fur trappers, miners, cattlemen, explorers, soldiers, and pioneer farmers—is to impart a flavor that makes the chronicle even more uniquely American. That is the purpose of this book.

The tale begins, as should all histories of the frontier, in the sixteenth and seventeenth centuries when Spanish and French and British frontiersmen established their outposts in what was to become the first of a succession of American wests—St. Augustine, Quebec, Jamestown, and Plymouth. They were true pioneers, even though they wore armor and ruffled collars rather than buckskin, even though they looked to their homelands for supplies and protection rather than living from the wilderness. For they were motivated by a thirst for adventure, or the hope of gain, or a compulsion toward change, and these were the impulses that led generations of their successors to forsake the comfort and security of established communities to venture into the unknown. Gradually these first pioneers learned how to live in a virgin country where men were few and lands plentiful, where nature was strong and society weak. So their beachheads became villages, and as newcomers flowed in, the perimeter of civilization advanced slowly over the coastal lowlands. The conquest of the continent had begun.

Its pace steadily accelerated. A century and a half were needed to reach the crest of the Appalachian Mountains—only a few hundred miles from the coast—and to push through the gaps into the great central valley of the continent. Another fifty years witnessed the peopling of the eastern half of the Mississippi Valley, until by 1850 that whole domain had been carved into states. Long before this date, venturesome frontiersmen were probing the secrets of the trans-Mississippi country, where they clashed with the Spaniards and British, who had already occupied the region. These previous settlers were pushed aside with as little respect for international good will as for humanitarianism, for nothing could halt the American frontiersman when good lands lay ahead. By 1890 the whole continent had been broken into by bodies of settlement, and the director of the census announced that an unbroken frontier line no longer existed.

When the story of this advance is told by the frontiersmen themselves, much is revealed of their nature and of the nature of the American civilization to which they contributed. Sometimes they use faulty grammar; often their eccentric spelling poses problems in interpretation for the modern reader. But their tale is worth telling, not alone because it chronicles the adventure, the bravery, the sacrifice of the early pioneers to whom we owe so much. It is worth telling because it speaks of the frontier spirit, the spirit of daring, of enterprise, of hope, that has become a part of the American tradition—and has not been completely weathered away by the substitution of an industrial-urban environment in the twentieth century.

For this reason, we begin this book with several observations by frontiersmen and their contemporaries on the manner in which the distinctive conditions of life along the frontiers altered those who lived there. From their words, one learns that elements of the American character that persist today emerged during the pioneering experience. This the reader should remember as he reads the entire pioneer story; too often the glamour and romance of the frontier obscures its significance as a continuing force in American life.

For the convenience of the reader, we have made a few minor changes in the documents. In all cases, u, v, i, and j have been altered to conform to modern usage; the old y has been changed to th; superior letters have been lowered; and contractions with superior letters have been spelled out. In all cases old style typography has been eliminated.

Most of the extensive reading in many hundreds of sources, ranging from government documents to the scrawled diaries of semiliterate backwoodsmen, needed to compile these pages was done in the Newberry Library of Chicago and the Henry E. Huntington Library, San Marino, California. To the staffs of those institutions who gave so generously of their time and knowledge to aid us in our quest for materials, we offer grateful thanks.

Bloomington, Ind.   M. R.
San Marino, Calif.   R. A. B.
February 1969

CONTENTS

	PREFACE	v
PART I	WESTWARD TO THE MISSISSIPPI	
Chapter 1	The Frontier and the American Character	2

Why Men Went West (John L. McConnel, *Western Characters* . . . , 1853) — 3

The Universal Hope of Self-Betterment (Christopher C. Andrews, *Minnesota and Dacotah* . . . , 1857) — 5

Frontier Types (James Flint, *Letters from America*, 1822) — 6

Emergence of Frontier Traits (Robert Baird, *View of the Valley of the Mississippi* . . . , 1834) — 8

The Frontier and American Democracy (Alexis de Tocqueville, *Democracy in America*, 1835) — 11

The Frontier and the National Character (Edwin L. Godkin, *North American Review*, 1865) — 13

The Significance of the Frontier (Frederick Jackson Turner, "The Significance of the Frontier in American History," 1893) — 16

Chapter 2 Spain and France Pioneer in America, 1492–1609 — 25

Admiral of the Ocean (Honors Claimed by Christopher Columbus, 1492) — 25

Explorations of Hernando de Soto (*True Relation of the Hardships Suffered by Governor Hernando de Soto* . . . , 1539) — 26

French-Spanish Rivalry in Florida (Narrative of Lemoyne on the Laudonnière-Ribaut Expeditions, 1565) — 32

Spanish Missions in Florida: The Uprising of 1597 (Luis Geronimo Oré, *The Martyrs of Florida*, 1597) — 39

Beginnings of the French Fur Trade (Samuel de Champlain, *Voyages of Samuel de Champlain*, 1611) — 42

Chapter 3 The English Southern Frontier, 1607–1700 — 46

The Occupation of Jamestown (Captain John Smith, "Description of Virginia," 1612) — 46

Problems of the First Settlers (Governor Thomas Gates, "A True Declaration . . . ," 1610) — 54

Bacon's Rebellion in Virginia ("Strange News from Virginia," 1677) — 56

Opening the Carolina Fur Trade (Dr. Henry Woodward's Report, 1674) — 59

Advertising the Carolina Frontier (Thomas Nairne, *A Letter from South Carolina*, 1710) — 62

Chapter 4 The English Northern Frontier, 1620–1700 — 65

London Backing for the Plymouth Colony (William Bradford, *History of Plimoth Plantation*, 1620) — 65

The Mayflower Compact (William Bradford, *History of Plimoth Plantation*, 1620) — 66

The Pilgrims Relations with the Indians (William Bradford, *History of Plimoth Plantation*, 1620) — 67

Settling the Plymouth Colony (Edward Winslow, Relation or Journal, 1622) — 69

Reasons for Leaving Massachusetts Bay (Thomas Lechford, "Plain Dealing or News from New England," 1641) — 71

Occupying the Connecticut Valley (John Winthrop, *Journal*, 1634) — 73

Rebellion Against Puritanism: New Hampshire ("Conditions of the Northern Provinces," 1665) — 74

News of Victory over the Pequots (John Winthrop to William Bradford, 1637) — 75

The Puritan Land System (Edward Johnson, *Wonder-Working Providence*, 1654) — 77

King Philip's War (Edward Randolph, "The Causes and Results of King Philip's War," 1675) — 79

Chapter 5 The Old West, 1675–1750 — 82

Exploring the Backcountry: John Lederer (John Lederer, *The Discoveries of John Lederer*, 1670) — 82

Exploring the Backcountry: James Needham (Abraham Wood's Narrative, 1673)   85
Trouble with the Piedmont Indians (Abraham Wood's Narrative, 1674)   86
Conquest of the Indians (John Fontaine, Description of Life at Christanna, 1716)   90
The Knights of the Golden Horseshoe (John Fontaine's Journal, 1716)   92
A German Settlement in the Virginia Upcountry (John Fontaine's Journal, 1716)   95
The Palatine Germans in New York (Petition of Palatines to the King, 1720)   96
Causes of Scotch-Irish Migration (*Letters Written by Hugh Boulter, D.D. . . . ,* 1749)   98
Life in the Old West (Joseph Doddridge, *Notes on the Settlement and Indian Wars,* 1750)   101

Chapter 6   *The French Barrier, 1630–1750*   107

La Salle Explores the Mississippi River (Narrative of Henry Tonty, 1682)   107
Settlement of the Illinois Country (Archives of the Sulpitian Seminary of Quebec, 1689–1699)   111
Establishment of Detroit (Report of the Intendant, Henry Tonty, 1727)   115
Detroit Twenty Years Later: The Problems of Authority (Letter to the French Ministry of Marine, 1749)   118
Conflicts over the Fur Trade, 1748 (Letter from French Ministry of Marine to Governor General of New France)   119
Louisiana Under the French Regime, 1751 (Jean-Bernard Bossu, *Travels in the Interior of North America,* 1751)   121

Chapter 7   *Colonial and Indian Wars, 1680–1763*   126

The British Alliance with the Iroquois (Peter Wraxall, *An Abridgement of the Indian Affairs,* 1684)   127
The Effect of the Treaty of Ryswick on the Frontiers (Cadwallader Colden, *The History of the Five Nations of Canada*)   131
Friction Following Queen Anne's War (Proceedings of the Council of Marine, 1717)   134
The British Threaten the French in the Ohio Country, 1748 (Letter from the Governor General of New France, 1749)   136
French Retaliation: The Blainville Expedition, 1749 (Céloron's Journal of the Campaign)   137

x   Contents

           An English View of the French Traders, 1755 (Edmond Atkin, Report of 1755)   141
           Border Fighting in the Seven Years' War (Major Robert Rogers, *Journal of Major Robert Rogers*)   145
           The War in the South: The Pacification of the Cherokee (Henry Timberlake, *Memoirs of Lieut. Henry Timberlake*, 1765)   149

Chapter 8   *Settlement Crosses the Mountains, 1763–1776*   156

           The Defeat of Chief Pontiac (George Croghan's Report to Sir William Johnson)   157
           Barriers to Expansion: The Proclamation Line (Proclamation of 1763)   161
           Formulation of a Western Policy (Report of the British Board of Trade)   163
           The Long-Hunters of Kentucky: Daniel Boone (John Filson, . . . *Present State of Kentucke*, 1784)   171
           The Founding of Boonesborough (John Filson, . . . *Present State of Kentucke*, 1784)   174
           The Impact of Lord Dunmore's War (J. Hector St. John de Crèvecoeur, *Letters from an American Farmer*, 1793)   175
           Cutting the Wilderness Road (John Filson, . . . *Present State of Kentucke*, 1784)   177
           The Quebec Act of 1774 (Peter Force, *American Archives*)   179

Chapter 9   *The West in the Revolution, 1776–1783*   181

           American-Indian Treaty Making: A British View (Henry Hamilton to General Guy Carleton, 1775)   182
           Indian Warfare in Kentucky (George Rogers Clark's Petition to the Virginia Legislature, 1776)   183
           Supplies for the Kentucky Garrison (Letter to Captain William Harrod, 1777)   184
           The Siege of Boonesborough (Daniel Boone, "Autobiography")   185
           Planning the American Attack on Detroit (Patrick Henry to George Rogers Clark, 1778)   188
           Clark's Attack on Vincennes (George Rogers Clark to George Mason)   189
           The War in the Ohio Country, 1780 (George Rogers Clark to Thomas Jefferson)   192
           The Battle of King's Mountain (Ensign Robert Campbell's Memoir of the Battle of King's Mountain)   194
           Boundary Provisions of the Treaty of Paris, 1783 (The Treaty of Paris)   197

Chapter 10	Government Policy in the West: Land and Diplomacy, 1783–1803	199

Transfer of the Western Lands to Congress (Statement of Congressional Policy, 1780)   199
Virginia Cedes Its Western Lands (Virginia Land Cession of 1784)   200
Western State-Making in the Post-Revolutionary Era (Declaration of Rights and Constitution of the State of Frankland)   202
Formulating a Western Policy: Land Sales (The Ordinance of 1785)   206
Land Speculation and Western Policy: The Ohio Company (Articles of Agreement of the Ohio Company, 1786)   207
The Ohio Company Secures Its Lands (Diary of the Reverend Manasseh Cutler, July 20 and July 21, 1787)   209
The Ordinance of 1787: Government for the West (Ordinance of 1787)   210
The Defeat of General Arthur St. Clair (Winthrop Sargent's Diary, 1791)   213
Wayne's Victory and the Treaty of Greenville (Address of Anthony Wayne to the Indians, 1794)   216
Land Speculation on the Southern Frontier (John Gordon to George Profit, 1785)   217
The Spanish Conspiracy (James Wilkinson's Memorial to Governor Esteban Miró, 1787)   219
Kentucky Petitions for Statehood, 1788 (Petition of the Danville Convention of August, 1788)   222
The Yazoo Speculations of 1789 (Alexander Moultrie to Alexander McGillivray, 1790)   223
The Treaty of New York (Alexander McGillivray to Don Carlos Howard, 1790)   226
The Genêt Conspiracy in Kentucky (Address of the Democratic Society of Kentucky, 1793)   228
American Occupation of Louisiana (Governor William C. Claiborne's Proclamation of 1803)   231

Chapter 11	Occupation of the Appalachian Plateau, 1796–1812	233

The Rush Westward in 1796 (Moses Austin, "A Memorandum of M. Austin's Journey . . . ," 1796)   233
Land Speculation on the New York Frontier: The "Hot House" Technique (Isaac Weld, *Travels through the States . . .* , 1797)   236
The Holland Land Company (Report of Joseph Ellicott to the Company, 1809)   238

	The Connecticut Land Company Settles the Western Reserve (Minutes of the Company Directors, 1798)	240
	The Ohio Valley Frontier in 1802 (F. A. Michaux, *Travels to the West of the Alleghany Mountains* . . . , 1805)	242
	Agitation for Cheaper Lands (Petition to Congress by Citizens of the Northwest Territory, 1799)	245
	Political Divisions on the Ohio Frontier (John Cleves Symmes to President Thomas Jefferson, 1802)	247
	The Ohio Constitution and Backwoods Democracy (John Bradbury, *Travels in the Interior of America* . . . , 1819)	248
Chapter 12	*The West in the War of 1812, 1812–1815*	252
	The United States Claims West Florida (Proclamation of President James Madison, 1810)	253
	Expansionist Sentiment in Georgia (Governor D. B. Mitchell to the Georgia Legislature, 1812)	254
	Land-Grabbing in the Northwest (The Fort Wayne Treaty of 1809)	256
	Indian Protest Against the Fort Wayne Treaty (Speech of Tecumseh, 1810)	258
	The Battle of Tippecanoe (Diary of Isaac Naylor, 1811)	260
	The Western Demand for War (Resolution of Kentucky Legislature, December 1811)	262
	Henry Clay Speaks for War (Speech of Henry Clay in Congress, December 1811)	264
	The American Invasion of Canada (Proclamation of General William Hull from Detroit, July 1812)	267
	The Battle of the Thames (William Henry Harrison to the Secretary of War, 1813)	268
	The Battle of Horseshoe Bend (Andrew Jackson to the Secretary of War, 1814)	270
Chapter 13	*Peopling the Interior Valley, 1815–1850*	274
	The Great Migration of 1816 (Morris Birkbeck, *Notes on a Journey in America*, 1818)	274
	Travel on the Old National Road (Charles F. Hoffman, *A Winter in the West, By A New Yorker*, 1835)	276
	Travel on the Ohio River (Timothy Flint, *Recollections of the Last Ten Years*, 1826)	278
	Englishmen Settle the Illinois Prairies (Morris Birkbeck, *Letters from Illinois*, 1818)	280
	Indian Removal: The Government Policy (John C. Calhoun, Secretary of War, to President James Monroe, 1825)	281

		Contents	xiii

The Tragedy of Indian Removal (Lieutenant J. T. Sprague's Report on Removal of the Creek Party)   283

The Black Hawk War (*Life of MA-KA-TAI-ME-SHE-KIA-KIAK, or Black Hawk*, 1833)   286

Routes to the West in the 1830s (Timothy Flint, *History and Geography of the Mississippi Valley*, 1832)   289

Travel on the Erie Canal (The Jacob Schramm Letters to Germany, 1836)   292

Causes for Migration: New England's Rural Decay (Charles C. Nott, "A Good Farm for Nothing," 1889)   294

Causes for Migration: Southern Soil Exhaustion (John H. Craven in *The Farmers Register*, 1833)   295

A South Carolina Planter Moves Westward (Eli H. Lide Reports on His Family's Migration to Alabama, 1836)   297

Frenzied Speculation in the Southwest (The Diary of James D. Davidson, 1836)   298

Frenzied Speculation in the Northwest (*Journals of Ralph Waldo Emerson*, 1857)   299

Land Promotion on the Prairies (Henry W. Ellsworth, *The Valley of the Upper Wabash*, 1838)   300

PART II   THE TRANS-MISSISSIPPI WEST

Chapter 14   Spanish Occupants of the Far West   342

Spanish Exploration: The Coronado Expedition (Francisco Vásquez de Coronado to the King of Spain, 1541)   342

Spanish Colonization: The Founding of New Mexico (Juan de Oñate to the Viceroy of New Spain, 1599)   345

The Pueblo Uprising of 1680 (Pedro Garcia's Testimony of August 25, 1680)   348

The Mission Frontier: Fray Eusebio Kino, S.J. (Eusebio Francisco Kino, S.J., "Diary of the Expedition to the North," 1700)   349

The Mission Frontier in California (Alexander Forbes, *California*, 1839)   352

Beginnings of International Conflict (Colonel Pedro Fermín de Mendinueta to the Viceroy of New Spain, 1768)   354

Chapter 15   The Explorers' Frontier, 1803–1840   357

Lewis and Clark Reach the Rocky Mountains (Journals of Lewis and Clark, May 26, 1805)   357

The Problems of River Travel (Journals of Lewis and Clark, June 15, 1805)   359

The Expedition Crosses the Divide (Journals of Lewis and Clark, August 12, 1805)   359

Meeting with Shoshoni Indians (Journals of Lewis and Clark, August 13, 1805)   361

Lewis and Clark Reach the Pacific (Journals of Lewis and Clark, November 15, 1805)   363

Zebulon Montgomery Pike Reaches the Rocky Mountains (Journals of Zebulon Montgomery Pike, November 15, 1806)   364

Pike's Party Crosses the Rockies (Journals of Zebulon Montgomery Pike, January 14, 1807)   365

Pike's Party Is Captured by the Spaniards (Journals of Zebulon Montgomery Pike, February 26, 1807)   369

Beginnings of the "Great American Desert" Legend (Report of Zebulon Montgomery Pike, 1810)   370

Journey Along the Red River (Edwin James, *Account of an Expedition* . . . , 1823)   371

The "Great American Desert" Legend Grows (Report of Major Stephen H. Long, 1821)   373

John C. Frémont Advertises the West: The Bumble Bee (John C. Frémont, *Report of the Exploring Expedition* . . . , 1845)   373

Chapter 16   **Traders and Trappers Open the Far West, 1820–1845**   376

Caravans on the Santa Fe Trail (Josiah Gregg, *Commerce of the Prairies*, 1844)   376

Fur Trade on the Upper Missouri (John C. Luttig, *Journal of a Fur-Trading Expedition on the Upper Missouri*, 1813)   379

William H. Ashley's Fight with the Arikara (The Diary of James Clyman, March 1823)   382

The Hudson's Bay Company Invades the Rockies (Peter Skene Ogden, Snake Country Journals, 1825)   386

Fur Trade in the Desert Southwest (James Ohio Pattie, *Personal Narrative* . . . , 1831)   389

Fur Trade and Rendezvous in the Central Rockies (George F. Ruxton, *Adventures in Mexico and the Rocky Mountains*, 1849)   393

Decline of the Fur Trade: The Final Rendezvous (Osburne Russell, *Journal of a Trapper* . . . , 1839)   396

Chapter 17   **The Mississippi Valley Frontier, 1810–1845**   399

Primitivism in the Lower Mississippi Valley (William Darby, *The Emigrant's Guide* . . . , 1818)   399

Frontier Society in the Mississippi Valley (Timothy Flint, *Recollections of the Last Ten Years*, 1826)   401

Migration to the Upper Valley: The Iowa Fever (Nathan H. Parker, *Iowa As It Is in 1855*, 1855) — 403
Demand for Land Reform: Pre-emption (Petition of the Iowa Territorial Convention, 1837) — 405
An Iowa Land Sale (John B. Newhall, *Sketches of Iowa, or the Emigrant's Guide*, 1841) — 406
Squatters Versus Speculators in Iowa (Hawkins Taylor, Reminiscences of the Burlington Land Sale, 1838) — 407
Frontier Claim Associations (Constitution of the Claim Association of Johnson County, Iowa, 1839) — 408
Operation of the Claim Associations (A Claim Association Trial in the Duck Creek Settlement; The Dahlonega War, 1843) — 410

Chapter 18 Texas: Colonization and Revolution, 1820–1845 — 414

Stephen F. Austin Advertises for Settlers (Stephen F. Austin, "Letter to Fellow Citizens," 1823) — 414
The Empresario System (Coahuila-Texas Colonization Act of 1825) — 416
Mexico's Distrust of the Texans (Report of General Manuel Mier y Terán, June 1828) — 419
Mexican Restrictions on Immigration (Mexican Decree of April 6, 1830) — 422
Cultural Conflict in Texas (Stephen F. Austin, "Address of the Central Committee to the Convention," 1833) — 423
Causes of the Texas Revolution (Report of Stephen F. Austin to the Texan People, 1835) — 426
Moving Toward Independence (Declaration of Causes Issued by the San Felipe de Austin Convention, November 1835) — 429
The Fall of the Alamo (Letter of Colonel William B. Travis from the Alamo, March 3, 1836) — 430
The Military Phase: The "Runaway Scrape" (W. B. Dewes, *Letters from an Early Settler of Texas*, 1852) — 432
Sam Houston Stands Firm (General Houston to the Secretary of War, March 29, 1836) — 433
The Battle of San Jacinto (General Sam Houston to G. G. Burnet, April 1836) — 434
Migration to the Texan Republic (J. A. Orr, "A Trip from Houston to Jackson, Mississippi," 1845) — 436

Chapter 19 The Occupation of Oregon, 1820–1845 — 439

Early Propaganda for Oregon (Dr. John Floyd's "Committee on the Occupation of the Columbia River," 1821) — 439

Propaganda for Oregon (Hall Jackson Kelley, "Advantages of Settling the Oregon Country," 1830)   441
The First American Invaders (Nathaniel J. Wyeth's Journal, October 29, 1832)   444
Failure of the First Invaders (Nathaniel J. Wyeth, "Statement of Facts," 1847)   445
Origin of the Missionary Invasion (Letter of William Walker to the *Christian Advocate*, 1833)   447
Founding the Jason Lee Mission, 1834 (Daniel Lee and J. H. Frost, *Ten Years in Oregon*, 1844)   449
The Hudson's Bay Company Reaction (Dr. John McLoughlin to the Deputy Governor, 1838)   450
Beginnings of the "Oregon Fever" in Iowa (Letter to the *National Intelligencer*, 1843)   452
Propaganda for Oregon: Peter H. Burnett (Edward H. Lenox, *Overland to Oregon* . . . , 1904)   453
The 1843 Migration: Organizing the Caravan (Peter H. Burnett to the *New York Herald*, January 5, 1845)   454
The Election of Officers (Correspondent of the *New Orleans Picayune*, November 21, 1843)   455
The Westward March, 1843 (Jesse Applegate, "A Day with the Cow Column," 1843)   456
Origins of Government in Oregon (Minutes of an Oregon "Wolf Meeting," February 1843)   460

Chapter 20   The American Invasion of California, 1820–1845   462

Life in California in the 1830s: The Ranchos (Guadalupe Vallejo, "Ranch and Mission Days in Alta California," 1890)   462
The American Hide and Tallow Trade (Richard Henry Dana, Jr., *Two Years Before the Mast*, 1840)   467
Suppression of the Americans: Isaac Graham (Charles Wilkes, *Narrative of the United States Exploring Expedition* . . . , 1845)   470
John A. Sutter and His Fort (Lansford W. Hastings, *The Emigrant's Guide to Oregon and California*, 1845)   472
The Bidwell-Bartleson Migration, 1841 (John Bidwell, "The First Emigrant Train to California," 1890)   477
Arrival of the Emigrants in California (Nicholas Dawson, *Narrative of Nicholas "Cheyenne" Dawson*, 1841)   482
The Tragedy of the Donner Party (Diary of Patrick Breen, February 1847)   484

Contents   xvii

Chapter 21   Expansion and War, 1844–1848   487

    British Designs on Texas (Ashbel Smith to Anson Jones, June 24, 1844)   487
    British Designs on California (Waddy Thompson, *Recollections of Mexico*, 1847)   489
    The Spirit of Manifest Destiny (John L. O'Sullivan in the *Democratic Review*, 1845)   490
    British Strength in the Oregon Country (James Douglas on the Hudson's Bay Company Establishment, 1839)   493
    The American Threat to the Hudson's Bay Company (Dr. John McLoughlin to the Hudson's Bay Company, 1844)   495
    The Demand for All Oregon: Thomas Hart Benton (Speech of Thomas Hart Benton in Senate, May 28, 1846)   497
    American Designs on California (President James K. Polk's Instructions to Thomas O. Larkin, October 1845)   498
    The Bear Flag Revolt (Simon Ide, *A Biographical Sketch of the Life of William B. Ide*, 1880)   501
    Origins of the Mexican War: The Nueces Skirmish (William S. Henry, *Campaign Sketches of the War with Mexico*, 1847)   503
    President Polk Decides for War (Diary of James K. Polk, May 9, 1846)   504
    Mexican View of the Mexican War (Ramon Alcaraz, *The Other Side . . .* , 1850)   506

Chapter 22   The Mormon Frontier, 1847–1860   509

    The Mormon Exodus from Nauvoo (Correspondent of *Daily Missouri Republican*, May 13, 1846)   509
    The Pioneer Band Reaches Utah (William Clayton's Journal for 1847)   512
    The Cooperative Experiment: The Economy (Speech of Brigham Young Recorded by Wilford Woodruff, July 25, 1847)   515
    The Cooperative Experiment: The Governmental System (J. W. Gunnison, *The Mormons, or Latter-Day Saints*, 1852)   517
    Mormon Expansion over the Great Basin (Howard Stansbury, *Exploration and Survey of the Valley of the Great Salt Lake*, 1852)   519
    Mormon Expansion: Parowan City (Frederick Piercy, *Route from Liverpool to Great Salt Lake Valley*, 1855)   520
    The Handcart Migration of 1856 (T. B. H. Stenhouse, *The Rocky Mountain Saints*, 1873)   521

	The Mountain Meadows Massacre (John D. Lee, *Mormonism Unveiled* . . . , 1877)	524
	The Mormon War of 1857 (Diary of John Pulsipher, March and April, 1877)	527
Chapter 23	**The Mining Frontier, 1849–1876**	**530**
	The Discovery of California Gold (James W. Marshall in *Hutching's California Magazine*, 1857)	530
	Spread of the Gold Fever in California (Walter Colton, *Three Years in California*, 1850)	531
	Gold Propaganda Reaches the East (Letter in *Daily Union*, September 22, 1848)	532
	Mining Techniques (Louise A. K. S. Clappe, *The Shirley Letters from the California Mines, 1851–52*)	533
	The Rush to the Fraser River Mines (Letter to *London Times*, June 16, 1858)	535
	Cultural Conflict on the Fraser River (Isaac J. Stevens to Lewis Cass, July 21, 1858)	536
	The Comstock Lode (J. Ross Browne, "A Peep at Washoe," 1861)	538
	The Rush of the "Fifty-Niners" (Correspondent of *Missouri Republican*, March 27, 1859)	541
	The First Major Colorado Gold Discovery (Henry Villard, *The Past and Present of the Pike's Peak Gold Regions*, 1860)	542
	Excitement in the Montana Gold Fields (Granville Stuart, *Forty Years on the Frontier* . . . , 1863–1864)	544
	Governmental Organization in the Mining Camps (Charles H. Shinn, *Mining Camps* . . . , 1884)	546
	Justice in the Mining Camps (Thomas J. Dimsdale, *The Vigilantes of Montana*, 1866)	548
Chapter 24	**The Transportation Frontier, 1850–1884**	**552**
	Freighting on the Great Plains (Alexander Majors, *Seventy Years on the Frontier*, 1893)	552
	A Mail Subsidy for Western Stagecoaching (Act of Congress of March, 1857)	554
	The Butterfield Overland Mail (Waterman L. Ormsby to the *New York Herald*, September–November, 1858)	555
	The Joys of Overland Coaching (Mark Twain, *Roughing It*, 1872)	558
	The Pony Express: Meeting a Rider on the Plains (Mark Twain, *Roughing It*, 1872)	561

Building the Union Pacific (Granville M. Dodge, "How We Built the Union Pacific Railway," 1910) — 562

The Symphony of Track-Laying (William A. Bell, *New Tracks in North America*, 1869) — 564

The "Hell on Wheels" of the Union Pacific (John H. Beadle, *The Undeveloped West . . .* , 1873) — 565

The Race Toward Promontory (Granville M. Dodge, "How We Built the Union Pacific Railway," 1910) — 567

Driving the Golden Spike (Sidney Dillon, "Historic Moment: Driving the Last Spike," 1892) — 568

The Thrill of Western Railroading (Helen Hunt Jackson, *Bits of Travel at Home*, 1878) — 570

Chapter 25 The Indian Barrier, 1860–1890 — 572

The Chivington Massacre (Testimony of Lieutenants Connor and Cramer before a Congressional Committee) — 572

The Congressional Peace Commission of 1867 (William T. Sherman, *Memoirs*, 1890) — 574

The Battle of the Washita (George A. Custer, *My Life on the Plains*, 1874) — 576

The Battle of the Little Big Horn (Interview with Sitting Bull, *New York Herald*, 1877) — 579

The Extermination of the Buffalo (Hamlin Russell, "The Story of the Buffalo," 1893) — 581

The Indian Problem: The Militarist's Solution (Nelson A. Miles, "The Indian Problem," 1879) — 583

The Indian Problem: The Humanitarian's Solution (Helen Hunt Jackson, *A Century of Dishonor*, 1881) — 585

The Emergence of Governmental Indian Policy (Chester A. Arthur to Congress, December 1881) — 587

The Formulation of Policy (The Dawes Severalty Act of 1887) — 588

Chapter 26 The Ranchers' Frontier, 1865–1890 — 592

The Beginnings of the Long Drive (Diary of George C. Duffield, 1866) — 592

First of the "Cow Towns," Abilene (Joseph G. McCoy, *Historic Sketches of the Cattle Trade*, 1874) — 595

The Long Drive (Charles N. Harger, "Cattle-Trails of the Prairies," 1892) — 597

Drovers "Hit" the Cow Towns (Andy Adams, *The Log of a Cowboy*, 1903) — 599

Range Law on the Cattle Frontier (National Live Stock Historical Association, *Prose and Poetry . . .* , 1904) — 602

Organization of the Cattlemen's Associations (Letter to the Montana Stockgrowers' Association, 1884) — 604
The Round-Up (John Baumann, "On a Western Ranche," 1887) — 606
Investment in the Range Cattle Industry (Walter Baron von Richthofen, *Cattle-Raising on the Plains of North America*, 1885) — 608
End of the Open Range: The Winter of 1886–1887 (John Clay, *My Life on the Range*) — 610

Chapter 27   Technology and the Farmers' Frontier, 1865–1890 — 613

The Problem of Fencing on the Great Plains (Report of the Commissioner of Agriculture, 1871) — 613
Mechanizing the Western Farm (*Year Book of the United States Department of Agriculture*, 1899) — 615
The Land System: The Problem of Speculation (Albert D. Richardson, *Beyond the Mississippi*, 1867) — 618
Propaganda for Immigrants: The Dakota Territory (George A. Batchelder, *A Sketch of the History and Resources of Dakota Territory*, 1870) — 619
Propaganda for Immigrants: Railroad Advertising (Circular of the Burlington and Missouri River Railroad) — 621
Propaganda for Immigrants: An America Letter (Letter of Gjert Gregoriussen Hovland) — 622
The Rush for Free Land, 1871 (E. Jeff Jenkins, *The Northern Tier: or, Life Among the Homestead Settlers*, 1880) — 623
Life on a Kansas Homestead, 1877 (Letters of Howard Ruede, 1877–1878) — 624
Bonanza Farming in Minnesota (C. C. Coffin, "Dakota Wheat Fields," 1880) — 630
The Oklahoma Land Rush ("The Rush to Oklahoma," *Harper's Weekly*, 1889) — 631

Chapter 28   The Twentieth-Century West: Problem and Promise — 636

The Indian Problem: A Military Viewpoint (J. L. Humfreville, *Twenty Years Among Our Hostile Indians*, 1899) — 637
A Revised Indian Policy (Indian Commissioner John Collier's Views, 1920s) — 638
The New Indian Policy Is Stated (Indian Commissioner Philleo Nash Summarizes Progress, 1961) — 641
Proposals for Western Irrigation Policies (John W. Powell, "Institutions for the Arid Lands," 1890) — 642
Changing Concepts of Land Policy (Henry A. Wallace's Report on the Western Range, 1936) — 644

Social Problems of the New West (Governor Cuthbert Olson Urges Reform Legislation, 1939) 647
The Frontier Heritage of Western Cities (Shelton Bissell on Revivalism, 1928) 653
The Persistence of the Frontier Influence (Frederick Jackson Turner Views the Future, 1903) 656

PART I

WESTWARD TO THE MISSISSIPPI

CHAPTER 1 | The Frontier and the American Character

Some who witnessed the westward expansion of the American people during the eighteenth and nineteenth centuries recognized that the frontier was more than a haven for the dispossessed of Europe and the East. They saw that as pioneers moved and adjusted themselves to their new environments something happened to them and their institutions. Living in a strange new world where men were few and land plentiful, where virgin natural resources awaited exploitation, where ancestral and hereditary distinctions were less valued than needed skills, and where no rigid social structure retarded the ambitious as they struggled to rise in wealth and status, frontiersmen developed habits and value-scales geared to life amidst unique opportunities for self-improvement. They were, some witnesses believed, being "Americanized" by living on the frontiers.

Such a transformation did not take place overnight. The first frontiersmen, those who left Spain and France and England in the sixteenth and seventeenth centuries to plant Europe's first beachheads along the Atlantic coast, were but slightly altered by their environment. For as long as they could remain dependent on their mother countries for supplies and social guidance, they lived and worked and thought as did their cousins at home. Traditional patterns were easier to follow than new ones. But slowly pioneers advanced toward the interior of the continent, breaking the bonds with Europe as they did so and subjecting themselves increasingly to America's environmental pressures. A century and a half were required to settle the coastal lowlands and hilly backcountry that were framed by the Appalachian Mountain system, another half-century to breach the mountains and advance to the Mississippi, still another to people the trans-Mississippi West. By the 1840s pioneers were at the shores of the Pacific; by the 1890s the Great Plains had been homesteaded. Each of these steps meant a deepening of the American experience.

As Americans observed their pioneering countrymen in this westward march, they learned a great deal about the way in which the frontier advanced, and they speculated occasionally about the effect of this expansion on the national character and institutions. They recognized that identifiable motives impelled some to leave the security and comfort of settled communities for the danger and discomfort of pioneer life. They saw that the pattern of settlement was duplicated on each successive frontier, although always with variations. They observed that standard types were emerging in the successive Wests—fur trappers, herdsmen, backwoodsmen, pioneer farmers, equipped farmers, and town planters, to name a few—and that these were present on all frontiers although seldom in the same proportion. They realized that life in a land of unusual opportunity for self-advancement endowed the pioneers with habits and values less prominently displayed by easterners.

WHY MEN WENT WEST

American and European travelers who visited the new settlements inquired often as to the reasons that impelled frontiersmen to abandon civilization for the wilderness. One set of answers was compiled by John L. McConnel, who lived much in the West during the 1830s and 1840s:[1]

Let us inquire what motives could induce men to leave regions, where the axe had been at work for many years—where the land was reduced to cultivation, and the forest reclaimed from the wild beast and the wilder savage—where civilization had begun to exert its power, and society had assumed a legal and determined shape—to depart from all these things, seeking a new home in an inhospitable wilderness, where they could only gain a footing by severe labor, constant strife, and sleepless vigilance? To be capable of doing all this, from *any* motive, a man must be a strange compound of qualities; but that compound, strange as it is, has done, and is doing, more to reclaim the west, and change the wilderness into a garden, than all other causes combined.

[1] John L. McConnel, *Western Characters or Types of Border Life in the Western States* (New York, 1853), pp. 108–114.

A prominent trait in the character of the genuine American, is the desire "to better his condition"—a peculiarity which sometimes embodies itself in the disposition to forget the good old maxim, "Let well-enough alone," and not unfrequently leads to disaster and suffering. A thorough Yankee—using that word as the English do, to indicate national, not sectional, character—is never satisfied with doing well; he always underrates his gains and his successes; and, though to others he may be boastful enough, and may, even truly, rate the profits of his enterprise by long strings of "naught," he is always whispering to himself, "I ought to do better." If he sees any one accumulating property faster than himself, he becomes emulous and discontented—he is apt to think, unless he goes more rapidly than any one else, that he is not moving at all. If he can find no one of his neighbors advancing toward fortune, with longer strides than he, he will imagine some successful "speculator," to whom he will compare himself, and chafe at his inferiority to a figment of his own fancy. If he possessed "a million a minute," he would cast about for some profitable employment, in which he might engage, "to pay expenses." He will abandon a silver-mine, of slow, but certain gains, for the gambling chances of a gold "placer"; and if any one within his knowledge dig out more wealth than he, he will leave the "diggings," though his success be quite encouraging, and go quixoting among the islands of the sea, in search of pearls and diamonds. With the prospect of improvement in his fortunes—whether that prospect be founded upon reason, be a naked fancy, or the offspring of mere discontent—he regards no danger, cares for no hardship, counts no suffering. Everything must bend before the ruling passion, "to better his condition."

His spirit is eminently encroaching. Rather than give up any of his own "rights," he will take a part of what belongs to others. Whatever he thinks necessary to his welfare, to that he believes himself entitled. To whatever point he desires to reach, he takes the straightest course, even though the way lie across the corner of his neighbor's field. Yet he is intensely jealous of his own possessions, and warns off all trespassers with an imperial menace of "the utmost penalty of the law." He has, of course, an excellent opinion of himself—and justly: for when not blinded by cupidity or vexed by opposition, no man can hold the scales of justice with a more even hand.

He is seldom conscious of having done a wrong: for he rarely moves until he has ascertained "both the propriety and expediency of the motion." He has, therefore, an instinctive aversion to all retractions and apologies. He has such a proclivity to the forward movement, that its opposite, even when truth and justice demand it, is stigmatized, in his vocabulary, by odious and ridiculous comparisons. He is very stubborn, and, it is feared, sometimes mistakes his obstinacy for firmness. He thinks a safe retreat worse than a defeat with slaughter. Yet he never rests under a reverse, and, though manifestly prostrate, will never acknowledge that he is beaten. A check enrages him more than a decided failure: for so long as his end is not accomplished, nor defeated, he can see no reason why he should not succeed. If his forces are driven back, shattered and destroyed, he is not cast down, but angry—he forthwith swears vengeance and another trial. He is quite insatiable—as a failure does not dampen him, success can never satisfy him. His plans are always on a great scale; and, if they sometimes exceed his means of execution, at least, "he who aims at the sun," though he may lose his arrow, "will not strike the ground." He is a great projector—but he is eminently practical, as well as theoretical; and if *he* cannot realize his visions, no other man need try.

He is restless and migratory. He is fond of change, for the sake of the change; and he will have it, though it bring him only new labors and new hardships. He is, withal, a little selfish—as might be supposed. He begins to lose his attachment to the advantages of his home, so soon as they are shared by others. He does not like near neighbors—has no affection for the soil; he will leave a place on which he has expended much time and labor, as soon as the region grows to be a "settlement." Even in a town, he is dissatisfied if his next neighbor lives so near that the women can gossip across the division-fence. He likes to be at least one day's journey from the nearest plantation.

I once heard an old pioneer assign as a reason why he must emigrate from western Illinois, the fact that "people were settling right under his nose"—and the farm of his nearest neighbor was twelve miles distant, by the section lines! He moved on to Missouri, but there the same "impertinence" of emigrants soon followed him; and, abandoning his half-finished "clearing," he packed his family and household goods in a little wagon, and retreated, across the plains to Oregon. He —or was, two years ago—living in the valley of the Willamette, where, doubtless, he is now chafing under the affliction of having neighbors in the same region, and nothing but an ocean beyond.

His character seems to be hard-featured. But he is neither unsocial, nor morose. He welcomes the stranger as heartily as the most hospitable patriarch. He receives the sojourner at his fireside without question. He regales him with the best the house affords: is always anxious to have him "stay another day." He cares for his horse, renews his harness, laughs at his stories, and exchanges romances with him. He hunts with him; fishes, rides, walks, talks, eats, and drinks with him. His wife washes and mends the stranger's shirts, and lends him a needle and thread to sew a button on his only pair of pantaloons. The children sit on his knee, the dog lies at his feet, and accompanies him into the woods. The whole family are his friends, and only grow cold and distant when they learn that he is looking for land, and thinks of "settling" within a few leagues. If nothing of the sort occurs—and this only "leaks out" by accident, for the pioneer never pries inquisitively into the business of his guest, he keeps him as long as he can; and when he can stay no longer, fills his saddle-bags with flitches of bacon and "pones" of corn-bread, shakes him heartily by the hand, exacts a promise to stop again on his return, and bids him "God-speed" on his journey.

THE UNIVERSAL HOPE OF SELF-BETTERMENT

While restlessness, a thirst for adventure, overcrowding, and idealism drove men toward the frontiers, the principal force impelling migration was the hope of gain. To the average pioneer, the West was a land of promise where fertile fields assured abundant harvests, where the extra quarter-section of farmland could be sold to a latecomer at a profit, where "growing up with the country" assured both affluence and an elevated social status. An easterner, Christopher C. Andrews, who visited the Minnesota frontier in the 1850s sensed this eagerness of the frontiersmen to better themselves:[2]

As I have looked abroad upon the vast domain of the West beyond the dim Missouri, or in the immediate valley of the Mississippi,

---

[2]Christopher C. Andrews, *Minnesota and Dacotah: Or Letters Descriptive of a Tour through the North-West* (Washington, 1857), pp. 114–117.

I have wondered at the contrast presented between the comparatively small number who penetrate to the frontier, and that great throng of men who toil hard for a temporary livelihood in the populous towns and cities of the Union. And I have thought if this latter class were at all mindful of the opportunities for gain and independence which the new territories afforded, they would soon abandon—in a great measure at least—their crowded alleys in the city, and aspire to be cultivators and owners of the soil. Why there has not been a greater emigration from cities I cannot imagine, unless it is owing to a misapprehension of Western life. Either it is this, or the pioneer is possessed of a very superior degree of energy.

It has been said that the frontier man always keeps on the frontier; that he continues to emigrate as fast as the country around him becomes settled. There is a class that do so. Not, however, for the cause which has been sometimes humorously assigned—that civilization was inconvenient to them—but because good opportunities arise to dispose of the farms they have already improved; and because a further emigration secures them cheaper lands. The story of the pioneer who was disturbed by society, when his nearest neighbor lived fifteen miles off, even if it be true, fails to give the correct reason for the migratory life of this class of men.

It almost always happens that wherever we go somebody else has preceded us. Accident or enterprise has led some one to surpass us. Many of the most useful pioneers of this country have been attracted hither by the accounts given of its advantages by some one of their friends who had previously located himself here. Ask a man why he comes, and he says a neighbor of his, or a son, or a brother, has been in the territory for so many months, and he likes it so well I concluded to come also. A very respectable gentleman from Maine, a shipowner and a man of wealth, who came up on the boat with me to St. Paul, said his son-in-law was in the territory, and he had another son at home who was bound to come, and if his wife was willing he believed the whole family would come. Indeed the excellent state of society in the territory is to be attributed very much to the fact that parents have followed after their children.

It is pretty obvious too why men will leave poor farms in New England, and good farms in Ohio, to try their fortunes here. The farmer in New England, it may be in New Hampshire, hears that the soil of Minnesota is rich and free from rocks, that there are other favorable resources, and a salubrious climate such as he has been accustomed to. He concludes that it is best to sell out the place he has, and try ploughing where there are no rocks to obstruct him. The farmer of Ohio does not expect to find better soil than he leaves; but his inducements are that he can sell his land at forty or fifty dollars an acre, and preempt as good in Minnesota for a dollar and a quarter an acre. This operation leaves him a surplus fund, and he becomes a more opulent man, with better means to adorn his farm and to educate his children.

Those who contemplate coming West to engage in agricultural employment should leave their families, if families they have, behind till they have selected a location and erected some kind of a habitation; provided, however, they have no particular friend whose hospitality they can avail themselves of till their preliminary arrangements are effected. It will require three months, I judge, for a man to select a good claim (a quarter section, being 160 acres), and fence and plough a part of it and to erect thereon a cabin. There is never a want of land to preempt in a new country. The settler can always get an original claim, or buy out the claim of another very cheap, near some other settlers.

The liberal policy of our government in regard to the disposal of public lands is peculiarly beneficial to the settler. The latter has the first chance. He can go on to a quarter section which may be worth fifteen dollars an acre, and preempt it before it is surveyed, and finally obtain it for $1.25 an acre. Whereas the speculator must wait till the land is surveyed and advertised for sale; and then he can get only what has not been preempted, and at a price which it brings at auction, not less than $1.25 an acre. Then what land is not sold at public sale is open to private entry at $1.25 an acre. It is such land that bounty warrants are located on. Thus it is seen the pioneer has the first choice. Why, I have walked over land up here that would now bring from ten to twenty dollars an acre if it was in the market, and which any settler can preempt and get for $1.25 an acre. I am strongly tempted to turn farmer myself, and go out and build me a cabin. The speculation would be a good one.

FRONTIER TYPES

As men moved farther west, distinctive frontier types emerged on the successive frontiers, each exhibiting the degree of change wrought by the pioneering experience. Some men became near-savages, resentful of their fellows, unhappy amidst human companionship, and content to live in isolated sloth; these were the backwoodsmen noted by all visitors to the successive Wests. Far more made no compromise with nature, and either as small, relatively capital-less farmers or as well-equipped estate-holders sought to hurry the coming of civilization. Contemporaries neglected numerous other types —fur trappers, herdsmen, miners, soldiers, missionaries, and a host more—who played important roles in the frontier process. The description of James Flint, a British traveler, who found three distinct types operating during the 1820s is accurate in spirit if not in detail:[3]

All who have paid attention to the progress of new settlements, agree in stating, that the first possession of the woods in America, was taken by a class of hunters, commonly called backwoodsmen. These, in some instances, purchased the soil from the government, and in others, placed themselves on the public lands without permission. Many of them, indeed, settled new territories before the ground was surveyed, and before public sales commenced. Formerly pre-emption rights were given to these squatters; but the irregularities and complicacy that the practice introduced into the business of the land-office, have caused its being given up, and squatters are now obliged to make way for regular purchasers. The improvements of a backwoodsman are usually confined to building a rude log cabin, clearing and fencing a small piece of ground for raising Indian corn. A horse, a cow, a few hogs, and some poultry, comprise his live-stock; and his farther operations are performed with his rifle. The formation of a settlement in his neighbourhood is hurtful to the success of his favourite pursuit, and is the signal for his removing into more remote parts of the wilderness. In the case of his owning the land on which he has settled, he is contented to sell it at a low price, and his establishment, though trifling, adds much to the comfort of his successor.

The next class of settlers differ from the former in having considerably less dependence on the killing of game, in remaining in the midst of a growing population, and in devoting themselves more to agriculture. A man of this class proceeds on a small capital; he either enlarges the clearings begun in the woods by his backwoodsman predecessor, or establishes himself on a new site. On his arrival in a settlement, the neighbours unite in assisting him to erect a cabin for the reception of his family. Some of them cut down the trees, others drag them to the spot with oxen, and the rest build up the logs. In this way a house is commonly reared in one day. For this well-timed assistance no immediate payment is made, and he acquits himself by working to his neighbours. It is not in his power to hire labourers, and must depend therefore on his own exertions. If his family is numerous and industrious, his progress is greatly accelerated. He does not clear away the forests by dint of labour, but girdles the trees. By the second summer after this operation is performed, the foliage is completely destroyed, and his crops are not injured by the shade. He plants an orchard, which thrives and bears abundantly under every sort of neglect. His live-stock soon becomes much more numerous than that of his back-wood predecessor; but, as his cattle have to shift for themselves in the woods, where grass is scanty, they are small and lean. He does not sow grass seeds to succeed his crops, so that his land, which ought to be pasturage, is overgrown with weeds. The neglect of sowing grass-seeds deprives him of hay; and he has no fodder laid up for the winter except the blades of Indian corn, which are much withered, and do not appear to be nutritious food. The poor animals are forced to range the forests in winter, where they can scarcely procure any thing which is green, except the buds of underwood on which they browse.—Trees are sometimes cut down that the cattle may eat the buds. Want of shelter in the winter completes the sum of misery. Hogs suffer famine during the droughts of summer, and the frosts and snows of winter; but they become fat by feeding on the acorns and

---

[3] James Flint, *Letters from America* (Edinburgh, 1822), pp. 206–209.

beech nuts which strow the ground in autumn. Horses are not exempted from their share in these common sufferings, with the addition of labour, which most of them are not very able to undergo. This second rate class of farmers are to be seen in the markets of towns, retailing vegetables, fruits, poultry, and dairy produce. One of them came lately into this place on horseback, with ten pounds of butter to sell; but as he could not obtain a price to his mind, he crossed the river to Louisville market. In going and returning he must have paid twenty-five cents to the ferryman—a considerable expense, when it is considered that he had travelled twelve miles with his little cargo. Another, who lives at the distance of eight miles from this place, brought a barrel of whisky, containing about thirty-three gallons. He employed neither horse nor vehicle in the transportation, but rolled the cask along the road, which, by the by, is none of the smoothest. Incidents of this kind may, perhaps, cause you to suppose that the condition of the second rate settler is similar to that of subtenants in the north of Scotland, or in Ireland; but the high price of labour in America explains the apparent parity. Men perform offices for themselves that, in Britain, would be done by hiring others. The American farmer, it must be observed, is commonly the proprietor of the land he occupies; and, in the *hauteur* of independence, is not surpassed by the proudest freeholders of Britain. The settler of the grade under consideration, is only able to bring a small portion of his land into cultivation, his success, therefore, does not so much depend on the quantity of produce which he raises, as on the gradual increase in the value of his property. When the neighbourhood becomes more populous, he in general has it in his power to sell his property at a high price, and to remove to a new settlement, where he can purchase a more extensive tract of land, or commence farming on a larger scale than formerly.

The next occupier is a capitalist, who immediately builds a larger barn than the former, and then a brick or a frame house. He either pulls down the dwelling of his predecessor, or converts it into a stable. He erects better fences, and enlarges the quantity of cultivated land; sows down pasture fields, introduces an improved stock of horses, cattle, sheep, and these probably of the Merino breed. He fattens cattle for the market, and perhaps erects a flour-mill, or a saw-mill, or a distillery. Farmers of this description are frequently partners in the banks; members of the State assembly, or of Congress, or Justices of the Peace. The condition of the people has necessarily some relation to the age and prosperity of the settlements in which they live. In Pennsylvania, for instance the most extensive farmers are prevalent. In the earliest settled parts of Ohio and Kentucky, the first and second rate farmers are most numerous, and are mixed together. In Indiana, backwoodsmen and second rate settlers predominate. The three conditions of settlers described, are not to be understood as uniformly distinct; for there are intermediate stages, from which individuals of one class pass, as it were, into another. The first invaders of the forest frequently become farmers of the second order; and there are examples of individuals acting their parts in all the three gradations.

EMERGENCE OF FRONTIER TRAITS

Whether regressing to the near-barbarism of the backwoodsman or clinging to the forms of civilization as a capitalist, all pioneers responded in some degree to the frontier environment. Techniques and skills had to be adjusted to an unfamiliar situation in which land was plentiful and men few. Opportunity was abundant in the West, and the limit of a man's progress was determined by his own capabilities rather than the dictates of society. To Europeans and easterners reared in a stabilized social order where class lines were firmly drawn, the most challenging feature of frontier life was the opportunity for individual self-advancement. Some observers recognized that the special circumstances of western life altered not only the behavior but also the character of the frontiersmen. They saw emerging in the successive Wests a national character which glorified characteristics that they labeled as typically "American." One of the first to note the emergence of these traits along the frontiers was Robert Baird, author of a standard guidebook to the West in the 1830s:[4]

The great difficulty in describing the character and manners of the West, taken in the general, arises from the fact that they do not *essentially* differ from those of the population of the Atlantic states. The shades of difference,—and they are only shades,—are such as have been created by causes and circumstances existing in the West alone. Every one who has seen much of the West, at once perceives these shades; but they are too attenuate and impalpable to admit of being very distinctly pourtrayed. I shall, however, endeavour to indicate some of the traits of difference, after having made the remarks which I am about to make, with regard to the mode in which the West has been peopled from the Atlantic states.

In travelling over the various states and territories of the West, I have been struck with a fact which is somewhat remarkable. It is the manner in which that country has been colonized. The emigration to the Valley of the Mississippi seems to have gone on in columns, moving from the East almost due West, from the respective states from which they originated. From New England the emigrating column advanced through New-York, peopling the middle and western parts of that state in its progress; but still continuing, it reached the northern part of Ohio, then Indiana, and finally Illinois. A part of the same column from New-England and New-York is diverging into Michigan. It is true also, that straggling companies, as it were, diverge to a more southerly direction, and scatter over the middle and southern parts of the Valley, and are to be found in every state, in every county and town, in greater or less numbers. The Pennsylvania and New Jersey column advanced within the parallels of latitude of those states into West Pennsylvania, and still continuing, advanced into the middle and southern parts of Ohio, and extends even into the middle parts of Indiana and Illinois. The Virginia column advanced first into the western part of that state and Kentucky,—which was long a constituent part of it,—thence into the southern parts of Indiana and Illinois, until it has spread over almost the whole of Missouri. The North Carolina column advanced first into East Tennessee, thence into West Tennessee, and also into Missouri. And the South Carolina and Georgia column has moved upon the extensive and fertile lands of Alabama, and has in some degree peopled Mississippi. Louisiana was a foreign colony. The American part of it is composed of emigrants from the upper part of the Valley, and from the southern and eastern states. The same remark is true of the small population of the state of Mississippi. In Arkansas the emigrating columns of Kentucky and Tennessee predominate. As was remarked of the New England column, it may be said that straggling

---

[4] Robert Baird, *View of the Valley of the Mississippi, or the Emigrant's and Traveller's Guide to the West* (Philadelphia, 1834), pp. 100–103.

parties from all the others have wandered from the main bodies, and have taken a more northerly or southerly direction. A hundred considerations of business or affinity, have operated to occasion this divergency.

The above mentioned fact furnishes a better key than any other that I know of, to furnish a correct knowledge of the diversities of customs and manners which prevail in the Valley of the Mississippi. For if one knows what are the peculiarities of the several states east of the Allegheny Mountains, he may expect to find them, with some shades of difference, occasioned by local circumstances, in the corresponding parallels in the West. Slavery keeps nearly within the same parallels. And so does every other peculiarity. The New England column is intelligent, industrious, economical, enterprising, moral, and fond of institutions for the promotion of knowledge and religion. The Pennsylvania column of Scotch, Irish, Germans, &c. partakes of all the characteristics of those worthy nations. The southern columns have a great degree of similarity, and are distinguished by high-mindedness, generosity, liberality, hospitality, indolence, and, too often, dissipation. The southern character, however, is a noble one, when moulded by good influences.

The peculiarities, or, to speak more properly, the developements of character, which may be said to distinguish the population of the West, may be readily enumerated; and they are all created by the peculiar circumstances in which the people have been placed in that new world. They are,

1. A *spirit of adventurous enterprise*: a willingness to go through any hardship or danger to accomplish an object. It was the spirit of enterprise which led to the settlement of that country. The western people think nothing of making a long journey, of encountering fatigue, and of enduring every species of hardship. The great highways of the West —its long rivers—are familiar to very many of them, who have been led by trade to visit remote parts of the Valley.

2. *Independence of thought and action.*— They have felt the influence of this principle from their childhood. Men who can endure any thing: that have lived almost without restraint, free as the mountain air, or as the deer and the buffalo of their forests—and who know that they are Americans all—will act out this principle during the whole of life. I do not mean that they have such an amount of it as to render them *really* regardless alike of the opinions and the feelings of every one else. But I have seen many who have the virtue of independence greatly perverted or degenerated, and who were not pleasant members of a society, which is a state requiring a compromising spirit of mutual co-operation in all, and a determination to bear and forbear.

3. An *apparent roughness*, which some would deem *rudeness of manners*.

These traits characterize, especially, the agricultural portions of the country, and also in some degree the new towns and villages. They are not so much the offspring of ignorance and barbarism, (as some would suppose), as the results of the circumstances of a people thrown together in a new country, often for a long time in thin settlements; where, of course, acquaintances for many miles around are soon, of necessity, made and valued from few adventitious causes. Where there is perfect equality in a neighbourhood of people who know but little about each other's previous history or ancestry—but where each is lord of the soil which he cultivates. Where a log cabin is all that the best of families can expect to have for years, and of course can possess few of the external decorations which have so much influence in creating a diversity of rank in society. These circumstances, have laid the foundation for that equality of intercourse, simplicity of manners, want of deference, want of reserve, great readiness to make acquaintances, freedom of speech, indisposition to brook real or imaginary insults, which one witnesses among the people of the West.

THE FRONTIER AND AMERICAN DEMOCRACY

Of the aspects of western character catalogued by visitors, none received greater attention than the social and political democracy of frontier communities. There equality of all men (save Indians and minority groups) was both a byword and a creed to be defended at any cost. This was recognized by the Frenchman Alexis de Tocqueville, one of the most astute observers to visit America, during this period. In "Democracy in America," first published in 1835, Tocqueville wrote of frontier democracy; he ascribed the democratic spirit that was so marked throughout the United States partly to the pioneering experience:[5]

The chief circumstance which has favored the establishment and the maintenance of a democratic republic in the United States, is the nature of the territory which the Americans inhabit. Their ancestors gave them the love of equality and of freedom; but God himself gave them the means of remaining equal and free, by placing them upon a boundless continent. General prosperity is favorable to the stability of all governments, but more particularly of a democratic one, which depends upon the will of the majority, and especially upon the will of that portion of the community which is most exposed to want. When the people rule, they must be rendered happy, or they will overturn the state: and misery stimulates them to those excesses to which ambition rouses kings. The physical causes, independent of the laws, which promote general prosperity, are more numerous in America than they ever have been in any other country in the world, at any other period of history. In the United States, not only is legislation democratic, but Nature herself favors the cause of the people. . . .

It would be difficult to describe the avidity with which the American rushes forward to secure this immense booty which fortune offers. In the pursuit, he fearlessly braves the arrow of the Indian and the diseases of the forest; he is unimpressed by the silence of the woods; the approach of beasts of prey does not disturb him; for he is goaded onwards by a passion stronger than the love of life. Before him lies a boundless continent, and he urges onward as if time pressed, and he was afraid of finding no room for his exertions. I have spoken of the emigration from the older States; but how shall I describe that which takes place from the more recent ones? Fifty years have scarcely elapsed since that of Ohio was founded; the greater part of its inhabitants were not born within its confines; its capital has been built only thirty years, and its territory is still covered by an immense extent of uncultivated fields; yet already the population of Ohio is proceeding westward, and most of the settlers who descend to the fertile prairies of Illinois are citizens of Ohio. These men left their first country to improve their condition;

---

[5] Alexis de Tocqueville, *Democracy in America* (Cambridge, 1863), vol. 1, pp. 371–372, 376–377, 378–380.

they quit their second, to ameliorate it still more; fortune awaits them everywhere, but not happiness. The desire of prosperity is become an ardent and restless passion in their minds, which grows by what it feeds on. They early broke the ties which bound them to their natal earth, and they have contracted no fresh ones on their way. Emigration was at first necessary to them; and it soon becomes a sort of game of chance, which they pursue for the emotions it excites, as much as for the gain it procures.

Sometimes the progress of man is so rapid that the desert reappears behind him. The woods stoop to give him a passage, and spring up again when he is past. It is not uncommon, in crossing the new States of the West, to meet with deserted dwellings in the midst of the wilds; the traveller frequently discovers the vestiges of a loghouse in the most solitary retreat, which bear witness to the power, and no less to the inconstancy, of man. In these abandoned fields, and over these ruins of a day, the primeval forest soon scatters a fresh vegetation; the beasts resume the haunts which were once their own; and Nature comes smiling to cover the traces of man with green branches and flowers, which obliterate his ephemeral track. . . .

In Europe, we are wont to look upon a restless disposition, an unbounded desire of riches, and an excessive love of independence, as propensities very dangerous to society. Yet these are the very elements which insure a long and peaceful future to the republics of America. Without these unquiet passions, the population would collect in certain spots, and would soon experience wants like those of the Old World, which it is difficult to satisfy; for such is the present good fortune of the New World, that the vices of its inhabitants are scarcely less favorable to society than their virtues. These circumstances exercise a great influence on the estimation in which human actions are held in the two hemispheres. What we should call cupidity, the Americans frequently term a laudable industry; and they blame as faintheartedness what we consider to be the virtue of moderate desires.

In France, simple tastes, orderly manners, domestic affections, and the attachment which men feel to the place of their birth, are looked upon as great guaranties of the tranquillity and happiness of the state. But in America, nothing seems to be more prejudicial to society than such virtues. The French Canadians, who have faithfully preserved the traditions of their ancient manners, are already embarrassed for room upon their small territory; and this little community, which has so recently begun to exist, will shortly be a prey to the calamities incident to old nations. In Canada, the most enlightened, patriotic, and humane inhabitants make extraordinary efforts to render the people dissatisfied with those simple enjoyments which still content them. There the seductions of wealth are vaunted with as much zeal as the charms of a moderate competency in the Old World; and more exertions are made to excite the passions of the citizens there, than to calm them elsewhere. If we listen to their accounts, we shall hear that nothing is more praiseworthy than to exchange the pure and tranquil pleasures which even the poor man tastes in his own country, for the sterile delights of prosperity under a foreign sky; to leave the patrimonial hearth, and the turf beneath which one's forefathers sleep,—in short, to abandon the living and the dead, in quest of fortune.

At the present time, America presents a field for human effort far more extensive than any sum of labor which can be applied to work it. In America, too much knowledge cannot be diffused; for all knowledge, whilst it may serve him who possesses it, turns also to the advantage of those who are without it. New wants are not to be feared there, since they can be satisfied without difficulty; the growth of human passions need not be dreaded, since all passions may find an easy and a legitimate object; nor can men there be made too free, since they are scarcely ever tempted to misuse their liberties.

The American republics of the present day are like companies of adventures, formed to explore in common the waste lands of the New World, and busied in a flourishing trade. The passions which agitate the Americans most deeply are not their political, but their commercial, passions; or, rather, they introduce the habits of business into their political life. They love order, without which affairs do not prosper; and they set an especial value upon regular conduct, which is the foundation of a solid business. They prefer the good sense which amasses large fortunes to that enterprising genius which frequently dissipates them; general ideas alarm their minds, which are accustomed to positive calculations; and they hold practice in more honor than theory.

THE FRONTIER AND THE NATIONAL CHARACTER

Even more observing than Tocqueville among the earlier appraisers of the frontier's influence was Edwin L. Godkin, editor of "The Nation," one of America's most influential magazines. In an essay prepared during the Civil War for the "North American Review," he anticipated many of the views later developed by historians to show that pioneering had been a major force in shaping the national character. Significantly, Godkin's opinions were based on actual observation and not on mere speculation:[6]

If we inquire what are those phenomena of American society which it is generally agreed distinguish it from that of older countries, we shall find, we are satisfied, that by far the larger number of them may be attributed in a great measure to what, for want of a better name, we shall call "the frontier life" led by a large proportion of the inhabitants, and to the influence of this portion on manners and legislation, rather than to political institutions, or even to the equality of conditions. In fact, we think that these phenomena, and particularly those of them which excite most odium in Europe, instead of being the effect of democracy, are partly its cause, and that it has been to their agency more than to aught else, that the democratic tide in America has owed most of its force and violence....

A society composed at the period of its formation mainly of young men, coming from all parts of the world in quest of fortune, released from the ordinary restraints of family, church, and public opinion, even of the civil law, naturally and inevitably acquires a certain contempt for authority and impatience of it, and individualism among them develops itself very rapidly. If you place this society, thus constituted, in the midst of a wilderness, where each member of it has to contend, tools in hand, with Nature herself for wealth, or even subsistence, the ties which bind him to his fellows will for a while at least be rarely anything stronger

---

[6] Edwin L. Godkin, "Aristocratic Opinions of Democracy," *North American Review*, CCVI (January, 1865), 194–232. Reprinted in Edwin L. Godkin, *Problems of Democracy* (New York, 1896). The extracts quoted here are from the latter version, pp. 25–26, 38–45, 50–52.

than that of simple contiguity. The only mutual obligation which this relation suggests strongly is that of rendering assistance occasionally in overcoming material difficulties—in other words, the simplest bond which can unite human beings. Each person is, from the necessity of the case, so absorbed in his own struggle for existence, that he has seldom occasion or time for the consideration and cultivation of his social relations. He knows nothing of the antecedents of his neighbors, nor they of his. They are not drawn together, in all probability, by a single memory or association. They have drifted into the same locality, it is true, under the guidance of a common impulse, and this a selfish one. So that the settler gets into the habit of looking at himself as an individual, of contemplating himself and his career separate and apart from the social organization. We do not say that this breeds selfishness—far from it; but it breeds individualism.

If the members of such a society are compelled to work hard for the gratification of their desires, to meet and overcome great difficulties and hardships and dangers, the result is naturally the production of great energy, of great audacity, and of a self-confidence that rises into conceit. In this self-confidence is almost always contained a prodigious contempt for experience and for theory. The ends which such men have had in view having all been attained without the aid of either, they cannot see the use of them. They have found their own wits sufficient for the solution of every problem that has presented itself to them, so that deference to the authority of general maxims framed by persons who never found themselves placed in similar circumstances, wears an air of weakness or absurdity.

The devotion to material pursuits, which is necessary at the outset, is made absorbing in a country like the West, by the richness of the prizes which are offered to shrewd speculation and successful industry. Where probable or even possible gains are so great, the whole community gives itself up to the chase of them with an eagerness which is not democratic, but human. It would not, we think, be difficult to show that the existence in old countries of an idle class, content with moderate and secured fortunes, and devoted solely to amusement and the cultivation of art or literature, is largely due to the immense difficulty of making profitable investments. In those countries the capital accumulated by past generations is so great, and every field of industry is so thronged, that a very large number of those who find themselves possessed of a sum of money are forced to relinquish all hope of increasing it. For we know that whenever, as during "the railway mania" in England, or Law's Mississippi scheme in France, the chance, real or imaginary, is offered of drawing such prizes as every day fall to the lot of hundreds in America, men of every grade and calling rush after them with an ardor which no training or tastes or antecedents seem sufficient to restrain. The desire for wealth is one of the constant forces of human society, and if it seems to assert its sway more imperiously here than in Europe, it is not because it is fostered by the equality of conditions, but because its gratification is surrounded by fewer obstacles.

If to strong individualism, contempt for experience, and eagerness in pursuit of material gain, we add want of respect for training, and profound faith in natural qualities, great indifference as to the future, the absence of a strong sense of social or national continuity, and of taste in art and literature and oratory, we have, we believe, enumerated the leading defects which European writers consider inherent in democratic society. But these, too, are marked peculiarities of all societies newly organized in a new country. We know them to be so by actual observation, for which modern colonization has afforded us abundant facilities; while it is safe to say that trustworthy illustrations of them have never been discovered in any society which was simply democratic and not new. There is no feature of life in new States in America more marked than the general belief of the people in their own originality, and their respect for this quality. The kind of man they most admire is one who has evolved rules for the conduct of life out of his own brain by the help of his own observation; and they entertain a strong distrust of men who have learned what they know by a fixed course of study, mainly because persons who have passed the early part of their lives in learning out of books or from teachers are generally found less fitted to grapple with the kind of difficulties which usually present themselves in Western life, than those who were compelled to learn to conquer them by actual contact with them. So that the "self-made man," as he is called, meaning the man who has surmounted, with little or no aid from education, those obstacles by which the larger portion of the community find themselves hampered and harassed, is looked on as a sort of type of merit and ability.

The process by which the ideas that govern private life are transferred to the conduct of public affairs, is not difficult to understand. In a new community, in which there is not much time for either study or reflection, it would be difficult always to convince the public, even if any other kind of man were to be had, that the kind of man who displays most ability in the conduct of his own business is not the fittest to take charge of that of the public. That other qualities than those necessary for success in the career in which everybody else is running should be needed for legislation, is an idea which meets with no acceptance until enforced by experience. And in a really frontier village, in which no disturbing influences are in operation, it will probably be found that the prosperous management of a dry-goods store will be taken as strong indication of ability to fill the post of Secretary of the Treasury, and deal with the most intricate problems of national finance. But the successful politician in a new country, where deference for experience or culture has not yet grown up, is, after all, the man who has most facility in expressing the ideas which are filling the heads of his neighbors.

It may be taken as a general rule, that those who cannot look very far back do not look very far forward. Experience is the nurse of forethought. Youth is rarely troubled about to-morrow. Age is far-seeing, because it remembers so much. And communities made of the materials we are describing, as they have no past, are apt to be very careless about the future. The sense of political continuity, of the identity, for political purposes, of each generation with the one which has preceded it and the one which is to follow it, and of the consequent responsibility of each for the acts and promises of the other, is rarely deeply rooted in a state which has no past to dwell on. We are therefore not surprised to find that the doctrine of the absence of all right on the part of one generation to enter into any obligations that would bind its successor—a doctrine utterly subversive of what is called "public faith," and which, if carried out to its full extent, would reduce the intercourse of civilized nations to the mere interchange of compliments or abuse—was first openly preached and acted on in Mississippi, the person who now represents Southern statesmanship to the world being its author. But it is a doctrine which grows naturally in a new society. The reverse of it conflicts strongly with the notions of the proper limits of accountability, which are derived from the relations of individuals. There is little in the analogies presented by the relations of a man either with his family or his fellows, in such a society, to suggest the expediency or propriety of his helping, as a citizen, to repay money which was borrowed before he was born. We think it will generally be found that, when a state formed by colonization, as carried on in modern times, displays a proper disposition with regard to the public liabilities, it is rather owing to the feeling of local pride than to a deep sense of responsibility. . . .

We need hardly say, that we are very far from asserting that the state of society which we have been describing as "Western" can be predicated literally either of the whole West or of any part of it. There is probably not a village in it of which our picture is true in every particular. There are doubtless to be found in every district many departures from the general type which we have sketched, many modifications effected by the presence of cultivated people, or by the extraordinary intelligence and unusually favorable antecedents of the inhabitants. What we have endeavored to portray is the general features of society in new countries which have been subjected to the ordinary agencies of frontier life, and exempted from the disturbing influences of older and more finished organizations. In so far as our sketch is inaccurate as applied to the new States of the Union, to the same extent will our description of their influence on the East require modification. The study of society is not one of the exact sciences; and the utmost that the most careful inquirer can hope for is an approximation to the truth. This is all that we pretend to have achieved in the present instance, but it is sufficient for our purpose.

In so far as the influence exercised by that portion of the population which is immersed in the cares and toils of frontier life on the national character, or manners, or politics, or literature, or oratory, has been deteriorating or obstructive, it is, of course, fair matter for regret to all friends of rational progress. But those who are most disheartened by the contemplation of its effects may find abundant consolation in the consideration that its action is but temporary, and that every day that passes weakens its force and hastens its disappearance. The greatest fault of new countries is their newness, and for this the great remedy is time. As soon as the population gets settled in its seat, and its attention has ceased to be distracted by a multiplicity of prizes, and its energies to be absorbed in the mere struggle for shelter and food, the polishing process begins. This struggle, if it have hardened the hands, and tanned the foreheads, and roughened the manners of those engaged in it, has also most certainly developed qualities which, if they do not themselves constitute national greatness, are its only sure and lasting foundation.

THE SIGNIFICANCE OF THE FRONTIER

While observations and speculations such as those of Godkin and Tocqueville testified that some contemporaries were aware of the frontier's influence in molding the national character, the average American did not realize that expansion had altered his habits or institutions. The individual who was to make his countrymen conscious of the significance of their pioneering past was Frederick Jackson Turner, a young historian at the University of Wisconsin. Rebelling against the current historical beliefs that all American institutions had evolved from their "germs" in medieval societies, Turner fastened upon the frontier as one reason for the observable differences between people of the United States and of Europe. His challenging views were embodied in "The Significance of the Frontier in American History," read before a meeting of the American Historical Association at Chicago in the summer of 1893:[7]

In a recent bulletin of the Superintendent of the Census for 1890 appear these significant words: "Up to and including 1880 the country had a frontier of settlement, but at present the unsettled area has been so broken into by isolated bodies of settlement that there can hardly be said to be a frontier line. In the discussion of its extent, its westward movement, etc., it can not, therefore, any longer have a place in the census reports." This brief official statement marks the closing of a great historic movement. Up to our own day American history has been in a large degree the history of the colonization of the Great West. The existence of an area of free land, its continuous recession, and the advance of American settlement westward, explain American development.

Behind institutions, behind constitutional forms and modifications, lie the vital forces that call these organs into life and shape them to meet changing conditions. The peculiarity of American institutions is, the fact that they have been compelled to adapt themselves to the changes of an expanding people—to the changes involved in crossing a continent, in winning a wilderness, and in developing at each area of this progress out of the primitive economic and political conditions of the frontier into the complexity of city life. Said Calhoun in 1817, "We are great, and rapidly—I was about to say fearfully—growing!" So saying, he touched the distinguishing feature of American life. All peoples show development; the germ theory of politics has been sufficiently emphasized. In the case of most nations, however, the development has occurred in a limited area; and if the nation has expanded, it has met other growing peoples whom it has conquered. But in the case of the United States we have a different phenomenon. Limiting our attention to the Atlantic coast, we have the familiar phenomenon of the evolution of institutions in a limited area, such as the rise of representative government; the differentiation of simple colonial governments into complex organs; the progress from primitive industrial society, without division of labor, up to manufacturing civilization. But we have in addition to this a recurrence of the process of evolution in each western area reached in the process of expansion. Thus American development has exhibited not merely advance along a single line, but a return to primitive conditions on a continually advancing frontier line, and a new development for that area. American social development has been continually beginning over again on the frontier. This perennial rebirth, this fluidity of American life, this expansion westward with its new opportunities, its continuous touch with the simplicity of primitive society, furnish the forces dominating American character. The true point of view in the history of this nation is not the Atlantic coast, it is the Great West. Even the slavery struggle, which is made so exclusive an object of attention by writers like Professor von Holst, occupies its important place in American history because of its relation to westward expansion.

---

[7] Frederick Jackson Turner, "The Significance of the Frontier in American History," *American Historical Association Annual Report for the Year 1893* (Washington, 1894), pp. 199–227. Reprinted in Frederick Jackson Turner, *The Frontier in American History* (New York, 1920), pp. 1–38. The extracts quoted here are from the latter version pp. 1–4, 22–32, 37–38.

In this advance, the frontier is the outer edge of the wave—the meeting point between savagery and civilization. Much has been written about the frontier from the point of view of border warfare and the chase, but as a field for the serious study of the economist and the historian it has been neglected.

The American frontier is sharply distinguished from the European frontier—a fortified boundary line running through dense populations. The most significant thing about the American frontier is, that it lies at the hither edge of free land. In the census reports it is treated as the margin of that settlement which has a density of two or more to the square mile. The term is an elastic one, and for our purposes does not need sharp definition. We shall consider the whole frontier belt, including the Indian country and outer margin of the "settled area" of the census reports. This paper will make no attempt to treat the subject exhaustively; its aim is simply to call attention to the frontier as a fertile field for investigation, and to suggest some of the problems which arise in connection with it.

In the settlement of America we have to observe how European life entered the continent, and how America modified and developed that life and reacted on Europe. Our early history is the study of European germs developing in an American environment. Too exclusive attention has been paid by institutional students to the Germanic origins, too little to the American factors. The frontier is the line of most rapid and effective Americanization. The wilderness masters the colonist. It finds him a European in dress, industries, tools, modes of travel, and thought. It takes him from the railroad car and puts him in the birch canoe. It strips off the garments of civilization and arrays him in the hunting shirt and the moccasin. It puts him in the log cabin of the Cherokee and Iroquois and runs an Indian palisade around him. Before long he has gone to planting Indian corn and plowing with a sharp stick; he shouts the war cry and takes the scalp in orthodox Indian fashion. In short, at the frontier the environment is at first too strong for the man. He must accept the conditions which it furnishes, or perish, and so he fits himself into the Indian clearings and follows the Indian trails. Little by little he transforms the wilderness, but the outcome is not the old Europe, not simply the development of Germanic germs, any more than the first phenomenon was a case of reversion to the Germanic mark. The fact is, that here is a new product that is American. At first, the frontier was the Atlantic coast. It was the frontier of Europe in a very real sense. Moving westward, the frontier became more and more American. As successive terminal moraines result from successive glaciations, so each frontier leaves its traces behind it, and when it becomes a settled area the region still partakes of the frontier characteristics. Thus the advance of the frontier has meant a steady movement away from the influence of Europe, a steady growth of independence on American lines. And to study this advance, the men who grew up under these conditions, and the political, economic, and social results of it, is to study the really American part of our history. . . .

We may next inquire what were the influences on the East and on the Old World. A rapid enumeration of some of the more noteworthy effects is all that I have time for.

First, we note that the frontier promoted the formation of a composite nationality for the American people. The coast was preponderantly English, but the later tides of continental immigration flowed across to the free lands. This was the case from the early colonial days. The Scotch-Irish and the Palatine Germans, or "Pennsylvania Dutch," furnished the dominant element in the stock of the colonial frontier. With these peoples were also the freed indented servants, or redemptioners, who at the expiration of their time of service passed to the frontier. Governor Spotswood of Virginia writes in 1717, "The inhabitants of our frontiers are composed generally of such as have been transported hither as servants, and, being out of their time, settle themselves where land is to be taken up and that will produce the necessarys of life with little labour." Very generally these redemptioners were of non-English stock. In the crucible of the frontier the immigrants were Americanized, liberated, and fused into a mixed race, English in neither nationality nor characteristics. The process has gone on from the early days to our own. Burke and other writers in the middle of the eighteenth century believed that Pennsylvania was "threatened with the danger of being wholly foreign in language, manners, and perhaps even inclinations." The German and Scotch-Irish elements in the frontier of the South were only less great. In the middle of the present century the German element in Wisconsin was already so considerable that leading publicists looked to the creation of a German state out of the commonwealth by concentrating their colonization. Such examples teach us to beware of misinterpreting the fact that there is a common English speech in America into a belief that the stock is also English.

In another way the advance of the frontier decreased our dependence on England. The coast, particularly of the South, lacked diversified industries, and was dependent on England for the bulk of its supplies. In the South there was even a dependence on the Northern colonies for articles of food. Governor Glenn, of South Carolina, writes in the middle of the eighteenth century: "Our trade with New York and Philadelphia was of this sort, draining us of all the little money and bills we could gather from other places for their bread, flour, beer, hams, bacon, and other things of their produce, all which, except beer, our new townships begin to supply us with, which are settled with very industrious and thriving Germans. This no doubt diminishes the number of shipping and the appearance of our trade, but it is far from being a detriment to us." Before long the frontier created a demand for merchants. As it retreated from the coast it became less and less possible for England to bring her supplies directly to the consumer's wharfs, and carry away staple crops; and staple crops began to give way to diversified agriculture for a time. The effect of this phase of the frontier action upon the northern section is perceived when we realize how the advance of the frontier aroused seaboard cities like Boston, New York, and Baltimore to engage in rivalry for what Washington called "the extensive and valuable trade of a rising empire."

The legislation which most developed the powers of the national government, and played the largest part in its activity, was conditioned on the frontier. Writers have discussed the subjects of tariff, land, and internal improvement as pendants to the slavery question. But when American history comes to be rightly viewed it will be seen that the slavery question is an incident. In the period from the end of the first half of the present century to the close of the Civil War, slavery rose to primary but far from exclusive importance. But this does not justify Professor von Holst, to take an example, in treating our constitutional history in its formative period down to 1828 in a single volume, giving six volumes chiefly to the history of slavery from 1828 to 1861, under the title of a *Constitutional History of the United States*. The growth of nationalism and the evolution of American political institutions were dependent on the advance of the frontier. Even so recent a writer as Rhodes, in his *History of the United States since the Compromise of 1850,* has treated the legislation called out by the western advance as incidental to the slavery struggle.

This is a wrong perspective. The pioneer needed the goods of the coast, and so the grand series of internal improvements and railroad legislation began, with potent nationalizing effects. But the West was not content with bringing the farm to the factory. Under the lead of Clay—"Harry of the West" —protective tariffs were passed, with the cry of bringing the factory to the farm.

The public domain has been a force of profound importance in the nationalization and development of the government. The effects of the struggle of the landed and the landless states, and of the Ordinance of 1787, need no discussion. Administratively the frontier called out some of the highest and most vitalizing activities of the general government. The purchase of Louisiana was perhaps the constitutional turning point in the history of the republic, inasmuch as it afforded both a new area for national legislation and the occasion of the downfall of the policy of strict construction. But the purchase of Louisiana was called out by frontier needs and demands. As frontier states accrued to the Union, the national power grew. In a speech on the dedication of the Calhoun monument, Mr. Lamar explained: "In 1789 the states were the creators of the federal government; in 1861 the federal government was the creator of a large majority of the states."

When we consider the public domain from the point of view of the sale and disposal of the public lands, we are again brought face to face with the frontier. The policy of the United States in dealing with its lands is in sharp contrast with the European system of scientific administration. Efforts to make this domain a source of revenue, and to withhold it from emigrants in order that settlement might be compact, were in vain. The jealousy and the fears of the East were powerless in the face of the demands of the frontiersmen. John Quincy Adams was obliged to confess: "My own system of administration, which was to make the national domain the inexhaustible fund for progressive and unceasing internal improvement, has failed." The reason is obvious; systems of administration were not what the West demanded; it wanted land. Adams states the situation as follows:

The slave-holders of the South have bought the cooperation of the Western country by the bribe of the Western lands, abandoning to the new Western States their own proportion of this public property, and aiding them in the design of grasping all the lands into their own hands. Thomas H. Benton was the author of this system, which he brought forward as a substitute for the American system of Mr. Clay, and to supplant him as the leading statesman of the West. Mr. Clay, by his tariff compromise with Mr. Calhoun, abandoned his own American system. At the same time he brought forward a plan for distributing among all the States of the Union the proceeds of the sales of the public lands. His bill for that purpose passed both houses of Congress, but was vetoed by President Jackson, who, in his annual message of December, 1832, formally recommended that all the public lands should be gratuitously given away to individual adventurers and to the States in which the lands are situated.

"No subject," said Henry Clay, "which has presented itself to the present, or perhaps any preceding, congress, is of greater magnitude than that of the public lands." When we consider the far-reaching effects of the government's land policy upon political, economic, and social aspects of American life, we are disposed to agree with him. But this legislation was framed under frontier influences, and under the lead of Western statesmen like Benton and Jackson. Said Senator Scott of Indiana in 1841: "I consider the preemption law merely declaratory of the custom or common law of the settlers."

It is safe to say that the legislation with regard to land, tariff, and internal improvements—the American system of the nationalizing Whig Party—was conditioned on frontier ideas and needs. But it was not merely in legislative action that the frontier worked against the sectionalism of the coast. The economic and social characteristics of the frontier worked against sectionalism. The men of the frontier had closer resemblances to the Middle region than to either of the other sections. Pennsylvania had been the seed plot of frontier emigration, and, although she passed on her settlers along the Great Valley into the west of Virginia and the Carolinas, yet the industrial society of these Southern frontiersmen was always more like that of the Middle region than like that of the tidewater portion of the South, which later came to spread its industrial type throughout the South.

The Middle region, entered by New York harbor, was an open door to all Europe. The tidewater part of the South represented typical Englishmen, modified by a warm climate and servile labor, and living in baronial fashion on great plantations; New England stood for a special English movement—Puritanism. The Middle region was less English than the other sections. It had a wide mixture of nationalities, a varied society, the mixed town and county system of local government, a varied economic life, many religious sects. In short, it was a region mediating between New England and the South, and the East and the West. It represented that composite nationality which the contemporary United States exhibits, that juxtaposition of non-English groups, occupying a valley or a little settlement, and presenting reflections of the map of Europe in their variety. It was democratic and nonsectional, if not national; "easy, tolerant, and contented;" rooted strongly in material prosperity. It was typical of the modern United States. It was least sectional not only because it lay between North and South but also because with no barriers to shut out its frontiers from its settled region, and with a system of connecting waterways, the Middle region mediated between East and West as well as between North and South. Thus it became the typically American region. Even the New Englander, who was shut out from the frontier by the Middle region, tarrying in New York or Pennsylvania on his westward march, lost the acuteness of his sectionalism on the way.

Until the spread of cotton culture into the interior gave homogeneity to the South, the western part of it showed tendencies to fall away from the faith of the fathers into internal improvement legislation and nationalism. In the Virginia convention of 1829–30, called to revise the constitution, Mr. Leigh, of Chesterfield, one of the tidewater counties, declared:

One of the main causes of discontent which led to this convention, that which had the strongest influence in overcoming our veneration for the work of our fathers, which taught us to condemn the sentiments of Henry and Mason and Pendleton, which weaned us from our reverence for the constituted authorities of the state, was an overweening passion for internal improvement. I say this with perfect knowledge; for it has been avowed to me by gentlemen from the West over and over again. And let me tell the gentleman from Albemarle (Mr. Gordon) that it has been another principal object of those who set this ball of revolution in motion, to overturn the doctrine of state rights, of which Virginia has been the very pillar, and to remove the barrier she has interposed to the interference of the federal government in that same work of internal improvement, by so reorganizing the legislature that Virginia, too, may be hitched to the federal car.

It was this nationalizing tendency of the West that transformed the democracy of Jefferson into the national republicanism of Monroe and the democracy of Andrew Jackson. The West of the War of 1812, the West of Clay, and Benton, and Harrison, and Andrew Jackson, shut off by the Middle states and the mountains from the coast sections, had a solidarity of its own with national tendencies. On the tide of the Father of Waters, North and South met and mingled into a nation. Interstate migration went steadily on—a process of cross-fertilization of ideas and institutions. The fierce struggle of the sections over slavery on the western frontier does not diminish the truth of this statement; it proves the truth of it. Slavery was a sectional trait that would not down, but in the West it could not remain sectional. It was the greatest of frontiersmen who declared: "I believe this government cannot endure permanently half slave and half free. It will become all of one thing, or all of the other." Nothing works for nationalism like intercourse within the nation. Mobility of population is death to localism, and the Western frontier worked irresistibly in unsettling population. The effects reached back from the frontier and affected profoundly the Atlantic Coast, and even the Old World.

But the most important effect of the frontier has been in the promotion of democracy here and in Europe. As has been pointed out, the frontier is productive of individualism. Complex society is precipitated by the wilderness into a kind of primitive organization based on the family. The tendency is anti-social. It produces antipathy to control, and particularly to any direct control. The tax-gatherer is viewed as a representative of oppression. Professor Osgood, in an able article, has pointed out that the frontier conditions prevalent in the colonies are important factors in the explanation of the American Revolution, where individual liberty was sometimes confused with absence of all effective government. The same conditions aid in explaining the difficulty of instituting a strong government in the period of the confederacy. The frontier individualism has from the beginning promoted democracy.

The frontier states that came into the Union in the first quarter of a century of its existence came in with democratic suffrage provisions, and had reactive effects of the highest importance upon the older states whose peoples were being attracted there. It was *western* New York that forced an extension of suffrage in the constitutional convention of that state in 1821; and it was *western* Virginia that compelled the tidewater region to put a more liberal suffrage provision in the constitution framed in 1830, and to give to the frontier region a more nearly proportionate representation with the tidewater aristocracy. The rise of democracy as an effective force in the nation came in with Western preponderance under Jackson and William Henry Harrison, and it meant the triumph of the frontier—with all of its good and with all of its evil elements. An interesting illustration of the tone of frontier democracy in 1830 comes from the debates in the Virginia convention already referred to. A representative from western Virginia declared:

But, sir, it is not the increase of population in the West which this gentleman ought to fear. It is the energy which the mountain breeze and western habits impart to those emigrants. They are regenerated, politically I mean, sir. They soon become *working politicians*; and the difference, sir, between a *talking* and a *working* politician is immense. The Old Dominion has long been celebrated for producing great orators; the ablest metaphysicians in policy; men that can split hairs in all abstruse questions of political economy. But at home, or when they return from congress, they have negroes to fan them asleep. But a Pennsylvania, a New York, an Ohio, or a western Virginia statesman, though far inferior in logic, metaphysics and rhetoric to an old Virginia statesman, has this advantage, that when he returns home he takes off his coat and takes hold of the plough. This gives him bone and muscle, sir, and preserves his republican principles pure and uncontaminated.

So long as free land exists, the opportunity for a competency exists, and economic power secures political power. But the democracy born of free land, strong in selfishness and individualism, intolerant of administrative experience and education, and pressing individual liberty beyond its proper bounds, has its dangers as well as its benefits. Individualism in America has allowed a laxity in regard to governmental affairs which has rendered possible the spoils system and all the manifest evils that follow from the lack of a highly developed civic spirit. In this connection may be noted also the influence of frontier conditions in permitting lax business honor, inflated paper currency and wild-cat banking. The colonial and revolutionary frontier was the region whence emanated many of the worst forms of an evil currency. The West in the War of 1812 repeated the phenomenon on the frontier of that day, while the speculation and wild-cat banking of the period of the crisis of 1837 occurred on the new frontier belt of the next tier of States. Thus each one of the periods of lax financial integrity coincides with periods when a new set of frontier communities had arisen, and coincides in area with these successive frontiers, for the most part. The recent Populist agitation is a case in point.

Many a State that now declines any connection with the tenets of the Populists, itself adhered to such ideas in an earlier stage of the development of the State. A primitive society can hardly be expected to show the intelligent appreciation of the complexity of business interests in a developed society. The continual recurrence of these areas of paper-money agitation is another evidence that the frontier can be isolated and studied as a factor in American history of the highest importance. . . .

From the conditions of frontier life came intellectual traits of profound importance. The works of travelers along each frontier from colonial days onward describe certain common traits, and these traits have, while softening down, still persisted as survivals in the place of their origin, even when a higher social organization succeeded. The result is that to the frontier the American intellect owes its striking characteristics. That coarseness and strength combined with acuteness and inquisitiveness; that practical, inventive turn of mind, quick to find expedients; that masterful grasp of material things, lacking in the artistic but powerful to effect great ends; that restless, nervous energy; that dominant individualism, working for good and for evil, and withal that buoyancy and exuberance which comes with freedom—these are traits of the frontier, or traits called out elsewhere because of the existence of the frontier. Since the days when the fleet of Columbus sailed into the waters of the New World, America has been another name for opportunity, and the people of the United States have taken their tone from the incessant expansion which has not only been open but has even been forced upon them. He would be a rash prophet who should assert that the expansive character of American life has now entirely ceased. Movement has been its dominant fact, and, unless this training has no effect upon a people, the American energy will continually demand a wider field for its exercise. But never again will such gifts of free land offer themselves. For a moment, at the frontier, the bonds of custom are broken and unrestraint is triumphant. There is not *tabula rasa*. The stubborn American environment is there with its imperious summons to accept its conditions; the inherited ways of doing things are also there; and yet, in spite of environment, and in spite of custom, each frontier did indeed furnish a new field of opportunity, a gate of escape from the bondage of the past; and freshness, and confidence, and scorn of older society, impatience of its restraints and its ideas, and indifference to its lessons, have accompanied the frontier. What the Mediterranean Sea was to the Greeks, breaking the bond of custom, offering new experiences, calling out new institutions and activities, that, and more, the ever retreating frontier has been to the United States directly, and to the nations of Europe more remotely. And now, four centuries from the discovery of America, at the end of a hundred years of life under the Constitution, the frontier has gone, and with its going has closed the first period of American history.

Frederick Jackson Turner's pronouncement of the "frontier hypothesis" endowed the study of western history with new purpose and new respectability. No longer was the Wild West simply a carnival of disorder and lawlessness; no longer were the pioneers merely colorful misfits whose stirring adventures excited readers of dime novels and pulp magazines. Rather, the frontier was a major force in the evolution of a distinctive American personality, and recognition of this was essential to understanding the evolution of the United States as a whole. Turner's essay conjured into being a major school of historical studies that down to the present has argued over the validity of his thesis and sought to prove or disprove his conclusions by re-examination of the evidence.

The pages that follow contain a sampling of the raw materials needed for such an examination. In them the story of America's westward expansion is told in the words of the men and women who carried civilization from the Atlantic to the Pacific. Some wrote well and some badly; some described uncommon adventures and others prosaic events, but all were seized with the pioneering spirit, that sent men in quest of the pot of gold at the western end of the rainbow. The records they left behind reveal the meaning of the frontier experience to those who participated and help to demonstrate that Frederick Jackson Turner's hypothesis deserves the attention of all who seek to understand why Americans behave as Americans.

CHAPTER 2

Spain and France Pioneer in America, 1492-1609

The discovery of America was only one aspect of Europe's efforts to expand the frontiers of faith, learning, and trade, which began in the centuries following the Crusades. Knowledge of exotic products, unique skills, and great wealth stirred the imagination of European adventurers and inspired them to seek easier and shorter routes to Asia. While the Portuguese pioneered the coast of Africa by sending Bartholomeu Diaz around the Cape of Good Hope in 1486, Spain waited only until the Moors had been driven out before financing a voyage that its rulers hoped would end costly dependence on Moslem traders for Oriental goods. That the world was round was no secret; that there might be islands between Europe and Asia was logical; but that two continents, offering Europeans greater economic and political opportunity than they had ever known, divided Western Europe and East Asia seemed beyond comprehension. Only in this sense was the discovery of America an accident.

ADMIRAL OF THE OCEAN

In 1492, Christopher Columbus, a Genoese sea captain, offered to open the markets of Asia for Spain by sailing westward across the Atlantic. Convinced that he had the courage, skill, and experience to lead the expedition, Columbus asked a high price for his services. Like most pathfinders, he wanted to share in the profits of his discoveries, but, like most investors, the Spanish rulers sought to maximize returns and minimize their risks. Reaching an agreement did not prove easy. Only when Columbus prepared to take his proposition to the king of France, did the Spanish monarchs yield to his demands. The titles and honors Columbus gained indicate the scope and magnitude of the claim Spain hoped to stake in Asia.[1]

Foreasmuch as you, Christopher Columbus are going by our Command, with some of our ships and with some of our subjects, to discover and acquire certain islands and mainland in the ocean, and it is hoped that, by the help of God some of the said islands and mainland in the said ocean will be discovered and acquired by your pains and industry; and therefore it is a just and reasonable thing that since you incur the said danger for our service you be rewarded for it, and as we desire to honor and favour you on account of what is aforesaid, it is our will

---

[1] *Christopher Columbus: His Own Book of Privileges, 1502,* compiled by Benjamin Franklin Stevens (London, 1893), pp. 53–54.

and pleasure that you the said Christopher Columbus after you have discovered and acquired the said islands and mainland in the said ocean or any of them whatsoever shall be our Admiral of the said islands and mainland which you may thus discover and acquire, and shall be our Admiral and Viceroy and Governor therein, and shall be empowered from that time forward to call and entitle yourself Don Christopher Columbus, and that your sons and successors in the said office and charge may likewise entitle and call themselves Don, and Admiral, and Viceroy and Governor thereof; and, that you may have power to use and exercise the said office of Admiral, together with the said office of Viceroy and Governor of the said islands and mainland which you may thus discover and acquire, by yourself or by your lieutenants, and to hear and determine all the suits and causes civil and criminal appertaining to the said office of Admiralty and Viceroy and Governor according as you shall find by law, and as the admirals of our kingdoms are accustomed to use and exercise it; and may have power to punish and chastise delinquents, and exercise the said offices of Admiralty, Viceroy and Governor, you and your said lieutenants, in all that concerns and appertains to the said offices and to each of them, and that you shall have and levy the fees and salaries annexed, belonging and appertaining to the said offices and to each one of them, according as our High Admiral in the Admiralty of our Kingdoms is accustomed to levy them. And ... we command Prince Don John, our very dear and beloved son, and Infantes, dukes, prelates, marquesses, counts, masters of orders, priors, commanders, and members of our council ... Mayors, and subcommanders, governors of castles, fortified and unfortified houses and all councillors and assistants, governors, alcaldes, bailiffs, judges, ... knights, esquires, officers and liege men of all the cities, towns, and places in our kingdoms and dominions, and of those which you may conquer and acquire, and the captains, masters, mates, officers, mariners and seamen, who now are or hereafter shall be our natural subjects, and each one and any one of them, that upon being discovered and the said islands and mainland in the said ocean acquired by you and the oath and formality requisite in such case having been made and done by you ... they shall have and hold you from thenceforth for the whole of your life, and your son and successor after you, and successor after successor for ever and ever, as our Admiral of the said ocean and as Viceroy and Governor of the said islands and mainland, which you the said Don Christopher Columbus may discover and acquire; and they shall treat with you, and with your said lieutenants whom you may place in the said offices of Admiral and Viceroy and Governor ... and shall pay and cause to be paid to you the salary, dues, and other things. ...

The Spanish explorers who followed Columbus proved that he had discovered a "new world." Lusting for gold and conquest, the Spaniards penetrated the jungles and climbed the mountains of Central and South America. They searched the coastline of the Gulf of Mexico in quest of a passage that would lead to the Pacific Ocean. Hernán Cortés invaded Mexico; Vasco Núñez de Balboa crossed the Isthmus of Panama; Francisco Pizarro conquered the Inca; and Juan Ponce de León, the first Spaniard to explore Florida, perished while searching for gold and a fountain of youth.

EXPLORATIONS OF HERNANDO DE SOTO

Hernando de Soto's expedition to Florida and the southeast frontier best illustrates the basic attitudes of the conquistador in the period of expansion and exploitation. There was no need to open prisons to find men willing to join him; many of his followers were gentlemen, lesser nobles of the sword—brave, reckless, and ruthless. Because they responded eagerly to his leadership, Soto never faced a mutiny or a threat of dissent. His expedition, carefully planned, showed the Spanish unmindful of danger, willing to face unknown hazards in strange lands, disdainful of a hostile native population, and capable of sustaining great physical hardships. But his expedition also revealed the Spanish frontiersman as taken in by fables of wealth, engaged in dastardly duplicity, victimized by incredible greed, and totally unaware of the ethical implications of his cruelty to the Indian. This account of Soto's journey by a member of his party, an anonymous Portuguese adventurer, vividly captures the spirit of the Spanish conquistador.[2]

On Sunday, May 18, of the year 1539, the *adelantado* [de Soto] left the Havana with his fleet consisting of nine ships—five vessels with topsails, two caravels, and two brigantines. For several days, they sailed attended by good weather. On Whitsunday, May 25, they sighted the land of Florida, and for fear of shoals anchored a league from shore. On Friday, May 30, they disembarked on the land of Florida, two leagues from the town of an Indian chief Ucita. They disembarked the two hundred and thirteen horses which they carried, in order to lighten the ships so that they would need less water. All the men landed and only the seamen stayed aboard, who in a week, by going up with the tide a short distance daily, brought the vessels near to the town. As soon as the men landed the camp was established on the shore near the bay which went up to the town. The captain general, Vasco Porcallo, taking with him seven horses, immediately over-ran the land for half a league round about and found six Indians who tried to oppose him with their arrows—the weapons with which they were accustomed to fight. The horsemen killed two of them and four [others] escaped, for the land being obstructed by woods and swamps, the horses, because of weakness from voyaging on the sea, became mired there and fell with their masters. That night following, the governor [de Soto] with one hundred men in brigantines came upon a town which he found without people, because the Christians were perceived as soon as they came within sight of the shore; and they saw many smokes along the whole coast, which the Indians make in order to give information to one another. On the following day, Luis de Moscoso, *maestre de campo*, set the men in order, those on horse in three squadrons—the vanguard, the battle line, and the rear guard—and in that way they marched that day and the next, going around great mud flats which come from the bay. They arrived at the town of Ucita, where the governor was, on Sunday, June first, the day of the Trinity. The town consisted of seven or eight houses. The chief's house stood near the beach on a very high hill which had been artificially built as a fortress. At the other side of the town was the temple and on top of it a wooden bird with its eyes gilded. Some pearls, spoiled by fire and of little value, were found there. The Indians bore them through in order to string them for beads, which are worn around the neck or arm, and they esteem them greatly. The houses were of wood and were covered with palm leaves. The governor was lodged in the houses of the chief and with him Vasco Porcallo and Luis de Moscoso; and in the other houses which

[2] James A. Robertson (trans. and ed.), *True Relation of the Hardships Suffered by Governor Hernando de Soto and certain Portuguese Gentlemen During the Discovery of the Province of Florida* (De Land, Fla.: The Florida Historical Society, 1933), vol. 1, pp. 31–38, 49–55, 72–73, 79–81, 91–97, 217–224, 226–229.

were located in the middle of the town, the chief constable, Baltasar de Gallegos. And apart in the same houses were placed the provisions carried on the ships. The other houses and the temple were destroyed, and a mess of every three or four built a small house in which they were lodged. The land round about was greatly encumbered and choked with a vast and lofty forest. The governor ordered it to be cut down for the space of a crossbow-shot about the town, in order that the horses might run and the Christians have the advantage of the Indians if the latter should by chance try to attack them by night. They posted footsoldiers as sentinels, in couples at each position along the roads and at proper places, who stood watch for four hours. The horsemen visited them and were ready to aid them if there should be an alarm. The governor appointed four captains over the horsemen and two over the footsoldiers. . . . While they were in the town of Ucita, the Indians whom Juan de Anasco had captured along the coast and whom the governor brought along as guides and interpreters escaped one night through the carelessness of two men who were guarding them. The governor and all were very sorry for this, for some forays had already been made, but no Indians could be captured, as the land was swampy and in many parts covered with lofty and thick woods.

The governor sent the chief constable, Baltasar de Gallegos, from the town of Ucita with forty horse and eighty foot into the interior to see whether any Indian could be captured; and in another direction, Captain Juan Rodriguez Lobillo, with fifty foot, most of them armed with swords and shields. . . . They went over swampy land where the horse could not go. A half league from camp they came upon some Indian huts near the river; [but] the people who were inside them plunged into the river. They captured four Indian women, and twenty Indians came at us and attacked us so stoutly that we had to retreat to the camp, because of their being (as they are) so skillful with their weapons. Those people are so warlike and so quick that they make no account of footsoldiers; for if these go for them, they flee, and when their adversaries turn their backs they are immediately on them. The farthest they flee is the distance an arrow is shot. They are never quiet but always running and crossing from one side to another so that the crossbows or the arquebuses cannot be aimed at them; and before a bowman can fire a shot, an Indian shoots three or four arrows, and very seldom does he miss what he shoots at. If the arrow does not find armor, it penetrates as deeply as a crossbow. The bows are very long and the arrows are made of certain reeds like canes, very heavy and so tough that a sharpened cane passes through a shield. Some are pointed with a fishbone, as sharp as an awl, and others with a certain stone like a diamond point. Generally when these strike against armor, they break off at the place where they are fastened in. Those of cane split and enter through the links of mail and are more hurtful. Juan Rodriguez Lobillo reached the camp with six men wounded, one of whom died. He brought the four Indian women whom he had captured in the quarters or huts. Baltasar de Gallegos, on going into the level terrain two leagues from the town, saw ten or eleven Indians. . . .

From the port of Espiritu Santo, where the governor was, he sent the chief constable, Baltasar de Gallegos, with fifty horse and thirty or forty foot to the province of Paracoxi, in order to note the disposition of the land that lay beyond and to send him word of what he found. . . . Baltasar de Gallegos reached Paracoxi and thirty Indians came to him on the part of the cacique who was absent from his town. . . . He asked them if they knew or had any information of any rich land where there was gold or silver. They said yes, that there was a province toward the west called Cale, and that the people of the land were hostile to others living in other lands where it was summer most of the year. That land had gold in abundance and when those people came to make war on the people of Cale, they wore hats of gold resembling helmets. . . . At this the governor and all those in the port with him received great joy, for they believed what the Indians said might be true. . . . He and all the rest of the men marched inland and reached Paracoxi . . . and from there . . . he took the road toward Cale. . . . He reached Cale and found the town without people. He seized three Indians who were spies. There he awaited the men who were coming behind, who were experiencing great hardship from hunger and bad roads as the land was very poor in maize, low, and very wet, swampy, and covered with dense forests, and the provisions brought from the port were finished. Wherever any village was found, there were some blites and he who came first gathered them and having stewed them with water and salt, ate them without anything else. Those who could not get any of them, gathered the stalks from the maize fields which being still young had no maize, and ate them. . . . As soon as they reached Cale, the governor ordered all the maize which was ripe in the fields to be taken, which was enough for three months. When they were gathering this, the Indians killed three Christians and one of two Indians who were captured told the governor that seven days journey farther on was a very large province with maize in abundance, called Apalache. He immediately set out from Cale with fifty horse. . . . [As for the men who were left behind] inasmuch as there was no one to serve them, the bread each one had to eat he ground in a mortar cannon or mortar made of a log, with a pestle like a window bar. Some sifted the meal though their coats of mail. The bread was baked in some flat pieces of earthern vessels which they set on fire, in the same way as I have already said was done in Cuba. It is so difficult to grind that many, who would not formerly eat it unless it was ground, ate the maize parched and sodden. . . . [After de Soto reached Apalache] a youth who said that he was not of that land, but that he was from another very distant one lying in the direction of the sunrise, and that some time ago he had come in order to visit [other] lands and that his land was called Yupaha and a woman ruled it; that the town where she lived was of wonderful size, and that the Chieftainess collected tribute from many of neighboring chiefs, some of whom gave her clothing and others gold in abundance. He told how it was taken from the mines, melted, and refined, just as if he had seen it done, or else the devil taught him; so that all who knew anything of this said it was impossible to give so good an account of it unless one had seen it; and all when they saw the signs he made believed whatever he said to be true.

On Wednesday, the 3d of March, 1540, the governor left Anhaica Apalacha. He ordered his men to provide themselves with maize for a journey of sixty leagues through uninhabited land. Those of horse carried the maize on their horses, and those of foot on their backs; for most of the Indians whom they had to serve them, being naked and in chains, died because of the hard life they suffered during that winter. . . . On April 4, the governor passed through a town, by name Altamaca; and on the tenth day of the month reached Ocute. The cacique sent him two thousand Indians bearing gifts, namely, many rabbits, partridges, maize bread, two hens and many dogs, which are esteemed among the Christians as if they were fat sheep because there was a great lack of meat and salt. Of this there was so much need and lack in many places and in many occasions that if a man fell sick, there was nothing with which to make him well; and he would waste away of an illness which could have been easily cured in any other place, until nothing but his bones were left and he would die of pure weakness, some saying: "If I had a bit of meat or some lumps of salt, I should not die." The Indians do not lack meat; for they kill many deer, hens, rabbits, and other game with their arrows. In this they have great skill, which the Christians do not have, and even if they had it, they had no time for it, for most of the time they were on the march, and they did not dare to turn aside from the paths. And because they lacked meat so badly, when the six hundred men of Soto arrived in any town, and found twenty or thirty dogs, he who got one and who killed it, thought he was not a little agile. And if he who killed one did not send his captain a quarter, the latter, if he learned of it, upbraided him and gave him to understand it in the watches or in any other matter of work that arose with which he could annoy him. . . .

[In early May, de Soto arrived at Cutifachiqui. The Chieftainess] came from the town in a carrying chair in which certain principal Indians carried her to the river. She entered a canoe with an awning at the stern and on the bottom of which was already spread a mat for her and above it two cushions one on top of the other, on which she seated herself. With her principal men and other canoes filled with Indians who accompanied her, she went to the place where the governor was. . . . And she presented him a quantity of clothing which she brought in the other canoes, namely blankets and skins. And from her neck drew a long string of pearl beads and threw it about the neck of the governor, exchanging with him many gracious words of affection and courtesy. . . . The cacica, observing that the Christians esteemed pearls, told the governor that he might order certain graves in that town to be examined, for he would find many, and that if he wished to send to the uninhabited towns, they could load all their horses. The graves of that town were examined and fourteen arrobas of pearls were found. . . . The youth told the governor that he was now beginning to enter the land of which he had spoken to him. . . . All the men were of the opinion that they should settle in that land as it was an excellent region, that if it were settled, all the ships from New Spain, and those from Peru, Santa Marta, and Tierra firme, on their way back to Spain, would come to take advantage of the stop there for their route passes by there; and as it is a good land and suitable for making profit. Since the governor's purpose was to seek another treasure like that of . . . Peru, he had no wish to content himself with good land or with pearls even though many of them were worth their weight in gold. . . . Thereupon, the governor determined to go in search of that land, and as he was a man, hard and dry of word, and although he was glad to listen and learn the opinion of all, after he had voiced his own opinion he did not like to be contradicted and always did what seemed best to him. Accordingly all conformed to his will, and although it seemed a mistake to leave the land, . . . no one had anything to say to him after his decision was learned. . . . [Led on by news of villages one beyond the other de Soto gradually traveled through the Southeast, eventually finding himself virtually lost, but on the banks of the Great River—the Mississippi.] The governor's grief was intense on seeing the small prospect he had for reaching the sea; and worse, according to the way in which his men and horses were diminishing, they could not be maintained in the land without succor. With that thought he fell sick, but before he took to his bed, he sent an Indian to tell the cacique of Quigaltam that he was the son of the sun and that wherever he went all obeyed him and did him service. He requested him to choose his friendship and come there where he was, for he would be glad to see him; and in token of love and obedience that he should bring him something of what was most estccmcd in that land. By the same Indian [the cacique] answered him saying that with respect to what he [de Soto] said about being the son of the sun, let him dry up the Great river and he would believe him. With respect to the rest [of what the governor had said], he was not accustomed to visit anyone. On the contrary, all of whom he had knowledge visited and served him and obeyed him and paid him tribute, either by force or their own volition. Consequently, if he [the governor] wished to see him, let him cross there. If he came in peace, he would welcome him with special good will; if he came in war he would await him in the town where he was, for not for him or any other would he move one foot backward. When the Indian came with this reply, the governor was already in bed, badly racked by fever. He was very angry that he was not in condition to cross the river forthwith and go in quest of him to see whether he could not lessen that arrogant demeanor. . . . In order that the Indians might fear him, the governor determined to send a captain to Nilco . . . in order that by treating them cruelly . . . [the Indians] should [not] dare to attack him. . . . The captain had order that no male Indian's life should be spared. So great was their confusion that not an Indian shot at a Christian. The cries of the women and little children were so loud that they deafened the ears of those who pursued them. A hundred or so Indians were killed there and many were badly wounded with the lances, who were let go in order that they might strike terror into those who did not happen to be there. There were men there so cruel and such butchers that they killed old men and young men and all they came upon without anyone offering them little or much resistance. . . . The governor realized within himself that the hour had come in which he must leave this present life. . . . Therefore he appointed Luis de Moscoso de Alavarado as their [the men of the party] captain general, and by all those who were present he was immediatly sworn and elected as governor. Next day, May 21, died the magnanimous, virtuous, and courageous captain, Don Hernando de Soto, governor of Cuba and *adelantado* of Florida, whom fortune exalted as she is wont to do with others, so that he might fall from a greater height. . . . Luis de Moscoso determined to conceal his death from the Indians, for Hernando de Soto had given them to understand that the Christians were immortal. Also because they knew him to be bold, wise, and courageous, if they should learn of his death, they would be emboldened to attack [the Spaniards] even though they were at peace. . . . Luis de Moscoso ordered him [de Soto's body] to be placed in a house where he was kept for three days; and . . . he ordered him to be buried at night inside at a gate of the town. And since the Indians had seen that he was sick and found him missing . . . and seeing he had been disturbed, looked and talked among themselves. Luis de Moscoso having learned this, ordered him disintered at night and a considerable quantity of sand was placed within the blankets in which he was shrouded, and he was taken in a canoe and cast into the middle of the river.

FRENCH-SPANISH RIVALRY IN FLORIDA

Despite Soto's ill-fated expedition, the Spanish, who wished to maintain their empire in the New World were compelled to defend Florida against foreign intruders. In 1564, ambitious French Protestant leaders, like the Huguenot Admiral Gaspard de Coligny, attempted to colonize Florida both to gain a foothold in Roman Catholic America and to provide a base from which to attack the Spanish treasure fleet. Hardly more than trespassers, inexperienced in living in the wilderness, and eager to enrich themselves at the expense of the Indians, the French found Florida inhospitable. The following account by the artist-cartographer Charles Lemoyne, who was taken to America to paint the landscape and the natives, tells of the conflicts between the Spanish and the French and demonstrates that the Indian was not the exclusive victim of European brutality on the frontier.[3]

Charles IX, King of France, having been notified by the Admiral de Chatillon [Coligny] that there was too much delay in sending forth the re-enforcements needed by the small body of French whom Jean Ribaud had left to maintain the French dominion in Florida, gave orders to the admiral to fit out such a fleet as was required for the purpose. The admiral, in the meanwhile, recommended to the king a noble man of the name of Renaud [Rebe] de Laudonnière; a person well known at court, and of varied abilities, though experienced not so much in military as in naval affairs. The king accordingly appointed him his own lieutenant, and appropriated for the expedition the sum of a hundred thousand francs. The admiral, who was a man endowed with all the virtues, and eminent for Christian piety, was so zealous for the faithful doing of the king's business, as to give special instructions to Laudonnière, exhorting him in particular to use all manner of diligence in doing his duty, and first of all, since he professed to be a religious man, to select the right sort of men, and such as feared God, to be of his company. He would do well, in the next place, to engage as many skilled mechanics of all kinds as possible. In order to give him better facilities for these purposes he received a royal commission, bearing the king's seal....

On the 20th of April, 1564, our three ships set sail from Havre de Grace, and steered directly for the Fortunate Islands, or as the seafaring men call them, the Canaries. Sailing thence, on the tropic we made the Antilles Islands, at one of which, called Dominica, we watered, losing however, two men. Making sail again, we reached the coast of Florida, or New France as it is called, on Thursday, 22d June.

M. de Laudonnière having reconnoitred the stream named by Ribaud the River May [Saint John's], and finding it easy of navigation for ships, and offering a suitable site for a fort, set promptly about preparing to erect one.... Meanwhile all the shore was occupied by immense numbers of men and women, who kept up fires, and against whom we naturally thought it necessary to be much on our guard. Gradually, however, it appeared that to injure us was the last thing in their thoughts: on the other hand, they showed numerous testimonies of friendship

---

[3]Frederick B. Perkins (trans.), *Narrative of Le Moyne, an Artist Who Accompanied the French Expedition to Florida under Laudonnière*, 1594 (Boston, 1875), pp. 1–5, 14–21.

and liking, being seized with great admiration at finding our flesh so different from their own. The commodities which we received from these new dealers were in great part such things as they valued most, being for the support of life or the protection of the body. Such were grains of maize roasted, or ground into flour, or whole ears of it; smoked lizards or other wild animals, such as they consider great delicacies; and various kinds of roots, some for food, and some for medicine. When they found out after a time that the French were more desirous of metals and minerals, some brought them. M. de Laudonnière, who soon perceived that our men were acting avariciously in their dealing, now forbade, on pain of death, any trading or exchange with Indians for gold, silver, or minerals, unless all should be put into a common stock for the benefit of all.

In the meantime several chiefs visited our commander, and signified to him that they were under the authority of a certain king named Saturioua, within the limits of whose dominions we were, whose dwelling was near us, and who could muster a force of some thousands of men. This information was thought good reason for hastening the completion of our fort. King Saturioua, himself, on his part, like a prudent commander, sent out his scouts from day to day, to see what we were about; and being advised by them that we had marked out a triangle by stretching cords, and were digging up the earth of the lines of it, he became desirous of seeing for himself. He sent forward, however, some two hours in advance of his own appearance, an officer with a company of a hundred and twenty able-bodied men, armed, with bows, arrows, clubs, and darts, and adorned, after the Indian manner, with their riches; such as feathers of different kinds, necklaces of a sort of shells, bracelets of fishes teeth, girdles of silver-colored balls, some round, some oblong; and having many pearls fastened on their legs. Many of them had also hanging to their legs round flat plates of gold, silver, or brass, so that in walking they tinkled like little bells. This officer, having made his announcement, proceeded to cause shelter to be erected on a small height near by, of branches of palms, laurels, mastics, and other odoriferous trees, for the accommodation of the king. From this point the king could see whatever was going on within our lines, and a few tents and military supplies and baggage, which we had not yet found time to get under cover; as our first business was to get our fort completed, rather than to put up huts, which could be easily erected at leisure afterwards.

M. de Laudonnière, upon receiving the message of the officer, so disposed his forces as to be prepared for a stout resistance in case of attack, although they had no ammunition on shore for their defence....

The king was accompanied by seven or eight hundred men, handsome, strong, well-made, and active fellows, the best-trained and swiftest of his force, all under arms as if on a military expedition. Before him marched fifty youths with javelins and spears; and behind these, and next to himself, were twenty pipers, who produced a wild noise, without musical harmony or regularity, but only blowing away with all their might, each trying to be the loudest. Their instruments were nothing but a thick sort of reeds, or canes, with two openings; ... like pipe-organs or whistles. On his right hand limped his soothsayer, and on the left was his chief counsellor: without which two personages he never proceeded on any matter whatever. He entered the place prepared for him alone, and sat down in it after the Indian manner; that is, by squatting on the ground like an ape or any other animal. Then having looked all around, and having observed our little force drawn up in line of battle, he ordered M. de Laudonnière and d'Ottigny [who acted as second in command] to be invited into his tabernacle, where he delivered to them a long oration, which they understood only in part. He did, however, inquire who we were, why we had landed on his territory rather than elsewhere, and what was our purpose. M. de Laudonnière replied by the mouth of Capt. La Caille, who, as was mentioned, had some knowledge of the language, that he was sent by a most powerful king, called the King of France, to offer a treaty by which he should become a friend to the king here, and to his allies, and an enemy to their enemies; an announcement which the chief received with much pleasure. Gifts were then exchanged in pledge of perpetual friendship and alliance. This done, the king approached nearer to our force, and greatly admired our arms, particularly the arquebuses. Upon coming up to the ditch of our fort, he took measurements both within and without; and perceiving that the earth was being taken from the ditch, and laid into a rampart, he asked what was the use of the operation. He was told in reply that we were going to put up a building that would hold all of us, and that many small houses were to be erected inside it; at which he expressed admiration, and a desire to see it completed as soon as possible. To this end, he was therefore asked to give us the help of some of his followers in work. He consented, and sent us eighty of his stoutest men, most used to labor, who were of great assistance to us, and much hastened the completion both of our fort and cabins. Having given his orders about this, he himself went away.

While all this was going on, every man of our force—noblemen, soldiers, artificers, sailors, and all—was hard at work to get our post in a state of defence against an enemy and to get up a shelter from the weather; and every man was making sure, from the amounts of the gifts and trading so far, that he would quickly become rich.

The fort now being completed, and a residence for himself, as well as a large building to contain the provisions and other indispensable military supplies, M. de Laudonnière proceeded to shorten the allowance of food and drink: so that, after three weeks, only one glass of spirit and water, half and half, was given out daily per man; and as for provisions, which it had hoped would be abundant in this New World, none at all were found; and unless the natives had not furnished us from their own stores from day to day, some of us must assuredly have perished from starvation, especially such as did not know how to use fire-arms in hunting.

In the meanwhile M. de Laudonnière ordered his chief artificer, Jean des Hayes of Dieppe, to build two shallops, to be, according to my recollection, of thirty-five or forty feet keel, for exploring in the upper waters of the river, and along the seacoast; which were in good season nearly completed.

But by this time the noblemen who had come from France to the New World from ambitious motive only, and with splendid outfits, began to be greatly dissatisfied at finding that they realized none of the advantages which they had imagined, and promised themselves; and complaints began daily to be made by many of them. On the other part M. de Laudonnière himself, who was a man too easily influenced by others, evidently fell into the hands of three or four parasites, and treated with contempt the soldiers, who were just those whom he should have considered. And what is far worse, indignation began to be felt by many who professed the desire of living according to the doctrine of the reformed gospel, for the reason that they found themselves with a minister of God's word.

But to return to King Saturioua. The chief

sent messengers to M. de Laudonnière, not only to confirm the league which had been made, but also to procure the performance of its conditions, namely, that the latter was to be the friend of the king's friends, and the enemy of his enemies; as he was now organizing an expedition against them. M. de Laudonnière gave an ambiguous reply to these ambassadors; for we had learned, in the course of an extended voyage up the main stream of the River of May, that the enemy of our neighbor King Saturioua was far more powerful than he; and that, moreover, his friendship was indispensable to us for reason that the road to the Apalatcy [the Appalachian] Mountains (which we were desirous of reaching, because we were informed that most of the gold and silver which we had received in trade was brought thence) lay through his dominions. Besides, some of our people were already with him, who had already sent the fort a good deal of gold and silver, and were negotiating with him; for M. de Laudonnière had orders to treat with this great king, Outina, on the same terms as above mentioned.

King Saturioua, having received this cold answer, now came to the fort, which was called Fort Carolina, with some twelve or fifteen hundred men; but finding to his surprise, that things were greatly changed, that he could no longer get across the ditch, but that there was only one entrance to the post, and that a very narrow one, he . . . found Capt. La Caille; who announced to him, that, for the purpose of an interview, he would not be admitted into the fort unless without his men, or at most with not more than twenty of such as he might select. In astonishment at this information, he, however, dissimulated, and entered the fort with twenty of his followers, when everything was exhibited to him. He was terribly frightened himself at the sound of the drums and trumpets, and at the reports of the brass cannon which were fired in his presence; and, when he was told that all his forces had run away, he readily believed it, as he would gladly have been farther off himself. This, indeed made our name very great through all those parts; and, in fact, much more than the reality was believed of us. He did, however, after all, notify M. de Laudonnière that his faith was pledged, that his own (King Saturioua's) forces were ready, that his supplies were at hand, and that his own subordinate chiefs were assembled. Failing, however, to obtain what he wished, he set out on his expedition with his own men. . . .

There was great scarcity with us, because for various reasons the Indians, both those near by and those farther off, all broke off their intercourse with us. One of these reasons was, that they obtained nothing from us in exchange for their provisions; another that they suffered much violence from our men in their expeditions after supplies. Some were even senseless, not to say malignant, enough to burn their houses, with the notion that by doing so we should be more promptly supplied. But the difficulty daily increased, until we had to go three or four miles before we could meet a single Indian. Then there took place moreover, a campaign against the powerful chief Outina. . . . In short . . . the condition of want to which they were reduced would be [described as] pitiful. . . .

After, however, some of us had actually perished of hunger, and all the rest of us were starved until our skin cleaved to our bones, M. de Laudonnière at last gave up hope of receiving reenforcements from France, for which he had now been waiting eighteen months, and called a general council to deliberate on the means of returning to France. It was herein finally concluded to refit as well as possible the third of our ships, and to raise her sides with planks so as to enlarge her capacity; and, while the artificers were employed on the work, the soldiers were to collect provisions along the coast....

After, however, we were quite ready for the voyage, and when we had been for only three weeks waiting for a fair wind to depart from the province, there unexpectedly arrived a fleet of seven ships, commanded by the famous Jean de Ribaud ... who was sent out to succeed M. de Laudonnière, and for the carrying on of the King's designs. This arrival so wholly unexpected, filled us all with joy.... But the joy was brief, as we quickly found....

Seven or eight days after Ribaud's arrival, while all the gentlemen, soldiers, and sailors, except a few men left in charge of the four larger ships, were on shore, and occupied about putting up houses, and rebuilding the fort, about four o'clock in the afternoon some soldiers were walking on the seashore saw six ships steering towards our four which were at anchor. They instantly sent information to Ribaud.... [Our ships] had at once cut their cables, and gone to sea under all sail; the six thereupon weighed anchor and sailed in pursuit.... This made us uneasy enough all the following night during which Ribaud ordered all the small craft to be made ready, and stationed five or six hundred arquebusiers on the shore in readiness to embark if needed. Thus the night passed away, and the next day until about noon, when the largest of our four ships, "The Trinity," came in sight, steering directly for us.... But Ribaud fearing that the enemy might have taken the ships, and were trying to trap us, would not risk his men, eager though they were to go aboard....

[Finding the ships in French hands], Ribaud at once called a council of his chief subordinates.... The more prudent part of this assembly would have preferred to complete the erection and arming of the fort as soon as possible, while Laudonnière's men, who knew the country, should be sent against the Spaniards; ... Ribaud, however, after perceiving this plan to be generally acceptable, said,

Gentlemen, I have heard your views, and desire now to state my own. First, however, you should be informed that, a little before our leaving France, I received a letter from the admiral, at the end of which he had written with his own hand as follows: "M. de Ribaud, we have advices that the Spaniard means to attack you. Do not yield a particle to him, and you will do right." I must therefore declare plainly to you that it may result from your plan that the Spaniards will not await any assault from our brave men, but will at once escape aboard ship, by which we should lose our opportunity of destroying those who are seeking to destroy us. The better plan seems to me to be, to put all our soldiers on board our four ships now at anchor, and seize at once upon their ships, while anchored where they have landed....

M. de Laudonnière, who was by this time familiar with the climate of the country, now suggested that the weather should be carefully taken into account before putting the men on board ship again; as at that time of the year a species of whirlwinds or typhoons, which sailors call "hourigan," from time to time come on suddenly, and inflict terrible damage on the coast. For this reason he favored the former of the purposed plans.... Ribaud alone, however, condemning all their reasons, persisted in his own determination. ... Not satisfied with his own force, M. de Ribaud asked for Laudonnière's captains and ensign, whom the latter could not well refuse to send with him; and all of Laudonnière's men, when they saw their standardbearer going, insisted on going with him....

All the troops being now on board, a fair wind for an hour or two was all that was needed to bring us up with the enemy; but just as the anchors were about to be weighed the wind changed, and blew directly against us, exactly from the point where the enemy were, for two whole days and nights, while we waited for it to become fair. . . . But just as they [Ribaud's ships] had weighed anchor, and set sail, there came up all at once so terrible a tempest that the ships had to put out to sea as quickly as possible for their own safety; and, the storm continuing, they were driven to the northward some fifty miles from the fort, where they were all wrecked on some rocks and destroyed. All the ships companies were, however, saved. . . . The Spanish ships were also wrecked and destroyed in the same gale.

As the storm continued, the Spaniards, who were informed of the embarkation of French forces, suspected, what was not so very far from the truth, that the troops had been cast away and destroyed, in it, and fancied that they could easily take our fort. Although the rains continued as constant and heavy as if the world was to be again overwhelmed with a flood, they set out, and marched all night towards us. On our part, those few who were able to bear arms were the same night on guard; for, out of about one hundred and fifty persons remaining in the fort, there were scarcely twenty in a serviceable condition, since Ribaud . . . had carried off with him all the able soldiers except fourteen or fifteen who were sick or mutilated, or wounded in the campaign against Outina. All the rest . . . had never even heard a gun fired, . . . and, besides, there were some women, whose husbands, most of them, had gone on board the ships. M. de Laudonnière himself was sick in bed.

When the day broke, . . . the officer of the guard, pitying the drenched and exhausted condition of the men, who were worn out with long watching permitted them to take a little rest; but they had scarcely time to go to their quarters, and lay aside their arms, when the Spaniards, guided by a Frenchman named Francois Jean, . . . attacked the fort at the double quick in three places at once, penetrated the works without resistance, and, getting possession of the place of arms, drew up their forces there. Then parties searched the soldier's quarters, killing all whom they found, so that awful outcries and groans arose from those who were being slaughtered. For my own part. . . . I saw that nothing was visible except slaughter, and that the place of arms itself was held by the Spaniards, I turned back at once and made for one of the embrasures, where I knew I could get out. . . . I leaped down into the ditch, crossed it, and went on alone for some distance over rising ground into a piece of woods, until, having reached a higher part of the hill . . . [I decided to] make for the seashore . . . and try . . . [to] discover something of the two small vessels which Ribaud sent into the river to be used in disembarking the provisions he brought from France.

I came upon a Frenchman from Rouen, La Crete by name, a Belgian called Elie des Planques, and M. de Laudonnière's maid-servant, who had been wounded in the breast. . . . We found M. de Laudonnière himself, and another man named Bartholomew, who had received a deep sword cut in the neck; and after a time we picked up others, until there were fourteen or fifteen of us in all . . . We travelled in water more than waist-deep for two days and two nights through swamps and reeds; . . . On the third day, by the blessing of God, and with the help of the sailors, we got safe on board. . . .

This done, we set sail from Florida, ill manned and ill provisioned. . . .

As for the fate of Ribaud after his shipwreck, as I was not present with him, I can only relate what I heard from a sailor of

Dieppe, who escaped from the Spaniards, as will be mentioned. . . . Although all their weapons had been lost in the wreck, Ribaud made a noble speech to his men, setting forth that it was their duty to bear with calmness the calamity which they had suffered by the will of God; for he was a man of piety, and a fine speaker. . . . It was decided to set out for the fort, from which they were about fifty miles away. . . . Having, however, courageously made their way through all obstacles, they finally reached a point some four or five miles, as well as the soldiers from Laudonnière's force could judge, from the fort. Ribaud now determined not to advance any nearer. . . . Upon hearing the story [that Fort Carolina was in Spanish hands], it may easily be imagined how great was the grief of Ribaud and all his company and how utterly he was at a loss what to say or do. . . . He foresaw the cruelty of the Spaniards; and yet perceived that most of his force would perish by starvation and exposure in the woods; but, before resolving on any definite step, it was decided to send some messenger to the fort, to learn something of the intentions of the Spaniards, and what disposal had been made of the Frenchmen in the fort. . . . [At a meeting between French and Spanish officers] the French asked what had become of the men left in the fort. The Spaniards replied that their commander, who was a humane and clement person, had sent them all to France in a large ship abundantly supplied, and that they might say to Ribaud that he and his men should be used equally well. . . . Ribaud, on hearing it, believed too hastily this story about his men having been sent back to France, and summoned another council. Here most of the soldiers began to cry out, "Let us go, let us go! What is to hinder our going over to them at once. . . . Others, more prudent, said that they could never put faith in Spaniards; for, they urged, if there were no other reason than the hatred which they bear to us on account of our religion, they assuredly will not spare us.

Ribaud . . . perceiving that most were of his mind, that it was best to surrender to the Spaniards, decided to . . . ask, in the name of the lieutenant of the king of France, for a safe-conduct, and to announce that, if the Spanish leader would make oath to spare all their lives, they would come in and throw themselves at his feet. . . . [The Spanish leader, Menendez] not only pledged his faith . . . but made oath in the presence of all his men, and drew up a writing sealed with his seal. . . .

Ribaud . . . having made an excellent speech to his people, and all having joined in offering prayer to God, gave orders to proceed, and with all his company came down to the bank of the river near the fort. Ribaud, himself, and d'Ottigny, Laudonnière's lieutenant, were first led into the fort by themselves; the rest were halted about a bowshot from the fort, and were all tied up in fours, back to back; from which and other indications, they quickly perceived that their lives were lost. Ribaud asked to see the governor . . . but he spoke to deaf ears. . . . A Spanish soldier finally came in, and asked if he were the French commander, "Ribaud." The answer was, "yes." The man asked again, if Ribaud did not expect, when he gave an order to his soldiers, that they should obey; to which he said again, "Yes."—"I propose to obey the orders of my commander also," replied the Spaniard; "I am ordered to kill you"; and with that he thrust a dagger into his breast. . . . When this was done men were detailed to kill all the rest . . . which they proceeded to do without delay meanwhile calling them Lutherans, and enemies of God. . . . In this manner they were all most cruelly murdered in violation of an oath, except a drummer . . . a fifer . . . a fiddler . . . and one sailor escaped . . . being the same who related to me this narrative.

The Laudonnière episode brought a bloody denouement to French aspirations for empire and fortune in Florida. Spain, shifting its emphasis from conquest to colonization, relied on what has been called the mission system. Across the borderlands of its vast empire, a network of priests labored to convert the native populations from "warlike pagans" to "docile Christians." The popular image of these priests varies between that of the benign friar in an era of tolling bells, praying Indians, and lovely missions to that of a group of grasping exploiters, eager to break down the cultural unity and identity of the Indians. But on the southeast frontier the friars, or the religious as they were called, debated and defended the Christian value system and with stoic calm, resignation, and intense personal bravery, faced the hazards of living among primitive people.

SPANISH MISSIONS IN FLORIDA:
THE UPRISING OF 1597

The chronicler here, Luis Oré, a Spanish-American born in Peru in 1554, achieved fame on both sides of the Atlantic for his work as a missionary. This account, although unpretentious in manner, ranks the Franciscan martyrs in Florida with the conquistadors. There is, of course, irony in the fact that the order of the gentle Saint Francis should find itself on the firing line of the frontier. The selection that follows tells of an uprising in Guale (Florida) in 1597.[4]

---

[4] Luis Geronimo Oré, *The Martyrs of Florida* ("Franciscan Studies," No. 18), translated and with notes by Maynard R. Geiger, O.F.M. (New York: J. F. Wagner, Inc., 1936), pp. 73–77, 91–92, 100–101.

These religious friars encountered great difficulty in reducing those Indians, because all had exchanged their women with those of others, and had two or more children by them during the time of their apostasy. They lived with them according to their desires more than with their lawful wives. Things were so bad that the friars could not get the Indians to an agreement. Some of the Christian women had gone to the pagans in the interior and had given birth as a result of these unions to two or three children. Their husbands had entered into relations with women here by whom they also had children. Because they were Christians and had been married by the Church, it was imperative that they give up the women and live as Christians. And in this manner there was more difficulty than if they had to be converted for the first time. The fathers told the Indians: "Leave this woman who is not yours." To this the Indian would reply: "Bring me mine who is among the pagans and make her love me and I shall leave this one." But the religious answered thus: "Until we bring her, leave this one." Again the Indian answered: "If I leave her, I will not have anyone to give me to eat and if I do not enter the house where my children are, and if I do not bring them food and wood they will perish." The religious were not able to solve the situation by any remedy for it was grave and onerous, so they were discouraged. They turned to God in prayer and besought Him to remedy the affair. He favored them so that gradually He brought them back and on His part evened out the difficulty, taking some of them out of this world to the other. Thus partners became free of their former alliance and were able to contract anew.

Two years after the friars arrived in Florida, namely in the year 1597, the Indians of Guale, instigated by the devil who is adverse to all good works, seized upon an occasion [to revolt]. One of the fathers would not permit an Indian youth, who was a Christian and heir to the caciquedom, to have more than one wife to whom he was married. Because he was a Christian, he should live as a Christian and not as a pagan. He was told that according to the Christian law, he could not have more than one wife and at that no other than the one to whom he was married.

This *cacique* and two other Indians, like him, given to the same immoral practice, went into the interior among the pagan, without saying anything or without obtaining permission as they were wont to do on other occasions. After a few days they returned at night with many other pagan Indians, painted and smeared with red paste, and with feathers on their heads. This among them is a sign of cruelty and slaughter.

That night when the Indians arrived neither the priest nor those in the town knew anything about it. When, in the morning, the Indians opened the priest's house, they found them praying; then without waiting to give any explanation, they killed the priest with a stone hatchet which they call *macana*, but which is known as *champi* in the language of the Incas of Cuzco. This happened at Tolomato, the chief place of the district. . . .

When this religious was dead, the Indians began to exchange women in order to give rein to their sensuality and unlawful pleasures. A command was given that the head of the dead religious be placed on the end of a lance and set up at the landing place, and that the body be taken by two Indians to the woods, to be hidden so that the Christians would not find it. Hence it is that the body has not been found.

Afterwards they sent notice to the isle of Guale, which was near, commanding the *cacique* to kill two friars who were in his territory. When the *cacique* heard of this, he was much grieved, nor did he wish to fulfill the command. Therefore he warned the lay brother of what he had learned about the Indians' deeds, advising him that he and the Father Commissary go to the Isle of San Pedro. . . .

The *cacique* advised the lay brother again the next day, but not being able to believe such a thing, the brother reacted the same as the first time. On the third day, the Indians of the conspiracy came and told the *cacique* that they were coming to have him kill the friars; otherwise they would have to kill the *cacique*. The *cacique* answered he had no reason for killing the friars and that if they cared to overlook them, and would leave them free, he would give the Indians as much as he had. The Indians agreed to answer that they had come to kill and that they intended to carry out their intention. The *cacique* then went to Fray Miguel and with tears told him what was happening and that he could not rescue them and that he and his people were going to the woods and to weep for them as if they were his own brothers.

When Fray Miguel and his companions saw this, they turned to prayer to await the critical hour of death. He said Mass and afterwards spent more than four hours in prayer. Presently the Indians sacked the house, then came first the lay brother and gave a blow with the hatchet or *macana*, from which he soon died. They did not dare approach Fray Miguel, owing to the respect they had for him. But a pagan Indian came and gave him a heavy blow with a *macana* and stunned him. All the faithful of the town came, wishing to defend and rescue him, but another pagan Indian came from behind and gave him another very heavy blow which cut his brains to pieces. This pagan Indian, within a few days, gave way to despair and hung himself from a height with a cord of his bow. This caused great wonder among the Indians.

The Christian Indians buried the body [of the priest] at the foot of a very high cross which he himself erected. Six years afterwards when [the Spaniards] came to look for his bones they found them at the foot of the cross, as the Indians told them.

Father Avila was at his mission whither the Indians went with the set determination to kill him. They arrived at night and since they found him already retired, they knocked at the door, feigning they were bringing a letter from his prelate. . . . Then the Indians commenced to open the door with violence, which they in fact finally succeeded [in doing]. . . . They shot at him with three arrows and left him for dead. . . . Soon there came to him an Indian, feigning charity, who took off his habit and said to him: "Take off this habit which is full of blood and I shall wash it for you."

The Indian took it off and put it on himself, so that the religious was naked. Nevertheless, the Indian was of use to him, in that he was a young chieftain, for he then liberated him from the fury of the others, and so the religious was not killed. The Chieftain persuaded the Indians that they should take the religious along with them and give him a more cruel form of death, or that he should remain a captive among them to serve them, since they had already left him for dead.

It is incredible what this religious experienced in the year of his captivity among those barbarians. He was naked in a climate which is as rigorous as that of Madrid, nor did he have anyone to heal his wounds, nor did he have any cloth for bandages to cover or bind them. . . . The Indians determined to burn him, tied to a stake which was to serve as a firebrand, with a great quantity of twigs and sticks which they had brought together for the purpose. In this predicament, an Indian woman came forth and freed the religious from the pillar, for she had a son among the hostages, held by the military. She declared: "This man I must have in place of my son, for he will bring my son to me; and if I deliver him from death, the governor will not order my son to be killed." At this, they delivered him from death after which he was somewhat more free.

Great was the persecution he sustained at the hands of the boys who many times came only short of killing or hanging him in view of the fact that when the religious had taught them Christian doctrine and reading, he had sometimes struck them. The Indians made him serve as a slave in the community house. . . . [Avila later recounted:] They tried to use force on me to make me abandon my law and accept that of the Indians, and marry an Indian after their manner. This I answered with contradiction and with great spirit and feeling, confounding the Indians in such a way that they marvelled at the spirit and liberty I used in speaking to them and contradicting them. . . . [But the Indians argued]

You will never see the Spaniards again, nor they you; leave your law and become an Indian and you will enjoy what we enjoy; you will have a wife or more if you wish; furthermore, in the other life you will enjoy what you enjoy here, for we know that he who has been miserable and mean in this life, will be the same in the other. This is our belief. Give up the things you teach us for they are foolish. Here we are bringing this Indian woman, young and beautiful; marry her and you will have a happy life and thus reward yourself.

While they were speaking and acting in this manner, the Indian girl brought decayed palm leaves from the woods, similar to straw, made a bed for [me] and called [me] to dine. As soon as I saw this, I perceived the persecution of the devil who did not leave any occasion pass, in order to tempt me and make me disconsolate. I had recourse to God in prayer on this occasion and with tears that fell from my eyes, begged him to give me grace to deliver me from so diabolical a temptation ... I fled to the woods. [Avila finally escaped this test. When the governor of Guale heard of the uprising he ordered a reprisal.] One hundred Spanish soldiers and two hundred friendly Indians went out ... and when they entered the towns [in Guale] they found the houses of the fathers burned, and many others destroyed or tenantless.... From an Indian whom they apprehended they learned that the whole population was where Father Avila ... was in captivity.... The governor rescued him and freed him from that miserable slavery in which the barbarous Indians held him.

Although the Spanish mission frontier suffered from occasional setbacks, such as the uprising in Guale, the priests steadily expanded their influence among the Indians. Franciscan friars established missions that, by 1650, made it possible for Spain to control the Southeast with only a few scantily manned forts. Where the conquistador failed, the friars succeeded.

BEGINNINGS OF THE FRENCH FUR TRADE

While the Spanish consolidated their holdings in the South, the French, eager to profit from the fishing and fur trades, directed their efforts toward the St. Lawrence Valley. Jacques Cartier had staked France's claim in 1534, but more than seventy years elapsed before a group of French merchant adventurers—lured by the royal promise of a monopoly of the fur trade—established a permanent settlement. The driving spirit in early French explorations was Samuel de Champlain, and under his direction Frenchmen gradually mastered the techniques for survival on the frontier. In 1608, after his first attempt at colonization at Ste. Croix had failed because of the harsh climate, Champlain selected the site for the city of Quebec.

Champlain's contributions were both positive and negative: he not only helped bring the first Jesuit missionaries to Canada but also alienated the Iroquois Indians by using firearms against them while a member of an Algonkin raiding party. The episode had enormous significance in the growth of the fur trade because it turned the upper Great Lakes region into a battleground where Iroquois and Algonkin fought for control. Champlain's journal, perceptive, imaginative, and lucid, dramatizes the personal lives and rivalries among the French in Canada. He recounted an episode of 1604, which shows how he formed Indian friendships:[5]

Now I will drop this discussion to return to the savages who had conducted me to the falls of the river ... [and] who went to notify Bessabez, their chief, and other savages, who in turn proceeded to another little river to inform their own, named Cabahis, and give him notice of our arrival.

The 16th of the month there came to us thirty savages on assurances given them by those who had served us as guides. There came also to us the same day the above named Bessabez with six canoes. As soon as the savages who were on land saw him coming they all began to sing, dance, and jump until he had landed. Afterwards, they all seated themselves in a circle on the ground, as is their custom, when they wished to celebrate a festivity, or an harangue is to be made. Cabahis, the other chief, arrived also a little later with twenty or thirty of his companions, who withdrew to one side and greatly enjoyed seeing us, as it was the first time they had seen Christians. A little while after, I

[5] William L. Grant (ed.), *The Voyages of Samuel De Champlain* (New York, 1907), pp. 49–50, 202–205, 208–211.

went on shore with my companions and two of our savages who served as interpreters. I directed the men in our barque to approach near the savages, and hold their arms in readiness to do their duty in case they notice any movement of these people against us. Bessabez, seeing us on land, bade us sit down, and began to smoke with his companions, as they usually do before an address. They presented us with venison and game.

I directed our interpreter to say to our savages that they should cause Bessabez, Cabahis, and their companions to understand that Sieur de Monts [Champlain's patron] had sent me to see them, and also their country, and that he desired to preserve friendship with them and to reconcile them with their enemies, the Souriquois . . . , and moreover that he desired to inhabit their country and show them how to cultivate it, in order that they might not continue to lead so miserable a life as they were doing, and some other words on the same subject. This our savages interpreted to them, at which they signified their great satisfaction, saying that no greater good could come to them than to have our friendship, and that they desired to live in peace with their enemies, and that we should dwell in their land, in order that they might in the future more than ever before engage in hunting beavers, and give us a part of them in return for our providing them with things which they wanted. After he finished his discourse, I presented them with hatchets . . . , caps, knives, and other little knickknacks, when we separated from each other. All the rest of this day and the following night, until break of day, they did nothing but dance, sing, and make merry, after which we traded for a certain number of beavers. Then each party returned, Bessabez with his companions on the one side, and we on the other, highly pleased at having made the acquaintance of this people. . . .

[By the time of Champlain's 1611 voyage not only were the Indians more sophisticated in the trade but also there was intense competition among French traders.] On going ashore [at Quebec] I found Sieur du Parc who had spent the winter at the settlement. He and all his companions were very well, and had not suffered any sickness. Game, both large and small, had been abundant during the entire winter, as they told me. I found there the Indian captain, named Batiscan, and some Algonquins, who said they were waiting for me, being unwilling to return to Tadoussac without seeing me. I proposed to them to take one of our company to the Trois Rivières to explore the place, but being unable to obtain anything from them this year I put it off until the next. Still I did not fail to inform myself particularly regarding the origin of the people living there, of which they told me with exactness. I asked them for one of their canoes, which they were unwilling to part with on any terms, because of their own need of it. . . .

Meanwhile I urged on the repairs to our barque. When it was ready, a young man from La Rochelle, named Tresart, asked me to permit him to accompany me to the above mentioned fall. This I refused, replying that I had special plans of my own, and that I did not wish to conduct any one to my prejudice, adding that there were other companies than mine there, and that I did not care to open up a way and serve as a guide, and that he could make the voyage well enough alone and without help.

The same day I set out from Quebec, and arrived at the great fall on the twenty-eighth of May. But I found none of the savages who had promised me to be there on this day. . . . After examining the two shores, both in the woods and on the river bank, in order to find a spot favorable for the location of a settlement, and get a place ready for building, I went some eight leagues by land along the great fall and through the woods, which are very open, as far as a lake, whither our savages, conducted me. Here I observed the country carefully. But in all that I saw, I found no place more favorable than a little spot to which barques and shallops can easily ascend, with the help of a strong wind or by taking a winding course, in consequence of the strong current. But above this place, which we named La Place Royale, at the distance of a league from Mount Royal, there are a great many little rocks and shoals, which are very dangerous. . . . Formerly savages tilled these lands, but they abandoned them on account of their wars, in which they were constantly engaged. There is also a large number of other fine pastures, where any number of cattle can graze. There are also various kinds of trees found in France, together with many vines, nut and plum trees, cherries, strawberries, and other kinds of good fruit. . . . Fish are very abundant, including all varieties we have in France, and many very good ones which we do not have. Game is also plenty, the birds being of various kinds. There are stags, hinds, does, caribous, rabbits, lynxes, bears, beavers, also other small animals, and all in such large numbers, that while we were at the fall we were abundantly supplied with them. . . .

On the first day of June, Pont Grave arrived at the fall, having been unable to accomplish anything at Tadoussac. A numerous company attended and followed after him to share in the booty, without the hope of which they would have been far in the rear. . . .

On the thirteenth day of the month two hundred Charioquois savages, together with the captains, Ochatequin, Iroquet, and Tregouaroti, brother of our savage, brought back my servant [apparently Étienne Brulé who had spent the winter with them]. . . . As they were approaching slowly and in order, our men prepared to salute them, with a discharge of arquebuses, muskets, and small pieces. When they were at hand they all set to shouting together, and one of the chiefs gave orders that they should make their harangue, in which they greatly praised us, commending us as truthful, inasmuch as I had kept the promise to meet them at this Fall. After they had made three more shouts, there was a discharge of musketry twice from thirteen barques . . . that were there. This alarmed them so, that they begged me to assure them that there should be no more firing, saying that the greater part of them had never seen Christians, not heard thunderings of that sort, and that they were afraid of its harming them, but that they were greatly pleased to see our savage in health, whom they supposed to be dead, as had been reported by some Algonquins. . . . The savage commended the treatment I had shown him in France, and the remarkable objects he had seen, at which all wondered, and went away quietly to their cabins, expecting that on the next day I would show them the place where I wished to have them dwell. . . .

The next day I showed them a spot for their cabins, in regard to which the elders and principal ones consulted very privately. After their long consultation they sent for me alone and my servant, who had learned their language very well. They told him they desired a close alliance with me, and were sorry to see here all these shallops [the boats of other French traders], and that our savage had told them he did not know them all nor their intentions, and that it was clear that they were attracted only by their desire of gain and their avarice, and that when their assistance was needed they would refuse it, and would not act as I did in offering to go with my companions to their country and assist them, all of which I had given them proofs in the past.... After considerable conversation, they made a present of a hundred castors [beaver skins], I gave them in exchange other kinds of merchandise. They told there were more than four hundred savages of their country who had purposed to come, but had been prevented by the following representations of an Iroquois prisoner, who had belonged to me, but had escaped to his own country. He had reported, they said, that I had given him his liberty and some merchandise, and that I purposed to go to the Fall with six hundred Iroquois to meet the Algonquin and kill them all, adding that the fear aroused by this intelligence had alone prevented them from coming. I replied that the prisoner in question had escaped without my leave, that our savage knew very well how he went away, and that there was no thought of abandoning their alliance ... since I had engaged in war with them, and sent my servant to their country to foster their friendship, which was still farther confirmed by my promise to them in so faithful a manner.

They replied that, so far as they were concerned, they had never thought of this, that they were well aware that all this talk was far from truth, and that if they had believed the contrary they would not have come, but that the others were afraid, never having seen a Frenchman except my servant. They told me also that three hundred Algonquin would come in five or six days, if we would wait for them, to unite with themselves in war against the Iroquois; that, however, they would return without doing so unless I went. I talked a great deal about the source of the great river and their country, and they gave me detailed information about their rivers, falls, lakes and lands, as also about the tribes living there, and what is to be found in the region. Four of them assured me that they had seen a sea at a great distance from their country, but that it was difficult to go there, not only on account of the wars, but of the intervening wilderness. They told me also that, the winter before, some savages had come from the direction of Florida, beyond the country of the Iroquois, who lived near our ocean, and were in alliance with these savages. In a word they made me a very exact statement, indicating by drawings all the places where they had been, and taking pleasure in talking to me about them; and for my part I did not tire of listening to them, as they confirmed points in regard to which I had been in doubt. After all this conversation was concluded, I told them that we would trade for the few articles they had, which was done the next day. Each one of the barques carried away its portion; we on our side had all the hardship and venture; the others, who had not troubled themselves about any exploration had the booty, the only thing that urges them to activity, in which they employ no capital and venture nothing.

By the opening of the seventeenth century, Europeans had established the first frontiers in Florida and Canada. Their hold was tenuous. The French settled the tiny village of Quebec, sheltered by the north bank of the St. Lawrence, where eager and competitive traders sought Indians rich in beaver to trade for Europe's tools and gimcracks. The Spanish held the town of St. Augustine, surrounded by mission stations that served restive Indians who were still uncertain of the meaning of the white man's coming. Both the Spanish and the French were developing their own techniques for survival and success on the frontier, but in each instance a high price was paid for this mastery. As the first French and Spanish experiences proved, the Europeans were compelled to make dramatic adjustments not only in their style of life but also in their value system.

CHAPTER 3 | *The English Southern Frontier, 1607-1700*

While the Spaniards and Frenchmen devised techniques for mastering the American frontier environment, the English, too, sought to share in the profits of the New World. English navigators searched for a Northwest Passage to Asia; English fishermen worked the foggy Newfoundland banks; and Sir Francis Drake's Elizabethan sea dogs turned pirate and privateer at the expense of Spain's treasure fleets. By the early 1580s, Queen Elizabeth, reaffirming England's claim to North America, granted Sir Walter Raleigh permission to establish a colony. His three unsuccessful ventures, including the so-called Lost Colony on Roanoke Island, helped to change the English attitude toward colonization. Obviously, no single individual could afford to finance a colony, and no colony could succeed without a cadre of settlers who understood the wilderness and were willing to make their homes there.

THE OCCUPATION OF JAMESTOWN

The merchants in the coastal cities of England quickly took advantage of this knowledge. Forming joint stock companies to limit their risks, they applied to the Crown for permission to settle colonies in America. In 1606, James I chartered the London Company. He extended to its members the right to establish a colony in Virginia, but he guaranteed the settlers the liberties and immunities of Englishmen. In the spring of 1607, three English ships dropped anchor in Chesapeake Bay. The land they found challenged and thwarted them. Captain John Smith, an adventurer and braggart, who can be credited with saving the colony from disastrous failure, provided one of the finest accounts of the country and the Indians:[1]

Virginia is a Country in America, that lyeth betweene the degrees of 34 and 44 of the north latitude. The bounds thereof on the East side are the great *Ocean*. On the South lyeth Florida: on the North nova Francia. As for the West thereof, the limits are unknowne. Of all this country wee purpose not to speake, but only of that part which was planted by the English men in the yeare of our Lord, 1606. And this is under the degrees 37, 38, and 39. The temperature of this countrie doth agree well with English con-

---

[1] Lyon Gardiner Tyler (ed.), *Narratives of Early Virginia* (New York, 1907), pp. 80-83, 90-101.

stitutions being once seasoned to the country. Which appeared by this, that though by many occasions our people fell sicke; yet did they recover by very small meanes and continued in health, though there were other great causes, not only to have made them sicke, but even to end their daies, etc.

The sommer is hot as in Spaine; the winter colde as in Fraunce or England. The heat of sommer is in June, Julie, and August, but commonly the coole Breeses asswage the vehemencie of the heat. The chiefe of winter is halfe December, January, February, and halfe March. The colde is extreame sharpe, but here the proverbe is true that no extreame long continueth.

In the yeare 1607, was an extraordinary frost in most of Europe, and this frost was founde as extreame in Virginia. But the next yeare for 8 or 10 daies of ill weather, other 14 daies would be as Sommer.

The windes here are variable, but the like thunder and lightning to purifie the aire, I have seldome either seene or heard in Europe. From the Southwest came the greatest gustes with thunder and heat. The Northwest winde is commonly coole, and bringeth faire weather with it. From the Northe is the greatest cold, and from the East and South-East as from the Barmadas, fogs and raines.

Some times there are great droughts, other times much raine, yet great necessity of neither, by reason we see not but that all the variety of needfull fruits in Europe may be there in great plenty by the industry of men, as appeareth by those we there planted.

There is but one entraunce by sea into this country, and that is at the mouth of a very goodly Bay, the widenesse whereof is neare 18 or 20 miles. The cape on the South side is called Cape Henry in honour of our most noble Prince. The shew of the land there, is a white hilly sand like unto the Downes, and along the shores great plentie of Pines and Firres.

The north Cape is called Cape Charles in honour of the worthy Duke of Yorke. Within is a country that may have the prerogative over the most pleasant places of Europe, Asia, Africa, or America, for large and pleasant navigable rivers: heaven and earth never agreed better to frame a place for mans habitation being of our constitutions, were it fully manured and inhabited by industrious people. Here are mountaines, hils, plaines, valleyes, rivers and brookes all running most pleasantly into a faire Bay compassed but for the mouth with fruitfull and delightsome land. In the Bay and rivers are many Isles both great and small, some woody, some plaine, most of them low and not inhabited. This Bay lieth North and South in which the water floweth neare 200 miles and hath a channell for 140 miles, of depth betwixt 7 and 15 fadome, holding in breadth for the most part 10 or 14 miles. From the head of the Bay at the north, the land is mountanous, and so in a manner from thence by a Southwest line; So that the more Southward, the farther of[f] from the Bay are those mounetaines. From which, fall certaine brookes, which after come to five principall navigable rivers. These run from the Northwest into the South east, and so into the west side of the Bay, where the fall of every River is within 20 or 15 miles one of an other.

The mountaines are of diverse natures, for at the head of the Bay the rockes are of a composition like miln-stones. Some of marble, &c. And many peeces of christall we found as throwne downe by water from the mountaines. For in winter these mountaines are covered with much snow, and when it dissolveth the waters fall with such violence, that it causeth great inundations in the narrow valleyes which yet is scarce perceived being once in the rivers. These waters wash from the rocks such glistering tinctures that the ground in some places seemeth as guilded, where both the rocks and the earth are so splendent to behold, that better judgements then ours might have beene perswaded, they contained more then probabilities. The vesture of the earth in most places doeth manifestly prove the nature of the soile to be lusty and very rich. The coulor of the earth we found in diverse places, resembleth *bole Armoniac, terra sigillata ad lemnia,* Fullers earth, marle, and divers other such appearances. But generally for the most part the earth is a black sandy mould, in some places a fat slimy clay, in other places a very barren gravell. But the best ground is knowne by the vesture it beareth, as by the greatnesse of trees or abundance of weedes, &c.

The country is not mountanous nor yet low but such pleasant plaine hils and fertle valleyes, one prettily crossing an other, and watered so conveniently with their sweete brookes and christall springs, as if art it selfe had devised them. By the rivers are many plaine marishes containing some 20, some 100, some 200 Acres, some more, some lesse. Other plaines there are fewe, but only where the Savages inhabit: but all overgrowne with trees and weedes being a plaine wildernes. . . .

Of Such Things Which Are Naturall in Virginia and How They Use Them

Virginia doth afford many excellent vegitables and living Creatures, yet grasse there is little or none but what groweth in lowe Marishes: for all the Countrey is overgrowne with trees, whose droppings continually turneth their grasse to weedes, by reason of the ranckness of the ground; which would soone be amended by good husbandry. The wood that is most common is Oke and Walnut: many of their Okes are so tall and straight, that they will beare two foote and a halfe square of good timber for 20 yards long. Of this wood there is 2 or 3 severall kinds. The Acornes of one kind, whose barke is more white than the other, is somewhat sweetish; which being boyled halfe a day in severall waters, at last afford a sweete oyle, which they keep in goards to annoint their heads and joints. The fruit they eate, made in bread or otherwise. There is also some Elme, some black walnut tree, and some Ash: of Ash and Elme they make sope Ashes. If the trees be very great, the ashes will be good, and melt to hard lumps: but if they be small, it will be but powder, and not so good as the other. Of walnuts there is 2 or 3 kindes: there is a kinde of wood we called Cypres, because both the wood, the fruit, and leafe did most resemble it; and of those trees there are some neere 3 fadome about at the root, very straight, and 50, 60, or 80 foot without a braunch. By the dwelling of the Savages are some great Mulbery trees; and in some parts of the Countrey, they are found growing naturally in prettie groves. There was an assay made to make silke, and surely the wormes prospered excellent well, till the master workeman fell sicke: during which time, they were eaten with rats.

In some parts, were found some Chesnuts whose wild fruit equalize the best in France, Spaine, Germany, or Italy, to their tasts that had tasted them all. Plumbs there are of 3 sorts. The red and white are like our hedge plumbs: but the other, which they call *Putchamins,* grow as high as a Palmeta. The fruit is like a medler; it is first greene, then yellow, and red when it is ripe: if it be not ripe it will drawe a mans mouth awrie with much torment; but when it is ripe, it is as delicious as an Apricock.

They have Cherries, and those are much like a Damsen; but for their tastes and colour, we called them Cherries. We see some few Crabs, but very small and bitter. Of vines, great abundance in many parts, that climbe the toppes of the highest trees in some places, but these beare but fewe grapes.

But by the rivers and Savage habitations where they are not overshadowed from the sunne, they are covered with fruit, though never pruined nor manured. Of those hedge grapes, wee made neere 20 gallons of wine, which was neare as good as your French Brittish wine, but certainely they would prove good were they well manured. There is another sort of grape neere as great as a Cherry, this they call *Messaminnes*; they bee fatte, and the juyce thicke: neither doth the tast so well please when they are made in wine. They have a small fruit growing on little trees, husked like a Chesnut, but the fruit most like a very small acorne. This they call *Chechinquamins*, which they esteeme a great daintie. They have a berry much like our gooseberry, in greatnesse, colour, and tast; those they call *Rawcomenes*, and doe eat them raw or boyled. Of these naturall fruits they live a great part of the yeare, which they use in this manner. The walnuts, Chesnuts, Acornes, and *Chechinquamens* are dryed to keepe. When they need them, they breake them betweene two stones, yet some part of the walnut shels will cleave to the fruit. Then doe they dry them againe upon a mat over a hurdle. After, they put it into a morter of wood, and beat it very small: that done, they mix it with water, that the shels may sinke to the bottome. This water will be coloured as milke; which they cal *Pawcohiscora*, and keepe it for their use. The fruit like medlers, they call *Putchamins*, they cast uppon hurdles on a mat, and preserve them as Pruines. Of their Chesnuts and *Chechinquamens* boyled 4 houres, they make both broath and bread for their chiefe men, or at their greatest feasts. Besides those fruit trees, there is a white populer, and another tree like unto it, that yeeldeth a very cleere and an odoriferous Gumme like Turpentine, which some called Balsom. There are also Cedars and Saxafras trees. They also yeeld gummes in a small proportion of themselves. Wee tryed conclusions to extract it out of the wood, but nature afforded more then our arts.

In the watry valleyes groweth a berry, which they call *Ocoughtanamnis*, very much like unto Capers. These they dry in sommer. When they will eat them, they boile them neare halfe a day; for otherwise they differ not much from poyson. *Mattoume* groweth as our bents do in meddows. The seede is not much unlike to rie, though much smaller. This they use for a dainty bread buttered with deare suet.

During Somer there are either strawberries which ripen in April; or mulberries which ripen in May and June, Raspises, hurtes, or a fruit that the Inhabitants call *Maracocks*, which is a pleasant wholsome fruit much like a lemond. Many hearbes in the spring time there are commonly dispersed throughout the woods, good for brothes and sallets, as Violets, Purslin, Sorrell, &c. Besides many we used whose names we know not.

The chiefe roote they have for foode is called *Tockawhoughe*. It groweth like a flagge in low muddy freshes. In one day a Savage will gather sufficient for a weeke. These rootes are much of the greatnes and taste of Potatoes. They use to cover a great many of them with oke leaves and ferne, and then cover all with earth in the manner of a colepit; over it, on each side, they continue a great fire 24 houres before they dare eat it. Raw it is no better then poison, and being roasted, except it be tender and the heat abated, or sliced and dried in the sun, mixed with sorrell and meale or such like, it will prickle and torment the throat extreamely, and yet in sommer they use this ordinarily for bread.

They have an other roote which they call *wighsacan*: as thother feedeth the body, so this cureth their hurts and diseases. It is a small root which they bruise and apply to the wound. *Pocones* is a small roote that groweth in the mountaines, which being dryed and beate in powder turneth red: and this they use for swellings, aches, annointing their joints, painting their heads and garments. They account it very pretious and of much worth. *Musquaspenne* is a roote of the bignesse of a finger, and as red as bloud. In drying, it will wither almost to nothing. This they use to paint their Mattes, Targets, and such like.

There is also Pellitory of Spaine, Sasafrage, and divers other simples, which the Apothecaries gathered, and commended to be good and medicinable.

In the low Marshes, growe plots of Onyons containing an acre of ground or more in many places; but they are small, not past the bignesse of the Toppe of ones Thumbe.

Of beastes the chief are Deare, nothing differing from ours. In the deserts towards the heads of the rivers, ther are many, but amongst the rivers few. There is a beast they call *Aroughcun*, much like a badger, but useth to live on trees as Squirrels doe. Their Squirrels some are neare as greate as our smallest sort of wilde rabbits; some blackish or blacke and white, but the most are gray.

A small beast they have, they call *Assapanick*, but we call them flying squirrels, because spreading their legs, and so stretching the largenesse of their skins that they have bin seene to fly 30 or 40 yards. An *Opassom* hath an head like a Swine, and a taile like a Rat, and is of the bignes of a Cat. Under her belly shee hath a bagge, wherein shee lodgeth, carrieth, and sucketh her young. *Mussascus* is a beast of the forme and nature of our water Rats, but many of them smell exceeding strongly of muske. Their Hares no bigger then our Conies, and few of them to be found.

Their Beares are very little in comparison of those of Muscovia and Tartaria. The Beaver is as bigge as an ordinary water dogge, but his legges exceeding short. His fore feete like a dogs, his hinder feet like a Swans. His taile somewhat like the forme of a Racket bare without haire; which to eate, the Savages esteeme a great delicate. They have many Otters, which, as the Beavers, they take with snares, and esteeme the skinnes great ornaments; and of all those beasts they use to feede, when they catch them.

There is also a beast they call *Vetchunquoyes* in the forme of a wilde Cat. Their Foxes are like our silver haired Conies, of a small proportion, and not smelling like those in England. Their Dogges of that country are like their Wolves, and cannot barke but howle; and their wolves not much bigger then our English Foxes. Martins, Powlecats, weessels and Minkes we know they have, because we have seen many of their skinnes, though very seldome any of them alive. But one thing is strange, that we could never perceive their vermine destroy our hennes, egges, nor chickens, nor do any hurt: nor their flyes nor serpents anie waie pernitious; where in the South parts of America, they are alwaies dangerous and often deadly.

Of birds, the Eagle is the greatest devourer. Hawkes there be of diverse sorts as our Falconers called them, Sparowhawkes, Lanarets, Goshawkes, Falcons and Osperayes; but they all pray most upon fish. Pattridges there are little bigger then our Quailes, wilde Turkies are as bigge as our tame. There are woosels or blackbirds with red shoulders, thrushes, and diverse sorts of small birds, some red, some blew, scarce so bigge as a wrenne, but few in Sommer. In winter there are great plenty of Swans, Craynes gray and white with blacke wings,

Herons, Geese, Brants, Ducke, Wigcon, Dotterell, Oxeies, Parrats, and Pigeons. Of all those sorts great abundance, and some other strange kinds, to us unknowne by name. But in sommer not any, or a very few to be seene.

Of fish we were best acquainted with Sturgeon, Grampus, Porpus, Seales, Stingraies whose tailes are very dangerous, Brettes, mullets, white Salmonds, Trowts, Soles, Plaice, Herrings, Conyfish, Rockfish, Eeles, Lampreyes, Catfish, Shades, Pearch of 3 sorts, Crabs, Shrimps, Crevises, Oysters, Cocles, and Muscles. But the most strange fish is a smal one so like the picture of S. George his Dragon, as possible can be, except his legs and wings: and the Todefish which will swell till it be like to brust, when it commeth into the aire.

Concerning the entrailes of the earth little can be saide for certainty. There wanted good Refiners: for these that tooke upon them to have skill this way, tooke up the washings from the mounetaines and some moskered shining stones and spangles which the waters brought down; flattering themselves in their own vaine conceits to have been supposed that they were not, by the meanes of that ore, if it proved as their arts and judgements expected. Only this is certaine, that many regions lying in the same latitude, afford mines very rich of diverse natures. The crust also of these rockes would easily perswade a man to beleeve there are other mines then yron and steele, if there were but meanes and men of experience that knew the mine from spare.

Of Their Planted Fruits in Virginia and How They Use Them

They divide the yeare into 5 seasons. . . . From September untill the midst of November are the chiefe Feasts and sacrifice. Then have they plenty of fruits as well planted as naturall, as corne greene and ripe, fish, fowle, and wild beastes exceeding fat.

The greatest labour they take, is in planting their corne, for the country naturally is overgrowne with wood. To prepare the ground they bruise the barke of the trees neare the roote, then do they scortch the roots with fire that they grow no more. The next yeare with a crooked peece of wood, they beat up the woodes by the rootes; and in that moulds, they plant their corne. Their manner is this. They make a hole in the earth with a sticke, and into it they put 4 graines of wheat and 2 of beanes. These holes they made 4 foote one from another. Their women and children do continually keepe it with weeding, and when it is growne midle high, they hill it about like a hop-yard.

In Aprill they begin to plant, but their chiefe plantation is in May, and so they continue till the midst of June. What they plant in Aprill they reape in August, for May in September, for June in October. Every stalke of their corne commonly beareth two eares, some 3, seldome any 4, many but one, and some none. Every eare ordinarily hath betwixt 200 and 500 graines. The stalke being green hath a sweet juice in it, somewhat like a suger Cane, which is the cause that when they gather their corne greene, they sucke the stalkes: for as wee gather greene pease, so doe they their corne being greene, which excelleth their old. They plant also pease. . . . Their Beanes are the same the Turkes call *Garnanses*, but these they much esteeme for dainties.

Their corne they rost in the eare greene, and bruising it in a morter with a Polt, lappe it in rowles in the leaves of their corne, and so boyle it for a daintie. They also reserve that corne late planted that will not ripe, by roasting it in hot ashes, the heat thereof drying it. In winter they esteeme it being boyled with beans for a rare dish, they call *Pausarowmena*. Their old wheat they first steep a night in hot water, in the morning pounding it in a morter. They use a small basket for their Temmes, then pound againe the great, and so separating by dashing their hand in the basket, receave the flower in a platter made of wood scraped to that forme with burning and shels. Tempering this flower with water, they make it either in cakes, covering them with ashes till they bee baked, and then washing them in faire water, they drie presently with their owne heat: or else boyle them in water eating the broth with the bread which they call *Ponap*. The grouts and peeces of the cornes remaining, by fanning in a Platter or in the wind away the branne, they boile 3 or 4 houres with water; which is an ordinary food they call *Ustatahamen*. But some more thrifty then cleanly, doe burne the core of the eare to powder which they call *Pungnough*, mingling that in their meale; but it never tasted well in bread, nor broth. Their fish and flesh they boyle either very tenderly, or broyle it so long on hurdles over the fire; or else, after the Spanish fashion, putting it on a spit, they turne first the one side, then the other, til it be as drie as their jerkin beefe in the west Indies, that they may keepe it a month or more without putrifying. The broth of fish or flesh they eate as commonly as the meat.

In May also amongst their corne, they plant Pumpeons, and a fruit like unto a muske millen, but lesse and worse; which they call *Macocks*. These increase exceedingly, and ripen in the beginning of July, and continue until September. They plant also *Maracocks* a wild fruit like a lemmon, which also increase infinitely: they begin to ripe in September and continue till the end of October. When all their fruits be gathered, little els they plant, and this is done by their women and children; neither doth this long suffice them: for neere 3 parts of the yeare, they only observe times and seasons, and live of what the Country naturally affordeth from hand to mouth, &c.

The Commodities in Virginia or That May Be Had by Industrie

The mildnesse of the aire, the fertilitie of the soile, and the situation of the rivers are so propitious to the nature and use of man as no place is more convenient for pleasure, profit, and mans sustenance. Under that latitude or climat, here will live any beasts, as horses, goats, sheep, asses, hens, &c. as appeared by them that were carried thither. The waters, Isles, and shoales, are full of safe harbours for ships of warre or marchandize, for boats of all sortes, for transportation or fishing, &c. The Bay and river have much marchandable fish and places fit for Salt coats, building of ships, making of iron, &c. . . . a practise for marriners, a trade for marchants, a reward for the good, and that which is most of all, a businesse (most acceptable to God) to bring such poore infidels to the true knowledge of God and his holy Gospell.

Of the Naturall Inhabitants of Virginia.

The land is not populous, for the men be fewe; their far greater number is of women and children. Within 60 miles of James Towne there are about some 5000 people, but of able men fit for their warres scarse 1500. To nourish so many together they have yet no means, because they make so smal a benefit of their land, be it never so fertill. 6 or 700 have beene the most [that] hath beene seene together. . . . As small as the proportion of ground that hath yet beene discovered, is in comparison of that yet unknowne. The people differ very much in stature, especially in language, as before is expressed. Some being very great as the Sesquesahamocks, others very little as the Wighcocomocoes: but generally tall and straight, of a comely proportion, and of a colour browne, when they are of any age, but they are borne white. Their haire is generally black; but few have any beards. The men weare halfe their heads shaven, the other halfe long. For Barbers they use their women, who with 2 shels will grate away the haire, of any fashion they please. The women are cut in many fashions agreeable to their ycarcs, but ever some part remaineth long. They are very strong, of an able body and full of agilitie, able to endure to lie in the woods under a tree by the fire, in the worst of winter, or in the weedes and grasse, in Ambuscado in the Sommer. They are inconstant in everie thing, but what feare constraineth them to keepe. Craftie, timerous, quicke of apprehension and very ingenuous. Some are of disposition fearefull, some bold, most cautelous, all Savage. Generally covetous of copper, beads, and such like trash. They are soone moved to anger, and so malitious, that they seldome forget an injury: they seldome steale one from another, least their conjurours should reveale it, and so they be pursued and punished. That they are thus feared is certaine, but that any can reveale their offences by conjuration I am doubtfull. Their women are carefull not to bee suspected of dishonesty without the leave of their husbands. Each houshold knoweth their owne lands and gardens, and most live of their owne labours. For their apparell, they are some time covered with the skinnes of wilde beasts, which in winter are dressed with the haire, but in sommer without. The better sort use large mantels of deare skins not much differing in fashion from the Irish mantels. Some imbrodered with white beads, some with copper, other painted after their manner. But the common sort have scarce to cover their nakednesse but with grasse, the leaves of trees, or such like. We have seen some use mantels made of Turky feathers, so prettily wrought and woven with threeds that nothing could bee discerned but the feathers, that was exceeding warme and very handsome. But the women are alwaies covered about their midles with a skin and very shamefast to be seene bare. They adorne themselves most with copper beads and paintings. Their women some have their legs, hands, brests and face cunningly imbrodered with diverse workes, as beasts, serpentes, artificially wrought into their flesh with blacke spots. In each eare commonly they have 3 great holes, whereat they hange chaines, bracelets, or copper. Some of their men weare in those holes, a smal greene and yellow coloured snake, neare halfe a yard in length, which crawling and lapping her selfe about his necke often times familiarly would kiss his lips. Others wear a dead Rat tied by the tail. Some on their heads weare the wing of a bird or some large feather, with a Rattell. Those Rattels are somewhat like the chape of a Rapier but lesse, which they take from the taile of a snake. Many have the whole skinne of a hawke or some strange fowle, stuffed with the wings abroad. Others a broad peece of copper, and some the hand of their enemy dryed. Their heads and shoulders are painted red with the roote *Pocone* braied to powder mixed with oyle; this they hold in somer to preserve them from the heate, and in winter from the cold. Many other formes of paintings they use, but he is the most gallant that is the most monstrous to behould.

Their buildings and habitations are for the most part by the rivers or not farre distant from some fresh spring. Their houses are built like our Arbors of small young springs bowed and tyed, and so close covered with mats or the barkes of trees very handsomely, that notwithstanding either winde raine or weather, they are as warme as stooves, but very smoaky, yet at the toppe of the house there is a hole made for the smoake to goe into right over the fire.

Against the fire they lie on little hurdles of Reedes covered with a mat, borne from the ground a foote and more by a hurdle of wood. On these round about the house, they lie heads and points one by thother against the fire: some covered with mats, some with skins, and some starke naked lie on the ground, from 6 to 20 in a house. Their houses are in the midst of their fields or gardens; which are smal plots of ground, some 20, some 40, some 100 some 200 some more, some lesse. Some times from 2 to 100 of these houses togither, or but a little separated by groves of trees. Neare their habitations is little small wood, or old trees on the ground, by reason of their burning of them for fire. So that a man may gallop a horse amongst these woods any waie, but where the creekes or Rivers shall hinder.

Men women and children have their severall names according to the severall humor of their Parents. Their women (they say) are easilie delivered of childe, yet doe they love children verie dearly. To make them hardy, in the coldest mornings they wash them in the rivers, and by painting and ointments so tanne their skins, that after year or two, no weather will hurt them.

The men bestowe their times in fishing, hunting, wars, and such manlike exercises, scorning to be seene in any woman like exercise, which is the cause that the women be verie painefull and the men often idle. The women and children do the rest of the worke. They make mats, baskets, pots, morters, pound their corne, make their bread, prepare their victuals, plant their corne, gather their corne, beare al kind of burdens, and such like.

PROBLEMS OF THE FIRST SETTLERS

The first English colonists, lacking the preparation for life in the Virginia wilderness, were unable to utilize the rich and luxuriant land that spread before them. Jamestown, the site of their first settlement, proved virtually uninhabitable because of marshes and swamps. The English failed to protect their supplies or to plant and care for their crops. A "starving time" followed. Even as the early governors attempted to enforce discipline and compel a practical adjustment to the frontier, the material and social culture of the English settlers declined. Governor Sir Thomas Gates failed to stop the trend toward social disorganization and advocated the abandonment of Jamestown. In his essay, "A True Declaration of the Estate of the Colonie of Virginia," published in 1610, Gates presented a harsh view of Virginia's first settlers:[2]

No man ought to judge of any Countrie by the fennes and marshes (such as is the place where James towne standeth) except we will condemne all England, for the Wilds and Hundreds of Kent and Essex. In our particular, wee have an infallible proofe of the temper of the Countrie. . . .

If any man shall accuse these reports of partiall falshood, supposing them to be but Utopian, and legendarie fables, because he cannot conceive, that plentie and famine, a tempareate climate, and distempered bodies,

---

[2] Albert B. Hart (ed.), *American History Told by Contemporaries* (New York, 1897), vol. 1, pp. 206–208.

felicities, and miseries can be reconciled together, let him now reade with judgement, but let him not judge before he hath read. . . .

Now, I demand whether Sicilia, or Sardinia, (sometimes the barnes of Rome) could hope for increase without manuring. A Colony is therefore denominated, because they should be Coloni, the tillers of the earth, and stewards of fertilitie: our mutinous loiterers would not sow with providence, and therefore they reaped the fruits of too deare bought repentance. An incredible example of their idlenes, is the report of Sir Thomas Gates, who affirmeth, that after his first coming thither, he had seen some of them eat their fish raw, rather than they would go a stones cast to fetch wood and dresse it, *Di j laboribus omnia vendunt*, God sels us all things for our labour, when Adam himselfe might not live in paradice without dressing the garden.

Unto idleness, you may joyne treasons, wrought by those unhallowed creatures that forsooke the Colony, and exposed their desolate brethren to extreame miserie. You shall know that 28 or 30 of the companie, were appointed (in the Ship called the Swallow) to truck for Corne with the Indians, and having obtained a great quantitie by trading, the most seditious of them conspired together, persuaded some, & enforced others to this barbarous project. They stole away the Ship, they made a league amongst themselves to be professed pirates, with dreames of mountaines of gold, and happy roberies: thus at one instant, they wronged the hopes, and subverted the cares of the Colony, who depended upon their returne, fore-slowed to looke out for further provision: they created the Indians our implacable enemies by some violence they had offered: they carried away the best Ship (which should have been a refuge, in extremities) they weakened our forces, by substraction of their armes, and succours. These are that scum of men that fayling in their piracy, that beeing pinched with famine and penurie, after their wilde roving upon the Sea, when all their lawlesse hopes failed, some remained with other pirates, they met upon the Sea, the others resolved to returne to England, bound themselves by mutuall oath, to agree all in one report, to discredit the land, to deplore the famyne, and to protest that this thier comming awaie, proceeded from desperate necessitie: . . .

Unto Treason, you may joyne covetousnesse in the Mariners, who for their private lucre partly imbezled the provisions, partly prevented our trade with the Indians, making the matches in the night, and forestalling our market in the day: whereby the Virginians were glutted with our trifles, and inhaunced the prices of their Corne and Victuall. That Copper which before would have provided a bushell, would not now obtaine so much as a pottle; *Non habet eventus fordida preda bones*, the consequent of sordid gaine is untimely wretchednesse.

Joyne unto these an other evill: there is great store of Fish in the river, especially of Sturgeon; but our men provided no more of them then for present necessitie, not barrelling up any store against that season the Sturgeon returned to the sea. And not to dissemble their folly, they suffered fourteene nets (which was all they had) to rot and spoile which by orderly drying and mending might have been preserved: but being lost, all help of fishing perished. *Quanto maiora timentur dispendis tanto promptior debet esse cautela*, fundamentall losses that cannot be repealed, ought with the greatest caution to be prevented.

The state of the Colony, by these accidents began to find a sensible declyning: which *Powhatan* (as a greedy Vulture) observing, and boyling with desire of revenge, he invited Captaine Ratclife, and about thirty others to trade for Corne, and under the colour of fairest friendship, he brought them within the compasse of his ambush, whereby they were cruelly murthered, and massacred....

Cast up this reckoning together: want of government, store of idlenesse, their expectations frustrated by the Traitors, their market spoyled by the Mariners, our nets broken, the deere chased, our boats lost, our hogs killed, our trade with the Indians forbidden, some of our men fled, some murthered, and most by drinking of the brackish water of James fort weakened, and indaungered, famyne and sicknesse by all these meanes increase, here at home the monies came in so slowly, that the Lo. Laware could not be dispatched, till the Colony was worne and spent with dificulties: Above all, having neither Ruler, nor Preacher, they neither feared God nor man, which provoked the wrath of the Lord of Hosts, and pulled downe his judgements upon them, *Discite justitiam moniti*, Now, (whether it were that God in mercie to us would weede out these ranke hemlockes; or whether in judgment to them he would scourge their impieties; or whether in wisedome he would trie our patience, *Vt magna desiseremus*, that wee may beg great blessins earnestly) our hope is that our Sunne shall not set in a cloude, since this violent storme is dispersed, Since all necessarie things are provided, an absolute and powerful government is setled, as by this insuing relation shall be described....

Despite the hardships and trials of these early years, the English gradually became seasoned to life on the frontier. But, unlike the Spanish who used their Florida colony as a base to guard their treasure fleet or the French who quickly developed the fur trade, the English found Virginia an economic loss until 1612, when John Rolfe began cultivating tobacco. Although a highly profitable crop, tobacco culture proved a mixed blessing. It damaged the free-labor system by making slavery advantageous and upset the land system by depleting the soil of resources. Settlers now eagerly voyaged to Virginia and sought to profit from tobacco produced on cheap or free land. But as the new plantations were established and a sense of increased security prevailed, Indians, fearful of the steady intrusion of white settlers, attacked the frontier in 1622. They killed 357 settlers and the remainder went eastward to more protected areas. The colonists struck back, almost driving the Indians from the Virginia tidewater and destroying their military potential.

Civil war, religious persecution, and economic unrest in England between 1620 and 1670 spurred heavy immigration to America. Many English immigrants came to Virginia, where the Indian attack of 1622 was followed by years of peace. Soil exhaustion and the large influx of immigrants seeking new lands pushed the frontier line into the piedmont, or foothills, of the Appalachian Mountains. As the new settlers pioneered in developing virgin land and faced the hazard of Indian attack, the tidewater emerged as a region with a new social order as wealthier planters, government officials, and commercial factors came more and more to assume the leadership of the colony. They took advantage of liberal land laws to acquire huge tracts of undeveloped western lands for speculation; and they dominated the House of Burgesses.

BACON'S REBELLION IN VIRGINIA

As long as tobacco prices were high, taxes bearable, and the Indian frontier peaceful, the pioneer farmers in the backcountry of Virginia and the new colony of Maryland busied themselves with the daily struggle for survival. But when trade regulations strangled the tobacco industry and the Indians grew restive in the 1670s, the colonists became aroused. The frontier planters complained of obvious grievances ranging from inadequate suffrage and infrequent elections to the ineffective system of Indian defense.

Their resentment flared into rebellion in 1676, when repeated Indian depredations went unpunished. The leader of the uprising, Nathaniel Bacon, was less interested in reform than in Indian war, but his ability to turn the upcountry settlers against the tidewater establishment proved that the unrest and sectional tension that had swelled up on the frontier could be focused against what had become the first East. "Strange News from Virginia," a report in a contemporary news sheet, was the earliest published account of Bacon's Rebellion. Although clearly hostile to Bacon's cause, it shows the furious response of the frontiersmen both to the Indian and to legal authority.[3]

That Plantation which he chose to settle in is generally known by the name of *Curles*, situate in the upper part of *James* River, and the time of his Revolt was not till the beginning of *March* 1675-6. At which time the *Susquo-hannan Indians* (a known Enemy to that Country) having made an Insurrection, and kild divers of the *English*, amongst whom it was his fortune to have a Servant slain; in revenge of whose death, and other dammages he received from those turbulent *Susquohanians*, without the Governour's Consent he furiously took up Arms against them, and was so fortunate as to put them to flight, but not content therewith; the aforesaid *Governour* hearing of his eager pursuit after the vanquisht *Indians*, sent out a select Company of Souldiers to command him to desist; but he instead of listning thereunto, persisted in his Revenge, and sent to the *Governour* to intreat his Commission, that he might more chearfully prosecute his design; which being denied him by the Messenger he sent for that purpose, he notwithstanding continued to make head with his own Servants, and other *English* then resident in *Curles* against them. In this interim the people . . . had returned him Burgess of their County; and he in order thereunto took his own Sloop and came down towards *James Town*, conducted by thirty odd Souldiers, . . . the Governour thereupon ordered an allarm to be beaten through the whole Town, which took so hot, that *Bacon* thinking himself not secure whilst he remained there within reach of their Fort, immediately commanded his men aboard, and tow'd his Sloop up the River; which the Governour perceiving, ordered the Ships which lay at *Sandy-point* to pursue and take him; and they by the industry of their Commanders succeeded so well in the attempt, that they presently stopt his passage; so that Mr. *Bacon* finding himself pursued both before and behind, after some capitulations, quietly surrendred himself Prisoner to the Governours Commissioners, to the great satisfaction of all his Friends; which action of his was so obliging to the Governour, that he granted him his liberty immediately upon Paroll, without confining him either to Prison or Chamber, and the next day, after some private discourse passed betwixt the Governour, the Privy Council, and himself, he was amply restored to all his former Honours and Dignities, and a Commission partly promised him to be General against the *Indian* Army; but upon farther enquiry into his Affairs it was not thought fit to be granted

---

[3] "Strange News from Virginia," in Harry Finestone (ed.), *Bacon's Rebellion: The Contemporary News Sheets* (Charlottesville, Va.: University Press of Virginia, 1957), pp. 9–17.

him; whereat his ambitious mind seem'd mightily to be displeas'd. . . . Afterwards he headed the same Runnagado *English* that he formerly found ready to undertake and go sharers with him in any of his Rebellions, and adding to them the assistance of his own Slaves and Servants, headed them so far till they toucht at the *Occonegies* [this and one variant spelling represent the author's version of Occaneechi] Town, where he was treated very civilly, and by the Inhabitants informed where some of the *Susquohanno's* were inforted, whom presently he assails, and after he had vanquished them, slew about seventy of them in their Fort: But as he returned back to the *Occoneges*, he found they had fortified themselves with divers more *Indians* than they had at his first arrival; wherefore he desired Hostages of them for their good behaviour, whilst he and his followers lay within command of their Fort. But those treacherous *Indians* grown confident by reason of their late recruit, returned him this Answer, *That their Guns were the only Hostages he was like to have of them, and if he would have them he must fetch them.* Which was no sooner spoke, but the *Indians* sallied out of the Fort and shot one of his Sentinels, whereupon he charged them so fiercely, that the Fight continued not only all that day, but the next also, till the approach of the Evening, at which time finding his men grow faint for want of Provision, he laid hold of the opportunity, being befriended by a gloomy night, and so made an honourable retreat homewards.

Howbeit we may judge what respect he had gain'd in *James-Town* by this subsequent transaction. When he was first brought hither it was frequently reported among the Commonalty that he was kept close Prisoner, which report caused the people of that Town, those of *Charles-City, Henrico,* and *New-Kent* Countries, being in all about the Number of eight hundred, or a thousand, to rise and march thitherwards in order to his rescue; whereupon the Governor was forced to desire Mr. *Bacon* to go himself in Person, and by his open appearance quiet the people.

This being past, Mr. *Bacon* about the 25*th* of *June* last, dissatisfied that he could not have a Commission granted him to go against the *Indians,* in the night time departed the Town unknown to any body, and about a week after got together between four and five hundred men of *New-Kent* County, with whom he marched to *James-Town,* and drew up in order before the House of State; and there peremptorily demanded of the Governor, *Council* and *Burgesses* (there then collected) a Commission to go against the *Indians,* which if they should refuse to grant him, he told them that neither he nor ne're a man in his Company would depart from their Doors till he had obtained his request; whereupon to prevent farther danger in so great an exigence, the Council and Burgesses by much intreaty obtain'd him a Commission Signed by the *Governor,* an Act for one thousand men to be Listed under his command to go against the *Indians,* to whom the same pay was to be granted as was allowed to them who went against the *Fort.* . . .

Having obtained these large Civilities of the *Governor,* &c. one would have thought that if the Principles of honesty would not have obliged him to peace and loyalty, those of gratitude should. But, alas, when men have been once flusht or entred with Vice, how hard is it for them to leave it, especially if it tends towards ambition or greatness, which is the general lust of a large Soul, and the common error of vast parts, which fix their Eyes so upon the lure of greatness, that they have no time left them to consider by what indirect and unlawful means they must (if ever) attain it. . . .

In fine, he continued (I cannot say properly in the Fields, but) in the Woods with a considerable Army all last Summer, and maintain'd several Brushes with the Governors Party: sometime routing them, and burning all before him, to the great damage of many of his Majesties loyal Subjects there resident; sometimes he and his Rebels were beaten by the Governor, &c. and forc't to run for shelter amongst the Woods and Swomps. In which lamentable condition that unhappy Continent has remain'd for the space of almost a Twelve-month, every one therein that were able being forc't to take up Arms for security of their own lives, and no one reckoning their Goods, Wives, or Children to be their own, since they were so dangerously expos'd to the doubtful Accidents of an uncertain War.

But the indulgent Heavens, who are alone able to compute what measure of punishments are adequate or fit for the sins or transgressions of a Nation, has in its great mercy saw fit to put a stop, at least, if not a total period and conclusion to these *Virginian* troubles, by the death of this *Nat. Bacon*, the great Molestor of the quiet of that miserable Nation; so that now we who are here in *England*, and have any Relations or Correspondence with any of the Inhabitants of that Continent, may by the arrival of the next Ships from that Coast expect to hear that they are freed from all their dangers, quitted of all their fears, and in great hopes and expectation to live quietly under their own Vines, and enjoy the benefit of their commendable labours.

Bacon's rebellion was doomed even before his death; Governor William Berkeley had summoned redcoats and warships from England to put down the insurrection. The rebels found no mercy at the hands of the lawful authorities. In fact, a royal commission later investigating the episode forced Berkeley's recall because of his vindictiveness.

OPENING THE CAROLINA FUR TRADE

Although reforms were instituted in Virginia, a widespread spirit of dissatisfaction existed on the frontier, which caused many pioneers to migrate to the South and West. They found, at least temporarily, greater freedom from restraint in Carolina. The population growth in this colony had been slow not only because of Spanish pressure but also because the Indians in the region fought off penetration. While the agricultural development around Charleston lagged, the inhabitants turned to the fur trade. Daring pathfinders, their packs loaded with "truck," hunted out Indians eager to barter their deer skins for the white man's goods. Dr. Henry Woodward first opened the trade with the Westos in 1674. His report of that expedition is one of the earliest accounts of a Carolina trader.[4]

Haveing received notice at Charles Towne from Mr. Percyvall that strange Indians were arrived at your Lordships Plantation, Immediately I went up in the yawle, w[h]ere I found according to my former conjecture in all probability that they were the Westoes not understanding ought of their speech, resolving nevertheless (they having first bartered their truck) to venture up into the maine with them they seeming very unwilling to stay the night yet very desireous that I should goe along with them. The tenth of October being Saturday in the afternoon I accordingly set forth, the weather raw and drizzling, they being ten of them and my selfe in Company. We travelled the remaining part of that afternoon West and by North thorough your Lordships land towards the head of Ashley River, passing divers tracks of excellent oake and Hickery land,

---

[4] Alexander S. Salley (ed.), *Narratives of Early Carolina* (New York, 1911), pp. 130–134.

with divers spatious Savanas, seeming to the best of my judgment good Pastorage. As we travelled this day I saw (as divers other times likewise in my journey) w[h]ere these Indians had drawne uppon trees (the barke being hewed away) the effigies of a bever, a man, on horseback and guns, Intimating thereby as I suppose, their desire for freindship, and comerse with us. The weather continuing wett wee took up our quarters, haveing steered exactly by compass from St. Giles Plantation according to the fore named Course. The Indian being diligent in makeing two barke-covered Hutts, to shelter us from the injury of the weather, this night as well as the afternoone proved tedious, having had soe large a vacation from my travels, the diet before almost naturalized now seemed unpleasant, and the ground altogether was uneasy for lodginge. Soe soon as the day appeared wee set forth sterring West and by South. After wee had passed the head of Ashley River I found the land indifferently good. In the afternoon wee entered a large tracke of Pines, which continued untill we came within two or three miles of that part of Aedistaw River w[h]ere wee crossed over. The land seemeth fertyl along the banks of this River, whose head they report to bee about four score mile up in the main from the part wee passed, being then twenty mile or something more distant from w[h]ere divideing himselfe he makes the pleasant plantation of Aedistawe. Here killing a large buck wee took up our rendeavouze with two mile of the river, glad of the opportunity of lying in two of their hunting hutts. Uppon Monday morning four of the company went to give notice of our comeing. Wee following steered West S. West, the land Piny except along the skirts of small rivulets, many of which wee passed this day. The weather all over cast. This evening wee provided shelter, the night proveing extreame wett. Wee supped with two fatt Turkeys to help out with our parcht corne flower broth. The following day proveing as bad as the night, wee forsooke not the benefitt of our hutts. Uppon Wednesday morneing wee sett forth, nothing at all varying our former course. This day wee had a sight of Aedistawe River bearing north west by north of us, the soyle very promiseing, and in some places excellently tymbered. In the afternoon wee shott a fatt doe which, proportionably divideing amongst them, was carried along by them for our better comons at night, quartering along the sides of a pleasant run. Thursday wee tooke our journey dew West, passing many large pastorable Savanas, the other land promising very well. This day wee shott two Bucks. The best of both with a fatt Turkey wee carried along with us, for our better accomodation at night. Fryday wee traveled West and by South, haveing towards three the afternoon a sight of the mountaines, which bore northwest of us, passing the head of Port Royall river over a tree, w[h]ere the river intricately runs through large vallies of excellent land, at the begining of the adjoyning Hills, along whose banks in a mighty thicke wood wee took up our Quarters. The ensuing day wee went over many fattigous hills, the land especially the vallies being excellent good, our course West a little Southwardly. In the afternoon wee mett two Indians with their fowling peeces, sent by their cheife to congratulate my arrivall into their parts, who himselfe awaited my comeing with divers others at the Westoe River. The ridge of hills through which the river runs then being in sight bore West and by North. The banks of this river seeme like white chalky cliffs and are at least one hundred foot perpendicular, opposite to which banks uppon a sandy poynt were two or three hutts under whose shelter was their cheife with divers others in his company. The two Indians wee met had a canoc ready to pass us over, w[h]ere soe soon as wee landed, I was carried to the Captains hutt, who courteously entertained mee with a good repast of those things they counte rarietys amonge them. The river here being very deep with a silent current trended North and by West and South and by East nearest. Soe soone as the raine ceased wee sett upp the fertyle banks of this spatious river. Haveing paddled about a league upp wee came in sight of the Westoe towne, *alias* the Hickauhaugau which stands uppon a poynt of the river (which is undoubtedly the river May) uppon the Westerne side soe that the river encompasseth two-thirds thereof. When we came within [sight] of the towne I fired my fowling peece and pistol which was answered with a hollow and imediately thereuppon they gave mee a volley of fifty or sixty small arms. Here was a concourse of some hundred of Indians, drest up in their anticke fighting garbe. Through the midst of whom being conducted to their cheiftaines house, the which not being capable to containe the crowd that came to see me, the smaller fry got up and uncouvered the top of the house to satisfy their curiosity. The cheife of the Indians made long speeches intimateing their own strength (and as I judged their desire of freindship with us). This night first haveing oyled my eyes and joynts with beares oyl, they presented mee divers deare skins, setting befoore me sufficient of their food to satisfy at least half a dozen of their owne appetites. Here taking my first nights repose, the next day I veiwed the Towne, which is built in a confused maner, consisting of many long houses whose sides and tops are both artifitially done with barke, upon the tops of most whereof fastened to the ends of long poles hang the locks of haire of Indians that they have slaine. The inland side of the towne being duble Pallisadoed, and that part which fronts the river haveing only a single one.

Under whose steep banks seldom ly less than one hundred faire canoes ready uppon all occasions. They are well provided with arms, amunition, tradeing cloath and other trade from the northward for which at set times of the year they truck drest deare skins furrs and young Indian Slaves. In ten daies time that I tarried here I viewed the adjacent part of the Country. They are Seated uppon a most fruitfull soyl. The earth is intermingled with a sparkling substance like Antimony, finding severall flakes of Isinglass in the paths. The soales of my Indian shooes in which I travelled glistened like sylver. The clay of which their pots and pipes are made is intermingled with the like substance. The wood land is abounding with various sorts of very large straite timber. Eight daies journey from the towne the River hath its first falls West N. West, w[h]ere it divides it selfe into three branches, amongst which dividing branches inhabit the Cowatoe and Chorakae Indians with whom they are at continual warrs. Forty miles distant from the towne northward they say lye the head of Aedistaw river being a great meer or lake. Two days before my departure arrived two Savana Indians living as they said twenty days journey West Southwardly from them. There was none here that understood them, but by signes they intreated freindship of the Westoes, showeing that the Cussetaws, Checsaws and Chiokees were intended to come downe and fight the Westoes. At which news they expeditiously repaired their pallisadoes, keeping watch all night. In the time of my abode here they gave me a young Indian boy taken from the falls of that River. The Savana Indians brought Spanish beeds and other trade as presents, makeing signes that they had comerce with white people like unto mee, whom were not good. These they civilly treated and dismissed before my departure. Ten of them prepared to accompany mee in my journey home, returning by the same ways that I came, killing much game with two large she beares uppon the way through much rain the fresshes being mightly encreased. The 5th of November wee our selfes carrying our trade upon barke logs swam over Aedistaw River and the 6th of that Instant in safety I arrived at your Honourables Plantation at the Head of Ashley River. For good reasons I permitted them not to enter your Plantation, but very well satisfyed dispatcht them homewards that evening, whom I againe expect in March with deare skins, furrs and younge slaves.

Before long English traders plunged deeper into the interior, flanking the Spanish and extending English influence among Indian tribes like the Creek. These welcomed the Carolina traders, who brought goods both better and cheaper than the Spanish could offer. Neither mission nor fort proved an effective bulwark against the Carolinians who, by 1690, gathered several hundred strong and with trains of pack animals carried guns, trinkets, and rum along the trail to the Creek villages. The only rivals the Carolinians encountered were Virginia traders who, equally eager to share in the profits, were willing to make the long trek down the piedmont and then westward to reach the Creeks.

ADVERTISING THE CAROLINA FRONTIER

Behind this shield of exploration came a force of Carolina's pioneer farmers. Once the Indian's power had been weakened and the Spanish northward thrust had been controlled, the proprietors of Carolina encouraged settlement and stressed the economic and social advantages of living in the colony. Any potential colonist, uncertain as to what he would find in the wilderness, or doubtful about how he would fare, or concerned about how much effort he would be forced to expend for a livelihood, could turn to numerous promotional tracts that circulated widely throughout England. The following excerpt from a tract written by a Swiss, Thomas Nairne, although referring to South Carolina, and describing land prices, land tenure, financial arrangements, and opportunities in that colony is fairly typical of the southern frontier:[5]

Nothing can be more reasonable than the Price of Lands in this Province; we must do their Lordships the Justice to say, they have always, in that Respect, dealt with great Favour and Gentleness. The first twenty Years they got little or nothing at all, and since not much more than is barely sufficient to support the necessary Charges of the Government. By this Conduct the Proprietors have advanc'd the Interest of the *English* Nation to their own present Loss. For if their Lordships had not remitted many Years Arrears of Rent, if they had not waited a great while for Money due for Lands, and suffer'd the People to supply themselves with Slaves, before they paid it; if they had not sold their Lands, and established their Rents, at so moderate a Rate; the Country had not been in Circumstances to purchase all the Effects brought yearly from *Great Britain*, in 22 Sail of Ships, as they now do.

The Method has hitherto often been for Men to settle themselves upon a Piece of Ground, improve it, build, raise stock, plant Orchards, and make such Commodities, which being sold, procur'd them Slaves, Horses, Houshold-Goods, and the like Conveniences; and after this was done, in seven

---

[5] Thomas Nairne, A *Letter from South Carolina* (London, 1710), pp. 46–51.

or eight Years they might begin to think it Time to pay the Lords something for their Land.

Free and common Soccage is the Tenure by which Lands are held, a small Quit-Rent being paid annually to the Proprietors, as Lords of the Fee, in lieu of all Services, Perquisites, and Demands whatsoever. There are two Ways of taking out Titles; one is by Purchase, at twenty Pounds a thousand Acres, paid to the Lords Reciever, the Grant whereof reserves to their Lordships an annual Rent of a Shilling for each hundred Acres; the other is without any Purchase-money paid down, but by taking out a Patent, upon Condition to pay yearly to the Lords Proprietors a Penny for each Acre. Every one is at Liberty to choose which of these Methods he will, tho' the former, being much preferable, is most common.

The Tenour of the Grants of Lands from the Proprietors, runs to this Purpose: First their Lordships Title by a Charter from K. *Charles* II is recited; then, in Consideration of so much Money there acknowledg'd to be received, they sell, alienate, and make over unto A. B. his Heirs, &c. a Plantation, containing so many Acres of Land, situate and lying in such a County, and having such a Form and Marks, as appear by the Plan of it annex'd, he or they paying for the same, the Sum of one Shilling yearly, for each hundred Acres, in lieu of all Dues or Demands whatsoever.

When a Person would take up Land, (as we term it) he first views the Place, and satisfies himself that no other has any Property there, and then goes to the Secretary, and takes out a Warrant for the Quantity he desires. Warrants ready sign'd by the Governour are left with proper Blanks in the Secretaries Office, and directed to the Surveyor, impowering him to measure and lay out such a Number of Acres for such a Person, and to return a Plan and Certificate thereof into the Secretaries Office. Then the Secretary files the Certificates, and writes a Grant (the Form where of is settled by Act of Assembly) which he annexes to the Plan, and carries it next Council Day, into the Council, to be sign'd by the Governour, and such of the Council as are Trustees for the Sale of Lands, and sealed with the publick Seal of the Colony. If the Grant is to be for Lands purchas'd, a Record of the Receipt of the Purchase-Money by the Lords Reciever, must be produced, as a Warrant for signing the Patent.

If any one designs to make a Plantation, in this Province, out of the Woods, the first thing to be done is, after having cutt down a few Trees, to split Palissades, or Clapboards, and therewith make small Houses or Huts, to shelter the Slaves. After that, while some Servants are clearing the Land, others are to be employed in squaring or sawing Wall-plats, Posts, Rafters, Boards and Shingles, for a small House for the Family, which usually serves for a Kitchin afterwards, when they are in better Circumstances to build a larger. During the Time of this Preparation, the Master Overseer, or white Servants, go every Evening to the next Neighbour's House, where they are lodg'd and entertain'd kindly, without any Charges. And if the Person have any Wife or Children, they are commonly left in some Friend's House, till a suitable dwelling Place and Conveniencies are provided, fit for them to live decently.

The properest Time to begin a Settlement is in *September*, or, at farthest, before the first of *December*. The Time between that and the first of *March* is spent in cutting down and burning the Trees, out of the Ground, design'd to be sowed that Year, splitting Rails, and making Fences round the Corn Ground, and Pasture. The smallest Computation usually made is, that each labouring Person will, in this Time, clear three Acres fit for Sowing.

In the second Fall, or Winter, after a Plantation is settled, they make Gardens, plant Orchards, build Barns, and other convenient Houses. The third or fourth Winter, Persons of any Substance provide Brick, Lime, or other Materials, in order to build a good House. The Lime here is all made of Oister-shells, burnt with Wood; of these there is great Plenty lying in and by all Creeks and Rivers, in great Heaps or Beds, where large Boats are loaden at low Water.

Our Cows graze in the Forests, and the Calves being separated from them, and kept in Pastures, fenced in, they return home at Night to suckle them. They are first milk'd, then shut up in a Fold all Night, milk'd again in the Morning, and then turn'd out into the Woods. Hogs rove several Miles over the Forests, eating such Nuts and Ground-Roots as they can find; but having a Shelter made at home to keep them warm, and something given them to eat, they generally return every Evening.

People who design to make their Fortunes in new Countries, should consider beforehand, what Method, or Course of Life, they purpose to follow, when they arrive there; and not flatter themselves with vain Fancies, as if Riches were to be got without Industry, or taking suitable Methods to attain them. 'Tis Encouragement sufficient for a rational Man to know, that when due Means are us'd, they seldom fail of obtaining the End. In this Province as little will serve to put a Person into a Way of living comfortably, as in any Place whatever, and perhaps less. That you and your Friends may be throughly convinc'd of this, without being led into any Mistakes, I shall here first insert an Account of what is necessary to settle a Planter to live with Comfort and Decency....

By the early years of the eighteenth century, the English were well established in the Carolinas and Virginia. Along the outer edge of the frontier were fur traders and pathfinders, steadily encroaching into areas of Spanish influence and seeking contact with western tribes. Behind this line, came pioneer farmers, too poor to buy land, making the basic investment of labor and hoping to produce a cash staple such as rice in Carolina or tobacco in Virginia. These people felt the constant pressure of established farmers with investment capital, who moved westward to buy good land because their old plantations were no longer profitable enough or because they wanted greater opportunity. A method of utilizing an undeveloped country had begun.

CHAPTER 4

The English Northern Frontier, 1620-1700

While English colonists were struggling to establish themselves in Virginia and Carolina, another group faced the hardships of New England. Like Virginia and Carolina, the region had been granted to a company of promoters, the Council of New England, but unlike the London Company or the Carolina proprietors, the Council failed to build a permanent settlement. In fact, its earliest efforts proved so unsatisfactory and its financial resources were so limited that the Council ultimately sold off its rights to small companies of settlers, who sought fishing and fur trading opportunities or a religious sanctuary.

LONDON BACKING FOR THE PLYMOUTH COLONY

The task of building the first permanent New England colony fell to the Separatists, or Pilgrims, a small group of religious dissenters who, having abandoned England and tried unsuccessfully to live in Holland, were determined to find a haven in America. Middle- and lower-middle-class people, unable to raise sufficient funds among their own members to underwrite their venture, the Pilgrims turned to London merchants for capital. William Bradford, the most noteworthy Pilgrim chronicler, explained how the contract terms were drawn and why they were accepted:[1]

To which the 2 agents sent from Leyden (or at least one of them who is most charged with it) did consente; seeing els that all was like to be dashte, & the opportunitie lost, and that they which had put of their estats and paid in their moneys were in hazard to be undon. They presumed to conclude with the marchants on those termes, in some things contrary to their order & comission, and without giving them notice of the same; yea, it was conceled least it should make any furder delay; which was the cause afterward of much trouble & contention.

It will be meete I here inserte these conditions, which are as foloweth.

Anno: 1620 July 1

1. The adventurers & planters doe agree, that every person that goeth being aged 16

---

[1] William Bradford, *Bradford's History of Plimoth Plantation* (Boston, 1901), pp. 56–58.

years & upward, be rated at 10 pounds, and ten pounds to be accounted a single share.

2. That he that goeth in person, and furnisheth him selfe out with 10 pounds either in money or other provissions, be accounted as haveing 20 pounds in stock, and in the devission shall receive a double share.

3. The persons transported & adventurers shall continue their joynt stock & partnership together, the space of 7 years, (excepte some unexpected impedimente doe cause the whole company to agree otherwise,) during which time, all profits & benifits that are gott by trade, traffick, trucking, working, fishing, or any other means of any person or persons, remaine still in the comone stock untill the division.

4. That at their coming ther, they chose out such a number of fitt persons, as may furnish their ships and boats for fishing upon the sea; imploying the rest in their severall faculties upon the land; as building houses, tilling, and planting the ground, & makeing shuch comodities as shall be most usefull for the collonie.

5. That at the end of the 7 years, the capitall & profits, viz. the houses, lands, goods and chatles, be equally devided betwixte the adventurers, and planters; which done, every man shall be free from other of them of any debt or detrimente concerning this adventure.

6. Whosoever cometh to the colonie herafter, or putteth any into the stock, shall at the ende of the 7 years be alowed proportionably to the time of his so doing.

7. He that shall carie his wife & children, or servants, shall be alowed for everie person now aged 16 years & upward, a single share in the devision, or if he provid them necessaries, a duble share, or if they be between 10 year old and 16, then 2 of them to be reconed for a person, both in trasportation and devision.

8. That such children as now goe, & are under the age of ten years, have noe other shar in the devision, but 50 acers of unmanured land.

9. That such persons as die before the 7 years be expired, their executors to have their parte or sharr at the devision, proportionably to the time of their life in the collonie.

10. That all such persons as are of this collonie, are to have their meate, drink, apparell, and all provissions out of the comon stock & goods of the said collonie.

The cheefe & principall differences betwene these & the former conditions, stood in those 2 points; that the houses, & lands improved, espetialy gardens & home lotts should remaine undevided wholy to the planters at the 7 years end. Secondly, that they should have had 2 days in a weeke for their owne private imploymente, for the more comforte of them selves and their families, espetialy such as had families.

The London capitalists could drive a hard bargain; the uncertainties of the expedition and the inexperience of the Pilgrim settlers freighted their thoughts. But the objection of the Pilgrims to being deprived of private holdings proved well founded. Only after a division of lands and the assurance of private landholdings did the colony successfully liquidate its debt.

THE MAYFLOWER COMPACT

A puzzling frontier experience confronted the Pilgrims when their ship, the "Mayflower," blown off course by heavy winds, came on the landfall of New England rather than Virginia where they had been granted permission to settle. The Pilgrims had neither land title nor power to govern in this region and, to protect their claims to both, wrote the first free-association-of-squatters document in American history. The

Mayflower Compact, introduced here by William Bradford, struck a compromise between a church covenant and a social contract:²

A combination made by them before they came ashore, being the first foundation of their govermente in this place; occasioned partly by the discontented & mutinous speeches that some of the strangers amongst them had let fall from them in the ship— That when they came a shore they would use their owne libertie; for none had power to comand them, the patente they had being for Virginia, and not for New-england, which belonged to an other Goverment, with which the Virginia Company had nothing to doe. And partly that shuch an acte by them done (this their condition considered) might be as firme as any patent, and in some respects more sure.

The forme was as followeth.

In the name of God, Amen. We whose names are underwriten, the loyall subjects of our dread soveraigne Lord, King James, by the grace of God, of Great Britaine, Franc, & Ireland king, defender of the faith, &c., haveing undertaken, for the glorie of God, and advancement of the Christian faith, and honour of our king & countrie, a voyage to plant the first colonie in the Northerne parts of Virginia, doe by these presents solemnly & mutualy in the presence of God, and one of another, covenant & combine our selves togeather into a civill body politick, for our better ordering & preservation & furtherance of the ends aforesaid; and by vertue hearof to enacte, constitute, and frame such just & equall lawes, ordinances, acts, constitutions, & offices, from time to time, as shall be thought most meete & convenient for the generall good of the Colonie, unto which we promise all due submission and obedience. In witnes wherof we have hereunder subscribed our names at Cap-Codd the 11 of November, in the year of the raigne of our soveraigne lord, King James, of England, France, & Ireland the eighteenth, and of Scotland the fiftie fourth. anno Domini 1620.

THE PILGRIMS RELATIONS
WITH THE INDIANS

Once ashore, the new colonists, trusting that they would prevail in the wilderness, pitted their Christian dedication and faith against the frontier. Illness cut them down, and human nature proved as susceptible to corruption among the members of the "Mayflower's" crew as it had among the settlers on the Virginia frontier at Jamestown. But the tightly organized, religiously integrated community tended to protect its members rather than distintegrate on the frontier. The Pilgrims were more fortunate than the Virginians also in dealing with the Indians. Even though fearful of the tribes, they quickly gleaned benefits from some Indians, who had been taken to Europe and returned by earlier English visitors. In terse prose, William Bradford illustrates the reaction of a Pilgrim leader to the earliest problems of survival:³

In these hard & difficulte beginings they found some discontents & murmurings arise amongst some, and mutinous speeches & carriags in other; but they were soone quelled & overcome by the wisdome, patience, and just & equall carrage of things by the Governor and better part, which clave faithfully togeather in the maine. But that which was most sadd & lamentable was, that in 2 or 3 monethts time halfe of their company dyed, espetialy in January & February, being the

---

² William Bradford, *Bradford's History of Plimoth Plantation* (Boston, 1901), pp. 109–110.

³ William Bradford, *Bradford's History of Plimoth Plantation* (Boston, 1901), pp. 111–112, 114–116.

depth of winter, and wanting houses & other comforts; being infected with the scurvie & other diseases, which this long vioage & their inacomodate condition had brought upon them; so as ther dyed some times 2 or 3 of a day, in the foresaid time; that of 100 & odd persons, scarce 50 remained. And of these in the time of most distres, ther was but 6 or 7 sound persons, who, to their great comendations be it spoken, spared no pains, night nor day, but with abundance of toyle and hazard of their owne health, fetched them woode, made them fires, drest them meat, made their beads, washed their lothsome cloaths, cloathed & uncloathed them; in a word, did all the homly & necessarie offices for them which dainty & quesie stomacks cannot endure to hear named; and all this willingly & cherfully, without any grudging in the least, shewing herein their true love unto their freinds & bretheren. A rare example & worthy to be remembred. Tow of these 7 were Mr. William Brewster, ther reverend Elder, & Myles Standish, ther Captein & military comander, unto whom my selfe, & many others, were much beholden in our low & sicke condition. And yet the Lord so upheld these persons, as in this generall calamity they were not at all infected either with sicknes, or lamnes. And what I have said of these, I may say of many others who dyed in this generall vissitation, & others yet living, that whilst they had health, yea, or any strength continuing, they were not wanting to any that had need of them. And I doute not but their recompence is with the Lord.

But I may not hear pass by an other remarkable passage not to be forgotten. As this calamitie fell among the passengers that were to be left here to plant, and were hasted a shore and made to drinke water, that the sea-men might have the more bear, and one in his sicknes desiring but a small cann of beere, it was answered, that if he were their owne father he should have none; the disease begane to fall amongst them also, so as allmost halfe of their company dyed before they went away. . . .

All this while the Indians came skulking about them, and would sometimes show them selves aloofe of, but when any aproached near them, they would rune away. And once they stoale away their tools wher they had been at worke, & were gone to diner. But about the 16 of March a certaine Indian came bouldly amongst them, and spoke to them in broken English, which they could well understand, but marvelled at it. At length they understood by discourse with him, that he was not of these parts, but belonged to the eastrene parts, wher some English-ships came to fhish, with whom he was aquainted, & could name sundrie of them by their names, amongst whom he had gott his language. He became proftable to them in aquainting them with many things concerning the state of the cuntry in the east-parts wher he lived, which was afterwards profitable unto them; as also of the people hear, of their names, number, & strength; of their situation & distance from this place, and who was cheefe amongst them. His name was *Samaset*; he tould them also of another Indian whos name was *Squanto*, a native of this place, who had been in England & could speake better English then him selfe. Being, after some time of entertainmente & gifts, dismist, a while after he came againe, & 5 more with him, & they brought againe all the tooles that were stolen away before, and made way for the coming of their great Sachem, called *Massasoyt*; who, about *4 or 5 days after*, came with the cheefe of his freinds & other attendance, with the aforesaid *Squanto*. With whom, after frendly entertainment, & some gifts given him, they made a peace with him (which hath now continued this 24 years) in these terms.

1. That neither he nor any of his, should injurie or doe hurte to any of their peopl.

2. That if any of his did any hurte to any of theirs, he should send the offender, that they might punish him.

3. That if any thing were taken away from any of theirs, he should cause it to be restored; and they should doe the like to his.

4. If any did unjustly warr against him, they would aide him; if any did warr against them, he should aide them.

5. He should send to his neighbours confederats, to certifie them of this, that they might not wrong them, but might be likewise comprised in the conditions of peace.

6. That when ther men came to them, they should leave their bows & arrows behind them.

After these things he returned to his place caled *Sowams*, some 40 mile from this place, but *Squanto* contiued with them, and was their interpreter, and was a spetiall instrument sent of God for their good beyond their expectation. He directed them how to set their corne, wher to take fish, and to procure other comodities, and was also their pilott to bring them to unknowne places for their profitt, and never left them till he dyed. He was a *native of this place*, & scarce any left alive besids him selfe. He was caried away with diverce others by one *Hunt*, a master of a ship, who thought to sell them for slaves in Spaine; but he got away for England, and was entertained by a marchante in London, & imployed to New-foundland & other parts, & lastly brought hither into these parts by one Mr. *Dermer*, a gentle-man imployed by Sr. Ferdinando Gorges....

Presidente & Counsell for New-England, that he made the peace betweene the salvages of these parts & the English; of which this plantation, as it is intimated, had the benefite.

SETTLING THE PLYMOUTH COLONY

Aided by knowledge gained from the Indians and willing to work hard, the hardy Pilgrims who survived the first dreadful December of 1620 learned to live on the edge of civilization. They took advantage of the richness of nature and harvested the products of both the land and the sea. Plymouth's colonists quickly attained self-sufficiency, attempted to repay their indebtedness, and offered shrewd advice to other Englishmen planning to settle in America. Within two years of their landing, Edward Winslow, a Pilgrim leader and later governor of the colony, explained how the pioneering process had been carried on and invited his friends to leave crowded places and join the Pilgrims in developing the new and vacant land:[4]

You shall understand that in this little time that a few of us have been here, we have built seven dwelling-houses and four for the use of the plantation, and have made preparation for divers others. We set the last spring some twenty acres of Indian corn, and sowed some six acres of barley and pease; and according to the manner of the Indians, we manured our ground with herrings, or rather shads, which we have in great abundance, and take with great ease at our doors. Our corn did prove well; and, God be praised, we had a good increase of Indian corn, and our barley indifferent good, but our pease not worth the gathering, for we feared they were too late sown. They came up very well, and blossomed; but the sun parched them in the blossom.

Our harvest being gotten in, our governor sent four men on fowling, that so we might,

---

[4] Albert B. Hart (ed.), *American History Told by Contemporaries* (New York, 1897), vol. 1, pp. 356–359.

after a special manner, rejoice together after we had gathered the fruit of our labors. They four in one day killed as much fowl as, with a little help beside, served the company almost a week. At which time, amongst other recreations, we exercised our arms; many of the Indians coming amongst us, and among the rest their greatest king, Massasoyt, with some ninety men, whom for three days we entertained and feasted; and they went out and killed five deer, which they brought to the plantation, and bestowed on our governor, and upon the captain and others. And although it be not always so plentiful as it was at this time with us, yet by the goodness of God we are so far from want, that we often wish you partakers of our plenty.

We have found the Indians very faithful in their covenant of peace with us, very loving, and ready to pleasure us. We often go to them, and they come to us. Some of us have been fifty miles by land in the country with them, the occasions and relations whereof you shall understand by our general and more full declaration of such things as are worth the noting. Yea, it hath pleased God so to possess the Indians with a fear of us and love unto us, that not only the greatest king amongst them called Massasoyt, but also all the princes and peoples round about us, have either made suit unto us, or been glad of any occasion to make peace with us; so that seven of them at once have sent their messengers to us to that end. Yea, an isle at sea, which we never saw, hath also, together with the former, yielded willingly to be under the protection and subject to our sovereign lord King James. So that there is now great peace amongst the Indians themselves, which was not formerly, neither would have been but for us; and we, for our parts, walk as peaceably and safely in the wood as in the highways in England. We entertain them familiarly in our houses, and they as friendly bestowing their venison on us. They are a people without any religion or knowledge of any God, yet very trusty, quick of apprehension, ripe-witted, just....

For the temper of the air here, it agreeth well with that in England; and if there be any difference at all, this is somewhat hotter in summer. Some think it to be colder in winter; but I cannot out of experience so say. The air is very clear, and not foggy, as hath been reported. I never in my life remember a more seasonable year than we have here enjoyed; and if we have once but kine, horses, and sheep, I make no question but men might live as contented here as in any part of the world. For fish and fowl, we have great abundance. Fresh cod in the summer is but coarse meat with us. Our bay is full of lobsters all the summer, and affordeth variety of other fish. In September we can take a hogshead of eels in a night, with small labor, and can dig them out of their beds all the winter. We have muscles and othus [others?] at our doors. Oysters we have none near, but we can have them brought by the Indians when we will. All the spring-time the earth sendeth forth naturally very good sallet herbs. Here are grapes, white and red, and very sweet and strong also; strawberries, gooseberries, raspas, &c.; plums of three sorts, white black, and red, being almost as good as a damson; abundance of roses, white, red and damask; single, but very sweet indeed. The country wanteth only industrious men to employ; for it would grieve your hearts if, as I, you had seen so many miles together by goodly rivers uninhabited; and withal, to consider those parts of the world wherein you live to be even greatly burthened with abundance of people. These things I thought good to let you understand, being the truth of things as near as I could experimentally take knowledge of, and that you might on our behalf give God thanks, who hath dealt so favorably with us....

When it pleaseth God we are settled and

fitted for the fishing business and other trading, I doubt not but by the blessing of God the gain will give content to all. In the mean time, that we have gotten we have sent by this ship; and though it be not much, yet it will witness for us that we have not been idle, considering the smallness of our number all this summer. We hope the merchants will accept of it, and be encouraged to furnish us with things needful for further employment, which will also encourage us to put forth ourselves to the uttermost.

Now because I expect your coming unto us, with other of our friends, whose company we much desire, I thought good to advertise you of a few things needful. Be careful to have a very good bread-room to put your biscuits in. Let your cask for beer and water be iron-bound, for the first tire, if not more. Let not your meat be dry-salted; none can better do it than the sailors. Let your meal be so hard trod in your cask that you shall need an adz or hatchet to work it out with. Trust not too much on us for corn at this time, for by reason of this last company that came, depending wholly upon us, we shall have little enough till harvest. Be careful to come by some of your meal to spend by the way; it will much refresh you. Build your cabins as open as you can, and bring good store of clothes and bedding with you. Bring every man a musket or fowling-piece. Let your piece be long in the barrel, and fear not the weight of it, for most of our shooting is from stands. Bring juice of lemons, and take it fasting; it is of good use. For hot waters, aniseed water is the best; but use it sparingly. If you bring any thing for comfort in the country, butter or sallet oil, or both, is very good. Our Indian corn, even the coarsest, maketh as pleasant meat as rice; therefore spare that, unless to spend by the way. Bring paper and linseed oil for your windows, with cotton yarn for your lamps. Let your shot be most for big fowls, and bring store of powder and shot. I forbear further to write for the present, hoping to see you by the next return.

REASONS FOR LEAVING MASSACHUSETTS BAY

Plymouth Colony grew slowly and the Pilgrims were soon engulfed by the Puritans, a vigorous group of dissenters who migrated from England to America between 1630 and 1640 because of their increasing hostility to the religious and political policies of Charles I. Puritan leadership was wealthy, influential, and educated. Whenever possible, in the early stages of migration and settlement, the Puritans attempted to substitute investment capital for labor. Not only could the Puritans raise money more easily than the Pilgrims, but also they could take advantage of pioneering techniques to subdue the wilderness which others had learned. The Puritans, too, came in large numbers.

The Puritans secured their American holdings by purchasing a grant from the Council of New England in 1628. They decided to take over the struggling fishing village of Salem, and with a royal charter formed the Massachusetts Bay Company. They were not above profit seeking, but the underlying purpose of the colony remained the establishment of a Zion where they could dictate their own religious practices as well as exclude others. When the Puritans set sail for America, they carried the charter of the Massachusetts Bay Company with them and quickly converted a corporation into an almost self-governing commonwealth. With its splendid harbor, Boston swiftly replaced Salem village as the center of the Puritan community.

The problems of their leaders centered on retaining the cohesive character of the sect, and they attempted to enforce doctrinal conformity in the settlement. But because the availability of land provided mobility, social control was difficult to exert. The Bay Colony had scarcely passed its first decade when several smaller settlements were established on its southern fringes. Roger Williams, who upheld the rights of Indians to their lands and advocated the separation of church and state, was banished and, after fleeing to live among the Indians, settled Providence. The region that is now Rhode Island soon filled with the exiled followers of John Wheelright, Anne Hutchinson, and Samuel Gorton—none of whom was acceptable in the Bay Colony. Opponents of Puritan rule continued to speak out vigorously against their policies, even at the risk of ostracism. Thomas Lechford, a Puritan lawyer, in writing "A Note of what things I mislike in the Country," aptly delineated many of the reasons why migration from Massachusetts to establish new communities continued during the long years of Puritan ascendancy:[5]

I doubt,

1. Whether so much time should be spent in the publique Ordinances, on the Sabbath day, because that thereby some necessary duties of the Sabbath must needs be hindered, as visitation of the sick, and poore, and family.

2. Whether matters of offence should be publiquely handled, either before the whole Church, or strangers.

3. Whether so much time should be spent in particular catechizing those that are admitted to the communion of the Church, either men or women; or that they should make long speeches; or when they come publiquely to be admitted, any should speak contradictorily, or in recommendation of any, unless before the Elders, upon just occasion.

4. Whether the censures of the Church should be ordered, in publique, before all the Church, or strangers, other then the denunciation of the censures, and pronunciation of the solutions.

5. Whether any of our *Nation* that is not extremely ignorant or scandalous, should bee kept from the Communion, or his children from *Baptisme*.

6. That many thousands of this Countrey have forgotten the very principles of Religion, which they were daily taught in *England*, by set forms and Scriptures read, as the Psalmes, first and second Lesson, the ten Commandments, the Creeds, and publique catechizings. And although conceived Prayer be good and holy, and so publike explications and applications of the Word, and also necessary both in and out of season: yet for the most part it may be feared they dull, amaze, confound, discourage the weake and ignorant, (which are the most of men) when they are in ordinary performed too tediously, or with the neglect of the Word read, and other premeditated formes inculcated, and may tend to more ignorance and inconvenience, then many good men are aware of.

7. I doubt there hath been, and is much neglect of endeavours, to teach, civilize, and convert the *Indian Nation*, that are about the Plantations.

8. Whether by the received principles, it bee *possible* to teach, civilize, or convert them, or when they are converted, to maintain Gods worship among them.

9. That electorie courses will not long be safe here, either in Church or Commonwealth.

10. That the civill government is not so equally administred, nor can be, divers orders or by-laws considered.

11. That unless these things be wisely and in time prevented, many of your usefullest men will remove and scatter from you.

---

[5] Albert B. Hart (ed.), *American History Told by Contemporaries* (New York, 1897), vol. 1, pp. 388–389.

OCCUPYING THE CONNECTICUT VALLEY

Voluntary removal from Massachusetts by distinguished and substantial citizens, who really shared Puritan goals but who may have disagreed on the means of achieving them, distressed the colony's leadership more than the exiled dissenters. This dispersal would not only weaken the Boston center but would also create potential rivals. The effort to keep the Reverend Thomas Hooker and the Newtown (Cambridge) congregation from moving to the Connecticut Valley, only four years after the Bay Colony was established, typified the problem. In his journal, John Winthrop, the leading Puritan magistrate, summarized a meeting of the Massachusetts General Court at Newtown in September 1634, conveying the sharpness of tempers and arguments in the discussion over Hooker's departure:[6]

The general court began at Newtown, and continued a week, and then was adjourned fourteen days. Many things were there agitated and concluded, as fortifying in Castle Island, Dorchester, and Charlestown; also against tobacco, and costly apparel, and immodest fashions; and committees appointed for setting out the bounds of towns; with divers other matters, which do appear upon record. But the main business, which spent the most time, and caused the adjourning of the court, was about the removal of Newtown. They had leave, the last general court, to look out some place for enlargement or removal, with promise of having it confirmed to them, if it were not prejudicial to any other plantation; and now they moved, that they might have leave to remove to Connecticut. This matter was debated divers days, and many reasons alleged pro and con. The principal reasons for their removal were, 1. Their want of accommodation for their cattle, so as they were not able to maintain their ministers, nor could receive any more of their friends to help them; and here it was alleged by Mr. Hooker, as a fundamental error, that towns were set so near each to other.

2. The fruitfulness and commodiousness of Connecticut, and the danger of having it possessed by others, Dutch or English.

3. The strong bent of their spirits to remove thither.

Against these it was said, 1. That, in point of conscience, they ought not to depart from us, being knit to us in one body, and bound by oath to seek the welfare of this commonwealth.

2. That, in point of state and civil policy, we ought not to give them leave to depart. 1. Being we were now weak and in danger to be assailed. 2. The departure of Mr. Hooker would not only draw many from us, but also divert other friends that would come to us. 3. We should expose them to evident peril, both from the Dutch (who made claim to the same river, and had already built a fort there) and from the Indians, and also from our own state at home, who would not endure they should sit down without a patent in any place which our king lays claim unto.

3. They might be accommodated at home by some enlargement which other towns offered.

4. They might remove to Merimack, or any other place within our patent.

5. The removing of a candlestick is a great judgment, which is to be avoided.

Upon these and other arguments the court being divided, it was put to vote; and, of the deputies, fifteen were for their departure, and ten against it. The governor and two assistants were for it, and the deputy and all the rest of the assistants were against it, (except

---

[6] James K. Hosmer (ed.), *Winthrop's Journal* (New York, 1908), vol. 1, pp. 132–134.

the secretary, who gave no vote;) whereupon no record was entered, because there were not six assistants in the vote, as the patent requires. Upon this grew a great difference between the governor and assistants, and the deputies. They would not yield the assistants a negative voice, and the others (considering how dangerous it might be to the commonwealth, if they should not keep that strength to balance the greater number of the deputies) thought it safe to stand upon it. So, when they could proceed no farther, the whole court agreed to keep a day of humiliation to seek the Lord, which accordingly was done, in all the congregations, the 18th day of this month; and the 24th the court met again. Before they began, Mr. Cotton preached, (being desired by all the court, upon Mr. Hooker's instant excuse of his unfitness for that occasion). He took his text out of Hag. ii. 4, etc., out of which he laid down the nature or strength (as he termed it) of the magistracy, ministry, and people, viz.,—the strength of the magistracy to be their authority; of the people, their liberty; and of the ministry, their purity; and showed how all of these had a negative voice, etc., and that yet the ultimate resolution, etc., ought to be in the whole body of the people, etc., with answer to all objections, and a declaration of the people's duty and right to maintain their true liberties against any unjust violence, etc., which gave great satisfaction to the company. And it pleased the Lord so to assist him, and to bless his own ordinance, that the affairs of the court went on cheerfully; and although all were not satisfied about the negative voice to be left to the magistrates, yet no man moved aught about it, and the congregation of Newtown came and accepted of such enlargement as had formerly been offered them by Boston and Watertown; and so the fear of their removal to Connecticut was removed.

At this court Mr. Goodwin, a very reverend and godly man, being the elder of the congregation of Newtown, having, in heat of argument, used some unreverend speech to one of the assistants, and being reproved for the same in the open court, did gravely and humbly acknowledge his fault, etc.

REBELLION AGAINST PURITANISM: NEW HAMPSHIRE

The continuing threatened serious losses of population, resulting from the incredible centrifugal power within the Puritan community, was only one reason why its leaders attempted to expand the colony's boundaries. An equally pressing problem stemmed from the presence of exiles or non-Puritan settlers who came in increasing numbers to establish fishing and trading villages in New England and who challenged the Bay Colony's hegemony. Responding to these threats, the Puritans laid claim to and occupied towns and vacant lands wherever they could. Members of the Anglican Church joined the chorus of exiled dissenters who denounced the Puritans and appealed to England for help. In the 1660s a commission sent from England to examine the charges—admittedly hostile to the Puritans—submitted this report with the purpose of restricting the expansion of Massachusetts:[7]

New Hampshire is the name of a Province granted to Captain Robert Mason about the yeare 1635 and was to begin on the Sea Coast 3 Miles easterly of Merimack River and reaches to Piscatoquay, and 60 miles of that Breath up into the Country, but now it is usurped by the Mattachusets who pretend that it is within their Bounds, and that the

---

[7] Albert B. Hart (ed.), *American History Told by Contemporaries* (New York, 1897), vol. 1, p. 428.

People Petitioned to be within their Protection, it is true that difference of Opinion made a Division amongst them, and a few who were for Congregationall Churches did Petition for their Assistance by which occasion partly by force, partly by Composition they have engrossed the whole and named it Norfolke.

When the Mattachusets Charter was first granted the Mouths only of the two Rivers Charles and Merimack were knowne to them, for they durst not travaile farre up into the Country, presently after there was an house erected 3 large Miles north from Merimack which was for 17 yeares called and knowne to be the bounds of the Matachusetts, and in that time was this Pattent graunted to Captain Mason.

Mr. Wheelewright was banished out of the Jurisdiction of the Mattachusetts and was permitted to inhabite immediatly beyond that bound house, as himselfe gave Testimony before the Commissioners.

Mr. Mason had a Pattent for some Land about Cape Anne before the Mattachusetts had their first Pattent, whereupon Captain Mason and Mr. Cradock, who was the first Governour of the Mattachusetts, and lived in London agreed that the Matachusetts should have that Land which was graunted to Captain Mason about Cape Anne, and Captain Mason should have that Land which was beyond Merimack River and graunted to the Matachusets. This agreement was sent to Mr. Henry Jocelin to get recorded at Boston, but before he could have leisure to goe thither he heard that Captain Mason was dead, and therefore went not, of this he made Affidavit before the Commissioners who forbore to doe any thing about the Limitts of this Province till this might more fully be proved, though the Generality of the People Petitioned to be taken from under the Matachusets Tyranny, as themselves styled it.

NEWS OF VICTORY OVER THE PEQUOTS

The rapid settlement of Massachusetts led to an early clash with the Indians of New England. Although many of the tribes had remained docile in the face of the Bay Colony's growth, the Pequot, an offshoot of the Mohawk, engaged in repeated attacks on isolated settlers and traders. Driven eastward by the Iroquois from upstate New York, the Pequot felt trapped and isolated. The tribe, linked by trade with the Dutch, who had planted a colony in New Amsterdam, attempted to rally the other Massachusetts tribes against English intrusion. Puritan leaders could not allow what they viewed as Indian arrogance to go unpunished. The wanton murder of English traders triggered the Pequot war, a ruthless attack on the Indians that reached a bloody climax in 1637. John Winthrop of Massachusetts hastily penned a joyous letter of victory to his good friend William Bradford of Plymouth and described the circumstances of the last fight. Little reading between the lines is necessary to understand the Puritan attitude toward the Indians:[8]

WORTHY SIR:

I received your loving letter, and am much provoked to express my affections towards you, but straitnes of time forbids me; for my desire is to acquainte you with the Lords greate mercies towards us, in our prevailing against his & our enimies; that you may rejoyce and praise his name with us. About 80 of our men, haveing costed along towards the Dutch plantation, (some times by water, but most by land,) mett hear & ther with some Pequents, whom they slew or tooke prisoners. 2 sachems they tooke, & beheaded; and not hearing of Sassacous, (the cheefe sachem,)

---

[8] William Bradford, *Bradford's History of Plimoth Plantation* (Boston, 1901), pp. 427–430.

they gave a prisoner his life, to goe and find him out. He wente and brought them word where he was, but Sassacouse, suspecting him to be a spie, after he was gone, fled away with some 20 more to the Mowakes, so our men missed of him. Yet, deviding them selves, and ranging up & downe, as the providence of God guided them (for the Indeans were all gone, save 3 or 4 and they knew not whither to guid them, or els would not), upon the 13 of this month, they light upon a great company of them, viz. 80 strong men, & 200 women & children, in a small Indean towne, fast by a hideous swamp, which they all slipped into before our men could gett to them. Our captains were not then come togeither, but ther was Mr. Ludlow and Captaine Masson, with some 10 of their men, & Captaine Patrick with some 20 or more of his, who, shooting at the Indeans, Captaine Trask with 50 more came soone in at the noyse. Then they gave order to surround the swampe, it being about a mile aboute; but Levetenante Davenporte & some 12 more, not hearing that comand, fell into the swampe among the Indeans. The swampe was so thicke with shrubwoode, & so boggie with all, that some of them stuck fast, and received many shott. Levetenant Davenport was dangerously wounded aboute his armehole, and another shott in the head, so as, fainting, they were in great danger to have been taken by the Indeans. But Sargante Rigges, & Jeffery, and 2 or 3 more, rescued them, and slew diverse of the Indeans with their swords. After they were drawne out, the Indeans desired parley, & were offered (by Thomas Stanton, our interpretour) that, if they would come out, and yeeld them selves, they should have their lives, all that had not their hands in the English blood. Wherupon the sachem of the place came forth, and an old man or 2 & their wives and children, and after that some other women & children, and so they spake 2 howers, till it was night. Then Thomas Stanton was sente into them againe, to call them forth; but they said they would selle their lives their, and so shott at him so thicke as, if he had not cried out, and been presently rescued, they had slaine him. Then our men cutt of a place of the swampe with their swords, and cooped the Indeans into so narrow a compass, as they could easier kill them throw the thickets. So they continued all the night, standing aboute 12 foote one from an other, and the Indeans, coming close up to our men, shot their arrows so thicke, as they pierced their hatte brimes, & their sleeves, & stockins, & other parts of their cloaths, yet so miraculously did the Lord preserve them as not one of them was wounded, save those 3 who rashly went into the swampe. When it was nere day, it grue very darke, so as those of them which were left dropt away betweene our men, though they stood but 12 or 14 foote assunder; but were presenly discovered, & some killed in the pursute. Upon searching of the swampe, the next morning, they found 9 slaine, & some they pulled up, whom the Indeans had buried in the mire, so as they doe thinke that, of all this company, not 20 did escape, for they after found some who dyed in their flight of their wounds received. The prisoners were devided, some to those of the river, and the rest to us. Of these we send the male children to Bermuda, by Mr. William Peirce, & the women & maid children are disposed aboute in the townes. Ther have been now slaine & taken, in all, aboute 700. The rest are dispersed, and the Indeans in all quarters so terrified as all their friends are affraid to receive them. 2 of the sachems of Long Iland came to Mr. Stoughton and tendered them selves to be tributaries under our protection. And 2 of the Neepnett sachems have been with me to seeke our frendship. Amonge the prisoners we have the wife

& children of Mononotto, a womon of a very modest countenance and behaviour. It was by her mediation that the 2 English maids were spared from death, and were kindly used by her; so that I have taken charge of her. One of her first requests was, that the English would not abuse her body, and that her children might not be taken from her. Those which were wounded were fetched of soone by John Galopp, who came with his shalop in a happie houre, to bring them victuals, and to carrie their wounded men to the pinass, wher our cheefe surgeon was, with Mr. Wilson, being aboute 8 leagues off. Our people are all in health, (the Lord be praised,) and allthough they had marched in their armes all the day, and had been in fight all the night, yet they professed they found them selves so fresh as they could willingly have gone to such another bussines.

This is the substance of that which I received, though I am forced to omite many considerable circomstances. So, being in much straitnes of time, (the ships being to departe within this 4 days, and in them the Lord Lee and Mr. Vane,) I hear breake of, and with harty saluts to, &c., I rest

Yours assured,
JOHN WINTHROP

THE PURITAN LAND SYSTEM

The destruction of the Pequot Indians brought forty years of precarious peace to the New England frontier and allowed for the systematic advance of settlers. Unlike the southern planters who moved as individuals and used the blank patent system to claim land, the Puritans moved in groups to establish communities because their socio-religious cohesiveness would have deteriorated in a distinctly rural and individualistic environment. This system reduced litigation over conflicting land claims, provided an orderly basis for expansion, and served the goals of the sect. But doubts quickly arose, both within and without the Puritan community, as to whether organized town planting assured the most equitable distribution of land. Edward Johnson, who helped establish Woburn, Massachusetts, described the Puritan land system when it operated at its best.[9]

But to begin, this Town, as all others, had its bounds fixed by the General Court, to the contenese [contents] of four miles square, (beginning at the end of Charles Town bounds). The grant is to seven men of good and honest report, upon condition, that within two year they erect houses for habitation thereon, and so go on to make a Town thereof, upon the Act of Court; these seven men have power to give and grant out lands unto any persons who are willing to take up their dwellings within the said precinct, and to be admitted to al common priviledges of the said Town, giving them such an ample portion, both of Medow and Upland, as their present and future stock of cattel and hands were like to improve, with eye had to others that might after come to populate the said Town; this they did without any respect of persons, yet such as were exorbitant, and of a turbulent spirit, unfit for a civil society, they would reject, till they come to mend their manners; such came not to enjoy any freehold. These seven men ordered and disposed of the streets of the Town, as might be best for improvement of the Land, and yet civil and religious society maintained; to which end those that had land neerest the place for Sabbath Assembly, had a lesser quantity at home, and more farther off to improve for corn, of all kinds; they refused

---

[9] J. Franklin Jameson (ed.), *Johnson's Wonder-Working Providence* (New York, 1910), pp. 213–214.

not men for their poverty, but according to their ability were helpful to the poorest sort, in building their houses, and distributed to them land accordingly; the poorest had six or seven acres of Medow, and twenty five of Upland, or thereabouts. Thus was this Town populated, to the number of sixty families, or thereabout, and after this manner are the Towns of New England peopled. The scituation of this Town is in the highest part of the yet peopled land, neere upon the head-springs of many considerable rivers, or their branches, as the first rise of Ipswitch river, and the rise of Shashin river, one of the most considerable branches of Merrimeck, as also the first rise of Mistick river and ponds, it is very full of pleasant springs, and great variety of very good water, which the Summers heat causeth to be more cooler, and the Winters cold maketh more warmer; their Medows are not large, but lye in divers places to particular dwellings, the like doth their Springs; their Land is very fruitful in many places, although they have no great quantity of plain land in any one place, yet doth their Rocks and Swamps yeeld very good food for cattel; as also they have Mast and Tar for shipping, but the distance of place by land causeth them as yet to be unprofitable; they have great store of iron ore; their meeting-house stands in a small Plain, where four streets meet; the people are very laborious, if not exceeding some of them.

Now to declare how this people proceeded in religious matters, and so consequently all the Churches of Christ planted in New-England, when they came once to hopes of being such a competent number of people, as might be able to maintain a Minister, they then surely seated themselves, and not before, it being as unnatural for a right N. E. man to live without an able Ministery, as for a Smith to work his iron without a fire. . . .

Johnson's view of the New England land system glossed over defects that gradually assumed importance. For example, in the early stages of community development the proprietors of towns willingly granted lands and political equality to morally acceptable newcomers. But as land became scarce, new settlers were either denied admission to a town or limited in their political and economic rights because the corporation owners saw the opportunity to profit by holding good lands for speculation. Even efforts taken in law courts to break the power of the proprietors proved unsuccessful. The Bay Colony's leadership never espoused equality and saw the land policy as a means of controlling the "natural liberty" of man. Land speculation in New England took two forms: holding lands within established towns and granting lands on the frontier to select members of the Puritan community who could wait for the advance of settlers before selling their holdings. The New England land scheme undoubtedly would have failed if the settlers had found an agricultural staple crop comparable to tobacco, but the lack of a staple and the intractable soil of the region compelled the Puritans to live in groups and share the burden of clearing hillsides of rocks and trees.

The march of New England settlers along the coast or into the interior river valleys followed in the footfalls of merchants who competed with the Dutch and the Swedes for control of the Indian trade. Initially the Hollanders had the best of the contest. From New Amsterdam, which they founded in 1624, the Dutch traders drove the English from the Delaware Valley in 1643 and in 1655, ousted the Swedes, who had pioneered in the area since 1638. But the major Anglo-Dutch confrontation focused on Fort Orange, later called Albany, in the upper Hudson Valley, where the New Englanders attempted to claim a share of the profitable Iroquois trade. The issue was resolved in 1664 when Peter Stuyvesant, the stormy governor of New Netherland, reluctantly surrendered control of the colony to an English fleet. Thereafter, New England and New York merchants clashed over the trade.

KING PHILIP'S WAR

The fast-moving traders and the steady expansion of towns left many New England Indian tribes surrounded and dependent upon the white settlers. Rigorous Puritan Indian regulations, systematically violated for the benefit of corrupt white men plus the avarice of land speculators, paved the way for King Philip's War (1675-1677), a bloody conflict that brought terror to thousands of pioneers and caused a general retreat into the major centers of population. Colonial losses so staggered the English that the home government sent Edward Randolph to America as a special agent to investigate the disaster. His views of the causes and results of King Philip's War help to explain not only Puritanism's built-in rationalizations for its defects but also the more practical considerations that led to the uprising:[10]

Eighth Enquiry. What hath been the originall cause of the present warre with the natives. What are the advantages or disadvantages arising thereby and will probably be the End?

Various are the reports and conjectures of the causes of the present Indian warre. Some impute it to an imprudent zeal in the magistrates of Boston to christianize those heathen before they were civilized and injoyning them the strict observation of their lawes, which, to a people so rude and licentious, hath proved even intollerable, and that the more, for that while the magistrates, for their profit, put the lawes severely in execution against the Indians, the people, on the other side, for lucre and gain, intice and provoke the Indians to the breach thereof, especially to drunkennesse, to which those people are so generally addicted that they will strip themselves to their skin to have their fill of rume and brandy, the Massachusets having made a law that every Indian drunke should pay 10s. or be whipped, according to the discretion of the magistrate. Many of these poor people willingly offered their backs to the lash to save their money; whereupon, the magistrates finding much trouble and no profit to arise to the government by whipping, did change that punishment into 10 days worke for such as could not or would not pay the fine of 10s. which did highly incense the Indians.

Some beleeve there have been vagrant and jesuiticall priests, who have made it their businesse, for some yeares past, to goe from Sachim to Sachim, to exasperate the Indians against the English and to bring them into a confederacy, and that they were promised supplies from France and other parts to extirpate the English nation out of the continent of America. Others impute the cause to some injuries offered to the Sachim Philip; for he being possessed of a tract of land called Mount Hope, a very fertile, pleasant and rich soyle, some English had a mind to dispossesse him thereof, who never wanting one pretence or other to attain their end, complained of injuries done by Philip and his Indians to their stock and cattle, whereupon Philip was often summoned before the magistrate, sometimes imprisoned, and never released but upon parting with a considerable part of his land.

But the government of the Massachusets (to give it in their own words) do declare

---

[10] Albert B. Hart (ed.), *American History Told by Contemporaries* (New York, 1897), vol. 1, pp. 458–460.

these are the great evils for which God hath given the heathen commission to rise against them: The wofull breach of the 5th commandment, in contempt of their authority, which is a sin highly provoking to the Lord: For men wearing long hayre and perewigs made of womens hayre; for women wearing borders of hayre and for cutting, curling and laying out the hayre, and disguising themselves by following strange fashions in their apparell: For profanesse in the people not frequenting their meetings, and others going away before the blessing be pronounced: For suffering the Quakers to live amongst them and to set up their threshholds by Gods thresholds, contrary to their old lawes and resolutions.

With many such reasons, but whatever be the cause, the English have contributed much to their misfortunes, for they first taught the Indians the use of armes, and admitted them to be present at all their musters and trainings, and shewed them how to handle, mend and fix their muskets, and have been furnished with all sorts of armes by permission of the government, so that the Indians are become excellent firemen. And at Natick there was a gathered church of praying Indians, who were exercised as trained bands, under officers of their owne; these have been the most barbarous and cruel enemies to the English of any others. Capt. Tom, their leader, being lately taken and hanged at Boston, with one other of their chiefs.

That notwithstanding the ancient law of the country, made in the year 1633, that no person should sell any armes or ammunition to any Indian upon penalty of 10*l*. for every gun, 5*l*. for a pound of powder, and 40*s*. for a pound of shot, yet the government of the Massachusets in the year 1657, upon designe to monopolize the whole Indian trade did publish and declare that the trade of furrs and peltry with the Indians in their jurisdiction did solely and properly belong to their commonwealth and not to every indifferent person, and did enact that no person should trade with the Indians for any sort of peltry, except such as were authorized by that court, under the penalty of 100*l*. for every offence, giving liberty to all such as should have licence from them to sell, unto any Indian, guns, swords, powder and shot, paying to the treasurer 3*d*. for each gun and for each dozen of swords; 6*d*. for a pound of powder and for every ten pounds of shot, by which means the Indians have been abundantly furnished with great store of armes and ammunition to the utter ruin and undoing of many families in the neighbouring colonies to inrich some few of their relations and church members.

No advantage but many disadvantages have arisen to the English by the warre, for about 600 men have been slaine, and 12 captains, most of them brave and stout persons and of loyal principles, whilest the church members had liberty to stay at home and not hazard their persons in the wildernesse.

The losse to the English in the severall colonies, in their habitations and stock, is reckoned to amount to 150,000*l*. there having been about 1200 houses burned, 8000 head of cattle, great and small, killed, and many thousand bushels of wheat, pease and other grain burned (of which the Massachusets colony hath not been damnifyed one third part, the great losse falling upon New Plymouth and Connecticot colonies) and upward of 3000 Indians men women and children destroyed, who if well managed would have been very serviceable to the English, which makes all manner of labour dear.

The warre at present is near an end. In Plymouth colony the Indians surrender themselves to Gov. Winslow, upon mercy, and bring in all their armes, are wholly at his disposall, except life and transportation; but for all such as have been notoriously cruell to women and children, so soon as discovered they are to be executed in the sight of their fellow Indians.

The government of Boston have concluded a peace upon these terms.

1. That there be henceforward a firme peace between the Indians and English.

2. That after publication of the articles of peace by the generall court, if any English shall willfully kill an Indian, upon due proof, he shall dye, and if an Indian kill an Englishman and escape, the Indians are to produce him, and he to passe tryall by the English lawes.

That the Indians shall not conceal any known enemies to the English, but shall discover them and bring them to the English.

That upon all occasions the Indians are to ayd and assist the English against their enemies, and to be under English command.

That all Indians have liberty to sit down at their former habitations without let.

King Philip's War was the last major frontier problem of the seventeenth century. The crushing defeat administered to the Indians, the renewed advance of English settlers, and the creation of pallisaded, or fortified, towns guaranteed the successful occupation of coastal lands and river bottoms. As the century drew to a close, the New Englander, like his counterpart in the southern tidewater, had developed and perfected the techniques that assured his survival in America.

CHAPTER 5 | *The Old West,*
1675-1750

The persistent expansion of English settlers along the coast and beyond the fall line resulted in the quick utilization of the best and most accessible lands for farms and towns. Where population pressure was low, prudent speculators bought huge tracts of land, patiently waiting for natural increase to spur the value of their holdings. Where population pressure was high, land prices jumped and newcomers labored as indentured servants, turned squatter, or looked for opportunity elsewhere. Meanwhile, accelerated changes in the economic, political, and religious conditions in Europe hurried a greater stream of immigrants to America; and in the colonies religious disagreement, economic regulation, political dissent, and slavery urged white settlers to seek new lands. In the South, even well-established and wealthy tidewater planters could not resist the temptation to think in terms of better and larger holdings farther west. In the North, an emerging group of domestic investors, their coffers filled with profits accrued from commerce or land, saw the West as a logical area for speculation.

At the time of King Philip's War little was known of the belt of land that lay west of the line of settlement. The chain of mountains, rugged uplands, and deep fertile valleys that ranged from New England to the Carolinas proved to be a unique physiographic province.

Called the Old West by historians, it ignored colonial boundaries and achieved a unity in the minds of the settlers. In the South, the Old West started in the piedmont and sloped swiftly upward to the Appalachian Mountains. At the eastern edge were the Blue Ridge Mountains, a rugged front of steep walled hills out of which tumbled rivers and small streams that flowed eastward across the coastal plain to the Atlantic. Beyond the Blue Ridge Mountains lay a chain of valleys and mountain belts in parallel ridges that taken together were called the Great Valley. At the western edge of the Great Valley were the Allegheny Mountains. In a sense the Great Valley extended from New England to the Carolinas. The primary differences in the regions were that the mountains in the North were higher, more difficult to cross, genuinely forbidding, and the rivers that flowed from them turned south rather than east as they cut gaps in the mountains and drained into the Atlantic.

EXPLORING THE BACKCOUNTRY:
JOHN LEDERER

Between the years 1675 and 1775, land-hungry settlers searched the Old West for rich soil, useful lumber, and good water, following the trails marked by Indian traders and the pathfinders in the service of wealthy speculators. Many of these earliest western explorers left no record; shadowy figures, they engaged in the Indian trade, climbed mountains for their own satisfaction, or perhaps even lost their lives to Indian warriors. One of the first official explorers was John Lederer, a twenty-six-year-old German medical student employed by Governor William Berkeley of Virginia to find a way through the Appalachian barrier and discover what lay beyond. Lederer made three journeys; and although his written account proved somewhat fanciful, his experience served as good advice for future traders and travelers:[1]

Two breaches there are in the *Apalataeen* Mountains, opening a passage into the Western parts of the Continent. One, as I am informed by Indians, at a place called *Zynodoa*, to the Norward; the other at *Sara*, where I have been my self: but the way thither being thorow a vast Forest, where you seldom fall into any Road or Path, you must shape your course by a Compass; though some, for want of one, have taken their direction from the North-side of the trees, which is dintinguished from the rest by quantities of thick Moss growing there. You will not meet with many hinderances on horseback in your passage to the Mountains, but where your course is interrupted by branches of the great Rivers, which in many places are not Fordable; and therefore if you be unprovided of means or strength to make a Bridge by felling trees across, you may be forced to go a great way about: in this respect company is necessary, but in others so inconvenient, that I would not advise above half a dozen, or ten at the most, to travel together; and of these, the major part Indians: for the Nations in your way are prone to jealousie and mischief towards Christians in a considerable Body, and as courteous and hearty to a few, from whom they apprehend no danger.

When you pass thorow an even level Country, where you can take no particular remarks from hill or waters to guide your self by when you come back, you must not forget to notch the trees as you go along with your small Hatchet, that in your return you may know when you fall into the same way which you went. By this means you will be certain of the place you are in, and may govern your course homeward accordingly.

In stead of Bread, I used the meal of parched *Mayz*, i.e. Indian Wheat; which when I eat, I seasoned with a little Salt. This is both more portable and strengthning then Biscuit, and will suffer no mouldiness by any weather. For other provisions, you may securely trust to your Gun, the Woods being full of Fallow, and *Savanae* of Red-Deer, besides great variety of excellent Fowl, as wilde Turkeys, Pigeons, Partridges, Phesants &c. But you must not forget to dry or barbecue some of these before you come to the Mountains: for upon them you will meet with no Game, except a few Bears.

Such as cannot lie on the ground, must be provided with light Hamacks, which hung in the trees, are more cool and pleasant then any bed whatsoever.

The Order and Discipline to be observed in this Expedition is, that an Indian Scout or two march as far before the rest of the company as they can in sight, both for the finding out provision, and discovery of Ambushes, if any should be laid by Enemies. Let your other Indians keep on the right and left hand, armed not onely with Guns, but Bills and Hatchets, to build small Arbours or Cottages of boughs and bark of trees, to

---

[1] William P. Cummings (ed.), *The Discoveries of John Lederer* (Charlottesville, Va.: The University Press of Virginia, 1958), pp. 38–43.

shelter and defend you from the injuries of the weather. At nights it is necessary to make great fires round about the place where you take up your lodging, as well to scare Wild-beasts away, as to purifie the air. Neither must you fail to go the Round at the close of the evening: for then, and betimes in the morning, the Indians put all their designes in execution: in the night they never attempt any thing.

When in the remote parts you draw near to an Indian Town, you must by your Scouts inform your self whether they hold any correspondence with the *Sasquesahana-ughs*: for to such you must give notice of your approach by a Gun; which amongst other Indians is to be avoided, because being ignorant of their use, it would affright and dispose them to some treacherous practice against you.

Being arrived at a Town, enter no house until you are invited; and then seem not afraid to be led in pinion'd like a prisoner: for that is a Ceremony they use to friend and enemies without distinction.

You must accept of an invitation from the Seniors, before that of young men; and refuse nothing that is offered or set afore you: for they are very jealous, and sensible of the least slighting or neglect from strangers, and mindful of Revenge....

If you barely designe a Home-trade with neighbour-Indians, for skins of Deer, Beaver, Otter, Wild-Cat, Fox, Racoon, &c. your best Truck is a sort of course Trading Cloth, of which a yard and a half makes a Matchcoat or Mantle fit for their wear; as also Axes, Hoes, Knives, Sizars and all sorts of edg'd tools. Guns, Powder and Shot, &c. are Commodities they will greedily barter for: but to supply the Indians with Arms and Ammunition, is prohibited in all English Governments.

In dealing with the Indians, you must be positive and at a word: for if they perswade you to fall any thing in your price, they will spend time in higgling for further abatements, and seldom conclude any Bargain. Sometimes you may with Brandy or Strong liquor dispose them to an humour of giving you ten times the value of your commodity; and at other times they are so hide-bound, that they will not offer half the Market-price, especially if they be aware that you have a designe to circumvent them with drink, or that they think you have a desire to their goods, which you must seem to slight and disparage.

To the remoter Indians you must carry other kinds of Truck, as small Looking-glasses, Pictures, Beads and Bracelets of glass, Knives, Sizars, and all manner of gaudy toys and knacks for children, which are light and portable. For they are apt to admire such trinkets, and will purchase them at any rate, either with their currant Coyn of small shells, which they call *Roanoack* or *Peack*, or perhaps with Pearl, Vermilion, pieces of Christal; and towards *Ushery*, with some odde pieces of Plate or Buillon, which they sometimes receive in Truck from the *Oestacks*.

Could I have foreseen when I set out, the advantages to be made by a Trade with those remote Indians, I had gone better provided; though perhaps I might have run a great hazard of my life, had I purchased considerably amongst them, by carrying wealth unguarded through so many different Nations of barbarous people: therefore it is vain for any man to propose to himself, or undertake a Trade at that distance, unless he goes with strength to defend, as well as an Adventure to purchase such Commodities: for in such a designe many ought to joyn and go in company.

EXPLORING THE BACKCOUNTRY: JAMES NEEDHAM

Quick on Lederer's heels were other explorers financed by Governor Berkeley or his agent, Abraham Wood, a frontier captain who, as early as 1650, had found the forks of the Roanoke River. In 1673, Wood recruited James Needham, a reliable Carolina trader, and Gabriel Arthur, probably an illiterate indentured servant, to trade in the southern piedmont. Neither these explorers nor their employer anticipated the outcome of their contact with the Cherokee Indians. Abraham Wood later retold their story to a friend in England.[2]

I sent out two English men and eight Indians, with accommodation for three moneths but by misfortune and unwillingness of the Indians before the mountaines, that any should discover beyond them my people returned effecting little, to be short, on the 17th of May: 1673 I sent them out againe, with the like number of Indians and four horses about the 25th of June they mett with the Tomahitans as they were journying from the mountains to the Occhonechees. The Tomahaitans told my men that if an English man would stay with them they would some of them com to my plantation with a letter which eleven of them did accordingly, and about fourty of them promised to stay with my men att Occhonechee untill the eleven returned: the effect of the letter was they resolved by Gods Blessing to goe through with the Tomahitans the eleven resolve to stay at my house three days to rest themselves. I hastned away another English man and a horse to Occhonechee to give them intelligence; but by the extremity of raine they could not bee expeeditious, so that through the instigation of the Occhonechees, and through the doubt they had, as I suppose, of the miscarrge of theire men att my plantations, being soe possest by the other Indians, the Tomihitans went away, and my two men with them, and as since I understand the eleven over tooke them, before they came to the mountains, with my letter, which rejoyced the two English men and one Appomattecke Indian for noe more durst to go a long with them; they jornied nine days from Occhonechee to Sitteree: west and by south, past nine rivers and creeks which all end in this side the mountaines and emty them selves into the east sea. Sitteree being the last towne of inhabitance and not any path further untill they came within two days jorney of the Tomahitans; they travell from thence up the mountaines upon the sun setting all the way, and in foure dayes gett to the toppe, some times leading theire horses sometimes rideing. The ridge upon the topp is not above two hundred paces over; the decent better then on this side. in halfe a day they came to the foot, and then levell ground all the way, many slashes upon the heads of small runns. The slashes are full of very great canes and the water runes to the north west. They pass five rivers and about two hundred paces over the fifth being the middle most halfe a mile broad all sandy bottoms, with peble stones, all foardable and all empties themselves north west, when they travell upon the plaines, from the mountains they goe downe, for severall dayes they see straged hilles on theire right hand, as they judge two days journy from them, by this time they have lost all theire horses but one; not so much by the badness of the way as by hard travell. not haveing time to feed. when they lost sight of those hilles they see a

---

[2] Clarence W. Alvord and Lee Bidgood (eds.), *The First Explorations of the Trans-Allegheny Region by the Virginians, 1650–1674* (Cleveland, 1912), pp. 210–213.

fogg or smoke like a cloud from whence raine falls for severall days on their right hand as they travell still towards the sun setting great store of game, all along as turkes deere, ellkes, beare, woolfe and other vermin very tame, at the end of fifteen dayes from Sitteree they arive at the Tomahitans river, being the 6th river from the mountains. this river att the Tomahitans towne seemes to run more westerly than the other five. This river they past in cannoos the town being seated in the other side about foure hundred paces broad above the town, within sight, the horse they had left waded only a small channell swam, they were very kindly entertained by them, even to addoration in their cerrimonies of courtesies and a stake was sett up in the middle of the towne to fasten the horse to, and aboundance of corne and all manner of pulse with fish, flesh and beares oyle for the horse to feed upon and a scaffold sett up before day for my two men and Appomattocke Indian that theire people might stand and gaze at them and not offend them by theire throng. This towne is seated on the river side, haveing the clefts of the river on the one side being very high for its defence, the other three sides trees of two foot over, pitched on end, twelve foot high, and on the topps scafolds placed with parrapits to defend the walls and offend theire enemies which men stand on to fight, many nations of Indians inhabitt downe this river, which runes west upon the salts which they are att warre withe and to that end keepe one hundred and fifty cannoes under the command of theire forte. the leaste of them will carry twenty men, and made sharpe at both ends like a wherry for swiftness, this forte is foure square; 300: paces over and the houses sett in streets, many hornes like bulls hornes lye upon theire dunghills, store of fish they have, one sort they have like unto stocke—fish cured after that manner.

TROUBLE WITH THE PIEDMONT INDIANS

Needham's success convinced him to report to Wood. And leaving Arthur with the Indians, he departed for Virginia and hoped to return with trading goods. But the men were not to meet again, as revealed in this portion of Wood's narrative.[3]

I suppose, it happened as they past Sarrah river an Indian lett his pack slip into the water whether on purpose or by chance I canot judge, upon this some words past betwine Needham and the Indian. Ochenechee Indian John took up Mr. Needham very short in words and soe continued scoulding all day untill they had past the Yattken towne and soe over Yattken river, not far from the river Mr. Needham alighted it not being far from the foot of the mountaines, and there tooke up theire quarters. Still Indian John continued his wailing and threating Mr. Needham tooke up a hatchet which lay by him, haveing his sword by him threw the hatchet on the ground by Indian John and said what John are you minded to kill me. Indian John imediately catched up a gunn, which hee him selfe had carried to kill meat for them to eate and shot Mr. Needham neare the burr of the eare and killd him not withstanding all the Tomahittans started up to rescue Needham but Indian John was too quick for them, soe died this heroyick English man whose fame shall never die if my penn were able to eternize it which had adventured where never any English man had dared to atempt before and with him died one hundred forty-four pounds star-

---

[3] Clarence W. Alvord and Lee Bidgood (eds.), *The First Explorations of the Trans-Allegheny Region by the Virginians, 1650–1674* (Cleveland, 1912), pp. 216–225.

ling of my adventure with him. I wish I could have saved his life with ten times the vallue. Now his companions the Tomahittans all fell a weepeing and cried what shall wee doe now you have killd the English man wee shall be cut of by the English. Indian John drew out his knife stept across the corpes of Mr. Needham, ript open his body, drew out his hart, held it up in his hand and turned and looked to the eastward, toward the English plantations and said hee vallued not all the English. The Tomahittans reployed, how dare you doe this, wee are all afraid of the English. Indian John reployed he was paid for what he had done and had receved his rewarde and then laid a command upon the Tomahittans that they should dispatch and kill the English man which Needham had left att the Tomahittans and immediately opened the packs tooke what goods he pleased, soe much as Needham's horse could carry and soe returned backe.

Now wee returne backe to my man Gabriell Arther. The Tomahittans hasten home as fast as they can to tell the newes the King or chife man not being att home, some of the Tomahittans which were great lovers of the Occheneechees went to put Indian Johns command in speedy execution and tied Gabriell Arther to a stake and laid heaps of combustible canes a bout him to burne him, but before the fire was put too the King came into the towne with a gunn upon his shoulder and heareing of the up rore for some was with it and some a gainst it. The King ran with great speed to the place, and said who is that that is goeing to put fire to the English man. a Weesock borne started up with a fire brand in his hand said that am I. The King forthwith cockt his gunn and shot the wesock dead, and ran to Gabriell and with his knife cutt the thongs that tide him and had him goe to his house and said lett me see who dares touch him and all the wesocks children they take are brought up with them as the Ianesaryes are a mongst the Turkes. this king came to my house upon the 21th of June as you will heare in the following discouerse.

Now after the tumult was over they make preparation for to manage the warr for that is the course of theire liveing to forage robb and spoyle other nations and the king commands Gabriell Arther to goe along with a party that went to robb the Spanyarrd, promising him that in the next spring hee him selfe would carry him home to his master. Gabriell must now bee obedient to theire commands. in the deploreable condition hee was in was put in armes, gun, tomahauke, and targett and soe marched a way with the company, beeing about fifty. they travelled eight days west and by south as he guest and came to a town of negroes, spatious and great, but all wooden buildings Heare they could not take any thing without being spied. The next day they marched along by the side of a great carte path, and about five or six miles as he judgeth came within sight of the Spanish town, walld about with brick and all brick buildings within. There he saw the steeple where in hung the bell which Mr. Needham gives relation of and harde it ring in the eveing. heare they dirst not stay but drew of and the next morning layd an ambush in a convenient place neare the cart path before mentioned and there lay allmost seven dayes to steale for theire sustenance. The 7th day a Spanniard in a gentille habitt, accoutered with gunn, sword and pistoll. one of the Tomahittans espieing him att a distance crept up to the path side and shot him to death. In his pockett were two pices of gold and a small gold chain. which the Tomahittans gave to Gabriell, but hee unfourtunately lost it in his venturing as you shall heare by the sequell. Here they hasted to the negro town where they had the advantage to meett with a lone negro. After him runs one of the Tomahittans with a dart in his hand, made with a pice of the blaide of Needhams sworde, and threw it after the negro, struck him thrugh betwine his shoulders soe hee fell downe dead. They tooke from him some toys. which hung in his eares, and bracelets about his neck and soe returned as expeditiously as they could to theire owne homes.

They rested but a short time before another party was commanded out a gaine and Gabrielle Arther was comanded out a gaine, and this was to Porte Royall, Here hee refused to goe saying those were English men and he would not fight a gainst his own nation, he had rather be killd. The King tould him they intended noe hurt to the English men, for he had promised Needham att his first coming to him that he would never doe violence a gainst any English more but theire buisness was to cut off a town of Indians which lived neare the English, I but said Gabriell what if any English be att that towne, a trading, the King sware by the fire which they adore as theire god they would not hurt them soe they marched a way over the mountains and came upon the head of Portt Royall river in six days. There they made perriaugers of bark and soe past down the streame with much swiftness, next coming to a convenient place of landing they went on shore and marched to the eastward of the south, one whole day and parte of the night. At length they brought him to the sight of an English house, and Gabriell with some of the Indians crept up to the house side and lisening what they said, they being talkeing with in the house, Gabriell hard one say, pox take such a master that will not alow a servant a bit of meat to eate upon Christmas day, by the meanes Gabriell knew what time of the yeare it was, soe they drew of secretly and hasten to the Indian town, which was not above six miles thence. about breake of day stole upon the towne. The first house Gabriell came too there was an English man. Hee hard him say Lord have mercy upon mee. Gabriell said to him runn for thy life. Said hee which way shall I run. Gabriell reployed, which way thou wilt they will not meddle with thee. Soe hee rann and the Tomahittans opened and let him pas cleare there they got the English mans snapsack with beades, knives and other petty truck in it. They made a very great slaughter upon the Indians and a bout sun riseing they hard many great guns fired off amongst the English. Then they hastened a way with what speed they could and in less then fourteene dayes arived att the Tomahittns with theire plunder.

Now the king must goe to give the monetons a visit which were his frends, mony signifing water and ton great in theire language. Gabriell must goe along with him. They gett forth with sixty men and travelled tenn days due north and then arived at the monyton towne situated upon a very great river att which place the tide ebbs and flowes. Gabriell swom in the river severall times, being fresh water, this is a great towne and a great number of Indians belong unto it, and in the same river Mr. Batt and Fallam were upon the head of it as you read in one of my first jornalls. This river runes north west and out of the westerly side of it goeth another very great river about a days journey lower where the inhabitance are an inumarable company of Indians, as the monytons told my man which is twenty days journey from one end to the other of the inhabitance, and all these are at warr with the Tomahitans. when they had taken theire leave of the monytons they marched three days out of thire way to give a clap to some of that great nation, where they fell on with great courage and were as curagiously repullsed by theire enimise.

And heare Gabriell received shott with two arrows, one of them in his thigh, which stopt his runing and soe was taken prisoner, for Indian vallour consists most in theire heeles for he that can run best is accounted the best man. These Indians thought this Gabrill to be noe Tomahittan by the length of his haire, for the Tomahittans keepe theire haire close cut to the end an enime may not take an advantage to lay hold of them by it. They tooke Gabriell and scowered his skin with water and ashes, and when they perceived his skin to be white they made very much of him and admire att his knife gunn and hatchett they tooke with him. They gave those thing to him a gaine. He made signes to them the gun was the Tomahittons which he had a disire to take with him, but the knife and hatchet he gave to the king. they not knowing the use of gunns, the king receved it with great shewes of thankfullness for they had not any manner of iron instrument that hee saw amongst them whilst he was there they brought in a fatt beavor which they had newly killd and went to swrynge it. Gabriell made signes to them that those skins were good a mongst the white people toward the sun riseing they would know by signes how many such skins they would take for such a knife. He told them foure and eight for such a hattchett and made signes that if they would lett him return, he would bring many things amongst them. they seemed to rejoyce att it and carried him to a path that carried to the Tomahittans gave him Rokahamony for his journey and soe they departed, to be short. when he came to the Tomahittans the king had one short voyage more before hee could bring in Gabriell and that was downe the river, they live upon in perriougers to kill hoggs, beares and sturgion which they did

incontinent by five dayes and nights. They went down the river and came to the mouth of the salts where they could not see land but the water not above three foot deepe hard sand. By this meanes wee know this is not the river the Spanyards live upon as Mr. Needham did thinke. Here they killd many swine, sturgin and beavers and barbicued them, soe returned and were fifteen dayes runing up a gainst the streame but noe mountainous land to bee seene but all levell.

After they had made an end of costing of it about the 10th day of May 1674, the king with eighteen more of his people laden with goods begin theire journey to come to Forte Henry att the falls of Appomattock river in Charles City County in Virginia, they were not disturbed in all theire travels untill they came to Sarah, w[h]ere the Occhenechees weare as I tould you before to waite Gabrills coming. There were but foure Occohenechees Indians there soe that they durst not adventure to attempt any violent acction by day. Heare they say they saw the small truck lying under foot that Indian John had scattered and thrown about when he had killd Mr. Needham. When it grew prity late in the night th Occhenee began to worke thire plot and made an alaram by an hubbub crying out the towne was besett with in numarable company of strange Indians this puts the towne people into a sodane fright many being betweene sleepeing and wakeing, away rune the Tomahittans and leave all behind them, and a mongst the rest was Gabrills two peices of gold and chaine in an Indian bagge away slipe Gabriell and the Spanish Indian boy which he brought with him and hide themselves in the bushes.

After the Tomahittans were gon the foure Occhenechees for there came no more to disturb them, made diligent search for Gabriell. the moone shining bright Gabriell saw them, but he lying under covert of the bushes could not be seene by that Indians. In the morning the Occhenechees haveing mist of thire acme passed home and Gabriell came into the town againe and foure of the Tomahittans packs hires foure Sarrah Indians to carry them to Aeno. Here he mett with my man I had sent out soe long ago before to inquire for news despratly sick of the flux, here hee could not gett any to goe forth with his packs for feare of the Occhenechees, soe he left them and adventured himselfe with the Spanish Indian boy. the next day came before night in sight of the Occhenechees towne undiscovered and there hid himselfe untill it was darke and then waded over into the iland where the Occhenechees are seated, strongly fortified by nature and that makes them soe insolent for they are but a handfull of people, besides what vagabonds repair to them it beeing a receptackle for rogues. Gabriell escapes cleaurely through them and soe wades out on this side and runs for it all night.

Gabriel Arthur was probably the first English trader to travel from the Gulf of Mexico to the Ohio and from the Tennessee River to the Carolinas.

CONQUEST OF THE INDIANS

By 1700, English traders moved easily through the Blue Ridge toward the Ohio Valley as well as into the southern piedmont to tap the Indian trade. Virginia pioneer farmers inched their way into the upcountry, grazing their scrawny cattle in the cowpens that surrounded their cabins and forcing a livelihood from their half-cleared fields. This constant push westward trapped many Indians behind the advancing frontier. Governor Alexander Spotswood gathered some of them at Christanna into what could be called an early reservation. John Fontaine's description of life at Christanna tragically reveals the pathos of the native American:[4]

We set out with a guide for Christanna, for this house is the most outward settlement on this side of Virginia, which is the south side. We have no roads here to conduct us, nor inhabitants to direct the traveller. We met with several Indians, and about twelve we came to Meherrin River opposite to Christanna Fort....

About half after twelve we crossed the river in a canoe, and went up to the Fort, which is built upon rising ground. It is an inclosure of five sides, made only with palisadoes, and instead of five bastions, there are five houses, which defend the one the other; each side is about one hundred yards long. There are five cannon, which were fired to welcome the Governor. There are twelve men here continually to keep the place. After all the ceremony was over, we came into the fort and were well entertained. The day proving wet and windy, we remained within doors, and employed ourselves in reading of Mr. Charles Griffin his observations on the benefit of a solitary life....

Mr. Griffin, who is an Englishman, is employed by the government to teach the Indian children, and to bring them to Christianity. He remains in this place, and teaches them the English tongue, and to read the Bible and Common Prayers, as also to write. He hath been now a year amongst them and hath had good success. He told the Governor that the Indian chiefs or great men, as they style themselves, were coming to the fort to compliment him. These Indians are called Saponey Indians, and are always at peace with the English: they consist of about two hundred persons, men, women, and children;

---

[4] Ann Maury, *Memoirs of a Huguenot Family* (New York, 1853), pp. 271–275, 278–279.

they live within musket-shot of the fort, and are protected by the English from the insults of the other Indians, who are at difference with the English; they pay a tribute every year to renew and confirm the peace, and show their submission. This nation hath no king at present, but is governed by twelve of their old men, which have power to act for the whole nation, and they will all stand to every thing that these twelve men agree to, as their own act.

About twelve of the clock the twelve old men came to the fort, and brought with them several skins, and as soon as they came to the Governor, they laid them at his feet, and then all of them as one man made a bow to the Governor: they then desired an interpreter, saying they had something to represent to him, notwithstanding some of them could speak good English. It is a constant maxim amongst the Indians in general, that even if they can speak and understand English, yet when they treat of any thing that concerns their nation, they will not treat but in their own language, and that by an interpreter, and they will not answer any question made to them without it be in their own tongue.

The Governor got an interpreter, after which they stood silent for a while, and after they had spit several times upon the ground, one of them began to speak, and assured the Governor of the satisfaction they had of seeing him amongst them, and of the good-will they had towards the English. They said that some of the English had wronged them in some things, which they would make appear, and desired he would get justice done to them, that they depended upon him for it: which the Governor promised he would, and he thanked them for the good opinion they had of his justice towards them; whereupon they all made a bow, and so sat down on the ground all around the Governor.

The first complaint they made was against another nation of Indians called Genitoes, who had surprised a party of their young men that had been out a hunting, and murdered fifteen of them, without any reason. They desired of the Governor to assist them to go out to war with these Genito Indians, until they had killed as many of them; but this the Governor could not grant. He told them he would permit them to revenge themselves, and help them to powder and ball, at which they seemed somewhat rejoiced. They also complained against some of the English, who had cheated them. The Governor paid them in full for what they could make out that they were wronged of by the English, which satisfied them, and afterwards he made them farewell presents, and so dismissed them.

About three of the clock, came sixty of the young men with feathers in their hair and run through their ears, their faces painted with blue and vermilion, their hair cut in many forms, some on one side of the head, and some on both, and others on the upper part of the head, making it stand like a cock's-comb, and they had blue and red blankets wrapped about them. They dress themselves after this manner when they go to war the one with the other, so they call it their war-dress, and it really is very terrible, and makes them look like so many furies. These young men made no speeches, they only walked up and down, seeming to be very proud of their most abominable dress.

After this came the young women; they all have long straight black hair, which comes down to the waist; they had each of them a blanket tied round the waist, and hanging down about the legs like a petticoat. They have no shifts, and most of them nothing to cover them from the waist upwards; others of them there were that had two deer skins sewed together and thrown over their shoulders like a mantle. They all of them grease their bodies and heads with bear's oil, which, with the smoke of their cabins, gives them an ugly smell. They are very modest and very true to their husbands. They are straight and well limbed, good shape, and extraordinary good features, as well the men as the women. They look wild, and are mighty shy of an Englishman, and will not let you touch them. The men marry but one wife, and cannot marry any more until she die, or grow so old that she cannot bear any more children; then the man may take another wife, but is obliged to keep them both and maintain them. They take one another without ceremony....

The Governor sent for all the young boys, and they brought with them their bows, and he got an axe, which he stuck up, and made them all shoot by turns at the eye of the axe, which was about twenty yards distant. Knives and looking-glasses were the prizes for which they shot, and they were very dexterous at this exercise, and often shot through the eye of the axe. This diversion continued about an hour. The Governor then asked the boys to dance a war dance, so they all prepared for it, and made a great ring; the musician being come, he sat himself in the middle of the ring; all the instrument he had was a piece of board and two small sticks; the board he set upon his lap, and began to sing a doleful tune, and by striking on the board with his sticks, he accompanied his voice; he made several antic motions, and sometimes shrieked hideously, which was answered by the boys. As the men sung, so the boys danced all round, endeavoring who could outdo the one the other in antic motions and hideous cries, the movements answering in some way to the time of the music. All that I could remark by their actions was, that they were representing how they attacked their enemies, and relating one to the other how many of the other Indians they had killed, and how they did it, making all the motions in this dance as if they were actually in the action. By this lively representation of their warring, one may see the base way they have of surprising and murdering the one the other, and their inhuman manner of murdering all the prisoners, and what terrible cries they have, they who are conquerors. After the dance was over, the Governor treated all the boys, but they were so little used to have a belly full, that they rather devoured their victuals than any thing else. So this day ended.

THE KNIGHTS OF THE GOLDEN HORSESHOE

To herald the opening of the Old West and to encourage large-scale investors and slave-owning planters to move into the backcountry, Governor Spotswood led an elaborate party of explorers into the Shenandoah Valley. When the men returned home, he presented each with a golden horseshoe. John Fontaine, one of these self-styled Knights of the Golden Horseshoe, dramatized the behavior and activities of Virginia's wealthy speculators:[5]

This first encampment was called Beverley Camp in honor of one of the gentlemen of our party. We made great fires, and supped, and drank good punch. By ten of the clock I had taken all of my ounce of Jesuit's Bark, but my head was much out of order.

30th In the morning about seven of the clock, the trumpet sounded to awake all the company and we got up. One Austin Smith, one of the gentlemen with us, having a fever,

---

[5] Ann Maury, *Memoirs of a Huguenot Family* (New York, 1853), pp. 284–289.

returned home. We had lain upon the ground under cover of our tents, and we found by the pains in our bones that we had not had good beds to lie upon. At nine in the morning, we sent our servants and baggage forward, and we remained, because two of the Governor's horses had strayed. At half past two we got the horses, at three we mounted, and at half an hour after four, we came up with our baggage at a small river, three miles on the way, which we called Mine River, because there was an appearance of a silver mine by it. We made about three miles more, and came to another small river, which is at the foot of a small mountain, so we encamped here and called it Mountain Run, and our camp we called Todd's Camp. We had good pasturage for our horses, and venison in abundance for ourselves, which we roasted before the fire upon wooden forks, and so we went to bed in our tents. Made 6 miles this day.

31st At eight in the morning, we set out from Mountain Run, and after going five miles we came upon the upper part of Rappahannoc River. One of the gentlemen and I, we kept out on one side of the company about a mile, to have the better hunting. I saw a deer, and shot him from my horse, but the horse threw me a terrible fall and ran away; we ran after, and with a great deal of difficulty got him again; but we could not find the deer I had shot, and we lost ourselves, and it was two hours before we could come upon the track of our company. About five miles further we crossed the same river again, and two miles further we met with a large bear, which one of our company shot, and I got the skin. We killed several deer, and about two miles from the place where we killed the bear, we encamped upon Rappahannoc River. From our encampment we could see the Appalachian Hills very plain. We made large fires, pitched our tents, and cut boughs to lie upon, had good liquor, and at ten we went to sleep. We always kept a sentry at the Governor's door. We called this Smith's Camp. Made this day fourteen miles.

1st September At eight we mounted our horses, and made the first five miles of our way through a very pleasant plain, which lies where Rappahannoc River forks. I saw there the largest timber, the finest and deepest mould, and the best grass that I ever did see. We had some of our baggage put out of order, and our company dismounted, by hornets stinging the horses. This was some hindrance, and did a little damage, but afforded a great deal of diversion. We killed three bears this day, which exercised the horses as well as the men. We saw two foxes but did not pursue them; we killed several deer. About five of the clock, we came to a run of water at the foot of a hill, where we pitched our tents. We called the encampment Dr. Robinson's Camp, and the river, Blind Run. We had good pasturage for our horses, and every one was cook for himself. We made our beds with bushes as before. On this day we made 13 miles.

2d At nine we were all on horseback, and after riding about five miles we crossed Rappahannoc River, almost at the head, where it is very small. We had a rugged way; we passed over a great many small runs of water, some of which were very deep, and others very miry. Several of our company were dismounted, some were down with their horses, others under their horses, and some thrown off. We saw a bear running down a tree, but it being Sunday, we did not endeavor to kill any thing. We encamped at five by a small river we called White Oak River, and called our camp Taylor's Camp.

3d About eight we were on horseback, and about ten we came to a thicket, so tightly laced together, that we had a great deal of trouble to get through; our baggage was injured, our clothes torn all to rags, and the saddles and holsters also torn. About five of the clock we encamped almost at the head of James River, just below the great mountains. We called this camp Colonel Robertson's Camp. We made all this day but eight miles.

4th We had two of our men sick with the measles, and one of our horses poisoned with a rattlesnake. We took the heaviest of our baggage, our tired horses, and the sick men, and made as convenient a lodge for them as we could, and left people to guard them, and hunt for them. We had finished this work by twelve, and so we set out. The sides of the mountains were so full of vines and briers, that we were forced to clear most of the way before us. We crossed one of the small mountains this side the Appalachian, and from the top of it we had a fine view of the plains below. We were obliged to walk up the most of the way, there being abundance of loose stones on the side of the hill. I killed a large rattlesnake here, and the other people killed three more. We made about four miles, and so came to the side of James River, where a man may jump over it, and there we pitched our tents. As the people were lighting the fire, there came out of a large log of wood a prodigious snake, which they killed; so this camp was called Rattlesnake Camp, but it was otherwise called Brooks' Camp.

5th A fair day. At nine we were mounted; we were obliged to have axe-men to clear the way in some places. We followed the windings of James River, observing that it came from the very top of the mountains. We killed two rattlesnakes during our ascent. In some places it was very steep, in others, it was so that we could ride up. About one of the clock we got to the top of the mountain; about four miles and a half, and we came to the very head spring of James River, where it runs no bigger than a man's arm, from under a large stone. We drank King George's health, and all the Royal Family's, at the very top of the Appalachian mountains. About a musket-shot from the spring there is another, which rises and runs down on the other side; it goes westward, and we thought we could go down that way, but we met with such prodigious precipices, that we were obliged to return to the top again. We found some trees which had been formerly marked, I suppose, by the Northern Indians, and following these trees, we found a good, safe descent. Several of the company were for returning; but the Governor persuaded them to continue on. About five, we were down on the other side, and continued our way for about seven miles further, until we came to a large river, by the side of which we encamped. We made this day fourteen miles. I, being somewhat more curious than the rest, went on a high rock on the top of the mountain, to see fine prospects, and I lost my gun. We saw, when we were over the mountains, the footing of elks and buffaloes, and their beds. We saw a vine which bore a sort of wild cucumber, and a shrub with a fruit like unto a currant. We eat very good wild grapes. We called this place Spotswood Camp, after our Governor.

6th We crossed the river, which we called Euphrates. It is very deep; the main course of the water is north; it is fourscore yards wide in the narrowest part. We drank some healths on the other side, and returned; after which I went a swimming in it. We could not find any fordable place, except the one by which we crossed, and it was deep in several places. I got some grasshoppers and fished; and another and I, we catched a dish of fish, some perch, and a fish they call chub. The others went a hunting, and killed deer and turkeys. The Governor had graving irons, but could not grave any thing, the stones were so hard. I graved my name on a tree by the river side; and the Governor buried a bottle with a paper inclosed, on which he writ that he took possession of this place in the name and for King George the First of England. We had a good dinner, and after it we got the men together, and loaded all their arms, and we drank the King's health in Champagne, and fired a volley—the Princess's health in Burgundy, and fired a volley, and all the rest of the Royal Family in claret, and a volley. We drank the Governor's health and fired another volley. We had several sorts of liquors, viz., Virginia red wine and white wine, Irish usquebaugh, brandy, shrub, two sorts of rum, champagne, canary, cherry, punch, water, cider, &c.

I sent two of the rangers to look for my gun, which I dropped in the mountains; they found it, and brought it to me at night, and I gave them a pistole for their trouble. We called the highest mountain Mount George, and the one we crossed over Mount Spotswood.

7th At seven in the morning we mounted our horses, and parted with the rangers, who were to go farther on, and we returned homewards; we repassed the mountains, and at five in the afternoon we came to Hospital Camp, where we left our sick men, and heavy baggage, and we found all things well and safe. We encamped here, and called it Captain Clouder's Camp.

Although English officials frowned on the creation of manorial estates and royal officers attempted to prevent the engrossment of the backcountry by speculators and planters, almost every colony gradually altered its land system under pressure from influential individuals. Tidewater planters of Carolina, Virginia, and Maryland defied royal advice and managed to acquire large tracts of land with the collusion of officials who were tired of opposition and desired to share in the profits of the West. New England's town planting system degenerated until by the 1740s single investors bought entire town sites far in advance of the line of settlement. By 1762, most of Massachusetts' land had been auctioned off. In New York, where Indian traders centered at Albany had long blocked settlement on the upper Hudson and Mohawk rivers, the lower Hudson Valley had been sliced into huge tracts where landowners paid low taxes and rented their holdings rather than selling them to settlers. When pressure forced the opening of upstate New York, land jobbers besieged royal officials, until by the 1760s, the forest-covered hills and lush valleys were prizes for the select few. Pennsylvania, that Quaker sanctuary for the oppressed of Europe, was not exempt from speculation; and the proprietors tried to collect rents and taxes from squatters and former indentured servants who pioneered in the backcountry.

A GERMAN SETTLEMENT IN THE VIRGINIA UPCOUNTRY

But the story of land speculation and engrossment was not so deplorable in fact as it appears in retrospect; colonists were welcomed everywhere. Marginal land, even good land, lay unclaimed on the frontier. Speculators encouraged settlers by offering incentives such as tax and rent forgiveness, roads, low prices, and long-term loans. Furthermore, in contrast with conditions in Europe, especially in the Rhine Palatinate, where the German Protestants suffered from war and famine, America was a land of opportunity. More than 250,000 Palatine Germans migrated first to England and then to America.

The Germans were attracted to Pennsylvania because of Quaker toleration. They settled peacefully among the Quakers or moved west, gradually filling in the eastern slopes of the Great Valley as far south as the Carolinas. Generally docile, hardworking, and apolitical, they contributed the Conestoga or covered wagon, and the big cattle barn to the material culture of the frontier. Most German settlers were poor and whether they lived in New York, Pennsylvania, or Virginia, they constituted a weak shield against the Indians. John Fontaine's terse prose describes a German settlement in Virginia's upcountry in November 1715:[6]

We continued on our way until we came five miles above this land, and there we went to see the Falls of Rappahannoc River. The water runs with such violence over the rocks and large stones that are in the river, that it is almost impossible for boat or canoe to go up or down in safety. After we had satisfied our curiosity, we continued on the road. About five we crossed a bridge that was made by the Germans, and about six we arrived at the German settlement. We went immediately to the minister's house. We found nothing to eat, but lived on our small provisions, and lay upon good straw. We passed the night very indifferently.

21st Our beds not being very easy, as soon as it was day, we got up. It rained hard, but notwithstanding, we walked about the town, which is palisaded with stakes stuck in the ground, and laid close the one to the other, and of substance to bear out a musket-shot. There are but nine families, and they have nine houses, built all in a line; and before every house, about twenty feet distant from it, they have small sheds built for their hogs and hens, so that the hog-sties and houses make a street. The place that is paled in is a pentagon, very regularly laid out; and in the very centre there is a blockhouse, made with five sides, which answer to the five sides of the great inclosure; there are loop-holes through it, from which you may see all the inside of the inclosure. This was intended for a retreat for the people, in case they were not able to defend the palisadoes, if attacked by the Indians.

They make use of this block-house for divine service. They go to prayers constantly once a day, and have two sermons on Sunday. We went to hear them perform their service, which was done in their own language, which we did not understand; but they seemed to be very devout, and sang the psalms very well.

This town or settlement lies upon Rappahannoc River, thirty miles above the Falls, and thirty miles from any inhabitants. The Germans live very miserably. We would tarry here some time, but for want of provisions we are obliged to go. We got from the minister a bit of smoked beef and cabbage, which were very ordinary and dirtily drest.

We made a collection between us three of about thirty shillings for the minister; and about twelve of the clock we took our leave, and set out to return; the weather hazy, and small rain.

THE PALATINE GERMANS IN NEW YORK

The abject poverty of the Virginia Germans was not atypical. In 1720, a group of Palatines who had been established in upstate New York petitioned the king for aid, explaining their pathetic history of broken promises, hardships,

---

[6] Ann Maury, *Memoirs of a Huguenot Family* (New York, 1853), pp. 267–269.

and abuse at the hands of the officials of New York.[7]

That, In the year 1709. The Palatines, & other Germans, being invited to come into England about Four Thousand of them were sent into New York in America, of whom about 1700 Died on Board, or at their landing in that Province, by unavoidable sickness

That before they went on Board, they were promised, those remaining alive should have forty acres of Land, & Five pounds sterling per Head, besides Cloths, Tools, Utensils & other necessaries, to Husbandry to be given at their arrival in America

That on their landing their they were quartered in Tents, & divided into six companies, having each a Captain of their own Nation, with a promise of an allowance of fifteen Pounds per annum to each commander

That afterwards they were removed on Lands belonging to Mr. Livingstone, where they erected small Houses for shelter during the winter season

That in the Spring following they were ordered into the woods, to make Pitch & Tar, where they lived about two years; But the country not being fit to raise any considerable quantity of Naval Stores, They were commanded to Build, to clear & improve the ground, belonging to a private person

That the Indians having yielded to Her late Majesty of pious memory a small Tract of Land called Schorie for the use of the Palatines, they in fifteen days cleared a way of fifteen miles through the woods & settled fifty Families therein

---

[7] Edmund Bailey O'Callaghan (ed.), *Documents Relative to the Colonial History of New York* (Albany, 1855), vol. 5, pp. 553–555.

That in the following Spring the remainder of the said Palatines joined the said fifty families so settled therein Schorie

But that country being too small for their encreasing families, they were constrained to purchase some Neighbouring Land of the Indians for which they were to give Three hundred pieces of Eight

And having built small Houses, & Hutts there about one year after the said purchase some gentlemen of Albani, declared to the Palatines, that themselves having purchased the said countrie of Schorie of the Governor of New York they would not permit them to live there, unless an agreement were also made with those of Albany; But that the Palatines having refused to enter into such an agreement, A Sheriff & some officers were sent from Albany to seize one of their Captains, who being upon his Guard; The Indians were animated against the Palatines; but these found means to appease the Savages by giving them what they would of their own substance.

That in the year 1717 the Governour of New York having summoned the Palatines to appear at Albani, some of them being deputed went thither accordingly, where they were told, that unless they did agree with the Gentlemen of Albany, the Governor expected an order from England to transport them to another place, And that he would send twelve men to view their works & improvements to appraise the same & then to give them the value thereof in money

But this not being done the Palatines to the number of about three Thousand, have continued to manure & to sew the Land that they might not be starved for want of Corn & food

For which manuring the Gentlemen of Albani have put in prison one man and one woman, & will not release them, unless they

have sufficient security of One Hundred Crowns for the former

Now in order that the Palatines may be preserved in the said Land of Schorie, which they have purchased of the Indians, or that they may be so settled in an adjoining Tract of Land, as to raise a necessary subsistance for themselves & their families, they have sent into England Three Persons one of whom is since dead humbly to lay their Case before His Majesty, not doubting but that in consideration of the Hardships they have suffered for want of a secure settlement, His Majestys Ministers and Council will compassionate those His faithful Subjects;

Who, in the first year after their arrival willingly and cheerfully sent Three Hundred men to the expedition against Canada, & afterwards to the Asistance of Albani which was threatened by the French and Indians, for which service they have never received One Penny tho' they were upon the Establishment of New York or New Jersey nor had they received one Penny of the five pounds per head promised at their going on board from England Neither have their commanders received anything of the allowance of fifteen pounds per Annum, and tho' the arms they had given them at the Canada expedition which were by special order from Her late Majesty, to be left in their possession, have been taken from them, yet they are still ready to fight against all the enemies of His Majesty & those countrys whenever there shall be occasion to shew their hearty endeavors for the prosperity of their generous Benefactors in England as well as in America

Therefore they hope from the Justice of the Right Honble the Lords Commissioners of Trade and Plantations, to whom their Petition to their Excellencies the Lords Justices has been referred That they shall be so supported by their Lordships Report, as to be represented fit objects to be secured in the Land they now do inhabit or in some near adjoining lands remaining in the right of the Crown in the said Province of New York

CAUSES OF SCOTCH-IRISH MIGRATION

Shortly after the Palatine Germans began arriving in America, a host of Scotch-Irish settlers entered the colonies, invading upcountry New England, moving into upstate New York, populating the Carolinas, settling backcountry Pennsylvania, and crossing the Great Valley establishing settlements between the Germans and the wilderness. Unlike the docile German refugees who eagerly sought asylum, the Scotch-Irish Presbyterians, armed perhaps with their experience in colonizing northern Ireland, militantly challenged the American environment. By the eve of the American Revolution, they had become a vital part of the "cutting edge" of the frontier. So heavy was the Scotch-Irish migration to America that alarmed English officials inquired about the "expelling factors" in northern Ireland. The following series of letters between the Bishop of London and the Duke of Newcastle illustrate why the Scotch-Irish were willing to face the American wilderness:[8]

DUBLIN, MAR. 13, 1728

TO THE BISHOP OF LONDON:

My Lord:—As we have had reports here that the Irish gentlemen in London would have the great burthen of tithes thought one of the chief grievances, that occasion such numbers of the people of the North going to America, I have for some time designed to write to your lordship on that subject.

But a memorial lately delivered in here by

---

[8] Hugh Boulter, *Letters Written by His Excellency Hugh Boulter, DD., Lord Primate of Ireland* . . . (Oxford, 1769), pp. 250–251, 260–261, 287–289, 289–295.

the Dissenting ministers of this place, containing the causes of this desertion, as represented to them by the letters of their brethren in the North (which memorial we have lately sent over to my lord lieutenant), mentioning the oppression of the ecclesiastical courts about tithes as one of their great grievances: I found myself under a necessity of troubling your lordship on this occasion with a true state of that affair, and of desiring your lordship to discourse with the ministry about it.

The gentlemen of this country have ever since I came hither been talking to others, and persuading their tenants, who complained of the excessiveness of their rents, that it was not the paying too much rent, but too much tithe that impoverished them: and the notion soon took among the Scotch Presbyterians, as a great part of the Protestants in the North are, who it may easily be supposed do not pay tithes with great cheerfulness. And indeed I make no doubt but the landlords in England might with great ease raise a cry amongst their tenants of the great oppression they lay under by paying tithes....

What the gentlemen want to be at is, that they may go on raising their rents, and that the clergy should still receive their old payments for their tithes. But as things have happened otherwise, and they are very angry with the clergy, without considering that it could not happen otherwise than it has, since if a clergyman saw a farm raised in its rent e.g., from 10 to 20 l. per annum, he might be sure his tithe was certainly worth double what he formerly took for it. Not that I believe the clergy have made a proportionable advancement in their composition for their tithes to what the gentlemen have made in their rents. And yet it is upon this rise of the value of the tithes that they would persuade the people to throw their distress.

In a conference I had with the Dissenting ministers here some weeks ago, they mentioned the raising the value of the tithes beyond what had been formerly paid as a proof that the people were oppressed in the article of tithes. To which I told them, that the value of tithes did not prove any oppression, except it were proved that that value was greater than they were really worth, and that even then the farmer had his remedy by letting the clergy take it in kind.

And there is the less in this argument, because the fact is, that about the years 1694 and 1695, the lands here were almost waste and unsettled, and the clergy in the last distress for tenants for their tithes, when great numbers of them were glad to let their tithes at a very low value, and that during incumbency, for few would take them on other terms: and as the country has since settled and improved, as those incumbents have dropped off, the tithe of those parties has been considerably advanced without the least oppression, but I believe your lordship will think not without some grumbling. The same, no doubt, has happened when there have been careless or needy incumbents, and others of a different character that have succeeded them.

I need not mention to your lordship that I have been forced to talk to several here, that if a landlord takes too great a portion of the profits of a farm for his share by way of rent (as the tithe will light on the tenant's share) the tenant will be impoverished: but then it is not the tithe but the increased rent that undoes the farmer. And indeed in this country, where I fear the tenant hardly ever has more than one third of the profit he makes of his farm for his share, and too often but a fourth or perhaps a fifth part, as the tenant's share is charged with the tithe, his case is no doubt hard, but it is plain from what side the hardship arises.

Another thing they complain of in their memorial is, the trouble that has been given them about their marriages and their schoolmasters. As to this I told them, that for some time they had not been molested about their marriages; and that as to their school-masters, I was sure they had met with very little trouble on that head, since I had never heard any such grievance so much as mentioned till I saw it in their memorial.

Another matter complained of is the sacramental test, in relation to which I told them, the laws were the same in England.

As for other grievances they mention, such as raising the rents unreasonably, the oppression of justices of the peace, seneschals, and other officers in the country, as they are by no ways of an ecclesiastical nature, I shall not trouble your lordship with an account of them, but must desire your lordship to talk with the ministry on the subject I have now wrote about, and endeavor to prevent their being prepossessed with any unjust opinion of the clergy, or being disposed, if any attempt should be made from hence to suffer us to be stript of our just rights.

DUBLIN, MAR. 13, 1728

TO THE DUKE OF NEWCASTLE:

My Lord:—As we are in a very bad way here, I think myself obliged to give your Grace some account of it.

The scarcity and dearness of provision still increases in the North. Many have eaten the oats they should have sowed their land with; and except the landlords will have the good sense to furnish them with seed, a great deal of land will lye idle this year....

The humour of going to America still continues, and the scarcity of provisions certainly makes many quit us. There are now seven ships at Belfast, that are carrying off about 1000 passengers thither; and if we knew how to stop them, as most of them can neither get victuals nor work, it would be cruel to do it....

The dissenting ministers here have lately delivered in a memorial, representing the grievances their brethren have assigned as the causes, in their apprehension of the great desertion in the North. As one of these causes relates to the ecclesiastical courts here, and as it is generally repeated here that the Irish gentlemen at London are for throwing the whole occasion of this desertion on the severity of tithes, I have by this post written to the Bishop of London a very long letter on that subject, and have desired him to wait on the ministry, and discourse with them on that head.

DUBLIN, JULY 16, 1728

TO THE DUKE OF NEWCASTLE:

My Lord:— ... We have hundreds of families (all Protestants) removing out of the North to America; and the least obstruction in the linen manufacture, by which the North subsists, must occasion greater numbers following; and the want of silver increasing, will prove a terrible blow to that manufacture, as there will not be money to pay the poor for their small parcels of yarn.

DUBLIN, Nov. 23, 1728

TO THE DUKE OF NEWCASTLE:

My Lord:—I am very sorry I am obliged to give your Grace so melancholy an account of the state of this kingdom, as I shall in this letter; but I thought it my duty to let his Majesty know our present condition in the North. For we have had three bad harvests together there, which has made oatmeal, which is their great subsistence, much dearer than ordinary; and as our farmers here are very poor, and obliged as soon as they have their corn to sell it for ready money to pay their rents, it is much more in the power of those who have a little money, to engross corn here, and make advantage of its scarceness, than in England.

We have had for several years some agents from the colonies in America, and several masters of ships, that have gone about the country and deluded the people with stories of great plenty, and estates to be had for going for, in those parts of the world; and they have been the better able to seduce people by reason of the necessities of the poor of late.

The people that go from here make great complaints of the oppressions they suffer here, not from the Government, but from their fellow-subjects, of one kind or another, as well as of the dearness of provisions, and they say these oppressions are one reason of their going.

But whatever occasions their going, it is certain that above 4000 men, women, and children have been shipped off from hence for the West Indies [*i. e.*, North America] within three years, and of these, above 3000 this last summer. Of these, possibly one in ten may be a man of substance, and may do well enough abroad; but the case of the rest is deplorable. The rest either hire themselves to those of substance for passage, or contract with the masters of ships for four years' servitude when they come thither; or, if they make a shift to pay for their passage, will be under the necessity of selling themselves for servants when they come there.

LIFE IN THE OLD WEST

Almost regardless of their ethnic background, the frontiersmen found a common social and material culture; a way of life marked by a weakening of formal institutions and a gradual reconstruction of society along lines more suitable to the pioneer's immediate needs. Undoubtedly, the settlers would have wished to enjoy the culture of the East and they reclaimed much of it as quickly as possible. But the frontiering process demanded not only a high degree of personal courage and skill but also a variety of collectivism and cooperation. Growing to manhood in the eighteenth century, Joseph Doddridge described the life of the small farmer who, skilled in the use of the ax and rifle, settled the Great Valley:[9]

On the frontiers, and particularly amongst those who were much in the habit of hunting, and going on scouts and campaigns, the dress of the men was partly Indian and partly that of civilized nations.

The hunting shirt was universally worn. This was a kind of loose frock, reaching half way down the thighs, with large sleeves, open before, and so wide as to lap over a foot or more when belted. The cap was large, and sometimes handsomely fringed with a ravelled piece of cloth of a different color from that of the hunting shirt itself. The bosom of this dress served as a wallet to hold a chunk of bread, cakes, jerk, tow for wiping the barrel of the rifle, or any other necessary for the hunter or warrior. The belt, which was always tied behind, answered several purposes, besides that of holding the dress together. In cold weather the mittens, and sometimes the bullet-bag, occupied the front part of it. To the right side was suspended the tomahawk and to the left the scalping knife in its leathern sheath. The hunting shirt was generally made of linsey, sometimes of coarse linen, and a few of dressed deer skins. These last were very cold and uncomfortable in wet weather. The shirt and jacket were of the common fashion. A pair of drawers or breeches and leggins were the dress of the thigh and legs; a pair of moc-

---

[9] Joseph Doddridge, *Notes on the Settlement and Indian Wars* (Pittsburgh, 1912), pp. 91–96, 109–110, 113–115.

casins answered for the feet much better than shoes. These were made of dressed deer skin. They were mostly made of a single piece with a gathering seam along the top of the foot, and another from the bottom of the heel, without gathers as high as the ankle joint or a little higher. Flaps were left on each side to reach some distance up the legs. These were nicely adapted to the ankles and lower part of the leg by thongs of deer skin, so that no dust, gravel or snow could get within the moccasin.

The moccasins in ordinary use cost but a few hours labor to make them. This was done by an instrument denominated a moccasin awl, which was made of the back-spring of an old claspknife. This awl with its buckshorn handle was an appendage of every shot pouch strap, together with a roll of buckskin for mending the moccasins. This was the labor of almost every evening. They were sewed together and patched with deer skin thongs, or whangs, as they were commonly called.

In cold weather the moccasins were well stuffed with deer's hair, or dry leaves, so as to keep the feet comfortably warm; but in wet weather it was usually said that wearing them was "a decent way of going barefooted;" and such was the fact, owing to the spongy texture of the leather of which they were made.

Owing to this defective covering of the feet, more than to any other circumstance, the greater number of our hunters and warriors were afflicted with the rheumatism in their limbs. Of this disease they were all apprehensive in cold or wet weather, and therefore always slept with their feet to the fire to prevent or cure it as well as they could. This practice unquestionably had a very salutary effect, and prevented many of them from becoming confirmed cripples in early life.

In the latter years of the Indian war our young men became more enamored of the Indian dress throughout, with the exception of the matchcoat. The drawers were laid aside and the leggins made longer, so as to reach the upper part of the thigh. The Indian breech clout was adopted. This was a piece of linen or cloth nearly a yard long, and eight or nine inches broad. This passed under the belt before and behind leaving the ends for flaps hanging before and behind over the belt. These flaps were sometimes ornamented with some coarse kind of embroidery work. To the same belts which secured the breech clout, strings which supported the long leggins were attached. When this belt, as was often the case, passed over the hunting shirt the upper part of the thighs and part of the hips were naked....

As the Indian mode of warfare was an indiscriminate slaughter of all ages and both sexes, it was as requisite to provide for the safety of the women and children as for that of the men.

The fort consisted of cabins, blockhouses and stockades. A range of cabins commonly formed one side, at least, of the fort. Divisions or partitions of logs separated the cabins from each other. The walls on the outside were ten or twelve feet high, the slope of the roof being turned wholly inward. A very few of these cabins had puncheon floors, the greater part were earthen. The blockhouses were built at the angles of the fort. They projected about two feet beyond the outer walls of the cabins and stockades. Their upper stories were about eighteen inches every way larger in dimension than the under one, leaving an opening at the commencement of the second story to prevent the enemy from making a lodgment under their walls. In some forts, instead of blockhouses, the angles of the fort were furnished with bastions. A large folding gate made of thick slabs, nearest the spring, closed the fort. The stockades, bastions, cabins and blockhouse walls, were furnished with port holes at proper heights and distances. The whole of the outside was made completely bullet proof.

It may be truly said that necessity is the mother of invention; for the whole of this work was made without the aid of a single nail or spike of iron, and for this reason, such things were not to be had.

In some places less exposed a single blockhouse, with a cabin or two, constituted the whole fort. Such places of refuge may appear very trifling to those who have been in the habit of seeing the formidable military garrisons of Europe and America; but they answered the purpose, as the Indians had no artillery. They seldom attacked, and scarcely ever took one of them.

The families belonging to these forts were so attached to their own cabins on their farms that they seldom moved into their fort in the spring until compelled by some alarm, as they called it; that is, when it was announced by some murder that the Indians were in the settlement.

The fort to which my father belonged was, during the first years of the war, three-quarters of a mile from his farm; but when this fort went to decay, and became unfit for defense, a new one was built at his own house. I well remember that, when a little boy, the family were sometimes waked up in the dead of night by an express with a report that the Indians were at hand. The express came softly to the door, or back window, and by a gentle tapping waked the family. This was easily done, as an habitual fear made us ever watchful and sensible to the slightest alarm. The whole family were instantly in motion. My father seized his gun and other implements of war. My stepmother waked up and dressed the children as well as she could, and being myself the oldest of the children I had to take my share of the burdens to be carried to the fort. There was no possibility of getting a horse in the night to aid us in removing to the fort. Besides the little children, we caught up what articles of clothing and provision we could get hold of in the dark, for we durst not light a candle or even stir the fire. All this was done with the utmost dispatch and the silence of death. The greatest care was taken not to awaken the youngest child. To the rest it was enough to say *Indian* and not a whimper was heard afterwards. Thus it often happened that the whole number of families belonging to a fort who were in the evening at their homes were all in their little fortress before the dawn of the next morning. In the course of the succeeding day their household furniture was brought in by parties of the men under arms.

Some families belonging to each fort were much less under the influence of fear than others, and who, after an alarm had subsided, in spite of every remonstrance, would remove home, while their more prudent neighbors remained in the fort. Such families were denominated *fool hardy* and gave no small amount of trouble by creating such frequent necessities of sending runners to warn them of their danger, and sometimes parties of our men to protect them during their removal....

The necessary labors of the farms along the frontiers were performed with every danger and difficulty imaginable. The whole population of the frontiers huddled together in their little forts left the country with every appearance of a deserted region; and such would have been the opinion of a traveler concerning it, if he had not seen, here and there, some small fields of corn or other grain in a growing state.

It is easy to imagine what losses must have been sustained by our first settlers owing to this deserted state of their farms. It was not the full measure of their trouble that they risked their lives, and often lost them, in subduing the forest, and turning it into fruitful fields; but compelled to leave them in a deserted state during the summer season, a great part of the fruits of their labors was lost by this untoward circumstance. Their sheep and hogs were devoured by the wolves, panthers and bears. Horses and cattle were often let into their fields, through breaches made in their fences by the falling of trees, and frequently almost the whole of a little crop of corn was destroyed by squirrels and raccoons, so that many families, and after an hazardous and laborious spring and summer, had but little left for the comfort of the dreary winter.

The early settlers on the frontiers of this country were like Arabs of the desert of Africa, in at last two repects; every man was a soldier, and from early in the spring till late in the fall, was almost continually in arms. Their work was often carried on by parties, each one of whom had his rifle and everything else belonging to his war dress. These were deposited in some central place in the field. A sentinel was stationed on the outside of the fence, so that on the least alarm the whole company repaired to their arms, and were ready for the combat in a moment. Here, again, the rashness of some families proved a source of difficulty. Instead of joining the working parties, they went out and attended their farms by themselves, and in case of alarm an express was sent for them, and sometimes a party of men to guard them to the fort. These families, in some instances, could boast that they had better crops, and were every way better provided for the winter than their neighbors. In other instances their temerity cost them their lives.

In military affairs, when every one concerned is left to his own will, matters are sure to be but badly managed. The whole frontiers of Pennsylvania and Virginia presented a succession of military camps or forts. We had military officers, that is to say, captains and colonels, but they, in many respects, were only nominally such. They could advise but not command. Those who chose to follow their advice did so to such an extent as suited their fancy or interest. Others were refractory and thereby gave much trouble. These officers would lead a scout or campaign. Those who thought proper to accompany them did so, those who did not remained at home. Public odium was the only punishment for their laziness or cowardice. There was no compulsion to the performance of military duties, and no pecuniary reward when they were performed.

It is but doing justice to the first settlers of this country to say that instances of disobedience of families and individuals to the advice of our officers were by no means numerous. The greater number cheerfully submitted to their directions with a prompt and faithful obedience.

Our clothing was all of domestic manufacture. We had no other resource for clothing, and this, indeed, was a poor one. The crops of flax often failed, and the sheep were destroyed by the wolves. Linsey, which is made of flax and wool, the former the chain and the latter the filling, was the warmest and most substantial cloth we could make. Almost every house contained a loom, and almost every woman was a weaver.

Every family tanned their own leather. The tan vat was a large trough sunk to the upper edge in the ground. A quantity of bark was easily obtained every spring, in clearing and fencing the land. This, after drying, was brought in and in wet days was shaved and pounded on a block of wood, with an axe or mallet. Ashes was used in place of lime for taking off the hair. Bear's oil, hog's lard and tallow, answered the place of fish oil. The leather, to be sure, was coarse; but it was substantially good. The operation of currying was performed by a drawing knife with its edge turned, after the manner of a currying knife. The blacking for the leather was made of soot and hog's lard.

Almost every family contained its own tailors and shoemakers. Those who could not make shoes could make shoepacks. These, like moccasins, were made of a single piece of leather with the exception of a tongue piece on the top of the foot. This was about two inches broad and circular at the lower end. To this the main piece of leather was sewed, with a gathering stitch. The seam behind was like that of a moccasin. To the shoepack a sole was sometimes added. The women did the tailor work. They could all cut out and make hunting shirts, leggins and drawers.

The state of society which existed in our country at an early period of its settlement is well calculated to call into action every native mechanical genius. This happened in this country. There was, in almost every neighborhood, some one whose natural ingenuity enabled him to do many things for himself and his neighbors, far above what could have been reasonably expected. With the few tools which they brought with them into the country they certainly performed wonders. Their plows, harrows with their wooden teeth, and sleds, were in many instances well made. Their cooper ware, which comprehended everything for holding milk and water, was generally pretty well executed. The cedar ware, by having alternately a white and red stave, was then thought beautiful. Many of their puncheon floors were very neat, their joints close and the top even and smooth. Their looms, although heavy, did very well. Those who could not exercise these mechanic arts were under the necessity of giving labor, or barter, to their neighbors in exchange for the use of them, so far as their necessities required.

An old man in my father's neighborhood had the art of turning bowls from the knots of trees, particularly those of the ash. In what way he did it, I do not know: or whether there was much mystery in his art. Be that as it may, the old man's skill was in great request as well turned wooden bowls were amongst our first rate articles of household furniture....

My father possessed a mechanical genius of the highest order, and necessity, which is the mother of invention, occasioned the full exercise of his talents. His farming utensils were the best in the neighborhood. After making his loom, he often used it as a weaver. All the shoes belonging to the family were made by himself. He always spun his own shoe thread. Saying that no woman could spin *shoe thread* as well as he could. His cooper ware was made by himself. I have seen him make a small, neat kind of wooden ware called set work, in which the staves were all attached to the bottom of the vessel by the means of a groove cut in them by a strong clasp knife, and small chisel, before a single hoop was put on. He was sufficiently the carpenter to build the best kind of houses then in use, that is to say first a cabin, and afterwards the hewed log house, with a shingled roof. In his latter years he became sickly, and not being able to labor he amused himself with tolerably good imitations of cabinet work.

Not possessing sufficient health for service on the scouts, and campaigns, his duty was that of repairing the rifles of his neighbors when they needed it. In this business he manifested a high degree of ingenuity. A small depression on the surface of a stump or log and a wooden mallet were his instruments for straightening the gun barrel when crooked. Without the aid of a bow string he could discover the smallest bend in a barrel. With a bit of steel, he could make a saw for deepening the furrows, when requisite. A few shots determined whether the gun might be trusted.

Although he never had been more than six weeks at school he was nevertheless a first rate penman, and a good arithmetician. His penmanship was of great service to his neighbors in writing letters, bonds, deeds of conveyance, etc.

Young as I was, I was possessed of an art which was of great use. It was that of weaving shot-pouch straps, belts and garters. I could make my loom and weave a belt in less than one day. Having a piece of board about four feet long, an inch auger, spike gimlet, and a drawing knife, I needed no other tools or materials for making my loom. It frequently happened that my weaving proved serviceable to the family, as I often sold a belt for a day's work, or making an hundred rails. So that, although a boy, I could exchange my labor for that of a full grown person for an equal length of time.

CHAPTER 6

The French Barrier, 1630-1750

As the English steadily expanded their colonial enclaves in America, attempting to overcome the physical environment that pinned them to the coast, the French suffered from too ready access to the interior of the continent. Long before the death of Champlain in 1635, his "young men," led by Etienne Brulé and Jean Nicolet, had already reached Wisconsin, Illinois, and Michigan in their search for Indians willing to exchange furs for tools, cloth, and guns. Jesuit missionaries, who arrived in New France in 1632, quickly learned Indian languages and eagerly labored among the tribes. The French appeared to have the capacity and the opportunity to satisfy their goals in America.

Success, however, did not breed success: the easy advance into the Great Lakes country excited intense anti-French feeling among the Iroquois Indians in upstate New York. Linked to the Dutch traders at Albany, the Iroquois felt seriously threatened when the French missionaries and traders bypassed them to deal with the less-sophisticated tribes. To protect their control of the trade, an absolute necessity for them, the Iroquois in 1642, launched the first major intertribal war where modern weapons were used. For more than a decade, Iroquois raiding parties, armed with guns, ravaged southern Canada and the upper lake states. When the Iroquois finally tired of the struggle and accepted a peace from the French in 1653, missionaries and traders once again began the patient process of rebuilding Indian alliances.

LA SALLE EXPLORES THE MISSISSIPPI RIVER

French policy shifted after 1665 when Jean Talon, the "Great Intendant," was named administrator of Canada. Crushing the Iroquois by force, because they had again launched attacks against the French lines of communication with the interior, Talon encouraged traders and missionaries to seek out tribes beyond Illinois and Wisconsin for profit and conversion. At Talon's request, Jacques Marquette, a Jesuit missionary, and Louis Jolliet, a trader, journeyed down the Colbert River, as the French dubbed the Mississippi, and returned with news of their findings. The Count de Frontenac, Louis de Buade, governor of New France, followed up the Jolliet-Marquette expedition by cooperating with

Robert La Salle, an empire-builder who conceived of a chain of trading posts that would assure the French control not only of the Northwest but also of the Mississippi Valley. To gather futher information, La Salle, in 1682, explored the Mississippi River. One of the best accounts of this journey was drafted by his aid, "Iron Hand," Henry Tonty, an indomitable soldier and trader who had suffered the loss of a hand and wore a metal one in its stead:[1]

We went in canoes to the River Chicaou, where there is a portage which joins that of the Islinois. The rivers being frozen we made sledges and dragged our baggage to a point thirty leagues below the village of Islinois, and there, finding the navigation open, we arrived at the end of January at the River Mississipy. The distance from Chicaou is estimated at 140 leagues. We descended this river and found, six leagues below, on the right, a great river, which comes from the west. There are numerous nations above. We slept at its mouth. The next day we went on to the village of the Tamaroas, six leagues off on the left. There was no one there, all the people being at their winter quarters in the woods. We made our marks to inform the savages that we had passed, and continued our route as far as the River Ouabache, which is eighty leagues from that of the Islinois. It comes from the east and is more than 500 leagues in length. It is by this river that the Iroquois advance to make war against the nations of the south. Continuing our voyage, we came to a place, about sixty leagues from there, which was named Fort Prudhomme, because one of our men, of that name, lost himself there when out hunting and was nine days in the woods without food. As they were looking for him they fell in with two Chicachas savages, whose village was three days' journey from there, in the lands along the Mississipy. They have 2,000 warriors, the greatest number of whom have flat heads, which is considered a beauty among them, the women taking pains to flatten the heads of their children, by means of a cushion which they put on their foreheads and bind with a band to the cradle, and thus make their heads take this form, and when they are fat their faces are as big as a large soupplate. All the nations on the seacoast have the same custom.

M. de La Salle sent back one of them with presents to his village, so that, if they had taken Prudhomme, they might send him back, but we found him on the tenth day, and as the Chicachas did not return, we continued our route as far as the village of Capa, fifty leagues off. We arrived there in foggy weather, and as we heard the beating of the drum we crossed over to the other side of the river, where in less than half an hour we made a fort. These savages, having been informed that we were coming down the river, came in their canoes to look for us. We made them land, and sent two Frenchmen as hostages to their village. The chief visited us with the calumet, and we went to visit them. They regaled us for five days with the best they had, and after having danced the calumet to M. de La Salle, they conducted us to the village of Tongengan, of their nation, eight leagues from Capa. These received us in the same manner, and from thence they went with us to Toriman, two leagues further on, where we met with the same reception.

It should be remarked that these villages, with another called Osotouy, which is six leagues to the right descending the river, are

---

[1] Louise Phelps Kellogg (ed.), *Early Narratives of the Northwest 1634–1699* (New York: Charles Scribner's Sons, 1917), pp. 296–304. Reprinted by permission of Barnes and Noble, Inc., New York, N.Y.

commonly called Arkansas. The first three villages are situated on the Great River. M. de La Salle erected the arms of the king there. They have cabins made with the bark of cedar; they have no worship, adoring all sorts of animals. Their country is very beautiful, having abundance of peach, plum, and apple trees. Vines flourish there. Buffaloes, deer, stags, bears, turkeys, are very numerous. They even have domestic fowls. They have very little snow duing the winter, and the ice is not thicker than an *écu*. They gave us guides to conduct us to their allies, the Taensas, sixty leagues distant.

The first day we began to see and to kill alligators, which are numerous, and from fifteen to twenty feet long. When we had arrived opposite to the village of the Taenças, M. de La Salle ordered me to go to it and inform the chief of his arrival. I went with our guides. We had to carry a bark canoe for ten arpents, and to launch it on a small lake on which their village was placed. I was surprised to find their cabins made of mud and covered with cane mats. The cabin of the chief was forty feet square, the wall about ten feet high and a foot thick, and the roof, which was of a dome shape, about fifteen feet high. I was not less surprised when, on entering, I saw the chief seated on a camp bed, with three of his wives at his side, surrounded by more than sixty old men, clothed in large white cloaks, which are made by the women out of the bark of the mulberry tree, and are tolerably well worked. The women were clothed in the same manner, and every time the chief spoke to them, before answering him, they howled and cried out several times—"Oh! Oh! Oh!"—to show their respect for him, for their chiefs are held in as much consideration as our kings. No one drinks out of the chief's cup, nor eats out of his dishes; no one passes before him; when he walks they clean the path before him.

When he dies they sacrifice his principal wife, his principal housesteward, and a hundred men of the nation, to accompany him into the other world.

They have a form of worship, and adore the sun. They have a temple opposite the house of the chief, and similar to it, except that three eagles are placed on this temple who look towards the rising sun. . . . When I wished to see what was inside, the old men prevented me, giving me to understand that their God was there; but I have since learnt that it is the place where they keep all their treasure. . . .

Let us return to the chief. When I was in his cabin he told me with a smiling countenance the pleasure he felt at the arrival of the French. I saw that one of his [chief's] wives wore a pearl necklace. I presented her with ten yards of blue glass beads in exchange for it. She made some difficulty, but the chief having told her to let me have it, she did so. I carried it to M. de La Salle, giving him an account of all that I had seen and told him that the chief intended to visit him the next day—which he did. He would not have done this for savages, but the hope of obtaining some merchandise induced him to act thus. He came the next day to our cabins, to the sound of the drum and the music of the women, who had embarked in wooden canoes. The savages of the river use no other boats than these. M. de La Salle received him with much politeness, and gave him some presents; they gave us, in return, plenty of provisions and some of their robes. The chief returned well satisfied. . . .

The next day we saw a canoe. M. de La Salle ordered me to chase it, which I did, and when I was just on the point of taking it, more than 100 men appeared on the banks of the river, with bows bent, to defend their people. M. de La Salle shouted to me to come back, which I did. We went on and encamped opposite them. Afterwards, M. de La Salle expressing to me a wish to meet them peacefully, I offered to carry to them the calumet. I embarked, and crossed to the other side. At first they joined their hands, as a sign that they wished to be friends; I, who had but one hand, told our men to do the same thing.

I made the chief men among them cross over to M. de La Salle, who accompanied them to their village, three leagues inland, and passed the night there with some of his men. The next day he returned with the chief of the village where he had slept, who was a brother of the great chief of the Naché; he conducted us to his brother's village, situated on a hill-side near the river, at six leagues distance. We were very well received there. This nation counts more than 3,000 warriors. These men cultivate the ground as well as hunt, and they fish as well as the Taensa, and their customs are the same....

We continued our journey, and crossed a great canal, which went towards the sea on the right.

Thirty leagues further on we saw some fishermen on the bank of the river, and sent to reconnoitre them. It was the village of the Quinipissa, who let fly arrows upon our scouts, who retired in consequence, as ordered. As M. de La Salle did not wish to fight against any nation, he made us embark....

M. de La Salle sent canoes to inspect the channels. Some went to the channel on the right hand, some to the left, and M. de La Salle chose that in the centre. In the evening each made his report, that is to say, that the channels were very fine, wide, and deep. We encamped on the right bank, erected the arms of the King, and returned several times to inspect the channels. The same report was made.

This river is 800 leagues long, without rapids, to wit, 400 from the country of the Sioux, and 400 from the mouth of the Islinois River to the sea. The banks are almost uninhabitable, on account of the spring floods. The woods are chiefly poplar, the country one of canes and briars and of trees torn up by the roots; but a league or two from the river, is the most beautiful country in the world, prairies, open woods of mulberry trees, vines, and fruits that we are not acquainted with. The savages gather the Indians corn twice in the year. In the lower course of the river, the part which might be settled, is where the river makes a course north and south, for there, in many places, every now and then it has bluffs on the right and left.

The river is only navigable for ships as far as the village of Nadesche, for above that place the river winds too much; but this would not prevent one's setting out from the country above with pirogues and flatboats, to proceed from the Ouabache to the sea. There are but few beavers, but to make amends, there is a large number of buffaloes or bears, large wolves, stags, *sibolas*, hinds, and roe deer in abundance; and some lead mines, with less than one-third refuse. As these savages are stationary, and have some habits of subordination, they might be obliged to make silk in order to procure necessaries for themselves, if the eggs of silkworms were brought to them from France, for the forests are full of mulberry trees. This would be a valuable trade....

Let us return to the sea coast, where, provisions failing, we were obliged to leave sooner than we wished, in order to seek provisions in the neighboring villages. We did not know how to get anything from the village of the Quinipissa, who had received us badly as we went down the river. We lived on potatoes until six leagues from their village, when we saw smoke. M. de La Salle went to reconnoitre at night. Our people reported that they had seen some women. We went there at daybreak and taking four of the women, encamped on the other bank, opposite their village. One of the women was sent with merchandise, to show this tribe that we had no evil design against them and wished for their alliance and for provisions. She made her report. One of them came immediately and invited us to encamp on the other bank, which we did. We sent back the three other women, keeping, however, constant guard. They brought us some provisions in the evening, and the next morning, at daybreak, the scoundrels attacked us. . . .

We left in the evening in order to reach the village of the Nachés where we had left a quantity of grain as we passed down. When we arrived there the chief came out to meet us. M. de La Salle made them a present of the scalps we had taken from the Quinipissa. They had already heard the news, for they had resolved to betray and kill us. We went up to their village armed, and, as we saw no women there, we had no doubt of their having some evil design. In a moment we were surrounded by more than 1,500 men. They brought us something to eat, and we ate with our guns in our hands. As they are afraid of firearms, they did not dare to attack us. The chief of the nation begged M. de La Salle to go away, as his young men had not much sense, which we very willingly did—the game not being equal, we having only fifty men, French and savages. . . .

From thence we came to Fort Prudhomme, where M. de La Salle fell dangerously ill, which obliged him to send me forward, with five others, to arrange his affairs at Missilimakinak. In passing toward the Ouabache, I found four Iroquois, who told us that there were 100 men of their nation coming on after them. This gave us some alarm, for there is no pleasure in meeting warriors on one's road, especially when they have been unsuccessful. . . .

I presented the calumet to them. They laid down their arms and conducted us to their village without doing us any harm. The chiefs held a council, and, taking us for Iroquois, had already resolved to burn us; and, but for some Islinois who were among them, we should have fared ill. They let us proceed. We arrived about the end of June, at the River Chicacou, and, by the middle of July, at Missilimakinak. M. de La Salle, having recovered, joined us in September. Resolving to go to France. . . .

In France, La Salle, confident that he could develop the entire valley and block the intrusions of either England or Spain, recruited money and men to establish a post at the mouth of the Mississippi. He sailed for America in 1684. But fortune turned an angry face toward La Salle's expedition. The river's mouth eluded his ships, and he landed in Texas. His men rebelled and some elected to live among the Indians. In the end, he was murdered by his disgruntled followers. La Salle's failure sorely slowed French occupation of the lower Mississippi Valley.

SETTLEMENT OF
THE ILLINOIS COUNTRY

But in the upper valley, the missionaries also pushed to extend the domain of the French flag. The settlement of Cahokia, Illinois, demonstrated the various influences present on the mission frontier. The accounts that follow were located in the Archives of the Sulpician Seminary at Quebec:[2]

---

[2] John Francis McDermott (ed.), *Old Cahokia* (St. Louis: Missouri Historical Society, 1949), pp. 68–74, 76–78.

In the years 1698 and 1699 the Seminary of the Foreign Missions of Quebec sent three missionaries, namely, Messrs. de Monttigny, Davion and St. Côsme [to locate] in the upper Mississippi [country] below the mouth of the Missouri River. [They were directed to establish themselves] beyond the [territory of the] Illinois [Indian tribes] in order to avoid any complaint from the Jesuits, who might be inclined to object that the missions conducted by that Order were being invaded. The Seminary of Quebec expended between twenty and twenty five thousand *livres* to equip the missionaries, for wages and rations of the boatmen, and to support the missionaries for several years. M. de Montigny, who is still living at the Seminary in Paris, can testify to all this. The Gentlemen of the Foreign Missions of Paris, on learning of the expedition, sent through the courtesy of M. d'Iberville, at the end of 1698, between a thousand and twelve hundred *livres* of clothing, linens and other provisions to assist the missionaries in their work.

A second expedition was dispatched from Quebec in 1700, consisting of M. Fouccaut, a priest from Paris and M. de Bouteville, a priest from Canada. This effort again cost the Seminary of Quebec about ten thousand *livres*. Finally, in 1703, the Seminary sent out M. Bergier, a priest of the Diocese of Vienne in Dauphin, and of the city of Thain on the Rhone. He went by the same route to the Mississippi [country]. On this venture the Seminary expended about two thousand crowns.

M. de St. Côsme settled among the Tamaroa, M. Montigny among the Natchez, M. Davion among the Tonicas, and M. de St. Côsme with a tribe still lower down the river [towards the sea]. All of these nations along the Mississippi had not been evangelized by the Jesuits. That Order found it difficult enough to supply missionaries for all the Indians between Quebec and the Illinois country as well as other missions in the north. M. de St. Valier, Bishop of Quebec, and M. de Frontenac, Governor General of Canada, had [therefore] authorized the Missionaries of the Foreign Missions to establish themselves in those places.

It would seem that having expended so much effort no one would wish to interfere with the Missionaries of the Seminary of Quebec. Yet, Father Lamberville, Procurator of the Jesuits in Canada, so importuned Father de la Chaise that he named . . . as members of a royal commission to examine the facts and to determine whether the Missionaries of Quebec should enter this mission field and whether they were impairing [the work] of any of the Jesuit missions. The focal point of the problem was the mission among the Tamaroa, which the Jesuits maintained to be a dependency of their territory of the Illinois.

At one of these gatherings held at the residence of the Archbishop of Auch, the Bishop of Marseilles, now Archbishop of Paris, asked the Sieur Tremblay, who was there with Father Lamberville, whether the location in question might have gold or silver mines or deposits of precious stones. The Sieur Tremblay replied that the only riches to be won were sufferings. As a matter of fact Messrs. Foucaut and St. Côsme lost their lives in this mission. M. Bergier wore himself out there, dying the death worthy of a missionary. Messrs. de Montigny and Davion have often been in danger of losing their lives. . . .

Louis XIV, of glorious memory, at the end of 1703 granted to the Foreign Missions of Quebec an order for three thousand *livres* on his royal treasury for the support of the Indian missions which they had established along the Mississippi. At the end of 1704 His Majesty again granted a similar order for fifteen hundred *livres* to support a pastor and a vicar among the Indians as well as for the French on the lower Mississippi. These two grants were donated annually until 1717. But payment was made in paper money or treasury notes and the largest amount was tendered in bank notes in 1720. Probably not more than a thousand crowns in actual money was received from all the grants. In spite of this, it was necessary to meet bills in actual cash for all the expeditions made between 1705 and 1724 in which year the Missionaries of the Foreign Mission gave up the field.

Little protection was offered [to the Missionaries of the Seminary of Quebec] in all the good they desired to accomplish. The Sieur de la Vente was recalled. They have never been able to obtain funds to build rectories and churches (at Mobile they built at their own expense) or for decorations and lighting [such as are usually given to missionaries]. On the contrary they have carried on divine services at their own expense. They were even refused chalices and church ornaments which were always granted to other missionaries. These obstacles did not prevent them from sending M. Varlet, Doctor of the Sorbonne, in 1711 or 1712, to replace M. Bergier who died among the Tamaroa. When he realized the need for more missionaries, he induced the Seminary of Quebec, early in 1718, to send Messrs. Calvarin, Thaumur, and Mercier. The three priests, who came by land, supplied the missionary needs of the Tamaroa and planned to evangelize the Indians of the Missouri [country]. They arrived among the Tamaroa in 1719. This venture cost the Seminary of Quebec more than ten thousand *livres*. M. Varlet was ordered to return to France.

The Letters Patent of the Company of the Indies placed on that organization the obligation of supporting missionaries, both those who served the Indians and those who cared for the French in the lower Mississippi [country]. The Gentlemen of the Foreign Missions several times during 1718 and 1719 petitioned the Directors of the Company for the fees due the missionaries to the Indians and to the French. His Majesty annually assigned a sum of three thousand *livres* to the Indian Missionaries and a sum of fifteen hundred *livres* to those who worked among the French. The Honorable Directors, whom M. Varlet visited personally after his consecration as Bishop of Babylon, made similar promises, but not even a *sou* was ever paid. And this, despite the fact that the Company [spent a great deal of money to transport] thousands of miserable [wretches] to the country where they died of hunger. It was Messrs. Davion, Le Maire, and Huvé who succored these poor people, administering the sacraments to them and endangering their very lives to help them. In spite of all this, the Gentlemen of the Foreign Missions never received a *sou* of revenue. This is why they refrained from continuing to send missionaries to the country. It also explains why the Company [of the Indies] encouraged the Capuchins to undertake the field as the priests of the Foreign Missions were withdrawn.

M. Raudot, Director of the Company [of the Indies] was presented a memorandum in 1723 or 1724, requesting six hundred *livres* for each year of service given by Messrs. Davion, Le Maire, and Huvé up to the time they were recalled. A similar request was made for the services of Messrs. Calvarin, Thaumur, and Mercier, who were among the Tamaroa, the first of these until his death, and the others up to the date of the memorandum....

Concerning what was due Messrs. Calvarin, Thaumur, and Mercier, the Director of the Company at Fort de Chartres was unwilling to pay these three missionaries anything from the date of their departure from Quebec in 1718 to the death of M. Calvarin and for the five or six years Messrs. Thaumur and Mercier cared for the mission among the Tamaroa. The Director was not even willing to approve payment to M. Mercier for his services to M. de Bourgmont on his journey of discovery of the Missouri though M. Mercier was with the expedition the whole time it was out. [1724]

Number thirty-two shows the domain we have reserved for ourselves in the prairie of the Kaokias. It has six *arpents* frontage. In the prairie where the mill is built we have reserved another domain of 20 *arpents* in the very place where the mill is situated, leaving it in about the center of the second domain, the depth of which shall run from the bluffs to the Mississippi, or from the Mississippi to the bluffs, taking for direction a line running north north west. On both sides of the said first domain seven pieces of land have been granted by warranty deeds to 7 settlers of whom four only, the nearest to the French village, are in full possession; the other three, as well as ourselves, sow in the farther part of their fields fifteen to twenty *minots* of wheat for this year in uncultivated fields that they have bought from said Indians and which have three *arpents* frontage. Our domain as well as three fields belonging to settlers being occupied by the Kaokias whom we have been unable to persuade to move farther than a league away, because they fear that they might be attacked by some tribe who would destroy them if they went too far from the French, we can only sow in the farther end of our fields, where we have land enough for sowing 200 *minots*. More than 3 weeks ago we placed 170 *minots* in the earth. The twelve *arpents* of land, granted without title, on this side of our domain, that is, on the side near our village, belong to the men named Pichard, Blondin, Louis gault, La Source; the nine *arpents* on the other side of the said domain belong to Rolet, Francois Mercier, and Robillard, who is the farthest away. All these fields should run north north west, we think, which may be changed a trifle, when a sworn surveyor, of which there are none yet in the country, shall come to make an official survey.

The said *habitants* having absolutely insisted that their lands begin at the bank of the little river that separates the island from this prairie and that they must be granted in depth to the bluffs, as they have been granted by all the concessioners or *seigneurs* to all the settlers of the Illinois, we could not refuse them, not only so that we would not live alone at this mission, which would not be expedient for us, but also not to give occasion of crying out against us, which would not have failed to happen. As for the *cens et rentes* no settler has yet paid any in all this country; that will no doubt to done later.

The whole extent of the land belonging to the mission on the bluffs is almost exclusively covered with white oak; the woods there are quite open and there are many little prairies of from 5 or 6 *arpents* to 20 or 25. These who are good judges say that the grape would thrive admirably on those slopes; if we had a vine-dresser, we would make an attempt, for wild grapes of several varieties are not lacking in this country. It is said also that sheep would find fat pasturage here, to which I agree. In that case, one could bring them up from the sea [Gulf], where there is no lack of them, nevertheless that would mean considerable expense for transport by water.

The former village of the Kaskaskias is rightly considered a very advantageous spot to place the stone fort which the crown has ordered built in the Illinois country. The limestone, the stone and wood for building, a river in which to shelter boats, the view on the Mississippi for about two leagues above and below, the rock which slopes gently almost to the Mississippi, a beautiful prairie which adjoins the rock, the Mississippi which would be protected by this fort as well as the Missouri which empties into this river from the west five leagues from here, and the river of the Illinois which there mixes its waters eleven leagues from here on the eastern side—all that would seem indeed to invite the building of the said fort in that place, as is much spoken of, and in that case it is not difficult to foresee that the seigniory of the Tamaroa will soon be settled from one end to the other.

You will find, gentlemen, several erasures in this common letter which we wrote more than a month ago. These erasures come in part from changes in *habitants* who take land today and leave it tomorrow. If the messenger who leaves tomorrow gave us more time we should have recopied it, but he is so pressed that we have not even time to write several private letters. As for the plan which we have the honor of sending you, we have drawn it the best we could, it is sufficiently correct for the distances from one place to another. If M. Renault had not been sick, he would have done us the pleasure to draw it himself and without doubt it would have been better done. However that may be, it can always give you an idea of the location of your seignory of the Tamaroa. We have the honor to be, with much respect and submission. [1735]

ESTABLISHMENT OF DETROIT

The problems of the clergy in establishing missions were no more complex than were those of the civil officials of New France. In an effort to create fortified centers, stimulate trade, and develop agriculture, the government granted trade monopolies and large landholdings to various individuals, if they promised to colonize the land. The system, semifeudal in character, divided the colonists into two classes: first, a petty nobility of soldiers, landholders, and traders; and second, farmers called habitants. The relationship between the classes proved scarcely amicable. The new nobility boasted no lineage: their titles had been earned in the struggle against the wilderness. Along the major rivers of Canada and at strategic sites, the petty nobility labored to prosper as landlords and traders. Jealous of the special privileges extended to the nobles, the habitants incessantly complained to the authorities, who proved to be willing listeners because of their determination to strengthen the French hold in America. The following account, drafted by Jean Talon in 1727, explains Henry Tonty's problems in establishing Detroit:[3]

I had not then an exact idea of the Post of Detroit, when I had the honor of laying before you the representations of the Habitants of Detroit, That the Exclusive right to Trade granted to the Commandant was detrimental to the growth of that place. I thought that, since the Time when this Post was Established, a sufficient number of families had gone thither to allow of the habitants dividing into two Classes; and that some would remain to cultivate the Land, while the others by means of Trade—which really ought to be free in a Colony—would go to a distance to seek what the former required.

I have reconsidered that too General opinion, in consequence of the Explanation that has since been given me. That is, that in fact

---

[3] Reuben Gold Thwaites (ed.), *Collections of the State Historical Society of Wisconsin* (Madison, 1902), vol. 16, pp. 471–475.

there are as Yet only twenty-eight or thirty Habitants; And that Corn that sells at forty sols a minot in the Colony has been worth at that Place as much as 25 livres A minot, and at present is worth 22 livres, and other articles in proportion. As Regards the Exclusive right to Trade, it must also be understood that this Privilege relates only to the goods for the fur Trade; and in no wise concerns any of the other Goods handled in more general Commerce, for the needs of the Habitants. Accordingly, the Habitants are free to go and come, and to procure the same for themselves.

One of the Complaints that I Found in memorials that had been Sent to me Was, Moreover, that the Sieur de Tonty had sublet His Exclusive privilege to several persons, and that he should Exploit it himself rather than allow it to be exercised by several, thus increasing the number of persons to obtain an advantage Over Them.

The three objects of those representations are, therefore: The Exclusive right to the Fur Trade; The subletting of the same by Monsieur de Tonty; And the Trade in other goods. With regard to the Exclusive Privilege, it would have been Impossible to Enact anything here respecting it, [because] First: It has been granted by the King and it must continue until the King be pleased to revoke it. The Sieur de Tonty holds it under an onerous Title, which consists in his Being charged with all the expense of the Post—not only for the Officers and Soldiers who may be in Garrison there (to whom the King will pay only their allowances and salary, and their Clothing Taken from His warehouses), but for the support of the chaplain and of the Surgeon, and for the presents to be given the savages. To all this the King Is not obliged to contribute in any manner—as is expressly set forth in the King's memorial to Messieurs de Vaudreuil and Begon, dated June 15, 1722.

Secondly: It affects only the goods for the fur trade, And This has nothing in Common with what will more or less facilitate the Establishment of the Habitants. The fact that these fur-Trade Goods are Solely in the hands of Monsieur de Tonty can Interest only the Merchants of Montreal, who thereby lose the sale of some Outfits; but it is Not from their Mouths that these complaints come—we owe these attentions only to The personal Interests of the Detroit Habitants. But, as the Sieur de Tonty and his Sub-farmers must always obtain at Quebec or at Montreal their supply of merchandise suited to the fur Trade (and even other Kinds of merchandise), or have the same brought out from France, this does no Injury to either the Kingdom or the Colony.

Whether the Sieur de Tonty Exploits His privilege himself or causes it to be Exploited, the fact is Still of no interest—because, as it relates to fur-Trade Goods, it is a personal matter that concerns only the Savages, and not the Habitants of the Country, who are free to provide Themselves with everything needed for their subsistence. The question whether one should Exploit a privilege oneself, or allow it to be Exploited by several Sub-farmers, applies only in the case of taxes Imposed; since the sub-farmers of these frequently disturb the administration by Harassing the people, through Coercive acts and costs, more than the farmers Themselves would have done. And there is here no question of a right whose Extension to several Agents might be prejudicial to the public. It is quite the Contrary. And it may be said that the number of sub-farmers for that Trade, constituting a greater number of Merchants, thus places the goods in more hands, and causes them to lower the price, for the reason that a larger number of Merchants are supplied with the goods.

But, since Monsieur de Tonty and his sub-farmers are, through the opportunity afforded by the Fur-Trade, enabled to Trade in the other goods needed at Detroit, This is a point which must be considered, to see whether they do not take advantage of it. With regard to this the following reflection may be made. Either the people of Detroit are in a Position themselves to engage in Commerce and to go for their goods at a distance, or they are not. If They Are in such a Position they are at perfect liberty to do so—provided, nevertheless, that it be Solely with the produce of their Lands. Once more, the Exclusive privilege granted to the Sieur de Tonty only applies to Goods for the Fur-Trade. Why do they not go and get the other goods with the Corn And other fruits that they harvest?

If that be impossible, owing to The Enormous distance between the Places and the Inadequacy of their number, Is it not an advantage to them that some one should supply Himself with these goods, in order that they may Find them when Necessary; That some one should incur the expense and Run the risks?

Accordingly, it would only remain to Consider the question of the prices at which the goods should be Held; and Whether Sieur de Tonty or his sub-farmers have not taken Too great an advantage of the Impossibility or of the few Opportunities that the Detroit Habitants would find for going themselves to a distance to obtain what they need. Now that the habitants should be able to do so is impossible, and would even tend to Defeat the object of their establishment. In fact, how can it be possible that out of 28 or 30 Habitants, who are some two or Three hundred Leagues Distant from the towns of the Colony, a portion should detach themselves for the purpose of bringing provisions, Cloths, materials, and Implements to their Fellow-Habitants, and that they should purchase this merchandise with the mere products of their Farms—as they had been commanded to do, in order that they should not abandon Farming? How could they carry grain for the Distance of at least two Hundred leagues that separates Detroit from Montreal, and Across all the Portages, in order to provide themselves with Linens, Stuffs, and other Articles to bring back with Them? That is not possible. The Intention in this was, to allow them to Trade only between Themselves, in their own produce, in order to Encourage them to Settle at Detroit, where the Climate is the finest in Canada. This nevertheless, they do not do. And we are Informed that those people carry on only the Commerce of the fur Trade, And will not be dependent on the Commandant.

The excessive Price of Corn in that Quarter shows how little progress has hitherto been made by that Settlement, and the little possibility that exists, on the Habitants' part, of procuring there for Themselves what they Need; we also see how Important it is that the few Habitants there should not be diverted from the Cultivation of the Soil.

I have been shown invoices of Goods, as sold by Sieur de Tonty's People. They did not appear to me to be dear; and you will observe, Monseigneur, that the Detroit Habitants admit that the goods have been offered to them on fairly advantageous Terms; and that they merely say, in this respect, that the goods were offered to them at a Time when they could not take advantage of them.

I have not seen a person at Montreal who has corroborated their complaints; but since my departure from Montreal I have learned that Monsieur The Governor-General has relieved Sieur de Tonty of his Post, for reasons which he will most probably have given you.

Sieur de Tonty's farmers have since come to represent to me that they, as well as Sieur de Tonty, were Disturbed in the exercise of his privilege. They stated that they advanced supplies for the Post; and that, even if Sieur de Tonty had deserved to be relieved, owing to dereliction from duty, his Exclusive privilege should always remain Executory in the persons of his farmers—who have entered upon the undertaking on the faith of a privilege that was given by the King, and rests solely with the King. Notwithstanding this, permits have been given in virtue of this revocation, whereby as many as Five Canoes have been sent up, and their Trade has been Broken up. As Sieur de Tonty had been relieved, and this makes the case a more private one, I did not wish to take Cognizance of it.

DETROIT TWENTY YEARS LATER: THE PROBLEMS OF AUTHORITY

French authorities, always plagued by habitants who refused to remain on the land but fled into the wilderness to become "coureurs de bois" or illicit traders, continued to wrestle with the problem of establishing a stable population in Canada. Even at highly strategic points where settlers were essential for defense and for control of the Indian trade, neither missionaries nor privileged military officers could provide a complete solution. The following letter to the French minister describing conditions in Detroit twenty years after the Tonty episode affords an excellent illustration of the problems:[4]

---

[4] Reuben Gold Thwaites (ed.), *Collections of the State Historical Society of Wisconsin* (Madison, 1908), vol. 18, pp. 30–32.

Regarding the post of Detroit.

This post has with much reason at all times been considered very interesting and important, not only from its position with reference to the savage Nations it controls, but Also as a barrier to the Encroachment of the English and because of the provisions it can supply to the Voyageurs of the Southern posts; moreover it Is very advantageous for the fur Trade.

All these Considerations Led Messieurs de La Galissoniere and Bigot to take upon Themselves to Send to that post as early as last spring as many families as they could get, to whom they promised a provision of flour for two years with all the necessary implements for clearing and hoeing the soil. This number is not as large as they would have wished, only 46 persons having gone there, including men, women and Children. It Was Neccessary, Monseigneur, not to lose a year while waiting for your answer as we Were convinced It would be in Accordance with your ideas, And next spring we will Send up others of we can get them.

It Is Necessary to populate Detroit. If we could have a strong militia there with some regular troops the savage Nations would never dare to make disturbances. And to succeed in this and have Proper discipline in that country, it was necessary to send families there and to Establish a resident Commandant, As has just Been done In favor of Monsieur de Celoron. He will Keep them in hand and make them settle on the land he will give them to clear in consideration of the aid they receive from the King. That officer cannot go there before next spring as he Has not Yet returned from la belle riviere whither he was Sent by Monsieur de La Galissoniere.

Monsieur de Lajonquiere will not forget to make him feel How greatly he should Be flattered by such a proof of Confidence in him, and impress upon him the attention he must devote to increase the population of that post and make the inhabitants sedentary. As regards ourselves, we can Induce only the habitants of the government of Montreal to go there by giving them the same advantages as were given the others last spring. Those of the other governments will not emigrate.

Messieurs de la Galissoniere and Bigot had arranged that the houses should Be built In Villages only, with half a League between so that the habitants may be stronger at Home and have less Fear of the savage. We even Sent Our ordinance to that effect. But Monsieur The Chevalier de Longueuil who Commanded there and who has recently returned has assured us that nobody would build on those Conditions, each One wishing to take a Concession where he can find good Soil, or an advantageous situation according to his own ideas; and that if they were hindered in this regard, Detroit would not be Settled.

We are obliged to rely on the reports of those who have lived in that country, but we will decide nothing on the subject until Monsieur de Celoron is able to look into the matter himself and Report on it to us.

Monsieur de Lajonquiere will Arrange with Monsieur Bigot the instructions to be given that officer.

Father La Richardie, Missionary of the hurons at the said post, has asked as urgently as possible for help in restoring his mission that Was destroyed by the rebellious savages; Messieurs de La Galissoniere and Bigot considered such restoration necessary, and The latter gave the said Missionary the 5000 livres he asked. We know that the repairs of this Mission are well advanced. One can get even the slightest amount of work done in that country only by dint of cash payments; the workmen being unwilling to Be paid in Montreal.

CONFLICTS OVER THE FUR TRADE, 1748

Governmental problems of staggering complexity confronted the French in America; arguments of geographic unity, religion, economic interest, military urgency, and political necessity were all frequently raised when officials attempted to locate boundaries and determine zones of political and economic regulation. The problem of antagonistic religious groups, endlessly wrangling about who should serve the Indian, paled in significance when compared with the rivalry of the merchants in New Orleans and Quebec for control of the highly prized Indian trade in Illinois. At the outset, Illinois and the upper river system fell within the administration of Quebec, but when the scheme of the master financier John Law to stimulate settlement on the lower river by forming a special company captured the imagination of the French, the New Orleans traders gained ascendancy. A thoughtful reading of the following letter from the French minister to the governor of Canada written in 1748 discloses the plight of French officials in trying to reconcile the various conflicting interests on this frontier:[5]

Monsieur

You are no doubt aware that the Illinois post was formerly an immediate dependency of the general government of Canada, and that it was only in 1717 that it was taken

---

[5] Reuben Gold Thwaites (ed.), *Collections of the State Historical Society of Wisconsin* (Madison, 1908), vol. 18, pp. 14–17.

from it to be united to and incorporated with the particular government of Louisiana. The reasons for such change were that, in consequence of the desire then prevailing to favor the concessions of the company of the Occident, the addition of the Illinois country to the latter colony would be all the more advantageous to it that such country would supply fresh materials for its commerce, both through the trade with the Savages, and through the products of its cultivation. The working of the mines was also brought forward as an abundant source of wealth. And it was considered that there would be better opportunities of utilizing those advantages in Louisiana than in Canada.

But in the first place, the chief reason that then led to such decision no longer exists, since the King has taken over the colony of Louisiana, for it is indifferent to the King's service and to that of the State whether that colony or Canada benefits by the advantages the Illinois establishment can give; and the only question at issue is to know which of the two can derive the greatest benefit from it or is most in need thereof.

In the second place, if we consider the circumstances which must lead to the decision of this question, they all seem to be in favor of Canada.

In fact, the Illinois post can be considered only as a burdensome establishment for Louisiana. It is 400 leagues distant from New Orleans. It serves but to divide and consequently to weaken the forces of that colony. It entails considerable expenditure on the King for the maintenance of the two companies in garrison there, owing to the difficulties of transport, and for the same reason causes the death of many soldiers. The greater portion of the proceeds of the fur-trade with the savages passes into Canada. And everybody knows that the hopes that had been raised with regard to the mines have vanished, since the whole thing is reduced to getting a little from those of lead.

By reuniting that post to Canada, Louisiana would, in the first place, gain the two companies of troops stationed there, which might be more usefully employed for the defense of the chief posts of that colony. The King would be spared the expense occasioned by that garrison there. It would be sufficient to send there from Canada a detachment of a few soldiers with an officer to be commandant, and the farmer of the trade of the post or the traders to whom licenses would be granted should be obliged to transport the necessary provisions for that detachment and other requisites, according to the practice for the remote posts of Canada. So that this post, far from being a burden upon the King, might, on the contrary, increase the revenues of that colony, which would be in a much better position than Louisiana to exploit that post, although it is farther from Montreal than from New Orleans, owing to the people of Canada being accustomed to journeys of that kind.

It does not appear either that the removal of the two companies of troops forming the garrison can injuriously affect the safety of the post. Besides the fact that the French are there in sufficient number to have nothing to fear from the savages, it is probable that the latter will be better satisfied and quieter under the immediate command of an officer from Canada, because it is certain that they fear the French and savages of that country much more than those of Louisiana.

The separation of the post could not injure the defence of Louisiana. The habitants of the Illinois country could hardly be in a position to aid in it. And if an occasion arose, the officer of Canada in command there, would always be obliged to execute the orders that would be given him in the matter by the governor of Louisiana.

There is only the article of flour which the latter colony obtains from the Illinois, that can deserve attention. But could not that branch of trade, the only one from which it derived any benefit, continue to be carried on notwithstanding the reunion of that post to Canada? And could not the convoys that transport such flour go on doing it as usual?

It is true that the goods that would not fail to be sent there from Louisiana might give rise to difficulties in connection with the trade of that post. But could not arrangements be made to conciliate all such matters?

I beg you to weigh all these reasons and such others as may occur to you and consider whether it would in fact be advisable to unite the Illinois to Canada, or leave that post a dependency of Louisiana. In communicating your opinion on the subject to me, you will also please explain the new arrangements you think should be made in consequence of the decision you may propose. I am also writing on this matter to Monsieur de Vaudreuil, the Governor of Louisiana, and when I shall have received your answer and his, I will take the King's orders on the subject and communicate them to both of you.

LOUISIANA UNDER THE FRENCH REGIME, 1751

In 1751, a young military officer, Jean-Bernard Bossu, sailed to New Orleans under orders to serve in the Mississippi Valley. The French had been active in the lower valley since the days of La Salle. To Bossu, New Orleans proved to be an exciting and cosmopolitan city, dominated by its merchants and politicians; in the backcountry, Negro slaves, imported by John Law's company, labored in the fields. The French at this time wrote their first black codes, which restricted white masters as much as Negro slaves. But Bossu, neither a philosopher nor a scholar, simply wrote clear buoyant letters describing many of the things that he witnessed and experienced. Traveling upriver he sensed a turning back of the clock of civilization. The following selections, taken from his letters, not only depict the nature of the French settlements on the lower river but also demonstrate the intense profit motive so evident in colonial administrations:[6]

In 1698, Le Moine d'Iberville, a Canadian gentleman, discovered the mouth of the river which La Salle had missed in 1684. Our ship ran aground on a bar; we fired a cannon to summon the pilot, and at the same time the captain unloaded the artillery pieces and landed the two hundred regular troops who had been sent to serve in the colony of Louisiana. This lightened the ship enough to float her again.

On April 4, eighteen officers landed at Fort Balize, where Monsieur de Santilly is in command. He entertained us as royally as possible during our stay at his post, which is isolated and surrounded by swamps filled with snakes and alligators.

The Marquis de Vaudreuil, having heard of our arrival, sent out several boats to get us and to bring us refreshments. After having assigned our soldiers to the ships, we sailed and rowed until we arrived at New Orleans on Easter Sunday. The Marquis de Vaudreuil is supposed to receive twenty-four more naval companies in Louisiana. These troops are to arrive on merchant vessels outfitted by the King. There are also girls, recruited in France, coming to populate the

---

[6] From *Bossu's Travels in the Interior of North America, 1751–1762*, translated and edited by Seymour Feiler. Copyright 1962 by the University of Oklahoma Press. Pp. 21–25, 29–30, 68–69, 91–92.

land. Industrious soldiers who want to marry them are discharged from the service. The King grants them a certain number of acres of land to clear and supports them for three years. He also has them furnished with a rifle, a half pound of powder and two pounds of lead each month, an ax, a pick, seed, a cow, a calf, chickens, a rooster, etc.

The Marquis de Vaudreuil has assigned the twenty-four new companies to different parts of the colony, without favor to anyone, so that everyone can share and share alike. Lots were drawn for the Illinois post, which is five hundred leagues from New Orleans, and the company to which I was assigned received that assignment. I have the honor of being among those officers whom Monsieur Rouillé, the naval minister, has recommended to the Marquis de Vaudreuil, and I am fully aware of the benefits of such a recommendation. I can assure you that the General's table is of great comfort to me at the present time, as it is to all those who have just arrived and have not yet had the time to find permanent lodging. There is such abundance that we are served too well. The Governor does the honors of his table with such nobility and generosity that he has gained the esteem and admiration of all the officers, who rightly call him the Father of the Colony. Monsieur Michel de la Rouvillière, the director of markets, has contributed to making life agreeable for us by his fine control over staple products as well as everything else with which his office is concerned....

My visit to the different nations during this long trip will enable me to give you a detailed description of the beautiful Mississippi and of the people who inhabit its shores.

In the meantime, I shall describe the capital of Louisiana, but I do not think that it is necessary to speak of the city at length, since you are doubtless familiar with most of the maps and articles published on it. I simply want to call to your attention that New Orleans, with its well-laid-out streets, is bigger and more heavily populated today than formerly. There are four types of inhabitants: Europeans, Indians, Africans or Negroes, and half bloods, born of Europeans and savages native to the country.

Those born of French fathers and French, or European, mothers are called Creoles. They are generally very brave, tall, and well built and have a natural inclination toward the arts and sciences. Since these studies cannot be pursued very well because of the shortage of good teachers, rich and well-intentioned fathers send their children to France, the best school for all things.

As for the fair sex, whose only duty is to please, they are already born with that advantage here and do not have to go to Europe to acquire it artificially.

New Orleans and Mobile are the only cities where there is no *patois*; the French spoken here is good.

Negroes are brought over from Africa to clear the land, which is excellent for growing indigo, tobacco, rice, corn, and sugar cane; there are sugar plantations which are already doing very well. This country offers a delightful life to the merchants, artisans, and foreigners who inhabit it because of its healthful climate, its fertile soil, and its beautiful site. The city is situated on the banks of the Mississippi, one of the biggest rivers in the world, which flows through eight hundred leagues of explored country. Its pure and delicious waters flow forty leagues among numerous plantations, which offer a delightful scene on both banks of the river, where there is a great deal of hunting, fishing, and other pleasures of life.

The Capuchins were the first monks to go to New Orleans as missionaries in 1723. The superior of these good monks, who are concerned solely with their religious work, is vicar of the parish. The Jesuits settled in Louisiana two years later, and these shrewd politicians managed to exploit the richest plantation in the colony, obtained through their intrigues. The Ursulines were sent over at about the same time. These pious women, whose zeal is certainly to be commended, educate young ladies; they also take orphans into their school, for each of whom they receive fifty crowns from the King. These same nuns were in charge of the military hospital....

This trip is made by rowing against the current of the winding Mississippi, which flows between two great forests of timber trees as old as the world.

The first things encountered are two German villages dating back to the grant which the King gave Law in 1720. This group was to consist of 1,500 Germans and Provençals. Their four square leagues of land, forming a duchy, was in the territory of an Indian nation called the Arkansas. Enough equipment for a company of dragoons and merchandise worth more than one million pounds had already been brought there. But Law failed, and the India Company, which owned Louisiana at that time, took possession of all the equipment and merchandise.

The colonists separated, and the Germans settled ten leagues above New Orleans. These very industrious people supply the capital with food. The two villages are commanded by a Swedish captain.

Two leagues farther there are the Acolapissas, who are well known for their loyalty to the French. The true name of this small tribe is *Aquelon Pissas*, meaning "nation of men who hear and see."

Then there are the Humas, who are sun worshippers. Like almost all the other American nations, these people believe that the Supreme Being lives in the sun and wants to be worshiped in this life-giving star as Author of Nature. They say that there is nothing on earth which can be compared to the wonderful sun, which lights up the universe, spreading joy and abundance. They have dedicated a cult to the sun as the visible symbol of the greatness and goodness of a God who deigns to make himself known to man by showering him with blessings.

Fifteen leagues upriver from the Humas is Pointe Coupée, a post which is about forty leagues from New Orleans. The land here is very fertile and is covered with fruit trees. There are many Frenchmen in this area who raise tobacco, cotton, rice, corn, and other products. These colonists also sell building timber, which they float down to New Orleans on rafts....

Here I am at last, thank God, at Fort de Chartres, after a long, hard, and dangerous trip. We left the Arkansas Indians on November 7 and traveled three hundred leagues to get here without seeing a single village or house. Since this stretch of land is absolutely uninhabited, it is fortunate that there are herds of buffalo and many deer, especially in this dry season. We often killed many buffalo, deer, and bear as they crossed the river to which they had come in flocks for water. When the French are on the march, they usually hire Arkansas Indians to keep them supplied with game. These hunters go out in their canoes in the morning and kill buffalo along the river's edge. The meat is left along the shore and is later picked up by the boats of the convoy.

The Indians carefully cut the tongues and the steaks from the animals they have killed and offer them as gifts to the commander and the officers of the convoy. After this, a sergeant or a corporal distributes the meat to the soldiers in each boat. Sometimes they have so much that they make a consommé soup out of it. The pleasure we get from hunting makes up for the hardships encountered on the trip. Game is so plentiful near the St. Francis River that, when we camped on its banks, we found it impossible to sleep because of the constant coming and going all night long of swans, cranes, geese, bustards, and ducks. Near the territory of the Illinois Indians, there are doves, which are a type of wild wood pigeon, in such thick clouds that they eclipse the sun. These birds, which live only on beech tree seeds and acorns, are excellent in the fall. Sometimes you can kill up to eighty of them with a single rifle shot. It is too bad that only a few savages inhabit such beautiful country.

Monsieur de Macarty, the Irish leader of the convoy, had an attack of the gout and did not want to spend the winter en route. He decided to set out before the others when we were still at the juncture of the Ohio and the Mississippi, thirty leagues from the Illinois. He took with him the best rowers without worrying the least about those he left behind, contrary to the orders of the Marquis de Vaudreuil. Yet the law of nature requires every man to lend his assistance in case of enemy attacks or other misfortunes, such as the one which occurred to my ship, the *St. Louis*. It got stuck on a sand bank, and we had to unload it almost entirely before we could get it afloat again. I lost two days and was not able to rejoin the convoy.

To make matters worse, three days after the accident, when I had only fourteen leagues more to get to the Illinois, my ship struck a tree which emerged from the water like a flying buttress. The Mississippi is full of such trees, especially in the dry season. Water rushed in through the large hole caused by the accident, and the ship sank in less than an hour. I lost everything that I owned and came close to dying. I jumped into a canoe so loaded down with things that had been salvaged from the wreck that it overturned. Several soldiers drowned and I would have too if a brave Arkansas, disregarding the severe weather, had not jumped into the water and seized me by the hooded coat I was wearing. . . .

In June, I arrived at the capital of Louisiana where I found your letter waiting for me. I was happy to hear that you are in good health. That makes up in a way for my sadness in learning that our dear governor had left for France. Even a greater misfortune is Monsieur Michel de la Rouvillière's death, brought on by a stroke. He had written me that he had learned of the sad loss of my boat and that he would gladly do all he could to help me, although one was not usually reimbursed by the King for such losses. I would have to make out an exact report of my losses, certified by Monsieur Macarty, commander of the convoy. He said that this report would be absolutely necessary to justify the expenditure and that as soon as he had received these papers, he would see to it that I was reimbursed. Before he left, the Marquis de Vaudreuil advised me to see his successor, Monsieur de Kerlérec, who has paid absolutely no attention to the Marquis' recommendation. His character is exactly the opposite of his predecessor's. The new governor says that he has not come all this way just for a change of air. He kept me in New Orleans and did not allow me to rejoin my garrison before 1754, when I left with the convoy headed by Monsieur de Faverot. The King's boats were so loaded down with packs of trinkets that there was no room for the provisions I had to take along for the trip. I complained to Monsieur de Kerlérec, who was rather disagreeable about it. He asked me what I was taking along to trade with the Indians, and I answered that I understood nothing about commerce since I was a military man, that the

King had sent me to Louisiana to serve him, and that it was my duty to do so. Finally, Monsieur de Kerlérec permitted me to join my garrison.

I left New Orleans on August 17, but the boats, as I have already said, were so loaded down with merchandise that we were caught by cold weather and ice and could not go on to the Illinois territory. We had to spend the winter en route and did not arrive at our destination until January, 1755. All of this caused a great deal of damage and added immensely to the King's expenses.

Even Bossu's somewhat naïve observations, made on the basis of visits to only a small portion of New France's far-flung outposts, reveal the extent of the French hold on the continent's hinterland. This expansion indicated the dynamism of France's religious, business, and military leaders, the relative simplicity of the geography of the frontier, and the economic opportunity that challenged its investors. But the documents prove also that Indians, Spaniards, and English rivals, no less than problems of internal organization, combined to disrupt French efforts to subdue and exploit North America. The non-Indian population of Canada probably never exceeded 150,000 at one time, and even though many were farmers, traders, priests, and merchants, the colony was virtually an armed camp. Had French civilization remained unchallenged, it would unquestionably have made a different adjustment to the American environment. That civilization was challenged, however, by a British juggernaut destined to destroy New France.

CHAPTER 7

Colonial and Indian Wars, 1680-1763

Successful French colonization of North America, coupled with apparent high profits in the Indian trade of Canada, excited English officials and angered merchants and traders of the English colonies. Why, they asked, should the trade of the interior be surrendered to the French: English trading goods were better and cheaper; English traders were equally willing to brave the dangers of the wilderness; and English investors were eager to pour capital into a potentially lucrative market. Admittedly the risks were great: hostile Indians prowling the forests liked nothing better than a chance meeting with a trader and the opportunity to make off with scalp, goods, and liquor. French missionaries encouraged Indians to drive the English out by force, and French traders would fight to the death rather than lose control of key posts or Indian tribes.

By the end of the seventeenth century, the French were establishing themselves from Quebec to New Orleans and the English settlers were groping their way through the passes into the Old West. The stage was being set for a series of bloody frontier fights. Had the monarchs of England and France been interested in peace, restraining the active and competitive traders would have proved difficult if not impossible, but neither France nor England really wanted peace. Religion, royal succession, honor, prestige, economic gain, and imperial aspirations drew the leaders of both countries into repeated wars of escalating magnitude. For virtually one hundred years, from 1689 until 1783, French and English soldiers faced each other on battlefields as far apart as India and America. If the leadership at home had a sense of perspective about where the best efforts should be made or where the greatest wealth should be expended, it proved unable to control the actions of petty royal officials, who, living at the fringes of power and empire, triggered costly and dangerous border clashes.

In America, the Iroquois country of upstate New York was the focal point of the Anglo-French confrontation. Originally armed by the Dutch and latently hostile to the French since the days of Champlain, the Iroquois became willing pawns of rival powers. The English needed the Iroquois; the tribesmen formed a bulwark against the intrusion of militant French traders, priests, and soldiers and provided an opportunity for trade. Of this the five nations that comprised the Iroquoian tribes understood little; and thus, goaded by the English, they eagerly accepted the war belt and raised the tomahawk.

THE BRITISH ALLIANCE WITH THE IROQUOIS

English reliance on and use of the Iroquois against the French on the eve of King William's War (1689-1697) is apparent in scattered and incomplete entries between 1684 and 1691 in Indian Secretary Peter Wraxall's "Abridgement of the Indian Affairs" (New York Collection of Indian Records).[1]

ALBANY COURT HOUSE 31 JULY 1684

The Right Honorable Francis Lord Howard Governor of Virginia &c. The Honorable Col Thomas Dongan Governor of New York for His Royal Highness The Duke of York. And Several other Gentleman

A Deputation of Sachems from the *Mohawks, Oneydas, Onnandagas & Cayouges.*

The Chief Subject of this Meeting was to bury the Ax & make a firm & lasting Peace between the Virginia & Maryland Indians & the aforesaid Nations, which was sollemnly Effected & agreed to.

The Above 4 Nations of Indians in a Speech they Made to Governor Dongan requested they might have the Duke of Yorks Arms to put up at each of their Castles as a mark of their Affection & Attachment.

Governor Dongan spoke as follows to the 4 Nations

That there be a good Understanding betwixt your Selves, and if there be any Difference to acccquaint me & I will compose it, and that you make no Covenant & Agreement with the French or any other Nation without my knowledge & Approbation. And that they say the same to the Sennekas. And I do give you the Great Duke of Yorks Arms to put upon each of the Castles as a Sign that you are under this Government.

The Mohawks during the above meeting offered to Governor Dongan for the use & Service of the Christians a Tract of Land belonging to them, which by Minutes Dated the first of August the Governor accepted & gave them for the same sundry goods therein Specified, & the Copy of a Deed is recorded, bearing Date the 1 day of August 1684 from the Mohawk Indians to Governor Dungan to his heirs & assigns forever, of a Tract or parcell of Land sittuated upon the Mohawk River, beginning where the Bounds & Limits of Schenecktady ends at a Place called by the Natives Cagguwarrioene & so runing up both sides of the River to a Creek or Kiln called & known by the name of Ottnawadase together with all the Pasture Meadows, Trees, Timber &c. (The Preamble of the Deed says we the underwritten Maquasse Sachems in consideration &c but no Signatures or Names appear to be signed in the Record).

ALBANY 2d AUGUST 1684

A Speech of the Onnondages & Cajouga Sachems made in the Court House at Albany to Colonel Thomas Dongan Governor of New York in the Presence of Lord Effingham Howard Governor of Virginia (Translated from this Vol of the Records from the Low Dutch Language by Peter Wraxall.)

Brother Corlaer, You are a Mighty Sachem & we but a Small People. When the English first came to New York to Virginia & Maryland, they were but a small People & we a large Nation; & we finding they were good People gave them Land & dealt Civilly by them; Now that that you are grown Numerous & we decreased, you must Protect us from the French, which if you dont we shall loose all our Hunting & Bevers: The French want all the Bevers & are Angry that we bring any to the English.

We have put all our Land & our Persons under the Protection of the Great Duke of York Brother to your Mighty Sachem. The Susqua-

---

[1] Reprinted by permission of the publishers from Charles H. McIlain, editor, *Wraxall's Abridgement of the New York Indian Affairs, 1678–1751.* Cambridge, Mass.: Harvard University Press, 1915. Pp. 10–17.

hanna River which we won with our Sword, we have given to this Government; And we desire it may be a Branch of that Great Tree which is Planted here, whose Top reaches to the Sun & under whose Branches We Shelter our Selves from the French or any other Enemy: Our Fire burns in your Houses & Your Fire in Ours & we desire it may ever so continue.

We will not consent that the Great Penn's People should settle on the Susquahanna River; Our Young Warriors are like the the Wolves of the Forrest as you Great Sachem of Virginia know, besides, we have no other Land to leave our Wives & Children.

We have submitted our Selves to the Great Sachem Charles who liveth on the other side of the Great Lake, And we now give you in token thereof Two white Buckskins to be sent to him, that He may write & put a great Red Seal thereto, that we put under the Protection of the Great Duke of York, the Susquahanna River above the Wasaghta or Falls together with all the rest of our Lands & to no one else. Our Brothers his People are as Fathers to our Wives & Children & gave us Bread in the time of Need, And we will neither give up our Selves nor our Lands to any other Government than this. And We desire that Corlaer (the Governor) will transmit these our Resolutions to the Great Sachem Charles who lives over the Great Lake, with this Belt of Wampum & this Smaller one to the Duke of York his Brother, & we present you Corlaer with a Bever Skin that you may fulfill our request.

And we let you know O Great Man of Virginia (meaning Lord Effingham) that Great Penn spoke to us in this House by his Agents, and begged us to sell him the Susquahanna River, but we would not listen to him, having already annexed it to this Government & we desire that you will bear Testimony of what we have now said & do now again confirm, which We desire you will let the Great Sachem over the Great Lake know, And also that we are a Free People & unite our Selves to the English, and it is therefore in our Power to dispose of our Land to whom we think proper, and We present you with a Bever.

COURT HOUSE AT ALBANY
5 AUGUST 1684

Present Lord Howard Governor Dongan & other Gentlemen

The Sennekas answered a Speech of Col Dongans which is not recorded, but their Answer contained some Complaints the Governor of Canada had made against them for Robbing some French Subjects—they Answer that whilst the French Governor stiled himself their Father & called them his Children his People & himself supplied their Enemies with Amunition to destroy them, & catching the French carrying some, they took it from them. In the Course of their Speech they thanked the Governor for the Duke of Yorks Arms which he sent them, They apply to him for his Protection of them against the French, acknowledging him to be the Governor of their Country & themselves under his Command.

ALBANY THE 5 AUGUST 1684
IN THE EVENING

My Lord Effingham having made his Speech to the Sennekas which is not recorded, they made their Answer. They consent to bury the Ax & make a perpetual Peace with the Virginia & Maryland Indians & return their Dutiful thanks to Governor Dongan for his Mediatorship.

In the conclusion of their Speech they address themselves to Governor Dongan & say, that the other Nations from the Mohawks to the Cayugas having given up to the Government of New York the Susquahannah River & All that Country [the Land as before Specified], they do confirm the same, & in token thereof (according to the Indian Custom) they make presents thereupon—At the Court House in Albany the 5th day of August 1687.

An Excellent Speech of Governor Dongan's to the 5 Nations who were at Warr with the French—

1. he tells them they brought this Warr on themselves by entering into a Correspondance with the French without his knowledge or Consent which as Subjects of His Britannick Majesty they ought not to have done.

2. he advises them to elect One or Two of their wisest Sachems & one or two Chief Warriors of each Nation to be a Council to manage all the Affairs of the War, for by taking all their Measures & Designs in public meetings they are liable to be betrayed. Also to advertise him of their Scheemes by a trusty Messinger.

3. To Strengthen themselves by an Alliance Offensive & Defensive with the Ottowaws & Twich Twicks & the farther Indians, lay the Path open for them to come & trade with us, when they will have every thing cheaper than from the French.

4. To Open a safe Path for the Northern Indians & Mehikanders who are at Ottowawa to come home & the Governor would use his best Endeavors to assist

5. To send Messengers in the Name of all the 5 Nations to invite the Christian Indians at Canada to come home to their Native Country.

6. Not to keep their Corn in their Castles but bury it some where in the Woods & that few People may know where it is.

7. Not to suffer any French Priest among them, for One that was at Onnondaga discovered to the French every thing that passed among them.

8. That the Cheifs keep their People Sober

(N.B. I find no Answer recorded to this Excellent Speech)

From this last Speech of Governor Dongans to the 2d of June 1691. I cannot find any Governors Speech or meeting with the Indians Recorded. the intermediate Space of Time in the Records is filled up with Transactions between the Magistrates of Albany & the Indians; in some parts They are entituled the Convention of Albany.

The Indians carried on a War against the French & sent several Deputations to Albany to invite us into the same, They were answered that a Revolution had happened in England & that the Prince of Orange was upon the Throne who was a Professed Enemy to the French King & therefore we expected a New Governor to arrive with a Declaration of war against the French.

The 3 February 1689. There is a full Account of a Grand Meeting of the 5 Nations at Onnondaga, to which it is said the Convention of Albany sent Arnout the Interpreter & one Saunders together with Two Indians to lay before the Assembly the Proposals of the Convention. At this Meeting were also Two Cayuoga Indians who were carried Prisoners to France & a Praying Onnondagu Indian in the French Interest.

These Last spoke to the Assembly in behalf of the French & invited & exhorted the 5 Nations to meet the Governor of Canada next Spring at Cadaraqui & to enter into an Alliance with him.

Next Spoke the Indians in the Name of the Convention of Albany whose Instructions consisted of 6 Articles That the Coalition of the 5 Nations with this Government as Subject to the Great King of England, so Solemnly, so long & so often acknowledged by them, doth not give them the Power to enter into any Treaties with the French against our Consent, & that such a proceeding would be Traiterous & Disloyal.—That They are Subjects of the King of England, that the French being His Enemies, & the Declaration of War against the French so long expected being now arrived, Should the 5 Nations now agree to a Cessation of Arms or make a Treaty of Peace with the French, the King of England will consider it as throwing off their Allegiance to him, & dissolving the Bond of Union which hath so long subsisted & been so often renewed in the most solemn Manner between this Government & the 5 Nations—&c. &c.

The Sennekas Spoke next, They gave the Assembly an Account, that they had entered into a Treaty of Peace & Alliance with the Wagenhaer Nation of Indians in behalf of themselves the Other 4 Nations & this Government & that the Three Wagenhaers were now present to ratify the same. This was accordingly accepted on all sides. The Wagenhaers promised to use their best endeavours to bring the Jenedadees & Ottowawaes into the Alliance.

An Onnondaga Sachem then rose up & said—Bretheren—We must govern our Selves by the Propositions from the Convention of Albany, & look on the French with Enmity, They are our Enemies & Deceitful.

The Speeker for the whole Assembly then Addressed himself to Arnout our Interpreter & desired him to lay before the Assembly the Instructions he brought from Albany This he did—They then all consulted together, & the said Speaker in behalf of the whole said. They were all determined to preserve their Coalition with us & to make War upon the French of Canada—and said, We are very Glad to hear our King (meaning the King of England) hath declared War against the French & that a new Governor is soon expected.

The Speaker then Addressed himself in behalf of the whole Assembly to the Deputies from the Governor of Canada & told them, The Five Nations were detirmined not to meet him at Cadaraquie, That they would make no Peace with him, but took up the Ax against him—they accquainted him that had made a Peace with the Wagenhaes—The Assembly then broke up.

ALBANY 2d DAY OF JUNE 1691

Extracts from the Answer of the Oneydas, Onnondagas, Cayouga & Sennekas by their Sachems to His Excellancy Col. Henry Slaughters Speech, (which I do not find Recorded).

You accquainted us that you were sent by their Majestys of England to Govern this Province. We are glad that you are safe arrived & that we have a Governor again.

We have been informed by our Forefathers, that in former times a Ship arrived here in this Country, which was matter of Great Admiration to us, especially our desire was to know what should be within her Belly. In that Ship were Christians & amongst the rest One Jaques with whom we made a Covenant of Friendship, which Covenant hath since been tyed together with a Chain, & always been kept inviolable both by the Brethren & us, in which Covenant it was agreed, that whosoever should hurt or prejudice the One, should be guilty of injuring the Other, all of us being comprehended in One Common League.

(in testimony here of they gave a Bever Skin)

You have made a Covenant with us wherein they of Boston & Virginia are included.

Your Excellency is the Great Governor of this Country, you command the Christians & us too.

ALBANY THE 4TH OF JUNE 1691.

The Mohawk Indians acquainted Governor [Fletcher] Slaughter, that some of their Nation had been to Cannada & spoke with the Governor there who was very desirous that the 5 Nations should make a lasting Peace with his Praying Indians, & had sent by them (the Mohawks) a Belt of Wampum to Corlaer the Governor of the Mohawks & the rest of the 5 Nations to consent to & make Peace with his Praying Indians. And they desire Now to know of the Governor what they shall do upon this Occasion—

His Excellency answered to all the 5 Nations. That he admired the Mohawks would admit of any Treaty with the Praying Indians of Canada, they being as much Enemies to the Bretheren as the French. Therefore he could not admit of any proposals from them, & must check the Bretheren for hearkening to any thing from them.

The Mohawks in the afternoon of the same day made a Speech to the Governor in which they renewed the Covenant, & said tho an Angry Dog (meaning the French) should come & endeavor to bite the Chain of Unity between us in peices with his Teeth, yet they would keep it firm both in Peace & War.—

After this an Oneyda Sachem rose up in the behalf of the 4 Nations & told the Mohawks, that as to the Belt of Wampum which the French Governor had sent, they rejected it as venemous & detestable & would prosecute the War as long as they lived.

Between the above date & the 5 August following I find the Mayor & Magistrates of Albany accquainted the Indians with the Death of Governor [Fletcher] Slaughter & that Major Ingolsby succeeded him as Commander in Chief.

King William's War, stemming from Louis XIV's refusal to accept William of Orange as king of England, increased the tempo and ferocity of the fighting that had begun in 1684. After 1689, however, the French became acutely aware of the threat to their control, and the Count de Frontenac returned as governor of Canada. The "Iron Governor," a European aristocrat with the incredible capacity to inflame Indians by leading them in self-intoxicating war-dances, rallied the pro-French Indians and marched boldly upon the Iroquois and the English in New York. Unprecedented savagery characterized the fighting on both sides. Gradually, the French gained the upper hand, especially after English colonial expeditions failed to seize Montreal and Quebec. In the Great Lakes country, only the intense rivalry between the Jesuits and the fur-trading interests, which led to a brief suspension in the trade, prevented Frontenac from winning complete control of the region. In the Hudson Bay area, where fighting had broken out even before the declaration of war, the French scored many victories, capturing the key base at York Factory.

THE EFFECT OF THE TREATY OF RYSWICK ON THE FRONTIERS

But victory or defeat for England or France would not be determined by what transpired in America. When the Anglo-French negotiators signed the Treaty of Ryswick in 1697, they agreed to restore each other's boundaries as they were in America before King William's War. The dynamics of the Anglo-French controversy in New York, however, did not easily yield to the stroke of a negotiator's pen. Cadwallader Colden, who as a member of the governor's council had access to the official records of New York, drafted an interesting description of what happened on the frontier when the news of the treaty reached America:[2]

Soon after the News of the Peace of Reswick reached New-York, the Governor sent an Express to Canada, to inform the Governor there of it, that Hostilities might cease. The Five Nations having an Account of the Peace earlier than they had it in Canada, took Advantage of it, in hunting Bever near Cadarsekui Fort. The Governor of Canada being informed of this, and believing that the Five Nations thought themselves secure by the general Peace, resolved to take his last Revenge of them. For this Purpose he sent a considerable Party of Adirondacks

[2] Cadwallader Colden, *The History of the Five Nations of Canada* (New York, 1904), pp. 253–262.

to surprise them, which they did, and killed several, but not without Loss of many of their own Men. The Loss of one of their greatest Captains at that Time gave the Five Nations the greatest Affliction. After he was mortally wounded, he cried out: "Must I, who have made the whole Earth tremble before me, now die by the Hands of Children?" for he despised the Adirondacks.

A Dispute at this Time arose, between the Government of New-York and Canada, about the French Prisoners which the Five Nations had in their Hands. The Earl of Bellamont, then Governor of New-York, would have the French receive those Prisoners from him, and directed the Five Nations to bring them to Albany for that Purpose. The French, on the other Hand, refused to own the Five Nations as subject to the Crown of Great-Britain and threatened to continue the War against the Five Nations, if they did not bring the Prisoners to Montreal, and deliver them there. The Count de Frontenac sent some of the Praying Indians with a Message to this Purpose, and to have all the French Allies included in the general Peace.

The Messenger on his Return told the Count, publickly in Presence of several Utawawas, that the Five Nations refused to include several of his Allies, but were resolved to revenge the Injuries they had received. The Utawawas were exceedingly discomposed at hearing this, and the Count, to recover their Spirits, assured them, that he never would make Peace without including all his Allies in it, and without having all their Prisoners restored. At the same Time he made Preparations to attack the Five Nations with the whole Force of Canada.

The Earl of Bellamont being informed of this, sent Captain John Schuyler (of the Militia) to tell the Count, that he had the Interest of the King his Master too much at Heart, to suffer the French to treat the Five Nations like Enemies, after the Conclusion of the general Peace; for which Reason he had ordered them to be on their Guard, and had furnished them with Arms and Ammunition; that he had ordered the Lieutenant-Governor, in Case they were attacked, either by the French or their Allies, to join them with the regular Troops; and that, if he found it necessary, he would raise the whole Force of his Government in their Defence.

This put a Stop to the French Threatening, and both sides made Complaint to their Masters. The two Kings ordered their respective Governors to be assisting to each other, in making the Peace effectual to both Nations, and to leave the Disputes, as to the Dependency of the Indian Nations, to be determined by Commissioners, to be appointed pursuant to the Treaty of Reswick.

It is exceedingly impolitick, when weaker Potentates, ingaged in a Confederacy against one powerful Prince, leave any Points to be determined after the Conclusion of a Peace; for if they cannot obtain a concession, while the Confederacy stands and their Force is united, how can a weaker Prince hope to obtain it, when he is left alone to himself, after the Confederacy is dissolved? The French have so often found the Benefit of this Piece of Imprudence, that in all their Treaties they use all the Cajoling, and every Artifice in their Power, to obtain this Advantage, and they seldom miss it.

About the Time of the Conclusion of the Peace at Reswick, the noted Therouet died at Montreal. The French gave him Christian Burial in a pompous Manner, the Priest, that attended him at his Death, having declared that he died a true Christian; for, said the Priest, while I explained to him the Passion of our Saviour, whom the Jews crucified, he cried out; "Oh! had I been there, I would have revenged his Death, and brought away their Scalps."

Soon after the Peace was known at Montreal, three considerable Men of the Praying Indians came to Albany; they had fine laced Coats given them, and were invited to return to their own Country. They answered, that they were young Men, and had not Skill to make a suitable Answer, and had not their ancient Men to consult with; but promised to communicate the Proposals to their old Men, and would bring back an Answer in the Fall. I find nothing more of this in the Register of Indian Affairs, though it might have been of great Consequence had it been pursued to Purpose; but such Matters, where there is not an immediate private Profit, are seldom pursued by the English with that Care and Assiduity, with which they are by the French. . . .

The Count de Frontenac died while these Disputes continued. Monsieur de Callieres, who succeeded him, put an End to them, by agreeing to send to Onondaga to regulate the Exchange of Prisoners there; for which Purpose Monsieur Maricour, Ioncaire, and the Jesuit Bruyas, were sent.

When the French Commissioners were come within less than a Mile of Onondaga Castle, they put themselves in Order and marched with the French Colours carried before them, and with as much Show as they could make. Decanesora met them without the Gate, and complimented them with three Strings of Wampum. By the first he wiped away their Tears for the French that had been slain in the War. By the second he opened their Mouths, that they might speak freely; that is, promised them freedom of Speech. By the third he cleaned the Matt, on which they were to sit, from the Blood that had been spilt on both Sides: The Compliment was returned by the Jesuit, then they entered the Fort, and were saluted with a general Discharge of all the fire Arms. They were carried to the best Cabin in the Fort, and there entertained with a Feast. The Deputies of the several Nations not being all arrived, the Jesuit, and Monsieur Maricour, passed the Time in visiting and conversing with the French Prisoners. The General Council being at last met, the Jesuit made the following Speech, which I take from the Relation the Five Nations afterwards made of it to the Earl of Ballamont.

1. I am glad to see the Five Nations, and that some of them went to Canada, notwithstanding Corlear forbid them: I am sorry for the Loss of your People killed by the remote Indians; I condole their Death, and wipe away the Blood by this Belt.

2. The War Kettle boiled so long, that it could have scalded all the Five Nations had it continued; but now it is overset, and turned upside down, and a firm Peace made.

3. I now plant the Tree of Peace and Welfare at Onondaga.

4. Keep fast the Chain you have made with Corlear, for now we have one Heart and one Interest with them; but why is Corlear against your corresponding with us, ought we not converse together when we are at Peace and in Friendship?

5. Deliver up the French Prisoners you have, and we shall deliver not only those of your Nation we have, but all those likewise taken by any of our Allies; and gave a Belt.

6. I offer myself to you to live with you at Onondaga, to instruct you in the Christian Religion, and to drive away all Sickness, Plagues and Diseases out of your Country, and gave a third Belt.

7. This last Belt, he said, is from the Rondaxe, or French Indians, to desire Restitution of the Prisoners taken from them.

The Jesuit in the Conclusion said;

Why does nor Corlear tell you what passes between the Governor of Canada and him? He keeps you in the Dark, while the Governor of Canada conceals nothing from his Children. Nor does the Governor of Canada claim your Land, as Corlear does.

The General Council immediately rejected the Belt by which the Jesuit offered to stay with them, saying, We have already accepted Corlear's Belt, by which he offers us Pastors to instruct us. Decanesora added, The Jesuits have always deceived us, for while they preached Peace, the French came and knocked us on the Head. To this the Jesuit replied, that if he had known that Corlear intended to send them Pastors, he would not have offered this Belt.

It is to be observed that the Indian Council refused to hear the French, or to give them an Answer, but in Presence of the Commissioners from Albany.

The French Commissioners having assured the Peace with the Five Nations, the Inhabitants of Canada esteemed it the greatest Blessing that could be procured for them from Heaven; for nothing could be more terrible than this last War with the Five Nations. While this War lasted, the Inhabitants eat their Bread in continual Fear and Trembling. No Man was sure, when out of his House, of ever returning to it again. While they laboured in the Fields, they were under perpetual Apprehensions of being killed or seized, and carried to the Indian Country, there to end their Days in cruel Torments. They many Times were forced to neglect both their Seed Time and Harvest. The Landlord often saw all his Land plundered, his Houses burnt, and the whole Country ruined, while they thought their Persons not safe in their Fortifications. In short, all Trade and Business was often at an intire Stand, while Fear, Despair, and Misery appeared in the Faces of the poor Inhabitants.

The French Commissioners carried several of the principal Sachems of the Five Nations back with them, who were received at Montreal with great Joy. They were saluted by a Discharge of all the great Guns round the Place, as they entered. The French Allies took this amiss, and asked if their Governor was entering. They were told, that it was a Compliment paid to the Five Nations, whose Sachems were then entering the Town. We perceive, they replied, that Fear makes the French shew more Respect to their Eenemies than Love can make them do to their Friends.

Monsieur de Callieres assembled all the French Allies, (who were then very numerous at Montreal) to make the Exchange of Prisoners, and they delivered the Prisoners they had taken, though the Five Nations had sent none to be exchanged for them. Thus we see a brave People struggle with every Difficulty, till they can get out of it with Honour; and such People always gain Respect, even from their most inveterate Enemies.

FRICTION FOLLOWING QUEEN ANNE'S WAR

King William's War ended in a tenuous truce. England and France gathered resources for another contest, and in America farseeing officials and Indian traders renewed their efforts to win strategic footholds before fighting resumed. By 1702, when problems of royal succession in Spain and England again provided an excuse for war, the French possessed a stronger grasp of the West. The new struggle, called Queen Anne's War, did not end until 1713. In America, fighting occurred primarily along the southern frontier and in New England. The governor of the Carolinas, eager to stave off an attack on the colony, sent troops storming toward the Spanish lands in Florida, where France's ally failed to blunt the English attack. Only two things stood between the English and their control of Louisiana: winning the friendship of the

Indians of the South, and gathering a fleet to strike at New Orleans. From 1703 to 1706, English traders reduced the influence of France and Spain among the tribes, but fear of an attack on Charleston prevented the Carolinians from mobilizing a fleet. Louisiana continued to be French. In the North, the Iroquois remained neutral, mindful of the heavy price they had paid in King William's War. This restricted the fighting. Nevertheless, the French wreaked such havoc on the New England frontier that a colonial army raised in Boston sailed to Port Royal and captured that powerful Acadian naval base. But one year later, in 1710, another colonial expedition failed to subdue Quebec and conquer Canada.

Unlike King William's War, which Cadwallader Colden declared to be a draw that worked to the advantage of the French, the English gathered spoils at the close of Queen Anne's War. The Treaty of Utrecht in 1713 forced France to yield Newfoundland, control of Hudson Bay, and any claim of sovereignty over the Iroquois. It failed, however, to define territorial boundaries. Increased friction in the West was inevitable. Three years after the war, the French ministry discussed the condition of the western frontier on the basis of a report from the governor of Canada.[3]

He has learned from Monsieur de Ramezay that the Outauois savages and other Nations of the upper country who are allies of the French, Have since last year been very peaceably disposed, that their relations with each other have been amicable, and that they have the sentiments which they ought to have toward the Renards.

Sieur de Vincennes, the officer stationed among the Miamis and Ouyatanons, has reported that the Iroquois have sent those Nations Collars Underground,—that is to say, Secret messages,—by which they invited them to come and get what they need at a post established on *the Oyo River*, which is a new settlement of the English of Carolina. They said that there they would find merchandise at half the prices asked by the French, who were tyrannizing over them.

Sieur de Vincennes Had the Miamis make the reply that from father to son they had been the Children of Onontio (this is the name which the Savages give to the Governor-general of Canada), and that they would not depart from their obedience to him.

The Ouyatanons have sent a young Slave to Sieur de Ramezay to reiterate the request they made to him last year to be present at their Councils, and to furnish a Missionary to teach them, and a blacksmith to repair their weapons.

Monsieur de Vaudreuil will provide what they ask, and will pay special attention to garrisoning all the posts. It is of the Utmost importance to establish those On the Southern frontier, where the English of Pensilvania, Carolina, and Virginia are anxious to introduce themselves, which would ruin the Commerce not only of Canada, but even of Louisiana, on account of the easy communication furnished by the Rivers that empty into the great river Mississipy.

In the years that followed, the French and Spanish faced increasing pressure from English traders who moved secretly along western trails to sell guns, tools, and cloth to the Indians. Carolina officials ceaselessly courted the friendship of southern tribes or destroyed them like the Yamessee who remained steadfastly pro-French. English intrigue contributed to the violent outbreak, in 1729, among the Natchez Indians that not only sent French prestige plunging but also upset French colonization schemes in the

---

[3] Reuben Gold Thwaites (ed.), *Collections of the State Historical Society of Wisconsin* (Madison, 1902), vol. 16, pp. 345–346.

lower Mississippi Valley. While the French exterminated the Natchez and many Chickasaw who sided with them, the English utilized these years of bloody frontier fighting to strengthen their hold in the South by establishing Georgia, a sanctuary for English prisoners as well as a slaveless, military bastion for defense against attacks from the west and south. By the early 1740s, undeclared war raged along the Georgia-Florida frontier, in a struggle that saw Spain's influence among the Indians dwindle until the English could threaten French control of the Southwest. France fared little better in the Northwest where the Fox Indians waged a bloody, decade-long conflict. Only the systematic and ruthless annihilation of the Fox and their allies, achieved at high cost, allowed the French to consolidate their rule in Michigan and Wisconsin.

By the mid 1740s, England and France were close to war. Indians, inspired by the French, raided deep into Massachusetts. Rival traders cut each other's routes in upstate New York and Pennsylvania, and Anglo-French disagreements fomented Indian disorders in the South. Yet the magnitude of the fighting scarcely increased in America when the two great colonial powers, at loggerheads over Frederick II of Prussia's seizure of Silesia, launched King George's War in 1744. Although the French achieved success in Europe, in America four years of fighting ended with a truce that included the restoration of all former boundaries.

THE BRITISH THREATEN THE FRENCH IN THE OHIO COUNTRY

During the brief truce that followed, the upper Ohio Valley became a center of controversy. English traders, following migrating Delaware and Shawnee tribes, dominated the trade in western Pennsylvania and eastern Ohio after 1740. Taking advantage of the critical shortage of goods suffered by the French in King George's War, they extended influence to the Miami River. By the close of the conflict in 1748, George Croghan, a shrewd Irish trader, built a palisaded post at Pickawillany, deep in French territory. The following selection, written by the governor of Canada, the Marquise de la Galissonière, explained his response to this threat in a letter to the French Minister of Marine:[4]

MONSEIGNEUR:

Since the English last autumn made some unseasonable movements, chiefly in the direction of Acadia, and since they also on the side of the lakes had much speech with the Indians tending to induce them to revolt, I have thought that I should take measures to check the results of their ill will, at least until I received new orders.

Consequently on one side I have sent the Sieur de Boishébert to the lower part of the river St. John with a small detachment to reassure the inhabitants against threats of the Sieur Gorham, the English officer who was sent by M. Mascarene to make these inhabitants renew an oath of fidelity that they should never have been obliged to take. I wrote at the same time to M. Mascarene. I annex my letter and his answer.

On the side of the lakes I have sent the Sieur de Céloron with a detachment of two hundred Frenchmen and thirty Indians. He has orders to go to the Beautiful River or Ohio River and descend it, both to drive out the Hurons who have assassinated the French and to win back some other Indians who have departed from their duty, as well as to remove the English who come to trade in those regions where they proposed this year to establish a post.

---

[4] Theodore C. Pease and Ernestine Jenison (eds.), *Collections of the Illinois State Historical Library* (Springfield, 1940), vol. 19, pp. 96–99.

This river which falls into the Wabash and thence into the Mississippi indubitably belongs to France, and if the English were to establish themselves there it would give them entry into all our posts and would open to them the way to Mexico. I have given orders to the Sieur de Céloron to take possession anew, and I have charged him to examine the region well and to see what settlements might be made there.

I have given him as chaplain the Reverend Father Bonnecamp, Jesuit and mathematician, who will afford us more exact and detailed information than we have hitherto had of those regions as well as those by which the detachment will pass going and coming.

The necessity of having similar information has induced me to send to Detroit the Sieur de Léry, *fils,* and to Mackinac the Sieur de Lotbinière. They have no other mission than to observe everything that may be useful to the service and to draw up memoirs. Father Bonnecamp has had made for the Sieur de Léry and for himself instruments to take the elevations and has graduated them, but the Sieur de Lotbinière has graduated his own, and I have much confidence in his workmanship.

To enter into the arrangements which I have taken with respect to Detroit, I sent this last spring some families amounting to about forty-five persons, and I have given to Sieur de Sabrevois, who is there to relieve M. le Chevalier de Longueuil, instructions which appear to me proper for augmenting that establishment.

That of the Illinois, which is not less important, has just lost M. le Chevalier de Bertet who died the ninth of January. He was an excellent officer as I had the honor to indicate to you last year. If you were to choose a successor to him from this colony, I know no one who would be more fit for it than the Sieur de Céloron.

I am with very profound respect, Monsieur,

Your very humble and obedient servant,

La Galissonière

FRENCH RETALIATION: THE BLAINVILLE EXPEDITION, 1749

Galissonière's orders proved easier to give than to enforce. Céloron de Blainville entered the Ohio Valley, buried lead plates indicating French sovereignty, tried to talk the Indians into returning to French posts, but retired without attacking the English traders. His journal illustrates the problems of Indian diplomacy confronting the French when they lacked the will to fight:[5]

The 27th I arrived at White River about ten o'clock at night. I knew that three leagues in the interior there were six cabins of Miamis, which caused me to camp at this place.

The 28th I sent Monsieur de Villiers and my son to these cabins to request those Savages to come and speak with me. They brought them and I engaged them to come with me to the village of la Demoiselle, where I was about to go to carry the message of their father Onontio. They consented to this and asked me to wait until the morrow in order to give them time to go and prepare for their journey. There are in this same village two cabins of Sonnontouans; the policy of these tribes is to always have some of the latter with them who are shields for them. I engaged one of the Sonnontouans who speaks miami well to come with me to the home of la Demoiselle. I had need of him, having no interpreter for that language,

---
[5] Reuben Gold Thwaites (ed.), *Collections of the State Historical Society of Wisconsin* (Madison, 1908), vol. 18, pp. 46–55.

and I had matters of consequence to treat of with the Miami chief.

The 29th I wrote to Monsieur Raimond, captain and commandant at the Miami fort, and begged him to send me a certain Roy, an interpreter, with as many horses as he possibly could to transport our baggage over a portage fifty leagues in length.

The 30th, the Savages of White River having come, I embarked in order to arrive at Rock River, at whose mouth I had a leaden plate buried and the arms of the King attached to a tree, concerning which I drew up an official report.

Year 1749, we Céloron, knight of the royal and military order of Saint-Louis, captain commanding a detachment sent by the orders of Monsieur the marquis de La Galissonière, commandant general of Canada upon the Beautiful River, otherwise called the Ohio, accompanied by the chief officers of the detachment, have buried on the point formed by the right bank of the Ohio and the left bank of Rock River, a leaden plate, and fastened to a tree the arms of the King, in witness whereof we have drawn up and signed with Messieurs the officers, the present official report.

This done, I embarked. The shallowness of the water in the river caused me to be thirteen days ascending it.

The 12th the Miamis of the village of la Demoiselle, having learned that I had arrived near them, sent four chiefs to me with peace calumets for me to smoke. As I had half of my people on land, there not being enough water in the river to float loaded canoes, I was informed by Monsieur de Courtemanche, officer of the detachment, of the arrival of these envoys. I disembarked at the place where they were, and when we had all sat down, they commenced their ceremony and presented to me the calumet; I accepted it. They carried it, thereupon, to Monsieur de Contrecoeur, captain second in command of the expedition, and to all the officers, and to the Canadians who, hungry, for a smoke, would have wished the ceremony to last longer. The time to camp having arrived, we slept at that place; the envoys remaining with us. I was obliged despite the scarcity of the provisions that I possessed to give them supper.

The 13th I arrived at the village of la Demoiselle, I had my camp pitched and sentinels placed, and awaited the arrival of the interpreter that I had requested of Monsieur de Raimond. During this time I sounded their minds to know if they were disposed to return to Kiskanon, this is the name of their ancient village. It seemed to me that they had no great repugnance to this. They had two English engagés in their village whom I made depart. Those who had passed the summer in trading there had already gone away with their effects by the land route; they have paths of communication from one village to the other.

The 17th, annoyed that the interpreter had not arrived and that my provisions were being consumed in waiting, I determined to speak with la Demoiselle by means of an Iroquois who spoke miami well. I showed them the magnificent presents on the part of Monsieur the General, in order to induce them to return to their village and explained to them his intentions in the following terms:

"My children, the manner that I have treated you, spite of what you have done to the French, what I have given you to maintain your wives and children, ought to prove to you the attachment that I have for you and the sincerity of my sentiments. I forget what you have done and I bury it in the depths of the earth, in order nevermore to recall it, persuaded that you have done nothing but at the instigation of people whose policy is to trouble the earth and to spoil the spirit of those with whom they communicate, and who, without appearing therein themselves, profiting by the unfortunate ascendency that you have allowed them to gain over you, have caused you to commit faults and engaged you in evil affairs, in order to ruin you in my estimation. It is to enlighten you that I send you my word, listen well and give good heed thereto, my children; it is the word of a father who loves you and has your interests at heart. By these two branches of porcelain I put out the two fires that you have lighted within the past two years at Rock River and White River, I extinguish them in such a manner that there will not appear even a single spark."

By a collar to la Demoiselle and one to le Baril

"My children, I come to say to you by these branches of porcelain that I extinguish the two fires that you have lighted within the past two years at Rock River and at White River. By these collars I raise you from your mats, and take you by the hand to bring you to Kikakon, where I relight your fire and make it more enduring than ever. It is in that land, my children, that you will enjoy perfect tranquility and that I shall be present at each instant to give you the marks of my friendship; it is in that land, my children, that you will enjoy the pleasures of life, being the *spot where repose the bones of your ancestors, and those of Monsieur de Vincennes, whom you loved so well and who governed you always* in such manner that your affairs always went well. If you have forgotten the counsels that they gave you these ashes will recall their memory to you. The bones of your ancestors suffer from your absence, have pity on your dead who desire you again in your village. Go thither with your wives and children; the chief whom I send you, carries my word, and will light your fire anew at Kiskakon in such manner that it will never be extinguished. I will give all the succor that you may expect from my friendship, and consider, my children, that I do for you what I have never done for any other nation."

Another word by four branches of porcelain and two to le Baril

"By these branches of porcelain I erect a barrier to all passage to the Beautiful River, so that you shall no longer go thither and so that the English who are the authors of all evil designs may not approach this territory which belongs to me. I make for you at the same time a beautiful road to conduct you to Kiskikon, where I relight your fire. I break off all trade with the English whom I have notified to retire from my lands, and if they come thither they shall have cause to repent."

By two branches of porcelain to la Demoiselle and two to le Baril

"When you have done, my children, what I request of you, which is solely for your advantage, I invite you to come and see me, next year, and to receive from me particular marks of my esteem; I give the same invitation to all your brothers of the Beautiful River. I hope that you have one and all sufficient spirit to respond to me as you should, and in order to begin to give you a proof of my friendship I send you these presents to cover your wives and children; I add to these gun-powder and balls that you may live more conveniently en route when you return to Kiskanon. Abandon the country where you are, it is pernicious for you, and profit by what I do for you."

The council finished, everyone retired. They carried the presents to their village where they assembled to deliberate on their replies. . . .

Reply of la Demoiselle, chief of the Miamis, established at Rock River, and of le Baril established at White River, the 18th of September 1749, by peace calumets

"It is an ancient custom among us, when we speak of pleasent matters first to present the calumets, we pray you to have the goodness to listen to us. We come to reply to what you have said to us. This calumet is a token of the pleasure that I have in smoking with you, and we hope to smoke this same calumet with our father next year."

By a collar

"My father, we have listened with pleasure to your words. We have truly seen that you come only with good intentions. You have brought to our memory the bones of our ancestors, who groan at seeing us in this place and who continually recall us. You prepare for us a fine road to return to our former mats. We thank you for it, our father, and we promise you to return thither the very beginning of next spring. We thank you for the kind words which you have given us, we see in truth that you have not forgotten us. Be persuaded that we shall endeavor always to have only pleasant relations with the Chaouanons. We recollect the good counsel which Monsieur de Vincennes gave us. My father, you address people without spirit and who cannot reply to you, perhaps, as you have hoped, but they speak sincerely to you. It is not with the tips of the lips that they speak to you, but from the bottom of the heart. You have bid us to reflect seriously on what you have said to us; we have done so, and shall continue to do so during the entire winter. We hope to have the pleasure of giving you a good word in the spring. If the hunting is abundant, we will repair our faults. We assure you, my father, we will listen no longer either to bad discourse or to evil rumors. Such at present is our intention."

Reply of Monsieur de Céloron to la Demoiselle and to le Baril in the same council

"I have listened to you, my children, and I have weighed well your words. Whether you have not well understood me, or whether you pretend not to have done so, you have not replied to what I said to you. I proposed to you, on the part of your father Ontonio, to come with me to Kiskanon in order there to relight your fire, and replace your mats; you postpone this until next spring. I should have been charmed to tell your father Onontio that I had brought you back; that would have given him pleasure because of the interest that he takes in whatever concerns you. You have given me your word to come there at the end of the winter; be faithful to your promise. You assure me of this in the strongest manner, and if you fail, fear the resentments of a father who has only too much reason to be irritated against you and who has offered you the means of regaining his good graces."

Reply to these words by la Demoiselle and le Baril

"My father, we will be faithful in executing the promise that we have given you; we will return at the end of the winter to our former abode, and, if the Master of life favors our hunting, we hope to repair our past faults. Be persuaded that we do not speak with the tips of our lips, but from the bottom of the heart. We could not at present, return whither you wish to conduct us, as the season is too far advanced."

The council finished, I detained several old

men to try and discover if what they had just said to me was sincere. While I spoke with these Savages, who assured me that all these two villages would return, in the spring to Kiskakon and that what detained them was not having any cabins built where I wished to conduct them, and that whilst hunting in the winter, they would approach their former village and would certainly return thither, Roy, whom I had requested of Monsieur de Raymond arrived the 19th. I waited to try, by means of Roy, to induce la Demoiselle with some other chiefs to go with me and relight their fires, and replace their mats at Kiskakon. In this I could not succeed. They kept saying always and assuring me that they would return next spring.

The 20th, all was ready for our departure; we broke camp. After having burned our canoes, of which we could no longer make use, we set out to march by land, each one carrying his own provisions and baggage, except Messieurs the officers, for whom I had procured horses and several men to carry their loads. I had arranged all my men in four companies, of which each had an officer at the right and one at the left. I conducted the right and Monsieur de Contrecoeur the left. We took only five and a half days to cover that route, which is estimated to be fifty leagues in length.

AN ENGLISH VIEW OF THE FRENCH TRADERS, 1755

Oddly enough, at the very time that a steady stream of English trade goods eroded French hegemony among western Indian tribes, the English traders felt themselves disadvantaged in competing against the French. Much that they had achieved stemmed from the efforts of private investors, sometimes even single individuals willing to risk themselves and their stock by invading the regions that the French governors had designated for favored post captains. But since men live by myths as well as facts, it is important to know how the English conceived of their French competitors in order to understand the motivation behind English policy. Unique in this regard is the 1755 report of Edmond Atkin, a long-time Indian trader and a confidant of the governor of South Carolina:[6]

Having taken this short view of the Posture of Indian Affairs, between our own and the French Colonies, it is worth while to consider, whence it comes to Pass that, possess'd as we are of vastly superior Advantages, by Situation on the Ocean, by our Conveniencies for the quick and easy introduction of our Goods to the Inland Parts, by the Quality and Cheapness of our Goods fit for Indians, and by the natural disposition of the Indians to prefer us, from a greater similarity between their and our Government, the French have notwithstanding, in spite of their own very great disadvantages in all those Respects, made so rapid a Progress even among Nations nearest to our Settlements, as hath lately surprized every Body. It is universally known, that the Indian [affairs] have been managed and conducted on one general plan, steadily pursued throughout Canada and Louisiana, under the immediate direction of the Crown; the chief object of which is, to exclude us not only from the Missisipi but from all the Indian Nations on this side of it. In the execution whereof are employed Men of the greatest Knowledge and Experience, by early and long Service, from among the Officers, and Missionaries; who are supported out of the

---

[6] Wilbur R. Jacobs (ed.), *Indians of the Southern Frontier* (Lincoln, Neb.: University of Nebraska Press, 1967), pp. 7–13.

Trade with the Indians, who rest their hopes of Preferment on their own Behaviour, and who on all Occasions support the Honour and Dignity of the French Nation, and watch all opportunities to turn every Occurrence to their own Advantage, or to the Disadvantage of great Britain and her Colonies. And in every Nation where the[y] can obtain the least opening for it, they fail not either by Consent or Compulsion, to place Forts and Garrisons howsoever small, under pretence of protecting those Indians against their Enemies, (which are sometimes of their own Creating for the Purpose), but with a real Intention to establish a Claim of Posession, and to fix Boundaries to us. Whereas on the other hand, the Conduct of our Colonies hath been as various as their different Interests, arising from their different Situations, which have been the Foundation of as many distinct local and partial Considerations. Without a mutual regard for the Interest of the whole, some of them relying for their Security and the Continuance of a friendly Commerce with the Indians, on its own Importance to them, have not extended their Care even to their own Frontiers, but have confined their object only to the keeping mischief from their doors. The French have accordingly taught the Indians to consider our Colonies, as so many separate independent Communities, having no Concern with each other. Whence it hath arisen that the Indians in Peace and Amity with one of them, have at the same time behaved as enemies towards the people of another. Some of the Colonies have made no regulations at all in the Indian Affairs; others have made different ones, and some but seldom if at all sent proper Persons to look into them. But the management of them hath often been left to Traders, who have no Skill in Public Affairs, are directed only by their own Interest, and being generally the loosest kind of People, are despis'd and held in great Contempt by the Indians as Liars, and Persons regarding nothing but their own Gain. All those things are pretty well known.

As it is commonly supposed, that the French have acquired their influence, and maintain their Power among the Indian Nations, intirely by their Forts;—it seems also to have been generally thought, that if they are not [to] be removed, yet our Building Forts in the same Places, and in such other places where the French still propose to do it, will be a Sufficient remedy to put an intire stop to the same, and to secure our own Interest. But this will be found on a more intimate accquaintance with that subject, to be a very great Error. How useful and necessary soever Forts really are, for establishing between the Crowns of Great Britain and France marks of Possession, or for the mutual protection of their Traders and Friends, and for fixing the doubtfull and wavering among the Indians; yet it is truly a great absurdity to imagine, that either the French or ourselves can maintain an Interest & Influence, more especially among the Inland Nations, barely by the Possession of Forts, without being at the same time possess'd of their *Affections*; Or that anything less than such a Wall as is built between China and Tartary can, when the Indians are our Enemies, secure our wide extended and exposed Colonies from their Incursions. Most of the French inland Forts are small, and very weak, having but few Men. And tho' the Indians are unskilled, and unprovided for the Attack of Forts, yet the Garrisons of the largest may easily be starv'd by them into a Surrender whenever they please. We must [look] therefore into the Conduct and Management of the French in those Forts, in order to discover by the *Arts* practiced therein the true causes from whence, under a Commerce clogged with a most hazardous Navigation & expensive Transportation of Goods, with the additional load of paying all the Charges of their Government, and under a total inability at any rate of supplying all the wants of the Indians, they have still gain'd their affections, and consequently that surprising Influence which we have felt. Those Arts will be found to be the most Simple, the most easy and certain, and the least expensive imaginable. The two Principal ones are, the Provision of *Gunsmiths*, and not so much valuable Presents as a judicious Application of them. We furnish the Indians with Guns enough in exchange for their deer skins and Furrs; but the French mend them and keep them in repair Gratis. We are sometimes almost lavish of presents on particular Occasions, which in the way they are given produce but little good effect with those that receive them, and still less with their Nation. But the French by a constant prudent Practice, make even Trifles productive of the most desirable National Consequences. When an Indian after undergoing the mortification of having a Gun (perhaps from trial and use become a favourite one) suddenly by some slight accident to the Lock, or Touch hole, render'd intirely useless to him, I say when he sees it afterwards as suddenly restored to its former State, and as useful as before, it gladdens his Heart more than a present of a new Gun would. He then looks on our Trader and the Frenchman with different Eyes. The former only Sold him the Gun (perhaps at an extravagant price); the latter when it is spoiled, hath as it were new made [it] for nothing. This endears the Frenchman to him. He is glad to have such a Friend near him. Their mutual Convenience unites them. Gratitude inclines the Indian to oblige him by any means in his Power. The presents to Indians are made at the expence of the Crown of France. Besides those given by the Governors at periodical Meetings, some are left in the occasional disposition of the Commanders of Forts the Year round. A present of any Value is never given by them but to an Indian of Sway and Consequence [among the Warriours], or as an Orator among the people. And then he comes by it easy, and without any Trouble. Whereas when such do receive Presents of some Value from us, they earn them much too dearly by tiresome tedious Journies of some hundred Miles, and the loss of time from their Hunts, which they know would have turn'd to better Account. Even trifles are put on the footing of things of Value at the French Forts, by bestowing them chiefly on the old Head Men of Note, who being past the fatigue of War and constant Hunting for their Livelyhood, but on Account of their Age held in great Veneration for their Wisdom and Experience, spend the remainder of their days almost intirely in the Town Round Houses, where the Youth and others daily report; relating to them the History of their Nation, discoursing of Occurrences, and delivering precepts and Instructions for their Conduct and Welfare. Which is all the Indian Education. To these old men who are unable to purchase Necessaries, or to perform long Journeys, when they visit those Forts the French give from time to time a Load or two of Powder and Ball, a Flint, a Knife, a little Paint, a flap or shirt, and the like. The Old Men repay the French largely for those Trifles, in their Harrangues at the round Houses, by great Encomiums on their kindness, and recommendations of them to favour; which often inculcated, make impressions on the Youth, that grow up with them into a confirm'd prejudice. On the other hand those old men complain, that our Traders, who confine their kindness and Civility almost wholly to the Young Hunters for the sake of their deerskins, shew Slights to them which lessen them in the Eyes of their People. The vast Quantity of Ammunition with which the French furnish the Indians every where by their Water Carriage more Conveniently than we can, hath strengthened their influence, that Article being the only means the Indians have to get everything else they stand in need of. Ammunition, especially Bulletts, being heavy and a Horse Load but of small Value, our Traders who are oblig'd to carry on their Trade in the Southern Parts, where the most numerous Indians are, many hundred Miles wholly by Horse Carriage, naturally consulting their own greatest profitt, have carried but scanty supplies of that Article, and in a great measure left it to the French; who have thereby imperceptably acquir'd an Addition to their Interest, in a manner which hath hitherto pass'd almost unnotic'd; But is of so much consequence to them, that the Governour of new Orleans in a letter to the French Secretary of State, (which being intercepted in the late War is now in my hands) gave it as his opinion,

That were it not for those great supplies of Ammunition, some Nations of Indians devoted to the English, would not suffer Frenchmen to remain among them. And therefore he propos'd even to restrain the Quantity, to make them more Submissive.

The same reason should lead us by some means or other to encrease it.

The National effects which the Skillfull application of little [presents] to particular Indians, and the providing Gunsmiths to mend the Guns of all in General hath produced, are scarce to be conceiv'd. The French in many places have made those two things alone as practices in their Forts, in conjunction with a better supply of Ammunition than our Traders carry, almost counterballance every other disadvantage they labour under. To illustrate fully the truth of this observation, because I think it of moment, I make choice of the Alabama Fort in the upper Creek Nation, on the Mobile River. That Fort being about 460 miles by Land from Charles Town, and about 300 miles by Water from Mobile, was built immediately upon the breaking out of the Indian War with Carolina in 1715, when that Province had Traders in every Town in the Nation, and was posess'd of the whole Indian Trade with the more Western Nations, the Chicasaws, Chactaws, Natchees, and others, to the [very] Banks of the Missisippi River, near 900 miles back. At that time the foundations of New Orleans were not laid; and but three Years before there were but 28 French Families Settled in all that was calld Louisiana. Ever since the peace which was made with the Indians in general in 1718, [our Traders] have resided as before in all the Creek Towns, and supplied them plentifully with all goods, except Ammunition. The French have never been able to supply the Goods necessary for them, except that Article. Insomuch that the Governor of Louisiana, in another Letter in 1744 to the French Secretary of State acknowledged, "That the Indians upbraided them therewith, and their breach of promises on that Head." They have constantly been obliged to draw all their Necessaries for that Garrison from the Indians; and during the late War, were under the Necessity of purchasing from our Traders the very presents they gave them. And yet at that time, those Creek Indian Chiefs being earnestly press'd to it in Charles Town by the So. Carolina Government, refused not only to assist us in attacking that Albama Fort, but even to stand neuter while we did it ourselves; and could only be prevailed on to give their Consent, that we might build a Fort also in their Nation. At their return home, intelligence was given immediately to the Commander of the Albama Fort, of our Intention; and the whole Nation kept under alarm a long time, by the War whoop sent from Town to Town. Such sort of Attachments to the French have surprised most people. But their true Springs are really those I have given.

It is no small addit[t]ion to the influence of the French, that their Officers allways on the spot, both prevent Abuses being offer'd to the Indians by particular Persons, and also never fail to demand immediate Satisfaction for any Injuries or Insults offer'd by them; which is the more readily complied with. Whereas we not being in the like Condition to demand such Satisfaction for any offences, are obliged to put up with them, and are therefore slighted—None dare to talk with the Indians about State affairs but standing Sworn Interpreters, and they only what is given in Charge; who occasionally throw out what is suitable for their Purposes. Whereas our Traders uncontrouled tell them every man what Story he pleases—I have nothing to add under this head but what all the World knows, the great hold the French Missionaries have in influencing the Indians, by means of their Superstition; whose service is such, that they have been esteemed almost of as much Consequence as Garrisons. They have been the means of gaining as much respect from the Indians to the French, as our Traders have caused disrespect to us, by their disolute Lives and Manners. And by accquiring their Confidence and Esteem, they have been able to penetrate the Thoughts and Designs of the Indians, when others could not; and when they could do no more, have at least given time to the Governors to take measures for disconcerting their Intrigues.

BORDER FIGHTING IN THE SEVEN YEARS' WAR

Atkin's appraisal may not have been entirely unjustified because in 1752, two years after Céloron de Blainville's ineffective display, the Marquis Duquesne, governor of New France, decided to oust the English from both the upper and lower Ohio Valley. In a two-pronged offensive, he first sent a strong force that quickly subdued the English traders in Ohio and carried off their trade goods; and second, he ordered the construction of a chain of forts on the upper river, including a post at the strategic fork of the Ohio that is now Pittsburgh. Duquesne's plan assured the French a shorter route to Ohio, threatened to keep the English south and east of the river, and overawed the Indians in the region.

Governor Robert Dinwiddie of Virginia, horrified by Duquesne's drive to control both the trade and the land north of the river, sent young George Washington hurrying west in mid-winter on an expedition that proved to be as fruitless as Blainville's. Ordering the French to leave the valley, Washington returned home to report that he had encountered polite but militant defiance. Determined to beat the French at their own game, Dinwiddie again sent Washington west—this time to build a post at the strategic fork—but the Virginians were too late. By the time their tiny army reached the West, a large French force was already building Fort Duquesne. Washington foolishly attacked a French scouting party. Fortunately for his men, a truce permitted their safe withdrawal.

Washington's blunder signaled a series of English failures. In 1755, an army of British regulars and Virginia militiamen commanded by General Edward Braddock cut a road to Fort Duquesne, only to suffer a staggering defeat at the hands of an inferior French force because of confusion and ineptitude. English soldiers also tasted defeat at Fort Crown Point and delay at Fort Oswego that same year. And Indians, convinced that the French were winning in the struggle, ravaged the frontier. By 1756, even Pennsylvania's Quakers yielded to backcountry demands for blockhouses to protect settlers from Indian depredation.

As in earlier years, the fighting on the frontier gradually developed into a major war: the Seven Years' War, or the Great War for Empire. Even though England poured money and men into American colonial defense, it remained unable to mobilize the colonies because of defective leadership. The French military commander, Marquis Louis Joseph de Montcalm, led a united but smaller force that smashed through the English barrier forts by capturing Oswego. Behind the French victories was the support of the Indians who terrorized the frontier and sent settlers fleeing eastward from Albany and the Lake Champlain region.

This kind of fighting demanded that the English organize semi-independent units or rangers that could wage frontier warfare. In his "Journal," Major Robert Rogers, who was well-known for his band of rangers, spelled out the rules of behavior for his men:[7]

These volunteers I formed into a company by themselves, and took the more immediate command and management of them to myself; and for their benefit and instruction reduced into writing the following rules or plan of discipline, which, on various occasions, I had found by experience to be necessary and advantageous, *viz.*:

I. All Rangers are to be subject to the rules and articles of war; to appear at roll-call every evening on their own parade, equipped, each with a fire-lock, sixty rounds of powder and ball, and a hatchet, at which time an officer from each company is to inspect the same, to see they are in order, so as to be ready on any emergency to march at a minute's warning; and before they are dismissed the necessary guards are to be draughted, and scouts for the next day appointed.

II. Whenever you are ordered out to the enemies forts or frontiers for discoveries, if your number be small, march in a single file, keeping at such a distance from each other as to prevent one shot from killing two men, sending one man, or more, forward, and the like on each side, at the distance of twenty yards from the main body, if the ground you march over will admit of it, to give the signal to the officer of the approach of an enemy, and of their number, &c.

III. If you march over marshes or soft ground, change your position, and march abreast of each other, to prevent the enemy from tracking you, (as they would do if you marched in a single file) till you get over such ground, and then resume your former order, and march till it is quite dark before you encamp, which do, if possible, on a piece of ground that may afford your centries the advantage of seeing or hearing the enemy at some considerable distance, keeping one half of your whole party awake alternately through the night.

IV. Some time before you come to the place you would reconnoitre, make a stand, and send one or two men, in whom you can confide, to look out the best ground for making your observations.

V. If you have the good fortune to take any prisoners, keep them separate, till they are examined, and in your return take a different rout from that in which you went out,

---

[7] Robert Rogers, *Journal of Major Robert Rogers* (Albany, 1883), pp. 82–86.

that you may the better discover any party in your rear, and have an opportunity, if their strength be superior to yours, to alter your course, or disperse, as circumstances may require.

VI. If you march in a large body of three or four hundred, with a design to attack the enemy, divide your party into three columns, each headed by a proper officer, and let these columns march in single files, the columns to the right and left keeping at twenty yards distance or more from that of the center, if the ground will admit, and let proper guards be kept in the front and rear, and suitable flanking parties at a due distance as before directed, with orders to halt on all eminences, to take a view of the surrounding ground, to prevent your being ambuscaded, and to notify the approach or retreat of the enemy, that proper dispositions may be made for attacking, defending, &c. And if the enemy approach in your front on level ground, form a front of your three columns or main body with the advanced guard, keeping out your flanking parties, as if you were marching under the command of trusty officers, to prevent the enemy from pressing hard on either of your wings, or surrounding you, which is the usual method of the savages, if their number will admit of it, and be careful likewise to support and strengthen your rear guard.

VII. If you are obliged to receive the enemy's fire, fall, or squat down, till it is over, then rise and discharge at them. If their main body is equal to yours, extend yourselves occasionally; but if superior, be careful to support and strengthen your flanking parties, to make them equal with theirs, that if possible you may repulse them to their main body, in which case push upon them with the greatest resolution, with equal force in each flank and in the centre, observing to keep at a due distance from each other, and advance from tree to tree, with one half of the party before the other ten or twelve yards. If the enemy push upon you, let your front fire and fall down, and then let your rear advance thro' them and do the like, by which time those who before were in front will be ready to discharge again, and repeat the same alternately, as occasion shall require; by this means you will keep up such a constant fire, that the enemy will not be able easily to break your order, or gain your ground.

VIII. If you oblige the enemy to retreat, be careful, in your pursuit of them, to keep out your flanking parties, and prevent them from gaining eminences, or rising grounds, in which case they would perhaps be able to rally and repulse you in their turn.

IX. If you are obliged to retreat, let the front of your whole party fire and fall back, till the rear hath done the same, making for the best ground you can; by this means you will oblige the enemy to pursue you, if they do it at all, in the face of a constant fire.

X. If the enemy is so superior that you are in danger of being surrounded by them, let the whole body disperse, and every one take a different road to the place of rendezvous appointed for that evening, which must every morning be altered and fixed for the evening ensuing, in order to bring the whole party, or as many of them as possible together, after any separation that may happen in the day; but if you should happen to be actually surrounded, form yourselves into a square, or, if in the woods, a circle is best, and, if possible, make a stand till the darkness of night favours your escape.

XI. If your rear is attacked, the main body and flankers must face about to the right or left, as occasion shall require, and form themselves to oppose the enemy, as before directed; and the same method must be observed, if attacked in either of your flanks, by which means you will always make a rear of one of your flank guards.

XII. If you determine to rally after a retreat, in order to make a fresh stand against the enemy, by all means endeavor to do it on the most rising ground you can come at, which will give you greatly the advantage in point of situation, and enable you to repulse superior numbers.

XIII. In general, when pushed upon by the enemy, reserve your fire till they approach very near, which will then put them into the greater surprise and consternation, and give you an opportunity of rushing upon them with your hatchets and cutlasses to the better advantage.

XIV. When you encamp at night, fix your centries in such a manner as not to be relieved from the main body till morning, profound secrecy and silence being often of the last importance in these cases. Each centry, therefore, should consist of six men, two of whom must be constantly alert, and when relieved by their fellows, it should be done without noise; and in case those on duty see or hear any thing which alarms them, they are not to speak, but one of them is silently to retreat, and acquaint the commanding officer thereof, that proper dispositions may be made; and all occasional centries should be fixed in like manner.

XV. At the first dawn of day, awake your whole detachment; that being the time when the savages chuse to fall upon their enemies, you should by all means be in readiness to receive them.

XVI. If the enemy should be discovered by your detachments in the morning, and their numbers are superior to yours, and victory doubtful, you should not attack them till the evening, as then they will not know your numbers, and if you are repulsed, your retreat will be favoured by the darkness of the night.

XVII. Before you leave your encampment, send out small parties to scout round it, to see if there be any appearance or track of an enemy that might have been near you during the night.

XVIII. When you stop for refreshment, chuse some spring or rivulet if you can, and dispose your party so as not to be surprised, posting proper guards and centries at a due distance, and let a small party waylay the path you came in, lest the enemy should be pursuing.

XIX. If, in your return, you have to cross rivers, avoid the usual fords as much as possible, lest the enemy should have discovered, and be there expecting you.

XX. If you have to pass by lakes, keep at some distance from the edge of the water, lest, in case of an ambuscade or an attack from the enemy, when in that situation, your retreat should be cut off.

XXI. If the enemy pursue your rear, take a circle till you come to your own tracks, and there form an ambush to receive them, and give them the first fire.

XXII. When you return from a scout, and come near our forts, avoid the usual roads, and avenues thereto, lest the enemy should have headed you, and lay in ambush to receive you, when almost exhausted with fatigues.

XXIII. When you pursue any party that has been near our forts or encampments, follow not directly in their tracks, lest you should be discovered by their rear-guards, who, at such a time, would be most alert; but endeavor, by a different route to head and meet them in some narrow pass, or lay in ambush to receive them when and where they least expect it.

XXIV. If you are to embark in canoes, battoes, or otherwise, by water, chuse the evening for the time of your embarkation, as you will then have the whole night before you, to pass undiscovered by any parties of the enemy, on hills or other places, which command a prospect of the lake or river you are upon.

XXV. In padling or rowing, give orders that the boat or canoe next the sternmost, wait for her, and the third for the second, and the fourth for the third, and so on, to prevent separation, and that you may be ready to assist each other on any emergency.

XXVI. Appoint one man in each boat to look out for fires, on the adjacent shores, from the numbers and size of which you may form some judgment of the number that kindled them, and whether you are able to attack them or not.

XXVII. If you find the enemy encamped near the banks of a river, or lake, which you imagine they will attempt to cross for their security upon being attacked, leave a detachment of your party on the opposite shore to receive them, while, with the remainder, you surprise them, having them between you and the lake or river.

XXVIII. If you cannot satisfy yourself as to the enemy's number and strength, from their fire, &c., conceal your boats at some distance, and ascertain their number by a reconnoitering party, when they embark, or march, in the morning, marking the course they steer, &c., when you may pursue, ambush, and attack them, or let them pass, as prudence shall direct you. In general, however, that you may not be discovered by the enemy on the lakes and rivers at a great distance, it is safest to lay by, with your boats and party concealed all day, without noise or shew, and to pursue your intended route by night; and whether you go by land or water, give out parole and countersigns, in order to know one another in the dark, and likewise appoint a station for every man to repair to, in case of any accident that may separate you.

Such in general are the rules to be observed in the Ranging service; there are, however, a thousand occurrences and circumstances which may happen, that will make it necessary, in some measure, to depart from them, and to put other arts and stratagems in practice; in which cases every man's reason and judgment must be his guide, according to the particular situation and nature of things; and that he may do this to advantage, he should keep in mind a maxim never to be departed from by a commander, *viz.*: to preserve a firmness and presence of mind on every occasion.

THE WAR IN THE SOUTH:
THE PACIFICATION OF THE CHEROKEE

The year 1758 rang the changes on French success. Despite Montcalm's brilliant defense of Fort Ticonderoga—it cost the English 2000 men—one British army under General Jeffrey Amherst and General James Wolfe reduced Louisbourg, a second force under Colonel John Bradstreet captured Fort Frontenac, and a third, led by General John Forbes built a road to Fort Duquesne and forced the French to abandon that strategic post. This swift changing power relationship produced equally rapid shifts in Indian allegiances; tribes that had scourged the colonial settlements now welcomed English war belts and traders. But the task of negotiating with the Indians still required a strong stomach and steel nerves. The following account, written by Lieutenant Henry Timberlake, explains his role in the pacification of the Cherokee.[8]

---

[8] Henry Timberlake, *The Memoirs of Lieut. Henry Timberlake* (London, 1765), pp. 2–6, 9–11, 28–41.

I made my first campaign in the year 1756, with a company of gentlemen called the Patriot Blues, who served the country at their own expence; but whether terrified by our formidable appearance, or superior numbers, the enemy still avoided us; so that, notwithstanding many recent tracks and fires, we never could come to an engagement. On our return, I made application for a commission in the Virginia regiment, then commanded by Col. Washington; but there being at that time no vacancy, I returned home.

In the year 1758, a new regiment was raised for that year's service, to be commanded by the Hon. William Byrd, Esq; from whom I not only received an ensigncy, but as subalterns were to be appointed to a troop of light-horse, he honoured me with the cornetcy of that also. I was soon after ordered on a escort, in which service I continued till July, when I joined the army at Ray's-Town, where I found General Forbes already arrived. The army then marched to Fort Ligonier, on the way to Fort Du Quesne. I was seized here by a violent fit of sickness, calght in searching for some of the troop-horses that were lost, by overheating myself with running and drinking a large quantity of cold water, which rendered me incapable of duty. I got something better about the time the troops marched for Fort Du Quesne, and could sit my horse when helped on, but was ordered back by General, who, however, on my telling the doctor I hoped to do duty in a day or two, permitted me to continue the march. We heard the French blow up their magazine, while yet some miles off; and, on our arrival, we found the barracks, and every thing of value in flames. My malady rather increased, so that I was at last compelled to petition for my return, I lost my horse at Fort Ligonier, the third I had lost during the campaign; and being obliged to mount a very weak one, I met with great difficulty in crossing the Allegany mountains; and before I reached Ray's Town my horse was entirely knocked up. I bought another, and proceeded to Winchester, where, in a little time, I got perfectly recovered.

Those light-horsemen that survived the campaign, were here in want of all necessaries; and no money being sent up from Williamsburg to pay them, I advanced upwards of an hundred pounds, intending to reimburse myself from the first that should arrive: meanwhile the troops I belonged to were disbanded, and I, in consequence, out of pay....

When Col. Byrd was appointed to the command of the old regiment, in the room of Col. Washington, who resigned; on which I was unfortunately induced to accept another commission. I served another campaign in the year 1759, under General Stanwix, in the same quarter: but on our arrival at Pittsburg, formerly Fort Du Quesne, I had little employment, except looking over the men at work, till the fall of the leaf, when the General gave me the command of Fort Burd, about sixty miles to the eastward of Pittsburg, where I continued about nine months at a very great expence partly through hospitality to those who passed to and from Pittsburg, and the dearness of necessaries and partly by building myself a house, and making several improvements, and finishing the half-constructed fort, for which I never received any gratuity. I was relieved by a company of the Pennsylvania regiment in the spring, and returned to Pittsburg, but found Col. Byrd with one half of the regiment ordered against the Cherokees, now become our most inveterate enemies; while the remainder under Col. Stephen were destined to serve on the Ohio....

In the spring 1761, I received orders to return to my division, which was to proceed to the southward, and join the other half against the Cherokee. Soon after this junction we began our march towards the Cherokee country. Col. Byrd parted from us at a place called Stalnarkeres, and returned down the country, by which the command developed on Col. Stephen. We marched, without molestation, to the great island on Holston's river, about 140 miles from the enemy's settlements, where we immediately applied ourselves to the construction of a fort, which was nearly completed about the middle of November, when Kanagatucko, the nominal king of the Cherokees, accompanied by about 400 of his people, came to our camp, sent by his countrymen to sue for peace, which was soon after granted by Col. Stephen, and finally concluded on the 19th instant. All things being settled to the satisfaction of the Indians, their king told Col. Stephen he had one more favour to beg of them, which was, to send an officer back with them to their country, as that would effectually convince the nation of the good intentions and sincerity of the English towards them. The Colonel was embarrased at the demand; he saw the necessity of some officer's going there, yet could not command any on so dangerous a duty. I soon relieved him from this dilemma, by offering my service; my active disposition, or, if I may venture to say, a love of my country, would not permit it's losing so great an advantage, for want of resolution to become hostage to a people, who, tho' savage, and unacquainted with the laws of war or nations, seemed now tolerably sincere, and had, seeing me employed in drawing up the articles of peace, in a manner cast their eyes upon me as the properest person to give an account of it to their countrymen. The Colonel seemed more apprehensive of the danger than I was myself, scarce giving any encouragement to a man whom he imagined going to make himself a sacrifice, lest he should incur the censure of any accident that might befall me.

The 28th was fixed for our departure; but, on making some inquiries about our intended journey, the Indians informed me that the rivers were, for small craft, navigable quite to their country; they strove, however, to deter me from thinking of that way, by laying before me the dangers and difficulties I must encounter; almost alone, in a journey so much further about, and continually infested with parties of northern Indians, who though at peace with the English, would not fail to treat, in the most barbarous manner, a person whose errand they knew to be so much against their interest. They professed themselves concerned for my safety, and intreated me to go along with them: but as I thought a thorough knowledge of the navigation would be of infinite service, should these people ever give us the trouble of making another campaign against them I formed a resolution of going by water; what much conduced to this, was the slowness they marched with when in a large body, and the little pleasure I could expect in such company....

[T]he old warrior, commonly called the Slave Catcher of Tennessee, invited us to his camp, treated us with dried venison, hominy, and boiled corn. He told us that he had been hunting some time thereabouts, and had only intended running in seven or eight days, but would now immediately accompany us. We set out with them next morning to pursue our voyage; but I was now obliged to give over taking the courses of the river, lest the Indians, who tho' very hospitable are very suspicious of things they cannot comprehend, should take unbrage at it....

Within four or five miles of the nation, the Slave Catcher sent his wife forward by land, partly to prepare a dinner, and partly to let me have her place in his canoe, seeing me in pain and unaccustomed to such hard labour, which seat I kept till about two o'clock, when we arrived at his house, opposite the mouth of Tellequo river, completing a twenty-two days course of continual fatigues, hardships, and anxieties.

Our entertainment from these people are as good as the country could afford, consisting of roast, boiled, and fried meats of several kinds, and very good Indian bread, baked in a very curious manner. After making a fire on the hearth-stone, about the size of a large dish, they sweep the embers off, laying a loaf smooth on it; this they cover with a sort of deep dish, and renew the fire upon the whole, under which the bread bakes to as great perfection as in any European oven.

We crossed the river next morning, with some Indians that had been visiting in that neighbourhood, and went to Tommontly, taking Fort Loudon in the way, to examine the ruins.

We were received at Tommontly in a very kind manner by Ostenaco, the commander in chief, who told me, he had already given me up for lost, as the gang I parted with at the Great Island had returned about ten days before, and that my servant was then actually preparing for his return, with the news of my death.

After smoking and talking some time, I delivered a letter from Colonel Stephen, and another from Captain M' Neil, with some presents from each, which were gratefully accepted by Ostenaco and his consort. He gave me a general invitation to his house, while I resided in the country; and my companions found no difficulty in getting the same entertainment, among an hospitable, tho' savage people, who always pay a great regard to any one taken notice of by their chiefs.

Some days after, the headmen of each town were assembled in the town-house of Chote, the metropolis of the country, to hear the articles of peace read, whither the interpreter and I accompanied Ostenaco.

The town-house, in which are transacted all public business and aversions, is raised with wood, and covered over with earth and has all the appearance of a small mountain at a little distance. It is built in the form of a sugar loaf and large enough to contain 500 persons, but extremely dark, having, besides the door, which is so narrow that but one at a time can pass, and that after much winding and turning, but one small aperture to let the smoke out, which is so ill contrived, that most of it settles in the roof of the house. Within it has the appearance of an ancient amphitheatre, the slats being raised one above another, leaving an area in the fire; the seats of the head warriors are nearest it.

They all seemed highly satisfied with the articles. The peace-pipe was smoked, and Ostenaco made an harangue to the following effect:

The bloody tommahawke, so long lifted against our brethren the English, must now be buried deep, deep in the ground, never to be raised again; and whoever shall act contrary to any of these articles, must expect a punishment equal to his offence. Should a strict observance of them be neglected a war must necessarily follow, and a second peace may not be so easily obtained. I therefore once more recommend to you, to take particular care of your behavior towards the English whom we must now look upon as ourselves, they have the French and Spaniards to fight, and we enough of our own colour, without medling with either nation. I desire likewise, that the white warrior, who has ventured himself here with us, may be well used and respected by all, wherever he goes amongst us.

The harrangue being finished, several pipes were presented me by the headsmen, to take a whiff. This ceremony I could have waved, as smoking was always very disagreeable to me; but as it was a token of their amity, and they might be offended if I did not comply, I put on the best face I was able, though I dared not even wipe the end of the pipe that came out of their mouths; which, considering their paint and dirtiness, are not of the most *ragoutant*, as the French term it.

After smoking, the eatables were produced, consisting chiefly of wild meat; such as venison, bear, and buffalo; tho' I cannot much commend their cookery, every thing being greatly overdone: there were likewise potatoes, pumpkins, homminy, boiled corn, beans, and pease, served up in small flat baskets, made of split canes which were distributed amongst the crowd; and water, which, except the spirituous liquor brought by the Europeans is their only drink, was handed about in small goards. What contributed greatly to render this feast disgusting, was eating without knives and forks, and being obliged to grope from dish to dish in the dark. After the feast there was a dance; but I was already so fatigued with the ceremonies I had gone through, that I retired to Kanagatucko's hot-house; but was prevented taking any repose by the smoke, with which I was almost suffocated, and the croud of Indians that came and sat on the bed-side; which indeed was not much calculated for repose to any but Indians, or those that had passed an apprenticeship to their ways, as I had done: it was composed of a few boards, spread with bear-skins, without any other covering; the house being so hot, that I could not endure the weight of my own blanket.

Some hours after I got up to go away, but met Ostenaco, followed by two or three Indians, with an invitation from the headman of Settico, to visit him the next day.

I set out with Ostenaco and my interpreter in the morning, and marched towards Settico, till we were met by a messenger, about half a mile from the town, who came to stop us till every thing was prepared for our reception: from this place I could take a view of the town, where I observed two stand of colours flying, one at the top, and the other at the door of the town-house; they were as large as a sheet, and white. Lest therefore I should take them for French, they took great care to inform me, that their custom was to hoist red colours as an emblem of war; but white, as a token of peace. By this time we were joined by another messenger, who desired us to move forward.

About 100 yards from the town-house we were received by a body of between three and four hundred Indians, ten or twelve of which were entirely naked, except a piece of cloth about their middle, and painted all over in a hideous manner, six of them with eagles tails in their hands, which they shook and flourished as they advanced, danced in a very uncommon figure, singing in concert with some drums of their own make, and those of the late unfortunate Capt. Damere; with several other instruments, uncouth beyond description. Cheulah, the headman of the town, led the procession, painted blood-red except his face, which was half black, holding an old rusty broad-sword in his right hand, and an eagle's tail in his left. As they approached, Cheulah, singling himself out from the rest, cut two or three capers, as a signal to the other eagle-tails, who instantly followed his example. This violent exercise, accompanied by the band of musick, and a loud yell from the mob, lasted about a minute, when the headman waving his sword over my head, struck it into the ground, about two inches from my left foot; then dircting himself to me, made a short discourse (which my interpreter told me was only to bid me a hearty welcome) and presented me with a string of beads. We then proceeded to the door, where Chuelah, and one of the beloved men, taking me each arm, led me in, and seated me in one of the first seats; it was so dark that nothing was perciptible till a fresh supply of canes were brought, which being burnt in the middle of the house answers both purposes of fuel and candle. I then discovered about five hundred faces; and Cheulah addressing me a second time, made a speech much to the same effect as the former, congratulating me on my safe arrival thro' the numerous parties of the northern Indians, that generally haunt the way I came. He then made some professions of friendship, concluding with giving me another string of beads, as a token of it. He had scarce finished, when four of those who had exhibited at the procession made their second appearance, painted milk-white; their eagle-tails in one hand, and small goards with beads in them in the other, which they rattled in time to the musick.

During this dance the peace-pipe was prepared; the bowl of it was of red stone, curiously cut with a knife, it being very soft, tho' extremely pretty when polished. Some of these are of black stone, and some of the same earth they make their pots with, but beautifully diversified. The stem is about three feet long, finely adorned with porcupine quills, dyed feathers, deers hair, and such like gaudy trifles.

After I had performed my part with this, I was almost suffocated with the pipes, presented me on every hand, which I dared not to decline. They might amount to about 170 or 180; which made me so sick, that I did not stir for several hours. The Indians entertained me with another dance, at which I was detained till about seven o'clock the next morning, when I was conducted to the house of Chucatah, then second in command, to take some refreshment. Here I found a white woman, named Mary Hughes, who told me she had been a prisoner there near a twelvemonth, and that there still remained among the Indians near thirty white prisoners more, in a very miserable condition for want of cloaths, the winter being particularly severe; and their misery was not a little heightened by the usage they received from the Indians. I ordered her to come to me to Ostenaco's, with her miserable companions, where I would distribute some shirts and blankets I had brought with me amongst them, which she did some days after.

After a short nap, I arose and went to the town-house, where I found the chiefs in consultation; after some time, I was called upon, and desired to write a letter for them to the Governor of South Carolina, which signified their desire of living in peace with the English, as long as the sun shone, or grass grew, and desired that a trade might be opened between them. These wrote, I sealed them up, with some wampum and beads in the inside. I was the same day invited to Chilhowey, where I was received and treated much in the same manner as at Settico. I wrote some letters; and one that Yachtino the headman had brought from Col. Stephen was interpreted to them, which seemed to give them great satisfaction. I found here a white man, who, notwithstanding the war, lived many years among them; he told me that the lower towns had been greatly distressed when attacked by Colonel Montgomery; being obliged to live many months upon horse-flesh, and roots out of the woods, occasioned partly by the numbers drove among them, and the badness of the crops that year.

Returning home with Ostenaco the next day, being the 2d of January 1762, I enquired whether he thought I should receive any more invitations? He told me he believed not, because the towns to which I had already been invited, having been our most inveterate enemies during the war, had done this, as an acknowledgment and reparation of their fault.

The loss of Indian allies weakened France's grasp in America. In the upper Mississippi Valley and the lake country, the warriors compelled the French to retreat to a few strongholds. And while Montcalm pleaded for additional aid and lamented the corruption of Canadian officials, Amherst reclaimed Fort Crown Point and Fort Ticonderoga. But the mortal blow fell at Quebec where both England and France sacrificed brilliant military leaders—Wolfe and Montcalm—in a battle that set well-trained British regulars against ill-trained French provincials. Quebec fell. In 1760, one year later, Montreal capitulated. At the Treaty of Paris in 1763, France surrendered its claims west of the Mississippi River to Spain, those east of the river to England. The Great War for Empire ended with France banished from North America as a major colonial power.

CHAPTER 8 | *Settlement Crosses the Mountains, 1763-1776*

The defeat of France provided an elixir to a large group of zealous Americans eager to exploit the West. It also hastened the day when Englishmen at home and in America would be forced to answer really searching questions about the frontier: Should the Indians be safeguarded for humanitarian reasons? How should land be taken from them for distribution to the settler? How should the fur trade be regulated? And to what degree should existing colonial governments exercise control over the unsettled West? But self-seeking Indian traders cared not a whit about the ultimate solutions to these problems. Loaded with trading goods, desirous of profit but ignoring the consequences of dealing with the tribes, they dogged the heels of the army that occupied the French forts. Land-hungry pioneers proved little better. They defied the orders of English military officers, who warned that the region west of the mountains was closed to settlement, and traveling along Forbes' military road, invaded the Pittsburgh region where they marked their land claims by notching trees with their tomahawks.

Farseeing men recognized the complexities of trying to reconcile the interests of traders, frontiersmen, land speculators, and humanitarians.

But, more especially, making the American solution compatible with imperial interests appeared an almost impossible task to English administrators. Although the Indian trade had long possessed an active lobby in England, land speculation gradually replaced it as the vital dynamic of western policy. As early as 1747, speculators employed skilled hunters to seek good lands far in advance of the area of settlement. These same speculators formed land companies that virtually besieged English cabinet officers who controlled colonial policy. Hardly an influential American remained completely aloof while companies were formed to petition for grants of millions of acres of land on the Ohio and Mississippi rivers.

Seeking an accommodation that would provide time for a continuous study of western problems, England's Board of Trade suggested a useful and integrated proposal. To separate the races, a demarcation line would be drawn at the point of their actual contact, and the movement of white settlers beyond it would be forbidden until the land question could be resolved. To ease population pressures, three new colonies—Quebec, East Florida, and West Florida—were planned. Such questions as the future of the Indian, the fur trade, and the army (England had 10,000 men stationed in America at the close of the war) remained for later analysis. But before the plan could be adopted, news from America forced an immediate change in policy.

THE DEFEAT OF CHIEF PONTIAC

On May 7, 1763, a group of Ottawa Indians led by Pontiac attacked Detroit. Although no overall planning had preceded the assault, a large-scale Indian uprising followed, and one fort after another, taken by surprise, fell to the Indians. Only the major posts at Niagara, Pittsburgh, and Detroit held out. Pontiac and his followers, smarting under the indignity of broken promises regarding their sacred hunting grounds, cheap goods, and presents of ammunition and weapons, proved responsive to the unscrupulous instigations of French traders eager to squeeze a final franc from the region before being driven out. In less than ninety days, the English had lost the West. But the Indians' fate was sealed. Lord Jeffrey Amherst, who despised the "savages" to the point of considering their extermination by spreading smallpox-ridden blankets among them, unleashed powerful relief forces that lifted the sieges at Detroit and Pittsburgh. By the summer of 1764, many Indians, aware of the cruel hoax worked by the French, willingly made peace at Fort Niagara. George Croghan, long experienced in the Ohio trade, who served as Deputy Superintendent for the northern tribes, undertook the dangerous task of finding Pontiac's band to make final peace terms. Croghan's account of his actions and his letter to his superior, Sir William Johnson, indicates that he was as much interested in land speculation opportunities and trade possibilities as he was in peace:[1]

[1] Reuben Gold Thwaites (ed.), *Early Western Travels, 1748–1846* (Cleveland, 1904), vol. 1, pp. 138–141.

8th At day-break we were attacked by a party of Indians, consisting of eighty warriors of the Kiccapoos and Musquattimes, who killed two of my men and three Indians, wounded myself and all the rest of my party, except two white men and one Indian; then made myself and all the white men prisoners, plundering us of every thing we had. A deputy of the Shawnesse who was shot through the thigh, having concealed himself in the woods for a few minutes after he was wounded—not knowing but they were Southern Indians, who are always at war with the northward Indians—after discovering what nation they were, came up to them and made a very bold speech, telling them that the whole northward Indians would join in taking revenge for the insult and murder of their people; this alarmed those savages very much, who began excusing themselves, saying their fathers, the French, had spirited them up, telling them that the Indians were coming with a body of southern Indians to take their country from them, and enslave them; that it was this that induced them to commit this outrage. After dividing the plunder, (they left great part of the heaviest effects behind, not being able to carry them,) they set off with us to their village at Ouattonon, in a great hurry, being in dread of pursuit from a large party of Indians they suspected were coming after me. Our course was through a thick woody country, crossing a great many swamps, morasses, and beaver ponds. We traveled this day about forty-two miles.

9th An hour before day we set out on our march; passed through thick woods, some highlands, and small savannahs, badly watered. Traveled this day about thirty miles.

10th We set out very early in the morning, and marched through a high country, extremely well timbered, for three hours; then came to a branch of the Ouabache, which we crossed. The remainder of this day we traveled through fine rich bottoms, overgrown with reeds, which make the best pasture in the world, the young reeds being preferable to sheaf oats. Here is great plenty of wild game of all kinds. Came this day about twenty-eight, or thirty miles.

11th At day-break we set off, making our way through a thin woodland, interspersed with savannahs. I suffered extremely by reason of the excessive heat of the weather, and scarcity of water; the little springs and runs being dried up. Traveled this day about thirty miles.

12th We passed through some large savannahs, and clear woods; in the afternoon we came to the Ouabache; then marched along it through a prodigious rich bottom, overgrown with reeds and wild hemp; all this bottom is well watered, and an exceeding fine hunting ground. Came this day about thirty miles.

13th About an hour before day we set out; traveled through such bottoms as of yesterday, and through some large meadows, where no trees, for several miles together, are to be seen. Buffaloes, deer, and bears are here in great plenty. We traveled about twenty-six miles this day.

14th The country we traveled through this day, appears the same as described yesterday, excepting this afternoon's journey through woodland, to cut off a bend of the river. Came about twenty-seven miles this day.

15th We set out very early, and about one o'clock came to the Ouabache, within six or seven miles of Port Vincent. On my arrival there, I found a village of about eighty or ninety French families settled on the east side of this river, being one of the finest situations that can be found. The country is level and clear, and the soil very rich, producing wheat and tobacco. I think the latter preferable to that of Maryland or Virginia. The French inhabitants hereabouts, are an idle, lazy people, a parcel of renegadoes from Canada, and are much worse than the Indians. They took a secret pleasure at our misfortunes, and the moment we arrived, they came to the Indians, exchanging trifles for their valuable plunder. . . .

23d Early in the morning we set out through a fine meadow, then some clear woods in the afternoon came into a very large bottom on the Ouabache, within six miles of Ouicatanon; here I met several chiefs of the Kickapoos and Musquattimes, who spoke to their young men who had taken us, and reprimanded them severely for what they had done to me, after which they returned with us to their village, and delivered us all to their chiefs.

The distance from port Vincent to Ouicatanon is two hundred and ten miles. This place is situated on the Ouabache. About fourteen French families are living in the fort, which stands on the north side of the river. The Kickapoos and the Musquattimes, whose warriors had taken us, live nigh the fort, on the same side of the river, where they have two villages; and the Ouicatanons have a village on the south side of the river. . . . They went immediately to the Kickapoos and Musquattimes, and charged them to take the greatest care of us, till their chiefs should arrive from the Illinois, where they were gone to meet me some time ago, and who were entirely ignorant of this affair, and said the French had spirited up this party to go and strike us.

The French have a great influence over these Indians, and never fail in telling them many lies to the prejudice of his majesty's interest, by making the English nation odious and hateful to them. I had the greatest difficulties in removing these prejudices. As these Indians are a weak, foolish, and credulous people, they are easily imposed on by a designing people, who have led them hitherto as they pleased. The French told them that as the southern Indians had for two years past made war on them, it must have been at the instigation of the English, who are a bad people. However I have been fortunate enough to remove their prejudice, and, in a great measure, their suspicions against the English. The country hereabouts is exceedingly pleasant, being open and clear for many miles; the soil very rich and well watered; all plants have a quick vegetation, and the climate very temperate through the winter. This post has always been a very considerable trading place. The great plenty of furs taken in this country, induced the French to establish this post, which was the first on the Ouabache, and by a very advantageous trade they have been richly recompensed for their labor.

On the south side of the Ouabache runs a big bank, in which are several fine coal mines, and behind this bank, is a very large meadow, clear for several miles. It is surprising what false information we have had respecting this country: some mention these spacious and beautiful meadows as large and barren savannahs. I apprehend it has been the artifice of the French to keep us ignorant of the country. These meadows bear fine wild grass, and wild hemp ten or twelve feet high, which, if properly manufactured, would prove as good, and answer all the purpose of the hemp we cultivate.

28th I set off for the Ilinois with the Chiefs of all those Nations when by the way we met with Pondiac together with the Deputies of the Six Nations, Delawares & Shawanese, which accompanied Mr. Frazier & myself down the Ohio & also Deputies with speeches from the four Nations living in the Ilinois Country to me & the Six Nations, Delawares & Shawanese, on which we return'd to Ouiatonon and there held another conference, in which I settled all matters with the Ilinois Indians—Pondiac & they agreeing to every thing the other Nations had done, all which they confirmed by Pipes & Belts, but told me the French had informed them that the English intended to take their Country from them, & give it to the Cherokees to settle on, & that if ever they suffered the English to take possession of their Country they would make slaves of them, that this was the reason of their Opposing the English hitherto from taking possession of *Fort Chartres* & induced them to tell Mr. La Gutrie & Mr. Sinnott that they would not let the English come into their Country. But being informed since Mr. Sinnott had retired by the Deputies of the Six Nations, Delawares & Shawanese, that every difference subsisting between them & the English was now settled, they were willing to comply as the other Nations their Brethren had done and desired that their Father the King of England might not look upon his taking possession of the Forts which the French had formerly possest as a title for his subjects to possess their Country, as they never had sold any part of it to the French, & that I might rest satisfied that whenever the English came to take possession they would receive them with open arms.

[Then Croghan wrote to Sir William Johnson.]

Sir:

In the scituation I was in at Ouiatonon, with great numbers of Indians about me, & no Necessaries such as Paper & Ink, I had it not in my power to take down all the speeches made by the Indian Nations, nor what I said to them, in so particular a manner as I could wish, but hope the heads of it as I have taken down will meet with your approbation.

In the Course of this Tour through the Indian Countrys I made it my study to converse in private with Pondiac, & several of the Chiefs of the different Nations, as often as oppertunity served, in order to find out the sentiments they have of the French & English, Pondiac is a shrewd sensible Indian of few words, & commands more respect amongst those Nations, than any Indian I ever saw could do amongst his own Tribe. He and all his principal men of those Nations seem at present to be convinced that the French had a view of interest in stirring up the late differance between his Majesties Subjects & them & call it a Bever War, for neither Pondiac nor any of the Indians which I met with, ever pretended to deny but the French were at the bottom of the whole, & constantly supplyed them with every necessary they wanted, as far as in their power, every where through that Country & notwithstanding they are at present convinced, that it was for their own Interest, yet it has not changed the Indians affections to them, they have been bred up together like Children in that Country, & the French have always adopted the Indians customs & manners, treated them civily & supplyed their wants generously, by which means they gained the hearts of the Indians & commanded their services, & enjoyed the benefit of a very large Furr Trade, as they well knew if they had not taken this measure they could not enjoy any of those Advantages. The French have in a manner taught the Indians in that Country to hate the English, by representing them in the worst light they could on all occasion, in particular they have made the Indians there believe lately, that the English would take their Country from them & bring the *Cherokees* there to settle & to enslave them, which report they easily gave credit to, as the Southern Indians had lately commenced war against them. I had great difficulty in remoeving this suspicion and convincing them of the falsity of this report, which I flatter myself I have done in a great measure, yet it will require some time, a very even Conduct in those that are to reside in their Country, before we can expect to rival the French in their affection, all Indians are jealous & from their high notion of liberty hate power, those Nations are jealous and prejudiced against us, so that the greatest care will be necessary to convince them of our honest Intention by our Actions. The French sold them goods much dearer than the English Traders do at present, in that point we have the advantage of the French, but they made that up in large presents to them for their services, which they wanted to support their Interest in the Country, & tho' we want none of their services, yet they will expect favours, & if refused look on it in a bad light, & very likely think it done to distress them for some particular Advantages we want to gain over them. They are by no means so sensible a People as the Six Nations or other Tribes this way, & the French have learned them for their own advantage a bad custom, for by all I could learn, they seldom made them any general presents, but as it were fed them with Necessaries just as they wanted them Tribe by Tribe, & never sent them away empty, which will make it difficult & troublesome to the Gentlemen that are to command in their Country for some time, to please them & preserve Peace, as they are a rash inconsiderate People and don't look on themselves under any obligations to us, but rather think we are obliged to them for letting us reside in their Country. As far as I can judge of their Sentiments by the several Conversations I have had with them, they will expect some satisfaction made them by Us, for any Posts that should be established in their Country for Trade. But you will be informed better by themselves next Spring, as Pondiac & some Chiefs of every Nation in that Country intend to pay you a visit. The several Nations on the Ouiabache, & towards the *Ilinois, St. Josephs, Chicago, Labaye, Sagina* & other places have applyed for Traders to be sent to their settlements, but as it is not in the power of any Officer to permit Traders to go from Detroit or *Michillimackinac*, either English or French, I am of opinion the Indians will be supplyed this year chiefly from the *Ilinois*, which is all French property & if Trading Posts are not established at proper Places in that Country soon the French will carry the best part of the Trade over the *Missisipi* which they are determined to do if they can, for I have been well informed that the French are preparing to build a strong trading Fort on the other side Missisipi, about 60 miles above *Fort Chartres*, and have this Summer in a private manner transported 26 pieces of small canon up the River for that purpose.

G. Croghan

BARRIERS TO EXPANSION: THE PROCLAMATION LINE

Before peace could be restored in the Northwest, the President of the Board of Trade, Lord Hillsborough, decided to enact a cheap, quick solution to the western problem that would provide a visible separation of the races. The result was the Proclamation of 1763:[2]

Whereas we have taken into our royal consideration the extensive and valuable acquisitions in America secured to our Crown by the late definitive treaty of peace concluded at Paris the 10th day of February last; and being desirous that all our loving subjects, as well of our kingdom as of our colonies in America, may avail themselves, with all convenient speed, of the great benefits and advantages which must accrue therefrom to their commerce, manufactures, and navigation; we have thought fit, with the advice of our Privy Council, to issue this our Royal Proclamation, hereby to publish and declare to all our loving subjects that we have, with the advice of our said Privy Council, granted our letters patent under our Great Seal of Great Britain, to erect within the countries and islands ceded and confirmed to us by the said treaty, four distinct and separate governments, styled and called by the names of Quebec, East Florida, West Florida, and Grenada, and limited and bounded as follows, viz.:

First, the Government of Quebec, bounded on the Labrador coast by the river St. John, and from thence by a line drawn from the head of that river, through the lake St. John, to the south end of the lake Nipissim; from whence the said line, crossing the river St. Lawrence and the lake Champlain in 45 degrees of north latitude, passes along the high lands which divide the rivers that empty themselves into the said river St. Lawrence from those which fall into the sea; . . .

Secondly, the Government of East Florida,

---

[2] Adam Shortt and Arthur G. Doughty (eds.), *Documents Relating to Constitutional History of Canada* (Ottawa, 1907–1914), vol. 1, pp. 163–165.

bounded to the westward by the gulf of Mexico and the Apalachicola river; to the northward, by a line drawn from that part of the said river where the Chatahoochee and Flint rivers meet, to the source of the St. Mary's river, and by the course of the said river to the Atlantic Ocean; . . .

Thirdly, the Government of West Florida, bounded to the . . . westward, by the lake Pontchartrain, the lake Maurepas, and the river Mississippi; to the northward, by a line drawn due east from that part of the river Mississippi which lies in 31 degrees north latitude, to the river Apalachicola or Chatahoochee; and to the eastward, by the said river. . . .

We have also, with the advice of our Privy Council aforesaid, annexed to our Province of Georgia all the lands lying between the rivers Altamaha and St. Mary's.

And whereas it is just and reasonable, and essential to our interest and the security of our colonies, that the several nations or tribes of Indians with whom we are connected, and who live under our protection, should not be molested or disturbed in the possession of such parts of our dominions and territories as, not having been ceded to or purchased by us, are reserved to them, or any of them, as their hunting-grounds; we do therefore, with the advice of our Privy Council, declare it to be our royal will and pleasure, that no Governor or commander in chief, in any of our colonies of Quebec, East Florida, or West Florida, do presume, upon any pretence whatever, to grant warrants of survey, or pass any patents for lands beyond the bounds of their respective governments as described in their commissions; as also that no Governor or commander in chief of our other colonies or plantations in America do presume for the present, and until our further pleasure be known, to grant warrants of survey or pass patents for any lands beyond the heads or sources of any of the rivers which fall into the Atlantic Ocean from the west or north west; or upon any lands whatever, which, not having been ceded to or purchased by us, as aforesaid, are reserved to the said Indians, or any of them.

And we do further declare it to be our royal will and pleasure, for the present as aforesaid, to reserve under our sovereignty, protection, and dominion, for the use of the said Indians, all the land and territories not included within the limits of our said three new governments, or within the limits of the territory granted to the Hudson's Bay Company; as also all the land and territories lying to the westward of the sources of the rivers which fall into the sea from the west and northwest as aforesaid; and we do hereby strictly forbid, on pain of our displeasure, all our loving subjects from making any purchases or settlements whatever, or taking possession of any of the lands above reserved, without our special leave and license for that purpose first obtained.

And we do further strictly enjoin and require all persons whatever, who have either wilfully or inadvertently seated themselves upon any lands within the countries above described, or upon any other lands which, not having been ceded to or purchased by us, are still reserved to the said Indians as aforesaid, forthwith to remove themselves from such settlements.

And whereas great frauds and abuses have been committed in the purchasing lands of the Indians, to the great prejudice of our interests, and to the great dissatisfaction of the said Indians; in order, therefore, to prevent such irregularities for the future, and to the end that the Indians may be convinced of our justice and determined resolution to remove all reasonable cause of discontent, we do, with the advice of our Privy Council, strictly enjoin and require, that no private person do presume to make any purchase from the said Indians of any lands reserved to the said Indians within those parts of our colonies where we have thought proper to allow settlement; but that if at any time any of the said Indians should be inclined to dispose of the said lands, the same shall be purchased only for us, in our name, at some public meeting or assembly of the said Indians, to be held for that purpose by the Governor or commander in chief of our colony respectively within which they shall lie: and in case they shall lie within the limits of any proprietary government, they shall be purchased only for the use and in the name of such proprietaries, conformable to such directions and instructions as we or they shall think proper to give for that purpose. And we do, by the advice of our Privy Council, declare and enjoin, that the trade with the said Indians shall be free and open to all our subjects whatever, provided that every person who may incline to trade with the said Indians do take out a license for carrying on such trade, from the Governor or commander in chief of any of our colonies respectively where such person shall reside, and also give security to observe such regulations as we shall at any time think fit, by ourselves or commissaries to be appointed for this purpose, to direct and appoint for the benefit of the said trade. And we do hereby authorize, enjoin, and require the Governors and commanders in chief of all our colonies respectively, as well those under our immediate government as those under the government and direction of proprietaries, to grant such licenses without fee or reward, taking especial care to insert therein a condition that such license shall be void, and the security forfeited, in case the person to whom the same is granted shall refuse or neglect to observe such regulations as we shall think proper to prescribe as aforesaid.

And we do further expressly enjoin and require all officers whatever, as well military as those employed in the management and direction of Indian affairs within the territories reserved as aforesaid, for the use of the said Indians, to seize and apprehend all persons whatever who, standing charged with treasons, misprisions of treason, murders, or other felonies or misdemeanors, shall fly from justice and take refuge in the said territory, and to send them under a proper guard to the colony where the crime was committed of which they shall stand accused, in order to take their trial for the same.

FORMULATION OF A WESTERN POLICY

The Proclamation Line of 1763 posed as many problems as it solved: the French settlers in the Northwest were left without government; the line of demarcation, already breached by settlers, caused bitter wrangling; and the Indian trade provisions opened the way for ruthless competition and exploitation. In the South, governors ignored the Proclamation and continued to sell Indian trading licenses for a profit. Illegal traders from Montreal and Albany swarmed through the West. But even the heavily financed Scotch-Irish and Jewish merchants of Philadelphia and Lancaster suffered losses when they established stores in Illinois. Land speculators, equally disturbed by the restrictions of the Proclamation, clamored for a liberalization of policy. That English officials yielded to American pressures was evident from a plan suggested in 1767, but all too frequent shifts in personnel within the British ministries brought sharp criticism of the new proposal. The following report of the Board of Trade summarizes the plan, the criticisms, and the deeper issues that influenced British policy:[3]

In obedience to your Majesty's commands signified to us by a letter from the Earl of Shelburne, one of your Majesty's principal Secretaries of State, dated the 5th of October last, we have taken into our most serious consideration the several memorials, letters, and other papers therewith referred to us, containing objections to, and observations upon the present Plan for the management of our commerce and connexions with the Indians in North America; stating the great expense attending as well that branch of service, as the present disposition of the troops for Indian purposes, and urging the expediency and propriety, in various lights, of establishing certain new governments upon the Mississippi, the Ohio, and at the Detroit, between the Lakes Erie and Huron. We have also conferred, upon this occasion, with such of your Majesty's military servants, as have been employed in North America, and with such merchants and others as are most intelligent in the North American and Indian trade.

Whereupon we humbly beg leave to represent to your Majesty, That the subject matter, to which these papers refer, and the questions arising thereupon, stated to us in the Earl of Shelburne's letter, appear to us to lead to a consideration of no less consequence and importance, than what system it may be now proper for your Majesty to pursue, with respect to that vast and extensive country in North America, which, on account of the Indian War raging within it, was made by the Proclamation of the 7 October 1763, the object of mere provisional arrangement.

The advantages arising from the Treaty of Paris, are in no part of it more distinguished than in those stipulations, which by obtaining from France and Spain cessions to your Majesty of those important possessions in North America, which, by their situation, gave most alarm and annoyance to the British Colonies, laid the foundation of lasting security to your Majesty's Empire in North America, and of relief to this country by a reduction of that heavy expense, with which it was necessarily burthen'd for the defence and protection of those colonies. And, although the unfavourable impressions left upon the minds of the Indians by the event of the war, and the representations of the French that we meant to extirpate them, did for sometime involve us in a war with them, that rendered necessary the continuance of a large military establishment; yet, that war being happily ended, the Treaties of Peace and Friendship to which all the various tribes have acceded, having been finally concluded, it is now become of immediate importance to examine, how far the alteration which has thus taken place in the state of your Majesty's Dominion in North America, may require or admit of any proportionable alteration in the system, by which that part of your Majesty's service is to be carried on for the future.

The parts of the Service for which we are more immediately called upon by the Earl of Shelburne's letter to give our attention, are, (1) the present Civil Establishment regarding the Indians; (2) the disposition of the troops for Indian purposes; and lastly, the establishment of certain new colonies.

. . . We are directed to state our opinion, how far the present expense of the civil establishment regarding the Indians may with

---

[3] Edmund Bailey O'Callaghan and Berthold Fernow (eds.), *Documents Relative to the Colonial History of New York* (Albany, 1856–1887), vol. 7, pp. 19–31.

safety and propriety be reduced, by entrusting the Indian trade, and all other Indian affairs, to the management of the several colonies.

In considering this question it may be proper to observe, that the institution of Superintendants for the affairs of Indians appears to have been a measure originally adopted principally with a view to counteract the designs of the French in 1754, who by sowing the seeds of jealousy amongst the Indians, and exciting them to resent injuries, for redress of which they had in vain solicited the colonies, had well nigh entirely weaned them from the British interest, and at the same time by uniting the force and conducting the enterprizes of the savages, had rendered them an overmatch for your Majesty's colonies standing single and disunited.

... Upon a careful examination into the state of Indian affairs after the conclusion of peace, it appears that the two principall causes of the discontent, that still rankled in the minds of the Indians and influenced their conduct, were the encroachments made upon lands which they claimed as their property, and the abuses committed by Indian traders and their servants. The necessity which appeared . . . induced the Proclamation of October 1763; which very prudently restrained all persons from trading with the Indians without licence; and forbid, by the strongest prohibitions, all settlement beyond the limits therein described as the boundary of the Indian hunting ground, putting both their commerce and property under the protection of officers acting under your Majesty's immediate authority, and making their intervention necessary in every transaction with those Indians.

These, however, being, as we have before observed, mere provisional arrangements adapted to the exigence of the time, it is become now necessary to consider what may be more permanently requisite in both the cases to which they apply.

The giving all possible redress to the complaints of the Indians in respect to encroachments on their lands, and a steady and uniform attention to a faithful execution of whatever shall be agreed upon for that salutary purpose, is a consideration of very great importance. It is a service of a general nature, in which your Majesty's interest, as Lord of the Soil of all ungranted lands which the Indians may be inclined to give up, is deeply and immediately concerned, and with which the general security of your Majesty's possessions there is in some measure connected. It is an object comprehensive of a variety of cases, to which the separate authority and jurisdiction of the respective colonies is not competent, and it depends upon negotiation, which has always been carried on between Indians and officers acting under your Majesty's immediate authority, and has reference to matters which the Indians would not submit to the discussion of particular colonies.

For these reasons we are of opinion, that the execution of all measures and services, respecting the complaints of the Indians touching their lands, should be continued to be entrusted to the Superintendants at present acting under commission from your Majesty, reserving to the Governor and Council of every particular colony, which may be interested in any measure that has reference to this general service, a right to interpose their advice, and making their concurrence necessary to the ratification of every compact that shall be provisionally made, until your Majesty's pleasure shall be known upon it. . . .

Upon the whole it does appear to us, that it will be greatly for your Majesty's interest as well as for the peace, security, and advantage of the colonies, that this boundary line should as speedily as possible be ratified by your Majesty's authority, and that the Superintendants should be instructed and impowered to make treaties in your Majesty's name with the Indians for that purpose, and enabled to make such presents to the Indians as the nature and extent of the concessions on their part shall appear to require. Care, however, should be taken in the settlement of this business, that the agreement for a boundary line be left open to such alterations as, by the common consent, and for the mutual interests of both parties, may hereafter be found necessary and expedient.

... We humbly submit whether it may not be further necessary that the colonies should be required to give every sanction to the measure in their power and to provide by proper laws for the punishment of all persons, who shall endanger the publick peace of the community, by extending settlements or occupying lands beyond such line.

... We humbly submit, that there are other branches of duty and service, which ... require the intervention of officers acting under your Majesty's immediate authority; and which ... cannot be provided for by the Provincial Laws. Such are the renewal of antient compacts or covenant chains made between the Crown and the principal tribes of savages in that country; the reconciling differences and disputes between one body of Indians and another; the agreeing with them for the sale or surrender of lands for public purposes not lying within the limits of any particular colony; and the holding interviews with them for these and a variety of other general purposes, which are merely objects of negotiation between your Majesty and the Indians....

Antecedent to the establishment of the present plan of Superintendants, the management of these interests was entrusted to the Governors of the colonies which were principally connected with the Indians. But when we consider the dependent state of such Governors; that the other duties of their stations must interfere with this very important one; how greatly the objects of this service are increased by alliances with those numerous nations heretofore under the dominion of France; and how necessary it is that a constant watch should be kept upon their motions and designs; and that your Majesty's servants should be constantly and regularly informed of the true state of affairs and of all transactions in the Indian country; we cannot but be of opinion ... that the office of Superintendants should for the present be continued for these purposes; and that they should be enabled by a stated annual establishment confined to a certain sum, to make such presents as have been usual and customary [and] therefore ... absolutely necessary upon all occasions of treaties held with the Indians for publick purposes; the expence of which, including salaries to the two Superintendants, need not, according to the calculations and estimates made by them, exceed eight thousand pounds annually....

It must be admitted that a proper plan of trade with the Indians is an object deserving great attention not only from the commercial benefit resulting from it, but also from the effect that it ... must have upon the temper and disposition of the savages. ... We are convinced, however, upon the whole of this consideration,

1. That no one general plan of commerce and policy is or can be applicable to all the different nations of Indians of different interests and in different situations.

2. That the confining trade to certain posts and places, which is the spirit and principal of the present system, however ex-

pedient and effectual with respect to the southern Indians, is of doubtfull policy with respect to those Indians more particularly connected with New York and Pensylvania; and that it is evidently disadvantageous, inconvenient, and even dangerous with respect to the much larger body of Indians, who possess the country to the westward, and with whom your Majesty's subjects in Quebec in particular do carry on so extensive a commerce.

3. That independent of this objection, and of any doubt that might attend the practicability of its execution in its full extent, the whole Plan does consist of such a variety of establishments, and necessarily leads to such extensive operations, as to bring on an increasing expence which in point of commerce, may exceed the value of the object to which it applies, and being greater than the trade can bear, must, if the present Plan should be permanent, either fall upon the colonies (in which case it will be impracticable to settle the proportion each colony should bear), or become a burthen upon this country, which we humbly conceive would be both unreasonable and highly inconvenient.

For these reasons therefore and under these circumstances, we are humbly of opinion that the laying aside that part of the present Plan which relates to the Indian trade, and intrusting the entire management of that trade to the colonies themselves, will be of great advantage to your Majesty's service, as a means of avoiding much difficulty, and saving much expense both at present and in future.

... But we trust, that the experience which the old colonies have had of the ill effects of such inattention and neglect, will induce all of them to use more caution and better management for the future; and particularly to adopt such of the regulations established by the present Superintendants as have evidently operated to the benefitt of the trade, and to the giving that satisfaction and content to the Indians. . . .

. . . We beg leave . . . to represent it to your Majesty as our humble opinion, that it will be in the highest degree expedient to reduce all such posts in the interior country, as are not immediately subservient to the protection of the Indian commerce and to the defeating of French and Spanish machinations among the Indians, or which . . . cannot be maintained but at an expence disproportioned to the degree of their utility. . . .

It is evident that . . . neither the trade of your Majesty's subjects can be protected, nor the connection and intercourse between Louisiana and the Indians prevented, by forts or military establishments.

In the Northern District the principal Indians form themselves into two great Confederacies; the one composed of the Six Nations and their allies and dependants, the other, called the Western Confederacy, composed of a great variety of powerfull tribes occupying that extensive country which lyes about the Lakes Huron, Michigan, and Superior, and to the West and Northwest.

The commerce and connection with the first of these bodies of Indians was, antecedent to the war, confined chiefly to the Province of New York, upon the teritories of which their principal hunting ground lyes, and the trade was carried on at fortified truck-houses upon the Lake Ontario. Since the peace a large share of this trade is carried on from Pennsylvania by the channel of the Ohio, and from thence by Venango and Rivière-aux-Bœufs into Lake Erie. The commerce and connection with those Indians which form the Western Confederacy, were . . . altogether confined to the French in Canada, and is now principally carried on from thence by your Majesty's subjects there, through the channel of the Ottawa River and by the lakes.

... It does appear to us that the keeping up military establishments at Detroit, Michilimacinac, and Niagara, and the having two, or at most three armed vessels on the Lakes Erie, Huron, Michigan, and Superior, may be necessary for keeping up and preserving that good correspondence with the Indians, which is essential to the safety, improvement, and extension of the trade with them.

All such forts as shall be judged necessary to be kept up for the security of your Majesty's dominions against a foreign enemy, or for forcing obedience to and a due execution of the Laws of Trade, ought to be garrisoned by troops in your Majesty's pay, commanded by officers appointed by your Majesty; as it would in our humble opinion be dangerous to publick safety, and inconsistent with the true principles of this Government, that forts and military establishments intended to answer such important objects, should be entrusted to any other hands. . . .

This consideration therefore naturally leads us to the last head of inquiry referred to us by the Earl of Shelburne's letter, viz. How far the establishment of new governments on the Mississippi, the Ohio, and at Detroit, would contribute to answer the purpose of lessening either the present civil or military expence or would procure the several other important advantages set forth in the papers referred to us.

Now, although it does not appear from the papers referred to us, that propositions have been made for the establishment of more than three new governments or colonies in the interior parts of America; viz. one at the Detroit between Lakes Erie and Huron; one at or near the mouth of the Ohio; and one in the Illinois country at or near the mouth of the river of that name; and therefore by the strict letter of his lordship's reference, the present consideration seems to be confined to these only; yet as it does appear . . . that they are meant to support the utility of colonizing in the interior country, as a general principle of policy; and that in fact they have nothing less in view than the entire possession and peopling of all that country, which has communications with the rivers Mississippi and St. Lawrence, it does in our humble opinion, open a much wider field of discussion than might at the first glance seem to be necessary.

The proposition of forming inland colonies in America is, we humbly conceive, entirely new; it adopts principles in respect to American settlements different from what has hitherto been the policy of this kingdom; and leads to a system which, if pursued through all its consequences, is in the present state of this country of the greatest importance.

The great object of colonizing upon the Continent of North America has been to improve and extend the commerce, navigation, and manufactures of this Kingdom, upon which its strength and security depend: (1) by promoting the advantageous fishery carried on upon the northern coast; (2) by encouraging the growth and culture of naval stores, and of raw materials to be transported hither in exchange for perfect manufacture and other merchandize; (3) by securing a supply of lumber, provisions, and other necessaries for the support of our establishments in the American islands.

In order to answer these salutary purposes it has been the policy of this Kingdom to confine her settlements as much as possible to the sea coast and not to extend them to places unaccessible to shipping and consequently more out of the reach of commerce, a plan which at the same time . . . had the further political advantage of guarding against all interfering of foreign powers and of enabling this Kingdom to keep up a superior naval force in those seas, by the actual possession of such rivers and harbours as were proper stations for fleets in time of war.

Such, may it please your Majesty, have been the considerations inducing that plan of policy hitherto pursued in the settlement of your Majesty's American colonies, with which the private interest and sagacity of the settlers co-operated from the first establishments.... It was upon these principles and with these views, that Government undertook the settling of Nova Scotia in 1749; and ... that it was so liberally supported by the aid of Parliament.

The same motives ... did, as we humbly conceive, induce the forming the colonies of Georgia, East Florida, and West Florida to the south, and the making those provisional arrangements in the Proclamation in 1763, by which the interior country was left to the possession of the Indians....

It is well known that, antecedent to the year 1749, all that part of the sea coast of the British Empire in America which extends north-east from the Province of Main to Cançeau in Nova Scotia, and from thence north to the mouth of St. Lawrence's River, lay waste and neglected, though naturally affording or capable by art of producing every species of naval stores, the seas abounding with whale, cod, and other valuable fish, and having many great rivers, bays, and harbours fit for the reception of ships of war.... [These considerations] induced that Plan for the settlement of Nova Scotia, to which we have been referred....

The establishment of Government in this part of America ... induced a zeal for migration; and associations were formed for taking up lands and making settlements in this Province by principal persons residing at those colonies. In consequence of these associations upwards of 10,000 souls have passed from those colonies into Nova Scotia, who have either engaged in the fisheries, or become exporters of lumber and provisions to the West Indies; and further settlements to the extent of 21 townships of 100,000 acres each, have been engaged to be made there by many of the principal persons in Pennsylvania, whose names and association for that purpose now lye before your Majesty in Council.

The Government of Massachusets Bay, as well as the proprietors of large tracts to the eastward of the Province of Main, excited by the success of these settlements, are giving every encouragement to the like settlements in that valuable country lying between them and Nova Scotia; and the proprietors of twelve townships, lately laid out there by the Massachusets Government, now solicit your Majesty for a confirmation of their title.

Such, may it please your Majesty is the present state of the progress making in the settlement of the northern parts of the sea coasts of North America, in consequence of what appears to have been the policy adopted by this Kingdom; and many persons of rank and substance here are proceeding to carry into execution the Plan, which your Majesty (pursuing the same principles of commercial policy) has approved for the settlement of the islands of St. John and Cape Breton, and of the new established colonies to the south; and therefore ... we cannot be of opinion that it would ... be adviseable to divert your Majesty's subjects in America from the persuit of these important objects, by adopting measures of a new policy at an expence to this Kingdom, which, in its present state, it is unable to bear....

The several arguments urged in support of the particular establishments now recommended, ... appear to us reducible to the following general propositions, viz.: (1) that such colonies will promote population, and increase the demands for, and consumption of, British manufactures; (2) that they will secure the furr trade, and prevent all illicit trade, or interfering of French or Spaniards with the Indians; (3) that they will be a defence and protection to the old colonies against the Indians; (4) that they will contribute to lessen the present heavy expence of supplying provisions to the distant forts and garrisons; lastly, that they are necessary in respect to the inhabitants already residing in those places where they are proposed to be established, who require some form of civil government. . . .

We admit, as an undeniable principle of true policy, that, with a view to prevent manufactures, it is necessary and proper to open an extent of territory for colonization proportioned to the increase of people; as a large number of inhabitants, cooped up in narrow limits, without a sufficiency of land for produce, would be compelled to convert their attention and industry to manufactures. But we submit whether the encouragement given to the settlement of the colonies upon the sea-coast, . . . has not already effectually provided for this object as well as for . . . consumption of British manufactures; an advantage which, in our humble opinion, would not be promoted by these new colonies, which being proposed to be established at the distance of above fifteen hundred miles from the sea, and in places which upon the fullest evidence are found to be utterly inaccessible to shipping, will, from their inability to find returns wherewith to pay for the manufactures of Great Britain, be probably led to manufacture for themselves; . . . The settlement of that extensive tract of sea-coast hitherto unoccupied, . . . together with the liberty that the . . . middle colonies will have (in consequence of the proposed boundary line with the Indians) of gradually extending themselves backwards, will more effectually and beneficially answer the object of encouraging population and consumption, than the erection of new governments. Such gradual extension might, through the medium of a continued population upon even the same extent of territory, preserve a communication of mutual commercial benefits between its extremest parts and Great Britain, impossible to exist in colonies separated by immense tracts of unpeopled desart. As to the effect which it is supposed the colonies may have to increase and promote the furr trade, and to prevent all contraband trade or intercourse between the Indians under your Majesty's protection and the French or Spaniards, it does appear to us: that the extension of the furr trade depends entirely upon the Indians being undisturbed in the possession of their hunting grounds; that all colonizing does in its nature, and must in its consequences operate to the prejudice of that branch of commerce; and that the French and Spaniards would be left in possession of a great part of what remained, as New Orleans would still continue the best and surest markett. As to the protection which it is supposed these new colonies may be capable of affording to the old ones, it will in our opinion appear upon the slightest view of their situation, that, so far from affording protection to the old colonies, they will stand most in need of it themselves. . . .

The present French inhabitants in the neighbourhood of the lakes will, in our humble opinion, be sufficient to furnish with provisions whatever posts may be necessary to be continued there. . . . There never has been an instance of a government instituted merely with a view to supply a body of troops with suitable provisions; nor is it necessary in these instances for the settlements already existing as above described; which . . . do not, in our humble opinion, require any other superintendance than that of the military commanding at these posts.

This careful analysis by the Board of Trade became the basis of British western policy, and even the entreaties of such influential Americans as Benjamin Franklin, George Washington, Patrick Henry, and Richard Henry Lee—all deeply involved in land speculation—were rejected. English policy rested on a fundamental misconception: the Board of Trade believed that westward expansion would cease unless genuinely encouraged from Britain. But curtailing the functions of Indian superintendents, redrawing the demarcation line, and attempting to divert population north and south only resulted in increased Indian tensions and efforts to circumvent the goals of the Board of Trade. The move to draw a new boundary led to an open fight between speculators and officials that resulted not only in unjust Indian treaties but also in fraudulent surveys. Furthermore, the older and larger companies, cognizant of the unstable character of English politics, renewed their determination to persuade the financially embarrassed ministries to reconsider and to sell tracts in the West for proprietary colonies. In addition, in the 1770s American speculators stumbled on the so-called Camden-Yorke decision, a ruling by England's Attorney General, the Earl of Camden, and the Solicitor General, Charles Yorke, intended to clarify the status of landholding privileges in India. Camden and Yorke held that land sales concluded between English citizens and Indian princes were legal. Pretending to believe that this ruling could be applied in America, the American investors sent agents hurrying westward to negotiate directly with the Indians.

THE LONG-HUNTERS OF KENTUCKY: DANIEL BOONE

The speculators had no difficulty finding men willing to do their bidding. For more than a decade hunters had clambered through the Cumberland Gap into Kentucky, searched their way into Tennessee, or drifted down the Ohio River. They knew the easiest routes to the most fertile basins and the best valleys. These skilled woodsmen vanished into the wilderness. They lived in the twilight zone between savagery and civilization, and emerged after a season or a year either loaded with a cache of fur or haggard and exhausted, sadly recounting a tale of Indian depredation. Daniel Boone belonged to this group of "long-hunters." His account of activities in Kentucky, although far too pompous to be of his own composition, typifies the risks, losses, and adventures of the long-hunter:[4]

It was on the first of May, in the year 1769, that I resigned my domestic happiness for a time, and left my family and peaceable habitation on the Yadkin River, in North-Carolina, to wander through the wilderness of America, in quest of the country of Kentucke, in company with John Finley, John Stewart, Joseph Holden, James Monay, and William Cool. We proceeded successfully, and after a long and fatiguing journey through a mountainous wilderness, in a westward direction, on the seventh day of June following, we found ourselves on Red-River, where John Finley had for merly been trading with the Indians, and, from the top of an eminence, saw with pleasure the beautiful level of Kentucke. Here let me observe, that for some time we had experienced the most uncomfortable weather as a prelibation of our future sufferings. At this place we encamped, and made a shelter to defend us from the inclement season, and began to hunt and reconnoitre the country. We found every where abundance of wild beasts of all sorts, through this vast forest. The buffaloes were more frequent than I have seen cattle

---

[4] John Filson, *The Discovery, Settlement, and Present State of Kentucke* (Wilmington, Del., 1784), pp. 50–57.

in the settlements, browzing on the leaves of the cane; or croping the herbage on those extensive plains, fearless, because ignorant, of the violence of man. Sometimes we saw hundreds in a drove, and the numbers about the salt springs were amazing. In this forest, the habitation of beasts of every kind natural to America, we practised hunting with great success until the twenty-second day of December following.

This day John Stewart and I had a pleasing ramble, but fortune changed the scene in the close of it. We had passed through a great forest, on which stood myriads of trees, some gay with blossoms, others rich with fruits. Nature was here a series of wonders, and a fund of delight. Here she displayed her ingenuity and industry in a variety of flowers and fruits, beautifully coloured, elegantly shaped, and charmingly flavoured; and we were diverted with innumerable animals presenting themselves perpetually to our view.—In the decline of the day, near Kentucke river, as we ascended the brow of a small hill, a number of Indians rushed out of a thick cane-brake upon us, and made us prisoners. The time of our sorrow was now arrived, and the scene fully opened. The Indians plundered us of what we had, and kept us in confinement seven days, treating us with common savage usage. During this time we discovered no uneasiness or desire to escape, which made them less suspicious of us; but in the dead of night, as we lay in a thick cane-brake by a large fire, when sleep had locked up their senses, my situation not disposing me for rest, I touched my companion and gently awoke him. We improved this favourable opportunity, and departed, leaving them to take their rest, and speedily directed our course towards our old camp, but found it plundered, and the company dispersed and gone home. About this time my brother, Squire Boon, with another adventurer, who came to explore the country shortly after us, was wandering through the forest, determined to find me, if possible, and accidentally found our camp. Notwithstanding the unfortunate circumstances of our company, and our dangerous situation, as surrounded with hostile savages, our meeting so fortunately in the wilderness made us reciprocally sensible of the utmost satisfaction. So much does friendship triumph over misfortune, that sorrows and sufferings vanish at the meeting not only of real friends, but of the most distant acquaintances, and substitutes happiness in their room.

Soon after this, my companion in captivity, John Stewart, was killed by the savages, and the man that came with my brother returned home by himself. We were then in a dangerous, helpless situation, exposed daily to perils and death amongst savages and wild beasts, not a white man in the country but ourselves.

Thus situated, many hundred miles from our families in the howling wilderness, I believe few would have equally enjoyed the happiness we experienced. I often observed to my brother, You see now how little nature requires to be satisfied. Felicity, the companion of content, is rather found in our own breasts than in the enjoyment of external things: And I firmly believe it requires but a little philosophy to make a man happy in whatsoever state he is. This consists in a full resignation to the will of Providence; and a resigned soul finds pleasure in a path strewed with briars and thorns.

We continued not in a state of indolence, but hunted every day, and prepared a little cottage to defend us from the Winter storms. We remained there undisturbed during the Winter; and on the first day of May, 1770, my brother returned home to the settlement by himself, for a new recruit of horses and ammunition, leaving me by myself, without bread, salt or sugar, without company of my fellow creatures, or even a horse or dog. I confess I never before was under greater necessity of exercising philosophy and fortitude. A few days I passed uncomfortably. The idea of a beloved wife and family, and their anxiety upon the account of my absence and exposed situation, made sensible impressions on my heart. A thousand dreadful apprehensions presented themselves to my view, and had undoubtedly disposed me to melancholy, if further indulged.

One day I undertook a tour through the country, and the diversity and beauties of nature I met with in this charming season, expelled every gloomy and vexatious thought. Just at the close of day the gentle gales retired, and left the place to the disposal of a profound calm. Not a breeze shook the most tremulous leaf. I had gained the summit of a commanding ridge, and, looking round with astonishing delight, beheld the ample plains, the beauteous tracts below. On the other hand, I surveyed the famous river Ohio that rolled in silent dignity, marking the western boundary of Kentucke with inconceivable grandeur. At a vast distance I beheld the mountains lift their venerable brows, and penetrate the clouds. All things were still. I kindled a fire near a fountain of sweet water, and feasted on the loin of a buck, which a few hours before I had killed. The sullen shades of night soon overspread the whole hemisphere, and the earth seemed to gasp after the hovering moisture. My roving excursion this day had fatigued my body, and diverted my imagination. I laid me down to sleep, and I awoke not until the sun had chased away the night. I continued this tour, and in a few days explored a considerable part of the country, each day equally pleased as the first. I returned again to my old camp, which was not disturbed in my absence. I did not confine my lodging to it, but often reposed in thick cane-brakes, to avoid the savages, who, I believe, often visited my camp, but fortunately for me, in my absence. In this situation I was constantly exposed to danger, and death. How unhappy such a situation for a man tormented with fear, which is vain if no danger comes, and if it does, only augments the pain. It was my happiness to be destitute of this afflicting passion, with which I had the greatest reason to be affected. The prowling wolves diverted my nocturnal hours with perpetual howlings; and the various species of animals in this vast forest, in the day time, were continually in my view.

Thus I was surrounded with plenty in the midst of want. I was happy in the midst of dangers and inconveniences. In such a diversity it was impossible I should be disposed to melancholy. No populous city, with all the varieties of commerce and stately structures, could afford so much pleasure to my mind, as the beauties of nature I found here.

Thus, through an uninterrupted scene of sylvan pleasures, I spent the time until the 27th day of July following, when my brother, to my great felicity, met me, according to appointment, at our old camp. Shortly after, we left this place, not thinking it safe to stay there longer, and proceeded to Cumberland river, reconnoitring that part of the country until March, 1771, and giving names to the different waters.

Soon after, I returned home to my family with a determination to bring them as soon as possible to live in Kentucke, which I esteemed a second paradise, at the risk of my life and fortune.

Long-hunters like Boone, the advance guard of civilization, left tomahawk-blazed trails through the mountains for other settlers to follow. More and more farmers moved into western

Pennsylvania, and cabins dotted the south bank of the Ohio River as far west as the mouth of the Great Kanawha. Still other pioneers moved south and west from Virginia or almost directly west from North Carolina to establish settlements on the banks of the Watauga, Holston, and Nolichucky—all tributaries of the Tennessee River. The settlers on the upper Tennessee River, aware that they had moved beyond the demarcation line, leased their lands from the Cherokee Indians. The settlers on the Watauga River drafted and signed Articles of Association, forming a government to legalize their landholdings, issue marriage licenses, try lawsuits, keep the peace, and enlist a militia. As Virginia and North Carolina gradually extended political jurisdiction in the areas, royal authorities challenged the extralegal practices of the settlers, setting aside the Indian treaties and declaring void many of the land sales.

THE FOUNDING OF BOONESBOROUGH

Although Daniel Boone was familiar with the upper Tennessee settlements, he turned to Kentucky when he decided to move his family west. He had no difficulty in recruiting a large party to join him in establishing a new settlement:[5]

I returned safe to my old habitation, and found my family in happy circumstances. I sold my farm on the Yadkin, and what goods we could not carry with us; and on the twenty-fifth day of September, 1773, bade a farewel to our friends, and proceeded on our journey to Kentucke, in company with five families more, and forty men that joined us in Powel's Valley, which is one hundred and fifty miles from the now settled parts of Kentucke. This promising beginning was soon overcast with a cloud of adversity; for upon the tenth day of October, the rear of our company was attacked by a number of Indians, who killed six, and wounded one man. Of these my eldest son was one that fell in the action. Though we defended ourselves, and repulsed the enemy, yet this unhappy affair scattered our cattle, brought us into extreme difficulty, and so discouraged the whole company, that we retreated forty miles, to the settlement on Clench river. We had passed over two mountains, viz. Powel's and Waiden's, and were approaching Cumberland mountain when this adverse fortune overtook us. These mountains are in the wilderness, as we pass from the old settlements in Virginia to Kentucke, are ranged in a S. west and N. east direction, are of a great length and breadth, and not far distant from each other. Over these, nature hath formed passes, that are less difficult than might be expected from a view of such huge piles. The aspect of these cliffs is so wild and horrid, that it is impossible to behold them without terror. The spectator is apt to imagine that nature had formerly suffered some violent convulsion; and that these are the dismembered remains of the dreadful shock; the ruins, not of Persepolis or Palmyra, but of the world!

I remained with my family on Clench until the sixth of June, 1774, when I and one Michael Stoner were solicited by Governor Dunmore, of Virginia, to go the Falls of the Ohio, to conduct into the settlement a number of surveyors that had been sent thither by him some months before; this country having about this time drawn the attention of many adventurers. We immediately complied with the Governor's request, and conducted in the surveyors, compleating a tour of eight hundred miles, through many difficulties, in sixty-two days.

---

[5] John Filson, *The Discovery, Settlement, and Present State of Kentucke* (Wilmington, Del., 1784), pp. 57–58.

THE IMPACT OF LORD DUNMORE'S WAR

Persistent white encroachment into Kentucky after Pontiac's surrender alarmed the Shawnee Indians of eastern Ohio and the Cherokee Indians of Tennessee. Both tribes claimed the "dark and bloody ground," Kentucky, where they hunted game and warred upon each other. The Shawnee were especially concerned because they had already been forced west by the advance of white settlers, and they saw in Kentucky a repetition of the settlers' pattern of expansion: the extermination of game animals, the land-seeking surveyors, the coming of pioneer farmers, and finally, the expulsion of the Indian. In an effort to blunt the thrust into Kentucky, the Shawnee sought alliances with the Cherokee and the Seneca, a powerful member tribe of the Iroquois group.

Because the Shawnee Indians believed that the loss of the Kentucky hunting grounds would be a tribal disaster and because the twin pressures of population and economics were pushing the English through the Cumberland Gap into this area, a frontier war seemed inevitable. Tensions along the frontier of western Pennsylvania and Kentucky were further heightened when the Virginia and Pennsylvania colonies disputed ownership of the land at the forks of the Ohio River. So long as Quaker-dominated Pennsylvania controlled the region, the settlers could not count upon unquestioned eastern support in their conflicts with the Indians. For this reason, the Shawnee remained at peace despite constant provocation by the white settlers. But in 1774, Virginia's governor Lord Dunmore claimed the area and appointed an unruly frontiersman, Dr. John Connolly, commander at Pittsburgh.

Fighting broke out almost immediately as Shawnee braves, infuriated by the numerous insults and murders inflicted upon the tribe, attacked and massacred the inhabitants of smaller settlements. Shrewd diplomacy kept both the Cherokee and the Iroquois neutral and allowed Lord Dunmore to plan a careful military operation against the virtually isolated Shawnee. But Virginia's luck rather than military skill left the Indians disheartened after a day-long battle at Point Pleasant on the Great Kanawha. The retreat of the Indians into Ohio and their fear that Dunmore would raze their villages and murder their women and children forced a quick surrender. In the Treaty of Camp Charlotte, the Shawnee relinquished their claim to Kentucky. Years later a Frenchman, J. Hector St. John de Crèvecoeur, who had served with Montcalm and decided to settle in Pennsylvania, attributed Lord Dunmore's War to certain deep-seated problems:[6]

But to return to our back settlers. I must tell you, that there is something in the proximity of the woods, which is very singular. It is with men as it is with the plants and animals that grow and live in the forests; they are entirely different from those that live in the plains. I will candidly tell you all my thoughts but you are not to expect that I shall advance any reasons. By living in or near the woods, their actions are regulated by the wildness of the neighbourhood. The deer often come to eat their grain, the wolves to destroy their sheep, the bears to kill their hogs, the foxes to catch their poultry. This surrounding hostility immediately puts the gun into their hands; they watch these animals, they kill some; and thus by defending their property, they soon become professed hunters; this is the progress; once hunters, farewell to the plough. The chase renders them ferocious, gloomy, and unsociable; a hunter wants no neighbour, he rather hates them, because he dreads the competition. In

---

[6] J. Hector St. John [de Crèvecoeur], *Letters from an American Farmer* (Philadelphia, 1793), pp. 55–58.

a little time their success in the woods makes them neglect their tillage. They trust to the natural fecundity of the earth, and therefore do little; carelessness in fencing often exposes what little they sow to destruction; they are not at home to watch; in order therefore to make up the deficiency, they go oftener to the woods. That new mode of life brings along with it a new set of manners, which I cannot easily describe. These new manners being grafted on the old stock, produce a strange sort of lawless profligacy, the impressions of which are indelible. The manners of the Indian natives are respectable, compared with this European medley. Their wives and children live in sloth and inactivity; and having no proper pursuits, you may judge what education the latter receive. Their tender minds have nothing else to contemplate but the example of their parents; like them they grow up a mongrel breed, half civilised, half savage, except nature stamps on them some constitutional propensities. That rich, that voluptuous sentiment is gone that struck them so forcibly; the possession of their freeholds no longer conveys to their minds the same pleasure and pride. To all these reasons you must add, their lonely situation, and you cannot imagine what an effect on manners the great distances they live from each other has! Consider one of the last settlements in its first view: of what is it composed? Europeans who have not that sufficient share of knowledge they ought to have, in order to prosper; people who have suddenly passed from oppression, dread of government, and fear of laws, into the unlimited freedom of the woods. This sudden change must have a very great effect on most men, and on that class particularly. Eating of wild meat, whatever you may think, tends to alter their temper: though all the proof I can adduce, is, that I have seen it: and having no place of worship to resort to, what little society this might afford is denied them. The Sunday meetings, exclusive of religious benefits, were the only social bonds that might have inspired them with some degree of emulation in neatness. Is it then surprising to see men thus situated, immersed in great and heavy labours, degenerate a little? It is rather a wonder the effect is not more diffusive. The Moravians and the Quakers are the only instances in exception to what I have advanced. The first never settle singly, it is a colony of the society which emigrates; they carry with them their forms, worship, rules, and decency: the others never begin so hard, they are always able to buy improvements, in which there is a great advantage, for by that time the country is recovered from its first barbarity. Thus our bad people are those who are half cultivators and half hunters; and the worst of them are those who have degenerated altogether into the hunting state. As old ploughmen and new men of the woods, as Europeans and new made Indians, they contract the vices of both; they adopt the moroseness and ferocity of a native, without his mildness, or even his industry at home. If manners are not refined, at least they are rendered simple and inoffensive by tilling the earth; all our wants are supplied by it, our time is divided between labour and rest, and leaves none for the commission of great misdeeds. As hunters it is divided between the toil of the chase, the idleness of repose, or the indulgence of inebriation. Hunting is but a licentious idle life, and if it does not always pervert good dispositions; yet, when it is united with bad luck, it leads to want: want stimulates that propensity to rapacity and injustice, too natural to needy men, which is the fatal gradation. After this explanation of the effects which follow by living in the woods, shall we yet vainly flatter ourselves with the hope of converting the Indians? We should rather begin with converting our backsettlers; and now if I dare mention the name of religion, its sweet accents would be lost in the immensity of these woods. Men thus placed are not fit either to receive or remember its mild instructions; they want temples and ministers, but as soon as men cease to remain at home, and begin to lead an erratic life, let them be either tawny or white, they cease to be its disciples.

Thus have I faintly and imperfectly endeavoured to trace our society from the sea to our woods! yet you must not imagine that every person who moves back, acts upon the same principles, or falls into the same degeneracy. Many families carry with them all their decency of conduct, purity of morals, and respect of religion; but these are scarce, the power of example is sometimes irresistible. Even among these backsettlers, their depravity is greater or less, according to what nation or province they belong. Were I to adduce proofs of this, I might be accused of partiality. If there happens to be some rich intervals, some fertile bottoms, in those remote districts, the people will there prefer tilling the land to hunting, and will attach themselves to it; but even on these fertile spots you may plainly perceive the inhabitants to acquire a great degree of rusticity and selfishness.

It is in consequence of this straggling situation, and the astonishing power it has on manners, that the backsettlers of both the Carolinas, Virginia, and many other parts, have been long a set of lawless people; it has been even dangerous to travel among them. Government can do nothing in so extensive a country, better it should wink at these irregularities, than that it should use means inconsistent with its usual mildness. Time will efface those stains: in proportion as the great body of population approaches them they will reform, and become polished and subordinate. Whatever has been said of the four New England provinces, no such degeneracy of manners has ever tarnished their annals; their backsettlers have been kept within the bounds of decency, and government, by means of wise laws, and by the influence of religion. What a detestable idea such people must have given to the natives of the Europeans! They trade with them, the worst of people are permitted to do that which none but persons of the best characters should be employed in. They get drunk with them, and often defraud the Indians. Their avarice, removed from the eyes of their superiors, knows no bounds; and aided by the little superiority of knowledge, these traders deceive them, and even sometimes shed blood. Hence those shocking violations, those sudden devastations which have so often stained our frontiers, when hundreds of innocent people have been sacrificed for the crimes of a few. It was in consequence of such behaviour, that the Indians took the hatchet against the Virginians in 1774. Thus are our first steps trod, thus are our first trees felled, in general, by the most vicious of our people; and thus the path is opened for the arrival of a second and better class, the true American freeholders; the most respectable set of people in this part of the world: respectable for their industry, their happy independence, the great share of freedom they possess, the good regulation of their families, and for extending the trade and the dominion of our mother country.

CUTTING THE WILDERNESS ROAD

The crushing terms the Shawnee were forced to accept at the close of Lord Dunmore's War virtually eliminated any threat to the rapid occupation of Kentucky. Judge Richard Henderson of North Carolina, a land speculator who frequently employed Boone, recognized a unique opportunity for fantastic profits if he could secure control of the region by leasing it from the Cherokee. In the late summer of 1774, Henderson and a group of North Carolina associates organized the Louisa Company and sought to gain possession of a parcel of land south of the Ohio River and west of the Great Kanawha along with the privilege of building a road through the Cumberland Gap. Even before an Indian agreement could be negotiated, the confident Henderson began advertising land for sale in 500-acre parcels at 20 shillings for each 100 acres and with an annual quitrent of 2 shillings.

Perhaps because he had learned of the Camden-Yorke ruling or perhaps because he understood the drift toward social upheaval on the eve of the Revolution, Henderson decided to purchase rather than lease the lands from the Cherokee. In January 1775, his reorganized company, now called the Transylvania Company, summoned the Indians to a treaty making. The result was the Treaty of Sycamore Shoals, signed on March 17. The Cherokee not only parted with the tracts that Henderson wanted but also allowed the settlers on the upper Tennessee River to convert their lease privileges into outright purchases. Although the Treaty of Sycamore Shoals could not lay claim to a shred of legality in the light of any English precedent in America, Henderson employed Boone to build what became known as the Wilderness Road. Originating at the Long Island of the Holston River, the Wilderness Road passed over the Cumberland Gap and emerged on the Kentucky River where Boone had constructed his crude settlement. The task was not so simple as Boone, recently returned from Lord Dunmore's War, hoped that it might be:[7]

---

[7] John Filson, *The Discovery, Settlement, and Present State of Kentucke* (Wilmington, Del., 1784), pp. 58–61.

Soon after I returned home, I was ordered to take the command of three garrisons during the campaign, which Governor Dunmore carried on against the Shawanese Indians: After the conclusion of which, the Militia was discharged from each garrison, and I being relieved from my post, was solicited by a number of North Carolina gentlemen, that were about purchasing the lands lying on the S. side of Kentucke River, from the Cherokee Indians, to attend their treaty at Wataga, in March, 1775, to negotiate with them, and, mention the boundaries of the purchase. This I accepted, and at the request of the same gentlemen, undertook to mark out a road in the best passage from the settlement through the wilderness to Kentucke, with such assistance as I thought necessary to employ for such an important undertaking.

I soon began this work, having collected a number of enterprising men, well armed. We proceeded with all possible expedition until we came within fifteen miles of where Boonsborough now stands, and where we were fired upon by a party of Indians that killed two, and wounded two of our number; yet, although surprised and taken at a disadvantage, we stood our ground. This was on the twentieth of March, 1775. Three days after, we were fired upon again, and had two men killed, and three wounded. Afterwards we proceeded on to Kentucke river without opposition; and on the first day of April began to erect the fort of Boonsborough at a salt lick, about sixty yards from the river, on the S. side.

On the fourth day, the Indians killed one of our men.—We were busily employed in building this fort, until the fourteenth day of June following, without any farther opposition from the Indians; and having finished the works, I returned to my family, on Clench.

In a short time, I proceeded to remove my family from Clench to this garrison; where we arrived safe without any other difficulties than such as are common to this passage, my wife and daughter being the first white women that ever stood on the banks of Kentucke river.

On the twenty-fourth day of December following we had one man killed, and one wounded, by the Indians, who seemed determined to persecute us for erecting this fortification.

On the fourteenth day of July, 1776, two of Col. Calaway's daughters, and one of mine, were taken prisoners near the fort. I immediately pursued the Indians, with only eight men, and on the sixteenth overtook them, killed two of the party, and recovered the girls. The same day on which this attempt was made, the Indians divided themselves into different parties, and attacked several forts, which were shortly before this time erected, doing a great deal of mischief. This was extremely distressing to the new settlers. The innocent husbandman was shot down, while busy cultivating the soil for his family's supply. Most of the cattle around the stations were destroyed. They continued their hostilities in this manner until the fifteenth of April, 1777, when they attacked Boonsborough with a party of above one hundred in number, killed one man, and wounded four—their loss in this attack was not certainly known to us.

On the fourth day of July following, a party of about two hundred Indians attacked Boonsborough, killed one man, and wounded two. They besieged us forty-eight hours; during which time seven of them were killed, and at last, finding themselves not likely to prevail, they raised the siege, and departed.

The Indians had disposed their warriors in different parties at this time, and attacked the different garrisons to prevent their assisting each other, and did much injury to the distressed inhabitants.

Henderson's problems were far more complicated than those posed by a sporadic Indian uprising. While Boone struggled to blaze a useful trail, Henderson tried to enforce the conditions of his ownership on the existing pioneers and force a toll from the immigrants moving westward to settle in Kentucky. But even Boone's men refused to be guided by the wishes of the Transylvania Company and spent much of their time hunting for the best lands. If Henderson hoped to take advantage of his claims, he would have to find some way of controlling the flood of settlers that now surged westward, elbowing their way into the older settlements and establishing new ones. The Transylvania Company found itself without any recourse to law. Henderson's own frame of government, hopelessly impractical, was ignored; appeal to royal authority was out of the question both because the Treaty of Sycamore Shoals was drafted in defiance of colonial authorities and because the Continental Congress was already in session to organize colonial opposition to English control. Discontent with Henderson's pretentions reached a climax in June 1776, when young George Rogers Clark, a turbulent frontiersman, guided the hostile element in Kentucky into establishing a revolutionary committee and asking Virginia to extend governmental control over the area. In 1777, the House of Burgesses acted upon this request. Henderson's plans collapsed, but he ultimately received almost 200,000 acres from Virginia and North Carolina as compensation. By that time, however, the Revolution was in flood tide.

THE QUEBEC ACT OF 1774

At almost the same time that Henderson was busy organizing the Louisa Company, the British Parliament passed the Quebec Act in an effort to rectify a mistake in the Proclamation of 1763—the failure to provide government for the French inhabitants in the Northwest:[8]

> Whereas His Majesty, by his Royal Proclamation bearing date the seventh day of October in the third year of his reign, thought fit to declare the provisions which had been made in respect to certain countries, territories and islands in America, ceded to His Majesty by the definitive Treaty of Peace, concluded at Paris on the tenth day of February 1763: And whereas by the arrangements made by the said Royal Proclamation, a very large extent of country, within which there were several colonies and settlements of the subjects of France, who claimed to remain therein under the faith of the said Treaty, was left without any provision being made for the administration of civil government therein; ... be it enacted ...
>
> That all the territories, islands and countries in North America belonging to the Crown of Great Britain, bounded on the South by a line from the Bay of Chaleurs, along the high lands which divide the rivers that empty themselves into the river Saint Lawrence from those which fall into the sea, to a point in forty-five degrees of northern latitude, on the eastern bank of the river Connecticut, keeping the same latitude directly west, through the lake Champlain, until, in the same latitude, it meets the river Saint Lawrence; from thence up the eastern bank of the said river to the Lake Ontario; thence through the Lake Ontario, and the river commonly called Niagara; and thence along by the eastern and south-eastern bank of Lake Erie, following the said bank, until the same shall be intersected by the northern boundary granted by the charter of the Province of Pensylvania, in case the same shall be so intersected; and from thence along the said northern and western boundaries of the said Province, until the said western boundary strike the Ohio; ... and along the bank of the said river, westward to the banks of the Mississippi, and northward to the southern boundary of the territory granted to the Merchants Adventurers of England trading to Hudson's Bay; ... are hereby, during His Majesty's pleasure, annexed to and made part and parcel of the Province of Quebec. ...
>
> Provided always, that nothing herein contained relative to the boundary of the Province of Quebec shall in any wise affect the boundaries of any other colony.
>
> And ... it is hereby declared, that His Majesty's subjects professing the religion of the Church of Rome of and in the said Province of Quebec, may have, hold and enjoy the free exercise of the religion of the Church of Rome, subject to the King's Supremacy; ... and that the clergy of the said Church may hold, receive and enjoy their accustomed dues and rights, with respect to such persons only as shall profess the said religion.

Ironically, this liberal toleration measure, construed by angry revolutionists as a means of establishing Roman Catholicism in the West and depriving the older English colonies of control of the region in favor of the French in Quebec, became an Intolerable Act—one of the immediate causes of the revolutionary conflict. Westerners themselves played almost no role in the coming of the Revolution. Only in the sense that they had become Americans far earlier than the colonists on the eastern seaboard did they contribute to the revolutionary spirit. For them, in an intellectual sense, the Revolution was over earlier than it was for the easterner.

---

[8] Peter Force, *American Archives* (Washington, 1837–1853), vol. 1, pp. 216–220.

CHAPTER 9

The West in the Revolution, 1776-1783

Although many frontiersmen were aware of the increasing tension between the colonies and England, few of them participated in the dialogue that terminated in revolution. Isolated, diffident, distrustful of eastern colonial administrators, and absorbed in developing the economic activities at hand, most backwoodsmen cared little about duties on tea, stamp taxes, or other issues that highlighted the emergence of American nationality. Those westerners who did share colonial hostility toward England were concerned with the failure of the home government to devise a successful policy for westward expansion—usually defined by Indian traders to mean a huge, easily exploited Indian and game reserve, and by settlers to mean a vast land reservoir freed from savages, accessible by good roads, and readily available for farming.

Yet even those who resented Britain's failure to formulate a viable western policy shied from open warfare, for all pioneers recognized the inevitable consequences of a conflict. Removal of British power, they knew, would once more expose the West to terrorizing Indian attacks and bloody fighting. They realized also that they, the American settlers, would be its principal victims, for the English not only commanded the loyalty of the red men, but were in a position to direct Indian war parties against any common enemy. Western posts from the Carolinas to New England were in British hands. The men most experienced in Indian negotiations were English officials. The sharpest critics of the land-grabbing tactics of ruthless frontiersmen were England's Indian agents. Inevitably the tribesmen looked more to England than to the colonies for leadership, and would be deadly pawns in the hands of British leaders.

These forebodings were justified, for had the British decided to arm the Indians and unleash them against the frontier settlements at the outbreak of the Revolutionary War, the backwoodsmen could have been driven from western Pennsylvania, Kentucky, and Tennessee. Such a policy of unrestrained savage warfare was, however, little to England's taste; British officers hesitated to launch an inhumane attack on women and children and had the good sense to realize that the Indians would not distinguish between loyal and disloyal settlers. If the red men were to be used—and they must if the West was to be won—they must be delicately handled and rigidly controlled.

AMERICAN-INDIAN TREATY MAKING: A BRITISH VIEW

Americans, on the other hand, would readily have enlisted the Indians in their cause had they not realized that this was as impossible as it was unwise: impossible because the red men were too bound to Britain to switch allegiance, unwise because they made uncertain allies unless kept loyal by constant gifts that were beyond the resources of the pioneers. Hence neutrality on the Indians' part became the foremost immediate goal of settlers in the West. Through the late summer of 1775 commissioners sought to negotiate treaties with a number of tribes, but only two—the Shawnee and Delaware near Pittsburgh—accepted this offer of friendship. These activities were carefully observed by Lieutenant Governor Henry Hamilton, Britain's principal agent in the West, from his post at Detroit. His report to his superiors showed how shrewdly he appraised the frontiersmen and the value of their treaties:[1]

... a Delaware savage, named Mahingan John arrived here 23d November from Pittsbourg where he had been present at a Council of the Virginians assembled there upon the design of engaging several nations to declare in their favor he came to this place in company with a frenchman (one Drouillard) whom Captain Lernoult has employed & who was within ten miles of Pittsburg. Drouillard's busyness was to enquire among the savages what was going forward, & to bring the earliest accounts to this place, as also to accompany any savage who might have got Belts to distribute, & to learn the result as well as to contradict false reports &ct. Mahingan John had got belts from the Virginians, which he was to deliver to a Huron chief called Old Calotte, who lives about 10 leagues from this place who is much in the English Interest, and who has declared he will not allow those Belts to go any further, but that they should be buried with him. We expect him here early in the Spring and shall endeavor to keep him in the same disposition. We have had accounts of your Excellency's success against the Rebels upon which I beg leave most sincerely to congratulate you. As Mahingan John is to be at a Council next Spring at Pitsburgh, he has been made acquainted with some of the particulars which are sufficient to undeceive the Delawares and Shawanese, which latter from the purport of the enclosed papers your Excellency will perceive are not likely to continue upon terms with the Virginians. Indeed any Peace between those people and any of the savage nations is liable to frequent interruptions from more causes than one. The Virginians are haughty Violent and bloody, the savages have a high opinion of them as Warriors, but are jealous of their encroachments, and very suspicious of their faith in treaties, the Virginians having furnished them with frequent cause, seizing their Chiefs & detaining them as hostages, during which time their treatment has not been as mild as good policy should have dictated. In the inroads of the Virginians upon the savages, the former have plundered, burnt and murdered without mercy. Tis to be supposed from the character of the savages, that opportunity only is wanting to retaliate, and that there can be but little cordiallity between them. If the affairs of the Colonials decline next year as I think we may reasonably expect, from all I can learn of the disposition of the savages, the frontier of Virginia in particular will suffer very severely. The nation of the Hurons is greatly respected by all the neighbouring nations, and it is probable the expence of presents to

---

[1] Reuben Gold Thwaites and Louise P. Kellogg (eds.), *The Revolution on the Upper Ohio* (Madison, 1908), pp. 127–135.

them next Spring will be pretty considerable. C[aptain] Lernoult tells me your Excellency had mentioned to him by letter that he should have by this fall or the next spring six Months provisions in addition for this post and that of Missilimalkinak, which considering the proposed addition of seamen, and the Necessity of providing the savages will be very necessary. Mr. Hay who acts as Engineer here, and who understands the Huron language, judges from what the savages say that if the Virginians and Delawares should cross the Ohio next Spring it will be as early as April. . . .

The following Paragraph is copied from the torn pieces of a paper which coverd the Talk of the Virginians to the savages at Fort Pitt, and which I suppose being deem'd by some of the council as too acrimonious has been corrected and crossed out as I have done exactly

I have sent this copy to your Excellency because tho not deliverd at the Council it shows how hardly they can restrain their inveteracy against the Savages, and how little cordiallity there can be in their Professions on either side. It does not appear that the savages have returned Belts or Strings for those presented them by the Commissioners, nor have we any account of the answer given by them to the Talk of the Commissioners. a copy of the minutes is sent to Niagara, & will be forwarded in the Spring to Missilimakinak

INDIAN WARFARE IN KENTUCKY

Hamilton could afford to watch and wait, hoping to restrain the Indians and prevent revolutionary bloodshed in the Northwest, but English officials on the southern frontier were less fortunate. No amount of pressure could dissuade the Cherokee from taking to the warpath against the settlers on the upper Tennessee River and by the end of 1776 a furious war was in progress there. Regular troops from North Carolina, South Carolina, and Virginia who came to the aid of the beleaguered pioneers waged such a ruthless campaign against the Cherokee villages and food supplies that by 1777 the Indians sued for peace, surrendering their claims to thousands of acres on the upper Tennessee. A temporary peace in the Carolina backcountry shifted the western center of warfare to Kentucky.

There Lieutenant Governor Henry Hamilton was cast in the role of a villain by the Americans. With only slightly more than a hundred soldiers to guard his own post at Detroit, and with fewer than three hundred scattered through the entire Northwest, he had no choice but to succumb when the Delaware, Shawnee, and Miami Indians demanded arms that could be used to drive settlers from Kentucky. As raids began in the summer of 1776, the Kentuckians fled to the safety of a few stockaded bastions—Boonesborough, Harrodsburg, and St. Asaph's Station—which were converted into forts that proved effective so long as the red men had no cannon to batter down the walls. This policy led to the surrender of the rest of Kentucky to the Indians; homes were burned, fields laid waste, isolated settlers killed. To end this carnage the "forted-up" settlers besieged the Virginia government for aid. Typical of their lament was a plea by George Rogers Clark sent eastward in the autumn of 1776:[2]

*To the Honourable
the Speaker & Gentlemen
of the House of Delegates*

The petition of John Gabriel Jones and George Rodgers Clark on behalf of the Inhabitants of the County of Kentuck humbly sheweth that the last Service that lies in their power prior to the return of your Petitioners to their Constituents which will be

---

[2] James A. James (ed.), *George Rogers Clark Papers* (Springfield, Ill., 1912), vol. 3, pp. 18–19.

tomorrow, is to acquaint this Honourable House of their Defenceless State, and imploreing their immediate Protection by sending such Forces as they think necessary. And they cannot but Observe how much it is to the Interest of Virginia to prevent the Inhabitants from abandoning that settlement and how necessary and advantageous it will be to the publick in Case of an Indian War, an event much to be Feared, with the Kiccapoos, Picts, and other Nations of Indians lying West of the River Ohio, as their Situation is so contiguous to those Nations that the Seat of War may be carried thither, and thus Secure the Frontiers effectually at once, Add to this that in this Service they can save the Public at least one-half of what an Army must Cost to be levyed any where else on the Frontier Counties, or any part of America. Perfectly satisfyed they have done all that laid in their Power, and happy would they be could they have done more for their Constituents, therefore Submitting their Case to this Honourable House no ways doubting but they in their great Wisdom and goodness will immediately send Aid to their Relief. and your Petitioners &c.
Friday October 1776

SUPPLIES FOR THE KENTUCKY GARRISON

The English knew that the Americans lacked gunpowder and even boasted to the Indians that the war could not last for long. But they did not anticipate that George Gibson, a young Indian trader experienced on the lower Ohio, planned to navigate the Mississippi River, buy powder from the Spanish, and return with it to Kentucky. Joined by William Linn and disguised as an innocent merchant, Gibson sailed a skiff to New Orleans. The British consul suspected that the Americans were spies, and Governor Bernardo de Galvez arrested Gibson to placate the English. When released from jail, Gibson sailed for Virginia with news that Linn had started upriver with almost 10,000 pounds of powder which he had secured through the efforts of Oliver Pollock, a leading New Orleans merchant who supported the Revolution. Alerted by Gibson, Dorsey Pentecost for the Virginia authorities wrote to William Harrod to search the river for Linn.[3]

SIR

I have received his Excellency the Governor's directions to endeavour to find out where Captain Gibsons Cargo of Powder is. In consequence of which I am to order that you do with all possible expedition raise a Company of Fifty privates in Conjunction and with the assistance of Lieutenant Nathan Hammond and Ensign Andrew Steel, with whom, and under your Command, you are Immediately to proceed down the Ohio, taking all possible Care to examine Strickly the mouth of all Creeks and Rivers which you pass, & when you arrive at the Mouth of Kentucke or at the Falls of Ohio, I think it would be advisable to send to Harrod's-Burgh, and make inquiry after Captain Linn & the said Cargoe, whom you are to conduct with the utmost Safety agreeable to these Instructions. If you should not fall in with Captain Linn (who superintends and Conducts the said Cargo) before you arrive at the Mouth of Ohio, I think it will be necessary that you pass up the Mississippi to the Kaskaskias Village, where you will make inquiry & probably meet with Captain Linn with his Cargo, & if you don't meet him before you get there, when you meet him, you

---

[3] Reuben Gold Thwaites and Louise P. Kellogg (eds.), *The Revolution on the Upper Ohio* (Madison, 1908), pp. 226–229.

will conduct him with the utmost Safety and the said Cargo up to the House of James Austurgass on the Monongahela River, & immediately advise me thereof. I desire that all possible care may be observed, as I have great reason to apprehend Danger from the Savages. If you hear nothing of Captain Linn at the aforesaid places, you will proceed on until you meet him. If you find it conducive to the good of the Service you are ordered upon, you will engage the necessary Interpreter or Interpreters, who should be worthy, Trusty persons. Colonel David Shepherd will furnish you with Beef, Pork, and Craft, at the mouth of Grave Creek; and your Lieutenant will apply to Joseph Parkison for flour & Salt, & send him to my house for the necessary Ammunition. You will not fail to leave proper Spies on the River Ohio, in case you move up to Harrod's-Burgh, & at the mouth of Ohio, in case you go up to the Kaskaskias Village, lest Captain Linn should Slip your Notice in the Interim. Depending on your Strict adherence to these Instructions, I have the pleasure of being

Sir Your most obedient Servant

DORSEY PENTECOST
County Lieutenant of Yohogania

P.S. If you run out of Provisions ammunition or any other article necessary for your Subsistance, or by any wise to Facilitate the Expedition, you will purchase it, & draw on Government or me for the Pay, which Shall Punctually be paid but I must once more recommend the utmost Frugality, Prudence and Good Conduct

THE SIEGE OF BOONESBOROUGH

Linn succeeded in delivering his precious cargo to the beleaguered garrison at Fort Henry, the site of Wheeling, West Virginia, but the Kentuckians were less well-cared for. There Chief Blackfish and his Shawnee warriors kept the forted settlers in a state of constant siege during the summer of 1777. This meant that they faced the winter of 1777-1778 with scant food supplies and no salt to relieve the monotony of an all-meat diet. One of their leaders, Daniel Boone, was determined to ease the situation by leading a salt-making party to Blue Licks on the Licking River but only met with more serious disaster. He described the events to his earliest biographer, John Filson:[4]

On the first day of January, 1778, I went with a party of thirty men to the Blue Licks, on Licking River, to make salt for the different garrisons in the country.

On the seventh day of February, as I was hunting, to procure meat for the company, I met with a party of one hundred and two Indians, and two Frenchmen, on their march against Boonsborough, that place being particularly the object of the enemy.

They pursued, and took me; and brought me on the eighth day to the Licks, where twenty-seven of my party were, three of them having previously returned home with the salt. I knowing it was impossible for them to escape, capitulated with the enemy, and, at a distance in their view, gave notice to my men of their situation, with orders not to resist, but surrender themselves captives.

The generous usage the Indians had promised before in my capitulation, was afterwards fully complied with, and we proceeded with them as prisoners to old Chelicothe, the principal Indian town, on Little Miami, where we arrived, after an uncomfortable journey, in very severe weather, on the eighteenth day of February, and received

[4] John Filson, *The Discovery, Settlement, and Present State of Kentucke* (Wilmington, Del., 1784), pp. 63–70.

as good treatment as prisoners could expect from savages—On the tenth day of March following, I, and ten of my men, were conducted by forty Indians to Detroit, where we arrived the thirtieth day, and were treated by Governor Hamilton, the British commander at that post, with great humanity.

During our travels, the Indians entertained me well; and their affection for me was so great, that they utterly refused to leave me there with the others, although the Governor offered them one hundred pounds Sterling for me, on purpose to give me a parole to go home. Several English gentlemen there, being sensible of my adverse fortune, and touched with human sympathy, generously offered a friendly supply for my wants, which I refused, with many thanks for their kindness; adding, that I never expected it would be in my power to recompense such unmerited generosity.

The Indians left my men in captivity with the British at Detroit, and on the tenth day of April brought me towards Old Chelicothe, where we arrived on the twenty-fifth day of the same month. This was a long and fatiguing march, through an exceeding fertile country, remarkable for fine springs and streams of water. At Chelicothe I spent my time as comfortably as I could expect; was adopted, accordin to their custom, into a family where I became a son, and had a great share in the affection of my new parents, brothers, sisters, and friends. I was exceedingly familiar and friendly with them, always appearing as chearful and satisfied as possible, and they put great confidence in me. I often went a hunting with them, and frequently gained their applause for my activity at our shooting-matches. I was careful not to exceed many of them in shooting; for no people are more envious than they in this sport. I could observe, in their countenances and gestures, the greatest expressions of joy when they exceeded me; and, when the reverse happened, of envy. The Shawanese king took great notice of me, and treated me with profound respect, and entire friendship, often enstructing me to hunt at my liberty. I frequently returned with the spoils of the woods, and as often presented some of what I had taken to him, expressive of duty to my sovereign. My food and lodging was, in common, with them, not so-good indeed as I could desire, but necessity made every thing acceptable.

I now began to meditate an escape, and carefully avoided their suspicions, continuing with them at Old Chelicothe until the first day of June following, and then was taken by them to the salt springs on Sciotha, and kept there, making salt, ten days. During this time I hunted some for them, and found the land, for a great extent about this river, to exceed the soil of Kentucke, if possible, and remarkably well watered.

When I returned to Chelicothe, alarmed to see four hundred and fifty Indians, of their choices warriors, painted and armed in a fearful manner, ready to march against Boonsborough, I determined to escape the first opportunity.

On the sixteenth, before sun-rise, I departed in the most secret manner, and arived at Boonsborough on the twentieth, after a journey of one hundred and sixty miles; during which, I had but one meal.

I found our fortress in a bad state of defence, but we proceeded immediately to repair our flanks, strengthen our gates and posterns, and form double bastions, which we compleated in ten days. In this time we daily expected the arrival of the Indian army; and at length, one of my fellow prisoners, escaping from them, arrived, informing us that the enemy had an account of my departure, and postponed their expedition three weeks.

—The Indians had spies out viewing our movements, and were greatly alarmed with our increase in number and fortifications. The Grand Councils of the nations were held frequently, and with more deliberation than usual. They evidently saw the approaching hour when the Long Knife would dispossess them of their desirable habitations; and anxiously concerned for futurity, determined utterly to extirpate the whites out of Kentucke. We were not intimidated by their movements, but frequently gave them proofs of our courage.

About the first of August, I made an incursion into the Indian country, with a party of nineteen men, in order to surprise a small town up Sciotha, called Paint-Creek-Town. We advanced within four miles thereof, where we met a party of thirty Indians, on their march against Boonsborough, intending to join the others from Chelicothe. A smart fight ensued betwixt us for some time: At length the savages gave way, and fled. We had no loss on our side: The enemy had one killed, and two wounded. We took from them three horses, and all their baggage; and being informed, by two of our number that went to their town, that the Indians had entirely evacuated it, we proceeded no further, and returned with all possible expedition to assist our garrison against the other party. We passed by them on the sixth day, and on the seventh, we arrived safe at Boonsborough.

On the eighth, the Indian army arrived, being four hundred and forty-four in number, commanded by Capt. Duquesne, eleven other Frenchmen, and some of their own chiefs, and marched up within view of our fort, with British and French colours flying; and having sent a summons to me, in his Britannick Majesty's name, to surrender the fort, I requested two days consideration, which was granted.

It was now a critical period with us.—We were a small number in the garrison:—A powerful army before our walls, whose appearance proclaimed inevitable death, fearfully painted, and marking their footsteps with desolation. Death was preferable to captivity; and if taken by storm, we must inevitably be devoted to destruction. In this situation we concluded to maintain our garrison, if possible. We immediately proceeded to collect what we could of our horses, and other cattle, and bring them through the posterns into the fort: And in the evening of the ninth, I returned answer, that we were determined to defend our fort while a man was living—Now, said I to their commander, who stood attentively hearing my sentiments, We laugh at all your formidable preparations: But thank you for giving us notice and time to provide for our defence. Your efforts will not prevail; for our gates shall for ever deny you admittance.—Whether this answer affected their courage, or not, I cannot tell; but, contrary to our expectations, they formed a scheme to deceive us, declaring it was their orders, from Governor Hamilton, to take us captives, and not to destroy us; but if nine of us would come out, and treat with them, they would immediately withdraw their forces from our walls, and return home peaceably. This sounded grateful in our ears; and we agreed to the proposal.

We held the treaty within sixty yards of the garrison, on purpose to divert them from a breach of honour, as we could not avoid suspicions of the savages. In this situation the articles were formally agreed to, and signed; and the Indians told us it was customary with them, on such occasions, for two Indians to shake hands with every white-man in the treaty, as an evidence of entire friendship. We agreed to this also, but were soon convinced their policy was to take us prisoners.—They immediately grappled us; but, although surrounded by hundreds of savages, we extricated ourselves from them, and escaped all safe into the garrison, except one that was wounded, through a heavy fire from their army. They immediately attacked us on every side, and a constant heavy fire ensued between us day and night for the space of nine days.

In this time the enemy began to undermine our fort, which was situated sixty yards from Kentucke river. They began at the water-mark, and proceeded in the bank some distance, which we understood by their making the water muddy with the clay; and we immediately proceeded to disappoint their design, by cutting a trench a-cross their subterranean passage. The enemy discovering our counter-mine, by the clay we threw out of the fort, desisted from that stratagem: And experience now fully convincing them that neither their power nor policy could effect their purpose, on the twentieth day of August they raised the siege, and departed.

During this dreadful siege, which threatened death in every form, we had two men killed, and four wounded, besides a number of cattle. We killed of the enemy thirty-seven, and wounded a great number. After they were gone, we picked up one hundred and twenty-five pounds weight of bullets, besides what stuck in the logs of our fort; which certainly is a great proof of their industry. Soon after this, I went into the settlement, and nothing worthy of a place in this account passed in my affairs for some time.

PLANNING THE AMERICAN ATTACK ON DETROIT

The famous siege of Boonesborough was lifted in mid-August, 1778, but the retreat of the Shawnee to north of the Ohio brought little peace to the frontier. That year Mohawk warriors led by Joseph Brant swept across upper New York laying waste the settlements; that year a thousand Indians and Tories surprised the nearly defenseless pioneers of Pennsylvania's Wyoming Valley and only retreated after hundreds had been killed or driven into the forest. With the exception of Pittsburgh and a few guarded sites on the upper Ohio, Americans from Albany to St. Asaph's Station were in constant fear of Indian attack. Clearly this condition of near-siege could not be endured long. Clearly, too, the backcountry could be saved only by launching an aggressive campaign against the British who supplied the red men and goaded them on. So reasoned George Rogers Clark, one of the proven leaders of the Kentucky colony. Fearful lest word of his plans leak to the British, he journeyed to Williamsburg to lay his case before Governor Patrick Henry, arriving just as the town throbbed with the hopeful news of the defeat of General John Burgoyne's British regulars at the Battle of Saratoga. Henry discussed Clark's proposal with Thomas Jefferson, then issued the following order:[5]

IN COUNCIL WILLIAMSBURG

JANUARY 2ND 1778

LIEUT COLONEL GEORGE ROGERS CLARK

You are to proceed with all convenient Speed to raise Seven Companies of Soldiers to consist of fifty men each officered in the usual manner & armed most properly for the Enterprise & with this Force attack the British post at Kaskasky.

It is conjectured that there are many pieces of Cannon & military Stores to considerable Amount at that place, the taking & preservation of which would be a valuable

---

[5] James A. James (ed.), *George Rogers Clark Papers* (Springfield, Ill., 1912), vol. 3, pp. 34–35.

acquisition to the State. If you are so fortunate therefore as to succeed in your Expectation, you will take every possible Measure to secure the Artillery & Stores & whatever may advantage the State.

For the Transportation of the Troops, provisions &c down the Ohio, you are to apply to the Commanding officer at Fort Pitt for Boats, &, during the whole Transaction you are to take especial Care to keep the true Destination of your Force secret. Its Success depends upon this. Orders are therefore given to Captain Smith to secure the two men from Kaskasky. Similar conduct will be proper in similar cases.

It is earnestly desired that you show Humanity to such British Subjects and other persons as fall in your hands. If the white Inhabitants at that post & the neighbourhood will give undoubted Evidence of their attachment to this State (for it is certain they live within its Limits) by taking the Test prescribed by Law & by every other way & means in their power, Let them be treated as fellow Citizens & their persons & property duly secured. Assistance & protection against all Enemies whatever shall be afforded them & the Commonwealth of Virginia is pledged to accomplish it. But if these people will not accede to these reasonable Demands, they must feel the miseries of War, under the direction of that Humanity that has hitherly distinguished Americans, & which it is expected you will ever consider as the Rule of your Conduct & from which you are in no Instance to depart.

The Corps you are to command are to receive the pay & allowance of Militia & to act under the Laws & Regulations of this State now in Force as Militia. The Inhabitants at this Post will be informed by you that in case they accede to the offers of becoming Citizens of this Commonwealth a proper Garrison will be maintained among them & every Attention bestowed to render their Commerce beneficial, the fairest prospects being opened to the Dominions of both France & Spain.

It is in Contemplation to establish a post near the Mouth of Ohio. Cannon will be wanted to fortify it. Part of those at Kaskasky will be easily brought thither or otherwise secured as circumstances will make necessary.

You are to apply to General Hand for powder & Lead necessary for this Expedition. If he can't Supply it the person who has that which Cap' Lynn bro' from Orleans can. Lead was sent to Hampshire by my Orders & that may be deliver'd you. Wishing you Success.

I am Sir your humble Servant

P. Henry

CLARK'S ATTACK ON VINCENNES

Clark's public orders concealed his true purpose; he planned to capture the British posts at Kaskaskia, Cahokia, and Vincennes in the Illinois country, thus placing the Indians of Ohio under his control and putting him in a position to move on Detroit. Spies had already told him that the French settlers there would welcome him, especially after the French alliance of 1778. With 175 men, Clark left the falls of the Ohio on July 4, and captured Kaskaskia and Cahokia without firing a shot. Vincennes capitulated as soon as the settlers there learned of his victory and of the French alliance. Hamilton retaliated at once, as he must or lose control of the Indians in the entire country north of the Ohio. Mobilizing militia and friendly Indians, he descended on Vincennes in December 1778, recapturing the post without difficulty when the French garrison fled. Once more the tide had turned in the struggle for domination of the Ohio Valley. The next move was up to George Rogers Clark. Several months later he described what happened to George Mason:[6]

We were now Sensible that St Vincents was in possession of the English; and consequently we might shortly expect an Attact though no danger at present, and had some time to make preparation for what we were certain of—I had reason to expect a Reinforcement on the presumption that Government ordered one on the Receipt of my first Letter; still encouraged each other and hoped for the best; But suffered more uneasiness than when I was certain of an immediate Attact, as I had more time to reflect: the Result of which was that the Illinois in a few months would be in the possession of the English except the Garrison which I knew would not be disposed to surrender without the greatest distress I sent off the Horsemen to St Vincents to take a Prisoner by which we might get intiligence, but found it impracticable, on account of the high waters; but in the hight of our anxiety on the evening of the 29th of January 1779 Mr. Vague [Vigo] a Spanish Merchant Arrived from St Vincents, and was there the time of its being taken, and gave me every Intiligence that I could wish to have. Governour Hamiltons Party consisted of about eight hundred when he took possession of that Post on the 17th day of december past: finding the Season too far spent for his intention against Kaskaskias had sent nearly the whole of his Indians out in different Parties to War: But to embody as soon as the weather would Permit and compleat his design: He had also sent messengers to the southern Indians, five hundred of whom he expected to join him. only eighty Troops in Garrisson (our Situation still appeared desperate, it was at this moment I would have bound myself seven years a Slave to have had five hundred Troops) I saw the only probability of our maintaining the Country was to take the advantage of his present weakness, perhaps we might be fortunate: I considered the Inclemency of the season, the badness of the Roads &c—as an advantage to us, as they would be more off their Guard on all Quarters. I collected the Officers, told them the probability I thought there was of turning the scale in our favour: I found it the sentiment of every one of them and eager for it. Our Plans immediately concluded on; and sent An Express to Cohos for the Return of Captain McCarthy & his Volunteers, and set about the necessary preparations in order to Transport my Artillery Stores &c.

I had a Large Boat prepared and Rigged mounting two four pounders six large swevels Manned with a fine Company Commanded by Lieut. Rogers: She set out in the evening of the 4th of January with orders to force her way if possible within ten Leagues of St Vincents and lay until further Orders. This Vessel when Compleat was much admired by the Inhabitants as no such thing had been seen in the Country before. I had great Expectations from her I conducted myself as though I was sure of taking Mr. Hamilton, instructed my Officers to observe the same Rule. In a day or two the Country seemed to believe it, many anctious to retrieve their Characters turned out, the Ladies began also to be spirited and interest themselves in the Expedition, which had great Effect on the Young men. By the 4th day of January I got every thing Compleat and on the 5th I marched being joined by two Volunteer Companies of the Principal Young Men of the Illinois Commanded by Captain McCarty & Francis Charlaville. Those of the Troops was Captains Bowman & William Worthingtons of the light Horse. we were

---

[6] James A. James (ed.), *George Rogers Clark Papers* (Springfield, Ill., 1912), vol. 3, pp. 138–141.

Conducted out of the Town by the Inhabitants: and Mr. Jeboth the Priest, who after a very suitable Discourse to the purpose, gave us all Absolution And we set out on a Forlorn hope indeed; for our whole Party with the Boats Crew consisted of only a little upwards of two hundred. I cannot account for it but I still had inward assurance of success; and never could when weighing every Circumstance doubt it: But I had some secret check. We had now a Rout before us of two hundred and Forty miles in length, though, I suppose one of the most beautiful Country in the world; but at this time in many parts flowing with water and exceading bad marching. my greatest care was to divert the Men as much as possible in order to keep up their spirits; the first obstruction of any consequence that I met with was on the 13th Arriveing at the two little Wabachces although three miles asunder they now make but one, the flowed water between them being at Least three feet deep, and in many places four: Being near five miles to the opposite Hills, the shallowest place, except about one hundred Yards was three feet. This would have been enough to have stop'ed any set of men that was not in the same temper that we was But in three days we contrived to cross, by building a large Canoe, ferried across the two Channels, the rest of the way we waded; Building scaffolds at each to lodge our Baggage on until the Horses Crossed to take them; it Rained nearly a third of our March; but we never halted for it; In the evening of the 17th we got to the low Lands of the River Umbara which we found deep in water, it being nine miles to St Vincents which stood on the East side of the Wabache and every foot of the way covered with deep water, we Marched down the little River in order to gain the Banks of the main which we did in about three Leagues, made a small Canoe and sent an Express to meet the Boat and hurry it up from the spot we now lay on was about ten miles to Town, and every foot of the way put together that was not three feet and upwards under water would not have made the length of two miles and a half and not a mouthful of Provision; To have waited for our Boat, if possible to avoid it, would have been Impolitic If I was sensible that You wou'd let no Person see this relation I would give You a detail of our suffering for four days in crossing those waters, and the manner it was done; as I am sure that You wou'd Credit it. but it is too incredible for any Person to believe except those that are as well acquainted with me as You are, or had experienced something similar to it I hope You will excuse me until I have the pleasure of seeing You personally. But to our inexpressible Joy in the evening of the 23rd we got safe on Terra firma within half a League of the Fort, covered by a small Grove of Trees had a full view of the wished for spot (I should have crossed at a greater distance from the Town but the White River comeing in just below us we were affraid of getting too near it) we had Already taken some Prisoners that was coming from the Town: Laying in this Grove some time to dry our Clothes by the Sun we took another Prisoner known to be a friend by which we got all the Intelligence we wished for: but would not suffer him to see our Troops except a few.

A thousand Ideas flashed in my Head at this moment I found that Governor Hamilton was able to defend himself for a considerable time, but knew that he was not able to turn out of the Fort; that if the Seige Continued long a Superior number might come against us, as I knew there was a Party of English not far above in the River: that if they found out our Numbers might raise the disaffected Savages and harass us. I resolved to appear as Darring as possible, that the Enemy might conceive by our behaviour that we were very numerous and probably discourage them. I immediately wrote to the Inhabitants in general. Informing them where I was and what I determined to do desireing the Friends to the States to keep close in their Houses those in the British Interest to repair to the fort and fight for their King: otherways there should be no mercy shewn them &c—&c—Sending the Compliments of several Officers that was known to be Expected to reinforce me, to several Gentlemen of the Town: I dispatched the Prisoner off with this letter waiting until near sunset, giving him time to get near the Town before we marched. As it was an open Plain from the Wood that covered us; I march'd time enough to be seen from the Town before dark but taking advantage of the Land, disposed the lines in such a manner that nothing but the Pavilions could be seen, having as many of them as would be sufficient for a thousand Men, which was observed by the Inhabitants, who had Just Receiv'd my letter counted the different Colours and Judged our number accordingly. But I was careful to give them no oppertunity of seeing our Troops before dark, which it would be before we could Arrive. The Houses obstructed the Forts observing us and were not Allarmed as I expected by many of the Inhabitants: I detached Lieutenant Bayley and party to Attact the Fort at a certain Signal, and took possession of the strongest Posts of the Town

THE WAR IN THE OHIO COUNTRY

Clark's plan of marching on Detroit failed when his short-term Virginia enlistees abandoned him, but elsewhere on the frontier American forces enjoyed unfamiliar triumphs during 1778 and 1779. The Iroquois villages of upper New York were ravaged by an army from Pittsburgh under Colonel Daniel Brodhead; a force under General John Sullivan defeated an Anglo-Indian raiding party near the village of Newton, ending fear of further attacks in central and northern Pennsylvania; in the South, Virginians and North Carolinians led by Colonel Evan Shelby destroyed the villages and grain supplies of the Cherokee and Chicamauga. These victories convinced the perennially optimistic westerners that the war was over in the West, and the frontier tide began to flow once more. By 1780, some 20,000 lived in Kentucky and a new settlement at Nashville on the Cumberland River was taking shape under the leadership of George Robertson. But the outlook was to change. The Continental Congress lacked money to buy Indian friendship or military power to command Indian respect and obedience; by the middle of 1780 warfare flamed along the borderlands once more. Harassing raids terrorized the outlying settlements from upper New York to Kentucky, where a party under Captain Henry Bird, armed with cannon, forced the surrender of several stockaded forts. Once more George Rogers Clark was called into action. With a thousand Kentuckians he launched a counterthrust against the Indian villages of Chillicothe and Piqua in Ohio, and this time he had a cannon to overawe the natives. He reported his success to Thomas Jefferson, who was by this time governor of Virginia:[7]

LOUISVILLE, AUGUST 22ND, 1780

By every possible exertion, and the aid of Col. Slaughter's corps, we completed the number of 1000, with which we crossed the

---

[7] James A. James (ed.), *George Rogers Clark Papers* (Springfield, Ill., 1912), vol. 3, pp. 451–453.

river at the mouth of Licking on the first day of August, and began our march on the 2nd. Having a road to cut for the artillary to pass, for 70 miles it was the 6th before we reached the first town, which we found vacated, and the greatest part of their effects carried off. The general conduct of the Indians, on our march, and many other corroborating circumstances, proved their design of leading us on to their own ground and time of action. After destroying the crops and buildings of Chillecauthy, we began our march for the Picaway settlements, on the waters of the Big Miami, the Indians keeping runners continually before our advanced guards. At half past two in the evening of the 8th, we arrived in sight of the town and forts, a plain of half a mile in width lying between us. I had an opportunity of viewing the situation and motion of the enemy near their works.

I had scarcely time to make those dispositions necessary, before the action commenced on our left wing, and in a few minutes became almost general, with a savage fierceness on both sides. The confidence the enemy had of their own strength and certain victory, or the want of generalship, occasioned several neglects, by which those advantages were taken that proved the ruin of their army, being flanked two or three different times, drove from hill to hill in a circuitous direction, for upwards of a mile and a half; at last took shelter in their strongholds and woods adjacent, when the firing ceased for about half an hour, until necessary preparations were made for dislodging them. A heavy firing again commenced, and continued severe until dark, by which time the enemy were totally routed. The cannon playing too briskly on their works they could afford them no shelter. Our loss was about 14 killed and thirteen wounded; theirs at least triple that number. They carried off their dead during the night, except 12 or 14 that lay too near our lines for them to venture. This would have been a decisive stroke to the Indians, if unfortunately the right wing of our army had [not] been rendered useless for some time by an uncommon chain of rocks that they could not pass, by which means part of the enemy escaped through the ground they were ordered to occupy.

By a French prisoner we got the next morning we learn that the Indians had been preparing for our reception ten days, moving their families and effects: That the morning before our arrival, they were 300 warriors, Shawanese, Mingoes, Wyandotts and Delawares. Several reinforcements coming that day, he did not know their numbers; that they were sure of destroying the whole of us; that the greatest part of the prisoners taken by Byrd, were carried to Detroit, where there were only 200 regulars, having no provisions except green corn and vegetables. Our whole store at first setting out being only 300 bushels of corn, and 1500 of flour; having done the Shawanese all the mischief in our power, after destroying Picawey settlements, I returned to this post, having marched in the whole 480 miles in 31 days. We destroyed upwards of 800 acres of corn, besides great quantities of vegetables, a considerable proportion of which appear to have been cultivated by white men, I suppose for the purpose of supporting war parties from Detroit. I could wish to have had a small store of provisions to have enabled us to have laid waste part of the Delaware settlements, and falling in at Pittsburg, but the excessive heat, and weak diet, shew the impropriety of such a step. Nothing could excel the few regulars and Kentuckyans, that composed this little army, in bravery, and implicit obedience to orders; each company vying with the other who should be the most subordinate.

THE BATTLE OF KING'S MOUNTAIN

The Indians had been punished, but the pro-English balance of power remained unchanged. As 1780 drew to a close, there was no certainty that mounting Indian hostility, increasing discontent among the French in the Illinois country, and growing British military strength would not erase Clark's achievements. Nor was the situation on the southern frontier more favorable. There Lord Cornwallis, who now commanded the English forces, was moving northward with a large army of regulars which had landed at Charleston. To protect his inland flank, he dispatched a brave and daring young Scottish officer, Major Patrick Ferguson, to gather a force of Tories and ravage the backcountry. Ferguson performed his task with skill, punishing patriots, destroying property, and driving the revolutionary frontiersmen either westward over the mountains or north and east into the path of Cornwallis' army. But when he decided to cross the mountains and fight the frontiersmen on their own ground he sealed his doom. As word spread, armed backwoodsmen from all over the Southwest gathered, determined to fight to the end. This show of force sent Ferguson eastward to rejoin Cornwallis, but before he could do so he was compelled to make a stand at King's Mountain in the North Carolina upcountry. One of the best accounts of the Battle of King's Mountain was written by Ensign Robert Campbell shortly after:[8]

In the fall of the year 1780, when the American cause wore a very gloomy aspect in the Southern States, Cols. Arthur and William Campbell, hearing of the advance of Colonel Ferguson along the mountains in the State of North Carolina, and that the Whigs were retreating before him, unable to make any effectual resistance, formed a plan to intercept him, and communicated it to the commanding officers of Sullivan and Washington Counties, in the State of North Carolina. They readily agreed to co-operate in any expedition against Col. Ferguson. Col. Arthur Campbell immediately ordered the militia of Washington Co., Virginia, amounting to near four hundred, to make ready to march under command of Col. Wm. Campbell, who was known to be an enterprising and active officer. Cols. Shelby and Sevier raised a party of three hundred, joined him on his march, and moved with forced marches toward Col. Ferguson. At the same time Cols. Williams, Cleveland, Lacey, and Brandon, of the States of North and South Carolina, each conducted a small party toward the same point, amounting to near three hundred. Col. Ferguson had notice of their approach by a deserter that left the army on the Yellow Mountain, and immediately commenced his march for Charlotte, dispatching at the same time different messengers to Lord Cornwallis with information of his danger. These messengers being intercepted on their way, no movement was made to favor his retreat.

These several corps of American volunteers, amounting to near one thousand men, met at Gilbert Town, and the officers unanimously chose Colonel Campbell to the command. About seven hundred choice riflemen mounted their horses for the purpose of following the retreating army. The balance being chiefly footmen, were left to follow on and come up as soon as they could. The pursuit was too rapid to render an escape practicable. Ferguson, finding that he must inevitably be over-taken, chose his ground,

---

[8] Lyman C. Draper, *King's Mountain and Its Heroes* (Cincinnati, 1881), pp. 537–540.

and waited for the attack on King's Mountain. On the 7th of October, in the afternoon, after a forced march of forty-five miles on that day and the night before, the volunteers came up with him. The forenoon of the day was wet, but they were fortunate enough to come on him undiscovered, and took his pickets, they not having it in their power to give an alarm. They were soon formed in such order as to attack the enemy on all sides. The Washington and Sullivan regiments were formed in the front and on the right flank; the North and South Carolina troops, under Cols. Williams, Sevier, Cleveland, Lacey, and Brandon, on the left. The two armies being in full view, the center of the one nearly opposite the center of the other—the British main guard posted nearly half way down the mountain —the commanding officer gave the word of command to raise the Indian war-whoop and charge. In a moment, King's Mountain resounded with their shouts, and on the first fire the guard retreated, leaving some of their men to crimson the earth. The British beat to arms, and immediately formed on the top of the mountain, behind a chain of rocks that appeared impregnable, and had their wagons drawn up on their flank across the end of the mountain, by which they made a strong breast-work.

Thus concealed, the American army advanced to the charge. In ten or fifteen minutes the wings came round, and the action became general. The enemy annoyed our troops very much from their advantageous position. Col. Shelby, being previously ordered to reconnoitre their position, observing their situation, and what a destructive fire was kept up from behind those rocks, ordered Robert Campbell, one of the officers of the Virginia Line, to move to the right with a small company to endeavor to dislodge them, and lead them on nearly to the ground to which he had ordered them, under fire of the enemy's lines and within forty steps of the same; but discovering that our men were repulsed on the other side of the mountain, he gave orders to advance, and post themselves opposite to the rocks, and near to the enemy, and then returned to assist in bringing up the men in order, who had been charged with the bayonet. These orders were punctually obeyed, and they kept up such a galling fire as to compel Ferguson to order a company of regulars to face them, with a view to cover his men that were posted behind the rocks. At this time, a considerable fire was drawn to this side of the mountain by the repulse of those on the other, and the Loyalists not being permitted to leave their posts. This scene was not of long duration, for it was the brave Virginia volunteers, and those under Col. Shelby, on their attempting rapidly to ascend the mountain, that were charged with the bayonet. They obstinately stood until some of them were thrust through the body, and having nothing but their rifles by which to defend themselves, they were forced to retreat. They were soon rallied by their gallant commanders, Campbell, Shelby and other brave officers, and by a constant and well-directed fire of their rifles, drove them back in their turn, strewing the face of the mountain with their assailants, and kept advancing until they drove them from some of their posts.

Ferguson being heavily pressed on all sides, ordered Capt. DePeyster to reinforce some of the extreme posts with a full company of British regulars. He marched, but to his astonishment when he arrived at the place of destination, he had almost no men, being exposed in that short distance to the constant fire of their rifles. He then ordered his cavalry to mount, but to no purpose. As quick as they were mounted, they were taken down by some bold marksmen. Being driven to desperation by such a scene of misfortune, Col. Ferguson endeavored to make his escape, and, with two Colonels of the Loyalists, mounted his horse, and charged on that part of the line which was defended by the party who had been ordered round the mountain by Col. Shelby, it appearing too weak to resist them. But as soon as he got to the line he fell, and the other two officers, attempting to retreat, soon shared the same fate. It was about this time that Col. Campbell advanced in front of his men, and climbed over a steep rock close by the enemy's lines, to get a view of their situation, and saw they were retreating from behind the rocks that were near to him. As soon as Capt. DePeyster observed that Col. Ferguson was killed, he raised a flag and called for quarters. It was soon taken out of his hand by one of the officers on horseback, and raised so high that it could be seen by our line, and the firing immediately ceased. The Loyalists, at the time of their surrender, were driven into a crowd, and being closely surrounded, they could not have made any further resistance.

In this sharp action, one hundred and fifty of Col. Ferguson's party were killed, and something over that number were wounded. Eight hundred and ten, of whom one hundred were British regulars, surrendered themselves prisoners, and one thousand five hundred stand of arms were taken. The loss of the American army on this occasion amounted to thirty killed, and something over fifty wounded, among whom were a number of brave officers. Col. Williams, who has been so much lamented, was shot through the body, near the close of the action, in making an attempt to charge upon Ferguson. He lived long enough to hear of the surrender of the British army. He then said, "I die contented, since we have gained the victory," and expired.

The third night after the action, the officers of the Carolinas complained to Col. Campbell, that there were among the prisoners a number who had, previous to the action on King's Mountain, committed cool and deliberate murder, and other enormities alike atrocious, and requested him to order a court-martial to examine into the matter. They stated that if they should escape, they were exasperated, and they feared they would commit other enormities worse than they had formerly done. Col. Campbell complied, and ordered a court-martial immediately to sit, composed of the Field Officers and Captains, who were ordered to inquire into the complaints which had been made. The court was conducted orderly, and witnesses were called and examined in each case. The consequence was that there were thirty-two condemned. Out of these, nine who were thought the most dangerous, and who had committed the most atrocious crimes, were executed. The others were pardoned by the commanding officer. One of the crimes proven against a Captain that was executed was, that he had called at the house of a Whig, and inquired if he was at home, and being informed by his son, a small boy, that he was not, he immediately drew out his pistol and shot him. The officers on the occasion acted from an honorable motive to do the greatest good in their power for the public service, and to check those enormities so frequently committed in the States of North and South Carolina at that time, their distress being almost unequaled in the annals of the American Revolution.

The westerners could take little joy in their victory, for the Cherokee had seized upon the opportunity provided by Ferguson's expedition to renew their raids on the southern frontier and were only subdued after another major campaign led by "Nulichucky Jack" Sevier. The next two years witnessed bitter fighting along the Ohio River, where raids and reprisals resulted in massacres, burned villages, wasted cornfields, and a slow but steady demoralization of the settlers. When peace negotiations were begun in Paris to end the American Revolution and secure independence for the colonies, the condition north of the Ohio had reached a nadir.

BOUNDARY PROVISIONS OF THE TREATY OF PARIS, 1783

Yet the Treaty of Paris that gave the Americans their freedom from British rule was surprisingly favorable to their cause. They secured not only independence, but certain commercial and fishing privileges, and above all such extensive boundaries that they were assured room for expansion for generations to come. These concessions they owed less to their military victories in the West than to the generosity of the English negotiators, who recognized that the new nation must grow in order to survive. Their farsightedness was shown especially in the provisions of the Treaty of Paris that established the borders of the United States:[9]

From the north west Angle of Nova Scotia, Viz. that Angle which is form'd by a Line drawn due north, from the Source of St. Croix River to the Highlands, along the said Highlands which divide those Rivers that empty themselves into the River St. Laurence, from those which fall into the Atlantic Ocean, to the northwesternmost Head of Connecticut River; thence down along the middle of that River to the 45th Degree of North Latitude; from thence by a Line due West on said Latitude, untill it strikes the River Iroquois, or Cataraquy; thence along the middle of said River into Lake Ontario; through the middle of said Lake, untill it strikes the Communication by Water between that Lake and Lake Erie; thence along the middle of said Communication into Lake Erie, through the middle of said Lake, untill it arrives at the Water Communication between that Lake and Lake Huron; thence along the middle of said water communication into the Lake Huron; thence through the middle of said Lake to the Water Communication between that Lake and Lake Superior; thence through Lake Superior northward of the Isles Royal & Phelipeaux, to the Long Lake; thence through the middle of said Long Lake, and the water Communication between it and the Lake of the Woods, to the said Lake of the Woods, thence through the said Lake to the most Northwestern point thereof, and from thence on a due west Course to the River Mississippi; thence by a Line to be drawn along the middle of the said River Mississippi, untill it shall intersect the northernmost part of the 31st Degree of North Latitude. South, by a Line to be drawn due East, from the Determination of the Line last mentioned, in the Latitude of 31 Degrees North of the Equator, to the middle of the River Apalachicola or Catahouche; thence along the middle thereof, to its junction with the Flint River; thence strait to the Head of St. Mary's River, and thence down along the middle of St. Mary's River to the Atlantic Ocean. East, by a Line to be drawn along the middle of the River St. Croix, from its Mouth in the Bay of Fundy to its Source; and from its Source directly North, to the aforesaid Highlands which divide the Rivers that fall into the Atlantic Ocean, from those which fall into the River St. Laurence; com-

---

[9] *Treaties, Conventions, International Protocals and Agreements Between the United States of America and Other Powers, 1776–1909*, compiled by William M. Malloy (Washington, 1910), vol. 1, pp. 587–588.

prehending all Islands within twenty Leagues of any part of the Shores of the united States, and lying between Lines to be drawn due East from the points where the aforesaid Boundaries between Nova Scotia on the one part and East Florida on the other shall respectively touch the Bay of Fundy, and the Atlantic Ocean; excepting such Islands as now are, or heretofore have been within the Limits of the said Province of Nova Scotia.

The Treaty of Paris of 1783 ushered in a new day in the history of the American frontier. Before the pioneers stretched a thousand miles of virgin wilderness, beckoning them on to the very shores of the Mississippi. Now, too, they could accept this invitation, for no meddling London ministers could say them nay. For the first time in generations they were ready to resume their march toward the Pacific, with no restraining hand upon them and limitless opportunity ahead.

CHAPTER 10

Government Policy in the West: Land and Diplomacy, 1783-1803

Independence was won, and the gateway to the West was no longer barred by an unsympathetic Parliament. But the Americans soon found that the problems of the region beyond the Appalachians were as insoluble for them as they had been for British ministers. How should the lands there be divided and sold? What type of government should be provided? And, most pressing of all, how could the warlike Indians be pacified and the foreign agents who goaded them on be removed? These were problems that had baffled experienced rulers. Yet now they had to be solved by a tiny new nation, inadequately governed by a powerless Congress under the Articles of Confederation, and so weak that European nations ruthlessly disregarded its rights, especially along the frontiers.

TRANSFER OF THE WESTERN
LANDS TO CONGRESS

Before Congress could grapple with these questions, a preliminary step was necessary. At the close of the Revolution the domain between the Appalachians and the Mississippi River was claimed by seven states on the basis of their colonial charters, many of which extended boundaries from sea to sea. Since 1776, pressure had been brought on these states to cede their western lands to the nation, partly because the joint holdings would form a bond of union needed to hold the quarreling states together, partly because sale of lands in the West would provide needed revenue, partly because the six landless states faced depopulation if their neighbors subsisted on land sales rather than taxation.

Complicating the situation further, influential land speculators from the landless states formed powerful companies that included some of the country's leading politicians and spearheaded the drive for cession, knowing that this was their only chance to secure western grants for development. Congress might be talked into selling them lands but the seven states would care for their own speculators first. These jobbers were centered in the middle states, and were especially strong in Maryland. Due partly to their influence, that state announced in 1778 that it would never ratify the Articles of Confederation until the landed states ceded their holdings. This move placed the landed states, and especially Virginia, in an awkward position. Its western claims, based on its 1609 charter, extended over most of the Northwest, and were larger than those of any other state. It was reluctant to cede such a rich domain to the national government for exploitation by speculators from other states. Yet few people realized that land-jobbing was involved; in the public eye Virginia was selfishly clinging to its lands and denying the nation a needed frame of government, for the Articles of Confederation required unanimous consent for adoption. Nor was the state's cause aided when Congress, on October 10, 1780, adopted a resolution pledging that all ceded lands would be used for the national good:[1]

Resolved, that the unappropriated lands that may be ceded or relinquished to the United States, by any particular States, pursuant to the recommendation of Congress of the 6 day of September last, shall be disposed of for the common benefit of the United States, and be settled and formed into distinct republican States, which shall become members of the Federal Union, and shall have the same rights of sovereignty, freedom and independence, as the other States: that each State which shall be so formed shall contain a suitable extent of territory, not less than one hundred nor more than one hundred and fifty miles square, or as near thereto as circumstances will admit;

That the necessary and reasonable expences which any particular State shall have incurred since the commencement of the present war, in subduing any of the British posts, or in maintaining forts or garrisons within and for the defence, or in acquiring any part of the territory that may be ceded or relinquished to the United States, shall be reimbursed;

That the said lands shall be granted and settled at such times and under such regulations as shall hereafter be agreed on by the United States in Congress assembled, or any nine or more of them.

VIRGINIA CEDES ITS WESTERN LANDS

This resolution multiplied the pressures on Virginia, as did New York's action in 1780 of ceding to the national government its very doubtful rights to all lands claimed by the Iroquois. Bowing but not buckling before the wind, the Virginia legislators agreed late in 1780 to turn over their western holdings, but only on condition that no earlier private purchases made there be recognized. This astute step, which would invalidate all speculative claims to the region, launched three years of political fencing and intrigue, with Virginia and the middle state land jobbers the antagonists, Congress the battleground, and the American people the losers. In the end Virginia's brand of justice prevailed when popular opinion forced Congress to accept the cession with all conditions attached. Virginia's cession, accepted by Congress on March 1, 1784, set a pattern that other states were to follow:[2]

Whereas the General Assembly of the Commonwealth of Virginia at their sessions begun on the twentieth day of October one

---

[1] Gaillard Hunt (ed.), *Journals of the Continental Congress, 1774–1789* (Washington, 1910), vol. 18, p. 1915.

[2] Clarence E. Carter (ed.), *The Territorial Papers of the United States. II, The Territory Northwest of the River Ohio, 1787–1803* (Washington, 1934), pp. 6–9.

thousand seven hundred & eighty three passed an Act entitled "an Act to authorize the delegates of this State in Congress to convey to the United States in Congress Assembled all the right of this Commonwealth to the Territory North-Westward of the River Ohio." in these words following to wit—

Whereas the Congress of the United States did by their Act of the sixth day of September in the year one thousand seven hundred and eighty recommend to the several States in the Union having claims to waste and unappropriated Lands in the Western Country a liberal Cession to the United States of a portion of their respective claims for the common Benefit of the Union. And Whereas this Commonwealth did on the second day of January in the year one thousand seven hundred & Eighty one yield to the Congress of the United States for the Benefit of the said States all right, title & claim which the said Commonwealth had to the Territory North-West of the River Ohio subject to the Conditions annexed to the said Act of Cession And Whereas the United States in Congress Assembled have by their Act of the thirteenth of September last stipulated the terms on which they agree to accept the Cession of this State should the Legislature approve thereof which Terms although they do not come fully up to the propositions of this Commonwealth are conceived on the whole to approach so nearly to them as to induce this State to accept thereof in full confidence that Congress will in justice to this State for the liberal Cession she hath made earnestly press upon the other States claiming large Tracts of waste and uncultivated Territory the propriety of making Cessions equally liberal for the common Benefit and support of the Union Be it enacted by the General Assembly that it shall and may be lawful for the delegates of this State to the Congress of the United States or such of them as shall be assembled in Congress and the said delegates or such of them so assembled are hereby fully authorized and empowered for and on behalf of this State by proper deeds or instrument in writing under their Hands and Seals to convey, transfer, assign and make over unto the United States in Congress Assembled for the Benefit of the said States all right title and claim as well of soil as jurisdiction which this Commonwealth hath to the Territory or Tract of Country within the limits of the Virginia Charter situate lying and being to the North-West of the River Ohio subject to the terms and conditions contained in the before recited Act of Congress of the thirteenth day of September last that is to say upon condition that the Territory so ceded shall be laid out and formed into States containing a suitable extent of Territory not less than one hundred nor more than one hundred and fifty miles square or as near thereto as circumstances will admit and that the States so formed shall be distinct Republican States and admitted members of the federal union, having the same rights of Sovereignty, Freedom and Independence as the other States —That the necessary and reasonable expences incurred by this State in subduing any British Posts or in maintaing Forts or Garrisons within and for the defence or in acquiring any part of the Territory so Ceded or relinquished shall be fully reimbursed by the United States and that one Commissioner shall be appointed by Congress one by this Commonwealth and another by those two Commissioners who or a majority of them shall be authorized and empowered to adjust and liquidate the account of the necessary and reasonable expences incurred by this State which they shall judge to be comprized within the intent and meaning of the Act of Congress of the tenth of October one thousand seven hundred and Eighty respecting such expences— That the French and Canadian Inhabitants and other Settlers of the Kaskaskies St Vincents and the neighbouring Villages who have professed themselves Citizens of Virginia shall have their possessions and titles confirmed to them and be protected in the enjoyment of their rights and liberties—That a quantity not exceeding one hundred and fifty thousand Acres of Land promised by this State shall be allowed and granted to the then Colonel now General George Rogers Clarke and to the Officers and Soldiers of his Regiment who marched with him when the posts of Kaskaskies and St Vincents were reduced and to the Officers and Soldiers that have been since incorporated into the said Regiment to be laid off in one Tract the length of which not to exceed double the breadth in such place on the North-West Side of the Ohio as a majority of the Officers shall choose and to be afterwards divided among the said Officers and Soldiers in due proportion according to the Laws of Virginia. That in case the quantity of good Lands on the South-East side of the Ohio upon the Waters of Cumberland River and between the Green River and Tenessee river which have been reserved by Law for the Virginia Troops upon Continental establishment should from the North Carolina line bearing in further upon the Cumberland Lands than was expected prove insufficient for their legal Bounties the deficiency should be made up to the said Troops in good Lands to be laid off between the Rivers Scioto & little Miami on the north-West Side of the River Ohio in such proportions as have been engaged to them by the Laws of Virginia—That all the Lands within the Territory so Ceded to the United States and not reserved for or appropriated to any of the before mentioned purposes or disposed of in bounties to the Officers and Soldiers of the American Army shall be considered as a common fund for the use and benefit of such of the United States as have become or shall become members of the Confederation or federal Alliance of the said States Virginia inclusive according to their usual respective proportions in the general charge and expenditure and shall be faithfully and bona fide disposed of for that purpose and for no other use or purpose whatsoever. Provided that the Trust hereby reposed in the delegates of this State shall not be executed unless three of them at least are present in Congress.

And Whereas the said General Assembly by their Resolution of June sixth one thousand seven hundred & Eighty three had constituted and appointed us the said Thomas Jefferson, Samuel Hardy, Arthur Lee and James Monroe delegates to represent the said Commonwealth in Congress for one year from the first Monday in November then next following which Resolution remains in full force. Now therefore Know Ye that we the said Thomas Jefferson, Samuel Hardy, Arthur Lee and James Monroe by virtue of the power and authority committed to us by the Act of the said General Assembly of Virginia before recited, and in the name & for & on behalf of the said Commonwealth do by these presents convey, transfer, assign and make over unto the United States in Congress Assembled for the benefit of the said States, Virginia inclusive all right, title and claim as well of soil as of jurisdiction which the said Commonwealth hath to the Territory or tract of Country within the limits of the Virginia Charter, situate, lying and being to the North-West of the River Ohio, to and for the uses & purposes and on the Conditions of the said recited Act. In Testimony whereof we have hereunto subscribed our Names and affixed our Seals in Congress the first day of March in the year of our Lord one thousand seven hundred & Eighty four and of the Independence of the United States the Eighth.

WESTERN STATE-MAKING IN THE POST-REVOLUTIONARY ERA

Virginia's cession broke the log jam, and one after another the remaining states fell into line. In so doing, each followed the pattern of reserving sizable areas to satisfy the claims of military bounty holders. In addition Massachusetts retained ownership of the western half of New York, and Connecticut held the northeast corner of Ohio, the so-called Connecticut or Western Reserve. The transfer of so much real estate inevitably stirred troubles along the borderlands, where pioneers had their own opinions of who should govern them. The situation was especially troublesome in North Carolina. When the legislature ceded the state's holdings in June 1784, the people of the backcountry rose in rebellion, insisting that they be granted immediate statehood to forestall the lawlessness that threatened in the interval between state and national rule. Meeting in convention in November 1785, delegates from the Tennessee settlements adopted a "Declaration of Rights" and a constitution for the State of Frankland which rings with democratic sentiments, as its opening paragraphs demonstrate:[3]

A Declaration of Rights made by the Representatives of the Freemen of the State of Frankland

1. That all political power is vested in and derived from the people only.

2. That the people of this State ought to have the sole and exclusive right of regulating the internal government and police thereof.

3. That no man, or set of men, are entitled to exclusive or separate emoluments or privileges from the community, but in consideration of public services.

4. That the Legislative, Executive and Supreme Judicial powers of government ought to be forever separate and distinct from each other.

5. That all powers of suspending laws, or the execution of laws, by any authority, without the consent of the representatives of the people, is injurious to their rights, and ought not to be exercised.

6. That elections of members to serve as representatives, in General Assembly, ought to be free.

7. That, in all criminal prosecutions, every man has a right to be informed of the accusation against him, and to confront the accusers and witnesses with other testimony, and shall not be compelled to give evidence against himself.

8. That no freeman shall be put to answer any criminal charge but by indictment, presentment, or impeachment.

9. That no freeman shall be convicted of any crime but by the unanimous verdict of a jury of good and lawful men, in open court, as heretofore used.

10. That excessive bail should not be required, nor excessive fines imposed, nor cruel nor unusual punishments inflicted.

11. That general warrants, whereby an officer or messenger may be commanded to search suspected places, without evidence of the fact committed, or to seize any person or persons not named, whose offences are not particularly described and supported by evidence, are dangerous to liberty, and ought not to be granted.

12. That no freeman ought to be taken, imprisoned, or disseized of his freehold, liberties, or privileges, or outlawed, or exiled, or in any manner destroyed or deprived of his life, liberty, or property, but by the law of the land.

13. That every freeman, restrained of his liberty, is entitled to a remedy, to enquire into the lawfulness thereof, and to remove the same, if unlawful; and that such remedy ought not to be denied or delayed.

14. That in all controversies at law, respecting property, the ancient mode of trial by jury is one of the best securities of the rights of the people, and ought to remain sacred and inviolable.

15. That the freedom of the press is one of the great bulwarks of liberty, and therefore ought never to be restrained.

16. That the people of this State ought not to be taxed, or made subject to payment of any impost or duty, without the consent of themselves, or their representatives, in General Assembly, freely given.

17. That the people have a right to bear arms for the defence of the State; and as

---

[3] J. G. M. Ramsey (ed.), *The Annals of Tennessee* (Philadelphia, 1853), pp. 325–328.

standing armies, in time of peace, are dangerous to liberty, they ought not to be kept up; and that the military should be kept under strict subordination to, and governed by, the civil power.

18. That the people have a right to assemble together, to consult for their common good, to instruct their representatives, and to apply to the Legislature for redress of grievances.

19. That all men have a natural and unalienable right to worship Almighty God according to the dictates of their own consciences.

20. That, for redress of grievances, and for amending and strengthening the laws, elections ought to be often held.

21. That a frequent recurrence to fundamental principles is absolutely necessary to preserve the blessings of liberty.

22. That no hereditary emoluments, privileges, or honours, ought to be granted or conferred in this State.

23. That perpetuities and monopolies are contrary to the genius of a free State, and ought not to be allowed.

24. That retrospective laws, punishing acts committed before the existence of such laws, and by them only declared criminal, are oppressive, unjust, and incompatible with liberty; therefore no *ex post facto* law ought to be made.

The Constitution or Form of Government Agreed to and Resolved upon by the Representatives of the Freemen of the State of Frankland, elected and chosen for that particular purpose, in Convention assembled, at Greeneville, the 14th November, 1785.

This State shall be called the *Commonwealth of Frankland*, and shall be governed by a General Assembly of the representatives of the freemen of the same, a Governor and Council, and proper courts of justice, in the manner following, *viz:*

Section 1. The supreme legislative power shall be vested in a single House of Representatives of the freemen of the commonwealth of Frankland.

Sec. 2. The House of Representatives of the freemen of this State shall consist of persons most noted for wisdom and virtue, to be chosen equally and adequately according to the number of freemen in the commonwealth; provided when the number amounts to one hundred it shall never exceed it, nor be ever afterwards reduced lower than eighty, and every county shall annually send the number apportioned to it by the General Assembly.

Sec. 3. No person shall be eligible to, or hold a seat in, the House of Representatives of the freemen of this commonwealth, unless he actually resides in, and owns land in the county to the quantity of one hundred acres, or to the value of fifty pounds, and is of the full age of twenty-one years. And no person shall be eligible or capable to serve in this or any other office in the civil department of this State, who is of an immoral character, or guilty of such flagrant enormities as drunkenness, gaming, profane swearing, lewdness, sabbath breaking, and such like; or who will, either in word or writing, deny any of the following propositions, *viz:*

1st. That there is one living and true God, the Creator and Governor of the universe.

2d. That there is a future state of rewards and punishments.

3d. That the scriptures of the Old and New Testaments are given by divine inspiration.

4th. That there are three divine persons in the Godhead, co-equal and co-essential.

And no person shall be a member of the House of Representatives, who holds a lucrative office either under this or other States;

that is, has a fixed salary or fees from the State, or is in actual military service and claiming daily pay, or minister of the gospel, or attorney at law, or doctor of physic.

Sec. 4. Every free male inhabitant of this State, of the age of *twenty-one* years, who shall have resided in this State six months immediately preceding the day of election, shall have a vote in electing all officers chosen by the people, in the county where he resides.

Sec. 5. The House of Representatives of this commonwealth shall be styled the *General Assembly of the Representatives of the Freemen of Frankland*; and shall have power to choose their own Speaker, and all other officers, Treasurer, Secretary of State, Superior Judges, Auditors, members to Congress. They shall have power to sit on their own adjournments; to prepare bills, and to enact them into laws; to judge of the elections of, and qualifications of, their own members. They may expel a member, but not a second time for the same cause; they may administer oaths on the examination of witnesses, redress grievances, impeach State criminals, grant charters of incorporation, constitute towns, cities, boroughs, and counties, and shall have all other powers necessary for the Legislature of a free State or commonwealth. But they shall have no power to add, alter, abolish, or infringe any part of the Constitution.

Two-thirds of the whole members elected shall constitute a House, (and the expense from the appointed time 'till they make a House, shall be laid on absentees, without a reasonable excuse,) and having met and chosen their Speaker, shall, each of them, before they proceed to business, take and subscribe, as well the oath of fidelity and allegiance hereafter directed, as the following oath—

"I, A. B., do swear, That, as a member of this Assembly, I will not propose or assent to any bill or resolution, which shall appear to me injurious to the people, nor do, nor consent to any act or thing whatever, that shall have a tendency to lessen or abridge the rights and privileges as declared in the Constitution of this State; but will in all things conduct myself as a faithful honest representative and guardian of the people, according to the best of my judgment and abilities. *So help me God.*"

The doors of the house in which the representatives of the freemen of this State shall sit in General Assembly, shall be and remain open, for the admission of all persons who shall behave decently; except when the good of the commonwealth requires them to be shut.

Sec. 6. The votes and proceedings of the General Assembly shall be printed weekly, during their sitting, with the Yeas and Nays on any question, vote, or resolution, (except when the vote is taken by ballot,) when any two members require it; and every member shall have a right to insert the reasons of his vote upon the Journals, if he desires it.

Sec. 7. That the laws, before they are enacted, may be more maturely considered, and the danger of hasty and injudicious determinations as much as possible prevented, all Bills of a public and general nature shall be printed for the consideration of the people, before they are read in the General Assembly the last time, for debate and amendment; and, except on occasions of sudden necessity, shall not be passed into laws before the next session of the Assembly: And, for the more perfect satisfaction of the public, the reasons and motives for making such laws shall be fully and clearly expressed in the preambles.

Sec. 8. The style of the laws of this commonwealth shall be, *Be it enacted, and it is hereby enacted, by the Representatives of the Freeman of the Commonwealth of Frankland, in General Assembly, and by the authority of the same.* And the General Assembly shall affix their Seal to every Bill as soon as it is enacted into a law; which seal shall be kept by the Assembly, and shall be called the *Seal of the Laws of Frankland,* and shall not be used for any other purpose.

Sec. 9. As in every free government the people have a right of free suffrage for all officers of government that can be chosen by the people, the freemen of this State shall elect Governor and Counsellors, Justices of the Peace for each county, and Coroner or Coroners, Sheriffs, and all other such officers, except such as the Assembly are empowered to choose.

Sec. 10. All the able bodied men in this State shall be trained for its defence, under such regulations, restrictions and exceptions as the General Assembly shall direct by law, preserving always to the people, from the age of sixteen, the right of choosing their colonels, and all other officers under that rank, in such manner and as often as shall be by the same laws directed.

FORMULATING A WESTERN POLICY: LAND SALES

The State of Frankland—or Franklin as it was soon called—was short-lived, for conflicting factions there created such turmoil that North Carolina revoked its cession. Not until 1789, when most land in Tennessee had been sold to the financial benefit of the state, was title finally transferred to Congress. In the meantime other northern states had ceded their lands, and other southern states followed, although Georgia did not complete its cession until 1802. Long before this Congress turned to the task of selling and governing its princely domain. Sales came first, for the new government was desperate for funds. The system of survey and sale that was adopted represented a compromise between the haphazard southern custom of occupying territory before it was surveyed and the orderly but cumbersome northern system by which areas were divided into rectangular lots and then sold. This combination made the Ordinance of 1785, which was adopted on May 20 of that year, one of the most enduring measures ever enacted by Congress:[4]

The Surveyors, as they are respectively qualified, shall proceed to divide the said territory into townships of six miles square, by lines running due north and south, and others crossing these at right angles, as near as may be, unless where the boundaries of the late Indian purchases may render the same impracticable, . . .

The first line, running due north and south as aforesaid, shall begin on the river Ohio, at a point that shall be found to be due north from the western termination of a line, which has been run as the southern boundary of the state of Pennsylvania; and the first line, running east and west, shall begin at the same point, and shall extend throughout the whole territory. Provided, that nothing herein shall be construed, as fixing the western boundary of the state of Pennsylvania. The geographer shall designate the townships, or fractional parts of townships, by numbers progressively from south to north; always beginning each range with number one; and the ranges shall be distinguished by their progressive numbers to the westward. The first range, extending from the Ohio to the lake Erie, being marked number one. The Geographer shall personally attend to the running of the first east and west line; and shall take the latitude of the ex-

---

[4] John C. Fitzpatrick (ed.), *Journals of the Continental Congress, 1774–1789* (Washington, 1933), vol. 28, pp. 375–378.

tremes of the first north and south line, and of the mouths of the principal rivers. . . .

The parts of the townships respectively, shall be marked by subdivisions into lots of one mile square, or 640 acres, in the same direction as the external lines, and numbered from 1 to 36; always beginning the succeeding range of the lots with the number next to that with which the preceding one concluded. . . .

The board of treasury shall transmit a copy of the original plats, previously noting thereon the townships, and fractional parts of townships, which shall have fallen to the several states, by the distribution aforesaid, to the Commissioners of the loan office of the several states, who, after giving notice . . . shall proceed to sell the townships or fractional parts of townships, at public vendue, in the following manner, viz.: The township, or fractional part of a township, N. 1, in the first range, shall be sold entire; and N. 2, in the same range, by lots; and thus in alternate order through the whole of the first range . . . provided, that none of the lands, within the said territory, be sold under the price of one dollar the acre, to be paid in specie, or loan office certificates, reduced to specie value, by the scale of depreciation, or certificates of liquidated debts of the United States, including interest, besides the expense of the survey and other charges thereon, which are hereby rated at thirty six dollars the township, . . . on failure of which payment the said lands shall again be offered for sale.

There shall be reserved for the United States out of every township the four lots being numbered 8, 11, 26, 29, and out of every fractional part of a township, so many lots of the same numbers as shall be found thereon, for future sale. There shall be reserved the lot N. 16, of every township, for the maintenance of public schools within the said township; also one third part of all gold, silver, lead and copper mines, to be sold, or otherwise disposed of as Congress shall hereafter direct.

LAND SPECULATION AND WESTERN POLICY: THE OHIO COMPANY

Congressional hopes of large land sales in the West did not materialize, partly because the orderly system of surveys established in the Ordinance of 1785 required time for completion, partly because the sizable minimum amount purchasable eliminated individual settlers as purchasers, and partly because Indian unrest on the frontiers kept would-be frontiersmen at home. So when a group of speculators expressed interest in buying a sizable tract in the Ohio country—even at a price well below that established by law—Congress was willing to listen. The adventurers who made the offer were New Englanders led by Brigadier General Rufus Putnam. Putnam knew that Revolutionary veterans had been paid for their military services in nearly worthless government securities, which still had to be accepted by Congress at face value. Why not pool a million dollars worth of these, and buy a million acres of land in eastern Ohio for a colony? This was the dream that led Putnam to issue an invitation to veterans to meet at Boston's Bunch of Grapes Tavern in March 1786. There they adopted the "articles of agreement" that gave birth to the Ohio Company:[5]

—On the first Day of March One thousand and seven hundred & Eighty Six Convened at the Bunch of Grapes Tavern in Boston as Delegates from several of the Coun-

---

[5] Archer B. Hulbert (ed.), *The Records of the Original Proceedings of the Ohio Company* (Marietta, Ohio: Marietta Historical Commission, 1917), vol. 1, pp. 4–9.

ties of the Commonwealth of Massachusetts to consider of the Expediency of forming an Association, or company to purchase lands and make a settlement in the Western Country, . . .

Elected General Rufus Putnam Chairman of the Convention and Maj. Winthrop Sargent Clerk—From the very pleasing Description of the Western Country given by Generals Putnam & Tupper and others it appearing expedient to form a settlement there, a Motion was made for chusing a Committee to prepare the Draught or Plan of an association into a Company to the said Purpose, for the Inspection and Approbation of this Convention—Resolved in the affirmative.—Also Resolved that this Committee shall consist of five.—General Putnam Mr. Cutler—Colonel Brooks, Major Sargent & Capt. Cushing were elected.—

Adjourned to half after 3 o'clock Thursday.—

Thursday 2d March—Convened agreably to adjournment at the Bunch of Grapes Tavern—& further adjourned till tomorrow morning half past 8 o'clock—then to meet at Bracketts Sign of Oliver Cromwell in School Street.—

Friday 3d March met agreably to adjournment and the Committee for Preparing a draught or Plan of association Reported that they had gone through the Business, and layd their Proceedings before the Convention, in form following—

Articles of agreement entered into by the Subscribers, for constituting an association, by the name of the Ohio Company.

The design of this association is to raise a fund in Continental Certificates, for the sole purpose, and to be appropriated to the entire use of purchasing Lands in the Western territory (belonging to the United States) for the benefit of the Company and to promote a settlement in that Country.—

That the fund shall not exceed One Million of Dollars, in Continental Specie Certificates, exclusive of One years Interest due thereon (except as hereafter provided) and that each share or subscription shall consist of One thousand Dollars as aforesaid, and also ten Dollars in gold or silver, to be paid into the hands of such agents as the Subscribers may elect.—

That whole fund of Certificates raised by this Association, except, One years Interest due thereon, mentioned under the first article, shall be apply'd to the purchase of Lands in some one of the proposed States, north westerly of the River Ohio, as soon as those lands are surveyed, and exposed for Sale by the Commissioners of Congress, according to the Ordinance of that Honourable Body, passed 20th May, 1785, or on any other plan that may be adopted by Congress not less advantageous to the Company. The One years interest shall be applied to the purpose of making a settlement in the Country, and assisting those who may be otherwise unable to remove themselves thither: The Gold and Silver is for defraying the expenses of those persons employed as Agents in purchasing the land and other contingent Charges that may arise in the prosecution of the business: The surplus (if any) to be appropriated as the One year's interest on the Certificates. . . .

That no person shall be permitted to hold more than five shares in the companies funds, and no subscription for less than a full share will be admitted; but this is not meant to prevent those who cannot, or chuse not to adventure a full share from associating amongst themselves, and by one of their number subscribing the sum required.—

That the directors shall have the sole disposal of the company's fund, for the purposes before mentioned: that they shall by themselves or such person or persons as they may think proper to intrust with the business, purchase lands for the benefit of the company, where, and in such way, either at publick or private sale, as they shall judge will be most advantageous to the company; they shall also direct the application of the one year's interest, and Gold and Silver mentioned in the first article, to the purposes mentioned under the 2nd article, in such way and manner as they shall think proper; for those purposes the directors shall draw on the treasurer from time to time, making themselves accountable for the application of the monies agreeably to this association.—

THE OHIO COMPANY SECURES ITS LANDS

The million dollars, even in depreciated securities, proved impossible to raise, but when $250,000 had been subscribed the Ohio Company dispatched its agent Reverend Manasseh Cutler to New York, where Congress was meeting, to negotiate a sale. Congressmen were accustomed to hard-bargaining New Englanders but Cutler's proposal went a little far; he asked for a million acres in the valley of the Muskingum River at a price considerably less than the dollar an acre set by the Ordinance of 1785—and with payment in depreciated securities. While Congress hesitated, Cutler received a call from Colonel William Duer, who explained that he represented some of the leading financial interests in New York—and was also secretary of the Board of Treasury which handled land sales. What happened was described by Cutler in his diary:[6]

Friday, July 20. This morning the Secretary of Congress furnished me with the Ordinance of yesterday, which states the conditions of a contract, but on terms to which I shall by no means accede. Informed the Committee of Congress that I could not contract on the terms proposed; should prefer purchasing lands of some of the States, who would give incomparably better terms, and therefore proposed to leave the City immediately. They appeared to be very sorry no better terms were offered, and insisted on my not thinking of leaving Congress until another attempt was made. I told them I saw no prospect of a contract, and wished to spend no more time and money on a business so unpromising. They assured me I had many friends in Congress who would make every exertion in my favor; that it was an object of great magnitude, and [I] must not expect to accomplish it in less than two or three months. If I desired it, they would take the matter up that day on different ground, and did not doubt they should still obtain terms agreeably to my wishes. Colonel Duer came to me with proposals from a number of the principal characters in the city, to extend our contract, and take in another Company, but that it should be kept a profound secret. He explained the plan they had concerted, and offered me generous conditions, if I would accomplish the business for them. The plan struck me agreeably. Sargent insisted on my undertaking, and both urged me not to think of giving the matter up so soon. I was convinced it was best for me to hold up the idea of giving up a contract with Congress, and making a contract with some of the States, which I did in the strongest terms, and represented to the Committee, and to Duer and Sargent, the difficulties I saw in the way, and the improbability of closing a bargain when we were so far apart; and told them I conceived it not worth while to say any thing further to Congress on the subject. This appeared to have the effect I wished. The

---
[6] William P. Cutler and Julia P. Cutler (eds.), *Life, Journals and Correspondence of Rev. Manasseh Cutler, LL.D.* (Cincinnati, 1888), vol. 1, pp. 294–296.

Committee were mortified, and did not seem to know what to say, but still urged another attempt. I left them in this state, but afterward explained my views to Duer and Sargent, who fully approved my plan. Promised Duer to consider his proposals.

We had agreed last evening to make a party to Brookline, on Long Island, which is a small village opposite New York, and divided only by a ferry across East River. Duer, Webb, Hammond, Sargent, and others were of the party. When we landed, we ordered a dinner of fried oysters at the Stone House Tavern. We took a walk on the high lands, and viewed several of the old forts erected by the British at the expense of immense labor. Here we had a fine prospect of New York, the shipping in the harbor, and of Staten Island. We dined at four. Our dinner was elegant. Oysters were cooked in every possible form, but the fried were most delicious. I spent the evening (closeted) with Colonel Duer, and agreed to purchase more land, if terms can be obtained, for another Company, which will probably forward the negotiations. Bill, 4s. 6d.

Saturday, July 21. Several members of Congress called on me early this morning. They discovered much anxiety about a contract, and assured me that Congress, on finding I was determined not to accept their terms, and had proposed leaving the City, had discovered a much more favorable disposition, and believed if I renewed my request I might obtain conditions as reasonable as I desired. I was very indifferent, and talked much of the advantages of a contract with some of the States. This I found had the desired effect. At length told them if Congress would accede to the terms I had proposed, I would extend the purchase to the tenth township from the Ohio, and to the Scioto inclusively, by which Congress would pay near four millions of the national debt;

that our intention was an actual, a large, and immediate settlement of the most robust and industrious people in America; and that it would be made systematically, which must instantly enhance the value of federal lands, and prove an important acquisition to Congress. On those terms I would renew the negotiations, if Congress was disposed to take the matter up again.

THE ORDINANCE OF 1787: GOVERNMENT FOR THE WEST

The resulting shady agreement launched one of the most spectacular land-jobbing schemes in history. It was agreed that the Ohio Company would ask for 1,500,000 acres at a price of $1,000,000. It would, in addition, request 5,000,000 acres for Colonel Duer and his associates, who would organize as the Scioto Company. For this favor they would loan the Ohio Company the money needed for a down payment on its grant. The Reverend Mr. Cutler had driven a hard bargain—more than a million acres of the best land in the West at about 8 cents an acre in cash, for all transactions were in depreciated securities—but he was still unsatisfied. The tract would be worthless, he told Congress, until some form of government was provided for the West. Colonists would hesitate to go there unless assured the eventual right to govern themselves. Under his prodding, Congress adopted a measure that it had long been considering, the Ordinance of 1787, or Northwest Ordinance:[7]

So soon as there shall be five thousand free male inhabitants of full age in the dis-

---

[7] Roscoe R. Hill (ed.), *Journals of the Continental Congress, 1774–1789* (Washington, 1936), vol. 32, pp. 337–343.

trict, upon giving proof thereof to the governor, they shall receive authority, with time and place, to elect representatives from their counties or townships to represent them in the general assembly, *Provided*, That, for every five hundred free male inhabitants, there shall be one representative, and so on progressively with the number of free male inhabitants shall the right of representation increase, until the number of representatives shall amount to twenty five; after which, the number and proportion of representatives shall be regulated by the legislature; *Provided*, That no person be eligible or qualified to act as a representative unless he shall have been a citizen of one of the United States three years, and be a resident in the district, or unless he shall have resided in the district, three years; and, in either case, shall likewise hold in his own right, in fee simple, two hundred acres of land within the same; *Provided, also*, That a freehold in fifty acres of land in the district having been a citizen of one of the states, and being resident in the district or the like freehold and two years residence in the district, shall be necessary to qualify a man as an elector of a representative.

The representatives thus elected, shall serve for the term of two years; and, in case of the death of a representative, or removal from office, the governor shall issue a writ to the county or township for which he was a member, to elect another in his stead, to serve for the residue of the term.

The general assembly or legislature shall consist of the governor, legislative council, and a house of representatives. The legislative council shall consist of five members, to continue in Office five years, unless sooner removed by Congress any three of whom to be a quorum and the members of the Councill shall be nominated and appointed in the following manner, to wit; As soon as representatives shall be elected, the Governor shall appoint a time and place for them to meet together, and when met they shall nominate ten persons residents in the district and each possessed of a freehold in five hundred acres of Land and return their names to Congress; five of whom Congress shall appoint and commission to serve as aforesaid; and whenever a vacancy shall happen in the council, by death or removal from office, the house of representatives shall nominate two persons qualified as aforesaid, for each vacancy, and return their names to Congress, one of whom Congress shall apoint and commisson for the residue of the term, and every five years, four months at least before the expiration of the time of service of the Members of Council, the said house shall nominate ten persons, qualified as aforesaid, and return their names to Congress, five of whom Congress shall appoint and commission to serve as Members of the council five years, unless sooner removed. And the Governor, legislative council, and house of representatives, shall have authority to make laws in all cases, for the good government of the district, not repugnant to the principles and Articles in this Ordinance established and declared. And all bills having passed by a majority in the house, and by a majority in the council, shall be referred to the Governor for his assent; but no bill or legislative Act whatever, shall be of any force without his assent. The governor shall have power to convene, prorogue, and dissolve the general assembly, when in his opinion, it shall be expedient.

[The Ordinance of 1787 also contained a Bill of Rights that is a landmark in the history of individual liberty:]

It is hereby ordained and declared by the authority aforesaid, That the following articles shall be considered as Articles of compact between the Original States and the people and States in the said territory and forever remain unalterable, unless by common consent, *to wit,*

Article the First. No person demeaning himself in a peaceable and orderly manner shall ever be molested on account of his mode of worship or religious sentiments in the said territory.

Article the Second. The Inhabitants of the said territory shall always be entitled to the benefits of the writ of habeas corpus, and of the trial by Jury; of a proportionate representation of the people in the legislature, and of judicial proceedings according to the course of the common law; all persons shall be bailable, unless for capital offences, where the proof shall be evident or the presumption great; all fines shall be moderate; and no cruel or unusual punishments shall be inflicted; no man shall be deprived of his liberty or property, but by the judgment of his peers or the law of the land; and, should the public exigencies make it necessary for the common preservation to take any persons property, or to demand his particular services, full compensation shall be made for the same; and in the just preservation of rights and property it is understood and declared; that no law ought ever to be made, or have force in the said territory, that shall in any manner whatever, interfere with or affect private contracts or engagements, bona fide, and without fraud previously formed.

Article the Third. Religion, morality, *and knowledge being necessary to good government and the happiness of mankind,* Schools and the means of education shall forever be encouraged. The utmost good faith shall always be observed toward the Indians, their lands and property shall never be taken from them without their consent; and, in their property, rights, and liberty, they shall never be invaded or disturbed, unless in just and lawful wars authorized by Congress; but laws founded in justice and humanity shall from time to time be made, for preventing wrongs being done to them, and for preserving peace and friendship with them.

Article the Fourth. The said territory, and the States which may be formed therein, shall forever remain a part of this Confederacy of the United States of America, subject to the Articles of Confederation, and to such alterations therein as shall be constitutionally made; and to all the Acts and Ordinances of the United States in Congress assembled, comformable thereto. The inhabitants and settlers in the said territory, shall be subject to pay a part of the federal debts contracted or to be contracted, and a proportional part of the expences of Government, to be apportioned on them by Congress, according to the same common rule and measure by which apportionments thereof shall be made on the other States; and the taxes for paying their proportion shall be laid and levied by the authority and direction of the legislatures of the district or districts or new States, as in the original States, within the time agreed upon by the United States in Congress assembled. The legislatures of those districts or new States, shall never interfere with the primary disposal of the Soil by the United States in Congress assembled, nor with any regulations Congress may find necessary for securing the title in such soil to the bona fide purchasers. No tax shall be imposed on lands the property of the United States; and in no case shall non resident proprietors be taxed higher than residents....

Article the Fifth. There shall be formed in the said territory, not less than three nor more than five states....

Article the Sixth. There shall be neither Slavery nor involuntary Servitude in the said territory otherwise than in the punishment of crimes, whereof the party shall have been duly convicted; Provided, always, That any person escaping into the same, from whom labor or service is lawfully claimed in any one of the original States, such fugitive may be lawfully reclaimed and conveyed to the person claiming his or her labor or service as aforesaid.

The Ordinance of 1787 was too conservative for western tastes, denying complete self-rule during the territorial period, but it did assure orderly government in the Old Northwest. So migration began. In the spring of 1788 recruits under the Ohio Company banner laid out the town of Marietta, soon to be followed by a badly managed colony of French innocents imported by the Scioto Company who founded Gallipolis. Another speculator, John Cleves Symmes, a New Jersey politician, obtained lands from Congress for an outpost on the site of Cincinnati. Others drifted in, until by the end of the 1780s a thin band of settlements extended along the north bank of the Ohio River from Marietta to the Great Miami River.

Migration lagged, however, for before life in the Ohio country could be made safe, pressing diplomatic problems had to be solved. The Indians there were resentful and restless, eager to take to the warpath against intruders on their lands. This was bad enough, but the situation was made worse by the meddling of European powers. Britain, France, and Spain were all eager to re-establish empires in the American West, knowing that the new government was too feeble to resist, and all were capable of using the Indians as pawns for their ambitions. England posed the most immediate threat, for at the close of the Revolution it retained possession of a string of armed posts along the Canadian border—at Oswego, Niagara, Detroit, and Mackinac—where traders and military men could seek red-skinned allies for their country's expansionistic programs.

THE DEFEAT OF GENERAL ARTHUR ST. CLAIR

The British were too wary to incite open warfare, but the activities of agents who urged the Indians to unite in a confederation that would hold back the Americans convinced many tribesmen that when war began they would again fight side-by-side with English regulars. Skirmishing began in 1789 after a series of treaty-making efforts failed and was heightened by Kentuckians who raided north of the Ohio River. The new government under President George Washington realized that military force was necessary and, in 1790, dispatched an expedition northward under the aging Josiah Harmar. When this met with disaster, a second force was hurriedly recruited and entrusted to Governor Arthur St. Clair of the Northwest Territory. With three thousand men St. Clair marched north from Cincinnati during the autumn of 1791, pausing on the way to build a chain of outposts. By November 3, 1791, the army was at a small tributary of the Wabash River, in the heart of the Indian country. What happened next was described by an officer in St. Clair's command, Winthrop Sargent:[8]

In the common order of duty the troops had been paraded every morning ten minutes before daylight, and continued under

---

[8] "Winthrop Sargent's Diary While with General Arthur St. Clair's Expedition Against the Indians," in *Ohio Archaeological and Historical Publications* (Columbus, 1925), vol. 33, pp. 258–262.

arms till near sunrise, but for the purpose of collecting the horses which were to be sent back to Fort Jefferson for ammunition and stores, and to refresh the men who were to be put generally on duty in erecting some works of deposit at this place, they were dismissed at an earlier hour than usual. It was in this opportunity that I visited the militia camp and was informed that the parties to have been ordered out had been altogether neglected. Colonel Oldham mentioned to me the loss of all his own horses, and the apprehension that we must have suffered much in this way, but gave me no reason to suppose that he had made any discoveries which might lead him to suppose the enemy were in force to fight us.

Immediately upon my return to headquarters, and about half an hour before sun-rising, the attack commenced upon the militia. Their position appeared to me (and I had reconnoitered it well) to have been a very defensible one. For four hundred yards in front the wood was open and afforded no cover to the enemy; it could hardly be supposed an attempt would be made upon their rear, for in that case the Indians must have been exposed to two fires—a situation they extremely dread—and besides, the bottom land in that direction, and which was just at the back of their tents, fell suddenly to near thirty feet, and men stepping off only a little distance from it must have put themselves under good cover. I regretted to the General upon the preceding evening that we could not occupy this ground, but the troops, much fatigued, had at that time got their camp, and it was too late to alter their disposition.

The firing of the enemy was preceded for about five minutes by the Indian yell, the first I ever heard; not terrible, as has been represented, but more resembling an infinitude of horse-bells suddenly opening to you than any other sound I could compare it to. The resistance of the militia deserves not the name of defense, but should be branded as the most ignominious flight. Except a very faint and feeble fire from their small guards, I can not learn that there was any opposition, or even to show of it. But dashing "helter skelter" into our camp, they threw the battalions, not then quite formed, into some confusion. And not conceiving even this a place of sufficient security, they broke through the second line, carrying with them a few men of Gaither's, and but for a fire they received from the enemy and which drove them back, there is no doubt but they would have been off. During the whole action their conduct was cowardly in the most shameful degree, a few instances to the contrary excepted.

Close upon the heels of the flying militia followed the Indians, who for a moment seemed as if determined to enter our camp with them; but the complexion of the troops, drawn up in tolerable order and with fixed bayonets, cooled their ardour a little, and they were fain to cover themselves behind logs and bushes at the distance of about seventy yards. From the very early attack upon the left of the front, and through the whole of the second line, there can be little doubt but that we were completely surrounded at the time of the first onset upon the militia. And though it may be impossible to ascertain with precision the numbers of the enemy, yet if we estimate them at upwards of a thousand, I am persuaded we shall not overrate them. Taking this for granted, and when it is known that our whole force (the militia excepted) amounted only to thirteen hundred and eighty men—eighty of whom were officers' servants, who are very seldom, if ever, brought into action—and that the various guards, equal to two hundred and twenty by being made up in the general detail from the corps, and dispersed in the suddenness of the attack (never after to be effectually collected), reducing our efficient numbers to one thousand and eighty of raw and undisciplined troops, ignorant totally of the Indian and indeed all other mode of fighting—for the whole army was constituted by new raised troops, engaged only for six months, the Second Regiment excepted, and this also was but of the moment, just brought into the field, without time for instruction and never having fired even a blank cartridge—whoever, I say, shall be acquainted with all these circumstances must acknowledge that we entertained an unequal war and long maintained the contest, too soon rendered doubtful by the superiority of the Indian mode of fighting. For though very early in the action we lost considerable number of officers, yet it was not until a severe service of more than two hours that a retreat was thought of. . . .

In this desperate situation of affairs, when even hope, that last consolation of the wretched, had failed the army, that the General took the resolution of abandoning his camp and attempting a retreat. There was a mere possibility that some of the troops might be brought off, though it could not be counted on among the probabilities. But there was no alternative. The men must either retreat, or be sacrificed without resistance, as the enemy were shooting them down at pleasure from behind trees and the most secure covers, whilst they could scarcely be led to discharge a single gun with effect.

Upon this occasion very extraordinary exertions were made to draw together men sufficient to give the appearance of efficiency. Feints were made in various directions and different parts of the encampment, and whilst they served in some measure to produce the first effect, they operated to deceive the enemy.

Having thus collected in one body the greatest part of the troops and such of our wounded as could possibly hobble along with us, we pushed out from the left of the rear line, sacrificing our artillery and baggage; and with them, we were compelled to leave some of our wounded.

In about one mile and a half, we gained the road, the enemy scarcely pursuing beyond that distance, and annoying us very little on our retreat. There can be no doubt they had it in their power to have cut us off, almost to a man; it is probable, however, that they might have been suspicious of the movement, and therefore thought it most eligible to embrace the opportunity to plunder, before possibly it could be snatched from them. Those unfortunate men also whom we were compelled to leave behind must for a time have engaged their attention. Although there were but a very few of them—all that were able to walk being brought off, and some of the officers on horses—yet the sympathy for those few is sufficient to torture the mind of sensibility. The soldier who has not been compelled to sacrifice his brave companion to all the torments which the most infernal invention can devise, knows not the extent of military sufferings, and is happily a stranger to the most agonizing motives of vengeance. But the determined resolution of our unfortunate friends (incapacitated from wounds to quit the field, yet who, as soon as the fate of the day became uncertain, charged their pieces with a coolness and deliberation that reflects the highest honor upon their memory) and the firing of musketry in camp after we quitted it, leaves us very little room for doubt that their latest efforts were professionally brave and that where they could pull a trigger they avenged themselves.

It is not probable that many of the Indians fell this day, though there are persons who pretend to have seen great numbers dead. I had myself an opportunity of making observations, but they were not correspondent with this assertion.

The conduct of the army after quitting the ground was in a most supreme degree disgraceful. Arms, ammunition and accoutrements were almost all thrown away, and even the officers in some instances divested themselves of their fusees and C——, exemplifying by this conduct a kind of authority for the most precipitate and ignominious flight.

It was half an hour past nine o'clock when we quitted the field of action, and by seven in the evening we had reached Fort Jefferson, a distance of twenty-nine miles.

WAYNE'S VICTORY AND THE TREATY OF GREENVILLE

St. Clair's crushing defeat greatly worsened the American position in the Ohio country, for the Indians were now confident and boldly predicted that the "Long Knives" would be driven back across the Ohio. This the United States would never accept. Plans were at once launched for a new military expedition, this one led by the experienced General Anthony Wayne. All through the winter of 1793–1794, Wayne drilled his army in the techniques of wilderness warfare. As he did so, the British agents at Detroit also prepared for the final act in their drama. Indian chiefs were entertained and supplied, encouraging speeches were given, and a new post, Fort Miami, was built on undisputably American territory on the lower Maumee River. These warlike activities meant that Wayne's expedition might launch an international conflict when it advanced in the summer of 1794, but when it met the Indians at the Battle of Fallen Timbers (August 20, 1794), the British did not dare come to the aid of their allies. The result was an American victory that ended Indian resistance in the Northwest for a generation. Realizing this, Wayne called the Indian chiefs together and on September 12 mixed threats with cajolery as he urged them to accept peace:[9]

Brothers—The President of the United States, General Washington, the Great Chief of America, once more speaks to you thro' me, his principal Warrior Major General and Commander in Chief of the Federal Army, and commissioner Plenipotentiary for settling a permanent and lasting Peace with all, and every Tribe or Tribes, Nations or Nation of Indians, North of the Ohio.

Brothers,—Summon your utmost powers of attention, and listen to the voice of Truth and Peace.

It is now one moon since I addressed you by a Flag from this place, inviting you to appoint Deputies, to meet me and my Army without delay, between this place and Roche de Bout, in order to settle the preliminaries of a lasting Peace. I also informed you that the United States loved Mercy and Kindness, more than War and Desolation. I likewise requested you to be no longer deceived, by the false promises and language of the bad white people, at the foot of the Rapids, but you were Deaf to this request and the voice of Peace, you again took the advice of those bad white men, and in place of meeting me as friends you preferred War; and instead of the Calumet of Peace, you suddenly presented from your Secret Coverts the Scalping Knife, and Tommahawk; but in return for the few *drops* of Blood we lost upon that occasion we caused *Rivers* of

---

[9] "Address of Wayne to the Indians, Grand Glaize, September 12, 1794," in *Historical Collections of the Michigan Pioneer and Historical Society* (Lansing, 1888), vol. 12, pp. 143–144.

yours to flow. I told you that the Arm of United States was strong, you only felt the weight of its little finger.—Informed you that the British had neither the power nor inclination to protect you, you have severely experienced the truth of that assertion; Be therefore no longer blind to your own true interests and happiness; but listen to the Voice of Peace, and permit me now to draw a veil over the late transaction and to bury in deep oblivion, and to obliterate from the mind all remembrance of past Injuries.

Eight moons are now passed since you sent Stephen Young, George White Eyes, and another Warrior with a flag to Greenville, accompanied by a Mr. Robert Willson as your Interpreter in order to know upon what terms I would consent to a general Peace with the Delawares, Shawanoes & Miamis &c I returned for answer that the Ears & heart of the President of the United States, General Washington, were ever open to the voice of Peace, & that he had instructed me his Chief Warrior to listen to that Welcome voice from whatever Quarter it Came, provided it was from proper authority & from the heart, The terms mentioned, were equitable, clear and implicit.

Brothers, If you now wish for Peace & to be restored to the possession of your cultivated lands and hunting grounds, come forward, with all the American Prisoners now in your hands, and in exchange, you shall receive all such Prisoners as I have, belonging to your nations.

Appoint a number of your Sachems, and Chief Warriors to attend them, bring with you some of your most Confidential Interpreters and I hereby pledge my Sacred honor, for your safe return, & for your kind treatment while with me.

Open your minds freely to me, and let us try to agree upon such fair, & equitable terms of Peace as shall be for the true interest and happiness of both the white, & red people; and that you may in future plant your Corn, & hunt in peace and safety, and that by an interchange of kindness and good offices towards each other we may cement that Brotherly love and affection, as shall endure to the end of time.

The Commanding Officer at this place has orders to receive and treat you with kindness, and to send with you one of his officers to Conduct you safe to Head Quarters, where you shall receive a sincere Welcome from your friend and Brother

The Indians had no choice; a year later their representatives signed the Treaty of Greenville, whereby they surrendered much of Ohio and a triangle in southeastern Indiana to the United States. At about the same time word arrived from abroad of Jay's Treaty (1794) in which Britain agreed to evacuate the northwestern posts by June 1, 1796. This diplomatic success, coupled with Wayne's victory, ended Indian resistance in the Northwest for fifteen years.

LAND SPECULATION
ON THE SOUTHERN FRONTIER

Not so the Southwest. There 14,000 warriors disputed the American advance, ably backed by Spanish officials in New Orleans and the Floridas. Moreover, Spain controlled the mouth of the Mississippi and could at any time close that stream to navigation by the Americans who lived in Kentucky, the Nashville and Holston settlements of Tennessee, and the Georgia backcountry. That was an effective weapon, for the 120,000 frontiersmen who lived in those outposts could be strangled economically if their exports were blocked. By threatening to use its control of the river, Spain hoped to force the United States to surrender its claims to the

"Yazoo Strip," a disputed area lying between the southern borders of the United States and West Florida, which was claimed by both countries under a poorly drawn clause of the Treaty of Paris.

This was a powder-keg situation, and an explosion was not long in coming. It was touched off by land speculators. To these bold adventurers, all the Southwest was fair game, even though occupied by Indians, Frenchmen, or Spaniards. Companies to secure lands there began blossoming in the early months of 1784, but not until a year later did they cause a major conflict. At that time Thomas Green and other southern land jobbers goaded the Georgia legislature into creating the whole region west to the Mississippi into Bourbon County, which was thrown open to sale. That this measure was planned by speculators, written by speculators, and designed solely to benefit speculators was obvious to all, even to Americans living in Bourbon County. One, John Gordon, a resident of Natchez, explained in a letter to a friend written in June 1785, not only what the jobbers accomplished but also why they failed:[10]

ESTEEMED FRIEND:

I have purposely omitted some opportunities to write you of late certain news of the above place which were then being spoken of softly, but which are to-day matters of open conversation. Thomas Green, went hence to Georgia, more than a twelvemonth ago, took, as is said, the liberty of presenting a memorial containing the names of various inhabitants of Natchez, petitioning the governor and state council of Georgia to take us of Natchez under their protection, which they graciously conceded to him, and have sent him with the title of lieutenant-colonel to establish a new county beginning at the Yasú River. and thence running down to the Mississippi, as far as the latitude of thirty-one degrees, and thence, east, etc. One Captain Davenport has arrived here. He is one of the four commissioners (Green is one). The other two are coming by way of the [Indian] nations, and are expected any day. At this point, the above-mentioned Captain Davenport has come to get me, and since for lack of a better, I am acting as interpreter of this post, I find myself under the necessity of accompanying them to see the commandant, to whom he must present his credentials to-morrow. A few people have come down with this captain, among them a doctor (a surgeon) and his family. The inhabitants here are more quiet than could be expected. They talk much of erecting a free, sovereign and independent state (if the Spaniards will cede it to them), and are determined under no consideration to become a county of the state of Georgia. It is reported that a thousand families are ready to come down as soon as the boundaries are known. The name of the new county is to be Bourbon. The name of the Congress has not been mentioned as yet, and it is only the state of Georgia which is making the demand. It is not believed among us that anything will be done or can be done for some time. At least you may take for granted that the inhabitants of Natchez will make no movement, since a number of them now talk of moving lower down if they are granted permission. The Georgians have made a code of laws for this recently formed county, one of the provisions of which is that no one may possess more than a thousand acres of land, and that all the Spanish decrees and concessions of land he annulled and [the lands] sold for the benefit of the state. He

---

[10] "Letter of John Gordon to George Profit, June 25, 1785," in Edmund C. Burnett (ed.), "Papers Relating to Bourbon County, Georgia," *American Historical Review*, XV (October, 1909), 96–97.

who has lived in possession of land for some time is given the preference of purchase at the rate of a half *peso fuerte* (half a dollar) per acre. There are still others which it makes me angry to mention. So far as I am concerned, I form no special opinion, but I must say that I shall prefer the Spanish government to the American, for the taxes give me the headache whenever I think of them.

I have been confined lately for seventeen days by the most severe attack of gout. The water has driven me from my first house with part of my effects, which, together with other losses, has been a great detriment to my sales. Captain Davenport, who is now with me, says that this place must of necessity belong to Georgia, and then afterward petition the government to become a free state. I hope that the two commissioners who are coming will bring something more solid after all that we have seen. While writing the above I have been interrupted twenty times. Davenport says that I have made a mistake in some of the laws above mentioned. May God keep us Spanish, with which supplication, I remain, although in great haste, yours,

John Gordon

THE SPANISH CONSPIRACY

The speculation had two predictable results: the Indians, led by the Creeks and their skillful Chief Alexander McGillivray, took to the warpath throughout the Southwest, and Spain closed the Mississippi River to navigation by Americans. Its next step was logical; an agent was hurried to the United States to extract a favorable treaty from that nation at the moment of the United States' greatest need. Don Diego de Gardoqui was too successful; the American negotiator John Jay, Secretary for Foreign Affairs, agreed to allow the Mississippi to stay closed for a quarter century in return for commercial concessions advantageous to eastern trading interests. This was going too far, even for the eastern-dominated Congress, which refused to ratify the Jay-Gardoqui Treaty. But the harm was done. The government had been willing to sell out to the hated Spanish and accept a treaty that would strangle the West economically. Why stay loyal to such a government? Through Kentucky and Tennessee talk of rebellion was heard. One who sought to capitalize on this disloyalty was James Wilkinson, a polished scoundrel with an insatiable thirst for power. Why not funnel Kentucky's discontent into creating a new western republic under Spain's protection, with himself as its George Washington? Wilkinson first enlisted a number of Kentuckians in his plot, then during the summer of 1787 started down the Mississippi with a fleet of flatboats laden with flour and tobacco. At New Orleans he was well-received by Governor Esteban Miró and D. Martin Navarro, the Intendant, who allowed him to sell his goods at a handsome profit. Then, on September 23, he delivered to Miró a proposal for a plan that would sever the Mississippi Valley from the Union:[11]

It will not be improper, Gentlemen, for me to explain clearly at this point, to your Honors, the purpose of my voyage in order that you may duly inform your August Sovereign thereof.

Be it known to your Honors that the Notables of Kentucky, the place of my residence, chafing under the inconveniences and privations they suffer through the restric-

---

[11] "James Wilkinson Memorial to Governor Esteban Miró, Governor of Louisiana, and D. Martin Navarro, Intendant of the Same. September 23, 1787," in Temple Bodley (ed.), *Reprints of Littell's Political Transactions in and Concerning Kentucky*, "Filson Club Publications," vol. 31 (Louisville, 1926), cxxxiv–cxxxvii.

tions placed on its commerce, suggested and pleaded that I make this voyage in order to penetrate, if this were possible, the attitude of Spain toward their country and to discover, if this were practicable, whether it would be agreeable to open a negotiation, *to admit us under its protection as vassals*, with certain privileges in matters of religion and politics in accordance with the temper, and necessary to the welfare of the present generation. These privileges would have been specifically defined, and I would have brought my commission in writing from Kentucky (about to become a free and independent State) were it not that it continues to be subordinated to the republic of Virginia, but as I observed above that the people of this district, after they have organized their government will make their representation to the Court of Spain upon the subject which I have just mentioned, and as I am convinced that its happiness and the peace of Louisiana depend on the success of this petition, I will with the greatest satisfaction employ all my abilities to this end, so as to merit those considerations which my services may make me deserving of. If this proposition is admitted, I will be ready to receive instructions from the Government, and return to Kentucky by the shortest and surest route, and on the way I will establish a confidential correspondence near Congress that will regularly procure for me information as to all the measures that may in any way have relation with our affair. If in the reply which I may receive to this memorial my propositions are admitted, I shall on my return to Kentucky proceed with careful deliberation, take advantage of my personal consideration and political influence in order to familiarize the people with whom I live with and make popular among them the aims that constitute the purpose of my present voyage, to which I have already fixed the sight of all that part that knows how to discern in this community, and I will bind myself to constantly send by confidential messenger, (who must be compensated for the perils and fatigue of the journey) exact accounts of the measures I may have adopted in this important business, the effect they produce as also of any procedure of Congress.

I hope, however, that no wrong will be surmised; if, at the same time I labor to further the work that may produce the agrandizement of Spain and the prosperity of thousands of souls, I should attempt to secure the stability and welfare of my own family. To this end, and in order to give the strongest proof and bond of the sincerity of my propositions, I beg to be allowed to send to a representative in this city who deals in negroes, cattle, tobacco, flour, bacon, tallow, fats and apples, the product of about fifty or sixty thousand dollars of principal in Kentucky, these articles to be sold for my account and the amount deposited with this government as a guarantee of my good conduct until the time we are advised of the success of our projects or that I may establish my residence in Louisiana.

Thus, Gentlemen, have I given to your Honors my opinion, prospects and purposes in an affair that I consider of the greatest importance to Louisiana, as also to the country in which I am now living: when I reflect that I have written this memorial with continuous interruptions, daily efforts and various other disadvantages, I know that it must be full of errors and imperfections. But in the midst of these painful reflections I comfort myself in thinking that I have the honor of addressing two gentlemen from whose candor and consideration I will experience the most ample protection.

After your Honors have duly examined these observations, they will be able to determine whether or no it will be useful to appoint an agent in Kentucky, and once this idea is approved your Honors will draw up the regulations necessary to the rendering of the more essential services to the Crown; it is clear that an agent in that country, without personal influence will be able to warn the government in time of any offensive action that could be attempted, a matter without doubt of the greatest importance, but I comprehend that it is not out of reason to conclude that a man of great popularity and political talents, co-operating with the causes above mentioned, *will be able to alienate the Western Americans from the United States, destroy the insiduous designs of Great Britain and throw those (Western Americans) into the arms of Spain.*

I am certain of one thing, and that is, that I have respected the sacred truth of the facts I have established and that I have made use of my greatest faculties in digesting my speculations, but let it be permitted to me to observe here that the events that appear so probable and which I have anticipated in these pages, may possibly never be accomplished; in this case may I again be permitted to remark that I do not pretend infallibility in my judgment, nor can I be held responsible for the uncertainty and changes in human fortune. My understanding may err; but my heart can never deceive, and if the success does not correspond to our hopes, we may justly exclaim with the poet:

"It does not pertain to mortals to be masters of success."

But we have done more, we have deserved it!

Before concluding, I beg the indulgence of being permitted to make a few other remarks. The interest of the inhabitants residing on the shores of the rivers that pour their waters into the Ohio being the same, their policy must in any event, and notwithstanding any temporary misunderstanding, be the same: for once the upper settlements see Kentucky flourish, enjoy peace and accumulate riches under the protection of Spain, they will find themselves impelled by the most powerful arguments that may be offered to the human intellect to embrace the policy that procured for Kentucky the referred to advantages. These districts extend themselves from the waters South of the Tennessee River up to the arms of the Northern Ohio for a distance of 500 miles more or less, situated west of the Apalachian Mountains and generally following their direction. It is not possible to assure the number of these large settlements, but I confine myself tightly within the truth when I say they contain 150,000 men capable of bearing arms.

Finally, Gentlemen, permit me to observe that it appears to me that the success of these propositions depends in a large measure on the following contingencies:

1st: The most inviolable secrecy, not only of the project but also of my name which is well known to Mr. Carmichael the American Charge d'Affaires at the Court of Madrid.

2nd: Of the continuation of Sr. de Miro in his present command, on account of the personal knowledge that both of us have formed, thus acquiring reciprocally a personal confidence that is essential to the negotiation, which would not be the case afterwards with his successor.

3rd: I am absolutely convinced that the appointment of D. Martin Navarro to be Minister to the American Government would be most advantageous for the promotion of the project. This gentleman, being near Congress, with the knowledge he possesses of this affair, would be able to take advantage of any occasion to further our aims, and through this means we would be able to establish direct communication from Congress to the western countries and from Louisiana to the Court.

Forgive the above remarks, prompted by the conviction of their usefulness, and by my zeal in the cause to which I have pledged myself. To you, Gentlemen, I have confided an affair of so important a nature that were it divulged it would destroy my fame and fortune forever; but I feel the greatest confidence in the discretion and silence of your Honors, and if in any event the project should be rejected by the Court, I must rely on the candor and high honor of a worthy Minister to bury all I have communicated in eternal forgetfulness.

KENTUCKY PETITIONS FOR STATEHOOD, 1788

Wilkinson's Spanish conspiracy could never succeed. The bulk of the Americans in the West were basically loyal to the United States and level-headed enough to realize that life under an autocratic Spanish monarch would be even more intolerable than life under a neglectful republic. Yet talk of rebellion was fired by genuine and justifiable discontent. Kentucky was inadequately governed, for it was still a county of Virginia, which was too absorbed in its affairs to pay attention to its over-mountain outpost. To westerners, there was only one acceptable solution: the region must be severed from Virginia and shape its own destiny as a separate state in the Union. This, not a separate republic under Spanish protection, was the goal of all but a small faction of extreme discontents led by Wilkinson. The ambitions of the majority were voiced at a series of conventions held almost annually through the 1780s. One, a meeting at Danville in August 1788, produced a petition that was typical of all as it demanded that the Virginia legislature allow the area separate statehood and recited the grievances that made this desirable:[12]

To the Honourable the General Assembly for the Commonwealth of Virginia

GENTLEMEN,

The representatives of the good people inhabiting the several counties composing the district of Kentucky, in convention met, beg leave again to address you on the great and important subject of their separation from the parent state, and being made a member of the federal union.

To repeat the causes which impel the inhabitants of this district to continue their application for a separation, will, in our opinion, be unnecessary. They have been generously acknowledged and patronized in former Assemblies, and met the approbation of that august body, whose consent was necessary towards the final completion of this desirable object, and who resolved that the measure was expedient and necessary, but which from their peculiar situation, they were inadequate to decide on.

As happiness was the object which first dictated the application for a separation, so it has continued to be the ruling principle in directing the good people of Kentucky to that great end, upon constitutional terms,

---

[12] "To the Honourable the General Assembly of Virginia. . . ," in Temple Bodley (ed.), *Reprints of Littell's Political Transactions in and Concerning Kentucky,* "Filson Club Publications," vol. 31 (Louisville, 1926), pp. 106–108.

and they conceive the longer that measure is delayed, the more will they lie exposed to the merciless savage, or (which is greatly to be feared) anarchy, with all the concomitant evils attendant thereon.

Being fully impressed with these ideas, and justified by frequent examples, we conceive it our duty as freemen, from the regard we owe to our constituents, and being encouraged by the resolutions of Congress, again to apply to your honourable body, praying that an act may pass at the present session, for enabling the good people of the Kentucky district, to obtain an independent government and be admitted into the confederation, as a member of the federal union, upon such terms and conditions as to you may appear just and equitable; and that you transmit such act to the president of this convention with all convenient dispatch, in order for our consideration and the final completion of this business.—This we are emboldened to ask, as many of the causes which produced former restrictions, do not now exist.—Finally, relying on the justice and liberality of your honourable house, so often experienced, and which we are even bound to acknowledge, we again solicit the friendly interposition of the parent state, with the congress of U. States for a speedy admission of the district into the federal union, and also to urge that honourable body, in the most express terms, to take effectual measures for procuring to the inhabitants of this district the free navigation of the River Mississippi, without which the situation of a large part of the community will be wretched and miserable, and may be the source of future evils.

Ordered, That the president sign and the clerk attest the said address, and that the same be enclosed by the president to the speaker of the house of delegates.

Resolved, That this convention highly approve the address presented by General James Wilkinson to the Governor Intendant of Louisiana, and that the President be requested to present him the thanks of the convention for the regard which he therein manifested for the interest of the western country.

Resolved, That when this convention doth adjourn, it will adjourn to the first Monday in August next.

THE YAZOO SPECULATIONS OF 1789

Despite these velvet-gloved threats, the Kentuckians were content to wait while statesmen east of the mountains fashioned a constitution and launched a new government in 1789, hoping that it would be powerful enough to solve their problems and understanding enough to grant them statehood. James Wilkinson still dreamed of a western empire and still plotted with Spanish officials, but the king's ministers in Madrid dashed his hopes; vetoing all plans that would separate Kentucky from the Union, they instead sought to quiet discontent by opening the Mississippi to navigation by all paying a 15 percent export duty. At the same time, they encouraged Americans to migrate into Louisiana or West Florida, whose citizens paid no such tax. These moves ended the Spanish conspiracy, but the discontent remained. It plagued the new government under President Washington that took office in the spring of 1789. The embers were fanned by an outrageous act of the Georgia legislature. Knowing that it would eventually have to cede the state's western lands to the federal government, in December 1789, it sold virtually all of them to three speculating companies: the South Carolina Yazoo Company, the Virginia Yazoo Company, and the Tennessee Yazoo Company. The grandiose plans of these jobbers—who had secured 25,400,000 acres of prime real estate for $207,580—were outlined by one of them, Alexander Moultrie, in a letter soliciting support from a friend:[13]

> CHARLESTON SOUTH CAROLINA
> 19TH FEBRUARY 1790
>
> SIR
>
> This will be accompanied by our mutual Friend Mr. Inglis, thro' whose Communication I take the Honour of addressing you.
>
> The Business of the 3 Georgia Grants to the three Companys, the one Called the South Carolina Yazou Company, the other the Virginia Yassou Company and the third the Tennessee Company, is a Matter to which at present I daresay you are no stranger, nor to the Magnitude and importance of the Many desirable effects which must arise from it. The first Company is the one of which I have the Honour at present to be director, the Territory beginning on Coles creek on the Mississippi Contains above five Millions of Acres extending from the Source of said Creek a due East Course to the Tombigby and thence up the Middle of Tombigby to the degree of Lat: 33 thence a due West Course to the Middle of Mississippi then down the Middle of the Mississippi including all Islands to the Mouth of Coles Creek. Of the very excellent quality of the Land, its Climate and Situation for Commerce, I am sure there will be no necessity to give any particular descriptive account. The Law passed last December in Augusta, in which by a very decided Majority Specifically described to each Company, on payment of the purchase Money and a right of preemption is given to us for 2 Years; but added to this give me leave to assure you as a Gentleman that a person of Character Setts off this day from Charleston for Augusta for the payment of the purchase Money being provided with it for that purpose and to return absolutely with the Grant in 15 or 20 days. The Gentlemans Name is Colonel Weld of Georgia. So far, Sir, the Contract is irrevocably perfected and Accomplished.
>
> A great deal has been attempted in Congress by some whose disappointed private views have led them into very improper extravagances of temper; but I trust that at this day, a body like Congress who has more her own importance and real dignity to Consult & to support, than the private disputes of a few Artful Speculators, will not hesitate to decide on the line of law, justice and propriety in such a Case; more especially when 'tis so generally ingrafted in the heart of Americans, how unequall the Authority of that Body is to the power of divesting the Citizen or State of their Rights of property or the Latter of its local Sovereignty. The last Georgia will never surrender and the former will be most tenaciously preserved. Any other idea I cannot forbear to laugh at. But this has all been only a puff Circulated with the wind, Shallow in its origin and weak in its effect.
>
> Some of the Lower Counties also in Georgia about two or three and not a Majority of Either, have attempted to be Consequential likewise on the occasion, but I believe they begin to be more Sensible of their inefficacy. Selfishness also was their Basis.
>
> We have an Agent in Kentucky, there will be another at Yazou, another at Orleans, and Another in East Georgia, as well as a Director in Carolina. Mr. Pereman and Mr. Inglis are amongst the Concerned here. Our Connexions in Europe and America as far

---

[13] Alexander Moultrie to Alexander McGillivray, February 19, 1790, from Charleston. In Arthur P. Whitaker (ed.), "The South Carolina Yazoo Company," *Mississippi Valley Historical Review*, XVI (December, 1929), 391–394.

as New York are powerfull and respectable. Governor Henry of Virginia is at the head of the Virginia Company, we are united in Measures and pursuits. The Virginia Territory's southern Boundary commences from our Northern and extend to the North Carolina Line, the Western and Eastern Limits are Co Extensive.

There is no doubt but in less than 3 Years each Company will be a Separate State. A very large Migration is now about to move on from the Waters above us; 30,000 makes a State by the Articles of Confederation. We have a Chactaw Grant for the Western front of our Territory & from Settlements will make everything Convenient and Satisfactory to them. Large Emigrations from Europe also will take place from Various parts, our Merchants abroad are Busy, and an African Trade on a very extensive Basis is now preparing for next Summer.

The vast extent, Sir, of the Furr & peltry Trade besides the Agricultural Staples from the whole Western Frontier of this Continent is an object of too much Magnitude to escape Your Observation and especially when added to the *friendly Commercial intercourse* which we will Cultivate with the Spaniards, and trust they will be Convinced it will be our Mutual interest to support & preserve.

Our Connexions in Europe and Elsewhere I say are powerful, but I think there will be two additional Circumstances which will render this Stupendous Business the Admiration of the World.

The first is to have the Nation of Creeks and Chactaws on a footing of such Amity & mutual interest with us and Georgia, that a plan be adopted to engage them on the Terms of Commerce and Civilization and every Means be recurred to to Support them, & that a person of Your Character Should take the lead in so brilliant a Scene,

which I think would give the Greatest eclat in the Civilized World and raise your already respected Character to everlasting fame. Your Acquiescence in these Measures will entitle You to a territorial Right amongst us of above (I think) four hundred thousand Acres which we have no doubt will soon bring a Guinea an Acre.

Your Connexions as a Citizen of America will then be amongst some of the Most influential Characters of our Continent, Your Nation will Rise and flourish amongst the sons of the Earth and live in peace and happiness.

Their next Generations may Shine in the Councils of America, you will be beheld as their Great patron and Friend, and will preside at the head of a System of Commerce which will soon be the most lucrative and extensive in the World.

Mr. Inglis reserves half a share for Your Acceptance (say 295 000 Acres) and I think your friend Osborn has done the same. The State of Georgia I am Sure will do every thing for You she can but you must Meet her half way. I trust you will soon see Dr. O'Fallon via Orleans who will proceed there from Kentuckey. He will make such Communications to you as will, I hope, demonstrate our great idea of the Business and our Anxiety for Your interest in the same.

If ever man had a most amazing extent of Power, wealth, influence & happiness within his Grasp, I think it is now you.

I have wrote to you rather in haste being just Returned from Court very busily employed and I have done it tho personally unknown to You, yet with the unrestrained freedom of a Friend. Pray let me hear as soon as possible your Judgement on the Matter; I hope My ideas will Meet with Yours, & that every blessed Fruit will attend you and us in so just and so Glorious a Work.

The Chactaws will soon have all their

Matters perfectly Regulated and accommodated. I have the Honor to be

Sir with Respect
Your Most Obedient Servant
A. MOULTRIE
Director of South Carolina Y. C.

Alexander McGillivray Esquire

THE TREATY OF NEW YORK

This speculator intrusion was deplored by President Washington, who realized that it would stir the Indian warfare that had ravaged the frontiers for a half-dozen years; but in the long run he was to benefit, for this turn of events brought problems in the Southwest to the boiling point. Clearly border raids there could be ended only by a massive invasion of the Indian territory such as that of General Anthony Wayne in the Northwest, or by convincing the tribal leaders that peace was to their advantage. Fortunately, world events allowed President Washington to pursue the latter course. These brought Spain and England to the point of war just at this time. The able Creek leader who was mapping Indian strategy, Chief Alexander McGillivray, saw the danger of his situation at once; his supply of arms and ammunition, normally obtained from England with Spanish funds, would be cut off, and his warriors would be at the mercy of the Americans. This realization led him to respond favorably to peace overtures from Washington's government, and on August 7, 1790, he signed the Treaty of New York which temporarily ended hostilities. The wily McGillivray explained the terms and purposes of the treaty in a letter to one of his Spanish overlords who was naturally displeased by his defection:[14]

---

[14] From *McGillivray of the Creeks*, by John Walton Caughey. Copyright 1938 by the University of Oklahoma Press. Pp. 273–276.

NEW YORK, AUGUST 11, 1790

DEAR SIR:

The serious illness which has troubled me ever since my arrival has prevented me until now, from replying to the subjects suggested in the paper that you put in my hands in Philadelphia. I now take advantage of this leisure moment to write you something in answer to that paper. Our friend Mr. Leslie has good reason for saying in his letter to me that Spain is the natural protector of the Southern Indian Nations. This is not only my opinion but also the general one of those who are fairly well informed about our situation; all consideration of a sane policy should dispose her to such a protection. It is of equal importance for the interests of the Indian Nations that they be closely connected with Spain; according to these principles I negotiated and concluded a treaty of peace and alliance, with the officials of the king authorized to that effect, which was founded on the permanent basis of reciprocal convenience; and it is not my intention or my desire to sacrifice said treaty to new projects.

I certainly should not have hastened to accept the invitation to make a treaty in this place if our situation were such as to encourage me to run the risk involved; anyway I am sanctioned in this measure by the advice of Governor Miro and others to whom I have always communicated our public affairs without reserve, and of whom I have asked at all times advice for my government. He has repeated to me his desires that I conclude peace with the Americans, respecting at all times our treaty with Spain; which treaty (I inform you in passing) was never confirmed or ratified, as he himself has confessed, and the aids and helps which have been given us to sustain and carry on our claims and rights were, after a fashion snatched by force; for on an urgent occasion, these aids were lent me scantily and with reluctance. Our trade, in truth, is put on an equal footing with the extension of our desires; and it has been of infinite utility to my nation.

For this we are duly grateful; nevertheless, having reflected on everything maturely, I feel justified in concluding a peace with the United States, although it is not equal to our claims and desires. My refusal of the American propositions of peace at Rock Landing last September came near to causing very serious consequences, and in spite of the fact that the proceedings of the Georgians toward us are generally condemned, my hasty refusal was considered by the President as an insult to the dignity of the United States, and if I had not come to this city, Congress would have undoubtedly declared war against us; in which circumstances we would have had much to fear situated as we were, especially since the new government is established on a basis which renders it capable of making war on us in a fashion that would assure them a complete success. In that case the terms prescribed to us by the Americans would leave us very little or nothing; and we could not very well count on the efficacious measures in our favor on your part, for as the offered and stipulated guaranty had never been confirmed we had no solid basis for supposing or hoping that Spain would go into a war in order to sustain our claims.

These motives have led me to agree to the following articles of peace to end our disputes. The first stipulation required of us was an unqualified recognition of the sovereignty of the United States over us. I opposed this article. After much debate it was modified, to extend over those parts of our nation which lie within the boundaries of the United States. It did not seem to me worth while to cavil on this point, being persuaded that Spain would sustain and maintain her claims against the pretension that the United States makes to 31° north latitude on the Mississippi, etc.; therefore, we would remain in our former state. Another stipulation was directed toward taking our trade from its present source. After much debate it was decided to defer the consideration of this point until the end of two years; and it seemed to me the best way to escape this article, the most difficult point to adjust. It occupied us several days, because the Georgians and other interested persons insisted that the cessions made to them should be confirmed on the part of our nation. These lands had been alienated and populated and could not be restored except by force, and force could not be employed against the citizens, nor their blood shed. I agreed that an arbitrary line should be drawn on the Oconee River for which the United States should make us immediately a compensation of ten thousand dollars in merchandise, and two thousand dollars annually; the United States surrendering all claims up to the new Georgian line, from the branch of the Alatamaya to the source of the St. Marys River and its various springs, the old British boundary over that river being included, and the United States being a guarantor of all future usurpations on the part of their citizens.

These articles, with some regulations to maintain good order between us, compose the treaty, and everything considered, I am thankful that it did not turn out worse.

Being in general little influenced by personal considerations I did not stipulate anything with respect to my estates in Georgia and South Carolina, although I will ask said states to return them to me, and if they do not do so the union will compensate me. Some time ago those of Carolina left my estate at my disposal. I resisted, as much as I decently could, accepting the honorary badge of Brigadier General; finally, tired of being repeatedly pressed to do so, I agreed to add this plumage to my cap.

The foregoing is an exact compendium of my negotiations here, which I give with candor and without reserve, and I flatter myself that no part of the treaty can give just motive for suspecting that I failed to fulfill my obligations. Now I must repeat a plea which I have made many times; to wit: that the true aims and dispositions of the ministry in respect to our affairs be communicated to me. The time is critical and it is absolutely necessary that there exist between us a clear, explicit, and confidential communication in place of the vague and ambiguous procedure which up to the present has existed between us, and which has only served to perplex my mind and to embarrass our public affairs. Let certain articles and stipulations be formed and agreed upon, which must be duly confirmed and ratified by the King; let us have a certain rule by which to govern ourselves to our satisfaction, through lack of which we have been induced to adopt certain measures which otherwise might not have been adopted. I refer to the stipulations, to the guaranty of offensive alliance and commerce of the Treaty of Pensacola of the year '84.

And let there be a liberal establishment of officials of the department in the nation. It is a well known fact that I am not greedy, but a former ruling hurt my feelings, when I was placed on the same basis as a common interpreter, a stipend which long ago I have refused to accept. We lack two interpreters with comfortable salaries.

I was almost forgetting to say that I protested strongly against the behavior of the new western companies, in the terms in which Georgia has formed them, and I have the word of the government that said companies will be broken up.

Having concluded all our affairs in this city, I desire to start my homeward journey at the end of this week for the St. Mary River. I end this letter wishing you a happy agreeable trip to St. Augustine, begging you to give my regards to our friend Mr. Leslie, since I have no time to write to him now. This letter is written in terms which will give you to understand that it was finished after various interruptions. With the most affectionate expression of esteem and attention, I remain, Dear Sir, yours as usual

ALEXANDER McGILLIVRAY

Señor Don Carlos Howard,
Captain of the Regiment of Hibernia, etc.

THE GENÊT CONSPIRACY IN KENTUCKY

The peace that descended on the over-mountain country when Alexander McGillivray called off his warriors was deceptive; the basic problems of the frontiersmen—self-government, adequate trade outlets, a stable land system—remained unsolved, and could be solved only with the passage of time. So the West remained discontented, and this meant that the spirit of rebellion could still be stirred among extreme hot-heads. The spark that touched off the next crisis was provided by Citizen Edmond Genêt, fiery disciple of the French revolutionary government, who reached the United States in 1793 and immediately began plotting to separate the West from the United Sates. George Rogers Clark was enlisted to form a legion of frontiersmen to attack New Orleans (Spain and Britain were allied against revolutionary France at this time), and other disciples formed Democratic societies throughout the West to preach revolution and the rights of man. One, the

Democratic Society of Kentucky, spoke for the West's persistent unrest when it addressed the over-mountain men and urged them to action:[15]

To the inhabitants of the United States, west of the Allegany and Apalachian mountains:

DECEMBER 13, 1793

FELLOW-CITIZENS:

The Democratic Society of Kentucky having had under consideration the measures necessary to obtain the exercise of your rights to the free navigation of the Mississippi, have determined to address you upon that important topic. In so doing they think that they only use the undoubted right of citizens to consult for their common welfare. This measure is not dictated by party or faction; it is the consequence of unavoidable necessity. It has become so from the neglect shown by the General government, to obtain for those of the citizens of the United States who are interested therein the navigation of that river.

In the present stage, when the rights of man have been fully investigated and declared by the voice of nations, and more particularly in America, where those rights were first developed and declared, it will not be necessary to prove that the free navigation of the Mississippi is the natural right of the inhabitants of the country watered by its streams. It cannot be believed that the beneficient God of nature would have blessed this country with unparalleled fertility, and furnished it with a number of navigable streams, and that that fertility should be consumed at home, and those streams should not convey its superabundance to other climes. Far from it: for if we examine the wise diversity of the earth as to climate and productions, lands, seas, and rivers, we must discover the glorious plan of infinite beneficence to unite by the exchange of their surplus, various nations, and connect the ends of the earth in the bands of commerce and mutual good offices. From the everlasting decrees of Providence, then, we derive this right; and it must be criminal either to surrender or suffer it to be taken from us, without the most arduous struggles. But this right is ours, not only from nature, but compact. We do not mean to urge this, as if a compact could give an additional sanction to a natural right, but to show that our claim is derived from every source which can give it validity. The navigation of the Mississippi was solemnly given and confirmed by Great Britain to the citizens of the United States, by the provisional articles entered into at Paris, between the two nations. More than eleven years have since elapsed, during which we have been denied the exercise of a right, founded upon such irrefragable grounds. What has been done by the former or present Government, during this period, on our behalf? In the former we have been able to learn of no attempt to procure from the King of Spain even an acknowledgment of our right. Repeated memorials were presented to Congress upon the subject, but they were treated with a neglect bordering on contempt. They were laid upon the table, there to rest in endless oblivion. Once, indeed, we know, this subject was introduced into Congress, under the former Government; but it was by an unwarrantable and disgraceful proposition to barter away our rights. The proposition was not adopted; the attempt being rendered abortive by the spirited and patriotic opposition of a part of the Union. The time at length came, when the voice of the people called for a change in the General Government, and the present constitution of the United States was adopted. We then flattered

---

[15] Address of the Democratic Society of Kentucky, December 13, 1793 in *American State Papers, Miscellaneous* (Washington, 1834), vol. 1, pp. 929–930.

ourselves that our rights would be protected; for we were taught to believe, that the former loose and weak confederation having been done away, the new Government would possess the requisite energy. Memorials upon the subject were renewed. Six years have passed away, and our right is not yet obtained. Money is to be taken from us by an odious and oppressive excise, but the means of procuring it by the exercise of our just right is denied. In the mean while, our brethren on the Eastern waters possess every advantage which nature or compact can give them. Nay, we do not know that even one firm attempt to obtain it has been made. Alas! Is the energy of our Government not to be exerted against our enemies? It is all to be reserved for her citizens?

Experience, fellow-citizens, has shown us that the General Government is unwilling that we should obtain the navigation of the river Mississippi. A local policy appears to have an undue weight in the councils of the Union. It seems to be the object of that policy to prevent the population of this country, which would draw from the Eastern States their industrious citizens. This conclusion inevitably follows from a consideration of the measures taken to prevent the purchase and settlement of the lands bordering on the Mississippi. Among those measures, the unconstitutional interference which rescinded sales, by one of the States, to private individuals, makes a striking object. And perhaps the fear of a successful rivalship, in every article of their exports, may have its weight. But, if they are not unwilling to do us justice, they are at least regardless of our rights and welfare. We have found prayers and supplications of no avail, and should we continue to load the table of Congress with memorials, from a part only of the Western country, it is too probable they would meet with a fate similar to those which have been formerly presented. Let us, then, all unite our endeavors in the common cause. Let all join in a firm and manly remonstrance to the President and Congress of the United States, stating our just and undoubted right to the navigation of the Mississippi, remonstrating against the conduct of Government with regard to that right, which must have been occasioned by local policy or neglect, and demanding of them speedy and effectual exertions for its attainment. We cannot doubt that you will cordially and unanimously join in this measure. It can hardly be necessary to remind you that considerable quantities of beef, pork, flour, hemp, tobacco, &c., the produce of this country, remain on hand for want of purchasers, or are sold at inadequate prices. Much greater quantities might be raised if the inhabitants were encouraged by the certain sale which the free navigation of the Mississippi would afford. An additional increase of those articles, and a greater variety of produce and manufactures, would be supplied, by means of the encouragement, which the attainment of that great object would give to emigration. But it is not only your own rights which you are to regard: remember that your posterity have a claim to your exertions to obtain and secure that right. Let not your memory be stigmatised with a neglect of duty. Let not history record that the inhabitants of this beautiful country lost a most invaluable right, and half the benefits bestowed upon it by a bountiful Providence, through your neglect and supineness. The present crisis is favorable. Spain is engaged in a war which requires all her forces. If the present golden opportunity be suffered to pass without advantage, and she shall have concluded a peace with France, we must then contend against her undivided strength.

But what may be the event of the proposed application is still uncertain. We ought, therefore, to be still upon our guard, and watchful to seize the first favorable opportunity to gain our object. In order to this, our union should be as perfect and lasting as possible. We propose that societies should be formed, in convenient districts, in every part of the Western country, who shall preserve a correspondence upon this and every other subject of general concern. By means of these societies we shall be enabled speedily to know what may be the result of our endeavors, to consult upon such further measures as may be necessary to preserve union, and, finally, by these means, to secure success.

Remember that it is a common cause which ought to unite us, that that cause is indubitably just, that ourselves and posterity are interested, that the crisis is favorable, and that it is only by union that the object can be achieved. The obstacles are great, and so ought to be our efforts. Adverse fortune may attend us, but it shall never dispirit us. We may for a while exhaust our wealth and strength, but until the all-important object is procured we pledge ourselves to you, and let us all pledge ourselves to each other, that our perseverance and our friendship will be inexhaustible.

JOHN BRECKENRIDGE, *Chairman*

Time and the international situation solved the problems that had grieved the Kentuckians. Genêt soon overstayed his welcome and was sent packing, while diplomats grappled with the basic problems that had ruffled Spanish-American relations for so long. From the American point of view the time was ripe for such ventures. Spain was in a pliant mood, partly because it realized that its plotting and its efforts to attract immigrants into Louisiana had failed, partly because setbacks in the then raging European war were so disastrous that it had to sue France for a separate peace—and perhaps precipitate a retaliatory attack by Spain's former ally, Great Britain. So Spain backed down completely. The Treaty of San Lorenzo (1795) gave Americans the perpetual right to navigate the Mississippi and awarded the disputed Yazoo strip to the United States.

AMERICAN OCCUPATION OF LOUISIANA

Nor had American statesmen reaped the full harvest of the turbulent European situation. Louisiana was to be their next plum. When Napoleon seized that colony from Spain in 1801, all American officialdom realized that a powerful neighbor in the Mississippi Valley would menace the whole borderland. They need not have feared; within two years the mercurial French dictator had changed his mind and decided to sell Louisiana outright. In 1803 this princely domain, embracing most of the area between the Mississippi and the Rocky Mountains, became the property of the United States for a payment of only about $15,000,000. On December 30, 1803, the French flag was lowered from the pole in the public square of New Orleans, and the Stars and Stripes raised in its place. Governor William C. Claiborne, newly named to the post, supervised these ceremonies. The proclamation that he issued to the people promised a new era of progress for them and their children:[16]

Whereas, by stipulations between the governments of France and Spain, the latter ceded to the former the Colony and Prov-

---

[16] Governor Claiborne's Proclamation of December 20, 1803 in *Message from the President of the United States, accompanying Sundry Documents Relative to a Delivery of Possession, on the 20th Ultimo, by the Commissioners of the French Republic, to the Commissioners of the United States of America, of the Territory of Louisiana* (Washington, 1804), pp. 8–10.

ince of Louisiana, with the same extent which it had at the date of the above mentioned Treaty in the hands of Spain, and that it had when France possessed it, and such as it ought to be after the Treaties subsequently entered into between Spain and other states; and whereas the government of France has ceded the same to the United States by a treaty duly ratified, and bearing date the 30th of April, in the present year, and the possession of said colony and province is now in the United States, according to the tenor of the last mentioned treaty; and whereas the Congress of the United States, on the 31st day of October, in the present year, did enact that until the expiration of the session of Congress then sitting, (unless provisions for the temporary government of the said territories be sooner made by Congress,) all the military, civil and judicial powers exercised by the then existing government of the same, shall be vested in such person or persons, and shall be exercised in such manner as the President of the United States shall direct, for the maintaining and protecting the inhabitants of Louisiana in the free enjoyment of their liberty, property and religion; and the President of the United States has by his commission, bearing date the same 31st day of October, invested me with all the powers, and charged me with the several duties heretofore held and exercised by the Governor General and Intendant of the Province:

I have, therefore, thought fit to issue THIS MY PROCLAMATION, making known the premises, and to declare, that the government heretofore exercised over the said province of Louisiana, as well under the authority of Spain as of the French Republic, has ceased, and that of the United States of America is established over the same; that the inhabitants thereof will be incorporated in the Union of the United States, and admitted as soon as possible according to the principles of the Federal Constitution, to the enjoyment of all the rights, advantages and immunities of citizens of the United States; that in the mean time they shall be maintained and protected in the free enjoyment of their liberty, property and the religion which they profess; that all laws and municipal regulations which were in existence at the cessation of the late government, remain in full force; and all civil officers charged with their execution, except those whose powers have been specially vested in me, and except also such officers as have been entrusted with the collection of the revenue, are continued in their functions, during the pleasure of the governor for the time being, or until provision shall otherwise be made.

And I do hereby exhort and enjoin all the inhabitants and other persons within the said province, to be faithful and true in their allegiance to the United States, and obedient to the laws and authorities of the same, under full assurance that their just rights will be under the guardianship of the United States, and will be maintained from all force or violence from without or within.

In testimony whereof I have hereunto set my hand.

With the Louisiana Purchase the United States won its final diplomatic victory in the long struggle for dominance in the Mississippi Valley. No longer could Europe's powers challenge the new Republic there; no longer could European agents goad Indians into raids on the backcountry settlements. For the first time in a generation the frontiers were relatively free from danger. The result was a rush to the overmountain country that dwarfed any migrations in America to this time.

CHAPTER 11

The Occupation of the Appalachian Plateau, 1796-1812

The workable land and governmental systems devised by Congress could not prove their worth until the diplomatic triumphs of 1794 and 1795 made life in the West relatively safe. That miracle was accomplished by the events of those years: Wayne's victory at Fallen Timbers, the Treaty of Greenville, Britain's evacuation of the northwestern posts following Jay's treaty, and Pinckney's treaty with its guarantees of free navigation of the Mississippi. For the first time in a dozen years men could move westward with their families, secure in the belief that the war whoop would not sound near their cabins. So they moved, by the thousands and tens of thousands, and the westering surge did not diminish until the troubled years preceding the outbreak of the War of 1812 revived the Indian menace. During those seventeen years between 1795 and 1812 Kentucky and Tennessee were comfortably filled, the hilly lands of western New York state were transformed into a land of tidy villages and farms, and much of southern Ohio and southeastern Indiana was occupied. Before the westward-moving tide diminished, three new states had been carved from the trans-Appalachian wilderness: Kentucky in 1792, Tennessee in 1796, and Ohio in 1803.

THE RUSH WESTWARD IN 1796

The migrations that began in 1795 and 1796 were of the first come-outers—the restless, the discontented, who were always on the cutting edge of the frontiers, but had been held back now for a generation. Their eagerness to reach the promised lands beyond the Appalachians was captured in words by one who traveled with them and recorded not only his own adventures but tales he heard along the way. Moses Austin, later to gain fame as the founder of Texas, crossed the Cumberland Gap into Kentucky in December 1796 on his way from Virginia to Missouri. His descriptions of the hardships of his journey included impressions of the pioneers who jammed the Wilderness Road, all bent on reaching the West "because every body says it's good land:"[1]

On the 8 day of December 1796 in the Evening I left Austin Ville on Hors Back

[1] Moses Austin, "A Memorandum of M. Austin's Journey from the Lead Mines of the County of Wythe in the State of Virginia to the Lead Mines in the Province of Louisiana West of the Mississippi," *American Historical Review*, V (April, 1900), 523–526.

233

takeing Jos. Bell as an assistant and a Mule to Pack my baggage and that night went to Mr. James Campbells who on the morning of the 9 started with me for Kentuckey. Nothing of note took place from Mr. Campbells to Captain Craggs where we arrived on the 11th at Eve furnishing ourselves with Blankets &c at Abington as we passed the Morning of the 12 I left Captain Cragg, in Companey with a Mr. Wills from Richmond bound to Nashvill in the State of Tennessee. that night I arrived at the Block Hous, so called from being some years past used as such but at this time in the hands of Colo Anderson, at whose Hous, it was Expected good accomedations, could be had, more so in Consiquence of his being a friend of Mr. Campbells. However, it was with great Trouble, that he admitted us under his Roof, or would allow us any thing for our Horses and Mules. Colo Andersons is 36 Miles from Cap' Craggs, which, I left by Day light, takeing the road Through Powells Valle. at this place I parted with Mr. Wills who took the road for Cumberland Which forked at this place. the road being Bad and the weather uncommonly Cold, I found it was with hard Traveling that we reached the foot of Wallons ridge that Night. from Andersons, to Benedict Yancy's is 34 Miles and an uncommon Mountainous road. Fifteen Miles from the Block Hous is Clynch mountain and the river of the same name. I the same Day passed a number of Mountains and ridges, the most considerable of which are Copper Creek Powells and Wallons, as also several large Creeks and Powells River. Mr Yancys is the enterence into Powells Valley. a Wagon road has lately been Opened into, and Down the Valley, and Notwithstanding great panes and Expence, the passage is so bad that at maney of the mountains the waggoners are obliged to lock all the wheels and make fast a Trunk of Tree Forty feet long to the back of the waggon to prevent it from Pressing on the Horses. in this manner many waggons have passed on to Kentuckey. It was late in the Evening of the 13th that I arrived at the Hous of this Mr Yancys, and the badness of the weather, had made Me Determin, not to go any Further, being then 8 OClock and snowing fast, however I found it was not so Easy a matter to bring the old Man and Woman to think as I did; For when I demanded or rather requested leave to stay, they absolutely refused me, saying, that we could go to a Hous six miles Down the Valley. Finding moderate words would not answer I plainly told Mr Yancy that I should not go any further, and that stay I would. Old Mrs Yancy had much to say about the liberties some Men take, and I replied by observing the Humanity of Others, and so ended our dispute. our Horse was stripped and some Corn and Fodder obtained. we soon Found ways and means to make the rough ways smooth, and takeing out our Provision Bag made a good supper, after which placing our Blanketts on the Floor with our feet to the fire I sleeped well. The 14 we started from Mr Yancys and the Day being bad with snow and rain, we stopped at a Mr Ewings five miles Below Lee Court Hous and Ten from Mr Yancys. at Mr. Ewing we reced the *'welcome'* of Mr and Mrs Ewing at whos Hous we staid, untill the morning of the 15, when after being furnished with Every thing we wanted and a Good Piece of Beef to take with us, we took leave of Mr and Mrs Ewing and family and that Night about Sun down arrived at Cumberland Mountain. about ½ a Mile before you pass this mountain you come into the road from Hawkins Courtt Hous and Knox Vill, which is said to be the Best road. after passing the Mountain which we did this Night, we stopped a[t] Mrs. Davis's who keeps

Tavern Down the mountain, and met with very good accomedations. Powells Vally has lately been made a County by the name of Lee, takeing all the Country from Washington County to the Kentucky line. The Court Hous is About Thirty miles up the Vally from the pass of Cumberland mountain at which place is a Small Town of Six or Ten Houses and Two Stores. Powells Vally is, I am informed about six miles Broad and 60 in length. its good land but so Inclosed with Mountains that it will be always Difficult to Enter with waggons. When the Vally becomes well improved it will be an Agreeable place but at this time its thinly settled and Small farms. On the 16th by Day light our Horses being ready we took our leave of Mrs Davis, who I must take the liberty to say may be Justly call Captain Molly of Cumberland Mountain, for she Fully Commands this passage to the New World. . . .

I cannot omitt Noticeing the many distressed families I passed in the Wilderness nor can any thing be more distressing to a man of feeling than to see woman and children in the Month of December Travelling a Wilderness Through Ice and Snow passing large rivers and Creeks with out Shoe or Stocking, and barely as maney raggs as covers their Nakedness, with out money or provisions except what the Wilderness affords, the Situation of such can better be Imagined then discribed. to say they are poor is but faintly express'g there Situation,—life *What is it, Or What can it give,* to make Compensation for such accumulated Misery. Ask these Pilgrims what they expect when they git to Kentuckey the Answer is Land. have you any. No, but I expect I can git it. have you any thing to pay for land, No. did you Ever see the Country. No but Every Body says its good land. can any thing be more Absurd than the Conduct of man, here is hundreds Travelling hundreds of Miles, they Know not for what Nor Whither, except its to Kentucky, passing land almost as good and easy obtained, the Proprietors of which would gladly give on any terms, but it will not do its not Kentuckey its not the Promised land its not the goodly inheratance the Land of Milk and Honey. and when arrived at this Heaven in Idea what do they find? a goodly land I will allow but to them forbiden Land. exausted and worn down with distress and disappointment they are at last Obliged to become hewers of wood and Drawers of water.

While the migratory column observed by Moses Austin moved from the uplands of Virginia, Maryland, and the Carolinas into Kentucky and Tennessee, another left the New England and Middle States to people western New York and Pennsylvania. This land of rolling hills and fertile valleys was opened in 1789 when the crushing defeat administered the Iroquois Indians during the Revolutionary War was translated into treaties that forced their removal to reservations or to Canada. Even before this time, in 1786, the two eastern states that claimed the area, Massachusetts and New York, settled their differences by dividing western New York between them, Massachusetts taking the western portion. Each was eager to sell at once to replenish coffers left empty by war. New York disposed of its domain over the next few years to large speculators who in turn parceled out farms to individual owners on the credit system. Massachusetts in 1788 marketed its 6,000,000 acres to two wealthy land jobbers with political connections—Oliver Phelps and Nathaniel Gorham—for about three cents an acre. Unable to meet payments even on this small sum, these speculators soon sold to other speculators, principally two firms from overseas, the Pulteney Estates of England and the Holland Land Company formed by four Dutch banking houses.

LAND SPECULATION ON THE NEW YORK FRONTIER: THE "HOT HOUSE" TECHNIQUE

Selling to foreign speculators introduced a new settlement pattern to the frontier. Unlike American speculators who operated on hope and credit, these concerns had money to develop their properties, thus making them more attractive to newcomers. The result was the "hot house" period in New York's settlement. The agent of the Pulteney Estates, Charles Williamson, built roads, grist and saw mills, distilleries, and towns; he deepened harbors on Lake Ontario, and even laid out a race track and theater at the town of Bath. This extravagent expenditure did attract pioneers in such numbers that within a few years Bath was a well-established community, complete with a thriving commercial life, cultural activities, cultivated gentlemen, and a swarm of smaller speculators who found profit in reselling the company's lands. A traveler, Isaac Weld, who visited there in 1796 described life on that frontier:[2]

The landed property of which this gentleman, who founded Bath, &c. has had the active management, is said to have amounted originally to no less than six millions of acres, the greater part of which belonged to an individual in England. The method he has taken to improve this property has been, by granting land in small portions and on long credits to individuals who would immediately improve it, and in larger portions and on a shorter credit to others who purchased on speculation, the lands in both cases being mortgaged for the payment of the purchase money; thus, should the money not be paid at the appointed time, he could not be a loser, as the lands were to be returned to him, and should they happen to be at all improved, as was most likely to be the case, he would be a considerable gainer even by having them returned on his hands; moreover, if a poor man, willing to settle on his land, had not money sufficient to build a house and to go on with the necessary improvements, he has at once supplied him, having had a large capital himself, with what money he wanted for that purpose, or sent his own workmen, of whom he keeps a prodigious number employed, to build a house for him, at the same time taking the man's note at three, four, or five years, for the cost of the house, &c. with interest. If the man should be unable to pay at the appointed time, the house, mortgaged like the lands, must revert to the original proprietor, and the money arising from its sale, and that of the farm adjoining, partly improved, will in all probability be found to amount to more than what the poor man had promised to pay for it; but a man taking up land in America in this manner, at a moderate price, cannot fail, if industrious, of making money sufficient to pay for it, as well as for a house, at the appointed time.

The numbers that have been induced by these temptations, not to be met with elsewhere in the States, to settle in the Genesee County, is astonishing; and numbers are still flocking to it every year, as not one third of the lands are yet disposed of. It was currently reported in the county, as I passed through it, that this gentleman, of whom I have been speaking, had, in the notes of the people to whom he had sold land payable at the end of three, or four, or five years, the immense sum of two millions of dollars. The original cost of the land was not more than a few pence per acre; what therefore must be the profits!

---

[2] Isaac Weld, *Travels through the States of North America, and the Provinces of Upper and Lower Canada, during the Years 1795, 1796, and 1797* (London, 1797), pp. 438–441.

It may readily be imagined, that the granting of land on such very easy terms could not fail to draw crowds of speculators (a sort of gentry with which America abounds in every quarter) to this part of the country; and indeed we found, as we passed along, that every little town and village throughout the country abounded with them, and each place, in consequence, exhibited a picture of idleness and dissipation. The following letter, supposed to come from a farmer, though somewhat ludicrous, does not give an inaccurate description of one of these young speculators, and of what is going on in this neighbourhood. It appeared in a newspaper published at Wilkesbarré, on the Susquehannah, and I give it to you verbatim, because, being written by an American, it will perhaps carry more weight with it than any thing I could say on the same subject.

To the Printers of the Wilkesbarré Gazette.

GENTLEMEN,

It is painful to reflect, that speculation has raged to such a degree of late, that honest industry, and all the humble virtues that walk in her train, are discouraged and rendered unfashionable.

It is to be lamented too, that dissipation is sooner introduced in new settlements than industry and economy.

I have been led to these reflections by conversing with my son, who has just returned from the Lakes or Genesee, though he has neither been to the one or the other;—in short, he has been to Bath, the celebrated Bath, and has returned both a speculator and a gentleman; having spent his money, swopped away my horse, caught the fever and ague, and, what is infinitely worse, that horrid disorder which some call the terra-phobia.

We can hear nothing from the poor creature now (in his ravings) but of the captain and Billy—of ranges—townships—numbers—thousands—hundreds—acres—Bath—fairs—races—heats—bets—purses—silk stockings—fortunes—fevers—agues, &c. &c. &c. My son has part of a township for sale, and it is diverting enough to hear him narrate its pedigree, qualities, and situation. In fine, it lies near Bath, and the captain himself once owned, and for a long time reserved it. It cost my son but five dollars per acre; he was offered six in half a minute after his purchase; but he is positively determined to have eight, besides some precious reserves. One thing is very much in my boy's favour—he has six years credit. Another thing is still more so—he is not worth a sous, nor ever will be at this rate. Previous to his late excursion the lad worked well, and was contented at home on my farm; but now work is out of the question with him. There is no managing my boy at home; these golden dreams still beckon him back to Bath, where, as he says, no one need either work or starve; where, though a man may have the ague nine months in the year, he may console himself in spending the other three fashionably at the races.

A FARMER

HANOVER, OCTOBER 25TH, 1796

The town of Bath stands on a plain, surrounded on three sides by hills of a moderate height. The plain is almost wholly divested of its trees; but the hills are still uncleared, and have a very pleasing appearance from the town. At the foot of the hills runs a stream of pure water, over a bed of gravel, which is called Conhocton Creek. There is a very considerable fall in this creek just above the town, which affords one of the finest seats for mills possible. Extensive saw and flour mills have already been erected upon it, the principal saw in the former of which gave, when we visited the mill, one hundred and twenty strokes in a minute, sufficient to cut, in the same space of time, seven square feet, superficial measure, of oak timber; yet the miller informed us, that when the water was high it would cut much faster.

THE HOLLAND LAND COMPANY

In the ten years that he directed the Pulteney Estates, Williamson spent a million dollars of his backers' money and collected less than $150,000 in cash—although more was due under the credit system that was universal on the frontier. This set of figures convinced the shrewd Dutch bankers who controlled the Holland Land Company that there would be no "hurrying of civilization" on their estates, which comprised the whole western end of New York state. This decision was justified; American frontiersmen counted on profits from the improvement of their lands and did not favor a company that skimmed those profits off for its own benefit. So the Holland Land Company holdings filled as rapidly as those of the Pulteney Estates and at far less expense to the backers; by 1810, western New York was so well occupied that the company was debating means of discouraging the small speculators who were grabbing up all land that was left on the theory that it would soon command a premium price. This situation was described by Joseph Ellicott, the company's agent, in a report to his backers that year:[3]

My Report of 1809 among other Things recommended that the same Plan for disposing of these Lands should be continued as had been the Practice for the greater Part of the Term of the Administration. However before the Expiration of the year I was compelled to the Necessity of abandoning a Part of the old System, viz: that Part denominated Provisional Sales. I found by Experience that there is a Period that a System of that kind must for the Benefit and Advantage of the Land holders be discontinued, because the Plan is so susceptible of Abuse that eventually more Injury arises from it than all the Benefits derived.

At the same Time I may be permitted to say that in my Opinion it is the best Plan that can be devised for the Commencement of new Settlements, and indeed until a Tract of Country becomes tolerably populated, but Experience has taught me that there is an Epoch that renders it necessary to abandon that System and resort to that contained in my First and original Instructions that is to make no Sales unless from 5 to 10 pr Cent of the Purchase Money is paid in hand, and enter(ed) immediately into the Article of Agreement. During the preceding twelve Months, a scene of retail Speculation, that is Speculation in a small Way, was all the Rage; Industry became paralized, every Settler and every Labourer on the Purchase as well as every Man who came into the Country (and they came in by Shoals) were taking up Lots on provisional Agreements without any Intention of making Settlements, or ever making any Payment for the Land; having no other Object in View than to dispose of that provisional Agreement to a second Person, a coming-in Settler at an Advance as high as he could obtain, and if he should not find some Person to give him one or two hundred Dollars for this *Chance* as he called it by the Period or Termination of the provisional Agreement, by a Trick of Cunning he would contrive to get the Land another Term, although I was very guarded to prevent that kind of jockeying and low Cunning that many People possess, and indeed is their whole Study until eventually they reduce it to a science. Our System was that where any Person who was a Settler on the

---

[3] Robert W. Bingham (ed.), *Holland Land Company Papers. Reports of Joseph Ellicott* (Buffalo: Buffalo and Erie Historical Society, 1941), pp. 74–78, 82–83.

Purchase—should take up a Lot of Land by provisional Agreement not comply with the Terms of that Agreement in the Period limited for Compliance not to give that same Person another Refusal of the same Lot but these People would generally by Means of a second Person, who would lend his Name, obtain another provisional Term, and so on until an Opportunity offered to make 50. 100. 150 or $ 200 for the Chance of the Lot to some coming in Settler, who, if the Lot had not been under and subject to that provisional Agreement, would have take up the Lot of us, and we should have received the Money that the provisional Purchaser obtained of the real Purchaser and eventually this real Purchasers and Settler having paid over all his Money to the provisional Purchaser, what we obtained was the Settler without any Money and the only advantage we got was that this Settler was increasing the value of the Territory by Means of his Improvement; and after he had effected his Settlement we were compelled to issue him an Article by paying from one to fifteen or twenty Dollars.

It is true however that the Settlements that are effected will increase the Value of the Land, and that ultimately the Money that the Land was sold for will be paid with the accruing Interest, but the getting little or no Money from many of this Description of Sales was not the only Injury we began to sustain by this Method of transacting Business, because such vast Quantities of Lands were already taken up in this Way, and Shoals of People at the Office from Monday morning until Saturday Night taking up Lands on provisional Agreement until at Length we had in many Townships scarcely a feasable Lot of Land for Sale and the coming on Settler was compelled, if he had got Land, to buy second handed of provisional Purchasers. The Evil did not end here, because it became at length difficult to ascertain the Lots that were settled, and those that had reverted, because in many Instances where Settlements were made the People grew neglectful of reporting their Improvements and Settlement, and some Person making the Discovery that the Settlers' provisional Term had expired he would call at the Office and obtain an Article for the Lot and then make the Settler, who had made the Improvements and was residing on the Lot pay him nearly the value of the Improvement he himself had made, or keep the Lot by Virtue of the Article of Agreement he had obtained. In short the Business in this large Extent of Country became so complex and confused that I was compelled to abandon provisional Sales altogether, and resort to real ones where the 5 or 10 pr Cent of the Purchase Money was paid in hand, and an Article of Agreement issued at once, or make no Sale. And indeed I have found this Amendment to be productive of the best Effects as it relates to the Receipt of Moneys; as we now receive more than double the Amount we formerly did on making provisional Sales, because those who ultimately complied with the Terms of the provisional Sale and made the Settlement and Improvement seldom could be prevailed upon after years had elapsed to pay more than ¼ of the 5 Pr Cent of the Purchase Money, as the Case might be, and on Examination of the Articles of Agreement accompanying this Report it will be seen that where there is endorsed on the Article a large Improvement a few Dollars only could be obtained in Part of 5 Pr Cent of the Purchase Money and few People when they come to purchase Lands but what are in a Situation to pay some where near 5 pr Cent of the Purchase Money on as much Land as they want for a Farm, but such is the Disposition of the greatest Part of the People that if they can obtain the Land for a given Time with making little or not any Payment they will not pay. . . .

The natural Population of the Inhabitants already on this Territory would without the Aid of Emigration settle the whole Territory in half a Century, but as the Emigration will treble the natural Population we may safely calculate without giving so much Encouragement as we have heretofore given, that the whole Territory at least the most inviting Parts will all be settled in a few years. In order to enable ourselves to form an Opinion of the Extent of Settlement we may reasonably calculate upon for the next ten Years, and Increase of Population, we may advert to the adjoining Country East of Genesee County, that is to say the County of Ontario. When the Census for 1800 was taken by Act of Congress of the Inhabitants of the United States, the whole number of Inhabitants within the Limits of the County of Ontario was only about 14000, and by the Census taken by Act of Congress in 1810 the Inhabitants of Ontario County amounted to rising 42000. In nearly that proportion has the Increase been in all the Counties Eastward until we arrive at Herkimer County, and in nearly the same proportion has the Value of wild or new Lands increased in Price. . . .

In some Parts Turnpike Roads are making from the Interior of the Country to Lake Ontario; one from the Village of Canandaigua in Ontario County to great Sodus Bay for the Purpose of transporting Produce to that Place with more Facility than it can be carried along the present Roads, which must from the Country being new, and of Course the Roads bad, be attended with more Expence than when the Roads are made good. The English Land Company who have a considerable Interest in that Country I have understood have subscribed liberally to the Stock to encourage the making of the Road. They have found by Experience that there is nothing so beneficial to the Sale of Land and for a good Price, as Roads, and the better they are made, the more they add to the Value of a County through which they pass.

Villages are erecting and other laying out on the Shore of Lake Ontario wherever there is a Probability of making a Harbour for such Craft as are used for the Navigation of the Lake; and the Time is not far distant when those who may navigate these inland seas will behold their Shores handsomely ornamented and chequered with the finest and best Farms, and thriving villages which already begin to display themselves to the Mariners of the Lakes.

I must take the Liberty to request that you will pardon this Digression, because to you who travelled through these Regions when the Country was almost one impenetrable extended Wilderness the Description I have given will appear more like Fable than Reality; but Sir, to me, who have been an Eye Witness to the growing Improvements going on in these Regions for these ten Years past it is very easy for me to anticipate what will take Place in that Respect at a future Period, more especially as Advantages of a permanent Nature regarding the great Interests of this Country, are annually presenting themselves to our View.

THE CONNECTICUT LAND COMPANY SETTLES THE WESTERN RESERVE

As western New York filled during the early years of the nineteenth century, another migratory column moved beyond to invade the

Ohio country. There two regions seemed especially attractive at this time. One was the Western Reserve, the tract in northeastern Ohio retained by Connecticut when it ceded its western holdings in 1786. This whole area was sold in 1795 to a syndicate of speculators organized as the Connecticut Land Company. These shrewd Yankees squandered no money on improvements as did their New York counterparts, but they did realize that lands, if not cash, could be used to encourage settlement. Tracts could be given away to grist mill operators, saw mill operators, distillers, and others who would provide services or markets essential to colony planting. This device, which proved singularly successful in encouraging migration to the Western Reserve, was to be imitated increasingly by large landholders on later frontiers. Its operations are described in the minutes of the Connecticut Land Company:[4]

January 30th 1798 The Meeting opened According to adjournment. At this Meeting the following report of a Committee appointed to Enquire into the Expediency of laying out and Cutting roads on the Reserve, was approved of, and Accepted

To the Gentleman Proprietors of the Connecticut Land Company in Meeting at Hartford

Your Committee appointed to Enquire into the Expediency of laying out and Cutting roads on the Reserve—Report, That in their opinion it will be expedient to lay out and Cut a Road from Pennsylvania to the City of Cleveland the Small Stuff to be cut out twenty five feet wide and the Timber to be girded thirty three feet wide, and Sufficient Bridges thereon, over Such Streams as are Not fordable, And the Said Road begin in Township number 13 in the first range at the Pennsylvania line, and to run Westerly through Townships number 12 in the 2nd range, number 12 in the third range, number 11 in the 4th range to the Indian ford at the bend of the Grand River thence through Township number 11 in the 5th range, number 10 in the Sixth range, number 10 in the Seventh range, number 10 in the 8th range, and the North west part of Number 9 in the 9th range, and to the Chagrin River near where a large Creek Enters it from the East, and from the Crossing the Chagrin the most direct way to the Middle highway leading from the City of Cleveland to the hundred Acre lots, also a highway to Start from the former in the Townships Number 10 in the 8th range and to pass through Township Number 9 in the 7th range, Number 8 in the 6th range Number 7 in the 6th range, Number 5 in the 5th range Number 4 in the fourth range and then direct to the Salt Spring in Number 3 in the third range, and that the Expense of opening Said Roads may Probably Cost two thousand Six hundred dollars. . . . On Reconsideration of the Acceptance of the within and foregoing Report. Voted that it be Accepted with the following additions viz: That the particular location of Roads through the Said Township Shall be Ascertained by an Agent or Agents to be appointed by the Directors for that purpose.

January 27th The Meeting opened according to Adjournment, When the following Vote Passed. Viz: Whereas the Directors of the Connecticut Land Company for the purpose of Encouraging Settlement on the Western Reserve and Compensating these persons who first settled in the Territory, for the risk and hardships they encountered Have given to Tabitha Cuma Stiles, wife of

---

[4] Claude L. Shepard, "The Connecticut Land Company: A Study of the Beginnings of Colonization of the Western Reserve," *Annual Report of the Western Reserve Historical Society (1915–1916). Pt. II, The Connecticut Land Company and Accompanying Papers* (Cleveland, 1916), pp. 180–184.

Job P. Stiles, one City, one Ten, and one hundred Acre Lot and to Anna Gunn wife of Elija Gunn one hundred Acre Lot, to James King and wife one hundred Acre lot, and to Nathaniel Doan one city Lot, he being obliged to reside thereon as a Black Smith and all in the City and Town of Cleveland —Therefore Voted, by the Connecticut Land Company that they do approve and Confirm the aforesaid Grants, and authorize the Directors to Carry the Same into Complete Effect,

[*Monday January 29th*]

V*oted* That the Directors be Authorized to Make donations of Such part of the lots in the City and Town of Cleveland as they Shall think expedient for the Encouragement of Useful Mechanics who Shall Actually Settle and reside in Said Town.

[*Dec. 5, 1798*]

V*oted* That the Directors be authorized to apply a Sum not exceeding three hundred dollars in Erecting works at the Salt Springs, And in manageing the Same in Such way and manner as they may Judge will be most for the interest of the Company.

Voted that the Directors be, and they are hereby authorized to Lease the Salt Springs in the Western Reserve with a Sufficient quantity of Land adjourning as will be necessary to improve the works for making Salt for a term of not exceeding five years.

[*Dec. 5, 1798*]

V*oted* That the Company grant as a Bounty a Sum not exceeding Two hundred dollars, or Loan the Sum Not Exceeding five hundred Dollars without interest untill the first day of April AD 1802, and three years after that time on interest annually at the Election of the Contractor unto any person or persons who Shall Contract with surety to the Satisfaction of the Directors, to erect by the first day of December Next a good Grist Mill in townships Number Nine in the Ninth range on the Western Reserve. Also a grant or Loan as aforesaid to any person who Shall Contract as aforesaid to erect a Grist Mill of the foregoing description within Said time in Township number Seven in the Seventh range And the Same Sum by way of grant or Loan as aforesaid to be granted or loaned from the first day of April 1800 untill the first day of April 1803, without interest, and three years longer on interest afterwards unto any Person or persons who Shall Contract with Surety to the Satisfaction of the Directors to build by the first day of December 1800 a good Grist Mill on the Nearest Suitable Mill Seat to the Corner between Townships number two in the Eighth range and Number three in the Seventh range. And the Same terms to any person who will Contract to build as aforesaid on the Nearest Mill Seat to the Center of townships Number four in the fourth range of Townships provided the Same be within Seven Miles of Said Center, And the Same terms to any person who Shall Contract to build as aforesaid on the Nearest Mill Seat to the Corner between Number Eleven in the Second range and Number two in the third range, and that the directors or Agent be empowered to carry this vote into effect.

V*oted* That a tax of Ten dollars be Assessed on Each of the Shares of the Company to be paid to the Clerk of the Directors by the 7th day of January Next.

THE OHIO VALLEY FRONTIER IN 1802

The second area in the Ohio country that lured pioneers at this time—the region south of the Greenville treaty line—was not blessed with speculating companies that built roads or granted plots to grist mill and flour mill operators, but the pace of growth there even surpassed that of the Western Reserve. Ease of access was responsible. Settlers had only to make their way to Pittsburgh or Wheeling on the Ohio River, buy a crude flatboat or barge, and drift down the river until they spotted an attractive homesite. Others moved inland from the Ohio, buying from small speculating companies or individual jobbers who appropriated most of the best land, then sold on credit. By 1802, the whole region south of the Greenville line was occupied. The bustle of life on this mushrooming frontier was mirrored by a traveler, F. A. Michaux, who journeyed down the Ohio River in 1802 and recorded his impressions of the primitive settlements along the banks and of the restless frontiersmen who were already looking westward to still newer frontiers:[5]

Till the years 1796 and 1797 the banks of the Ohio were so little populated that they scarcely consisted of thirty families in the space of four hundred miles; but since that epoch a great number of emigrants have come from the mountainous parts of Pennsylvania and Virginia, and settled there; in consequence of which the plantations now are so increased, that they are not farther than two or three miles distant from each other, and when on the river we always had a view of some of them.

The inhabitants on the borders of the Ohio, employ the greatest part of their time in stag and bear hunting, for the sake of the skins, which they dispose of. The taste that they have contracted for this kind of life is prejudicial to the culture of their lands; besides they have scarcely any time to meliorate their new possessions, that usually consist of two or three hundred acres, of which not more than eight or ten are cleared. Nevertheless, the produce that they derive from them, with the milk of their cows, is sufficient for themselves and families, which are always very numerous. The houses that they inhabit are built upon the borders of the river, generally in a pleasant situation, whence they enjoy the most delightful prospects; still their mode of building does not correspond with the beauties of the spot, being nothing but miserable log houses, without windows, and so small that two beds occupy the greatest part of them. Notwithstanding two men may erect and finish, in less than three days, one of these habitations, which, by their diminutive size and sorry appearance, seem rather to belong to a country where timber is very scarce, instead of a place that abounds with forests. The inhabitants on the borders of the Ohio do not hesitate to receive travellers who claim their hospitality; they give them a lodging, that is to say, they permit them to sleep upon the floor wrapped up in their rugs. They are accommodated with bread, Indian corn, dried ham, milk and butter, but seldom any thing else; at the same time the price of provisions is very moderate in this part of the United States, and all through the western country.

No attention is paid by the inhabitants to any thing else but the culture of Indian corn; and although it is brought to no great perfection, the soil being so full of roots, the stems are from ten to twelve feet high, and produce from twenty to thirty-five hundred weight of corn per acre. For the three first years after the ground is cleared, the corn springs up too strong, and scatters before it ears, so that they cannot sow in it for four or five years after, when the ground is cleared

---

[5] F. A. Michaux, *Travels to the West of the Alleghany Mountains. In the States of Ohio, Kentucky, and Tennessea* (London, 1805), pp. 108–114.

of the stumps and roots that were left in at first. The Americans in the interior cultivate corn rather through speculation to send the flour to the sea-ports, than for their own consumption; as nine tenths of them eat no other bread but that made from Indian corn; they make loaves of it from eight to ten pounds, which they bake in ovens, or small cakes baked on a board before the fire. This bread is generally eaten hot, and is not very palatable to those who are not used to it.

The peach is the only fruit tree that they have as yet cultivated, which thrives so rapidly that it produces fruit after the second year.

The price of the best land on the borders of the Ohio did not exceed three piastres per acre; at the same time it is not so dear on the left bank in the States of Virginia and Kentucky, where the settlements are not looked upon as quite so good.

The two banks of the Ohio, properly speaking, not having been inhabited above eight or nine years, nor the borders of the rivers that run into it, the Americans who are settled there, share but very feebly in the commerce that is carried on through the channel of the Mississippi. This commerce consists at present in hams and salted pork, brandies distilled from corn and peaches, butter, hemp, skins and various sorts of flour. They send again cattle to the Atlantic States. Tradespeople who supply themselves at Pittsburgh and Wheeling, and go up and down the river in a canoe, convey them haberdashery goods, and more especially tea and coffee, taking some of their produce in return.

More than half of those who inhabit the borders of the Ohio, are again the first inhabitants, or as they are called in the United States, the *first settlers*, a kind of men who cannot settle upon the soil that they have cleared, and who under pretence of finding a better land, a more wholesome country, a greater abundance of game, push forward, incline perpetually towards the most distant points of the American population, and go and settle in the neighbourhood of the savage nations, whom they brave even in their own country. Their ungenerous mode of treating them stirs up frequent broils, that brings on bloody wars, in which they generally fall victims; rather on account of their being so few in number, than through defect of courage.

Prior to our arrival at Marietta, we met one of these *settlers*, an inhabitant of the environs of Wheeling, who accompanied us down the Ohio, and with whom we travelled for two days. Alone in a canoe from eighteen to twenty feet long, and from twelve to fifteen inches broad, he was going to survey the borders of the Missouri for a hundred and fifty miles beyond its *embouchure*. The excellent quality of the land that is reckoned to be more fertile there than that on the borders of the Ohio, and which the Spanish government at that time ordered to be distributed *gratis*, the quantity of beavers, elks, and more especially bisons, were the motives that induced him to emigrate into this remote part of the country, whence after having determined on a suitable spot to settle there with his family, he was returning to fetch them from the borders of the Ohio, which obliged him to take a journey of fourteen or fifteen hundred miles, his costume, like that of all the American sportsmen, consisted of a waistcoat with sleeves, a pair of pantaloons, and a large red and yellow worsted sash. A carabine, a tomahawk or little axe, which the Indians make use of to cut wood and to terminate the existence of their enemies, two beaver-snares, and a large knife suspended at his side, constituted his sporting dress. A rug comprised the whole of his luggage. Every evening he encamped on the banks of the river, where, after having made a fire, he passed the night; and whenever he conceived the place favourable for the chace, he remained in the woods for several days together, and with the produce of his sport, he gained the means of subsistence, and new ammunition with the skins of the animals that he had killed.

Such were the first inhabitants of Kentucky and Tennessea, of whom there are now remaining but very few. It was they who began to clear those fertile countries, and wrested them from the savages who ferociously disputed their right; it was they, in short, who made themselves masters of the possessions, after five or six years' bloody war: but the long habit of a wandering and idle life has prevented their enjoying the fruit of their labours, and profiting by the very price to which these lands have risen in so short a time. They have emigrated to more remote parts of the country, and formed new settlements. It will be the same with most of those who inhabit the borders of the Ohio. The same inclination that led them there will induce them to emigrate from it. To the latter will succeed fresh emigrants, coming also from the Atlantic states, who will desert their possessions to go in quest of a milder climate and a more fertile soil. The money that they will get for them will suffice to pay for their new acquisitions, the peaceful delight of which is assured by a numerous population. The last comers instead of log-houses, with which the present inhabitants are contented, will build wooden ones, clear a greater quantity of the land, and be as industrious and persevering in the melioration of their new possessions as the former were indolent in every thing, being so fond of hunting. To the culture of Indian corn they will add that of other grain, hemp, and tobacco; rich pasturages will nourish innumerable flocks, and an advantageous sale of all the country's produce will be assured them through the channel of the Ohio.

AGITATION FOR CHEAPER LANDS

The speculators who controlled land sales in Ohio, New York, and elsewhere on the frontiers performed a basic service, but they also made themselves extremely unpopular with the frontiersmen. Why, the pioneers asked, should they be forced to support these nonworking parasites who did only two things: parceled out land in small lots needed by primitive farmers and sold on credit. Why did the federal government not sell in small quantities and allow time for payment? As the population in the West increased, so did the political influence of that region, and with it the first effective pressure to modify the conservative system of land sales inaugurated in the Ordinance of 1785. The westerners won a partial victory in the Land Act of 1796 which allowed a year's credit on half the purchase price, but their great triumph came four years later. The Land Act of 1800 reduced the smallest amount purchasable from 640 to 320 acres, provided for land offices in the West, and authorized initial payment of one-fourth of the price, the remainder to be paid in four years. The reason for this frontier triumph can be found in the flood of petitions frontiersmen showered on Congress in 1798 and 1799. Typical was one originating in the Ohio country:[6]

To the Honorable the Senate and House of Representatives of the United States in Congress Assembled, the Petition of the un-

---

[6] "Petition to Congress by Citizens of the Northwest Territory [1799]," in Clarence E. Carter (ed.), *The Territorial Papers of the United States. III, The Territory Northwest of the River Ohio, 1787–1803* (Washington, 1934), pp. 52–53.

dersign,d Citizens of the Territory of the United States North west of the River Ohio Humbly Sheweth That your petitioners having attentively examined a law passed by your Honorable body on the 18th day of May 1796 Entitled "An Act providing for the sale of the Lands of the United States in the Territory of the United States North West of the River Ohio &c" and feeling the highest respect for and Gratitude to the framers of the said Law for the care and Oeconomy over the property of their Common Country. Humbly beg leave to Offer their Objections thereto, your petitioners beg leave to Suggest it as their Opinions that the one Half of the said Lands are directed to be sold in too large Tracts as they Contain 5120 Acres exclusive of Reservations no doubt your Honorable body are not Strangers to the Scarcity of money which is at present Experienced in the United States. few persons will therefore be in a Situation to purchase any of these Tracts on the terms they are to be sold. Which under Existing Circumstances are your petitioners Conceive too severe and Calculated to impede the sale of the lands and risk the ruin of the purchaser—The terms your petitioners have reference to are as follows to wit. see the 7§ of the said law

Be it further enacted that the highest bidder for any Tract of land sold by Virtue of this Act Shall deposit at the time of sale one twentieth part of the amount of the purchase money, to be forfeited if a moiety of the sum bid including the said twentieth part is not paid within Thirty days to the Treasurer of the United States or to such person as shall be appointed by the President of the United States to attend the places of sale for that purpose and upon payment of a moiety of the purchase money within thirty days the purchaser shall have one years credit for the residue and shall receive from the Secretary of the Treasury or the Govenor of Western Territory as the case may be a certificate describing the land sold the sum paid an account of the ballance remaining due, the time when such ballance becomes payable and that the whole land Sold will be forfeited if the said ballance is not then paid, but if it shall be duly discharged the purchaser or his assinee or other legal Representative shall be entitled to a patent for the said land and on payment of the said Ballance to the Treasurer within the specified time and producing to the Secretary of state a receipt for the same—upon the aforesaid Certificate the President of the United States is hereby authorised to grant a patent for the lands to the said purchaser his heirs or assigns and all patents Shall be Countersigned by the Secretary of state and recorded in his office, but if there should be a failure in any payment the sale shall be void all the money theretofore paid on account of the purchase shall be forfeited to the United States, and the lands thus sold shall again disposed of in the same manner as if a sale had never been made

It is with the deepest regret that your petitioners see the impossibility of becoming purchasers on these terms In the course of human affairs disappointments are frequent and from the law a failure of one day. nay an Hour may Subject the purchaser to inevitable Ruin—When your Honorable body reflect on the very great change which has taken place in the United States since the passage of the aforesaid law and consider the dangerous situation in which the purchaser is placed you will no doubt see the necessity of taking the same into Consideration and to alter the terms of sale So as to give a longer time for the different payments and to secure those payments in such a manner as not to deter persons wishing to purchase or risk the ruin of those who become purchasers, Your petitioners further Humbly pray that the lands Bounded on the west by the Siota river and on the North by the United States Bounty lands on the East by the seventeenth Range line and on the South by the Ohio may be offered for sale at the Town of Chillicothe which lies on the west branch of the Siota Opposite to the large body of good lands within the boundary aforesaid as persons disposed to purchase can be Comfortably Accommodated at the said Town of Chillicothe and with Convenience Examine the lands aforesaid the advantage of such an arrangement would in the Opinion of your petitioners be advantagious to the United States and Satisfactory and Convenient to Purchasers—Your petitioners as in duty bound shall every pay &C &C

POLITICAL DIVISIONS ON THE OHIO FRONTIER

As essential as frontier pressure to the western victory in the Land Act of 1800 was the changing political climate in the East. There the commercially oriented Federalist party which had dominated during the administrations of George Washington and John Adams was swept from office in 1800, to be replaced by the Jeffersonian-Republican party under President Thomas Jefferson. The Jeffersonians were less mindful of the commercial interests of seaboard merchants than the Federalists, and more prone to champion agrarian programs in both East and West. This viewpoint explains their support of the Land Act of 1800; it also spelled the end of a clique of Federalist officials who had controlled politics in the new territories. Chief of these was Governor Arthur St. Clair of the Northwest Territory, a crotchety conservative with as little liking for the people he governed as for the democracy that they upheld. Something of the spleen that he inspired was shown in a letter by one of his political rivals, Judge John Cleves Symmes, written in 1802:[7]

To Thomas Jefferson esquire,
President of the United States

Pardon me Sir, if in this instance I depart from the prescribed mode of addressing the President on a subject of Territorial concern, through Mr Maddison the the proper organ of state business. My communication being of a delatory nature against the first Magistrate of the Northwestern Territory, whose prompt removal from office rests solely with the President: it would seem only necessary, Sir, correctly to inform the conscience of the President with regard to the mal-administration of Arthur St. Clair esquire governor of said territory, in order to invite a measure so desirable to thousands of the Inhabitants of the western country, as that of his being dismissed from his government. To incline the President to be propitious in this respect to the wishes of the people—I humbly conceive it my duty, sir, to sketch out some of the leading features in the public character of governor St. Clair.—A few of which are the following.

By constitution a despot, as well as from long imperious habits of commanding, he has become unsufferably arbitrary.

Like other tyrants, he places his confidence for advice and support, in the weak and the guileful of the citizens, who misguide and disgrace him.

The prosperity of the territory is, and always has been a secondary consideration with him. literally his will is law; and measures (however eligible, considered either as

---

[7] "Judge John Cleves Symmes to President Thomas Jefferson, January 23, 1802," in Clarence E. Carter (ed.), *The Territorial Papers of the United States. III, The Territory Northwest of the River Ohio, 1787–1803* (Washington, 1934), pp. 205–207.

convenient, honorary, or pecuniary) which do not concentrate their good effect, in his family or among his favorites, are altogether inadmissible with him.

He is at war with those who do not approach him with adulation on their tongue.

He hessitates not, to sacrifice the best interest of the territory, when they come in competition with his partial aims.

Though of courtly exterior; his heart, if judged of by the tongue, is illiberal beyond a sample.

Destitute of gratitude, he abhors the government that feeds him:—the public or private hand that relieves him in distress, confers no obligation.

Though a commentator of the sedition law,—is seditious himself.

Is he commissioned to guide the citizens confided to his charge, to their true interests? he wantonly misleads them.—to protect? he invades their rights.—to harmonize? he irritates dissension.—To revere a republican form of government? he raises the sneer and sends it round the board.

His pious frauds practised on the public, are not calculated for the meridian of his own altars.—there the presiding deities are of grecian Mythology.

Wanting application to his official duties, which lie neglected from year to year;—fain would he arrogate to himself the superintendency of the judiciary.

Outrageous, if a citizen charged with the murder of an Indian, be acquitted by a jury of the country.—he can calmly look on and see citizens Murdered by Indians, without one effort of the executive to bring the murderers to a trial.

Notorious for his military blunders,—if we believe him correct, and could he again command; his talents supersedes the necessity of three major, and six brigadier generals, although the Militia law requires them.

Wiser in his own conceit, than the other two branches of the Legislature, collective and unanimous; he withholds his assent to bills of the most salutary nature.

Under his long administration the people are not, nor have they ever been satisfied, and many detesting him, have fled the territory.

Although in a colonial situation, the people are proud of the right they have, to resort to the general government, as they now do, for relief from his oppressive and undue exercise of the executive power.

Do these imputations need proof?—let letters, prisons, flames, human-bones and tears bear testimony; while neglected frenchrights, imbecility of Magistrates of his appointment, executive deception, unequal tenures in office, his Usurped prerogatives, and ill placed patronage, fill the North western territory with murmurs, deep—awful—dangerous; while his distracted government totters to its foundation.

All of which, with sincerity and truth, to the President of the United states, is most respectfully submitted, by his Obedient humble servant.

JOHN CLEVES SYMMES

THE OHIO CONSTITUTION AND BACKWOODS DEMOCRACY

If Judge Symmes correctly mirrored the Jeffersonian-Republican attitude toward Governor St. Clair, the old Federalist's days as an officeholder were numbered. His faction was steadily losing strength as newcomers from Jefferson's party swelled the population, demanding more power in the territorial legislature, insisting on more offices, and pressing for statehood for the Ohio country. The Republicans won their first major victory in May 1800, when they succeeded in a measure dividing the Northwest Territory into two parts along lines favorable to their political ambitions. The next step was taken in April 1802, when a congressional enabling act authorized them to call a convention to frame a constitution for the new state. Ohio entered the Union in 1803 with a Jeffersonian-Republican slate of officers firmly in control. This democratic climate proved even more alluring to migrants; for the next decade the population increased steadily. Not until the outbreak of Indian troubles on the eve of the War of 1812 did the tide begin to slow. By this time southern Ohio was passing beyond the frontier stage, and even its northern fringes were receiving settlers. A traveler, John Bradbury, who journeyed widely in the backcountry there at this time understood the relationship between the democratic constitution and the distinctive regional character beginning to shape itself:[8]

The constitution of the state of Ohio declares that

1. All men are born equally free and independent.
2. All men have a natural right to worship God according to the dictates of their own conscience.
3. Trial by jury shall be inviolate.
4. Printing-presses shall be free.
5. Unwarrantable searches shall not be permitted.
6. Unnecessary rigor shall not be exercised.
7. Excessive bail shall not be required in bailable offences.
8. All penalties shall be proportioned to the nature of the offence.
9. The liberty of the people to assemble together, to consult for the public good, and to bear arms in their own defence, is guaranteed.
10. Hereditary emoluments, honours, and privileges are for ever prohibited.
11. Slavery is for ever prohibited, and it is declared that "No indenture of any negro or mulatto, hereafter made and executed out of the state, or if made in the state, where the term of service exceeds one year, shall be of the least validity, except those given in the case of apprenticeship."
12. "Religion, morality, and knowledge being essentially necessary to the good government and happiness of mankind, schools, and the means of instruction, shall be for ever encouraged by legislative provision, not inconsistent with the rights of conscience."

The government is legislative and executive, and regulates the judicial and military authorities.

The legislature consists of a senate and house of representatives. The senators are elected *biennially*, the representatives *annually*, by the people, and one half vacate their seats every year. Every free white male, who is a citizen of the United States, and has resided in that state one year, has a vote for a representative; if he has resided two years, he can vote for a senator.

Every citizen qualified to vote for a representative, and above twenty-five years of age, is also eligible to be himself elected: if above thirty years of age, he is eligible to become a senator.

The governor is also chosen by the people, and serves for two years: he cannot by law be elected more than three times in succession.

The election is carried on throughout the state on the same day, and during the same hours, viz. from ten to four o'clock. There is a poll in every township, and it is conducted by ballot; each elector hands in a slip of paper, containing the name of the candi-

---

[8] John Bradbury, *Travels in the Interior of America in the Years 1809, 1810, and 1811* (London, 1819), pp. 309–313.

date to whom he gives his vote, at which time his own name is registered. By this means, the whole business of election is begun and terminated in one day, without any noise or disturbance.

The justices are appointed by the people of their respective townships, and retain their office only three years, unless re-elected.

In the military of the state, the captains and the subaltern officers are chosen by those in their respective company districts, who are subject to military duty.

Majors are elected by captains and subalterns.

Colonels are elected by majors, captains, and subalterns.

Brigadier-generals are elected by the commissioned officers of their respective brigades.

Major-generals and quarter-master-generals are appointed by joint ballot of both houses of the legislature.

The governor is commander-in-chief, and appoints the adjutants.

In regard to the manners of the people west of the Alleghanies, it would be absurd to expect that a general character could be now formed, or that it will be for many years yet to come. The population is at present compounded of a great number of nations, not yet amalgamated, consisting of emigrants from every state in the Union, mixed with English, Irish, Scotch, Dutch, Swiss, Germans, French, and almost from every country in Europe. In some traits they partake in common with the inhabitants of the Atlantic States, which results from the nature of their government. That species of hauteur which one class of society in some countries show in their intercourse with the other, is here utterly unknown. By their constitution, the existence of a privileged order, vested by birth with hereditary privileges, honours, or emoluments, is for ever interdicted. If, therefore, we should here expect to find that contemptuous feeling in man for man, we should naturally examine amongst those clothed with judicial or military authority; but we should search in vain. The justice on the bench, or the officer in the field, is respected and obeyed whilst discharging the functions of his office, as the representative or agent of the law, enacted for the *good of all*; but should he be tempted to treat even the least wealthy of his neighbours or fellow-citizens with contumely, he would soon find that he could not do it with impunity. Travellers from Europe, in passing through the western country, or indeed any part of the United States, ought to be previously acquainted with this part of the American character, and more particularly if they have been in the habit of treating with contempt, or irritating with abuse, those whom accidental circumstances may have placed in a situation to administer to their wants. Let no one here indulge himself in abusing the waiter or hostler at an inn: that waiter or hostler is probably a citizen, and does not, nor can he, conceive that a situation in which he discharges a duty to society, not in itself dishonourable, should subject him to insult: but this feeling, so far as I have experienced, is entirely defensive. I have travelled near ten thousand miles in the United States, and never received the least incivility or affront.

The migratory stream had flowed steadily since the middle 1790s into Kentucky and Tennessee to extend the borders of settlement there almost to the Mississippi, across western New York and Pennsylvania, into the Ohio country and westward along the banks of the Ohio River into modern Indiana. It slowed to a halt in 1809 and 1810 because of a new Indian war. This conflict originated as did all major Indian wars when Americans intruded on the lands of the red men who had ultimately to decide to defend themselves or to be exterminated. But this war, like so many in the past, was intensified by the meddling of European powers. So it merged into a minor international conflict, the War of 1812 between Britain and the United States, which was destined to have a lasting effect on the West.

CHAPTER 12

The West in the War of 1812, 1812-1815

For the generation of Americans that elbowed its way westward after 1800, the Napoleonic Wars offered unique opportunities to demonstrate nationalism, overrun Canada, drive Spain from the Floridas, and sweep aside the remaining Indian barrier east of the Mississippi River. All the issues which generated Anglo-American conflict received warm welcome in the West because each could be used to further western goals. When the British, locked in a life-and-death-struggle with the French, ruthlessly violated the rights of neutrals on the seas, impressed American seamen, and tried to regulate American commerce with Europe, western spokesmen whose livelihood was only remotely affected by trade and whose knowledge of marine law was scanty outdid eastern mercantile interests in their denunciation of England and their insistence that American freedom of the seas be defended—if necessary, even by war. Since both Britain and its ally Spain could be most easily attacked by land through Canada and Florida, western rhetoric set forth many causes for war but always focused on the same techniques to resolve them. Spain must be ousted and England's hold on the tribes ended. Whether the War of 1812 should be attributed to the fight for neutral rights, land hunger for Florida and Canada, or a desire to crush the Indians is less important than the shared belief that the West played a significant part in bringing about the struggle.

Different issues provoked greater or lesser reactions in the West, for political sentiment, economic needs, and personal ambitions all tended to affect sectional attitudes. Thus, the primary concern of those who favored war to protect the nation's commerce and save the nation's honor was particularly strong in the South and West, partly because frontier nationalism helped shape sentiment there, partly because the Jeffersonian-Republicans who predominated were more inclined to support their President than the Federalists of the seaboard, and partly because westerners and southerners operated under a marginal economy that was easily injured by any interference with overseas trade. They wanted war to secure the right to ship cotton and cereals to Europe, and to defend the national honor that they singularly cherished. But they knew that England and Spain could not be attacked directly and could be hurt only by the conquest of Canada and the Floridas. The prospect of overrunning Canada seemed especially alluring; its conquest would wipe out the bases from which Indians raided the backcountry, and a conquered Canada could be used to force England to guarantee freedom of the seas by putting this as a price for its return.

THE UNITED STATES CLAIMS WEST FLORIDA

This expansionist sentiment operated first in the Southwest, with the Floridas as the objective. West Florida was especially tempting, for through it ran the rivers over which the Southwest must export is produce, and in it were hundreds of renegades, runaway slaves, and outlaw Indians whose raids across the border menaced life and property. Moreover, West Florida could be taken without straining international relations too badly; one interpretation of the Louisiana Treaty of 1803 held that the United States already had title to the region. This was sufficient excuse to spark a migration of expansionists to the Baton Rouge area, and to send this unruly crew into action when rumors of an impending war penetrated their outposts. In September 1810 they seized West Florida in a bloodless revolution. President Madison, who had watched these events with ill-concealed pleasure, knowing that Spain was too occupied on the Continent to interfere, issued on October 27, 1810, a proclamation formally adding West Florida to the United States:[1]

Whereas the territory south of the Mississippi Territory and eastward of the river Mississippi, and extending to the river Perdido, of which possession was not delivered to the United States in pursuance of the treaty concluded at Paris on the 30th April, 1803, has at all times, as is well known, been considered and claimed by them as being within the colony of Louisiana conveyed by the said treaty in the same extent that it had in the hands of Spain and that it had when France originally possessed it; and

Whereas the acquiescence of the United States in the temporary continuance of the said territory under the Spanish authority was not the result of any distrust of their title, as has been particularly evinced by the general tenor of their laws and by the distinction made in the application of those laws between that territory and foreign countries, but was occasioned by their conciliatory views and by a confidence in the justice of their cause and in the success of candid discussion and amicable negotiation with a just and friendly power; and

Whereas a satisfactory adjustment, too long delayed, without the fault of the United States, has for some time been entirely suspended by events over which they had no control; and

Whereas a crisis has at length arrived subversive of the order of things under the Spanish authorities, whereby a failure of the United States to take the said territory into its possession may lead to events ultimately contravening the views of both parties, whilst in the meantime the tranquillity and security of our adjoining territories are endangered and new facilities given to violations of our revenue and commercial laws and of those prohibiting the introduction of slaves;

Considering, moreover, that under these peculiar and imperative circumstances a forbearance on the part of the United States to occupy the territory in question, and thereby guard against the confusions and contingencies which threaten it, might be construed

---

[1] *Messages and Papers of the Presidents*, compiled by James D. Richardson (Washington, 1896), vol. 1, pp. 480–481.

into a dereliction of their title or an insensibility to the importance of the stake; considering that in the hands of the United States it will not cease to be a subject of fair and friendly negotiation and adjustment; considering, finally, that the acts of Congress, though contemplating a present possession by a foreign authority, have contemplated also an eventual possession of the said territory by the United States, and are accordingly so framed as in that case to extend in their operation to the same:

Now be it known that I, James Madison, President of the United States of America, in pursuance of these weighty and urgent considerations, have deemed it right and requisite that possession should be taken of the said territory in the name and behalf of the United States. William C. C. Claiborne, governor of the Orleans Territory, of which the said Territory is to be taken as part, will accordingly proceed to execute the same and to exercise over the said Territory the authorities and functions legally appertaining to his office; and the good people inhabiting the same are invited and enjoined to pay due respect to him in that character, to be obedient to the laws, to maintain order, to cherish harmony, and in every manner to conduct themselves as peaceable citizens, under full assurance that they will be protected in the enjoyment of their liberty, property, and religion.

EXPANSIONIST SENTIMENT IN GEORGIA

This was an open invitation to the frontiersmen in West Florida, and they responded predictably. By December, the Stars and Stripes floated over Baton Rouge, although the fort at Mobile remained in Spanish hands until the outbreak of war legitimatized its capture. East Florida was just as tempting a prize, but here the situation was different. No obscure clauses in treaties between the powers gave President Madison an excuse to annex the region, and he did not dare flaunt Spanish authority by overrunning the territory of a nation with whom the United States was supposedly on friendly terms. No such qualms restrained frontiersmen along the southern border. There a belligerent governor of Georgia, George Mathews, led an army against St. Augustine in March 1812, without any sanction whatever. President Madison was sufficiently aware of his legal obligations to dismiss his overenthusiastic disciple when the siege of St. Augustine failed, but the borderland still flamed with expansionist enthusiasm. Mathews' replacement as governor of Georgia, D. B. Mitchell, reflected this in his message to the state legislature in November 1812:[2]

After a forbearance to which there is scarcely a parallel to be found in the history of any independent nation, the United States have been at length compelled, in vindication of their honor and for the maintenance of their indubitable rights, to declare war against Great Britain. A detail of the causes which produced this act of our government, is, I presume, neither expected nor desired from me at this time; they have been communicated to congress by the constitutional organ, the president of the United States, in a lucid and dignified address which you have all seen and no doubt possess. The insolent and arbitrary domination, assumed by the British, to control by her naval power the rights of this country, and the measures adopted by our government with a view of bringing the corrupt and corrupting ministry of Great Britain to a sense of justice, have been felt by Georgia with as much severity

---

[2] *Niles' Weekly Register*, III (November 28, 1812), pp. 193–194.

as any other state in the union. Her planters had long been in the habit of raising articles for exportation, from which they derive their principal resources, and depended upon importation from abroad for their annual supplies: hence, they felt with peculiar effect the want of that intercourse from which they derived their greatest advantage; yet, no selfish views ever operated upon their minds, or impaired their confidence in the government or wisdom of their measures; on the contrary, they have under every difficulty and privation maintained a firm republican and constitutional character, which I am confident they will still maintain. No difficulties or privations will ever induce them to submit to degradation and dishonor. And permit me to ask, if a submission to the black catalogue of British aggression, would not be a submission to degradation and dishonor? It assuredly would: Let us therefore maintain the character we have acquired, and unite heart and hand in support of the government, and the contest in which our country is now engaged—it is a contest sanctioned by justice and prompted by necessity, and under the guidance of Divine Providence we shall obtain the objects for which we contend....

The confidence with which I anticipated the declaration of war against Great Britain, led me with equal confidence to anticipate an enlargement of the powers of the President, by congress, as the necessary consequence, having for its object the entire occupancy of East and West Florida. That this should have been the course pursued, I was extremely solicitious; knowing as I did, and still do, that the interests of Georgia would be effectually promoted by that event, and the views and wishes of the general government at the same time accomplished.—The senate of the United States, however, in their wisdom had different views of the subject, and the matter was permitted to remain as before the war.—It is nevertheless my sincere and candid opinion, that the peace and safety of this state will be hazarded, if the occupancy of East Florida, by our government, is relinquished, or much longer delayed. The present force in Augustine is of a description which we cannot tolerate, and the mode of warfare which the governor of that place has commenced, is so savage and barbarous, that it is impossible for an American to hear it without feeling the utmost indignation and resentment against the power who commands or even permits it. I recommend this subject in an especial manner to your most serious consideration, as involving, not only your immediate interest, but your future peace and happiness. It is with real pleasure that I assure you of my entire confidence in the disposition of the president to proceed in the business with the utmost decision, if he is authorised by congress. Copies of such documents as are calculated to give you a clear view of the subject and enable you to form correct conclusions, will accompany this communication: And should any additional information be desired during the session, if in the power of the executive, it will be furnished with pleasure. I have been the more particular upon this head because I feel its importance, and because too, the agency which I have had in it, has been grossly misrepresented, and conduct and motives attributed to me as malicious as they are unfounded. That agency will now be committed to another person.

The Spanish officers in Augustine, St. Marks and Pensacola are using every effort to stimulate the Creek Indians to commence hostilities against us.—As yet those within the United States' line, as I have before observed, profess peace and friendship; but, those of the Seminoles, whose towns are in Florida, have been guilty of such outrages as leave no doubt of their intention, and ought to satisfy us that no time is to be lost in applying that chastisement which their crimes deserve. In August last some parties of them made their appearance upon the frontier of Camden county, and killed and scalped a young man about seventeen years of age, the son of Mr. Thomas Wilder, who resided near Trader's hill on St. Mary's river; and, at the same time, shot another lad, and wounded him severely, but who had the good fortune to make his escape. As soon as I received information of these facts, and numerous others of less atrocity, I sent an order to brigadier general Floyd, to cause a block house to be erected on Trader's hill, and to put a small garrison in it for the protection of that part of the frontier, and if the Indians should again make their appearance, in a hostile manner, to collect a force, and pursue and punish them. I also wrote a letter to colonel Hawkins, demanding that the murderers would be apprehended and delivered up to the civil authority of Camden county, there to take their trial. Colonel Hawkins' answer, with subsequent information which I have received, fully convinces me that we have no satisfaction to expect from these Indians, and consequently that we ought to look to our own safety. With this view, I have given orders to have a stock of provender and provision contracted for and deposited at Trader's hill, for five hundred cavalry, and intended as soon as those supplies were procured, to order that number to take the field. This subject claims the immediate attention of the legislature.

LAND-GRABBING IN THE NORTHWEST

If the Southwest was eager to overrun the Floridas, the Northwest was even more determined to have Canada—at least until it could end the Indian wars that ravaged its borderland. Not a man there but was certain that this wilderness conflict, which began about 1809, was to be laid at the door of Britain; the Indians, so the frontiersmen believed, were armed and encouraged at British posts lying north of the international boundary. Actually this was not the case. Responsibility for the war could be placed squarely on Governor William Henry Harrison of Indiana Territory. Eager to provide lands for the pioneers from the East who began flooding into his territory early in the nineteenth century, he negotiated a whole series of land-grabbing treaties that drove the red men from their hunting grounds. His treaty-making techniques were as annoying as they were impossible to combat; Harrison used bribery, threats, and cajolery to persuade a few chiefs to cede the territory of an entire tribe, then occupied the region from which he could be dislodged only by force. Matters reached a climax in 1809 when he summoned 1100 Indians to a council at Fort Wayne. Again manipulation and bribery were used; again one faction was played off against another. The resulting Treaty of Fort Wayne transferred 3,000,000 acres of choice land to the United States for $7000 and annuities of $1750:[3]

James Madison, President of the United States, by William Henry Harrison, Governor and Commander in Chief of the Indiana territory, Superintendent of Indian Affairs, and Commissioner Plenipotentiary of the United States, for treating with the said Indian tribes, and the sachems, head-men, and warriors, of the Delaware, Pattawatamy, Miami, and Eel river tribes of Indians, have agreed and concluded upon the following treaty, which, when ratified by the said President, with the advice and consent of the Senate of the United States, shall be binding on said parties:

---

[3] *American State Papers, Indian Affairs* (Washington, 1832), vol. 1, p. 761.

Article 1. The Miami and Eel river tribes, and the Delawares and Pattawatamies, as their allies, agree to cede to the United States, all that tract of country which shall be included between the boundary line, established by the treaty of Fort Wayne, the Wabash, and a line to be drawn from the mouth of a creek called Racoon creek, emptying into the Wabash, on the southeast side, about twelve miles below the mouth of the Vermillion river, so as to strike the boundary line established by the treaty of Grouseland, at such a distance from its commencement, at the northeast corner of the Vincennes tract, as will leave the tract now ceded, thirty miles wide at the narrowest place; and also, all that tract which shall be included between the following boundaries, viz: Beginning at fort Recovery; thence, southwardly along the general boundary line, established by the treaty of Greenville, to its intersection with the boundary line established by the treaty of Grouseland; thence, along said line, to a point from which a line drawn parallel to the first mentioned line will be twelve miles distant from the same, and along the said parallel line to its intersection with a line to be drawn from fort Recovery, parallel to the line established by the said treaty of Grouseland.

Art. 2. The Miamies explicitly acknowledge the equal right of the Delawares, with themselves, to the country watered by the White river; but it is also to be clearly understood that neither party shall have the right of disposing of the same, without the consent of the other; and any improvements which shall be made on the said land by the Delawares, or their friends the Mohicans, shall be theirs forever.

Art. 3. The compensation to be given for the cession made in the first article, shall be as follows, viz. To the Delawares, a permanent annuity of five hundred dollars; to the Miamies, a like annuity of five hundred dollars; to the Eel river tribe, a like annuity of two hundred and fifty dollars; and to the Pattawatamies, a like annuity of five hundred dollars.

Art. 4. All the stipulations made in the treaty of Greenville, relatively to the manner of paying the annuities, and the right of the Indians to hunt upon the land, shall apply to the annuities granted and the land ceded by the present treaty.

Art. 5. The consent of the Wea tribe shall be necessary to complete the title to the first tract of land here ceded. A separate convention shall be entered into between them and the United States, and a reasonable allowance of goods given them in hand, and a permanent annuity, which shall not be less than three hundred dollars, settled upon them.

Art. 6. The annuities promised by the third article, and the goods now delivered, to the amount of five thousand two hundred dollars, shall be considered as a full compensation for the cession made in the first article.

Art. 7. The tribes who are parties to this treaty, being desirous of putting an end to the depredations which are committed by abandoned individuals of their own color, upon the cattle, horses, &c. of the more industrious and careful, agree to adopt the following regulations, viz. When any theft or other depredation shall be committed by any individual or individuals of one of the tribes, above mentioned, upon the property of any individual or individuals of another tribe, the chiefs of the party injured shall make application to the agent of the United States, who is charged with the delivery of the annuities of the tribe to which the offending party belongs, whose duty it shall be to hear the proofs and allegations on either side, and determine between them; and the amount of his award shall be immediately deducted from the annuity of the tribe to which the offending party belongs, and given to the person injured, or the chief of his village, for his use.

Art. 8. The United States agree to relinquish their right to the reserve at the old Ouiatanon towns, made by the treaty of Greenville, so far, at least, as to make no further use of it than for the establishment of a military post.

Art. 9. The tribes who are parties to this treaty, being desirous to shew their attachment to their brothers, the Kickapoos, agree to cede to the United States, the lands on the northwest side of the Wabash, from the Vincennes tract, to a northwardly extension of the line running from the mouth of the aforesaid Racoon creek, and fifteen miles in width from the Wabash, on condition that the United States, shall allow them an annuity of four hundred dollars; but this article is to have no effect, unless the Kickapoos will agree to it.

In testimony whereof, the said William Henry Harrison, and the sachems and war chiefs of the before mentioned tribes, have hereunto set their hands, and affixed their seals, at fort Wayne, this thirtieth of September, one thousand eight hundred and nine.

WILLIAM HENRY HARRISON [L. S.]

INDIAN PROTEST AGAINST THE FORT WAYNE TREATY

The Treaty of Fort Wayne, climaxing as it did a steady absorption of Indian lands in the Northwest, was sure to cause trouble. The resistance that followed was greater because of the presence among the Indians of two able leaders: the Shawnee chief Tecumseh and his brother the Prophet. For half a dozen years before 1809, they had been working quietly with the northwestern tribes, the Prophet displaying his allegedly mystical powers to persuade them to abandon the sins and liquor of the white man, Tecumseh urging them to unite in a confederation whose members were pledged to cede no land without the consent of all. At the time of the Treaty of Fort Wayne, Tecumseh was far from Indiana Territory, but he reached the territorial capital at Vincennes on August 10, 1810. Eight days later he delivered a moving speech, crying out against Harrison's land-grabbing tactics and warning that any attempt to occupy the ceded lands would result in war:[4]

Brother. Since the peace was made you have kill'd some of the Shawanese, Winebagoes Delawares and Miamies and you have taken our lands from us and I do not see how we can remain at peace with you if you continue to do so. You have given goods to the Kickapoos for the sale of their lands to you which has been the cause of many deaths amongst them. You have promised us assistance but I do not see that you have given us any.

You try to force the red people to do some injury. It is you that is pushing them on to do mischief. You endeavour to make destructions, you wish to prevent the Indians to do as we wish them to unite and let them consider their land as the common property of the whole you take tribes aside and advise them not to come into this measure and untill our design is accomplished we do not wish to accept of your invitation to go and visit the President.

The reason I tell you this is—You want

---

[4] Logan Esarey (ed.), *Messages and Letters of William Henry Harrison* ("Indiana Historical Collections," vol. 7) (Indianapolis, 1922), vol. 1, pp. 465–467.

by your distinctions of Indian tribes in allotting to each a particular track of land to make them to war with each other. You never see an Indian come and endeavour to make the white people do so. You are continually driving the red people when at last you will drive them into the great lake where they can't either stand or work.

Brother. You ought to know what you are doing with the Indians. Perhaps it is by direction of the President to make those distinctions. It is a very bad thing and we do not like it. Since my residence at Tippecanoe we have endeavoured to level all distinctions to destroy village chiefs by whom all mischief is done; it is they who sell our land to the Americans our object is to let all our affairs be transacted by Warriors.

Brother. This land that was sold and the goods that was given for it was only done by a few. The treaty was afterwards brought here and the Weas were induced to give their consent because of their small numbers. The treaty at Fort Wayne was made through the threats of Winamac but in future we are prepared to punish those chiefs who may come forward to propose to sell their land. If you continue to purchase of them it will produce war among the different tribes and at last I do not know what will be the consequence to the white people.

Brother. I was glad to hear your speech you said if we could show that the land was sold by persons that had no right to sell you would restore it, that that did sell did not own it it was *me*. These tribes set up a claim but the tribes with me will not agree to their claim, if the land is not restored to us you will soon see when we return to our homes how it will be settled. We shall have a great council at which all the tribes shall be present when we will show to those who sold that they had no right to sell the claim they set up and we will know what will be done with those Chiefs that did sell the land to you. I am not alone in this determination it is the determination of all the warriors and red people that listen to me.

I now wish you to listen to me. If you do not it will appear as if you wished me to kill all the chiefs that sold you this land. I tell you so because I am authorised by all the tribes to do so. I am at the head of them all. I am a Warrior and all the Warriors will meet together in two or three moons from this. Then I will call for those chiefs that sold you the land and shall know what to do with them. If you do not restore the land you will have a hand in killing them.

Brother. Do not believe that I came here to get presents from you if you offer us anything we will not take it. By taking goods from you you will hereafter say that with them you purchased another piece of land from us. If we want anything we are able to buy it, from your traders. Since the land was sold to you no traders come among us. I now wish you would clear all the roads and let the traders come among us. Then perhaps some of our young men will occasionally call upon you to get their guns repaired. This is all the assistance we ask of you.

Brother. I should now be very glad to know immediately, what is your determination about the land also of the traders I have mentioned.

Brother. It has been the object of both myself and brother from the beginning to prevent the lands being sold should you not return the land, it will occasion us to call a great council that will meet at the Huron Village where the council fire has already been lighted At which those who sold the land shall be call's and shall suffer for their conduct.

Brother. I wish you would take pity on all the red people and do what I have requested. If you will not give up the land

and do cross the boundary of your present settlement it will be very hard and produce great troubles among us. How can we have confidence in the white people when Jesus Christ came upon the earth you kill'd and nail'd him on a cross, you thought he was dead but you were mistaken. You have shaken among you and you laugh and make light of their worship.

Everything I have said to you is the truth the great spirit has inspired me and I speak nothing but the truth to you. In two moons we shall assemble at the Huron Village (addressing himself to the Weas and Pottawatomies) where the great belts of all the tribes are kept and there settle our differences.

Brother. I hope you will confess that you ought not to have listened to those bad birds who bring you bad news. I have declared myself freely to you and if you want any explanation from our Town send a man who can speak to us.

If you think proper to give us any presents and we can be convinced that they are given through friendship alone we will accept them. As we intend to hold our council at the Huron village that is near the British we may probably make them a visit. Should they offer us any presents of goods we will not take them but should they offer us powder and the tomhawk we will take the powder and refuse the Tomhawk.

I wish you *Brother* to consider everything I have said is true and that it is the sentiment of all the red people who listen to me.

THE BATTLE OF TIPPECANOE

Harrison, not to be intimidated, countered that the Fort Wayne treaty lands would be occupied. This was the last straw. All that winter of 1810–1811, war belts were passed from tribe to tribe as Tecumseh and the Prophet urged the Indians to unite in defense of their lands. In August 1811, Tecumseh started south to enlist southern tribes in his confederacy. This was Harrison's opportunity. He would not only occupy the forbidden territory, but would destroy the village of Prophetstown on the Upper Wabash River, the headquarters of Tecumseh and the Prophet. With a thousand troops he started northward from Vincennes in September 1811, reaching the village early in November. The attack came on November 7, a cold, rainy night, after the Prophet had endowed the Indians with supposedly magical protection against the white man's guns. A soldier in Harrison's army described the Battle of Tippecanoe:[5]

I awoke about four o'clock the next morning, after a sound and refreshing sleep, having heard in a dream the firing of guns and the whistling of bullets just before I awoke from my slumber. A drizzling rain was falling and all things were still and quiet throughout the camp. I was engaged in making a calculation when I should arrive at home.

In a few moments I heard the crack of a rifle in the direction of the point where now stands the Battle Ground house, which is occupied by Captain DuTiel as a tavern. I had just time to think that some sentinel was alarmed and had fired his rifle without a real cause, when I heard the crack of another rifle, followed by an awful Indian yell all around the encampment. In less than a minute I saw the Indians charging our line most furiously and shooting a great many rifle balls into our camp fires, throwing the live coals into the air three or four feet high.

At this moment my friend Warnock was shot by a rifle ball through his body. He ran a few yards and fell dead on the ground. Our

---

[5] Isaac Naylor, "The Battle of Tippecanoe," *Indiana Magazine of History*, II (December, 1906), pp. 165–167.

lines were broken and a few Indians were found on the inside of the encampment. In a few moments they were all killed. Our lines closed up and our men in their proper places. One Indian was killed in the back part of Captain Geiger's tent, while he was attempting to tomahawk the Captain.

The sentinels, closely pursued by the Indians, came to the lines of the encampment in haste and confusion. My brother, William Naylor, was on guard. He was pursued so rapidly and furiously that he ran to the nearest point on the left flank, where he remained with a company of regular soldiers until the battle was near its termination. A young man, whose name was Daniel Pettit, was pursued so closely and furiously by an Indian as he was running from the guard fire to our lines, that to save his life he cocked his rifle as he ran and turning suddenly round, placed the muzzle of his gun against the body of the Indian and shot an ounce ball through him. The Indian fired his gun at the same instant, but it being longer than Pettit's the muzzle passed by him and set fire to a handkerchief which he had tied round his head. The Indians made four or five most fierce charges on our lines, yelling and screaming as they advanced, shooting balls and arrows into our ranks. At each charge they were driven back in confusion, carrying off their dead and wounded as they retreated.

Colonel Owen, of Shelby county, Kentucky, one of General Harrison's volunteer aides, fell early in action by the side of the General. He was a member of the legislature at the time of his death. Colonel Davies was mortally wounded early in the battle, gallantly charging the Indians on foot with his sword and pistols, according to his own request. He made this request three times of General Harrison, before he permitted him to make the charge. This charge was made by himself and eight dragoons on foot near the angle formed by the left flank and front line of the encampment. Colonel Davies lived about thirty-six hours after he was wounded, manifesting his ruling passions in life—ambition, patriotism and an ardent love of military glory. During the last hours of his life he said to his friends around him that he had but one thing to regret—that he had military talents; that he was about to be cut down in the meridian of life without having an opportunity of displaying them for his own honor, and the good of his country. He was buried alone with the honors of war near the right flank of the army, inside of the lines of the encampment, between two trees. On one of these trees the letter 'D' is now visible. Nothing but the stump of the other remains. His grave was made here, to conceal it from the Indians. It was filled up to the top with earth and then covered with oak leaves. I presume the Indians never found it. This precautionary act was performed as a mark of peculiar respect for a distinguished hero and patriot of Kentucky.

Captain Spencer's company of mounted riflemen composed the right flank of the army. Captain Spencer and both his lieutenants were killed. John Tipton was elected and commissioned as captain of this company in one hour after the battle, as a reward for his cool and deliberate heroism displayed during the action. He died at Logansport in 1839, having been twice elected Senator of the United States from the State of Indiana.

The clear, calm voice of General Harrison was heard in words of heroism in every part of the encampment during the action. Colonel Boyd behaved very bravely after repeating these words: "Huzza! My sons of gold, a few more fires and victory will be ours!"

Just after daylight the Indians retreated across the prairie toward their town, carrying off their wounded. This retreat was from the right flank of the encampment, commanded by Captains Spencer and Robb, having retreated from the other portions of the encampment a few minutes before. As their retreat became visible, an almost deafening and universal shout was raised by our men. "Huzza! Huzza! Huzza!" This shout was almost equal to that of the savages at the commencement of the battle; ours was the shout of victory, theirs was the shout of ferocious but disappointed hope.

The morning light disclosed the fact that the killed and wounded of our army, numbering between eight and nine hundred men, amounted to one hundred and eight. Thirty-six Indians were found near our lines. Many of their dead were carried off during the battle. This fact was proved by the discovery of many Indian graves recently made near their town. Ours was a bloody victory, theirs a bloody defeat.

THE WESTERN DEMAND FOR WAR

Tippecanoe helped elect Harrison President in 1840, but it fanned rather than quenched the flames of war. From that day on raiding parties roamed the frontiers, killing and burning. Every westerner was sure that they had been armed and inspired by British agents in Canada, and especially at Fort Malden near Detroit. War with England would allow the United States to wipe out this nest and bring peace to the backcountry. This belief intensified the demand for war in the West, but it was by no means fundamental; only the thinly settled fringes of the frontier were affected, and they had little political influence. Instead westerners were eager to take up cudgels against Great Britain for two basic reasons: to secure freedom of the seas and to avenge national honor. This was made clear in the dozens of resolutions passed by western legislatures, by the hundreds of like resolutions adopted by villages or organizations, and by the even larger number of speeches given by western orators and politicians. Few mentioned the Indian danger or the desire for Canada. All stressed the urgency of reopening trade with Europe to end the depression that burdened the Ohio Valley, and all bristled with indignation at insults to the national honor of which England was guilty in its impressment policy. Typical was a resolution adopted by the Kentucky legislature on December 16, 1811:[6]

Whereas it is deemed by the legislature of this state, that they have, in the name, and on behalf of their constituents, at all times, a right to express, so far as their knowledge and information will enable them, the sense of the good people of this state, respecting the measures of the national government. And a crisis in our public affairs having arrived, which in the opinion of this legislature calls for the expression of her public sentiment respecting the course to be adopted, in order to resist the repeated, long continued and flagrant violations of our rights, as a free and independent nation, by Great Britain and France, and by the former especially—whose pretensions are an insult to our sovereignty, and which if yielded to, must end in our entire submission to whatever they may think proper to impose.

The people of this state, though not immediately exposed to those piratical depredations, which vex, and destroy the commerce of their eastern brethren on the ocean, cannot be less deeply interested in their effects. They look to the sufferings and wrongs of a single member as intimately affecting the whole body. But when an evil becomes so general and inveterate in its deleterious ef-

---

[6] *Niles' Weekly Register*, I (January 11, 1812), pp. 337–338.

fects, as to threaten dissolution, unless a proper and forcible remedy is applied—The state of Kentucky, yielding to none in patriotism; in its deep rooted attachment to the sacred bond of the union; in its faithful remembrance of the price of our freedom, and in the heartfelt conviction that our posterity have a sacred claim upon us, to transmit to them unimpaired, this God-like inheritance, cannot fail to be penetrated, with any event which threatens even to impair it; much less then, can she be insensible to those daring wrongs of a foreign power, which lead to its immediate destruction.

If the people of this state have looked up with confidence to the general government, whose functions empowered, and whose duty imperiously called for a remedy to the evils so intolerable in their progress, and in their consequences so menacing—(and redress for which, has been so long delayed) it has not been without a firm, and settled purpose, not always to bear the lash, nor finally to become beasts of burthen.

Forbearance beyond a certain point, ceases to be moderation, and must end in entire subjection.

It is not the purpose of this legislature to recapitulate, or enter into any argument to prove the existence and extent of those injuries, sustained from both the great belligerents of Europe. Those who feel, need not reason to produce the conviction of unjust suffering—and those, who cannot feel wrongs so palpable, no reasoning will convince.

We wish we could have it in our power to say, *when* Great Britain has ceased to harass and injure us—*when* she has shewn towards us an amicable disposition in the true spirit of justice—*when* she has ceased her efforts to diminish that security and prosperity, which are the eternal barriers of separation from her power, and to impair that liberty and independence forced from her reluctant grasp.

We could willingly have hailed a friend in a former unnatural parent, and from the experience of her regard to principles of justice, and reciprocal good offices, have ceased to recall those wanton cruelties that alienated us forever from her family.

But when we have discovered a systematic course of injury from her towards our country, evidencing too strongly to be mistaken, an utter disregard of almost every principle of acknowledged rights between independent nations, endeavouring by almost every act of violence on the high seas—on the coasts of foreign powers with whom we were in amity—and even in sight of our own harbours by capturing and destroying our vessels: confiscating our property: forcibly imprisoning and torturing our fellow-citizens: condemning some to death: slaughtering others, by attacking our ships of war: impressing all she can lay her hand upon, to man her vessels: bidding defiance to our seaports: insulting our national honour by every means that lawless force and brutality can devise: inciting the savages to murder the inhabitants on our defenceless frontiers: furnishing them with arms and ammunition lately, to attack our forces: to the loss of a number of brave men: and by every art of power and intrigue, seeking to dispose of our whole strength and resources, as may suit her unrestrained ambition or interest—and when her very offers of redress, go only to sanction her wrongs, and seek merely a removal of those obstacles interposed by our government, to the full enjoyment of her iniquitous benefits; we can be at no loss what course should be pursued.

Should we tamely submit, the world ought to despise us—We should despise ourselves —She herself would despise us.

When she shall learn to respect our rights,

we shall hasten to forget her injuries. Wherefore:

1. Resolved, by the general assembly for the state of Kentucky, that this state feel deeply sensibly, of the continued, wanton, and flagrant violations by Great Britain and France, of the dearest rights of the people of the United States, as a free and independent nation: that those violations if not discontinued, and ample compensation made for them, ought to be resisted with the whole power of our country.

2. Resolved, that as war seems probable so far as we have any existing evidence of a sense of justice on the part of the government of Great Britain, that the state of Kentucky, to the last mite of her strength and resources, will contribute them to maintain the contest and support the right of their country against such lawless violations; and that the citizens of Kentucky, are prepared to take the field when called on.

3. Resolved, that (while they have full and undiminished confidence in the administration and general government of the United States) in their opinion, the crisis calls for energetic measures; and that a temporising policy, while it might seem to remove the evil to a greater distance, would serve only to secure its continuance.

4. Resolved, that we will most readily lend our support also to any measures which may be adopted by the general government, to counteract the arbitrary restrictions, or unjust violations of our commerce by France.

HENRY CLAY SPEAKS FOR WAR

These western demands were impressed on Washington by a handful of aggressive young congressmen who held the balance of power in the Congress that assembled in December 1811. The War Hawks as they were derisively labeled, elected Henry Clay speaker of the House of Representatives, packed most of the important House committees with their members, and raised their voices for war. They were few in numbers—of the 61 members of the House who eventually voted for war only 7 were from the West and 29 from the South—but they spoke a language that was tuned to a mounting national sentiment. The nation's honor could be preserved, they insisted, and the nation's economy sustained, only by forcing Britain to its knees. Henry Clay typified their appeal in a speech that he gave on December 30, 1811:[7]

What are we to gain by war, has been emphatically asked? In reply, he would ask, what are we not to lose by peace?—commerce, character, a nation's best treasure, honor! If pecuniary considerations alone are to govern, there is sufficient motive for the war. Our revenue is reduced, by the operation of the belligerent edicts, to about six million of dollars, according to the Secretary of the Treasury's report. The year preceding the embargo, it was sixteen. Take away the Orders in Council it will again mount up to sixteen millions. By continuing, therefore, in peace, if the mongrel state in which we are deserve that denomination, we lose annually, in revenue only, ten millions of dollars. Gentlemen will say, repeal the law of non-importation. He contended that, if the United States were capable of that perfidy, the revenue would not be restored to its former state, the Orders in Council continuing. Without an export trade, which those orders prevent, inevitable ruin would ensue, if we imported as freely as we did prior to the

---

[7] *Annals of Congress*, 12th Congress, 1st Session, pp. 599–602.

embargo. A nation that carries on an import trade without an export trade to support it, must, in the end, be as certainly bankrupt, as the individual would be, who incurred an annual expenditure, without an income.

He had no disposition to swell, or dwell upon the catalogue of injuries from England. He could not, however, overlook the impressment of our seamen; an aggression upon which he never reflected without feelings of indignation, which would not allow him appropriate language to describe its enormity. Not content with seizing upon all our property, which falls within her rapacious grasp, the personal rights of our countrymen—rights which forever ought to be sacred, are trampled upon and violated. The Orders in Council were pretended to have been reluctantly adopted as a measure of retaliation. The French decrees, their alleged basis, are revoked. England resorts to the expedient of denying the fact of the revocation, and Sir William Scott, in the celebrated case of the Fox and others, suspends judgment that proof may be adduced of it. And, at the moment when the British Ministry through that judge, is thus affecting to controvert that fact, and to place the release of our property upon its establishment, instructions are prepared for Mr. Foster to meet at Washington the very revocation which they were contesting. And how does he meet it? By fulfilling the engagement solemnly made to rescind the orders? No, sir, but by demanding that we shall secure the introduction into the Continent of British manufactures. England is said to be fighting for the world, and shall we, it is asked, attempt to weaken her exertions? If, indeed, the aim of the French Emperor be universal dominion (and he was willing to allow it to the argument.) what a noble cause is presented to British valor. But, how is her philanthropic purpose to be achieved? By scrupulous observance of the rights of others; by respecting that code of public law, which she professes to vindicate, and by abstaining from self-aggrandizement. Then would she command the sympathies of the world. What are we required to do by those who would engage our feelings and wishes in her behalf? To bear the actual cuffs of her arrogance, that we may escape a chimerical French subjugation! We are invited, conjured to drink the potion of British poison actually presented to our lips, that we may avoid the imperial dose prepared by perturbed imaginations. We are called upon to submit to debasement, dishonor, and disgrace—to bow the neck to royal insolence, as a course of preparation for manly resistance to Gallic invasion! What nation, what individual was ever taught, in the schools of ignominious submission, the patriotic lessons of freedom and independence? Let those who contend for this humiliating doctrine, read its refutation in the history of the very man against whose insatiable thirst of dominion we are warned. The experience of desolated Spain, for the last fifteen years, is worth volumes. Did she find her repose and safety in subserviency to the will of that man? Had she boldly stood forth and repelled the first attempt to dictate to her Councils, her Monarch would not now be a miserable captive at Marseilles. Let us come home to our own history. It was not by submission that our fathers achieved our independence. The patriotic wisdom that placed you, Mr. Chairman, said Mr. C., under that canopy, penetrated the designs of a corrupt Ministry, and nobly fronted encroachment on its first appearance. It saw beyond the petty taxes, with which it commenced, a long train of oppressive measures terminating in the total annihilation of liberty; and, contemptible as they were, did not hesitate to resist them. Take the experience of the last four or five years, and which, he was sorry to say, exhibited in appearance, at least, a different kind of spirit. He did not wish to view the past further than to guide us for the future. We were but yesterday contending for the indirect trade—the right to export to Europe the coffee and sugar of the West Indies. To-day we are asserting our claim to the direct trade—the right to export our cotton, tobacco, and other domestic produce to market. Yield this point, and to-morrow intercourse between New Orleans and New York—between the planters on James river and Richmond, will be interdicted. For, sir, the career of encroachment is never arrested by submission. It will advance while there remains a single privilege on which it can operate. Gentlemen say that this Government is unfit for any war, but a war of invasion. What, is it not equivalent to invasion, if the mouths of our harbors and outlets are blocked up, and we are denied egress from our own waters? Or, when the burglar is at our door, shall we bravely sally forth and repel his felonious entrance, or meanly skulk within the cells of the castle?

He contended that the real cause of British aggression, was not to distress an enemy but to destroy a rival. A comparative view of our commerce with England and the continent, would satisfy any one of the truth of this remark. Prior to the embargo, the balance of trade between this country and England, was between eleven and fifteen millions of dollars in favor of England. Our consumption of her manufactures was annually increasing, and had risen to nearly $50,000,000. We exported to her what she most wanted, provisions and raw materials for her manufactures, and received in return what she was most desirous to sell. Our exports to France, Holland, Spain, and Italy, taking an average of the years 1802, 3, and 4, amounted to about $12,000,000 of domestic, and about $18,000,000 of foreign produce. Our imports from the same countries amounted to about $25,000,000. The foreign produce exported consisted chiefly of luxuries from the West Indies. It is apparent that this trade, the balance of which was in favor, not of France, but of the United States, was not of very vital consequence to the enemy of England. Would she, therefore, for the sole purpose of depriving her adversary of this commerce, relinquish her valuable trade with this country, exhibiting the essential balance in her favor—nay, more; hazard the peace of the country? No, sir, you must look for an explanation of her conduct in the jealousies of a rival. She sickens at your prosperity, and beholds in your growth—your sails spread on every ocean, and your numerous seamen—the foundations of a Power which, at no very distant day, is to make her tremble for naval superiority. He had omitted before to notice the loss of our seamen, if we continued in our present situation. What would become of the one hundred thousand, (for he understood there was about that number) in the American service? Would they not leave us and seek employment abroad, perhaps in the very country that injures us?

It is said, that the effect of the war at home will be a change of those who administer the Government, who will be replaced by others that will make a disgraceful peace. He did not believe it. Not a man in the nation could really doubt the sincerity with which those in power have sought, by all honorable, pacific means, to protect the interests of the country. When the people saw exercised towards both belligerents, the utmost impartiality; witnessed the same equal terms tendered to both; and beheld the Government successively embracing an accommodation with each in exactly the same spirit of amity, he was fully persuaded, now that war was the only alternative left to us by the injustice of one of the Powers, that the support and confidence of the people would remain undiminished. He was one, however, who was prepared (and he would not believe that he was more so than every other member of the Committee) to march on in the road of his duty, at all hazards. What! shall it be said that our *amor patriæ* is located at these desks—that we pusillanimously cling to our seats here, rather than boldly vindicate the most inestimable rights of the country? Whilst the heroic Daviess and his gallant associates, exposed to all the perils of treacherous savage warfare, are sacrificing themselves for the good of their country, shall we shrink from our duty?

THE AMERICAN INVASION OF CANADA

The War Hawks, with the support of most southerners and a surprisingly large number of easterners, carried the day; when the reluctant President James Madison was brow-beaten into sending a war message to Congress, that body responded with enthusiasm on June 18, 1812. The West was overjoyed. Canada would be overrun in a few weeks, and Fort Malden destroyed. This would end the Indian war, and force England to repeal the maritime decrees that were ruining American shipping. So westerners planned, and their plans led to disaster. Instead of attacking Montreal and separating east Canada from west Canada, strategists were forced by frontier demands to launch the first assault on Fort Malden. This was entrusted to the aging General William Hull, who reached Detroit in July 1812 with 2000 men, all eager to storm across the border and reduce Malden to ashes. Their tone was reflected by General Hull, who on July 13 issued a proclamation that breathed fire and brimstone for the redskins and the redcoats who aided them:[8]

Proclamation

Inhabitants of Canada! After thirty years of Peace and Prosperity, the United States have been driven to Arms. The injuries and agressions, the insults and indignities of Great Britain have *once more* left them no alternative but manly resistance or unconditional submission. The Army under my command has invaded your Country and the standard of the United States waves on the territory of Canada To the peaceable unoffending inhabitant, It brings neither danger nor difficulty. I come to find enemies not to *make* them. I come to *protect* not to *injure* you.

Separated by an immence ocean and an extensive Wilderness from Great Britain you have no participation in her Councils no interest in her Conduct; You have felt her Tyranny, you have seen her injustice, but I do not ask *you* to avenge the one or to redress the other. The United States are sufficiently powerful to afford you every security consistent with their rights & your expectations, I tender you the invaluable blessings of Civil, Political, & Religious Liberty, and their necessary results, individual, and General prosperity; That liberty which gave decision to our Councels and energy to our conduct in our struggle for Independence, and which conducted us safely and triumphantly thro' the stormy period of the Revolution.

---

[8] *Historical Collections of the Michigan Pioneer and Historical Society* (Lansing, 1890), vol. 15, pp. 106–107.

The Liberty which has raised us to an elevated rank among the Nations of the world and which has afforded us a greater measure of Peace & security wealth and prosperity than ever fell to the Lot of any people.

In the name of my *Country* and by the Authority of my Government I promise you protection to your *persons, property, and rights.* Remain at your homes, pursue your Customary and peaseful avocations, Raise not your hands against your bretheren, Many of your fathers fought for the freedom & *Independence* we now enjoy, Being Children therefore of the same family with us, and heirs to the same heritage, the arrival of an army of Friends must be hailed by you with a Cordial Welcome, You will be emancipated from Tyranny and oppression and restored to the dignified station of freemen. Had I any doubt of eventual success I might ask your assistance but I do not. I come prepared for every Contingency. I have a force which look down all opposition and that force is but the vanguard of a much greater. If contrary to your own interests & the just expectation of my country, you should take part in the approaching contest, you will be considered and treated as enemies and the horrors, and calamities of war will stalk before you.

If the barbarous and Savage policy of Great Britain be pursued, and the savages are let loose to murder our Citizens and butcher our women and children, this war will be a war of extermination.

The first stroke with the Tomahawk the first attempt with the scalping Knife will be the signal for one indiscriminate scene of desolation, *No White man found fighting by the side of an Indian will be taken prisoner* Instant destruction will be his lot. If the dictates of reason, duty, justice, and humanity, cannot prevail the employment of a force, which respects no rights & Knows no wrong, it will be prevented by a severe and relentless system of retaliation.

I doubt not your courage and firmness; I will not doubt your attachment to + + Liberty. If you tender your services voluntarily they will be accepted readily.

The United States offer you *Peace, Liberty,* and *Security* your choice lies between these, & *War, Slavery, and destruction,* Choose then, but choose wisely; and may he who knows the justice of our cause, and who holds in his hands the fate of Nations, guide you to a result the most compatible, with your rights and interests, your peace and prosperity.

WM HULL

THE BATTLE OF THE THAMES

These belligerent hopes were soon dashed. General Hull's supply lines were stretched too thin to maintain his army, and were in constant danger of being severed. Haunted by this fear, he delayed his attack so long that a force of British regulars under General Isaac Brock seized the initiative. Crossing the Detroit River on August 16, 1812, they stormed into the village, forcing Hull to surrender his entire army. Over the next weeks the fort at Mackinac and Fort Dearborn fell. Yet the West was not ready to give up. William Henry Harrison, who replaced Hull as commander, found recruits plentiful, but he was wise enough not to make his move until the United States won control of Lake Erie, thus protecting his supply lines. This came in September 1813, when Oliver Hazard Perry's fleet bested the English at the Battle of Lake Erie. With news of this victory, Harrison ferried his army across the lake and began his march toward Fort Malden. Now came Britain's turn to flee; the defending army under Colonel Henry Proctor started eastward along the Thames River toward the safety of Niagara. Harrison followed, and on October 5, 1813, overtook his prey. He described what happened next in a letter to the Secretary of War, written four days later:[9]

From the place where our army was last halted, to the Moravian Towns, a distance of about three and a half miles, the road passes through a beech forest without any clearing and for the first two miles near to the bank of the River. At from two to three hundred yards from the river a swamp extends parallel to it, throughout the whole distance. The intermediate ground is dry and although the trees are tolerably thick, it is in many places clear of underbrush. Across this strip of land its left appayed upon the river supported by artillery placed in the wood, their right in the swamp covered by the whole of their Indian force, the British Troops were drawn up. The troops at my disposal consisted of about one hundred and twenty regulars of the 27th regiment, five brigades of Kentucky Volunteer Militia Infantry under his Excellency Gov. Shelby, averaging less than five hundred men and Col. Johnson's Regiment of Mounted Infantry making in the whole an aggregate something above three thousand. No disposition of an army opposed to an Indian force can be safe unless it is secured on the flanks and in the rear. I had therefore no difficulty in arranging the Infantry conformably to my general order of battle. Genl. [George] Trotter's brigade of five hundred men formed the front line, his right upon the road and his left upon the swamp Genl. [John Edward] King's brigade as a second line one hundred and fifty yards in the rear of Trotter's and [David] Chiles' brigade as a *corps de reserve* in the rear of it these three brigades formed the command of Major Genl. [William] Henry. the whole of Genl. [Joseph] Deshai's Division consisting of two brigades were formed *en potence* upon the left of Trotter.

Whilst I was engaged in forming the Infantry I had directed Col. Johnson's Regiment which was still in front, to be formed in two lines opposite to the enemy and upon the advance of the Infantry to take ground to the left and forming upon that flank to endeavour to turn the right of the Indians. A moments reflection however convinced me that from the thickness of the woods and swampiness of the ground, they would be unable to do anything on horseback and there was no time to dismount them and place their horses in security. I therefore determined to refuse my left to the Indians and to break the British lines at once by a charge of the Mounted Infantry. the measure was not sanctioned by anything that I had seen or heard of but I was fully convinced that it would succeed. The American backwoodsmen ride better in the woods than any other people. A musket or rifle is no impediment to them being accustomed to carry them on horseback from their earliest youth. I was persuaded too that the enemy would be quite unprepared for the shock and that they could not resist it. Conformably to this idea I directed the regiment to be drawn up in close column with its right at the distance of fifty yards from the road, (that it might be in some measure protected by the trees from the artillery) its left upon the swamp and to charge at full speed as soon as the enemy delivered their fire. The few regular troops of the 27th Regiment under their Col.

---

[9] Logan Esarey (ed.), *Messages and Letters of William Henry Harrison* ("Indiana Historical Collections," vol. 9) (Indianapolis, 1922), vol. 2, pp. 561–563.

[George] (Paul) occupied in column of sections of four, the small space between the road and the river for the purpose of seizing the enemy's artillery and some ten or twelve friendly Indians were directed to move under the bank. The *Crotchet* formed by the front line and Genl. Desha's division was an important point. At that place, the venerable Governor of Kentucky was posted, who at the age of sixty-six preserves all the vigor of youth, the ardent zeal which distinguished him in the Revolutionary War and the undaunted bravery which he manifested at King's Mountain, with my aids de camp the acting assistant adjutant General Capt. [Robert] Butler my gallant friend Commodore Perry who did me the honour to serve as my volunteer aid de camp and Brigadier General Cass who having no command tendered me his assistance. I placed myself at the head of the front line of Infantry, to direct the movements of the Cavalry and give them the necessary support. The army had moved on in this order but a short distance, when the mounted men received the fire of the British line and were ordered to charge, the horses in the front of the column recoiled from the fire, another was given by the enemy and our column at length getting in motion broke through the enemy with irresistible force. in one minute the contest in front was over. the British officers seeing no hopes of reducing their disordered ranks to order, and our mounted men wheeling upon them and pouring in a destructive fire immediately surrendered. it is certain that three only of our troops were wounded in this charge (upon the left however the contest was more severe with the Indians. Col. Johnson, who commanded on that flank of his regiment received a most galling fire from them, which was returned with great effect). The Indians still further to the right advanced and fell in with our front line of Infantry near its junction with Desha's division and for a moment made an impression upon it. His Excellency Gov. Shelby however brought up a regiment to its support and the enemy receiving a severe fire in front, and a part of Johnson's Regiment having gained their rear, retreated with precipitation their loss was very considerable in the action and many were killed in their retreat.

THE BATTLE OF HORSESHOE BEND

The Battle of the Thames was one of the decisive victories of the War of 1812, not because the British were overwhelmingly defeated, but because the spirit of the Indians was broken. Tecumseh was killed, and his followers lost the will to resist, realizing that again their British allies had failed them. Southern tribesmen experienced a similar change of heart. There indecisive skirmishes went on through 1813 with heavy American losses; at the Fort Mims Massacre on the lower Alabama River five hundred frontiersmen were killed or captured. The turning point came in 1814 when Andrew Jackson of Tennessee was placed in command and led an army into the Indian country. By March 27 he and 3000 men were camped outside the village of Tohopeka, at the horseshoe bend of the Tallapoosa River. Jackson's own account of the battle that followed mirrored the brutality of backwoods warfare:[10]

I took up the line of march from this place on the morning of the 21st inst. and having opened a passage of 52 1-2 miles over the ridges which divide the waters of the two rivers, I reached the bend of the Tallapoosa three miles beyond where I had the engagement of the 22d of January, and

---

[10] *Niles' Weekly Register*, VI (April 30, 1814), pp. 146–147.

at the southern extremity of New-Youka, on the morning of the 27th. This bend resembles in its curvature that of a horse shoe, and is thence called by that name among the whites. Nature furnishes few situations so eligible for defence, and barbarians have never rendered one more secure by art. Across the neck of the bend which leads into it from the north they had erected a breastwork of the greatest compactness and strength, from five to eight feet high, and prepared with double port holes very artfully arranged. The figure of this wall manifested no less skill in the projection of it, than its construction; an army could not approach it without being exposed to a double and cross fire from the enemy, who lay in perfect security behind it. The area of this peninsula, thus bounded by the breastwork, includes I conjecture, eighty or hundred acres.

In this bend the warriors from Oakfuska, Oakehagu, New Youka, Hillabeen, the Fish ponds, and Eufauta towns, apprised of our approach, had collected their strength. Their exact number cannot be ascertained; but it is said by the prisoners we have taken to have been a thousand. It is certain they were very numerous, and that relying with the utmost confidence upon their strength, their situation and the assurances of their prophets, they concluded on repulsing us with great ease.

Early on the morning of the 27th, having encamped the preceding night at the distance of five miles from them—I detailed general Coffee with the mounted men and nearly the whole of the indian force, to cross the river at a ford about three miles below their encampment, and to surround the bend in such a manner that none of them should escape by attempting to cross the river. With the remainder of the forces I proceeded along the point of land which leads to the front of their breast-work; and at half past ten o'clock A. M. I had planted my artillery on a small eminence, distant from its nearest point about 80 yards, and from its farthest about two hundred and fifty; from whence I immediately opened a brisk fire upon its centre. With the musketry and rifles I kept up a galling fire wherever the enemy shewed themselves behind their works, or ventured to approach them. This was continued with occasional intermissions for about two hours, when captain Russell's company of spies, and a part of the Cherokee force, headed by their gallant chieftain colonel Richard Brown, and conducted by the brave colonel Morgan, crossed over to the peninsula in canoes, and set fire to a few of their buildings there situated. They then advanced with great gallantry towards the breast-work, and commenced firing upon the enemy who lay behind it.

Finding that this force, notwithstanding the determination they displayed, was wholly insufficient to dislodge the enemy, and that general Coffee had secured the opposite banks of the river, I now determined upon taking possession of their works by storm. Never were men better disposed for such an undertaking than those by whom it was to be effected. They had entreated to be led to the charge with the most pressing importunity, and received the order which was now given with the strongest demonstrations of joy. The effect was such as this temper of mind foretold. The regular troops, led on by their intrepid and skilful commander, colonel Williams, and by the gallant major Montgomery, were presently in possession of the nearer side of the breast-work; and the militia accompanied them in the charge with a vivacity and firmness which could not have been exceeded, and has seldom been equalled by troops of any description. A few companies of general Doherty's brigade on the right, were led on with gallantry by colonel

Russell—the advance guard, by the adjutant-general, colonel Sisler, and the left extremity of the line by captain Gordon of the spies, and captain M'Murry of general Johnson's brigade of West Tennessee militia.

Having maintained for a few minutes a very obstinate contest, musket to musket, through the port holes, in which many of the enemy's balls were welded to the bayonets of our muskets, our troops succeeded in gaining possession of the opposite side of the works. The event could no longer be doubtful. The enemy, although many of them fought to the last, with that kind of bravery which desperation inspires, were at length entirely routed and cut to pieces. The whole margin of the river which surrounds the peninsula was strewed with the slain. Five hundred and fifty-seven were found by officers of great respectability, whom I had ordered to count them; besides a great number who were thrown into the river by their surviving friends, and killed in attempting to pass it, by general Coffee's men, stationed on the opposite banks. Capt. Hammonds, who with his company of spies occupied a favorable position opposite the upper extremity of the breastwork, did great execution—and so did lieut. Bean, who had been ordered by general Coffee to take possession of a small island pointing to the lower extremity.

Both officers and men, who had the best opportunities on judging, believe the loss of the enemy in killed, not to fall short of eight hundred; and if their number was as great as it is represented to have been, by the prisoners, and as it is believed to have been by col. Carroll and others, who had a fair view of them, as they advanced to the breastworks, their loss must even have been more considerable—as it is quite certain that not more than twenty can have escaped. Among the dead was found their famous prophet Monahell—shot in the mouth by a grape shot, as if heaven designed to chastise his impostures by an appropriate punishment. Two other prophets were also killed—leaving no others, as I can learn, on the Tallapoosa. I lament that two or three women and children were killed by accident. I do not know the exact number of prisoners taken, but it must exceed three hundred—all women and children except three.

The battle may be said to have contínned with severity for about five hours; but the firing and slaughter continued until it was suspended by the darkness of the night. The next morning it was resumed, and sixteen of the enemy slain, who had concealed themselves under the banks. Our loss was twenty-six whitemen killed, and one hundred and seven wounded. Cherokees eighteen killed, and thirty-six wounded—friendly Creeks, five killed and eleven wounded.

The loss of col. Williams's regiment of regulars, is seventeen killed, fifty-five wounded, three of whom have since died. Among the former were major Montgomery, lieut. Sommerville and lieut. Moulton, who fell in the charge which was made on the works. No men ever acted more gallantly or fell more gloriously.

Of the artillery commanded by capt. Parish, 11 were wounded; one of whom, Samuel Garner, has since died. Lieuts. Allen and Ridley were both wounded. The whole company acted with its usual gallantry. Capt. Bradford of the 39th U. S. infantry, who acted as chief engineer, and superintended the firing of the cannon, has entitled himself by his good conduct to my warmest thanks. To say all in a word, the whole army who has achieved this fortunate victory, have merited by their good conduct the gratitude of their country. So far as I can, or could learn, there was not an officer or soldier who did not perform his duty with the utmost fidelity. The conduct of the militia, on this occasion, has gone far towards redeeming the character of that description of troops. They have been as orderly in their encampment, and on their line of march, as they have been signally brave in the day of battle.

The Battle of Horseshoe Bend played the role in the South that the Battle of the Thames played in the North. The Indians, their spirit broken, withdrew to their villages, no longer willing to resist American expansion. General Jackson took advantage of their weakness by forcing on the Creeks the Treaty of Fort Jackson (August 1814) which robbed them of about half of their lands. These dual victories assured peaceful expansion of the frontier for the next generation.

Elsewhere the War of 1812 was less satisfactory for the American cause. All attempts to overrun Canada failed, while British forces ravaged the capital of the nation, burning government buildings in retaliation for the destruction of York (now Toronto). The most decisive victory—that of Andrew Jackson at New Orleans in January 1815—was won after the peace treaty had been signed. This unsatisfactory record was reflected in the Treaty of Ghent; each nation agreed to restore all conquests made during the fighting, while the neutral rights that Americans hoped to secure by fighting were not even mentioned. Technically the United States lost the War of 1812 by failing to win its objectives; actually the nation won an important victory. With its national honor satisfied, with its borders safe, with the Indians of the backcountry cowed, its pioneers were free to sweep westward in unparalleled numbers as they overran the Mississippi Valley during the next quarter century.

CHAPTER 13

Peopling the Interior Valley, 1815-1850

The end of the War of 1812 signaled the start of the largest mass migration to the West that the United States had known. By that time, men who had been held back by the Indian wars were eager to move on, as men always were after such halts. But the main forces impelling their migration were the attractions that lay ahead. The West was the garden of the world, the Eden of their dreams. The eastern half of the Mississippi Valley was level or gently rolling, with no mountains to stand plows on edge. Forests were less dense than in the East, and more easily removed; they were interlaced with prairies assuring good pasturage. Everywhere rivers coursed the countryside, promising an economical outlet for the corn and tobacco and cotton that could be grown. This was a land to tempt the most laggard—a land that would shower its bounties on all. So they came, in such numbers that by 1850 the whole region east of the Mississippi had been carved into states.

THE GREAT MIGRATION OF 1816

Those in the van were the restless who were always first into each new wilderness—the perennially unsuccessful, the drifters, and the unfortunates without energy to match their ambition. Many were from the upland regions of the Appalachian area: the hilly backcountry of Virginia and Maryland, the interior of Pennsylvania and New York, the New England highlands. The principal gateway to the land of promise was at Pittsburgh, where the journey would begin down the Ohio toward the cheap lands ready to blossom under care. Men of this ilk, unambitious and with few resources, swarmed over the wilderness trails between 1816 and 1819, their scant belongings in wagons or handcarts or carried on their backs, their ill-clad families trudging beside them. An English traveler, Morris Birkbeck, witnessed this procession as he traveled across Pennsylvania:[1]

We have now fairly turned our backs on the old world, and find ourselves in the very stream of emigration. Old America seems to be breaking up, and moving westward. We are seldom out of sight, as we travel on this grand track, towards the Ohio, of family groups, behind and before us, some with a view to a particular spot; close to a brother perhaps, or a friend, who has gone before,

---

[1] Morris Birkbeck, *Notes on a Journey in America* (London, 1818), pp. 25–28, 31–33.

and reported well of the country. Many like ourselves, when they arrive in the wilderness, will find no lodge prepared for them.

A small waggon (so light that you might almost carry it, yet strong enough to bear a good load of bedding, utensils and provisions, and a swarm of young citizens,—and to sustain marvellous shocks in its passage over these rocky heights) with two small horses; sometimes a cow or two, comprises their all; excepting a little store of hard-earned cash for the land office of the district; where they may obtain a title for as many acres as they possess half-dollars, being one fourth of the purchase-money. The waggon has a tilt, or cover, made of a sheet, or perhaps a blanket. The family are seen before, behind, or within the vehicle, according to the road or the weather, or perhaps the spirits of the party.

The New Englanders, they say, may be known by the cheerful air of the women advancing in front of the vehicle; the Jersey people, by their being fixed steadily within it; whilst the Pennsylvanians creep lingering behind, as though regretting the homes they have left. A cart and single horse frequently affords the means of transfer, sometimes a horse and pack-saddle. Often the back of the poor pilgrim bears all his effects and his wife follows, naked-footed, bending under the hopes of the family. . . .

May 26 We have completed our third day's march to general satisfaction. We proceed nearly as fast as our fellow-travellers in carriages, and much more pleasantly, so that we have almost forgotten our indignation against the pitiful and fraudulent stage-master, of George Town; so apt are we to measure the conduct of other people, by the standard of our convenience, rather than its own merit.

This is a land of plenty, and we are proceeding to a land of *abundance*, as is proved by the noble droves of oxen we meet, on their way from the western country, to the city of Philadelphia. They are kindly, well-formed, and well-fed animals, averaging about six cwt. . . .

The taverns in the great towns, east of the mountains, which lay in our route, afford nothing in the least corresponding with our habits and notions of convenient accommodation: the only similarity is in the expence.

At these places all is performed on the gregarious plan: every thing is public by day and by night;—for even night in an American inn affords no privacy. Whatever may be the number of guests, they must receive their entertainment *en masse*, and they must sleep *en masse*. Three times a-day the great bell rings, and a hundred persons collect from all quarters, to eat a hurried meal, composed of almost as many dishes. At breakfast you have fish, flesh and fowl; bread of every shape and kind, butter, eggs, coffee, tea—every thing, and more than you can think of. Dinner is much like the breakfast, omitting the tea and coffee; and supper is the breakfast repeated. Soon after this meal, you assemble once more, in rooms crowded with beds, something like the wards of a hospital; where, after undressing in public, you are fortunate if you escape a partner in your bed, in addition to the myriads of bugs, which you need not hope to escape.

But the horrors of the kitchen, from whence issue these shoals of dishes, how shall I describe, though I have witnessed them. —It is a dark and sooty hole, where the idea of cleanliness never entered, swarming with negroes of all sexes and ages, who seem as though they were bred there: without floor, except the rude stones that support a raging fire of pine logs, extending across the entire place; which forbids your approach, and which no being but a negro could face.

In your reception at a western Pennsylvania tavern there is something of hospitality combined with the mercantile feelings of your host. He is generally a man of property, the head man of the village perhaps, with the title of Colonel, and feels that he confers, rather than receives, a favour by the accommodation he affords; and rude as his establishment may be, he does not perceive that you have a right to complain: what he has you partake of, but he makes no apologies; and if you shew symptoms of dissatisfaction or disgust, you will fare the worse; whilst a disposition to be pleased and satisfied will be met by a wish to make you so.

At the last stage, our party of eight weary pilgrims, dropping in as the evening closed, alarmed the landlady, who asked the ladies if we were not English, and said, she would rather not wait upon us,—we should be "difficult." However, she admitted us, and this morning, at parting, she said she liked to wait on "such" English; and begged we would write to our friends and recommend her house. We were often told that we were not "difficult," like the English; and I am sure our entertainment was the better, because they found us easy to please.

TRAVEL ON THE OLD NATIONAL ROAD

Most of the immigrants who went west just after the War of 1812 followed the traditional route to the interior: by road or trail to Pittsburgh at the Forks of the Ohio, then down that stream to their destination. Others took advantage of a new route made possible by government largess. This was the Old National Road, or Cumberland Road, built with federal funds and opened in 1818 between Cumberland on the Potomac and Wheeling on the Ohio. For the first time, the Appalachian Mountains could be crossed on a smooth highway. Hence from the day it was opened the National Road was crowded with travelers: immigrants hurrying westward, freighters with their lumbering wagons, stagecoaches threading their way with their passengers, drivers with their herds of cattle. An easterner, Charles F. Hoffman, who journeyed westward at this time described the bustle of traffic:[2]

About thirty miles from Wheeling we first struck the national road. It appears to have been originally constructed of large, round stones, thrown without much arrangement on the surface of the soil, after the road was first levelled. These are now being ploughed up, and a thin layer of broken stones is in many places spread over the renovated surface. I hope the roadmakers have not the conscience to call this Macadamizing. It yields like snow-drift to the heavy wheels which traverse it, and the very best parts of the road that I saw are not to be compared with a Long Island turnpike. Two-thirds indeed of the extent traversed were worse than any artificial road I ever travelled, except perhaps the log causeways among the new settlements in northern New-York. The ruts are worn so broad and deep by heavy travel, that an army of pigmies might march into the bosom of the country under the cover they would afford. Perhaps I was the more struck with the appearance of this celebrated highway from the fact of much of the road over the mountains having been in excellent condition.—There is one feature, however, in this national road which is truly fine,—I allude to the massive stone bridges which form a part of it. They occur, as the road crosses a winding creek, a dozen times within as many miles. They consist either of one, two, or three arches; the centre arch

---

[2] Charles F. Hoffman, *A Winter in the West, by a New Yorker* (New York, 1835), vol. 1, pp. 42–49.

being sprung a foot or two higher than those on either side. Their thick walls projecting above the road, their round stone buttresses, and carved key-stones combine to give them an air of Roman solidity and strength. They are monuments of taste and power that will speak well for the country when the brick towns they bind together shall have crumbled in the dust.

These frequently recurring bridges are striking objects in the landscape, where the road winds for many miles through a narrow valley. They may be seen at almost every turn spanning the deep bosom of the defile, and reflected with all their sombre beauty in the stream below....

By far the greatest portion of travellers one meets with, not to mention the ordinary stage-coach passengers, consists of teamsters and the emigrants. The former generally drive six horses before their enormous wagons—stout, heavy-looking beasts, descended, it is said, from the famous draught horses of Normandy. They go about twenty miles a day. The leading horses are often ornamented with a number of bells suspended from a square raised frame-work over their collars, originally adopted to warn these lumbering machines of each other's approach, and prevent their being brought up all standing in the narrow parts of the road.

As for the emigrants, it would astonish you to witness how they get along. A covered one-horse wagon generally contains the whole worldly substance of a family consisting not unfrequently of a dozen members. The tolls are so high along this western turnpike, and horses are so comparatively cheap in the region whither the emigrant is bound, that he rarely provides more than one miserable Rosinante to transport his whole family to the far west. The strength of the poor animal is of course half the time unequal to the demand upon it, and you will, therefore, unless it be raining very hard, rarely see any one in the wagon, except perhaps some child overtaken by sickness, or a mother nursing a young infant. The head of the family walks by the horse, cheering and encouraging him on his way. The good woman, when not engaged as hinted above, either trudges along with her husband, or, leading some weary little traveller by the hand behind, endeavours to keep the rest of her charge from loitering by the wayside. The old house-dog—if not chained beneath the wagon to prevent the half-starved brute from foraging too freely in a friendly country—brings up the rear. I made acquaintance with more than one of these faithful followers in passing, by throwing him a biscuit as I rode by, and my canine friend, when we met at an inn occasionally afterward, was sure to cultivate the intimacy. Sometimes these invaluable companions give out on the road, and in their broken-down condition are sold for a trifle by their masters. I saw several fine setters which I had reason to suspect came into the country in this way; and the owner of a superb brindled greyhound which I met among the mountains, told me that he had bought him from an English emigrant for a dollar. He used the animal with great success upon deer, and had already been offered fifty dollars for him.

The hardships of such a tour must form no bad preparatory school for the arduous life which the new settler has afterward to enter upon. Their horses, of course, frequently give out on the road; and in companies so numerous, sickness must frequently overtake some of the members. Nor should I wonder at serious accidents often occurring with those crank conveyances among the precipices and ravines of the mountains. At one place I saw a horse, but recently dead, lying beneath a steep, along the top of which the road led; and a little farther in advance, I picked up a pocketbook with some loose leaves floating near the edge of the precipice.

TRAVEL ON THE OHIO RIVER

When the westward-moving immigrants reached the Ohio—whether by the National Road at Wheeling or the trails and highways that led to Pittsburgh—they usually took to the rivers for the last stages of their journey. They could choose between a variety of craft, most of them ungainly, but all admirably designed for the task to be performed. Some travelers took passage on the keelboats and commercial vessels that regularly plied the western rivers. Others purchased space on the barges and flatboats that carried bulky farm produce to the New Orleans markets and could always accommodate a few passengers. More built or bought their own crude flatboats, loaded their families, livestock, and household goods aboard, and kept house as they floated to their new homes. These flimsy craft often ran aground or disintegrated in a violent storm, but they offered cheap transportation and ready-made housing. The boats were usually knocked apart when the pioneer reached his destination and the lumber used for the first dwelling place. Timothy Flint, a westerner by adoption and spirit, saw these craft as they waited at Pittsburgh to carry settlers to their new homes:[3]

Many travellers and emigrants to this region, view the first samples of the modes of travelling in the western world, on the Allegany at Oleanne point, or the Monongahela at Brownsville. These are but the retail specimens. At Pittsburg, where these rivers unite, you have the thing in gross, and by wholesale. The first thing that strikes a stranger from the Atlantic, arrived at the boat-landing, is the singular, whimsical, and amusing spectacle, of the varieties of watercraft, of all shapes and structures. There is the stately barge, of the size of a large Atlantic schooner, with its raised and outlandish looking deck. This kind of craft, however, which required twenty-five hands to work it up stream, is almost gone into disuse, and though so common ten years ago, is now scarcely seen. Next there is the keelboat, of a long, slender, and elegant form, and generally carrying from fifteen to thirty tons. This boat is formed to be easily propelled over shallow waters in the summer season, and in low stages of the water is still much used, and runs on waters not yet frequented by steam-boats. Next in order are the Kentucky flats, or in the vernacular phrase, "broadhorns," a species of ark, very nearly resembling a New England pig-stye. They are fifteen feet wide, and from forty to one hundred feet in length, and carry from twenty to seventy tons. Some of them, that are called family-boats, and used by families in descending the river, are very large and roomy, and have comfortable and separate apartments, fitted up with chairs, beds, tables and stoves. It is no uncommon spectacle to see a large family, old and young, servants, cattle, hogs, horses, sheep, fowls, and animals of all kinds, bringing to recollection the cargo of the ancient ark, all embarked, and floating down on the same bottom. Then there are what the people call "covered sleds," or ferry-flats, and Alleganyskiffs, carrying from eight to twelve tons. In another place are pirogues of from two to four tons burthen, hollowed sometimes from one prodigious tree, or from the trunks of two trees united, and a plank rim fitted to the upper part. There are common skiffs, and other small craft, named, from the man-

---

[3] Timothy Flint, *Recollections of the Last Ten Years* (Boston, 1826), pp. 13–16.

ner of making them, "dug-outs," and canoes hollowed from smaller trees. These boats are in great numbers, and these names are specific, and clearly define the boats to which they belong. But besides these, in this land of freedom and invention, with a little aid perhaps, from the influence of the moon, there are monstrous anomalies, reducible to no specific class of boats, and only illustrating the whimsical archetypes of things that have previously existed in the brain of inventive men, who reject the slavery of being obliged to build in any received form. You can scarcely imagine an abstract form in which a boat can be built, that in some part of the Ohio or Mississippi you will not see, actually in motion. The New York canal is beginning, indeed, to bring samples of this infinite variety of water-craft nearer to the inspection of the Atlantic people.

This variety of boats, so singular in form, and most of them apparently so frail, is destined in many instances to voyages of from twelve hundred to three thousand miles. Keel-boats, built at this place, start on hunting expeditions for points on the Missouri, Arkansas, and Red River, at such distances from Pittsburg as these. Such are the inland voyages on these long streams, and the terms of the navigation are as novel as are the forms of the boats. You hear of the danger of "riffles," meaning probably, ripples, and planters, and sawyers, and points, and bends, and shoots, a corruption, I suppose, of the French "chute." You hear the boatmen extolling their prowess in pushing a pole, and you learn the received opinion, that a "Kentuck" is the best man at a pole, and a Frenchman at the oar. A firm push of the iron-pointed pole on a fixed log, is termed a "reverend" set. You are told when you embark, to bring your "plunder" aboard, and you hear about moving "fernenst" the stream; and you gradually become acquainted with a copious vocabulary of this sort. The manners of the boatmen are as strange as their language. Their peculiar way of life has given origin not only to an appropriate dialect, but to new modes of enjoyment, riot, and fighting. Almost every boat, while it lies in the harbour has one or more fiddles scraping continually aboard, to which you often see the boatmen dancing. There is no wonder that the way of life which the boatmen lead, in turn extremely indolent, and extremely laborious; for days together requiring little or no effort, and attended with no danger, and then on a sudden, laborious and hazardous, beyond Atlantic navigation; generally plentiful as it respects food, and always so as it regards whiskey, should always have seductions that prove irresistible to the young people that live near the banks of the river. The boats float by their dwellings on beautiful spring mornings, when the verdant forest, the mild and delicious temperature of the air, the delightful azure of the sky of this country, the fine bottom on the one hand, and the romantic bluff on the other, the broad and smooth stream rolling calmly down the forest, and floating the boat gently forward,—all these circumstances harmonize in the excited youthful imagination. The boatmen are dancing to the violin on the deck of their boat. They scatter their wit among the girls on the shore who come down to the water's edge to see the pageant pass. The boat glides on until it disappears behind a point of wood. At this moment perhaps, the bugle, with which all the boats are provided, strikes up its note in the distance over the water. These scenes, and these notes, echoing from the bluffs of the beautiful Ohio, have a charm for the imagination, which, although I have heard a thousand times repeated, and at all hours, and in all positions, is even to me always new, and always delightful.

ENGLISHMEN SETTLE THE ILLINOIS PRAIRIES

The destination of those who descended the Ohio was no longer Kentucky or Ohio, but the newer lands of Indiana and Illinois. There they filled the river bottoms first, then pushed over the uplands as they carved the southern portions of those territories into farms. Like their pioneer ancestors before them, they selected wooded areas for settlement, knowing that a dense forest growth meant rich soil. More recent arrivals from Europe harbored no such traditional prejudices, and were able to capitalize on another of nature's bounties. As the frontier advanced across the Lake Plains province, pioneers began to emerge from the woodlands and settle the prairies of interior America. These level or gently rolling grasslands were ideal for farming, with soils that were rich and deep, timber nearby for fencing and housing, and freedom from the back-breaking task of clearing. One of the first to realize the advantages of the prairie was Morris Birkbeck, a wealthy English farmer, who established a colony for his fellow countrymen on the prairies of southern Illinois near today's Albion and Wanborough. Birkbeck described the plan for his settlement and extolled the virtues of the region in a letter published in England in 1818:[4]

I have secured a considerable tract of land, more than I have any intention of holding, that I may be able to accommodate some of our English friends. Our soil appears to be rich, a fine black mould, inclining to sand, from one to three or four feet deep, lying on sandstone or clayey loam; so easy of tillage as to reduce the expense of cultivation below that of the land I have been accustomed to in England, notwithstanding the high rates of human labour. The wear of plough-irons is so trifling, that it is a thing of course to sharpen them in the spring once for the whole year. Our main object will be live stock, cattle, and hogs, for which there is a sure market at a good profit. Twopence a pound you will think too low a price to include a profit; but remember, we are not called upon, after receiving our money for produce, to refund a portion of it for rent, another portion for tithe, a third for poor's rates, and a fourth for taxes; which latter are here so light as scarcely to be brought into the nicest calculation. You will consider also, that money goes a great deal farther here, so that a less profit would suffice. The fact is, however, that the profits on capital employed any way in this country are marvellous: in the case of livestock the outgoings are so small, that the receipts are nearly all clear.

The idea of exhausting the soil by cropping, so as to render manure necessary, has not yet entered into the estimates of the western cultivator. Manure has been often known to accumulate until the farmers have removed their yards and buildings out of the way of the nuisance. They have no notion of making a return to the land, and as yet there seems no bounds to its fertility.

For about half the capital that is required for the mere cultivation of our worn-out soils in England, a man may establish himself as a proprietor here, with every comfort belonging to a plain and reasonable mode of living, and with a certainty of establishing his children as well or better than himself—such an approach to certainty at least as would render *anxiety* on that score unpardonable.

Land being obtained so easily, I had a fancy to occupy here just as many acres as

---

[4] Morris Birkbeck, *Letters from Illinois* (London, 1818), pp. 17–19.

I did at Wanborough; and I have added 160 of timbered land to the 1,440 I at first concluded to farm. I shall build and furnish as good a house as the one I left, with suitable outbuildings, garden, orchard, &c. make 5,000 rods of fence, chiefly bank and ditch, provide implements, build a mill, support the expenses of housekeeping and labour until we obtain returns, and pay the entire purchase-money of the estate, for less than half the capital employed on Wanborough farm. At the end of fourteen years, instead of an expiring lease, I or my heirs will probably see an increase in the value of the land equal to fifteen or twenty times the original purchase.

In the interval my family will have lived handsomely on the produce, and have plenty to spare, should any of them require a separate establishment on farms of their own.

Thus I see no obstruction to my realising all I wished for on taking leave of Old England. To me, whose circumstances were comparatively easy, the change is highly advantageous; but to labouring people, to mechanics, to people in general who are in difficulties, this country affords so many sure roads to independence and comfort, that it is lamentable that any, who have the means of making their escape, should be prevented by the misrepresentation of others, or their own timidity.

INDIAN REMOVAL: THE GOVERNMENT POLICY

The massive migration of the years 1815 to 1819 was directed largely toward the Old Northwest, and reached such proportions that Indiana became a state in 1816 and Illinois in 1818. It declined after the Panic of 1819 and the depression that followed. Yet those years were significant in the history of expansion, for they witnessed the tragic expulsion of the Indians who clung to their homes east of the Mississippi River, thus opening the way for a later and more vigorous westward thrust during the 1830s and 1840s. The policy of uprooting the eastern Indians was officially launched in the middle 1820s, but its foundations had been laid during the War of 1812 when the battles of the Thames and Horseshoe Bend broke their power and left them at the mercy of the white men. For a decade thereafter they were allowed to live in relative peace, but when population pressures mounted, the government was ready to respond. The official policy was pronounced in January 1825, when Secretary of War John C. Calhoun sketched for President James Monroe the steps needed to assure peaceful relations between the two civilizations for all time to come:[5]

Of the four southern tribes, two of them (the Cherokees and Choctaws) have already allotted to them a tract of country west of the Mississippi. That which has been allotted to the latter is believed to be sufficiently ample for the whole nation, should they emigrate; and if an arrangement, which is believed not to be impracticable, could be made between them and the Chickasaws, who are their neighbors, and of similar habits and dispositions, it would be sufficient for the accommodation of both. A sufficient country should be reserved to the west of the Cherokees on the Arkansas, as a means of exchange with those who remain on the east. To the Creeks might be allotted a country between the Arkansas and the Canadian river, which limits the northern boun-

---

[5] "Report of John C. Calhoun to President James Monroe, January 24, 1825" in *American State Papers, Indian Affairs* (Washington, 1834), vol. 2, pp. 543-544.

dary of the Choctaw possessions in that quarter. There is now pending with the Creeks a negotiation, under the appropriation of the last session, with a prospect that the portion of that nation which resides within the limits of Georgia may be induced, with the consent of the nation, to cede the country which they now occupy for a portion of the one which it is proposed to allot for the Creek nation on the west of the Mississippi. Should the treaty prove successful, its stipulations will provide for the means of carrying it into effect, which will render any additional provision, at present, unnecessary. It will be proper to open new communications with the Cherokees, Choctaws, and Chickasaws, for the purpose of explaining to them the views of the Government, and inducing them to remove beyond the Mississippi, on the principles and conditions which may be proposed to the other tribes. It is known that there are many individuals of each of the tribes who are desirous of settling west of the Mississippi, and, should it be thought advisable, there can be no doubt that (if, by an adequate appropriation, the means were afforded the Government of bearing their expense) they would emigrate. Should it be thought that the encouragement of such emigration is desirable, the sum of $40,000, at least, would be required to be appropriated for this object, to be applied under the discretion of the President of the United States. The several sums which have been recommended to be appropriated, if the proposed arrangement should be adopted, amount to $95,000. The appropriation may be made either general or specific, as may be considered most advisable.

I cannot, however, conclude without remarking, that no arrangement ought to be made which does not regard the interest of the Indians as well as our own; and that, to protect the interest of the former, decisive measures ought to be adopted to prevent the hostility which must almost necessarily take place, if left to themselves, among tribes hastily brought together, of discordant character, and many of which are actuated by feelings far from being friendly towards each other. But the preservation of peace between them will not alone be sufficient to render their condition as eligible in their new situation as it is in their present. Almost all of the tribes proposed to be affected by the arrangement are more or less advanced in the arts of civilized life, and there is scarcely one of them which has not the establishments of schools in the nation, affording, at once, the means of moral, religious, and intellectual improvement. These schools have been established, for the most part, by religious societies, with the countenance and aid of the Government; and, on every principle of humanity, the continuance of similar advantages of education ought to be extended to them in their new residence. There is another point which appears to be indispensable to be guarded, in order to render the condition of this race less afflicting. One of the greatest evils to which they are subject is that incessant pressure of our population, which forces them from seat to seat, without allowing time for that moral and intellectual improvement, for which they appear to be naturally eminently susceptible. To guard against this evil, so fatal to the race, there ought to be the strongest and the most solemn assurance that the country given them should be theirs, as a permanent home for themselves and their posterity, without being disturbed by the encroachments of our citizens. To such assurance, if there should be added a system, by which the Government, without destroying their independence, would gradually unite the several tribes under a simple but enlightened system of government and laws formed on the principles of our own, and to which, as their own people would partake in it, they would, under the influence of the contemplated improvement, at no distant day, become prepared, the arrangements which have been proposed would prove to the Indians and their posterity a permanent blessing. It is believed that, if they could be assured that peace and friendship would be maintained among the several tribes; that the advantages of education, which they now enjoy, would be extended to them; that they should have a permanent and solemn guaranty for their possessions, and receive the countenance and aid of the Government for the gradual extension of its privileges to them, there would be among all the tribes a disposition to accord with the views of the Government. There are now, in most of the tribes, well educated, sober, and reflecting individuals, who are afflicted at the present condition of the Indians, and despondent at their future prospects. Under the operation of existing causes, they behold the certain degradation, misery, and even the final annihilation of their race, and, no doubt, would gladly embrace any arrangement which would promise to elevate them in the scale of civilization, and arrest the destruction which now awaits them. It is conceived that one of the most cheap, certain, and desirable modes of effecting the object in view, would be for Congress to establish fixed principles, such as have been suggested, as the basis of the proposed arrangement; and to authorize the President to convene, at some suitable point, all of the well-informed, intelligent, and influential individuals of the tribes to be affected by it, in order to explain to them the views of the Government, and to pledge the faith of the nation to the arrangements that might be adopted. Should such principles be established by Congress, and the President be vested with suitable authority to convene the individuals as proposed, and suitable provision be made to meet the expense, great confidence is felt that a basis of a system might be laid, which, in a few years, would entirely effect the object in view, to the mutual benefit of the Government and the Indians; and which, in its operations, would effectually arrest the calamitous course of events to which they must be subject, without a radical change in the present system. Should it be thought advisable to call such a convention, as one of the means of effecting the object in view, an additional appropriation of $30,000 will be required; making, in the whole, $125,000 to be appropriated.

All of which is respectfully submitted.

J. C. CALHOUN

THE TRAGEDY OF INDIAN REMOVAL

As Calhoun suggested, the principal impact of this policy of removal would be on the southern tribes, for by this time the northern Indians had been so scattered and broken that they could readily be transplanted to reservations in present-day Kansas and Nebraska. In the South, however, the Five Civilized Tribes—the Creeks, Cherokee, Choctaw, Chickasaw, and Seminole—were firmly established on tribal lands they had owned for centuries; moreover they showed every sign of adopting the white man's civilization, with farms, slaves, cotton mills, and in some cases their own written language and newspapers. Yet they stood in the path of the advancing frontiersmen, with no humanitarian spokesman to plead their case. So they must go. Beginning in 1826, treaty after treaty was forced on the tribes, first in Georgia and then in Alabama and Mississippi, requiring them to cede their lands in return for reservations in the Indian Territory beyond the Mississippi, as modern Oklahoma was then known. Some read the handwriting on the wall and left voluntarily; others were marched westward in gangs under the guns of troops. The record of one such Creek Indian party, kept by Lieutenant J. T. Sprague who was in charge, revealed the depths to which the nation could descend in dealing with a powerless minority:[6]

The 3rd of September I placed all the Indians under my charge in care of Mr. Felix G. Gibson and Charles Abercrombie, members of the Alabama Emigrating Company, and on the morning of the 5th the Party started for Arkansas, arranged to waggons according to the contract. The train consisted of forty-five waggons of every description, five hundred ponies and two thousand Indians. The moving of so large a body necessarily required some days to effect an arrangement to meet the comfort and convenience of all. The marches for the first four or five days were long and tedious and attended with many embarrasing circumstances. Men, who had ever had claims upon these distressed beings, now preyed upon them without mercy. Fraudulent demands were presented and unless some friend was near, they were robbed of their horses and even clothing. Violence was often resorted to to keep off these depredators to such an extent, that unless forced marches had been made to get out of this and the adjoining counties, the Indians would have been wrought to such a state of desperation that no persuasion would have deterred them from wreaking their vengeance upon the innocent as well as the guilty.

As soon as time and circumstances would permit, proper arrangements were made to secure to the Indians, regularly, their rations and transportation. A large herd of cattle were driven ahead of the train which supplied the Party with fresh beef. Two days rations were issued every other day, while corn was issued every day. The Party moved on without any serious inconvenience, other than the bad state of the roads and frequent drunken broils, until the 22nd, when from the warmth of the weather and the wearied condition of the Indians, I deemed it expedient to halt for a days rest. Tuck-e-batch-e-hadjo, the principal chief, had been desirous of stopping sooner, and had expressed his determination to do so. The situation of the camp at the time was not a desirable one for a halt, nor was I inclined to indulge him. I ordered the train to proceed. He with reluctance, came on.

From the first days march, I saw a disposition in the Indians, among both old and young, to remain behind. From their natural indolence and from their utter disregard for the future, they would straggle in the rear, dependent upon what they could beg, steal or find for support. I used every entreaty to induce them to keep up but finding this of no avail I threatened them with soldiers and confinement in irons. This had a salutary effect, and was the means of bringing most of them into camp in good season. On the night of the 24th inst. the party encamped at Town Creek, Al., after twenty days march averaging about twelve miles a day. I waited on the contractors and requested them to halt the party the following day. To this they expressed their unqualified disapprobation and denied my authority to exercise such a power. Their expenses they said were from six to seven hundred dollars per day, and if such authority was given or implied in the Contract, their hopes of making anything were gone. I assured them, that from the condition of the Indians, the common calls of humanity required it, and that one of the stipulations of the Contract was that they should treat the Indians with humanity and forbearance. I ordered the Indi-

---

[6] From *Indian Removal* by Grant Foreman. Copyright 1932 by the University of Oklahoma Press. Pp. 167–169, 171–173.

ans to halt, and told the Contractors they could act on their own pleasure; either go on with their empty waggons—or remain. The party halted and resumed the journey on the following morning, the 25th. The Indians and horses were evidently much relieved by the days rest.

From this period to the fifth of October our marches were long, owing to the great scarcity of water; no one time, however, exceeding twenty miles. The Indians in large numbers straggled behind, and many could not get to Camp till after dark. These marches would not have been so burdensome had proper attention been paid to the starting of the Party in the morning. It was necessary that their baggage, as well as their children, should be put in the waggons, and the sick and feeble sought out in the different parts of the Camp. But this was totally disregarded. I reminded the Contractors that the party now required the utmost attention, that unless they were strictly seen to, we should not at night have more than half the Indians in Camp. To this they were indifferent, saying, that "they must keep up or be left." Early in the morning the waggons moved off, the Agents at the head, leaving those behind to take care of themselves. Its an absurdity to say, that the Indians must take care of themselves; they are men it is true, but it is well known that they are totally incapable of it, and its proverbial that they will never aid each other....

On the 5th of October I again halted the party and rested one day. To this the contractors objected and seemed determined to drive the Indians into their measures. The 7th the party again moved and on the 9th inst. encamped near Memphis, Tenn. Great inconvenience was experienced upon this entire route for the want of Depots of provisions. There was no time when the proper rations were not issued, but from the frequent necessity of gathering and hauling corn, the Indians were often obliged to take their rations after dark. This caused great confusion and many were deprived of their just share....

The Mississippi Swamp at this season was impassable for waggons and it was agreed that the horses should go through while the women and children with their baggage took steam boats to Rock Roe. This place was attained by descending the Mississippi, about one hundred miles to the mouth of White River, and ascending this river about seventy miles, and thereby avoiding a swamp about fifty miles in breadth.

Finding that the embarkation of the parties that proceeded mine would cause much delay, a mutual agreement was effected between the Chiefs, the contractors and myself, to take the party up the Arkansas river to Little Rock. The advantages to be gained by this were evident; it put us ahead of all the other parties, secured us an abundant supply of provisions, and avoided a tedious journey of one hundred and fifty miles on foot. A commodious steam boat was procured and upon this and two flat boats I put as near as could be estimated fifteen hundred women and children and some men, with their baggage. The men amounting to some six or seven hundred passed through the swamp with their horses, in charge of my Assistant Agent Mr. Freeman. I received every assurance that upon this route the necessary provision was made for them. On board the boats, an abundance of corn and bacon were stored for the party to subsist upon until we should reach Little Rock. On the 27th the boat started. The Indians were comfortably accommodated, sheltered from the severity of the weather and from the many sufferings attending a journey on foot. The boats stopped at night for them to cook and sleep, and in the morning, resumed the journey.

The current of the Arkansas being so

strong at this time, it was found expedient to leave a part of the Indians until the boat could go up and return. These were left in the care of an Agent with the necessary supplies. On the 3rd of November we arrived at Little Rock. The larger portion of the party which passed through the Swamp, joined us the 4th. Many remained behind and sent word, that "when they had got bear skins enough to cover them they would come on." Here, they felt independent, game was abundant and they were almost out of the reach of the white-men. At first, it was my determination to remain at Little Rock until the whole party should assemble. But from the scarcity of provisions and the sale of liquor, I determined to proceed up the country about fifty miles and there await the arrival of all the Indians. Tuck-e-batch-e-hadjo refused to go. "He wanted nothing from the white-men and should rest." Every resting place with him was where he could procure a sufficiency of liquor. The petulant and vindictive feeling which this Chief so often evinced, detracted very much from the authority he once exercised over his people. But few were inclined to remain with him.

The 12th we encamped at Potts, the place designated for the concentration of the whole party. My Assistant Agent, together with three Agents of the Company, returned immediately to bring up and subsist all in the rear. Some of them went as far back as the Mississippi Swamp. They collected, subsisted and transported all they could get to start by every argument and entreaty. . . . A body of Indians under a secondary Chief, Narticher-tus-ten-nugge expressed their determination to remain in the swamp in spite of every remonstrance. They evinced the most hostile feelings and cautioned the white-men to keep away from them. The 14th the steam boat that had returned from Little Rock to bring up those left on the Arkansas, arrived at our encampment with Tuck-e-batch-e-hadjo and his few adherents on board. On this boat the following day, I put all the sick, feeble and aged, placed them in charge of Doctor Hill, the surgeon of the party, with instructions to proceed to Fort Gibson, and then be governed by the proper officer at that place. This party arrived at their place of destination on the 22nd instant and were received by the officer of the proper department. The Agents bringing up the rear, arrived at camp on the 17th. Those in the Swamp still persisted in their determination to remain. Neither the Agents or myself had any means by which we could force them into proper measures, most conducive to their comfort and progress. The season being far advanced and the weather daily becoming more severe, I ordered the party to proceed the following morning.

The sufferings of the Indians at this period were intense. With nothing more than a cotton garment thrown over them, their feet bare, they were compelled to encounter cold, sleeting storms and to travel over hard frozen ground. Frequent appeals were made to me to clothe their nakedness and to protect their lacerated feet. To these I could do no more than what came within the provisions of the Contract. I ordered the party to halt on the 22nd and proceeded again on the 23rd. The weather was still severe, but delay only made our condition worse. The steam boat, on its return from Fort Gibson, fortunately found us encamped near the river Spadra. On board of her I succeeded in getting nearly the whole party, amounting now to some sixteen hundred souls.

THE BLACK HAWK WAR

The removal of the Indians to beyond the Mississippi was one of the most tragic events in the history of the United States, but it did end conflict between the races for the time being—with one exception. This occurred in the Old Northwest, where a band of Fox and Sauk Indians, after removal to Iowa, returned to their farms in northern Illinois for no other purpose than to till the rich soil and harvest their corn. This was little to the liking of whites who were already appropriating their lands. So the alarm was raised, and troops soon appeared to harry the red men back across the river. But the Indians found a leader in the person of Chief Black Hawk and fled eastward into southern Wisconsin, pillaging as they went. On their heels were the soldiers. "Black Hawk's Rebellion" was no war, for the Indians were poorly supplied and inadequately armed and were concerned more with slipping safely back to Iowa than with killing. Yet its last stages, as Black Hawk led his people down the Wisconsin River toward safety with the army constantly menacing, formed another sad chapter in the saga of Indian-white relations in the United States. Black Hawk mirrored that sadness in the account of these events that he recorded in his "autobiography":[7]

During our encampment at the Four Lakes, we were hard put to, to obtain enough to eat to support nature. Situate in a swampy, marshy country, (which had been selected in consequence of the great difficulty required to gain access thereto,) there was but little game of any sort to be found—and fish were equally scarce. The great distance to any settlement, and the impossibility of bringing supplies therefrom, if any could have been obtained, deterred our young men from making further attempts. We were forced to dig *roots* and *bark trees*, to obtain something to satisfy hunger and keep us alive! Several of our old people became so much reduced, as actually to *die with hunger!* And, finding that the army had com-menced moving, and fearing that they might come upon and surround our encampment, I concluded to remove my women and children across the Mississippi, that they might return to the Sac nation again. Accordingly, on the next day, we commenced moving, with five Winnebagoes acting as our guides, intending to descend the Ouisconsin.

Ne-a-pope, with a party of twenty, remained in our rear, to watch for the enemy, whilst we were proceeding to the Ouisconsin, with our women and children. We arrived, and had commenced crossing them to an island, when we discovered a large body of the enemy coming towards us. We were now compelled to fight, or sacrifice our wives and children to the fury of the whites! I met them with fifty warriors, (having left the balance to assist our women and children in crossing,) about a mile from the river, when an attack immediately commenced. I was mounted on a fine horse, and was pleased to see my warriors so brave. I addressed them in a loud voice, telling them to stand their ground, and never yield it to the enemy. At this time I was on the rise of a hill, where I wished to form my warriors, that we might have some advantage over the whites. But the enemy succeeded in gaining this point, which compelled us to fall back into a deep ravine, from which we continued firing at them and they at us, until it began to grow dark. My horse having been wounded twice during this engagement, and fearing from his loss of blood, that he would soon give out—and finding that the enemy would not come near enough to receive our fire, in the dusk of the evening—and knowing that our women and children had had sufficient time to reach the island in the Ouisconsin, I ordered my warriors to return, in different routes, and meet me at the Ouisconsin—and were astonished to find that the enemy were not disposed to pursue us.

In this skirmish, with fifty braves, I de-

---

[7] *Life of MA-KA-TAI-ME-SHE-KIA-KIAK, or Black Hawk* (Cincinnati, 1833), pp. 130–136.

fended and accomplished my passage over the Ouisconsin, with a loss of only six men; though opposed by a host of mounted militia. I would not have fought there, but to gain time for my women and children to cross to an island. A warrior will duly appreciate the embarrassments I labored under —and whatever may be the sentiments of the *white people*, in relation to this battle, my nation, though fallen, will award to me the reputation of a great brave, in conducting it.

The loss of the enemy could not be ascertained by our party; but I am of opinion, that it was much greater, in proportion, than mine. We returned to the Ouisconsin, and crossed over to our people.

Here some of my people left me, and descended the Ouisconsin, hoping to escape to the west side of the Mississippi, that they might return home. I had no objection to their leaving me, as my people were all in a desperate condition—being worn out with travelling, and starving from hunger. Our only hope to save ourselves, was to get across the Mississippi. But few of this party escaped. Unfortunately for them, a party of soldiers from Prairie du Chien, was stationed on the Ouisconsin, a short distance from its mouth, who fired upon our distressed people. Some were killed, others drowned, several taken prisoners, and the balance escaped to the woods and perished with hunger. Among this party were a great many women and children.

I was astonished to find that Ne-a-pope and his party of *spies* had not yet come in— they having been left in my rear to bring the news, if the enemy were discovered. It appeared, however, that the whites had come in a different direction, and intercepted our trail but a short distance from the place where we first saw them—leaving our spies considerably in the rear. Ne-a-pope, and one other, retired to the Winnebago village, and there remained during the war! The balance of his party, being *brave men*, and considering our interest as their own, returned, and joined our ranks.

Myself and band having no means to descend the Ouisconsin, I started, over a rugged country, to go to the Mississippi, intending to cross it, and return to my nation. Many of our people were compelled to go on foot, for want of horses, which, in consequence of their having had nothing to eat for a long time, caused our march to be very slow. At length we arrived at the Mississippi, having lost some of our old men and little children, who perished on the way with hunger.

We had been here but a little while, before we saw a steam boat (the "Warrior,") coming. I told my braves not to shoot, as I intended going on board, so that we might save our women and children. I knew the captain, and was determined to give myself up to him. I then sent for my *white flag*. While the messenger was gone, I took a small piece of white cotton, and put it on a pole, and called to the captain of the boat, and told him to send his little canoe ashore, and let me come on board. The people on the boat asked whether we were Sacs or Winnebagoes. I told a Winnebago to tell them that we were Sacs, and wanted to give ourselves up! A Winnebago on the boat called to us *"to run and hide, that the whites were going to shoot!"* About this time one of my braves had jumped into the river, bearing a white flag to the boat—when another sprang in after him, and brought him to shore. The firing then commenced from the boat, which was returned by my braves, and continued for some time. Very few of my people were hurt after the first fire, having succeeded in getting behind old logs and trees, which shielded them from the enemy's fire.

The Winnebago, on the steam boat, must

either have misunderstood what was told, or did not tell it to the captain correctly; because I am confident that he would not have fired upon us, if he had known my wishes. I have always considered him a good man, and too great a brave to fire upon an enemy when sueing for quarters.

After the boat left us, I told my people to cross, if they could, and wished: that I intended going into the Chippewa country. Some commenced crossing, and such as had determined to follow them, remained—only three lodges going with me. Next morning, at daybreak, a young man overtook me, and said that all my party had determined to cross the Mississippi—that a number had already got over safe, and that he had heard the white army last night within a few miles of them. I now began to fear that the whites would come up with my people, and kill them, before they could get across. I had determined to go and join the Chippewas; but reflecting that by this I could only save myself, I concluded to return, and die with my people, if the Great Spirit would not give us another victory! During our stay in the thicket, a party of whites came close by us, but passed on without discovering us!

Early in the morning a party of whites, being in advance of the army, came upon our people, who were attempting to cross the Mississippi. They tried to give themselves up—the whites paid no attention to their entreaties—but commenced *slaughtering* them! In a little while the whole army arrived. Our braves, but few in number, finding that the enemy paid no regard to age or sex, and seeing that they were murdering helpless women and little children, determined to *fight until they were killed!* As many women as could, commenced swimming the Mississippi, with their children on their backs. A number of them were drowned, and some shot, before they could reach the opposite shore.

One of my braves, who gave me this information, piled up some saddles before him, (when the fight commenced,) to shield himself from the enemy's fire, and killed three white men! But seeing that the whites were coming too close to him, he crawled to the bank of the river, without being perceived, and hid himself under it, until the enemy retired. He then came to me and told me what had been done. After hearing this sorrowful news, I started, with my little party, to the Winnebago village at Prairie La Cross. On my arrival there, I entered the lodge of one of the chiefs, and told him that I wished him to go with me to his father—that I intended to give myself up to the American war chief, and *die,* if the Great Spirit saw proper! He said he would go with me. I then took my *medicine bag,* and addressed the chief. I told him that it was "the soul of the Sac nation—that it never had been dishonored in any battle—take it, it is my life—dearer than life—and give it to the American chief!" He said he would keep it, and take care of it, and if I was suffered to live, he would send it to me.

During my stay at the village, the squaws made me a white dress of deer skin. I then started, with several Winnebagoes, and went to their agent, at Prairie du Chien, and gave myself up.

ROUTES TO THE WEST
IN THE 1830s

Black Hawk's War and the sorrowful saga of Indian removal may stir the consciences of today's Americans, but to the frontiersmen the end justified any means. Now all the West was open to the Mississippi River, and once more they could resume their westward march. They were eager, and able, to do so. Returning prosperity during the early 1830s assured them a ready market for the bountiful crops they could produce in the West and accentuated their normal restlessness. Also improvements in transportation promised easier access to the frontier, as well as better markets. The Old National Road was extended across Ohio and into Indiana in the 1830s. Steamboats were plying the Mississippi and its tributaries in ever increasing numbers. Turnpikes, some of them improved, were linking East and West. These internal improvements, as they were then called, help explain the volume and direction of the westward migration of the period from the 1830s to the 1850s. An observer, Timothy Flint, noted their extent and influence as he traveled across the backcountry at this time:[8]

After the long vexed question whether to remove or not, is settled, by consulting friends, travellers and books, the next step is to select the route, and arrange the preparations for it. The universality and cheapness of steam boat and canal passage and transport, have caused, that more than half the whole number of immigrants now arrive in the West by water. This remark applies to nine tenths of those that come from Europe and the northern states. They thus escape much of the expense, slowness, inconvenience and danger of the ancient cumbrous and tiresome journey in wagons. They no longer experience the former vexations of incessant altercation with landlords, mutual charges of dishonesty, discomfort from new modes of speech and reckoning money, from breaking down carriages and wearing out horses.

But the steam boats and canal boats have their disadvantages. Cast perhaps for the first time among a mixed company of strangers, the bashful mother and the uneasy and curious children present an ample specimen of their domestic training; and how much they have profited by that universal education, about which every one talks. But though they may mutually annoy, and be annoyed, their curiosity is constantly excited, and gratified; their hunger abundantly appeased; and they occasionally form pleasant intimacies with their fellow travellers. If travelling be a mode of enjoyment, these unsated and unhackneyed travellers probably find, on the whole, a balance of enjoyment in favor of the journey of immigration.

The chances are still more favorable for the immigrants from Virginia, the two Carolinas and Georgia, who, from their habits and relative position, still immigrate, after the ancient fashion, in the southern wagon. This is a vehicle almost unknown at the north, strong, comfortable, commodious, containing not only a movable kitchen, but provisions and beds. Drawn by four or six horses, it subserves all the various intentions of house, shelter and transport; and is, in fact, the southern ship of the forests and prairies. The horses, that convey the wagon, are large and powerful animals, followed by servants, cattle, sheep, swine, dogs, the whole forming a primitive caravan not unworthy of ancient days, and the plains of Mamre. The procession moves on with power in its dust, putting to shame and uncomfortable feelings of comparison the northern family with their slight wagon, jaded horses and subdued, though jealous countenances. Their vehicle stops; and they scan the strong southern hulk, with its chimes of bells, its fat black drivers and its long train of concomitants, until they have swept by.

Perhaps more than half the northern immigrants arrive at present by way of the New York canal and lake Erie. If their destination be the upper waters of the Wa-

---

[8] Timothy Flint, *History and Geography of the Mississippi Valley* (Cincinnati, 1832), vol. 1, pp. 184–186.

bash, they debark at Sandusky, and continue their route without approaching the Ohio. The greater number make their way from the lake to the Ohio, either by the Erie and Ohio, or the Dayton canal. From all points, except those west of the Guyandot route and the national road, when they arrive at the Ohio, or its navigable waters, the greater number of the families 'take water.' Emigrants from Pennsylvania will henceforward reach the Ohio on the great Pennsylvania canal, and will 'take water' at Pittsburgh. If bound to Indiana, Illinois or Missouri, they build, or purchase a family boat. Many of these boats are comfortably fitted up, and are neither inconvenient, nor unpleasant floating houses. Two or three families sometimes fit up a large boat in partnership, purchase an 'Ohio pilot,' a book that professes to instruct them in the mysteries of navigating the Ohio; and if the Ohio be moderately high, and the weather pleasant, this voyage, unattended with either difficulty or danger, is ordinarily a trip of pleasure. We need hardly add, that a great number of the wealthier emigrant families take passage in a steam boat.

While the southerner finds the autumnal and vernal season on the Ohio too cool, to the northerner it is temperate and delightful. When the first wreaths of morning mist are rolled away from the stream by the bright sun, disclosing the ancient woods, the hoary bluffs, and the graceful curves and windings of the long line of channel above and below, the rich alluvial belt and the fine orchards on its shores, the descending voyagers must be destitute of the common perceptions of the beautiful, if they do not enjoy the voyage, and find the Ohio, in the French phrase, La belle riviere.

After the immigrants have arrived at Cincinnati, Lexington, Nashville, St. Louis, or St. Charles, in the vicinity of the points, where they had anticipated to fix themselves, a preliminary difficulty, and one of difficult solution is, to determine to what quarter to repair. All the towns swarm with speculating companies and land agents; and the chance is, that the first inquiries for information in this perplexity will be addressed to them, or to persons who have a common understanding and interest with them. The published information, too, comes directly or indirectly from them, in furtherance of their views. One advises to the Wabash, and points on the map to the rich lands, fine mill seats, navigable streams and growing towns in their vicinity. Another presents a still more alluring picture of the lands in some part of Illinois, Missouri, the region west of the lakes, and the lead mines. Another tempts him with White River, Arkansas, Red River, Opelousas, and Attakapas, the rich crops of cotton and sugar, and the escape from winter, which they offer. Still another company has its nets set in all the points, where immigrants congregate, blazoning all the advantages of Texas, and the Mexican country. In Cincinnati, more than in any other town, there are generally precursors from all points of the compass, to select lands for companies, that are to follow. There are such here at present both from Europe and New England; and we read advertisements, that a thousand persons are shortly to meet at St. Louis to form a company to cross the Rocky Mountains, with a view to select settlements on the Oregon.

When this slow and perplexing process of balancing, comparing and fluctuating between the choice of rivers, districts, climates and advantages, is fixed, after determination has vibrated backwards and forwards according to the persuasion and eloquence of the last adviser, until the purpose of the immigrant is fixed, the northern settler is generally borne to the point of debarkation, nearest his selected spot, by water. He thence hires the transport of his family and movables to the spot; though not a few northern emigrants move all the distance in wagons. The whole number from the north far exceeds that from the south. But they drop, in noiseless quietness, into their position, and the rapidity of their progress in settling a country is only presented by the startling results of the census.

The southern settlers who immigrate to Missouri and the country south west of the Mississippi, by their show of wagons, flocks and numbers create observation, and are counted quite as numerous, as they are. Ten wagons are often seen in company. It is a fair allowance, that a hundred cattle, beside swine, horses and sheep, and six negroes accompany each. The train, with the tinkling of an hundred bells, and the negroes, wearing the delighted expression of a holiday suspension from labor in their countenances, forming one group, and the family slowly moving forward, forming another, as the whole is seen advancing along the plains, it presents a pleasing and picturesque spectacle.

TRAVEL ON THE ERIE CANAL

As Flint noted, no improvement in transportation had a greater impact than the Erie Canal. This waterway, stretching from Albany to Buffalo across New York state and providing an all-water route between the Hudson River and Lake Erie, was opened in 1825 and immediately revolutionized travel and trade between the coast and the interior. Now would-be settlers could journey cheaply and comfortably from Albany to Buffalo, carrying their household goods with them, then transfer to one of the Great Lakes steamers that plied to such ports as Cleveland, Detroit, or Chicago. The result was to deflect migration from the Ohio Valley to the northern portions of the Old Northwest and to hurry the peopling of upper Indiana and Illinois, Michigan, and Wisconsin. What travel on the Erie Canal was like at this time was described by a newly arrived German immigrant Jacob Schramm who made the journey in 1836 and recorded his experiences in letters to his family:[9]

We arranged for the trip to Buffalo in a canalboat: sleeping quarters, and meals with the captain, 8 dollars each. This is a distance of 360 English miles, or 72 German ones, and the trip lasted 7 days. The boats are suitably fitted up. There are three cabins: a small one where the women passengers sleep; a second, with benches, which at night are put together and made into beds for the men; and a third where meals are served. Next to the dining room is the kitchen, where the sailors and the cook have their quarters. In the middle is the large space for goods. The boats are not very large, about 50 feet long and 10 wide, with the lower deck just high enough so a man can stand upright; nevertheless everything is surprisingly well managed. People of this region, therefore, make constant use of these boats, and it never occurs to anyone to go by foot, to ride, or travel by carriage. If one wants to live cheaply he can, if he takes care of his own provisions. In that case a person pays just half for the trip, and is allowed 50 lbs. free. When we went aboard this canalboat at Albany it was already nightfall; still, goods and people were being taken on and

[9] Emma S. Vonnegut (ed. and trans.), *The Schramm Letters: Written by Jacob Schramm and Members of His Family from Indiana to Germany in the Year 1836* ("Indiana Historical Society Publications," vol. 12, No. 4.) (Indianapolis, 1935), pp. 249–254.

continued to be until 11 o'clock. Everything was weighed. The passengers who boarded themselves went into the back room, but those who ate with us at the captain's table, into the cabin itself....

That night the boat lay at Albany, and in the morning it was taken into the lock and weighed; then the canal toll was paid. How high the amount was, I could not discover, with my lack of English, but the toll must stand at such a figure in relation to the freight rates as to allow profit to the boat owners, the shippers, and the state of New York, which built the canal, for there is a tremendous, continuous line of boats coming and going; indeed, as I learned later in German, the canal is long since paid for, and now has a big balance.

The weighing of the boat was done in this fashion. The boat is taken into a lock, which has the same water level as the canal and is an extension of it. When the boat is at the right spot, the entrance to the lock from the canal is closed by a gate that reaches the bottom, and fits so tight that no water can come through. The lock is then opened on the other side so that the water runs out. When it is out, the boat rests on a scaffold connected with big scales above, and in 5 minutes the weighing is finished. Thereupon the lock is again opened so that the water can rush back. In a few minutes it is back as it was before, and the boat returns to the canal.

The boat is drawn by horses, usually in relays of two, and day and night they keep up a sharp pace. The canal is only 4 or 5 feet deep, and of course the boats are built in accordance. For the most part they are the property of companies in New York or Albany, or other cities along the way, and have connections at all the landings. There are companies that have 300 such boats, which continually take goods and people to the western states, and bring produce to the eastern states. This output from the interior consists chiefly of cornmeal, barley, tobacco, and hides. There are also people who use the canals independently, but they cannot take passengers, because they have to have their own horses with them all the way. When one pair is tired, they are brought aboard and fed while the other team is hitched to the boat, and so they alternate. Every boat has to have a man to drive the horses. The companies that have so many boats have farms at different stations, where they keep a large number of horses, and where the horses are changed and fresh drivers provided. There are also many mail packets, likewise company owned, which expedite light packages, letters and passengers. They are narrower and longer than freight boats, and constructed less for heavy loads than for speed. A trip can be made very quickly on one of these, for the horses keep at a trot as they do with a German express, but they are more expensive.

The first day we traveled through beautiful, settled country, with the Mohawk River, which by means of locks supplies the water for the middle section of the canal, on the right. It is a good-sized stream, but hasn't enough water for steamships. Beyond are heavily wooded mountains, and the whole view is splendid. Along the canal is a chain of inns and stores where a person can get in one place what, in Germany, he would have to look for in many shops and workshops.

The first day we passed many locks, and that delayed the trip. The canal is for the most part laid out where the country is flattest, but as all the hills cannot be avoided, locks have to be built, which must cost frightful sums. There are perhaps 200 between Albany and Buffalo. At the entrance into one of these locks, built from quarried stone, there is a pair of gates, which is closed when the boat is once inside. The upper section of the canal, perhaps 10 or 15 feet higher, is held by another gate, which is closed while one is going through the lower gate, and then opened as soon as the lower one is closed. As the water comes rushing through the gate of the lock, the water and the boat at the closed door are lifted, rising to the height of the upper level. This process is repeated till one is up the hill. Sometimes the rise is small, and only 1 or 2 such locks are needed, but sometimes it is greater, and 4, 6, 8, 10, or even 12 locks follow one after the other. The boat that wants to descend must wait meanwhile until the lock gate of the lower level is opened....

So the journey proceeded as far as Buffalo, which we reached Sunday morning at three o'clock.

CAUSES FOR MIGRATION: NEW ENGLAND'S RURAL DECAY

The Erie Canal played another, and less obvious, role in the story of America's westward expansion. As goods grown cheaply on the virgin soils of the Great Lakes country flooded eastern markets, farmers in New England and the Middle States found themselves in an impossible situation. Their own soils, depleted by centuries of cropping, could not produce cereals at a price competitive with grains and flour produced in the West and shipped on the Erie Canal to New York or Boston. Hence they could do one of two things. They could move into the cities that were mushrooming throughout the Northeast, or they could migrate to the West themselves. Thousands did the latter, many simply abandoning their worn-out New England farms. A New Englander, Charles C. Nott, writing a few years later, described what happened in terms that could just as well have been applied to the 1830s and 1840s:[10]

Midway between Williamstown and Brattleboro, a few years ago, I saw on the summit of a hill against the evening sky what seemed a large cathedral. Driving thither, I found a huge, old-time two-story church, a large academy (which had blended in the distance with the church), a village with a broad street, perhaps 150 feet in width. I drove on and found that the church was abandoned, the academy dismantled, the village deserted. The farmer who owned the farm on the north of the village lived on one side of the broad street, and he who owned the farm on the south lived on the other, and they were the only inhabitants. All of the others had gone—to the manufacturing villages, to the great cities, to the West. Here had been industry, education, religion, comfort, and contentment, but there remained only a drear solitude of forsaken homes.

And here I have placed before you the three distinctive and essential facts of this New England problem—the farm of Mr. Foster, the boom in Williamstown, the deserted village in Vermont.

The deserted village was the old-fashioned "Centre" of the town; on a high hill, remote from railways and mill-streams, unknown to summer boarders—an agricultural village, dependent upon the agriculture around it and from which it sprang. The causes which operated upon Mr. Foster's farm and the surrounding agriculture struck it, and indeed seemed to strike it sooner, and a more effective blow.

The ruin of New England agriculture is

---

[10] *The Nation*, XLIX (November 21, 1889), pp. 406–407.

due to a combination of causes, the chief of which are these:

For many years the Government has been paying the most extraordinary bounty that the world ever knew for agricultural products. It has not paid this bounty upon agriculture to farmers in general, but only to those who would live in the West, and largely, if not chiefly, to the peasants and peasant-farmers and younger sons of Europe. To them it has said in substance, "Come over here and undersell American farmers east of the Alleghanies, and we will give you for nothing citizenship and a farm. Land which in your own country is a monopoly, the property of the great, beyond the hope of the poor, shall be yours without price, without rent, in fee simple absolute."

At the same time the Government has likewise been giving another set of bounties in land and guaranteed bonds to such railroads as should carry the immigrant farmers to their free farms without their being subjected to the dangers and delays and hardships which beset the "first settlers" of the olden time, and which should bring their agricultural products to the overstocked markets of the world for as nearly nothing as possible, and certainly at freight rates lower than the world ever dreamed of.

Accordingly, under this artificial bounty system, we have seen what was inevitable and what might have been expected, viz., that the most industrious and frugal class in the country, the farmers east of the Alleghanies, is the only class which has not shared in the general prosperity. Instead of letting our agriculture grow by natural causes—hard work, improved methods, better culture, and slowly extending area—we have seized the new land which properly belongs to the next century, and have squandered the riches which nature garnered for mankind with a waste and prodigality for which future generations, if they have any sense, may well curse their fathers....

It may be asked whether the sons of New England farmers have not as individuals shared in the benefits of the land system; whether they have not had easier times, worn better clothes, and smoked cigars instead of pipes. To this it must be answered that we are now considering New England and her agricultural conditions. What we do know is, first, that the old nursery of good and great and useful men is, under existing causes, being destroyed, or, to quote from the columns of the *Nation*, "The forest, like a rising tide, encroaches upon the former fields; population in the mountain towns diminishes; taxes increase; civilization recedes; the Celtic immigrant succeeds the Pilgrim stock"; second, that there is no rural New England in the West rearing a posterity worthy of the old stock; that the youth who was starved out of his birthplace in consequence of the land policy of the Government, has not been replaced there by a wiser or a better man, and that, in his new habitat, material wealth has been the only gain. The admonition to his fathers was, "*Go forth for freedom and for conscience' sake*"; to him, "*Go West, young man, go West, to make money to buy land to grow corn to fat hogs to make more money to buy more land to grow more corn to fat more hogs.*"

CAUSES FOR MIGRATION:
SOUTHERN SOIL EXHAUSTION

The rural decay of the Northeast was matched in the Southeast by the problem of soil depletion. There farms had been planted to tobacco or cotton for generations, with no attempt at fertilization or crop rotation. The result was desolation, with fields gullied, soils stripped of their mineral wealth, and yields declining alarmingly. This was especially the situation in the hilly piedmont area, where heavy rains washed away humus soils. A letter from a planter, John H. Craven, to one of the leading farm papers of the South described the problems facing farmers in the Virginia backcountry in the middle 1830s:[11]

At that time the whole face of the country presented a scene of desolation that baffles description—farm after farm had been worn out, and washed and gullied, so that scarcely an acre could be found in a place fit for cultivation. It will be well to observe here, that there is a ridge of red land passing through the counties of Albemarle and Orange, whose soil was of the very best quality, and susceptible of the highest degree of improvement, but which had at the same time been *butchered* by that most horrible mode of culture adopted by the first settlers of this country. The practice then was to clear the land, to put it in tobacco for three or four years in succession, according to the strength of the soil, afterwards in corn and wheat alternately, or corn and oats so long as it was capable of producing any thing. They never ploughed in those days, but simply scratched the ground, and this too, right up and down the steepest hills, instead of horizontally, with those little one horse half share or shovel ploughs, until the whole of the virgin soil was washed and carried off from the ridges into the valleys. This is a very imperfect description of the face of the country at the time of my settlement here; I believe it would not be saying too much, if I were to affirm, that there had not been before that period, one good plough in the county. Col. Thomas Mann Randolph, had commenced the horizontal ploughing on his farm; but, for the want of good ploughs, it was a long time before he could succeed sufficiently well to induce others to adopt the same plan. Indeed, there were many who, though considered at that time good practical farmers, were disposed to ridicule it for years after Col. Randolph had adopted it. And here, since there has been some little discussion of late in regard to the question, who first introduced this mode of ploughing, I will take the liberty of saying, that there is no person in Albemarle who ever doubted, nor do I myself doubt, that although some considerable improvement may have been made by others since that gentleman adopted it, yet he is entitled to the whole credit of its original introduction, and for which he deserves a monument to his memory.

Suffice it to say, in regard to the condition of the country at the time I speak of, that it wore the most haggard, frightful, poverty-stricken appearance imaginable, never having had upon it either plaster or clover, or, as one might naturally judge from its looks, vegetation of any kind. We had but one alternative in this state of things, either to improve and restore the soil, or to remove to some new and better country; which latter course was the most common—the majority of farmers, after they had impoverished their lands, preferring to leave the improvement of them to others, rather than undertake it themselves. There is here, as in all other places, a great variety of opinions in regard to the best mode of improvement—the manner of ploughing, whether deep or shallow—the time of ploughing—the time and manner of applying manure—questions which must be decided according to circumstances, and not by a single invariable rule. There are some things, however, which may be considered as all important—such as a rotation of

---

[11] *The Farmers Register*, I (August, 1833), p. 50. Letter of John H. Craven dated June 12, 1833.

crops, a rigid and scrupulous attention to the collection and preservation of all the manure that can be obtained, and great care in ploughing; for good ploughing, in my estimation, is the first step towards the improvement of an exhausted farm.

A SOUTH CAROLINA PLANTER MOVES WESTWARD

Why stay in the East amid such decay when good lands lay to the west? So many a planter reasoned. The attraction was the rich bottom land of Alabama and Mississippi, recently cleared of Indians and ideal for the production of cotton. So the migration began, with pioneer farmers leading the way, and well-to-do planters following on their heels. The latter seldom ventured into virgin areas, for their investment in slaves and equipment was too heavy to risk save on soil of proven fertility. So they normally purchased several smaller farms from the first occupants, consolidated them into a plantation, and moved westward, traveling in caravans with their families, their slaves, their livestock, and their household goods. Despite their comparative wealth, these planters were truly pioneers. They were required to build log cabins, cut down trees, roll the logs together for burning, and generally follow the clearing patterns common to all frontiersmen save for one difference: much of their labor was performed by slaves. Eli H. Lide described this process in a letter to a friend written in March 1836. He had moved from South Carolina to Carlowville, Alabama, the previous winter with his father, his mother, his brothers and sisters, and a number of slaves:[12]

[12] Fletcher M. Green (ed.), *The Lides Go South. . . . and West. The Record of a Planter Migration in 1835* (Columbia, South Carolina: University of South Carolina Press, 1952), pp. 15–17.

We are all very busily engaged in clearing and planting, repairing &c. having not long since gotten thro: with building as many negro houses as will answer present purposes, untill we can steal a little time from other matters, which indeed seems hard to do, for there are so many things pressing upon us and wedging themselves upon every moment of time, that some times I dislike to take the necessary time to eat. Father has a house, but I have one to build for myself or put up with rather a poor chance of a house offered me by Major Lee as a place of refuge in case I shall not find time to build. Indeed I am affraid I shall not be able to get up cabbins sufficient, for I must attend to clearing land for I have but little open, and have not been able to rent more than about from 30 to 35 acres and some of that poor, and have to give $4 per acre rent for a part and five dollars for a part, which looks like buying land. My man Rowell made but a poor out clearing land last year, that which he pretended to clear he only fell the smallest trees, without cutting up or trimming and deaded but very few acres and a great many trees were cut half round and left.

I had to do all this work over and indeed what he had done was but of little advantage, if he had done his duty I should have been able to have cleared 75 or 80 acres more than I shall under existing circumstances. I expect to get 80 acres under fence this week, forty of which is now ready for the plough, on the remaining forty the logs are yet to roll and burn. I have nearly twenty acres more cut down and am now burning the brush. Tomorrow however I stop to plant potatoes. I have planted about 25 acres of corn on rented land and in a few days shall plant about five acres more, on which last mentioned I hope to make 60 or seventy bushels per acre. I shall be obliged to plant the greater part of my land this year in corn as it is almost all new, and of such growth as will not die the first year say 140 acres corn and about 90 in cotton so you see I can not do much this year. I expect to keep about four or five hands clearing all summer, by doing this I hope to get in as much land as I can cultivate another year.

I have been all this while holding up to your view the dark side of the subject. I will now let you take peep at what I call the bright side, we live in a delightful neighborhood a kind of village place something like Society Hill not quite so dense a population but far more numerous which in point of intelligence is inferiour to none. As to health from all the information which I can gather it must be equal to the hills of Chesterfield the people here say equal to any in the world, of this however I prefer to be no judge but can see no local cause for sickness. Here is natural scenery which is grand and sublime, entirely superior to any thing I saw on the Blue Ridge, as to the *soil* it would do your very heart good to look at it.

I am often very much diverted to see Father, he is indeed the most busy man you ever saw, and he lets nothing keep him from his farm he is all the time among his negroes in the field and seems to be as active about his business as he could be at eighteen, he seems to have forgotten that he is old. He has a valuable tract of land and he can get double (as I was told to day) what it cost him. Some days ago I was walking with him over some of his beautiful hammocks and he said it appeared to him that land could not be any better than that was. He also says he has better prospects before him *now*, than he ever had and that a man might live here clear and aboveboard, he is fully as well pleased with the country as I am.

I have between 1800 and two thousand acres of land here which is too much for me. I some times think of selling 480 acres but am affraid to offer it for fear some one will want to purchase it. I put out a negro boy to learn the Blacks[mith] trade for whom I get $150 dollars a year hire. Corn is worth from 75/100 to 1.00 per bushel and scarce at that price.

FRENZIED SPECULATION IN THE SOUTHWEST

As the Lides, and thousands like them, turned their faces toward the West during the 1830s, the migration assumed stampede proportions. Each new fragment of land was snatched up by eager buyers as soon as it was cleared of its Indian occupants; everywhere in Alabama and Mississippi the forests rang with the sound of axes, and a pall of smoke from burning logs hazed the air. Speculators who watched this rush were elated; with times good, business booming, money plentiful, and a spirit of adventure in the air, they were justified in spending any amount to buy lands, knowing that a buyer would soon appear willing to pay a hundred percent more. In this heady atmosphere, land prices in the Southwest skyrocketed at a pace that bore no relationship to reason. A diarist at Vicksburg, James D. Davidson, in 1836 witnessed the wild bidding that went on and the astronomical prices that accompanied the land frenzy:[13]

November 1st We are now approaching Vicksburg—the famous Vicksburg of Lynching memory. As I approach it, I hail with pleasure the Hills on which it is situated. They are the first Hills I have seen in 1300

---

[13] Herbert A. Keller (ed.), "A Journey through the South in 1836: Diary of James D. Davidson," *Journal of Southern History*, I (August, 1935), p. 355. Copyright 1935 by the Southern Historical Association. Reprinted by permission of the Managing Editor.

miles travel, and I long to climb one of them. They are the only things like home that I have seen, since I left the Mountains of Va.

Vicksburg. I reached here at 12 oclock A.M. I was met on the shore by two acquaintances from Rockbridge who left there after I did, and by one of my travelling companions who left me at Louisville. Vicksburg is a busy place. The people here are run mad with speculation. They do business in . . . a kind of phrenzy. Money is scarce, but credit is plenty, and he who has no money can do as much business as he who has. There is an enormous value set upon every thing here. Every[thing] is sold as if they were precious relics—so extravagant is their cost. Lots of 22 by 70 feet sell at $10,000 & $15,000—Houses rent at $2000—A wagon and team hire at $16 a day—a horse at $2.50—a pair of Turkies at $5.00. A pair of chickens or ducks at $1.00. Wood at $10 a load—butter at 75 cts—Eggs at $1.50 a dozen, and cabbage at 50 cts a head—

There will be a tremendous failure here some day, and that not far hence. And Vicksburg, I am told, is the State in Miniature. It will be a fine field for Lawyers in two or three years.

FRENZIED SPECULATION IN THE NORTHWEST

That same speculative enthusiasm sent prices in the Northwest to the same fantastic heights. Ralph Waldo Emerson heard tales of the manner in which Chicago real estate boomed during the 1830s when he visited that frontier city a short time later:[14]

'Tis very droll to hear the comic stories of the rising values here, which, ludicrous though they seem, are justified by facts presently. Mr. Corwin's story of land offered for $50,000, and an hour given to consider it. The buyer made up his mind to take it, but he could not have it; it was five minutes past the hour, and it was now worth $60,000. After dinner, he resolved to give the price, but he had overstayed the time again, and it was already $70,000; and it became $80,000, before night,—when he bought it. I believe it was Mr. Corwin's joke, but the solemn citizens who stood by, heard it approvingly, and said, "Yes, that is about the fair growth of Chicago *per hour.*" However, a quite parallel case to this, I am told, actually occurred in the sale of the "American House" lot, which rose in a day from perhaps $40,000 to 50, 60, 70, 80, or 90,000, at which price it was sold. Mr. Foster, of Evansville, when I asked about the once rival towns which competed with Chicago, said, "Yes, at New City they once thought there was to be the great centre, and built sixty houses." "Was there not a river and harbor there?" "Oh, yes, there was a guzzle out of a sandbank, but now there are still the sixty houses, and when I passed by the last time, there was one owl, which was the only inhabitant."

Mr. W. B. Ogden told me that he came here from New York twenty-one years ago. In New York he had, in association with some others, made a large purchase here to the amount of $100,000. He had never been here, but wished to have a reason for coming beyond merely seeing the country; had never then been beyond Buffalo westward.

He arrived here one morning, June 11, 1836. He learned that one of the parties of whom he had purchased was in the house, on his arrival at the tavern or fort, and this person sent for him to come up and see him. This Mr. Bronson had heard some rumor that his brother had sold the land to a company in New York, but hoped it was not so.

---

[14] Ralph Waldo Emerson, *Journals of Ralph Waldo Emerson* (Boston, 1913), vol. 9, pp. 76–80.

Mr. Ogden showed him his deed. Bronson said it was all right, but it was injudicious in his brother. Ogden said he was glad to hear that, for he had feared he had made a foolish bargain. While he was in Bronson's room, somebody tapped at the door, and wished to know if the man who represented *Block No. 1* was here? Mr. Ogden knew nothing of it; but Bronson told the man, Yes, Ogden represented that purchase. "Well, will you sell Block No. 1?" Ogden replied he knew nothing of it, but after breakfast he would go and see the land. After breakfast, they crossed in a little boat, and looked about in the swamp and woods, and came to a stake. "Here," said Bronson, "is Block No. 1." Well, they were followed by several persons, and, among others, the one he had seen. These came up, and the man said, "What will you take for this property?" Ogden said he knew nothing of its value, but if they would make him an offer, he would inform himself, and answer. The man said, "We will give you $35,000 for eight blocks from No. 1 to No. 8." Ogden said, "I never altered a muscle of my face, but I looked him in the face, to see if he were joking, and expected they would all laugh; but they all looked solemn, and the speaker no more crazy than the rest. So I took Bronson's arm, and walked apart, and said, 'Is this a joke, or are they crazy, or is this the value of the land?' 'Yes, this is the supposed value.' 'Is it worth more?' 'Perhaps, but you must wait.' So I went back, and said, as gravely as I could, that I would take it; but I expected them to laugh, but that would not harm me. But the man said, 'Well we will pay 10 per cent down, and we will pay it now.' But I said, 'We will go back to the tavern.' But the man was uneasy, and wished to pay now. I said, 'I shall not vary from what I have said.' But the man inclined to pay now. So he took out of his pocket ten $1000 notes of the U. S. Bank, and I put them in my waistcoat pocket."

And from that time Mr. Ogden proceeded to sell piece after piece of the land (about 150 acres) till in one year he had nearly sold the whole for $1,000,000.

LAND PROMOTION ON THE PRAIRIES

This extravaganza of speculation ended when the Panic of 1837 ushered in a five-year period of hard times. During those years few could afford to move to the frontier, yet interest in the region did not die. It was kept alive partly by eastern investors who were searching for an outlet for their funds safer than the factories and railroads that had gone bankrupt during the depression. They found this in the prairies of Indiana and Illinois. The principal propagandist of these grasslands was a Connecticut businessman, Henry W. Ellsworth, who visited the area in 1832 and was impressed by the beauty and fertility of the countryside between the Wabash and Kankakee valleys of Indiana. Here were farms ready for the plow, where the soil was deep and good, and where no backbreaking task of clearing hindered immediate productivity. Ellsworth moved to the prairies in 1835 and immediately began amassing large holdings. Thus he was ready to capitalize on the postpanic psychology among eastern investors seeking an outlet for funds. His invitation to them was issued in 1838 in the form of a small book, "The Valley of the Upper Wabash," which not only pictured the grasslands as modern Edens, certain to increase in value at a spectacular rate, but outlined a plan that would assure investors a sure 25 percent yearly:[15]

No finer grass land can be found, than that along the borders of the Wabash. Crops

---

[15] Henry W. Ellsworth, *The Valley of the Upper Wabash* (New York, 1838), pp. 65–68, 173–174.

of two tons to the acre, could be raised with certainty, and arks constructed for the transportation of the hay, when pressed, to New Orleans. An estimate of the cost and cultivation of one thousand acres, would give the following result:

One thousand acres in account with the cultivator

DR.
To 1,000 acres of land, at $1 25 per acre	$ 1,250 00
To breaking up the same, at $2 25 per acre	2,250 00
To ditching and fencing the same at 15 cents per acre	150 00
To harrowing and sowing seed, at 60 cents per acre	600 00
To mowing, raking, and pressing 2,000 tons of hay, at $2 50 per ton, is	5,000 00
To expense of transportation on 2,000 tons to New Orleans, at $8 per ton	16,000 00
Amount	$25,250 00

CR.
By sale of 2,000 tons of hay, at $25, (average price per ton,) is	$50,000 00
Income derived from sales, &c.	$50,000 00
Expenditures	25,250 00
Profit	$24,750 00

Again, calculating at the rate of only one ton to the acre, and the price of $20 to the ton, we shall have:

Cash received for 1,000 tons of hay, at $20 per ton, is	$20,000 00
Expenditures	14,750 00
Profit	$ 5,250 00

Or allowing in the first calculation, the sum of $10,000 for contingencies, we should have:

Apparent profit	$24,750 00
Allowance for contingencies	10,000 00
Profit	$14,750 00

Another estimate of the cost of 640 acres, fenced in the ordinary method, and containing a house upon it like the plan, would stand as follows:

Six hundred and forty acres, in account with the cultivator

DR.
To 640 acres of land, at $1 25, is	$ 800 00
Four miles, or 1,280 rods, at 20 rails to the rod, gives 25,600 rails, to which add for enclosures, cribs, &c., 1,400 rails. Total of rails is 27,000, which, at $3 50 per hundred, gives	945 00
Breaking up 640 acres, at $2 25 per acre	1,440 00
House like plan, laying up fence, and well	300 00
Harrowing and sowing seed, at 60 cents per acre	384 00
Mowing, raking, and pressing 960 tons, (*one and a half* ton per acre,) at $2 50	2,400 00
Transportation of 960 tons of hay to New Orleans, at $8 per ton, is	7,680 00
Amount	$13,949 00

CR.
By sale of 960 tons of hay, at $20 per ton, is	$19,200 00
Income, as above	$19,200 00
Expenditures	13,949 00
Profit	$ 5,251 00

We have, then, a profit of $5,251 on six hundred and forty acres, *after paying for the land, with a good house, fencing in the ordinary manner, and calculating the product at only one and a half tons to the acre, and the price at the very lowest sum of* $20.

The reader must also bear in mind that the expenditures of the *second* year are materially diminished, and the profits consequently increased. The original cost of the land, and nearly the whole expense of breaking up the sod, are saved. In many cases no ploughing of the ground, *at first*, will be required. After burning the prairie grass in the spring, the seed may be sowed and *harrowed in at once*.

The following estimate exhibits the profits and expenditures of the *second* year:

Six hundred and forty acres in account with the cultivator

	DR.
To harrowing and sowing seed, at 60 cents per acre	$ 384 00
To mowing, making, and pressing, 1,280 tons, (2 tons per acre,) at $2 50 per ton	3,200 00
To freight on 1,280 tons to New Orleans, at $8 per ton	10,240 00
Amount	$13,824 00
	CR.
By sale of 1,280 tons of hay, at $25, (average price at New Orleans,) is	$32,000 00
Income, as above	$32,000 00
Deduct expenditures	13,824 00
Profit	$18,176 00

Another material reduction, of the expense attending the cultivation of hay and other crops, will be found in the use of some of the mowing and reaping machines recently invented. . . .

Circular

The undersigned have entered into partnership, by the name of Curtis and Ellsworth, for the transaction of a General Agency in the Wabash and Maumee valley, and opened an office in Lafayette, the county seat of Tippecanoe county, in the State of Indiana. They propose to purchase of Government and individuals, lands in Indiana and Illinois, for such persons as are desirous to make investments, and to take charge of the same, or of *other lands* already purchased; pay taxes, and, when requested, to put lands into cultivation, and generally, to promote, in the best possible manner, the interests of their employers. . . .

The richest prairie land can still be secured at Government prices; and, by the aid of newly invented ditching, reaping, and mowing machines, it is believed that the land entered can in two years be made to pay, without expense to the owner, an interest of $50 per acre.

The undersigned will take capital to invest in new lands, and allow the capitalist the legal title and a deduction of 8 or 10 per cent. interest, and divide the extra profits, which, it is confidently believed, will not be less than 25 per cent. more. Any quantity of land enclosed, with the accommodation of a small cabin, can be rented, and one-third of the crops allowed by the tenant. Sixty bushels of corn, thirty bushels of wheat, forty bushels of oats, two tons of hay, is the usual crop. More can be obtained by particular attention. Corn can be raised at six cents per bushel by contract; and this is fed to swine, which are fully fattened without further trouble, by turning the same into the fields when the grain is ripe. Several large landed proprietors have hired land ploughed, and the corn planted and well attended, for $3 to $3 50 per acre, and raised from 70 to 75 bushels on the same.

This was persuasive propaganda, and eastern capitalists responded with such enthusiasm that within a few years much of central Indiana was owned by absentee investors. This was unfortunate, for most made no attempt to occupy their lands, thus slowing the peopling of the area. Not until the 1850s did mounting taxes and the pressure of population force them to unload their holdings, and not until then was the settling of Indiana completed. The last virgin lands of Illinois were overrun at the same time. These were in the Grand Prairie in the central part of the state—a grassland so extensive that pioneers could not settle there until railroads were built to supply them with lumber and fuel, and to carry out their crops. The frontier there advanced with the Illinois Central Railroad as it built across the Grand Prairie in the 1850s.

This was the final act in the drama of the frontier's expansion east of the Mississippi. With the conquest of the Indiana and Illinois prairies, the last forests had been cut away, the last grasslands turned by the plow, the last fertile lands placed under cultivation. Wisconsin became a state in 1848, completing the political organization of the area. The frontier was only a memory now to the farmers and planters of the Mississippi Valley, but to others it was a way of life. For beyond the Mississippi venturesome pioneers were already busily engaged in the conquest of a new wasteland, in advancing their nation's borders to the Pacific.

Wagon train moving through Ute Pass, Colorado, *ca.* 1870.

PICTURE PORTFOLIO:
AMERICA'S FRONTIER PEOPLE

Covered wagon on prairie, possibly near Colorado Springs, *ca.* 1870s.

PIONEER FARMERS

Couple in front of sod house, Nebraska, *ca.* 1880.

Family in farmyard, Wisconsin, *ca.* 1890s.

The Spees family were musicians and entertainers who homesteaded near Westerville, Custer County, Nebraska, *ca.* 1887.

Two brothers and neighboring homesteaders eating watermelon and playing cards, Custer County, *ca.* 1880s.

A group with accordion near wooden cabin, northern Wisconsin.

Coffee break for threshing crew near Minto, Walsh County, North Dakota, *ca.* 1890.

Men showing horses near sheep pen, Black River Falls, Wisconsin.

Barn raising on the Rainy River, Minnesota, *ca.* 1890.

Cowboy rescuing a calf in a snowstorm.

CATTLEMEN

Watering the cattle, Rosata Lake, New Mexico, *ca.* 1901.

Cowboys, Bonham, Texas, *ca.* 1909.

Chuck wagon, JA Ranch, Texas, 1907.

Branding, LS Ranch, Texas, 1908.

LS Ranch, Texas, 1908.

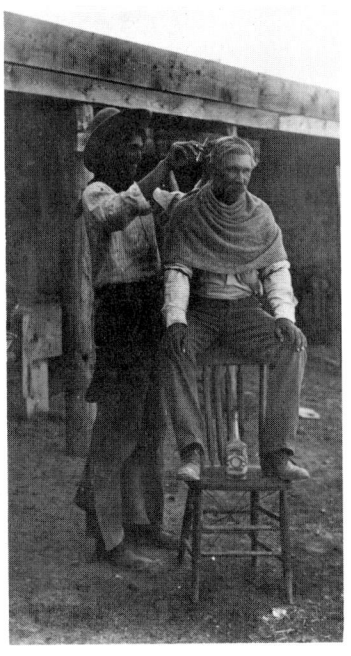

BarW Ranch, Texas, *ca.* 1901.

Entertainment, Texas, *ca.* 1901.

Creede, Colorado. One of the last of the boom towns, it was founded in 1890 by Nicholas Creede, who made his strike while stopping for lunch in the area. The population was 8000 by 1893 but then declined sharply with the drop in the price of silver.

MINERS

Placer mining among the boulders, Tuolumne County, California, 1866.

Pandora miners, Telluride, Colorado, *ca.* 1880.

Timbering in mine, Cripple Creek, Colorado, *ca.* 1890s.

Head of Auburn ravine, California, 1852.

Gould & Curry Mine, Virginia City, Nevada.

Miners and mule train. Goldfield, Nevada.

Ocean Grove Dining Rooms on San Miguel River, Colorado, July 17, 1897.

Miners' cabin on Gore Range, Colorado, *ca.* 1880s.

The *Willamette* discharging freight at Skagway, Alaska.

Crossing the Dyea River, Yukon Trail, Alaska, 1895.

Scales and summit of Chilkoot Pass, 1898.

Women prospectors on their way to Klondike, 1898.

St. Croix boom, near Stillwater, Minnesota, 1886. Logs from many companies on the St. Croix River were corralled, secured into rafts, marked with the company's name, and sent down into the Mississippi.

(*Opposite*) Breaking a log jam, Minnesota, 1865.

LUMBERMEN

Hay Creek, Kanabec County, Minnesota, March 1, 1894.

Lumber camp kitchen, northern Minnesota, *ca.* 1890s.

Lumber camp, violin trio in cook house, August Mason Camp, 1902.

Two views of Indian encampments near Deadwood, South Dakota, 1891.

SOLDIERS
IN INDIAN COUNTRY

Indian School, Omaha, Nebraska, 1879.

Apache prisoners in transit to Fort Sam Houston, San Antonio, Texas. Front row from left: Fun and Perico (half brothers of Geronimo), Naiche, Geronimo, Chappo (son to Geronimo), Chappo's wife, 1886.

Waiting for the run to begin at 4:30 A.M. into Cheyenne and Arapaho country. This was the third of five runs made in the settlement of the Oklahoma Territory.

Opening of the Cherokee Strip, September 16, 1893.

OKLAHOMA:
THE RUSH FOR LAND

Law office set up on the prairie at the opening of Guthrie, April 22, 1889.

Guthrie's first bank.

Peter Pearson, a first-hour arrival on April 22, holds his town lot against all contenders.

Bennett Avenue, Cripple Creek, Colorado, July 4, 1893.

LIFE IN THE TOWN

Black River Falls, Wisconsin.

Prairie town, Wisconsin, *ca.* 1890s.

Small town store, Marion, Minnesota, *ca.* 1890s.

Saloon, Telluride, Colorado, *ca.* 1895.

The lynching of George Wetherell by the "respectable citizens" of Canon City, December 4, 1888. Wetherell was a notorious murderer whose victims were all shot at night.

Schoolgirls at lunch, Oregon.

Farm family, Wisconsin, *ca.* 1890.

PART II

THE TRANS-
MISSISSIPPI
WEST

CHAPTER 14 | Spanish Occupants of the Far West

The pioneers who tamed the forests and prairies of the Mississippi Valley frontier were all unwittingly fashioning a staging area for the venturesome frontiersmen whose destiny lay in America's Far West. Exploration of that vast hinterland began soon after the Louisiana Purchase of 1803, when government-financed expeditions sought to determine the resources hidden in Thomas Jefferson's bargain in real estate. Their reports stimulated later invasions, first of fur trappers who roamed the Rocky Mountain country from the 1820s to the 1840s, then of miners, cattlemen, and farmers. The American frontier of settlement reached the Pacific during the 1840s, and by the 1890s the whole giant region was occupied.

The rapidity of this conquest was remarkable, for in the Far West pioneers faced obstacles unknown to their eastern counterparts: an unfamiliar natural environment, Indian tribesmen so skilled in warfare that they outmatched the best troops sent against them, and rival European powers so firmly established that their dislodgement seemed impossible.

SPANISH EXPLORATION: THE CORONADO EXPEDITION

Of the Europeans who occupied the Far West, the most formidable were the Spaniards. Spain's conquest of the New World began with Columbus' landfall and soon centered in Mexico, where in the sixteenth century hardy conquistadors unearthed the Aztec fortunes in gold and silver that spelled wealth and power for the mother country. Once firmly in possession of this rich domain, Spanish explorers inevitably turned their attention to the north, for surely, they thought, that unknown land concealed treasures as rich as those of Mexico itself. Of the several expeditions sent to test this belief, none was more colorful than that commanded by Francisco Vásquez de Coronado. Between 1540 and 1542, he and his faithful followers endured incredible hardships as they threaded their way across New Mexico, Texas, and Kansas in a vain quest for fabled cities and treasure-troves of precious metals. A letter written by Coronado to his ruler, Charles V of Spain, on October 20, 1542, described the last stages of his journey toward the mythical city of Quivera (he had learned of Quivera from tall-tales of the Indians) and of his heartbreak on finding a cluster of primitive grass huts rather than a gleaming metropolis with streets of silver and houses of gold:[1]

I started from this province on the twenty-third of last April, for the place

---

[1] Parker Winship (ed.), *Coronado's Journey to New Mexico and the Great Plains, 1540–1542*, in A. B. Hart and Edward Channing (eds.), "American History Leaflets" (New York, 1894), No. 13.

which the Indians wanted to guide me to. In nine days' march I reached some plains, so vast that I did not find their limit anywhere that I went, although I travelled more than three hundred leagues through them. And I found such a quantity of cows in these, of the kind that I wrote Your Majesty about, that they have in this country, that it is impossible to number them, for while I was journeying through these plains, until I returned to where I first found them, there was not a day when I lost sight of them. And after seventeen days' march I came across a settlement of Indians who travel round with these cows, who are called Querechos, who do not plant, and who eat the raw flesh and drink the blood of the cows they kill, and they tan the skins of the cows, with which all the people of this country dress themselves here. They have little field tents made of the hides of the cows, tanned and greased, very well made, in which they live as they travel around near the cows, changing with these. They have dogs which they load, which carry their tents and poles and small things. These are the best formed people that I have seen in the Indies. They could not give me any account of the country where the guides were taking me. I travelled five days more as the guides wished to lead me, until I reached some plains, as completely without landmarks as if we had been swallowed up in the sea, where they strayed about, because there was not a stone, nor a bit of rising ground, nor a tree, nor a shrub, nor anything to go by. There is much very fine pasture land with good grass. And while we were lost in these plains, some horsemen who went off to hunt cows fell in with some Indians who were also out hunting, who are enemies of those that I came across in the last settlement, and of another sort of people, who are called Teyas; they have their bodies and faces all painted, are a large people like the others, of a very good build; they eat the flesh raw just like the Querechos, and live and travel round with the cows in the same way as these. I got an account of the country where the guides were taking me from these, which was not like what they had told me, because these made out that the houses there were of straw and skins and not of stones, with stories, as the guides I had, had made it, and the supply of corn in it small. This news troubled me greatly, to find myself on these limitless plains, where I was in great need of water, and often had to drink it so poor that it was more mud than water. Here the guides confessed to me that they had not told the truth, but that it was only in regard to the size of the houses, because they were of straw, but that they had told the truth about the large number of inhabitants and the other things about their habits. The Teyas were against this, and on account of this division between some of the Indians and the others, and also because many of the men I had with me had not eaten anything except meat for some days, because we had reached the end of the corn which we carried from this province and because they made it out more than forty days' journey from where I fell in with the Teyas to the country where the guides were taking me, although I appreciated the trouble and danger there would be in the journey from the lack of water and corn, it seemed to me best, in order to see if there was anything there of service to Your Majesty, to go forward with only thirty horsemen, until I should come where I could see the country, so as to give Your Majesty a true account of what was to be seen in it. And I sent all the rest of the force I had with me to this province, with Don Tristan de Arellano in command, because it would have been impossible to prevent the loss of many men, if all should go on, owing to the lack of water and, besides, the fact that they had to kill bulls and cows on which to sustain themselves. And with only the thirty horsemen whom I took for my escort, I travelled forty-two days after I left the force, living all this while solely on the flesh of the bulls and cows which we killed, at the cost of several of our horses which they killed, because, as I wrote Your Majesty, they are very brave and fierce animals, and going many days without water, and cooking the food with cow dung, because there is not any kind of wood in all these plains, away from the gullies and rivers, which are very few.

It pleased Our Lord that, after having journeyed across these deserts seventy-seven days, I arrived at the province they call Quivira, to which the guides were conducting me, and where they had described to me houses of stone, with many stories, and not only are they not of stone, but of straw, but the people in them are as barbarous as all those whom I have seen and passed before this; they do not have cloaks, nor cotton of which to make them, but use the skins of the cattle they kill, which they tan, because they are settled on a very large river among these. They eat the raw flesh like the Querechos and Teyas; they are enemies of each other, but are all of the same sort of people, and these at Quivira have the advantage in the houses they have and in planting corn. In this province, which the guides who brought me are natives of, they received me peaceably, and although they told me when I set out for it that I could not succeed in seeing it all in two months, there are not more than twenty-five villages of straw houses in it and in all the rest that I saw and knew about, which gave their obedience to Your Majesty and placed themselves under Your Royal Overlordship. The people here are large. I had several Indians measured and found that they were ten palms in height; the women are well proportioned and their features are more like Moorish women than Indians. The natives here gave me a piece of copper which a chief Indian wore hung around his neck; I sent it to the Viceroy of New Spain, because I have not seen any other metal in these parts except this and some little copper bells which I sent him, and a bit of metal which looks like gold, which I don't know where it came from, except that I believe that the Indians who gave it to me got it from those whom I brought here in my service, because I cannot find its origin anywhere else nor where it came from. The diversity of languages they have in this country and my not having any one who understood them, because they speak their own language in each village, has hindered me, because I have been forced to send captains and men in many directions to find out whether there was anything in this country which could be of service to Your Majesty. And although I have searched with all diligence I have not found or heard of anything, unless it be these provinces, which is a very small affair. The province of Quivira is nine hundred and fifty leagues from Mexico. Where I reached it, it is in the fortieth degree. The country itself is the best I have ever seen for producing all the products of Spain, for besides the land itself being very fat and black and being very well watered by the rivulets and springs and rivers, I found prunes like those of Spain and nuts and very good sweet grapes and mulberries. I have treated the natives of this province and the others I fell in with where I went, as well as was possible, agreeably to what Your Majesty had commanded, and they have received no harm in any way from me or from those who went in my company. I remained twenty-five days in this province of Quivira, both so as to see and explore the country and to find out whether there was anything beyond which could be of service to Your Majesty, because the guides who had brought me had given me an account of other provinces beyond this. And what I am sure of is that there is not any gold nor any other metal in all that country, and the other things of which they had told me are nothing but little villages and in many of these they do not plant anything and do not have any houses except of skins and sticks, and they wander around with the cows, so that the account they gave me was false, because they wanted to get me to go there with the whole force, believing that as the way was through such uninhabited deserts, and from the lack of water, they would get us where our horses and we would die of hunger. And the guides confessed this and said they had done it by the advice and orders of the natives of these provinces. At this, after having heard the account of what was beyond, which I have given above, I returned to these provinces to provide for the force I had sent back here and to give Your Majesty an account of what this country amounts to, because I wrote Your Majesty that I would do so when I went there. I have done all that I possibly could to serve Your Majesty and to discover a country where God our Lord might be served and the Royal Patrimony of Your Majesty increased, as your loyal servant and vassal.

SPANISH COLONIZATION: THE FOUNDING OF NEW MEXICO

Coronado's failure convinced Spain that the barren land north of Mexico concealed neither treasure nor civilized peoples, but it did not permanently stifle interest in the region. Above all, the Spanish could not allow other Europeans to settle there, lest they threaten the rich province of Mexico and menace the trade routes that funneled the wealth of South America and the Orient through Mexico City. In 1578 and 1579, when Britain's Francis Drake braved the Straits of Magellan to enter the Pacific and raid ports and treasure galleons almost at will, horrified Spaniards decided that he must have discovered the fabled Northwest Passage. Future raids could be blocked only by planting a colony far to the north. A rich Mexican mine owner, Juan de Oñate, was assigned the honor of sacrificing his fortune and perhaps his life for the glory of the empire. He recruited a force of 130 soldier-settlers, a like number of slaves, and 8 Franciscan missionaries, and with this sizable crew he started northward in February 1598, driving 7000 cattle. In a letter to the Viceroy of New Spain written on March 2, 1599, Oñate described the fate of his expedition:[2]

Sir, I left the Nombre de Dios river on March 16 with the great train of carts, women, and children, as is well known to your lordship, rejected by all my opponents and with all the dire predictions that suited their wishes and not the mercy of God. His majesty was pleased to satisfy my desires and to have pity on my great hardships, sufferings, and expenses, leading me to these provinces of New Mexico with the entire army of his majesty in perfect health. . . . I came to gather firsthand information on the location and nature of the land, the character and customs of the people, and to take the most suitable measures for the army which I had left about twenty-two leagues from the first pueblos after crossing the Río del Norte. There I had

---

[2] George P. Hammond and Agapito Rey (eds.), *Don Juan de Oñate, Colonizer of New Mexico, 1595–1628* (Albuquerque, N. M.: University of New Mexico Press, 1953), vol. 1, pp. 480–485.

taken possession for his majesty of all these kingdoms and pueblos, which I examined with the aid of scouting parties before leaving. Not until August 19 of last year did the army catch up with me at the place chosen for it and where I had settled in this province of the Teguas.

During this time I traveled through sixty-one leagues of settled country directly to the north, and thirty-five more in an east-west direction. All of this area is studded with pueblos, large and small, close together. Thus, by the end of August, I began to prepare the people of the army for the rigorous winter of which the Indians and the nature of the land warned us. And the devil, who has always tried to prevent the great loss that he would suffer through our coming, resorted to one of his usual tricks with the mutiny of more than forty-five soldiers and officers, who in anger at not finding bars of silver on the ground right away and resentful because I did not allow them to abuse the natives either in their persons or property, became dissatisfied with the land, or rather with me. They tried to band together and escape to New Spain, or so they said, but their intention, as became clear later, was rather to take slaves and clothing, and to commit other outrages. I seized two captains and a soldier, who were said to be responsible, and was ready to garrote them, but, having ascertained that their offense was not so great, and considering my situation and the insistent requests of the friars and of the entire army, I gave up the idea of punishing them and closed the matter with the punishment already inflicted.

Thus, by the middle of September, I had completely calmed and pacified my army, although a spark of this great fire remained hidden in the ashes, for four dissimulating soldiers of that group fled at this time and stole some of the horses. This injured not only one, but many of the parties who held commissions from his majesty, in this cause and others, for improving the land. As this deed violated royal orders, it seemed to me that I should not let them go unpunished. So with all haste I dispatched Captain and Procurator General Gaspar Pérez de Villagrá and Artillery Captain Gerónimo Márquez with express orders to pursue and overtake them. They set out in the middle of September, as I have said, but their commission lasted longer than either they or I had anticipated. The result your lordship already knows, I have been told, from a letter they wrote at Santa Bárbara about two of the evildoers. The other two who escaped must have received their due punishment at the hands of your lordship.

I awaited their return for some days, and meanwhile I sent my sargento mayor to find the buffalo and to obtain supplies of meat. He traveled toward the east, where he found a multitude of them. What befell him, I relate in a special report. He and his men tarried so long that, in order not to lose more time, I went on. This was early in October, after the founding of this first church, where the first mass was said on September 8 and the friars were distributed to the various provinces and doctrinas. I went in person to the provinces of Abó and the Xumanas, and to those great and famous salines in this land, which must be some twenty leagues to the east of here. From there I crossed to the west through the province of Puaray to the discovery of the South sea in order to be able to report to your lordship. On the return of Captain Villagrá, whom I brought along for this purpose, I will report upon all that human effort was able to attain in such a short time, which is in brief what I shall tell you in the following chapter, day by day and event by event. This will deal particularly with the death of my nephew and maese de campo, who was following as my rearguard on the way to the South sea. The legal proceedings of his death, together with many other papers that I am sending to your lordship, were unavoidably delayed.

I have, then, discovered and inspected to date the following provinces: the province of the Tziguis, which one passes on the way from New Spain; the province of the Xumanas; the province of the Chiguas, which we Spaniards call Puaray; the province of the Cheres; the province of Tzia; the province of the Emmes; the province of the Teguas; the province of the Picuríes; the province of the Taos; the province of the Peccos; the province of Abbó and the Salines; the province of Tzuñi; and the province of Mohoce. These last two are at some distance to the west of the others. This is where I have now discovered the rich lodes, as set forth in the papers that your lordship will see. I was not able to work or exploit them because of the death of my maese de campo, Don Juan de Zaldívar, and the need to remedy the situation resulting therefrom, which I finished late last month; nor was I able to carry out my trip to the South sea, which was what brought me to the said provinces, having left my army at this province of the Teguas, from where I am writing at present.

Here and in the other above-mentioned provinces there must be, being conservative in my reckoning, sixty thousand Indians, with towns like ours and with houses built around rectangular plazas. They have no streets. At the pueblos where there are many plazas or large houses, they are joined by narrow passageways between the buildings. Where there are fewer people, the houses are two and three storeys high, of an estado and a half each, or an estado and a third, but there are some houses and even entire pueblos with four, five, six, and seven storeys.

The dress of the Indians consists of cotton or agave blankets, well decorated, white or black; it is very good clothing. Others dress in buffalo skins, of which there is a great abundance. These furs have a beautiful wool; I am sending you some samples of what they make of it. This land is plentiful in meat of the buffalo, sheep with huge antlers, and native turkeys. At Mohoce and Zuñi there is game of all kinds. There are many wild animals and beasts: lions, bears, tigers, wolves, penicas, ferrets, porcupines, and others. The natives tan and use their skins. To the west there are bees and very white honey, of which I am sending a sample. Their corn and vegetables, and their salines, are the best and largest to be found anywhere in the world.

There is great abundance and variety of ores; those I mentioned above are very rich. Some discovered around here do not seem so, although we have hardly started to examine the many things that they are. There are fine grape vines, rivers, and woods with many oak and some cork trees; there are also fruits, melons, grapes, watermelons, Castilian plums, capulins, piñon, acorns, native nuts, *coralejo*, which is a delicate fruit, and other wild plants. There are also many fine fish in this Río del Norte and other streams. From the metals that we find here, we can obtain all colors and the finest.

The people are as a rule of good disposition, generally of the color of those of New Spain, and almost the same in customs, dress, grinding of meal, food, dances, songs, and in many other respects. This is not true of their languages, which here are numerous and different from those in Mexico. Their religion consists in worshiping of idols, of which they have many; in their temples they worship them in their own way with fire, painted reeds, feathers, and general offerings of almost everything: little animals, birds, vegetables, etc. Their government is one of complete freedom, for although they have some chieftains they obey them badly and in very few matters.

We have seen other nations, such as the Querechos or Vaqueros, who live among the Cíbola cattle in tents of tanned hides. The Apaches, some of whom we also saw, are extremely numerous. Although I was told that they lived in rancherías, in recent days I have learned that they live in pueblos the same as the people here. They have a pueblo eighteen leagues from here with fifteen plazas. They are a people that has not yet publicly rendered obedience to his majesty, as I had the other provinces do, which cost us much labor, diligence, and care, traveling long distances with arms on our shoulders, with much watching and wariness. Because of failure to exercise as much caution as was necessary, my maese de campo and twelve companions were killed at a fortress pueblo named Acoma, which must have contained three thousand Indians, more or less. In punishment of their wickedness and treason to his majesty, to whom they had previously rendered obedience in a public ceremony, and as a warning to the others, I razed and burned their pueblo in a manner that your lordship will see by the legal proceedings of this trial. I have seen all of these provinces with my own eyes.

THE PUEBLO UPRISING OF 1680

Oñate planted his colony of San Juan in the upper Rio Grande Valley of today's New Mexico and lived to see it expand into a permanent outpost; by 1630, some 250 Spaniards and twice that many loyal Indians lived in several scattered communities including Santa Fe. During the next years the settlement grew steadily, largely through the efforts of missionaries who converted the Pueblo Indians of the region to the ways as well as the faith of Spain. This was certain to lead to native opposition, as Europeans of every race discovered when they sought to alter the cultural patterns of American Indians. In New Mexico this opposition took the form of the Pueblo revolt of 1680, an episode not only colorful and important in itself but with implications for the future. During that year the Pueblo Indians, suddenly and seemingly without reason, rose against the Spanish missionaries and soldiers in village after village, slaying priests and civilians with impartial savagery. Pedro Garcia, a Christian Indian of the Tagno nation, testified before Spanish authorities on August 25, 1680, on the uprising in his own pueblo of San Cristobal:[3]

The deponent said that he was in the service of Captain Joseph Nieto, because he was born and has been brought up in his house; and that some days ago he heard it said that two Teguas Indians, natives of the pueblo of Tesuque, had arrived at the pueblo of San Cristóbal, sent by the said Teguas, telling them to rebel, and that all the rest of the pueblos were now in this conspiracy. This word was passed to all the captains of the Tagnos, and that night those of San Cristóbal advised those of San Lázaro and of Galisteo, the father custodian also learning of it. The said father custodian notified the master of this witness and the other Spaniards, who assembled in the said pueblo of Galisteo; and the next day this witness, while weeding part of a cornfield on his master's estancia, which is something like a league from the pueblo of Galisteo, saw

---

[3] Charles W. Hackett (ed.), *Revolt of the Pueblo Indians of New Mexico and Otermín's Attempted Reconquest, 1680–1682* (Albuquerque, N.M.: University of New Mexico Press, 1942), vol. 1, pp. 24–25.

coming to the place where he was an Indian named Bartolomé, the cantor mayor of the pueblo of Galisteo. He came up weeping and said to him,

What are you doing here? The Indians want to kill the custodian, the fathers, and the Spaniards, and have said that the Indian who shall kill a Spaniard will get an Indian woman for a wife, and he who kills four will get four women, and he who kills ten or more will have a like number of women; and they have said that they are going to kill all the servants of the Spaniards and those who know how to speak Castilian, and they have also ordered that rosaries be taken away from every one and burned. Hurry! Go! Perhaps you will be lucky enough to reach the place where the Spaniards are and will escape with your wife and an orphan girl that you have.

Asked why they were plotting such treason and rebellion, he said that the said cantor told him that they were tired of the work they had to do for the Spaniards and the religious, because they did not allow them to plant or do other things for their own needs; and that, being weary, they had rebelled. Later he [the witness] learned from another of his comrades that in the said pueblo of Galisteo they had killed the father custodian, Fray Domingo de Vera, and in the fields in view of the pueblo, Fathers Fray Fernando de Velasco and Fray Manuel Tinoco, ministers guardianes of Pecos and San Marcos, and he saw that the said Indians took possession of the cattle and property of the convent. The said Indians also killed Captain Joseph Nieto, Juan de Leiva, and Nicolás de Leiva, robbed their haciendas, and killed their wives and children, keeping three of the said women. After this the said Indians of all the pueblos of Los Tagnos, Pecos, and San Marcos went to fight at the villa. Because six Tagnos Indians of Galisteo were killed and many were wounded, receiving broken arms and legs and other wounds, the Indians of the pueblo became enraged and killed the said three women, mistresses of this witness, named Lucía, María, and Juana. He knows also that they killed another young woman named Dorotea, daughter of Maestre de Campo Pedro de Leiva. The said cantor also told him that they had brought from the Teguas an order from them, and from the Taos, Pecuríes, and Yutas Indians, saying that they would destroy the Indian or pueblo that refused to rebel; and for this reason and because of being a Christian he [the witness] went along the road from Santo Domingo to overtake the señor governor and captain-general and the people who were marching with his lordship. In sight of the camp the Indians of Santo Domingo came out against him on horseback and took away his wife and the other woman, and he escaped because the Spaniards who were in the rear guard came out to help him. What he has said is the truth, and is what he knows and has seen, under the oath that he took. This, his said declaration, being read to him, he affirms and ratifies it. He states that he does not know his age or how to sign. Apparently he is about thirty years old.

THE MISSION FRONTIER: FRAY EUSEBIO KINO, S.J.

The Pueblo revolt underlined Spain's principal problem as a colonizing power in North America: the sparseness of its homeland population and the vastness of its empire decreed that it must utilize converted natives as settlers, yet these could be used only under a close supervision that bred rebellion. Spain found a partial answer in a frontier device that became its principal instrument for expansion: the mission station. Patient friars, sometimes alone but sometimes protected by a handful of soldiers, advanced steadily northward from Mexico, founding missions wherever tribesmen would have them and teaching their wards not only Christianity but the arts of husbandry and civilization. By the end of the seventeenth century, the mission frontier extended across northern Mexico in a giant arc that occasionally touched the present international boundary. The missionary who was to thrust it still farther outward into the present United States was Fray Eusebio Francisco Kino, S.J., a zealot whose eagerness to win souls was matched only by his thirst for geographic knowledge. Using the mission that he built at Nuestra Señora de los Dolores in northern Sonora as a base, Fray Kino ventured into the deserts of modern Arizona where he found friendly natives and lands suitable for pasturage. This was enough to kindle in him a desire to plant a new mission there. In April 1700, he led a little band of missionaries and settlers out of the Mission Dolores and a few weeks later planted the Mission San Xavier de Bac not far south of today's Tucson. His "Diary of the Expedition to the North" describes the journey and the founding of this remote outpost:[4]

April 26, 1700 Having arrived at this great ranchería of San Xavier del Baac of these Sobaiporis of the west, which are those of the Rio de Santa Maria (the Sobaypuris of the Rio de San Joseph living thirty leagues farther to the east) I heard the news which also I had heard on the road two or three days before, that some soldiers had gone into the Pimeria of Soba and of the west, and finding myself with so many Indians in this great valley, who were close to three thousand, and also in view of the many prayers of the natives that I should stay with them, I determined not to go farther. And from this great valley of San Xavier, by way of the Rio Grande westward as far as the Cocomaricopas and Yumas, and even to the Rio Colorado, as I desired, I tried to take and did take measures to find out whether the blue shells came from any other region than the opposite coast of California. To that end I despatched various messengers in all directions, some to the east to call Captain Humaric; others to the north to call those of Santa Catalina, and those of La Encarnacion and of San Andres, of the Rio Grande, with their justices, governors, and captains; and especially others to the west and northwest to call various Pima, Opa, and Cocomaricopa governors from near the Rio Colorado, to learn with all possible exactness in regard to the blue shells and the passage by land to California. During the seven days that we were here, while most of those whom I sent with the invitations were on the way, we catechized the people and taught them the Christian doctrine every day, morning and afternoon. We killed six beeves of the three hundred which they were tending for me here, with forty head of sheep and goats, and a small drove of mares. They had also a good field of wheat which was beginning to head; and during the following days they planted for the church a large field of maize, which they had previously cleared.

27 On the twenty-seventh they gave me five little ones to baptize.

28 On the twenty-eighth we began the foundations of a very large and capacious church and house of San Xavier del Baac, all the many people working with much pleasure and zeal, some in digging for the foundations, others in hauling many and very

---

[4] Reprinted by permission of the publishers, The Arthur H. Clark Company, from *Kino's Historical Memoir of Pimería Alta*, edited by Herbert E. Bolton. Vol. 1, pp. 234–238.

good stones of *tezontle* from a little hill which was about a quarter of a league away. For the mortar for these foundations it was not necessary to haul water, because by means of the irrigation ditches we very easily conducted the water where we wished. And that house, with its great court and garden near by, will be able to have throughout the year all the water it may need, running to any place or work-room one may please, and one of the greatest and best fields in all Nueva Biscaya.

29 On the twenty-ninth we continued laying the foundations of the church and of the house. Today and yesterday Captain Humaric and his son, named Oracio Police, arrived from the Sobaiporis of the east; the other and elder son, named Francisco Xavier, had remained behind to guard their country, which is on the Apache frontier. Many other justices also came, and among them an alcalde to whom the soldiers in the last expedition, which they made in November, 1699, had given the staff of office.

30 On the thirtieth, at sunrise, various letters from Nuestra Señora de los Dolores were brought me by a courier of this Pimeria, who, it appeared, must have made the sixty leagues which intervenes in a day and a half and the two nights. After mass I went down to the ranchería of San Cosme, a three leagues' journey, and to that of San Agustin, two leagues farther, to see whether there were any sick or little ones to baptize. At San Cosme they gave me six children to baptize, and one adult, a sick woman; and at San Agustin I baptized three more little ones. In the afternoon we returned to San Xavier del Baac, and at nightfall various justices arrived from the northwest and from Santa Catalina and from the Rio and Casa Grande, among them being the captain and governor of La Encarnacion, thirty-five leagues away. Immediately, and also at night, we had long talks, in the first place in regard to our holy faith, and in regard to the peace, and quietude, and love, and happiness of Christians, and they promised, as we requested of them, to carry these good news and teachings to other rancherías and nations much farther on, to the Cocomaricopas, Yumas, etc. At the same time I made further and further inquiries as to whence came the blue shells, and all asserted that there were none in this nearest Sea of California, but that they came from other lands more remote.

We discussed also what means there might be whereby to penetrate to the Moquis of New Mexico, and we found that by going straight north the entry would be very difficult, since these Pimas were on very unfriendly terms with the Apaches who live between, although the distance and the journey was probably not more than sixty or seventy leagues, for this valley of San Xavier del Baac is in thirty-two and a half degrees of north latitude, and the Moquis and Zuñis in thirty-six degrees.

May 1, 1700 On the first of May, in the afternoon and at nightfall, many justices, captains, and governors arrived from the west, from San Francisco del Addi, and from San Serafin, some coming forty and fifty leagues. We talked with them a great part of the night, as we had done the night before, in regard to the eternal salvation of all those nations of the west and the northwest, at the same time continuing various inquiries in regard to the blue shells which were brought from the northwest and from the Yumas and Cutganes, which admittedly came from the opposite coast of California and from the sea which is ten or twelve days' journey farther than this other Sea of California, on which there are shells of pearl and white, and many others, but none of those blue ones which they gave us among the Yumas and sent me with the holy cross to Nuestra Señora de los Remedios.

THE MISSION FRONTIER IN CALIFORNIA

Over the next years, as the Arizona missions slowly grew, religious interest shifted to another borderland of even greater significance. The conquest of California had long intrigued Spaniards, but its distance from Mexico City, the difficulty of the desert routes that led to it, and the perverse nature of the Pacific's winds and currents which blocked coastal navigation long closed that tempting land to colonizers. Those who surmounted these barriers were the Franciscans, who, in 1767, were authorized to plant their missions there to forestall Russian intruders who were advancing southward from Alaska. Two years later Fray Junípero Serra founded the first California mission at San Diego. Others followed rapidly—around San Francisco Bay, at Monterey and Santa Barbara, in the San Gabriel Valley—until by 1821, when Spanish overlords were replaced by Mexicans, no less than twenty-one missions linked Baja California with the San Francisco area. Each was a center for civilizing as well as converting the Indians, each mission possessing giant herds of cattle and horses, and thriving home industries producing hides, tallow, soap, brandy, and other items for trade. A British visitor, Alexander Forbes, described them at the height of their influence:[5]

Each mission has allotted to it, in the first instance, a tract of land of about fifteen miles square, which is generally fertile and well suited for husbandry. This land is set apart for the general uses of the mission, part being cultivated, and part left in its natural condition and occupied as grazing ground. The buildings of the mission are, like the Presidio, all on the same general plan, but are varied according to the locality and number of the inhabitants. Most of the missionary villages or residences are surrounded by a high wall enclosing the whole; others have no such protection but consist of open rows of streets of little huts built of bricks: some of these are tiled and whitewashed and look neat and comfortable; others are dirty and in disrepair and in every way uncomfortable. In the mission of Santa Clara, which in several respects excels the others, the houses of the Indians form five rows or streets, which compared with the old straw huts must be considered really comfortable: and this is the greatest improvement that has taken place in the domestic civilization of these people at the missions. The buildings are generally built in the form of a square or part of a square, the church usually forming a portion of the elevation. The apartments of the fathers, which are often spacious, the granaries and work-shops compose the remainder. The Indian population generally live in huts at about two hundred yards distant from the principal edifices; these huts are sometimes made of *adobes*, but the Indians are often left to raise them on their own plan; viz. of rough poles erected into a conical figure, of about four yards in circumference at the base, covered with dry grass and a small aperture for the entrance. When the huts decay, they set them on fire, and erect new ones; which is only the work of a day. In these huts the married part of the community live, the unmarried of both sexes being kept, each sex separate, in large barn-like apartments, where they work under strict supervision.

---

[5] Alexander Forbes, *California* (London, 1839), pp. 210–216.

The storehouses and workshops, at some of the larger missions, are of great extent and variety. There may be seen a place for melting tallow, one for making soap, workshops for smiths, carpenters, &c., storehouses for the articles manufactured, and the produce of the farms: viz. stores for tallow, soap, butter, salt, wool, hides, wheat, peas, beans, &c. &c. &c. Four or five soldiers have their residence a few yards further off, and are meant to watch the Indians, and to keep order; but they are generally lazy, idle fellows; and often give the missionary more trouble than all his Indians; and instead of rendering assistance increase his troubles. But in all Spanish countries, nothing can possibly be done without soldiers, and the idea of having any public establishment without a guard of soldiers would appear quite ridiculous.

The church is, of course, the main object of attraction at all the missions, and is often gaudily decorated. In some of the missions where there is good building-stone in the vicinity, the external appearance of the sacred building is not unseemly; in other missions the exterior is very rude. In all of them the interior is richer than the outside promises. In several there are pictures, and the subject of these is generally representations of heaven or hell, glaringly coloured purposely to strike the rude senses of the Indians. Pérouse says that the picture of hell in the church of San Carlos has, in this way, done incalculable service in promoting conversion; and well remarks that the protestant mode of worship, which forbids images and pompous ceremonies, could not make any progress among these people. He is of opinion that the picture of paradise in the same church, has exerted comparatively little effect on account of its tameness: but Langsdorff tells of wonders in this way wrought by a figure of the virgin represented as springing from the coronal of leaves of the *Agave Americana,* or great American aloe, instead of the ordinary stem! The priests also take care to be provided with rich dresses for the same purpose of inspiring awe.

The object of the whole of the Californian or missionary system being the conversion of the Indians and the training of them up, in some sort, to a civilized life, the constant care of the fathers is and ever has been directed towards these ends. The children born in the missions are, of course, devoted to the missionary discipline from their infancy; but the zeal of the fathers is constantly looking out for converts from among the wild tribes on the borders of their territories. Formerly when the missionaries were strangers in the land, and the natives were numerous, and spread around their settlements, there was no lack of materials on which to exercise their converting zeal. But for a good many years the case has been different; the natives have become fewer in number and have been gradually receding from the missionary territory: the very progress of conversion has necessarily occasioned this. New means of obtaining converts have been therefore had recourse to; and there can be no doubt that some of these means go far beyond the bounds of legitimate persuasion. It would be injustice to tax the Fathers with openly sanctioning, much less directing the more severe of these means; yet they cannot be altogether ignorant of them, and must be regarded as encouraging them indirectly. And, indeed, it must be admitted that with their particular views of the efficacy of baptism and ceremonial profession of christianity in saving souls, the conversion of the Indians even by force, can hardly be otherwise regarded by them than as the greatest of benefits conferred on these people and therefore justifying some severity in effecting it. No one who has seen or known any thing of the singular humanity and benevolence of these good Fathers will for a moment believe that they could sanction the actual cruelties and bloodshed occasionally wrought in their name by the military and more zealous converts. Certain it is, however, that every encouragement is held out to all, who shall bring in *Gentiles* for conversion. Converts that can be depended on are stationed in the vicinity of the haunts occupied by their wild brethren, whose business it is to represent their own condition in the most favourable light possible, with the view of inducing them to join the missionary fold. Others are permitted to pay visits to their kindred of more distant tribes, with the same views, and are almost expected to bring back converts with them. "At a particular period of the year also" we are told by Captain Beechey, "when the Indians can be spared from the agricultural concerns of the establishment, many of them are permitted to take the launch of the mission and make excursions to the Indian territory. On these occasions the padres desire them to induce as many of their unconverted brethren as possible to accompany them back to the mission, of course implying that this is to be done only by persuasion; but the boat being furnished with a cannon and musketry, and in every respect equipped for war, it too often happens that the neophytes and the *gente de razón*, who superintend the direction of the boat, avail themselves of their superiority, with the desire of ingratiating themselves with their masters and of receiving a reward. There are, besides, repeated acts of aggression which it is necessary to punish, all of which furnish proselytes. Women and children are generally the first objects of capture, as their husbands and parents sometimes voluntarily follow them into captivity."

BEGINNINGS OF INTERNATIONAL CONFLICT

With the founding of the California missions, New Spain's northern empire stretched in a giant arc from eastern Texas across New Mexico and Arizona to San Francisco Bay. Every point along this perimeter was vulnerable. Supplied by distant Mexico City over desert trails a thousand miles long and often neglected between 1810 and 1821 as Mexico endured the throes of revolution, the thin line of missions, presidios, and pueblos was so poorly guarded that it could be penetrated almost at will by properly equipped foes. Nor were these lacking. Savage nonmission Indians were always eager to sack the stations and villages, and during the waning years of the eighteenth century showed an increasing tendency to do so. The reason for their aggressiveness was readily observable; frequenting their villages now were French traders from Canada and Anglo-American traders from the Mississippi Valley, all of them willing to supply the red men with firearms and to goad them into assaults on Spain's borderlands. The handwriting on the wall was revealed by Colonel Pedro Fermín de Mendinueta, governor of the province of New Mexico, when in a letter written during the fall of 1768 to the Viceroy of New Spain he described what was apparently a commonplace Indian attack. His letter sounded a note of alarm: the attackers were armed with British weapons:[6]

Most excellent Sir: Under date of December 20 of the last year of '67, I gave an account to your excellency of the condition of this province under my charge and how I

---

[6] Alfred B. Thomas (ed.), *The Plains Indians and New Mexico, 1751–1778* (Albuquerque, N.M.: University of New Mexico Press, 1940), pp. 159–162.

found myself with some hope of achieving peace with the Comanche nation, although with some fear of the reliability of the Comanches and their wary and astute nature. This same fear moved me to order, at the end of May, the establishment of fifty men, presidial troops, militia, and Indians, on the hill of San Antonio to protect the weak frontier of Ojo Caliente, with orders that their advance scouts keep under observation the ford of the Rio del Norte, which is precisely the spot which the Comanches must cross to reach *Ojo Caliente.*

The first day of June, at four in the afternoon, I received a letter from the alcalde mayor of Taos in which he gave me an account of how, on May 31, at five in the afternoon, six Comanche chiefs entered that pueblo carrying a white flag. They said they were coming to ask for peace, and that their ranchería would arrive at that pueblo on June 2, bringing to Taos a young man whom they had captive. They added that they were coming very rapidly and could remain only long enough to carry on trade in the goods they brought.

With this information, I ordered the horse herd assembled for the troop and militia of this villa to march at once. At twelve noon on the second, we reached the place where the horse herd pastured, seven leagues distant to the south of this villa. At the same hour, I began the march and made ten leagues during the rest of the day. At midnight I received notice that the Comanches, a little before daybreak on the second, had declared war, and, without more delay than saddling my horse, I continued the march with all speed possible. At four in the morning, having advanced four or five leagues over bad terrain, I learned that the Comanches had retreated after having killed five settlers and a Taos Indian, who, against the orders of the alcalde mayor, had gone to the ranchería to carry on a very little trade at the cost of the lives of the settlers, who, in their own defense, killed four Comanches. Notwithstanding this news, I reached the pueblo, which is twenty-five leagues from this villa over rough and rocky hills, which make haste to reach there totally impossible.

There I learned of the crafty strategem of the coming of these barbarians. At the Rio de la Costilla, which is fifteen leagues distant to the north of Taos, they dispatched one hundred men to attack Ojo Caliente, confident that, at the news of peace and trade which they had announced at Taos, the people would attend, and thus they would find no opposition to their design upon Ojo Caliente. Meanwhile, those who arrived at Taos, numbering four hundred, were provided with muskets and munitions and some necessary things for peace and trade. Knowing ahead of time what was taking place at Ojo Caliente, they could be much more expeditious in trading, and then, by retreating, would leave me in a ridiculous position. But the fifty men stationed on the hill of San Antonio went out to meet the Comanches, who, after crossing the river, marched for Ojo Caliente. The unexpected event of meeting the troops put them into precipitate flight without waiting to join battle. Pursued constantly, they were not overtaken. They threw themselves into the river, in which some part of them perished, and those who got out advised those who were in Taos of the outcome. As this did not correspond to what they had planned, and aware of my proximity, they took their vengeance out on those six who were in their ranchería and fled with such speed that they left dead horses along the trail, together with supplies, saddles, buffalo skins, and bits of clothing. It was not possible for me to overtake them because of the speed of their departure; the long distance and such bad terrain made it impossible for the horse herd to travel. Indeed, to be able to return to this villa, it was necessary to recondition the horse herd for three days and send parties to collect the exhausted ones left on the road. The irreparable weakness of the horse makes long expeditions impossible, especially in the springtime, the season of intemperate weather, whereas the indispensable daily duties of the troop make them possible accordingly after the middle of July.

For the defense of this important frontier, which cannot be reinforced with the promptness it demands, I have dispatched two cannons of artillery with powder and munitions and an artillery soldier so that he may handle them in any event that occurs. At the same time, I am prepared to set out on a campaign to search for these barbarians. I shall take with me the young Taos Indian, whom, before the outbreak of war, the alcalde mayor of that pueblo had ransomed from the Comanches. He can give me some information of the lands in which these Comanches usually live.

This same young man tells me that the guns which the Comanche have they get from the Jumanos, a tribe which lives in pueblos located at the junction of the Napestle and Colorado rivers which is, according to conjecture, more than two hundred leagues to the southwest of this villa. He also assures me that not many months ago the Jumanos brought seventeen loads of guns and munitions to the Comanches and that they bought all of this material with horses. As there are no French to trade with the Jumanos, and since Louisiana is under our sovereign, these arms, I fear, are from the English, who, by navigating the Mississippi, may have established this trade so menacing to this province.

These skirmishes along New Spain's borderlands presaged the fall of one empire and the rise of another. The British traders who supplied the Plains Indians were more or less controlled by a strict government and strong commercial companies, but when Americans replaced them after the Louisiana Purchase of 1803 these safeguards were removed. The American frontiersmen were restless, eager, aggressive, and too profit-hungry to be hindered by distant federal officials, even if the new Republic was powerful enough to control them. Their destiny was to mount a sustained assault on all who stood in the way of their westward march, whether Indians, British, or Spaniards. Before their pressure the mission frontier of New Spain crumbled away, until by the 1840s the borders of the United States extended to the Pacific. The firstcomers to carry the American flag into alien territory were the official explorers, sent by a curious government to investigate its unknown holdings beyond the Mississippi.

CHAPTER 15

The Explorers' Frontier, 1803-1840

The strategy of American exploration in the trans-Mississippi West was mapped by President Thomas Jefferson. Long interested in the region as a scientist and as a practical American concerned with the extent of his nation's resources, he was not long in office before he asked Congress for a secret appropriation to explore westward "even to the Western Ocean." When the grant was forthcoming, Jefferson chose two competent leaders: Meriwether Lewis, who had been trained in frontier ways in the Virginia backwoods, and William Clark, a younger brother of George Rogers Clark. Before they started, welcome news reached Washington: Napoleon had agreed to sell Louisiana to the United States. Now exploration was even more imperative, for the West might offer new fur-trading opportunities to replace those that were disappearing with the pacification of eastern tribes as well as yield priceless scientific information.

LEWIS AND CLARK REACH THE ROCKY MOUNTAINS

Aware of these responsibilities, Lewis and Clark started for St. Louis during the summer of 1803, gathering a crew of forty-eight husky young frontiersmen as they went. The winter was spent in planning and in hardening the party for the trials ahead; when the group started up the Missouri in the spring of 1804, they were well-equipped to face the unknown. All that summer and fall the men worried a large keelboat and two pirogues up the swift-flowing river, then went into winter quarters at the Mandan villages near modern Bismarck, North Dakota. When the ice melted early in 1805 they were off again. They sent the keelboat back to St. Louis and traveled now in lighter Indian craft, guided by a talented Shoshoni woman Sacájawea, who had been a captive of the Mandan Sioux. She had promised to lead Lewis and Clark westward if they would return her to her own people. For six weeks they battled the ever-swifter current of the Missouri before they sighted the towering peaks of the Rocky Mountains. Lewis described that exciting moment in his journal:[1]

Sunday May 26th, 1805. Set out at an early hour and proceeded principally by the toe line, using the oars mearly to pass the river in order to take advantage of the shores.

---

[1] Reuben Gold Thwaites (ed.), *Original Journals of the Lewis and Clark Expedition, 1804–1806* (New York, 1904), vol. 2, pp. 78–80.

scarcely any bottoms to the river; the hills high and juting in on both sides, to the river in many places. the stone tumbleing from these clifts and brought down by the rivulets as mentioned yesterday became more troublesome today. the black rock has given place to a very soft sandstone which appears to be washed away fast by the river, above this and towards the summits of the hills a hard freestone of a brownish yellow colour shews itself in several stratas of unequal thicknesses frequently overlain or incrusted by a very thin strata of limestone which appears to be formed of concreted shells. Capt. Clark walked on shore this morning and ascended to the summit of the river hills he informed me on his return that he had seen mountains on both sides of the river runing nearly parrallel with it and at no great distance; also an irregular range of mountains on larboard about 50 miles distant; the extremities of which boar W. and N.W. from his station. he also saw in the course of his walk, some Elk several herds of the Big horn, and the large hare; the latter is common to every part of this open country. scarcely any timber to be seen except the few scattering pine and spruce which crown the high hills, or in some instances grow along their sides. In the after part of the day I also walked out and ascended the river hills which I found sufficiently fortieguing. on arriving to the summit [of] one of the highest points in the neighbourhood I thought myself well repaid for my labour; as from this point I beheld the Rocky Mountains for the first time, I could only discover a few of the most elivated points above the horizon, the most remarkable of which by my pocket compass I found bore N. 65.° W. being a little to the N. of the N.W. extremity of the range of broken mountains seen this morning by Captain C. these points of the Rocky Mountains were covered with snow and the sun shone on it in such manner as to give me the most plain and satisfactory view. while I viewed these mountains I felt a secret pleasure in finding myself so near the head of the heretofore conceived boundless Missouri; but when I reflected on the difficulties which this snowey barrier would most probably throw in my way to the Pacific, and the sufferings and hardships of myself and party in thim, it in some measure counterballanced the joy I had felt in the first moments in which I gazed on them; but as I have always held it a crime to anticipate evils I will believe it a good comfortable road untill I am compelled to believe differently. saw a few Elk & bighorns at a distance on my return to the river I passed a creek about 20 yards wide near its entrance it had a handsome little stream of runing water; in the creek I saw several softshelled Turtles which were the first that have been seen this season; this I believe proceeded reather from the season than from their non existence in the portion of the river from the Mandans hither. on the Starboard shore I killed a fat buffaloe which was very acceptable to us at this moment; the party came up to me late in the evening and encamped for the night on the Larboard side; it was after Dark before we finished butchering the buffaloe, and on my return to camp I trod within [a] few inches of a rattle snake but being in motion I passed before he could probably put himself in a striking attitude and fortunately escaped his bite, I struck about with my espontoon being directed in some measure by his nois untill I killed him. Our hunters had killed two of the Bighorned Anamals since I had left them. we also passed another creek a few miles from Turtle Creek on the Starboard 30 Yards in width which also had runing water bed rockey. late this evening we passed a very bad rappid which reached quite across the river; the party had considerable difficulty in ascending it altho' they doubled their crews and used both the rope and the pole. while they were passing this rappid a female Elk and it's fawn swam down through the waves which ran very high, hence the name of Elk rappids which they instantly gave this place, these are the most considerable rappids which we have yet seen on the missouri and in short the only place where there has appeared to be a suddon decent. opposite to these rappids there is a high bluff and a little above on Larboard a small cottonwood bottom in which we found sufficient timber for our fires and encampment. here I rejoined the party after dark. The appearances of coal in the face of the bluffs, also of birnt hills, pumice stone salts and quarts continue as yesterday. This is truly a desert barren country and I feel myself still more convinced of it's being a continuation of the black hills. we have continued every day to pass more or less old stick lodges of the Indians in the timbered points, there are two even in this little bottom where we lye.

THE PROBLEMS OF RIVER TRAVEL

As glamorous as the Rockies might be to the explorers, the thrill of discovery soon gave way to less pleasant emotions as the crewmen battled the swift waters of the upper Missouri. In the now frequent rapids the men had to stand waist-deep in the foaming stream to warp the heavy boats over rocky passages. Clark, in his journal entry for June 15, 1805, described a bit of travel that was altogether too typical of this stage of the journey:[2]

a fair morning and worm, we set out at the usial time and proceeded on with great dificuelty as the river is more rapid we can hear the falls this morning verry distinctly.

our Indian woman sick & low spirited I gave her the bark & apply it exteranely to her region which revived her much. the current excessively rapid and dificuelt to assend great numbers of dangerous places, and the fatigue which we have to encounter is incretiatable the men in the water from morning untill night hauling the cord & boats walking on sharp rocks and round sliperery stones which alternately cut their feet & throw them down, notwith standing all this dificuelty they go with great chearfulness, aded to those dificuelties the rattle snakes [are] inumerable & require great caution to prevent being bitten. we passed a small river on the Lard Side about 30 yards wide verry rapid which heads in the mountains to the S.E. I sent up this river 5 miles, it has some timber in its bottoms and a fall of 15 feet at one place, above this river the bluffs are of red earth mixed with stratums of black stone, below this little [river], we pass a white clay which mixes with water like flour in every respect, the Indian woman much wors this evening, she will not take any medison, her husband petetions to return &c., river more rapid late in the evening we arrived at a rapid which appeared so bad that I did not think it prudent to attempt passing of it this evening as it was now late.

THE EXPEDITION CROSSES THE DIVIDE

Such hardships foretold more to come, for ahead lay the Great Falls of the Missouri. For a solid month—between June 16 and July 15, 1805—the men labored as they carried boats and goods over the seventeen-mile portage around this barrier to reach navigable waters. Now they were in Shoshoni country and eager to establish contact with the Indians who would

---

[2] Reuben Gold Thwaites (ed.), *Original Journals of the Lewis and Clark Expedition, 1804–1806* (New York, 1904), vol. 2, pp. 161–162.

supply them with horses for the journey across the mountains. They reached the Three Forks of the Missouri late in July without sighting any red men and in mid-August were at the continental divide. Lewis, in his diary entry for that day, described their sensations as they crossed the top of the continent:[3]

This morning I sent Drewyer out as soon as it was light, to try and discover what rout the Indians had taken. he followed the track of the horse we had pursued yesterday to the mountain wher it had ascended, and returned to me in about an hour and a half. I now determined to pursue the base of the mountains which form this cove to the S.W. in the expectation of finding some Indian road which lead over the Mountains, accordingly I sent Drewyer to my right and Shields to my left with orders to look out for a road or the fresh tracks of horses either of which we should first meet with I had determined to pursue. at the distance of about 4 miles we passed 4 small rivulets near each other on which we saw som recent bowers or small conic lodges formed with willow brush. near them the indians had geathered a number of roots from the manner in which they had toarn up the ground; but I could not discover the root which they seemed to be in surch of. I [saw] several large hawks that were nearly black. near this place we fell in with a large and plain Indian road which came into the cove from the N.E. and led along the foot of the mountains to the S.W. o[b]liquely approaching the main stream which we had left yesterday. this road we now pursued to the S.W. at 5 miles it passed a stout stream which is a principal fork of the ma[i]n stream and falls into it just above the narrow pass between the two clifts before mentioned and which we now saw below us. here we halted and breakfasted on the last of our venison, having yet a small peice of pork in reserve. after eating we continued our rout through the low bottom of the main stream along the foot of the mount[a]ins on our right the valley for 5 miles further in a S.W. direction was from 2 to 3 miles wide the main stream now after discarding two stream[s] on the left in this valley turns abruptly to the West through a narrow bottom betwe[e]n the mountains. the road was still plain, I therefore did not dispair of shortly finding a passage over the mountains and of taisting the waters of the great Columbia this evening. we saw an animal which we took to be of the fox kind as large or reather larger than the small wolf of the plains. it's colours were a curious mixture of black, redis[h] brown and yellow. Drewyer shot at him about 130 yards and knocked him dow[n] bet [but] he r[e]covered and got out of our reach. it is ce[r]tainly a different animal from any that we have yet seen. we also saw several of the heath cock with a long pointed tail and an uniform dark brown colour but could not kill one of them. they are much larger than the common dunghill fowls, and in their [h]abits and manner of flying resemble the growse or prarie hen. at the distance of 4 miles further the road took us to the most distant fountain of the waters of the Mighty Missouri in surch of which we have spent so many toilsome days and wristless nights. thus far I had accomplished one of those great objects on which my mind has been unalterably fixed for many years, judge then of the pleasure I felt in all[a]ying my thirst with this pure and ice-cold water which issues from the base of a low mountain or hill of a gentle ascent for ½ a mile. the mountains are high on either hand leave this gap at the head of this rivulet through

---

[3] Reuben Gold Thwaites (ed.), *Original Journals of the Lewis and Clark Expedition, 1804–1806* (New York, 1904), vol. 2, pp. 333–336.

which the road passes. here I halted a few minutes and rested myself. two miles below McNeal had exultingly stood with a foot on each side of this little rivulet and thanked his god that he had lived to bestride the mighty & heretofore deemed endless Missouri. after refreshing ourselves we proceeded on to the top of the dividing ridge from which I discovered immence ranges of high mountains still to the West of us with their tops partially covered with snow. I now decended the mountain about ¾ of a mile which I found much steeper than on the opposite side, to a handsome bold runing Creek of cold Clear water. here I first tasted the water of the great Columbia river. after a short halt of a few minutes we continued our march along the Indian road which lead us over steep hills and deep hollows to a spring on the side of a mountain where we found a sufficient quantity of dry willow brush for fuel, here we encamped for the night having traveled about 20 Miles.

MEETING WITH SHOSHONI INDIANS

A day later, on August 13, the explorers finally discovered a band of Shoshoni Indians and with some difficulty convinced them that they were not a Blackfoot raiding party. Lewis' diary describes the events of that important day:[4]

we had proceeded about four miles through a wavy plain parallel to the valley or river bottom when at the distance of about a mile we saw two women, a man and some dogs on an eminence immediately before us. they appeared to v[i]ew us with attention and two of them after a few minutes set down as if to wait our arrival we continued our usual pace towards them. when we had arrived within half a mile of them I directed the party to halt and leaving my pack and rifle I took the flag which I unfurled and a[d]vanced singly towards them the women soon disappeared behind the hill, the man continued untill I arrived within a hundred yards of him and then likewise absconded. tho' I frequently repeated the word *tab-ba-bone* sufficiently loud for him to have heard it. I now haistened to the top of the hill where they had stood but could see nothing of them. the dogs were less shye than their masters they came about me pretty close I therefore thought of tying a handkerchief about one of their necks with some beads and other trinkets and then let them loose to surch their fugitive owners thinking by this means to convince them of our pacific disposition towards them but the dogs would not suffer me to take hold of them; they also soon disappeared. I now made a signal fror the men to come on, they joined me and we pursued the back track of these Indians which lead us along the same road which we had been traveling. the road was dusty and appeared to have been much traveled lately both by men and horses. these praries are very poor the soil is of a light yellow clay, intemixed with small smooth gravel, and produces little else but prickly pears, and bearded grass about 3 inches high. the prickley pear are of three species that with a broad leaf common to the missouri; that of a globular form also common to the upper pa[r]t of the Missouri and more especially after it enters the Rocky Mountains, also a 3rd peculiar to this country. it consists of small circular thick leaves with a much greater number of thorns. these thorns are stronger and appear to be barbed. the leaves grow from the margins of each other as in the broad leafed pear of the missouri, but are so

---

[4] Reuben Gold Thwaites (ed.), *Original Journals of the Lewis and Clark Expedition, 1804–1806* (New York, 1904), vol. 2, pp. 337–341.

slightly attatched that when the thorn touches your mockerson it adhears and brings with it the leaf covered in every direction with many others. this is much the most troublesome plant of the three. we had not continued our rout more than a mile when we were so fortunate as to meet with three female savages. the short and steep ravines which we passed concealed us from each other untill we arrived within 30 paces. a young woman immediately took to flight, an Elderly woman and a girl of about 12 years old remained. I instantly laid by my gun and advanced towards them. they appeared much allarmed but saw that we were to near for them to escape by flight they therefore seated themselves on the ground, holding down their heads as if reconciled to die which the[y] expected no doubt would be their fate; I took the elderly woman by the hand and raised her up repeated the word *tab-ba-bone* and strip[ped] up my shirt sleve to s[h]ew her my skin; to prove to her the truth of the ascertion that I was a white man for my face and ha[n]ds which have been constantly exposed to the sun were quite as dark as their own. they appeared instantly reconciled, and the men coming up I gave these women some beads a few mockerson awls some pewter looking-glasses and a little paint. I directed Drewyer to request the old woman to recall the young woman who had run off to some distance by this time fearing she might allarm the camp before we approached and might so exasperate the natives that they would perhaps attack us without enquiring who we were. the old woman did as she was requested and the fugitive soon returned almost out of breath. I bestoed an equ[i]volent portion of trinket on her with the others. I now painted their tawny cheeks with some vermillion which with this nation is emblematic of peace. after they had become composed I enformed them by signs that I wished them to conduct us to their camp that we wer anxious to become acquainted with the chiefs and warriors of their nation. they readily obeyed and we set out, still pursuing the road down the river. we had marched about 2 miles when we met a party of about 60 warriors mounted on excellent horses who came in nearly full speed, when they arrived I advanced towards them with the flag leaving my gun with the party about 50 paces behi[n]d me. the chief and two others who were a little in advance of the main body spoke to the women, and they informed them who we were and exultingly shewed the presents which had been given them these men then advanced and embraced me very affectionately in their way which is by puting their left arm over you[r] wright sholder clasping your back, while they apply their left cheek to yours and frequently vociforate the word *áh-hí-e, áh-hí-e* that is, I am much pleased, I am much rejoiced. bothe parties now advanced and we wer all carressed and besmeared with their grease and paint till I was heartily tired of the national hug. I now had the pipe lit and gave them smoke; they seated themselves in a circle around us and pulled of[f] their mockersons before they would receive or smoke the pipe. this is a custom among them as I afterwards learned indicative of a sacred obligation of sincerity in their profession of friendship given by the act of receiving and smoking the pipe of a stranger. or which is as much as to say that they wish they may always go bearfoot if they are not sincere; a pretty heavy penalty if they are to march through the plains of their country. after smoking a few pipes with them I distributed some trifles among them, with which they seemed much pleased particularly with the blue beads and vermillion. I now informed the chief that the object of our visit was a friendly one, that after we should reach his camp I would undertake to explain to him fully those objects, who we wer, from whence we had come and w[h]ither we were going; that in the mean time I did not care how soon we were in motion, as the sun was very warm and no water at hand. they now put on their mockersons, and the principal chief Ca-me-âh-wait made a short speech to the warriors. I gave him the flag which I informed him was an emblem of peace among whitemen and now that it had been received by him it was to be respected as the bond of union between us. I desired him to march on, which [he] did and we followed him; the dragoons moved on in squadron in our rear. after we had marched about a mile in this order he halted them and gave a second harang; after which six or eight of the young men road forward to their encampment and no further regularity was observed in the order of march. I afterwards understood that the Indians we had first seen this morning had returned and allarmed the camp; these men had come out armed cap a pe for action expecting to meet with their enimies the Minnetares of Fort de Prarie whome they Call Pâh'-kees. they were armed with b[o]ws arrow and Shields except three whom I observed with small pieces such as the N.W. Company furnish the natives with which they had obtained from the Rocky Mountain Indians on the Yellow stone river with whom they are at peace.

LEWIS AND CLARK REACH THE PACIFIC

For three days Lewis and the advance party waited for Clark to arrive with the canoes and the Shoshoni woman Sacájawea, who had guided them on their journey. When they joined forces on August 17, 1805, the Indians were summoned to a conference where peace talks were exchanged and gifts distributed; in return the Shoshoni promised the explorers horses, supplies, and guides to lead them across the mountains. The groups set out on August 29 and soon met a band of Flathead Indians who led them across Lolo Pass and through rugged countryside to the Clearwater River. Now the route to the Pacific was open before them, broken only by the rapids where the Columbia River passed through the Cascade Mountains. On November 15, 1805, they sighted the ocean. Clark's diary describes their thrill, and the discomforts they endured amidst the rain and fog of an Oregon winter:[5]

Rained all the last night at intervals of sometimes of 2 hours, This morning it became cold & fair, I prepared to set out at which time the wind sprung up from the S. E. and blew down the River & in a fiew minits raised such swells and waves brakeing on the Rocks at the Point as to render it unsafe to proceed. I went to the point in an empty canoe and found it would be dangerous to proceed even in an empty *canoe* The sun shown untill 1 oClock P. M. which gave an oppertunity for us to dry some of our bedding & examine our baggage, the greater Part of which I found wet. some of our Pounded fish spoiled I had all the arms put in order & amunition examined.

The rainey weather continued without a longer intermition than 2 hours at a time, from the 5th in the morning untill the 16th is *eleven* days rain, and the most disagreeable time I have experenced confined on a tempiest coast wet, where I can neither git

---

[5] Reuben Gold Thwaites (ed.), *Original Journals of the Lewis and Clark Expedition, 1804–1806* (New York, 1904), vol. 3, pp. 223–224.

out to hunt, return to a better situation, or proceed on: in this situation have we been for Six days past. fortunately the wind lay about 3 oClock we loaded I in great haste and set out passed the blustering Point below which is a sand beech, with a small marshey bottom for 3 miles on the Starboard Side, on which is a large village of 36 houses deserted by the Inds & in full possession of the flees, a small creek fall[s] in at this village, which waters the Country for a few miles back; Shannon & 5 Indians met me here, Shannon informed me he met Captain Lewis some distance below & he took Willard with him & sent him to meet me, the Indians with him wer rogues, they had the night before stold both his and Willards guns from under their heads, Captain Lewis & party arrived at the camp of those Indians at so timely a period that the Indians were allarmed & delivered up the guns &c. The tide meeting of me and the emence swells from the Main Ocian (imedeately in front of us) raised to such a hite that I concluded a form a camp on the highest spot I could find in the marshey bottom, and proceed no further by water as the Coaste becomes verry [dangerous] for crafts of the size of our Canoes, and as the Ocian is imedeately in front and gives us an extensive view of it from Cape disapointment to Point addams, except 3 small Islands off the mouth and SW of us. my situation is in the upper part of Haleys Bay S. 86°. W. course miles to Cape Disapointment and S. 35°. W. course miles from Point Addams.

The River here at its mouth from Point addams to the enterance of Haley Bay above is [blank space in MS.] miles or thereabouts, a large Island the lower point of which is immediately in the mouth above

4 Indians in a canoe came down with *papto* [wapatoo] roots to sell, for which they asked blankets or robes, both of which we could not spare I informed those Indians all of which understood some English that if they stole our guns &c the men would certainly shute them, I treated them with great distance, & the sentinal which was over our Baggage allarmed them verry much, they all Promised not to take any thing, and if any thing was taken by the squars & bad boys to return them &c. the waves became verry high Evening fare & pleasent, our men all comfortable in the camps they have made of the boards they found at the Town above

ZEBULON MONTGOMERY PIKE REACHES THE ROCKY MOUNTAINS

Before Lewis and Clark returned safely to St. Louis in the fall of 1806, President Jefferson had dispatched a second major exploring party into the Far West, this one under the command of Zebulon Montgomery Pike. His force of twenty-three men started up the Missouri and Osage rivers in July 1806 with instructions to explore the Southwest as Lewis and Clark had investigated the Northwest. Pike's principal objective was the unknown country between the Arkansas and Red rivers; hence he cut across country to the Big Bend of the Arkansas and followed that stream westward. On November 15, the explorers thrilled at their first sight of the Rocky Mountains:[6]

Nov. 15th. Marched early. Passed two deep creeks and many high points of rocks; also, large herds of buffalo.

At two o'clock in the afternoon I thought

---

[6] Elliott Coues (ed.), *The Expeditions of Zebulon Montgomery Pike* (New York, 1895), vol. 2, pp. 443–447.

I could distinguish a mountain to our right, which appeared like a small blue cloud; viewed it with the spy glass, and was still more confirmed in my conjecture, yet only communicated it to Dr. Robinson, who was in front with me; but in half an hour they appeared in full view before us. When our small party arrived on the hill they with one accord gave three cheers to the Mexican mountains. Their appearance can easily be imagined by those who have crossed the Alleghenies; but their sides were whiter, as if covered with snow, or a white stone. Those were a spur of the grand western chain of mountains which divide the waters of the Pacific from those of the Atlantic ocean; and it divides the waters which empty into the Bay of the Holy Spirit from those of the Mississippi, as the Alleghenies do those which discharge themselves into the latter river and the Atlantic. They appear to present a natural boundary between the province of Louisiana and New Mexico, and would be a defined and natural boundary.

Before evening we discovered a fork on the south side bearing S. 25° W.; and as the Spanish troops appeared to have borne up it, we encamped on its banks, about one mile from its confluence, that we might make further discoveries on the morrow, Killed three buffalo. Distance 24 miles.

Sunday, Nov. 16th. After ascertaining that the Spanish troops had ascended the right branch or main river, we marched at two o'clock. The Arkansaw appeared at this place to be much more navigable than below, where we first struck it; and for any impediment I have yet discovered in the river, I would not hesitate to embark in February at its mouth and ascend to the Mexican mountains, with crafts properly constructed. Distance 11½ miles.

Nov. 17th. Marched at our usual hour; pushed on with an idea of arriving at the mountains, but found at night no visible difference in their appearance from what we did yesterday. One of our horses gave out and was left in a ravine, not being able to ascend the hill; but I sent back for him and had him brought to the camp. Distance 23½ miles.

Nov. 18th. As we discovered fresh signs of the savages, we concluded it best to stop and kill some meat, for fear we should get into a country where we could not kill game. Sent out the hunters; walked myself to an eminence whence I took the courses to the different mountains, and a small sketch of their appearance. In the evening, found the hunters had killed without mercy, having slain 17 buffalo and wounded at least 20 more.

Nov. 19th. Having several buffalo brought in, gave out sufficient to last this month. I found it expedient to remain and dry the meat, as our horses were getting very weak, and the one died which was brought up on the 17th. Had a general feast of marrow-bones, 136 of them furnishing the repast.

Nov. 20th. Marched at our usual hour; but as our horses' loads were considerably augmented by the death of one horse and the addition of 900 lbs. of meat, we moved slowly and made only 18 miles. Killed two buffalo and took some choice pieces.

PIKE'S PARTY CROSSES THE ROCKIES

Winter was on them now, so Pike and his men established a base camp at the site of modern Pueblo, Colorado, while he and three companions vainly tried to climb the peak that bears his name. For a time they rested, but the lure of the unknown could not long be resisted. Despite bitter cold and raging blizzards, they pushed westward into the mountains to seek the source of the Arkansas River. In the end winter conquered. Pike left most of his men at today's Cañon City while he and a few companions set out on January 14, 1807, to cross the range and find a warmer camp site. The hardships endured in a winter crossing of the Rockies were vividly described in Pike's journal:[7]

Jan. 14th. We marched our party, consisting of 18 soldiers, the doctor, and myself, each of us carrying 45 pounds and as much provision as he thought proper, which, with arms, etc., made on an average 70 pounds. Left Baroney and one man, Patrick Smith.

We crossed the first ridge, leaving the main branch of the river to the north of us, and struck on the south fork, on which we encamped, intending to pursue it through the mountains, as its course was more southerly. Distance 13 miles.

Jan. 15th. Followed up this branch and passed the main ridge of what I term the Blue mountains. Halted early. The doctor, myself, and one hunter went out with our guns; each killed a deer, and brought them into camp. Distance 19 miles.

Jan. 16th. Marched up the creek all day. Encamped early, as it was snowing. I went out to hunt, but killed nothing. Deer on the hill; the mountains lessening. Distance 18 miles.

Jan. 17th. Marched about four miles, when the great White mountain presented itself before us, in sight of which we had been for more than one month, and through which we supposed lay the long-sought Red river. We now left the creek on the north of us, and bore away more east, to a low place in the mountains. About sunset we came to the edge of a prairie which bounded the foot of the mountains. As there was no wood or water where we were, and the woods from the skirts of the mountains appeared to be at no great distance, I thought proper to march for it; in the middle of said prairie crossed the creek, which now bore east. Here we all got our feet wet. The night commenced extremely cold, when we halted at the woods at eight o'clock, for encampment. After getting fires made, we discovered that the feet of nine of our men were frozen; and, to add to this misfortune, both of those whom we called hunters were among the number. This night we had no provision. Reaumer's thermometer stood at 18½° below zero. Distance 28 miles.

Sunday, Jan. 18th. We started two of the men least injured; the doctor and myself, who fortunately were untouched by the frost, also went out to hunt something to preserve existence. Near evening we wounded a buffalo with three balls, but had the mortification to see him run off notwithstanding. We concluded it was useless to go home to add to the general gloom, and went amongst some rocks, where we encamped and sat up all night; from the intense cold it was impossible to sleep. Hungry and without cover.

Jan. 19th. We again took the field, and after crawling about one mile in the snow, got to shoot eight times among a gang of buffalo; we could plainly perceive two or three to be badly wounded, but by accident they took the wind of us, and to our great mortification all were able to run off. By this time I had become extremely weak and

---

[7] Elliott Coues (ed.), *The Expeditions of Zebulon Montgomery Pike* (New York, 1895), vol. 2, pp. 482–495.

faint, it being the fourth day since we had received sustenance, all of which we were marching hard, and the last night had scarcely closed our eyes to sleep. We were inclining our course to a point of woods, determined to remain absent and die by ourselves rather than return to our camp and behold the misery of our poor lads, when we discovered a gang of buffalo coming along at some distance. With great exertions I made out to run and place myself behind some cedars. By the greatest of good luck, the first shot stopped one, which we killed in three more shots; and by the dusk had cut each of us a heavy load, with which we determined immediately to proceed to the camp, in order to relieve the anxiety of our men and carry the poor fellows some food.

We arrived there about twelve o'clock, and when I threw my load down, it was with difficulty I prevented myself from falling; I was attacked with a giddiness of the head, which lasted for some minutes. On the countenances of the men was not a frown, nor a desponding eye; all seemed happy to hail their officer and companions, yet not a mouthful had they eaten for four days. On demanding what were their thoughts, the sergeant replied that on the morrow the most robust had determined to set out in search of us and not return unless they found us, or killed something to preserve the lives of their starving companions.

Jan. 20th. The doctor and all the men able to march; returned to the buffalo to bring in the balance of the meat. On examining the feet of those who were frozen we found it impossible for two of them to proceed, and two others only without loads, by the help of a stick. One of the former was my waiter, a promising young lad of twenty, whose feet were so badly frozen as to present every probability of losing them. The doctor and party returned toward evening, loaded with the buffalo meat.

Jan. 21st. This day we separated the four loads which we intended to leave, and took them some distance from camp, where we secured them. I went up to the foot of the mountain to see what prospect there was of being able to cross it, but had not more than fairly arrived at its base when I found the snow four or five feet deep; this obliged me to determine to proceed and *côtoyer* the mountain to the south, where it appeared lower, until we found a place where we could cross.

Jan. 22d. I furnished the two poor lads who were to remain with ammunition, made use of every argument in my power to encourage them to have fortitude to resist their fate, and gave them assurance of my sending relief as soon as possible. We parted, but not without tears.

We pursued our march, taking merely sufficient provisions for one meal, in order to leave as much as possible for the two poor fellows who remained. They were John Sparks and Thomas Dougherty. We went on eight miles and encamped on a little creek, which came down from the mountains. At three o'clock went out to hunt, but killed nothing. Little snow....

Jan. 24th. We sallied out in the morning, and shortly after perceived our little band marching through the snow about two and a half feet deep, silent and with downcast countenances. We joined them and learned that, finding the snow to fall so thickly that it was impossible to proceed, they had encamped about one o'clock the preceding day. As I found all the buffalo had quit the plains, I determined to attempt the traverse of the mountain, in which we persevered until the snow became so deep that it was impossible to proceed; when I again turned my face to the plain, and for the first time in the voyage found myself discouraged.

This was also the first time I heard a man express himself in a seditious manner; he exclaimed that "it was more than human nature could bear, to march three days without sustenance, through snows three feet deep, and carry burdens only fit for horses," etc. As I knew very well the fidelity and attachment of the majority of the men, and even of this poor fellow (only he could not endure fasting), and that it was in my power to chastise him when I thought proper, I passed it unnoticed for the moment, determined to notice it at a more auspicious time.

We dragged our weary and emaciated limbs along until about ten o'clock. The doctor and myself, who were in advance, discovered some buffalo on the plain, when we left our loads on the snow, and gave orders to proceed to the nearest woods to encamp. We went in pursuit of the buffalo, which were on the move. The doctor, who was then less reduced than myself, ran and got behind a hill and shot one down, which stopped the remainder. We crawled up to the dead one and shot from him as many as 12 or 14 times among the gang, when they removed out of sight. We then proceeded to butcher the one we had shot; and after procuring each of us a load of the meat, we marched for the camp, the smoke of which was in view. We arrived at the camp, to the great joy of our brave lads, who immediately feasted sumptuously....

Jan. 27th. We marched, determined to cross the mountains, leaving Menaugh encamped with our deposit. After a bad day's march through snows, in some places three feet deep, we struck on a brook which led west. This I followed down, and shortly came to a small stream, running west, which we hailed with fervency as the waters of Red river. Saw some sign of elk. Distance 14 miles.

Jan. 28th. Followed down the ravine and discovered after some time that there had been a road cut out; on many trees were various hieroglyphics painted. After marching some miles, we discovered through the lengthy vista, at a distance, another chain of mountains; and nearer by, at the foot of the White mountains which we were then descending, sandy hills. We marched on the outlet of the mountains, left the sandy desert to our right, and kept down between it and the mountain. When we encamped, I ascended one of the largest hills of sand, and with my glass could discover a large river, flowing nearly N. by W. and S. by E., through the plain....

Jan. 29th. Finding the distance too great to attempt crossing immediately to the river, in a direct line, we marched obliquely to a copse of woods, which made down a considerable distance from the mountains. Saw sign of horses. Distance 17 miles.

Jan. 30th. We marched hard, and arrived in the evening on the banks of the Rio del Norte, then supposed to be Red River. Distance 24 miles.

Jan. 31st. As there was no timber here we determined on descending until we found timber, in order to make transports to descend the river with, where we might establish a position that four or five might defend against the insolence, cupidity, and barbarity of the savages, while the others returned to assist the poor fellows who had been left behind at different points. We descended 18 miles, when we met a large west branch emptying into the main stream, about five miles up which branch we took our station. Killed one deer. Distance 18 miles.

Sunday, Feb. 1st. Laid out the place for our works, and went out hunting.

PIKE'S PARTY IS CAPTURED BY THE SPANIARDS

Pike and his men endured their hardships in vain, for they had not emerged as they thought in the Red River Valley but in the San Luis Valley, in the basin of the Rio Grande. On the banks of this stream they established winter quarters and sent back for those who had been left east of the mountains. There they were discovered by Spanish troops:[8]

Feb. 26th. In the morning was apprized of the approach of strangers by the report of a gun from my lookout guard. Immediately afterward two Frenchmen arrived. My sentinel halted them, and ordered them to be admitted, after some questions. They informed me that his Excellency, Governor Allencaster, had heard it was the intention of the Utah Indians to attack me; had detached an officer with 50 dragoons to come out and protect me; and that they would be here in two days. To this I made no reply: but shortly after the party came in sight, to the number, as I afterward learned, of 50 dragoons and 50 mounted militia of the province, armed in the same manner with lances, escopates, and pistols. My sentinel halted them at the distance of about 50 yards. I had the works manned. I thought it most proper to send out the two Frenchmen to inform the commanding officer that it was my request he should leave his party in the small copse of woods where he was halted, and that I would meet him myself in the prairie in which our work was situated. This I did, with my sword on me only. I was then introduced to Don Ignatio Saltelo and Don Bartholemew Fernandez, two lieutenants, the former the commandant of the party. I gave them an invitation to enter the works, but requested the troops might remain where they were. This was complied with. When they came round and discovered that to enter they were obliged to crawl on their bellies over a small draw-bridge, they appeared astonished, but entered without further hesitation.

We first breakfasted on deer, meal, goose, and some biscuit which the civilized Indian who came out as a spy had brought me. After breakfast the commanding officer addressed me as follows:

"Sir, the governor of New Mexico, being informed you had missed your route, ordered me to offer you, in his name, mules, horses, money, or whatever you might stand in need of to conduct you to the head of Red river; as from Santa Fe to where it is sometimes navigable is eight days' journey, and we have guides and the routes of the traders to conduct us."

"What," said I, interrupting him, "is not this the Red river?"

"No, Sir! The Rio del Norte."

I immediately ordered my flag to be taken down and rolled up, feeling how sensibly I had committed myself in entering their territory, and conscious that they must have positive orders to take me in.

He now added that he "had provided 100 mules and horses to take in my party and baggage, and how anxious his Excellency was to see me at Santa Fe." I stated to him the absence of my sergeant [Meek, with Miller], the situation of the balance of the party [Vasquez and Smith in the stockade on the Arkansaw; Dougherty and Sparks in the mountains with frozen feet], and that my orders would not justify my entering into the Spanish territory. He urged still further, until I began to feel myself a little heated in

---

[8] Elliott Coues (ed.), *The Expeditions of Zebulon Montgomery Pike* (New York, 1895), vol. 2, pp. 508–510.

the argument; and told him, in a peremptory style, that I would not go until the arrival of my sergeant with the balance of the party. He replied, "that there was not the least restraint to be used; that it was only necessary his Excellency should receive an explanation of my business on his frontier; that I could go now, or on the arrival of my party; that, if none went in at present, he should be obliged to send in for provisions; but that, if I would now march, he would leave an Indian interpreter and an escort of dragoons to conduct the sergeant [Meek, and the five other absentees—Miller of the relief-party, Vasquez, Smith, Sparks, Dougherty] into Santa Fe." His mildness induced me to tell him that I would march, but must leave two men [Jackson and Carter] to meet the sergeant and party, to instruct him as to coming in, as he never would come without a fight, if not ordered.

I was induced to consent to this measure by the conviction that the officer had positive orders to bring me in; and as I had no orders to commit hostilities, and indeed had committed myself, although innocently, by violating their territory, I conceived it would appear better to show a will to come to an explanation than to be in any way constrained; yet my situation was so eligible, and I could so easily have put them at defiance, that it was with great reluctance I suffered all our labor to be lost without once trying the efficacy of it. My compliance seemed to spread general joy through their party, as soon as it was communicated; but it appeared to be different with my men, who wished to have "a little dust," as they expressed themselves, and were likewise fearful of treachery.

My determination being once taken, I gave permission for the Spanish lieutenant's men to come to the outside of the works, and some of mine to go out and see them. The hospitality and goodness of the Creoles and Metifs began to manifest itself by their producing their provision and giving it to my men, covering them with their blankets, etc.

BEGINNINGS OF THE "GREAT AMERICAN DESERT" LEGEND

Probably Pike was not as hopelessly lost as he pretended to be, but his insistence that he was on the Red River did him no good. The Mexican troops marched him and his men into Mexico, confiscated his papers, and finally deposited him in the United States, having given him an admirable opportunity to observe the defenses of northern Mexico. His report, written largely from memory in 1810, was widely read. In it he planted the seeds of one of the most influential legends in western history: that of a "Great American Desert" embracing most of the western Great Plains:[9]

Numerous have been the hypotheses formed by various naturalists to account for the vast tract of untimbered country which lies between the waters of the Missouri, Mississippi, and the Western Ocean, from the mouth of the latter river to 48° north latitude. Although not flattering myself to be able to elucidate that which numbers of highly scientific characters have acknowledged to be beyond their depth of research, still I would not think I had done my country justice did I not give birth to what few lights my examination of those internal deserts has enabled me to acquire. In that vast country of which I speak, we find the soil generally dry and sandy, with gravel, and discover that the moment we approach a stream the land becomes more humid, with

---

[9] Elliott Coues (ed.), *The Expeditions of Zebulon Montgomery Pike* (New York, 1895), vol. 2, pp. 524–525.

small timber. I therefore conclude that this country never was timbered; as, from the earliest age the aridity of the soil, having so few water-courses running through it, and they being principally dry in summer, has never afforded moisture sufficient to support the growth of timber. In all timbered land the annual discharge of the leaves, with the continual decay of old trees and branches, creates a manure and moisture, which is preserved from the heat of the sun not being permitted to direct his rays perpendicularly, but only to shed them obliquely through the foliage. But here a barren soil, parched and dried up for eight months in the year, presents neither moisture nor nutrition sufficient to nourish the timber. These vast plains of the western hemisphere may become in time as celebrated as the sandy deserts of Africa; for I saw in my route, in various places, tracts of many leagues where the wind had thrown up the sand in all the fanciful form of the ocean's rolling wave, and on which not a speck of vegetable matter existed.

But from these immense prairies may arise one great advantage to the United States, viz.: The restriction of our population to some certain limits, and thereby a continuation of the Union. Our citizens being so prone to rambling and extending themselves on the frontiers will, through necessity, be constrained to limit their extent on the west to the borders of the Missouri and Mississippi, while they leave the prairies incapable of cultivation to the wandering and uncivilized aborigines of the country.

JOURNEY ALONG THE RED RIVER

Interest in exploration slackened as the nation drifted into the War of 1812 and ended during the course of that conflict. But many mysteries remained, including the source of the Red River, and in 1820 a new expedition under Major Stephen H. Long was dispatched to solve the riddle of that illusive stream. He started on June 6, 1820, with nineteen men. One of them, Dr. Edwin James, doubled as botanist and chronicler. Reaching the Rocky Mountains, the party turned southward and divided into two groups. One under Captain John R. Bell descended the Arkansas River, enduring a succession of disasters that cost them their notes and scientific instruments. The other, led by Long, started south to seek the Red River. Happening on a likely looking stream, they turned eastward through a barren country, where they suffered hunger and thirst, and were constantly menaced by Indians. James describes their hardships in an entry in his diary for August 3, 1820:[10]

Thursday, 3d. Little delay was occasioned by our preparations for breakfast. The fourth part of a biscuit, which had been issued to each man on the preceding evening, and which was to furnish both supper and breakfast, would have required little time had all of it remained to be eaten, which was not the case. We were becoming somewhat impatient on account of thirst, having met with no water which we could drink for near twenty-four hours; accordingly, getting upon our horses at an early hour, we moved down the valley, passing an extensive tract, whose soil is a loose red sand, intermixed with gravel and small pebbles, and producing nothing but a few sunflowers and sand cherries, still unripe. While we should remain upon a soil of this description, we could scarcely expect to meet with water or wood, for both of which we began to feel the most urgent necessity; and as the prospect of the country before us promised no

---

[10] Edwin James, *Account of an Expedition from Pittsburgh to the Rocky Mountains, Performed in the Years 1819, 1820* (London, 1823), vol. 2, pp. 281–283.

change, it is not surprising we should have felt a degree of anxiety and alarm, which, added to our sufferings from hunger and thirst, made our situation extremely unpleasant. We had travelled great part of the day enveloped in a burning atmosphere, sometimes letting fall upon us the scorching particles of sand, which had been raised by the wind, sometimes almost suffocating by its entire stagnation, when we had the good fortune to meet with a pool of stagnant water, which, though muddy and brackish, was not entirely impotable, and afforded us a more welcome treat than it is in the power of abundance to supply. Here was also a little wood, and our badger, with the addition of a young owl, was very hastily cooked and eaten.

Numbers of cow buntings had been seen a little before we arrived at this encampment, flying so familiarly about the horses that the men killed several with their whips.

August 4th. We were still passing through a barren and desolate region, affording no game, and nearly destitute of wood and water. Its soil is evidently the detritus of a stratum of red sandstone and coarse conglomeratic, which is still the basis and prevailing rock. It appears to contain a considerable proportion of lime, and fragments of plaster stone and selenite are often seen intermixed with it.

Our morning's ride of sixteen miles brought us to a place where the water of the river emerges to view, rising to the surface of that bed of sand beneath which it had been concealed for a distance of more than one hundred miles. The stream is still very inconsiderable in magnitude; the water brackish, and holds suspended so large a quantity of red earth as to give it the colour of florid blood. The general direction of its course inclining still towards the south-east, we were now induced to believe it must be one of the most considerable of the upper tributaries of Red river. A circumstance tending to confirm this opinion was our falling in with a large and much frequented Indian trace, crossing the creek from the west, and following down along the east bank. This trace consisted of more than twenty parallel paths, and bore sufficient marks of having been recently travelled, affording an explanation of the cause of the alarming scarcity of game we had for some time experienced. We supposed it to be the road leading from the Pawnee Piqua village on Red river to Santa Fé....

The hunters were kept constantly out during the day, but nothing was killed until evening, when Verplank brought in a young buck, which enabled us to make a full meal, the first we had eaten for several days.

Game in this portion of the country is extremely scarce, and few traces of bisons are to be seen; and as we were travelling along a frequented road, we had some reason to fear this want of game might continue.

A few wild horses had been observed in the course of the day, and towards evening one was seen following the party, but keeping at a distance. At night, after our horses had been staked in the usual manner, near our camp, we perceived him still lingering about, and at length approaching the tent so closely, that we began to entertain some hopes of capturing him alive. In attempting this we stationed a man with a long-noosed rope in the top of a cotton-wood tree, under which we tied a few of our horses; but this plan did not succeed.

On the following morning one of our hunters fortunately discovered the same horse standing asleep under the shade of a tree, and having shot him, returned immediately to camp with the intelligence. We had all suffered so severely from hunger, and our present want of provisions was so great, that instead of questioning whether we should eat the flesh of a horse, we congratulated ourselves on the acquisition of so seasonable a supply. We felt a little regret at killing so beautiful an animal, who had followed us several miles on the day before, and had lingered with a sort of confidence about our camp; but our scruples all yielded to the loud admonitions of hunger.

THE "GREAT AMERICAN DESERT" LEGEND GROWS

Long's failure to locate the Red River (the stream he was following proved to be the Canadian River, which led him back to the Arkansas) and the barrenness of the country he traversed fixed in his mind an image of all the Far West as an uninhabitable desert. His report, which was widely read, helped fasten this belief in the public mind for a generation:[11]

In regard to this extensive section of country, I do not hesitate in giving the opinion, that it is almost wholly unfit for cultivation, and of course uninhabitable by a people depending upon agriculture for their subsistence. Although tracts of fertile land considerably extensive are occasionally to be met with, yet the scarcity of wood and water, almost uniformly prevalent, will prove an insuperable obstacle in the way of settling the country. This objection rests not only against the section immediately under consideration, but applies with equal propriety to a much larger portion of the country. Agreeably to the best intelligence that can be had, concerning the country both northward and southward of the section, and especially to the inferences deducible from the account given by Lewis and Clarke of the country situated between the Missouri and the Rocky Mountains above the river Platte, the vast region commencing near the sources of the Sabine, Trinity, Brases, and Colorado, and extending northwardly to the forty-ninth degree of north latitude, by which the United States' territory is limited in that direction, is throughout of a similar character. The whole of this region seems peculiarly adapted as a range for buffaloes, wild goats, and other wild game; incalculable multitudes of which find ample pasturage and subsistence upon it.

This region, however, viewed as a frontier, may prove of infinite importance to the United States, inasmuch as it is calculated to serve as a barrier to prevent too great an extension of our population westward, and secure us against the machinations or incursions of an enemy that might otherwise be disposed to annoy us in that part of our frontier.

JOHN C. FRÉMONT ADVERTISES THE WEST: THE BUMBLE BEE

The harshly realistic impressions of Pike and Long, branding the plains as a "Great American Desert," served for a generation as a deterrent to the occupation of the Far West. Fortunately they were offset by the opposite views of a later explorer whose enthusiasm more than matched their pessimism. John C. Frémont, whose most notable expeditions were in 1842 and 1843, saw not a single foot of land that was not already known to frontiersmen, but still his contributions to the westward expansion of the United States were significant.

---

[11] Edwin James, *Account of an Expedition from Pittsburgh to the Rocky Mountains, Performed in the Years 1819, 1820* (London, 1823), vol. 3, pp. 237–238.

His glowing reports, written in a vivid style and depicting the most barren wastelands as Edens flowing with milk and honey, were published just as the westward-moving tide was beginning to flow and stimulated migration as did few other forces. Typical was Frémont's account of a flag-planting ceremony on his 1842 expedition. This occurred when his party of twenty-one men, having followed the well-traveled Oregon Trail westward along the Platte River and into South Pass, turned northward to the Wind River mountains and climbed what he believed to be the highest peak of the Rockies. Few gestures could have been more futile—he might better have spent his time mapping the trail for future immigrants—but the episode fired the national imagination and focused interest on the West:[12]

When we had secured strength for the day by a hearty breakfast, we covered what remained, which was enough for one meal, with rocks, in order that it might be safe from any marauding bird; and, saddling our mules, turned out faces once more towards the peaks. This time we determined to proceed quietly and cautiously, deliberately resolved to accomplish our object if it were within the compass of human means. We were of opinion that a long defile which lay to the left of yesterday's route would lead us to the foot of the main peak. Our mules had been refreshed by the fine grass in the little ravine at the Island camp, and we intended to ride up the defile as far as possible, in order to husband our strength for the main ascent. Though this was a fine passage, still it was a defile of the most rugged mountains known, and we had many a rough and steep slippery place to cross before reaching the end. In this place the sun rarely shone; snow lay along the border of the small stream which flowed through it, and occasional icy passages made the footing of the mules very insecure, and the rocks and ground were moist with the trickling waters in this spring of mighty rivers. We soon had the satisfaction to find ourselves riding along the huge wall which forms the central summits of the chain. There at last it rose by our sides, a nearly perpendicular wall of granite, terminating 2,000 to 3,000 feet above our heads in a serrated line of broken, jagged cones. We rode on until we came almost immediately below the main peak, which I denominated the Snow peak, as it exhibited more snow to the eye than any of the neighboring summits. Here were three small lakes of a green color, each of perhaps a thousand yards in diameter, and apparently very deep. These lay in a kind of chasm; and, according to the barometer, we had attained but a few hundred feet above the Island lake. The barometer here stood at 20.450, attached thermometer 70°.

We managed to get our mules up to a little bench about a hundred feet above the lakes, where there was a patch of good grass, and turned them loose to graze. During our rough ride to this place, they had exhibited a wonderful surefootedness. Parts of the defile were filled with angular, sharp fragments of rock, three or four and eight or ten feet cube; and among these they had worked their way, leaping from one narrow point to another, rarely making a false step, and giving us no occasion to dismount. Having divested ourselves of every unnecessary encumbrance, we commenced the ascent. This time, like experienced travellers, we did not press ourselves, but climbed leisurely, sitting down so soon as we found breath beginning to fail. At intervals we

---

[12] John C. Frémont, *Report of the Exploring Expedition to the Rocky Mountains in the Year 1842, and to Oregon and Northern California in the Years 1843–'44* (Washington, 1845), pp. 68–69.

reached places where a number of springs gushed from the rocks, and about 1,800 feet above the lakes came to the snow line. From this point our progress was uninterrupted climbing. Hitherto I had worn a pair of thick moccasins, with soles of *parflêche*; but here I put on a light thin pair, which I had brought for the purpose, as now the use of our toes became necessary to a further advance. I availed myself of a sort of comb of the mountain, which stood against the wall like a buttress, and which the wind and the solar radiation, joined to the steepness of the smooth rock, had kept almost entirely free from snow. Up this I made my way rapidly. Our cautious method of advancing in the outset had spared my strength; and, with the exception of a slight disposition to headache, I felt no remains of yesterday's illness. In a few minutes we reached a point where the buttress was overhanging, and there was no other way of surmounting the difficulty than by passing around one side of it, which was the face of a vertical precipice of several hundred feet.

Putting hands and feet in the crevices between the blocks, I succeeded in getting over it, and, when I reached the top, found my companions in a small valley below. Descending to them, we continued climbing, and in a short time reached the crest. I sprang upon the summit, and another step would have precipitated me into an immense snow field five hundred feet below. To the edge of this field was a sheer icy precipice; and then, with a gradual fall, the field sloped off for about a mile, until it struck the foot of another lower ridge. I stood on a narrow crest, about three feet in width, with an inclination of about 20° N. 51° E.

As soon as I had gratified the first feelings of curiosity, I descended, and each man ascended in his turn; for I would only allow one at a time to mount the unstable and precarious slab, which it seemed a breath would hurl into the abyss below. We mounted the barometer in the snow of the summit, and, fixing a ramrod in a crevice, unfurled the national flag to wave in the breeze where never flag waved before. During our morning's ascent, we had met no sign of animal life, except the small sparrow-like bird already mentioned. A stillness the most profound and a terrible solitude forced themselves constantly on the mind as the great features of the place. Here, on the summit, where the stillness was absolute, unbroken by any sound, and the solitude complete, we thought ourselves beyond the region of animated life; but while we were sitting on the rock, a solitary bee (*bromus, the humble bee*) came winging his flight from the eastern valley, and lit on the knee of one of the men.

Frémont's literary skill outshone his abilities as an explorer; his deft symbolism of the humble bee that "came winging his flight from the eastern valley" typified the manner in which his vivid writing captured the nation's imagination and whetted interest in the Far West. Actually Frémont, and to a lesser degree Long and Pike, contributed little to man's geographical knowledge. Others had preceded them into the Rocky Mountain country and beyond, driven not by a thirst for glory but by the urge for humdrum profits. These were the fur trappers, who more than any other group explored and publicized the Far West.

CHAPTER 16

Traders and Trappers Open the Far West, 1820-1845

The true pioneers of the far western frontier were not the government explorers who crisscrossed its vastness between 1803 and the 1840s; with the exception of Lewis and Clark, they saw scarcely a single foot of countryside not already known to Anglo-Americans. Instead the real heralds of expansion were traders and fur trappers. Impelled by a thirst for adventure no less than by an urge for profits, these frontiersmen paved the way for the coming of the settlers. They sought out the fertile valleys, marked the trails, advertised the riches of the West, and broke down the self-sufficiency of the Indian occupants by reducing them to dependence on the white man's weapons and infecting them with the white man's vices and diseases. By the time the traders and trappers began to disappear from the mountains in the 1840s, the western country was ready to receive its first permanent American occupants.

CARAVANS ON THE SANTA FE TRAIL

One group of traders played an additional role in the drama of conquest. When Mexico won its independence from Spain in 1821, its northern provinces were opened to merchants from the United States. First to capitalize on this opportunity was William Becknell, who returned to the Mississippi Valley in January 1822 with bags of silver coins to prove that the people of Santa Fe were eager to trade precious metals, furs, and mules for Yankee merchandise. From that year, caravans of covered wagons annually lumbered across the 900 miles of plains, deserts, and mountains between Independence or Westport in Missouri and the New Mexican capital or cities within Mexico itself. The Santa Fe trade not only vitalized frontier economy but revealed the weakness of the mother country's hold on its northern provinces and taught pioneers the techniques of wagon travel across the plains. One of the traders, Josiah Gregg, whose "Commerce of the Prairies" is a classic of western literature, describes the organization of a caravan for its long journey:[1]

Early on the 26th of May we reached the long looked-for rendezvous of Council Grove,

---

[1] Josiah Gregg, *Commerce of the Prairies* (New York, 1844), vol. 1, pp. 42-49.

where we joined the main body of the caravan. Lest this imposing title suggest to the reader a snug and thriving village, it should be observed that on the day of our departure from Independence we passed the last human abode upon our route; therefore, from the borders of Missouri to those of New Mexico not even an Indian settlement greeted our eyes.

This point is nearly a hundred and fifty miles from Independence, and consists of a continuous strip of timber nearly half a mile in width, comprising the richest varieties of trees; such as oak, walnut, ash, elm, hickory, etc. and extending all along the valleys of a small stream known as Council Grove Creek, the principal branch of the Neosho River. This stream is bordered by the most fertile bottoms and beautiful upland prairies, well adapted to cultivation: such, indeed, is the general character of the country from thence to Independence. All who have traversed these delightful regions look forward with anxiety to the day when the Indian title to the land shall be extinguished and flourishing white settlements dispel the gloom which at present prevails over this uninhabited region. Much of this prolific country now belongs to the Shawnees and other Indians of the border, though some portion of it has never been allotted to any tribe.

Frequent attempts have been made by travelers to invest the Council Grove with a romantic sort of interest, of which the following fabulous vagary, which I find in a letter that went the rounds of our journals, is an amusing sample: "Here the Pawnee, Arapaho, Comanche, Loup, and Eutaw Indians, all of whom were at war with each other, meet and smoke the pipe once a year." Now it is more than probable that not a soul of most of the tribes mentioned above ever saw the Council Grove. Whatever may be the interest attached to this place, however, on account of its historical or fanciful associations, one thing is very certain, that the novice, even here, is sure to imagine himself in the midst of lurking savages. These visionary fears are always a source of no little merriment to the veteran of the field, who does not hesitate to travel with a single wagon and a comrade or two, or even alone, from the Arkansas River to Independence.

The facts connected with the designation of this spot are simply these. Messrs. Reeves, Sibley, and Mathers, having been commissioned by the United States in the year 1825 to mark a road from the confines of Missouri to Santa Fé, met on this spot with some bands of Osages, with whom they concluded a treaty whereby the Indians agreed to allow all citizens of the United States and Mexico to pass unmolested, and even to lend their aid to those engaged in the Santa Fé trade; for which they were to receive a gratification of eight hundred dollars in merchandise. The commissioners on this occasion gave to the place the name of Council Grove.

But, although the route examined by the Commissioners named above was partially marked out as far as the Arkansas by raised mounds, it seems to have been of but little service to travelers, who continued to follow the trail previously made by the wagons, which is now the settled road to the region of the short buffalo grass.

The designation of Council Grove, after all, is perhaps the most appropriate that could be given to this place; for *we* there held a grand council, at which the respective claims of the different aspirants to office were considered, leaders selected, and a system of government agreed upon, as is the standing custom of these promiscuous caravans. One would have supposed that electioneering and party spirit would hardly have penetrated so far into the wilderness: but so it was. Even in our little community we had our office-seekers and their political adherents, as earnest and as devoted as any of the modern school of politicians in the midst of civilization. After a great deal of bickering and wordy warfare, however, all the candidates found it expedient to decline, and a gentleman by the name of Stanley, without seeking or even desiring the office, was unanimously proclaimed captain of the caravan. The powers of this officer were undefined by any constitutional provision, and consequently vague and uncertain: orders being only viewed as mere requests, they are often obeyed or neglected at the caprice of the subordinates. It is necessary to observe, however, that the captain is expected to direct the order of travel during the day and to designate the camping ground at night; with many other functions of a general character, in the exercise of which the company find it convenient to acquiesce. But the little attention that is paid to his commands in cases of emergency, will leave the reader to become acquainted with, as I did, by observing their manifestations during the progress of the expedition.

But after this comes the principal task of organizing. The proprietors are first notified by proclamation to furnish a list of their men and wagons. The latter are generally apportioned into four divisions, particularly when the company is large—and ours consisted of nearly a hundred wagons, besides a dozen of dearborns and other small vehicles and two small cannons (a four and six pounder), each mounted upon a carriage. To each of these divisions a lieutenant was appointed, whose duty it was to inspect every ravine and creek on the route, select the best crossings, and superintend what is called in prairie parlance the "forming" of each encampment.

Upon the calling of the roll we were found to muster an efficient force of nearly two hundred men, without counting invalids or other disabled bodies, who, as a matter of course, are exempt from duty. There is nothing so much dreaded by inexperienced travelers as the ordeal of guard duty. But no matter what the condition or employment of the individual may be, no one has the smallest chance of evading the common law of the prairies. The amateur tourist and the listless loafer are precisely in the same wholesome predicament—they must all take their regular turn at the watch. There is usually a set of genteel idlers attached to every caravan, whose wits are forever at work in devising schemes for whiling away their irksome hours at the expense of others. By embarking in these trips of pleasure they are enabled to live without expense; for the hospitable traders seldom refuse to accommodate even a loafing companion with a berth at their mess without charge. But then these lounging attachés are expected at least to do good service by way of guard duty. None are even permitted to furnish a substitute, as is frequently done in military expeditions, for he that would undertake to stand the tour of another besides his own would scarcely be watchful enough for the dangers of the prairies. Even the invalid must be able to produce unequivocal proofs of his inability, or it is a chance if the plea is admitted. For my own part, although I started on the sick list, and though the prairie sentinel must stand fast and brook the severest storm (for then it is that the strictest watch is necessary), I do not remember ever having missed my post but once during the whole journey.

The usual number of watches is eight, each standing a fourth of every alternate night. When the party is small the number is greatly reduced, while in the case of very small bands they are sometimes compelled for safety's sake to keep one watch on duty half the night. With large caravans the captain usually appoints eight sergeants of the guard, each of whom takes an equal portion of men under his command.

The heterogeneous appearance of our company, consisting of men from every class and grade of society, with a little sprinkling of the softer sex, would have formed an excellent subject for an artist's pencil. It may appear, perhaps, a little extraordinary that females should have ventured across the prairies under such forlorn auspices. Those who accompanied us, however, were members of a Spanish family who had been banished in 1829 in pursuance of a decree of the Mexican congress and were now returning to their homes in consequence of a suspension of the decree. Other females, however, have crossed the prairies to Santa Fé at different times, among whom I have known two respectable French ladies, who now reside in Chihuahua.

The wild and motley aspect of the caravan can be but imperfectly conceived without an idea of the costumes of its various members. The most fashionable prairie dress is the fustian frock of the city-bred merchant furnished with a multitude of pockets capable of accommodating a variety of extra tackling. Then there is the backwoodsman with his linsey or leather hunting-shirt—the farmer with his blue jean coat—the wagoner with his flannel-sleeve vest—besides an assortment of other costumes which go to fill up the picture.

In the article of firearms there is also an equally interesting medley. The frontier hunter sticks to his rifle, as nothing could induce him to carry what he terms in derision "the scatter-gun." The sportsman from the interior flourishes his double-barreled fowling-piece with equal confidence in its superiority. The latter is certainly the most convenient description of gun that can be carried on this journey; as a charge of buckshot in night attacks (which are the most common) will of course be more likely to do execution than a single rifle-ball fired at random. The repeating arms have lately been brought into use upon the prairies and they are certainly very formidable weapons, particularly when used against an ignorant savage foe. A great many were furnished beside with a bountiful supply of pistols and knives of every description, so that the party made altogether a very brigand-like appearance.

FUR TRADE
ON THE UPPER MISSOURI

While Santa Fe traders softened the Southwest readying it for the day of American occupation, this process was accomplished for the Far West as a whole by fur trappers. These venturesome pioneers began their invasion soon after Lewis and Clark brought back word of an all-water route to the northern Rockies, where streams teemed with beaver. Beginning in 1807, trappers ascended the Missouri River in cumbersome keelboats laden with trading goods, but they found the obstacles almost insurmountable. Distances were so great that travel expenses absorbed most profits; hostile Indians along the Big Muddy endangered lives and property; and trading in the northern Rockies was rendered hazardous by the constant threat of attack from the ever-hostile Blackfoot Indians. By the spring of 1813, the firm that dominated this phase of the trade, the Missouri Fur Company under Manuel Lisa, was ready to admit defeat. A company clerk, John C. Luttig, described the events leading to evacuation of the principal outpost, Fort Manuel:[2]

---

[2] John C. Luttig, *Journal of a Fur-Trading Expedition on the Upper Missouri, 1812–1813*, edited by Stella M. Drumm (St. Louis: Missouri Historical Society, 1920), pp. 121–128.

Sunday the 21 Clear and cold, this day is the coldest we have had this winter, at 12 oclock this Day Charbonneau and I Engagee arrived from the Bigbellies, himself and Woahl had traded out of 492 Plus only 168, the Chief named Borne was thrown off by the Nation only 5 Lodges remaining with him, and had a seperate Village, he persuaded Charbonneau to come with some Powder & to his Village to trade, he went and took 25 lb Powder and 50 lb Ball of which he was robbed off when Charbonneau was informed by the Chief Cheveux de Loup who [was] first Chief among them that 4 or 5 Days after his Arrival from hence in December last, 2 Men from the N. W. Company had been with them, they came under pretext to trade dressd Buffaloe Skins, and made some Presents to the Chiefs, and began to harangue against the american traders, told them we would give them nothing, but a little powder, and that they the N. W. Company would furnish them with every thing without Pay if they would go to war, and rob and Kill the Americans, this had the desired effect on Borne, and he made several Speeches to the Nation to that purpose, but being disgraced and not liked he retired without Success, though himself fulfilled his promise to rob, but was afraight to Kill, thus are those Bloodhounds the British constantly employed and do every thing in their Power to annoy and destroy the Americans and their trade, they have nothing to fear on Account and in Respect of our Government, all though in our territories, and in fact our Government does not care to meddle with them, nor how many Citizens are sacrificed by the British influence with the Indians, if there was a fort at the River St Peters as was promised by Liet Pike and another in these Parts of the Missouri, it would do infinitively good to hunters and traders, and bring great wealth to the States, but this is out of question, they have a strong Garrison at Bellefontaine, and that is enough, the soldiers parade, eat and drink and spent their time in Idleness, is there any necessity to keep so many idle fellows in a settled Country, they do not even prevent and cannot protect our Settlers about 80 or 90 Miles above, and we have seen outrages committed by the Indians, horrid to relate, there was after the Sheep were destroyed by the Wolves, a small Garrison errected on Salt River, Mississippi which will do more good than all Bellefontaine, and if one was to be erected about 500 Leagues up the Missouri it would be very good to Keep the Indians in their Bounds, Provisions are plenty and the other necessaries could be sent by the traders, but it has been frequently the Case, and has been said our Citizens have no Business to go among the Indians to trade but the profits thereof are not considered, and this Branch of Business will never succeed if not protected by Government, to seat of the British Traders. When Charbonneau passed the Chajennes which are above us about 4 Leagues, they warned him to be cautious and take care of his Life, that they had discovered 27 Men lurking about, supposing to be the Saunies Sioux, he arrived however without accident.

Monday the 22d Fine weather and cold some Buffaloe in Sight, 7 Men went across the River to hunt, and returned about noon, having Killed but 1 Cow 2 Bulls the weather being to cold, to pursue the Buffaloe, at 1 oclock 45 Mi. P. M. we were alarmed by the Cry *to Arms*, Archambeau is Killed and by sorting found us surrounded by Indians on all Sides, out the reach of our Guns, Archambeau was hawling hay with a Sleigh from the other Side, and just on coming on the River he was shot and Killed Immediatly he was a very good Men and had been 6 years on the Missouri, we put ourselves immediatly in Defence, and placed two swivels on the Bank of the River, but unfortunaly our

Balls did not reach across, and those on this Side Kept out of Reach of our fire, and dare not come to an open Attack, their Numbers was between 4 a 500, they took the Scalp and cut him nearly to pieces, they marched off about 4 oclock, leaving us to lament the Death of fellow Citizen unrevenged, a party of our Men went across to bring the Corps which they found terrible mangled, they brought 29 Arrows which were sticking in his body and a good many more had been brocken to pieces, his Head Broken the Brains scattered about his nose and ears cut off, his teeth Knocked out and more terrible Deeds which I will not express with my Pen. We mustered in the Evening and found ourselves 26 Men strong, selected Guards for to night, divided in 5 Watches, 4 Men in each and 2 in each Bastion, gave the Boys a Dram and every one was in Readiness for defence to the last Moment our situation in general is not very pleasing at this time menaced by the Sioux, below, and we dare not trust too much to Chajennes above, they have made a vast quantity of Robes and wish to augment the trade we are told and they shewed a Horn which they made which holds 40 Loads of Powder, instead of giving 20 Load for a Plus, I hope we will have no Row with them as to the Rees we fear nothing, they are a sett of lying and good for nothing fellows.

Thuesday the 23d Passed a quiet night, and our Guards saw nothing, after Breakfast Immel and four Men went out reconnoitring on swift horses, returned at noon and reported they had found the tracks of the war party and judged by the Size of the Road they had made to have been about 400, the Road went right across the Hills and the party which was stationed above the fort say about 60 had met them at right angles, about 2 Miles west of the fort, we interred the Remains of our poor fellow Citizen Archambeau, and guarded in the afternoon saw some Buffaloe chased on the other Side, supposed by the same Party, we also saw Dogs on the Ice which returned to the Woods at the point above us, and made us certain there was some hid in the Woods, as also by a track which we found, descending the Coast on our Side 1 Mile below the fort, set guard for the Night had a fine Day but cold and cloudy evening.

Wednesday the 24th Passed a tranquil night, but saw some running fires, the Signal of Indians after Battle, 3 Men went to Langue de Buche's Camp to hear of their Situation a fine Day but cold, set all our Dogs out of fort for guard.

Thursday the 25th Passed a quiet night, I guarded till 4 oclock in the morning the 3 Men went out yesterday did not Return, Dogs out guarding, dark and cloudy evening.

Friday the 26th Snowed last night and this Morning we are constant watching in our careful Situation, we hear and see nobody from all around us, and are like Prisoners in Deserts to expect every moment our fate.

At 3 oclock P. M. our 3 Men returned with Machecou, the whites and Indians who camp above us had heard nothing of the fracas which had happened, the Chajennes had the next Day after the affair, 24 horses stolen by the Sioux, undoubtedly the same party who attacked us there Scheme was to plunder the fort, expecting that we would divide and a party would run across the River to rescue the Man which was Killed, and then come between us and plunder and Kill those in the fort. cleared up towards evening and cold.

Saturday the 27th Passed another tranquil Night cloudy at Sunrise, cleared up at 8 A. M. cold weather.

Sunday the 28 Snowed last night and this Morning the most which has fell this Winter about 4 Inches deep, cleared up in the afternoon with cold weather. nothing remarkable these 2 Days past.

Monday the 1st of March, 1813 Clear and cold, after dinner Charbonneau and Leclair set off for their Stations at the Bigbellies took some Powder and Ball to compleat his Equipment, they were escorted by 5 of our Men, untill he would be out of Danger, at Sunset it began to Snow.

Thuesday the 2d A vast deal of snow had fell last night, but was clear and cold in the Morning, cloudy afternoon, at 2 P. M. 7 Men and 2 Women of the Rees arrived at the fort, the first which made their appearance since Goshé left us, 4 Men 1 Women went to Langue de Buche the others remained.

Wednesday the 3d Clear and cold, the Indians which arrived yesterday said that the upper Village of the Rees would come this Day to trade, which however proved to be a lie, at noon 7 Rees arrived from above as also our party which had escorted Charbonneau, with Latour, Machecou, Duroche and Laderoute, 2 Squaws and 3 Children, a party of Men went over the River to cut firewood, had a fine warm Day and cloudy evening.

Thursday the 4th Last night about 3 inches of snow had fell cloudy and cold Morning, in the afternoon 4 Mandans arrived from their village on their way to the Rees, no news.

Friday the 5th Snowstorm last night and continued snowing all this Day, the Mandans pursued their Route.

WILLIAM H. ASHLEY'S FICHT WITH THE ARIKARA

Because profits were dearer to some frontiersmen than life itself, the northern Rockies did not long remain unoccupied. By 1822, fur trappers were back again, this time led by William Henry Ashley of Missouri, who was destined to become one of the West's dominant leaders over the next years. With a hundred "enterprising young men," Ashley traded in the upper Missouri River country that year, but the expedition sent to reinforce his party in 1823 taught him the dangers of the river route. Near present-day Bismarck, North Dakota, Ashley's keelboats were suddenly attacked by Arikara Indians. One of the party, James Clyman, described the assault in his diary, a document as noted for its ingenious spelling as for its colorful detail:[3]

On the 8th of March 1824 [1823] all things ready we shoved off from the shore fired a swivel which was answered by a Shout form the shore which we returned with a will and porceed up stream under sail

A discription of our crew I cannt give but Fallstafs Battallion was genteel in comparison I think we had about (70) seventy all told Two Keel Boats with crews of French some St Louis gumboes as they ware called

We proceeded slowly up the Misourie River under sail wen winds ware favourable and towline when not Towing or what was then calld cordell is a slow and tedious method of assending swift waters It is done by the men walking on the shore and hawling the Boat by a long cord Nothing of importance came under wiew for some months except loosing men who left us from time to time & engaging a few new men of a much better appearance than those we lost The Missourie is a monotinous crooked stream with large cottonwood forest trees on one side and small young groth on the other with a bare Sand Barr intervening I will state one circumstanc only which will show

---

[3] Charles L. Camp (ed.), "James Clyman, His Diaries and Reminiscences," *California Historical Society Quarterly*, IV (June, 1925), 111–116.

something of the character of Missourie Boats men

The winds are occasionally very strong and when head winds prevail we are forced to lay by this circumstanc happened once before we left the Settlements the men went out gunning and that night came in with plenty of game Eggs Fowls Turkeys and what not Haveing a fire on shore they dressed cooked and eat untill midnight being care full to burn all the fragments the wind still Blowing in the morning several Neighbours came in hunting for poultry liberty was given to search the boats but they found nothing and left the wind abateing somewhat the cord was got out amd pulling around a bend the wind became a farir sailing breeze and [the sails] wa[r]e ordred unfurled when out droped pigs and poultry in abundance

A man was ordred to Jump in the skiff and pick up the pigs and poultry

Ariveing at Council Bluffs we m[a]de several exchanges (8) eight or Ten of our men enlisting and 2 or 3 of the Soldier whose [terms of enlistment] was nearly expired engageing with us The officers being verry liberal furnished us with a Quantity of vegetables here we leave the last appearance of civilization and [enter] fully Indian country game becomeing more plenty we furnished ourselvs with meat daily

But I pass on to the arickaree villages whare we met with our defeat on ariveing in sight of the villages the barr in front was lined with squaws packing up water thinking to have to stand a siege

For a better understanding it is necessay that I state tha[t] the Missourie furr company have established a small trading house some (60) or (80) miles below the arrickree villages the winter previous to our assent and the arrickarees haveing taken some Sioux squaws prisoners previously one of these Squaws got away from them and made for this trading post and they persuing come near overtaking her in sight of the post the men in the house ran out and fired on the Pesucing arrickarees killing (2) others so that Rees considered war was fully declared between them and the whites But genl. Asley thought he could make them understand that his [company] was not resposable for Injuries done by the Missourie fur company But the Rees could not make the distiction they however agreed to receive pay for thier loss but the geeneral would make them a present but would not pay the Misourie fur companies damages

After one days talk they agreed to open trade on the sand bar in front of the village but the onley article of Trade they wantd was ammunition For feare of a difficulty, the boats ware kept at anchor in the streame, and the skiffs were used for communications Betteen the boats and the shore we obtained twenty horses in three d[a]ys trading, but in doing this we gave them a fine supply of Powder and ball which on [the] fourth day wee found out to [our] Sorrow

In the night of the third day Several of our men without permition went and remained in the village amongst them our Interperter Mr Rose about midnight he came runing into camp & informed us that one of our men was killed in the village and war was declared in earnest We had no Military organization diciplin or Subordination Several advised to cross over the river at once but thought best to wait untill day light But Gnl. Ashley our imployer Thought best to wait till morning and go into the village and demand the body of our comrade and his Murderer Ashley being the most interested his advice prevailed We laid on our arms e[x]pecting an attact as their was a continual Hubbub in the village

At length morning appeared every thing still undecided finally one shot was fired into our camp the distance being however to great for certain aim Shortly firing became Quite general we seeing nothing to fire at Here let me give a Short discription of an Indian City or village as it is usually called Picture to your self (50) or (100) large potatoe holes as they are usuly caled in the west (10) to (15) feet in diameter and 8 to 10 feet high in the center covered on the outside with small willow brush then a (a) layer of coarse grass a coat of earth over all a hole in one side for a door and another in the top to let out the smoke a small fire in the center *all Told* The continual wars between them and Sioux had caused them to picket in their place You will easely prceive that we had little else to do than to Stand on a bear sand barr and be shot at, at long range Their being seven or Eigh hundred guns in village and we having the day previously furnished them with abundance of Powder and Ball [There were] many calls for the boats to come ashore and take us on board but no prayers or threats had the [slightest effect] the Boats men being completely Parylized Several men being wounded a skiff was brought ashore all rushed for the Skiff and came near sinking it but it went the boat full of men and water the shot still coming thicker and the aim better we making a brest work of our horses (most) they nerly all being killed the skiffs having taken sevarl loads on Board the boats at length the shot coming thicker and faster one of the skiffs (was turned) was let go the men clambering on Board let the skiff float off in their great eaganess to conceal themselves from the rapid fire of the enemy I seeing no hopes of Skiffs or boats comeing ashore left my hiding place behind a dead hors, ran up stream a short distance to get the advantage of the current and concieving myself to be a tolerable strong swimer stuck the muzzle of my rifle in [my] belt the lock ove my head with all my clothes on but not having made sufficien calculation for the strong current was carried passed the boat within a few feet of the same one Mr Thomas Eddie [saw me] but the shot coming thick he did not venture from behin the cargo Box and so could not reach me with a setting pole which [he] held in his hands K[n]owing now or at [least] thinking that I had the river to swim my first aim was to rid myself of all my encumbraces and my Rifle was the greatest in my attempt to draw it over my head it sliped down the lock ketching in my belt comeing to the surface to breathe I found it hindred worse than it did at first making one more effort I turned the lock side ways and it sliped through which gave me some relief but still finding myself to much encumbred I next unbucled my belt and let go my Pistols still continueing to disengage my self I next let go my Ball Pouch and finally one Sleeve of my Hunting shirt which was buckskin and held an immence weight of water when rising to the surface I heard the voice of encoragemnt saying hold on Clyman I will soon relieve you. This [from] Reed Gibson who had swam in and caught the skiff the men had let go afloat and was but a few rods from me I was so much exausted that he had to haul me into the skiff wh[ere] I lay for a moment to catch breath when I arose to take the only remaing ore when Gibson caled oh, god I am shot and fell forward in the skiff I encouraged him and [said] Perhaps not fatally give a few pulls more and we will be out of reach he raised and gave sevreral more strokes with the oar using it as a paddle when [he] co[m]plained of feeling faint when he fell forward again and I took his plac in the sterm and shoved it across to the East shore whare we landed I hauled the skiff up on the shore and told Gibson to remain in the Skiff and I would go upon the high land whare I could see if any danger beset us thair. After getting up on the river bank and looking around I Discovered sevral Indian in the water swimming over [some] of whoom ware nearly across the stream I spoke to Gibson telling him of the circumstance he mearly said save yourself Clyman and pay no attention to me as I am a dead man and they can get nothing of me but my Scalp My first Idea was to get in the skiff and meet them in the water and brain them with the oar But on second look I conconcluded there ware to many of them and they ware too near the shore then I looked for some place to hide But there being onley a scant row of brush along the shore I concluded to take to the open Pararie and run for life by this time Gibson had scrambled up the bank and stood by my side and said run Clyman but if you escape write to my friends in Virginia and tell them what has become of me I [ran] for the open Prarie and Gibson for the brush to hide at first I started a little distance down the river but fearing that I might be headed in some bend I steered directly for the open Prarie and looking Back I saw three Inians mount the bank being intirely divested of garments excepting a belt aroun the waist containing a Knife and Tomahawk and Bows and arrows in their [hands] they made but little halt and started after me one to the right the other to the left while the third took direct after me I took direct for the rising ground I think about three miles of[f] there being no chanc for dodging the ground being smooth and level but haveing the start of some 20 or 30 rods we had appearantle an even race for about one hour when I began to have the palpitation of the heart and I found my man was gaining on me I had now arived at a moderately roling ground and for the first time turned a hill out of sight I turned to the right and found a hole was[h]ed in the earth some 3 feet long 1½ feet wide and Pehaps 2 feet deep with weeds and grass perhaps one foot high surrounding it into this hole I droped and persuer immediatle hove in sight and passed me about fifty yards distant both my right an left hand persuers haveing fallen cosiderably in the rear and particularly the one on my right here fortune favoured me for my direct persuer soon passed over some uneven ground got out of sight when I arose and taking to the right struck into a low ground which covered me and following it soon came into a moderately steep ravine in all this time I gained breath and I did not see my persuers until I gained the top of the ridge over a Quarter of a mile from my friend when I gained this elevation I turned around [and saw] the three standing near togather I made them a low bow with both my hand and thanked god for my present Safety and diliveranc

But I did not remain long here wishing to put the gratest possible distance between me and the Arrickarees I still continued Southward over a smoothe roling ground But what ware my reflection being at least Three Hundred miles from any assistanc unarmed and u[n]provided with any sort of means of precureing a subsistance not even a pocket Knife I began to feel after passing So many dangers that my pro[s]pects ware still verry slim mounting some high land I saw ahed of me the river and Quite a grove of timber and being verry thirsty I made for the water intending to take a good rest in the timber I took one drink of water and setting down on a drift log a few minuits I chanced to look [at] the [river] and here came the boats floating down the stream the [men] watcing along the shores saw me about as soon as I saw them the boat was laid in and I got aboard

I spoke of my friend Gibson whe[n] I was informed he was on board I immediately wen[t] to the cabin whare he lay but he did not recognize me being in the agonies of Death the shot having passed through his bowels I could not refrain from weeping over him who lost his lifee but save mine he did not live but an hour or so and we buried him that evening the onley one of (12) that ware killed at the arrickarees Eleven being left on the sand bar and their Scalps taken for the Squaws to sing and dance over

Before meeting with this defeat I think few men had Stronger Ideas of their bravery and disregard of fear than I had but standing on a bear and open sand barr to be shot at from bihind a picketed Indian village was more than I had contacted for and some what cooled my courage.

THE HUDSON'S BAY COMPANY INVADES THE ROCKIES

As though the Indians were not a sufficient menace, American trappers in the northern Rockies came face-to-face with a formidable rival. Britain's venerable Hudson's Bay Company in 1824 established Fort Vancouver on the banks of the Columbia River in modern-day Oregon and from there sent its "brigades" into the interior. These colorful caravans of traders, trappers, and Indians roamed far and wide in their quest for beaver pelts, exploring the central valleys of California, venturing into the Great Basin country, and invading the northern Rocky Mountains. There in 1825 one of the most capable brigade leaders, Peter Skene Ogden, recorded in his journal a meeting with a party of American traders—a meeting that forecast the bitter rivalry that was to come:[4]

Monday 23rd Remd. in Camp in expectation of the arrival of our absent party, early in the day a party of 15 men Canadians & Spaniards headed by one Provost & Francois one of our deserters, arrived, and also in the afternoon arrived in Company with 14 of our absent men a party of 25 Americans with Colours flying the latter party headed by one Gardner they encamped within 100 yards of our encampment & lost no time in informing all hands in the Camp that they were in the United States Territories & were all free indebted or engaged & to add to this they would pay Cash for their Beaver 3½ dollars p. lb., & their goods cheap in proportion our Freemen in lieu of Seeking Beaver have been with the Americans no doubt plotting.

Tuesday 24th This morning Gardner came to my Tent & after a few words of no import, he questioned me as follows Do you know in whose Country you are? to which I made answer that I did not as it was not determined between Great Britain & America to whom it belonged, to which he made answer that it was that it had been ceded to the latter & as I had no licence to trap or trade to return from whence I came to this I made answer when we receive orders from the British Government we Shall obey, then he replied remain at your peril, he then departed & seeing him go into John Grey an American & half Iroquois Tent one of my Freemen I followed him, on entering this Villain Grey said I must now tell you that all the Iroquois as well as myself have long wished for an opportunity to join the Amer-

---

[4] E. E. Rich and A. M. Johnson (eds.), *Peter Skene Ogden's Snake Country Journals, 1824–26* (London: Hudson's Bay Record Society, 1950), pp. 51–56. Reprinted by permission of the Hudson's Bay Record Society.

icans & if we did not Sooner it was owing to our bad luck in not meeting with them, but now we go & all you Can Say Cannot prevent us, Gardner was Silent having only made one remark as follows, you have had these men already too long in your Service & have most Shamefully imposed on them selling them goods at high prices & giving them nothing for their Skins on which he retired, Grey then said that is true and alluding to the gentlemen he had been with in the Columbia they are Says he the greatest Villains in the World & if they were here this day I would Shoot them but as for you Sir you have dealt fair with me & with us all, but go we will we are now in a free Country & have Friends here to Support us & if every man in the Camp does not leave you they do not Seek their own interest, he then gave orders to his Partners to raise Camp & immediately all the Iroquois were in motion, & made ready to Start this example was Soon followed by others at this time the Americans headed by Gardner & accompanied by two of our Iroquois who had been with them the last two years advanced to Support & assist all who were inclined to desert, Lazard an Iroquois now Called out we are Superior in numbers to them let us fire & pillage them on Saying this he advanced with his Gun Cocked & pointed at me but finding I was determined not to allow him or others to pillage us of our Horses as they had already taken two say Old Pierres which had been lent him, they desisted & we Secured the ten Horses but not without enduring the most opprobious terms they could think of from both Americans & Iroquois all this time with the exception of Messrs. Kittson & McKay & two of the engaged men & the latter not before they were Called Came to our assistance thus we were overpowered by numbers & these Villains 11 in number with Duford, Perrault and Kanota escaped with their Furs in fact some of them had conveyed theirs in the night to the American Camp. A Carson & Annance paid their debts & followed the example of the others, I cannot but Consider it a fortunate Circumstance I did not fire for had I I have not the least doubt all was gone, property & furs indeed this was their plan that I should fire & assuredly they did all they Could to make me but I was fully aware of their plan & by that means Saved what remains—they Started & encamped about half a mile from us. From the above affair I am now Convinced the 6 absent men they have Secured & it would be folly in me to delay my departure for their arrival, indeed I fear many of the Freemen will yet leave us.

Wednesday 25th Late last evening I was informed the Iroquois & Americans intended to attack & pillage the Camp on hearing this I conversed with Some of the Freemen & engaged men to know if they would assist in defending the Company's property in Case of attack and they Said they would we made all necessary preparations in Case of *attack* & kept Strict guard during the Night, at day light I gave the Call to raise Camp, scarcely had we begun loading our Horses, when the Americans & three of our Iroquois Came to our Camp but finding us prepared kept quiet Soon after Mr. Montour, Clement & Prudhomme came forward & told me they intended joining the Americans that they were free & not indebted I endeavoured to reason with Mr. Montour but all in vain, the reasons he gave for his villany were the Company turned me out of doors they have £260 of my money in their hands which they intend to defraud me of as they have refused to give me interest for but they may keep it now for my debt & Prudhoms. which we have Contracted in the Columbia as for Clement he has a Balce. in the Compys. Book; go we will where we shall be paid for our Furs &

not be imposed & cheated as we are in the Columbia—they were immediately Surrounded by the Americans who assisted them in loading & like all Villains appeared to exult in their Villany we then Started but on my mounting my Horse Gardner Came forward & Said you will See us shortly not only in the Columbia but at the Flat Heads & Cootanies as we are determined you Shall no longer remain in our Territory, to this I made answer when we Should receive orders from our Government to leave the Columbia we would but Not before to this he replied our Troops will make you this Fall we then parted & proceeded to our encampment of the 19th Inst. and encamped. Here I am now with only 20 Trappers Surrounded on all Sides by enemies & our expectations & hopes blasted for returns this year, to remain in this quarter any longer it would merely be to trap Beaver for the Americans for I Seriously apprehend there are Still more of the Trappers who would Willingly join them indeed the tempting offers made them independant the low price they Sell their goods are too great for them to resist & altho' I represented to them all these offers were held out to them as so many baits Still it is without effect I have now no other alternative left but direct my Course towards of Salmon River without loss of time to follow up my Second intentions in proceeding by the Walla Walla *route* is now in a manner rendered impracticable as our numbers are by far too few, as nearly one half of the Trappers are determined to return to Fort des Prairies so if we divide again neither party would Stand a chance of ever reaching the Columbia, there is now No alternative I must bend & Submit to the will of the party.

Thursday 26th   Late last evening two of the six absent men joined us they had Seen nothing of the remaining four By their accounts as they were on their return to the Camp yesterday they fell in an American party from 30 to 40 men as they Say Troops, who on Seeing them Called to them to advance which they did, their traps 15 in number 16 Beaver & their two Horses were taken from them they were then told if they would remain with them & not return & Join me their property would be restored to them otherwise not, they were Strictly guarded during the day & while in the act of changing Watches about midnight last night they effected their escape leaving all behind them how far this is Correct I cannot Say it may be probably made to Suit intentions as they have both Women & Horses perhaps they will now Watch an opportunity to return if they do which they Can easily effect without their Furs both day & night we shall however watch them, we raised Camp & encamped at our encampment of the 14th. 5 Beavers were taken.

May—Friday 27th   Raised Camp & came to our encampment of the 9th. Cloudy weather rain during the day only 1 Beaver altho' many Traps in the Water, it does not appear from our success now that we left many behind as we went along. Our Camp is now dull & gloomy.

Saturday 28th   We Strongly suspect this morning that a party is forming to desert this they Can easily effect at any time but with their Furs not conveniently we raised Camp & came to our Encampment of the 3d on Bear River here we found the Water had risen three feet since we were last here we lost no time in making rafts of rushes & had the greater part of the Freemens furs & Traps Crossed over Strongly guarded.

Sunday 29th   Three men deserted leaving all behind them Women, Children Horses, Traps & Furs so greatly are they prepossessed in favor of the Americans that they sacrificed all to join them. I cannot make too great progress otherwise I apprehend many more will leave us, our Numbers are now So few that if any war party Comes across us we shall Stand a poor chance of escaping, we Crossed over the remainder of our property & Horses & proceeded in a north west Course direct to the Snake River. Weather fair. 2 Beavers—we Came 18 miles & encamped on a Small Creek destitute of Beaver.

FUR TRADE IN THE DESERT SOUTHWEST

If trade in the northern Rockies was plagued by hostile Indians and stubborn Britishers, trade in the southern Rockies revealed an even more insurmountable obstacle. Americans began to invade the region in the 1820s, venturing westward from Taos and Santa Fe into the Gila River country and as far as California. There they found no troublesome rivals comparable to the Hudson's Bay Company employees and no Indians as savage as the Blackfoot, but the arid deserts of the Southwest proved to be an even deadlier foe. A glimpse of the hardships faced by trappers as they struggled to cross the barren wastes near modern Yuma is given in the chronicles of James Ohio Pattie, one of the most colorful if not the most accurate recorders of events on the southwestern frontier:[5]

We started on the 26th, with our two [Indian] guides, neither of whom could speak Spanish, and of course we had nothing to do but follow them in silence. We struck off a south west course, which led in the direction of the snow covered mountain, which still loomed up in its brightness before us. Our guides made signs that we should arrive at the foot about midnight, though the distance appeared to us to be too great to be travelled over in so short a time. We were yet to learn, that we should find no water, until we drank that of the melted snow. We perceived, however, that their travelling gait, worn as we were, was more rapid than ours. We pushed on as fast as we could a league further, when we were impeded by a high hill in our way, which was about another league to the summit, and very precipitous and steep. When we reached the top of it we were much exhausted, and began to be thirsty. We could then see the arid salt plain stretching all the way from the foot of this hill to the snow covered mountains.

We thought it inexpedient to enquire of our guides, if there was no water to be found between us and the mountain. It appeared but too probable, that such was the fact. To know it to a certainty, would only tend to unnerve and dishearten us. If there was any, we were aware that we should reach it by travelling no more distance than as if we knew the fact. We found it best to encourage the little hope that remained, and hurried on through the drifted sand, in which we sank up to our ankles at every step. The cloudless sun poured such a blaze upon it, that by the scorching of our feet, it might have seemed almost hot enough to roast eggs in. What with the fierce sun and the scorching sand, and our extreme fatigue, the air seemed soon to have extracted every particle of moisture from our bodies. In this condition we marched on until nearly the middle of the day, without descrying any indication of water in any quarter. A small shrubby tree stood in our way, affording a tolerable shade. We laid ourselves down to get a few minutes rest. The Indians sternly beckoned us to be up and onward, now for the first time clearly explaining to us, that there was no water until we reached the mountains in view. This

---

[5] James Ohio Pattie, *Personal Narrative of James O. Pattie of Kentucky* (Cincinnati, 1831), pp. 158–165.

unseasonable and yet necessary information, extinguished the last remainder of our hope, and we openly expressed our fears that we should none of us ever reach it.

We attempted to chew tobacco. It would raise no moisture. We took our bullets in our mouths, and moved them round to create a moisture, to relieve our parched throats. We had travelled but a little farther before our tongues had became so dry and swollen, that we could scarcely speak so as to be understood. In this extremity of nature, we should, perhaps, have sunk voluntarily, had not the relief been still in view on the sides of the snow covered mountains. We resorted to one expedient to moisten our lips, tongue and throat, disgusting to relate, and still more disgusting to adopt. In such predicaments it has been found, that nature disburdens people of all conditions of ceremony and disgust. Every thing bends to the devouring thirst, and the love of life. The application of this hot and salt liquid seemed rather to enrage than appease the torturing appetite. Though it offered such a semblance of what would satisfy thirst, that we economized every particle. Our amiable Dutchman was of a sweetness of temper, that was never ruffled, and a calmness and patience that appeared proof against all events. At another time, what laughter would have circulated through our camp, to hear him make merry of this expedient! As it was, even in this horrible condition, a faint smile circulated through our company as he discussed his substitute for drink. 'Vell, mine poys, dis vater of mein ish more hotter as hell, und as dick as boudden, und more zalter as de zeas. I can't drink him. For Cod's sake, gif me some of yours, dat is more tinner.'

Having availed ourselves to the utmost of this terrible expedient, we marched on in company a few miles further. Two of our companions here gave out, and lay down under the shade of a bush. Their tongues were so swollen, and their eyes so sunk in their heads, that they were a spectacle to behold. We were scarcely able, from the condition of our own mouths, to bid them an articulate farewell. We never expected to see them again, and none of us had much hope of ever reaching the mountain, which still raised its white summit at a great distance from us. It was with difficulty that we were enabled to advance one foot before the other. Our limbs, our powers, even our very resolutions seemed palsied. A circumstance that added to our distress, was the excessive and dazzling brightness of the sun's rays, so reflected in our eyes from the white sand that we were scarcely able to see our way before us, or in what direction to follow our guides. They, accustomed to go naked, and to traverse these burning deserts, and be unaffected by such trials, appeared to stand the heat and drought, like camels on the Arabian sands. They, however, tried by their looks and gestures to encourage us, and induce us to quicken our pace. But it was to no purpose. However, we still kept moving onward, and had gained a few miles more, when night brought us shelter at least from the insupportable radiance of the sun, and something of coolness and moisture.

But it was so dark, that neither we or our guides could discover the course. We stopped, and made a large fire, that our companions, if yet living, and able to move, might see where we were, and how to direct ther own course to reach us. We also fired some guns, which, to our great relief and pleasure, they answered by firing off theirs. We still repeated firing guns at intervals, until they came up with us. They supposed that we had found water, which invigorated their spirits to such a degree, that it aroused them to the effort they had made. When they had arrived, and found that we had reached no water, they appeared to be angry, and to complain that we had disturbed their repose with false hopes, and had hindered their dying in peace. One of them in the recklessness of despair, drew from his package a small phial, half full of laudanum, and drank it off, I suppose in the hope of sleeping himself quietly to death. We all expected it would have that effect. On the contrary, in a few moments he was exhilarated like a man in a state of intoxication. He was full of talk, and laughter, and gaiety of heart. He observed, that he had taken it in hopes that it would put him to sleep, never to wake again, but that in fact, it had made him as well, and as fresh, as in the morning when he started; but that if he had imagined that it would prove such a sovereign remedy for thirst, he would cheerfully have shared it with us. We scraped down beneath the burning surface of the sand, until we reached the earth that was a little cool. We then stripped off all our clothing and lay down. Our two Indians, also lay down beside us, covering themselves with their blankets. My father bade me lay on the edge of one of their blankets, so that they could not get up without awakening me. He was fearful that they would arise, and fly from us in the night. I implicitly conformed to my father's wish, for had this event happened, we should all undoubtedly have perished. But the Indians appear to have meditated no such expedient, at any rate, they lay quiet until morning.

As soon as there was light enough to enable us to travel we started, much refreshed by the coolness of the night, and the sleep we had taken. We began our morning march with renewed alacrity. At about ten in the forenoon we arrived at the foot of a sand hill about a half a mile in height, and very steep. The side was composed of loose sand, which gave way under our feet, so that our advancing foot steps would slide back to their former places. This soon exhausted our little remaining strength; though we still made many an unavailing effort to ascend. The sun was now so high, as to beam upon us with the same insufferable radiance of yesterday. The air which we inhaled, seemed to scald our lungs. We at length concluded to travel towards the north, to reach, if we might, some point where the hill was not so steep to ascend. At two in the afternoon we found a place that was neither so steep nor so high, and we determined here to attempt to cross the hill. With great exertions and infinite difficulty, a part of us gained the summit of the hill; but my father and another of our company, somewhat advanced in years, gave out below, though they made the most persevering efforts to reach the summit of the hill with the rest. Age had stiffened their joints, and laid his palsying hand upon their once active limbs, and vigorous frames. They could endure this dreadful journey no longer. They had become so exhausted by fruitless efforts to climb the hill, that they could no longer drag one foot after the other. They had each so completely abandoned the hope of ever reaching the water, or even gaining the summit of the hill, that they threw themselves on the ground, apparently convinced of their fate, and resigned to die. I instantly determined to remain with my father, be it for life or death. To this determination he would by no means consent, as he remarked it would bring my destruction, without its availing him. On the contrary, he insisted, that I should go on with the rest, and if I found any water near at hand, that I should return with my powder horn full. In this way he assured me, I might be instrumental in saving my own life, and saving him at the same time. To this I consented, and with much fatigue gained the summit of the hill, where my companions were seated waiting for us. They seemed undetermined, whether to advance onward, or wait for my father, until I related his determination. My purpose was to proceed onward only so far, as that, if the Almighty should enable us to reach water, I might be able to return with a powder horn full to him and Mr. Slover, (for that was the name of the elderly companion that remained with him.)

This resolution was agreed to by all, as a proper one. Being satisfied by our consciences as well as by the reasoning of my father and his companion, that we could render them no service by remaining with them, except to increase their sufferings by a view of ours; and aware, that every moment was precious, we pushed on once more for the mountain. Having descended this hill, we ascended another of the same wearying ascent, and sandy character with the former. We toiled on to the top of it. The Eternal Power, who hears the ravens when they cry, and provideth springs in the wilderness, had had mercy upon us! Imagine my joy at seeing a clear, beautiful running stream of water, just below us at the foot of the hill! Such a blissful sight I had never seen before, and never expect to see again. We all ran down to it, and fell to drinking. In a few moments nothing was to be heard among us, but vomiting and groaning. Notwithstanding our mutual charges to be cautious, we had overcharged our parched stomachs with this cold snow water.

Notwithstanding I was sick myself, I emptied my powder horn of its contents, filled it with water, and accompanied by one companion, who had also filled his powder horn, I returned towards my father and Mr. Slover, his exhausted companion, with a quick step. We found them in the same position in which we had left them, that is, stretched on the sand at full length, under the unclouded blaze of the sun, and both fast asleep; a sleep from which, but for our relief, I believe they would neither of them ever have awakened. Their lips were black, and their parched mouths wide open. Their unmoving posture and their sunken eyes so resembled death, that I ran in a fright to my father, thinking him, for a moment, really dead. But he easily awakened, and drank the refreshing water. My companion at the same time bestowed his horn of water upon Mr. Slover. In the course of an hour they were both able to climb the hill, and some time before dark we rejoined the remainder of our company. They had kindled a large fire, and all seemed in high spirits. As for our two Indians, they were singing, and dancing, as it seemed to us, in a sort of worship of thankfulness to the Great Spirit, who had led them through so much peril and toil to these refreshing waters. We roasted some of our beaver meat, and took food for the first time in forty-eight hours, that is to say, from the time we left our Indian friends, until we reached this water. Our Dutchman insisted that the plain over which we passed, should be named the devil's plain, for he insisted, that it was more hotter as hell, and that none but teyvils could live upon it. In fact, it seemed a more fitting abode for fiends, than any living thing that belongs to our world. During our passage across it, we saw not a single bird, nor the track of any quadruped, or in fact any thing that had life, not even a sprig, weed or grass blade, except a single shrubby tree, under which we found a little shade. This shrub, though of some height, resembled a prickly pear, and was covered thick with thorns. The prickly pears were in such abundance, that we were often, dazzled as our eyes were with the sun's brightness, puzzled to find a path so as neither to torment our feet or our bodies with the thorns of these hated natives of the burning sands. This very extensive plain, the Sahara of California, runs north and south, and is bounded on each side by high barren mountains, some of which are covered with perpetual snow.

On the 28th, we travelled up this creek about three miles, and killed a deer, which much delighted our two Indian guides. At this point we encamped for the night. Here are abundance of palm trees and live oaks, and considerable of mascal. We remained until the 3d of March, when we marched up this creek, which heads to the south, forming a low gap in the mountain. On the 7th, we arrived at the point, and found some of the Christian Indians from the Mission of St. Catharine. They were roasting mascal and the tender inside heads of the palm trees for food, which, when prepared and cooked after their fashion, becomes a very agreeable food. From these Indians we learned that we were within four days' travel of the mission mentioned above.

FUR TRADE AND RENDEZVOUS IN THE CENTRAL ROCKIES

With the northern and southern hunting grounds both too dangerous to provide assured profits, American trappers turned naturally to the central Rockies. The trading genius who first developed this area was William Henry Ashley who, after his defeat by the Arikara in 1823, sent an overland party under Jedediah Strong Smith westward to investigate rumors of a beaver-rich river beyond the mountains. Crossing the Rockies through South Pass, Smith and his men stumbled on the Green River, which proved to be all that rumor had proclaimed it. A jubilant Ashley started west as soon as the news reached him and there solved the principal problem of the fur trade in the Far West: that of supply. Instead of sending out parties of trappers each spring he proposed that the trappers stay in the mountains, to be supplied by an annual caravan from St. Louis. Thus originated the most colorful of the West's institutions, the "rendezvous." Each year thereafter a lengthy train of pack mules laden with ammunition, traps, knives, sugar, coffee, tea, alcohol, and other necessities that nature could not provide reached a designated point where several hundred "mountain men" and as many more friendly Indians awaited its arrival. For a week or more trading went on as the trappers exchanged their "hairy bank notes," the beaver pelts, for the long-forgotten goods of civilization. George F. Ruxton, a British writer who enjoyed a long love affair with the American West and vividly described the mountain men, attended a typical rendezvous during the heyday of the fur trade:[6]

The trappers of the Rocky Mountains belong to a "genus" more approximating to the primitive savage than perhaps any other class of civilized man. Their lives being spent in the remote wilderness of the mountains, with no other companion than Nature herself, their habits and character assume a most singular cast of simplicity mingled with ferocity, appearing to take their colouring from the scenes and objects which surround them. Knowing no wants save those of nature, their sole care is to procure sufficient food to support life, and the necessary clothing to protect them from the rigorous climate. This, with the assistance of their trusty rifles, they are generally able to effect, but sometimes at the expense of great peril and hardship. When engaged in their avocation, the natural instinct of primitive man is ever alive, for the purpose of guarding against danger and the provision of necessary food. Keen observers of nature, they rival the beasts of prey in discovering the haunts and

---

[6] George F. Ruxton, *Adventures in Mexico and the Rocky Mountains* (London, 1849), pp. 241–246.

habits of game, and in their skill and cunning in capturing it. Constantly exposed to perils of all kinds, they become callous to any feeling of danger, and destroy human as well as animal life with as little scruple and as freely as they expose their own. Of laws, human or divine, they neither know nor care to know. Their wish is their law, and to attain it they do not scruple as to ways and means. Firm friends and bitter enemies, with them it is "a word and a blow," and the blow often first. They may have good qualities, but they are those of the animal; and people fond of giving hard names call them revengeful, bloodthirsty, drunkards (when the wherewithal is to be had), gamblers, regardless of the laws of *meum* and *tuum*—in fact, "White Indians." However, there are exceptions, and I *have* met honest mountain-men. Their animal qualities, however, are undeniable. Strong, active, hardy as bears, daring, expert in the use of their weapons, they are just what uncivilised white man might be supposed to be in a brute state, depending upon his instinct for the support of life. Not a hole or corner in the vast wilderness of the "Far West" but has been ransacked by these hardy men. From the Mississippi to the mouth of the Colorado of the West, from the frozen regions of the North to the Gila in Mexico, the beaver-hunter has set his traps in every creek and stream. All this vast country, but for the daring enterprise of these men, would be even now a *terra incognita* to geographers, as indeed a great portion still is; but there is not an acre that has not been passed and repassed by the trappers in their perilous excursions. The mountains and streams still retain the names assigned to them by the rude hunters; and these alone are the hardy pioneers who have paved the way for the settlement of the western country.

Trappers are of two kinds, the "hired hand" and the "free trapper:" the former hired for the hunt by the fur companies; the latter, supplied with animals and traps by the company, is paid a certain price for his furs and peltries.

There is also the trapper "on his own hook;" but this class is very small. He has his own animals and traps, hunts where he chooses, and sells his peltries to whom he pleases.

On starting for a hunt, the trapper fits himself out with the necessary equipment, either from the Indian trading-forts, or from some of the petty traders—coureurs des bois —who frequent the western country. This equipment consists usually of two or three horses or mules—one for saddle, the others for packs—and six traps, which are carried in a bag of leather called a *trap-sack*. Ammunition, a few pounds of tobacco, dressed deer-skins for mocassins, &c., are carried in a wallet of dressed buffalo-skin, called a possible-sack. His "possibles" and "trap-sack" are generally carried on the saddle-mule when hunting, the others being packed with the furs. The costume of the trapper is a hunting-shirt of dressed buckskin, ornamented with long fringes; pantaloons of the same material, and decorated with porcupine-quills and long fringes down the outside of the leg. A flexible felt hat and mocassins clothe his extremities. Over his left shoulder and under his right arm hang his powder-horn and bullet-pouch, in which he carries his balls, flint and steel, and odds and ends of all kinds. Round the waist is a belt, in which is stuck a large butcher-knife in a sheath of buffalo-hide, made fast to the belt by a chain or guard of steel; which also supports a little buckskin case containing a whetstone. A tomahawk is also often added; and, of course, a long heavy rifle is part and parcel of his equipment. I had nearly forgotten the pipe-holder, which hangs round his neck, and is generally a gage d'amour, and a triumph of squaw workmanship, in shape of a heart, garnished with beads and porcupine-quills.

Thus provided, and having determined the locality of his trapping-ground, he starts to the mountains, sometimes alone, sometimes with three or four in company, as soon as the breaking up of the ice allows him to commence operations. Arrived on his hunting-grounds, he follows the creeks and streams, keeping a sharp look-out for "sign." If he sees a prostrate cotton-wood tree, he examines it to discover if it be the work of beaver—whether "thrown" for the purpose of food, or to dam the stream. The track of the beaver on the mud or sand under the bank is also examined; and if the "sign" be fresh, he sets his trap in the run of the animal, hiding it under water, and attaching it by a stout chain to a picket driven in the bank, or to a bush or tree. A "float-stick" is made fast to the trap by a cord a few feet long, which, if the animal carry away the trap, floats on the water and points out its position. The trap is baited with the "medicine," an oily substance obtained from a gland in the scrotum of the beaver, but distinct from the testes. A stick is dipped into this and planted over the trap; and the beaver, attracted by the smell, and wishing a close inspection, very foolishly puts his leg into the trap, and is a "gone beaver."

When a lodge is discovered, the trap is set at the edge of the dam, at the point where the animal passes from deep to shoal water, and always under water. Early in the morning the hunter mounts his mule and examines the traps. The captured animals are skinned, and the tails, which are a great dainty, carefully packed into camp. The skin is then stretched over a hoop or framework of osier-twigs, and is allowed to dry, the flesh and fatty substance being carefully scraped (grained). When dry, it is folded into a square sheet, the fur turned inwards, and the bundle, containing about ten to twenty skins, tightly pressed and corded, and is ready for transportation.

During the hunt, regardless of Indian vicinity, the fearless trapper wanders far and near in search of "sign." His nerves must ever be in a state of tension, and his mind ever present at his call. His eagle eye sweeps round the country, and in an instant detects any foreign appearance. A turned leaf, a blade of grass pressed down, the uneasiness of the wild animals, the flight of birds, are all paragraphs to him written in nature's legible hand and plainest language. All the wits of the subtle savage are called into play to gain an advantage over the wily woodsman; but with the natural instinct of primitive man, the white hunter has the advantages of a civilised mind, and, thus provided, seldom fails to outwit, under equal advantages, the cunning savage.

Sometimes, following on his trail, the Indian watches him set his traps on a shrub-belted stream, and, passing up the bed, like Bruce of old, so that he may leave no track, he lies in wait in the bushes until the hunter comes to examine his carefully-set traps. Then, waiting until he approaches his ambushment within a few feet, whiz flies the home-drawn arrow, never failing at such close quarters to bring the victim to the ground. For one white scalp, however, that dangles in the smoke of an Indian's lodge, a dozen black ones, at the end of the hunt, ornament the camp-fires of the rendezvous.

At a certain time, when the hunt is over, or they have loaded their pack-animals, the trappers proceed to the "rendezvous," the locality of which has been previously agreed upon; and here the traders and agents of the fur companies await them, with such assortment of goods as their hardy customers may require, including generally a fair supply of alcohol. The trappers drop in singly and in small bands, bringing their packs of beaver to this mountain market, not unfrequently to the value of a thousand dollars each, the produce of one hunt. The dissipation of the "rendezvous," however, soon turns the trapper's pocket inside out. The goods brought by the traders, although of the most inferior quality, are sold at enormous prices:—Coffee, twenty and thirty shillings a pint-cup, which is the usual measure; tobacco fetches ten and fifteen shillings a plug; alcohol, from twenty to fifty shillings a pint; gunpowder, sixteen shillings a pint-cup; and all other articles at proportionably exorbitant prices.

The "beaver" is purchased at from two to eight dollars per pound; the Hudson's Bay Company alone buying it by the pluie, or "plew," that is, the whole skin, giving a certain price for skins, whether of old beaver or "kittens."

The rendezvous is one continued scene of drunkenness, gambling, and brawling and fighting, as long as the money and credit of the trappers last. Seated, Indian fashion, round the fires, with a blanket spread before them, groups are seen with their "decks" of cards, playing at "euker," "poker," and "seven-up," the regular mountain-games. The stakes are "beaver," which here is current coin; and when the fur is gone, their horses, mules, rifles, and shirts, hunting-packs, and *breeches*, are staked. Daring gamblers make the rounds of the camp, challenging each other to play for the trapper's highest stake,—his horse, his squaw (if he have one), and, as once happened, his scalp. There goes "hos and beaver!" is the mountain expression when any great loss is sustained; and, sooner or later, "hos and beaver" invariably find their way into the insatiable pockets of the traders. A trapper often squanders the produce of his hunt, amounting to hundreds of dollars, in a couple of hours; and, supplied on credit with another equipment, leaves the rendezvous for another expedition, which has the same result time after time; although one tolerably successful hunt would enable him to return to the settlements and civilised life, with an ample sum to purchase and stock a farm, and enjoy himself in ease and comfort the remainder of his days.

An old trapper, a French Canadian, assured me that he had received fifteen thousand dollars for beaver during a sojourn of twenty years in the mountains. Every year he resolved in his mind to return to Canada, and, with this object, always converted his fur into cash; but a fortnight at the "rendezvous" always cleaned him out, and, at the end of twenty years, he had not even credit sufficient to buy a pound of powder.

These annual gatherings are often the scene of bloody duels, for over their cups and cards no men are more quarrelsome than your mountaineers. Rifles, at twenty paces, settle all differences, and, as may be imagined, the fall of one or other of the combatants is certain, or, as sometimes happens, both fall to the word "fire."

DECLINE OF THE FUR TRADE: THE FINAL RENDEZVOUS

Colorful as were the rendezvous, the days of this "Rocky Mountain fair" were numbered. The profits of as much as 2000 percent earned by the first caravans to carry trade goods westward brought a flood of competitors into the field, each interested in immediate returns rather than in preserving the fur-bearing animals. The ruthless quest for beaver that they encouraged led to overtrapping, until by the 1840s profits were declining precipitously. The sense of impending doom that presaged the near-extermination of the beaver quieted the rambunctious mountain men who attended the last of the rendezvous, turning those formerly rip-roaring gatherings into sober trading conclaves. One of these was described by Osburne Russell, perhaps the most reliable chronicler among the trappers:[7]

Here we found the hunting parties all assembled waiting for the arrival of supplies from the States. Here presented what might be termed a mixed multitude. The whites were chiefly Americans and Canadian French, with some Dutch, Scotch, Irish, English, halfbreed and fullblood Indians of nearly every tribe in the Rocky Mountains. Some were gambling at cards, some playing the Indian game of "hand" and others horse racing, while here and there could be seen small groups collected under shady trees relating the events of the past year, all in good spirits and health, for sickness is a stranger seldom met with in these regions. Sheep, elk, deer, buffalo and bear skins mostly supply the mountaineers with clothing, lodges and bedding, while the meat of the same animals supply them with food. They have not the misfortune to get any of the luxuries from the civilized world but once a year, and then in such small quantities that they last but a few days.

We had not remained in this quiet manner long before something new arose for our amusement. The Bannock Indians had for several years lived with the whites on terms partly hostile, frequently stealing horses and traps, and in one instance killed two white trappers. They had taken some horses and traps from a party of French trappers who were hunting Bear River in April previous, and they were now impudent enough to come with the village of sixty lodges and encamp within three miles of us in order to trade with the whites as usual, still having the stolen property in their possession and refusing to give it up. On the 15th of June four or five whites and two Nez Perce Indians went to their village and took the stolen horses (whilst the men were out hunting buffalo) and returned with them to our camp. About three o'clock p. m. of the same day thirty Bannocks came riding at full gallop up to the camp, armed with their war weapons. They rode into the midst and demanded the horses which the Nez Perces had taken saying they did not wish to fight with the whites. But the Nez Perces, who were only six in number, gave the horses to the whites for protection, which we were bound to give, as they were numbered among our trappers and far from their own tribe. Some of the Bannocks, on seeing this, started to leave the camp. One of them as he passed me observed that he did not come to fight the whites; but another, a fierce looking savage, who still stopped behind, called out to the others, saying, "We came to get our horses or blood and let us do it." I was standing near the speaker and understood what he said. I immediately gave the whites warning to be in readiness for an attack. Nearly all the men in camp were under arms. Mr. Bridger was holding one of the stolen horses by the bridle when one of the Bannocks rushed through the crowd, seized the bridle and attempted to drag it from Mr. Bridger by force, without heeding the cocked rifles that surrounded him any more than if they had been so many reeds in the hands of children. He was a brave Indian, but his bravery proved fatal to himself, for the moment he seized the bridle two rifle balls whistled through his body. The others wheeled to run, but twelve of them were shot

---

[7] Osburne Russell, *Journal of a Trapper, or Nine Years in the Rocky Mountains, 1834–1843* (Boise, Idaho: Syms-York Company, 1921), pp. 62–64.

from their horses before they were out of reach of rifle. We then mounted horses and pursued them, destroyed and plundered their village, and followed and fought them three days, when they begged us to let them go and promised to be good Indians in future. We granted their request and returned to our camp, satisfied that the best way to negotiate and settle disputes with hostile Indians is with the rifle, for that is the only pen that can write a treaty which they will not forget. Two days after we left them three white trappers, ignorant of what had taken place, went into their village and were treated in the most friendly manner. The Indians said, however, they had been fighting with the Blackfeet.

July 5th a party arrived from the States with supplies. The cavalcade consisted of forty-five men and twenty carts drawn by mules, under the direction of Mr. Thomas Fitzpatrick, accompanied by Capt. William Stewart on another tour of the Rocky Mountains.

Joy now beamed in every countenance. Some received letters from their friends and relations; some received the public papers and news of the day; others consoled themselves with the idea of getting a blanket, a cotton shirt or a few pints of coffee and sugar to sweeten it just by way of a treat, gratis, that is to say, by paying 2,000 per cent on the first cost by way of accommodation. For instance, sugar $2 per pint, coffee the same, blankets $20 each, tobacco $2 per pound, alcohol $4 per pint, and common cotton shirts $5 each, etc. And in return paid $4 or $5 per pound for beaver. In a few days the bustle began to subside. The furs were done up in packs ready for transportation to the States and parties were formed for the hunting the ensuing year. One party, consisting of 110 men, was destined for the Blackfoot country, under the direction of L. B. Fontanelle as commander and James Bridger as pilot. I started, with five others to hunt the headwaters of the Yellowstone, Missouri and Big Horn Rivers, a portion of the country I was particularly fond of hunting.

The decline of the fur trade coincided with the beginning of overland migration to the Far West. This was no coincidence. By the 1840s when the mountain men faded from the scene they had explored and advertised the whole trans-Missouri country until its features were known to every venturesome American on the Mississippi Valley frontier. Already propagandists were preaching the advantages of life in Oregon or California over a humdrum existence in Missouri or Illinois. The fur trappers who shuffled from the pages of history had no choice but to seek employment as "pilots" of the caravans of covered wagons that were ready to advance toward the Pacific. They had played their role in the drama of expansion; now they must yield the stage to the less glamorous farmers who would win all the Far West for the United States.

CHAPTER 17

The Mississippi Valley Frontier, 1810-1845

The Mississippi Valley was the staging area for the occupation of the Far West. There, in the tier of states bordering the Father of Waters, geographic, economic, and social conditions conspired during the 1830s and 1840s to create an atmosphere conducive to emigration and to develop a breed of men hardy and reckless enough to brave the dangers and hardships that lay ahead. The difficulties of migration to the remote Far West were so great that unusual conditions were necessary to set the tide rolling and unusual pioneers needed to survive the journey.

The settlement pattern within the valley helped explain the composition of the migrating stream. American frontiersmen began moving there shortly after the Louisiana Purchase, concentrating first about the commercial city of New Orleans with its predominantly French and Spanish population. By 1812, enough had arrived to justify statehood. Over the next few years, newcomers not only swelled Louisiana's population but engulfed the entire lower valley of the Mississippi, overrunning Missouri which entered the Union in 1821 and gradually filling Arkansas which followed in 1836. Thus the lower portions of the valley were comfortably filled even before the northern territories were opened to settlement. The great competition for good lands in the lower valley meant that most of those who migrated to the Far West were from this region.

PRIMITIVISM IN THE LOWER MISSISSIPPI VALLEY

The migrants were ideally suited to the conquest of a new frontier. Nearly all boasted the principal ingredient for success in a virgin land: experience in pioneering, for they or their fathers had moved from the East to the Mississippi Valley before deciding to move again. William Darby, who journeyed westward across Louisiana from New Orleans to the Sabine River in 1813, found every stage of civilization represented, from the highest to the most primitive, despite the state's 75,000 inhabitants:[1]

---

[1] William Darby, *The Emigrant's Guide to the Western and Southwestern States and Territories* (New York, 1818), pp. 61–62.

399

A journey from New Orleans to the mouth of the Sabine, exhibits man in every stage of his progress, from the palace to the hut, and inversely. To an observing eye, the rapid transition from the superb mansions of the wealthy citizens of New Orleans and its vicinity, to the rudely constructed log cabin, on the Sabine and Calcasiu, will suggest matter for the deepest reflection. In the short period of ten or fifteen days, can be viewed the moral revolutions of all ages. On a space of three hundred miles can be found human beings from the most civilized to the most savage. In the city of New Orleans, four or five of the most elegant of the living languages of the earth are now spoken in all their purity; and there is now enjoyed all that luxury and learning can bestow. Upon the banks of the Mississippi many of the sugar and cotton planters live in edifices, where, within and without, are exhibited all that art, aided by wealth, can produce. In Attacapas and Opelousas the glare of expensive luxury vanishes, and is followed by substantial independence. Often the loom occupies one part of the common sitting room or parlour of families that are really wealthy. The farm houses are generally rough, but solid buildings, in which the inhabitant enjoys good, wholesome, and abundant food, and excellent beds.

In the western parts of Opelousas are found those pastoral hunters, who recall to our imagination the primitive times of history. Their flocks and the chase furnish them with subsistence and occupation. Lodged in cabins rudely and hastily constructed, and really enjoying safety and plenty, it cannot be an illusion of fancy to consider these people as in possession of that object, *happiness*, that too often eludes the pursuit of men more highly cultivated. This is not a fancied picture; the writter often has, and particularly between the 3d and 15th of January, 1813, passed from the Sabine through Opelousas to New Orleans, and beheld, in reality, all the various gradations, to the contemplation of which he now invites his reader.

In the deep and solemn gloom of the Sabine woods, and the more imposing immensity of its prairies, has he often reflected upon the slow, but certain advance of the descendants of Europe in America. He considered himself as upon or near the line of contact, between two of those masses of civilized men, who have changed the political, religious, and moral state of this continent. The few inhabitants to be seen upon this confine of two empires, seem to indicate the utmost verge of inhabited earth, and the earliest dawn of human improvement. It is but justice to those men to say, that as far as the experience of the writer can enable him to judge of their character, they do ample justice to the long received opinion of the natural hospitality of man. He never once, in the course of many years, was turned away hungry from the door, or denied a nightly shelter under the roof of one of those apparently uncultivated sons of the forest. Oftentimes has he experienced from them, when weary and exhausted, a warm and generous reception, that many who repose on beds of down might blush to behold. From this honourable and true character, the much and very unjustly abused inhabitant of the Spanish Presidios is no exception. On an immense extent of territory these latter pursue exactly the same modes of life with the western people of Opelousas, and are distinguished by the same virtues.

There is a common and a vulgar observation very prevalent, in which the frontier inhabitants of Louisiana, the Spanish internal provinces, and even those of the United States, are assimilated to the native savage tribes, whose former residence these frontier men now occupy. Disgusting expressions, such as "they are just as bad as Indians"—"they are worse than savages"—"I would rather live amongst Choctaws or Shawnees," may be heard daily in some of the most polished circles, when speaking of the men that compose that hardy phalanx, whose generous bravery has oftentimes saved those declaimers from the tomahawk, scalping knife, or fire-brand of these same savages.

It may be asserted, without danger of contradiction, that the frontier men of the United States, the pastoral creole of Louisiana, and the horsemen of the Spanish internal provinces, are in a much greater degree superior to the aboriginal savages of America, in point of improvement, than they are inferior in mental endowments to the most polished society in Philadelphia, New-York, London, Paris, Rome, or Berlin. Whatever may be the cause, it is a fact, that the moral qualities of the American savages have been extolled far above their real merits, and the character of the pioneers of wealth, commerce, and education, depreciated in about the same ratio; and in both instances, pretended philosophy has made inductions in direct opposition to the facts upon which those inductions are supposed to be founded.

FRONTIER SOCIETY IN THE MISSISSIPPI VALLEY

Frontiering in the Mississippi Valley endowed pioneers with a restless energy, a foolhardy bravery, and a cocksure self-confidence that gave them a reputation unlike that earned by any other frontiersmen in history. To the rest of the nation they were fierce brawlers who settled every dispute with bowie knives and outdid the Indians in savagery and bloodthirsiness. Although unjustified, this image was easy to understand. In the past, the nonconformists who peopled the outer edges of frontiers had ranged far ahead of the settled areas, living as outlaws or squatters in the remote forests well beyond the reach of observers. Now they were hemmed in by the inhospitable environment that lay ahead and formed a disproportionate group within the population. Their numbers were augmented by the lawless elements who always concentrated in river valleys: raftsmen, gamblers, wood-lot operators, and the like. While the better elements far outnumbered the half-horse, half-alligator reprobates who gave the valley its bad name, the latter did bulk larger than normal in the social scene. And these outcasts made uncommonly fine colonizers. Timothy Flint, a New England minister who lived for a time in Missouri, accurately appraised their role in society:[2]

In approaching the country, I heard a thousand stories of gougings, and robberies, and shooting down with the rifle. I have travelled in these regions thousands of miles under all circumstances of exposure and danger. I have travelled alone, or in company only with such as needed protection, instead of being able to impart it; and this too, in many instances, where I was not known as a minister, or where such knowledge would have had no influence in protecting me. I never have carried the slightest weapon of defence. I scarcely remember to have experienced any thing that resembled insult, or to have felt myself in danger from the people. I have often seen men that had lost an eye. Instances of murder, numerous and horrible in their circumstances, have occurred in my vicinity. But they were such lawless rencounters, as terminate in murder every where, and in which the drunkenness, brutality, and violence were mutual. They

---

[2] Timothy Flint, *Recollections of the Last Ten Years* (Boston, 1826), pp. 175–178.

were catastrophes, in which quiet and sober men would be in no danger of being involved. When we look round these immense regions, and consider that I have been in settlements three hundred miles from any court of justice, when we look at the position of the men, and the state of things, the wonder is, that so few outrages and murders occur. The gentlemen of the towns, even here, speak often with a certain contempt and horror of the backwoodsmen. I have read, and not without feelings of pain, the bitter representations of the learned and virtuous Dr. Dwight, in speaking of them. He represents these vast regions, as a grand reservoir for the scum of the Atlantic states. He characterizes in the mass the emigrants from New England, as discontented coblers, too proud, too much in debt, too unprincipled, too much puffed up with self-conceit, too strongly impressed that their fancied talents could not find scope in their own country, to stay there. It is true there are worthless people here, and the most so, it must be confessed, are from New England. It is true there are gamblers, and gougers, and outlaws; but there are fewer of them, than from the nature of things, and the character of the age and the world, we ought to expect. But it is unworthy of the excellent man in question so to designate this people in the mass. The backwoodsman of the west, as I have seen him, is generally an amiable and virtuous man. His general motive for coming here is to be a freeholder, to have plenty of rich land, and to be able to settle his children about him. It is a most virtuous motive. And notwithstanding all that Dr. Dwight and Talleyrand have said to the contrary, I fully believe, that nine in ten of the emigrants have come here with no other motive. You find, in truth, that he has vices and barbarisms, peculiar to his situation. His manners are rough. He wears, it may be, a long beard. He has a great quantity of bear or deer skins wrought into his household establishment, his furniture, and dress. He carries a knife, or a dirk in his bosom, and when in the woods has a rifle on his back, and a pack of dogs at his heels. An Atlantic stranger, transferred directly from one of our cities to his door, would recoil from a rencounter with him. But remember, that his rifle and his dogs are among his chief means of support and profit. Remember, that all his first days here were passed in dread of the savages. Remember, that he still encounters them, still meets bears and panthers. Enter his door, and tell him you are benighted, and wish the shelter of his cabin for the night. The welcome is indeed seemingly ungracious: "I reckon you can stay," or "I suppose we must let you stay." But this apparent ungraciousness is the harbinger of every kindness that he can bestow, and every comfort that his cabin can afford. Good coffee, corn bread and butter, venison, pork, wild and tame fowls are set before you. His wife, timid, silent, reserved, but constantly attentive to your comfort, does not sit at the table with you, but like the wives of the patriarchs, stands and attends on you. You are shown to the best bed which the house can offer. When this kind of hospitality has been afforded you as long as you choose to stay, and when you depart, and speak about your bill, you are most commonly told with some slight mark of resentment, that they do not keep tavern. Even the flaxen-headed urchins will turn away from your money.

In all my extensive intercourse with these people, I do not recollect but one instance of positive rudeness and inhospitality. It was on the waters of the Cuivre of the upper Mississippi; and from a man to whom I had presented bibles, who had received the hospitalities of my house, who had invited me into his settlement to preach. I turned away indignantly from a cold and reluctant reception here, made my way from the house of this man,—who was a German and comparatively rich,—through deep and dark forests, and amidst the concerts of wolves howling on the neighbouring hills. Providentially, about midnight, I heard the barking of dogs at a distance, made my way to the cabin of a very poor man, who arose at midnight, took me in, provided supper, and gave me a most cordial reception.

With this single exception, I have found the backwoodsmen to be such as I have described; a hardy, adventurous, hospitable, rough, but sincere and upright race of people. I have received so many kindnesses from them, that it becomes me always to preserve a grateful and affectionate remembrance of them. If we were to try them by the standard of New England customs and opinions, that is to say, the customs of a people under entirely different circumstances, there would be many things in the picture, that would strike us offensively. They care little about ministers, and think less about paying them. They are averse to all, even the most necessary restraints. They are destitute of the forms and observances of society and religion; but they are sincere and kind without professions, and have a coarse, but substantial morality, which is often rendered more striking by the immediate contrast of the graceful bows, civility, and professions of their French Catholic neighbours, who have the observances of society and the forms of worship, with often but a scanty modicum of the blunt truth and uprightness of their unpolished neighbours.

In the towns of the upper country on the Mississippi, and especially in St. Louis, there is one species of barbarism, that is but too common; I mean the horrid practice of duelling. But be it remembered, this is the barbarism only of that small class that denominate themselves "the gentlemen." It cannot be matter of astonishment that these are common here, when we recollect, that the fierce and adventurous spirits are naturally attracted to these regions, and that it is a common proverb of the people, that when we cross the Mississippi, "we travel beyond the Sabbath."

MIGRATION TO THE UPPER VALLEY: THE IOWA FEVER

If the character of the settlers from the lower Mississippi Valley helped shape the settlement pattern in the Far West, so did the geographic distribution of population along the entire river valley. By the early 1830s, when Louisiana and Missouri had achieved statehood and Arkansas was soon to follow, the northern regions—later to become Iowa and Minnesota—were still virtually without permanent settlers. Hence the movement of pioneers out from the southern valley into the Far West was paralleled by a movement of newcomers into these virgin territories. Iowa was opened to settlement in 1833 when its eastern portions were purchased from the Indians; as the area filled, subsequent purchases made more and more land available. The "Iowa Fever" raged, infecting thousands upon thousands of men and women in the Old Northwest, the South, and Europe. This migratory stream was fed by effective propaganda, for newspaper editors and guidebook writers promoted the scattered forests and undulating prairies of the new territory as the garden of the world. A modern reader can understand the strength of their appeal in the eloquent prose of one guidebook author, Nathan H. Parker:[3]

---

[3] Nathan H. Parker, *Iowa As It Is in 1855* (Chicago, 1855), pp. 20–21, 25–28.

This State is located in the healthiest latitude of our continent; reaching only to latitude 43° 30′ on its northern boundary. Its winters are comparatively mild and pleasant, and its summers free from the long scorching rays of a southern sun and the epidemics so common in such climates. By the medical journals, Iowa is ranked as second only in point of health; and no doubt it will be *first*, when she has a settled and acclimated population, as free from toil, privations, and exposure as other states. . . .

The novelty of the prairie country is striking, and never fails to cause an exclamation of surprise from those who have lived amid the forests of Ohio and Kentucky, or along the wooded shores of the Atlantic, or in sight of the rocky barriers of the Allegheny ridge. The extent of the prospect is exhilarating. The outline of the landscape is undulating and graceful. The verdure and the flowers are beautiful; and the absence of shade, and consequent appearance of a profusion of light, produces a gaiety which animates every beholder.

These plains, although preserving a general level in respect to the whole country, are yet, in themselves, *not flat*, but exhibit a gracefully waving surface, swelling and sinking with easy, graceful slopes, and full, rounded outlines, equally avoiding the unmeaning horizontal surface, and the interruption of abrupt or angular elevations.

The attraction of the prairie consists in its extent, its carpet of verdure and flowers, its undulating surface, its groves, and the fringe of timber by which it is surrounded. Of all of these, the latter is the most expressive feature. It is that which gives character to the landscape, which imparts the shape, and marks the boundary of the plain. If the prairie be small, its greatest beauty consists in the vicinity of the surrounding margin of woodland, which resembles the shore of a lake indented with deep vistas, like bays and inlets, and throwing out long points, like capes and headlands.

In the spring of the year, when the young grass has just covered the ground with a carpet of delicate green, and especially if the sun is rising from behind a distant swell of the plain and glittering upon the dewdrops, no scene can be more lovely to the eye. The groves, or clusters of timber, are particularly attractive at this season of the year. The rich undergrowth is in full bloom. The rosewood, dogwood, crab-apple, wild plum, the cherry, and the wild rose are all abundant, and in many portions of the State the grape-vine abounds. The variety of wild fruit and flowering shrubs is so great, and such the profusion of the blossoms with which they are bowed down, that the eye is regaled almost to satiety.

The gaiety of the prairie, its embellishments, and the absence of the gloom and savage wildness of the forest, all contribute to dispel the feeling of loneliness which usually creeps over the mind of the solitary traveller in the wilderness. Though he may not see a house or a human being, and is conscious that he is far from the habitations of men, the traveller upon the prairie can scarcely divest himself of the idea that he is travelling through scenes embellished by the hand of art. The flowers, so fragile, so delicate, and so ornamental, seem to have been tastefully disposed to adorn the scene.

In the summer, the prairie is covered with long, coarse grass, which soon assumes a golden hue, and waves in the wind like a fully ripe harvest. The prairie-grass never attains its highest growth in the richest soil; but in low, wet, or marshy land, where the substratum of clay lies near the surface, the centre or main stem of the grass—that which bears the seed—shoots up to the height of eight and ten feet, throwing out long, coarse leaves or blades. But on the rich, undulating prairies, the grass is finer, with less of stalk and a greater profusion of leaves. The roots spread and interweave, forming a compact, even sod, and the blades expand into a close, thick grass, which is seldom more than eighteen inches high, until late in the season, when the seed-bearing stem shoots up. The first coat is mingled with small flowers—the violet, the bloom of the wild strawberry, and various others, of the most minute and delicate texture. As the grass increases in height, these smaller flowers disappear, and others, taller and more gaudy, display their brilliant colors upon the green surface; and still later, a larger and coarser succession arises with the rising tide of verdure. It is impossible to conceive a more infinite diversity, or a richer profusion of hues, "from grave to gay," than graces the beautiful carpet of green throughout the entire season of summer.

DEMAND FOR LAND REFORM: PRE-EMPTION

The influx of settlers lured by such paeans of praise posed problems at first, for no land office was established in Iowa until 1838. Unable to buy from the government, newcomers were forced to resort to the usual frontier practice of "squatting" on the plot they wanted, hoping that they would be able to purchase it when surveys were completed and auctions held. This was by no means assured, for wealthy speculators might overbid, robbing them of the years of labor that had gone into their "improvements." This could be prevented only by federal legislation that would allow pioneers to "pre-empt" land by settling on it, then buy their holdings at the minimum price. Nowhere was the demand for a "Pre-emption Law" more vocal than in Iowa, as a memorial adopted by the Territorial Convention which met in Burlington in November 1837 testified:[4]

A convention of citizens representing all the counties in that part of Wisconsin Territory lying west of the Mississippi river, have assembled at Burlington, the present seat of government of said Territory, for the purpose of taking into consideration several measures immediately affecting their interests and prosperity. Among the most important of these is the passage by your honorable bodies, at the session about to be commenced, of a preemption law by which the settlers on the public land shall have secured to them at the minimum price, the lands on which they live, which they have improved and cultivated without fear of molestation, or over-bidding on the part of the rich capitalist and speculator. It is a fact well known to your honorable bodies, that none of the land in Wisconsin, west of the Mississippi river, in what is called the "Iowa District," has yet been offered for sale by the government. It is equally true that that tract of country is now inhabited by twenty-five thousand souls, comprising a population as active, intelligent, and worthy as can be found in any other part of the United States. The enterprise of these pioneers has converted what was but yesterday a solitary and uncultivated waste, into thriving towns and villages, alive with the engagements of trade and commerce, and rich and smiling farms, yielding their bountiful return to the labors of the husbandman. This district has been settled and improved with a rapidity unexampled in the history of the country; emigrants from all parts of the United States, and from Europe, are daily adding to our numbers and importance. An attempt to force these lands thus occupied and im-

[4] *The History of Polk County, Iowa* (Des Moines, Iowa, 1880), pp. 149–150.

proved into market, to be sold to the highest bidder, and to put the money thus extorted from the hard earnings of an industrious and laborious people into the coffers of the public treasury, would be an act of injustice to the settlers, which would scarcely receive the sanction of your honorable bodies. In most cases the labor of years and the accumulated capital of a whole life has been expended in making improvements on the public land, under the strong and firm belief that every safeguard would be thrown around them to prevent their property, thus dearly earned by years of suffering, privation and toil, from being unjustly wrested from their hands. Shall they be disappointed? Will Congress refuse to pass such laws as may be necessary to protect a large class of our citizens from systemized plunder and rapine? The members comprising this convention, representing a very large class of people, who delegated them to speak in their stead, do most confidently express an opinion that your honorable bodies will at your present session, pass some law removing us from danger, and relieving us from fear on this subject. The members of this convention, for themselves, and for the people whose interests they are sent here to represent, do most respectfully solicit that your honorable bodies will, as speedily as possible, pass a pre-emption law, giving to every actual settler on the public domain, who has made improvements sufficient to evince that it is *bona fide* his design to cultivate and occupy the land, the right to enter at the minimum government price, one-half section for that purpose, before it shall be offered at public sale.

AN IOWA LAND SALE

By special act of Congress, pre-emption became a reality for Iowa in 1838 and for the entire West in 1841, but still the settlers were not properly protected. Some were unable to raise money to purchase the plots they had pre-empted; others fell victim to "claim jumpers," or were forced to borrow from the loan sharks who attended all government auctions with money to loan at from 3 to 6 percent a month. Clients unable to meet these exhorbitant fees risked having their hard-won lands taken from them by foreclosure. A land sale attended by these unwelcome characters was held in Iowa in 1840, and described by John B. Newhall:[5]

The great mass of people east of the Alleghanies, I apprehend, have but little idea of a western land sale. Many are the ominous indications of its approach among the "settlers." Every dollar is sacredly treasured up. The precious "mint drops" take to themselves wings, and fly away from the merchant's till to the farmer's cupboard. Times are dull in the towns; for the settler's home is dearer and *sweeter* than the merchant's sugar and coffee. At length the wished-for day arrives. The suburbs of the town present the scene of a military camp. The settlers have flocked from far and near. The hotels are thronged to overflowing. Barrooms, dining-rooms, and wagons, are metamorphosed into bedrooms. Dinners are eaten from a table or a stump; and thirst is quenched from a bar or a brook. The sale being announced from the land office, the township bidder stands near by with the registry book in hand, and each settler's name attached to his respective quarter or half section, and thus he bids off in the name of the whole township for each respective claimant. A thousand settlers are standing by, eagerly listening when *their* quarter shall be called off. The crier has passed the well-known numbers. His home is secure. He feels relieved. The

---

[5] John B. Newhall, *Sketches of Iowa, or the Emigrant's Guide* (New York, 1841), pp. 57–58.

litigation of "claim-jumping" is over forever. He is lord of the soil. With an independent step he walks into the land-office, opens the time-worn saddle-bags, and counts out the 200 or 400 dollars, silver and gold, takes his certificate from the general government, and goes his way rejoicing.

Such a scene have I witnessed which continued for three successive weeks, in which time nearly half a million of money was taken from the actual settlers of Iowa. It is an interesting sight to witness thousands of our fellow-beings, who, having planted themselves in a new country, are patiently waiting for the hour to arrive when they can *buy* the homes and the land from which they earn their bread—when they can say in truth, this is my own "vine and fig-tree." These are the embryo scenes consequent in commencing the settlement of this new country; occurrences that, to the uninformed European, would seem incomprehensible,—but the commencing landmarks which have marked the progress of the western pioneer, who, but as yesterday, verging upon the forests of Ohio and Kentucky, is now beyond the western shore of the Mississippi; and still his adventurous spirit looks onward, until nought shall remain save the boundless expanse of the vast Pacific.

SQUATTERS VERSUS SPECULATORS IN IOWA

As usual on the frontier, pioneers who could not depend on the government to protect their rights took the law into their own hands. With the force of public opinion solidly behind all local claimants, whether actual settlers or small-scale speculators, and against all outsiders, whether large speculators, claim jumpers, or loan sharks, extralegal activity was not only accepted but approved. The fate of a speculator who bid on a tract of land claimed by a squatter at the first land sale held at Burlington, Iowa, in 1838 was remembered by a pioneer, Hawkins Taylor, who attended:[6]

There were thousands of settlers at the sale at Burlington, in the fall of 1838; the officers could sell but one or two townships each day, and when the land in any one township was offered, the settlers of that township constituted the army on duty for that day, and surrounded the office for their own protection, with all the other settlers as a reserve force, if needed. The hotels were full of speculators of all kinds, from the money loaner, who would accommodate the settler at fifty per cent, that is, he would enter the settler's land, in his own name, and file a bond for a deed at the end of two years, by the settler paying him double the amount the land cost. At these rates, Dr. Barrett, of Springfield, Illinois, and Louis Benedict, of Albany, New York, loaned out one hundred thousand dollars each, and Lyne Sterling, and others, at least, an equal amount, at the same, or higher rates of interest. The men who come to Iowa now cannot realize what the early settlers had to encounter. The hotels were full of this and a worse class of money sharks. There was a numerous class who wanted to rob the settlers of their lands and improvements entirely, holding that the settler was a squatter and trespasser, and should be driven from his lands. You would hear much of this sort of talk about the hotels, but none about the settlers' camps. Amongst the loudest talkers of this kind was an F.F.V. a class that has now about "give out." This valiant gentleman was going to invest his money as he pleased, without reference to settlers' claims. When the town-

---

[6] Hawkins Taylor, "Squatters and Speculators at the First Land Sales," *Annals of Iowa*, 1st Series, VIII (July, 1870), 271–272.

ship of West Point was sold it was a wet, rainy day; I was bidder, and the officers let me go inside of the office. Just when I went into the office, Squire John Judy, who lived on section thirty-two or thirty-three, whispered to me that he had been disappointed in getting his money, at the last moment, and asking me to pass over his tract and not bid it off. I did so, but this Virginian bid it off. I was inside, and could not communicate to any one until the sale was through, and, as I did not bid on the tract, the outsiders supposed that it was not claimed by a settler, and the moment the bid was made, the bidder left for his hotel. As soon as I could get out, which was in a few minutes, and make known that Judy's land had been bid off by a speculator, within five minutes time, not less than fifteen hundred of as desperate and determined a set of men as ever wanted homes, started for the bold bidder. Prominent in the lead was John G. Kennedy, of Fort Madison, who enjoyed such sport. Col. Patterson, now of Keokuk, a Virginian by birth, but a noble, true-hearted friend of the settler, and who had been intimate with the Virginian, made a run across lots, and reached the hotel before Kennedy and his army. The Colonel informed the bidder of the condition of affairs, and advised him at once to abandon his bid, which he did, or rather, he authorized the Colonel to do it for him. The Colonel went out and announced to the crowd that the bid was withdrawn, and that the bidder had also withdrawn himself. Both offers were accepted, but the latter was bitterly objected to, and only acquisced in when it was found that the party had escaped the back way, and could not be found; there was no other remedy. This was the last outside bid given during that sale, and you heard no more talk about outside bidding, about the hotels. The squatters' rights were respected at that sale.

FRONTIER CLAIM ASSOCIATIONS

Something more than spontaneous action was needed in Iowa to protect local settlers and small-scale speculators from eastern speculators and moneylenders. In this situation, the pioneers followed the example of their ancestors who since the days of the Mayflower Compact of 1620 had erected their own extralegal law-enforcement machinery whenever the government was unable or unwilling to act for them. This took the form of "claim associations"; by 1840 more than one hundred were operating to protect squatters from claim jumpers, loan sharks, and outside speculators who might manipulate them out of their lands. Others were formed by small speculators to guard their holdings from settlers and large speculators. The constitution of one claim association, that of Johnson County adopted in March 1839, typified their purposes and methods. After designating the officers and their duties, it continued:[7]

1. All members. of the association shall be required in making claims to stake them off or blaze them in such a maner that the lines of such claims can be easily traced or followed and all claims thus made in order to be respected must be entered on record and there as fully and accurately described as practacable giving the names of the creek River or branch where such shall be the boundrys on any side and where bounded by other claims give the owners name of such claim if known and where the lands have been surveyed they shall be required to give the range Township and qr section as is custimary in describing surveyed Lands. and further persons making claims shall be re-

---

[7] Benjamin F. Shambaugh (ed.), *Constitution and Records of the Claim Association of Johnson County, Iowa* (Iowa City, 1894), pp. 7–12.

quired to put the initials of there names either on a tree or stake at each corner of there claims, no person shall hold more than 480 acres or three quarter sections of land by making claim thereto. and this quantity shall in all cases be recognized and constitute a claim let the same lye in a boddy or detached parcels. provided however that said claim is not in more than three separate and detached parcels. all persons wishing there claims recorded shall hand them in to the recorder in writing with there signature there to All Deeds of conveyance shall be admited to record and all assignments of Deeds and the first on record or admited for Record shall have the prefferance persons purchasing claims or parts of claims shall in all cases be required before the clerk to state on honour. that the amount specifyed in the deed or transfer is the actual a mount paid for such claim or part of claim as the case may be and that the purchase is valid and in good faith and that it has not been made to evade the law restricting persons in making claims to 480 acres or three quarter sections. this clause shall not be so construed as to deprive persons who sells there claims or a part there of taking another or a part as the case may be nor shall it be so construed that persons purchasing shall be deprived of the privalege of making a claim. nor shall any person or persons be intitled to make a claim from the fact of there having swaped or exchanged claims any person purchasing a claim and refusing to pay for it shall forfeit all claim there to and such claim thus forfeited shall revert back to the person selling such claim

Article 3 1. All persons having sold or purchased claims previous to the organization of this association and the adoption of the laws for the government of said association shall be entitled to all the privaleges and rights the laws of this association extend to those selling or purchasing after the adoption of said laws.

2. Any white male person over the age of eighteen can become a member of this association by signing the laws rules and regulations governing the association. no member of the association. shall have the privalege of voting on a question to change any article of the constitution or laws of the association unless he is a resident. citizen of the county and a claimholder. nor shall any member be entitled to vote for officers of this association unless they are claimholders. Actual citizens of the County. over the age of seventeen who are acting for them selves and dependent on their own exertions, and labour, for a lively hood, and whoos parents doe not reside with in the limits of the Territory can become members. of this association and entitled to all the privaleges of members.

no member can be declared elected an officer of the association unless such person shall have received a majority of the votes of the members presant, entitled to vote when such election shall take place Any law or article of the constitution of this association may be altered at the semianual meetings and at no other meetings provided however. that three fifths of the members presant who are resident citizens of the county and actual claim holders shall be in favour of such change or ammendment, *except that section fixing the quantity of land that every member is entitled to hold by claim and that section shall remain unaltered.* ....

6. Members of the association who are not citizens of the County shall be required in making claims to expend in improvements on each claim he or they may have made or may make the amount of fifty Dollars with in six months of the date of making such claim or claims and fifty Dollars everry six months there after until such person or persons becomes citizens of the county or forfeit the same—

7. All persons residing in the county at the adoption of the foregoing laws shall be

entitled to the privalege of voting at this meeting but after this it shall require two months residence to become a citizen of the county.

8. All claims made after the adoption of the foregoing laws shall be registered or offered for record within ten days after the making there of and all persons making claims after the adoption of the foregoing laws. shall be required in presenting his or there claim for record to state on honour before the recorder that such claim or claims has not been previously made or if made that they have been forfeited by the laws of this association to his or there personal knowledge.

9. All resident members whoos claims has been made previous to the adoption of the forigoing laws shall have the privalege of thirty days to have the same recorded in— And those who have made claims previous to the adoption of the forigoing laws. who are not citizens of the county shall have ninety days to have the same recorded in. And no person or persons shall have the privalege of registering claims in the name of nonresident persons

10. All trials or disputed cases shall be brought before the judicial Court in the following manner. any member of the association or the agent of any member of the association who is authorised to act as agent in writing for such person or persons beliveing their rights have been intruded on shall apply to any one of the seven judges who compose the judicial court and the judge so applyed to shall appoint a place and time for a meeting of the court and in writing authorise the marshalls to summons a sufficient number of judges to attend to compose a court at such place as he may deem most expedient to hold said court and further the judge so applyed to shall in writing authorise the marshall to summons all persons whoos testimony may be be nesasary in said case

and to authorise the marshalls to notify the defendant. in such case of the place and time of holding such court and summons all witnesses that either of the parties may require the court may previous to there proceding to investigate any case require the plaintiff and defendant to deposit a sufficient sum of money in there hands to defraay the expenses of said sut or the costs of said suit. and should either party refuse to deposit such sum of money the court may render judgment against such person refusing to doe the court shall in all cases brought before them be governed in their decissions by the laws of this association equity and justice

11. Any member refusing to be governed by the laws of the association or decission of the court shall no longer be considered a member and his name shall be striken from the association for the faithfull observance and mantanance of all the foregoing laws we mutualy pledge our honours, and subscribe our names here unto.

OPERATION OF THE CLAIM ASSOCIATIONS

Pioneers—in Iowa and elsewhere on the frontier—told dozens of stories of the "justice" meted out to claim jumpers or speculators who were rash enough to occupy land claimed by a member of an association. Two such incidents will demonstrate both the effectiveness of the associations, and the harshness of the punishment that they inflicted on their victims:[8]

Some trouble occurred this year among claim-holders. The new comers, in some instances, were unwilling to go over Duck Creek to take claims, and considered the

---

[8] Willard Barrows, "History of Scott County, Iowa," *Annals of Iowa*, 1st Series, I (January, 1863), 61.

Squatter Sovereignty too liberal in giving to each man three hundred and twenty acres, while none of it was improved. Individuals, not in actual possession, were liable to have their claims jumped. Several cases of this kind occurred, when the Society, which had been organized in March of this year, interfered. Having tried one man by the name of Stephens, who had jumped a claim of Maj. Wilson's, (now of Rock Island,) where the Ladies' College now stands, or a part of "Fulton's addition," and he refusing to vacate the premises, on application of the Major, the Sheriff of Du Buque county was sent for, there being then no nearer seat of Justice than Du Buque. On the arrival of Sheriff Cummings, he found Mr. Stephens snugly ensconced in the Major's cabin, armed with the instruments that would terminate life if properly handled, and threatening entire annihilation to any and all who might dare to touch him. The Sheriff soon summoned his posse, and with them came a yoke of oxen, which were soon hitched to one corner of the log cabin, and as the timbers began to show signs of parting, Mr. Stephens very willingly vacated the premises, and was shown the most feasible, as well as the quickest route to Stephenson, and never afterward made any attempt to recover his claim on this side of the river.

More serious was the so-called Dahlonega War, which was colorfully described by a participant, L. T. Stuart, in his reminiscences:[9]

Dahlonega township was settled on the first day of May 1843. Before sunset of that day, the prairie lying between Little Cedar Creek and the Des Moines River timber, was dotted with the white covers of wagons that had borne the scanty gear of our first settlers from their old and distant homes. Horses and oxen were feeding on the first sweet grass of May, while their owners were busily engaged in selecting claims. These settlers soon formed a club for mutual protection as in other localities, and enacted a code of "claim laws," with the usual provisions and penalties for "claim jumpers" and speculators.

Among the settlers were a few pretty hard cases. A big ugly fellow, with a countenance that one would think was inclined to quarrel with day-light for exposing its bad qualities, Martial must have been thinking of him when he wrote,

With all these tokens of a knave complete,
Should'st thou be honest thou'st a devlish cheat,

who emigrated from Georgia to this place, and who gloried in the name of James Woody, was destined to give his neighbors a deal of trouble. His wife Betsy was also a bit of a character when the spirit of Donnybrook Fair came over her. Old Jim, as his neighbors discourteously called him, had taken a claim just east of where the village of Dahlonega was located, which he sold during the summer to Martin Koontz, Sen., for two hundred and sixteen dollars, ready money. Now, James having a notion of his own about "Squatter Sovereignty," was not long in concluding that he would relieve some of his brother squatters of their claims without being at the little inconvenience of paying them for their good will, which he frankly admitted was not over-estimated by him. He only awaited for the completion of the township survey when he intended to preempt eighty acres of the claim he had sold to Koontz, with the money that he had received for the aforesaid claim. He had cut and hauled a lot of house-logs upon the north part of Koontz's claim, and might have suc-

---

[9] G. D. R. Boyd, "Sketches of History and Incidents Connected with the Settlement of Wapello County, from 1843 to 1859, Inclusive," *Annals of Iowa*, 1st Series, VI (January, 1868), 38–41.

ceeded in pre-empting it if he had not overdone the thing, by making an effort to take another eighty acre tract that was claimed by Joseph Kight. Peter White was covering a house that Koontz had built upon the south part of his claim, when on looking towards Kight's claim, was astonished to see a claim house standing upon Kight's land with several men about it as if at work. Peter was not long in getting himself down and over to Kight's cabin, which stood at the south-east corner of the public square in Doholonega. Kight on hearing that his claim was "jumped," swore vengeance against the intruders, and accompanied by a few friends started for the new claim-house, where they found old Jim Woody, Alex. Crawford, Bill Crawford, a man by the name of Brock, and others of the Woody tribe, celebrating their success at house-raising after the old fashion of having a little "sunthin to take," and perhaps were jubilating under the inspiration of "sod-corn whisky." Be that as it may, their gratulations were soon to be interrupted.

While they were all seated within the house they had just built, Kight and his company came upon them with the stealthiness of the panther, pulled the new and temporary roof down upon their heads, smashing their bottle and greatly endangering their persons with falling boards, weight-poles, &c. When they found that their house had been helped to tumble in upon them, they showed fight, but the attacking party having armed themselves with the handspikes used in raising the house, forced them to *"vamose the ranche."* Then tearing down and completely demolishing the house, Kight and his friends returned to Dahlonega. The Woody faction were not satisfied to remain vanquished, and swore that they could whip their opponents. The two Crawfords and Brock threw down their gloves, which were taken up by Elias Kitterman, Joseph Kight and Peter Kitterman, who after a bloody fight convinced them that they had been reckoning without their host. Betty Woody, like Joan of Arc, was a leader in the fight. Her shrill voice could be heard high above the battle's roar, encouraging her friends, and breathing imprecations dire upon her enemies. Kight had one of the Crawfords *hors du combat*, getting home a succession of trip-hammer licks in good style, when Betsy put a period to his fun by thrusting a huge stick into the hands of old man Crawford, conjuring him to strike for the honor of the Woody cause and the salvation of his own son who was being beat to a jelly. The old man needed no further prompting but brought the stick down with a right good will. Kight threw up his arm to protect his head, but the lick came with sufficient force to fracture the bone of his arm. Just at that moment a rock thrown by some one of the belligerents fell at Kight's feet, which he laid hold of and threw, unfortunately striking his clubbed antagonist in the eye, hiding the light of this earth from the aforesaid orb forevermore.

After the fight had subsided, old Jim Woody rushed out from his cabin with a rifle in his hands, swearing that Peter White was the meanest man of the lot, and he would shoot him right then and there. Peter was marching to time called "quick-step," when Jack Woody was heard to exclaim: "D—n it Dad, that gun is'nt loaded." "Shut yer mouth, Jack, Pete doesn't know it," was the reply. But the admonition came too late, Pete did know it, and laying hold of an axe threw it at old Jim with such accuracy that it scarcely missed his head, causing him to take shelter in his cabin. Jack snatched the gun from his father's hands and broke it to pieces,—done it we suppose, to prove his disapprobation of such conduct, and that he was of Georgia's chivalry, although his sire had shown the white feather.

Despite these teapot-tempest conflicts between settlers and speculators, Iowa's appeal was so compelling that the region filled rapidly, becoming a state in 1846. By this time the population tide was running northward toward Minnesota's forested acres. Lumbermen were first on the scene there, beginning their invasion in the 1830s, but farmers soon followed to grow food for the lumbermen, and townspeople to supply their commercial wants. As the forests were cut away, the influx of farmers and tradesmen swelled to major proportions, filling the valley of the Minnesota River first, then spilling over on either side. By 1858, when Minnesota became a state, its population had passed the 150,000 mark.

Long before this time, the Mississippi Valley frontier was feeding the population streams that were trickling toward the Far West. The Valley's settlement pattern determined the composition of this migration. Good lands were still available in the north, but from Missouri southward the best sites were already occupied. The perennially dissatisfied younger sons of farmers and freshly arrived newcomers were forced to take poorer sites, or move on. Thousands chose to move. They could not shift a short distance to an adjacent frontier, for stretching along the backcountry of the states that fringed the Mississippi were the chain of Indian reservations used to house the transplanted tribes from the East. Beyond this "permanent Indian Frontier" were the Great Plains, believed at this time to be an uninhabitable desert. Only by leapfrogging over these barriers to the valleys of the Oregon country and California could they find lands comparable to those that they coveted. This explains the fact that a majority of those who followed the Oregon and California trails westward, or who peopled Texas, came from the southern Mississippi Valley.

Many were driven from their homes there by the Panic of 1837, which was not fully felt in the West until the early 1840s. This devastating depression not only dropped the bottom from agricultural prices, but cast a pall over the future, for the Mississippi Valley states had gone heavily into debt during the precrash boom years to finance internal improvements and banking enterprises. All were burdened with obligations that could be met only by years of taxation. Why stay in a bankrupt land where farm values would be depressed for a generation when opportunity beckoned westward? So reasoned thousands of pioneers as they sold their small holdings, converted the farm wagons into "prairie schooners," and began the migration that would carry the American frontier to the shores of the Pacific.

CHAPTER 18

Texas: Colonization and Revolution, 1820-1845

Americans had long cast covetous eyes on Texas, but not until the Adams-Onís Treaty of 1819 between the United States and Spain did expansionist interest reach serious proportions. This treaty gave Florida to the United States, but it also set the western limits of the Louisiana Purchase at the Sabine River and the Rocky Mountains, awarding all of Texas to Spain. Many political leaders, and virtually all westerners, viewed this as a disgraceful surrender. Why accept the Sabine boundary when all of that rich province belonged rightfully to the American people? If craven Washington politicians were cowardly enough to give away territory, it must be won back. So reasoned many a western expansionist, and a sizable number of political leaders agreed.

Fortunately for those with such ambitions, Mexico's policy played directly into their hands. The United States must use its most effective weapon—the instinct of frontiersmen to invade new territories—and overrun Texas as a prelude to annexation. The Mexican government was eager to welcome American settlers. Since at least 1801, it had been concerned with the sparse population of its northern province; that immense domain was peopled by less than 4000 ranchers and townsmen. Government policy called for the admission of newcomers to bolster the military strength and economic potential of the region. It required only that those admitted profess the Roman Catholic faith and that they become Mexican citizens. When Spain controlled Mexico, no such steps could be taken. But when the Mexicans won their independence in 1821, they were ready to throw open the doors of Texas to acceptable immigrants.

STEPHEN F. AUSTIN ADVERTISES FOR SETTLERS

The American who was fortunate enough to capitalize on this opportunity was Moses Austin. Having spent much of his life in Spanish Louisiana, he used his Spanish citizenship to request permission to establish a colony of 300 Americans in Texas. This was readily granted, but Moses Austin died of exhaustion and exposure on his return journey from Mexico City in 1821. His son, Stephen F. Austin, was ready to pick up the reins. Selecting a site for his colony in the valleys of the Colorado and Brazos rivers, he began recruiting settlers in New Orleans. The first 150 who arrived late that year were plagued by the difficulties that beset all new frontiers, intensified now by the fact that Austin's grant was under attack. Austin hurried to Mexico City in 1822 to right matters, returning in 1823 with assurances of legal title plus authority to import an additional 300 colonizers. Now he was ready to recruit in earnest. A letter to his "Fellow Citizens" which was widely circulated typified the propaganda that was to make his venture a success:[1]

I have once more the pleasure of addressing you a few lines from the Colorado—My absence has been protracted greatly beyond my calculations and has been in the highest degree unpleasant to me, as it has retarded the progress of the most favourite enterprise I ever engaged in in my life; but I now flatter myself with the hope of receiving a full compensation for the difficulties I have encountered by witnessing the happiness of those who compose this Colony. I assure you that if my own private and personal interest had been the only incentive to induce me to persevere I should probably have abandoned the enterprise rather than surmounted the difficulties produced by the constant state of revolution in which the country has been, since my arrival in the city of Mexico. But I was animated by the gratifying hope of providing a home for a number of meritorious citizens and of placing them and their families in a situation to make themselves happy the balance of their lives. One of the greatest pleasures a virtuous mind can receive in this world is the consciousness of having benefited others, this pleasure I now have in prospect. The titles to your land is indisputable—the original grant for this settlement was made by the Spanish Government before the Revolution, it was then confirmed and the quantity of land designated by the decree of the Emperor Augustin Iturbide on the 18th of February last, and the whole was again approved and confirmed by the Sovereign Congress of the Mexican Nation on the 14 of April last after the fall of the Emperor. The titles are made by me and the Commissioner of the Government, and are then perfect and complete for ever, and each settler may sell his land the same as he could do in the United States.

All that depends on me, towards the advancement of the Colony will be executed in good faith, so far as my abilities extend, and with all the promptness in my power; but to enable me to benefit them to the full extent that I wish, it is necessary that the settlers should have confidence in me, and be directed by me I have a better opportunity of knowing what will be advantageous to them as regards their conduct and intercourse with the Government than any of them could have had, and I feel almost the same interest for their prosperity that I do for my own family—in fact I look upon them as one great family who are under my care. I wish the settlers to remember that the Roman Catholic is the religion of this nation, I have taken measures to have *Father Miness* formerly of Nachitoches, appointed our Curate, he is a good man and acquainted with the Americans—we must all be particular on this subject and respect the Catholic religion with all that attention due to its sacredness and to the laws of the land.

I have so far paid all the expenses attending this enterprise out of my own funds. I have spent much time and lost much property on the coast in my absence—I am now engaged in surveying the land and must pay money to the surveyors and hands employed

---

[1] Eugene C. Barker (ed.), "The Austin Papers," in the American Historical Association's, *Annual Report for the Year 1919* (Washington, 1924), vol. 2, pp. 679–681.

besides which I have to pay the expenses of the Commissioner, and heavy expenses attending the completion and recording of the titles. A moments reflection will convince the settlers that all this cannot be done without some aid from them, but as regards this point they may expect all the indulgence possible. Those who have the means must pay me a little money on receipt of their titles; from those who have not money I will receive any kind of property that will not be a dead loss to me, such as horses, mules, cattle, hogs, peltry, Furs, bees wax, home made cloth, dressed deer skins, etc. Only a small part will be required in hand, for the balance I will wait one, two, and three years, according to the capacity of the person to pay—In fact I will accomodate the settlers to the greatest extent in my power. I think that those who know me can state that my disposition is not to oppress any man; it is a pleasure for me to benefit my fellow citizens and I will sacrifice my own interest rather than distress them for one cent of money. But I have many sacred duties to attend which cannot be executed without money. The most of what I receive from the settlers will be applied for their own benefit, and I think they must all agree that it is also my duty to provide for my own family, and that in justice I ought to be compensated for the losses and fatigues I have sustained in this business, particularly when my labors secure handsome fortunes to my followers. I could exact the payment of all the expenses in hand before the titles are delivered, but shall not do so, the settlers may all rely on the terms above stated The smallest quantity of land a family will receive is one thousand yards square which may be increased by me and the Commissioner without limit in proportion to the size of the family.

Young men must join and take land in the name of one. All thus united will be ranked as one family, they can then divide the land amongst themselves—

I shall proceed immediately to the mouth of this River, and on my return go to the Brazos The settlers have now nothing to fear, there is no longer any cause for uneasiness. they must not be discouraged at any little depradations of Indians, they must remember that *American blood* flows in their veins, and that they must not dishonor that noble blood by yielding to trifling difficulties. I shall adopt every possible means for their security and defence, I have brought some powder from Bexar, a part of which will be sent to Capt. Robison for the use of the militia when needed—*Let every man do his duty, and we have nothing to fear—Let us be united as one man—discord must be banished from amongst us, or those who cause it will meet with most severe treatment*

Hoping to meet you soon in peace and happiness, I am Resptlly your friend and fellow citizen

THE EMPRESARIO SYSTEM

Austin's appeals attracted 272 settlers to his colony by the end of 1824 and helped convince the Mexican government that colonization was a feasible means of converting Texas from a wasteland to a valuable economic asset. This required the importation of newcomers on a larger scale. To encourage this, the Mexican congress that year decreed that all acceptable newcomers would be given free land, and that speculators, or "empresarios," who arranged for their importation would be awarded grants of thousands of acres. Individual states were encouraged to embody these principles in legislation. The legislature of Coahuila-Texas responded in March 1825 with a major colonization act that set the pattern for Texas migration over the next years:[2]

Invitation to Foreigners. All foreigners who, in virtue of the general law of the 18th of August, 1824, which guarantees the security of their persons and property in this republic, shall wish to emigrate to any of the settlements of the state of Coahuila and Texas, are permitted to do so; and the said state invites and calls them.

2. *Same Protected*. Those who shall thus emigrate, far from being molested, shall be admitted by the local authorities of said settlements, and permitted by the same freely to engage in any honest pursuit, provided they respect the general laws of the republic and the laws of the state.

3. *Domiciliation*. Any foreigner, already arrived in the state of Coahuila and Texas, who shall resolve to establish himself and become domiciliated therein, shall make a declaration to that effect before the ayuntamiento of the place he shall select as his residence, by which, in that case, he shall be sworn to obey the federal and state constitution, and to observe the religion prescribed in the former; and his name, and those of his family, if he have any, shall be registered in a book to be kept for the purpose, specifying the place he is from, his age, occupation, whether he is married, and that he has taken the oath prescribed, considering him henceforth, and not before, as domiciliated.

4. *Right To Land*. Any foreigner, from the time he is domiciliated agreeably to the foregoing article, shall be permitted to specify any vacant land, and it shall be the duty of the respective political authority to forward the instrument that shall be drawn to the executive for his approval, should he consider the applicant the same as the natives of the country, conforming to the existing laws on the subject....

8. *Settlements of One Hundred Families*. Projects for new settlements, wherein one or more persons shall offer to bring, at their own expense, one hundred families or more, shall be presented to the executive; who, on finding them in conformity to this law, shall admit the same, and immediately designate to the contractors the land whereon they shall establish themselves, and the term of six years, within which they shall present the number of families for which they contracted, under the penalty of losing the rights and privileges offered in their favor, in proportion to the number of families they shall fail to introduce, and of the contract becoming absolutely null should they not present one hundred families at the least.

9. *Contracts Of Empresarios*. Contracts made by the contractors or empresarios with the families which come at their expense, shall be guaranteed by this law, so far as they are in conformity with the provisions thereof....

11. *Measurement Of Land*. A square of land measuring one league, consisting of five thousand varas on each side, or, what is the same thing, a superficies containing twenty-five million varas, shall be called a sitio, and this shall be the unit for enumerating one, two or more sitios, in the same manner as one million square varas, or one thousand varas on each side, which shall constitute a labor, shall be the unit for counting one, two or more labors. The vara for this measure shall consist of three geometrical feet.

12. *Distribution Of Lands*. Adopting the aforesaid unit as a standard, and observing the distinction to be made on distrib-

---

[2] John Sayles and Henry Sayles (eds.), *Early Laws of Texas* (St. Louis, 1888), vol. 1, pp. 64–70.

uting lands between grazing lands or those suitable for raising stock, and irrigable tillage land, and that which is not irrigable, this law shall grant to the contractor or contractors for forming new settlements five sitios of grazing land and five labors, of which at least one-half shall be land not irrigable, for every hundred families they shall introduce and establish in the state; but they shall receive this premium only for eight hundred families, although they should introduce more; and no fraction whatever, not completing one hundred, shall entitle them to a premium, not even proportionally.

13. *Rights Of Contractors*. Should any contractor or contractors, on account of the families they shall have introduced, be entitled, according to the foregoing article, to more than eleven square leagues of land, it shall be granted them, but they shall be obligated to alienate the excess within twelve years; and should they not, it shall be done by the respective political authority at public sale, delivering the proceeds to the owners thereof, after deducting the costs of sale.

14. *Farming And Grazing Lands*. One labor shall be granted to each family included in the contract, whose only occupation is the cultivation of the soil; and should the same also raise stock, grazing land shall be added to complete a sitio; and should the raising of stock be the exclusive occupation, the family shall receive a superficies of twenty-four million square varas (being a sitio lacking one labor)....

22. *Payments By New Settlers*. The new settlers shall pay to the state, as an acknowledgment for each sitio of grazing land, thirty dollars; for each labor, not irrigable, two and a half; and for each that is irrigable, three and a half; and so on, proportionally, according to the class and quantity of land distributed to them; but the payment thereof need not be completed under six years from settlement, and in three installments; the first in four, the second in five, and the third in six years, under a penalty of forfeiting the land for a failure in any of the said payments; the contractors and the military mentioned in article 10 shall be exempt from this payment; the former, as regards the lands granted them as a premium, and the latter, for that which they obtain agreeably to their patents....

26. *Failure To Cultivate*. It shall be understood that the new settlers who shall not, within six years from the date of their possession, have cultivated or occupied, agreeably to their class, the lands that shall be granted them, have renounced the same; and the respective political authority shall immediately proceed to take back from them the lands and titles.

27. *Right To Alienate Lands*. The contractors and the military, already mentioned, in their turn, and those who have acquired lands by purchase, can alienate the same at any time, provided the successor obligates himself to cultivate the same within the same term as was obligatory on the part of the original proprietor, likewise reckoning the term from the date of the primitive titles. The other settlers shall be authorized to alienate their land when they shall have completed the cultivation thereof, and not before.

28. *Devise—Descent*. Every new settler, from the time of his settlement, shall be permitted to dispose of his land, although it shall not be cultivated, by testament made in conformity to the laws that are now, or shall hereafter be, in force; and should he die intestate, his lawful heir or heirs shall succeed him in the enjoyment of his rights and property, assuming in both cases the obligations and conditions incumbent on the respective grantee....

30. *Rights Of Emigrants*. New settlers

who shall resolve to leave the state to establish themselves in a foreign country, shall be at liberty to do so with all their property; but, after thus leaving, they shall no longer hold their land; and should they not have previously disposed of the same, or should not the alienation be in conformity to Art. 27, it shall become entirely vacant.

31. *Naturalization.* Foreigners who shall have obtained land according to this law, and established themselves in the new settlements, shall from that time be considered naturalized in the country; and by marrying natives of the republic, they shall possess a special merit for obtaining letters of citizenship of the state, saving what the constitution of the state, on either subject, shall provide.

32. *Taxes On New Settlements.* During the first ten years from the time the new settlements are founded, the same shall be free from all taxes of whatever denomination, except such as shall be generally imposed to prevent or repel foreign invasion, neither shall the products and effects of agriculture and industry pay excise, or other kinds of impost, in any part of the state, except only the duties to which the following article refers; after the expiration of the aforesaid term, the new settlements shall be liable to the same burdens as the old, and the colonists the same as the other inhabitants of the state.

MEXICO'S DISTRUST OF THE TEXANS

The Colonization Act of 1825 attracted settlers; a virtually free grant of twenty-five "labors" of land—4428 acres—was a magnet that few frontiersmen could resist. During the next four years fifteen "empresario" contracts were signed for the settlement of nearly 5500 families. Few succeeded; newcomers preferred the safety of Austin's colony to the uncertainties of another. But by 1830, some 4428 persons lived on Austin's grant and almost as many more in other colonies. Mexico was peopling its northern province, but Mexican officialdom was beginning to wonder if this was an unmixed blessing. Its colonization policy was attracting only Americans, rather than the mixture of nationalities hoped for, and these Americans were showing a distressing inability to integrate. The government was alarmed when a disgruntled "empresario" whose grant had been canceled staged the unsuccessful Fredonian Revolt in 1826, and linked this with a revived effort of the United States to buy Texas through diplomatic channels. Was the influx of Americans a plot to wrest Texas from Mexico? To find out, the government in the fall of 1827 sent an able official, General Manuel Mier y Terán, northward to investigate. The letter that Terán wrote from Nacogdoches on June 30, 1828, revealed him as both a good observer and a sound prophet:[3]

As one covers the distance from Béjar to this town, he will note that Mexican influence is proportionately diminished until on arriving in this place he will see that it is almost nothing. And indeed, whence could such influence come? Hardly from superior numbers in population, since the ratio of Mexicans to foreigners is one to ten; certainly not from the superior character of the Mexican population, for exactly the opposite is true, the Mexicans of this town comprising what in all countries is called the lowest class—the very poor and very ignorant. The naturalized North Americans in the town maintain an English school, and send their children north for further education; the poor

---

[3] Alleine Howren, "Causes and Origin of the Decree of April 6, 1830," *Southwestern Historical Quarterly,* XVI (April, 1913), 395–398.

Mexicans not only do not have sufficient means to establish schools, but they are not of the type that take any thought for the improvement of its public institutions or the betterment of its degraded condition. Neither are there civil authorities or magistrates; one insignificant little man—not to say more —who is called an *alcalde,* and an *ayuntamiento* that does not convene once in a lifetime is the most that we have here at this important point on our frontier; yet, wherever I have looked, in the short time that I have been here, I have witnessed grave occurrences, both political and judicial. It would cause you the same chagrin that it has caused me to see the opinion that is held of our nation by these foreign colonists, since, with the exception of some few who have journeyed to our capital, they know no other Mexicans than the inhabitants about here, and excepting the authorities necessary to any form of society, the said inhabitants are the most ignorant of negroes and Indians, among whom I pass for a man of culture. Thus, I tell myself that it could not be otherwise than that from such a state of affairs should arise an antagonism between the Mexicans and foreigners, which is not the least of the smoldering fires which I have discovered. Therefore, I am warning you to take timely measures. Texas could throw the whole nation into revolution.

The colonists murmur against the political disorganization of the frontier, and the Mexicans complain of the superiority and better education of the colonists; the colonists find it unendurable that they must go three hundred leagues to lodge a complaint against the petty pickpocketing that they suffer from a venal and ignorant *alcalde,* and the Mexicans with no knowledge of the laws of their own country, nor those regulating colonization, set themselves against the foreigners, deliberately setting nets to deprive them of the right of franchise and to exclude them from the *ayuntamiento.* Meanwhile, the incoming stream of new settlers is unceasing; the first news of these comes by discovering them on land already under cultivation, where they have been located for many months; the old inhabitants set up a claim to the property, basing their titles of doubtful priority, and for which there are no records, on a law of the Spanish government; and thus arises a lawsuit in which the *alcalde* has a chance to come out with some money. In this state of affairs, the town where there are no magistrates is the one in which lawsuits abound, and it is at once evident that in Nacogdoches and its vicinity, being most distant from the seat of the general government, the primitive order of things should take its course, which is to say that this section is being settled up without the consent of anybody.

The majority of the North Americans established here under the Spanish government—and these are few—are of two classes. First, those who are fugitives from our neighbor republic and bear the unmistakable earmarks of thieves and criminals; these are located between Nacogdoches and the Sabine, ready to cross and recross this river as they see the necessity of separating themselves from the country in which they have just committed some crime; however, some of these have reformed and settled down to an industrious life in the new country. The other class of early settlers are poor laborers who lack the four or five thousand dollars necessary to buy a *sitio* of land in the north, but having the ambition to become landholders—one of the strong virtues of our neighbors—have come to Texas. Of such as this latter class is Austin's colony composed. They are for the most part industrious and honest, and appreciate this country. Most of them own at least one or two slaves. Unfortunately the emigration of such is made under difficulties, because they lack the means of transportation, and to accomplish this emigration it has become necessary to do what was not necessary until lately: there are empresarios of wealth who advance them the means for their transportation and establishment.

The wealthy Americans of Louisiana and other western states are anxious to secure land in Texas for speculation, but they are restrained by the laws prohibiting slavery. If these laws should be repealed—which God forbid—in a few years Texas would be a powerful state which could compete in productions and wealth with Louisiana. The repeal of these laws is a point toward which the colonists are directing their efforts. They have already succeeded in getting from the Congress of Coahuila a law very favorable to their prosperity: the state government has declared that it will recognize contracts made with servants before coming to this country, and the colonists are thus assured of the employment of ample labor, which can be secured at a very low price in the United States. This law, according to the explanation made to me by several, is going to be interpreted as equivalent to permission to introduce slaves.

In spite of the enmity that usually exists between the Mexicans and the foreigners, there is a most evident uniformity of opinion on one point, namely the separation of Texas from Coahuila and its organization into a territory of the federal government. This idea, which was conceived by some of the colonists who are above the average, has become general among the people and does not fail to cause considerable discussion. In explaining the reasons assigned by them for this demand, I shall do no more than relate what I have heard with no addition of my own conclusions, and I frankly state that I have been commissioned by some of the colonists to explain to you their motives, notwithstanding the fact that I should have done so anyway in the fulfillment of my duty.

They claim that Texas in its present condition of a colony is an expense, since it is not a sufficiently prosperous section to contribute to the revenues of the state administration; and since it is such a charge it ought not to be imposed upon a state as poor as Coahuila, which has not the means of defraying the expenses of the corps of political and judicial officers necessary for the maintenance of peace and order. Furthermore, it is impracticable that recourse in all matters should be had to a state capital so distant and separated from this section by deserts infected by hostile savages. Again, their interests are very different from those of the other sections, and because of this they should be governed by a separate territorial government, having learned by experience that the mixing of their affairs with those of Coahuila brings about friction. The native inhabitants of Texas add to the above other reasons which indicate an aversion for the inhabitants of Coahuila; also the authority of the *comandante* and the collection of taxes is disputed.

That which most impressed me in view of all these conditions is the necessity of effective government in Nacogdoches at least, since it is the frontier with which the Republic is most in contact. Every officer of the federal government has immense districts under his jurisdiction, and to distribute these effectively it is necessary to give attention to economy as well as to government and security. The whole population here is a mixture of strange and incoherent parts without parallel in our federation: numerous tribes of Indians, now at peace, but armed and at any moment ready for war, whose steps toward civilization should be taken under the close supervision of a strong and intelligent government; colonists of another people, more progressive and better informed than the Mexican inhabitants, but also more shrewd and unruly; among these foreigners are fugitives from justice, honest laborers, vagabonds and criminals, but honorable and dishonorable alike travel with their political constitution in their pockets, demanding the privileges, authority and officers which such a constitution guarantees. The most of them have slaves, and these slaves are beginning to learn the favorable intent of the Mexican law toward their unfortunate condition and are becoming restless under their yoke, and the masters, in the effort to retain them, are making that yoke even heavier; they extract their teeth, set on the dogs to tear them in pieces, the most lenient being he who but flogs his slaves until they are flayed.

In short, the growing population, its unusual class, the prosperity and safety of the nation, all seem to me to demand the placing at this point of a *jefe politico* subordinate to the one at Béjar, and also a court of appeals. This done, I do not believe so radical a step as the separation of Texas from Coahuila, now desired by the inhabitants, would be necessary.

MEXICAN RESTRICTIONS ON IMMIGRATION

Alarmed by the state of affairs in the American colonies of Texas and warned by Terán's reports, the Mexican government decided to check further migration from the United States, while at the same time encouraging immigration from Mexico and Europe. But how could this be done without offending the powerful neighbor to the north? The ingenious answer was contained in an adroitly worded decree pronounced on April 6, 1830:[4]

1. *The Entry of Those Descriptions of Cotton Goods,* prohibited by the law of the twenty-second of May last, shall be permitted in the ports of the republic generally, until the last of June, 1831.

2. *Duties Appropriated.* The duties arising from the importation of such goods shall be appropriated to maintaining the indivisibility of the Mexican territory, to the formation of a fund of reserve, to be used in case of a Spanish invasion, and to the encouragement of national industry.

3. *Commissioners and Their Duties.* The government shall appoint one or more commissioners, whose duty it shall be to visit the colonies of the frontier states; to contract with the legislatures of said states for the purchase, by the nation, of lands suitable for the establishment of new colonies of Mexicans and foreigners; to enter into such arrangements as they may deem proper, for the security of the republic, with the colonies already established; to watch over the exact compliance of the contracts on the entrance of new colonists, and to investigate how far the contracts already made have been complied with.

4. *Lands for Fortifications, etc.* The executive is empowered to take possession of such lands as may be suitable for fortifications and arsenals, and for the new colonies, indemnifying the state in which such lands are situated by a deduction from the debt due from such state to the federation. . . .

7. *Mexican Families* Who may voluntarily desire to become colonists shall be conveyed free of expense, subsisted during the first year, and receive a grant of land and the necessary implements of husbandry.

---

[4] John Sayles and Henry Sayles (eds.), *Early Laws of Texas* (St. Louis, 1888), vol. 1, pp. 55–57.

8. *Must Conform to all Laws.* The individuals spoken of in the anterior articles shall conform to the laws of colonization of the federation, and the state in which they are settled.

9. *Foreigners Must Have Passport.* The entrance of foreigners by the frontiers of the north, under any pretense whatsoever, is prohibited, unless furnished with a passport, signed by an agent of the republic in the country from which the individual may come.

10. *No Change Will Be Made* with respect to the colonies already established, nor with respect to the slaves which they now contain; but the general government, and that of each particular state, shall exact, under the strictest responsibilities, the observance of the colonization laws and the prevention of the further introduction of slaves.

11. *Certain Foreigners Prohibited From Settling.* In the exercise of the right reserved to the general congress, by the seventh article of the law of the eighteenth of August, 1824, the citizens of foreign countries, lying adjacent to the Mexican territory, are prohibited from settling as colonists in the states or territories of the republic adjoining such countries. These contracts of colonization, the terms of which are opposed to the present article, and which are not yet complied with, shall consequently be suspended.

CULTURAL CONFLICT IN TEXAS

This decree sent a tremor of alarm through the American colonists. The stricter supervision threatened in the measure and the prohibition of further immigration from the United States brought the settlers face to face with a disturbing problem: did they really intend to become good Mexican citizens, or had they always believed that a preponderance of their fellow-countrymen in Texas would eventually swing that province into the orbit of their beloved United States? The answer was clear; the vast majority were and would remain Americans. Once this was realized, they became more acutely conscious of the cultural gulf that separated them from the Mexicans. As Americans they were accustomed to one system of law, government, and religion; as citizens of Mexico they would be forced to adopt another that was completely different. The attitude toward the right of citizens to petition their government and the right of the accused to be confronted by their accusers in law courts brought home to them the wide gulf between their cultures. Stephen F. Austin expressed the opinion of his fellow-countrymen on these basic points in an "Address of the Central Committee to the Convention" of Texan leaders who met early in 1833:[5]

The whole of this country, with the exception of the small towns of Bexar and Goliad, has been settled and redeemed from the wilderness within a few years by the enterprise of immigrants who removed to it in consequence of the express and earnest invitation of the government, contained in the national and state colonization laws. Those immigrants have uniformly evinced their gratitude to the government and nation of their adoption for all the acts of kindness and liberality that have been extended towards them, and they have faithfully performed their duty as Mexican citizens, and fulfilled the intention and spirit of the colonization laws, by settling the country, defending it from hostile indians, or other enemies, and developing its resources, thus

---

[5] Eugene C. Barker (ed.), "The Austin Papers," in the American Historical Association's, *Annual Report for the Year 1922* (Washington, 1928), vol. 2, pp. 935–938.

giving value and character to a large section of the Mexican territory which was before wild and almost unknown. They have introduced agriculture and the useful arts and commerce, and if as has been said by a celebrated author "that man deserves well of his country who makes a blade of grass grow where none grew before", how much more do the people of Texas deserve from their country who have so materially added to the national grandeur, phisical force and resources. The people of Texas ought therefore to rely with confidence on the government for protection, and to expect that an adequate remedy will be applied to the many evils that are afflicting them.

The invitations in virtue of which they came here, and the guarantees of the constitution and laws, evidently contain a pledge on the part of the government, that they should be governed in accordance with the spirit of the free political institutions of the Mexican republic, and in the manner best adapted to the local situation and necessities of Texas. The *right* of the people of Texas to represent their wants to the government, and to explain in a respectfull manner the remedies that will relieve them cannot therefore be doubted or questioned. It is not merely a right, it is also a sacred and bounden duty which they owe to themselves and to the whole Mexican nation, for should evils of great and desolating magnitude fall upon Texas for the want of competent remedies, the people here would have cause to accuse themselves of neglect for not making an effort to procure such remedies, and the government would also have cause to complain, that a full and frank and timely representation had not been made and a remedy solicited.

It is very evident that these considerations have influenced the people of Texas in all they have done up to the present time. They have been governed by the desire to do their duty faithfully to the Mexican nation and to themselves. In the discharge of this duty the people and civil authorities of Austins Colony made a respectfull and humble petition to the General and State governments on the 18 day of Feby 1832 setting forth the evils that were afflicting this country. The inhabitants and civil authorities of Bexar, the ancient and present capital of Texas, also made a very able and energetic represention on the same subject on the 19th of December last, Numerous other representatives have been made at various times by all the Ayuntamientos of Texas, and on the first of October last delegates of the people of Texas met in convention at this Town and unanimously resolved that it was expedient that the political union between Coahuila and Texas should be dissolved and that Texas should be organised as a separate State of the Mexican confederation as soon as the approbation of the General government to the effect could be obtained. That convention accordingly memorialised congress on the subject, and elected an agent to go to Mexico in order to forward the views of the people of Texas in obtaining the sanction of the general government. But the continuation of the intestine commotions which have raged within the bosom of the Mexican republic for more than twelve months past, and which threaten'd a total overthrow of the established institutions of the country, prevented the memorial from being presented in accordance with the intentions of the October convention.

That convention adopted many other memorials and resolutions, amongst the most important of which was the provisional organization of the militia, as a precaution against contemplated attacks upon our exposed frontier by the many tribes of hostile indians who inhabit the northern and western parts of Texas; and the establishment of the central and sub-committees of safety and correspondence throughout the country all of which were rendered inoperative by the decree of the governor of the state of Coahuila and Texas, who declared the proceedings of the convention null and void, and ordered the several committees to dissolve.

At the time when this committee determined to convoke the present convention, they took an impartial survey of our federal relations and of our local affairs.

They beheld the Mexican confederation torn and broken asunder by political parties each of which sustained its pretentions to the supreme executive power of the nation by force of arms. Civil war raged in every part of the Mexican territory and in looking upon the face of the nation nothing was to be seen but confusion and bloody discord—Brother contending with brother in deadly strife for mastery in political power. They saw that the constitution of the republic, that instrument which they had been taught to look upon as the sacred charter of their liberties was alternately violated and set aside by all parties, and that all the constitutional guarantees were merged for the time being in military power. They saw the constitutional period for the election of President and vice President of the nation and of members of Congress, pass by, and at least one third of the states refuse or neglect to hold the elections. The future presented the gloomy prospect that the days of constitutional freedom had been numbered to the Mexicans, and that we should ere long see the waves of anarchy and confusion close forever over the wreck of that Mexican republic. The disorganization of the government was so extreem, that even the leaders of the liberal party who have been contending for the restoration of constitutional liberty, and whose cause was espoused by the people of Texas, and generously defended with their blood and treasure, found themselves compelled to lay aside all the established forms, and to renovate the constitution by violent and unconstitutional means.

The committee turned from this view of our national affairs to that of the local internal situation of Texas which has not materially changed since the last convention. The political system under which Texas has heretofore been governed, tends to check the growth of the country, and to produce confusion and insecurity, rather than to extend protection to lives liberty and property. The unnatural annexation of what was formerly the province of Texas to Coahuila by the constituent congress of the Mexican nation, has forced upon the people of Texas a system of laws which they do not understand and which cannot be administered so as to suit their condition or to supply their wants.

The Alcaldes who are the highest judicial officers in Texas and have unlimited jurisdiction in all cases, are elected annually by the people, and those who are ignorant and corrupt and without responsibility are as liable to be chosen as the wise, the virtuous and the responsible. This remark is justified by the fact that the office is without emolument and is extreemly burdensome, and will therefore seldom be sought by those who are best qualified to fill it. In all civil cases there is an appeal to the supreme tribunal of the state at Saltillo a distance of near seven hundred miles from the inhabited parts of Texas. There are but few men in Texas who are qualified to prepare cases for the supreme court and when appeals have been taken they have generally been sent back several times to be reformed so that decissions in such cases are seldom had. It has become proverbial in Texas, that an appeal to Saltillo is a payment of the debt. It amounts to a total denial of justice especially to the poor, and this is the frail tenure by which the most important rights of the people of Texas are suspended.

The manner of trying culprits for high

criminal offences is such that it amounts to no tryal at all. The tryal by jury is not sanctioned by law, and the rights of the accused are committed to an alcalde who is ignorant of the formulas of the laws, and of the language in which they are written who prepares the cause for the judgment of the supreme tribunal in Saltillo, thus the lives, liberty and honor of the accused are suspended upon the tardy decission of a distant tribunal which knows not nor cares not for his suffering, and the rights of the community to bring offenders to speedy and exemplary punishment are sacrificed to forms equally uncertain and unknown. The formula required by law in the prosecution of criminals is so difficult to be pursued that most of the courts in Texas have long since ceased to attempt its execution. The tryal by jury has been attempted in some of the municipalities, but being unsupported by the sanction of law it also has failed of success. A total interegnum in the administration of justice in criminal cases may be said to exist. A total disregard of the laws has become so prevalent, both amongst the officers of justice, and the people at large, that reverence for laws or for those who administer them has almost intirely disappeared and contempt is fast assuming its place, so that the protection of our property our persons and lives is circumscribed almost exclusively to the moral honesty or virtue of our neighbor.

CAUSES OF THE TEXAS REVOLUTION

The cultural gap recognized by Austin was too wide to be bridged by impatient frontiersmen; the Texan-Americans could remain loyal to Mexico only if they were delegated such complete authority over their own local and state governments that the differences no longer intruded into their daily lives. This meant the separation of the state of Texas from the state of Coahuila-Texas, a step that the Mexican government would never allow. Conflicts resulting from this impasse began in 1832 and might have goaded the Texans into a revolution at that time had not a rebellion within Mexico elevated to the presidency of that Republic General Antonio López de Santa Anna, who seemed sympathetic to their cause. With Santa Anna in power, the time seemed ripe to settle a whole Pandora's box of grievances that had developed during the past years, over immigration, government, customs duties, slavery, and a host more. This was the inspiration for a convention of delegates from the American settlements that assembled at San Felipe de Austin on October 1, 1832, to press for a number of reforms including separate statehood. When Santa Anna showed no inclination to respond, a second convention met in 1833 to prepare similar demands, which were entrusted to Stephen F. Austin for delivery. After waiting months for an audience, Austin presented his petition to the Mexican President on November 5, 1833, and started back, well satisfied with the assurances given him. At Saltillo he was arrested and hurried back to Mexico City, where he learned that an angry letter written during his long wait had fallen into the hands of the officials. For this indiscretion he cooled his heels in a Mexican jail until July 1835, when he was allowed to return. The report that he presented the Texans summarized their grievances, and at the same time reflected the changing mood of Austin as he moved toward the conclusion that a revolution was necessary:[6]

I left Texas in April, 1833, as the public agent of the people, for the purpose of applying for the admission of this country into the Mexican confederation as a state separate from Coahuila. This application was based upon the constitutional and vested rights of Texas, and was sustained by me in the City

---
[6] Dudley G. Wooten, *A Comprehensive History of Texas, 1685–1897* (Dallas, 1898), vol. 1, pp. 501–504.

of Mexico to the utmost of my abilities. No honorable means were spared to effect the objects of my mission, and to oppose the forming of Texas into a territory, which was attempted. I rigidly adhered to the instructions and wishes of my constituents, so far as they were communicated to me. My efforts to serve Texas involved me in the labyrinth of Mexican politics: I was arrested, and have suffered a long persecution and imprisonment. I consider it to be my duty to give an account of these events to my constituents, and will, therefore, at this time, merely observe that I have never, in any manner, agreed to anything, or admitted anything, that would compromise the constitutional or vested rights of Texas. These rights belong to the people, and can only be surrendered by them.

I fully hoped to find Texas at peace and in tranquillity, but regret to find it in commotion; all disorganized, all in anarchy, and threatened with immediate hostilities. This state of things is deeply to be lamented; it is a great misfortune, but it is one which has not been produced by any acts of the people of this country; on the contrary, it is the natural and inevitable consequence of the revolution that has spread all over Mexico, and of the imprudent and impolitic measures of both the state and general governments with respect to Texas. The people here are not to blame, and cannot be justly censured. They are farmers, cultivators of the soil, and are pacific from interest, from occupation, and from inclination. They have uniformly endeavored to sustain the Constitution and the public peace by pacific means, and have never deviated from their duty as Mexican citizens. If any acts of imprudence have been committed by individuals, they evidently resulted from the revolutionary state of the whole nation, the imprudent and censurable conduct of the state authorities, and the total want of a local government of Texas.

It is, indeed, a source of surprise and creditable congratulation that so few acts of this description have occurred under the peculiar circumstances of the times. It is, however, to be remembered that acts of this nature were not the acts of the people, nor is Texas responsible for them. They were, as I before observed, the natural consequences of the revolutionary state of the Mexican nation; and Texas certainly did not originate that revolution, neither have the people, as a people, participated in it. The consciences and hands of the Texans are free from censure, and clean.

The revolution in Mexico is drawing to a close. The object is to change the form of government, destroy the Federal Constitution of 1824; and establish a central or consolidated government. The states are to be converted into provinces.

Whether the people of Texas ought or ought not to agree to this change, and relinquish all or a part of their constitutional and vested rights under the Constitution of 1824 is a question of the most vital importance; one that calls for the deliberate consideration of the people, and can only be decided by them, fairly convened for the purpose. As a citizen of Texas, I have a right to an opinion on so important a matter,—I have no other right, and pretend to no other. In the report which I consider it my duty to make to my constituents, I intend to give my views on the present situation of the country, and especially as to the constitutional and natural rights of Texas, and will, therefore, at this time merely touch on this subject.

Under the Spanish government Texas was a separate and distinct province. As such, it had a separate and distinct local organization. It was one of the unities that composed the general mass of the nation, and as such participated in the war of the revolution, and was represented in the Constituent Congress of Mexico that formed the Constitution of

1824. This Constituent Congress, so far from destroying this unity, especially recognized and confirmed it by the law of May 7, 1824, which united Texas with Coahuila provisionally, under the especial guarantee of being made a state of the Mexican confederation as soon as it possessed the necessary elements. That law and the Federal Constitution gave to Texas a specific political existence, and vested in its inhabitants special and defined rights, which can only be relinquished by the people of Texas, acting for themselves as a unity, and not as a part of Coahuila, for the reason that the union with Coahuila was limited, and only gave power to the state of Coahuila and Texas to govern Texas for the time being, but always subject to the vested rights of Texas. The state, therefore, cannot relinquish those vested rights by agreeing to the change of government, or by any other act, unless expressly authorized by the people of Texas to do so; neither can the general government of Mexico legally deprive Texas of them without the consent of this people. These are my opinions.

An important question now presents itself to the people of this country.

The Federal Constitution of 1824 is about to be destroyed, the system of government changed, and a central or consolidated one established. Will this act annihilate all the rights of Texas, and subject this country to the uncontrolled and unlimited dictation of the new government?

This is a subject of the most vital importance. I have no doubt the Federal Constitution will be destroyed and a central government established, and that the people will soon be called upon to say whether they agree to this change or not. This matter requires the most calm discussion, the most mature deliberation, and the most perfect union. How is this to be had? I see but one way, and that is by a general consultation of the people by means of delegates elected for that purpose, with full powers to give such an answer, in the name of Texas, to this question as they may deem best, and to adopt such measures as the tranquillity and salvation of the country may require.

It is my duty to state that General Santa Anna verbally and expressly authorized me to say to the people of Texas that he was their friend, that he wished for their prosperity, and would do all he could to promote it; and that, in the new Constitution, he would use his influence to give the people of Texas a special organization suited to their education, habits, and situation. Several of the most intelligent and influential men in Mexico, and especially the Ministers of Relations and War, expressed themselves in the same manner. These declarations afford another and more urgent necessity for a general consultation of all Texas, in order to inform the general government, and especially General Santa Anna, what kind of organization will suit "the education, habits, and situation of the people."

It is also proper for me to state that in all my conversation with the President and ministers and men of influence, I advised that no troops should be sent to Texas, nor cruisers along the coast. I gave it as my decided opinion that the inevitable consequence of sending an armed force to this country would be war. I stated that there was a sound and correct moral principle in the people of Texas that was abundantly sufficient to restrain or put down all turbulent or seditious movements, but that this moral principle could not, and would not, unite with any armed force sent against this country; on the contrary, it would resist and repel it, and ought to do so. This point presents another strong reason why the people of Texas should meet in consultation. This country is now in anarchy, threatened with hostilities, armed vessels are capturing everything they can catch on the coast, and acts of piracy are said to be committed under cover of the Mexican flag. Can this state of things exist without precipitating the country into a war? I think it cannot, and therefore believe that it is our bounden and solemn duty as Mexicans and as Texans to represent the evils that are likely to result from this mistaken and most impolitic policy in the military movements.

My friends, I can truly say that no one has been, or is now, more anxious than myself to keep trouble away from this country. No one has been, or now is, more faithful to his duty as a Mexican citizen, and no one has personally sacrificed or suffered more in the discharge of this duty. I have uniformly been opposed to having anything to do with the family political quarrel of the Mexicans. Texas needs peace and a local government; its inhabitants are farmers, and they need a calm and quiet life. But how can I, or any one, remain indifferent when our rights, our all, appear to be in jeopardy, and when it is our duty, as well as our obligation as good Mexican citizens, to express our opinions on the present state of things and to represent our situation to the government? It is impossible. The crisis is such as to bring it home to the judgment of every man that something must be done, and that without delay. The question will perhaps be asked, What are we to do? I have already indicated my opinion. Let all personalities or divisions, or excitements, or passion, or violence be banished from among us. Let a general consultation of the people of Texas be convened as speedily as possible, to be composed of the best, and most calm, and intelligent, and firm men in the country, and let them decide what representations ought to be made to the general government, and what ought to be done in future.

With these explanatory remarks I will give as a toast, "The constitutional rights and security and peace of Texas,—they ought to be maintained; and jeopardized, as they now are, they demand a general consultation of the people."

MOVING TOWARD INDEPENDENCE

Austin correctly diagnosed Mexico's ailment and accurately predicted the future. Santa Anna might camouflage himself in a garb of liberalism, but he was a would-be dictator who would trample all who stood between him and despotic control of the nation. In April 1834, he repudiated most of his liberal reforms and that fall abolished all state governments to proclaim himself dictator. Anticipating Texan resentment, he ordered garrisons established at Anahuac and the mouth of the Brazos River; at the same time he started northward with an army of subjugation to repress rebellions that had flamed everywhere. These threats goaded a few hotheads among the Texans into action. One group of forty under William B. Travis fell on the Mexican garrison at Anahuac on June 30, 1835, and a larger self-styled army under Austin forced the surrender of Santa Anna's troops in San Antonio, but the majority of the people still hoped for something short of complete revolution. Their representatives, meeting at San Felipe de Austin on November 3, 1835, voted overwhelmingly against independence. Instead they issued a "Declaration of Causes" for taking up arms, hoping in this fashion to attract liberal Mexicans to the common cause of deposing Santa Anna:[7]

Whereas, General Antonio Lopez de Santa Anna, and other military chieftains, have, by force of arms, overthrown the federal institutions of Mexico, and dissolved the social

---

[7] Eugene C. Barker, "The Texan Declaration of Causes for Taking Up Arms against Mexico," *Quarterly of the Texas State Historical Association*, XV (January, 1912), 182–183.

compact which existed between Texas and the other members of the Mexican confederacy; now the good people of Texas, availing themselves of their natural rights, solemnly declare,

1st. That they have taken up arms in defence of their rights and liberties, which were threatened by the encroachments of military despots, and in defence of the republican principles of the federal constitution of Mexico, of eighteen and twenty-four.

2d. That Texas is no longer morally or civilly bound by the compact of union; yet, stimulated by the generosity and sympathy common to a free people, they offer their support and assistance to such of the members of the Mexican confederacy as will take up arms against military despotism.

3d. That they do not acknowledge that the present authorities of the nominal Mexican republic have the right to govern within the limits of Texas.

4th. That they will not cease to carry on war against the said authorities whilst their troops are within the limits of Texas.

5th. That they hold it to be their right during the disorganization of the federal system, and the reign of despotism, to withdraw from the union, to establish an independent government, or to adopt such measures as they may deem best calculated to protect their rights and liberties, but that they will continue faithful to the Mexican government so long as that nation is governed by the constitution and laws that were formed for the government of the political association.

6th. That Texas is responsible for the expenses of her armies now in the field.

7th. That the public faith of Texas is pledged for the payment of any debts contracted by her agents.

8th. That she will reward, by donations in lands, all who volunteer their services in her present struggle, and receive them as citizens.

These declarations we solemnly avow to the world, and call God to witness their truth and sincerity, and invoke defeat and disgrace upon our heads, should we prove guilty of duplicity.

THE FALL OF THE ALAMO

While waving an olive branch toward Mexican liberals, the Texans prepared for war. Sam Houston was named commander of the army and was assigned the thankless task of whipping raw recruits into an effective military machine. While he did so the situation deteriorated rapidly; Santa Anna was at their door breathing defiance with every pronouncement, nor was there any tendency for Mexicans to rally to the Texan cause. There was no choice now but to declare independence, a step taken on March 1, 1836. From this time on, the sole concern of Texas was to defeat the 2400 troops under the Mexican dictator who were moving into the province. Only one small force threatened Santa Anna's progress; some 180 men under Colonel William B. Travis occupied the abandoned Alamo mission in San Antonio, and had to be dislodged before his army could advance. The Texans knew that they would be no match for the Mexican army, but they were well supplied and could account for more than their share of the enemy. Travis' last letter, smuggled through the enemy lines on the night of March 3, 1836, revealed the spirit that eventually won Texas its independence:[8]

From the twenty-fifth to the present date the enemy have kept up a bombardment

---

[8] Amelia Williams, "A Critical Study of the Siege of the Alamo and of the Personnel of Its Defenders," *Southwestern Historical Quarterly*, XXXVII (July, 1933), 22–24.

from two howitzers, one a five and a half inch, and the other an eight inch,—and a heavy cannonade from two long nine-pounders, mounted on a battery on the opposite side of the river, at a distance of four hundred yards from our wall. During this period the enemy have been busily employed in encircling us in with entrenched encampments on all sides, at the following distances, to wit: In Bexar, four hundred yards west; in Lavillita, three hundred yards south; at the powder-house, one thousand yards east of south; on the ditch, eight hundred yards northeast, and at the old mill, eight hundred yards north. Notwithstanding all this, a company of thirty-two men from Gonzales, made their way in to us on the morning of the first inst. at three o'clock, and Colonel J. B. Bonham (a courier from Gonzales) got in this morning at eleven o'clock without molestation. I have fortified this place, so that the walls are generally proof against cannon balls; and I shall continue to entrench on the inside, and strengthen the walls by throwing up dirt. At least two hundred shells have fallen inside of our works without having injured a single man; indeed, we have been so fortunate as not to lose a man from any cause, and we have killed many of the enemy. The spirits of my men are still high although they have had much to depress them. We have contended for ten days against an enemy whose numbers are variously estimated from fifteen hundred to six thousand men, with General Ramirez—Sesma and Colonel Batres, the aid-de-camp of Santa Anna, at their head. A report was circulated that Santa Anna himself was with the enemy, but I think it was false. A reinforcement of about one thousand men is now entering Bexar from the west, and I think it more than probable that Santa Anna is now in town, from the rejoicing we hear.

Col. Fannin is said to be on the march to this place with reinforcements, but I fear it is not true, as I have *repeatedly* sent to him for aid without receiving any. Colonel Bonham, my special messenger, arrived at La Bahia fourteen days ago, with a request for aid, and on the arrival of the enemy in Bexar, ten days ago, I sent an express to Colonel F., which arrived at Goliad on the next day, urging him to send us reinforcements; none have yet arrived. I look to the colonies alone for aid; unless it arrives soon, I shall have to fight the enemy on his own terms. I will, however, do the best I can under the circumstances; and I feel confident that the determined valor and desperate courage, heretofore exhibited by my men, will not fail them in the last struggle; and although they may be sacrificed to the vengeance of a Gothic enemy, the victory will cost the enemy so dear, that it will be worse for him than defeat. I hope your honorable body will hasten on reinforcements, ammunitions and provisions to our aid so soon as possible. We have provisions for twenty days for the men we have. Our supply of ammunition is limited. At least five hundred pounds of cannon powder, and two hundred rounds of six, nine, twelve, and eighteen pound balls, ten kegs of rifle powder and a supply of lead should be sent to this place without delay, under a sufficient guard.

If these things are promptly sent and large reinforcements are hastened to this frontier, this neighborhood will be the great and decisive ground. The power of Santa Anna is to be met here or in the colonies; we had better meet them here than to suffer a war of devastation to rage in our settlements. A blood red banner waves from the church of Bejar, and in the camp above us, in token that the war is one of vengeance against rebels; they have declared us as such; demanded that we should surrender at discretion, or that this garrison should be put to the sword. Their threats have no influence on me or my men, but to make all fight with desperation and that high-souled courage that characterizes the patriot, who is willing to die in defence of his country's liberty and his own honor.

The citizens of this municipality are all our enemies, except those who have joined us heretofore. We have three Mexicans now in the fort; those who have not joined us in this extremity, should be declared public enemies, and their property should aid in paying the expenses of the war.

The bearer of this will give your honorable body a statement more in detail, should he escape through the enemy's lines.

God and Texas—Victory or Death

THE MILITARY PHASE: THE "RUNAWAY SCRAPE"

The aid implored by Travis never arrived, and on the grey morning of March 6, 1836, the Mexicans attacked. By nightfall all defenders of the Alamo were dead. This defeat, and another at Goliad, not only cost Santa Anna heavily, but rallied the Texans to a common cause. Victory seemed unlikely at that moment, with nothing blocking the path of the Mexican army as it began its eastward march across Texas. Houston fell back slowly, shaping his recruits into the semblance of an army as he did so. Among the people, this retreat bred panic as the word spread that the Mexican barbarians would slaughter them all. Hurriedly they gathered their belongings and fled toward the Louisiana border, in a "runaway scrape" that was described by an observer, W. B. Dewes:[9]

---

[9] W. B. Dewes, *Letters from an Early Settler of Texas* (Louisville, 1852), pp. 203–205.

DEAR FRIEND:

In my last I promised to give you a sketch of "the runaway scrape," as the retreat of the families in last March, is called. The description which I shall give you will indeed be but a sketch, for 'tis beyond the power of pen to give anything but a faint idea of that dreadful time. Tongue cannot tell nor words reveal the horrors of that period. It seemed as though the whole country was panic struck. Every family in the country immediately left their homes as soon as the army commenced its retreat. Those who lived farthest east, and who were of course in the least danger, seemed to be the most alarmed, and fled with the greatest haste. Here we saw the old saying, "it grows as it goes," verified. Those who were most easily frightened, and the first to fly without waiting to know the truth of the situation, had gone on and in their flight had given exaggerated accounts of the danger which passed from mouth to mouth, till the people of Eastern Texas believed the whole force of the enemy were close upon them. The panic and fear increased; the roads were literally crowded with wagons, men, women, and children, hurrying on with the greatest speed to a place of safety. On they went, one after another, through woods and across prairies, seeming to have nothing in view but to go eastward. Here might be seen delicate ladies wading through mud and dirt, striving to hasten their footsteps and free themselves from the marshes; but at every step they would bog in deeper and deeper, till at last after toiling long they would succeed in getting out tired and wearied, yet still they would press on, hoping soon to reach a place of safety. Again, loaded wagons rolled on one after another in the greatest haste, till they came near the crossing of a stream, then each would strive to be first and foremost, in order that they might be soonest across the stream; now you might behold children falling from the wagons which still kept on leaving the children behind, till another wagon came along and picked them up. Mothers have in this manner been separated from their children for days, and some for weeks, as the wagons would often take a different course; all seemed to look out for themselves alone: the fountain of benevolence seemed dried up: on, on they pressed, regardless of all, save them-selves. So great was the alarm that families seated in happiness at their meals, on hearing that the Mexican army were approaching, wildly rushed from their houses and leaving all their property exposed to the incursions of the enemy, fled from their homes to save themselves from the approaching danger.

Every manner of crossing rivers was resorted to at this time; there being but few ferries and the watercourses very high. We were frequently obliged to tax our inventive faculties to find methods for crossing. To give you an example of our difficulties, I will tell you the manner in which we crossed the San Jacinto river. There were about seventy-five wagons in the company, and on arriving at the river we found no way to cross; the river was up to the top of the banks, and there was no ferry; the question now arose how are we to get across! we might construct rafts but the stream was so rapid that it would be hazardous to cross on them! yet cross we must, and some way must be thought of. But, thanks to the invention of two Yankees, the difficulty was soon obviated. They proposed that we should look us out a couple of very tall pine trees, so that their length might be sufficient to reach across the river, cut them down, peal the bark from them and then lay them across the river so near to each other that we might place the wagons on them and pull them across the river with a rope. This we did, upon each loaded wagon we placed a number of women and children, and the seventy-five wagons were all drawn over in the course of half a day.

You may perhaps imagine that the people all returned immediately to their homes upon the departure of the Mexicans from the country, but such is not the case; many of them have not yet returned. When I returned home there were no persons west of the Colorado river. I therefore was obliged to hire a couple of young men to remain with us and assist in protecting us from the Indians; but in a short time several families returned who resided on the river both above and below Columbus.

SAM HOUSTON STANDS FIRM

Amidst this chaos one man who kept his head was General Sam Houston. Knowing that time was essential to train his army, and realizing that every mile advanced by the Mexican force lengthened its supply lines and sapped its resources, he was content to retreat until he found exactly the right spot to make his stand. His confidence in this strategy was shown in a letter written to the Secretary of War on March 29, 1836, from the Brazos River:[10]

SIR:

On my arrival on the Brazos, had I consulted the wishes of all, I should have been like the ass between two stacks of hay. Many wished me to go below, others above. I con-

---

[10] Amelia Williams and E. C. Barker (eds.), *The Writings of Sam Houston* (Austin, Texas: University of Texas Press, 1938–1943), vol. 1, pp. 384–385.

sulted none—I held no councils of war. If I err, the blame is mine. I find Colonel Hockley, of my staff, a sage counsellor and true friend. My staff are all worthy, and merit well of me.

There was on yesterday, as I understood, much discontent in the lines, because I would not fall down the river. If it should be wise for me to do so, I can cross over at any time, and fall down to greater advantage and safety. I apprehend, in consequence of my falling back, that the enemy may change their route to Matagorda. I ordered all the men residing on the coast, and those arriving from United States at, or south of Velasco, to remain and fortify at some safe point; and, on yesterday, I sent Colonel Harcourt as principal engineer of the army, down to the coast, to erect fortifications at the most eligible point of defence. I place at his disposal the resources of the lower country for its defence and protection.

I pray God that you would get aid, speedy aid, from the United States; or, after all inducements, we must suffer. I hope to-day to receive ninety men from the Redlands. I can not now tell my force, but will soon be able. The enemy must be crippled by the fights they have had with our men. I have ordered D. C. Barrett and E. Gritton to be arrested and held subject to the future order of the government. I do think they ought to be detained and tried as traitors and spies.

For Heaven's sake, do not drop back again with the seat of government! Your removal to Harrisburg has done more to increase the panic in the country than anything else that has occurred in Texas, except the fall of the Alamo. Send fifty agents, if need be, to the United States. Wharton writes me from Nashville, that the ladies of that place have fitted out, at their own expense, no less than two hundred men.

If matters press upon us, for God's sake let the troops land at Galveston bay, and by land reach the Brasos! Let no troops march with baggage-wagons, or wagons of any kind.

THE BATTLE OF SAN JACINTO

By April 20, 1836, Houston was ready to make his stand. With an army of 783 men and a strong defensive position on the banks of the San Jacinto River, he felt that he could hold his own against Santa Anna's force, even though outnumbered three to one. The battle of San Jacinto, fought the next day, ended in complete victory for the Texans. Houston described his success in a letter to G. G. Burnet, president of the Republic of Texas, written a few days later:[11]

I have the honor to inform you that on the evening of the 18th inst., after a forced march of 55 miles, which was effected in two and a half days, the army arrived opposite Harrisburgh; that evening a courier of the enemy was taken, from which I learned that Gen. Santa Anna, with one division of his troops, had marched in the direction of Lynch's ferry, on the San Jacinto, burning Harrisburgh as he passed down. The army was ordered to be in readiness to march early the next morning. The main body effected a crossing over Buffalo Bayou, below Harrisburgh, on the morning of the 19th, having left the baggage, the sick, and a sufficient camp guard in the rear. We continued the march throughout the night, and without refreshment. At daylight we resumed the line of march, and in a short distance our scouts encountered those of the enemy, and we received information that Gen. Santa Anna was at New Washington, and would that day take up the line of march for Anahuac, cross-

---
[11] Chester Newell, *History of the Revolution in Texas* (New York, 1838), pp. 212–215.

ing at Lynch's. The Texan army halted within half a mile of the ferry, in some timber, and were engaged in slaughtering beeves, when the army of Santa Anna was seen approaching in battle array having been encamped at Clopper's Point, 8 miles below. Disposition was immediately made of our forces, and preparation for his reception. He took a position, with his infantry and artillery in the centre, occupying an island of timber, his cavalry covering the left flank. The artillery then opened on our encampment, consisting of one double fortified medium brass 12-pounder.

The infantry, in columns, advanced with the design of attacking our lines, but were repulsed by a discharge of grape and canister from our artillery, consisting of two six-pounders. The enemy had occupied a piece of timber within rifle shot of the left wing of our army, from which an occasional interchange of small arms took place between the troops, until the enemy withdrew to a position on the bank of the San Jacinto, about three quarters of a mile from our encampment, and commenced a fortification. A short time before sun-set, our mounted men, about 85 in number, under the special command of Col. Sherman, marched out for the purpose of reconnoitering the enemy. Whilst advancing, they received a volley from the left of the enemy's infantry, and after a sharp rencontre with their cavalry, in which ours acted well, and performed some feats of daring chivalry, they retired in good order, having had two men severely wounded, and several horses killed. In the mean time the infantry, under the command of Lieut. Col. Millard, and Col. Bush's regiment, with the artillery, had marched out for the purpose of covering the retreat, if necessary. All those fell back in good order to our encampment about sun-set, and remained without any ostensible action until the 21st at half past 3 o'clock, taking the first refreshment which they had enjoyed for two days. The enemy, in the mean time, extended the right flank of their infantry so as to occupy the extreme point of a skirt of timber on the bank of the San Jacinto, and screened their left by a fortification about five feet high, constructed of packs and baggage, leaving an opening in the centre of the breastwork, in which their artillery was placed—the cavalry upon the left wing.

About 9 o'clock on the morning of the 21st, the enemy were reinforced by 500 choice troops, under the command of Gen. Cos, increasing their effective force to upwards of 1500 men, while our aggregate force for the field numbered 783. At half past 3 o'clock in the morning, I ordered the officers of the Texan army to parade their respective commands, having in the mean time ordered the bridges on the only road communicating with the Brazos, distant 8 miles from our encampment, to be destroyed, thus cutting off all possibility of escape. Our troops paraded with alacrity and spirit, and were anxious for the contest. Their conscious disparity in numbers only seemed to increase their enthusiasm and confidence, and heightened their anxiety for the contest. Our situation afforded me the opportunity of making the arrangements preparatory to the attack, without exposing our designs to the enemy. The 1st regiment, commanded by Col. Burleson, was assigned to the centre; the 2d regiment, under the command of Col. Sherman, formed the left wing of the army; the artillery, under the special command of Col. G. W. Herkley, Inspector General, was placed on the right of the 1st regiment; and four companies of infantry, under the command of Lieut. Col. Millard, sustained the artillery upon the right. Our cavalry, 61 in number, commanded by Col. Mirabeau B. Lamar, (whose gallant and daring conduct, on the previous day had attracted the admiration of his comrades, and called him to that station,) placed on our extreme right, completed our line. Our cavalry was first despatched to the front of the enemy's left, for the purpose of attracting their notice, whilst an extensive island of timber afforded us an opportunity of concentrating our forces, and deploying from that point, agreeably to the previous design of the troops. Every evolution was performed with alacrity, the whole advancing rapidly in line, and through an open prairie, without any protection whatever for our men. The artillery advanced and took station within 200 yards of the enemy's breastwork, and commenced an effective fire with grape and canister.

Col. Sherman, with his regiment, having commenced the action upon our left wing, the whole line, at the centre and on the right, advancing in double quick time, rung the war cry "Remember the Alamo," received the enemy's fire, and advanced within point-blank shot before a piece was discharged from our lines. Our line advanced without a halt, until they were in possession of the woodland and the enemy's breastwork. The right wing of Burleson's, and the left of Millard's, taking possession of the breastwork; and our artillery having gallantly charged up within 70 yards of the enemy's cannon, when it was taken by our troops. The conflict lasted about 18 minutes from the time of the close of the action until we were in possession of the enemy's encampment, taking one piece of cannon, (loaded,) four stand of colors, all their camp equipage, stores, and baggage. Our cavalry had charged and routed that of the enemy upon the right, and given pursuit to the fugitives, which did not cease until they arrived at the bridge which I mentioned before. Capt. Karnes, always among the foremost in danger, commanded the pursuers. The conflict in the breastwork lasted but a few moments; many of the troops encountered hand to hand, and not having the advantage of bayonets on our side, our riflemen used their pieces as war clubs, breaking many of them off at the breech. The rout commenced at half past 4, and the pursuit by the main army continued until twilight. A guard was then left in charge of the enemy's encampment, and our army returned with their killed and wounded. In the battle our loss was 2 killed and 23 wounded, six of whom mortally. The enemy's loss was 630 killed, among which was 1 general officer, 4 colonels, 2 lieut. colonels, 7 captains, 12 lieutenants; wounded 280, of which were 3 colonels, 3 lieut. colonels, 2 second lieut. colonels, 7 captains, 1 cadet. Prisoners 730—President Santa Anna, Gen. Cos, 4 colonels, aids to Gen. Santa Anna, 6 lieut. colonels, the private secretary of Gen. Santa Anna, and the colonel of the Guerrero Battalion, are included in the number. Gen. Santa Anna was not taken until the 22d, and Gen. Cos on yesterday, very few having escaped. About 600 muskets, 300 sabres, and 200 pistols, have been collected since the action; several hundred mules and horses were taken, and near twelve thousand dollars in specie. For several days previous to the action, our troops were engaged in forced marches, exposed to excessive rains, and the additional inconvenience of extremely bad roads, ill supplied with rations and clothing; yet, amid every difficulty, they bore up with cheerfulness and fortitude, and performed their marches with speed and alacrity—there was no murmuring.

MIGRATION TO THE TEXAN REPUBLIC

Texan independence was won at San Jacinto, for while Mexico refused to recognize the new republic, it made no further attempt at conquest.

As an independent nation, Texas grew rapidly during its brief existence, attracting settlers by favorable land laws, a revival of the "empresario" system, and an open-handed welcome to all newcomers. Its population grew from 30,000 in 1836 to 142,000 in a single decade. This increase can be explained both by the attractiveness of the Republic of Texas and by the impact of the Panic of 1837 on the American Southwest. Bankrupt planters, large and small, suddenly discovered that the new nation was a haven against creditors as well as a place to begin life anew. A traveler through Mississippi at this time noted the spread of the "Texas Fever" there, and the reasons for the contagion:[12]

It is a beautiful and fertile country through Holmes, Yazoo and Madison Counties, over which we traveled. Many plantations had been recently opened, and on some of them elegant residences had been erected. The owners had freely indorsed for each other in the banks, and hundreds of thousands of dollars had been invested in negroes, brought from Virginia and the Carolinas. When the storm broke over the banks the suits were so numerous in the courts that some of the lawyers had their declarations in *assumpsit* printed by the quire, leaving blanks only for the names of the debtor, creditor and the amounts. In each of these counties an immense number of judgments had been obtained and the aggregate indebtedness had run into millions. A great number of these plantations in 1845 were uncultivated. The fences had fallen down, the homes and outhouses were tenantless and bespoke widespread desolation. We learned the history of the times from the lawyers at Lexington, Yazoo City and Canton. With these General Featherston talked as to his candidacy before the coming convention. We were told that as a general thing on the evening before abandonment those large plantations would present no unusual appearance. The stock would be in the stables, properly attended to; the cows would be in the cowpen; the hogs would be called and fed; the sheep would be herded; the plantation negroes would be in their proper places, and over all the hush of evening and the stillness of night would fall. On the morning following the smoke would curl from the chimneys, from residence and quarters, the cows would be lowing in the pen, the sheep bleating in the fold, the hogs in their place; not a wagon gone, not a vehicle missing; the meat left in the smokehouse, the poultry raising their usual disturbance—and not a human being, nor horse, nor mule, nor saddle, nor bridle on the whole place. Every negro, every horse, every mule spirited away in the darkness of the night—the negro women and children on horses and mules, the men on foot, all, all in a double-quick march for Texas, then a foreign government. The first object was to get across the county line, the next to cross the Mississippi River, and the next to cross the line of the Republic of Texas. All this had to be done before the executions could issue and be placed in the hands of the sheriffs of the different counties. Family carriages were left motionless to avoid creating any suspicion, the white families having taken their trips to neighboring towns, where the stage lines would convey them to points of safety—generally steamboat landings on the Mississippi—on their way to Texas. Even in the city of Columbus there remain on file in the circuit clerk's office printed declarations, containing not only the names of the plaintiff's banks, but in some cases the names of the defendants. This will convey

---

[12] J. A. Orr, "A Trip from Houston to Jackson, Miss., in 1845," in *Publications of the Mississippi Historical Society* (Oxford, Mississippi, 1906), vol. 9, pp. 175–176.

an idea of the immense indebtedness to the banks of the country and of the universality of endorsements and personal securities. The immovable property was all that the executions could reach. After this came hundreds of suits by holders of bank notes.

As an independent republic, Texas faced three alternatives, only one of which was to the liking of the majority of the people. It could exist as a small nation under the protection of France or England; it could expand over northern Mexico to become a sizable nation; or it could seek annexation by the United States. The latter alternative was favored from the outset, but Texans found to their annoyance that the United States was not willing to annex them. The prospect of additional slave territory, combined with the fear that annexation might touch off a war with Mexico, quenched for a time the expansionist thirst of the American government and people. Texas remained independent for a decade, until the United States changed its opinion. This transformation was hurried by the prospect of acquiring even more western lands into which pioneers were advancing. Of these, one of the most tempting was the Oregon country.

CHAPTER 19

The Occupation of Oregon, 1820-1845

The expansionist compulsion that peopled Texas with American frontiersmen was to find another outlet in the Oregon country. That distant domain had, since the early nineteenth century, been claimed by both England and the United States on the basis of discovery and exploration. At the outset neither nation was eager to resolve the conflict for each was confident that its own weapon could bring ultimate victory: westward expansion for the Americans, commercial enterprise for the British. Hence they agreed in 1818 on a treaty of joint occupation, opening the area between 42° and 54°40' to settlement and trade by the citizens of both nations. This agreement was renewed in 1827; it could be terminated on six month's notice by either party. Each was free to win Oregon by the most effective use of its own resources.

In this contest Britain gained the upper hand, with traders as its agents of conquest. A futile American attempt to occupy the region was made when John Jacob Astor in 1813 founded a trading post at Astoria on the Columbia River, but when Britain cleared the seas of American vessels during the War of 1812, he was unable to supply his outpost and surrendered it to an English rival, the North West Company. For a time, this trading concern disputed with the equally powerful Hudson's Bay Company for the commerce of the Pacific Northwest, with the battle for trade reaching open warfare at times. Eventually the crown in 1821 forced the two concerns to merge under the name of the Hudson's Bay Company. From that date on, this giant enterprise controlled the Oregon country, planting forts and trading posts at strategic points, and dominating both the sea lanes and the interior so completely that intruders were soon discouraged. This was especially the case after 1825 when Fort Vancouver was built, and Dr. John McLoughlin was placed in command. Recognizing that self-sufficiency was essential to profits, he directed the establishment of farms, orchards, and ranches that gave a look of permanent occupancy to the countryside. By the 1820s, the British monopoly was almost complete and had to be broken, or the United States would be forced to surrender the region by default.

EARLY PROPAGANDA FOR OREGON

A few who recognized the need for action in Oregon raised their voices in behalf of an aggressive American policy. None was more strid-

439

ent than that of Dr. John Floyd, a member of the House of Representatives from Virginia. His agitation forced Congress to name a "Committee on the Occupation of the Columbia River" under his chairmanship, and on January 25, 1821, Floyd told his colleagues of the purposes and ambitions of his committee:[1]

The committee, from carefully examining all the facts connected with the subject referred to them, are well persuaded that the situation of the United States is such as to enable it to possess all the benefits derived from this trade, which, in the hands of others, amounts to millions; many of whose trading establishments east of the Rocky Mountains are within the acknowledged limits of this Republic, as fixed by the Convention of London of the 20th of October, 1818; and, it is believed, that no Power, with the exception of Spain, has any just claim to territory west of them, or on the Pacific. The dependence for subsistence of many of those establishments, is upon the buffalo beef hunted by the Assiniboin Indians, who inhabit the country between the river of that name and the Missouri; their hunting ground is far within our boundary. To succeed in procuring to the people of the United States all the wealth flowing from this source, it is only necessary to occupy with a small trading guard the most northeastern point upon the Missouri river, and confine the foreigners to their own territory; at the same time occupying, with a similar guard, the mouth of Columbia. The great profit derived from this trade by the Canadian companies, when we know the distance and obstructions in their rivers, and in the various streams they ascend in carrying it on, the advance of price consequent upon it becomes rather a matter of amazement that otherwise, and inclines us to examine our own rivers with a view to the same object. Instead, however, of those formidable obstructions, we find a smooth and deep river running through a boundless extent of the most fertile soil on this continent, containing within its limits all those valuable furs which have greatly enriched others; a certain, safe, and easy navigation, with a portage of only two hundred miles, uniting it with another river, equally smooth, deep, and certain, running to the great Western ocean. Thus are those two great oceans separated by a single portage of two hundred miles! The practicability of a speedy, safe, and easy communication with the Pacific, is no longer a matter of doubt or conjecture: from information not to be doubted, the Rocky Mountains at this time, in several places, are so smooth and open that the labor of ten men for twenty days would enable a wagon with its usual freight to pass with great facility from the navigable water of the Missouri to that of the Columbia; the actual distance from river to river several hundred miles from their source, that is, from the great Falls of Missouri to the fork of Clark's river, is one hundred and forty-nine miles; the distance, therefore, of two hundred miles is to good navigation on the Columbia, which is the only river of any magnitude upon that whole coast, north of the Colorado of California, though there are several good harbors, secure and safe for vessels of any size.

The region of country from the ocean to the head of tide water, which is about two hundred miles, is heavily timbered, with a great variety of wood well calculated for ship building, and every species of cabinet or carpenter's work; though there is a heavily timbered country thence for two hundred miles further, yet it is of a lesser growth, and quality not so durable; at that point commences the plain country, when the soil becomes more thin, and almost without wood,

---

[1] *Annals of Congress*, 16th Congress, 2nd Session, pp. 954–955.

until it arrives at the table lands below the mountain. Though the soil of this region is not so good as in any other part of this great valley, yet it produces grass of the finest quality, and is emphatically called the region favorable to the production of the horse; this noble animal, so far surpassing all others in usefulness, courage, and swiftness, is here produced in greater perfection than even in Andalusia or Virginia. But, independent of all the wealth which may be derived from the fur trade of that river and the Missouri, the security too which the peace of this country would find in the influence which the American traders would obtain over the native, is the increasing commerce in the Western ocean. There is no employment so well calculated to make good seamen as the whale fisheries, which are known to be more profitable on this coast than any other; at the same time the oil is far preferable to that taken on any other coast, being clear and transparent as rock water. While so many of our citizens are industriously engaged in the various branches of trade in those seas, more valuable to this country, it is believed, than any other; while all nations who have claims upon that coast, and some who have none, are anxious to occupy some position upon it, even at a vast expense, to enable them to participate in its benefits, we have neglected to extend to it any portion of our care, though it appears, from the best information, that there is at this time eight millions of property owned by citizens of this Republic in the Pacific ocean.

PROPAGANDA FOR OREGON

The Oregon country was promoted by a few farseeing congressmen such as Dr. Floyd during the 1820s and 1830s, but a more effective propagandist was an eccentric Boston schoolteacher named Hall Jackson Kelley. Kelley's interest in the region was aroused by reports of the Lewis and Clark expedition; immersing himself in the subject he was ready by 1830 to publish the first of a succession of pamphlets and articles urging the immediate occupation of Oregon. His first, a sixty-seven page effusion titled "A Geographical Sketch of that Part of North America Called Oregon," described the topography and geography in glowing terms, and argued that commercial profits were to be garnered there as well as fortunes for farmers. His concluding section, "Advantages of Settling the Oregon Country," summarized and drove home his arguments:[2]

The local position of that country; its physical appearance and productions; its qualities of soil and climate, suggest, not only the practicability of founding a colony in it; but the consequent beneficial results to our Republic; and the many valuable blessings it might be made to yield to the settlers, and to their posterity. The expense of the project could not much exceed that of the present South Sea expedition, though the profits would be, in the proportion of one hundred to one. It is the object of these remarks to notice some of the advantages, which would inevitably accrue to the government of the United States from a colonization of that country.

First The occupancy of it, by three thousand of the active sons of American freedom, would secure it from the possession of another nation, and from augmenting the power and physical resources of an enemy. It might save that and this country, from the disastrous consequences of a foreign and corrupt population; and benefit mankind by a race of people, whose past lives, affording

---

[2] *A Geographical Sketch of that Part of North America Called Oregon* (Boston, 1830), reprinted in Fred W. Powell (ed.), *Hall J. Kelley on Oregon* (Princeton, 1932), pp. 60–67.

the most honourable testimony of their characters, would be a pledge for their future conduct, and a full indemnity for all expenses incurred in their behalf.

It is not a doubtful hypothesis, that unless our legitimate rights on the waters and in the territory of Oregon, are protected by planting a colony in it, or by other means no less effectual; they will in a few years more, become entirely lost to our merchants, or to the benefits of our country.

England is desirous of possessing the whole country, with all its invaluable privileges. She has evinced this, by that bold and lawless spirit of enterprise, by which she has acquired so great a monopoly in the Indian trade; by which, in the year 1812, she took from American citizens, the town of Astoria, (now called Fort George,) and still retains it; by which she built and scattered along the Columbia and its tributaries, on the Tatooche, and at other places, her trading towns. In this presumptuous way; in defiance to treaties and obligations, to the paramount claims of this country, and by alliances with the Indians, she hopes to secure a hold upon it, which the physical power of the American Republic, exerted in the plenitude of its energies, cannot break. She is provident in these things; and wisely anticipates that awful catastrophe, which will terminate on the Eastern Continent her long and brilliant career. She, therefore, selects this fair tract of earth, where to rebuild her empire, and again make it resplendent in wealth and power. Nature has provided every material on the spot, necessary to make it, as permanent and lasting in foundation, as stupendous in structure.

Second A free and exclusive trade with the Indians, and with a colony in Oregon, would very considerably increase the resources, and promote the commercial and manufacturing interests of our country.

The fur trade has been and still is found, vastly lucrative to those who pursue it. The contemplated colony would find it productive of great pecuniary advantage, and a fruitful source of their prosperity. The traffic carried on with the Indians will become more reciprocal, and equal in the diffusion of its comforts, as industry and the peaceful arts are sustained by them; for a trade with any people is commensurate with their real wants; these, with Indians, must naturally increase, as they assimilate their customs and habits to those of their refined and civilized neighbours....

English traders, by a proper circumspection and deportment of conduct, and by honest and honourable dealing, have conciliated the friendship of the natives, and secured a profitable trade with them, which consists chiefly in beads and many other articles of no value; in some coarse broad cloths, blankets, and a vast variety of iron and tin wares, which are exchanged principally for skins and furs, the productions of trapping and the chase. Economy has suggested to the Indians, a less valuable and a less cumbersome dress, than the beautiful and rich skin of the sea otter. They are now generally clad and decorated in articles of English merchandize. The exclusive privilege, therefore, of supplying these articles, would be alike beneficial to the merchant and the manufacturer, and would contribute to the wealth and prosperity of the country. Were not the Indian trade a source of great advantage, and the country valuable for colonization, that shrewd and eagle-eyed nation, without justice, would not have made it so long the theatre of commercial enterprise; nor would she have been so eager to possess and make it her own.

Third The fisheries might be more extensively and profitably pursued. They have long constituted a valuable branch of our commerce, and a perennial and vital source of our comforts and prosperity. Fish, in vast shoals and of the most useful kinds, abound in the Western ocean. Whales, both the black and spermaceti, throng those waters, and sport in the very seas and bays of Oregon....

Fourth A port of entry, and a naval station at the mouth of the Columbia, or in De Fuca straits, would be of immense importance to a protection of the whale and other fisheries, and of the fur trade; and to a general control over the Pacific ocean, where millions of our property, are constantly afloat. The great abundance of excellent timber for ship building; and the small comparative expense, at which ships of war might be built on the banks of the Columbia, would justify the making of navy yards, and building, in them, the principal part of our public and private vessels. Incalculable would be the advantages of some safe place, on that part of the globe, where to build, repair vessels, and get supplies;—where in time of war, to enter with prizes, and make preparation for common defence. The prizes taken by Commodore Porter, in that ocean and necessarily destroyed by him, for the want of some port, were more than equal, to any expense that might necessarily accrue, in making the proposed establishment, fortifying and strengthening it with three thousand settlers.

Fifth It is an object, worthy the attention of government, to secure the friendship of the Indians, and prevent alliances between them and other nations.

By cultivating a friendly intercourse, and coalition with them, they might not only be prevented from cooperating with an enemy; but if desirable, be induced to oppose his attacks. The American people, at present, are too far remote, to effect this purpose. The English are on the ground; their traders do business among them; and their interests, in a measure, commingle together. They are, therefore, in a better situation to direct the policy, and command the obedience of the Indians; to excite, in them, jealousies and a hatred implacable, fatal and eternal; and to expose our frontier settlements to the encroachments and abuses of an uncivilized, treacherous people. The Indians, at present are peaceable, and wish nothing more, than fair dealing; the free and undisturbed enjoyment of their rights. Satisfied of this, white men, may pursue in quiet and security, the various business of civilized life....

How consistent with the prosperity of the Indians, and the best good of our country, would such a state of things be. The Republic planting and protecting a colony; that colony cherishing the interest, and welfare of the Indians, who in turn contribute to the security of the Republic.

Sixth The settlement of the Oregon country, would conduce to a freer intercourse, and a more extensive and lucrative trade with the East Indies.

Commerce would break away from its present narrow and prescribed limits, and spread into new and broader channels, embracing within its scope China, Corea, the Phillipine and Spice islands, Japan and its provinces. These Countries possess an extremely dense population, and articles of merchandise, the richest in the world. The colony located on a shore of easy access; and measuring its conduct by a policy, liberal and universal, will find no difficulties in opening with that civilized people, a free intercourse, and consequently, inexhaustible sources of wealth and prosperity. Improvements and facilities in trade with China, resulting in a state of social and commercial relations, and connecting the interests of that Empire, with those of a government the most liberal, refined and free, will be sufficient motives on their part to form, on just and reciprocal principles, a commercial alliance, and to receive with all due consideration of respect, and favours our ministers.

These are subjects vast and valuable; and, it is believed, may be attained at an inconsiderable expense. The power of the Mandarines, would be restricted, and that of the Hoang agency suppressed. Other advantages would accrue; our trade would be disenthralled from the monopolies, the vexations and the bondage of the East India Company, should it be rechartered. The acquisition of just privileges, and a full participation in a trade, so exceedingly rich, deserves some attempt on the part of our government.

Such an extension and enjoyment of the East India trade, would provoke the spirit of American enterprize, to open communications from the Mississippi valley, and from the gulf of Mexico to the Pacific ocean, and thus open *new channels*, through which the products of America and the Eastern world, will pass in mutual exchange, saving in every voyage, a distance of ten thousand miles; *new channels*, which opening across the bosom of a wide spread ocean; and intersecting islands, where health fills the breeze and comforts spread the shores, would conduct the full tide of a golden traffic, into the reservoir of our national finance.

Seventh Many of our seaports would be considerably benefited by taking emigrants from their redundant population. It is said, and truly so, that business of all kinds is over done; that the whole population cannot derive a comfortable support from it; hence the times are called hard, which generally press the hardest upon those who pursue the useful occupations of laborious industry. Multitudes of such persons, sustaining the character of worthy citizens, cast out of employment, into idleness and poverty, might wisely emigrate to a country, where they could pursue useful occupations, to which they are competent, with profit. This reduction of population would promote the interests and prosperity of those who remain at home; industry with them would be more encouraged; agriculture, commerce and manufactories, mutually supplying each other, would be better supported, and unite in yielding in greater abundance, the necessary comforts and conveniences of life. . . .

These hastily written observations must be concluded by the remark, that all nations, who have planted colonies, have been enriched by them. England acquired a supremacy of the ocean, and all her national influence by it. America has a better opportunity, and fairer prospects of success, to emulate such examples. She can set up in business, her full grown and more affectionate children nearer home; and on a richer inheritance; and can receive to herself greater benefits. The present period is propitious to the experiment. The free governments of the world are fast progressing to the consummation of moral excellence; and are embracing within the scope of their policies, the benevolent and meliorating principles of humanity and reform. The most enlightened nation on earth will not be insensible to the best means of national prosperity. Convinced of the utility and happy consequences of establishing the Oregon colony, the American Republic will found, protect and cherish it; and thus enlarge the sphere of human felicity, and extend the peculiar blessings of civil polity, and of the Christian religion, to distant and destitute nations.

THE FIRST AMERICAN INVADERS

Kelley's extensive writings on Oregon bore fruit, sometimes in strange form. Nathaniel J. Wyeth, a well-to-do ice dealer in Cambridge, Massachusetts, read them and was determined to capitalize on the commercial prospects that had been so temptingly described. To this end he formed a joint stock company and advertised for adventurers who were willing to pay their own way from Boston to St. Louis, journey overland to Oregon, and engage in such business activities there as circumstances dictated. In March 1832 Wyeth led westward the thirty-one who responded. Meanwhile a ship he had sent loaded with trading supplies was rounding the Horn to meet them at the mouth of the Columbia. Thanks to the help of friendly mountain men, the party reached Fort Vancouver that fall, only to learn that their vessel had been wrecked. Wyeth was still determined to trade and was misled by Dr. John McLoughlin's warm greeting into believing that he would be welcome. He described his reactions and his reception at Fort Vancouver in his journal for October 29, 1832:[3]

29th Started at 10 ock and arrived at the fort of Vancouver at 12, 4 miles Here I was received with the utmost kindness and Hospitality by Doct. McLauchland [McLoughlin] the acting Gov. of the place MrMcDonald MrAllen and MrMckay gentlemen resident here Our people were supplied with food and shelter from the rain which is constant they raise at this fort 6000 bush. of wheat 3 of Barley 1500 potatoes 3000 peas a large quantity of punkins they have coming on apple trees, peach Do. and grapes. Sheep, Hogs, Horses, Cows, 600 goats, grist 2, saw mill 2. 24 lb guns powder magazine of stone the fort is of wood and square they are building a Sch. of 70 Tons there are about 8 settlers on the Multnomah they are the old engages of the Co. who have done trapping. I find Doct. McLauchland a fine old gentleman truly philanthropic in his Ideas he is doing much good by introducing fruits into this country which will much facilitate the progress of its settlement (Indian corn 3000 bush) The gentlemen of this Co. do much credit to their country and concern by their education deportment and talents. I find myself involved in much difficulty on acc. of my men some of whom wish to leave me and whom the Co. do not wish to engage no[r] to have them in the country without being attached to some Co. able to protect them alledging that if any of them are killed they will be obliged to aveng[e] it at an expense of money and amicable relations with the Indians. And it is disagreeable for me to have men who wish to leave me. The Co. seem disposed to render me all the assistance they can they live well at these posts they have 200 acres of land under cultivation the land is of the finest quality.

30th to 5th Nov remained at Vancouver and except the last day rain.

6th started down the river to look with a view to the Salmon buisness we decended the river at about 4 mils per hours and accomplished the journey in parts of 4 days the river is full of islands but they are all too low for cultivation being occasionally overflowed as also the praries (what few there are) on the main land with the exception of these small levells the country is so rough that a great part of the earth must be inhabited before this but the soil is good and the timber is heavy and thick and almost impenetrable from underbrush and fallen trees

FAILURE OF THE FIRST INVADERS

The sanguine hopes that launched Wyeth on his venture were soon scattered. He found his trading goods scant and overpriced when compared with the lavish supplies of the Hudson's

---

[3] Francis G. Young (ed.), *The Correspondence and Journals of Captain Nathaniel J. Wyeth, 1831–1836* (Eugene, Oregon, 1899), pp. 176–177.

Bay Company. The Indians were uninterested in breaking an alliance that had proven profitable to them, and the British traders were always at hand to compete for furs. Wyeth returned to Boston that year a sadder and poorer man but still convinced that trade with the Oregon country could be profitable. He tried again in 1834, and this time his vessel reached the Columbia safely. Here his good fortune ended, for again the quiet opposition of the Hudson's Bay Company and the expense of operating at such a distance from his source of supply left him near bankruptcy. He recited his difficulties in a "Statement of Facts" presented to Congress in 1847, when he sought reimbursement for his losses:[4]

On the 10th day of March 1832 I left Boston in a vessel with 20 men for Baltimore where I was joined by four more, and on the 27th left by Rail Road for Frederic Md from thence to Brownsville we marched on foot, and took passage from that place to Liberty Mo. on various steamboats, which place we left for the prairies on the 12th of May with 21 men, three having deserted, and on the 27th of May three more deserted. On the 8th of July we reached Pierre's Hole at the head of Lewis River where was then a rendezvous of Trappers and Indians. We remained at this place until the 17th at which time my party had been reduced by desertion and dismissial to 11 men, and then started for the Columbia arriving at Cape Disappointment on the 8th Nov. 1832, one man having died on the route. There I learned that a vessel on which I relied for supplies had been wrecked at the Society Islands. This intelligence discouraged the party so much that all but two requested a discharge. Of the 8 who then left me 5 returned to the U. S. by sea, one died there in 1834 and two remained as settlers. In the Spring of 1833 I commenced my return to the states with the two remaining men. When I reached the mouth of the Yellowstone one left me to remain with some of the trappers until I should return. With the other I reached the States, and soon after fitted out a vessel for the Columbia, and on the 7th Feb. 1834 left Boston for St. Louis where I organised a party of 70 men for the overland trip arriving at the head waters of the Snake or Lewis river in July 1834, and on the 15th of that month commenced to build Fort Hall, and after placing it in a defensive condition left it on the 7th August following for the mouth of the Columbia. On the 15th of Sept. I reached Oak Point 75 miles from its mouth where I met my vessel just arrived after a voyage of 8½ months, having been struck by lightening at sea and so injured as to be obliged to go into Valparaiso to repair. This vessel was fitted for the salmon fishing of that season. Her late arrival caused me to detain her until the following year. During the winter of 1835 this vessel went to the Sandwich Islands with timber & card returned in the Spring with cattle sheep goats & hogs which were placed on Wappatoo Island where in the mean time I had built an establishment called Fort William on the southwesterly side of the island and about 8 miles from the H. B. Co's post of Vancouver. At this post we grazed all the animals obtained from the Islands California and from the Indians, planted wheat corn potatoes peas beans turnips, grafted & planted apples and other fruits, built dwelling house and shops for working iron and wood, and in fact made a permanent location which has never been abandoned. I made this my personal residence during the Winter and Summer of 1835. In the autumn of that year I pro-

---

[4] Francis G. Young (ed.), *The Correspondence and Journals of Captain Nathaniel J. Wyeth, 1831–1836* (Eugene, Oregon, 1899), pp. 254–256.

ceeded to Fort Hall with supplies, having sent some previous to that time. During the winter of 1836 I resided at my post of Fort Hall, and in the Spring of that year returned to Fort William of Wappatoo Island whence I carried more supplies to Fort Hall arriving there the 18th June, and on the 25th left for the U. S. by way of Taos and the Arkansas river and arrived home early in the Autumn of 1836. The commercial distress of that time precluded the further prosecution of our enterprise, that so far had yielded little but misfortunes. It remained only to close the active business which was done by paying every debt, and returning every man who desired, to the place whence he was taken, and disposing of the property to the best advantage. All the property in the interior including Fort Hall was sold, it being necessary in order to retain that post, to keep up a garrison for its defense against the Indians, and to forward annual supplies to it, an operation at that time beyond our means. Fort William at Wappatoo Island requiring nothing of that kind was retained, and the gentleman then in charge Mr C. M. Walker was directed to lease it to some trusty person for 15 years unless sooner reclaimed. Nothing having been heard from Mr Walker for a long time I sent a request to John McLaughlin Esq. for the same purpose and also to have the island entered in my name at the land office established by the provisional government. That the original enterprise contemplated a permanent occupation is clearly shown by the instructions to the master of the brig Capt Lambert When I arrived on the lower Columbia in the Autumn of 1832 as her[e] in before stated there were no Americans there nor any one having an American feeling. So far as I know there had not been since Mr. Astor retired from the coast. Of the 11 men which I had then with me three remained until I again arrived in the Autumn of 1834 and 19 of those who then accompanied me including the missionaries remained permanently in the country.

ORIGIN OF
THE MISSIONARY INVASION

The efforts of politicians such as Dr. John Floyd, publicists like Hall Jackson Kelley, and commercial traders such as Nathaniel J. Wyeth kept Oregon before the nation but sparked no outburst of enthusiasm for the occupation or annexation of that remote land. The peopling of the Pacific Northwest resulted from an unlikely sequence of events. In October 1831, four Indians from the Oregon Country visited St. Louis with a band of returning fur traders. The red men—three Nez Percés and a Flathead —were impelled only by curiosity, but a more appealing motive was assigned them by another Indian who happened to be in St. Louis while they were there. William Walker, an educated Wyandot who had journeyed westward to help arrange the migration of his tribe to a reservation beyond the Mississippi, described the visitors from the Far West in a letter to a leading religious newspaper:[5]

I will here relate an anecdote, if I may so call it. Immediately after we landed in St. Louis, on our way to the West, I proceeded to Gen. Clark's, superintendent of Indian affairs, to present our letters of introduction from the Secretary of War, and to receive the same from him to the different Indian agents in the upper country. While in his office and transacting business with him, he informed

---

[5] *The Christian Advocate and Journal and Zion's Herald*, March 1, 1833, reprinted in Hiram M. Chittenden, *The American Fur Trade in the Far West* (New York, 1902), vol. 2, pp. 914–918.

me that three chiefs from the Flathead nation were in his house, and were quite sick, and that one (the fourth) had died a few days ago. They were from the west of the Rocky mountains. Curiosity prompted me to step into the adjoining room to see them, having never seen any, but often heard of them. I was struck with their appearance. They differ in appearance from any tribe of Indians I have ever seen: small in size, delicately formed, small limbs, and the most exact symmetry throughout, except the head. I had always supposed from their being called "Flatheads," that the head was actually flat on top; but this is not the case. The head is flattened thus:

From the point of the nose to the apex of the head, there is a perfect straight line, the protuberance of the forehead is flattened or leveled. You may form some idea of the shape of their heads from the rough sketch I have made with the pen, though I confess I have drawn most too long a proboscis for a flat-head. This is produced by a pressure upon the cranium while in infancy. The distance they had traveled on foot was nearly three thousand miles to see Gen. Clark, their great father, as they called him, he being the first American officer they ever became acquainted with, and having much confidence in him, they had come to consult him as they said, upon very important matters. Gen. C. related to me the object of their mission, and, my dear friend, it is impossible for me to describe to you my feelings while listening to his narrative. I will here relate it as briefly as I well can. It appeared that some white man had penetrated into their country, and happened to be a spectator at one of their religious ceremonies, which they scrupulously perform at stated periods. He informed them that their mode of worshipping the supreme Being was radically wrong, and instead of being acceptable and pleasing, it was displeasing to him; he also informed them that the white people *away* toward the rising of the sun had been put in possession of the true mode of worshipping the great Spirit. They had a book containing directions how to conduct themselves in order to enjoy his favor and hold converse with him; and with this guide, no one need go astray; but every one that would follow the directions laid down there could enjoy, in this life, his favor, and after death would be received into the country where the great Spirit resides, and live for ever with him.

Upon receiving this information, they called a national council to take this subject into consideration. Some said, if this be true, it is certainly high time we were put in possession of this mode, and if *our* mode of worshipping be wrong and displeasing to the great Spirit, it is time we had laid it aside. We must know something about this, it is a matter that cannot be put off, the sooner we know it the better. They accordingly deputed four of the chiefs to proceed to St. Louis to see their great father, Gen. Clark, to inquire of him, having no doubt but he would tell them the whole truth about it.

They arrived at St. Louis, and presented themselves to Gen. C. The latter was somewhat puzzled being sensible of the responsibility that rested on him; he, however, proceeded by informing them that what they had been told by the white man in their own country was true. Then went into a succinct history of man, from his creation down to the advent of the Saviour; explained to them all the moral precepts contained in the Bible, expounded to them the decalogue; informed them of the advent of the Saviour, his life, precepts, his death, resurrection, ascension, and the relation he now stands to man as a mediator—that he will judge the world, etc.

Poor fellows, they were not all permitted to return home to their people with the intelligence. Two died in St. Louis, and the remaining two, though somewhat indisposed, set out for their native land. Whether they reached home or not is not known. The change of climate and diet operated very severely upon their health. Their diet when at home is chiefly vegetables and fish.

If they died on their way home, peace be to their manes! They died inquirers after the truth. I was informed that the Flatheads, as a nation, have the fewest vices of any tribe of Indians on the continent of America.

FOUNDING THE JASON LEE MISSION, 1834

The Walker letter galvanized America's religious community into action. As contributions poured in, the Methodist Missionary Society voted to establish a mission among the Flatheads, and on July 17, 1833, the Reverend Jason Lee was named its head. Accompanied by his nephew Daniel Lee and two helpers, Jason Lee joined a fur-trading brigade traveling westward in the spring of 1834, and that fall was warmly welcomed to Fort Vancouver by Dr. John McLoughlin. Once more this canny Hudson's Bay Company agent hid more than he revealed by the cordiality of his greeting; he was determined to prevent the missionaries from settling in the Flathead country where they would interfere with the fur trade. His eloquence was partly responsible for convincing Lee to found his mission in the Willamette Valley, where Indians were few but agricultural prospects were ideal. Daniel Lee, in his account of the expedition, suggests that McLoughlin's influence was not alone in leading to this decision; Jason Lee was already thinking of his outpost as a nucleus for an American colony and was interested in a fertile site:[6]

---

[6] Daniel Lee and J. H. Frost, *Ten Years in Oregon* (New York, 1844), pp. 125, 127–128.

The Occupation of Oregon, 1820-1845   449

About two miles above Mr. Gervais's, on the east bank of the river, and sixty miles from its mouth, a location was chosen to commence our mission. Here was a broad, rich bottom, many miles in length, well watered, and supplied with timber, oak, fir, cotton-wood, white maple, and white ash, scattered along the borders of its grassy plains, where hundreds of acres were ready for the plough. We now hastened back to Vancouver, obtained horses of the company in exchange for those we had left at Wallah-wallah, and oxen and cows in loan; men to drive the cattle to the place, and a boat and crew to transport our supplies. . . .

In treating of the occasion in which the Oregon mission originated, it was shown that the supposed claim of the Flathead Indians on the first missionary efforts made in the country were unfounded; and subsequent inquiries had furnished reasons to the missionaries that could not justify even the attempt to commence their mission among them. 1. The means of subsistence in a region so remote and so difficult of access, were, to say the least, very doubtful. It was not a small matter to transport all necessary implements and tools to build houses and raise our provisions six hundred miles. 2. The smallness of their number. Their perpetual wars with Blackfeet Indians had prevented their increase; and they were, for their safety, confederated with the Nez Percés. 3. Their vicinity to the Blackfeet, as well the white man's enemy as theirs, and who would fall upon the abettors of their foes with signal revenge. 4. A larger field of usefulness was contemplated as the object of the mission than the benefiting of a single tribe. The wants of the whole country, present and prospective, so far as they could be, were taken into the account, and the hope of meeting these wants, in the progress of their work, led to the choice of the Walamet location, as a starting point, a place to stand on, and the centre of a wide circle of benevolent action. Here any amount of supplies could be produced from the soil that might be required in the enlargement of the work; and here the first blow was struck by the pioneer missionaries in Oregon; and here they began their arduous and difficult toil to elevate and save the heathen from moral degradation and ruin.

The rainy season was fast approaching, and a house was wanted to shelter us when it arrived. But first we had to prepare our tools, and gear our oxen. We handled axes and augurs, hung a grind stone, split rails, made yokes and bows for the oxen, and made a yard to catch them in, for some of them were not half tamed, and then to yoke them—"ay, there's the rub"—our wits, and ropes, physical might, all took hold—no flinching, no backing out. When we had succeeded in this, then came the all-day business of driving them. Men never worked harder and performed less. Our house advanced but slowly, and we were caught in one violent storm of wind and rain, which was near drenching all we had, the tent which we occupied being but a poor protection. When it cleared away, the wet articles were taken out and carefully dried. Before the next storm came on we had a roof on a part of our house, and a piece of floor laid, on which we could lie thankfully secure from the pelting storm without. A few weeks, all the time hard at it, and the roof was completed; a good chimney made of sticks and clay, and a fire-place in one end; floors laid of plank split from the fir, and hewn on the upper side; doors procured in the same way, and hung on wooden hinges. Then a table, then stools, and finally the luxury of chairs added to our self-made comforts. Our good mansion was built of logs, twenty by thirty feet, divided into two apartments by a partition across the middle, and lighted by four small windows, the sashes partly made by Mr. Jason Lee with his jack-knife. As to a living, we had brought a supply of flour from Vancouver, and made unleavened cakes, baked before the fire, and from the settlers we bought some peas, which, with the pork we had sent along in our outfit from Boston, made good soup, to which was sometimes added a small quantity of barley.

THE HUDSON'S BAY
COMPANY REACTION

Lee's careful explanation of the decision to settle in the Willamette Valley concealed one fact of which he was doubtless scarcely aware: he had been subjected to subtle pressure by Dr. John McLoughlin. McLoughlin was aware that some day the Oregon Country must be divided between Britain and the United States; he also knew that in such a settlement the Americans would almost surely secure the area south of the Columbia River. Hence his purpose was to divert newcomers to that region, at the same time strengthening the Hudson's Bay Company's hold on the disputed country north of the Columbia. McLoughlin explained and justified his policy toward traders and missionaries in a letter written on November 16, 1838, to the Deputy Governor of the company:[7]

An Important point for consideration is Whether the trappers and Engaged Servants Who retire from the Service should be allowed to settle in the country or Not; and Whatever way we View it—it is attended with difficulties. Governor Simpson Writes me not to Allow any of our people to settle

[7] E. E. Rich (ed.), *The Letters of John McLoughlin from Fort Vancouver to the Governor and Committee First Series, 1825–38* (Toronto, Champlain Society, and London, Hudson's Bay Record Society, 1941), pp. 172–175. Reprinted by permission of Hudson's Bay Record Society.

and of course I will obey the order. It is true I Know and Every One Knows who is acquainted with the Fur trade that as the country becomes settled the Fur trade Must Diminish and I therefore Discouraged our people from settling as long as I could without exciting ill Will towards the Company. And in 1828 formed the party of trappers Under Mr. Chief trader Alex. R. McLeod to hunt towards the Bonaventura in the hope that we would find a place Where we could Employ our Willamette freemen so as to remove them from a place where they were Anxious to begin to farm. One of them Lucier had applied to me for implements for farming but I did not give them and Dissuaded him from it and to get Rid of him Granted him and his family a passage to Canada and on his failing in his Attempt to get across the Mountains fall 1828 Inconsequence of the Express coming in so late, Gov. Simpson May perhaps recollect my Mentioning to him One of My Reasons for forming Mr. McLeods party and for Granting a passage to Lucier and his family to Canada and that on that Account Lucier was sent to join Mr. McLeods party. In 1829 Capt. Dominis came to Oppose us and Went away in 1830, and that year Lucier repeated his application for farming implements and as Dominis had Given out that he would be here the latter End of 1831 or beginning of 1832 I considered it but prudent to acceed to his Demand as I was afraid if I refused him he would join the first opposition which came here. In 1832 Wyeth came and returned in 1834. With these opponents alongside of Us if we had refused leave to these men to settle or refused them assistance to accomplish their object It would have Disaffected them to the Company, Excited their ill Will towards us, and Encouraged our opponents to persist in their Endeavours to get a footing in the country—still I Allowed none to settle but such as had Means to Enable them to Equip themselves with implements Except One Man who had been Wounded in a Battle with the Black feet and who was too infirm to follow the hunting party and I beg to state as My opinion that I consider this plan as the best the company can follow—By refusing the trappers or Servants Leave to settle they become disaffected and I may say hostile to the Interest of their Employers and by Allowing them to settle with families It serves as an Encouragement to them to behave Well—By Requiring them to have fifty pounds (the sum I have Made it a Rule a man must have if he wishes to settle) It makes them Exert themselves and when A Man is Arrived at their time of life and has his family (None But Men with families are Allowed to settle) about him he will not leave his farm to join an opposition, and you may Depend that the country Along the coast from Pugets Sound to St. Francisco is a much finer Country than Canada or New York. The soil is better in Many places and the Climate is Milder and as such a country will not remain long without settlers It Remains for your Honors to Decide whether you will Allow the Old Servants of the company to settle in it—Who with their children Will Look on the Company as their Benefactors or to prevent them and consequently keep the country to be settled by a people who will most probably feel very differently Inclined towards the Company, and I would therefore recommend to continue the plan I have hitherto followed and as we can get a Market for their Grain we might Make it a Branch of our Business—confer a Benefit on these men and Raise a population which would join us in opposition to that which is likely to come.

In Regard to the Missionaries they have given me to understand that they had written to their Board to settle with your Honors about getting their Supplies from us or to get freight from you and import their Wants from England. If I may be Allowed to give an opinion I would Recommend to Agree to let them have their supplies at the present or even a Lower Rate of Advance or give them freight, as if you refuse them they will get their supplies from Wahou as they are connected with the Missionaries at the Sandwich Islands Who have a Vessel of their own, and if they send her here We may be sure that some Adventurers will avail themselves of the opportunity to come and open shop in opposition to us, Give us an Immensity of trouble, and Make us Incur great Expence. Some people are Averse to the Missionaries Attempting to Civilize Indians on the plea that Indians can never be Civilized. Allowing for the sake of Avoiding Argument that it is so, can we prevent Missionaries dispersing themselves Among these Indians? I say we cannot even if we were so Inclined and as if they should succeed in civilizing these Indians it can in no way be an injury to us. We ought in policy to secure their Good Will and that of those who support them in their Laudable Endeavours to do Good, to afford them the countenance of our support and such assistance as we can give without Incurring Expence and this is the plan I have followed. The Methodists came in 1834, I gave them the little assistance they required from Me and for Which they paid—the Presbytarians came this year and I did the same —on the same Conditions, and I would recommend the same plan to be followed Without Distinction of Sect.

BEGINNINGS OF THE "OREGON FEVER" IN IOWA

The English policy was to backfire, for there was no holding back the American frontiersmen once they learned of the riches of the Willamette Valley. This news was spread by the missionaries—Jason Lee and the Methodists first, Presbyterians such as the Reverend Marcus Whitman later. Their constant pleas for financial aid, voiced in letters to religious papers and on speaking tours in the East, painted a tempting picture of the agricultural prospects of the Oregon Country, and such an inducement was all the pioneers needed. Sensing this, Senator Lewis F. Linn of Missouri urged the Senate to organize the territory there and to stimulate immigration by offering 640 acres to every settler. The Linn bill mustered few votes, but the prospect of a free farm in a rich valley spread an infection among the restless souls who were always on the cutting edge of the frontier. A letter from Iowa Territory, written in 1843, described the beginnings of the "Oregon Fever" there:[8]

I suppose you of the East consider the present residents of Iowa the very pioneers of the West. Never was a greater mistake; the true western pioneers have pushed on beyond us, or if here and there one still lingers, it is only that he may dispose of his farm and "improvements" to push for a "new country."

Strange, restless beings are the genuine pioneers. Among them you may find some who have helped to lay the foundations of every state from the "old thirteen" hither; men who have successfully held seats in every legislature, from Virginia to Iowa, inclusive, but who are now moving to a new country again to "make a claim;" again to act a conspicuous part in the community in which they live; again to run the political race, become the members of the legislature of some future state, find themselves thrown in the

---

[8] *National Intelligencer*, April 18, 1843, reprinted in *Oregon Historical Quarterly*, III (September, 1902), 311–312.

shade by those of greater attainments who follow in their wake, and again to push for the "new purchase."

Fearlessness, hospitality, and independent frankness, united with restless enterprise and unquenchable thirst for novelty and change, are the peculiar characteristics of the western pioneers. With him there is always a land of promise further west, where the climate is milder, the soil more fertile, better timber and finer prairies; and on, on, on, he goes, always seeking and never attaining the Pisgah of his hopes. You of the old states can not readily conceive the every-day sort of business an "old settler" makes of selling out his "improvements," hitching the horses to the big wagon, and, with his wife and children, swine and cattle, pots and kettles, household goods and household gods, starting on a journey of hundreds of miles to find and make a new home.

Just now Oregon is the pioneer's land of promise. Hundreds are already prepared to start thither with the spring, while hundreds of others are anxiously awaiting the action of congress in reference to that country, as the signal for their departure. Some have already been to view the country, and have returned with a flattering tale of the inducements it holds out. They have painted it to their neighbors in the brightest colors; these have told it to others; the Oregon fever has broke out, and is now raging like any other contagion. Mr. Calhoun was right when he told the senate that the American people would occupy that country independent of all legislation; that in a few years the pioneers of the West would overrun it and hold it against the world. "Wilson," said I a few days since to an old settler, "so you are going to Oregon." "Well, I is, horse. Tice Pitt was out looking at it last season, and he says it is a leetle the greatest country on the face of the earth. So I'm bound to go." "How do the old woman and the girls like the idea of such a long journey?" "They feel mighty peert about it, and Suke says she shan't be easy till we start."

PROPAGANDA FOR OREGON:
PETER H. BURNETT

Iowa was not unique. "The Oregon fever," reported "Niles' Weekly Register" a few months later, "is raging in almost every part of the Union." The effect of the virus on one Missouri family was remembered by a pioneer who as a small boy was taken by his father to Platte City to hear an Oregon enthusiast, Peter H. Burnett, rhapsodize on the milk and honey awaiting those who dared make the journey:[9]

One Saturday morning father said that he was going in to Platte City to hear Mr. Burnett talk about Oregon. I said. "Father, I want to go too," to which he replied, "all right son, come on," and together we went. When the hour for the address came, Mr. Burnett hauled a box out into the sidewalk, took his stand upon it, and began to tell us about the land flowing with milk and honey on the shores of the Pacific. Of his address that day, I remember this much, that he told of the great crops of wheat which it was possible to raise in Oregon, and pictured in glowing terms the richness of the soil and the attraction of the climate, and then with a little twinkle of humor in his eye, he said, "and they do say, gentlemen, they do say, that out in Oregon the pigs are running about under the great acorn trees, round and fat, and already cooked, with knives and

---

[9] Edward H. Lenox, *Overland to Oregon in the Tracks of Lewis and Clarke* (Oakland, California, 1904), pp. 10–14.

forks sticking in them so that you can cut off a slice whenever you are hungry." Of course at this everybody laughed. Burnett was a rather striking looking man of about ordinary height, with a very keen eye, a rather sloping forehead, light complexion, and was very ready of speech. He was a popular stump speaker, as his political campaign in California years after, abundantly showed.

Father was so moved upon by what he had heard at Fort Leavenworth and what he heard from Mr. Burnett, that he decided to join the company that was going west to Oregon. So when Mr. Burnett said, "Now gentlemen, as many of you as would like to go, walk right into my store and put down your names in the book which I have there," father was the first to respond and the first to sign his name, whereupon Mr. Burnett slapped him heartily on the shoulder and said, "Well, Davy, if you are going, I know who to tie to." And the event justified his words.

THE 1843 MIGRATION: ORGANIZING THE CARAVAN

Propaganda such as this set the migration tide rolling. Small parties began pioneering the Oregon Trail in 1840 and 1841, but not until 1843 did a mass movement begin. By May of that year, no less than a thousand persons with 1800 cattle waited to begin the journey at Independence, Missouri. On May 22 they set off, traveling haphazardly at first for pasturage was plentiful and Indians absent on this first stage of the migration. Near the Kansas River where the trail left the rich bottom lands some organization was necessary. In common with all frontiersmen who found themselves temporarily beyond the reach of legal governmental machinery, their first need was a compact in which all bound themselves to obey the majority will. Peter H. Burnett, who was destined to lead the caravan westward, reproduced this compact in a letter he wrote a New York newspaper shortly after his arrival in Oregon:[10]

Resolved, Whereas we deem it necessary for the government of all societies, either civil or military, to adopt certain rules and regulations for their government, for the purpose of keeping good order and promoting civil and military discipline. In order to insure union and safety, we deem it necessary to adopt the following rules and regulations for the government of the said company:—

Rule 1. Every male person of the age of sixteen, or upward, shall be considered a legal voter in all affairs relating to the company.

Rule 2. There shall be nine men elected by a majority of the company, who shall form a council, whose duty it shall be to settle all disputes arising between individuals, and to try and pass sentence on all persons for any act for which they may be guilty, which is subversive of good order and military discipline. They shall take especial cognizance of all sentinels and members of the guard, who may be guilty of neglect of duty, or sleeping on post. Such persons shall be tried, and sentence passed upon them at the discretion of the council. A majority of two thirds of the council shall decide all questions that may come before them, subject to the approval or disapproval of the captain.

---

[10] *New York Herald*, January 5, 1845, reprinted in Peter H. Burnett, "Letters of Peter H. Burnett," *Oregon Historical Quarterly*, III (December, 1902), 406–407.

If the captain disapprove of the decision of the council, he shall state to them his reasons, when they shall again pass upon the question, and if the same decision is again made by the same majority, it shall be final.

Rule 3. There shall be a captain elected who shall have supreme military command of the company. It shall be the duty of the captain to maintain good order and strict discipline, and as far as practicable, to enforce all rules and regulations adopted by the company. Any man who shall be guilty of disobedience of orders shall be tried and sentenced at the discretion of the council, which may extend to expulsion from the company. The captain shall appoint the necessary number of duty sergeants, one of whom shall take charge of every guard, and who shall hold their offices at the pleasure of the captain.

Rule 4. There shall be an orderly sergeant elected by the company, whose duty it shall be to keep a regular roll, arranged in alphabetical order, of every person subject to guard duty in the company; and shall make out his guard details by commencing at the top of the roll and proceeding to the bottom, thus giving every man an equal tour of guard duty. He shall also give the member of every guard notice when he is detailed for duty. He shall also parade every guard, call the roll, and inspect the same at the time of mounting. He shall also visit the guard at least once every night, and see that the guard are doing strict military duty, and may at any time give them the necessary instructions respecting their duty, and shall regularly make report to the captain every morning, and be considered second in command.

Rule 5. The captain, orderly sergeant, and members of the council shall hold their offices at the pleasure of the company, and it shall be the duty of the council, upon the application of one third or more of the company, to order a new election for either captain, orderly sergeant, or new member or members of the council, or for all or any of them, as the case may be.

Rule 6. The election of officers shall not take place until the company meet at Kansas River.

Rule 7. No family shall be allowed to take more than three loose cattle to every male member of the family of the age of sixteen and upward.

THE ELECTION OF OFFICERS

After another day's march cooled tempers that had been inflamed by conflict over the adoption of this constitution, the Oregon-bound emigrants paused again to name officers for their traveling republic. Peter H. Burnett was chosen captain and J. W. Nesmith orderly sergeant. Then candidates for the Council of Ten were nominated. The choice among these nominees was pleasantly described by a correspondent of the "New Orleans Picayune" who was present:[11]

The Oregonians were assembled here to the number of six or eight hundred, and when we passed their encampment they were engaged in the business of electing officers to regulate and conduct their proceedings. It was a curious and unaccountable spectacle to us as we approached. We saw a large body of men wheeling and marching about the prairie, describing evolutions neither recognizable as savage, civic or military. We soon knew they were not Indians, and were

---

[11] *New Orleans Picayune,* November 21, 1843, reprinted in *Oregon Historical Quarterly,* I (December, 1900), 399–401.

not long in setting them down for the emigrants, but what in the name of mystery they were about our best guessing could not reduce to anything in the shape of a mathematical probability.

On arriving among them, however, we found they were only going on with their elections in a manner perhaps old enough, but very new and quizzical to us. The candidates stood up in a row behind the constituents, and at a given signal they wheeled about and marched off, while the general mass broke after them "lick-a-ty-split", each man forming in behind his favorite so that every candidate flourished a sort of a tail of his own, and the man with the longest tail was elected! These proceedings were continued until a captain and a council of ten were elected; and, indeed, if the scene can be conceived, it must appear as a curious mingling of the whimsical with the wild. Here was a congregation of rough, bold, and adventurous men, gathered from distant and opposite points of the Union, just forming an acquaintance with each other, to last, in all probability, through good or ill fortune, through the rest of their days. Few of them expected, or thought, of ever returning to the states again. They had with them their wives and children, and aged, depending relatives. They were going with stout and determined hearts to traverse a wild and desolate region, and take possession of a far corner of their country destined to prove a new and strong arm of a mighty nation. These men were running about the prairie, in long strings; the leaders,—in sport and for the purpose of puzzling the judges, doubling and winding in the drollest fashion; so that, the all-important business of forming a government seemed very much like the merry schoolboy game of "snapping the whip." It was really very funny to see the candidates for the solemn council of ten, run several hundred yards away, to show off the length of their tails, and then cut a half circle, so as to turn and admire their longitudinal popularity *in extenso* themselves. "Running for office" is certainly performed in more literal fashion on the prairie than we see the same sort of business performed in town. To change the order of a town election, though for once, it might prove an edifying exhibition to see a mayor and aldermen start from the town pump and run around the court house square, the voters falling in behind and the rival ticket running the other way, while a band in the middle might tune up for both parties, playing "O, What a Long Tail Our Cat's Got;" which we surmise some popular composer may have arranged for such an occasion.

THE WESTWARD MARCH, 1843

As the emigrants found before they had progressed far along the Platte River, even these democratic safeguards did not assure harmony. Some without cattle complained that they were being held back by the slow-moving herds and might be snowbound before reaching Oregon. The disputes grew so acrimonious that the party broke into two, those without cattle moving ahead rapidly, and the "cow column" following. The leader of the latter, Jesse Applegate, later penned a classic description of life along the Oregon Trail as he remembered it in his "A Day with the Cow Column":[12]

It is four o'clock, A. M.; the sentinels on duty have discharged their rifles—the signal that the hours of sleep are over; and every

---

[12] Jesse Applegate, "A Day with the Cow Column," *Transactions of Fourth Annual Re-union of the Oregon Pioneer Association, for 1876* (Salem, Oregon, 1877), pp. 58–65.

wagon and tent is pouring forth its night tenants, and slow-kindling smokes begin largely to rise and float away on the morning air. Sixty men start from the corral, spreading as they make through the vast herd of cattle and horses that form a semi-circle around the encampment, the most distant perhaps two miles away.

The herders pass to the extreme verge and carefully examine for trails beyond, to see that none of the animals have strayed or been stolen during the night. This morning no trails lead beyond the outside animals in sight, and by five o'clock the herders begin to contract the great moving circle, and the well-trained animals move slowly towards camp, clipping here and there a thistle or tempting bunch of grass on the way. In about an hour, five thousand animals are close up to the encampment, and the teamsters are busy selecting their teams and driving them inside the "corral" to be yoked. The corral is a circle one hundred yards deep, formed with wagons connected strongly with each other; the wagon in the rear being connected with the wagon in front by its tongue and ox chains. It is a strong barrier that the most vicious ox cannot break, and in case of an attack of the Sioux would be no contemptible entrenchment.

From six to seven o'clock is a busy time; breakfast is to be eaten, the tents struck, the wagons loaded, and the teams yoked and brought up in readiness to be attached to their respective wagons. All know when, at seven o'clock, the signal to march sounds, that those not ready to take their proper places in the line of march must fall into the dusty rear for the day.

There are sixty wagons. They have been divided into fifteen divisions or platoons of four wagons each, and each platoon is entitled to lead in its turn. The leading platoon of to-day will be the rear one of to-morrow, and will bring up the rear unless some teamster, through indolence or negligence, has lost his place in the line, and is condemned to that uncomfortable post. It is within ten minutes of seven; the corral but now a strong barricade is everywhere broken, the teams being attached to the wagons. The woman and children have taken their places in them. The pilot (a borderer who has passed his life on the verge of civilization, and has been chosen to the post of leader from his knowledge of the savage and his experience in travel through roadless wastes) stands ready in the midst of his pioneers, and aids to mount and lead the way. Ten or fifteen young men, not to-day on duty, form another cluster. They are ready to start on a buffalo hunt, are well mounted and well armed as they need be, for the unfriendly Sioux have driven the buffalo out of the Platte, and the hunters must ride fifteen or twenty miles to reach them. The cow-drivers are hastening, as they get ready, to the rear of their charge, to collect and prepare them for the day's march.

It is on the stroke of seven; the rushing to and fro, the cracking of whips, the loud command to oxen, and what seemed to be the inextricable confusion of the last ten minutes has ceased. Fortunately every one has been found and every teamster is at his post. The clear notes of a trumpet sound in the front; the pilot and his guards mount their horses; the leading division of wagons move out of the encampment, and take up the line of march; the rest fall into their places with the precision of clockwork, until the spot so lately full of life sinks back into that solitude that seems to reign over the broad plain and rushing river as the caravan draws its lazy length towards the distant El-Dorado....

They (the wagons) form a line three-quarters of a mile in length; some of the teamsters ride upon the front of their wagons, some march beside their teams; scattered along the line companies of women and children are taking exercise on foot; they gather bouquets of rare and beautiful flowers that line the way; near them stalks a stately grey hound or an Irish wolf dog, apparently proud of keeping watch and ward over his master's wife and children. Next comes a band of horses; two or three men or boys follow them, the docile and sagacious animals scarce needing this attention, for they have learned to follow in the rear of the wagons, and know that at noon they will be allowed to graze and rest. Their knowledge of time seems as accurate as of the place they are to occupy in the line, and even a full-blown thistle will scarce tempt them to straggle or halt until the dinner hour has arrived. Not so with the large herd of horned beasts that bring up the rear; lazy, selfish and unsocial, it has been a task to get them in motion, the strong always ready to domineer over the weak, halt in the front and forbid the weaker to pass them. They seem to move only in fear of the driver's whip; though in the morning full to repletion, they have not been driven an hour, before their hunger and thirst seem to indicate a fast of days' duration. Through all the long day their greed is never sated nor their thirst quenched, nor is there a moment of relaxation of the tedious and vexatious labors of their drivers, although to all others the march furnishes some season of relaxation or enjoyment. For the cow-drivers there is none. . . .

The pilot, by measuring the ground and timing the speed of the wagons and the walk of his horses, has determined the rate of each, so as to enable him to select the nooning place, as nearly as the requisite grass and water can be had at the end of five hours' travel of the wagons. To-day, the ground being favorable, little time has been lost in preparing the road, so that he and his pioneers are at the nooning place an hour in advance of the wagons, which time is spent in preparing convenient watering places for the animals, and digging little wells near the bank of the Platte. As the teams are not unyoked, but simply turned loose from the wagons, a corral is not formed at noon, but the wagons are drawn up in columns, four abreast, the leading wagon of each platoon on the left—the platoons being formed with that view. This brings friends together at noon as well as at night.

To-day, an extra session of the Council is being held, to settle a dispute that does not admit of delay, between a proprietor and a young man who has undertaken to do a man's service on the journey for bed and board. Many such engagements exist, and much interest is taken in the manner this high court, from which there is no appeal, will define the rights of each party in such engagements. The Council was a high court in the most exalted sense. It was a Senate, composed of the ablest and most respected fathers of the emigration. It exercised both legislative and judicial powers, and its laws and decisions proved it equal and worthy the high trust reposed in it. Its sessions were usually held on days when the caravan was not moving. It first took the state of the little commonwealth into consideration; revised or repealed rules defective or obsolete, and exacted such others as the exigencies seemed to require. The common weal being cared for, it next resolved itself into a court to hear and settle private disputes and grievances. The offender and the aggrieved appeared before it; witnesses were examined, and the parties were heard by themselves and sometimes by council. The judges thus being made fully acquainted with the case, and being in no way influenced or cramped by technicalities, decided all cases according to their merits. There was but little use for lawyers before this court, for no plea was entertained which was calculated to hinder or defeat the ends of justice. Many of these judges have since won honors in higher spheres. They have aided to establish on the broad basis of right and universal liberty two of the pillars of our great Republic in the Occident. Some of the young men who appeared before them as advocates have themselves sat upon the highest judicial tribunals, commanded armies, been Governors of States, and taken high positions in the Senate of the nation.

It is now one o'clock; the bugle has sounded, and the caravan has resumed its westward journey. It is in the same order, but the evening is far less animated than the morning march; a drowsiness has fallen apparently on man and beast; teamsters drop asleep on their perches and even when walking by their teams, and the words of command are now addressed to the slowly creeping oxen in the softened tenor of women or the piping treble of children, while the snores of the teamsters make a droning accompaniment....

The sun is now getting low in the west, and at length the pains-taking pilot is standing ready to conduct the train in the circle which he has previously measured and marked out, which is to form the invariable fortification for the night. The leading wagons follow him so nearly round the circle, that but a wagon length separates them. Each wagon follows in its track, the rear closing on the front, until its tongue and ox-chains will perfectly reach from one to the other, and so accurate the measurement and perfect the practice, that the hindmost wagon of the train always precisely closes the gateway, as each wagon is brought into position. It is dropped from its team, (the teams being inside the circle) the team unyoked, and the yokes and chains are used to connect the wagon strongly with that in its front. Within ten minutes from the time the leading wagon halted, the barricade is formed, the teams unyoked and driven out to pasture. Every one is busy preparing fires of buffalo chips to cook the evening meal, pitching tents and otherwise preparing for the night....

All able to bear arms in the party have been formed into three companies, and each of these into four watches; every third night it is the duty of one of these companies to keep watch and ward over the camp, and it is so arranged that each watch takes its turn of guard duty through the different watches of the night. Those forming the first watch to-night will be second on duty, then third and fourth, which brings them through all the watches of the night. They begin at eight o'clock, P.M., and end at four o'clock A.M.

It is not yet eight o'clock when the first watch is to be set; the evening meal is just over, and the corral now free from the intrusion of cattle or horses, groups of children are scattered over it. The larger are taking a game of romps; "the wee toddling things" are being taught that great achievement that distinguishes man from the lower animals. Before a tent near the river a violin makes lively music, and some youths and maidens have improvised a dance upon the green; in another quarter a flute gives its mellow and melancholy notes to the still night air, which as they float away over the quiet river, seem a lament for the past rather than a hope for the future. It has been a prosperous day; more than twenty miles have been accomplished of the great journey.

ORIGINS OF GOVERNMENT IN OREGON

The "Great Migration" of 1843 demonstrated that the Oregon Trail was safe for large parties, and over the next three years long caravans of covered wagons regularly plodded westward. By the middle 1840s some 6000 Americans lived in the Oregon Country, nearly all of them clustered about the Methodist mission in the Willamette Valley. Being Americans, they soon manifested a strong desire to rejoin the United States; even as early as 1840 the handful of settlers then in the region petitioned Congress for annexation. The United States was unable to act on such requests so long as the territory was jointly held with Great Britain, but the pioneers suffered no such inhibitions. During the winter of 1842-1843 they met regularly in a Pioneer Lyceum and Literary Club to debate their course and by February were ready to act. When they assembled in a "wolf meeting" called to discuss means of ridding the land of predatory beasts, they seized the opportunity to deal with the whole problem of government. The minutes of that meeting reveal the ingenious technique employed by the settlers to convert an innocent gathering into a revolutionary body that threatened to undermine relations between the United States and England:[13]

The committee appointed to notify a general meeting and report business, made the following report, to wit:—

Your committee beg leave to report as follows: It being admitted by all that bears, wolves, panthers, etc., are destructive to the useful animals owned by the settlers of this colony,

---

[13] William H. Gray, *A History of Oregon, 1792–1849, Drawn from Personal Observation and Authentic Information* (Portland, Oregon, 1870), pp. 264–267.

your committee would submit the following resolutions, as the sense of this meeting, by which the community may be governed in carrying on a defensive and destructive war against all such animals.

Resolved, 1st. That we deem it expedient for this community to take immediate measures for the destruction of all wolves, panthers, and bears, and such other animals as are known to be destructive to cattle, horses, sheep, and hogs.

2d. That a treasurer be appointed, who shall receive all funds, and dispense the same, in accordance with drafts drawn on him by the committee appointed to receive the evidences of the destruction of the above-named animals; and that he report the state of the treasury, by posting up public notices, once in three months, in the vicinity of each of the committee.

3d. That a standing committee of eight be appointed, whose duty it shall be, together with the treasurer, to receive the proofs, or evidences, of the animals for which a bounty is claimed having been killed in the Wallamet Valley.

4th. That a bounty of fifty cents be paid for the destruction of a small wolf; three dollars for a large wolf; one dollar and fifty cents for a lynx; two dollars for a bear; and five dollars for a panther.

5th. That no bounty be paid unless the individual claiming said bounty give satisfactory evidence, or present the skin of the head with the ears of all animals for which he claims a bounty.

6th. That the committee and treasurer form a Board of advice to call public meetings, whenever they may deem it expedient, to promote and encourage all persons to use their vigilance in destroying all the animals named in the fourth resolution.

7th. That the bounties specified in the fourth resolution be limited to whites and their descendants.

8th. That the proceedings of this meeting be signed by the chairman and secretary, and a copy thereof be presented to the recorder of this colony.

On motion, the report was accepted.

[These routine proceedings were upset when one member of the audience rose to put a troublesome question to the group:]

How is it, fellow-citizens, with you and me, and our children and wives? Have we any organization upon which we can rely for mutual protection? Is there any power or influence in the country sufficient to protect us and all we hold dear on earth from the worse than wild beasts that threaten and occasionally destroy our cattle? Who in our midst is authorized at this moment to call us together to protect our own, and the lives of our families? True, the alarm may be given, as in a recent case, and we may run who feel alarmed, and shoot off our guns, while our enemy may be robbing our property, ravishing our wives, and burning the houses over our defenseless families. Common sense, prudence, and justice to ourselves demand that we act consistent with the principles we have commenced. We have mutually and unitedly agreed to defend and protect our *cattle and domestic animals*; now, fellow-citizens, I submit and move the adoption of the two following resolutions, that we may have protection for our persons and lives as well as our cattle and herds:—

Resolved, That a committee be appointed to take into consideration the propriety of taking measures for the civil and military protection of this colony.

Resolved, That said committee consist of twelve persons.

The motion was adopted unanimously, but even its backers realized that it was meaningless so long as American authority could not be extended over Oregon. They knew also that the United States could be goaded into demanding a favorable boundary settlement with Great Britain only if they applied continuous pressure. So the Willamette Valley buzzed with political activity over the next years. Meeting at Champoeg on May 2, 1843, the settlers named a committee to draw up the "First Organic Law" for the region. This, when adopted on July 5, created a simple governmental machinery to administer "Oregon Territory" until "such time as the United States of America extend their jurisdiction over us." At the same time petitions were showered on Washington demanding expulsion of the British from the whole region. The next move was up to Congress and the President. Fortunately for the settlers both the situation in the West and the public attitude toward expansion were changing rapidly. Partially responsible were developments in California.

CHAPTER 20

The American Invasion of California, 1820-1845

Unlike the occupation of the Oregon Country, the peopling of California by Americans involved the displacement of a European civilization. The firstcomers there were Franciscan missionaries; between 1769 and 1776 they completed twenty-one mission stations on the coastal lowlands lying between San Diego and San Francisco. Each was a harbinger of civilization as well as of Christianity; Indians were encouraged to settle nearby, where they could be taught the arts of husbandry and housekeeping. By the early nineteenth century each mission had become the center of a vast ranch, counting its cattle in thousands of head and supporting a stabilized Indian civilization.

LIFE IN CALIFORNIA IN THE 1830s: THE RANCHOS

Eventually the prosperity of the stations spelled their downfall, for Mexican landholders realized that only through secularization could they obtain the Franciscan estates. The Mexican Congress responded to their pressure in 1833 when a Secularization Act released the neophytes from all controls and threw the mission lands open to settlement. As the adobe churches crumbled, giant "ranchos" displaced mission stations as the typical California institution. Their owners lived an idyllic existence, supported by the labor of semi-enslaved natives and virtually free of all interference by the Mexican government in distant Mexico City. One of them, Guadalupe Vallejo, nostalgically described that pastoral era in his reminiscences:[1]

> In the old days every one seemed to live out-doors. There was much gaiety and social life, even though people were widely scattered. We traveled as much as possible on horseback. Only old people or invalids cared to use the slow cart, or *carreta*. Young men would ride from one ranch to another for parties, and whoever found his horse tired

---

[1] Guadalupe Vallejo, "Ranch and Mission Days in Alta California," *Century Magazine*, XLI (December 1890), 189–192.

would let him go and catch another. In 1806 there were so many horses in the valleys about San José that seven or eight thousand were killed. Nearly as many were driven into the sea at Santa Barbara in 1807, and the same thing was done at Monterey in 1810. Horses were given to the runaway sailors, and to trappers and hunters who came over the mountains, for common horses were very plenty, but fast and beautiful horses were never more prized in any country than in California, and each young man had his favorites. A kind of mustang, that is now seldom or never seen on the Pacific coast, was a peculiar light cream-colored horse, with silver-white mane and tail. Such an animal, of speed and bottom, often sold for more than a horse of any other color. Other much admired colors were dapple-gray and chestnut. The fathers of the Mission sometimes rode on horseback, but they generally had a somewhat modern carriage called a *volante*. It was always drawn by mules, of which there were hundreds in the Mission pastures, and white was the color often preferred.

Nothing was more attractive than the wedding cavalcade on its way from the bride's house to the Mission church. The horses were more richly caparisoned than for any other ceremony, and the bride's nearest relative or family representative carried her before him, she sitting on the saddle with her white satin shoe in a loop of golden or silver braid, while he sat on the bear-skin covered *anquera* behind. The groom and his friends mingled with the bride's party, all on the best horses that could be obtained, and they rode gaily from the ranch house to the Mission, sometimes fifteen or twenty miles away. In April and May, when the land was covered with wild-flowers, the light-hearted troop rode along the edge of the uplands, between hill and valley, crossing the streams, and some of the young horsemen, anxious to show their skill, would perform all the feats for which the Spanish-Californians were famous. After the wedding, when they returned to lead in the feasting, the bride was carried on the horse of the groomsman. One of the customs which was always observed at the wedding was to wind a silken tasseled string or a silken sash, fringed with gold, about the necks of the bride and groom, binding them together as they knelt before the altar for the blessing of the priest. A charming custom among the middle and lower classes was the making of the satin shoes by the groom for the bride. A few weeks before the wedding he asked his betrothed for the measurement of her foot, and made the shoes with his own hands; the groomsman brought them to her on the wedding-day.

But few foreigners ever visited any of the Missions, and they naturally caused quite a stir. At the Mission San José, about 1820, late one night in the vintage season a man came to the village for food and shelter, which were gladly given. But the next day it was whispered that he was a Jew, and the poor Indians, who had been told that the Jews had crucified Christ, ran to their huts and hid. Even the Spanish children, and many of the grown people, were frightened. Only the missionary father had ever before seen a Jew, and when he found that it was impossible to check the excitement he sent two soldiers to ride with the man a portion of the way to Santa Clara.

A number of trappers and hunters came into Southern California and settled down in various towns. There was a party of Kentuckians, beaver-trappers, who went along the Gila and Colorado rivers about 1827, and then south into Baja California to the Mission of Santa Catalina. Then they came to San Diego, where the whole country was much excited over their hunter clothes, their rifles, their traps, and the strange stories they told of the deserts, and fierce Indians, and things that no one in California had ever seen. Captain Paty was the oldest man of the party, and he was ill and worn out. All the San Diego people were very kind to the Americans. It is said that the other Missions, such as San Gabriel, sent and desired the privilege of caring for some of them. Captain Paty grew worse, so he sent for one of the fathers and said he wished to become a Catholic, because, he added, it must be a good religion, for it made everybody so good to him. Don Pio Pico and Doña Victoria Dominguez de Estudillo were his sponsors. After Captain Paty's death the Americans went to Los Angeles, where they all married Spanish ladies, were given lands, built houses, planted vineyards, and became important people. Pryor repaired the church silver, and was called "Miguel el Platero." Laughlin was always so merry that he was named "Ricardo el Buen Mozo." They all had Spanish names given them besides their own. One of them was a blacksmith, and as iron was very scarce he made pruning shears for the vineyards out of the old beaver traps.

On Christmas night, 1828, a ship was wrecked near Los Angeles, and twenty-eight men escaped. Everybody wanted to care for them, and they were given a great Christmas dinner, and offered money and lands. Some of them staid, and some went to other Missions and towns. One of them who staid was a German, John Gronigen, and he was named "Juan Domingo," or, because he was lame, "Juan Cojo." Another, named Prentice, came from Connecticut, and he was a famous fisherman and otter hunter. After 1828 a good many other Americans came in and settled down quietly to cultivate the soil, and some of them became very rich. They had grants from the governor, just the same as the Spanish people.

It is necessary, for the truth of the account, to mention the evil behavior of many Americans before, as well as after, the conquest. At the Mission San José there is a small creek, and two very large sycamores once grew at the Spanish ford, so that it was called *la aliso*. A squatter named Fallon, who lived near the crossing, cut down these for firewood, though there were many trees in the cañon. The Spanish people begged him to leave them, for the shade and beauty, but he did not care for that. This was a little thing, but much that happened was after such pattern, or far worse.

In those times one of the leading American squatters came to my father, Don J. J. Vallejo, and said: "There is a large piece of your land where the cattle run loose, and your vaqueros have gone to the gold mines. I will fence the field for you at my expense if you will give me half." He liked the idea, and assented, but when the tract was inclosed the American had it entered as government land in his own name, and kept all of it. In many similar cases American settlers in their dealings with the rancheros took advantage of laws which they understood, but which were new to the Spaniards, and so robbed the latter of their lands. Notes and bonds were considered unnecessary by a Spanish gentleman in a business transaction, as his words was always sufficient security.

Perhaps the most exasperating feature of the coming-in of the Americans was owing to the mines, which drew away most of the servants, so that our cattle were stolen by thousands. Men who are now prosperous farmers and merchants were guilty of shooting and selling Spanish beef "without looking at the brand," as the phrase went. My father had about ten thousand head of cattle, and some he was able to send back into the hills until there were better laws and officers, but he lost the larger part. On one occasion I remember some vigilantes caught two cattle-thieves and sent for my father to appear against them, but he said that although he wanted them punished he did not wish to have them hanged, and so he would not testify, and they were set free. One of them afterward sent conscience money to us from New York, where he is living in good circumstances. The Vallejos have on several occasions received conscience money from different parts of the country. The latest case occurred last year (1889), when a woman wrote that her husband, since dead, had taken a steer worth twenty-five dollars, and she sent the money.

Every Mission and ranch in old times had its *calaveras*, its "place of skulls," its slaughter-corral, where cattle and sheep were killed by the Indian butchers. Every Saturday morning the fattest animals were chosen and driven there, and by night the hides were all stretched on the hillside to dry. At one time a hundred cattle and two hundred sheep were killed weekly at the Mission San José, and the meat was distributed to all, "without money and without price." The grizzly bears, which were very abundant in the country,— for no one ever poisoned them, as the American stock raisers did after 1849,—used to come by night to the ravines near the slaughter-corral where the refuse was thrown by the butchers. The young Spanish gentlemen often rode out on moonlight nights to lasso these bears, and then they would drag them through the village street, and past the houses of their friends. Two men with their strong rawhide reatas could hold any bear, and when they were tired of this sport they could kill him. But sometimes the bears would walk through the village on their way to or from the corral of the butchers, and so scatter the people. Several times a serenade party, singing and playing by moonlight, was suddenly broken up by two or three grizzlies trotting down the hill into the street, and the gay *caballeros* with their guitars would spring over the adobe walls and run for their horses, which always stood saddled, with a reata coiled, ready for use, at the saddle bow. It was the custom in every family to keep saddled horses in easy reach, day and night.

Innumerable stories about grizzlies are traditional in the old Spanish families, not only in the Santa Clara Valley, but also through the Coast Range from San Diego to Sonoma and Santa Rosa. Some of the bravest of the young men would go out alone to kill grizzlies. When they had lassoed one they would drag him to a tree, and the well-trained horse would hold the bear against it while the hunter slipped out of the saddle, ran up, and killed the grizzly with one stroke of his broad-bladed machete, or Mexican hunting knife. One Spanish gentlemen riding after a large grizzly lassoed it and was dragged into a deep *barranca*. Horse and man fell on the bear, and astonished him so much that he scrambled up the bank, and the hunter cut the reata and gladly enough let him go. There were many cases of herdsmen and hunters being killed by grizzlies, and one could fill a volume with stories of feats of courage and of mastery of the reata. The governor of California appointed expert bear hunters in different parts of the country, who spent their time in destroying them, by pits, or shooting, or with the reata. Don Rafael Soto, one of the most famous of these men, used to conceal himself in a pit, covered with heavy logs and leaves, with a quarter of freshly killed beef above. When the grizzly bear walked on the logs he was shot from beneath. Before the feast-days the hunters sometimes went to the foothills and brought several bears to turn into the bull-fighting corral.

The principal bull-fights were held at Easter and on the day of the patron saint of the Mission, which at the Mission San José was March 19. Young gentlemen who had trained for the contest entered the ring on foot and on horseback, after the Mexican manner. In the bull and bear fights a hindfoot of the bear was often tied to the forefoot of the bull, to equalize the struggle, for a large grizzly was more than a match for the fiercest bull in California, or indeed of any other country. Bull and bear fights continued as late as 1855. The Indians were the most ardent supporters of this cruel sport.

The days of the *rodeos*, when cattle were driven in from the surrounding pastures, and the herds of the different ranches were separated, were notable episodes. The ranch owners elected three or five *juezes del campo* to govern the proceedings and decide disputes. After the rodeo there was a feast. The great feast-days, however, were December 12 (the day of our Lady Guadalupe), Christmas, Easter, and St. Joseph's Day, or the day of the patron saint of the Missions.

Family life among the old Spanish pioneers was an affair of dignity and ceremony, but it did not lack in affection. Children were brought up with great respect for their elders. It was the privilege of any elderly person to correct young people by words, or even by whipping them, and it was never told that any one thus chastised made a complaint. Each one of the old families taught their children the history of the family, and reverence towards religion. A few books, some in manuscript, were treasured in the household, but children were not allowed to read novels until they were grown. They saw little of other children, except their near relatives, but they had many enjoyments unknown to children now, and they grew up with remarkable strength and healthfulness.

In these days of trade, bustle, and confusion, when many thousands of people live in the Californian valleys, which formerly were occupied by only a few Spanish families, the quiet and happy domestic life of the past seems like a dream. We, who loved it, often speak of those days, and especially of the duties of the large Spanish households, where so many dependents were to be cared for, and everything was done in a simple and primitive way.

There was a group of warm springs a few miles distant from the old adobe house in which we lived. It made us children happy to be waked before sunrise to prepare for the "wash-day expedition" to the *Agua Caliente*. The night before the Indians had soaped the clumsy carreta's great wheels. Lunch was placed in baskets, and the gentle oxen were yoked to the pole. We climbed in, under the green cloth of an old Mexican flag which was used as an awning, and the white-haired Indian *ganan*, who had driven the carreta since his boyhood, plodded beside with his long *garrocha*, or ox-goad. The great piles of soiled linen were fastened on the backs of horses, led by other servants, while the girls and women who were to do the washing trooped along by the side of the carreta. All in all, it made an imposing cavalcade, though our progress was slow, and it was generally sunrise before we had fairly reached the spring. The oxen pulled us up the slope of the ravine, where it was so steep that we often cried, "Mother, let us dismount and walk, so as to make it easier." The steps of the carreta were so low that we could climb in or out without stopping the oxen. The watchful mother guided the whole party, seeing that none strayed too far after flowers, or loitered too long talking with the others. Sometimes we heard the howl of coyotes, and the noise of other wild animals in the dim dawn, and then none of the children were allowed to leave the carreta.

A great dark mountain rose behind the hot spring, and the broad, beautiful valley, unfenced, and dotted with browsing herds, sloped down to the bay as we climbed the cañon to where columns of white steam rose among the oaks, and the precious waters, which were strong with sulphur, were seen flowing over the crusted basin, and falling down a worn rock channel to the brook. Now on these mountain slopes for miles are the vineyards of Josiah Stanford, the brother of Senator Leland Stanford, and the valley below is filled with towns and orchards

We watched the women unload the linen and carry it to the upper spring of the group, where the water was best. Then they loosened the horses, and let them pasture on the wild oats, while the women put home-made soap on the clothes, dipped them in the spring, and rubbed them on the smooth rocks until they were white as snow. Then they were spread out to dry on the tops of the low bushes growing on the warm, windless, southern slopes of the mountain. There was sometimes a great deal of linen to be washed, for it was the pride of every Spanish family to own much linen, and the mother and daughters almost always wore white. I have heard strangers speak of the wonderful way in which Spanish ladies of the upper classes in California always appeared in snow-white dresses, and certainly to do so was one of the chief anxieties of every household. Where there were no warm springs the servants of the family repaired to the nearest *arroyo*, or creek, and stood knee-deep in it, dipping and rubbing the linen, and enjoying the sport. In the rainy season the soiled linen sometimes accumulated for several weeks before the weather permitted the house mistress to have a wash-day. Then, when at last it came, it seemed as if half the village, with dozens of babies and youngsters, wanted to go along too and make a spring picnic.

The group of hot sulphur-springs, so useful on wash-days, was a famed resort for sick people, who drank the water, and also buried themselves up to the neck in the soft mud of the slope below the spring, where the waste waters ran. Their friends brought them in litters and scooped out a hole for them, then put boughs overhead to shelter them from the hot sun, and placed food and fresh water within reach, leaving them sometimes thus from sunrise to sunset. The Paso Robles and Gilroy Springs were among the most famous on the coast in those days, and after the annual *rodeos* people often went there to camp and to use the waters. But many writers have told about the medicinal virtues of the various California springs, and I need not enlarge upon the subject. To me, at least, one of the dearest of my childish memories is the family expedition from the great thick-walled adobe, under the olive and fig trees of the Mission, to the *Agua Caliente* in early dawn, and the late return at twilight, when the younger children were all asleep in the slow carreta, and the Indians were singing hymns as they drove the linen-laden horses down the dusky ravines.

THE AMERICAN HIDE
AND TALLOW TRADE

From the viewpoint of American expansion, California's pastoral period was important for two reasons: first, indolence bred of plenty prompted such indifference to social improvement and such disrespect for Mexican authority that the social structure was gravely weakened and the area made ripe for conquest, and second, the economic activity of the "rancheros" focused American attention on the area. Yankee shipowners soon discovered that hides and tallow from the vast herds of cattle commanded ready markets—the hides in New England where they were used in the burgeoning shoe industry, the tallow in Peru where it was converted into candles for use in silver mines. Traders from the eastern seaboard regularly visited the coast after the 1820s; owners soon found it to their advantage to establish agents at shipping points to purchase and store hides. Every ship from the East carried back word of California's balmy climate and economic potential; every agent became a self-appointed promoter bent on luring his fellow Americans to the Eden he had discovered. One of the sailors on a hide-and-tallow ship, Richard Henry Dana, Jr., described the trade in a book that made his fame: "Two Years Before the Mast" (1840):[2]

In the middle of this crescent, directly opposite the anchoring ground, lie the mission and town of Santa Barbara, on a low, flat plain, but little above the level of the sea, covered with grass, though entirely without trees, and surrounded on three sides by an amphitheatre of mountains, which slant off to the distance of fifteen or twenty miles. The mission stands a little back of the town, and is a large building, or rather collection of buildings, in the center of which is a high tower, with a belfry of five bells; and the whole, being plastered, makes quite a show at a distance, and is the mark by which vessels come to anchor. The town lies a little nearer to the beach—about half a mile from it—and is composed of one-story houses built of brown clay—some of them plastered—with red tiles on the roofs. I should judge that there were about an hundred of them; and in the midst of them stands the Presidio, or fort, built of the same materials, and apparently but little stronger. The town is certainly finely situated, with a Bay in front, and an amphitheatre of hills behind. The only thing which diminishes its beauty is, that the hills have no large trees upon them, they having been all burnt by the great fire which swept them off about a dozen years before, and they had not yet grown up again. The fire was described to me by an inhabitant, as having been a very terrible and magnificent sight. The air of the whole valley was so heated that the people were obliged to leave the town and take up their quarters for several days upon the beach.

Just before sun-down the mate ordered a boat's crew ashore, and I went as one of the number. We passed under the stern of the English brig, and had a long pull ashore. I shall never forget the impression which our first landing on the beach of California made upon me. The sun had just gone down; it was getting dusky; the damp night wind was beginning to blow, and the heavy swell of the Pacific was setting in, and breaking in loud and high "combers" upon the beach. We lay on our oars in the swell, just outside the surf, waiting for a good chance to run in, when a boat, which had put off from the Ayacucho just after us, came alongside of us, with a crew of dusky Sandwich Islanders, talking and hallooing in their outlandish tongue. They knew that we were novices in this kind of boating, and waited to see us go in. The second mate, however, who steered our boat, determined to have the advantage of their experience, and would not go in first. Finding, at length, how matters stood, they gave a shout, and taking advantage of a

---

[2] Richard Henry Dana, Jr., *Two Years Before the Mast* (New York, 1840). Dana's narrative has often been reprinted. These extracts have been copied from a Boston, 1895 edition, pp. 54–57.

great comber which came swelling in, rearing its head, and lifting up the stern of our boat nearly perpendicular, and again dropping it in the trough, they gave three or four long and strong pulls, and went in on top of the great wave, throwing their oars overboard, and as far from the boat as they could throw them, and jumping out the instant that the boat touched the beach, and then seizing hold of her and running her up high and dry upon the sand. We saw, at once, how it was to be done, and also the necessity of keeping the boat "stern on" to the sea; for the instant the sea should strike upon her broad-side or quarter, she would be driven up broad-side on, and capsized. We pulled strongly in, and as soon as we felt that the sea had got hold of us and was carrying us in with the speed of a race-horse, we threw the oars as far from the boat as we could, and took hold of the gun-wale, ready to spring out and seize her when she struck, the officer using his utmost strength to keep her stern on. We were shot up upon the beach like an arrow from a bow, and seizing the boat, ran her up high and dry, and soon picked up our oars, and stood by her, ready for the captain to come down.

Finding that the captain did not come immediately, we put our oars in the boat, and leaving one to watch it, walked about the beach to see what we could, of the place. The beach is nearly a mile in length between the two points, and of smooth sand. We had taken the only good landing-place, which is in the middle; it being more stony towards the ends. It is about twenty yards in width from high-water mark to a slight bank at which the soil begins, and so hard that it is a favorite place for running horses. It was growing dark, so that we could just distinguish the dim outlines of the two vessels in the offing; and the great seas were rolling in, in regular lines, growing larger and larger as they approached the shore, and hanging over the beach upon which they were to break, when their tops would curl over and turn white with foam, and, beginning at one extreme of the line, break rapidly to the other, as a long card-house falls when the children knock down the cards at one end. The Sandwich Islanders, in the meantime, had turned their boat round, and ran her down into the water, and were loading her with hides and tallow. As this was the work in which we were soon to be engaged, we looked on with some curiosity. They ran the boat into the water so far that every large sea might float her, and two of them, with their trowsers rolled up, stood by the bows, one on each side, keeping her in her right position. This was hard work, for beside the force they had to use upon the boat, the large seas nearly took them off their legs. The others were running from the boat to the bank, upon which, out of the reach of the water, was a pile of dry bullocks' hides, doubled lengthwise in the middle, and nearly as stiff as boards. These they took upon their heads, one or two at a time, and carried down to the boat, where one of their number stowed them away. They were obliged to carry them on their heads, to keep them out of the water, and we observed that they had on thick woollen caps. "Look here, Bill, and see what you're coming to!" said one of our men to another who stood by the boat. "Well, D——," said the second mate to me, "this does not look much like Cambridge college, does it?—This is what I call 'head work.'" To tell the truth, it did not look very encouraging.

After they had got through with the hides, they laid hold of the bags of tallow, (the bags are made of hide, and are about the size of a common meal bag,) and lifting each upon the shoulders of two men, one at each end, walked off with them to the boat, and prepared to go aboard. Here, too, was something for us to learn. The man who steered, shipped his oars and stood up in the stern, and those that pulled the after oars sat upon their benches with their oars shipped, ready to strike out as soon as she was afloat. The two men at the bows kept their places; and when, at length, a large sea came in and floated her, seized hold of the gunwale, and ran out with her till they were up to their armpits, and then tumbled over the gunwale into the bow, dripping with water. The men at the oars struck out, but it wouldn't do; the sea swept back and left them nearly high and dry. The two fellows jumped out again; and the next time they succeeded better, and, with the help of a deal of outlandish hallooing and bawling, got her well off. We watched them till they were out of the breakers, and saw them steering for their vessel, which was now hidden in the darkness.

SUPPRESSION OF THE AMERICANS: ISAAC GRAHAM

Both explorers and traders eventually brought back word from California not only of a rich land but of Mexico's weak hold on its northern provinces. By the 1830s, turbulence within the mother country, combined with the vast distances separating Mexico City from California, reduced California's government to near anarchy. Revolution followed revolution, until even the more stable Mexican-Californians despaired of protecting their property without aid from an orderly neighbor such as the United States. This carnival of disorder reached a high point in 1840 when the governor, Juan Bautista Alvarado, hearing rumors that Americans were plotting his overthrow, suddenly ordered one hundred of them thrown into jail. Their alleged leader, a raw-boned fur trapper named Isaac Graham, was eventually sent in chains to Mexico with fifty of his supposed fellow conspirators. The dissatisfaction bred of this incident was described by Charles Wilkes, an official explorer from the United States, who was in California at the time:[3]

After a short time, it was found that the customs did not produce the required revenue; and the new government, fearing to tax the people and missions too openly, resorted to a renewal of the double duties, before more than two vessels had touched on the coast. Every day produced some restrictions upon the foreigners, who had now become estranged from the existing government that they had assisted to establish. Alvarado, finding his acts disapproved of by them, grew suspicious and jealous of their presence; for he well knew, from the manner of his own elevation, what an effective body they were

This state of things continued until the month of April, 1840, when Alvarado, anticipating an insurrectionary movement, and knowing the confidence that the aid of the foreigners would give the malcontent Californians, determined to rid the territory of them. For the purpose of obtaining some colour for the violence he intended, an Englishman, by the name of Gardner, was found, who deposed that all the foreigners, from San Francisco to San Diego, or from one extreme of California to the other, a distance of six or seven hundred miles, had conspired to murder the governor and take possession of the country: that an American, by the name of Graham, a trapper from the

---

[3] Charles Wilkes, *Narrative of the United States Exploring Expedition During the Years 1838, 1839, 1840, 1841, 1842* (Philadelphia, 1845), vol. 5, pp. 169–172.

state of Kentucky, was their leader; and that they were to rendezvous, for the purpose, at Nativetes, the residence of Graham. Colonel Castro was accordingly sent thither, with the prefect, two inferior officers, and fifteen armed soldiers. They proceeded to Nativetes, which is about twenty miles from Monterey; but, as they well knew that Graham was a resolute, strong, and brave man, it was necessary to take great precautions. They therefore chose midnight for their attack, at which hour they reached his farm. On their arrival they forced open the door, and at once fired a volley into the bed where he lay asleep, and so close to it that they set fire to his blankets. Graham was wounded in several places, and badly burnt.

On being thus awakened, he attempted to defend himself, but was overpowered by numbers, inhumanly beaten, and then tied hand and foot. A working-man, who attended the cattle with him, by the name of Shard, also an American, was held down by two men while a third deliberately cut the tendons of his legs with a butcher's knife, and left him to die. Graham was then tied upon a horse, and carried to Monterey, where he was loaded with irons, and placed in a filthy cell;—torn from the property he had accumulated, amounting to four or five thousand dollars in specie, and about ten thousand dollars in /cattle, which he had reared and bought, through his own industry: this, it is supposed, fell into the hands of the governor, who was much in want of funds at the time, and could conceive of no way by which his coffers could be so readily replenished as by such a wholesale robbery.

After the arrest of Graham, more than sixty foreigners were taken up immediately, put into irons, and cast into prison with him. At the same time, orders were issued to apprehend every foreigner found upon the coast; and in case of their not giving bonds for their appearance, they were to be thrust into prison.

Forty-seven of these men were embarked in a vessel called the Guipuzcoa, loaded with irons, nearly half of whom are said to have been citizens of the United States. One of these died from the treatment he received; and the hardships they were obliged to undergo on their journey to Tepic, are almost past belief.

The Guipuzcoa was eleven days on her passage to San Blas, during which time the prisoners were kept in the hold of this small vessel, without light or air, and endured every description of ill treatment. On their arrival at San Blas, they were landed without delay, and immediately marched, in the short space of two days, to Tepic, a distance of sixty miles.

The thermometer was at 90°; the road was mountainous and rough; they were barefooted, heavily ironed, and without any food, except what was given them from charity. They were urged forward by lashes inflicted on their naked bodies, and one who sank under the fatigue was severely beaten with the but-end of a musket.

At Tepic, they found in the English and American consuls kind friends, who exerted themselves to relieve their wants, and finally, through their remonstrances, and those of the English and American ministers, they were allowed to return to California; and orders were given that they should produce certificates of their losses, and be paid for them. All the Englishmen have returned, with every necessary document to establish their claims, and obtain redress for their wrongs; but on the part of the Americans, this is far from being the case. Of them none but Graham have returned, and he is broken both in health and spirits. What remuneration he has received, I did not learn; but the French and English have all obtained indemnity, through the attention their governments have paid to their wrongs. Ours alone has failed in the prompt protection of its citizens; and many complaints are made by our countrymen abroad that the government at home seems to have very little regard for their lives or property.

It would appear by this want of attention on the part of our government, that it had not been fully satisfied that the conduct of its citizens had been correct; at least, that is the feeling among them abroad. I have little testimony on this subject, except the protestations of many of those who have been more or less suspected of taking part in the expected revolt. I can say, that all the accounts I received invariably spoke of the foreigners as having had nothing to do with the intended outbreak, even if it were organized; and every one should be satisfied that they were innocent, by the fact that in Mexico they were all adjudged to be entirely guiltless of the charges brought against them, and that they were sent back at the expense of the Mexican government, with letters of security, and an order making it obligatory on the Governor of California to assist them in procuring evidence of the damages they had sustained. Although this may have been ample satisfaction, so far as mere remuneration goes, yet for the barbarous conduct shown to them by the authorities, some punishment ought to have been inflicted, and an example made. But such has not been the case, and those officers are still kept in their high places, with the power to repeat like barbarities. There is no other way to account for this not being insisted upon, than by supposing that the Mexicans hold so little authority over this territory as to make them extremely scrupulous how they take any measures that may cause the dismemberment of the state, and the loss of even the nominal dominion they now possess.

The situation of Upper California will cause its separation from Mexico before many years. The country between it and Mexico can never be any thing but a barren waste, which precludes all intercourse except that by sea, always more or less interrupted by the course of the winds, and the unhealthfulness of the lower or seaport towns of Mexico. It is very probable that this country will become united with Oregon, with which it will perhaps form a state that is destined to control the destinies of the Pacific. This future state is admirably situated to become a powerful maritime nation, with two of the finest ports in the world,—that within the straits of Juan de Fuca, and San Francisco. These two regions have, in fact, within themselves every thing to make them increase, and keep up an intercourse with the whole of Polynesia, as well as the countries of South America on the one side, and China, the Philippines, New Holland, and New Zealand, on the other. Among the latter, before many years, may be included Japan. Such various climates will furnish the materials for a beneficial interchange of products, and an intercourse that must, in time, become immense; while this western coast, enjoying a climate in many respects superior to any other in the Pacific, possessed as it must be by the Anglo-Norman race, and having none to enter into rivalry with it but the indolent inhabitants of warm climates, is evidently destined to fill a large space in the world's future history.

JOHN A. SUTTER AND HIS FORT

As tensions mounted and authority disintegrated in California, ambitious adventurers recognized an opportunity to make their fortunes. Of those who drifted in during the 1830s and early 1840s, two were to play essential roles in the events that followed: John Marsh and John A. Sutter. Marsh, a Harvard graduate and self-proclaimed physician, obtained a 50,000-acre "rancho" at Mount Diablo in the lower San Joaquin Valley; Sutter's principality was a short distance away on the Sacramento River. Both sought to increase the value of their real estate by attracting settlers from the United States; their persuasive letters to the eastern press made "Sutter's Fort" and the "Mount Diablo Ranch" well known among Mississippi Valley frontiersmen with an inclination to move. A guide book later used by "emigrants" from the "States" mirrored the importance of these bases in luring settlers, just as its picture of the indolent Mexicans helped whet the appetite of land-hungry Americans for a conquest that clearly offered no difficulties:[4]

The settlements and improvements are, chiefly, in connection with the different forts, military posts, and missionary stations, and at the various towns, all of which are confined entirely, to the Western section. Of these, I shall first notice, the forts and military posts, of the former of which, there are but two, one of which, is called New Helvetia, and the other is called Ross. Both of these are now in the possession of, and owned by, Captain Sutter, the former of which he built, and the latter he purchased of the Russians. New Helvetia, the most important of these, is situated in a well chosen position, on the south side of the Sacramento, about one mile from its south bank, 100 miles, east by north, from Yerba Buena, at latitude 38° 45' 42" north. In form, it is a sexangular oblong, its greatest length being 428 feet, and its greatest width, 178 feet; 233 feet of its length being 178 feet wide, and the residue but 129 feet wide. It is inclosed by permanent "adobie" walls, which are 18 feet high, and three feet thick, with bastions at the corners, the walls of which, are five feet thick. It is entered by three large swinging gates, one of which, is on the north, another on the south side, and the third at the east end.—The first of these, is entirely inaccessible from without, because of a deep, and impassable ravine, which extends the whole length of the fort, on the north; on each side of the second, is a platform, upon each of which, a nine-pounder is planted, and the third is completely commanded, by one of the bastions. There are two bastions, each of which has four guns, two nine-pounders, and two six-pounders; and in all, there are twelve guns, of different caliber. The inner building of this fort, consist of a large and commodious residence, for the various officers, in connection with which, is a large kitchen, a dining room, two large parlors, the necessary officers, shops and lodging apartments. Besides these, there is also a distillery, a horse-mill and a magazine, together with barracks, for the accommodation of, at least, one thousand soldiers. In connection with the fort, there are one thousand acres of land, under a good state of cultivation, and upon which are all the necessary buildings, together with an extensive tannery. Of this fort, Captain Sutter has charge, in person; he has about one hundred men, constantly in his employment, who annually sow one thousand acres of wheat, and have charge of his numerous herds, which, in all, amount to about twenty thousand head. Those, having charge of the various herds, are, generally, Indians, but his building and farming, are superintended chiefly by foreigners. He also has, a large number of experienced trappers, in his service, who have charge of about one thousand traps, and

---

[4] Lansford W. Hastings, *The Emigrant's Guide to Oregon and California* (Cincinnati, 1845), pp. 102–104, 124–127. A modern edition, with an historical note by Charles H. Carey, was published at Princeton in 1932.

from whose services, he annually realizes several thousand dollars.

Besides the business thus carried on, by the Captain, he is also doing a very extensive business, in a military way. All the usual military formalities, are regularly observed; sentinels are always kept out, day and night, who invariably give the captain, timely notice of the approach of persons, during the day, or of the slightest movement, of any thing, in the human form, during the night. Here too, the natives are being instructed, in the art of war; forty or fifty of them, are taken and instructed, for several months, and until they have acquired, a general knowledge, of military tactics; when they are turned off, and forty or fifty others are taken, who are drilled and trained, in the same manner, when they are also dismissed, and others taken in their stead, and so on continually.— The Mexicans, not being able to divine the cause, of all this military parade, at one time, became very suspicious, that all was not right; and finally, their suspicions were increased to such an extent, that they determined to effect the captain's unceremonious expulsion, from the country, of which determination, he was duly advised. The captain took the matter under consideration, and soon determined, to resist any attempted encroachment, upon his rights, and accordingly, informed the government of his determination. The government, however, proceeded to make its preliminary arrangements, for his expulsion, preparatory to which, a spy was sent, in the disguise of a friend, to the captain's fort, in order to ascertain his true position, as to vulnerableness, and means of resistance.—Upon the arrival of this mysterious visitor, an enemy in disguise, "a wolf in sheep's clothing," or a *Mexican* in *man's clothing*, the captain soon suspected his object, and informed him, that he must immediately depart, or he would, at once, order him to be put in irons, and, at the same time, informed him, that if the government, whose spy he was, thought proper to attempt his expulsion from the country, he was perfectly willing, at any time, to test its ability to accomplish that object.—This hypocritical visitor, now made rather an irregular disappearance, amid the jeers, taunts and threats, of the captain's men, and if he was not prepared to report to his *owners*, that the captain *was* invincible, he was fully prepared to report, that the captain *thought* himself invincible, which would be precisely the same thing, as far as Mexicans were concerned. The government, finding, that the captain was not to be deterred, and that an attempt to effect his expulsion, would be attended with dangerous consequences, of *course*, abandoned the undertaking. Ever since that time, the government has treated the captain with extraordinary kindness, bestowing upon him, the office of alcalde, and other little governmental favors, designed to repair the cloak of hypocrisy, which had been so seriously lacerated, in the above transaction. The truth, however, is, that the Mexicans look upon the captain, with much more than ordinary suspicion, notwithstanding their pretended friendship; but whether they are justified, in veiwing the captain, with some little suspicion, I do not pretend to say, as to that, each will judge for himself. Having heard thus much, in reference to this gentleman, many might be led to inquire more particularly, as to the captain; I will therefore remark, that he is a Swede by birth; he emigrated, at an early day, to the United States, where he resided for several years, residing most of the time, at St. Louis and St. Charles, in Missouri, and in 1839, he emigrated to California, where he has since remained. His military taste, as well as his military title, was derived from his service in Bonapart's army, to which he was attached, for several years. A more kind and hospitable gentleman, it has seldom been my fortune to meet. Such is his treatment of all foreigners, who visit him, that when they leave him, they are compelled to do so, with much regret, and under many obligations, for his continued, untiring and gentlemanly attentions. . . .

The Mexicans here, are a peculiar people, not only in reference to their intelligence, government, and all other particulars before mentioned, but also in reference to their manners and customs. The lower order of them live in mere huts, the walls of which are constructed of poles, which are set upright, side by side, one end being permanently fixed in the ground; the other ends are attached with raw hide ropes to a pole, which is placed horizontally on each side of the walls thus constructed, and about six or seven feet from the ground. The four walls being thus erected, poles are then placed transversely from one wall to the other, which are covered either with hay, flags, or cornstalks, constituting the roof, when the hut is completed, having neither floor nor chimney.—The second and higher orders, occupy such buildings as those which have been described upon a former page, most of which are also without either chimneys or floors. No furniture is generally found in or about the houses of the lower orders, excepting here and there a raw bullock's hide spread upon the ground, which, together with a blanket or two, constitutes their beds and bedding. Their clothing generally consists of nothing more than a shirt and a pair of pantaloons, yet some of them also have a kind of rude, primitive hat, and sandals. The chase and servitude to the higher orders, furnish them a livelihood; they subsist almost entirely upon meat, fish, oats and edible roots. Those of the second and higher orders, who reside in the interior, although they have "adobie" houses, yet they generally have neither beds, chairs, tables, nor any other furniture, excepting such beds as those before described, and a raw hide spread upon the ground, which constitutes a table, with a few stools or bullock's heads, which answer as chairs. Their apparel consists of a shirt, a pair of pantaloons, some kind of a hat and and shoes, or sandals, in addition to which, some have a pair of breeches and a blanket, with a perforation in the middle, through which they put their heads, and thus form, as they think, a very convenient coat or cloak. Meat, fish, beans, bread and fruit, constitute their food. But they subsist chiefly upon the former, as a matter of preference. Should you call at the residence of one of these Mexicans, even of the highest class residing in the interior, you would not only be received very kindly, but you would also be annoyed with continued proffers, of all the luxuries which they possess. And should you remain until noon, a large quantity of beef will be roasted before the fire, which, when done, will be attached to a few sticks, which are driven into the ground for that purpose, in the middle of the room, when you are invited to sit down with them, and partake of the rich repast; at the same time, you are offered a stool or beef's head as a substitute for a chair, if there happens to be one convenient, if not, you are expected to sit upon the ground. Being thus located, you now commence the dissection and mastication of the half, or quarter of a beef, as the case may be, with which you are now confronted; but in this operation, you labor under the disadvantage, of having none of the ordinary instruments, used upon such occasions; hence you are under the necessity of using your pocket knife, or such other knife as you may chance to have in your possession. Among some of these people, in addition to the roasted beef, you would also be furnished with a little bean soup, and, perhaps, some bread; but they all view plates, knives and forks, and the like, as mere useless appendages.—Should you call upon those of the lower order, with the view of obtaining a dinner, the presumption is, that the whole affair would result in a disgusting failure, if not on their part, in an attempt to procure something for you to eat, at least, upon your part, in your attempt to eat what they have succeeded in procuring; but whatever they have, they will readily offer you, with much apparent anxiety to accommodate. The higher order of those who reside in the different towns, and at the missions, generally live very well, much, in fact, as the foreigners do, who are equally as abundantly supplied with all the necessaries and luxuries of life, as citizens of our own country, or those of any other. All classes of the Mexicans are unusually kind and hospitable to foreigners, as far as it relates to their reception and treatment as guests. Whatever attention and kindness you may receive at their hands, while guests, and however long you may remain with them, they will receive no compensation, but to your proposition to remunerate them, they invariably reply, "God will pay."

Labor of all kinds is performed by the Indians and the lower order of the Mexicans, but those who are not bound in servitude to others, labor very little, as a competency of food and raiment, is readily acquired, with very little exertion. Among all classes, oxen are principally used for the draught, drawing by their horns, instead of their necks, as in the ordinary manner; a strong piece of timber about as large as an ordinary yoke, is placed upon the necks of the oxen, just back of the horns, to which it is permanently attached, by means of a raw-hide rope. To the middle of this new-fashioned yoke, a strong raw-hide rope is affixed, to which the cart, plough, or whatever else is to be drawn, is attached, when all is in readiness for actual service. Those oxen, yoked in this manner, draw most extremely large draughts, but by no means as large draughts as they could draw, if yoked in the ordinary manner.—The plough, which is in use among the Mexicans, is certainly among the most simply constructed, and cheapest of farming utensils, being, generally, a mere forked stick, one prong of which, being pointed, answers, as the share, and the other having a notch cut at the end, to which a rope may be attached, constitutes the beam, while the main stalk, extending back a few feet from the union of the two prongs, constitutes the handle. This is the California plough, which is in general use, throughout the entire country; but as an improvement upon this plough, some of the Mexicans construct one in a different manner, though with the same regard to cheapness, being two sticks of timber, so attached as to form a plough, very much like that just described; and designed only as a substitute for that, when a natural fork cannot be conveniently found.—Horses are seldom used otherwise than as saddle-horses, but we frequently see large draughts, drawn by them, which, instead of being harnessed in the ordinary manner, are put under the saddle, the girth of which is drawn extremely tight, when one end of a strong raw-hide rope, is attached to the stone, wood, or whatever else is to be drawn, while the other end is firmly attached to the pommel of the saddle. Every thing being thus arranged, the Mexican, with his heels loaded down with ponderous, gingling spurs, now mounts his steed, to whose sides he plies his heels with such *pointed* exactness, such force and confused gingling, that, as the only alternative, he leaps and darts away with his immense load, notwithstanding its very great ponderosity. With horses harnessed in this manner, it is quite common to see Mexicans on their way to market, their vehicles being a dry bullock's hide, to which one end of a long raw-hide rope is attached, the other end of which, is attached to the pommel of the saddle, of their riding horses. Upon this hide, thus dragging upon the ground, are heaped vegetables, fowls, and whatever else they may have in readiness for the market, as well as two or three women and children, which, from all appearances, are not designed for the market, or, at all events, it would seem that they would not sell to a very good advantage, without the preparatory expense of a thorough scouring. Upon arriving in market, I have frequently seen these inventive geniuses, with their strange omnibuses, and omnifarious loading, passing about from place to place, until they disposed of all their load, excepting that part of it which partook somewhat of humanity, when they also disposed of their extraordinary vehicles, and returned to their homes as they best could, some on horse back, some on foot, and others, I knew not how, unless by "*steam*," to raise which, they appeared to be making some efforts, which I thought, would most likely succeed. These are the vehicles in common use, among the Mexicans, but many of the foreigners, as well as some of the higher order of the Mexicans, have carts, wagons, and even carriages, but these are very seldom seen, and especially the latter; as traveling is, as yet, almost entirely on horseback and by water, the former of which methods, is, however, much the most generally adopted, both by the Mexicans and foreigners.

THE BIDWELL-BARTLESON MIGRATION, 1841

The diet of fact and fancy fed Mississippi Valley pioneers by propagandists for California inspired the inevitable migration. In 1841, the first overland party took off from the Missouri River—a pitifully small band of thirty-two men, one woman, and one child—ineptly led at first by John Bartleson and capably guided later by John Bidwell. Leaving the well-trodden Oregon Trail at Soda Springs in Idaho, the Bidwell-Bartleson group blundered westward to the Humboldt River, followed this stream to the Sierra Nevada, scaled those formidable peaks, and in November arrived at Marsh's Mount Diablo Ranch. Late in his life, John Bidwell wrote a memorable account of that journey, based on diaries kept at the time. The extracts that follow describe the start of the expedition, the trip across unknown deserts to the Humboldt, and the crossing of the Sierras:[5]

In November or December of 1840, while still teaching school in Platte County, I came across a Frenchman named Roubidoux, who said he had been to California. He had been a trader in New Mexico, and had followed the road traveled by traders from the frontier of Missouri to Santa Fé. He had probably gone through what is now New Mexico and Arizona into California by the Gila River trail used by the Mexicans. His description of California was of the superlative degree favorable, so much so that I resolved if possible to see that wonderful land, and with others helped to get up a meeting at Weston and invited him to make a statement before it in regard to the country. At that time when a man moved West, as soon as he was fairly settled he wanted to move again, and naturally every question imaginable was asked in regard to this wonderful country. Roubidoux described it as one of perennial spring and boundless fertility, and laid stress on the countless thou-

---

[5] John Bidwell, "The First Emigrant Train to California," *Century Magazine*, XLI (November, 1890), 109–111, 113–114, 125, 127–129.

sands of wild horses and cattle. He told about oranges, and hence must have been at Los Angeles or the mission of San Gabriel, a few miles from it. Every conceivable question that we could ask him was answered favorably. Generally the first question which a Missourian asked about a country was whether there was any fever and ague. I remember his answer distinctly. He said there was but one man in California that had ever had a chill there, and it was a matter of so much wonderment to the people of Monterey that they went eighteen miles into the country to see him shake. Nothing could have been more satisfactory on the score of health. He said that the Spanish authorities were most friendly, and that the people were the most hospitable on the globe; that you could travel all over California and it would cost you nothing for horses or feed. Even the Indians were friendly. His description of the country made it seem like a paradise.

The result was that we appointed a corresponding secretary and a committee to report a plan of organization. A pledge was drawn up in which every signer agreed to purchase a suitable outfit and to rendezvous at Sapling grove in what is now the state of Kansas, on the ninth of the following May, armed and equipped to cross the Rocky Mountains to California. We called ourselves the Western Emigration Society, and as soon as the pledge was drawn up every one who agreed to come signed his name to it, and it took like wildfire. In a short time, I think within a month, we had about 500 names; we also had correspondence on the subject with people all over Missouri, and even as far east as Illinois and Kentucky, and as far south as Arkansas. As soon as the movement was announced in the papers we had many letters of inquiry and we expected people in considerable numbers to join us.

About that time we heard of a man in Jackson County, Missouri, who had received a letter from a person in California named Dr. Marsh speaking favorably of the country, and a copy was published.

Our ignorance of the route was complete. We knew that California lay west, and that was the extent of our knowledge. Some of the maps consulted, supposed of course to be correct, showed a lake in the vicinity of where Salt Lake now is; it was represented as a long lake, three or four hundred miles in extent, narrow and with two outlets, both running into the Pacific Ocean, either apparently larger than the Mississippi River. An intelligent man with whom I boarded—Elam Brown, who until recently lived in California, dying when over ninety years of age—possessed a map that showed these rivers to be large, and he advised me to take tools along to make canoes, so that if we found the country so rough that we could not get along with our wagons we could descend one of these rivers to the Pacific. Even Frémont knew nothing about Salt Lake until 1843, when for the first time he explored it and mapped it correctly, his report being first printed, I believe, in 1845....

When we reached Sapling Grove, the place of rendezvous, in May, 1841, there was but one wagon ahead of us. For the next few days one or two wagons would come each day, and among the recruits were three families from Arkansas. We organized by electing as captain of the company a man named Bartleson from Jackson County, Missouri. He was not the best man for the position, but we were given to understand that if he was not elected captain he would not go; and he had seven or eight men with him, and we did not want the party diminished, so he was chosen. Every one furnished his own supplies. The party consisted of sixty-nine, including men, women, and children. Our teams were of oxen, mules, and horses. We had no cows, as the later emigrants usually had, and the lack of milk was a great privation to the children. It was understood that every one should have not less than a barrel of flour, with sugar and so forth to suit, but I laid in one hundred pounds of flour more than the usual quantity, besides other things. This I did because we were told that when we got into the mountains we probably would get out of bread and have to live on meat alone, which I thought would kill me even if it did not others. My gun was an old flint-lock rifle, but a good one. Old hunters told me to have nothing to do with cap or percussion locks, that they were unreliable, and that if I got my caps or percussion wet I could not shoot, while if I lost my flint I could pick up another on the plains. I doubt whether there was one hundred dollars in the whole party, but all were enthusiastic and anxious to go.

In five days after my arrival we were ready to start, but no one knew where to go, not even the captain. Finally a man came up, one of the last to arrive, and announced that a company of Catholic missionaries were on their way from St. Louis to the Flathead nation of Indians with an old Rocky Mountaineer for a guide, and that if we would wait another day they would be up with us. At first we were independent, and thought we could not afford to wait for a slow missionary party. But when we found that no one knew which way to go, we sobered down and waited for them to come up; and it was well that we did, for otherwise probably not one of us would ever have reached California, because of our inexperience. Afterwards, when we came in contact with Indians, our people were so easily excited that if we had not had with us an old mountaineer the result would certainly have been disastrous.

The name of the guide was Captain Fitzpatrick; he had been at the head of trapping parties in the Rocky Mountains for many years. He and the missionary party went with us as far as Soda Springs, now in Idaho, whence they turned north to the Flathead nation. The party consisted of three Roman Catholic priests—Fathers De Smet, Point and Mengarini—and ten or eleven French Canadians, and accompanying them were an old mountaineer named John Gray and a young Englishman named Romaine, and also a man named Baker. They seemed glad to have us with them, and we certainly were glad to have their company....

[All went well until the Bidwell-Bartleson party abandoned the Oregon Trail to strike westward from Soda Springs toward the rumored Humboldt River.]

We now got into a country where there was no grass nor water, and then we began to catechize the men who had gone to Fort Hall. They repeated, "If you go too far south you will get into a desert country and your animals will perish; there will be no water nor grass." We were evidently too far south. We could not go west, and the formation of the country was such that we had to turn and go north across a range of mountains. Having struck a small stream we camped upon it all night, and next day continued down its banks, crossing from side to side, most of the time following Indian paths or paths made by antelopes and deer. In the afternoon we entered a cañon, the walls of which were precipitous and several hundred feet high. Finally the pleasant bermy banks gave out entirely, and we could travel only in the dry bed of what in the wet season was a raging river. It became a solid mass of stones and huge boulders, and the animals became tenderfooted and sore so that they could hardly stand up, and as we continued the way became worse and worse. There was no place for us to lie down and sleep, nor could our animals lie down; the water had given out, and the prospect was indeed gloomy—the cañon had been leading us directly north.

All agreed that the animals were too jaded and worn to go back. Then we called the men: "What did they tell you at Fort Hall about the northern region?" They repeated, "You must not go too far north; if you do you will get into difficult cañons that lead toward the Columbia River, where you may become bewildered and wander about and perish." This cañon was going nearly north; in fact it seemed a little east of north. We sent some men to see if they could reach the top of the mountain by scaling the precipice somewhere and get a view, and they came back about ten or eleven o'clock saying the country looked better three or four miles farther ahead. So we were encouraged; even the animals seemed to take courage, and we got along much better than had been thought possible, and by one o'clock that day came out on what is now known as the Humboldt River. It was not until four years later (1845) that General Frémont first saw this river and named it Humbolt....

[The Humboldt was followed until it vanished into the desert at the Humboldt Sink; from there the weary journeyers made their way toward the Sierras, which towered before them.]

We were now camped on Walker River, at the very eastern base of the Sierra Nevadas, and had only two oxen left. We sent men ahead to see if it would be possible to scale the mountains, while we killed the better of the two oxen and dried the meat in preparation for the ascent. The men returned toward evening and reported that they thought it would be possible to ascend the mountains, though very difficult. We had eaten our supper and were ready for the climb in the morning. Looking back on the plains we saw something coming, which we decided to be Indians. They traveled very slowly, and it was difficult to understand their movements. To make a long story short, it was the eight men that had left us nine days before. They had gone farther south than we, and had come to a lake, probably Carson Lake, and there had found Indians, who supplied them plentifully with fish and pine nuts. Fish caught in such water are not fit to eat at any time, much less in the fall of the year. The men had eaten heartily of fish and pine nuts and had got something akin to cholera morbus. We ran out to meet them and shook hands, and put our frying pans on and gave them the best supper we could. Captain Bartleson, who when we started from Missouri was a portly man, was reduced to half his former girth. He said: "Boys, if ever I get back to Missouri I will never leave that country. I would gladly eat out of the troughs with my hogs." He seemed to be heartily sick of his late experience, but that did not prevent him from leaving us twice after that.

We were now in what is at present Nevada, and probably within forty miles of the present boundary of California. We ascended the mountain on the north side of Walker River to the summit, and then struck a stream running west which proved to be the extreme source of the Stanislaus River. We followed it down for several days and finally came to where a branch ran into it, each forming a cañon. The main river flowed in a precipitous gorge, in places apparently a mile deep, and the gorge that came into it was but little less formidable. At night we found ourselves on the extreme point of the promontory between the two, very tired, and with neither grass nor water. We had to stay there that night. Early the next morning two men went down to see if it would be possible to get down through the smaller cañon. I was one of them, Jimmy Johns was the other. Benjamin Kelsey, who had shown himself expert in finding the way, was now, without any election, still recognized as leader, as he had been during the absence of Bartleson. A party also went back to see how far we should have to go around before we could pass over the tributary cañon. The understanding was that when we went down the cañon if it was practicable to get through we were to fire a gun so that all would follow; but if not, we were not to fire, even if we saw game. When Jimmy and I got down about three-quarters of a mile I came to the conclusion that it was impossible to get through and said to him, "Jimmy, we might as well go back; we can't go here." "Yes, we can," said he, and insisting that we could, he pulled out a pistol and fired.

It was an old dragoon pistol, and reverberated like a cannon. I hurried back to tell the company not to come down, but before I reached them the captain and his party had started. I explained, and warned them that they could not get down; but they went on as far as they could go and then were obliged to stay all day and all night to rest the animals, and had to go among the rocks and pick a little grass for them, and go down to the stream through a terrible place in the cañon to bring water up in cups and camp kettles, and some of the men in their boots, to pour down the animals' throats in order to keep them from perishing. Finally, four of them pulling and four pushing a mule, they managed to get them up one by one, and then carried all the things up again on their backs—not an easy job for exhausted men.

In some way, nobody knows how, Jimmy got through that cañon and into the Sacramento Valley. He had a horse with him—an Indian horse that was bought in the Rocky Mountains, and which could come as near climbing a tree as any horse I ever knew. Jimmy was a character. Of all men I have ever known I think he was the most fearless; he had the bravery of a bulldog. He was not seen for two months—until he was found at Sutter's, afterwards known as Sutter's Fort, now Sacramento City.

We went on, traveling as near west as we could. When we killed our last ox we shot and ate crows or anything we could kill, and one man shot a wildcat. We could eat anything. One day in the morning I went ahead, on foot of course, to see if I could kill something, it being understood that the company would keep on as near west as possible and find a practicable road. I followed an Indian trail down into the cañon, meeting many Indians on the way up. They did not molest me, but I did not quite like their looks. I went about ten miles down the cañon, and then began to think it time to strike north to intersect the trail of the company going west. A most difficult time I had scaling the precipice. Once I threw my gun ahead of me, being unable to hold it and climb, and then was in despair lest I could not get up where it was, but finally I did barely manage to do so, and make my way north. As the darkness came on I was obliged to look down and feel with my feet, lest I should pass over the trail of the party without seeing it. Just at dark I came to an immense fallen tree and tried to go around the top, but the place was too brushy, so I went around the butt, which seemed to me to be about twenty or twenty-five feet above my head. This I suppose to have been one of the fallen trees in the Calaveras Grove of *sequoia gigantea* or mammoth trees, as I have since been there, and to my own satisfaction identified the lay of the land and the tree. Hence I concluded that I must have been the first white man who ever saw *sequoia gigantea*, of which I told Frémont when he came to California in 1845. Of course sleep was impossible, for I had neither blanket nor coat, and burned or froze alternately as I turned from one side to the other before the small fire which I had built, until morning, when I started eastward to intersect the trail, thinking the company had turned north. But I traveled until noon and found no trail; then striking south, I came to the camp which I had left the previous morning.

The party had gone, but not where they said they would go; for they had taken the same trail I followed into the cañon, and had gone up the south side, which they had found so steep that many of the poor animals could not climb it and had to be left. When I arrived, the Indians were there cutting the horses to pieces and carrying off the meat. My situation, alone among strange Indians killing our poor horses, was by no means comfortable. Afterwards we found that these Indians were always at war with the Californians. They were known as the Horse Thief Indians, and lived chiefly on horse flesh; they had been in the habit of raiding the ranches even to the very coast, driving away horses by the hundreds into the mountains to eat. That night I overtook the party in camp.

A day or two later we came to a place where there was a great quantity of horse bones, and we did not know what it meant; we thought that an army must have perished there. They were, of course, horses that the Indians had driven in and slaughtered. A few nights later, fearing depredations, we concluded to stand guard—all but one man, who would not. So we let his two horses roam where they pleased. In the morning they could not be found. A few miles away we came to a village; the Indians had fled, but we found the horses killed and some of the meat roasting on a fire.

We were now on the edge of the San Joaquin Valley, but we did not even know that we were in California. We could see a range of mountains lying to the west—the Coast Range—but we could see no valley. The evening of the day we started down into the valley we were very tired, and when night came our party was strung along for three or four miles, and every man slept where darkness overtook him. He would take off his saddle for a pillow and turn his horse or mule loose, if he had one. His animal would be too poor to walk away, and in the morning he would find him, usually within fifty feet. The jaded horses nearly perished with hunger and fatigue. When we overtook the foremost of the party the next morning we found they had come to a pond of water, and one of them had killed a fat coyote. When I came up it was all eaten except the lights and the windpipe, on which I made my breakfast.

ARRIVAL OF THE EMIGRANTS IN CALIFORNIA

Members of the Bidwell-Bartleson party and of other groups that followed them were disappointed by the scene that awaited them when they reached the San Joaquin Valley. Instead of a land of milk and honey pictured by the propagandists, they found semiarid deserts where burned vegetation testified to the lack of summer rainfall. "Cheyenne" Dawson, a young man who accompanied the 1841 caravan, remembered the shock of the first view when he wrote his memoirs:[6]

We had expected to find civilization—with big fields, fine houses, churches, schools, etc. Instead, we found houses resembling unburnt brick kilns, with no floors, no chim-

---

[6] Nicholas Dawson, *Narrative of Nicholas "Cheyenne" Dawson (Overland to California in '41 and '49, and Texas in '51)* (San Francisco: Grabhorn, 1933), pp. 29–33. These reminiscences were first printed in a small edition in 1901, but are more readily available in the volume published in 1933.

neys, and with the openings for doors and windows closed by shutters instead of glass. There were no fields or fencing in sight—only a strong lot made of logs, called a corral. Cattle and horses were grazing everywhere; but we soon found that there was nothing to eat but poor beef. The season before had been exceptionally dry, and no crops had been made except at the missions, where they irrigated; and, as many of the missions were on a rapid decline, but little had been raised at them.

Marsh was very kind and asked us what we craved most. We told him something fat. He had a fat hog. This he killed for us, and divided it among the messes. We relished it greatly. He also had a small quantity of seed wheat that he was saving to plant. A part of this he had made into tortillas for us. He told us that if we wished we could sleep in the house. This novel experience some of us tried, but we were much disturbed by fleas, and sick-stomached men crawling over us to get out. They had eaten too much pork.

At that time Sutter was on the Sacramento, and wanted colonists; but I, with ten or twelve others who were in a hurry to get into employment, decided to try the Spanish settlements south of us, and after a day or two's stay at Marsh's, set off. Marsh told us that we might meet with difficulties on account of having no passports from our government, and advised us to leave our guns behind. This all did but me. He gave us a letter of introduction to the next ranch ahead, and said no complaint would be made if we killed a beef occasionally.

We found very dim roads and got lost by taking a cattle trail up Mount Diablo. Finding out our mistake as night was approaching, we stopped and tried to kill a beef, but failed; we had nothing for supper but a hawk which I had shot. The next day we reached the ranch, presented our letter, and waited for our meal. It was a pot of stewed beef in the ranchman's kitchen, to which he invited us with a courtly bow. We squatted around the pot and ate all that was in it, then finished our meal by toasting and eating some of the fleece tallow hanging on poles in the kitchen. Marsh had told us that Californians never charged for entertainment; so when we had finished our repast we signed, as well as we could our thanks, and left.

We passed the Mission of San Jose, saw the bay on our right, but no ocean as yet—intervening mountains hid it from view. Just beyond the mission we came to a ranch, and concluded to put up there for the night, expecting to get supper, lodging and breakfast. We took off our packs in the yard and waited. None of us could speak Spanish, but we made our host understand that we were hungry. After a while we saw some men driving cattle toward the house. When they came near, one man threw a rope over the head of a beef, another roped his hind feet; the first roper then fastened his riata to the saddle horn, backed his horse to tighten the rope, jumped down, and by a quick jerk of its tail threw the animal, then immediately killed it by sticking. The two then began stripping the hide off. Shortly the ranchero came, and pointing to the beef, signed that there was something to eat. We cut off some of the flesh, and finding some wood, cooked and ate our supper. At the usual time we made our beds on the ground for the night; but before going to sleep we heard several guns fired and shouting, and the galloping of horses. We sprang up in alarm. In a few minutes horses began to gallop up, each horse bearing two riders—a woman in front on a man's saddle and a man on the crupper behind her, who, reaching both arms around the lady, had hold of the reins. They dismounted, and music striking up in the interior, they were soon dancing. Our battle was only a fandango.

The proprietor soon came out and almost

dragged us into the ballroom, seating us on benches against the wall. In a few minutes a lady approached and clapped her hands in in front of me. I did not understand this, but the host came and pulled me out, then signed me to clap out some other man if I did not wish to dance. We soon got into the hang of it and had a jolly time. This was the only dancing I ever did in my life, and it was only a few kicks. By and by the host came, and with many bows invited all into an adjoining room. Here we found a table, with a nice cloth and dishes, and on it delicious frijolas, tortillas, and roast beef! Wine, too!

The next day while we were traveling on toward the Pueblo de San Jose, we met a squad of men armed with muskets. They turned about when they met us, and escorted us into San Jose and up to a building into which they led us. It was the calaboose, or jail. They sent off our animals and left us—prisoners. That day an American by the name of Tom Bowen visited us, and told us we were arrested for entering the country without passports. He promised to intercede for us, and did, persuading the alcalde, by whose orders we had been arrested, to set us at liberty and return our animals to us, Bowen agreeing to feed us and keep us in San Jose until a messenger could be sent to the governor at Monterey to get orders what to do with us. So we were liberated, but remained in the town, eating beef which Bowen supplied, and faring very well.

THE TRAGEDY OF THE DONNER PARTY

Initial dissatisfaction vanished as the newcomers found work at Sutter's Fort or Marsh's ranch. Their enthusiastic letters home, describing the balmy climate and long growing season, encouraged others to follow; during the next half-dozen years caravans regularly made their way along the California Trail with only the usual allotment of hardships. One, however, gained immortality through suffering. Led by two Illinois farmers, Jacob and George Donner, this well-equipped party reached South Pass without difficulty in the summer of 1846. Beyond this point its eighty-nine members left the regular route to follow a short cut recommended by Lansford W. Hastings. This proved so nearly impassable that they did not reach the Sierras until winter was at hand. Near the crest of the mountains a blizzard roared in upon them, ending all hope of reaching the San Joaquin Valley. The hardships endured in that winter camp have become legend. They are etched boldly in a simple diary kept by one of the members, Patrick Breen:[7]

Frid. [*February*] *5th* Snowd. hard all untill 12 o'clock at night wind still continud to blow hard from the S. W: to day pretty clear a few clouds only Peggy very uneasy for fear we shall all perrish with hunger we have but a little meat left & only part of 3 hides has to support Mrs. Reid she has nothing left but one hide & it is on Graves shanty Milt is livig there & likely will keep that hide Eddys child died last night.

Satd. 6th It snowd. faster last night & to day than it has done this winter & still continues without an intermission wind S. W Murphys folks or Keysburgs say they cant eat hides I wish we had enough of them Mrs Eddy very weak.

Sund. 7th Ceasd. to snow last after one

---

[7] Patrick Breen, "Diary of Patrick Breen. One of the Donner Party," *Academy of Pacific Coast History Publications*, I (July, 1910), pp. 281–284. Most of the Breen diary was earlier printed in the *California Star*. This complete copy was edited by Frederick J. Teggart.

of the most severe storms we experienced this winter the snow fell about 4 feet deep. I had to shovel the snow off our shanty this morning it thawd so fast & thawd. during the whole storm. to day it is quite pleasant wind S. W. Milt here to day says Mrs Reid has to get a hide from Mrs. Murphy & McCutchins child died 2nd of this month.

Mond. 8th Fine clear morning wind S. W. froze hard last. Spitzer died last night about 3 o clock to we will bury him in the snow Mrs Eddy died on the night of the 7th.

Tuesd. 9th Mrs. Murphy here this morning Pikes child all but dead Milt at Murphys not able to get out of bed Keyburg never gets up says he is not able. John went down to day to bury Mrs Eddy & child heard nothing from Graves for 2 or 3 days Mrs Murphy just now going to Graves fine morning wind S. E. froze hard last night begins to thaw in the sun.

Wednsd. 10th Beautiful morning wind W: froze hard last night, to day thawing in the sun Milt Elliot died las night at Murphys shanty about 9 o'clock P: M: Mrs Reid went there this morning to see after his effects. J Denton trying to borrow meat for Graves had none to give they have nothing but hides all are entirely out of meat but a little we have our hides are nearly all eat up but with Gods help spring will soon smile upon us.

Thursd 11th Fine morning wind W. froze hard last night some clouds lying in the E: looks like thaw John Denton here last night very delicate. John & Mrs Reid went to Graves this morning.

Frid. 12th A warm thawey morning wind S. E. we hope with the assistance of Almighty God to be able to live to see the bare surface of the earth once more. O God of Mercy grant if it it be thy holy will Amen.

Sat. 13th Fine morning clouded up yesterday evening snowd a little & continued cloudy all night, cleared off about day light wind about S: W Mrs Reid has headacke the rest in health.

Sund 14th Fine morning but cold before the sun got up, now thawing in the sun wind S E Ellen Graves here this morning John Denton not well froze hard last night John & Edwd. E burried Milt. this morning in the snow.

Mond. 15 Moring cloudy untill 9 o clock then cleared off wam & sunshine wind W. Mrs Graves refusd. to give Mrs Reid any hides put Suitors pack hides on her shanty would not let her have them says if I say it will thaw it then will not, she is a case.

Tuesd. 16th Commencd. to rain yesterday evening turned to snow during the night & continud untill after daylight this morning it is now sun shine & light showers of hail at times wind N.W by W. we all feel very weakly to day snow not geting much less in quantity.

Wedsd. 17th Froze hard last night with heavy clouds runing from the N. W. & light showers of hail at times to day same kind of weather wind N. W. very cold & cloudy no sign of much thaw.

Thrsd 18th Froze hard last night to day clear & warm in the sun cold in the shanty or in the shade wind S. E all in good health Thanks be to Almighty God Amen.

Frid. 19th Froze hard last night 7 men arrived from Colifornia yesterday evening with som provisions but left the greater part on the way to day clear & warm for this region some of the men are gone to day to Donnos Camp will start back on Monday.

Saturd. 20th Pleasant weather.

Sund 21st Thawey warm day.

Mond 22nd The Californians started this morning 24 in number some in a very weak state fine morning wind S. W. for the 3 last days Mrs Keyburg started & left Keysburg here unable to go I burried Pikes child this morning in the snow it died 2 days ago, Paddy Reid & Thos. came back Messrs Graves & Mutry.

Tuesd. 23 Froze hard last night to day fine & thawey has the appearance of spring all but the deep snow wind S:S.E. shot Towser to day & dressed his flesh Mrs Graves came here this morning to borrow meat dog or ox they think I have meat to spare but I know to the contrary they have plenty hides I live principally on the same.

Wend. 24th Froze hard last night to day cloudy looks like a storm wind blows hard from the W. Commenced thawing there has not any more returned from those who started to cross the mts.

Thursd. 25th Froze hard last night fine & sunshiny to day wind W. Mrs Murphy says the wolves are about to dig up the dead bodies at her shanty, the nights are too cold to watch them, we hear them howl.

Frid 26th Froze hard last night today clear & warm Wind S: E: blowing briskly Marthas jaw swelled with the toothache; hungry times in camp, plenty hides but the folks will not eat them we eat them with a tolerable good apetite. Thanks be to Almighty God. Amen Mrs Murphy said here yesterday that thought she would commence on Milt. & eat him. I dont that she has done so yet, it is distressing The Donnos told the California folks that they commence to eat the dead people 4 days ago, if they did not succeed that day or next in finding their cattle then under ten or twelve feet of snow & did not know the spot or near it, I suppose they have done so ere this time.

Satd. 27th Beautiful morning sun shineing brilliantly, wind about S. W. the snow has fell in debth about 5 feet but no thaw but the sun in day time it freezeing hard every night, heard some geese fly over last night saw none.

Sund. 28th Froze hard last night to day fair & sunshine wind S.E. 1 solitary Indian passed by yesterday come from the lake had a heavy pack on his back gave me 5 or 6 roots resembleing onions in shape taste some like a sweet potatoe, all full of little tough fibres.

Mond. March the 1st So fine & pleasant froze hard last night there has 10 men arrived this morning from Bear Valley with provisions we are to start in two or three days & cash our goods here there is amongst them some old they say the snow will be here until June.

The hardships of the Donner party and the lesser sacrifices of all who braved the California Trail were to pay dividends for the United States. By 1846 the number of Americans living in California was not large—probably a thousand had reached there in the past half-dozen years—but their potential as agitators was enormous. Concentrated about Sutter's Fort and other rallying spots, sprinkled with former mountain men who were always spoiling for a fight, and thrust into a land where turbulence reigned instead of law, the American newcomers helped generate a tinderbox atmosphere that could be ignited by a single spark. Thus was the stage set for the Bear Flag Revolt that was to array the immigrants against their Mexican hosts and help add California to the United States.

CHAPTER 21

Expansion and War, 1844-1848

In 1844, the American people were forced to decide whether they were willing to expand their nation's borders at the risk of war with Mexico and possibly with England. By this time frontiersmen had blustered their way into California and waited only for an opportunity to wrest that troubled land from Mexico. Others filled the Willamette Valley of Oregon and daily made clear their eagerness to add that disputed territory to the United States. Still others in Texas openly sought annexation, even at the risk of war between Americans and Mexicans. Only the go-ahead signal from Washington was needed to bring open conflict and extend the national boundaries to the Pacific. Yet Washington officialdom hesitated to move without public approval.

The people were allowed to speak in the election of 1844, but the result was indecisive. James K. Polk, a Democrat, handily defeated Henry Clay, the perennial Whig candidate, on a platform calling for the "re-annexation of Texas and the re-occupation of Oregon," but sober observers realized that his election was no clear-cut mandate for expansion. Several northern states openly hostile to the acquisition of more slave territories sided with Polk, while such jingoistic states as Kentucky and Tennessee voted for Clay. Polk entered the White House loudly proclaiming his intention to add Texas, Oregon, and probably California to the Union, but he and his advisers recognized that he would be risking political suicide unless majority opinion shifted toward expansion.

BRITISH DESIGNS ON TEXAS

That public opinion did change over the next months was due largely to unwitting and unwilling aid from England and France. Both of those nations hoped to check the American advance westward, partly because they disliked the emergence of a nation powerful enough to challenge their supremacy, partly for more immediate reasons. England especially was ready to challenge Polk's ambitions, for its national interest would best be served by retaining the Oregon Country as a trading area, keeping California in Mexican hands, and assuring the continuation of the Republic of Texas. The latter offered a customs-free market for British manufactured goods and a source of cotton for its textile mills. Yet any overt act by Great Britain aimed at frustrating American ambitions was certain to solidify public opinion and quicken the demand for annexation. Ashbel Smith, an official diplomat of the Republic of Texas in England, recognized this when he gleefully reported to his government a conversation on June 24, 1844, with Lord Aberdeen, the British Foreign Secretary:[1]

I have had an interview to day with Lord Aberdeen at his request concerning the relations of Texas and chiefly in reference to the negotiations at Washington in the United States for 'annexation.' The unfavorable impression relative to the course of Texas entertained by his Lordship previously to my late interview with him appears to have been entirely removed; and Her Majesty's Government perceive that Texas in agreeing to treat for annexation has been influenced only by the wish to obtain in this way honorable peace after the total avowed failure of the Mediation of friendly Powers.

Lord Aberdeen observed that Her British Majesty's Government and that of France had communicated with each other touching the "annexation";—that, entire harmony of opinion subsists and that they will act in concert in relation to it:—that, though the rejection of the Annexation Treaty by the American Senate was regarded as nearly or quite certain, nothing would be done by these Governments until the American Congress shall have finally disposed of the subject for the present session. He stated that then the British and French Governments would be willing, if Texas desired to remain independent, to settle the whole matter by a "Diplomatic Act:"—this diplomatic act in which Texas would of course participate would ensure peace and settle boundaries between Texas and Mexico, guarantee the separate independence of Texas, etc., etc.;— the American Government would be invited to participate in the "Act" as one of the parties guaranteeing etc., equally with the European Governments;—that Mexico, as I think I clearly understood his Lordship, would be invited to become a party to the Diplomatic Act, and in case of her refusal, would be forced to submit to its decisions:— and lastly, in case of the infringement of the terms of settlement by either of the parties, to wit, Texas or Mexico, the other parties would be authorized under the Diplomatic Act, to compel the infringing party to a compliance with the terms.

Lord Aberdeen did not as I remember use the word Treaty, but employed the phrase Diplomatic Act. It would however have all the obligations of a treaty, and the rights of all the parties under it would of course be *perpetual*. I say, of course; for the other parties could not be expected to make a treaty of this nature limited for such a period as would suit the convenience of Texas. Such act would too, as you will have already remarked give to the European Governments, parties to it, a perfect right to forbid for all time to come the annexation of Texas to the United States, as also even the peaceful incorporation of any portion of Mexico beyond the boundary to be settled, which might hereafter wish to unite itself with Texas.

Lord Aberdeen observed that France will be guided in this matter by the counsels of England he suggested therefore that if such diplomatic act shall be passed, it shall be done at London.

I remarked to Lord Aberdeen in reply, that I had received no instructions from home since our interview a few days ago; that I had transmitted a memorandum of our conversation at that time to my Government

---

[1] Ashbel Smith to Anson Jones, June 24, 1844, in George P. Garrison (ed.), "Diplomatic Correspondence of the Republic of Texas," *Annual Report of the American Historical Association for 1908* (Washington, 1911), vol. 2, pp. 1153–1156.

with a request for instructions and information; and that until I should receive these I did not well see what further observations I could make. To avoid all possible misconception, I again stated that my remarks at our late interview were intirely inofficial.

The permanent perpetual character of a diplomatic act of the nature spoken of by Lord Aberdeen, appears to me as it will doubtless to you, worthy of our gravest consideration before acceding to it; and the inviting of European Governments to make compulsory settlement of dissensions between the countries of America and the conferring on them of the right to interfere in our affairs may lead to the greatest inconveniences on our side of the Atlantic; as such interference and settlements have been the pretexts for inflicting atrocious wrongs and oppressions on the smaller states of Europe. I have believed that the objections to a Diplomatic Act as mentioned above will be deemed by our Government greater perhaps than the inconveniences of our unsettled relations with Mexico.

I am clearly of opinion that these Govts. will not urge on Mexico to make peace, except in some such manner as I have stated above or on such conditions and guarantees as shall insure the permanent independence of Texas. Further, I should not be surprised were they to counsel Mexico not to make peace under present circumstances except with such conditions and guarantees, lest by so doing annexation should be facilitated by removing one of the obstacles to its accomplishment on the part of the United States.

Lord Aberdeen more than once made observations to the effect that he regretted the agitation of the abolition of Slavery in Texas, as it had created so much feeling and dissatisfaction on our side of the Atlantic; and that hereafter he would have nothing to say or do in relation to this subject.

The tone of Lord Aberdeen's remarks towards Texas was very friendly; and I believe a sincere desire exists on the part of his Government to foster our interests provided we remain independent; and, that Lord Aberdeen is prepared to adopt any proper course and to take promptly and efficiently all proper steps to bring about a peace with Mexico, if he felt assured that our annexation to the American Union would in that event be prevented.

For this purpose he would be satisfied with nothing less than a diplomatic act, the stringency of whose terms would be settled by negotiation.

BRITISH DESIGNS ON CALIFORNIA

If England pictured itself as the guardian of the Republic of Texas, some Englishmen, at least, were eager to play a comparable role in California. Their opportunity stemmed from the perennial poverty of the Republic of Mexico; that troubled nation had borrowed heavily from British and French creditors and was now unable to pay its debts. Promoters in London and Paris sensed opportunity in this situation, for Mexico might be persuaded to part with most or all of California to satisfy its obligations. Colonies planted there would eventually shower handsome returns on their founders. The dream of these schemers and the undercover support given them by officials of their governments was described by Waddy Thompson, American minister to Mexico City at the time:[2]

I will not say what is our policy in regard to California. Perhaps it is that it remain in the hands of a weak power like Mexico, and that all the maritime powers may have the advantage of its ports. But one thing I will

---

[2] Waddy Thompson, *Recollections of Mexico* (New York, 1847), pp. 234–236.

say, that it will be worth a war of twenty years to prevent England acquiring it, which I have the best reasons for believing she desires to do and just as good reasons for believing that she will not do if it costs a war with this country. It is, perhaps, too remote from us to become a member of the Union. It is yet doubtful whether the increase of our territory will have a federal or a centralizing tendency. If the latter, we have too much territory; and I am by no means sure that another sister Republic there, with the same language, liberty and laws, will not, upon the whole, be the best for us. If united in one government, the extremities may be so remote as not to receive a proper heat from the centre—so, at least, thought Mr. Jefferson, who was inspired on political questions if mortal man ever was. I am not one of those who have a rabid craving for more territory; on the contrary, I believe that we have enough. I know of no great people who have not been crowded into a small space— the Egyptians, the Romans, the Greeks, and another people who have exercised a greater influence upon man and his destiny than all others, the Jews; and, in our own time, the English. I want no more territory, for we have already too much. If I were to make an exception to this remark, it would be to acquire California. But I should grieve to see that country pass into the hands of England, or any other of the great powers.

Whenever the foreigners in California make the movement of separation, it must succeed. The department of Sonora, not half the distance from Mexico, has been in a state of revolt for the last four years, and the government has been unable to suppress it. The civil war there has been marked by acts of horrible atrocity, which are almost without precedent in any country. It is true that they do not eat the flesh of their enemies, but they leave them hanging on the trees to feast the birds of prey. There is scarcely a road in the whole department where such spectacles are not daily exhibited.

There is a great mistake, I think, in the opinion which is general in this country of the great ascendency of English influence in Mexico. It is true that Mr. Packenham had much influence there, which his great worth and frank and honorable character will give him anywhere; but my opinion is, that the general feeling of the Mexicans towards the English is unfriendly. They have a well-grounded jealousy of the great and increasing power which their large capital gives them; and, if the feelings of the Mexican people were consulted, or the opinions of their most enlightened men, England is the very last power to which the Mexicans would transfer California, or any other portion of their territory. I am quite sure that they would prefer that it should be an independent power, than to have any connection or dependence of any sort upon England. The most valuable of the Mexican mines are owned and worked by English companies, and at least two-thirds of the specie which is exported goes into the hands of the English. The British Government keeps two officers, or agents, in Mexico, with high salaries, to attend to this interest alone. It is with the money thus derived that the English establishments on this continent and in the West Indies are supported.

THE SPIRIT OF MANIFEST DESTINY

Exaggerated tales of British designs on Texas and California marvelously transformed American public opinion. Overnight the people awakened to their destiny: they must occupy the entire continent to protect its inhabitants from British despotism and Mexican peonage. A beneficent Diety obviously did not intend the perfect democratic institutions with which He had endowed the United States to be confined within narrow borders. The God-given duty of Americans was to overrun the continent and plant their flag at the Pacific. This flamboyant new spirit was sensed by John L. O'Sullivan, the nationalistic editor of the "Democratic Review," who coined the phrase Manifest Destiny to describe it and who admirably mirrored its purposes in an article for his journal written in 1845:[3]

Why, were other reasoning wanting, in favor of now elevating this question of the reception of Texas into the Union, out of the lower region of our past party dissensions, up to its proper level of a high and broad nationality, it surely is to be found, found abundantly, in the manner in which other nations have undertaken to intrude themselves into it, between us and the proper parties to the case, in a spirit of hostile interference against us, for the avowed object of thwarting our policy and hampering our power, limiting our greatness and checking the fulfilment of our manifest destiny to overspread the continent allotted by Providence for the free development of our yearly multiplying millions. This we have seen done by England, our old rival and enemy; and by France, strangely coupled with her against us, under the influence of the Anglicism strongly tinging the policy of her present prime minister, Guizot. The zealous activity with which this effort to defeat us was pushed by the representatives of those governments, together with the character of intrigue accompanying it, fully constituted that case of foreign interference, which Mr. Clay himself declared should, and would unite us all in maintaining the common cause of our country against the foreigner and the foe. We are only astonished that this effect has not been more fully and strongly produced, and that the burst of indignation against this unauthorized, insolent and hostile interference against us, has not been more general even among the party before opposed to Annexation, and has not rallied the national spirit and national pride unanimously upon that policy. We are very sure that if Mr. Clay himself were now to add another letter to his former Texas correspondence, he would express this sentiment, and carry out the idea already strongly stated in one of them, in a manner which would tax all the powers of blushing belonging to some of his party adherents.

It is wholly untrue, and unjust to ourselves, the pretence that the Annexation has been a measure of spoliation, unrightful and unrighteous—of military conquest under forms of peace and law—of territorial aggrandizement at the expense of justice, and justice due by a double sanctity to the weak. This view of the question is wholly unfounded, and has been before so amply refuted in these pages, as well as in a thousand other modes, that we shall not again dwell upon it. The independence of Texas was complete and absolute. It was an independence, not only in fact but of right. No obligation of duty towards Mexico tended in the least degree to restrain our right to effect the desired recovery of the fair province once our own—whatever motives of policy might have prompted a more deferential consideration of her feelings and her pride, as involved in the question. If Texas became peopled with an American population, it was by no contrivance of our government, but on the express invitation of that of Mexico herself; accompanied with such guaranties of State independence, and the maintenance of a federal system analogous to our own, as con-

---

[3] *Democratic Review*, XVII (July–August, 1845), 5–6, 9–10.

stituted a compact fully justifying the strongest measures of redress on the part of those afterwards deceived in this guaranty, and sought to be enslaved under the yoke imposed by its violation. She was released, rightfully and absolutely released, from all Mexican allegiance, or duty of cohesion to the Mexican political body, by the acts and fault of Mexico herself, and Mexico alone. There never was a clearer case. It was not revolution; it was resistance to revolution; and resistance under such circumstances as left independence the necessary resulting state, caused by the abandonment of those with whom her former federal association had existed. What then can be more preposterous than all this clamor by Mexico and the Mexican interest, against Annexation, as a violation of any rights of hers, any duties of ours? ...

California will, probably, next fall away from the loose adhesion which, in such a country as Mexico, holds a remote province in a slight equivocal kind of dependence on the metropolis. Imbecile and distracted, Mexico never can exert any real governmental authority over such a country. The impotence of the one and the distance of the other, must make the relation one of virtual independence; unless, by stunting the province of all natural growth, and forbidding that immigration which can alone develop its capabilities and fulfil the purposes of its creation, tyranny may retain a military dominion which is no government in the legitimate sense of the term. In the case of California this is now impossible. The Anglo-Saxon foot is already on its borders. Already the advance guard of the irresistible army of Anglo-Saxon emigration has begun to pour down upon it, armed with the plough and the rifle, and marking its trail with schools and colleges, courts and representative halls, mills and meeting-houses. A population will soon be in actual occupation of California, over which it will be idle for Mexico to dream of dominion. They will necessarily become independent. All this without agency of our government, without responsibility of our people—in the natural flow of events, the spontaneous working of principles, and the adaptation of the tendencies and wants of the human race to the elemental circumstances in the midst of which they find themselves placed. And they will have a right to independence—to self-government—to the possession of the homes conquered from the wilderness by their own labors and dangers, sufferings and sacrifices—a better and a truer right than the artificial title of sovereignty in Mexico a thousand miles distant, inheriting from Spain a title good only against those who have none better. Their right to independence will be the natural right of self-government belonging to any community strong enough to maintain it—distinct in position, origin and character, and free from any mutual obligations of membership of a common political body, binding it to others by the duty of loyalty and compact of public faith. This will be their title to independence; and by this title, there can be no doubt that the population now fast streaming down upon California will both assert and maintain that independence. Whether they will then attach themselves to our Union or not, is not to be predicted with any certainty. Unless the projected railroad across the continent to the Pacific be carried into effect, perhaps they may not; though even in that case, the day is not distant when the Empires of the Atlantic and Pacific would again flow together into one, as soon as their inland border should approach each other. But that great work, colossal as appears the plan on its first suggestion, cannot remain long unbuilt. Its necessity for this very purpose of binding and holding together in its iron clasp our fast settling Pacific region with that of the Mississippi valley—the natural facility of the route—the ease with which any amount of labor for the construction can be drawn in from the overcrowded populations of Europe, to be paid in the lands made valuable by the progress of the work itself—and its immense utility to the commerce of the world with the whole eastern coast of Asia, alone almost sufficient for the support of such a road—these considerations give assurance that the day cannot be distant which shall witness the conveyance of the representatives from Oregon and California to Washington within less time than a few years ago was devoted to a similar journey by those from Ohio; while the magnetic telegraph will enable the editors of the "San Francisco Union," the "Astoria Evening Post," or the "Nootka Morning News" to set up in type the first half of the President's Inaugural, before the echoes of the latter half shall have died away beneath the lofty porch of the Capitol, as spoken from his lips.

Away, then, with all idle French talk of *balances of power* on the American Continent. There is no growth in Spanish America! Whatever progress of population there may be in the British Canadas, is only for their own early severance of their present colonial relation to the little island three thousand miles across the Atlantic; soon to be followed by Annexation, and destined to swell the still accumulating momentum of our progress. And whosoever may hold the balance, though they should cast into the opposite scale all the bayonets and cannon, not only of France and England, but of Europe entire, how would it kick the beam against the simple solid weight of the two hundred and fifty or three hundred millions —and American millions—destined to gather beneath the flutter of the stripes and stars, in the fast hastening year of the Lord 1945!

BRITISH STRENGTH IN THE OREGON COUNTRY

Amidst this wave of sentiment for the nation's Manifest Destiny, expansionists had their day. Texas was their first prize. During the closing days of President John Tyler's term, Congress adopted a joint resolution inviting the infant republic to join the Union, and Texas hesitated only briefly before accepting. On December 29, 1845, President Polk signed the measure admitting this new state. The "re-occupation of Oregon" proved more difficult. Several thousand Americans lived there by 1845, but all were in the Willamette Valley, south of the Columbia River. This region was never in dispute; England recognized the prior rights of the United States there and was content to accept the Columbia River as Canada's southern boundary. The Americans, in turn, talked of "Fifty-four Forty or Fight," but were ready to settle for a westward extension of the 49th parallel to the sea. Thus the region actually claimed by both powers lay between the Columbia and the 49th parallel. Here the Hudson's Bay Company was firmly in control. Over the past years, Dr. John McLoughlin, the company's principal factor in the Northwest, had encouraged retired trappers to settle there as farmers and herdsmen, building up a stable population that would be almost impossible to dislodge. McLoughlin's policy and the extent of the agricultural establishments that he planted were described as early as 1839 in a letter written by his second in command, James Douglas:[4]

---

[4] James Douglas to the Governor and Committee of the Hudson's Bay Company, October 14, 1839, in E. E. Rich (ed.), *The Letters of John McLoughlin from Fort Vancouver to the Governor and Committee Second Series, 1839–44* (Toronto, Champlain Society, and London, Hudson's Bay Record Society, 1943), pp. 216–217, 220–222. Reprinted by permission of the Hudson's Bay Record Society.

By our latest dates of 21st July, the Salmon fishery was yeilding abundantly, and the crops looked remarkably well, the season having been in that quarter rather favourable. I may be permitted to mention here as a matter likely to interest the friends of our native population and all who desire to trace the first dawn and early progress of civilization, that the Cowegins around Fort Langley, influenced by the Council and example of the Fort, are beginning to cultivate the soil, many of them having with great perseverance and industry cleared patches of forrest land of sufficient extent to plant each 10 Bushels of Potatoes; the same spirit of enterprise extends, though less generally to the Gulf of Georgia and De Fuca's Straits, where the very novel sight of flourishing fields of potatoes satisfies our Missionary visitors, that the Honble. Company neither oppose, nor feel indifferent to the march of improvement.

We have been pursuing at Fort Nisqually the identical line of policy traced out in my report of last year; that is to say, in general terms, maintaining peace and confirming the industry of the Natives; and the increasing prosperity of the business, shows that our exertions have not been fruitless. Mr. Kittson's last letter of 11th Septr. states that the trade was then doing well, keeping, as it has done, since the beginning of the year considerably in advance of last Outfit. He has also been more successful than usual in farming: all former attempts in this way were in a measure defeated, through the unproductive character of the soil, which is hardly fit for tillage, in its natural state, the produce having been seldom found to exceed two to one of seed: This year Mr. Kittson contrived to manure a small wheat field, and was rewarded with a crop of 250 Bushels, a result attesting the capabilities of the soil when materials for enriching it are within reach. I mention this circumstance because it is not generally supposed that provisions to maintain a large establishment of people could be raised at this Post, and because it may have reference to future plans, should it ever become desirable to extend our timber transactions, by improving the natural advantages of the country which as it were, invite such views. Within 16 miles of Fort Nisqually there is a good mill seat, on the Chûte River at a distance of only four miles from Pugets Sound, with a clear open passage into it and abundance of fine timber in the vicinity. As such a place will be of great value hereafter, I have taken possession of it in the Company's name so that we may turn it to account or not, according to your wishes, and the future circumstances of the country.

We sent Seventy head of Cattle to this place in August last, and if they keep well in winter, we shall continue, from time to time, as means permit, to send more. The sheep are doing as well as expected, the increase of last spring being 174 lambs. . . .

The intentions expressed in my letter of March, with respect to the Cowelitz Farm, were closely followed out. The chief and all engrossing object to which our attention was called, being the production of the greatest possible quantity of grain, during the present year, every local improvement, unconnected with agriculture, was suspended on the earliest approach of spring, and we turned with undivided means to the plough and harrow, breaking up and smoothing the tough surface of the plain until the arrival of summer necessarily brought these operations to a close, when we had about 230 acres under seed. The tillage notwithstanding our utmost exertions was imperfect; it being absolutely beyond our power, to destroy the sward by any possible mechanical means, and our fields presented a rough unseemly appearance to the last. This circumstance caused the less pain, as the case was unavoidable, and we know from frequent trials that new land, never yields so well as that which has been repeatedly cropped. Being thus assured that there was no prospect of a good crop unless, as experience has shown, we enjoyed a moist summer, I felt, equally anxious by extending our cultivation through the utmost exertion of our means, to seize that chance should it happen, and if not, to secure, at least, the important advantage of having a considerable extent of land, in course of preparation for next year, when the turf, through the natural process of decay, will, in a great measure, be converted into soil, and the land mellowed to a degree that appears indispensable for the growth of weighty crops.

Seed time being over, and our fields lying open and exposed, they were next all encircled by substantial wooden fences, and afterwards we resumed the plough, with seven double teams having each a ploughman and driver, making in all 14 hands to fallow land for next year, in accordance with the plan I have now in view, of sowing 710 acres for the crop of 1840. I expected in course of the present summer to accomplish, the breaking up of about 480 acres to form with the 230 already under tillage, the extent above mentioned: but we fell short of our aim, and have fallowed since seed time only 320 acres, in consequence of the uncommon heat and dryness of summer which exhausting the soil of moisture, hardened it to a degree almost impervious to the plough. The same cause was productive of fatal injury to the new land crops, which were very inferior; but housed in fine condition.

This has been a year of trial at the Cowelitz, abounding in difficulties, amidst which the Gentleman in charge (Chief Trader Tod) has done all that could be expected; but we have now made good our footing and things will I hope go on more smoothly in future. To the two buildings of 40 × 30 feet, alluded to in my last letter, we have, this summer added a spacious barn; a great extent of enclosure is made, and there is 550 acres of land actually under tillage; we have also, a number of working oxen, and 40 horses broke to the Collar. It is my intention to sow 200 acres with wheat this autumn and 250 acres more in spring, together with about 260 acres of other grain and esculents. We will be dreadfully perplexed about the means of securing this immense crop without heavy loss; but the trial shall notwithstanding be made, and perhaps we may be relieved from embarrassment by chance succour, or by the assistance of Indians, who though lazy, unskilful workmen, requiring also very cautious and particular management, may be brought to lend their aid.

THE AMERICAN THREAT
TO THE HUDSON'S BAY COMPANY

The firm hold of the Hudson's Bay Company on the disputed area created a potentially explosive situation, for Polk was committed to winning "all of Oregon or none" and with an inflamed public opinion behind him could not retreat, while the British government knew that capitulation meant political suicide. For a time war seemed certain. Then, on January 1, 1845, the Hudson's Bay Company opened the door to a solution by shifting its principal operations and supplies from Fort Vancouver in the disputed region to Fort Victoria on Vancouver Island. The reasons for this move were outlined by McLoughlin in a letter to his London superiors in which he stressed the danger to the company supplies at Fort Vancouver because of the well-organized American settlers in the Willamette Valley:[5]

The Legislature of the Wallamette Settlement, assembled a few days ago, made some amendments in the Organic Law which is to serve as basis for a Constitution, and drew out a Petition to the Congress of the United States, which they sent by Dr. White, who left the Wallamette 13th Instant for the United States by way of the Snake Country & Missouri, copy of which for your information I take the liberty to forward, and you will see by this Document they now admit that we have an equal right to the Country with themselves, though when they first came they held out we had no right to be here, as this was United States Territory. But we avoided entering into discussion with them on this subject, as it would have had a bad effect, but contented ourselves with observing, as the Settlement of the Boundary was an affair of Government and not ours, and that we had to take it as they settled it, we did not trouble ourselves about it, as they would settle it as they thought proper without asking our opinion, and much less our consent; and they were so strongly prepossessed against us, that they expected when they left the States they would have to fight with us on arriving here, and to build Forts to protect themselves from the Indians whom we would, they supposed, excite against them. These apprehensions proceed from the false statements of the American Traders who have been obliged to retire from the Snake Country, Captn. Spaulding's Report, the speeches of the late Dr. Lynn and those of Messrs. Benton & Buchanan in the United States Senate, which are in the possession of some of the Immigrants, in which speeches they state, the British (alluding to us) have murdered or caused to be murdered by their Servants and by Indians under their control five hundred American Citizens. Last Spring I sent a copy of Mr. Buchanan's Speech to Sir George Simpson, and I will by the Vessel send you Messrs. Lynn & Benton's Speeches on the Oregon Question, which I presume you have not got or else you would have mentioned these statements to me. But I send you an Extract from the "Times" of December 1843, which perhaps you have not seen, in which an Extract from an Illinois Journal makes an attack on the Hudson's Bay Company, and grossly misrepresents my conduct, as I have done nothing but what every Settler in the Country does, and even now, though every American knows these Reports against us to be false, yet there are many among them, who it seems cannot overcome these feelings of national hostility. One of them speaking a few days ago to a person on whose veracity we can depend, observed, "It is true these are good folks and treat me kindly, but somehow or other I cannot like them, and moreover do not like those who like them." Another who left this to go to the States, observed that the only regret he had in leaving the Country, was that he did not burn Vancouver, as he had left the States with that intention. On being asked why he wished to do this, he could give no answer; and though the large mass of the Immigrants are friendly to us, as expressed in the Petition, yet it is certain there are several among them who have an antipathy to us (it does not deserve a severer name) merely from national feeling.

---

[5] E. E. Rich (ed.), *The Letters of John McLoughlin from Fort Vancouver to the Governor and Committee Third Series, 1844–46* (Toronto, Champlain Society, and London, Hudson's Bay Record Society, 1944), pp. 85–87. Reprinted by permission of the Hudson's Bay Record Society.

THE DEMAND FOR ALL OREGON: THOMAS HART BENTON

As the Oregon pioneers intensified their pressure for annexation, American public opinion swung rapidly to their support. With the cry of "Fifty-four Forty or Fight" resounding through the nation, President Polk served notice on Great Britain that the treaty of joint occupation was to be abrogated, at the same time making threatening gestures that seemed to portend war. Typical of this defiant spirit was a speech that Senator Thomas Hart Benton of Missouri delivered on May 28, 1846:[6]

The value of the country—I mean the Columbia River and its valley—(I must repeat the limitation every time, lest I be carried up to 54° 40′)—has been questioned on this floor and elsewhere. It has been supposed to be of little value—hardly worth the possession, much less the acquisition; and treated rather as a burden to be got rid of, than as a benefit to be preserved. This is a great error, and one that only prevails on this side of the water: the British know better; and if they held the tithe of our title, they would fight the world for what we depreciate. It is not a worthless country, but one of immense value, and that under many respects, and will be occupied by others, to our injury and annoyance, if not by ourselves for our own benefit and protection. Forty years ago it was written by Humboldt, that the banks of the Columbia presented the only situation on the northwest coast of America fit for the residence of a civilized people. Experience has confirmed the truth of this wise remark. All the rest of the coast, from the Straits of Fuca out to New Archangel, (and nothing but a fur trading post there,) remains a vacant waste, abandoned since the quarrel of Nootka Sound, and become the derelict of nations. The Columbia only invites a possessor; and for that possession, sagacious British diplomacy has been weaving its web. It is not a worthless possession; but valuable under many and large aspects; to the consideration of some of which I now proceed.

It is valuable, both as a country to be inhabited, and as a position to be held and defended. I speak of it, first, as a position, commanding the North Pacific ocean, and overlooking the eastern coast of Asia. The North Pacific is a rich sea, and is already the seat of a great commerce: British, French, American, Russian, and ships of other nations, frequent it. Our whaling ships cover it: our ships of war go there to protect our interest; and, great as that interest now is, it is only the beginning. Futurity will develop an immense, and various, commerce on that sea, of which the far greater part will be American. That commerce, neither in the merchant ships which carry it on, nor in the military marine which protects it, can find a port, to call its own, within twenty thousand miles of the field of its operations. The double length of the two Americas has to be run—a stormy and tempestuous cape to be doubled—to find itself in a port of its own country: while here lies one in the very edge of its field, ours by right, ready for use, and ample for every purpose of refuge and repair, protection and domination. Can we turn our back upon it? and, in turning the back, deliver it up to the British? Insane, and suicidal would be the fatal act!

To say nothing of the daily want of such a port in time of peace, its want, in time of war, becomes ruinous. Commodore Porter has often told me that, with protection from

---

[6] *Congressional Globe*, 29th Congress, 1st Session, p. 914.

batteries in the mouth of the Columbia, he never would have put himself in a condition to be attacked under the weak, or collusive guns of a neutral port. He has told me that, with such a port for the reception of his prizes, he would not have sunk in the ocean, or hid in islands where it was often found, the three millions of British property captured in his three years daring and dauntless cruise. Often has he told me, that, with such a port at his hand, he would never have been driven to spill upon the waters, that oil, for want of which, as a member of the British Parliament said, London had burnt darkly—had been in the dark—for a whole year. What happened to Commodore Porter and his prizes—what happened to all our merchant ships, driven from the North Pacific during the war—all this to happen again, and upon a far larger scale, is but half the evil of turning our backs now upon this commanding position; for, to do so, is to deliver it into the hands of a Power that knows the value of positions—the four quarters of the globe, and our own coasts attest that—and has her eye on this one. The very year after the renewal of the delusive convention of 1818—in the year 1819—a master ship-carpenter was despatched from London to Fort Vancouver, to begin there the repair of vessels, and even the construction of small ones; and this work has been going on ever since. She resists our possession now! If we abandon, she will retain! And her wooden walls, bristling with cannon, and issuing from the mouth of the Columbia, will give the law to the North Pacific, permitting our ships to sneak about in time of peace—sinking, seizing, or chasing them away, in time of war. As a position, then, and if nothing but a rock, or desert point, the possession of the Columbia is invaluable to us; and it becomes our duty to maintain it at all hazards.

AMERICAN DESIGNS ON CALIFORNIA

Sword rattling such as this proved effective. Lord Aberdeen, the Tory Foreign Minister in England, had a low opinion of the commercial prospects of the Oregon Country and was anxious to effect a settlement that would symbolize the peaceful intentions of his party. When the Hudson's Bay Company abandoned the region, he began an intensive campaign to convince the opposition Whig Party and the British public that surrender of the disputed region was justifiable, and by June 1846 he was ready to act. His offer to settle the controversy on the basis of the extension of the 49th parallel boundary was accepted by President Polk and affirmed by the Senate on June 10, 1846. Polk's aggressive policies had added hundreds of thousands of miles to the Republic, but more was to come. The thousand Americans who peopled the interior valleys of California were as vocal as the Willamette pioneers in demanding annexation, and the President and nation were in the mood to listen. California, however, was indisputably Mexican property, and had to be acquired by more devious tactics than those employed in Oregon. These were adopted by President Polk when in October 1845 he sent instructions to the American counsel in Monterey, Thomas O. Larkin, which hinted broadly that if California could be separated from Mexico by intrigue, it would be welcomed into the United States:[7]

I feel much indebted to you for the information which you have communicated to the Department from time to time in relation to California. The future destiny of that Country is a subject of anxious solicitude for the Government and people of the

---

[7] George P. Hammond (ed.), *The Larkin Papers* (Berkeley, Calif.: University of California Press, 1951–1964), vol. 4, pp. 44–47.

United States. The interests of our Commerce and our Whale fisheries on the Pacific Ocean, demand that you should exert the greatest vigilance in discovering and defeating any attempts which may be made by Foreign Governments to acquire a control over that Country. In the contest between Mexico and California we can take no part, unless the former should commence hostilities against the United States; but should California assert and maintain her independence, we shall render her all the kind offices in our power as a Sister Republic. This Government has no ambitious aspirations to gratify and no desire to extend our Federal system over more Territory than we already possess, unless by the free and spontaneous wish of the Independent people of adjoining Territories. The exercise of compulsion or improper influence to accomplish such a result, would be repugnant both to the policy and principles of this Government. But whilst these are the sentiments of the President, he could not view with indifference the transfer of California to Great Britain or any other European Power. The system of colonization by foreign Monarchies on the North American continent must and will be resisted by the United States. It could result in nothing but evil to the Colonists under their dominion who desire to secure for themselves the blessings of liberty by means of Republican Institutions; whilst it would be highly prejudicial to the best interests of the United States. Nor would it in the end benefit such foreign Monarchies. On the contrary, even Great Britain by the acquisition of California would sow the seeds of future War and disaster for herself; because there is no political truth more certain than that this fine Province could not long be held in vassalage by any European Power. The emigration to it of people from the United States would soon render this impossible.

I am induced to make these remarks in consequence of the information communicated to this Department in your Despatch of the 10th of July last. From this it appears that Mr. Rea, the Agent of the British Hudson Bay Company furnished the Californians with arms and money in October and November last, to enable them to expel the Mexicans from the Country: and you state that this policy has been reversed and now no doubt exists there, but that the Mexican troops about to invade the Province have been sent for this purpose at the instigation of the British Government: and that "it is rumored that two English Houses in Mexico have become bound to the new General to accept his drafts for funds to pay his troops for eighteen months". Connected with these circumstances, the appearance of a British Vice Consul and a French Consul in California, at the present crisis, without any apparent Commercial business, is well calculated to produce the impression, that their respective Governments entertain designs on that Country which must necessarily be hostile to its interests. On all proper occasions, you should not fail prudently to warn the Government and people of California of the danger of such an interference to their peace and prosperity—to inspire them with a jealousy of European dominion and to arouse in their bosoms that love of liberty and independence so natural to the American Continent. Whilst I repeat that this Government does not, under existing circumstances, intend to interfere between Mexico and California, they would vigorously interpose to prevent the latter from becoming a British or French Colony. In this they might surely expect the aid of the Californians themselves.

Whilst the President will make no effort and use no influence to induce California to become one of the free and independent States of this Union, yet if the People should desire to unite their destiny with ours, they would be received as brethren, whenever this can be done, without affording Mexico just cause of complaint. Their true policy, for the present, in regard to this question, is to let events take their course, unless an attempt should be made to transfer them, without their consent, either to Great Britain or France. This they ought to resist by all the means in their power as ruinous to their best interests and destructive of their freedom and independence.

I am rejoiced to learn that "our Countrymen continue to receive every assurance of safety and protection from the present Government" of California, and that they manifest so much confidence in you as Consul of the United States. You may assure them of the cordial sympathy and friendship of the President, and that their conduct is appreciated by him as it deserves.

In addition to your Consular functions, the President has thought proper to appoint you a Confidential Agent in California: and you may consider the present Despatch as your authority for acting in this character. The confidence which he reposes in your patriotism and discretion is evinced by conferring upon you this delicate and important trust. You will take care not to awaken the jealousy of the French and English Agents there by assuming any other than your Consular character. Lieutenant Archibald H. Gillespie of the Marine Corps will immediately proceed to Monterey and will probably reach you before this Despatch. He is a Gentleman in whom the President reposes entire confidence. He has seen these instructions and will co-operate as a confidential agent with you, in carrying them into execution.

You will not fail by every safe opportunity to keep the Department advised of the progress of events in California, and the disposition of the authorities and people toward the United States and other Governments. We should, also, be pleased to learn what is the aggregate population of that Province, and the force it can bring into the field: what is the proportion of Mexican, American, British and French Citizens, and the feelings of each class toward the United States; the names and character of the principal persons in the Executive, Legislative, and judicial Departments of the Government, and of other distinguished and influential Citizens; Its financial system and resources, the amount and nature of its commerce with Foreign Nations, its productions which might with advantage be imported into the United States, and the productions of the United States which might with advantage be received in exchange.

It would, also, be interesting to the Department to learn on what part of California the principal American settlements exist, the rate at which the number of Settlers have been and still are increasing, from what portions of the Union they come and by what routes they arrive in the Country.

These specifications are not intended to limit your enquiries. On the contrary it is expected that you will collect and communicate to the Department all the information respecting California which may be useful or important to the United States.

Your compensation will be at the rate of Six dollars per day from the time of the arrival of this Despatch or of Lieutenant Gillespie at Monterey. You will also be allowed your necessary travelling and other expenses incurred in accomplishing the objects of your appointment; but you will be careful to keep an accurate account of these expenditures and procure vouchers for them in all cases where this is practicable without interfering with the successful performance of your duties. For these expenses and your per diem allowance, you are authorised to draw from time to time on the Department. I am, Sir, Respectfully Your obedient Servant

THE BEAR FLAG REVOLT

Polk's none too subtle ambitions, combined with Mexico's turbulent internal situation which doomed California to a succession of corrupt and inefficient governors, touched off a powder keg of revolution before Larkin could win the province by intrigue. The American settlers, grouped about Sutter's Fort where their unity gave them confidence, were encouraged to act by the arrival of Captain John C. Frémont with sixty frontier-hardened followers. In June 1846, a band of them "appropriated" two hundred horses belonging to the Mexican army. Sensing that retribution was certain, they set off for nearby Sonoma, where they planned to capture the well-to-do rancher, Mariano G. Vallejo. After an all-night ride, the Americans reached the Sonoma plaza just at sunrise. One of their leaders, William B. Ide, recorded what happened:[8]

Fully impressed with the importance of this mission of benevolence and good will towards the sleeping and unsuspecting gentlemen to whom we were about to pay our respects, we took timely precaution to swear certain of our number against the commission of violence against either of those gentlemen. This step was considered proper, as we were aware there were certain *breathings of vengeance* against some of them, in the minds of a few of our party.

It was known that Doct. Semple, who was an active and conspicuous leading man of the host, was in favor of Independence, *instanter*; but we knew of none willing to *push* the measure. Under these circumstances it was thought prudent not to broach the subject generally, until some crisis should call the principle into immediate action.

Thus circumstanced, we arrived at Sonoma; and, after reconnoitering the place, and notifying our friends of our object in seizing the aforesaid gentlemen, and having secured the captain of the guard whom we found a little way out of town, we surrounded the house of Gen. M.G. Vallejo just at daybreak, on the 14th. William Merritt, Doct. Semple and Mr. Knight (who took wise care to have it understood on all hands that he was forced into the scrape as an interpreter), entered the house to secure their prisoners.

Jacob P. Leese, an American by birth, and brother-in-law of Gen. Vallejo, who lived near by, was soon there, to soothe the fears, and otherwise as far as possible assist his friends. Doct. Salvadore was also found there, and Col. Prudshon was also soon arrested and brought there. After the first surprise had a little subsided, as no immediate violence was offered, the General's generous *spirits* gave proof of his usual hospitality—as the richest wines and brandies sparkled in the glasses, and those who had thus unceremoniously met soon became merry companions; more especially—the weary visitors.

While matters were going on thus happily in the house, the main force sat patiently guarding it without. They appeared to understand that they had performed all the duty required of them, and only waited, that the said prisoners might be prepared and brought forth for their journey, and—waited still. The sun was climbing up the heavens an hour or more, and yet no man, nor voice, nor sound of violence came from the house to tell us of

---

[8] Simon Ide, *A Biographical Sketch of the Life of William B. Ide* (n.p., 1880), reissued (Oakland, Calif., 1944), pp. 89–93.

events within: patience was ill, and lingered ill. "Let us have a captain," said one—a *captain*, said all. Capt. Grigsby was elected, and went immediately into the house. The men still sat upon their horses—patience grew faint; an hour became an age. "Oh! go into the house, *Ide*, and come out again and let us know what is going on there!" No sooner said than done. There sat Doct. S., just modifying a long string of articles of capitulation. There sat Merritt—his head fallen: there sat Knight, no longer able to interpret; and there sat the new made Captain, as mute as the seat he sat upon. The bottles had well nigh vanquished the captors. The Articles of Capitulation were seized hastily, read and thrown down again, and the men outside were soon informed of their contents. Pardon us, dear Doctor—we will not make an exposition. It is sufficient to say, that by the rule of opposition, they gave motion and energy to the waiting mass, and all that was necessary was to direct the torrent and guide the storm.

No one hitherto in authority had thought of seizing the fortress, or disarming its guard. Capt. Grigsby was hastily called, and the men demanded of him that the prisoners should be immediately conveyed to the Sacramento Valley. Capt. G. inquired, "What are the orders of Capt. Fremont in relation to these men?" Each man looked on his fellow, yet none spake. "But have you not got Capt. Fremont's name in black and white to authorize you in this you have done?" cried the enraged Captain—and immediately we demanded, that if there were any one present who had orders from him, either written or verbal, he declare the same. All declared, one after another, that they had no such orders. Thereupon the Captain was briefly but particularly informed, that the people whom he knew had received from Gen. Castro, and others in authority, the most insolent indignities—had been, on point of death, ordered to leave the country; and that they had resolved to take the redress of grievances into their own hands; that we could not claim the protection of any government on earth, and were alone responsible for our conduct; that—Here the Captain's "fears of doing wrong" overcame his patriotism, and he interrupted the speaker by saying, "*Gentlemen, I have been deceived; I cannot go with you; I resign and back out of the scrape*. I can take my family to the mountains as cheap as any of you"—and Doct. S. at that moment led him into the house. Disorder and confusion prevailed. One swore he would not stay to guard prisoners—another swore we would all have our throats cut—another called for fresh horses, and all were on the move—every man for himself; when the speaker [Mr. Ide] resumed his effort, raising his voice louder and more loud, as the men receded from the place, saying: "We need no horses; we want no horses. *Saddle no horse for me. I* can go to the Spaniards, and make freemen of them. I will give myself to them. I will lay my bones here, before I will take upon myself the ignomiy of commencing an honorable work, and then flee like cowards, like thieves, when no enemy is in sight. In vain will you say you had honorable motives; Who will believe it? *Flee this day, and the longest life cannot wear off your disgrace*! Choose ye! choose ye this day, what you will be! We are robbers, or we *must be conquerors!*"—and the speaker in despair turned his back upon his receding companions.

With new hope they rallied around the desponding speaker—made him their Commander, their Chief; and his next words commanded the taking of the Fort. Joy lighted up every mind, and in a moment all was secured; 18 prisoners, 9 brass cannon, 250 stands of arms, and tons of copper, shot, and other public property, of the value of 10 or 1200 dollars, was seized and held in trust for the public benefit.

ORIGINS OF THE MEXICAN WAR: THE NUECES SKIRMISH

The Bear Flag Revolt had its beginning in Sonoma and progressed as Frémont and an assortment of other rebels marched on Monterey, but when they reached there they found that their comic opera war had merged into a more serious struggle. Ever since the annexation of Texas, Mexico had shouted defiance at the United States, charging that the colossus of the north was bent on dismembering its provinces one by one. The American government was scarcely less hostile to Mexico for its failure to repay debts and compensate citizens for losses suffered in its periodic revolutions. In this charged atmosphere, only a spark was needed to set off a major explosion. Texas provided this. It entered the Union insisting that its southern border extended to the Rio Grande, not the Nueces River as was actually the case. President Polk chose to take this claim seriously, and on January 12, 1846, sent an army under General Zachary Taylor to occupy the north bank of the Rio Grande, directly across from Matamoros where a Mexican force was camped. Now the only question was who would fire the first shot. On the morning of April 25, 1846, a detachment of Mexican troops crossed the river and clashed with an American scouting party. This engagement, and its effect on the soldiers, was colorfully described by an officer who was present:[9]

April 25th About 10 A.M. a grand review took place among the enemy; great military rejoicing; Arista arrived. He communicated that fact in a note, couched in courteous and gentlemanly terms, transmitted to the general by one of his staff. In the afternoon reports reached us that the enemy were crossing the river, above and below, in great force. Captain Thornton was sent out in the evening with a squadron of the 2d Dragoons to ascertain the fact of their crossing above. Captain Hardee and Lieutenants Kane and Mason were the officers of the party. Every one was on the "qui vive" to ascertain its truth, as, for several days past, matters were assuming a more hostile appearance.

April 26th The camp was electrified by the news brought by Chapita, the Mexican guide who accompanied Captain Thornton. He returned, and stated Captain Thornton had an engagement with a large body of Mexicans, and all had been either cut to pieces or taken prisoners. The excitement which prevailed in camp can hardly be imagined: the report was passed from tent to tent, and an immediate engagement was thought not improbable. About 11 o'clock a wounded dragoon was brought in on a cart; he was sent by General Torrejon, the commander of the force engaged with Captain Thornton, with a note to General Taylor, stating "that, on the score of humanity, he claimed the right of sending him two dragoons, wounded in the affair of to-day (26th), as he had no *flying hospital*; that the officers and men would be treated with all the rights of prisoners of war, by order of his chief." The man who was brought in had a very confused idea of the affair; knew that Captain Hardee was a prisoner, but was uncertain about the rest; reporting Captain Thornton and Lieutenant Kane killed. Increased activity was used in pressing forward the work; the general himself, for hours at a time, superintending it. All idea of there being *no fight* has ceased. W*ar has commenced,*

---

[9] William S. Henry, *Campaign Sketches of the War with Mexico* (New York, 1847), pp. 82–84.

and we look for a conflict within a few days. The train now at Point Isabel is ordered to remain.

General Taylor dispatched a messenger this evening with a requisition on the governors of Louisiana and Texas for five thousand men; three thousand from the former, two thousand from the latter. There is no doubt the enemy are crossing the river, and that all communication with Point Isabel is extremely hazardous. The troops sent for on General Taylor's requisition are expected to be used "to carry the war into Africa." We expect to *whip the Africans back to their country* before their arrival. In anticipation of an attack, the utmost vigilance is used at "the lines." An intrenchment has been thrown up around the camp, and the troops are lying in it under arms before daylight every morning.

April 27th The general received Captain Hardee's report of the fight. He states that after the guide refused to go any further, on account of the proximity of the enemy, they advanced about three miles, and came to a large plantation surrounded by a very high chaparral fence; that the whole squadron entered the field through the open bars, and advanced about two hundred yards to a house. While there the alarm was given of the enemy. "Our gallant commander ordered a charge, and led it in person; they dashed toward the bars again, but found them occupied by a large body of Infantry. They dashed to the right, under a galling fire, to endeavor to find a passage." Captain Thornton here fell; and Captain Hardee, taking command, called on his men to follow, and dashed toward the river, intending to swim it, but found the banks too boggy. He returned and formed his men out of range of Infantry. Perceiving they were completely hemmed in, he determined, if he could get honorable terms, to surrender; if not, to die fighting. He rode forward; met an officer; his terms were granted, and he surrendered his party, forty-five, prisoners. He states "that Captain Thornton was unhorsed," and, "I hear, died in a personal conflict with Romano Falcon." "Lieutenant Mason was not seen, but died, no doubt, fighting gallantly." "The gallant Sergeant Tredor fell in the first charge, and Sergeant Smith was unhorsed and killed." They were taken to Matamoras. Captain Hardee and Lieutenant Kane live at the hotel of General Ampudia, eat at his table, and are treated with the greatest kindness. General Arista "received them most graciously," put them on half pay, and gave them a ration, or, in lieu thereof, twenty-five cents per day. On Captain Hardee's declining, for himself and Lieutenant Kane, to receive the half pay, and requesting permission to send for some money, he refused, stating he would take the best of care of them. He speaks in high terms of their kind treatment. It was certainly unexpected, and is highly creditable to the enemy.

PRESIDENT POLK DECIDES FOR WAR

Even before this skirmish, President Polk had decided to force a declaration of war against Mexico, using as an excuse its failure to meet international obligations. In his famous "Diary" he told of the cabinet meeting on May 9, 1846, in which this decision was reached and of the dramatic arrival of dispatches telling of fighting along the Rio Grande:[10]

Saturday, 9th May, 1846 The Cabinet held a regular meeting to-day; all the members present. I brought up the Mexican

---

[10] Milo M. Quaife (ed.), *The Diary of James K. Polk* (New York, 1910), vol. 1, pp. 384–386.

question, and the question of what was the duty of the administration in the present state of our relations with that country. The subject was very fully discussed. All agreed that if the Mexican forces at Matamoras committed any act of hostility on Gen'l Taylor's forces I should immediately send a message to Congress recommending an immediate declaration of War. I stated to the Cabinet that up to this time, as they knew, we had heard of no open act of aggression by the Mexican army, but that the danger was imminent that such acts would be committed. I said that in my opinion we had ample cause of war, and that it was impossible that we could stand in *statu quo*, or that I could remain silent much longer; that I thought it was my duty to send a message to Congress very soon & recommend definitive measures. I told them that I thought I ought to make such a message by Tuesday next, that the country was excited and impatient on the subject, and if I failed to do so I would not be doing my duty. I then propounded the distinct question to the Cabinet and took their opinions individually, whether I should make a message to Congress on Tuesday, and whether in that message I should recommend a declaration of War against Mexico. All except the Secretary of the Navy gave their advice in the affirmative. Mr. Bancroft dissented but said if any act of hostility should be committed by the Mexican forces he was then in favour of immediate war. Mr. Buchanan said he would feel better satisfied in his course if the Mexican forces had or should commit any act of hostility, but that as matters stood we had ample cause of war against Mexico, & he gave his assent to the measure. It was agreed that the message should be prepared and submitted to the Cabinet in their meeting on Tuesday. A history of our causes of complaint against Mexico had been at my request previously drawn up by Mr. Buchanan. I stated that what was said in my annual message in December gave that history as succinctly and satisfactorily as Mr. Buchanan's statement, that in truth it was the same history in both, expressed in different language, and that if I repeated that history in [a] message to Congress now I had better employ the precise language used in my message of December last. without deciding this point the Cabinet passed to the consideration of some other subjects of minor importance....

About 6 o'clock P.M. Gen'l R. Jones, the Adjutant General of the army, called and handed to me despatches received from Gen'l Taylor by the Southern mail which had just arrived, giving information that a part of [the] Mexican army had crossed ... the Del Norte, and attacked and killed and captured two companies of dragoons of Gen'l Taylor's army consisting of 63 officers & men. The despatch also stated that he had on that day (26th April) made a requisition on the Governors of Texas & Louisiana for four Regiments each, to be sent to his relief at the earliest practicable period. Before I had finished reading the despatch, the Secretary of War called. I immediately summoned the Cabinet to meet at 7½ O'Clock this evening. The Cabinet accordingly assembled at that hour; all the members present. The subject of the despatch received this evening from Gen'l Taylor, as well as the state of our relations with Mexico, were fully considered. The Cabinet were unanimously of opinion, and it was so agreed, that a message should be sent to Congress on Monday laying all the information in my possession before them and recommending vigorous & prompt measure[s] to enable the Executive to prosecute the War.

MEXICAN VIEW OF THE MEXICAN WAR

Mexico's inadequacies as a neighbor were now forgotten by Polk. The war message that he hurried to Congress on May 10 was based almost entirely on Taylor's brief skirmish on the Rio Grande. "After repeated menaces," wrote the President, "Mexico has passed the boundary of the United States, has invaded our territory and shed American blood upon the American soil. . . . War exists, and notwithstanding all our efforts to avoid it, exists by act of Mexico itself." Such stirring words left Congress no alternative; two days later its members voted enthusiastically for war. This declaration gave Mexico legal justification for hostilities against the United States. The war, its people believed, cloaked a cold-blooded determination to seize Mexican territory. National survival, no less than national honor, demanded resistance to the last man. Mexico's attitude was revealed in a book by a group of writers which was widely circulated in the United States just after the war, causing many Americans to suffer sober second thoughts on the duty of a good neighbor:[11]

To explain then in a few words the true origin of the war, it is sufficient to say that the insatiable ambition of the United States, favored by our weakness, caused it. But this assertion, however veracious and well founded, requires the confirmation which we will present, along with some former tranactions, to the whole world. This evidence will leave no doubt of the correctness of our impressions.

In throwing off the yoke of the mother country, the United States of the North appeared at once as a powerful nation. This was the result of their excellent elementary principles of government established while in colonial subjection. The Republic announced at its birth, that it was called upon to represent an important part in the world of Columbus. Its rapid advancement, its progressive increase, its wonderful territory, the uninterrupted augmentation of its inhabitants, and the formidable power it had gradually acquired, were many proofs of its becoming a colossus, not only for the feeble nations of Spanish America, but even for the old populations of the ancient continent.

The United States did not hope for the assistance of time in their schemes of aggrandizement. From the days of their independence they adopted the project of extending their dominions, and since then, that line of policy has not deviated in the slightest degree. This conduct, nevertheless, was not perceptible to the most enlightened: but reflecting men, who examined events, were not slow in recognising it. Conde de Aranda, from whose perception the ends which the United States had resolved upon were not concealed, made use of some celebrated words. These we shall now produce as a prophecy verified by events. "This nation has been born a pigmy: in the time to come, it will be a giant, and even a colossus, very formidable in these vast regions. Its first step will be an appropriation of the Floridas to be master of the Gulf of Mexico."

The ambition of the North Americans has not been in conformity with this. They desired from the beginning to extend their dominion in such manner as to become the absolute owners of almost all this continent. In two ways they could accomplish their ruling passion: in one by bringing under their laws and authority all America to the Isthmus of Panama; in another, in opening

---

[11] Ramon Alcaraz, et. al. (eds.), *The Other Side: or Notes for the History of the War between Mexico and the United States* translated by Albert C. Ramsey (New York, 1850), pp. 2–3, 30–32.

an overland passage to the Pacific Ocean, and making good harbors to facilitate its navigation. By this plan, establishing in some way an easy communication of a few days between both oceans, no nation could compete with them. England herself might show her strength before yielding the field to her fortunate rival, and the mistress of the commercial world might for a while be delayed in touching the point of greatness to which she aspires.

In the short space of some three quarters of a century events have verified the existence of these schemes and their rapid development. The North American Republic has already absorbed territories pertaining to Great Britain, France, Spain, and Mexico. It has employed every means to accomplish this—purchase as well as usurpation, skill as well as force, and nothing has restrained it when treating of territorial acquisition. Louisiana, the Floridas, Oregon, and Texas, have successively fallen into its power. . . .

While the United States seemed to be animated by a sincere desire not to break the peace, their acts of hostility manifested very evidently what were their true intentions. Their ships infested our coasts; their troops continued advancing upon our territory, situated at places which under no aspect could be disputed. Thus violence and insult were united: thus at the very time they usurped part of our territory, they offered to us the hand of treachery, to have soon the audacity to say that our obstinacy and arrogance were the real causes of the war.

To explain the occupation of the Mexican territory by the troops of General Taylor, the strange idea occurred to the United States that the limits of Texas extended to the Rio Bravo del Norte. This opinion was predicated upon two distinct principles: one, that the Congress of Texas had so declared it in December, in 1836; and another, that the river mentioned had been the natural line of Louisiana. To state these reasons is equivalent at once to deciding the matter; for no one could defend such palpable absurdities. The first, which this government prizing its intelligence and civilization, supported with refined malice, would have been ridiculous in the mouth of a child. Whom could it convince that the declaration of the Texas Congress bore a legal title for the acquisition of the lands which it appropriated to itself with so little hesitation? If such a principle were recognised, we ought to be very grateful to these gentlemen senators who had the kindness to be satisfied with so little. Why not declare the limits of the rebel state extended to San Luis, to the capital, to our frontier with Guatemala?

The question is so clear in itself that it would only obscure by delaying to examine it further. We pass then to the other less nonsensical than the former. In the first place to pretend that the limits of Louisiana came to the Rio Bravo, it was essential to confound this province with Texas, which never can be tolerated. In the beginning of this article we have already shown the ancient and peaceable possession of Spain over the lands of the latter. Again, this same province, and afterwards State of Texas, never had extended its territory to the Rio Bravo, being only to the Nueces, in which always had been established the boundary. Lastly, a large part of the territory situated on the other side of the Bravo, belonged, without dispute or doubt, to other states of the Republic—to New Mexico, Tamaulipas, Coahuila, and Chihuahua.

Then, after so many and such plain proceedings, is there one impartial man who would not consider the forcible occupation of our territory by the North American arms a shameful usurpation? Then further, this power desired to carry to the extreme the sneer and the jest. When the question had resolved itself into one of force which is the *ultima ratio* of nations as well as of kings, when it had spread desolation and despair in our populations, when many of our citizens had perished in the contest, the bloody hand of our treacherous neighbors was turned to present the olive of peace. The Secretary of State, Mr. Buchanan, on the 27th of July, 1846, proposed anew, the admission of an Envoy to open negotiations which might lead to the concluding of an honorable peace. The national government answered that it could not decide, and left it to Congress to express its opinion of the subject. Soon to follow up closely the same system of policy, they ordered a commissioner with the army, which invaded us from the east, to cause it to be understood that peace would be made when our opposition ceased. Whom did they hope to deceive with such false appearances? Does not the series of acts which we have mentioned speak louder than this hypocritical language? By that test then, as a question of justice, no one who examines it in good faith can deny our indisputable rights. Among the citizens themselves, of the nation which has made war on us, there have been many who defended the cause of the Mexican Republic. These impartial defenders have not been obscure men, but men of the highest distinction. Mexico has counted on the assistance, ineffectual, unfortunately, but generous and illustrious, of a Clay, an Adams, a Webster, a Gallatin; that is to say, on the noblest men, the most appreciated for their virtues, for their talents, and for their services. Their conduct deserves our thanks, and the authors of this work have a true pleasure in paying, in this place, the sincere homage of their gratitude.

Such are the events that abandoned us to a calamitous war; and, in the relation of which, we have endeavored not to distort even a line of the private data consulted, to prove, on every occasion, all and each of our assertions.

From the acts referred to, it has been demonstrated to the very senses, that the real and effective cause of this war that afflicted us was the spirit of aggrandizement of the United States of the North, availing itself of its power to conquer us. Impartial history will some day illustrate for ever the conduct observed by this Republic against all laws, divine and human, in an age that is called one of light, and which is, notwithstanding, the same as the former—one of *force and violence*.

Future generations of Americans might agree with these Mexican publicists and deplore their country's imperialistic land-grabbing, but those of that time were too happy celebrating victory to be plagued by a bad conscience. A three-pronged attack brought weak Mexico to its knees. General Zachary Taylor continued south to capture Monterrey and Buena Vista; an "Army of the West" under General Stephen Watts Kearny conquered the "northern provinces" of New Mexico and California (aided in the latter province by the Bear Flaggers); and a principal force commanded by General Winfield Scott marched from Vera Cruz to Mexico City to subdue the capital in September 1847. The Treaty of Guadalupe Hidalgo mirrored the success of American arms; Mexico was forced to accept the Rio Grande boundary for Texas, and to surrender to the United States not only California but all of its territories north of the Gila River. The ratification of this treaty on March 10, 1848, ended territorial expansion into adjacent regions, save for the Gadsden Purchase of a strip in northern Mexico needed for a railroad route. The road to the Pacific now lay open to American frontiersmen.

CHAPTER 22

The Mormon Frontier, 1847-1860

While American troops were plundering Mexico of its northern provinces, the trickle of pioneers into the Far West continued, uninterrupted by the machinations of diplomats or the clash of arms. The Oregon Country and California attracted their share of newcomers during the war years, but more dramatic was the opening of a new frontier. Those responsible were not seasoned frontiersmen seeking greater opportunity but members of a religious community fleeing persecution. Their objective was not a hospitable Eden adjacent to established neighbors but the most isolated spot in all the West, where they could worship as they chose. The Mormons, or members of the Church of Jesus Christ of Latter-day Saints, found their haven in the valley of the Great Salt Lake. There they built a desert Zion, and there they established a new frontier outpost.

THE MORMON EXODUS FROM NAUVOO

Members of the Church of Jesus Christ of Latter-day Saints suffered persecution virtually from the day in 1830 when their church was founded by its prophet Joseph Smith. For a time they endured the hostility of their countrymen in Kirtland, Ohio, then in western Missouri, before mobs drove them eastward to find temporary peace and prosperity at Nauvoo, Illinois. By 1844, Nauvoo, with a population of 15,000, was the state's largest city and the Saints seemed to have found a permanent harbor. In that year, however, Joseph Smith received a revelation allowing plural marriage for some church members. This doctrine not only stirred Gentile wrath but split the faithful into two warring camps. With his followers divided, Joseph Smith fell victim to mobs that beset Nauvoo, dying a martyr's death on June 27, 1844. His followers, realizing that they must again flee as an aroused countryside intensified its attack upon them, chose Brigham Young as their leader and sadly prepared to begin their wanderings anew. During the next year, they sold their property at a fraction of its value, built wagons, and in well-organized bands made their way across Iowa to the Missouri River. A correspondent for a Missouri newspaper who visited the nearly deserted Nauvoo in the spring of 1846 described the departure of the last of the Mormons in terms that revealed the cruelty of their tormentors:[1]

---

[1] *Daily Missouri Republican*, May 13, 1846, reprinted in William Mulder and A. Russell Mortensen (eds.), *Among the Mormons* (New York: Knopf, 1958), pp. 168–174.

The city and country presents a very altered appearance since last fall. Then, the fields were covered with, or the barns contained, the crops of the season. Now, there are no crops, either growing or being planted. In many instances, the fences have been destroyed, houses have been deserted, and the whole aspect of the country is one of extreme desolation and desertion. At nearly every dwelling, where the owners have not sold out and moved off, preparations were making to go. Nearly every workshop in the city has been converted into a wagon maker's shop. Even an unfinished portion of the Temple is thus used, and every mechanic appears to be employed in making, repairing or finishing wagons, or other articles necessary for the trip. Generally, they are providing themselves with light wagons, with strong, wide bodies, covered with cotton cloth—in some instances painted, but mostly white. These are to be met with in every direction, and contribute greatly to the singular and mournful appearance of the country.

They appear to be going in neighborhoods, or companies, of four to six and ten wagons, and some of them are tolerably well provided with teams and provisions, but a very large portion present the appearance of being illy provided for so long a trip. Many of them are going with poor teams, and an amount of provisions insufficient for their subsistence for two months, if so long. Indeed, the stock of provisions for the whole company, so far as one may judge from appearance, cannot sustain the crowd until the fall, much less support them through the coming winter. If they should fail to make a good crop this year, at the stopping place, it cannot be otherwise than that many of them, especially the women and children, and the aged and decrepit, must be sorely pressed by starvation, if many of them do not literally perish from famine in the plains. They take with them their milch cows and their teams, being chiefly oxen. These will furnish food in the last resort. But, even with this resource, they have a very scanty supply. Of those whose condition is calculated to arouse sympathy, are a number of women, many of whom have large families of children, inadequately provided with provisions, &c., and without the assistance or protection of any male person. How they expect to get through the journey, we cannot conceive. The Church may give them some protection and assistance, but in all the preliminary preparations, and in setting out on the journey, these women seemed to rely upon themselves and their children, when they happened to be of age to render any aid whatever.

In the midst of this scene, in which there is presented an abandonment of their homes, the breaking up of social relations, a sacrifice of property, and inability to procure the necessary equipments and provisions—with an indefinite journey before them, a journey of months, probably years through plains and over mountains, occupied by Indians, and destitute of the assistance which might be expected in a civilized country—the spectator cannot fail to be struck with the lightness of heart, apparent cheerfulness, and sanguine hopes with which families bid adieu to their friends, and set out on their journey. Occasionally, the reverse of this is met with, but the great mass go forth, sustained and cheered by the promises of their leaders, and, strange as it may seem, a most devout conviction of the truth of their religion, and the rewards which they are to receive from heaven for their present sacrifice. No sect of religious enthusiasts were ever more firmly convinced of the entire truth of their creed than these people. Their trials and privations they regard as a species of martyrdom, which they must not shrink from, and for which they will be spiritually and temporally rewarded in due season. Their enthusiasm, or fanaticism, is stimulated by songs and hymns, in which their men, women and children join, and containing allusions to their persecutions; and the names of Oregon and California, and the hopes that await them, are mingled with their religious belief and expectations.

As a stranger passes through he will find himself frequently beset, mostly by women and children, with inquiries, "Do you wish to purchase a house and lot?" "Do you wish to buy a farm?" and thereupon, if any disposition is signified, he will be pressed and entreated to go and examine, and all the advantages, cheapness, &c., will be fully explained. The frequency and earnestness manifested everywhere, in the city and country, indicate the great anxiety which they entertain to get off. They are effecting some sales, but, from the sacrifices they are making, one would suppose the number and amount of transfers would be greater than they are. In the city, houses and lots are selling at from two to five and ten hundred dollars, which must have cost the owners double that sum. They are willing to sell for cash, or oxen or cattle, or to exchange for such articles of merchandise as they can barter or carry away with them. The most cases, they can give good titles. The number of purchasers is not in proportion to the property in market, nor near as large as was anticipated, from the profitable speculations which they offer, and the kind of property which they are willing to receive in payment. Farmers in other sections, it appears to us, would make profitable investments by exchanging their surplus stock for houses and lots in Nauvoo, or for farms. . . . Authority has been given to the Trustees to sell the Temple itself. Their original purpose was to lease it for a term of years, for some religious or literary purpose. Now they propose to sell it, and thus cut off the last and only motive which could exist to induce them to stay at Nauvoo, or return to it at any future time. The Temple is a stupendous building. . . . So far as room and convenience are requisite, it would answer well for a college or an asylum.

The members of the Church are not at peace even among themselves. A number, including Mrs. Emma Smith, the widow of Joe Smith, and his brother, deny the jurisdiction, and complain greatly of the conduct of the Council of Twelve—who have assumed and exercised the supreme authority since the death of the Prophet. This party, we believe, recognize the spiritual power of the new Prophet, [James J.] Strang, of Voree, Wisconsin Territory, but look forward to the time when a son of Joe, a lad of twelve or fourteen years of age, shall assume the position in the Church which his father occupied. This party do not contemplate removing with the other, but most of them will either join Strang, in Wisconsin Territory, or go to other parts.

They are crossing the river every day from Nauvoo, and a large number cross at Madison. Bad roads and high waters have detained them. It is difficult to arrive at the number who have crossed and are on the way. The first party, which crossed the river in February, have progressed as far as the east fork of Grand river, about 200 miles west of Nauvoo, within the Territory of Iowa. This party are styled the *Camp of Israel*, and have with them the Council of Twelve and most of the leading men of the Church. From the best information we could obtain, this Camp includes about 3000 souls. Between the Camp and the Mississippi river, there is said to be about 1500 wagons. Major Warren, who, on Friday last, visited the Camps within ten miles of Montrose, estimates the number of teams at about one thousand. Allowing five or six souls to a wagon—and the estimate is a reasonable one—it would give about seven thousand persons between the Mississippi and Grand river.

The first party have selected a temporary resting place on the east fork of Grand river, in the edge of a grove, which is free from underbrush. The soil is said to be very rich, and easily broken up and cultivated. Here they will enclose a large field—about 2300 acres—and leave that portion of their people who are not prepared to travel further, to plant and cultivate a crop, which is to be gathered for the subsistence of those who come on later in the season. Another portion of the camp will move two or three hundred miles further on, and select a second site, and put in a crop of buckwheat, and such roots and plants as grow rapidly, and will mature late in the season. After sowing this, those having provisions to subsist themselves through the winter, and teams sufficiently strong, will move further westward, or cross the mountains, if practicable. A body of several hundred, having the stoutest teams and the most ample supply of provisions, have been sent forward, with instructions to push directly across the mountains, and explore the territories of Oregon, California and Vancouver's Island, and upon their report it will depend where the Church will be re-established. This party, it is believed, have crossed the Missouri about sixty miles above St. Josephs, and are already some distance on the road to Oregon. From the camp on Grand river—says a letter from the Twelve to the Church at Nauvoo—the trading men have been sent out into Platte and the adjoining counties, to exchange whatever they can spare for oxen, cows and provisions. They complain, however, that the price of everything is high.

In and about Nauvoo, and throughout Hancock county, there is every indication that the citizens, or Anti-Mormons, with few exceptions, are satisfied that the Mormons are going, and are disposed to let them get off without further difficulty. There are, however, some few turbulent spirits in the county—for these broils have not been without their effects on the morals of individuals—and particularly some young men, who are willing, at any sacrifice, to keep up the excitement. A few nights ago, a Mr. Rea was dragged from his bed by four or five persons, stripped, and most severely beaten, but whether it was the act of the Anti-Mormons, or of one of the divisions of the Mormon church, we understood from the officers, was doubtful. The doors of other individuals have been placarded with notices to leave, &c., and on Saturday evening last, a number of persons assembled at Pontosuc, reported at about one hundred and fifty, who are said to have been under much excitement, and resolved to visit Nauvoo on the 16th inst. and burn down the houses and drive out all those who had not already left. These proceedings were universally condemned by the more intelligent and respectable portion of the Anti-Mormon party, and the movement appeared to excite no uneasiness on the part of Major W. D. Warren who had had the command of the State troops stationed in the county for the past seven months. Maj. Warren is well satisfied, that a large majority of the Mormons will leave as soon as they can dispose of their property.

THE PIONEER BAND REACHES UTAH

The Saints spent a miserable winter on the site of today's Council Bluffs, Iowa, while their leaders plotted the next step. They must, Brigham Young advised them, move beyond the United States where in some remote Mexican valley they could find peace. Guide books and travel accounts that described the Far West convinced them that the valley of the Great Salt Lake was properly isolated, yet capable of sustaining life. With this decided, the Mormons busied themselves preparing for the long overland journey, building wagons, storing supplies, and rehearsing the techniques of plains travel. By April 9, 1847, the first Pioneer Band of 143 men, 3 women, and 2 children was ready to start the trek. Blazing a new trail along the north bank of the Platte to avoid Missouri ruffians on the Oregon Trail, they crossed the continental divide at South Pass, turned southward to Fort Bridger, and followed the eastern valley of the Wasatch Range until they located a defile suitable for their crossing. The last stages of their journey through the mountains and the first sight of their future home were described by William Clayton, who kept a careful journal of the expedition:[2]

After traveling four miles, halted about half an hour to water teams and eat dinner. The road over which we have traveled is through an uneven gap between high mountains and is exceedingly rough and crooked. Not a place to be met with scarcely where there would be room to camp for the dense willow groves all along the bottom. We then proceeded on and traveled over the same kind of rough road till a little after 5:00 p. m. then camped on a ridge, having traveled today seven and a quarter miles. The last three miles has been the worst road of the two, it being through willow bushes over twenty feet high, also rose and gooseberry bushes and shaking poplar and birch timber. Although there has been a road cut through, it is yet scarcely possible to travel without tearing the wagon covers. We have crossed this creek which Elder Pratt names Canyon Creek eleven times during the day and the road is one of the most crooked I ever saw, many sharp turns in it and the willow stubs standing making it very severe on wagons. As we proceed up, the gap between the mountains seems to grow still narrower until arriving at this place where there is room to camp, but little grass for teams. There are many springs along the road but the water is not very good. In one place about a mile back there is a very bad swamp where the brethren spent some time cutting willows and laying them in to improve it. We have got along today without much damage which is somewhat favorable for the road is awful. At this place the ground around is represented as being swampy and dangerous for cattle. It is reported that there is no place to camp beyond this till where Elder Pratt's company camped and this is so small they have to huddle the wagons together. The soil continues sandy, except in the low moist places where it looks black and good. There is some pine occasionally in sight on the mountains, but timber here is scarce. We have passed through some small patches today where a few house logs might be cut, but this is truly a wild looking place.

Wednesday, 21st We started onward at half past six, the morning fine and pleasant. We crossed the creek once more and about a half a mile from where we camped, the road turns to the right leaving the creek and ascending the mountains gradually. Much time was necessarily spent cutting down stumps, heaving out rocks and leveling the road. It is an exceedingly rough place. There are several springs at the foot of the mountain and one a mile from the top which runs above the ground a little distance, then sinks under again. The last half mile of the ascent is very steep and the nearer the top the

---

[2] "William Clayton's Journal," in the *Deseret News* (Salt Lake City, 1921), pp. 303–309. Reprinted with permission from the *Deseret News*.

steeper it grows. There is considerable timber up this gap but mostly destroyed by fire. We saw a prairie pheasant while going up and some wild gooseberries. At eleven o'clock, the teams began to arrive on the dividing ridge and in less than an hour, all were safely up. From this ridge we can see an extensive valley to the west but on every other side high mountains, many of them white with snow. It seems as though a few hours' travel might bring us out from the mountains on good road again. We halted on the ridge a little while and then prepared to descend, many locking both hind wheels, a precaution not at all unnecessary. We found the road down exceedingly steep and rendered dangerous by the many stumps of trees left standing in the road. The brethren cut up many of them which delayed us much. About a mile down is a bridge formed of small trees laid one on another to fill up a deep ravine. It is steep on both sides and here Joseph Rooker turned his wagon over, however, without much damage. A mile and a half from the top is a spring and small stream of very good cold water where we halted to let teams drink. This would make a tolerably good camp ground in case of necessity. After this, the road is not so steep but is very rough and winds between high hills or mountains through willows and brush wood and over soft places, crossing the creek a number of times. At four and a half miles from the top of the ridge, we arrived at a good spring of cold water, plenty of grass and a good place to camp. Our teams have now been in the harness about ten hours without eating and the feeling of many was to stay here, but some wanted to go on and we continued. Turning suddenly to the right a little below this spring we began to ascend another high ridge and while ascending some of the teams began to fail. There are a great many service berries on this ridge growing on what we supposed to be wild apple trees. The berries are good and rich when ripe. The descent from this ridge is not nearly so steep as the other one, yet many locked both hind wheels. After descending, we found another small creek and a very rough road again. At 7:30, we formed our encampment near the creek, having traveled fourteen miles in thirteen hours. There is but little grass here and a poor chance for cattle. Orson Pratt's company are camped a half a mile ahead of us and our camp was formed by Colonel Markham. He says they have had many new cases of sickness but mostly getting better. The cannon is left back on the other side of the mountains. About a mile back from this place there is a small grove of sugar maple and considerable other timber along the creek. There are also beds of nice green rushes in several places.

Thursday, 22nd This morning is cloudy and some like for rain. We started on at 8:30 and soon came up with Elder Pratt's company. There were several bad places in the road where the brethren spent considerable time fixing them. As we near the mouth of the canyon, there is a small grove of elder bushes in bloom and considerable oak shrubbery. We named this a canyon because of the very high mountains on each side leaving but a few rods of a bottom for the creek to pass through and hardly room for a road. It is evident that the emigrants who passed this way last year must have spent a great deal of time cutting a road through the thickly set timber and heavy brush wood. It is reported that they spent sixteen days in making a road through from Weber River which is thirty-five miles but as the men did not work a quarter of their time much less would have sufficed. However, it has taken us over three days after the road is made although a great many hours have been spent in improving it. In this thick brush wood and around here there are many very large rattlesnakes lurking, making it necessary to use caution while passing through. After traveling one and three-quarters miles, we found the road crossing the creek again to the north side and then ascending up a very steep, high hill. It is so very steep as to be almost impossible for heavy wagons to ascend and so narrow that the least accident might precipitate a wagon down a bank three or four hundred feet,—in which case it would certainly be dashed to pieces. Colonel Markham and another man went over the hill and returned up the canyon to see if a road cannot be cut through and avoid this hill. While passing up, a bear started near them but soon was out of sight amongst the very high grass. Brother Markham says a good road can soon be made down the canyon by digging a little and cutting through the bushes some ten or fifteen rods. A number of men went to work immediately to make the road which will be much better than to attempt crossing the hill and will be sooner done.

Agreeable to President Young's instructions, Elder Pratt acompanied by George A. Smith, John Brown, Joseph Mathews, John Pack, O.P. Rockwell and J.C. Little started on this morning on horses to seek out a suitable place to plant some potatoes, turnips, etc., so as to preserve the seed at least. While the brethren were cutting the road, I followed the old one to the top of the hill and on arriving there was much cheered by a handsome view of the Great Salt Lake lying, as I should judge, from twenty-five to thirty miles to the west of us; and at eleven o'clock I sat down to contemplate and view the surrounding scenery. There is an extensive, beautiful, level looking valley from here to the lake which I should judge from the numerous deep green patches must be fertile and rich. The valley extends to the south probably fifty miles where it is again surrounded by high mountains. To the southwest across the valley at about twenty to twenty-five miles distance is a high mountain, extending from the south end of the valley to about opposite this place where it ceases abruptly leaving a pleasant view of the dark waters of the lake. Standing on the lake and about due west there are two mountains and far in the distance another one which I suppose is on the other side the lake, probably from sixty to eighty miles distance. To the northwest is another mountain at the base of which is a lone ridge of what I should consider to be rock salt from its white and shining appearance. The lake does not show at this distance a very extensive surface, but its dark blue shade resembling the calm sea looks very handsome. The intervening valley appears to be well supplied with streams, creeks and lakes, some of the latter are evidently salt. There is but little timber in sight anywhere, and that is mostly on the banks of creeks and streams of water which is about the only objection which could be raised in my estimation to this being one of the most beautiful valleys and pleasant places for a home for the Saints which could be found.

THE COOPERATIVE EXPERIMENT: THE ECONOMY

William Clayton's optimistic estimate of the valley of the Great Salt Lake concealed the fact that the Mormons must make the desert bloom if they were to survive. They had chosen to settle on an arid plateau, ringed by hills and mountains, where the rainfall virtually ceased between April and November. Even their plows were shattered when they first attempted to break the sun-baked soil. Undaunted, the Saints dammed a small stream and flooded the land to soften it. Thus began their practice of irrigating the land, and with it the necessity for a social order radically different from that on other frontiers. Normally, pioneers were irrationally individualistic, refusing to obey authorities who sought to elevate the needs of society above those of the individual. Brigham Young realized that the Mormons' desert community could never endure without cooperative enterprise, for this was essential if the limited water supply was to be shared by all. In a sermon preached to the Pioneer Band on July 25, 1847, two days after they reached the valley, he laid down the rules that were to govern them for years to come. His words were recorded by Wilford Woodruff in his journal, which also described the early exploration of the valley:[3]

He told the brethren, that they must not work on Sunday; that they would lose five times as much as they would gain by it. None were to hunt or fish on that day; and there should not any man dwell among us who would not observe these rules. They might go and dwell where they pleased, but should not dwell with us. He also said, no man should buy any land who came here; that he had none to sell; but every man should have his land measured out to him for city and farming purposes. He might till it as he pleased, but he must be industrious, and take care of it.

On Monday ten men were chosen for an exploring expedition. I took President Young into my carriage, and, traveling two miles towards the mountain, made choice of a spot for our garden.

We then returned to camp, and went north about five miles, and we all went on to the top of a high peak, on the edge of the mountain, which we considered a good place to raise an ensign. So we named it 'Ensign Peak.'

I was the first person who ascended this hill, which we had thus named. Brother Young was very weary, in climbing to the peak, from his recent fever.

We descended to the valley, and started north to the Hot Sulphur Springs, but we returned two miles to get a drink of cold water, and then went back four miles to the Springs. We returned to the camp quite weary with our day's explorations. Brothers Mathews and Brown had crossed the valley in the narrowest part, opposite the camp, to the west mountain, and found it about fifteen miles.

Next day Amasa Lyman came into camp, and informed us that Capt. Brown's detachment of the Mormon battalion would be with us in about two days.

We again started on our exploring expedition. All the members of the quorum of the Twelve belonging to the pioneers, eight in number, were of the company. Six others of the brethren, including Brannan of San Francisco, were with us.

We started for the purpose of visiting the great Salt Lake, and mountains on the west of the valley. We traveled two miles west from Temple Block, and came to the outlet of the Utah Lake; thence fourteen miles to the west mountain, and found that the land was not so fertile as on the east side.

We took our dinner at the fresh water pool, and then rode six miles to a large rock, on the shore of the Salt Lake, which we named Black Rock, where we all halted and bathed in the salt water. No person could sink in it, but would roll and float on the surface like a dry log. We concluded that the Salt Lake was one of the wonders of the world.

After spending an hour here, we went west

---

[3] Edward W. Tullidge, *Life of Brigham Young* (New York, 1876), pp. 175–178.

along the lake shore, and then returned ten miles to our place of nooning, making forty miles that day.

In the morning we arose refreshed by sleep in the open air. Having lost my carriage whip the night before, I started on horseback to go after it. As I approached the spot where it was dropped, I saw about twenty Indians. At first they looked to me in the distance like a lot of bears coming towards me. As I was unarmed I wheeled my horse and started back on a slow trot.

But they called to me, and one, mounting his horse, came after me with all speed. When he got within twenty rods I stopped and met him. The rest followed. They were Utes, and wanted to trade. I told them by signs that our camp was near, so he went on with me to the camp. From what we had yet seen of the Utes they appeared friendly, though they had a bad name from the mountaineers. The Indian wanted to smoke the pipe of peace with us, but we soon started on and he waited for his company.

We traveled ten miles south under the mountain. The land laid beautifully, but there was no water, and the soil was not so good as on the east. We saw about a hundred goats, sheep and antelope playing about the hills and valleys. We returned, weary, to the pioneer encampment, making thirty miles for the day.

THE COOPERATIVE EXPERIMENT: THE GOVERNMENTAL SYSTEM

Brigham Young's words were heeded by the Mormons, as well they might be for they believed that he voiced the will of God. Their zealous faith, no less than the inhospitable natural environment, compelled them to forsake individual gain for the community's good, laboring together to build homes, fence their fields, construct irrigation ditches, and plant new outposts. The result was one of the most successful experiments in cooperative enterprise in the nation's history. Basic to this success was the power of the church, voiced through its leaders. A traveler, J. W. Gunnison, who visited the Mormon settlements two years after their founding painted an accurate "picture of the governmental system that was" evolving under the paternalistic control of Brigham Young:[4]

While professing a complete divorce of church and state, their political character and administration is made subservient to the theocratical or religious element. They delight to call their system of government, a "Theo-Democracy;" and that, in a civil capacity, they stand as the Israelites of old under Moses. For the rule of those not fully imbued with the spirit of obedience, and sojourners not of the faith, as well as for things purely temporal, tribunals of justice, and law-making assemblies, are at present rendered necessary. But the rules and regulations vouchsafed from the throne of Heaven are fixed and unchangeable, which have preceded all present necessities, and by them are they guided in the manner of providing for, and executing temporal affairs:—so that those holding the revelations of God's Will, are the ones who make laws according to Truth, and the rulers or executors are clothed in Righteousness, and the end is Peace. In fact, their President of the church is the temporal civil governor, *because* he is the Seer of the Lord, and rules in virtue of that prophetic right over the home and Catholic

---

[4] J. W. Gunnison, *The Mormons, or Latter-Day Saints* (Philadelphia, 1852), pp. 23–25, 31–32.

"Latter-Day Saints of the Church of Jesus Christ," usually styled the Mormons. And should one be assigned to them, not of their creed, or other than their chief, he would find himself without occupation. He probably would be received with all due courtesy as a dintinguished personage, cordially received in social intercourse so long as his demeanor pleased the influential members and people:—but as Governor—to use their own expressive phrase,—"he would be let severely alone." Were he to convoke an assembly, and order an election, no attention would be paid to it, and he would be subjected to the mortification of seeing a legislature, chosen at a different time, enacting statutes, or else the old ones continued, and those laws enforced and the cases arising from their conflict adjudicated, by the present tribunals of justice, under their own judges. This certainly has been proclaimed as their determined policy, though there might arise circumstances that would cause them to dissemble for a time; and the peaceful character of the people would be assigned as the reason why no other burden was thrown upon foreign functionaries than the labor of drawing their salaries from the distant treasury. The dignity and the form of courts might easily obtain, to which Gentile sojourners or emigrants could resort, but the members of the Latter-Day Church would know nothing about them; their causes are to be settled in the church and not go to law out of it. The church is the court for doctrinal error—for other offences they have the statutes of Deserét, and what they call "Common Mountain Law."

For, among themselves, all disputes are to be settled under a "church" organization, to which is attached the civil jurisdiction, with officers, from the inferior justice of the peace up to the Governor. But the justice is a Bishop of a ward in the city or precinct of the town or county; the Judges on the bench of the superior courts are constituted from the High Priests, from the quorums of seventies, or from the college of the Apostles; and the Seer is the highest ruler and consulting Judge. A double name is therefore required, by which the same persons execute the functions in their different official capacities, according as they relate to prescribed civil or spiritual matters, except on opinions, or purity of faith. Even the legislature can make no law upon, or regulating what is given in "Revelations" to the prophet, only so far as is necessary to carry them into effect in social transactions.

The entire management is under the Presidency, which consists of three persons, the Seer and two counsellors. It is this board that governs their universal church; called universal because they claim to have preached in almost every nation, and in the United States in each congressional district; and have gathered societies called "Stakes of Zion," arranged on the model of their home assembly, on the islands of the ocean and either continent—and all are to obey the Presidency; at home in all things, and abroad in spiritual things, independent of every consideration—and the converts are commanded "to gather, gather, gather to the mountains," as fast as convenient and compatible with their character and situation....

Their admirable system of combining labor, while each has his own property, in land and tenements, and the proceeds of his industry, the skill in dividing off the lands, and conducting the irrigating canals to supply the want of water, which rarely falls between April and October,—the cheerful manner in which every one applies himself industriously, but not laboriously:—the complete reign of good neighborhood and quiet in house and fields, form themes for admiration to the stranger coming from the dark and sterile recesses of the mountain gorges into this flourishing valley:—and he is struck with wonder at the immense results, produced in so short a time by a handful of individuals.

This is the result of the guidance of all those hands by one master mind; and we see a comfortable people residing where, it is not too much to say, the ordinary mode of subduing and settling our wild lands could never have been applied.

To accomplish this, there was required religious fervor, with the flame fanned by the breezes of enthusiasm—the encircling of bands into the closest union, by the outward pressure of persecution—the high hopes of laying up a prospective reward, and returning to their deserted homes in great prosperity—the belief of reenacting the journey of the Israelitish church under another Moses, through the Egypt already passed, to arrive at another Jerusalem, more heavenly in its origin, and beautiful in its proportions and decorations.

Single families on that line of travel would have starved or fallen by the treachery of the Sioux, the cunning of the Crows and Shoshones, or the hatred of the savage Utahs. Concert and courage of the best kind were required and brought into the field, and the result is before us—to their own minds as the direct blessing and interposition of Providence, to others the natural reward of associated industry and perseverance.

MORMON EXPANSION OVER THE GREAT BASIN

The remarkable efficiency of the Mormon's "Theo-democracy" not only allowed them to build the handsome city of Salt Lake in the heart of their Zion, but to colonize smaller outposts over the entire Great Basin frontier, and beyond. Colony planting was developed to a fine art. When a new community was to be established, an exploring party was first dispatched to locate a site suitable for irrigation or adjacent to mineral wealth. Then the colonists were carefully selected to assure the right proportion of farmers, tradesmen, artisans, and professional men. All chosen for these ventures cheerfully sold their property and joined the cavalcade into the wilderness, assured that they were obeying the will of God. Howard Stansbury, a visitor to Salt Lake City in 1852, described the process:[5]

Near the eastern shores of Lake Utah, a site for a city has been selected on the left bank of the Provaux or Timpanogas River, an affluent of the lake, which is to be called *Provaux City*. From Ogden City on the north, all the way to this latter "Stake of Zion," the base of the Wahsatch range is studded with flourishing farms, wherever a little stream flows down the mountain-side with water sufficient for irrigating purposes; while in the gorges and cañons of the mountain are erected the saw and grist mills. Of the former, sixteen, and of the latter, eleven have been completed, and others are in the process of erection.

To the south of Lake Utah, on one of its tributaries, another city has been founded, called *Paysan*, and a hundred and thirty miles farther, on the road to California, another, named *Manti*, in what is called San Pete Valley. Still farther south, near Little Salt Lake, two hundred and fifty miles south of the city, a fourth, called *Cedar City*, has been laid out, in a spot possessing the advantages of excellent soil and water, plenty

---

[5] Howard Stansbury, *Exploration and Survey of the Valley of the Great Salt Lake* (Philadelphia, 1852), pp. 142–143.

of wood, iron ore, and alum, with some prospect of coal. It is the ultimate object of the Mormons, by means of stations, wherever the nature of the country will admit of their settling in numbers sufficient for self-defence, to establish a line of communication with the Pacific, so as to afford aid to their brethren coming from abroad, while on their pilgrimage to the land of promise. These stations will gradually become connected by farms and smaller settlements wherever practicable, until the greater part of the way will exhibit one long line of cultivated fields from the Mormon capital to San Diego.

The mode adopted for the founding of a new town is peculiar and highly characteristic. An expedition is first sent out to explore the country, with a view to the selection of such points as, from their natural advantages, offer facilities for a settlement. These being duly reported to the authorities, an elder of the church is appointed to preside over the little band designated to make the first improvement. This company is composed partly of volunteers and partly of such as are selected by the presidency, due regard being had to a proper intermixture of mechanical artisans, to render the expedition independent of all aid from without. In this way the settlement at San Pete was begun, sixty families leaving in a body, under one of the high officers of the church, and that in the month of October, undergoing all the rigours of cold and snow, to establish another "stake" in the wilderness. In December of the following year, another expedition, similarly composed and commanded, succeeded, with one hundred and thirty men and families, in planting the settlement at *Little Salt Lake*, which is represented as being now in a very flourishing condition. The succeeding March, a third party, with a hundred and fifty wagons, left the capital for the purpose of establishing a settlement in the southern part of California. It was to be situated at no great distance from San Diego, and near Williams's *ranche* and Cahone Pass, between which and Little Salt Lake it is designed to establish other settlements as speedily as possible. By means of these successive places of refreshment, the incoming emigration from the Pacific will be enabled to "go from strength to strength" till they reach the Zion of their hopes.

MORMON EXPANSION: PAROWAN CITY

Typical of the colonization technique was the building of Parowan City, which was established in 1851 to provide farm produce for a projected iron works that was being planned twenty miles away. Frederick Piercy, one of the company selected to pioneer this community, left a revealing account of the events of the first year:[6]

After looking out and selecting a location, we formed our waggons into two parallel lines, some seventy paces apart. We then took our boxes from the wheels, and planted them about a couple of paces from each other, so securing ourselves that we could not easily be taken advantage of by any unknown foe. This done, we next cut a road up the kanyon, opening it to a distance of some eight miles, bridging the creek in some five or six places, making the timber and poles (of which there is an immense quantity) of easy access. We next built a large meeting-house in the form of two rectangles, lying transversely, two stories high, of large pine trees,

---

[6] Frederick Piercy, *Route from Liverpool to Great Salt Lake Valley*, edited by James Linforth (Liverpool, 1855), p. 100.

all well hewn and neatly jointed together. We next built a large square fort, with a commodious cattle carrel inside the inclosure. The houses built were some of hewn logs, and some of adobies, all neat, comfortable and convenient. We next inclosed a field some five by three miles square, with a good ditch and pole fence. We dug canals and water ditches to the distance of some 30 or 40 miles. One canal to turn the water of another creek upon the field, for irrigating purposes, was seven miles long. We built a saw and grist mill the same season. I have neither time nor space to tell you of one-half of the labours we performed here in one season. Suffice it to say that, when the Governor came along in the spring, he pronounced it the greatest work done in the mountains by the same amount of men.

THE HANDCART MIGRATION OF 1856

Brigham Young's plans were as well organized as the town-planting procedures that he perfected: he would not only fill the Great Basin with Saints but would extend a "Mormon corridor" westward to the sea at San Diego. Only in this way, he reasoned, would the Mormons boast the power to ward off enemies and develop the trade that would elevate them to an independent position in the hierarchy of nations. Expansion on such a scale required settlers in ever-greater numbers. Many converts were brought from Europe by a highly efficient transportation system, their expenses paid by a Perpetual Emigration Fund. The cost was still heavy, however, and to ease the burden on his people Young decided to experiment with hand-carts that could be pulled by the emigrants. The first handcart brigades started west in June 1856 and, traveling at about fifteen miles a day, reached Salt Lake City in September with no serious difficulty. Two other brigades that did not start until August suffered a different fate. High in South Pass they were stopped by a blizzard, and by the time a rescue train from Salt Lake City reached them, 225 of the 1000 were dead. One of the survivors, T. B. H. Stenhouse, who later left the church and bitterly opposed Mormonism, left an account of their suffering:[7]

When we arrived at Iowa City, the great out-fitting point for the emigration, we found that three hand-cart companies had already gone forward, under the respective captaincy of Edmund Ellsworth, Daniel McArthur, and—Bunker, all Valley elders returning from missions to England. These companies reached Salt Lake City in safety before cold weather set in. No carts being ready for us, nor indeed anything necessary for our journey, we were detained three weeks at Iowa Camp, where we could celebrate the Fourth of July.

A few days after this we started on our journey, organized as follows: James G. Willie, captain of the company, which numbered about five hundred. Each hundred had a sub-captain, thus: first, Millen Atwood; second, Levi Savage; third, William Woodward; fourth, John Chislett; fifth,——Ahmensen. The third hundred were principally Scotch; the fifth, Scandinavians. The other hundreds were mostly English. To each hundred there were five round tents, with twenty persons to a tent; twenty hand-carts, or one to every five persons; and one Chicago wagon, drawn by three yoke of oxen, to haul provisions and tents. Each person was limited to *seventeen pounds of clothing and bedding*, making eighty-five pounds of luggage to each cart. To this were added such cooking utensils as the little mess of five re-

---

[7] T. B. H. Stenhouse, *The Rocky Mountain Saints* (London, 1873), pp. 314–316, 323–326.

quired. But their *cuisine* being scanty, not many articles were needed, and I presume the average would not exceed fifteen to twenty pounds, making in all a little over a hundred pounds on each cart. The carts being so poorly made, could not be laden heavily, even had the people been able to haul them.

The strength of the company was equalized as much as possible by distributing the young men among the different families to help them. Several carts were drawn by *young girls* exclusively; and two tents were occupied by them and such females as had no male companions. The other tents were occupied by families and some young men; all ages and conditions being found in one tent. Having been thrown closely together on shipboard, all seemed to adapt themselves to this mode of tent-life without any marked repugnance.

As we travelled along, we presented a singular, and sometimes an affecting appearance. The young and strong went along gaily with their carts, but the old people and little children were to be seen straggling a long distance in the rear. Sometimes, when the little folks had walked as far as they could, their fathers would take them on their carts, and thus increase the load that was already becoming too heavy as the day advanced. But what will parents not do to benefit their children in time of trouble? The most affecting scene, however, was to see a mother carrying her child at the breast, mile after mile, until nearly exhausted. The heat was intense, and the dust suffocating, which rendered our daily journeys toilsome in the extreme.

Our rations consisted of ten ounces of flour to each adult per day, and half that amount to children under eight years of age. Besides our flour we had occasionally a little rice, sugar, coffee, and bacon. But these items (especially the last) were so small and infrequent that they scarcely deserve mentioning. Any hearty man could eat his daily allowance for breakfast. In fact, some of our men did this, and then worked all day without dinner, and went to bed supperless or begged food at the farmhouses as we travelled along. . . .

[Despite their problems, all went well with the brigade until they climbed into South Pass. There, with rations running low, bone-biting cold, and snow piled deep along the trail, they were sustained only by the hope that a relief party was on its way:]

After untold toil and fatigue, doubling teams frequently, going back to fetch up the straggling carts, and encouraging those who had dropped by the way to a little more exertion in view of our soon-to-be improved condition, we finally, late at night, got all to camp—the wind howling frightfully and the snow eddying around us in fitful gusts. But we had found a good camp among the willows, and after warming and partially drying ourselves before good fires, we ate our scanty fare, paid our usual devotions to the Deity and retired to rest with hopes of coming aid.

In the morning the snow was over a foot deep. Our cattle strayed widely during the storm, and some of them died. But what was worse to us than all this was the fact that *five persons* of both sexes lay in the cold embrace of death. The pitiless storm and the extra march of the previous day had been too much for their wasted energies, and they had passed through the dark valley to the bright world beyond. We buried these five people in one grave, wrapped only in the clothing and bedding in which they died. We had no materials with which to make coffins, and even if we had, we could not have spared time to make them, for it required all the efforts of the healthy few who remained to perform the ordinary camp duties and to look after the sick—the number of whom increased daily on our hands, notwithstanding so many were dying.

The morning before the storm, or, rather, the morning of the day on which it came, we issued the last ration of flour. On this fatal morning, therefore, we had none to issue. We had, however, a barrel or two of hard bread which Captain Willie had procured at Fort Laramie in view of our destitution. This was equally and fairly divided among all the company. Two of our poor broken-down cattle were killed and their carcasses issued for beef. With this we were informed that we would have to subsist until the coming supplies reached us. All that now remained in our commissary were a few pounds each of sugar and dried apples, about a quarter of a sack of rice and a small quantity (possibly 20 or 25 lbs.) of hard bread. The brother who had been our commissary all the way from Liverpool had not latterly acted in a way to merit the confidence of the company; but it is hard to handle provisions and suffer hunger at the same time, so I will not write a word of condemnation. These few scanty supplies were on this memorable morning turned over to me by Captain Willie, with strict injunctions to distribute them only to the sick and to mothers for their hungry children, and even to them in as sparing a manner as possible. It was an unenviable place to occupy, a hard duty to perform; but I acted to the best of my ability, using all the discretion I could.

Being surrounded by snow a foot deep, out of provisions, many of our people sick, and our cattle dying, it was decided that we should remain in our present camp until the supply-train reached us. It was also resolved in council that Captain Willie with one man should go in search of the supply-train and apprise its leader of our condition, and hasten him to our help. When this was done we settled down and made our camp as comfortable as we could. As Captain Willie and his companion left for the West, many a heart was lifted in prayer for their success and speedy return. They were absent three days—three days which I shall never forget. The scanty allowance of hard bread and poor beef, distributed as described, was mostly consumed the first day by the hungry, ravenous, famished souls.

We killed more cattle and issued the meat; but, eating it without bread, did not satisfy hunger, and to those who were suffering from dysentery it did more harm than good. This terrible disease increased rapidly amongst us during these three days, and several died from exhaustion. Before we renewed our journey the camp became so offensive and filthy that words would fail to describe its condition, and even common decency forbids the attempt. Suffice it to say that all the disgusting scenes which the reader might imagine would certainly not equal the terrible reality. It was enough to make the heavens weep. The recollection of it unmans me even now—those three days! During that time I visited the sick, the widows whose husbands died in serving them, and the aged who could not help themselves, to know for myself where to dispense the few articles that had been placed in my charge for distribution. Such craving hunger I never saw before, and may God in his mercy spare me the sight again....

The storm which we encountered, our brethren from the Valley also met, and, not knowing that we were so utterly destitute, they encamped to await fine weather. But when Captain Willie found them and explained our real condition, they at once hitched up their teams and made all speed to come to our rescue. On the evening of the third day after Captain Willie's departure, just as the sun was sinking beautifully behind the distant hills, on an eminence immediately west of our camp several covered wagons, each drawn by four horses, were seen coming towards us. The news ran through the camp like wildfire, and all who were able to leave their beds turned out *en masse* to see them. A few minutes brought them sufficiently near to reveal our faithful captain slightly in advance of the train. Shouts of joy rent the air; strong men wept till tears ran freely down their furrowed and sunburnt cheeks, and little children partook of the joy which some of them hardly understood, and fairly danced around with gladness. Restraint was set aside in the general rejoicing, and as the brethren entered our camp the sisters fell upon them and deluged them with kisses. The brethren were so overcome that they could not for some time utter a word, but in choking silenced repressed all demonstration of those emotions that evidently mastered them. Soon, however, feeling was somewhat abated, and such a shaking of hands, such words of welcome, and such invocation of God's blessing have seldom been witnessed.

THE MOUNTAIN MEADOWS MASSACRE

As a result of such sacrifices, more than 8000 Saints lived in the valley of the Great Salt Lake by the middle 1850s, enjoying freedom from persecution and a degree of economic self-sufficiency for the first time in the history of the church. By this time, however, their isolation was threatened. The Great Basin country was organized as the Territory of Utah in 1850, with Brigham Young as its first governor and the Mormon church in undisputed control, but five years later Washington officialdom decided to inflict at least a measure of authority over the region. The three territorial judges sent westward with this responsibility were poorly chosen; all were bitterly anti-Mormon and soon returned to spread highly distorted tales of the Saints' rebellion against their attempted rule. President James Buchanan accepted their emotion-charged statements at face value. Insurrection must be suppressed, and by force. Hence in May 1857, about 2500 troops under Colonel Albert Sidney Johnston marched toward Utah. As they approached near-panic spread through the Mormon communities, which were already heated by a religious revival that was under way. Tensions exploded in September 1857, when a band of 140 Arkansas emigrants bound for California were attacked by Indians while camped in a valley known as Mountain Meadows. A scout sent by the band to obtain help was killed by a fanatical Mormon, who convinced his fellow Saints that his misdeed could be concealed only by slaughtering the entire party. John D. Lee, the leader in this savage design, later confessed and described the tragic history of the Mountain Meadows Massacre:[8]

When I entered the corral, I found the emigrants engaged in burying two men of note among them, who had died but a short time before from the effect of wounds received by them from the Indians at the time of the first attack on Tuesday morning. They wrapped the bodies up in buffalo robes, and buried them in a grave inside the corral. I was then told by some of the men that seven men were killed and seventeen others were wounded at the first attack made by the Indians, and that three of the wounded men

---

[8] John D. Lee, *Mormonism Unveiled; or the Life and Confessions of the Late Mormon Bishop, John D. Lee* (St. Louis, 1877), pp. 239–242.

had since died, making ten of their number killed during the siege.

As I entered the fortifications, men, women and children gathered around me in wild consternation. Some felt that the time of their happy deliverance had come, while others, though in deep distress, and all in tears, looked upon me with doubt, distrust and terror. My feelings at this time may be imagined (but I doubt the power of man being equal to even imagine how wretched I felt.) No language can describe my feelings. My position was painful, trying and awful; my brain seemed to be on fire; my nerves were for a moment unstrung; humanity was overpowered, as I thought of the cruel, unmanly part that I was acting. Tears of bitter anguish fell in streams from my eyes; my tongue refused its office; my faculties were dormant, stupefied and deadened by grief. I wished that the earth would open and swallow me where I stood. God knows my suffering was great. I cannot describe my feelings. I knew that I was acting a cruel part and doing a damnable deed. Yet my faith in the godliness of my leaders was such that it forced me to think that I was not sufficiently spiritual to act the important part I was commanded to perform. My hesitation was only momentary. Then feeling that duty compelled *obedience to orders*, I laid aside my weakness and my humanity, and became an instrument in the hands of my superiors and my leaders. I delivered my message and told the people that they must put their arms in the wagon, so as not to arouse the animosity of the Indians. I ordered the children and wounded, some clothing and the arms, to be put into the wagons. Their guns were mostly Kentucky rifles of the muzzle-loading style. Their ammunition was about all gone—I do not think there were twenty loads left in their whole camp. If the emigrants had had a good supply of ammunition they never would have surrendered, and I do not think we could have captured them without great loss, for they were brave men and very resolute and determined.

Just as the wagons were loaded, Dan. McFarland came riding into the corral and said that Major Higbee had ordered great haste to be made, for he was afraid that the Indians would return and renew the attack before he could get the emigrants to a place of safety.

I hurried up the people and started the wagons off towards Cedar City. As we went out of the corral I ordered the wagons to turn to the left, so as to leave the troops to the right of us. Dan. McFarland rode before the women and led them right up to the troops, where they still stood in open order as I left them. The women and larger children were walking ahead, as directed, and the men following them. The foremost man was about fifty yards behind the hindmost woman.

The women and children were hurried right on by the troops. When the men came up they cheered the soldiers as if they believed that they were acting honestly. Higbee then gave the orders for his men to form in single file and take their places as ordered before, that is, at the right of the emigrants.

I saw this much, but about this time our wagons passed out of sight of the troops, over the hill. I had disobeyed orders in part by turning off as I did, for I was anxious to be out of sight of the bloody deed that I knew was to follow. I knew that I had much to do yet that was of a cruel and unnatural character. It was my duty, with the two drivers, to kill the sick and wounded who were in the wagons, and to do so when we heard the guns of the troops fire. I was walking between the wagons; the horses were going in a fast walk, and we were fully half a mile from Major Higbee and his men, when we heard the firing. As we heard the guns, I ordered a halt and we proceeded to do our part.

I here pause in the recital of this horrid story of man's inhumanity, and ask myself the question, Is it honest in me, and can I clear my conscience before my God, if I screen myself while I accuse others? No, never! Heaven forbid that I should put a burden upon others' shoulders, that I am unwilling to bear my just portion of. I am not a traitor to my people, nor to my former friends and comrades who were with me on that dark day when the work of death was carried on in God's name, by a lot of deluded and religious fanatics. It is my duty to tell facts as they exist, and I will do so.

I have said that all of the small children were put into the wagons; that was wrong, for one little child, about six months old, was carried in its father's arms, and it was killed by the same bullet that entered its father's breast; it was shot through the head. I was told by Haight afterwards, that the child was killed by accident, but I cannot say whether that is a fact or not. I saw it lying dead when I returned to the place of slaughter.

When we had got out of sight, as I said before, and just as we were coming into the main road, I heard a volley of guns at the place where I knew the troops and emigrants were. Our teams were then going at a fast walk. I first heard one gun, then a volley at once followed.

McMurdy and Knight stopped their teams at once, for they were ordered by Higbee, the same as I was, to help kill all the sick and wounded who were in the wagons, and to do it as soon as they heard the guns of the troops. McMurdy was in front; his wagon was mostly loaded with the arms and small children. McMurdy and Knight got out of their wagons; each one had a rifle. McMurdy went up to Knight's wagon, where the sick and wounded were, and raising his rifle to his shoulder, said: "*O Lord, my God, receive their spirits, it is for thy Kingdom that I do this.*" He then shot a man who was lying with his head on another man's breast; the ball killed both men.

I also went up to the wagon, intending to do my part of the killing. I drew my pistol and cocked it, but somehow it went off prematurely, and I shot McMurdy across the thigh, my pistol ball cutting his buck-skin pants. McMurdy turned to me and said:

"Brother Lee, keep cool, you are excited; you came very near killing me. Keep cool, there is no reason for being excited."

Knight then shot a man with his rifle; he shot the man in the head. Knight also brained a boy that was about fourteen years old. The boy came running up to our wagons, and Knight struck him on the head with the butt end of his gun, and crushed his skull. By this time many Indians reached our wagons, and all of the sick and wounded were killed almost instantly. I saw an Indian from Cedar City, called Joe, run up to the wagon and catch a man by the hair, and raise his head up and look into his face; the man shut his eyes, and Joe shot him in the head. The Indians then examined all of the wounded in the wagons, and all of the bodies, to see if any were alive, and all that showed signs of life were at once shot through the head. I did not kill any one there, but it was an accident that kept me from it, for I fully intended to do my part of the killing, but by the time I got over the excitement of coming so near killing McMurdy, the whole of the killing of the wounded was done. There is no truth in the statement of Nephi Johnson, where he says I cut a man's throat.

Just after the wounded were all killed I

saw a girl, some ten or eleven years old, running towards us, from the direction where the troops had attacked the main body of emigrants; she was covered with blood. An Indian shot her before she got within sixty yards of us. That was the last person that I saw killed on that occasion.

THE MORMON WAR OF 1857

Had the American army entered the valley when passions were inflamed by the Mountain Meadows Massacre, a mass slaughter would almost certainly have occurred. Fortunately the troops were delayed, largely by Mormon bands that burned the grass needed for fodder, and wintered east of the Wasatch Range. Terror still stalked the valley in the Spring, as preparations were made for the coming of the soldiers. Everywhere Saints packed their belongings and prepared to flee southward, even into Mexico if necessary, to escape capture. The diary of John Pulsipher, a young soldier who stood guard that winter on the Wasatch barrier and then returned home to sense the panic that prevailed there, gives an accurate picture of the emotional tensions that persisted in the Mormon community:[9]

Thursday 3 We arose from our wet blankets & beds of snow so cold we could not sleep so packed up & started eating a bit of frozen bread as we walked along the icy path—making ten miles before daylight over little Mountain & so on into town passing the Governors office about 11 o'clock. The governor Bro. Brigham came out & viewed us as we past looking very clever and good. We were halted on the Temple Block—after a short speech & the Lords blessing on us we were dismissed to the hands of majors who marched the battalions to the wards where they lived—When we were dismissed, took baggage from wagon & were soon at home & found folks well.

The Lord has accepted our offering has confused & stopped our enemies & we have not had to kill them or even fire a gun at them but we have showed them that we would stand for our rights, & would not submit to such unlawful & unjust demands as they were determined to force upon us.

Brother Brigham has written to them showing the unjust & unconstitutional course government is taking in making war on us without a cause—yet it was of no effect —they were determined we would not let them in with their present hostile feelings to kill or drive us from our homes as in the past.

I went right to work on Fathers farm repairing fences getting out manure & etc. & hauling fire wood from the Mountains.

By the first week in March I had about 20 acres of wheat oats & barley put in Bro. Wm. was with me some of the time.

About this time, Bro. Brigham proclaimed to the people that it was the will of the Lord that we should move Southward. All the Settlements north of Utah Valley.

The policy was to get the people nearer together so they could be defended & the cuntry could be desolated behind us & we then are ready if U.S. does reenforce the army & determine on a big war.

I had made my calculations to go into farming quite largely for one of my size but with me as with others—individual plans much change when the public good requires

---

[9] Reprinted by permission of the publishers, The Arthur H. Clark Company, from "Diary of John Pulsipher" in *The Utah Expedition, 1857–1858,* edited by LeRoy R. Hafen and Ann W. Hafen. Pp. 211–214.

it. So we are very willing to leave our homes —& to our tents again. . . .

The U.S. army East of us have wintered very well, & are threatening to come upon us & make a final end of all that will not join them. Truly this is a trying time—Destruction stares us in the face which ever way we turn—They that have not the holy Ghost the comforter in them, are beginning to tremble. The prophet Brigham is as calm as if there was no danger—says *move South & see the Salvation of God*. And almost the entire people say Amen to it & are as happy as were the children of Israel led by Moses, anciently when they passed thru the red Sea.

April 6 This is the birthday of the Church. The U.S. Army are preparing to make a start for the Valley so it is necessary for us to be ready to stop them. I met with the Nauvoo Legion at 8:O'clock—attended Drill & inspection of arms, & at 11:O'clock the Legion marched into the Tabernacle where the women & children & a few men were holding Conference—When we were seated Br. Brigham arose & spoke about an hour—felt first rate—perfectly satisfied as to the triumph of Israel.

Said it is all I can do to hold back from killing those Infernal scoundrels out yonder at Bridger, sent by Government to destroy this people. Pres. Buchanan has violated his oath of office in sending that army against us, as peaceable citizens as are in the union.

They are determined not to pay us one dime of what they owe us—But are paying thousands & hundreds of thousands of dollars to hire the Indians to kill us.

I need a breeching as strong as that of Dutch harness to enable me to hold back from killing every Devil of that army—But it is best to hold back & let them whip themselves. It is the will of the Lord that we leave this city & the north country—Move south—& if our enemies come upon us, when we are doing all we can to get away we will send them to hell across lots—& if they hire the Indians to help them, we are good for all of them. AMEN.

At 12 o'clock the Legion Paraded again & men were selected to go to the Mountains & keep the army from coming upon us before we could get the families moved away—I was one of the number chosen to go.

Ten men have been between us & the enemy thru the winter—relieved once in two weeks now as spring has come & the enemy are preparing to come—a stronger guard is needed.

We have to go on foot as the snow is too deep to get teams over the Mountains yet our packs were of considerable size—arms—ammunition—blankets & provisions—my bundle weighed fifty 50 pounds.

April 7 I left my wife on the farm alone to take care of two little children, four horses, a few head of cattle & four cows to milk.

I leave them in care of the Lord & shouldered my pack & started thru mud then climbing over Mountains wallowing thro deep snow—then mud again—then wading the rushing streams of cold water or crawling along the brushey steeps to avoid the crossing of the crooked stream.

The enforced armistice during the winter of 1857–1858 allowed peacemakers to do their work. One especially, a private citizen named Thomas L. Kane who was respected by Mormons and Gentiles alike, talked with both parties and convinced Brigham Young to accept a Washington-appointed governor for the territory providing troops did not enter the valley. Thus ended the tragic and useless "Mormon War." Gradually the Saints who had fled southward drifted back to their homes. Bitterness persisted on both sides, and conflict between Mormons and civilian authorities sent from Washington remained a fact of life for another generation. Fortunately, the federal officials named to govern the territory were wise enough to realize that Brigham Young alone could control the Saints, and allowed him to do so. Under his capable direction the settlements expanded to embrace most of the usable areas of the Great Basin country, as Utah passed from the frontier stage to become a new nucleus of western civilization.

CHAPTER 23 | *The Mining Frontier, 1849-1876*

Despite migration to Oregon, California, and the Great Basin, only a handful of Americans were in the Far West at the close of the war with Mexico. This was understandable. The vast distances to be bridged between the Mississippi Valley frontier and the fertile coastal or mountain valleys and the hazards and expense of the journey deterred all but the boldest pioneers. Before the West could lure more than a token population, some additional attracting force must operate. This magnet was gold. From the January day in 1848 when dust and nuggets were found in California's American River until the 1870s when prospectors overran the Black Hills of South Dakota, precious metals touched off a series of "rushes" that filled the West's most remote areas with permanent settlers. The advance of the mining frontier—first westward with the rush of the forty-niners to California and then eastward from that state over the entire mountain West—speeded the peopling of the Far West as did no other event in history.

THE DISCOVERY OF CALIFORNIA GOLD

The individual whose happenstance discovery set this chain of events in motion was a "queer old codger" named James W. Marshall. His employer, Captain John A. Sutter, sent Marshall to the foothills of the Sierra Nevada Mountains during the winter of 1847–1848 to supervise the building of a sawmill on the American River. Tests showed that the first designs were faulty; the millrace would have to be deepened by flowing water through it before the wheel could be installed. Marshall, a decade later, in an account more notable for its color than its accuracy, recalled this operation and its aftermath:[1]

While we were in the habit at night of turning the water through the tail race we had dug for the purpose of widening and deepening the race, I used to go down in the morning to see what had been done by the water through the night; and about half past seven o'clock on or about the 19th of January—I am not quite certain to a day, but it was between the 18th and 20th of that month—1848, I went down as usual, and after shutting off the water from the race I stepped into it, near the lower end, and there, upon the rock, about six inches beneath the surface of the water, I DISCOVERED THE GOLD. I was entirely alone at the time. I picked up one or two pieces and examined them attentively; and having some general

---

[1] *Hutchings' California Magazine*, II (November, 1857), 200–201.

knowledge of minerals, I could not call to mind more than two which in any way resembled this—*sulphuret of iron,* very bright and brittle; and *gold,* bright, yet malleable; I then tried it between two rocks, and found that it could be beaten into a different shape, but not broken. I then collected four or five pieces and went up to Mr. Scott (who was working at the carpenter's bench making the mill wheel) with the pieces in my hand, and said, "I have found it."

"What is it?" inquired Scott.

"Gold," I answered.

"Oh! no," returned Scott, "that can't be."

I replied positively,—"I know it to be nothing else."

Mr. Scott was the second person who saw the gold. W.J. Johnston, A. Stephens, H. Bigler, and J. Brown, who were also working in the mill yard, were then called up to see it. Peter L. Wimmer, Mrs. Jane Wimmer, C. Bennet, and J. Smith, were at the house; the latter two of whom were sick; E. Persons and John Wimmer, (a son of P. L. Wimmer), were out hunting oxen at the same time. About 10 o'clock the same morning, P. L. Wimmer came down from the house, and was very much surprised at the discovery, when the metal was shown him; and which he took home to show his wife, who, the next day, made some experiments upon it by boiling it in strong lye, and saleratus; and Mr. Bennet by my dirertions beat it very thin.

Four days afterwards I went to the Fort for provisions, and carried with me about three ounces of the gold, which Capt. Sutter and I tested with *nitric acid.* I then tried it in Sutter's presence by taking three silver dollars and balancing them by the dust in the air, then immersed both in water, and the superior weight of the gold satisfied us both of its nature and value.

About the 20th of February, 1848, Capt. Sutter came to Coloma, for the first time, to consummate an agreement we had made with this tribe of Indians in the month of September previous, to wit:—that we live with them in peace, on the same land.

About the middle of April the mill commenced operation, and, after cutting a few thousand feet of lumber was abandoned; as all hands were intent upon gold digging.

SPREAD OF THE GOLD FEVER IN CALIFORNIA

Sutter tried to keep the discovery a secret, but as well curb the whirlwind. As the news swept California's coastal cities, the gold fever spread. By the end of May the whole countryside was infected with the fatal malady. At San Francisco, at Sonoma, at Santa Cruz and San José, men dropped their tools or deserted their jobs to rush for the gold fields. The excitement at Monterey was captured by John Colton, that town's sophisticated alcalde, in his diary:[2]

Tuesday, June 20 My messenger sent to the mines, has returned with specimens of the gold; he dismounted in a sea of upturned faces. As he drew forth the yellow lumps from his pockets, and passed them around among the eager crowd, the doubts, which had lingered till now, fled. All admitted they were gold, except one old man, who still persisted they were some Yankee invention, got up to reconcile the people to the change of flag. The excitement produced was intense; and many were soon busy in their hasty preparations for a departure to the mines. The family who had kept house for me caught the moving infection. Husband and wife were both packing up; the blacksmith dropped his

---

[2] Walter Colton, *Three Years in California* (New York, 1850), pp. 246–249.

hammer, the carpenter his plane, the mason his trowel, the farmer his sickle, the baker his loaf, and the tapster his bottle. All were off for the mines, some on horses, some on carts, and some on crutches, and one went in a litter. An American woman, who had recently established a boarding-house here, pulled up stakes, and was off before her lodgers had even time to pay their bills. Debtors ran, of course. I have only a community of women left, and a gang of prisoners, with here and there a soldier, who will give his captain the slip at the first chance. I don't blame the fellow a whit; seven dollars a month, while others are making two or three hundred a day! that is too much for human nature to stand.

Saturday, July 15 The gold fever has reached every servant in Monterey; none are to be trusted in their engagement beyond a week, and as for compulsion, it is like attempting to drive fish into a net with the ocean before them. Gen. Mason, Lieut. Lanman, and myself, form a mess; we have a house and all the table furniture and culinary apparatus requisite; but our servants have run, one after another, till we are almost in despair: even Sambo, who we thought would stick by from laziness, if no other cause, ran last night; and this morning, for the fortieth time, we had to take to the kitchen, and cook our own breakfast. A general of the United States Army, the commander of a man-of-war, and the Alcalde of Monterey, in a smoking kitchen, grinding coffee, toasting a herring, and pealing onions! These gold mines are going to upset all the domestic arrangements of society, turning the head to the tail, and the tail to the head. Well, it is an ill wind that blows nobody any good: the nabobs have had their time, and now comes that of the "niggers." We shall all live just as long, and be quite as fit to die.

Tuesday, July 18 Another bag of gold from the mines, and another spasm in the community. It was brought down by a sailor from Yuba river, and contains a hundred and thirty-six ounces. It is the most beautiful gold that has appeared in the market; it looks like the yellow scales of the dolphin, passing through his rainbow hues at death. My carpenters, at work on the school-house, on seeing it, threw down their saws and planes, shouldered their picks, and are off for the Yuba. Three seamen ran from the Warren, forfeiting their four years' pay; and a whole platoon of soldiers from the fort left only their colors behind. One old woman declared she would never again break an egg or kill a chicken, without examining yolk and gizzard.

GOLD PROPAGANDA REACHES THE EAST

Californians succumbed overnight to the gold virus, but the rest of the nation caught the infection more slowly. News of the discovery reached the East in a letter published in the "New York Herald" on August 19, 1848. Other stories followed, each more extravagant than the last; dispatches told of miners who scooped up gold by the bucketful, of a single mine that paid its owners $20,000 in six days, of children who made their fortunes by a turn of a shovel. Tall tales such as these were not apt to encourage complacency, and as they were repeated over and over again in the press during the autumn of 1848 a sizable segment of the population abandoned all sanity. Typical was a letter from Monterey published in a Washington newspaper that September:[3]

---

[3] *Daily Union* (Washington, D.C.), September 22, 1848. Reprinted in Ralph P. Bieber (ed.), *Southern Trails to California in 1849*, "Southwest Historical Series" (Glendale, Calif.: The Arthur H. Clark Co., 1937), pp. 90–92.

MONTEREY, UPPER CALIFORNIA,
JULY 3, 1848

DEAR SIR:

In my last letter I gave you some account of the mineral wealth of California. Silver, quicksilver, lead, and zinc have been found in our mountains, and now it has been discovered that the sands which lie along Feather river, on the American Fork, branches of the Sacramento, are richly impregnated with gold. It is found in a shape resembling snowflakes and is washed from the sand with great ease. A person with a basin or bowl will wash out from one to two ounces a day. Some who have been more fortunate in the selection of their spots, have more than quadrupled this amount. There is a man in Monterey who washed out five hundred dollars' worth in six days. Everybody is now going or gone to this gold region. Some thousands are on the spot and more are on the way. All Oregon, as soon as the news reaches there, will be down upon us. You can hardly hire a laborer here for $10 a day, and on the gold river he charges $50. Mechanics, lawyers, and doctors have all left for the gold region. Soldiers run from their camps, sailors from their decks, and women from their nurseries; their cradles answer for machines to wash out gold. San Francisco, Sonoma, Santa Cruz, and San José are deserted of their inhabitants, and the mass is beginning to move from Monterey. I shall soon be in the condition of a colonel with his regiment disbanded. The tract of country in which the gold is found extends over a hundred miles in one direction and some forty in the other. It is supposed that ten thousand persons might work for years and not exhaust it. As yet they have worked only on the margin of the streams, on account of its convenience to the water; but gold has been found leagues distant and even on the mountains. Bowls and basins have been in great demand among the gold washers. Tin pans have found a ready sale at $8 each; shovels at $10; a trough scooped out of a log, with a willow sieve on it, $100; and boards at the rate of $500 for a thousand feet. The price of board on the gold streams is $3 a day. For this the boarder gets coarse bread, beef, and beans, a tree to sleep under, and an owl to hoot in his ear at night. The gold is sold here for $14 the ounce and is worth $18 at any mint. I know a little boy only twelve years of age who washes out his ounce of gold a day, while his mother makes root beer and sells it at a dollar a bottle.

The fighting is all over with us here; people have no time to pick their flints; they are too much engrossed in picking for gold. This placer was discovered some time since by a Mormon but kept a secret till May last, when the golden chicken burst its shell; and [it] is now a full-grown cock, whose crowing has woke up all California and will yet disturb the slumbers of other lands. The El Dorado of fiction never prompted dreams that revelled in gold like the streams which shout their way from the mountains of California. They roll with an exulting bound, as if conscious that their pathway was paved with gold.

MINING TECHNIQUES

Such propaganda had its inevitable effect, and by mid-winter the rush of the forty-niners had begun. First to leave were those who could afford to purchase passage on ships bound for California around the Horn or via the Panama route; far more followed that spring as some 50,000 would-be miners crowded the overland trails. In all, nearly 80,000 persons spread themselves over the mother lode country that year, searching every stream and canyon of the Sierra's western foothills for the glint of yellow metal. Few knew mining techniques, but they learned quickly from Mexicans and Australians who were already schooled in the use of the "washing pan," the "cradle," the "sluice box," and more sophisticated devices for extracting precious metals from sand and gravel. The evolution of their techniques was described by Mrs. Louise A. K. S. Clappe, one of the most literate observers of the California scene, whose "Shirley Letters" were first printed in "The Pioneer: or California Monthly Magazine" during 1854 and 1855:[4]

Having got our gold-mines discovered and claimed, I will try to give you a faint idea of how they work them. Here, in the mountains, the labor of excavation is extremely difficult, on account of the immense rocks which form a large portion of the soil. Of course no man can work out a claim alone. For that reason, and also for the same that makes partnerships desirable, they congregate in companies of four or six, generally designating themselves by the name of the place from whence the majority of the members have emigrated; as, for example, the Illinois, Bunker Hill, Bay State, etc., companies. In many places the surface soil, or in mining phrase, the top dirt, pays when worked in a long-tom. This machine (I have never been able to discover the derivation of its name) is a trough, generally about twenty feet in length and eight inches in depth, formed of wood, with the exception of six feet at one end, called the "riddle" (query, why "riddle"?), which is made of sheet-iron perforated with holes about the size of a large marble. Underneath this colanderlike portion of the long-tom is placed another trough, about ten feet long, the sides six inches, perhaps, in height, which, divided through the middle by a slender slat, is called the riffle-box. It takes several persons to manage properly a long-tom. Three or four men station themselves with spades at the head of the machine, while at the foot of it stands an individual armed "wid de shovel an' de hoe." The spadesmen throw in large quantities of the precious dirt, which is washed down to the riddle by a stream of water leading into the long-tom through wooden gutters or sluices. When the soil reaches the riddle, it is kept constantly in motion by the man with the hoe. Of course, by this means, all the dirt and gold escapes through the perforations into the riffle-box below, one compartment of which is placed just beyond the riddle. Most of the dirt washes over the sides of the rifflebox, but the gold, being so astonishingly heavy, remains safely at the bottom of it. When the machine gets too full of stones to be worked easily, the man whose business it is to attend to them throws them out with his shovel, looking carefully among them as he does so for any pieces of gold which may have been too large to pass through the holes of the riddle. I am sorry to say that he generally loses his labor. At night they pan out the gold which has been collected in the riffle-box during the day. Many of the miners decline washing the top dirt at all, but try to reach as quickly as possible the bedrock, where are found the richest deposits of gold. The river is supposed to have formerly flowed over this bed-rock, in the crevices of which it left, as it passed away, the largest portions of the so eagerly sought for ore. The group of mountains amidst which we are living is a spur of the Sierra Nevada, and the bed-rock, which in this vicinity is of slate, is said to run through the entire range, lying, in distance varying from a few feet to eighty or ninety, beneath the surface of the soil. On Indian Bar the bed-rock falls in almost perpendicular benches, while at Rich

---

[4] Louise A. K. S. Clappe, *The Shirley Letters from the California Mines in 1851–52* (San Francisco, 1922), pp. 213–217.

Bar the friction of the river has formed it into large, deep basins, in which the gold, instead of being found, as you would naturally suppose, in the bottom of it, lies, for the most part, just below the rim. A good-natured individual bored *me*, and tired *himself*, in a hopeless attempt to make me comprehend that this was only a necessary consequence of the undercurrent of the water, but with my usual stupidity upon such matters I got but a vague idea from his scientific explanation, and certainly shall not mystify *you* with my confused notions thereupon.

When a company wish to reach the bedrock as quickly as possible, they sink a shaft (which is nothing more nor less than digging a well) until they "strike it." They then commence drifting coyote-holes, as they call them, in search of crevices, which, as I told you before, often pay immensely. These coyote-holes sometimes extend hundreds of feet into the side of the hill. Of course they are obliged to use lights in working them. They generally proceed until the air is so impure as to extinguish the lights, when they return to the entrance of the excavation and commence another, perhaps close to it. When they think that a coyote-hole has been faithfully worked, they clean it up, which is done by scraping the surface of the bed-rock with a knife, lest by chance they have overlooked a crevice, and they are often richly rewarded for this precaution.

THE RUSH TO THE FRASER RIVER MINES

Technological progress doomed the lone prospector; as capital flowed from the East and San Francisco into the mother lode country, heavy machinery replaced hand labor in building tunnels and crushing the quartz rock to extract the gold. While some miners stayed to operate this equipment, and more turned to farming or trade, thousands who were too badly infected with the gold fever to abandon prospecting swarmed out of California to search the entire Far West for mineral wealth. Most among this army of prospectors wandered in vain, but now and then one struck it rich. Whenever this occurred, a rush followed. One of the first major rushes was to the Fraser River country of British Columbia, where gold was discovered in the fall of 1857. The effect of this discovery on California's miners was described by a correspondent of the "London Times":[5]

Only a very inconsiderable quantity of gold has come down to San Francisco in the regular channels of trade—there have been but very trifling consignments, the bulk having come in private hands; but the paucity of consignments, although it has caused some suspicion of the truth of the reported wealth of the mines in the mind of the more cautious (I must confess a small class with us), yet the stories of what was seen and heard, and could be earned, have sufficed to unhinge the masses, and to produce an excitement which results in an unparalleled exodus.

From the 1st of this month till to-day (June 17th), seven sailing vessels and four steamers have left San Francisco, all for the new mines. They all went to Victoria except two of the sailing vessels, which went to Port Townsend and Bellingham Bay, but the final destination of all was the same,—'Frazer River.' All took passengers in crowds. One of the steamers carried away 1000 per-

---

[5] Letter of *London Times* correspondent, dated at San Francisco June 16, 1858 and printed in William C. Hazlitt, *British Columbia and Vancouver Island* (London, 1858), pp. 146–148.

sons, and another upwards of 1200, and multitudes are left behind waiting for the next departure. There are still thirteen vessels on the berth for the same destination, all filling with passengers and goods. One of these is a steamer, five of them are large clippers, three ships of considerable size, and the rest barks, brigs, and schooners, so that if the next news from the North is favourable this fleet will carry away a goodly crowd.

From San Francisco itself a great many have gone, and more are going. Common labourers, bricklayers, carpenters, printers, cabinet-makers, &c.—in short, all the mechanical arts are already represented in Vancouver's Island. Other classes go as well; in fact, the major portion whose interests can permit are going. People seem to have suddenly come to the conclusion that it is their fate to go. 'Going to Frazer's River?' 'Yes; oh, of course, I must go.' 'You going?' 'Yes, sir; I'm bound to go.' None are too poor and none too rich to go. None too young and none too old to go;—even the decrepit go. Many go with money, many go without; some to invest in 'real estate,' that arrant representative of humbug and swindling on this continent; some to see what may turn up—these are men cunning in the 'Micawber' theory; some out of curiosity, some to gamble, and some to steal, and, unquestionably, some to die.

Merchandize of all sorts, building materials, mules, and sundry necessaries to supply immediate wants, are, of course, being sent on in ample quantities. People of all nations are going. Men who can't speak a word of English are going, accompanied by interpreters.

This feverish state of the public mind cannot last long. As the rivers had risen so that the 'bars' could not be worked after the latter part of May, and as the waters will not abate till the beginning or middle of August, and as thousands of miners who went up without spare money are idle on the coast, we shall, no doubt, soon hear that many of them are dying of hunger. This will cool the ardour of many in this country.

The fares up by the steamers are—for the 'nobs' $60, and for the 'roughs' $30; the fare so so; and the attendance and other comforts can easily be guessed when I state that the decks of the steamer which I left to-day were so crowded with passengers that it was almost impossible to move through them. I suppose the waiters will have to fight their way when serving 'the quality.'

A gentleman who went down to the wharf and on board to see the sight, says the crush actually lifted him off the deck. It resembled a crowd at one of the London theatres on a 'star' night. The paper of to-day says, 'She appeared perfectly black with human beings, crowded in every part of her when she drew away from the wharf.' Her proper complement is 800, and she would not be comfortable with more than 600 passengers. She took to-day 1600 'at least,' it is commonly said. Persons in the way of knowing the fact estimate that of the labourers in every class in the State, all the unemployed and one-half the employed have already gone.

CULTURAL CONFLICT ON THE FRASER RIVER

Mining on the Fraser River differed sharply from that in California, which was characterized by haphazard prospecting, lawless mining camps, and an almost total lack of government supervision. The Fraser River miners were strictly regulated by an efficient governmental organization under the direction of James Douglas, governor of the crown colony of British Columbia. Each miner was forced to pay a monthly license fee of $5 and to conform with correct standards of behavior, which were enforced by a "gold commissioner" in each camp. This unaccustomed regulation aroused American miners there to near rebellion. Their spokesman was Isaac J. Stevens, the delegate to Congress from Washington Territory, who on July 21, 1858, addressed a letter to Secretary of State Lewis Cass demanding that the United States force Britain to abandon its licensing system. This unusual document mirrored the belief of American miners that gold should be available to all comers and that the government should keep a strictly hands-off attitude:[6]

The object of the present communication is to exhibit to the government of the United States the enormity and absolute illegality of the impositions placed upon the citizens of the United States by the British authorities assuming to exercise jurisdiction over the whole territory in which the late gold discoveries have been made, and to ask the interposition of the government in behalf of our citizens seeking to enter that territory.

On the 28th of December, 1857, his Excellency James Douglas, styling himself Governor of Vancouver's Island and its dependencies, issued a proclamation declaring that all mines of gold in its natural place of deposit within the districts of Frazer River and of Thompson River, belong to the crown of Great Britain, and that no person will be permitted to dig, search for, or remove gold on or from any lands, public or private (within said district), without first taking out and paying for a license in the form annexed.

The form of license annexed is as follows:

---

[6] Kinahan Cornwallis, *The New Eldorado; or, British Columbia* (London, 1858), pp. 322–324, 326–327.

The bearer having paid to me the sum of twenty-one shillings on account of the territorial revenue, I hereby license him to dig, search for, and remove gold on and from any such crown land within the —— of —— as I shall assign to him for that purpose during the month of ——, 185—.

This license must be produced whenever demanded by me or any other person acting under the authority of the government.

A. B., Commissioner

On the 8th of May, 1858, Governor Douglas issued the following proclamation:

Proclamation

By his Excellency James Douglas, Governor and Commander-in-Chief of the colony of Vancouver's Island and its dependencies, and Vice Admiral of the same, &c. &c.

Whereas it is commonly reported that certain boats and other vessels have entered Frazer River for trade; and whereas, there is reason to apprehend that other persons are preparing and fitting out boats and vessels for the same purpose.

Now, therefore, I have issued this my proclamation, warning all persons that such acts are contrary to law, and infringements upon the rights of the Hudson's Bay Company, who are legally entitled to trade with the Indians in the British possessions on the north-west coast of America, to the exclusion of all other persons, whether British or foreign.

And also that after fourteen days from the date of this, my proclamation, all ships, boats, and vessels, together with the goods laden on board found in Frazer River, or in any of the bays, rivers, or creeks of the said British possessions on the north-west coast of America, not having a license from the Hudson's Bay Company, and a sufferance from the proper officer of the Customs at

Victoria, shall be liable to forfeiture, and will be seized and condemned according to law.

Given under my hand and seal at Government House, Victoria, this eighth day of May, in the year of our Lord one thousand eight hundred and fifty-eight, and in the twenty-first of her Majesty's reign.

James Douglas, Governor....

I have no hesitation in declaring this opinion, that these proclamations have been made without any legal or binding authority which should be respected by the citizens or government of the United States.

The two important questions presented are, the authority of the Governor of Vancouver's Island to impose a tax of twenty-one shillings per month upon every person searching for gold on Frazer or Thompson Rivers, and the right to compel all persons in those territories to purchase their supplies from the Hudson's Bay Company. The first question which I propose to consider is the right to impose the tax, and demand a license....

The late discoveries in Siberia, California, and Australia, have shown that the most extensive deposits of gold are not in mines proper, but are diffused through the soil. Mines proper, in which it was anciently supposed gold was to be found, being entered by simple shafts, and developed by adits and levels beneath the ground, could be worked without disturbing the superficial soil. The enjoyment of the ancient prerogative of the crown in the "gold placers" would be totally inconsistent with private rights in the soil, and from consideration of public policy cannot be exercised in such "placers."

The crown undoubtedly possesses the right to prohibit or regulate by law the digging for gold in its possessions, just as it might prohibit or regulate by law the cutting of timber or using the soil; but in the absence of positive law prohibiting such occupation and use, it is believed to be the natural right of every man who enters a totally unoccupied country, to cut timber and wood, to consume the fruits of the earth, and gather all the products of the soil, which have not before been appropriated. It is believed that, while the jurisdiction simply of the British crown over the territory of Frazer and Thompson Rivers is not questioned, the crown has made no appropriation of that territory by law, and has exercised no acts restricting the natural rights of man in a wild and unoccupied country. Until the passage of such positive laws by proper authority, every man possesses the right to dig gold in that country, just as much as he has the right to cut timber or appropriate the fruits of the earth.

It is further believed that the acts of Governor Douglas, before referred to, in no respect constitute a legal and authorized prohibition to enter the gold-bearing country of New Caledonia, and that his demand of payment of money for a license to dig gold is a high-handed usurpation of power.

THE COMSTOCK LODE

The Fraser River boom collapsed within a few months, as American miners fled to escape overregulation and as the river's sand bars were robbed of their gold, but by this time attention was focused on a more promising site. Early in 1859, prospectors on the slopes of Mount Davidson in western Nevada stumbled on one of the richest mining finds in history: the Comstock Lode. Ore taken to California for assay proved to be worth $3876 a ton, an unbelievable figure. The inevitable rush followed to Virginia City, a ramshackle mining camp that mushroomed near the lode. A few experienced miners with capital quickly monopolized the gold-bearing rocks of the Comstock—and were soon to become multimillionaires. Thousands of others had nothing to do but prospect in nearby ravines for another gold-bearing vein, or to trade "feet" in untested mining claims for other "feet" in equally unproven mines. "Washoe," as the district was called, was peopled for a time by penniless millionaires, all living in a dream world that might be realized—or shattered—when mining machinery was imported. This intoxicating atmosphere was captured by a visiting journalist, J. Ross Browne, who described the camp and its inhabitants:[7]

On a slope of mountains speckled with snow, sage-bushes, and mounds of upturned earth, without any apparent beginning or end, congruity or regard for the eternal fitness of things, lay outspread the wondrous city of Virginia.

Frame shanties, pitched together as if by accident; tents of canvas, of blankets, of brush, of potato-sacks and old shirts, with empty whisky barrels for chimneys; smoky hovels of mud and stone; coyote holes in the mountain-side forcibly seized and held by men; pits and shafts with smoke issuing from every crevice; piles of goods and rubbish on craggy points, in the hollows, on the rocks, in the mud, in the snow, every where, scattered broadcast in pell-mell confusion, as if the clouds had suddenly burst overhead and rained down the dregs of all the flimsy, rickety, filthy little hovels and rubbish of merchandise that had ever undergone the process of evaporation from the earth since the days of Noah. The intervals of space, which may or may not have been streets, were dotted over with human beings of such sort, variety, and numbers that the famous ant-hills of Africa were as nothing in the comparison. To say that they were rough, muddy, unkempt and unwashed, would be but faintly expressive of their actual appearance; they were all this by reason of exposure to the weather; but they seemed to have caught the very diabolical tint and grime of the whole place. Here and there, to be sure, a San Francisco dandy of the "boiled shirt" and "stove-pipe" pattern loomed up in proud consciousness of the triumphs of art under adverse circumstances; but they were merely peacocks in the barn-yard.

A fraction of the crowd, as we entered the precincts of the town, were engaged in a lawsuit relative to a question of title. The arguments used on both sides were empty whisky-bottles, after the fashion of the *Basilinum*, or club law, which, according to Addison, prevailed in the colleges of learned men in former times. Several of the disputants had already been knocked down and convinced, and various others were freely shedding their blood in the cause of justice. Even the bull-terriers took an active part—or, at least, a very prominent part. The difficulty was about the ownership of a lot, which had been staked out by one party and "jumped" by another. Some two or three hundred disinterested observers stood by, enjoying the spectacle, several of them with their hands on their revolvers, to be ready in case of any serious issue; but these dangerous weapons are only used on great occasions—a refusal to drink, or some illegitimate trick at monte.

Upon fairly reaching what might be considered the centre of the town, it was interesting to observe the manners and customs of the place. Groups of keen speculators were huddled around the corners, in earnest consultation about the rise and fall of stocks; rough customers, with red and blue flannel

---

[7] J. Ross Browne, "A Peep at Washoe," *Harper's New Monthly Magazine*, XXII (January, 1861), 154–156.

shirts, were straggling in from the Flowery Diggings, the Desert, and other rich points, with specimens of croppings in their hands, or offering bargains in the "Rogers," the "Lady Bryant," the "Mammoth," the "Woolly Horse," and Heaven knows how many other valuable *leads,* at prices varying from ten to seventy-five dollars a foot. Small knots of the knowing ones were in confidential interchange of thought on the subject of every other man's business; here and there a loose man was caught by the button, and led aside behind a shanty to be "stuffed;" every body had some grand secret, which nobody else could find out; and the game of "dodge" and "pump" was universally played. Jew clothing-men were setting out their goods and chattels in front of wretched-looking tenements; monte-dealers, gamblers, thieves, cut-throats, and murderers were mingling miscellaneously in the dense crowds gathered around the bars of the drinking saloons. Now and then a half-starved Pah-Ute or Washoe Indian came tottering along under a heavy press of fagots and whisky. On the main street, where the mass of the population were gathered, a jaunty fellow who had "made a good thing of it" dashed through the crowds on horseback, accoutred in genuine Mexican style, swinging his *reata* over his head, and yelling like a devil let loose. All this time the wind blew in terrific gusts from the four quarters of the compass, tearing away signs, capsizing tents, scattering the grit from the gravel-banks with blinding force in every body's eyes, and sweeping furiously around every crook and corner in search of some sinner to smite. Never was such a wind as this—so scathing, so searching, so given to penetrate the very core of suffering humanity; disdaining overcoats, and utterly scornful of shawls and blankets. It actually seemed to double up, twist, pull, push, and screw the unfortunate biped till his muscles cracked and his bones rattled—following him wherever he sought refuge, pursuing him down the back of the neck, up the coat-sleeves, through the legs of his pantaloons, into his boots—in short, it was the most villainous and persecuting wind that ever blew, and I boldly protest that it did nobody good.

Yet, in the midst of the general wreck and crash of matter, the business of trading in claims, "bucking," and "bearing" went on as if the zephyrs of Virginia were as soft and balmy as those of San Francisco.

This was surely— No matter; nothing on earth could aspire to competition with such a place. It was essentially infernal in every aspect, whether viewed from the Comstock Ledge or the summit of Gold Hill. Nobody seemed to own the lots except by right of possession; yet there was trading in lots to an unlimited extent. Nobody had any money, yet every body was a millionaire in silver claims. Nobody had any credit, yet every body bought thousands of feet of glittering ore. Sales were made in the Mammoth, the Lady Bryant, the Sacramento, the Winnebunk, and the innumerable other "outside claims," at the most astounding figures—but not a dime passed hands. All was silver underground, and deeds and mortgages on top; silver, silver every where, but scarce a dollar in coin. The small change had somehow gotten out of the hands of the public into the gambling saloons.

Every speck of ground covered by canvas, boards, baked mud, brush, or other architectural material, was jammed to suffocation; there were sleeping houses, twenty feet by thirty, in which from one hundred and fifty to two hundred solid sleepers sought slumber at night, at a dollar a head; tents, eight by ten, offering accommodations to the multitude; any thing or any place, even a stall in a stable, would have been a luxury.

The chief hotel, called, if I remember, the "Indication," or the "Hotel de Haystack," or some such euphonious name, professed to accommodate three hundred live men, and it doubtless did so, for the floors were covered from the attic to the solid earth—three hundred human beings in a tinder-box not bigger than a first-class hencoop! But they were sorry-looking sleepers as they came forth each morning, swearing at the evil genius who had directed them to this miserable spot—every man a dollar and a pound of flesh poorer. I saw some, who perhaps were short of means, take surreptitious naps against the posts and walls in the bar-room, while they ostensibly professed to be mere spectators.

In truth, wherever I turned there was much to confirm the forebodings with which I had entered the Devil's Gate. The deep pits on the hill-sides; the blasted and barren appearance of the whole country; the unsightly hodge-podge of a town; the horrible confusion of tongues; the roaring, raving drunkards at the bar-rooms, swilling fiery liquids from morning till night; the flaring and flaunting gambling-saloons, filled with desperadoes of the vilest sort; the ceaseless torrent of imprecations that shocked the ear on every side; the mad speculations and feverish thirst for gain—all combined to give me a forcible impression of the unhallowed character of the place.

THE RUSH OF THE "FIFTY-NINERS"

While a few shrewd capitalists were being enriched by the Comstock's wealth—which yielded more than $300,000,000 in gold and silver before being exhausted—the attention of the wandering army of prospectors was directed elsewhere. The Pike's Peak country lured them first; a party of experienced miners made the first strike in the Rocky Mountains in the spring of 1858 near modern Denver. This proved disappointing, but exaggerated rumors of rich "diggings" began reaching the Mississippi Valley, not losing in their telling by local editors. There they were believed, for the Panic of 1857 burdened the land and thousands upon thousands of the jobless were eager to grasp at any straw that promised better times. The result was the "Rush of the Fifty-niners" in the spring of 1859—a mass exodus of a hundred thousand souls. A Kansas City correspondent for the "Missouri Republican" described the excitement as they departed:[8]

Here they come by every steamboat, hundreds after hundreds from every place—Hoosiers, Suckers, Corn crackers, Buckeyes, Red-horses, Arabs and Egyptians—some with ox wagons, some with mules, but the greatest number on foot, with their knap-sacks and old-fashioned rifles and shot-guns; some with their long-tailed blues, others in jeans and bob-tailed jockeys; in their roundabouts, slouched hats, caps and sacks. There are a few hand-carts in the crowd. They form themselves into companies of ten, twenty, and as high as forty-five men have marched out, two-and-two, with a captain and clerk, eight men to a hand-cart, divided into four reliefs, two at a time pulling the cart, which contains all the provisions, camp equipments, working tools, et cetera, for the eight persons thus arranged. Onward they move, in solemn order, day after day, old and young, tall and slender, short and fat, handsome and ugly, the strong and the weak, the red-faced rumbruiser and the lean, lank Jonathan, with grimmage sour, striding among

---

[8] *Missouri Republican*, March 27, 1859. Reprinted in LeRoy R. Hafen (ed.), *Colorado Gold Rush. Contemporary Letters and Reports, 1858–1859*, "Southwest Historical Series" (Glendale, Calif.: The Arthur H. Clark Co., 1941), pp. 285–287.

saints and sinners, heads up and still upper lips, march forward as "lords of creation," and seeming "monarchs of all they survey." Nothing daunted, and nothing short of the trip will satisfy their mighty imaginations, air castles and visionary hopes of immense wealth they are to receive for their pains. Enthusiastic, merry, with light hearts and a thin pair of breeches, they calculate to accomplish all their fondest hopes. Many have sold out all their homes, all their valuables, to furnish themselves with an outfit for Pike's Peak mines. Others left their wives and children behind with no protecting arm or support but what Providence may give, and blindly rush headlong into the wild delusion of glittering sands full of golden eggs. 425 arrived on the *Alonzo Child* to-day.

The runners and drummers for hotels and express wagons are thick as hail, with the cry, "$40 for passage to Pike's Peak from here; charge $50 at Leavenworth." "Shortest route, best roads, fine eating houses, good camping grounds—only 550 miles." Some stop, while others go on to Leavenworth, and take the Junction City road. The city of Leavenworth is full of them, who tarry but a little while after landing, fall into line, and take their march onward, without expending a solitary dime. Most of them are entirely out of money, but their means are invested in the mess—their money is all to come from the mines. Poor deluded creatures, running after shadows and phantoms, and bitter will be their cup when riches have taken wings— out of provisions, away from home, sick, sore and disappointed, they look homeward to cheerful faces and happy little ones, and exclaim, "no balm in Gilead." Only think of 100,000 persons scattered over a few miles of territory, digging and tearing up the ground in search of wealth.

Eating greasy meat, sleeping on the cold ground, in rain, snow and hail, hot and cold, wet and dry—up early and late—striving like giants to turn upside down the earth for the sake of gain, away from the cheering hearthstone, joyous laugh and happy home, among wolves and savage beasts, working out their lives for naught, when, with one half that energy, industry and perseverence, at home on their farms, they would have full pockets, good health, be with their family and friends, enjoying happiness, comfort, and peace.

THE FIRST MAJOR COLORADO GOLD DISCOVERY

The fifty-niners found no pot of gold at the end of their rainbow; fully half of them lost heart and turned back before reaching the mountains, and almost none who remained in the Pike's Peak country discovered pay dirt. Yet seasoned prospectors knew that precious metals were there, and some continued to search. The turning point came in May 1859, when John H. Gregory made a rich strike on the North Branch of Clear Creek. The news of this find electrified the speculators and tradesmen who were waiting in the newly founded town of Denver for the discovery that would transform their hamlet into a city. Henry Villard, a visitor, described their reaction when they heard of the success at "Gregory Gulch":[9]

Thus affairs stood, when in the course of the afternoon of the second Sunday in May, we were seated in the log-house that then represented the express office, in company with Dr. J. M. Fox, the general agent of the Express Company, and Mr. Joseph Hey-

---

[9] Henry Villard, *The Past and Present of the Pike's Peak Gold Regions* (St. Louis, 1860), pp. 35–37.

wood, a well known Californian, and formerly resident of Cincinnati. The trio were just discussing the unpromising aspect of things, when a short, slender, heavily bearded individual, in miner's garb, entered the room and inquired for letters. He was invited to a seat, and soon got to talking about the resources of the country. Contrary to expectation, he seemed to believe firmly in its mineral wealth. Being asked for his experience in the mountains from which he claimed to have just arrived, he stated, after a few moments of apparent hesitation, that a little more than a week ago, while following up the North fork of Clear Creek, in company with John H. Gregory and several others, he had discovered gold-bearing dirt in the vicinity of streaks of quartz rock, that ran over the mountains, in a ravine adjoining the valley of the Creek. The dirt, he asserted, had yielded him as much as a dollar's worth of gold to the pan. Perceiving a manifestation of incredulity on the part of his listeners, he produced, in corroboration of his statement, a bottle containing about forty dollars' worth of flour gold, and also several fragments of a hard substance which he designated as decomposed gold-bearing quartz. Mr. Heywood stepped outdoors with one of the pieces for the purpose of examining it with a magnifying glass. He soon called out Dr. Fox, whom he told that the specimen he held in his hand was as fine quartz as he had seen in the richest quartz veins in California. Several persons having, in the meantime, entered the office and showing upon hearing the miner's tale, a disposition to doubt its truthfulness, the latter grew rather excited, repeated what he had said, and asserted most emphatically that he would warrant one dollar to the pan of dirt to any number of men that would follow him to the locality in question, and added that they might bring a rope along and swing him up in case he should be found a liar.

This was the first news of the discovery of the Gregory mines that reached us. Its bearer, who had come to the Cherry Creek towns for a new supply of provisions returned to the mountains on the following day, in company with several others, who intended to sift his story by a visit to the scene of the alleged discovery.

A few more dull days elapsed without throwing any further light on the subject, and the spark of hope kindled by the miner's apparently earnest story had nearly been lost sight of amidst the surrounding darkness, when on the fifth day a Mr. Bates, late of Dubuque, Iowa, made his appearance in Auraria with a vial full of gold, representing a value of about eighty dollars, which he claimed to have washed out of thirty-nine pans of dirt, obtained not far from the spot on which Gregory had made his discovery. Mr. Bates being known as a reliable man, his story was at once credited and he and his bottle taken from cabin to cabin. The sight of his gold forthwith produced an intense excitement, and the news of his luck spread like wild-fire and at once moved the hearts of the denizens of the two towns with gladdening sensations. Individuals could be heard every [where] on the streets shouting to each other, "We are all right now," "the stuff is here after all," "the country is safe," &c.

On the following day an universal exodus took place in the direction of North Clear Creek. Whoever could raise enough provisions for a protracted stay in the mountains, sallied out without delay. Traders locked up their stores; bar-keepers disappeared with their bottles of whiskey, the few mechanics that were busy building houses, abandoned their work, the county judge and sheriff, lawyers and doctors, and even the editor of the *Rocky Mountain News*, joined in the general rush.

EXCITEMENT IN THE MONTANA GOLD FIELDS

The find at Gregory diggings portended the future; over the next months and years a succession of discoveries launched the Rocky Mountain country on the road to enduring growth and prosperity. Gold was also the lodestone that peopled the northern Rockies, where the states of Idaho and Montana were to be carved from the wilderness. Prospectors from the Fraser River fields explored that region in 1860, making their first strike on the Clearwater River. Others followed, to establish the first permanent settlements in Idaho. The pioneers in Montana were James and Granville Stuart, who in 1862 prospected near the headwaters of the Missouri River. Their richest strike was in Alder Gulch, where the mining camp of Virginia City established an international reputation for its rip-roaring lawlessness. Granville Stuart described that nineteenth-century Gomorrah as it appeared when only a few months old, revealing as he did so the wild fever of excitement that infected most prospectors:[10]

The winter of 1863–64 was a mild one, building and mining operations were carried on with but little interruption all winter and before spring every branch of business was represented. Gold was coming out in large quantities. The district extended from the foot of Old Baldy to twelve miles down the creek. The bed of the creek and the bars on both sides were uniformly rich; the bed rock being literally paved with gold. The Alder gulch diggings were the richest gold placer diggings ever discovered in the world.

Freight teams from Salt Lake arrived until late in the fall, bringing in supplies; and while we were not provided with luxuries there was no suffering from food shortage. Molasses was considered by us, a great delicacy and it was both scarce and dear. Sam Hauser hit upon a plan all his own whereby he kept the only one gallon of molasses in our mess all to himself. Returning home one evening tired and hungry, we found Sam sitting at the table holding a mouse suspended by the tail: the little animal had every appearance of having been drowned in the molasses. Sam didn't say that he had taken the mouse from the molasses, we just reached that conclusion by inference and immediately lost our fondness for molasses—not so with Hauser—he continued to spread molasses on his bread every meal until it was all gone. One day, in an inquiring mood, he asked us why we all quit on molasses. James replied that he liked molasses but not well enough to eat it after a mouse had drowned in it: whereupon Hauser informed us that he had killed the mouse and smeared it with molasses later just to see how we would take it.

There was a great number of saloons and each dispenser of liquid refreshments had the formula for making "tanglefoot:"—a quantity of boiled mountain sage, two plugs tobacco steeped in water, box cayenne pepper, one gallon water; so if any one got low in whiskey he promptly manufactured more. Saloons, gambling houses, public dance halls (hurdy gurdies) ran wide open and here, as

---

[10] Reprinted by permission of the publishers, The Arthur H. Clark Company, from *Forty Years on the Frontier as Seen in the Journals and Reminiscences of Granville Stuart* edited by Paul C. Phillips. Vol. 1, pp. 264–266, 270–272.

in California, gold dust flowed in a yellow stream from the buckskin bags of the miners into the coffers of the saloons, dance halls, and gambling dens. Gold dust was the sole medium of exchange and it was reckoned at $18.00 an ounce. Every business house had gold scales for weighing the dust. If a man was under the influence of liquor, the bar keepers were not averse to helping themselves liberally to the man's dust, when paying himself for drinks and he more often took $1.00 for a drink than the going price of twenty-five cents. A dance at one of the hurdy gurdies cost one dollar and as each dance wound up with an invitation to visit the bar where drinks for self and partner were expected, the cost of a waltz, schottische, or quadrille was usually $1.50. Dances kept up all night long but were usually orderly. If a man was found to be getting too much under the influence of liquor, some obliging friend would expel him from the hall. Every sort of gambling game was indulged in and it was no uncommon thing to see one thousand dollars staked on the turn of a monte card. The miner who indulged in gambling usually worked six days, then cleaned up his dust; and placing it in a buckskin sack hied himself to the nearest gambling house where he remained until he had transferred the contents of the sack to the professional gambler. If he played in luck he could usually stay in the game twenty-four hours. He would then return to his "diggins" without money and often with little grub; a sadder but no wiser man, for he would repeat the same thing over and over as long as his claim lasted and would then start out, blankets on his back, in search of new "diggins". . . .

About the middle of January, 1864, a regular stampede craze struck Virginia City. The weather had been quite cold and work in the mines was temporarily suspended. A large number of idle men were about town and it required no more than one man with an imaginative mind to start half the population off on a wild goose chase. Somebody would say that somebody said, that somebody had found a good thing and without further inquiry a hundred or more men would start out for the reported diggings.

One report of a discovery on Gallatin river started a large party out in that direction. Every horse that could be found fit to ride was made ready. We had some horses on a ranch near town and brought them in and in less than an hour we had sold them all for about twice what they would have sold for at any other time. Four hundred men left town in mid-winter, with the ground covered with snow, for some place on the Gallatin river; no one seemed to know exactly where they were going, but most of them brought up at Gallatin City. Many, who could not get horses, started on foot. The first night out brought them to a realization of the futility of such a trip and they turned back.

Late in the evening on January 22, a rumor started that a big discovery had been made on Wisconsin creek, a distance of thirty miles from Virginia City. The report said that as much as one hundred dollars to the pan had been found; and away the people flew all anxious to be first on the ground, where they could "just shovel up gold." Virginia City was almost deserted: men did not stop for horses, blankets, or provisions, the sole aim was to get there first and begin to shovel it out at the rate of one hundred to the pan. Fortunately the distance was not great and the weather was mild. Robert Dempsey had a ranch nearby and the stampeders got a supply of beef from him to last them back to town. It is needless to say that they found no diggings and all returned to Virginia in a few days.

The next great excitement was caused by a rumor of new rich discoveries on Boulder creek, a branch of the Jefferson. We sold every horse that we would spare at about three times its real value. Reece Anderson was among those taken with the fever and he joined the expedition. He had a good saddle and pack horses and plenty of food and blankets. There were so many in this stampede who started with little or nothing that those who had good outfits were obliged to share food with those who had none to keep them from starving and in the long run those with good outfits did not fare much better than those who started with none. Our friend, Reece Anderson, returned in about two weeks without having found any big thing in the way of gold mines, but he had accumulated quite a valuable stock of experience and got his nose, ears, and fingers badly frost-bitten.

The next big excitement started right in town. Somebody reported a "find" at the edge of town and in the morning claims were being staked off the main streets and on the rear of all of our lots. One enthusiastic man began to sink a hole in the street, just above the store and it began to look like we would be dug up and washed out without ceremony. Of course there was no gold found and mining operations in the streets and back yards was soon suspended.

A grand stampede to the Prickley Pear valley in which more than six hundred people took part was the last of the season. Away they went, crossing the hills into Boulder valley. They found the snow very deep, but fortunately not cold. Some good mines had been discovered on one bar about six hundred feet long, but all good ground had been taken when the stampeders arrived. The little army of disappointed men turned around and returned home once more.

GOVERNMENTAL ORGANIZATION IN THE MINING CAMPS

The rapid spread of the mining frontier— even into the Black Hills of South Dakota where the last major mining rush took place in 1876— posed serious problems. How could claims be protected, criminals controlled, and property secured in a thinly settled backcountry peopled only by transient miners? Like all frontiersmen who had temporarily ventured beyond the protection of traditional law-enforcement agencies, the miners took matters into their own hands. No sooner was a new mining camp established than its occupants met, chose officers, and laid out a "district" over which they would exert control. Each district adopted elaborate rules governing the size of claims, mining techniques, and the administration of justice. Charles H. Shinn, a journalist who lived among the California miners, produced a classic work on mining camps that described the function of the districts as they first evolved:[11]

As regards the important question of the number of mining-districts which have been governed by local laws of their own devising, the United-States Reports on Mineral Resources state that in 1866 there were over five hundred organized districts in California, two hundred in Nevada, and one hundred each in Arizona, Idaho, and Oregon. There were, perhaps, fifty each in Montana, New Mexico, and Colorado. Here is a total of more than eleven hundred camps in the Far West, as late as 1866. Since then the number of districts has diminished in the older mining-regions, and increased in the newer ones; but State and National legisla-

---

[11] Charles H. Shinn, *Mining Camps. A Study in American Frontier Government* (New York, 1884), pp. 236–240.

tion has in a great degree restricted the field for local enactments. The number of actual placer-camps in California during its "flush period" is not recorded; but it could not have fallen below five hundred, and probably exceeded that figure. Mining was carried on vigorously in twelve large counties, and to some extent in three others.

The first camp to which we shall invite the attention of our readers was situated five miles from Sonora, the county-seat of Tuolumne County, Cal., and was in one of the richest ravines known to the early miners. It bore the homely appellation of "Jackass Gulch" from the days of its first organization in 1848, but its earliest laws were not committed to writing. A square of ten feet of ground "often yielded ten thousand dollars from the surface dirt," and ten feet square was the maximum size of the claim allowed. After 1851 the laws, as adopted and enforced by the camp, were as follows:—

First, That each person can hold one claim by virtue of occupation, but it must not exceed one hundred feet square.

Second, That a claim or claims, if held by purchase, must be under a bill of sale, and certified to by two disinterested persons as to the genuineness of signature and of the consideration given.

Third, That a jury of five persons shall decide any question arising under the previous article.

Fourth, That notices of claims must be renewed every ten days until water to work the said claims is to be had.

Fifth, That, as soon as there is sufficiency of water for working a claim, five days' absence from said claim, except in case of sickness, accident, or reasonable excuse, shall forfeit the property.

Sixth, That, these rules shall extend over Jackass and Soldier Gulches, and their tributaries.

The greatly lessened value of the mining-ground is shown by the size of the claim being increased from ten feet square to one hundred feet square. Requirement of claim-notice renewals during the idle season was common in most of the camps, unless a miner lived upon his claim. Thriving though the camp was in 1851, still crowded with miners by the hundred, it was rapidly exhausted; and in 1856, according to the Tuolumne Directory of that year, had only twenty-two voters.

Springfield District, whose leaders were men of New England, trained in town-meetings and local self-government, was able to create an organic law far superior to that of the preceding camp. Its laws were adopted in written form at a mass-meeting of the miners, April 13, 1852; were revised Aug. 11, and again Dec. 22, 1854. After describing the boundaries with great minuteness, the preamble (of 1852) declares—

That California, is and shall be, governed by American principles; and as Congress has made no rules and regulations for the government of the mining-districts of the same, and as the State legislature of California has provided by statute, and accorded to the miners of the United States, the right of making all laws, rules, and regulations that do not conflict with the constitution and laws of California, in all actions respecting mining-claims; therefore we, the miners of Springfield District, do ordain and establish the following rules and regulations.

There are sixteen articles. The size of the claim is fixed at one hundred feet square, no person under any circumstances to hold more than one; work must be performed upon it at least one day out of three during the season for mining. Claims must have substantial stakes at each corner, and must be "registered and described in the book of the precinct registry," to which the owner or owners shall sign their names. Several persons, each owning a single claim, may concentrate their labor upon one of those claims.

Disputes are to be referred to a standing committee of five miners, or to any member or members of this committee, as arbitrators; or a miners' jury may be summoned. Each member of the standing committee shall in each case be paid two dollars for his service. It is easy to see that a single arbitrator was in many cases entirely satisfactory for both disputants. The laws proceed to further define the process of arbitration. The head of the committee is to be sworn by a justice of the peace, provided such an officer be appointed in this mining-district, and is to administer the oath to his associates and to the witnesses. In some of the early camps, the alcalde administered this oath "to honestly arbitrate," to his deputies. The decision arrived at in either jury-trial or arbitration must be received as conclusive and binding upon the parties thereto, and be deemed and considered final in all such cases. Either party may compel the other to come to trial, by giving three days' notice of time and place. Costs shall be paid in the same way as in magistrate's courts. Disputes over water-privileges are especially named for arbitration.

Thirty days' desertion of a claim during the working-season results in forfeiture without remedy.

Article thirteen reads as follows:—

No person not an American citizen, or where there is a reasonable doubt of his being entitled to the privileges of an American citizen, shall be competent to act on any arbitration, or trial by jury.

The next article provides that "companies which go to great expense running tunnels" are allowed "two claims for each member of the company." The first code of "tunnel-claim laws" adopted in this region was several years later,—Jan. 20, 1855; and it defined a legal tunnel-claim as "one hundred feet along the base, and running from base to base through the mountain."

Article fifteen provides for the election of a district recorder, who is to have fifty cents for recording the title of each mining-claim.

The last article provides that "all claims held by foreigners who have failed to secure their State license" shall be forfeited. This was to aid in the enforcement of the State Act of April 13, 1850, passed at San José. A list of the unnaturalized foreigners was to be kept in each county. The recorders of the different districts usually aided in its preparation.

These laws of Springfield District show plainly how much dependence was placed upon the arbitration—or, as the Spanish termed it, the *conciliacion*—plan. We shall find equal care in this regard in many other districts. Springfield is said to have been the first district in the Sierra Nevada that built a church before it built a gambling-house. It has remained an orderly, flourishing, and energetic community, since the days of its first organization.

JUSTICE IN THE MINING CAMPS

Mining districts protected claims and provided camps with a primitive form of government, but the administration of justice proved more difficult. Outlaws flocked to the mines in droves, attracted by the abundant wealth and relative lack of law-enforcement machinery. For a time they were tolerated, but when they became too numerous the lawful citizens took action, usually by forming a Vigilance Committee or a Peoples' Court to apprehend, try, and punish offenders. The operation of such a Peoples' Court in Virginia City, Montana, was amusingly described by an observer, Thomas J. Dimsdale. There a notorious criminal, Henry Plummer, had been chosen sheriff;

he in turn had named three hardened law-breakers—Buck Stinson, Haze Lyons, and Charley Forbes—as deputies, plus one honest deputy named Dillingham. When the latter informed a stagecoach driver that he was to be robbed by the other three deputies, they murdered him in cold blood. A Peoples' Court was promptly organized and sentenced two of the killers, Buck Stinson and Haze Lyons, to death. The trial of Charley Forbes gave Dimsdale a chance to reveal the ineffectiveness of these courts when emotion was allowed to rule.[12]

In the meantime Charley Forbes' trial went on. An effort was made to save Charley on account of his good looks and education, by producing a fully loaded pistol, which they proved (?) was his. It was, however, Buck Stinson's, and had been "set right" by Gallagher. The miners had got weary, and many had wandered off when the question was put; but his own masterly appeal, which was one of the finest efforts of eloquence ever made in the mountains, saved him.

Forbes was a splendid looking fellow—straight as a ramrod; handsome, brave, and agile as a cat in his movements. His friends believed that he excelled Plummer in quickness and dexterity at handling his revolver. He had the scabbard sewn to the belt, and wore the buckle always exactly in front, so that his hand might grasp the butt, with the forefinger on the trigger and the thumb on the cock, with perfect certainty, whenever it was needed, which was pretty often.

Charley told a gentleman of the highest respectability that he killed Dillingham, and he used to laugh at the "softness" of the miners who acquitted him. He moreover warned the gentleman mentioned that he would be attacked on his road to Salt Lake;

but the citizen was no way scary, and said, "You can't do it, Charley; your boys are scattered and we are together, and we shall give you—, if you try it." The party made a sixty-mile drive the first day, and thus escaped molestation. Charley had corresponded with the press, some articles on the state and prospects of the Territory having appeared in the California papers, and were very well written.

Charley was acquitted by a nearly unanimous vote. Judge Smith, bursting into tears, fell on his neck and kissed him, exclaiming, "My boy! my boy!" Hundreds pressed round him, shaking hands and cheering, till it seemed to strike them all at once that there were two men to hang, which was even more exciting, and the crowd "broke" for the "jail."

A wagon was drawn up by the people to the door in which the criminals were to ride to the gallows. They were then ordered to get into the wagon, which they did, several of their friends climbing in with them.

At this juncture Judge Smith was called for, and then, amidst tremendous excitement and confusion, Haze Lyons crying and imploring mercy, a number of ladies, much affected, begged earnestly to "Save the poor young boys' lives." The ladies admit the crying, but declare that they wept in the interest of fair play. One of them saw Forbes kill Dillingham, and felt that it was popular murder to hang Stinson and Lyons, and let off the chief desperado because he was good-looking. She had furnished the sheet with which the dead body was covered.

We cannot blame the gentle-hearted creatures; but we deprecate the practice of admitting the ladies to such places. They are out of their path. Such sights are unfit for them to behold, and in rough and masculine business of every kind women should bear no part. It unsexes them, and destroys the

---

[12] Thomas J. Dimsdale, *The Vigilantes of Montana* (Virginia City, Montana, 1866), pp. 68–71.

most lovely parts of their character. A woman is a queen in her own home; but we neither want her as a blacksmith, a ploughwoman, a soldier, a lawyer, a doctor, nor in any such professions or handicraft. As sisters, mothers, nurses, friends, sweethearts, and wives, they are the salt of the earth, the sheet anchor of society, and the humanizing and purifying element in humanity. As such, they cannot be too much respected, loved, and protected. From Blue Stockings, Bloomers, and strong-minded she-males generally, "Good Lord, deliver us."

A letter (written by other parties to suit the occasion), was produced, and a gentleman—a friend of Lyons—asked that "The letter which Haze had written to his mother might be read." This was done, amid cries of "Read the letter," "—the letter"; while others who saw how it would turn out shouted, "Give him a horse and let him go to his mother." A vote was taken again, after it had all been settled, as before mentioned— the first time by ayes and noes. Both parties claimed victory. The second party was arranged so that the party for hanging should go up-hill, and the party for clearing should go down-hill. The down-hill men claimed that the prisoners were acquitted, but the up-hills would not give way. All this time confusion confounded reigned around the wagon. The third vote was differently managed. Two pairs of men were chosen. Between one pair passed those who were for carrying the sentence into execution, and between the other pair marched those who were for setting them at liberty. The latter party ingeniously increased their votes by the simple but effectual expedient of passing through several times, and finally an honest Irish miner, who was not so weak-kneed as the rest shouted out, "Be ——, there's a bloody naygur voted three times." The descendant of Ham broke for the willows at top speed, on hearing this announcement. This vote settled the question, and Gallagher, pistol in hand, shouted, "Let them go, they're cleared." Amidst a thousand confused cries of "Give the murderers a horse," "Let them go," "Hurrah!" etc., one of the men, seeing a horse with an Indian saddle, belonging to a Blackfoot squaw, seized it, and mounting both on the same animal, the assassins rode at a gallop out of the Gulch. One of the guard remarked to another— pointing at the same time to the gallows— "There is a monument of disappointed justice."

While all this miserable farce was being enacted, the poor victim of the pardoned murderers lay stark and stiff on a gambling table, in a brush wakiup, in the Gulch. Judge Smith came to X, and asked if men enough could not be found to bury Dillingham. X said there were plenty, and, obtaining a wagon, they put the body into a coffin, and started up the "Branch," towards the present graveyard on Cemetery Hill, where the first grave was opened in Virginia to receive the body of the murdered man. As the party proceeded, a man said to Judge Smith, "Only for my dear wife and daughter, the poor fellows would have been hanged." A citizen, seeing that the so-called ladies had not a tear to shed for the *victim*, promptly answered, "I take notice that your dear wife and daughter have no tears for poor Dillingham, but only for two murderers." "Oh," said the husband, "I cried for Dillingham." "Darned well you thought of it," replied the mountaineer. A party of eight or ten were around the grave, when one asked who would perform the burial service. Some one said, "Judge, you have been doing the talking for the last three days, and you had better pray." The individual addressed knelt down and made a long and appropriate prayer; but it must be stated that he was so intoxicated that kneeling was, at least, as much a convenience as it was a necessity. Some men never "experience religion" unless they are drunk. They pass through the convivial and the narrative stages into the garrulous, from which they sail into the religious, and are deeply affected. The scene closes with the lachrymose or weeping development, ending in pig-like slumbers. Any one thus moved by liquor is not reliable.

The disorder that characterized Virginia City and other mining camps in their early years lasted but a short time. The great body of miners were respectable citizens who wanted nothing less than governmental supervision exerted by nation and state, and they worked rapidly to achieve that goal. They succeeded remarkably, for as mining entered its permanent era, with the advent of heavy machinery and quartz-crushing mills, the restless minority drifted on to be replaced by farmers, tradesmen, professional men, and others who came to grow up with the community. This transition was symbolized by the achievement of first territorial and then state government in district after district throughout the Far West, as occurred in Nevada, Colorado, Idaho, Montana, and Arizona. The mining frontier had played its role in the saga of American expansion; it had also posed problems that could only be solved by the creation of a transportation system which hurried the coming of civilization to all the West.

CHAPTER 24 || *The Transportation Frontier, 1850-1884*

The advance of the mining frontier posed a major problem. How could the widely scattered camps be supplied with the essentials of life? And, more important, how could the miners be reunited with their government in the "states" and the separatist tendencies usual on isolated frontiers be defeated. Not only the welfare of the miners but the perpetuation of a united nation depended on forging links connecting the Far West with the Mississippi Valley. Yet these would be difficult to fashion. Nearly a thousand miles of unsettled prairies and plains separated the commercial towns of Missouri and Iowa from the nearest mining camps in the Rocky Mountains. To construct supply lines across this wasteland where way traffic was nonexistent would exhaust the resources of the most affluent private concern.

Fortunately precedents pointed the way to a solution. Every major transportation development in the nation's history, from the early turnpikes and canals through the newfangled railroads then being built in the East, had been financed with government funds. To win the capital that private enterprise could not produce, the entrepreneurs who sought to enrich themselves by reuniting East and West had only to persuade Congress that the national welfare was at stake.

FREIGHTING ON THE GREAT PLAINS

First to get government aid were the overland freighters, whose great trains of ox-drawn covered wagons were already a familiar sight among the remote settlements of the Mississippi Valley frontier. They had a sensible proposition to offer: if the government would pay them to carry supplies to the military posts that had been scattered over the Far West after the Mexican War, they would be assured a financial backlog that would allow them to extend their operations to the nonmilitary communities. A number of small freighting concerns benefited from such contracts, but one soon surpassed all others. Three men—William H. Russell, William B. Waddell, and Alexander Majors—operating as the firm of Russell, Majors & Waddell, used army contracts to underwrite their major expenses so successfully that they built a giant transportation empire during the

1850s, sending their trains of lumbering freight wagons over most of the West. Alexander Majors, a devoted plainsman who was happier traveling with one of his "outfits" than counting profits in an eastern office, described in his reminiscences the operations of the company:[1]

The organization of a full-fledged train for crossing the plains consisted of from twenty-five to twenty-six large wagons that would carry from three to three and a half tons each, the merchandise or contents of each wagon being protected by three sheets of thin ducking, such as is used for army tents. The number of cattle necessary to draw each wagon was twelve, making six yokes or pairs, and a prudent freighter would always have from twenty to thirty head of extra oxen, in case of accident to or lameness of some of the animals. In camping or stopping to allow the cattle to graze, a corral or pen of oblong shape is formed by the wagons, the tongues being turned out, and a log chain extended from the hind wheel of each wagon to the fore wheel of the next behind, etc., thus making a solid pen except for a wide gap at each end, through which gaps the cattle are driven when they are to be yoked and made ready for travel, the gaps then being filled by the wagon-master, his assistant, and the extra men, to prevent the cattle from getting out. When the cattle are driven into this corral or pen, each driver yokes his oxen, drives them out to his wagon, and gets ready to start. The entire train of cattle, including extras, generally numbered from 320 to 330 head and usually from four to five mules for riding and herding. The force of men for each train consisted of a wagonmaster, his assistant, the teamsters, a man to look after the extra cattle, and two or three extra men as a reserve to take the places of any men who might be disabled or sick, the latter case being a rare exception, for as a rule there was no sickness. I think perhaps there was never a set of laboring men in the world who enjoyed more uninterrupted good health than the teamsters upon the plains. They walked by the side of their teams, as it was impossible for them to ride and keep them moving with regularity. The average distance traveled with loaded wagons was from twelve to fifteen miles per day, although in some instances, when roads were fine and there was a necessity for rapid movement, I have known them to travel twenty miles. But this was faster traveling than they could keep up for any length of time. Returning with empty wagons they could average twenty miles a day without injury to the animals.

Oxen proved to be the cheapest and most reliable teams for long trips, where they had to live upon the grass. This was invariably the case. They did good daily work, gathered their own living, and if properly driven would travel 2,000 miles in a season, or during the months from April to November; traveling from 1,000 to 1,200 miles with the loaded wagons, and with plenty of good grass and water, would make the return trip with the empty wagons in the same season. However, the distance traveled depended much upon the skill of the wagonmasters who had them in charge. For if the master was not skilled in handling the animals and men, they could not make anything like good headway and success. To make everything work expeditiously, thorough discipline was required, each man performing his duty and being in the place assigned him without confusion or delay. I remember once of timing my teamsters when they commenced to yoke their teams after the cattle had been driven

---

[1] Alexander Majors, *Seventy Years on the Frontier* (Chicago, 1893), pp. 102–105.

into their corral and allowed to stand long enough to become quiet. I gave the word to the men to commence yoking, and held my watch in my hand while they did so, and in sixteen minutes from the time they commenced, each man had yoked six pairs of oxen and had them hitched to their wagons ready to move. I state this that the reader may see how quickly the men who are thoroughly disciplined could be ready to "pop the whip" and move out, when unskilled men were often more than an hour doing the same work. The discipline and rules by which my trains were governed were perfect, and as quick as the men learned each one his place and duty, it became a very pleasant and easy thing for him to do. Good moral conduct was required of them, and no offense from man to man was allowed, thus keeping them good-natured and working together harmoniously. They were formed into what they called "messes," there being from six to eight men in a mess, each mess selecting the man best fitted to serve as cook, and the others carrying the water, fuel, and standing guard, so that the cook's sole business when in camp was to get his utensils ready and cook the meals.

We never left the cattle day or night without a guard of two men, the teamsters taking turns, and arranging it so that each man was on guard two hours out of the twenty-four, and sometimes they were only obliged to go on guard two hours every other night. This matter they arranged among themselves and with the wagonmaster. The duty of the wagonmaster was about the same as that of a captain of a steamboat or ship, his commands being implicitly obeyed, for in the early stages of travel upon the plains the men were at all times liable to be attacked by the Indians; therefore the necessity for a perfect harmony of action throughout the entire band. The assistant wagonmaster's duty was to carry out the wagonmaster's instructions, and he would often be at one end of the train while the master was at the other, as the train was moving. It was arranged, when possible, that no two trains should ever camp together, as there was not grass and water sufficient for the animals of both, and thus all confusion was avoided.

A MAIL SUBSIDY FOR WESTERN STAGECOACHING

Freighting supplied the minimum material needs of pioneers living in the Far West, but the slow-moving caravans failed to satisfy the emotional urge of westerners to be closely united to their homeland. Nothing would please them but continuous stagecoach service, with the coaches traveling day and night to span the continent in less than a month. Both East and West agreed on the need for such service, and both accepted the fact that it could be maintained only by generous contracts to carry the mails. Congress must authorize these, and this Congress was unable to do, for its members were so torn by the North-South conflict of the 1850s that they could not agree on a route. They finally resolved the problem by dumping the whole question on the Postmaster General, with authority to decide. The bill that resolved the issue, adopted in March 1857, made clear that the mail subsidy was the one essential feature of the contract between the government and the private concern that would operate the coaches:[2]

Sec. And be it further enacted, That the Postmaster General be, and he is hereby, authorized to contract for the conveyance of the entire letter mail from such point on the

---

[2] *Congressional Globe,* 34th Congress, 3rd Session, Appendix, p. 321.

Mississippi river as the contractors may select to San Francisco, in the State of California, for six years, at a cost not exceeding $300,000 per annum for semi-monthly, $450,000 for weekly, or $600,000 for semi-weekly service: to be performed semi-monthly, weekly, or semi-weekly, at the option of the Postmaster General.

Sec. And be it further enacted, That the contract shall require the service to be performed with good four-horse coaches or spring wagons, suitable for the conveyance of passengers, as well as the safety and security of the mails.

Sec. And be it further enacted, That the contractors shall have the right of preëmption to three hundred and twenty acres of any land not then disposed of or reserved, at each point necessary for a station, not to be nearer than ten miles from each other: *Provided,* That no mineral lands shall thus be preëmpted.

Sec. And be if further enacted, That the said service shall be performed within twenty-five days for each trip; and that, before entering into such contract, the Postmaster General shall be satisfied of the ability and disposition of the parties *bona fide* and in good faith to perform the said contract, and shall require good and sufficient security for the performance of the same; the service to commence within twelve months after the signing of the contract.

THE BUTTERFIELD OVERLAND MAIL

With a handsome subsidy assured, competition for the right of establishing the overland mail was spirited. The contract finally went to a syndicate of experienced coachers headed by John Butterfield, largely because they agreed to follow any route acceptable to the postmaster, a southerner. The route decided upon ran from the railroad at Tipton, Missouri, southward through Fort Smith, Arkansas, to El Paso and then to San Francisco—a distance of 2812 miles. The contract signed on September 16, 1857, bound the company to deliver mails regularly twice weekly within the twenty-five day period specified by Congress. Its signing plunged John Butterfield and his men into a flurry of activity; roads were marked, stations constructed where relays of horses could await arriving coaches, wagons and stagecoaches built, livestock purchased, and countless other details arranged. Finally, on September 16, 1858, the first coaches pulled out of Tipton and San Francisco. The lone through passenger on the westbound coach was Waterman L. Ormsby, a correspondent of the "New York Herald," whose reports painted a lively picture of the journey. The extracts that follow tell of the start of the trip from Tipton, the difficulties of travel in the remote Texas area, and the journey's end:[3]

The Pacific Railroad train, carrying the first overland mail, arrived at Tipton, the western terminus of the road, situated in Moniteau County, Mo., at precisely one minute after six o'clock P.M. of Thursday, the 16th inst., being several minutes behind time. We there found the first coach ready, the six horses all harnessed and hitched, and Mr. John Butterfield, Jr., impatient to be off.

The town contains but a few hundred inhabitants, and all these seemed to have turned out for the occasion, though they made no demonstration on account of it. The place is, however, but a few months old, having been built since the completion of this end of the line, and doubtless excitements are too rare to be appreciated. They

---

[3] *New York Herald*, September 26 to November 19, 1858. Reprinted in Waterman L. Ormsby, *The Butterfield Overland Mail*, edited by Lyle H. Wright and Josephine M. Bynum (San Marino, Calif.: The Huntington Library, 1942), pp. 10–13, 53–56, 128–130.

looked on with astonishment as the baggage and packages were being rapidly transferred from the cars to the coach. The latter was entirely new and had not yet held a load of passengers. It very much resembled those heavy coaches which are used in New York to convey passengers between the steamboats, car depots, and the hotels, and appeared to be quite as expensively built. In large letters over the side was the following: OVERLAND MAIL COMPANY.

The time occupied in shifting the baggage and passengers was just nine minutes, at which time the cry of "all aboard," and the merry crack of young John Butterfield's whip, denoted that we were off. I took a note of the "following distinguished persons present," as worthy of a place in history: Mr. John Butterfield, president of the Overland Mail Company; John Butterfield, Jr., on the box; Judge Wheeler, lady, and two children, of Fort Smith; Mr. T. R. Corbin, of Washington; and the correspondent of the *Herald*. It had been decided to take no passengers but the last named gentleman, on the first trip, but Mr. Butterfield made an exception in favor of Judge Wheeler, agreeing to take him to Fort Smith, where he intended to go himself. You will perceive, therefore, that your correspondent was the only through passenger who started in the first overland coach for San Francisco, as all the rest of the party dropped off by the time we reached Fort Smith. Not a cheer was raised as the coach drove off, the only adieu being, "Good bye, John," addressed to John, Jr., by one of the crowd. Had they have been wild Indians they could not have exhibited less emotion.

Our road for the first few miles was very fair, coursing through several small prairies, where for the first time I noticed those travelling hotels so commonly seen in the western country. These are large covered wagons, in which the owner and his family, sometimes numbering as high as a dozen, emigrate from place to place, travelling in the daytime, and camping near wood, water, and grass at night. All along the wildest western roads these hotels may be met in every direction, enlivening the way by their camp fires at night, and presenting pictures of domestic felicity which might well be emulated in certain quarters more comfortable and less homely. We rode along at a somewhat rapid pace, because John, Jr., was determined that the overland mail should go through his section on time; and, though his father kept calling out, "Be careful, John," he assured him that it was "all right," and drove on.

The first stopping place was at "Shackleford's," about seven miles distant, and we seemed hardly to have become comfortably seated in the coach before our attention was attracted to the illumination of our destination—a recognition of the occasion which seemed quite cheering after the apparent previous neglect. The team wheeled up in fine style, and we found the change of horses ready harnessed and supper waiting. Mr. Shackleford assured us that he would have fired a gun for us, but he could not get it to go off. We took the will for the deed, however, and hustled in to supper, which was soon despatched. After taking leave of Mr. Corbin and the others, we were off again to the next station, having been detained, in all, twenty minutes....

Some little delay was experienced, here, before the wild mules could be caught and harnessed, by which several hours of our advance time was lost. Mr. J. B. Nichols of Mr. Crocker's division was to drive, and Mr. Mather of Mr. Glover's division, which commences at Chadbourne and ends at Franklin on the Rio Grande, was to proceed on horseback, point out the road, and maintain a general supervision. Whether from the inefficiency of Mr. Nichols' driving, or because Mr. Mather's furious riding frightened the mules, or because the mules were wild, or that the boys had been having a jolly good time on the occasion of the arrival of the first stage, or by a special dispensation of Providence—or from a combination of all these causes—I will not pretend to say, but certainly, from some unforeseen and vexatious cause, we here suffered a detention of some hours. The mules reared, pitched, twisted, whirled, wheeled, ran, stood still, and cut up all sorts of capers. The wagon performed so many evolutions that I, in fear of my life, abandoned it and took to my heels, fully confident that I could make more progress in a straight line, and with much less risk of breaking my neck.

Mr. Lee, sutler at the fort, who, with others, had come out on horseback to see us start, kindly offered to take me up behind him—to which, though not much of an equestrian, I acceded with the view of having a little better sight of the sport at a safe distance. In this I was eminently gratified, for the gyrations continued to considerable length, winding up with tangling all the mules pretty well in the harness, the escape of one of the leaders into the woods, and the complete demolition of the top of the wagon; while those in charge of it lay around loose on the grass, and all were pretty well tired out and disgusted, except those who had nothing to do but look on.

For my part, I thought it the most ludicrous scene I ever witnessed, though it seemed a great pity that time which was needed on other parts of the route should be thus wasted or lost here. Both of the leading mules having escaped, and Mr. Mather having become completely anxious that every one should go to the d——l, and understand that he did not care a d——n for anyone, I thought the progress of the mail, for that night at least, was stopped; but Nichols averred that the mail should go on if he went alone with the two wheel-mules; and, sure enough, he started off after getting the harness once more disentangled, and kept the road in fine style. I had fully made up my mind by this time that it would be as much as my life was worth to go under the existing circumstances, but, seeing him go off, I rode up to him, and, finding persuasion of no avail, overcame my strong objections and concluded to go, though if I had had any property I certainly should have made a hasty will. When I had become seated I thought I would ascertain all the chances, and the following dialogue ensued between myself and Mr. Nichols:

"How far is it to the next station?"
"I believe it is thirty miles."
"Do you know the road?"
"No."
"How do you expect to get there?"
"There's only one road; we can't miss it."
"Have you any arms?"
"No, I don't want any; there's no danger."

Whether there was danger or not, I felt as if I had a little rather have started under other circumstances; but I was bound to go with the mail, though I had not much confidence that our two mules could make the thirty miles. Fortunately our course was a clear and straight one, leading across an apparently boundless prairie, with not a tree or shrub to be seen, the parched grass almost glistening in the light of the moon.

The night was clear and bright, the road pretty level, and the mules willing, and I soon ceased to regret having started. I alternately drove while Nichols slept, or slept while he drove, or rode horseback for the man who accompanied us to take back the team, and, altogether, passed a very pleasant night, though our progress was necessarily slow. But about 2 A.M. we came to a steep and stony hill, obstinately jutting from the prairie, right in our path and impossible of avoidance. One mule could neither be coaxed or driven up, so we had to camp until morning, when, after much difficulty, we ascended the hill and discovered the station fire, miles distant—a mere speck among the trees. We soon reached it and found it to be a corral, or yard, for the mules, and tents erected inside for the men, under charge of Mr. Henry Roylan. They had seen us coming and were herding the mules as we drove up. Their corral was built of upright rough timber, planted in the ground. They had pitched their tents inside, for fear of the Indians, and took turns standing guard, two hours on and two hours off. ...

From San José the road leads, through San Mateo and San Francisco counties, to the city, having prosperous ranches ranged all along the line, with the flourishing little villages of Redwood and Santa Clara en route. I was very sorry to be obliged to pass through this interesting part of the journey in the night—and a dark night at that; but the overland mail was on board and we made no stoppages other than to change horses at stations about ten miles apart. It was just after sunrise that the city of San Francisco hove in sight over the hills, and never did the night traveller approach a distant light, or the lonely mariner descry a sail, with more joy than did I the city of San Francisco on the morning of Sunday, October 10. As we neared the city we met milkmen and pleasure seekers taking their morning rides, looking on with wonderment as we rattled along at a tearing pace.

Soon we struck the pavements, and, with a whip, crack, and bound, shot through the streets to our destination, to the great consternation of everything in the way and the no little surprise of everybody. Swiftly we whirled up one street and down another, and round the corners, until finally we drew up at the stage office in front of the Plaza, our driver giving a shrill blast of his horn and a flourish of triumph for the arrival of the first overland mail in San Francisco from St. Louis. But our work was not yet done. The mails must be delivered, and in a jiffy we were at the post office door, blowing the horn, howling and shouting for somebody to come and take the overland mail.

I thought nobody was ever going to come —the minutes seemed days—but the delay made it even time, and as the man took the mail bags from the coach, at half-past seven A.M. on Sunday, October 10, it was just twenty-three days, twenty-three hours and a half from the time that John Butterfield, the president of the company, took the bags as the cars moved from St. Louis at 8 A.M. on Thursday, 16th of September, 1858. And I had the satisfaction of knowing that the correspondent of the New York *Herald* had kept his promise and gone through with the first mail—the sole passenger and the only one who had ever made the trip across the plains in less than fifty days.

THE JOYS OF OVERLAND COACHING

The Butterfield Overland Mail offered swift and efficient service between Tipton and San Francisco, but criticism of the round-about route that it followed mounted steadily, especially in the North and West. This seemed to spell opportunity to the freighting firm of Russell, Majors & Waddell, which was eager to fatten on mail contracts as well as army-supply contracts. If the partners could demonstrate that the "central route" through South Pass was faster than the "ox-bow" route of the Butterfield, the subsidy might be theirs. Having sharpened their knowledge of coaching by operating the stage between Leavenworth and Denver during the Pike's Peak gold rush, they formed the Central Overland, California, & Pike's Peak Express to run to San Francisco, planning to nurture the venture on freighting profits until a mail contract was secured. The firm soon established a world-wide reputation for fast and efficient service. Its most famous passenger was Samuel L. Clemens, who traveled westward to Carson City with his brother, Orin Clemens, newly appointed secretary of the territorial government of Nevada. Mark Twain's description of his trip is a classic of western literature:[4]

By eight o'clock everything was ready, and we were on the other side of the river. We jumped into the stage, the driver cracked his whip, and we bowled away and left "the States" behind us. It was a superb summer morning, and all the landscape was brilliant with sunshine. There was a freshness and breeziness, too, and an exhilarating sense of emancipation from all sorts of cares and responsibilities, that almost made us feel that the years we had spent in the close, hot city, toiling and slaving, had been wasted and thrown away. We were spinning along through Kansas, and in the course of an hour and a half we were fairly abroad on the great Plains. Just here the land was rolling—a grand sweep of regular elevations and depressions as far as the eye could reach—like the stately heave and swell of the ocean's bosom after a storm. And everywhere were cornfields, accenting with squares of deeper green, this limitless expanse of grassy land. But presently this sea upon dry ground was to lose its "rolling" character and stretch away for seven hundred miles as level as a floor!

Our coach was a great swinging and swaying stage, of the most sumptuous description —an imposing cradle on wheels. It was drawn by six handsome horses, and by the side of the driver sat the "conductor," the legitimate captain of the craft; for it was his business to take charge and care of the mails, baggage, express matter, and passengers. We three were the only passengers, this trip. We sat on the back seat, inside. About all the rest of the coach was full of mail bags—for we had three days' delayed mails with us. Almost touching our knees, a perpendicular wall of mail matter rose up to the roof. There was a great pile of it strapped on top of the stage, and both the fore and hind boots were full. We had twenty-seven hundred pounds of it aboard, the driver said—"a little for Brigham, and Carson, and 'Frisco, but the heft of it for the Injuns, which is powerful troublesome 'thout they get plenty of truck to read." But as he just then got up a fearful convulsion of his countenance which was suggestive of a wink being swallowed by an earthquake, we guessed that his remark was intended to be facetious, and to mean that we would unload the most of our mail matter somewhere on the Plains and leave it to the Indians, or whosoever wanted it.

We changed horses every ten miles, all day long, and fairly flew over the hard, level road. We jumped out and stretched our legs every time the coach stopped, and so the night found us still vivacious and unfatigued.

[The travelers soon settled into a routine, making themselves comfortable by spreading the mail sacks to form a level bed on which they could lounge or sleep. When well out on the plains, Mark Twain sang the praises of stagecoaching in a memorable passage:]

---

[4] Samuel L. Clemens, *Roughing It* (Hartford, Conn., 1872), pp. 25–26, 37–39.

As the sun went down and the evening chill came on, we made preparation for bed. We stirred up the hard leather letter-sacks, and the knotty canvas bags of printed matter (knotty and uneven because of projecting ends and corners of magazines, boxes and books). We stirred them up and redisposed them in such a way as to make our bed as level as possible. And we *did* improve it, too, though after all our work it had an upheaved and billowy look about it, like a little piece of a stormy sea. Next we hunted up our boots from odd nooks among the mail-bags where they had settled, and put them on. Then we got down our coats, vests, pantaloons and heavy woolen shirts, from the arm-loops where they had been swinging all day, and clothed ourselves in them—for, there being no ladies either at the stations or in the coach, and the weather being hot, we had looked to our comfort by stripping to our underclothing, at nine o'clock in the morning. All things being now ready, we stowed the uneasy Dictionary where it would lie as quiet as possible, and placed the water-canteens and pistols where we could find them in the dark. Then we smoked a final pipe, and swapped a final yarn; after which, we put the pipes, tobacco and bag of coin in snug holes and caves among the mail-bags, and then fastened down the coach curtains all around, and made the place as "dark as the inside of a cow," as the conductor phrased it in his picturesque way. It was certainly as dark as any place could be—nothing was even dimly visible in it. And finally, we rolled ourselves up like silk-worms, each person in his own blanket, and sank peacefully to sleep.

Whenever the stage stopped to change horses, we would wake up, and try to recollect where we were—and succeed—and in a minute or two the stage would be off again, and we likewise. We began to get into country, now, threaded here and there with little streams. These had high, steep banks on each side, and every time we flew down one bank and scrambled up the other, our party inside got mixed somewhat. First we would all be down in a pile at the forward end of the stage, nearly in a sitting posture, and in a second we would shoot to the other end, and stand on our heads. And we would sprawl and kick, too, and ward off ends and corners of mail-bags that came lumbering over us and about us; and as the dust rose from the tumult, we would all sneeze in chorus, and the majority of us would grumble, and probably say some hasty thing, like: "Take your elbow out of my ribs!—can't you quit crowding?"

Every time we avalanched from one end of the stage to the other, the Unabridged Dictionary would come too; and every time it came it damaged somebody. One trip it "barked" the Secretary's elbow; the next trip it hurt me in the stomach, and the third it tilted Bemis's nose up till he could look down his nostrils—he said. The pistols and coin soon settled to the bottom, but the pipes, pipe-stems, tobacco and canteens clattered and floundered after the Dictionary every time it made an assault on us, and aided and abetted the book by spilling tobacco in our eyes, and water down our backs.

Still, all things considered, it was a very comfortable night. It wore gradually away, and when at last a cold gray light was visible through the puckers and chinks in the curtains, we yawned and stretched with satisfaction, shed our cocoons, and felt that we had slept as much as was necessary. By and by, as the sun rose up and warmed the world, we pulled off our clothes and got ready for breakfast. We were just pleasantly in time, for five minutes afterward the driver sent the weird music of his bugle winding over the grassy solitudes, and presently we detected a low hut or two in the distance. Then the rattling of the coach, the clatter of our six horses' hoofs, and the driver's crisp commands, awoke to a louder and stronger emphasis, and we went sweeping down on the station at our smartest speed. It was fascinating—that old overland stagecoaching.

THE PONY EXPRESS: MEETING A RIDER ON THE PLAINS

Mark Twain and the nation might applaud the service of the Overland but praise could not be translated into profits, and no stagecoaching venture in the Far West could succeed without government subsidy. Russell, Majors & Waddell knew that they could survive only if they won the contract to carry the mails. Hence they decided on a desperate gamble to focus attention on the superiority of the central route. They would found a "Pony Express" in which fast horseback riders, operating in relays, would carry mail across the continent in ten days. The Pony Express that began service between St. Joseph and San Francisco on April 3, 1860, was one of the West's most glamorous enterprises, as Mark Twain testified. He described his impressions when his stagecoach met the Pony Express rider:[5]

In a little while all interest was taken up in stretching our necks and watching for the "pony-rider"—the fleet messenger who sped across the continent from St. Joe to Sacramento, carrying letters nineteen hundred miles in eight days! Think of that for perishable horse and human flesh and blood to do! The pony-rider was usually a little bit of a man, brimful of spirit and endurance. No matter what time of the day or night his watch came on, and no matter whether it was winter or summer, raining, snowing, hailing, or sleeting, or whether his "beat" was a level straight road or a crazy trail over mountain crags and precipices, or whether it led through peaceful regions or regions that swarmed with hostile Indians, he must be always ready to leap into the saddle and be off like the wind! There was no idling-time for a pony-rider on duty. He rode fifty miles without stopping, by daylight, moonlight, starlight, or through the blackness of darkness—just as it happened. He rode a splendid horse that was born for a racer and fed and lodged like a gentleman; kept him at his utmost speed for ten miles, and then, as he came crashing up to the station where stood two men holding fast a fresh, impatient steed, the transfer of rider and mail-bag was made in the twinkling of an eye, and away flew the eager pair and were out of sight before the spectator could get hardly the ghost of a look. Both rider and horse went "flying light." The rider's dress was thin, and fitted close; he wore a "roundabout," and a skull-cap, and tucked his pantaloons into his boot-tops like a race-rider. He carried no arms—he carried nothing that was not absolutely necessary, for even the postage on his literary freight was worth *five dollars a letter*. He got but little frivolous correspondence to carry—his bag had business letters in it, mostly. His horse was stripped of all unnecessary weight, too. He wore a little wafer of a racing-saddle, and no visible blanket. He wore light shoes, or none at all. The little flat mail-pockets strapped under the rider's thighs would each hold about the bulk of a child's primer. They held many and many an important business chapter and newspaper letter, but these were written on paper as airy and thin as gold-leaf, nearly, and thus bulk and weight were economized. The stage-coach traveled about a hundred to a hundred and twenty-five miles

---

[5] Samuel L. Clemens, *Roughing It* (Hartford, Conn., 1872), pp. 70–72.

a day (twenty-four hours), the pony-rider about two hundred and fifty. There were about eighty pony-riders in the saddle all the time, night and day, stretching in a long, scattering procession from Missouri to California, forty flying eastward, and forty toward the west, and among them making four hundred gallant horses earn a stirring livelihood and see a deal of scenery every single day in the year.

We had had a consuming desire, from the beginning, to see a pony-rider, but somehow or other all that passed us and all that met us managed to streak by in the night, and so we heard only a whiz and a hail, and the swift phantom of the desert was gone before we could get our heads out of the windows. But now we were expecting one along every moment, and would see him in broad daylight. Presently the driver exclaims:

"HERE HE COMES!"

Every neck is stretched further, and every eye strained wider. Away across the endless dead level of the prairie a black speck appears against the sky, and it is plain that it moves. Well, I should think so! In a second or two it becomes a horse and rider, rising and falling, rising and falling—sweeping toward us nearer and nearer—growing more and more distinct, more and more sharply defined—nearer and still nearer, and the flutter of the hoofs comes faintly to the ear—another instant a whoop and a hurrah from our upper deck, a wave of the rider's hand, but no reply, and man and horse burst past our excited faces, and go winging away like a belated fragment of a storm!

BUILDING THE UNION PACIFIC

The Pony Express was more romantic than profitable and helped drive its parent firm into bankruptcy when a mail contract failed to materialize. Its days, moreover, were numbered, for weird new devices that used electricity and mechanical power rather than horse flesh were invading the West. The first electric telegraph line across the continent was completed in October 1861, dooming the Pony Express. Only a year later, Congress chartered the Central Pacific Railroad to build eastward from California and the Union Pacific Railroad to construct westward from Omaha, with the understanding that they meet at the California-Nevada line. Again a generous government subsidy made construction possible: a four-hundred foot right of way, twenty alternate sections of land for each mile of track, and loans varying from $16,-000 to $48,000 a mile. Spurred by this promised largess, both roads began construction in the middle 1860s. Granville M. Dodge, the engineer in charge of building the Union Pacific, later described to a congressional committee the track-laying techniques that allowed this monumental task to be completed on schedule:[6]

The organization for work on the plains away from civilization was as follows: Each of our surveying parties consisted of a chief, who was an experienced engineer, two assistants, also civil engineers, rodmen, flagmen, and chainmen, generally graduated civil engineers but without personal experience in the field, besides axmen, teamsters, and herders. When the party was expected to live upon the game of the country a hunter was added. Each party would thus consist of from eighteen to twenty-two men, all armed. When operating in a hostile Indian country they were regularly drilled, though after the civil war this was unnecessary, as most of them had been in the army. Each party entering a country occupied by hostile Indians was generally furnished with

---

[6] Granville M. Dodge, "How We Built the Union Pacific Railway," 61st Congress, 2nd Session, *Senate Document No. 477* (Washington, 1910), pp. 13–15.

a military escort of from ten men to a company under a competent officer. The duty of this escort was to protect the party when in camp. In the field the escort usually occupied prominent hills commanding the territory in which the work was to be done, so as to head off sudden attacks by the Indians. Notwithstanding this protection, the parties were often attacked, their chief or some of their men killed or wounded, and their stock run off.

In preliminary surveys in the open country a party would run from 8 to 12 miles of line in a day. On location in an open country 3 or 4 miles would be covered, but in a mountainous country generally not to exceed a mile. All hands worked from daylight to dark, the country being reconnoitered ahead of them by the chief, who indicated the streams to follow, and the controlling points in summits and river crossings. The party of location that followed the preliminary surveys had the maps and profiles of the line selected for location and devoted its energies to obtaining a line of the lowest grades and the least curvature that the country would admit.

The location party in our work on the Union Pacific was followed by the construction corps, grading generally 100 miles at a time. That distance was graded in about thirty days on the plains, as a rule, but in the mountains we sometimes had to open our grading several hundred miles ahead of our track in order to complete the grading by the time the track should reach it. All the supplies for this work had to be hauled from the end of the track, and the wagon transportation was enormous. At one time we were using at least 10,000 animals, and most of the time from 8,000 to 10,000 laborers. The bridge gangs always worked from 5 to 20 miles ahead of the track, and it was seldom that the track waited for a bridge. To supply 1 mile of track with material and supplies required about 40 cars, as on the plains everything, rails, ties, bridging, fastenings, all railway supplies, fuel for locomotives and trains, and supplies for men and animals on the entire work, had to be transported from the Missouri River. Therefore, as we moved westward, every hundred miles added vastly to our transportation. Yet the work was so systematically planned and executed that I do not remember an instance in all the construction of the line of the work being delayed a single week for want of material. Each winter we planned the work for the next season. By the opening of spring, about April 1, every part of the machinery was in working order, and in no year did we fail to accomplish our work. After 1866 the reports will show what we started out to do each year, and what we accomplished....

It was not until after November, 1867, when we had been at work two years, that we got railroad communication with the East at Council Bluffs, Iowa, the initial point of the Union Pacific Railway, by the completion of the Northwestern Railway. Till then the Missouri River had been the sole route over which supplies could be had. It was available only about three months of the year, and our construction was limited by the quantities of rail and equipment that could be brought to us by boat in that time. In twelve months of work after we had rail communication, we located, built, and equipped 587 miles of road, working only from one end, transporting everything connected with it an average distance of 800 miles west of the Missouri River. This feat has not yet been surpassed. In accomplishing it we crossed the divide of the continent and two ranges of mountains, one of which was the Wasatch, where in the winter of 1868–69 we had to blast the earth the same as the rocks.

Our Indian troubles commenced in 1864 and lasted until the tracks joined at Promontory. We lost most of our men and stock while building from Fort Kearney to Bitter Creek. At that time every mile of road had to be surveyed, graded, tied, and bridged under military protection. The order to every surveying corps, grading, bridging, and tie outfit was never to run when attacked. All were required to be armed, and I do not know that the order was disobeyed in a single instance, nor did I ever hear that the Indians had driven a party permanently from its work. I remember one occasion when they swooped down on a grading outfit in sight of the temporary fort of the military some 5 miles away, and right in sight of the end of the track. The government commission to examine that section of the completed road had just arrived, and the commissioners witnessed the fight. The graders had their arms stacked on the cut. The Indians leaped from the ravines, and, springing upon the workmen before they could reach their arms, cut loose the stock and caused a panic. Gen. Frank P. Blair, General Simpson, and Doctor White were the commissioners, and they showed their grit by running to my car for arms to aid in the fight. We did not fail to benefit from this experience, for, on returning to the East the commission dwelt earnestly on the necessity of our being protected.

THE SYMPHONY OF TRACK-LAYING

To an outsider less concerned with the hazards and toil of track-laying than General Dodge, the swift advance of the steel rails across the endless plains seemed to epitomize the epic of America, while the coordinated movements of the construction crews assumed symphonic dimensions:[7]

One can see all along the line of the now completed road the evidences of ingenious self-protection and defence which our men learned during the war. The same curious huts and underground dwellings which were a common sight along our army lines then, may now be seen burrowed into the sides of the hills, or built up with ready adaptability in sheltered spots. The whole organisation of the force engaged in the construction of the road is, in fact, semi-military. The men who go ahead, locating the road, are the advance guard. Following these is the second line, cutting through the gorges, grading the road, and building bridges. Then comes the main line of the army, placing the sleepers, laying the track, spiking down the rails, perfecting the alignment, ballasting the rail, and dressing up and completing the road for immediate use. This army of workers has its base, to continue the figure, at Omaha, Chicago, and still farther eastward, from whose markets are collected the material for constructing the road. Along the line of the completed road are construction trains constantly 'pushing forward to the front' with supplies. The company's grounds and workshops at Omaha are the arsenal, where these purchases, amounting now to millions of dollars in value, are collected and held ready to be sent forward. The advanced limit of the rail is occupied by a train of long box cars, with hammocks swung under them, beds spread on top of them, bunks built within them, in which the sturdy, broad-shouldered pioneers of the great iron highway sleep at

[7] William A. Bell, *New Tracks in North America* (London, 1869), vol. 2, pp. 253–255.

night and take their meals. Close behind this train come loads of ties and rails and spikes, &c., which are being thundered off upon the roadside, to be ready for the track-layers. The road is graded a hundred miles in advance. The ties are laid roughly in place, then adjusted, gauged, and levelled. Then the track is laid.

Track-laying on the Union Pacific is a science, and we pundits of the Far East stood upon that embankment, only about a thousand miles this side of sunset, and backed westward before that hurrying corps of sturdy operatives with mingled feelings of amusement, curiosity, and profound respect. On they came. A light car, drawn by a single horse, gallops up to the front with its load of rails. Two men seize the end of a rail and start forward, the rest of the gang taking hold by twos until it is clear of the car. They come forward at a run. At the word of command the rail is dropped in its place, right side up, with care, while the same process goes on at the other side of the car. Less than thirty seconds to a rail for each gang, and so four rails go down to the minute! Quick work, you say, but the fellows on the U. P. are tremendously in earnest. The moment the car is empty it is tipped over on the side of the track to let the next loaded car pass it, and then it is tipped back again; and it is a sight to see it go flying back for another load, propelled by a horse at full gallop at the end of 60 or 80 feet of rope, ridden by a young Jehu, who drives furiously. Close behind the first gang come the gaugers, spikers, and bolters, and a lively time they make of it. It is a grand Anvil Chorus that those sturdy sledges are playing across the plains. It is in triple time, three strokes to a spike. There are ten spikes to a rail, four hundred rails to a mile, eighteen hundred miles to San Francisco. That's the sum, what is the quotient?

Twenty-one million times are those sledges to be swung—twenty-one million times are they to come down with their sharp punctuation, before the great work of modern America is complete!

THE "HELL ON WHEELS" OF THE UNION PACIFIC

As the Union Pacific tracks advanced westward, they left behind a chain of towns that became notorious throughout the world. These evolved from the temporary halting-places that housed the construction crews—Julesburg, Cheyenne, Laramie City—and to them flocked riffraff from all the West to prey on the workers. This "Hell on Wheels" was shifted periodically to keep pace with the advancing steel rails, but its appearance and occupants changed little. A traveler, John H. Beadle, described that peregrinating Hades while it was at Benton, 698 miles west of Omaha, in August 1868:[8]

Westward the grassy plain yields rapidly to a desert; at Medicine Bow we took final leave of the last trace of fertility, and traversed a region of alkali flats and red ridges for fifty miles. In the worst part of this desert, just west of the last crossing of the Platte, we found Benton, the great terminus town, six hundred and ninety-eight miles from Omaha. Far as they could see around the town not a green tree, shrub, or spear of grass was to be seen; the red hills, scorched and bare as if blasted by the lightnings of an angry God, bounded the white basin on the north and

---

[8] John H. Beadle, *The Undeveloped West; or, Five Years in the Territories* (Philadelphia, 1873), pp. 87–88, 90–92.

east, while to the south and west spread the gray desert till it was interrupted by another range of red and yellow hills. All seemed sacred to the genius of drought and desolation. The whole basin looked as if it might originally have been filled with lye and sand, then dried to the consistency of hard soap, with glistening surface tormenting alike to eye and sense.

Yet here had sprung up in two weeks, as if by the touch of Aladdin's Lamp, a city of three thousand people; there were regular squares arranged into five wards, a city government of mayor and aldermen, a daily paper, and a volume of ordinances for the public health. It was the end of the freight and passenger, and beginning of the construction, division; twice every day immense trains arrived and departed, and stages left for Utah, Montana, and Idaho; all the goods formerly hauled across the plains came here by rail and were reshipped, and for ten hours daily the streets were thronged with motley crowds of railroad men, Mexicans and Indians, gamblers, "cappers," and saloon-keepers, merchants, miners, and mulewhackers. The streets were eight inches deep in white dust as I entered the city of canvas tents and polehouses; the suburbs appeared as banks of dirty white lime, and a new arrival with black clothes looked like nothing so much as a cockroach struggling through a flour barrel.

It was sundown, and the lively notes of the violin and guitar were calling the citizens to evening diversions. Twenty-three saloons paid license to the evanescent corporation, and five dance-houses amused our elegant leisure. In this place I wasted my time for two weeks, waiting for something to turn up, and lounged about the places most dangerous to pocket and morals with the happy indifference of a man who has nothing to lose.

It cannot be denied, I think, that the man who has nothing is much braver than he who has plenty; and I further suspect the bravest of our soldiers will admit, that if, about the time he was ready to advance on Vicksburg or Richmond, he had learned that some obliging old relative had conveniently died, after leaving him $50,000, his appetite for fight would suddenly have lost much of its edge....

The great institution of Benton was the "Big Tent," sometimes, with equal truth but less politeness, called the "Gamblers' Tent." This structure was a nice frame, a hundred feet long and forty feet wide, covered with canvass and conveniently floored for dancing, to which and gambling it was entirely devoted. It was moved successively to all the mushroom terminus "cities," and during my stay was the great public resort of Benton. A description of one of these towns is a description of all; so let us spend one evening in the "Big Tent," and see how men amuse their leisure where home life and society are lacking.

As we enter, we note that the right side is lined with a splendid bar, supplied with every variety of liquors and cigars, with cut glass goblets, ice-pitchers, splendid mirrors, and pictures rivalling those of our Eastern cities. At the back end a space large enough for one cotillon is left open for dancing; on a raised platform, a full band is in attendance day and night, while all the rest of the room is filled with tables devoted to monte, faro, rondo coolo, fortune-wheels, and every other species of gambling known. I acknowledge a morbid curiosity relating to everything villainous, and, though I never ventured a cent but once in my life, I am never weary of watching the game, and the various fortunes of those who "buck against the tiger."

During the day the "Big Tent" is rather

quiet, but at night, after a few inspiring tunes at the door by the band, the long hall is soon crowded with a motley throng of three or four hundred miners, ranchmen, clerks, "bullwhackers," gamblers and "cappers." The brass instruments are laid aside, the string-music begins, the cotillons succeed each other rapidly, each ending with a drink, while those not so employed crowd around the tables and enjoy each his favorite game. To-night is one of unusual interest, and the tent is full, while from every table is heard the musical rattle of the dice, the hum of the wheel, or the eloquent voice of the dealer. Fair women, clothed with richness and taste, in white and airy garments, mingle with the throng, watch the games with deep interest, or laugh and chat with the players. The wife of the principal gambler—a tall, spiritual and most innocent looking woman —sits by his side, while their children, two beautiful little girls of four and six years, run about the room playing and shouting with merriment, climbing upon the knees of the gamblers and embraced in their rude arms, like flowers growing on the verge of frightful precipices. We take our stand near the monte table, where a considerable crowd gathers, silently intent on the motions of the dealer. He throws three cards upon the cloth, points out one as the "winning card," then turns them face downward, and proceeds to toss them about, talking fluently all the time.

"Now, then, here we go; my hand against your eyes. Watch the ace! The ace is your winning card. The eight and ten spot win for me. Here is the ace, the winning card (turning it face up occasionally). Watch it close! I have two chances to your one unless you watch the ace. Now, then, I'll bet any man twenty dollars, as they lie, that he can't pick up the ace, and I'll not touch the cards again. Will you go twenty dollars on it, sir?"

THE RACE TOWARD PROMONTORY

Even the attractions of the Big Tent could not slow construction. By the spring of 1868, the Central Pacific had bridged the Sierras and was winging its way across Nevada while the Union Pacific was battling its way through the Rockies just below South Pass. Each sought to win for itself as much of Utah as possible, to qualify for the generous loans and land grants that went with every mile of track. General Dodge later described the last furious pace of the race to the point where the two roads would meet:[9]

We made our plans to build to Salt Lake, 480 miles, in 1868, and to endeavor to meet the Central Pacific at Humboldt Wells, 219 miles west of Ogden, in the spring of 1869. I had extended our surveys during the years 1867 and 1868 to the California state line, and laid my plans before the company, and the necessary preparations were made to commence work as soon as frost was out of the ground, say about April 1. Material had been collected in sufficient quantities at the end of the track to prevent any delay. During the winter ties and bridge timber had been cut and prepared in the mountains to bring to the line at convenient points, and the engineering forces were started to their positions before cold weather was over, that they might be ready to begin their work as soon as the temperature would permit. I remember that the parties going to Salt Lake crossed the Wasatch Mountains on sledges, and that the snow covered the tops of the telegraph poles. We all knew and appreciated

---

[9] Granville M. Dodge, "How We Built the Union Pacific Railway," 61st Congress, 2nd Session, *Senate Document No. 477* (Washington, 1910), pp. 23–24.

that the task we had laid out would require the greatest energy on the part of all hands. About April 1, therefore, I went onto the plains myself and started our construction forces, remaining the whole summer between Laramie and the Humboldt Mountains. I was surprised at the rapidity with which the work was carried forward. Winter caught us in the Wasatch Mountains, but we kept on grading our road and laying our track in the snow and ice at a tremendous cost. I estimated for the company that the extra cost of thus forcing the work during that summer and winter was over $10,000,000, but the instructions I received were to go on, no matter what the cost. Spring found us with the track at Ogden, and by May 1 we had reached Promontory, 534 miles west of our starting point twelve months before. Work on our line was opened to Humboldt Wells, making in the year a grading of 754 miles of line.

The Central Pacific had made wonderful progress coming east, and we abandoned the work from Promontory to Humboldt Wells, bending all our efforts to meet them at Promontory. Between Ogden and Promontory each company graded a line, running side by side, and in some places one line was right above the other. The laborers upon the Central Pacific were Chinamen, while ours were Irishmen, and there was much ill-feeling between them. Our Irishmen were in the habit of firing their blasts in the cuts without giving warning to the Chinamen on the Central Pacific working right above them. From this cause several Chinamen were severely hurt. Complaint was made to me by the Central Pacific people, and I endeavored to have the contractors bring all hostilities to a close, but, for some reason or other, they failed to do so. One day the Chinamen, appreciating the situation, put in what is called a "grave" on their work, and when the Irishmen right under them were all at work let go their blast and buried several of our men. This brought about a truce at once. From that time the Irish laborers showed due respect for the Chinamen, and there was no further trouble.

When the two roads approached in May, 1869, we agreed to connect at the summit of Promontory Point, and the day was fixed so that trains could reach us from New York and California. We laid the rails to the junction point a day or two before the final closing.

DRIVING THE GOLDEN SPIKE

Finally, in mid May 1869, the two roads met at Promontory, Utah, where an assemblage of notables and workers gathered to watch the laying of the last tie, the placing of the last rail, and the driving of the last spike—especially cast in gold for the occasion. The scene was described by Sidney Dillon, a visiting journalist:[10]

It was not a large crowd. In brass bands, fireworks, procession, and oratory, the demonstration, when ground was broken at Omaha, less than five years before, was much more imposing. A small excursion party, headed by Governor Stanford, had come from San Francisco; while on our side, besides our own men, there were only two or three persons present, among whom was the Rev. Dr. Todd, of Pittsfield. Not more than five or six hundred, all told, comprised the whole gathering, nearly all of whom were

---

[10] Sidney Dillon, "Historic Moment: Driving the Last Spike," *Scribner's Magazine*, XII (August, 1892), pp. 258–259.

officials of the two companies—contractors, surveyors, and employees.

The point of junction was in a level circular valley, about three miles in diameter, surrounded by mountains. During all the morning hours the hurry and bustle of preparation went on. Two lengths of rails lay on the ground near the opening in the road-bed. At a little before eleven the Chinese laborers began levelling up the road-bed preparatory to placing the last ties in position. About a quarter past eleven the train from San Francisco, bringing Governor Stanford and party arrived and was greeted with cheers. In the enthusiasm of the occasion there were cheers for everybody, from the President of the United States to the day-laborers on the road.

The two engines moved nearer each other, and the crowd gathered round the open space. Then all fell back a little so that the view should be unobstructed. Brief remarks were made by Governor Stanford on one side, and General Dodge on the other. It was now about twelve o'clock noon, local time, or about 2 P.M. in New York. The two superintendents of construction—S. B. Reed of the Union Pacific, and S. W. Strawbridge of the Central—placed under the rails the last tie. It was of California laurel, highly polished, with a silver plate in the centre bearing the following inscription: "The last tie laid on the completion of the Pacific Railroad, May 10, 1869," with the names of the officers and directors of both companies.

Everything being then in readiness the word was given, and "Hats off" went clicking over the wires to the waiting crowds at New York, Philadelphia, San Francisco, and all the principal cities. Prayer was offered by the venerable Rev. Dr. Todd, at the conclusion of which our operator tapped out: "We have got done praying. The spike is about to be presented," to which the response came back: "We understand. All are ready in the East." The gentlemen who had been commissioned to present the four spikes, two of gold, and two of silver, from Montana, Idaho, California, and Nevada, stepped forward, and with brief appropriate remarks discharged the duty assigned them.

Governor Stanford, standing on the north, and Dr. Durant on the south side of the track, received the spikes and put them in place. Our operator tapped out: "All ready now; the spike will soon be driven. The signal will be three dots for the commencement of the blows." An instant later the silver hammers came down, and at each stroke in all the offices from San Francisco to New York, and throughout the land, the hammer of the magnet struck the bell.

The signal "Done" was received at Washington at 2.47 P.M., which was about a quarter of one at Promontory. There was not much formality in the demonstration that followed, but the enthusiasm was genuine and unmistakable. The two engines moved up until they touched each other, and a bottle of champagne was poured on the last rail, after the manner of christening a ship at the launching.

The event was celebrated in all the large cities, and everywhere hailed with demonstrations of delight. In New York, Trinity Church was thrown open at mid-day, an address was delivered by Rev. Dr. Vinton, and a large crowd united "to tender thanks to God for the completion of the greatest work ever undertaken by man." In Philadelphia bells were rung and cannon fired. At Chicago a great impromptu demonstration took place, in which all citizens joined; at Buffalo a large crowd gathered to hear the telegraph signals, sang the "Star-Spangled Banner," and listened to speeches from distinguished citizens; and at every important point the announcement of the completion of the work was received with unbounded joy.

THE THRILL OF WESTERN RAILROADING

Modern Americans, living in a day of supersonic planes and outer-space rockets, have difficulty understanding the impact of the first transcontinental railroad on the public mind. Yet few events in transportation history have been so significant. For the first time the nation's outposts could be reached without a grueling month of travel; now the ordinary citizen could journey from New York to San Francisco in a week, living in a style to which he was usually unaccustomed. A traveler on the Union Pacific in the early 1870s captured in her account of the trip something of the breathless excitement of those who ventured into the unknown West—an excitement rivaled today only by astronauts venturing into equally unknown worlds:[11]

We cross the Missouri at Council Bluffs; begin grumbling at the railroad corporations for forcing us to take a transfer train across the river; but find ourselves plunged into the confusion of Omaha before we have finished railing at the confusion of her neighbor. Now we see for the first time the distinctive expression of American overland travel. Here all luggage is weighed and rechecked for points further west. An enormous shed is filled with it. Four and five deep stand the anxious owners, at a high wooden wall, behind which nobody may go. Everybody holds up checks, and gesticulates and beckons.

---

[11] Helen Hunt Jackson, *Bits of Travel at Home* (Boston, 1878), pp. 6–9.

There seems to be no system; but undoubtedly there is. Side by side with the rich and flurried New-Yorker stands the poor and flurried emigrant. Equality rules. Big bundles of feather-beds, tied up in blue check, red chests, corded with rope, get ahead of Saratoga trunks. Many languages are spoken. German, Irish, French, Spanish, a little English, and all varieties of American, I heard during thirty minutes in that luggage-shed. Inside the wall was a pathetic sight,—a poor German woman on her knees before a chest, which had burst open on the journey. It seemed as if its whole contents could not be worth five dollars,—so old, so faded, so coarse were the clothes and so battered were the utensils. But it was evidently all she owned; it was the home she had brought with her from the Fatherland, and would be the home she would set up in the prairie. The railroad-men were good to her, and were helping her with ropes and nails. This comforted me somewhat; but it seemed almost a sin to be journeying luxuriously on the same day and train with that poor soul.

"Lunches put up for people going West." This sign was out on all corners. Piles of apparently ownerless bundles were stacked all along the platforms; but everybody was too busy to steal. Some were eating hastily, with looks of distress, as if they knew it would be long before they ate again. Others, wiser, were buying whole chickens, loaves of bread, and filling bottles with tea. Provident Germans bought sausage by the yard. German babies got bits of it to keep them quiet. Murderous-looking rifles and guns, with strapped rolls of worn and muddy blankets, stood here and there; murderous, but jolly-looking miners, four-fifths boots and the rest beard, strode about, keeping one eye on their weapons and bedding. Well-dressed women and men with polished shoes, whose goods were already comfortably bestowed in palace-cars, lounged up and down, curious, observant, amused. Gay placards, advertising all possible routes; cheerful placards, setting forth the advantages of travellers' insurance policies; insulting placards, assuming that all travellers have rheumatism, and should take "Unk Weed;" in short, just such placards as one sees everywhere,—papered the walls. But here they seemed somehow to be true and merit attention, especially the "Unk Weed." There is such a professional croak in that first syllable; it sounds as if the weed had a diploma.

"All aboard!" rung out like the last warning on Jersey City wharves when steamers push off for Europe; and in the twinkling of an eye we were out again in the still, soft, broad prairie, which is certainly more like sea than like any other land.

Again flowers and meadows, and here and there low hills, more trees, too, and a look of greater richness. Soon the Platte River, which seems to be composed of equal parts of sand and water, but which has too solemn a history to be spoken lightly of. It has been the silent guide for so many brave men who are dead! The old emigrant road, over which they went, is yet plainly to be seen; at many points it lies near the railroad. Its still, grass-grown track is strangely pathetic. Soon it will be smooth prairie again, and the wooden headboards at the graves of those who died by the way will have fallen and crumbled.

Dinner at Fremont. The air was sharp and clear. The disagreeable guide-book said we were only 1,176 feet above the sea; but we believed we were higher. The keeper of the dining-saloon apologized for not having rhubarb-pie, saying that he had just sent fifty pounds of rhubarb on ahead to his other saloon. "You'll take tea there to-morrow night."

"But how far apart are your two houses?" said we.

"Only eight hundred miles. It's considerable trouble to go back an' forth, an' keep things straight; but I do the best I can."

Two barefooted little German children, a boy and girl, came into the cars here, with milk and coffee to sell. The boy carried the milk, and was sorely puzzled when I held out my small tumbler to be filled. It would hold only half as much as his tin measure, of which the price was five cents.

"Donno's that's quite fair," he said, when I gave him five cents. But he pocketed it, all the same, and ran on, swinging his tin can and pint cup, and calling out, "Nice fresh milk. Last you'll get! No milk any further west." Little rascal! We found it all the way; plenty of it too, such as it was. It must be owned, however, that sage-brush and prickly pear (and if the cows do not eat these, what do they eat?) give a singularly unpleasant taste to milk; and the addition of alkali water does not improve it.

As western travel became more commonplace, and as the West itself became better known, the American people gradually awakened to the realization that they were living in a new age. Now hitherto remote parts of the continent could be visited and used by man. This became especially true during the next decade as other transcontinental railroads reached their destinations: the Southern Pacific, the Atchison, Topeka and Santa Fe, the Kansas Pacific, and the Northern Pacific. All were completed by 1884, placing formerly inaccessible areas within reach of settlers and markets. The way was open now for the final conquest of the Far West by pioneers. Before this advance could be launched, however, the prior occupants had to be dislodged. The completion of the transcontinental railroads doomed the American Indian and opened one of the most tragic chapters in the history of the United States.

CHAPTER 25

The Indian Barrier, 1860-1890

Even before the completion of the transcontinental railroads, the fate of thousands of Indians who occupied the Far West was sealed. To the frontiersmen and to the government alike the red men stood in the way of "progress"; their "wasteful" economy withheld from "civilized" users millions of acres of productive land that could be better employed. To travelers westward they were a hovering menace, threatening the stage and wagon routes that threaded the center of the continent. So they must go. Between 1854 and 1859, alternately by persuasion and force, the tribes that occupied the Kansas and Nebraska territories were pushed to one side, some onto small reservations north or south of the transportation routes, others westward to mingle with the plains Indians.

THE CHIVINGTON MASSACRE

The shaky peace that followed resettlement of the Indians was upset when the Pike's Peak gold rush sent a hundred thousand miners across the Indian lands. The Cheyenne and Arapaho, watching the scattering of the buffalo herds that were their staff of life, struck back to preserve their traditional culture. Between 1861 and 1864, they raided outlying settlements in the Colorado country, burning farmhouses and stage stations and killing a number of settlers. The climax of this "war" came in 1864, when a force of Colorado militiamen marched against the Indian reservation at Sand Creek in the southeastern corner of the territory. By this time the red men had sued for peace and believed themselves under federal protection. So they were caught unawares when the troops, commanded by the Indian-hating Colonel J. M. Chivington, fell upon their camp in the early morning of November 29, 1864. Within a few hours nearly 500 lay dead, many of them women and children, and some of them horribly mutilated. Even seasoned soldiers were horrified by this slaughter, as two of them testified later before a congressional investigating committee:[1]

Personally appeared before me Lieutenant James Connor First New Mexico Volunteer Infantry, who, after being duly sworn, says: That on the 28th day of November, 1864, I was ordered by Major General Scott J. An-

[1] 39th Congress, 2nd Session, U.S. Senate, *Reports of Committees*, No. 156, pp. 53, 73–74.

thony to accompany him on an expedition (Indian) as his battalion adjutant; the object of that expedition was to be a thorough campaign against hostile Indians, as I was led to understand. I referred to the fact of there being a friendly camp of Indians in that immediate neighborhood and remonstrated against simply attacking that camp, as I was aware that they were resting there, in fancied security under promises held out to them of safety from Major E. W. Wynkoop, former Commander of the post of Fort Lyon, as well as by Major J. S. Anthony, then in command.

Our battalion was attached to the command of Colonel J. M. Chivington, and left Fort Lyon on the night of the 28th of November, 1864; about daybreak on the morning of the 29th of November we came in sight of the camp of the friendly Indians aforementioned, and were ordered by Colonel Chivington to attack the same, which was accordingly done. The command of Colonel Chivington was composed of about one thousand men; the village of the Indians consisted of from one hundred to one hundred and thirty lodges, and, as far as I am able to judge, of from five hundred to six hundred souls, the majority of which were woman and children; in going over the battle-ground the next day I did not see a body of man, woman, or child but was scalped, and in many instances their bodies were mutilated in the most horrible manner —men, women, and children's privates cut out, &c; I heard one man say that he had cut out a woman's private parts and had them for exhibition on a stick; I heard another man say that he had cut the fingers off an Indian to get the rings on the hand; according to the best of my knowledge and belief these atrocities that were committed were with the knowledge of J. M. Chivington, and I do not know of his taking any measures to prevent them; I heard of one instance of a child a few months old being thrown in the feed-box of a wagon, and after being carried some distance left on the ground to perish; I also heard of numerous instances in which men had cut out the private parts of females and stretched them over the saddle-bows, and wore them over their hats while riding in the ranks. All these matters were a subject of general conversation, and could not help being known by Colonel J. M. Chivington.

Lieutenant Cramer Sworn: I am stationed at this post, First lieutenant, Company C, veteran battalion, Colorado Cavalry. I was at this post when Colonel Chivington arrived here, and accompanied him on his expedition. He came into the post with a few officers and men, and threw out pickets, with instructions to allow no one to go beyond the line. I was then in command of company K. He brought some eight or nine hundred men with him, and took from his post over a hundred men, all being mounted. My company was ordered along to take part. We arrived at the Indian village about daylight. On arriving in sight of the village a battalion of the 1st cavalry and the Fort Lyon battalion were ordered on a charge to surround the village and the Indian herd. After driving the herd towards the village, Lieutenant Wilson's battalion of the 1st took possession of the northeast side of the village, Major Anthony's battalion took position on the south, Colonel Chivington's 3d regiment took position in our rear, dismounted, and after the fight had been commenced by Major Anthony and Lieutenant Wilson, mounted, and commenced firing through us and over our heads. About this time Captain John Smith, Indian interpreter, attempting to come to our troops, was fired on by our men, at the command of some one in our rear, "To shoot the damned old son of a bitch." One of my men rode forward to save him, but was killed. To get out of the fire from the rear, we were ordered to the left. About this time Colonel Chivington moved his regiment to the front, the Indians retreating up the creek, and hiding under the banks. There seemed to be no organization among our troops; every one on his own hook, and shots flying between our own ranks. White Antelope ran towards our columns unarmed, and with both arms raised, but was killed. Several other of the warriors were killed in like manner. The women and children were huddled together, and most of our fire was concentrated on them. Sometimes during the engagement I was compelled to move my company to get out of the fire of our own men. Captain Soule did not order his men to fire when the order was given to commence the fight. During the fight, the battery on the opposite side of the creek kept firing at the bank while our men were in range. The Indian warriors, about one hundred in number, fought desperately; there were about five hundred all told. I estimated the loss of the Indians to be from one hundred and twenty-five to one hundred and seventy-five killed; no wounded fell into our hands, and all the dead were scalped. The Indian who was pointed out as White Antelope had his fingers cut off. Our force was so large that there was no necessity of firing on the Indians. They did not return the fire until after our troops had fired several rounds. We had the assurance from Major Anthony that Black Kettle and his friends should be saved, and only those Indians who had committed depredations should be harmed. During the fight no officer took any measures to get out of the fire of our own men. Left Hand stood with his arms folded, saying he would not fight the white men, as they were his friends. I told Colonel Chivington of the position in which the officers stood from Major Wynkoop's pledges to the Indians, and also Major Anthony's, and that it would be murder, in every sense of the word, if he attacked those Indians. His reply was, bringing his fist down close to my face, "Damn any man who sympathizes with Indians." I told him what pledges were given the Indians. He replied, "That he had come to kill Indians, and believed it to be honorable to kill Indians under any and all circumstances"; all this at Fort Lyon. Lieutenant Dunn went to Colonel Chivington and wanted to know if he could kill his prisoner, young Smith. His reply was, "Don't ask me; you know my orders; I want no prisoners." Colonel Chivington was in position where he must have seen the scalping and mutilation going on. One of the soldiers was taking a squaw prisoner across the creek, when other soldiers fired on him, telling him they would kill him if he did not let her go. On our approach to the village I saw some one with a white flag approaching our lines, and the troops fired upon it; and at the time Captain Smith was fired upon, some one wearing a uniform coat was fired upon approaching our lines. Captain Smith was wearing one. After the first I saw the United States flag in the Indian camp. It is a mistake that there were any white scalps found in the village. I saw one, but it was very old, the hair being much faded. I was ordered to burn the village, and was through all the lodges. There was not any snow on the ground, and no rifle-pits.

THE CONGRESSIONAL PEACE COMMISSION OF 1867

As word of American brutality at the Chivington Massacre spread among the plains Indians, war flamed anew. Fighting now spread northward, where the Sioux were rallied by an attempt of the United States to build the Powder River Road between Fort Laramie on the California Trail and the Montana mining camps. In this savage conflict one party of eighty-two soldiers under Captain W. J. Fetterman was ambushed and slaughtered. This senseless bloodshed stirred such resentment among eastern humanitarians that Congress felt called upon to reappraise the nation's entire Indian policy. The result was the creation in 1867 of a Congressional Peace Commission to survey the situation, negotiate with dissatisfied tribesmen, and seek a solution to the whole problem. One of the members of this commission, General William T. Sherman of Civil War fame, described its purposes and results in his memoirs:[2]

On the 20th of July, 1867, President Johnson approved an act to establish peace with certain hostile Indian tribes, the first section of which reads as follows: "Be it enacted, etc., that the President of the United States be and is hereby authorized to appoint a commission to consist of three (3) officers of the army not below the rank of brigadier-general, who, together with N. G. Taylor, Commissioner of Indian Affairs, John B. Henderson, chairman of the Committee of Indian Affairs of the Senate, S. F. Tappan, and John B. Sanborn, shall have power and authority to call together the chiefs and head men of such bands or tribes of Indians as are now waging war against the United States, or committing depredations on the people thereof, to ascertain the alleged reasons for their acts of hostility, and in their discretion, under the direction of the President, to make and conclude with said bands or tribes such treaty stipulations, subject to the action of the Senate, as may remove all just causes of complaint on their part, and at the same time establish security for person and property along the lines of railroad now being constructed to the Pacific and other thoroughfares of travel to the Western Territories, and such as will most likely insure civilization for the Indians, and peace and safety for the whites."

The President named as the military members Lieutenant-General Sherman, Brigadier-Generals A. H. Terry and W. S. Harney. Subsequently, to insure a full attendance, Brigadier-General C. C. Augur was added to the commission, and his name will be found on most of the treaties. The commissioners met at St. Louis and elected N. G. Taylor, the Commissioner of Indian Affairs, president; J. B. Sanborn, treasurer; and A. S. H. White, Esq., of Washington, D. C., secretary. The year 1867 was too far advanced to complete the task assigned during that season, and it was agreed that a steamboat (St. John's) should be chartered to convey the commission up the Missouri River, and we adjourned to meet at Omaha. In the St. John's the commission proceeded up the Missouri River, holding informal "talks" with the Santees at their agency near the Niobrara, the Yanktonnais at Fort Thompson, and the Ogallallas, Minneconjous, Sans Arcs, etc., at Fort Sully. From this point runners were sent out to the Sioux occupying the country west of the Missouri River, to meet us in council at the Forks of the Platte that fall, and to Sitting Bull's band of outlaw Sioux, and the Crows on the upper Yellowstone, to meet us in May, 1868, at Fort Laramie. We proceeded up the river to the mouth of the Cheyenne and turned back to Omaha, having ample time on this steamboat to discuss and deliberate on the problems submitted to our charge.

We all agreed that the nomad Indians

---

[2] William T. Sherman, *Memoirs of General William T. Sherman* (New York, 1890), vol. 2, pp. 434–436.

should be removed from the vicinity of the two great railroads then in rapid construction, and be localized on one or other of the two great reservations south of Kansas and north of Nebraska; that agreements, not treaties, should be made for their liberal maintenance as to food, clothing, schools, and farming implements for ten years, during which time we believed that these Indians should become self-supporting. To the north we proposed to remove the various bands of Sioux, with such others as could be induced to locate near them; and to the south, on the Indian Territory already established, we proposed to remove the Cheyennes, Arapahoes, Kiowas, Comanches, and such others as we could prevail on to move thither.

At that date the Union Pacific construction had reached the Rocky Mountains at Cheyenne, and the Kansas Pacific to about Fort Wallace. We held council with the Ogallallas at the Forks of the Platte, and arranged to meet them all the next spring, 1868. In the spring of 1868 we met the Crows in council at Fort Laramie, the Sioux at the North Platte, the Shoshones or Snakes at Fort Hall, the Navajos at Fort Sumner, on the Pecos, and the Cheyennes and Arapahoes at Medicine Lodge. To accomplish these results the commission divided up into committees, General Augur going to the Shoshones, Mr. Tappan and I to the Navajos, and the remainder to Medicine Lodge. In that year we made treaties or arrangements with all the tribes which before had followed the buffalo in their annual migrations, and which brought them into constant conflict with the whites.

Mr. Tappan and I found it impossible to prevail on the Navajos to remove to the Indian Territory, and had to consent to their return to their former home, restricted to a limited reservation west of Santa Fé, about old Fort Defiance, and there they continue unto this day, rich in the possession of herds of sheep and goats, with some cattle and horses; and they have remained at peace ever since.

THE BATTLE OF THE WASHITA

General Sherman and the other commissioners were whistling in the dark when they believed that the Indians would now live in peace with the whites. They were asking the principal tribes to crowd themselves into two large reservations, one in the Black Hills country, the other in the Indian Territory of modern Oklahoma. This meant the complete abandonment of one culture and the forced adoption of another; it meant forsaking the buffalo hunt and nomadic wandering for a sedantary existence as wards of the United States. No human being would make this transition willingly, and the red men were no exception. By the fall of 1868, the war was in full swing again, and once more the savagry on both sides shocked the civilized world. The most significant engagement occurred when General Philip H. Sheridan decided on a winter campaign and sent a sizable force under Colonel George A. Custer against a camp of the "hostiles" on the Washita River. The Indians, never expecting a winter attack, were taken by surprise when Custer's men struck at daybreak on November 26, 1868. The commander, who seldom underestimated his own accomplishments, later described how he divided his men in four columns for the assault, and the result:[3]

We had approached near enough to the village now to plainly catch a view here and there of the tall white lodges as they stood in irregular order among the trees. From the openings at the top of some of them we

---

[3] George A. Custer, *My Life on the Plains* (New York, 1874), pp. 163–165.

could perceive faint columns of smoke ascending, the occupants no doubt having kept up their feeble fires during the entire night. We had approached so near the village that from the dead silence which reigned I feared the lodges were deserted, the Indians having fled before we advanced. I was about to turn in my saddle and direct the signal for attack to be given—still anxious as to where the other detachments were—when a single rifle shot rang sharp and clear on the far side of the village from where we were. Quickly turning to the band leader, I directed him to give us "Garry Owen." At once the rollicking notes of that familiar marching and fighting air sounded forth through the valley, and in a moment were reechoed back from the opposite sides by the loud and continued cheers of the men of the other detachments, who, true to their orders, were there and in readiness to pounce upon the Indians the moment the attack began. In this manner the battle of the Washita commenced. The bugles sounded the charge, and the entire command dashed rapidly into the village. The Indians were caught napping; but realizing at once the dangers of their situation, they quickly overcame their first surprise and in an instant seized their rifles, bows, and arrows, and sprang behind the nearest trees, while some leaped into the stream, nearly waist deep, and using the bank as a rifle-pit, began a vigorous and determined defence. Mingled with the exultant cheers of my men could be heard the defiant war-whoop of the warriors, who from the first fought with a desperation and courage which no race of men could surpass. Actual possession of the village and its lodges was ours within a few moments after the charge was made, but this was an empty victory unless we could vanquish the late occupants, who were then pouring in a rapid and well-directed fire from their stations behind trees and banks. At the first onset a considerable number of the Indians rushed from the village in the direction from which Elliot's party had attacked. Some broke through the lines, while others came in contact with the mounted troopers, and were killed or captured.

Before engaging in the fight, orders had been given to prevent the killing of any but the fighting strength of the village; but in a struggle of this character it is impossible at all times to discriminate, particularly when, in a hand-to-hand conflict, such as the one the troops were then engaged in, the squaws are as dangerous adversaries as the warriors, while Indian boys between ten and fifteen years of age were found as expert and determined in the use of the pistol and bow and arrow as the older warriors. Of these facts we had numerous illustrations. Major Benteen, in leading the attack of his squadron through the timber below the village, encountered an Indian boy, scarcely fourteen years of age; he was well mounted, and was endeavoring to make his way through the lines. The object these Indians had in attempting this movement we were then ignorant of, but soon learned to our sorrow. This boy rode boldly toward the Major, seeming to invite a contest. His youthful bearing, and not being looked upon as a combatant, induced Major Benteen to endeavor to save him by making "peace signs" to him and obtaining his surrender, when he could be placed in a position of safety until the battle was terminated; but the young savage desired and would accept no such friendly concessions. He regarded himself as a warrior, and the son of a warrior, and as such he purposed to do a warrior's part. With revolver in hand he dashed at the Major, who still could not regard him as anything but a harmless lad. Levelling his weapon as he rode, he fired, but either from excitement or the changing positions of both parties, his aim was defective and the shot whistled harmlessly by Major Benteen's head. Another followed in quick succession, but with no better effect. All this time the dusky little chieftain boldly advanced, to lessen the distance between himself and his adversary. A third bullet was sped on its errand, and this time to some purpose, as it passed through the neck of the Major's horse, close to the shoulder. Making a final but ineffectual appeal to him to surrender, and seeing him still preparing to fire again, the Major was forced in self-defence to level his revolver and to despatch him, although as he did so it was with admiration for the plucky spirit exhibited by the lad, and regret often expressed that no other course under the circumstances was left him. Attached to the saddle bow of the young Indian hung a beautifully wrought pair of small moccasins, elaborately ornamented with beads. One of the Major's troopers afterward secured these and presented them to him. These furnished the link of evidence by which we subsequently ascertained who the young chieftain was—a title which was justly his, both by blood and bearing.

We had gained the centre of the village, and were in the midst of the lodges, while on all sides could be heard the sharp crack of the Indian rifles and the heavy responses from the carbines of the troopers. After disposing of the smaller and scattering parties of warriors, who had attempted a movement down the valley, and in which some were successful, there was but little opportunity left for the successful employment of mounted troops. As the Indians by this time had taken cover behind logs and trees, and under the banks of the stream which flowed through the centre of the village, from which stronghold it was impracticable to dislodge them by the use of mounted men, a large portion of the command was at once ordered to fight on foot, and the men were instructed to take advantage of the trees and other natural means of cover, and fight the Indians in their own style. Cook's sharpshooters had adopted this method from the first, and with telling effect. Slowly but steadily the Indians were driven from behind the trees, and those who escaped the carbine bullets posted themselves with their companions who were already firing from the banks. One party of troopers came upon a squaw endeavoring to make her escape, leading by the hand a little white boy, a prisoner in the hands of the Indians, and who doubtless had been captured by some of their war parties during a raid upon the settlements. Who or where his parents were, or whether still alive or murdered by the Indians, will never be known, as the squaw, finding herself and prisoner about to be surrounded by the troops, and her escape cut off, determined, with savage malignity, that the triumph of the latter should not embrace the rescue of the white boy. Casting her eyes quickly in all directions, to convince herself that escape was impossible, she drew from beneath her blanket a huge knife and plunged it into the almost naked body of her captive. The next moment retributive justice reached her in the shape of a well-directed bullet from one of the troopers' carbines. Before the men could reach them life was extinct in the bodies of both the squaw and her unknown captive.

The desperation with which the Indians fought may be inferred from the following: Seventeen warriors had posted themselves in a depression in the ground, which enabled them to protect their bodies completely from the fire of our men, and it was only when the Indians raised their heads to fire that the troopers could aim with any prospect of success. All efforts to drive the warriors from this point proved abortive, and resulted in severe loss to our side. They were only vanquished at last by our men securing positions under cover and picking them off by sharpshooting as they exposed themselves to get a shot at the troopers. Finally the last one was despatched in this manner. In a deep ravine near the suburbs of the village the dead bodies of thirty-eight warriors were reported after the fight terminated. Many of the squaws and children had very prudently not attempted to leave the village when we attacked it, but remained concealed inside their lodges. All these escaped injury, although when surrounded by the din and wild excitement of the fight, and in close proximity to the contending parties, their fears overcame some of them, and they gave vent to their despair by singing the death song, a combination of weird-like sounds which were suggestive of anything but musical tones. As soon as we had driven the warriors from the village, and the fighting was pushed to the country outside, I directed "Romeo," the interpreter, to go around to all the lodges and assure the squaws and children remaining in them that they would be unharmed and kindly cared for; at the same time he was to assemble them in the large lodges designated for that purpose, which were standing near the centre of the village. This was quite a delicate mission, as it was difficult to convince the squaws and children that they had anything but death to expect at our hands.

THE BATTLE OF THE LITTLE BIG HORN

Custer gained his fame at the Battle of the Washita, but he was to lose his life in a more serious war that followed on the northern plains. There the Sioux grew increasingly restless in their Black Hills reservation, and with reason. Corrupt agents pocketed their annuities, appropriated their supplies, and alloted them moldy flour and spoiled beef. When some bands reached the point of near starvation, warriors began drifting back to their old hunting grounds along the eastern slopes of the Big Horn mountains, where game was plentiful. When ordered to return, they gathered about two powerful chiefs, Sitting Bull and Crazy Horse, and declared that they would fight to preserve their fathers' way of life. This was a declaration of war. Three columns of troops were sent to converge on the Big Horn country during the summer of 1876. The commander of one, General Alfred H. Terry, sent a small force under Custer to scout the enemy position. Instead of returning to Terry's command when he located a large Sioux and Cheyenne village, this foolhardy commander attacked on June 25, 1876. His recklessness cost the lives of 265 men but won them enduring fame, for few battles captured the national imagination as did that on the Little Big Horn River. No white man survived to describe that engagement, but Sitting Bull was interviewed a year later by a correspondent of the "New York Herald," and told this story:[4]

"When the fight commenced here," I asked, pointing to the spot where Custer advanced beyond the Little Big Horn, "what happened?"

"Hell!"

"You mean, I suppose, a fierce battle?"

"I mean a thousand devils."

"The village was by this time thoroughly aroused?"

"The squaws were like flying birds; the bullets were like humming bees."

"You say that when the first attack was made, up here on the right of the map, the old men and the squaws and children ran down the valley toward the left. What did they do when this second attack came from up here toward the left?"

"They ran back again to the right, here and here," answered Sitting Bull, placing his

---

[4] *New York Herald*, November 16, 1877. Reprinted in W. A. Graham, *The Custer Myth. A Source Book of Custeriana* (Harrisburg, Penn.: Stackpole, 1953), pp. 70–72.

swarthy finger on the place where the words "Abandoned Lodges" are.

"And where did the warriors run?"

"They ran to the fight—the big fight."

"So that, in the afternoon, after the fight, on the right hand side of the map was over, and after the big fight toward the left hand side began, you say that the squaws and children all returned to the right hand side, and that the warriors, the fighting men of all the Indian camps, ran to the place where the big fight was going on?"

"Yes."

"Why was that? Were not some of the warriors left in front of these intrenchments on the bluffs, near the right side of the map? Did not you think it necessary—did not your war chiefs think it necessary—to keep some of your young men there to fight the troops who had retreated to those intrenchments?"

"No."

"Why?"

"You have forgotten."

"How?"

"You forget that only a few soldiers were left by the Long Hair on those bluffs. He took the main body of his soldiers with him to make the big fight down here on the left."

"So there were no soldiers to make a fight left in the intrenchments on the right hand bluffs?"

"I have spoken. It is enough. The squaws could deal with them. There were none but squaws and pappooses in front of them that afternoon."

"Well then," I inquired of Sitting Bull, "Did the cavalry, who came down and made the big fight, fight?"

Again Sitting Bull smiled.

"They fought. Many young men are missing from our lodges. But is there an American squaw who has her husband left? Were there any Americans left to tell the story of that day? No."

"How did they come on to the attack?"

"I have heard that there are trees which tremble."

"Do you mean the trees with trembling leaves?"

"Yes."

"They call them in some parts of the western country Quaking Asps; in the eastern part of the country they call them Silver Aspens."

"Hah! A great white chief, whom I met once, spoke these words 'Silver Aspens,' trees that shake; these were the Long Hair's soldiers."

"You do not mean that they trembled before your people because they were afraid?"

"They were brave men. They were tired. They were too tired."

"How did they act? How did they behave themselves?"

At this Sitting Bull again arose. I also arose from my seat, as did the other persons in the room, except the stenographer.

"Your people," said Sitting Bull, extending his right hand, "were killed. I tell no lies about deadmen. These men who came with the Long Hair were as good men as ever fought. When they rode up their horses were tired and they were tired. When they got off from their horses they could not stand firmly on their feet. They swayed to and fro—so my young men have told me—like the limbs of cypresses in a great wind. Some of them staggered under the weight of their guns. But they began to fight at once; but by this time, as I have said, our camps were aroused, and there were plenty of warriors to meet them. They fired with needle guns. We replied with magazine guns—repeating rifles. It was so (and here Sitting Bull illustrated by patting his palms together with the rapidity of a fusilade). Our young men rained lead across the river and drove the white braves back."

"And then?"

"And then, they rushed across themselves."

"And then?"

"And then they found that they had a good deal to do."

"Was there at that time some doubt about the issue of the battle, whether you would whip the Long Hair or not?"

"There was so much doubt about it that I started down there (here again pointing to the map) to tell the squaws to pack up the lodges and get ready to move away."

"You were on that expedition, then, after the big fight had fairly begun?"

"Yes."

"You did not personally witness the rest of the big fight? You were not engaged in it?"

"No. I have heard of it from the warriors."

"When the great crowds of your young men crossed the river in front of the Long Hair what did they do? Did they attempt to assault him directly in his front?"

"At first they did, but afterward they found it better to try and get around him. They formed themselves on all sides of him except just at his back."

"How long did it take them to put themselves around his flanks?"

"As long as it takes the sun to travel from here to here" (indicating some marks upon his arm with which apparently he is used to gauge the progress of the shadow of his lodge across his arm, and probably meaning half an hour. An Indian has no more definite way than this to express the lapse of time).

"The trouble was with the soldiers," he continued; "they were so exhausted and their horses bothered them so much that they could not take good aim. Some of their horses broke away from them and left them to stand and drop and die. When the Long Hair, the General, found that he was so outnumbered and threatened on his flanks, he took the best course he could have taken. The bugle blew. It was an order to fall back. All the men fell back fighting and dropping. They could not fire fast enough, though. But from our side it was so," said Sitting Bull, and here he clapped his hands rapidly twice a second to express with what quickness and continuance the balls flew from the Henry and Winchester rifles wielded by the Indians. "They could not stand up under such a fire," he added.

"Were any military tactics shown? Did the Long Haired Chief make any disposition of his soldiers, or did it seem as though they retreated all together, helter skelter, fighting for their lives?"

"They kept in pretty good order. Some great chief must have commanded them all the while. They would fall back across a *coulee* and make a fresh stand beyond on higher ground. The map is pretty nearly right. It shows where the white men stopped and fought before they were all killed. I think that is right—down there to the left, just above the Little Big Horn. There was one part driven out there, away from the rest, and there a great many men were killed. The places marked on the map are pretty nearly the places where all were killed."

"Did the whole command keep on fighting until the last?"

"Every man, so far as my people could see. There were no cowards on either side."

THE EXTERMINATION OF THE BUFFALO

"Custer's last stand" stirred the nation but did the Indians little good. Hopelessly outnumbered and woefully undersupplied, they were driven eastward until forced to surrender in

October 1876. Only Sitting Bull and some of his defiant warriors resisted, fleeing to Canada where they remained until 1881. Other Indian wars were fought during the next years, against Chief Joseph and his Nez Percé warriors in the Northwest, against Geronimo and his Apache in the Southwest, against the Sioux in the Black Hills reservation during the Ghost Dance outbreak of the 1890s. But the backbone of the red man's power had been broken, not by troops, but by the extermination of the buffalo. This was the Indians' staff of life, supplying him with food, clothing, shelter, and fuel. The opening of the West by railroads brought a small army of professional hunters who systematically slaughtered the great herds for their hides. By 1878, the southern herd was gone, and five years later that in the north had been exterminated. Hamlin Russell described this carnage as he observed it:[5]

The Union Pacific Railroad was completed in 1869, other railroads began to reach out their iron arms across the Kansas and Nebraska plains, and from that hour the fate of the buffalo was sealed. For several years to come he could be hunted, shot from horseback, driven into enclosures and slaughtered, or perhaps forced over precipices after the manner described in old geographies and school-books. The animals seem to have divided into two great herds towards the close of their career, for we hear of "the great Southern herd" and "the great Northern herd." The Southern herd was the first to go. Buffalo Bill and his kind, with English "sportsmen" and American army officers, vied with each other in the wanton slaughter. During three short years—1872-3-4—the number so killed has been estimated in millions. It matters not how accurate this estimate is, or whether the number so slain was one million or ten millions, the fact remains that at the close of 1874 the great Southern herd was extinct.

In the North the conditions were more favorable, but the relentless hunter was hot upon the trail of the diminishing herds. In 1876 Fort Benton alone sent eighty thousand hides to market. In 1883 two car-loads of hides were shipped from Dickinson, North Dakota. In 1884 Fort Benton sent none at all. In 1879 a little band of the animals were known to be grazing near Fort Totten, on Devil Lake, North Dakota, and it is believed that these animals furnished the two car-loads of robes which came eastward to St. Paul from Dickinson in 1883. This was the last year of the Buffalo—1883. A herd, numbering perhaps eighty thousand, crossed the Yellowstone River in that year, and went north towards the British line. "They never came back," is the pitiful refrain which one hears from the Indians along the border from Winnipeg in Manitoba to St. Mary's Lakes in Alberta. No, they never came back, and last summer and fall, while riding with the officers of the Canadian mounted police through Alberta, they told me the story of this last year of the buffalo, but it was never told twice alike by any two men, for a strange mystery seemed to hang over the closing scene of the great crime which annihilated the mighty herds. Some think that in the far North, in a great sheltered valley where the climate is tempered by the Chinook winds, the remnant of the "Old Guard" still remain, and refuse to make the attempt of another Southern migration. Frank A. Dowd, formerly a locomotive engineer on the Northern Pacific Railroad, but now the customs officer at the Sweet Grass Hills on the northern line of Montana, holds to this theory. He says: "They *couldn't* all have

---

[5] Hamlin Russell, "The Story of the Buffalo," *Harper's New Monthly Magazine*, LXXXVI (April, 1893), 796–798.

been killed so quickly. I saw them crossing the Yellowstone River. They darkened the plains with their numbers. Some of them must be living in the North. I don't believe that they were all killed." There are many others who hold with Mr. Dowd, but I cannot think the theory sound, for while all agree that many thousands of the herds reached the British line, and disappeared in the "great lone land" beyond, the weight of testimony is with those who hold that disease and the hard winter which followed annihilated the herd. A Roman Catholic priest, who has passed nearly all his life in the Northwest, said to me:

I remember that at Calgary, in 1881 and 1882, the Indians found the buffalo very poor and lean. It was all they could do to live on the meat during those years, and they complained that the animals were dying rapidly because of the unprecedentedly deep snows and severe winters. The hunters and Indians killed many of them, but the hard winter gave them the *coup de grâce*.

Other men were found who were ready to support both of these theories, for the subject furnishes an ever-present and interesting topic of conversation in all the wide territory north of the Northern Pacific Railroad to the lonely barracks of the mounted police force, far north of the Canadian Pacific line.

There was one fact, however, which the Canadian officers never lost an opportunity to speak of when discussing the subject. I remember seeing on the plains a great stack of whitening bones. There were perhaps fifty or a hundred tons of skulls and leg bones in the heap, which had been gathered by some of the northern Cree Indians. I had previously seen a pile of bones at Minot on the Great Northern Railroad which was estimated at over five thousand tons. This is all that is left of the buffalo now out of which the Indian can find profit. Once he obtained food, clothing, building material for his tepees, bones from which he could fashion weapons, and hides which he could sell or use in the making of canoes, and for many other purposes. Now the Eastern sugar-refineries purchase the bones found scattered all over the plains, to be used in clarifying sugar. The Indian picks them up, and he gets for them whatever the teamsters, commission men, brokers, railroad companies, and the other middle-men who stand between the starving savage on the plains and Claus Spreckles's representative choose to give him.

I said to the red-coated inspector who rode with me, "Do the Indians make a living gathering these bones?"

"Yes, in a way," was his reply; "but it is a mercy that they can't eat bones. We were never able to control the savages until their supply of meat was cut off. We have had no trouble worth speaking of since 1883, however."

There is a whole chapter in that remark. As long as the buffalo roamed through the Indian country, the settlement of the land and the extinction of the Indian title was practically an impossibility. With his food supply cut off, the Indian became suddenly tame and easy to handle. The West could not have been settled as rapidly as it has been since 1883 if the migratory herds of buffalo had continued their annual marches across the country. If one pities the poor Indian, he is also at liberty to pity the sad fate of the buffalo.

THE INDIAN PROBLEM:
THE MILITARIST'S SOLUTION

The sad plight of the Indians, crowded on reservations, the victims of corrupt agents, harassed by the military at every excuse, and forced to "walk the white man's road" when they preferred their own cultural patterns, stirred the national conscience during the 1880s and led the eastern half of the country into a period of unpleasant soul-searching. Were the Americans justified in reducing the noble red men to near peonage simply because the Indian definition of civilization differed from that of the majority of whites? And if not, what new policy could be substituted for the old? Disagreement on this point was violent. A sizable segment of the population held for the solution advocated by the "military"; control of Indian policy should be removed from the Office of Indian Affairs and vested in the army, thus eliminating the division of authority that had cost the red men so heavily. One able advocate of this viewpoint was General Nelson A. Miles, who expressed himself in strong language:[6]

It is held, first, that we as a generous people and liberal Government are bound to give to the Indians the same rights that all other men enjoy, and if we deprive them of these privileges we must then give them the best government possible. Without any legitimate government, and in a section of country where the lawless are under very little restraint, it is useless to suppose that thousands of wild savages thoroughly armed and mounted can be controlled by moral suasion. Even if they were in the midst of comfortable and agreeable surroundings, yet when dissatisfaction is increased by partial imprisonment and quickened by the pangs of hunger, a feeling that is not realized by one man in a thousand in civilized life, it requires more patience and forbearance than savage natures are likely to possess to prevent serious outbreaks.

The experiment of making a police force composed entirely of Indians is a dangerous one, unless they are under the shadow and control of a superior body of white troops, and, if carried to any great extent, will result in rearming the Indians and work disastrously to the frontier settlements. There would be a slight incongruity in a government out on the remote frontier, composed of a strictly non-combatant for chief, with a *posse comitatus* of red warriors, undertaking to control several thousand wild savages!

The available land that can be given to the Indians is being rapidly diminished; they can not be moved farther West; and some political party or administration must take the responsibility of protecting the Indians in their rights of person and property.

The advantage of placing the Indians under some government strong enough to control them and just enough to command their respect is too apparent to admit of argument. The results to be obtained would be:

First They would be beyond the possibility of doing harm, and the frontier settlements would be freed from their terrifying and devastating presence.

Second They would be under officials having a knowledge of the Indian country and the Indian character.

Third Their supplies and annuities would be disbursed through an efficient system of regulations.

Fourth Besides being amenable to the civil laws, these officers would be under strict military law, subject to trial and punishment for any act that would be "unbecoming a gentleman, or prejudicial to good order."

It is therefore suggested and earnestly recommended that a system which has proved to be eminently practicable should receive at least a fair trial. As the Government has in its employ men who by long and faithful service have established reputations for integrity, character, and ability which can not be disputed—men who have commanded armies,

---

[6] Nelson A. Miles, "The Indian Problem," *North American Review*, CXXVIII (March, 1879), 309–311.

reconstructed States, controlled hundreds of millions of public property, and who during years of experience on the frontier have opened the way for civilization and Christianty—it is believed that the services of these officials, in efforts to prevent war and elevate the Indian race, would be quite as judicious in their employment when inexperience and mismanagement have culminated in hostilities. Allowing the civilized and semi-civilized Indians to remain under the same supervision as at present, the President of the United States should have power to place the wild and nomadic tribes under the control of the War Department. Officers of known character, integrity, and experience, who would govern them and be interested in improving their condition, should be placed in charge of the different tribes. One difficulty has been, that they have been managed by officials too far away, and who knew nothing of the men they were dealing with. The Indians, as far as possible, should be localized on the public domain, in sections of country to which they are by nature adapted.

THE INDIAN PROBLEM:
THE HUMANITARIAN'S SOLUTION

Ranged against the military were reformers organized as the Indian Rights Association. Their solution was to abolish the reservation system and merge the Indians into the broader stream of American culture through education and land ownership. By far the most effective spokesman for this group was Helen Hunt Jackson, whose "Century of Dishonor" (1881) did more to plague the nation's conscience than any book since "Uncle Tom's Cabin":[7]

---

[7] Helen Hunt Jackson, *A Century of Dishonor* (New York, 1881), pp. 337–338, 340–342.

There is not among these three hundred bands of Indians one which has not suffered cruelly at the hands either of the Government or of white settlers. The poorer, the more insignificant, the more helpless the band, the more certain the cruelty and outrage to which they have been subjected. This is especially true of the bands on the Pacific slope. These Indians found themselves of a sudden surrounded by and caught up in the great influx of gold-seeking settlers, as helpless creatures on a shore are caught up in a tidal wave. There was not time for the Government to make treaties; not even time for communities to make laws. The tale of the wrongs, the oppressions, the murders of the Pacific-slope Indians in the last thirty years would be a volume by itself, and is too monstrous to be believed.

It makes little difference, however, where one opens the record of the history of the Indians; every page and every year has its dark stain. The story of one tribe is the story of all, varied only by differences of time and place; but neither time nor place makes any difference in the main facts. Colorado is as greedy and unjust in 1880 as was Georgia in 1830, and Ohio in 1795; and the United States Government breaks promises now as deftly as then, and with an added ingenuity from long practice.

One of its strongest supports in so doing is the wide-spread sentiment among the people of dislike to the Indian, of impatience with his presence as a "barrier to civilization," and distrust of it as a possible danger. The old tales of the frontier life, with its horrors of Indian warfare, have gradually, by two or three generations' telling, produced in the average mind something like an hereditary instinct of unquestioning and unreasoning aversion which it is almost impossible to dislodge or soften....

To assume that it would be easy, or by any one sudden stroke of legislative policy possible, to undo the mischief and hurt of the long past, set the Indian policy of the country right for the future, and make the Indians at once safe and happy, is the blunder of a hasty and uninformed judgment. The notion which seems to be growing more prevalent, that simply to make all Indians at once citizens of the United States would be a sovereign and instantaneous panacea for all their ills and all the Government's perplexities, is a very inconsiderate one. To administer complete citizenship of a sudden, all round, to all Indians, barbarous and civilized alike, would be as grotesque a blunder as to dose them all round with any one medicine, irrespective of the symptoms and needs of their diseases. It would kill more than it would cure. Nevertheless, it is true, as was well stated by one of the superintendents of Indian Affairs in 1857, that, "so long as they are not citizens of the United States, their rights of property must remain insecure against invasion. The doors of the federal tribunals being barred against them while wards and dependents, they can only partially exercise the rights of free government, or give to those who make, execute, and construe the few laws they are allowed to enact, dignity sufficient to make them respectable. While they continue individually to gather the crumbs that fall from the table of the United States, idleness, improvidence, and indebtedness will be the rule, and industry, thrift, and freedom from debt the exception. The utter absence of individual title to particular lands deprives every one among them of the chief incentive to labor and exertion—the very mainspring on which the prosperity of a people depends."

All judicious plans and measures for their safety and salvation must embody provisions for their becoming citizens as fast as they are fit, and must protect them till then in every right and particular in which our laws protect other "persons" who are not citizens.

There is a disposition in a certain class of minds to be impatient with any protestation against wrong which is unaccompanied or unprepared with a quick and exact scheme of remedy. This is illogical. When pioneers in a new country find a tract of poisonous and swampy wilderness to be reclaimed, they do not withhold their hands from fire and axe till they see clearly which way roads should run, where good water will spring, and what crops will best grow on the redeemed land. They first clear the swamp. So with this poisonous and baffling part of the domain of our national affairs—let us first "clear the swamp."

However great perplexity and difficulty there may be in the details of any and every plan possible for doing at this late day anything like justice to the Indian, however hard it may be for good statesmen and good men to agree upon the things that ought to be done, there certainly is, or ought to be, no perplexity whatever, no difficulty whatever, in agreeing upon certain things that ought not to be done, and which must cease to be done before the first steps can be taken toward righting the wrongs, curing the ills, and wiping out the disgrace to us of the present condition of our Indians.

Cheating, robbing, breaking promises—these three are clearly things which must cease to be done. One more thing, also, and that is the refusal of the protection of the law to the Indian's rights of property, "of life, liberty, and the pursuit of happiness."

When these four things have ceased to be done, time, statesmanship, philanthropy, and Christianity can slowly and surely do the rest. Till these four things have ceased to be done, statesmanship and philanthropy alike must work in vain, and even Christianity can reap but small harvest.

THE EMERGENCE OF GOVERNMENTAL INDIAN POLICY

In the end, the humanitarians had their way. As pressures mounted from reform groups, and as congressmen fell into line, national authorities had no choice but to listen—and act. One of the first to do so was President Chester A. Arthur, who in his message to Congress on December 6, 1881, summarized the arguments of the reformers such as Helen Hunt Jackson and recommended the three steps that they urged to solve the Indian problem: citizenship for the red men, allotment of land in severalty to them, and an educational program that would equip them to live as equals with white Americans:[8]

It has been easier to resort to convenient makeshifts for tiding over temporary difficulties than to grapple with the great permanent problem, and accordingly the easier course has almost invariably been pursued.

It was natural, at a time when the national territory seemed almost illimitable and contained many millions of acres far outside the bounds of civilized settlements, that a policy should have been initiated which more than aught else has been the fruitful source of our Indian complications.

I refer, of course, to the policy of dealing with the various Indian tribes as separate nationalities, of relegating them by treaty stipulations to the occupancy of immense reservations in the West, and of encouraging them to live a savage life, undisturbed by any earnest and well-directed efforts to bring them under the influences of civilization.

The unsatisfactory results which have sprung from this policy are becoming apparent to all.

As the white settlements have crowded the borders of the reservations, the Indians, sometimes contentedly and sometimes against their will, have been transferred to other hunting grounds, from which they have again been dislodged whenever their new-found homes have been desired by the adventurous settlers.

These removals and the frontier collisions by which they have often been preceded have led to frequent and disastrous conflicts between the races.

It is profitless to discuss here which of them has been chiefly responsible for the disturbances whose recital occupies so large a space upon the pages of our history.

We have to deal with the appalling fact that though thousands of lives have been sacrificed and hundreds of millions of dollars expended in the attempt to solve the Indian problem, it has until within the past few years seemed scarcely nearer a solution than it was half a century ago. But the Government has of late been cautiously but steadily feeling its way to the adoption of a policy which has already produced gratifying results, and which, in my judgment, is likely, if Congress and the Executive accord in its support, to relieve us ere long from the difficulties which have hitherto beset us.

For the success of the efforts now making to introduce among the Indians the customs and pursuits of civilized life and gradually to absorb them into the mass of our citizens, sharing their rights and holden to their responsibilities, there is imperative need for legislative action.

My suggestions in that regard will be chiefly such as have been already called to the attention of Congress and have received to some extent its consideration.

First. I recommend the passage of an act

---

[8] *A Compilation of the Messages and Papers of the Presidents, 1789–1897*, compiled by James D. Richardson (Washington, 1898), vol. 8, pp. 55–56.

making the laws of the various States and Territories applicable to the Indian reservations within their borders and extending the laws of the State of Arkansas to the portion of the Indian Territory not occupied by the Five Civilized Tribes.

The Indian should receive the protection of the law. He should be allowed to maintain in court his rights of person and property. He has repeatedly begged for this privilege. Its exercise would be very valuable to him in his progress toward civilization.

Second. Of even greater importance is a measure which has been frequently recommended by my predecessors in office, and in furtherance of which several bills have been from time to time introduced in both Houses of Congress. The enactment of a general law permitting the allotment in severalty, to such Indians, at least, as desire it, of a reasonable quantity of land secured to them by patent, and for their own protection made inalienable for twenty or twenty-five years, is demanded for their present welfare and their permanent advancement.

In return for such considerate action on the part of the Government, there is reason to believe that the Indians in large numbers would be persuaded to sever their tribal relations and to engage at once in agricultural pursuits. Many of them realize the fact that their hunting days are over and that it is now for their best interests to conform their manner of life to the new order of things. By no greater inducement than the assurance of permanent title to the soil can they be led to engage in the occupation of tilling it.

The well-attested reports of their increasing interest in husbandry justify the hope and belief that the enactment of such a statute as I recommend would be at once attended with gratifying results. A resort to the allotment system would have a direct and powerful influence in dissolving the tribal bond, which is so prominent a feature of savage life, and which tends so strongly to perpetuate it.

Third. I advise a liberal appropriation for the support of Indian schools, because of my confident belief that such a course is consistent with the wisest economy.

THE FORMULATION OF POLICY

The reform impulse generated by President Arthur's message culminated in 1887 when Congress wrote into law the Dawes Severalty Act, which was fathered by Senator Henry L. Dawes of Massachusetts on behalf of the humanitarians. This measure ended one chapter in the history of Indian relations, and opened another only slightly less tragic. Under its terms, certain Indians were to be granted land for farming or grazing, tribal government was to end, and the red men forced to walk the white man's road:[9]

Sec. 1 That in all cases where any tribe or band of Indians has been, or shall hereafter be, located upon any reservation created for their use, either by treaty stipulation or by virtue of an Act of Congress, or Executive order setting apart the same for their use, the President of the United States be, and he hereby is, authorized, whenever in his opinion any reservation, or any part thereof, of such Indians is advantageous for agricultural or grazing purposes, to cause said reservation, or any part thereof, to be surveyed, or resurveyed, if necessary, and to allot to each Indian located thereon one-eighth of a section of land:

Provided, That in case there is not suffi-

---

[9] Charles J. Kappler (ed.), *Indian Affairs: Laws and Treaties* (Washington, 1903), vol. 1, pp. 33–35, 56–57.

cient land in any of said reservations to allot lands to each individual in quantity as above provided the land in such reservation or reservations shall be allotted to each individual pro rata, as near as may be, according to legal subdivisions:

Provided further, That where the treaty or act of Congress setting apart such reservation provides for the allotment of lands in severalty to certain classes in quantity in excess of that herein provided the President, in making allotments upon such reservation, shall allot the land to each individual Indian of said classes belonging thereon in quantity as specified in such treaty or act, and to other Indians belonging thereon in quantity as herein provided:

Provided further, That where existing agreements or laws provide for allotments in accordance with the provisions of said act of February eighth, eighteen hundred and eighty-seven, or in quantities substantially as therein provided, allotments may be made in quantity as specified in this act, with the consent of the Indians, expressed in such manner as the President, in his discretion, may require:

And provided further, That when the lands allotted, or any legal subdivision thereof, are only valuable for grazing purposes, such lands shall be allotted in double quantities.

Sec. 2 That all allotments set apart under the provisions of this act shall be selected by the Indians, heads of families selecting for their minor children, and the agents shall select for each orphan child, and in such manner as to embrace the improvements of the Indians making the selection. Where the improvements of two or more Indians have been made on the same legal subdivision of land, unless they shall otherwise agree, a provisional line may be run dividing said lands between them, and the amount to which each is entitled shall be equalized in the assignment of the remainder of the land to which they are entitled under this act:

Provided, That if any one entitled to an allotment shall fail to make a selection within four years after the President shall direct that allotments may be made on a particular reservation, the Secretary of the Interior may direct the agent of such tribe or band, if such there be, and if there be no agent, then a special agent appointed for that purpose, to make a selection for such Indian, which selection shall be allotted as in cases where selections are made by the Indians, and patents shall issue in like manner.

Sec. 3 That the allotments provided for in this act shall be made by special agents appointed by the President for such purpose, and the agents in charge of the respective reservations on which the allotments are directed to be made, under such rules and regulations as the Secretary of the Interior may from time to time prescribe, and shall be certified by such agents to the Commissioner of Indian Affairs, in duplicate, one copy to be retained in the Indian Office and the other to be transmitted to the Secretary of the Interior for his action, and to be deposited in the General Land Office....

Sec. 5 That upon the approval of the allotments provided for in this act by the Secretary of the Interior, he shall cause patents to issue therefor in the name of the allottees, which patents shall be of the legal effect, and declare that the United States does and will hold the land thus allotted for the period of twenty-five years, in trust for the sole use and benefit of the Indian to whom such allotment shall have been made, or, in case of his decease, of his heirs according to the laws of the State or Territory where such land is located, and that at the expiration of said period the United States will convey the same by patent to said Indian, or his heirs as aforesaid, in fee, discharged of said trust and free of all charge or incumbrance whatsoever: *Provided,* That the President of the United States may in any case in his discretion extend the period.

And if any conveyance shall be made of the lands set apart and allotted as herein provided, or any contract made touching the same, before the expiration of the time above mentioned, such conveyance or contract shall be absolutely null and void:

Provided, That the law of descent and partition in force in the State or Territory where such lands are situate shall apply thereto after patents therefor have been executed and delivered, except as herein otherwise provided; and the laws of the State of Kansas regulating the descent and partition of real estate shall, so far as practicable, apply to all lands in the Indian Territory which may be allotted in severalty under the provisions of this act:

And provided further, That at any time after lands have been allotted to all the Indians of any tribe as herein provided, or sooner if in the opinion of the President it shall be for the best interests of said tribe, it shall be lawful for the Secretary of the Interior to negotiate with such Indian tribe for the purchase and release by said tribe, in conformity with the treaty or statute under which such reservation is held, of such portions of its reservation not allotted as such tribe shall, from time to time, consent to sell, on such terms and conditions as shall be considered just and equitable between the United States and said tribe of Indians, which purchase shall not be complete until ratified by Congress, and the form and manner of executing such release shall also be prescribed by Congress:

Provided however, That all lands adapted to agriculture, with or without irrigation so sold or released to the United States by any Indian tribe shall be held by the United States for the sole purpose of securing homes to actual settlers and shall be disposed of by the United States to actual and bona fide settlers only in tracts not exceeding one hundred and sixty acres to any one person, on such terms as Congress shall prescribe, subject to grants which Congress may make in aid of education:

And provided further, That no patents shall issue therefor except to the person so taking the same as and for a homestead, or his heirs, and after the expiration of five years occupancy thereof as such homestead; and any conveyance of said lands so taken as a homestead, or any contract touching the same, or lien thereon, created prior to the date of such patent, shall be null and void.

And the sums agreed to be paid by the United States as purchase money for any portion of any such reservation shall be held in the Treasury of the United States for the sole use of the tribe or tribes of Indians to whom such reservations belonged; and the same, with interest thereon at three per cent per annum, shall be at all times subject to appropriation by Congress for the education and civilization of such tribe or tribes of Indians or the members thereof.

The patents aforesaid shall be recorded in the General Land Office, and afterward delivered, free of charge, to the allottee entitled thereto.

And if any religious society or other organization is now occupying any of the public lands to which this act is applicable, for religious or educational work among the Indians, the Secretary of the Interior is hereby authorized to confirm such occupation to such society or organization, in quantity not exceeding one hundred and sixty acres in any one tract, so long as the same shall be so occupied, on such terms as he shall deem just;

but nothing herein contained shall change or alter any claim of such society for religious or educational purposes heretofore granted by law.

And hereafter in the employment of Indian police, or any other employes in the public service among any of the Indian tribes or bands affected by this act, and where Indians can perform the duties required, those Indians who have availed themselves of the provisions of this act and become citizens of the United States shall be preferred.

Sec. 6 That upon the completion of said allotments and the patenting of the lands to said allottees, each and every member of the respective bands or tribes of Indians to whom allotments have been made shall have the benefit of and be subject to the laws, both civil and criminal, of the State or Territory in which they may reside; and no Territory shall pass or enforce any law denying any such Indian within its jurisdiction the equal protection of the law.

And every Indian born within the territorial limits of the United States to whom allotments shall have been made under the provisions of this act, or under any law or treaty, and every Indian born within the territorial limits of the United States who has voluntarily taken up, within said limits, his residence separate and apart from any tribe of Indians therein, and has adopted the habits of civilized life, [*and every Indian in Indian Territory,*] is hereby declared to be a citizen of the United States, and is entitled to all the rights, privileges, and immunities of such citizens, whether said Indian has been or not, by birth or otherwise, a member of any tribe of Indians within the territorial limits of the United States without in any manner impairing or otherwise affecting the right of any such Indian to tribal or other property.

Laudable as were the motives of the humanitarians, the Dawes Severalty Act proved no panacea. Its effect, no less than that of the policy advocated by the militarists, was to sever the red men from cultural patterns in which they had been reared and plunge them unprepared into an alien civilization for which many had little liking. This transition, carried out over the next years by Indian agents and military leaders who were often hostile to the Indians and sometimes corrupt, spelled a succession of tragedies that lasted well into the twentieth century. From the viewpoint of the frontiersmen, however, the act was an unqualified success. Not only were the red men rendered powerless by the outlawing of their tribal system, but their reservation lands were placed on the market as the stipulated divisions among tribesmen took place. No longer would "hostiles" block the westward march of pioneers; no longer would millions of acres be withheld from the plow. The Indian wars, cruel though they were, and the Indian policy, tragic though it proved, opened the Great Plains to settlement by cattlemen and farmers.

CHAPTER 26 || *The Ranchers' Frontier, 1865-1890*

Indian removal opened the way to the conquest of America's last frontier: the Great Plains country. This began soon after the close of the Civil War. When that conflict ended, pioneers were already pushing westward across eastern Kansas and Nebraska, filling the river valleys first, then spilling into the upcountry. Beyond the 100th meridian, however, the buffalo herds were still in undisputed control, for there the ingredients of civilization were lacking: navigable streams for the export of surpluses, wood for housing and fuel, fencing materials, and water. Over most of this region average annual rainfall was less than the 20 inches needed for normal agriculture. To the frontiersmen, the upper Great Plains were the "Great American Desert."

During the late 1860s and 1870s this situation changed. Railroads were primarily responsible. As they pushed slowly westward, they brought the plains country into the orbit of the American economy; now settlers there could not only import lumber, farm machinery, building materials, fencing, and other essentials, but could ship their produce to markets at Chicago or St. Louis or Kansas City. Over the next years, as a result, this last unpeopled West was occupied to close an era in the history of the frontier.

THE BEGINNINGS OF THE LONG DRIVE

The firstcomers were cattlemen, attracted by a land where grass was abundant and free, and where no fences hindered the free movement of herds. The cradle of the ranching industry was Texas. Spanish cattle had been allowed to multiply until some five million roamed there in 1865. Many were wild and could be had for the taking; even those owned by Mexican or American ranchers could be purchased for a few dollars each. At this same time cattle at Sedalia, Missouri, the farthest western point reached by a railroad, sold at $35 a head. This price differential was noted by a few enterprising drovers, who during the winter of 1865–1866 began accumulating herds in Texas to drive to the railhead that spring. Most were to pay heavily for their boldness. One typical entrepreneur was George C. Duffield of Iowa, who with a partner bought a thousand Texan cattle in March, and by the end of April was ready to start them north. The hardships experienced on the drive across Texas to the Red River during an unusually wet spring were graphically described in his diary:[1]

29 Settled up & Recd last cattle started in evening from Salt Creek & travelled 5 miles to Alexanders gap between Colorado & Brazos

30 Mo All well in my Heard Travelled through Pansgath & to Bennett Creek 18 miles

May 1st Travelled 10 miles to Corryell co Big Stamped lost 200 head of cattle

2ond Spent the day hunting & found but 25 Head it has been Raining for three days these are dark days for me.

3rd Day Spent in hunting cattle found 23 hard rain and wind lots of trouble

4th Continued the hunt found 40 head day pleasant Sun shone once more. Heard that the other Herd has stampeded & lost over 200

5 Cloudy damp Morning rode 16 Miles & back to see the other Boys found them in trouble with cattle all scattered over the country

6th Started once More on My journey left Cow House River & got to Leon crossed & camped in prairie 5 miles north of River dark & Gloomey night hard rain Stampeded & lost 200 head of cattle (Milts Herd)

7th Hunt cattle is the order of the day— found most of our Cattle & drove 12 miles & camped on a large creek in Bosque Co

8th All 3 heards are up & ready to travel off together for the first time travelled 6 miles rain pouring down in torrents & here we are on the banks of a creek with 10 or 12 ft water & raising crossed at 4 Oclock & crossed into the Bosque Bottom found it 20 ft deep Ran my Horse into a ditch & got my Knee badly sprained—15 Miles

9th Still dark & gloomy River up everything looks *Blue* to me no crossing to day cattle behaved well

10th Crossed Bosque at Maridian & travelled to Brasos River & find it very high 14 Miles Pleasant day

11th Beautiful warm day lay in camp waiting on R Rode 3 Miles to Kimbleville & back. viewed River & Killed Beefe

12th Lay around camp visited River & went Bathing

13th Big Thunder Storm last night Stampede lost 100 Beeves hunted all day found 50 all tired. Every thing discouraging

14th Concluded to Cross Brazos swam our cattle & Horses & built Raft & Rafted our provisions & blankets &c over Swam River with rope & then hauled wagon over lost Most of our Kitchen furniture such as camp Kittles Coffee Pots Cups Plates Canteens &c &c

15 back at River bringing up wagon Hunting Oxen & other *lost* property. Rain poured down for one Hour. It does nothing but rain got all our *traps* together that was not lost & thought we were ready for off dark rainy night cattle all left us & in morning not one Beef to be seen

16th Hunt Beeves is the word—all Hands discouraged. & are determined to go 200 Beeves out & nothing to eat

17th No Breakfast pack & off is the order. all Hands gave the Brazos one good harty dam & started for Buchanan travelled 10 miles & camped found 50 Beeves (nothing to eat)

---

[1] George C. Duffield, "Driving Cattle from Texas to Iowa, 1866," *Annals of Iowa*, 3rd Series, XIV (April, 1924), pp. 250–253.

18th Every thing gloomey four best hands left us got to Buchanon at noon & to Rock Creek in Johnston Co distance 14th

19th Traveled 6 Miles to Mr Bs Ranch & Camped to wait for some of the other party to come up bought some flour & meat two pleasant days Killed Beefe

20th Rain poured down for two hours Ground in a flood Creeks up—Hands leaving Gloomey times as ever I saw drove 8 miles with 5 hands (359 Head) passed the night 6 miles S.W. from Fort Worth in Parker Co

21st drove 6 miles & crossed clear fork of Trinity in Tarrant Co Other Herd came up divided all the cattle into two Herds. & divided Hands

22nd This day has been spent in crossing the West Trinity & a hard & long to be remembered day to me we swam our cattle & Horses I swam it 5 times upset our wagon in River & lost Many of our cooking utencils again drove 3 miles & camped

23rd Travelled 10 Miles over a beautiful Prairie country such as I expected to see before I came here stopped for dinner on Henrietta Creek & then on to Elisabeth Town & creek & stopped for the night—Hard rain that night & cattle behaved very bad—ran all night—was on my Horse the whole night & it raining hard

24th Glad to see Morning come counted & found we had lost none for the first time —feel very bad. travelled 14 miles crossed Denton Creek

25 Travelled across Clear fork & Elm fork of Trinity passed through cross Timbers Passed the town of Denton County seat of Denton & camped one Mile from Pilot Point Traveled 20 mi (Lost my Knife today)

26th Passed through Pilot Point & travelled through a high rolling Prairie country—some fine wheat fields—wheat is ripe & being Harvested—14 miles

27th drove over Prairie road & passed some fine fields of wheat came in sight of Sherman in Grason Co 13 miles

28 Cold Morning wind blowing & all hands shivering are within 12 Miles of Red River moved up 6 Miles

29th Moved up to River & after many difficulties got all my Drove over but 100

30th worked in River all day & 50 Beeves on this side of River yet—am still in Texas

31st Swimming Cattle is the order We worked all day in the River & at dusk got the last Beefe over—& am now out of Texas— This day will long be remembered by me— There was one of our party Drowned to day (Mr Carr) & Several narrow escapes & I among the no.

June [1]st Stampede last night among 6 droves & a general mix up and loss of Beeves. Hunt Cattle again Men all tired & want to leave. am in the Indian country am annoyed by them believe they scare the Cattle to get pay to collect them—Spent the day in seperating Beeves & Hunting—Two men & Bunch Beeves lost—Many Men in trouble. Horses *all* give out & Men refused to do anything.

2ond Hard rain & wind Storm Beeves ran & had to be on Horse back all night Awful night. wet all night clear bright morning. Men still lost quit the Beeves & go to Hunting Men is the word—4 P.M. Found our men with Indian guide & 195 Beeves 14 Miles from camp. allmost starved not having had a bite to eat for 60 hours got to camp about 12 M *Tired*

3rd Dividing cattle & seperating is the order of the day. 4 Oclock all tired & Ponies give out. through dividing & have counted & found ourselves minus 55 Beeves

4th Concluded to start the Hurd & leave men to hunt with other who have lost Beeves crossed Blue River & camped 13 Miles further on our way Indians very troublesome

5th Oh! what a night—Thunder Lightning & rain—we followed our Beeves *all* night as they wandered about—put them on the road at day break found 90 Beeves of an other mans Herd travelled 18 Miles over the worst road I ever saw & come to Boggy Depot & crossed 4 Rivers It is well Known by that name We Hauled cattle out of the Mud with oxen half the day

FIRST OF THE "COW TOWNS," ABILENE

By the time Duffield and his partner reached a railhead, their herd of a thousand cattle had shrunk to a few hundred. The hardships and losses that he suffered, and that were suffered by all drovers that spring, convinced cattlemen that the drive northward could succeed only if a better trail could be pioneered. This must avoid all settled areas where farmers came out in force to repel the herds, as well as the hilly, wooded sections of eastern Texas and Missouri where the cattle became unmanageable. Such a trail was laid out that fall by Joseph G. McCoy, an Illinois meat dealer, who described his experiences in his reminiscences:[2]

After spending a few days investigating, Abilene, then as now, the county seat of Dickinson county, was selected as the point of location for the coming enterprise. Abilene in 1867 was a very small, dead place, consisting of about one dozen log huts, low, small, rude affairs, four-fifths of which were covered with dirt for roofing; indeed, but one shingle roof could be seen in the whole city. The business of the burg was conducted in two small rooms, mere log huts, and of course the inevitable saloon also in a log hut, was to be found.

The proprietor of the saloon was a corpulent, jolly, good-souled, congenial old man of the backwoods pattern, who, in his younger days, loved to fish and hunt, and enjoyed the life of the frontiersman. For his amusement a colony of pet prairie dogs were located on his lots, and often the old gentleman might be seen feeding his pets. Tourists and others often purchased one or more of these dogs, and took them East as curiosities. . . .

A tract of land adjoining the town was purchased for the location of the stock yards, hotel, offices, etc.

Abilene was selected because the country was entirely unsettled, well watered, excellent grass, and nearly the entire area of country was adapted to holding cattle. And it was the farthest point east at which a good depot for cattle business could have been made. Although its selection was made by an entire stranger to the country adjoining, and upon his practical judgment only, time has proved that no other so good point can be found in the State for the cattle trade. The advantages and requirements were all in its favor. After the point had been decided upon, the labor of getting material upon the ground began.

From Hannibal, Missouri, came the pine lumber, and from Lenape, Kansas, came the hard wood, and work began in earnest and with energy. In sixty days from July 1st a shipping yard, that would accommodate three thousand cattle, a large pair of Fairbank's scales, a barn and an office were completed, and a good three story hotel well on the way toward completion.

When it is remembered that this was accomplished in so short a time, notwithstand-

---

[2] Joseph G. McCoy, *Historic Sketches of the Cattle Trade* (Kansas City, 1874), pp. 44, 50–53.

ing the fact that every particle of material had to be brought from the East, and that, too, over a slow moving railroad, it will be seen that energy and a determined will were at work.

We should have mentioned sooner that when the point at which to locate the shipping yards was determined upon, a man well versed in the geography of the country and accustomed to life on the prairie, was sent into Southern Kansas and the Indian Territory with instructions to hunt up every straggling drove possible, (and every drove was straggling, for they had not where to go,) and tell them of Abilene, and what was being done there toward making a market and outlet for Texan cattle. Mounting his pony at Junction City, a lonely ride of almost two hundred miles was taken in a southwesterly direction, crossing the Arkansas River at the site of the present city of Wichita, thence far down into the Indian country; then turning east until trails of herds were found, which were followed until the drove was overtaken, and the owner fully posted in that, to him, all-absorbing topic, to-wit: a good, safe place to drive to, where he could sell or ship his cattle unmolested to other markets.

This was joyous news to the drover, for the fear of trouble and violence hung like an incubus over his waking thoughts alike with his sleeping moments. It was almost too good to be believed; could it be possible that some one was about to afford a Texan drover any other reception than outrage and robbery? They were very suspicious that some trap was set, to be sprung on them; they were not ready to credit the proposition that the day of fair dealing had dawned for Texan drovers, and the era of mobs, brutal murder, and arbitrary proscription ended forever.

Yet they turned their herds toward the point designated, and slowly and cautiously moved on northward, their minds constantly agitated with hope and fear alternately.

The first herd that arrived at Abilene was driven from Texas by a Mr. Thompson, but sold to Smith, McCord & Chandler, Northern men, in the Indian Nation, and by them driven to Abilene. However, a herd owned by Colonel O. W. Wheeler, Wilson and Hicks, all Californians, en route for the Pacific States, were stopped about thirty miles from Abilene for rest, and finally disposed of at Abilene, was really the first herd that came up from Texas, and broke the trail, followed by the other herds. About thirty-five thousand head were driven in 1867.

It should be borne in mind that it was fully the first of July before it was decided to attempt a cattle depot at Abilene or elsewhere, which, of course, was too late to increase the drive from Texas that year, but time enough only to gather together at that point such herds as were already on the road northward. Not until the cattle were nearly all at Abilene would the incredulous K. P. Railway Company build the requisite switch, and then not until a written demand was made for it, after which, an order was issued to put in a twenty-car switch, and particular direction was given to use "cull" ties, adding that they expected to take it up next year. It was with great difficulty that a hundred car switch was obtained instead of the twenty-car one. Nor were the necessary transfer and feed yards at Leavenworth put in until plans were made and a man to superintend their construction furnished by the same parties that were laboring so hard to get their enterprise on foot at Abilene. But in a comparatively brief time all things were ready for the shipment of the first train.

As we have before stated, about 35,000 head of cattle arrived at Abilene in 1867. In 1860 we believe that the United States Census gave Texas 3,500,000 head of cattle.

We are not sure that this is correct, but believe it is.

The drive of 1867 was about one per cent. of the supply. Great hardships attended driving that year on account of Osage Indian troubles, excessive rain-storms, and flooded rivers. The cholera made sad havoc with many drovers, some of whom died with the malady and many suffered greatly. The heavy rains caused an immense growth of grass, too coarse and washy to be good food for cattle or horses, and but little of the first years' arrivals at Abilene were fit to go to market. However, on the 5th of September, 1867, the first shipment of twenty cars was made to Chicago. Several Illinois stock men and others, joined in an excursion from Springfield, Ill., to Abilene, to celebrate by feast, wine and song, the auspicious event.

Arriving at Abilene in the evening, several large tents, including one for dining purposes, were found ready for the reception of guests. A substantial repast was spread before the excursionists, and devoured with a relish peculiar to camp life, after which wine, toasts, and speechifying were the order until a late hour at night.

Before the sun had mounted high in the heavens on the following day, the iron horse was darting down the Kaw Valley with the first train load of cattle that ever passed over the Kansas Pacific Railroad, the precursor to many thousands destined to follow.

THE LONG DRIVE

The founding of Abilene and the marking of the "Chisholm Trail" that reached it from Texas launched the era of the long drives. Herds of cattle, usually numbering about a thousand, were regularly driven northward thereafter. Between 1868 and 1871 nearly 1,500,000 cattle reached Abilene; by that time the westward advance of farmers forced a shifting of the trail westward, first to Ellsworth and Newton in central Kansas, then to Dodge City in the western limits of that state. In all more than four million longhorns reached these "cow towns" in the decade before 1879, to be shipped eastward via the Kansas Pacific or Santa Fe railroads to Chicago's stockyards. The efficient techniques used in handling herds on the long drive were described by Charles N. Harger, a contemporary observer:[3]

The drover secured, besides camp equipage and eatables, about eight men to the thousand cattle as drivers, and from six to ten horses to the man, according to the quality of the equines. After 1883–84, when Indians were less dangerous and fewer herds were on the trails, four to six men to the thousand head were considered sufficient. Having "cut out" the cattle one by one with lassoes (long rawhide ropes attached to the cow-boys' saddles and thrown with great accuracy by the riders), the steers and cows all received a "road brand," a supplementary mark to prevent confusion on the way to market. All was then ready for the long march.

Spring was the usual starting time, and during the seasons of the large drives, May, June, July, and August saw almost a solid procession passing over the great trails. So near were the herds that the drivers could hear one another urging along the stock, and frequently even the utmost care could not prevent two companies stampeding together, entailing a loss of much time and labor in separating them.

Once started, it was remarkable the orderly manner in which a herd took its way across the plains. A herd of a thousand beeves would string out to a length of two miles, and a larger one still longer. It made a

[3] Charles N. Harger, "Cattle-Trails of the Prairies," *Scribner's Magazine*, XI (June, 1892), pp. 738–741.

picturesque sight. The leaders were flanked by cow-boys on wiry Texas ponies, riding at ease in great saddles with high backs and pommels. At regular distances were other riders, and the progress of the cavalcade was not unlike that of an army on a march. There was an army-like regularity about the cattle's movements, too. The leaders seemed always to be especially fitted for the place, and the same ones would be found in the front rank throughout the trip; while others retained their relative positions in the herd day after day.

At the start there was hard driving, twenty to thirty miles a day, until the animals were thoroughly wearied. After that twelve to fifteen miles was considered a good day's drive, thus extending the journey over forty to one hundred days. The daily programme was as regular as that of a regiment on the march. From morning until noon the cattle were allowed to graze in the direction of their destination, watched by the cow-boys in relays. The cattle by this time were uneasy and were turned into the trail and walked steadily forward eight or ten miles, when, at early twilight, they were halted for another graze. As darkness came on they were gathered closer and closer into a compact mass by the cow-boys riding steadily in constantly lessening circles around them, until at last the brutes lay down, chewing their cuds and resting from the day's trip. Near midnight they would usually get up, stand awhile, and then lie down again, having changed sides. At this time extra care was necessary to keep them from aimlessly wandering off in the darkness. Sitting on their ponies, or riding slowly round and round their reclining charges, the cow-boys passed the night on sentinel duty, relieving one another at stated hours.

When skies were clear and the air bracing, the task of cattle-driving was a pleasant and healthful one. But there came rainy days, when the cattle were restless, and when it was anything but enjoyable riding through the steady downpour. Then especially were the nights wearisome, and the cattle were ready at any time to stampede.

No one could tell what caused a stampede, any more than one can tell the reason of the strange panics that attack human gatherings at times. A flash of lightning, a crackling stick, a wolf's howl, little things in themselves, but in a moment every horned head was lifted, and the mass of hair and horns, with fierce, frightened eyes gleaming like thousands of emeralds, was off. Recklessly, blindly, in whatever direction fancy led them, they went, over a bluff or into a morass, it mattered not, and fleet were the horses that could keep abreast of the leaders. But some could do it, and lashing their ponies to their best gait the cow-boys followed at breakneck speed. Getting on one side of the leaders the effort was to turn them, a little at first, then more and more, until the circumference of a great circle was being described. The cattle behind blindly followed, and soon the front and rear joined and "milling" commenced. Like a mighty mill-stone, round and round the bewildered creatures raced until they were wearied out or recovered from their fright.

To stop the herd from milling, either after a stampede or when in the cattle-yards at the end of the trip, was a necessary but difficult task. As in a stampede, it was death to an animal who failed to keep up with his comrades, for in a moment his carcass would be flattened by thousands of trampling hoofs. The human voice seemed the most powerful influence that could be used to affect the brutes, force being entirely out of the question. As soon as the "milling" began the cow-boys began to sing. It mattered not what so long as there was music to it, and it was not uncommon to hear some profane and heartless bully doling out camp-meeting hymns to soothe the ruffled spirits of a herd of Texas steers, a use which might have astonished the fathers and mothers of the churches "back in God's country," could they have known of it.

A stampede always meant a loss, and rendered the herd more likely to be again panic-stricken. Certain hysterical leaders were frequently shot because of their influence on the remainder of the column. Another danger was that of the mingling of two herds; while in the earlier days the presence of buffalo was a decided peril. A herd of buffalo roaring and tearing its way across the plain was almost certain to cause a panic, if within hearing, and outriders were necessary to watch for these enemies and turn their course from the trail. Besides, marauding Indians were always to be feared, and many a skirmish was had between the cow-boys and red-skins. An understanding with the chiefs was, however, usually sufficient to insure safety. Thus accompanied by incidents that brought into play all the strength and strategy of their guards, the horned host moved on. Rivers were crossed by swimming in the same order that had been followed on land.

Reaching the outskirts of the shipping-station the herd was held on the plains until the drover effected a sale or secured cars for shipment. Then the animals were driven into the stockades, dragged or coaxed into the cars, and were sent off to meet their fate in the great packing-houses. The journey had been a strange one to them, often accompanied by savage cruelties at the hands of heartless drivers, and the end of the trip with close confinement of yard and car, the first they had ever known, was strangest of all.

DROVERS "HIT" THE COW TOWNS

Cowboys who reached the end of the trail after three months of deadly monotony turned the cow towns into palaces of sin, sex, and corruption. Normally the cowboy was a sober, hard-working individual with little inclination to lawlessness or unsocial behavior, but his wearisome days in the saddle during the long drive made him eager to forget, and the towns provided him with the means of doing so. So Abilene and Newton and Dodge were kept in an almost constant state of turmoil during the summer months as herd after herd "hit town." One of the few authentic accounts of life on the range written by a cowboy, Andy Adams, describes one such blowout:[4]

On reaching Dodge, we rode up to the Wright House, where Flood met us and directed our cavalcade across the railroad to a livery stable, the proprietor of which was a friend of Lovell's. We unsaddled and turned our horses into a large corral, and while we were in the office of the livery, surrendering our artillery, Flood came in and handed each of us twenty-five dollars in gold, warning us that when that was gone no more would be advanced. On receipt of the money, we scattered like partridges before a gunner. Within an hour or two, we began to return to the stable by ones and twos, and were stowing into our saddle pockets our purchases, which ran from needles and thread to .45 cartridges, every mother's son reflecting the art of the barber, while John Officer had his blond mustaches blackened, waxed, and curled like a French dancing master. "If some of you boys will hold him," said Moss Strayhorn,

---

[4] Andy Adams, *The Log of a Cowboy* (New York, 1903), pp. 198–207.

commenting on Officer's appearance, "I'd like to take a good smell of him, just to see if he took oil up there where the end of his neck's haired over." As Officer already had several drinks comfortably stowed away under his belt, and stood up strong six feet two, none of us volunteered.

After packing away our plunder, we sauntered around town, drinking moderately, and visiting the various saloons and gambling houses. I clung to my bunkie, The Rebel, during the rounds, for I had learned to like him, and had confidence he would lead me into no indiscretions. At the Long Branch, we found Quince Forrest and Wyatt Roundtree playing the faro bank, the former keeping cases. They never recognized us, but were answering a great many questions, asked by the dealer and lookout, regarding the possible volume of the cattle drive that year. Down at another gambling house, The Rebel met Ben Thompson, a faro dealer not on duty and an old cavalry comrade, and the two cronied around for over an hour like long lost brothers, pledging anew their friendship over several social glasses, in which I was always included. There was no telling how long this reunion would have lasted, but happily for my sake, Lovell—who had been asleep all the morning—started out to round us up for dinner with him at the Wright House, which was at that day a famous hostelry, patronized almost exclusively by the Texas cowmen and cattle buyers. . . .

Along early in the evening, Flood advised us boys to return to the herd with him, but all the crowd wanted to stay in town and see the sights. Lovell interceded in our behalf, and promised to see that we left town in good time to be in camp before the herd was ready to move the next morning. On this assurance, Flood saddled up and started for the Saw Log, having ample time to make the ride before dark. By this time most of the boys had worn off the wire edge for gambling and were comparing notes. Three of them were broke, but Quince Forrest had turned the tables and was over a clean hundred winner for the day. Those who had no money fortunately had good credit with those of us who had, for there was yet much to be seen, and in Dodge in '82 it took money to see the elephant. There were several variety theatres, a number of dance halls, and other resorts which, like the wicked, flourish best under darkness. After supper, just about dusk, we went over to the stable, caught our horses, saddled them, and tied them up for the night. We fully expected to leave town by ten o'clock, for it was a good twelve mile ride to the Saw Log. In making the rounds of the variety theatres and dance halls, we hung together. Lovell excused himself early in the evening, and at parting we assured him that the outfit would leave for camp before midnight. We were enjoying ourselves immensely over at the Lone Star dance hall, when an incident occurred in which we entirely neglected the good advice of McNulta, and had the sensation of hearing lead whistle and cry around our ears before we got away from town.

Quince Forrest was spending his winnings as well as drinking freely, and at the end of a quadrille gave vent to his hilarity in an old-fashioned Comanche yell. The bouncer of the dance hall of course had his eye on our crowd, and at the end of a change, took Quince to task. He was a surly brute, and instead of couching his request in appropriate language, threatened to throw him out of the house. Forrest stood like one absent-minded and took the abuse, for physically he was no match for the bouncer, who was armed, moreover, and wore an officer's star. I was dancing in the same set with a red-headed, freckled-faced girl, who clutched my arm and wished to know if my friend was armed. I assured her that he was not, or we would have had notice of it before the bouncer's invective was ended. At the conclusion of the dance, Quince and The Rebel passed out, giving the rest of us the word to remain as though nothing was wrong. In the course of half an hour, Priest returned and asked us to take our leave one at a time without attracting any attention, and meet at the stable. I remained until the last, and noticed The Rebel and the bouncer taking a drink together at the bar,—the former apparently in a most amiable mood. We passed out together shortly afterward, and found the other boys mounted and awaiting our return, it being now about midnight. It took but a moment to secure our guns, and once in the saddle, we rode through the town in the direction of the herd. On the outskirts of the town, we halted. "I'm going back to that dance hall," said Forrest, "and have one round at least with that woman-herder. No man who walks this old earth can insult me, as he did, not if he has a hundred stars on him. If any of you don't want to go along, ride right on to camp, but I'd like to have you all go. And when I take his measure, it will be the signal to the rest of you to put out the lights. All that's going, come on."

There were no dissenters to the programme. I saw at a glance that my bunkie was heart and soul in the play, and took my cue and kept my mouth shut. We circled round the town to a vacant lot within a block of the rear of the dance hall. Honeyman was left to hold the horses; then, taking off our belts and hanging them on the pommels of our saddles, we secreted our six-shooters inside the waistbands of our trousers. The hall was still crowded with the revelers when we entered, a few at a time, Forrest and Priest being the last to arrive. Forrest had changed hats with The Rebel, who always wore a black one, and as the bouncer circulated around, Quince stepped squarely in front of him. There was no waste of words, but a gun-barrel flashed in the lamplight, and the bouncer, struck with the six-shooter, fell like a beef. Before the bewildered spectators could raise a hand, five six-shooters were turned into the ceiling. The lights went out at the first fire, and amidst the rush of men and the screaming of women, we reached the outside, and within a minute were in our saddles. All would have gone well had we returned by the same route and avoided the town; but after crossing the railroad track, anger and pride having not been properly satisfied, we must ride through the town.

On entering the main street, leading north and opposite the bridge on the river, somebody of our party in the rear turned his gun loose into the air. The Rebel and I were riding in the lead, and at the clattering of hoofs and shooting behind us, our horses started on the run, the shooting by this time having become general. At the second street crossing, I noticed a rope of fire belching from a Winchester in the doorway of a store building. There was no doubt in my mind but we were the object of the manipulator of that carbine, and as we reached the next cross street, a man kneeling in the shadow of a building opened fire on us with a six-shooter. Priest reined in his horse, and not having wasted cartridges in the open-air shooting, returned the compliment until he emptied his gun. By this time every officer in the town was throwing lead after us, some of which cried a little too close for comfort. When there was no longer any shooting on our flanks, we turned into a cross street and soon left the lead behind us.

RANGE LAW ON THE CATTLE FRONTIER

The cow towns, and the long drives that sustained them, captured the imagination of the nation—and the world—but they were doomed to die young. Their malady was economic. Herds lost weight on the trail, lowering their price, while at the end of the drive the seller was at the mercy of the buyer. These disadvantages could be offset by raising cattle near the railroads. As this was realized, ranches sprang up across the northern plains, where the grass was better than in Texas and where markets were accessible through the expanding network of steel rails. By the middle 1870s, the whole vast countryside from Kansas to the Dakotas was one giant pasture, peopled by ranchers who used the public domain to pyramid fortunes for themselves and by cowboys who tended their herds. This remarkable expansion of the cattle kingdom was possible only because the growers followed a traditional frontier practice. Operating as they were beyond the pale of the law and using government land to which they had no legal right, they drafted their own codes and enforced them as rigidly as did police forces in eastern cities. The result was an orderly expansion of the frontier, in which "grazing rights" were as respected as private property in the East. This process was described by cattlemen who compiled the records of the National Live Stock Historical Association:[5]

The first impulse of a pioneer cattleman who had entered a virgin district with his herd and established his headquarters there, was mentally to claim everything within sight and for a long distance beyond. But when the second one appeared with his stock the two would divide the district, and each keep on his side of the division line as agreed upon. As others came in the district would be still further divided, until, according to the very broad views our pioneer friends held as to the length and breadth of land each should have for "elbow room," it had become fully occupied. There was nothing to prevent them appropriating the country in this manner and arbitrarily defining the boundaries of their respective ranges, and with this practice there developed the theory of "range rights"—that is, of a man's right to his range in consequence of priority of occupation and continuous possession, although none asserted actual ownership of the range-land, nor did any of them really own as much as a square yard of it. Still, under the circumstances, the theory of "range rights" was not an unreasonable proposition.

For a district to become "fully occupied" did not at that time imply that the cattle outfits in it were near neighbors. In making claim to a range each stockman kept far over on the safe side by taking to himself a-plenty, and therefore their ranch buildings were anywhere from fifteen to thirty miles apart, and sometimes even farther. As a common rule, each man recognized and respected the range-rights of his neighbors in frank good faith, but occasionally there were conflicts, such as appear to have occurred from similar causes in the range live-stock business from a high antiquity in its history.

Encroachments upon what were considered to be "rights" of any kind, but especially of "range-rights," not only provoked much calling on the name of the Lord among our cattlemen in these times, but if persisted in after warning against them had been given, they usually brought on clashes, in which rifles and revolvers were used without hesitation. Such conflicts, which were more frequent in the Southern country than

---

[5] National Live Stock Historical Association, *Prose and Poetry of the Live Stock Industry of the United States* (Kansas City, 1904), pp. 588–591.

elsewhere, if not at once terminated in the favor of one or the other parties to them, sometimes took on the character of a feud that resulted in much trouble and loss of life. However, they seldom occurred between men who had come in before the district had become what was regarded as fully and sufficiently occupied, but usually were in consequence of some new man attempting to push in with his herd and "crowd" the range, and perhaps to put up ranch buildings as near as eight or ten miles to those of one of the established outfits. . . .

The pioneer ranch outfits as to buildings or shelters were rather primitive affairs that proclaimed yesterday's occupation of the land. At the outset almost anything that could be made to serve the purpose was considered good enough. Where timber was available a roughly-built house of unhewn logs with a "dirt roof" was the quickest and easiest building of a permanent character to construct, but many a man who began business in a small way got through his first year or two in a lean-to "shack" or in a "dug-out." In the southerly parts of the country, "after things became settled," if not before, the ranch buildings usually were either of logs or adobe. The latter, built with thick walls and having a deep dirt-roof, were very comfortable the year 'round, being cool in summer and warm when warmth was needed. In parts of the range country where there were matted growths of grass, sod was used as a building material, the sod cut to proper size being laid up in stone-wall fashion. By the stock-raising as well as by other, pioneers in Kansas, Nebraska, and Colorado many of these sod-houses were used for years, and were almost the equals of adobe structures. In the northern country logs were almost exclusively used, but the dirt roof was common everywhere from the Rio Grande to the headwaters of the Missouri.

Ranch headquarters were located as centrally in the range as practicable; by the side of a stream, and in a clump of trees if the locality were favored with such growths of timber; or under the brow of a hill, or in a widened ravine where there would be some shelter from winter's blasts. But as the nearness of surface-water was the first consideration in the times before the windmill came to help out the western stockman, and as the timber-growths along the streams often were thin and frequently absent in many parts of the range country, it happened even oftener than otherwise that the buildings stood out in the open without any protection from the full glare of the summer sun or from the driving winds of winter storms.

The typical headquarters establishment of a ranch in the period we are considering here was what was known as "a double cabin" by American pioneers from the beginning. This was a two-room building, the rooms being separated by an open space between, but the roof was continuous over all. In other words, two cabins, ten or fifteen feet apart with a common roof that spanned the division between them; this intermediate space sometimes being left open only on one side. In a ranch-building this between-place came handy for hanging up saddles, bridles, ropes, and so on, on pegs in the logs. One of the rooms was the cook's kingdom, in which he worked and slept and suffered his subjects to eat their meals from a long table; a bench on each side enabling them to seat themselves while eating. Aside from the cook's bunk, his stove and its belongings, the table and its benches, this "mess-room" seldom had any other "furniture." The other room, which usually was much the larger, was sitting-room and sleeping-room combined, with a yawning fireplace at one end. Sleeping bunks were built along the side walls, and the men stowed their personal belongings where they could, hanging their clothing on pegs in the logs. Nearly everything in and around the establishment was primitive. The mess-table and its benches, the bunks and chairs, often were made from "lumber" hewn out on the spot. But as boxes and barrels in which provisions were brought in accumulated, these or their materials were utilized in improving the furniture and fittings of the outfit. Late hours seldom were kept. The men were too tired for that. The rule of the ranch was the old one of early to bed and early to rise.

Near by the ranch-house there was a corral, and also a small pound or chute, both of which were used chiefly for handling fat cattle that were about to be started away to the market—as for putting the "road brand" on them.

All of these headquarters structures were put together roughly and seemingly in a careless way. Interest was centered on the cattle. They were "the main thing."

ORGANIZATION OF THE CATTLEMEN'S ASSOCIATIONS

Primitive means of protecting property sufficed so long as herds were small, but by the early 1880s capital investment in ranching was reaching astronomical figures. A rancher with a "spread" of thousands of acres and herds worth a quarter of a million dollars wanted more reliable protection than that carried on the hip. Moreover, as the range filled and the necessity of living near other ranchers multiplied problems, all manner of difficulties demanded solution. Herds had to be kept separated, water rights allotted, Indians and rustlers warded off, marketing procedures devised, and other problems solved. This was the situation that underlay the growth of Cattlemen's Associations throughout the range country, to serve as law enforcement agencies in a region where there was no formal government. Granville Stuart, who turned from mining to become president of the Montana Stockgrowers' Association when it was organized in July 1884, described the Association's purposes and obligations in a letter sent to all members a year later:[6]

DEAR SIR:

At the Convention of Stockmen from all parts of the Territory, held in Helena in July 1884, which resulted in the organization of the Montana Stock Growers, the unprotected and exposed condition of the livestock interests of the Territory from theft and disease were fully discussed and in pursuance of the resolutions adopted, the President of the Association called a meeting of the Executive Committee in Helena, January 12th, 1885, to which meeting Stockmen from all parts of the Territory were invited, the object being to secure the passage of better stock laws.

The Executive Committee was in session during the entire session of the Legislature, and while it was acknowledged by all that the stock interests needed protection from dangers, both present and prospective, yet it was unanimously determined that although a majority of both branches of the Legislature were favorably inclined toward this great and rapidly increasing industry, no legislation would be asked for except such as would commend itself, not only to stockmen generally, but to every citizen of the Territory. To the President and Secretary of the Association, assisted by such stockmen as could be present, was assigned the duty of preparing bills in accordance with these

[6] Robert H. Fletcher, *Free Grass to Fences* (New York, 1960), pp. 69–71. Published for the Historical Society of Montana by University Publishers.

views. This was done with the following result.

A bill was passed and became a law authorizing the Governor to appoint a Territorial Veterinarian Surgeon whose duty it should be to examine and report upon all cases of disease among horses, cattle, and mules, and where said disease is generally fatal and liable to become epidemic, he shall have the diseased animals appraised and may order them killed and burned, the owner receiving two-thirds of the value thereof.

The Surgeon also has power to quarantine all stock shipped or driven into the Territory that are diseased or that he has reason to believe may be diseased. The necessity for this law becomes apparent when we consider the impossibility of arresting a disease of a contagious and fatal nature, when once started among cattle and horses roaming at will over large districts, the only safety in such cases being in using all possible precautions against any disease obtaining a foothold.

A law was also passed authorizing the Governor to appoint six Live Stock Commissioners, being one each for the counties of Dawson, Custer, Yellowstone, Meagher, Chouteau, and Lewis and Clark, who should in turn appoint and employ such inspectors and detectives as they may deem necessary to best protect the livestock interests of the territory. Said Commissioners receive no pay or mileage and the inspectors and detectives employed by them are to be paid out of a special tax levy of one and one-half mills on the dollar, to be levied upon the cattle, horses, mules, and asses in the counties named. The other counties, being excepted from the provisions of the bill, have no inspectors.

This law is one of importance and is intended to put a stop to the stealing of livestock, which has grown to be an evil of great magnitude, and also to assist the Veterinarian Surgeon in finding and stamping out diseases of a contagious and fatal nature.

A law was also passed prohibiting the branding of cattle upon the public ranges during the month of August and from November 15th to May 15th, next succeeding; but the bill provides that any owner of stock may brand cattle on his own premises at any time if done in the presence of two responsible citizens. The exemptions from the provisions of this bill are the counties of Missoula, Deer Lodge, Silver Bow, Beaverhead, Madison, Jefferson, and all of Gallatin County lying west of the Belt or Bridger range of mountains.

A law was also passed to enable persons attaching or attempting in any other manner by legal process to take possession of livestock running at large on the public ranges of the Territory, to attach and hold the same, between the first of November and the next succeeding fifteenth day of May, by filing and recording with the county Clerk or Recorder of the County, wherein the property is roaming, a copy of such process, with a notice appended, giving the number, description, marks and brands of the animals. Such copy of the process, with the notice appended, after it has been so recorded, has the same effect as if the actual custody of the property had been taken. But the law requires that the *actual custody* of the property attached must be taken prior to the first day of August. This law applies in the same way and manner to the taking possession of the property under the foreclosure of a chattel mortgage on stock running at large on the public ranges. The intention of this law is to prevent the handling or collecting together of live stock on any range in winter because of the great injury and damage that would result, not only to the stock gathered, but to all other stock on the same range.

The enactment of these laws will go far

towards preventing great losses from theft, disease, and other causes, hitherto sustained by the owners of livestock in this Territory, and we urge upon every citizen the necessity of aiding in their enforcement.

We prepared a bill in regard to the payment for stock killed or injured by railroads, which was in the main satisfactory to the stockmen and the representatives of the railroads, it being to a considerable extent a compromise measure, but owing to the long discussion over it in the endeavor to harmonize conflicting interests, it passed a short time before the close of the session, and to our great surprise the Governor held and thus prevented it from becoming a law, a result the more to be regretted because it was a law for the protection of the farmer and small stock owners along the lines of railroads, who are much greater sufferers from the loss of stock killed and injured than the large owners whose stock, being wild, are less liable to be run over and injured.

Stockmen can best serve their own interests, and at the same time secure greater protection and other advantages, by joining the Montana Stock-growers Association and we most earnestly urge them to cooperate with us by doing so at once, if not already members of the Association. It costs but fifteen dollars ($15) to secure a membership, and the annual dues, after the first year, are ten dollars ($10).

Among the many advantages offered by the Association, one of the most important is the publication of a Brand Book each year, giving the brands, range, postoffice address, and other necessary information concerning members. Each member of the Association is entitled to one copy of the Brand Book and as many additional copies as are desired can be obtained at a nominal price. Application for membership in the Association should be sent to the Secretary accompanied by a check, draft, or P. O. order for fifteen dollars ($15), the initiation fees and annual dues for the first year.

THE ROUND-UP

One of the many functions of the stock growers' associations was to regulate the semiannual "round-ups" that were one of the most colorful institutions of the cattle kingdom. At an agreed-upon time herds from an entire district that had mingled on the unfenced range were brought together, and held while each rancher "cut out" his own beasts. The calves were then branded with the distinctive mark of their mother, and marketable beeves singled out for shipment to the railroad. John Baumann, participant in one of these events, left a vivid description:[7]

At last we are ready; our boss gives final instructions with regard to the circle each man will have to ride, and the exact spot towards which we are to converge by midday. No, we are not off yet; look at yon dun broncho ridden by a young hand; his stride is short and jerky, he is fetching at his bridle in an ominous manner, his ears laid back, and his long tail tight between his hind quarters; should he succeed in getting his head down or detect the slightest symptom of nervousness in his rider, we shall see some fun. He stops, shies half round, and with a vicious squeal pitches high into the air; his rider is already clutching the horn of his saddle, another buck and he is hanging on by the mane, yet another, and he is sprawling on the ground. Yoicks, gone away! We all gallop after the riderless brute, swinging our lassoes

[7] John Baumann, "On a Western Ranche," *The Fortnightly Review*, New Series, XLI (March, 1887), pp. 523–525.

exultingly round our heads, and in a few minutes he is dragged sullenly back to his crestfallen rider, who with his blood now fairly roused, remounts full of vengeful resolve, and this time succeeds in proving himself master.

But now to our work. We cross the river at a wild spot where its banks are formed by steep bluffs studded with cactus and prickly pear; cypress, cedar, and maple nestling at their base. A steep, narrow gorge leads to wide plains, bounded by a low range of flat-topped antelope hills. Up this gorge the circle-riders make their way, and dividing into couples, start at a lope for the lurking-places of the cattle. Creek, shady cañon, and arroyo are searched, and after many a chase after wilful calf or sullen bull, a goodly round up of seven or eight hundred head is formed.

"So—o, so—o, so gently lads; hold them together! Gallop round them; head back that little column led by a frightened steer. Quick! quick! or by the powers the whole herd will be off." Good! our little cow-ponies can go like the wind for a short distance; can turn and twist, and stop in the twinkling of an eye (sharper, indeed, than suits the seat of an awkward horseman); the fugitives are pressed back, bellowing loud protest the while. But now the whole mass is violently agitated; a couple of sharp-horned Texan bulls have come foul of each other. Quickly a space is cleared around them; they stand face to face glaring and snorting, with heads lowered, and defiantly tearing up clouds of dust till one or the other rushes to the attack. With a crash their heads meet; they sway about for a moment with locked horns; separate, retreat, and dash together again forehead to forehead, with all their strength and fury concentrated into that ferocious collision, until at length, after a combat lasting several minutes, the weaker turns tail and leaves his victor triumphant.

It is a wild and variegated spectacle, this mass of tangled and tossing horns. Rough, poor-looking cows, with calves as pretty as paint; savage, long-horned Texans; handsome, bald-faced Herefords; big, black, hornless Galloways; broad-browed shorthorn bulls, all thoroughbreds, intermingle with nondescript grades of all sizes and ages. They have not yet quite shed their winter coats, or the big brands on shoulder, side, and hip would stand out more distinctly. They are earmarked in every conceivable manner, from the becoming underslope to the disfiguring grub, which leaves a mere stump in the place of an ear. All are in lean condition, not having filled out yet on the juicy and fattening grasses which will shortly ripen as the season advances, but they look bright-eyed, clean, and healthy, with the exception of a few locoed beasts, whose dull, stupid eyes, mangy coats, and clumsy, purposeless movements, prove them to have indulged in orgies of the fatal plant. . . .

Tom Connor, range foreman of some fifty thousand head of cattle, is for the moment our "big chief," for it is on his ground that we are working. Tall, good-looking, and somewhat of a prairie "dude" in appearance, he is now the centre of a group of men awaiting his instructions. Some half-a-dozen of these, mounted on well-trained cutting-ponies, proceed quietly to enter the herd and wind their way in and out among the cattle until they mark one of their own brands. With a smart cut from the raw-hide quirt a young steer is set in motion; whichever way he twists or turns he finds the relentless horseman at his heels, and is forced against his will to the outskirts of the herd. Why should he leave his companions? He makes a sudden desperate turn, and rushes among them again. Before the eager little pony has had time to follow, he has succeeded in diving well into their midst. Leave him there for the present; he is on the alert now, and will be "mean to cut"; these youngsters, be they bull, heifer, or steer, always are. Others have been more successful; animals are being separated from the main bunch on all sides, and sent trotting in the direction of the respective cuts.

It is an animated, blood-stirring scene. The cuts are "held" by cowboys, who are tearing about in their endeavours to keep the beasts together. The cutting-ponies are dodging and turning with marvellous rapidity and sagacity, appearing almost to anticipate the movements of the pursued. The air is filled with smoke-like clouds of dust and the ground trembles with the thunder of many hoofs. By the time the sun nears the horizon the big round-up has been divided into several bunches, which are being slowly moved to their respective bedding-grounds, there to be held by night guards until the following day, when they will be day-herded and driven to our next camping-place. Both men and horses are dog-tired. We have changed our mounts after the mid-day meal, it is true, but the ground is rough, the work has been fast and furious. Our wiry little ponies, standing barely over fourteen hands, have to carry saddles weighing full forty pounds, and in many cases big, strapping fellows who, riding purely by balance and with a loose seat, are all over their backs, when the clever little animals dart about after cattle. They are, besides, roughly used, getting no praise or encouragement for work willingly done, but whip, spurs, and oaths for the slightest mistake. One form of suffering so common to their kind they certainly do escape. Their riders are light of hand, the enormous Mexican spade-bit hangs loosely in their mouths, and it is but rarely that they are made to realise its full power. Their heads are now turned towards camp, and they make an effort to gallop in gaily. We off-saddle and coil up our lariats to catch our night-horses out of the bunch which the horse-rustler is holding in readiness for us, saddle them, stake them out, and leave them there until our turn comes to go out on "night guard"; hobble the remainder of the bunch and let them wander off at their own sweet will. The day's work is done!

INVESTMENT IN THE RANGE CATTLE INDUSTRY

Stock grower's associations conducted efficient round-ups, but not even their well-run organizations could save the cattle kingdom from disaster brought on by the ranchers' own greed. Escalating profits were responsible. First-comers who stocked their ranges cheaply with Texas longhorns and fattened them at little cost on free grass reported returns of astronomical proportions on their investments. As word of their fortunes flooded the East and Europe, capital flowed westward in ever mounting volume to buy more cattle, and place more of the range under pasturage. Largely responsible for this overexpansion were a number of books and magazine articles filled with solid statistics on profits being earned by ranchers. Typical was a volume by Walter Baron von Richthofen, "Cattle-Raising on the Plains of North America" (1885), which painted an irresistible picture of the economic future of ranching:[8]

The immense profits which have been universally realized in the Western cattle business for the past, and which will be increased in the future, owing to the more economical methods pursued, so long as ranges can be purchased at present prices, may seem incredible to many of my readers, who, no

---

[8] Walter Baron von Richthofen, *Cattle-Raising on the Plains of North America* (New York, 1885), pp. 62–66.

doubt, have considered the stories of the fortunes realized as myths. Yet it is true that many men who started only a few years ago with comparatively few cattle, are now wealthy, and, in some cases, millionaires. They certainly did not find the gold upon the prairies, nor did they have any source of revenue beyond the increase of their cattle. The agencies producing this immense wealth are very natural and apparent.

The climate of the West is the healthiest on the earth; the pure, high mountain air and dry atmosphere are the natural remedies, or rather preventives, against sickness among cattle in general, and against all epidemic diseases in particular; for "nowhere in the Western States do we find any traces of pleuro-pneumonia, foot or mouth, and such like contagious diseases."

The pure clear water of the mountain rivers affords to cattle another health preserver, and the fine nutritious and bountiful grasses, and in winter the naturally-cured hay, furnish to them the healthiest natural food.

Formerly these pastures cost nothing, and at present only a trifle, as I explained in a former chapter, so that the interest on the investment in purchasing land is of little importance in the estimate of the cost of keeping a herd. In fact, ownership of land is now indispensable for a herd-owner. This land in less than ten years will be a considerable factor in the profits of the cattle business, as the value of pastures will constantly increase.

The principal cost of raising cattle is only the herding and watching the cattle by herders, without any cost for sheltering or feeding. In time even these expenses will be reduced, as now already herds are kept in large fenced ranges, and many of the herders are dispensed with.

The losses of cattle, as shown by statistics, are larger among Eastern and European herds, which are sheltered in stables and fed the whole year round, than among the shelterless herds of the West.

The losses in the West, to the causes whereof I shall devote a chapter, are practically reduced by long experience to a certain percentage, which enables the stockmen to calculate infallibly the profits and losses of their business.

This annual loss is found to average two to three per cent. We may safely put the loss in the extreme Northern States at about three per cent, and in the more Southern and temperate districts at two or less per cent.

The annual cost of herding the cattle, as I have shown in a previous chapter, is about seventy cents per head; adding the other expenses, such as taxes, loss of interest on the purchase-money of land, etc., we find that the entire annual expense is less than $1.50 per head.

It takes a heifer-calf, say, three years to mature, and a steer-calf will be ready for the market in four years. The latter will then bring forty dollars; deducting the six dollars of expense for his rearing, we have a net profit of thirty-four dollars on each steer.

Now let me illustrate the profits realized from one Texas cow, worth thirty dollars. In ten years she will have eight calves, which, if they are all steers, will have produced at the end of fourteen years $320, or a profit of $272. The cow herself still remains, and is worth about her original cost for the butcher. These figures are made without reference to any increase in the value of cattle or beef, and without reference to any improvement of the stock by crossing it with better blood.

The next thing to consider is the natural increase of cattle. I will give my opinion first, and then state those of some of the most experienced cattlemen.

I think that seventy-five or eighty per cent of the cows will drop one calf each every year, and that the mortality among these calves will be affected by the mildness or rigor of the climate. The loss of winterborn calves is very small in the Southern portion of the country, but increases as you go North. Therefore I conclude that, for breeding purposes, a more southerly located range is preferable. With the liberal use of bulls, which means at least one bull for every twenty-five cows, which should be strong and well developed, this increase of seventy-five to eighty per cent may be relied upon. Besides this, the barren and aged cows should be sold at once.

This percentage is to be understood with reference to cows and heifers which are three years of age or more when they drop their first calf.

It is estimated that forty per cent of heifers when only two years old will produce calves, but I hold this increase to be detrimental to the interest of stock-raising, and I would, when managing a herd, try all means possible to prevent such premature increase.

Few persons realize how rapidly cattle would multiply if all the female progeny were allowed to breed each year. If one hundred cows and their female progeny be kept at breeding for ten years, the result would be as follows:

Estimating the natural increase at eighty per cent, of which forty per cent of the cows would have heifers, which would, beginning when two years old, in their turn have young:

					Heifers
100 cows in first	year drop			. . . .	40
100	"	" second	"	"	40
140	"	" third	"	"	56
180	"	" fourth	"	"	72
236	"	" fifth	"	"	94
308	"	" sixth	"	"	123
402	"	" seventh	"	"	161
525	"	" eighth	"	"	210
686	"	" ninth	"	"	274
896	"	" tenth	"	"	358

Total, ten years 1,428

The number of steers would be the same as that of heifers, 1,428. Total increase, 2,856.

From this deduct an annual loss of three per cent of the number of cattle on hand, and make another deduction for the reason that cows will only average eight calves in ten years; take your original price of one hundred cows, deduct for the keeping of the same $1.50 per head per annum, and you will find an enormous increase and an immense sum representing the value of the cattle on hand, and will learn at what rate the capital in the live-stock business increases.

END OF THE OPEN RANGE: THE WINTER OF 1886–1887

Great profits were made in the late 1870s and early 1880s when grass was plentiful and a favorable weather cycle drenched the Great Plains with adequate rainfall. But by 1885 the situation had changed. The influx of eastern and European capital meant a spectacular increase in the number of cattle, and a corresponding decrease in the area of grazing land available for each. The herds could be sustained only so long as rainfall was plentiful; a cycle of dry years would spell disaster. To make matters worse, the abundance of beef drove prices steadily downward at the Chicago markets. Old-time cattlemen who read the signs of danger in these developments were proven right in 1886–1887. That summer was hot and dry, leaving grass sparse and streams empty. By autumn millions of cattle were so poorly fed that they were unprepared to resist winter's blasts. Yet that winter was one of the worst in history, with snow blanketing the northern plains from November onward and temperatures tumbling to sixty degrees below zero. A Montana rancher, John Clay, recorded in his reminiscences the tragedy that followed, not in terms of suffering endured by the freezing longhorns, but in the language of dollar-and-cent losses:[9]

> We rounded up one day near to Wind River and as the cattle came in they were almost exhausted from want of water and quite a few of them had not shed their winter coats. It was the same everywhere. On the Belle Fourche, a heavily grassed country, it was dry as a bone. The same condition existed on the Little Missouri and over on the Powder. In the spring of 1886 Dorr Clark had resigned from his position with the VVV outfit. Duncan Plumb had organized the Dominion Cattle Co., taking up a range on Grand River in South Dakota, and Clark became manager. Robert Robinson, son of the late Mr. J. M. Robinson and a half brother of Mr. Charles O. Robinson, took his place. Bobby had had a varied experience. He had worked in the yards, had seen a lot of the range, working for a while for Mr. Charles Coffey, now of Chadron, Nebraska. He was a man of the best kind of judgment and admirably suited for managing a large outfit. He was exceedingly economical, a fine judge of men and he had the faculty of gathering around him a capable bunch of cowpunchers, sobriety being his first requirement. Added to all this he was an excellent judge of range cattle, a gift possessed by very few men on the range, although it is their daily business. From him I learned many a lesson. In his daily life and work he was the exact opposite of his predecessor. About the first thing we had to decide was the important question about putting up our usual number of young steers. May was dry, June did not bring the usual rains, and by July 4th it looked so bad that we finally decided to do nothing. By August it was hot, dry, dusty and grass closely cropped. Every day made it apparent that even with the best of winters cattle would have a hard time and "through" cattle would only winter with a big percentage of loss.
>
> Meantime a cattle owner of those days when he had money was anxious to spend it. Fortunately when in New York during August I met Mr. George Dixon Fisher, a director of the Cedar Valley Land & Cattle Co., a well known outfit in the Panhandle. Fisher was anxious to sell his steer yearlings and we traded for 2,000 head to be delivered next season as two-year-olds. The price was $14.00 per head. We paid $2.50 for wintering and allowed a loss of 5 per cent during the winter. This made a sure thing. We spent our money but escaped the coming winter. As events turned out the trade was a life saver. Some people will say good luck, others good management. The reader can judge for himself. Our neighbors kept piling cattle onto the bone dry range. The Continental Cattle Co. drove up 32,000 head of steers. The Worsham Cattle Co., with no former holdings turned loose 5,000 head or thereabouts. Major Smith, who had failed to sell 5,500 southern three-year-old steers, was forced to drive them to his range on Willow Creek near to Stoneville, now Alzada, Mont. The Dickey Cattle Co., as previously related, had brought up 6,000 mixed cattle from the Cheyenne and Arapahoe country and turned them over to their outfit whose headquarters were twenty or twenty-five miles below the above hamlet on the Little Missouri. Thousands of other cattle were spread over the western and northwestern country in the most reckless way, no thought for the morrow. Even with the best of winters it would have been a case of suicide. As things turned out it was simple murder, at least for the Texas cattle. Winter came early and it stayed long. The owners were mostly absent and even those

---

[9] John Clay, *My Life on the Range* (New York: Antiquarian Press, Ltd., 1961), pp. 176–179.

who remained could not move about or size up the situation.

It was not till the spring round-ups that the real truth was discovered and then it was only mentioned in a whisper. Bobby Robinson, acute judge of conditions, estimated the loss among through cattle at less than 50 per cent. It turned out to be a total loss among this class of cattle and the wintered herds suffered from thirty to sixty per cent. I had gone to Europe in June, just as the round-ups had commenced. I got back the first days of August and for the first time heard of the terrific slaughter. It was simply appalling and the cowmen could not realize their position. From Southern Colorado to the Canadian line, from the 100th Meridian almost to the Pacific slope it was a catastrophe which the cowmen of today who did not go through it can never understand. Three great streams of ill-luck, mismanagement, greed, met together. In other words, recklessness, want of foresight and the weather, which no man can control. The buffalo had probably gone through similar winters with enormous losses and thus natural conditions were evened up in the countless years they had grazed the prairie and in the survival of the fittest their constitutions had been built up to stand the rigors of winter and the drought of summer.

As actual facts are better than surmise, here are some striking ones. The Continental Company was a shadow of its former self. The Worsham folks never attempted to gather their remnant. We gathered Major Smith's four-year-olds. Out of the 5,500 three-year-olds we got about 100 head. In this connection there was a rather strange coincidence to show how wintered steers will go through extraordinary hardship. Mr. D. W. Smith of Springfield, Illinois, had bought and turned loose under his brother's care about 1,200 two-year old JJ steers (Prairie Cattle Co.) in 1885. These had gone up early in the season, partly by rail, and had got a good start. We gathered these cattle and had only a 10 per cent loss in two years on the range, whereas his brother's bunch were short 98 per cent. There could be no mistake, as both lots were counted in and out. The VVV outfit had the same experience. The steers sent up during 1885 shipped with even a smaller loss, but they had the advantage of drifting eastward onto the Indian reservation lying west of the Missouri, and there we found lots of them in the spring and summer of 1887.

The cowmen of the West and Northwest were flat broke. Many of them never recovered. They had not the heart to face another debacle such as they had gone through and consequently they disappeared from the scene. Most of the eastern men and the Britishers said "enough" and went away.

The winter of 1886–1887 ended one period in the history of cattle raising. Dollar losses were hard enough to bear, but even worse was the sight of the thousands upon thousands of carcasses that covered the ground when the spring thaw came. Cattlemen realized that for humanitarian as well as practical reasons the day of the open range was over; they must fence their fields and provide winter feed for their stock. No longer would giant herds drift from pasture to pasture; now cowboys spent their time digging post holes or harvesting hay rather than with lassoes and branding irons. The cattle kingdom was emerging from its frontier stage, and by contracting, opening the Great Plains to the small farmers who were to subdue America's last great West.

CHARTER 27

Technology and the Farmers' Frontier, 1865-1890

Before farmers could challenge cattlemen for a share of the Great Plains, inventors had to equip them with the tools needed for the conquest. Many were essential. Cheap fencing was necessary in a land where wood for split rails was lacking. Well-digging equipment was needed to bring water to the surface for use by men and livestock. Efficient farm machinery had to be devised, for in the semiarid West a farmer had to till double the number of acres required in the East for the same return. New agricultural techniques were demanded, and new crops were essential for successful farming in a region where the average rainfall was less than the 20 inches needed for traditional agriculture. If these tools and techniques could be perfected, a vast new farming frontier lay open to the pioneers. This was a challenge that sent eastern inventors to their drawing boards and eastern scientists to their laboratories. Within a remarkably short time they had developed the machines and methods that opened the Great Plains and underlay the greatest mass migration of pioneers in the history of the American frontier.

THE PROBLEM OF FENCING ON THE GREAT PLAINS

Good fencing was a first need. The farming frontier could advance only at the expense of cattlemen, whose herds trampled fields and ruined crops and had to be contained. In 1871, the Commissioner of Agriculture dramatically demonstrated the profits that would await the inventor of a successful cheap fence, by showing that the nation's bill for building and maintaining inefficient wooden fences was almost two billion dollars, a sum only a shade smaller than the national debt in those days:[1]

It has been a mooted point, in the past, whether fences were intended to avert the destruction of corn by the cattle of neighbors, or to restrain one's own stock from similar depredations. For a long time the popular idea, logically interpreted, appeared to be that corn should be restrained to pre-

[1] *Report of the Commissioner of Agriculture for the Year 1871* (Washington, 1872), pp. 497, 511–512.

613

vent depredations upon cattle. Another question, of which a solution has been desired, is whether the money invested in farm-stock or that in farm fences is the greater sum. It is certain that the fence investment is a large one, and strongly suspected that much of it is avoidable and unprofitable. While rapidly paying the national debt, it is possible that the American people may discover a means of reducing another of almost equal proportions. In the one case the annual tax is a fixed sum, which is less than legal interest upon the entire principal; in the other; it is legal interest on the whole amount, and a still larger tax for depreciation of the principal, thus more than doubling the tax, and rendering the fence debt a heavier burden than the war debt.

It is beginning to be seen that our fence laws are inequitable in a greater degree than is required by the principle of yielding something of personal right, when necessary, for the general good. When a score of young farmers "go West," with strong hands and little cash in them, but a munificent promise to each of a homestead worth $200 now, and $2,000 in the future, for less than $20 in land-office fees, they often find that $1,000 will be required to fence scantily each farm, with little benefit to themselves, but mainly for mutual protection against a single stock-grower, rich in cattle, and becoming richer by feeding them without cost upon the unpurchased prairie. This little community of twenty families cannot see the justice of the requirement which compels the expenditure of $20,000 to protect their crops from injury by the nomadic cattle of their unsettled neighbor, which may not be worth $10,000 altogether. There is also inequality in the tax which fencing levies upon the farmers, the rate of which increases with the decrease of the area; for example, a farmer inclosing a section of land, 640 acres, with a cheap fence costing but $1 per rod, pays $1,280 for as many rods of fence, or $2 per acre; another, with a quarter section, 160 acres, pays $640, or $4 per acre; while a third, who is only able to hold 40 acres, must pay $320, or $8 per acre. Thus the fencing system is one of differential mortgages, the poor man in this case being burdened with an extra mortgage of $6 per acre which his richer neighbor is not compelled to bear. All these acres are of equal intrinsic and productive value, but those of the larger farm have each but a fourth of the annual burden thrown upon the smaller homestead, and the whole expense may be for protection against trespassing cattle owned by others. . . .

Cost of material.—A great variety of material is used for board-fences. Of course, inferior qualities of lumber are taken—that which is rough and knotty, or those kinds of wood less in request for house-finishing or furniture-making. Where oak is abundant, it is often employed; hemlock and spruce are used largely in New England, New York, and elsewhere, as other timber increases in value; and the cheaper grades of pine are extensively used in the Northwest, and culls from oak, poplar, ash, and other woods.

The average cost, as reported, is given in the accompanying table, from which it appears that boards used for fences are dearest in Texas, costing $29.53; $28.95 in Kansas; $27.88 in Nebraska; $27 in Delaware, and $25.66 in Rhode Island. The cost is least in Georgia, $12; $12.37 in Oregon; and $12.85 in Florida. The cost of rails are highest in New Jersey; next in order, Nevada, Rhode Island, Massachusetts, and Connecticut. The lowest figure is $8.12 per M, in Florida; then Georgia, Alabama, South Carolina, and Mississippi. . . .

This exhibit makes the cost of fences

nearly equal to the total amount of the national debt on which interest is paid, and about the same as the estimated value of all the farm animals in the United States. For every dollar invested in live stock, another dollar is required for the construction of defenses to resist their attacks on farm production. Experiment has proved that at least half this expense is unnecessary. Wherever it has been tried, wherever farm-animals are restrained, and their owners are placed under (fence) bonds for the good behavior of their restless dependents, the system is regarded with general and growing satisfaction, capital is released from unprofitable investment and made available for farm improvement, soiling is encouraged, the manurial resources of stock husbanded, and the way prepared for larger production and higher profit. Even where a herd law of some sort has not been enacted, the tendency is strong, as many correspondents assert, toward the reduction of the amount of fencing; as repairs are needed, division fences are taken down and the material used to keep outside fences in repair; fields are almost everywhere becoming larger; in the younger States, a single field often answers all requirements, and sometimes a single inclosure embraces within its bounds many farms. The entire town of Greeley, in Colorado, with its suburbs for gardens and small market farms, is surrounded with a single fence, the cattle being excluded and kept outside upon the illimitable plains. It is possible to dispense with fencing to the value of one thousand million dollars, and the advantages of the change would greatly overbalance the inconvenience of it. Let the farmers discuss the subject in the light of actual experiment, rather than under the influence of ancient prejudice, and their views will soon coincide with their true interests.

MECHANIZING THE WESTERN FARM

This cold array of figures sent dozens of would-be inventors to work; the fortunate individual who won the basic patents was Joseph F. Glidden of De Kalb, Illinois, with the principle of barbed-wire fencing. This cheap and efficient material was soon moving west by the freight-car load, to build a protective barrier between farmers and cattlemen. Farmers needed more than fencing, for to conquer the Great Plains, they had to have machinery suitable for agriculture in a subhumid environment. Nor did inventors fail them; by the end of the 1870s a whole arsenal of usable machines awaited buyers: steel gang plows that would turn several furrows at once, spring-toothed harrows to pulverize the prairie soil, grain drills to seed dozens of furrows, reapers and binders to cut and bundle wheat mechanically, headers to capture only the kernels of grain, steam-driven threshers, and more. By adopting these innovations, a farmer could care for a dozen acres for every one he had cultivated by older methods. The Department of Agriculture, surveying this revolution at the end of the 1890s, reported on the remarkable saving of manpower that had been achieved:[2]

Much remains to be said with regard to the evolution of agriculture in the United States, but only a brief reference can be made to some of the more important results of the investigation of hand and machine labor and processes as applied to agriculture, with a contrast between farming as it was practiced fifty to seventy years ago and farming as it is now carried on with the advantage of the

---

[2] *Year Book of the United States Department of Agriculture, 1899* (Washington, 1900), pp. 331–334.

labor-saving and perfecting implements and machines of the present time as well as with the improvements contributed by the chemist, the "book farmer," and the more enlightened experience of the last half century.

Corn Cultivation and Harvesting

Between 1855 and 1894 the following changes took place in the cultivation of corn. The time of human labor required to produce one bushel of corn on an average declined from 4 hours and 34 minutes to 41 minutes, and the cost of the human labor to produce this bushel declined from 35¾ cents to 10½ cents.

In the earlier years the plow and harrow of that period were used; the check rows were marked with the shovel plow; the seed was dropped by hand from a bucket or pouch carried by the farmer and covered with a hoe; the cultivating was done with a shovel plow; knives were used for cutting the stalks from the ground by hand; husking pegs were worn on the hand in husking; the stalks, husks, and blades were cut into fodder with an old-time machine turned by hand, and the corn was shelled by hand, either on a frying-pan handle or on a shovel or by rubbing the cob against the unshelled ears.

A radical change had taken place in 1894. The earth was loosened with a gang plow, and a disk harrow very thoroughly pulverized it. A corn planter drawn by a horse planted the corn, and the top soil was pulverized afterwards with a four-section harrow.

When it came to harvesting the corn, a self-binder drawn by horses cut the stalks and bound them, and the shocks of stalks were then hauled to a machine, which removed the husks from the ears, and in the same process cut the husks and the stalks and the blades into fodder, the power of the machine being supplied by a steam engine.

Then came the shelling of the corn, which is one of the marvels of the changes that have been wrought by machines. In this case, the machine operated by steam shelled 1 bushel of corn per minute, while in the old way the labor of one man was required for 100 minutes to do the same work.

Wheat Cultivation and Harvesting

The use of steam as a substitute for horse power in plowing, in harvesting, and in thrashing wheat has not materially contributed to economy except from a saving due to the elimination of animal power, so the more common power supplied by horses is here selected for the comparison. The years in contrast are 1830 and 1896.

It is one of the marvels of the age that the amount of human labor now required to produce a bushel of wheat from beginning to end is on an average only 10 minutes, whereas, in 1830, the time was 3 hours and 3 minutes. During the interval between these years the cost of the human labor required to produce this bushel of wheat declined from 17¾ cents to 3⅓ cents.

In the contrast thus presented the heavy, clumsy plow of the day was used in 1830; the seed was sown by hand, and was harrowed into the ground by the drawing of bushes over it; the grain was cut with sickles, hauled to a barn, and at some time before the following spring was thrashed with flails; the winnowing was done with a sheet attached to rods, on which the grain was placed with a shovel and then tossed up and down by two men until the wind had blown out the chaff.

In the latter year, on the contrary, the ground was plowed and pulverized in the same operation by a disk plow; the seed was sown with a mechanical seeder drawn by horses; the reaping, thrashing, and sacking of the wheat was done with the combined reaper and thrasher drawn by horses, and then the wheat was ready to haul to the granary.

The comparisons might be extended throughout many of the crops produced by the farmer, with a constantly recurring illustration of the saving of human labor and of the diminution of the cost of production by the dimunition of human labor. With regard to animal labor alone it often appears that an increased time is required in production, but where there is an increased cost it is principally due to the increased value of the labor of animals.

Saving in the Cost of Producing Crops

The potential saving in the cost of human labor on account of improved implements, machines, and processes, at the rate per bushel or ton, as the case may be, has been computed for seven of the principal crops of 1899; the comparison is between the old-time methods of production, in which hand labor was assisted only by the comparatively rude and inefficient implements of the day and the present time, when hand labor has not only the assistance of highly efficient and perfected implements and machines, but has been considerably displaced by them. The saving in the cost of human labor in cents, per unit of product, permits a very forcible statement of its equivalent in money by means of a computation consisting of the multiplication of the saving per unit into the crop of 1899. The result expresses the potential labor saving in the production of seven crops of that year, and is not an aggregate of the saving of human labor in the cost of producing the crops for all of the years between the earlier and the later ones, during which time this economizing and displacement of human labor has taken place. In the case of the crop of corn, the money measure of the saving of human labor required to produce it in 1899 in the most available economic manner, as compared with its production in the old-time manner, was $523,276,642; wheat, $79,194,867; oats, $52,866,200; rye, $1,408,950; barley, $7,323,480; white potatoes, $7,366,820; hay, $10,034,868.

The total potential saving in the cost of human labor for these seven crops of 1899, owing to the possible utilization of the implements, machines, and methods of the present time, in place of the old-time manner of production, reaches the stupendous amount of $681,471,827 for this one year.

It would be idle to claim that the progress of the agriculture of the United States and its evolution from the primitive scope and conditions in which it was found by the settlers who came from Europe have been set forth adequately, even in its important topics and details, in the foregoing pages, but perhaps enough has been presented to explain in their main features the causes and opportunities which in combination have led to an agricultural production actually too great to be grasped by the human mind.

As great as has been the growth of manufactures, mining, the fisheries, and trade and transportation, all of which tend to draw population from agriculture, yet more than one-third of the population of the country is engaged in agriculture or dependent upon agriculturists. This element in our population has proved to be a strong one. It has been conservative with regard to those things that experience has demonstrated to be good. It has been an industrial element upon which all other elements of the population have needed to depend as the cornerstone of the social and industrial structure.

The agricultural element is the one independent element in our society. Let whatever betide that may, this element has a degree of independence in subsistence and in living that no other element has, and still, as in the past, remains the chief mainstay of the nation.

THE LAND SYSTEM: THE PROBLEM OF SPECULATION

Technological innovations allowed the agricultural conquest of the Great Plains, but the magnet that attracted farmers westward was free land. When their advance began shortly after the close of the Civil War, farms on the public domain could be secured in three ways: by pre-empting 160 acres and paying at the long-established rate of $1.25 an acre, by purchasing from a speculator or railroad, or by homesteading a quarter-section. Actually far more pioneers purchased from speculators than from the government, but the Homestead Act of 1862 did more to advertise the West and lure the downtrodden from the East and from Europe than any other measure. "Free land for the homeless" was a slogan that captured the interest of both continents. Once in the West, newcomers found that this well-intentioned measure was subject to a variety of abuses, and that it was used by small speculators to obtain the best acreage for resale at advanced prices. A traveler, Albert D. Richardson, amusingly reported the ingenious devices that were used to bilk the government of its public domain:[3]

During this fall many residents were pre-empting their claims. The law contemplates a homestead of one hundred and sixty acres at a nominal price for each actual settler and no one else; but land is plenty and everybody preempts. A young merchant, lawyer, or speculator, rides into the interior, to the unoccupied public lands, pays some settler five dollars to show him the vacant 'claims,' and selects one upon which he places four little poles around a hollow square upon the ground, as children commence a cob-house. Then he files a notice in the land-office that he has laid the foundation of a house upon this claim and begun a settlement for actual residence. He does not see the land again until ready to 'prove up,' which he may do after thirty days. Then he revisits his claim, possibly erects a house of rough slabs, costing from ten to twenty dollars, eats one meal and sleeps for a single night under its roof. More frequently, however, his improvements consist solely of a foundation of four logs. He goes to the land-office with a witness, and certifies under oath his desire to preempt the northwest quarter of section twenty-four, township ten, range thirteen, (or whatever the tract may be,) for his 'own exclusive use and benefit.' The witness also swears that the preemptor settled upon the land at the time stated, and erected 'a habitable dwelling,' in which he still resides. Sometimes he is interrogated closely; but he can reply under oath to as many questions as the officer can ask; so the preemptor 'locates' a land-warrant upon the claim—i.e., leaves one in payment for it, as warrants can always be bought for less than one dollar twenty-five cents per acre, which must be given for Government lands when paid for in money. In return, he receives a preliminary title or 'duplicate.' ...

After the lapse of a few months, required for reporting the preemption to the General Land-office at Washington, upon the surrender of his duplicate he obtains a final title or 'patent' from the Government, inscribed on parchment....

In three cases out of four, after 'proving

---

[3] Albert D. Richardson, *Beyond the Mississippi* (Hartford, 1867), pp. 137–141.

up,' the preemptor never visits his land again unless for the purpose of selling it. Says the Spanish proverb, 'Oaths are words, and words are wind.' Thus this unequivocal perjury is regarded upon the frontier. The general feeling is that it wrongs no one, and that the settlers have a right to the land.

Hundreds of men whose families are still in the East find witnesses to testify that their wives and children are residing upon the land. I have known men to preempt who had never been within twenty miles of their claims, facile witnesses swearing with the utmost indifference that they were residing upon them.

The preemptors must state under oath that they have made no agreement direct or indirect for selling any part of the land. But in numberless instances these statements are falsehoods, connived at by the officers.

In most land-offices a man cannot preempt unless he has a house at least twelve feet square. I have known a witness to swear that the house in question was 'twelve by fourteen,' when actually the only building upon the claim was one whittled out with a penknife, twelve *inches* by fourteen.

Some offices require that the house must have a glass window. While traveling in the interior, I stopped at a little slab cabin, where I noticed a window-sash without lights hanging upon a nail. As I had seen similar frames in other cabins, I asked the owner what it was for.

'To preempt with,' was the reply.

'How?'

'Why, don't you understand? To enable my witness to swear that there is *a window in my house!*'

Sometimes the same cabin is moved from claim to claim, until half a dozen different persons have preempted with it. In Nebraska a little frame house, like a country daguerrean car, was built for this purpose *on wheels*, and drawn by oxen. It enabled the preemptor to swear that he had a bona fide resident upon his claim. It was let at five dollars a day, and scores of claims were proved up and preempted with it. The discovery of any such malpractice and perjury would invalidate the title. But I never knew of an instance where the preemptor was deprived of his land after once receiving his title.

PROPAGANDA FOR IMMIGRANTS:
THE DAKOTA TERRITORY

Defects in the homestead and pre-emption laws cost the pioneers heavily; speculators managed to engross most of the best land for resale at prices substantially above those sanctioned by the government. But even these were far lower than in the East or Europe, and this differential served as an irresistible attraction. Just as important in luring would-be settlers was the effective propaganda campaign launched by speculators, railroads, and state or territorial immigration bureaus. All flooded the eastern half of the nation and much of Europe with circulars, broadsides, newspaper advertisements, and books depicting the Great Plains as an Eden beyond compare. Typical was a persuasive volume issued by Dakota Territory in 1870 and written by George A. Batchelder:[4]

Think of it young men, you who are "rubbing" along from year to year, with no great hopes for the future, can you accept for a little while the solitude of nature and bear a few hard knocks for a year or two? Lay aside

---

[4] George A. Batchelder, A *Sketch of the History and Resources of Dakota Territory* (Yankton, 1870). Reprinted in *South Dakota Historical Collections* (1928), vol. 14, pp. 248–250.

your paper collars and kid gloves. Work a little. Possess your soul with patience and hold on your way with a firm purpose. Do this, and there is a beautiful home for you out here. Prosperity, freedom, independence, manhood in its highest sense, peace of mind and all the comforts and luxuries of life are awaiting you. The fountain of perennial youth is in the country, never in the city. Its healing, beautifying and restoring waters do not run through aqueducts. You must lie down on the mossy bank beneath trees, and drink from gurgling brooks and crystal streams.

Nine out of every ten young men without fortune in Boston and elsewhere, have high hopes for the future. They are going to do something by and by. When they get on a little farther they will show us what they can accomplish; but the chances are they never get that little farther on. The tide is against them. We are liable to forget that we measure ourselves by what we are going to do, whereas the world estimates us by what we have already done.

The young man who has measured off ribbon several years, in all probability is doing no better to-day than he was five years ago; and will be no farther along, except in years, five years hence than he is now.

How can any young man of spirit settle himself down to earning a bare existence, when all this vast region of the Northwest, with its boundless, undeveloped resources before him, is inviting him on? They will be nobodies where they are—they can be somebodies in building up a new society.

Young men predominate in the West, while maidens are scarce; therefore I say to you, get yourself a wife and bring her with you. You will be happier and more contented, and, I have no doubt, make money faster.

To young women I would say just a word. Out here

> "There is no goose so gray,
>   but, soon or late,
> Will find some honest gander
>   for a mate."

Therefore, attach yourself to some family emigrating, and if you are over 21 years, your 160 acres of land, to which you are entitled, and your other attractions, will soon find you a nest and a mate.

The West grows apace—more rapidly than you in the East get an idea of. It is said that, like a pumpkin vine, you can almost see it grow. Emigration travels fast. As fires blown by winds sweep through the dried grass of the prairies, so civilization spreads along the frontier.

Nine years ago the site of Yankton was covered with Indian lodges where now stand 400 houses with 2,000 inhabitants.

Our next neighbor east, the State of Minnesota, the future central state of the future American Continental Republic, twenty years ago had scarcely a population of five thousand, and now has over half a million. Eighteen years ago her whole total valuation in real and personal property was eight hundred thousand dollars, and now it is considerably over one hundred millions of dollars, and yet only about one-hundredth part of her area under cultivation. Think of the future and measure it by the advancement already made.

It is undoubtedly hard for many persons who would like to come West, to pull up their stakes in their own homes, and cut loose from old associations, and strike out alone upon the prairie. The human race is gregarious and prefers society to solitude, therefore I would advise the emigration of families together. Coming as a colony they will bring the moral atmosphere of their old homes with them. Within a week of their arrival they will have established a school and a church, and on a Sunday morning will ascend, yet lingering on the summer air, sweeter than the lays of birds amid the flowers, the songs of the Sunday school established in their new home....

It is the glory of our civilization that it adapts itself to all the circumstances of life.

The future of Dakota is not chimerical. Utah, Kansas and Nebraska have magnificent prairies and an exceedingly fertile soil, but they lack moisture. There are no rivers, ponds, wood-fringed lakes or gurgling brooks. In contrast to this is the domain of the great Northwest. For a few years the tide of emigration may flow, as it does now, into the more central States; but when the lands there along the rivers and streams are taken up, the great river of human life setting toward the Pacific, will be turned up the Missouri, the Red River of the North and the rivers of that country on and near the Northern Pacific Railroad.

Formerly the individual was the pioneer of civilization; now, the railroad is the pioneer, and the individual follows, or is only slightly in advance. Before the flowers bloom another year, Dakota will have her railroads; they will bring more towns, villages, churches, school houses, newspapers, and thousands of new and free people. The wild roses are blooming today, and the sod is yet unturned, and the prairie chicken rears her brood in quiet and safety, where, in a year or two will be heard the screech of the locomotive and the tramp of the approaching legions, another year will bring the beginning of the change; towns and cities will spring into existence, and the steam whistle and the noise of saws and hammers, and the click and clatter of machinery, the sound of industry will be heard. The prairies will be golden with the ripening harvest, and the field and the forest, the mine and the river, will all yield their abundance to the ever growing multitude.

PROPAGANDA FOR IMMIGRANTS: RAILROAD ADVERTISING

Among the propaganda agencies luring new settlers westward during the 1870s and 1880s, none was more effective than the railroad. Most of the lines that spanned the Great Plains had been allotted alternate sections of land along their right of way which they were eager to sell. Even those with no grants were anxious to encourage the occupation of adjacent lands to create way traffic. Hence all maintained promotional staffs and land offices which kept agents in European and eastern cities, distributed literature widely, and offered free trips to the West to prospective purchasers. A circular of the Burlington and Missouri River Railroad used by local agents to advertise its land was typical of many:[5]

Ho for the West! Nebraska ahead! The truth will out! The best farming and stock raising country in the world! The great central region, not too hot or too cold.

The facts about Western Iowa and Southern Nebraska are being slowly but surely discovered by all intelligent men. The large population now pouring into this region, consists of shrewd and well-informed farmers, who know what is good, and are taking advantage of the opportunities offered.

The crops of Southern Nebraska are as fine as can be; a large wheat and barley crop

---

[5] Reproduced in Richard C. Overton, *Burlington West* (Cambridge, 1941), p. 345.

has been harvested; corn is in splendid condition and all other crops are equally fine. The opportunities now offered to buy B. & M. R. R. lands on long credit, low interest, twenty percent rebate for improvements, low freights and fares, free passes to those who buy, &c., &c., can never again be found.

There are plenty of lands elsewhere, but they are in regions which can never be largely prosperous. Southern Nebraska, with its fine soil, pure water, and moderate climate is the right country for a new home. Go and see for yourself. You will be convinced as thousands have been before you. Low round-trip rates to all points and return, and the amount paid is refunded to those who buy.

I am now prepared to sell round trip tickets to Nebraska and return. The General Office of the B. & M. R. R. is at Lincoln, the Capitol of the State. I will sell tickets from Grinnell to Lincoln and return for $12.75, and the fare is refunded to those who buy. Write to me or call for a circular and for full information or for tickets to Lincoln or other points.

E. R. Potter, Grinnell, Iowa

PROPAGANDA FOR IMMIGRANTS: AN AMERICAN LETTER

Deliberate propaganda helped to swell the tide of settlers flowing toward the Great Plains country, but so did glowing reports written by recent arrivals to their home communities. Thousands of these were sent from Kansas, Nebraska, and the Dakotas to friends or relatives in the East and Europe, each dwelling, in extravagent language, on the good life provided by western plenty. These "America letters," as they are called by students of immigration history, were particularly effective in attracting immigrants from the poorer sections of Europe, especially from the Scandinavian countries. The following was written by Gjert Gregoriussen Hovland to friends in Norway:[6]

I must take this opportunity to let you know that we are in the best of health, and that we—both my wife and I—find ourselves exceedingly satisfied. Our son attends the English school, and talks English as well as the native born. Nothing has made me more happy and contented than the fact that we left Norway and journeyed to this country. We have gained more since our arrival here than I did during all the time that I lived in Norway, and I have every prospect of earning a livelihood here for myself and my family— even if my family were larger—so long as God gives me good health.

Such excellent plans have been developed here that, even though one be infirm, no one need suffer want. Competent men are elected whose duty it is to see that no needy persons, either in the cities or in the country, shall have to beg for their living. If a man dies and is survived by a widow and children who are unable to support themselves— as is so often the case—they have the privilege of petitioning these officials. To each one will then be given every year as much as is needed of clothes and food, and no discrimination will be shown between the native-born and those from foreign countries. These things I have learned through daily observation, and I do not believe there can be better laws and arrangements ... in the whole world. I have talked with a sensible person who has traveled in many countries, who has lived here twenty-six years, and has a full knowledge of the matter; both of him and of other reliable persons I have made

---

[6] Theodore C. Blegen (ed.), "A Typical America Letter," *Mississippi Valley Historical Review*, IX (June, 1922), pp. 71-72.

inquiries, for I wish to let everyone know the truth.

When assemblies are held to elect officials who are to serve the country, the vote of the common man carries just as much authority and influence as does that of the rich and powerful man. Neither in the matter of clothes nor in seats are distinctions to be observed, whether one be a farmer or a clerk. The freedom which one enjoys is just as good as that of the other. So long as he comports himself honestly he will be subjected to no interference. Everybody has the liberty to travel about in the country, wherever he wishes, without any passports or papers. Everyone is permitted to engage in whatever business he finds most desirable, in trade or commerce, by land or by water. But if anyone is found guilty of crime, he will be prosecuted and severely punished for it.

No duties are levied upon goods which are produced in the country and brought to the city by water or by land. In case of death, no registration is required; the survivor, after paying the debts, is free to dispose of the property for himself and his family just as he desires. . . . It would heartily please me if I could learn that every one of you who are in need and have little chance of gaining support for yourselves and your families would make up your mind to leave Norway and come to America, for, even if many more were to come, there would still be room here for all. For all those who are willing to work there is no lack of employment and business here. It is possible for all to live in comfort and without suffering want. I do not believe that any of those who suffer under the oppression of others and who must rear their children under straitened circumstances could do better than to help the latter to come to America. But alas, many persons, even though they want to come, lack the necessary means and many others are so stupid as to believe that it is best to live in the country where they have been brought up even if they have nothing but hard bread to satisfy their hunger. It is as if they should say that those who move to a better land, where there is plenty, commit a wrong. But I can find no place where our Creator has forbidden one to seek one's food in an honorable manner. I should like to talk to many persons in Norway for a little while, but we do not wish to live in Norway. We lived there altogether too long. Nor have I talked with any immigrant in this country who wished to return.

THE RUSH FOR FREE LAND, 1871

"America letters," railroad and territorial propaganda, the dream of free land—these were the lures that set in motion the mightiest migration in the history of the American frontier. Between 1870 and 1900 no less than 430,000,000 acres in the West were occupied, and 225,000,000 placed under cultivation—more than in all the years between 1607 and 1870. From the East, from neighboring states, from Europe came the settlers, some penniless, some affluent, all with the compelling dream of a farm of their own. Land—free land—was the magnet. So when they arrived they stormed the land offices seeking homestead or pre-emption rights. E. Jeff Jenkins, a visitor to Kansas in 1871, described a scene that was duplicated again and again in the Great Plains states over the next years:[7]

January 16, 1871, the date fixed for the opening of the United States Land Office for business, was a lively day for the little village of Concordia, with its half-dozen houses

[7] E. Jeff Jenkins, *The Northern Tier: or, Life Among the Homestead Settlers* (Topeka, Kansas, 1880), pp. 133–136.

surrounded with prairie grass. The creaking of the snow beneath the feet of the pedestrians, and the grating sound of the wagon wheels over the frozen ground, were evidence that the mercury was but a trifle above zero. The white covered wagons and smouldering camp-fires occupied every available space adjacent to the Land Office building.

A large number of settlers had collected in front of the building, waiting patiently for the office to open for business. One stalwart fellow had been holding to the doorknob since early dawn with as much tenacity as if life or death depended upon his being the first to enter the office when the door should be opened. Lawyers and land agents, with overcoat pockets crammed with papers, were passing to and fro among that vast throng of weather-beaten settlers and immigrants. That crowd of waiting people embraced persons of several nationalities, and native-born citizens from many of the States of the Union. They were of all ages, from the veteran farmer of threescore and ten, down to the young man who had just reached his majority. They were the frontiersmen whose energy and muscular power were well calculated to settle and improve a new country, and drive the Indians and buffalo westward. They were the men for whose benefit the homestead law was enacted, in return for which the Government was assured that the monotonous stillness of the frontier would be broken by every sound of civilization. They were men who could endure the hardships incident to the settlement of a new country and frontier life—men who could rear the cabin, construct the *"dug-out,"* and overturn the prairie sod that had been the grazing-ground of the buffalo, covered by the snows of winter and watered by the showers of summer for ages. . . .

The door was opened—a shout—a rush—a scramble over each other—a confused shouting of the number of the range and township, as a half-dozen or more simultaneously presented their papers to the officers, who, in the tumult, could as well have told which animal was the first taken into the ark, as to have designated which one of the settlers was prior in time with the presentation of his papers to the proper officer. One thing was manifest, however—the land office for the Republican Land District was open for business.

I never shall forget that scene. The space outside the railing or counter was instantly filled with settlers, until there was scarcely standing room, and yet a very large number of the applicants failed to gain admittance. Throughout the entire day, during office hours, the number of applicants increased, and, at the close of business for the day, a large number had failed to gain admittance. The day's work footed up one hundred and six homesteads entered, and one hundred and eighty preemption declaratory statements filed. The officers and their clerks were obliged to work until a late hour at night to transcribe the business transacted through the day. The following day was a repetition of the previous one, and the rush continued for months.

A plan was finally adopted by which, at the close of the office in the evening, a series of numbers, from one to nearly one hundred, were made upon a piece of paper, attached to the outside of the door, upon which the settlers wrote their names opposite the numbers. By this means only a certain number of applicants were admitted at one time, and the tumult and confusion of a promiscuous admission were avoided.

LIFE ON A KANSAS HOMESTEAD, 1877

The land was there, but using that land posed problems. The handicaps were staggering: no wood for housing or fuel, no water for man or beast, no protection against the searing heat of summer or the numbing cold of winter, no companionship among nearby neighbors, no roads or navigable rivers to allow an escape to settled communities. Some idea of the difficulties encountered by pioneers on the Great Plains can be realized by following the career of Howard Ruede, a young Pennsylvania-German who came to Kansas in 1877 to homestead a claim and in a series of letters home described each step as he brought his farm under cultivation, from the time he hired out to earn money for a stove that would heat his sod house until he produced his first crop:[8]

THURSDAY, APRIL 5, 1877
AT SNYDER'S, KILL CREEK, KANSAS

This was another hot day, and we had heavy work too, laying up sod. Snyder broke a lot for us this A.M. and we began laying up the wall. It is 20 inches thick. These "Kansas brick" are from 2 to 4 inches thick, 12 wide and 20 long, and the joints between them we fill with ground. Just before sunset we got the ridgepole into position on the crotches, so that the room will be about 7 feet high. We expect to get the roof in and have the place in condition to live in by the end of the week. The sod is heavy and when you take 3 or 4 bricks on a litter or hand barrow, and carry it 50 to 150 feet, I tell you it is no easy work. We quit just before sunset. Had supper about 7:30. I could hardly walk today—the result of that bareback ride. It was awfully hot right after dinner, and Levin fetched water from Snyder's in a jug. That water tasted good.

FRIDAY, APRIL 6, 1877

Plenty of air stirring today, so it was not so hot. We finished off the gable ends of the dugout and got the boards on the rafters, ready for the straw. A lot more sod to carry tomorrow for the roof. Had jack rabbit for supper. They dress 7 lb. sometimes and I tell you they are big ones, almost twice as big as ordinary rabbits. You ought to hear the prairie roosters. This is the pairing season, and they strut around and keep up a constant humming, and you can hear them ¼ mile, and farther if the wind is right. There are lots of them on my claim.

SATURDAY, APRIL 7, 1877

Used part of the straw on the roof, and covered the whole roof with a layer of sod, and then threw dirt on it, and the "House" was finished. We had not enough rafters, so L. & J. went to Rook and cut the balance of the top of that tree I let lie when I went to work at Heiser's the other day, and bought another tree and split it into rafters. Then they got Rook to haul the two loads of wood and a lot of straw to my claim, and for the entire job he charged $1. Cheap, wasn't it? The trades are pretty well represented here: Snyder and Heiser are coopers; Rook was a pawnbroker in England; Smith, a clerk in a store; Stevens, a gas meter maker; and then we three. I have a boil on my left lower jaw, and it troubles me not a little. And my heel isn't well yet, and won't be till I am fixed better to take care of it, which will not be for some days yet—till we get a well dug at the residence....

We are anxious to get into our place, for we can board ourselves for about one half what it costs us to board somewhere else. And when we work out, we get board and lodging, both being included in the day's wages. I am going to get a stove for work if I can, and I think it is possible. Tomorrow Jim and L. are going to Osborne and Schweitzer's for the well auger.... They will bring hinges for the door, and then we can hang the door and make the bunks in

---

[8] Howard Ruede, *Sod-House Days. Letters from a Kansas Homesteader, 1877–78,* edited by John Ise. (New York: Columbia University Press, 1937), pp. 39–43, 48, 51, 103–105, 131–132, 172, 194, 203–204, 212, 214–215, 229, 233, 239.

a day. I'd like to see you all, but I like this place better than Bethm and after I get you all here I'll be O.K. You would like it as much as I do if you were here. I am going to have a stone house in two years—not live in a dugout all the time, like a good many folks here. But I'll have to go in debt for breaking, I think. I'll make a bargain like this: get a man to break for me, and I will pay him in work during harvest and corn husking. I would like to have a paper once in a while. Direct to Kill Creek P. O.

MONDAY, APRIL 9, 1877

First thing this morning was to look for a second hand stove. For this I went to a man named Greenfield, who lives about 2½ miles east of here. He was not at home, not having arrived from Hays, to which place he had gone with a load. His wife, however, was home, but she didn't know whether the stove was for sale, and told me to come tomorrow. On the way back stopped at Guyer's, where I had seen two stoves, but only one belonged to them. Then I went to Rook's. He will break sod for me for $2.50 per acre, and take his pay in work. But I made no bargain....

I made out an estimate of the cost of our house. This does not include what was paid for in work: Ridgepole and hauling (including two loads of firewood) $1.50; rafters and straw, 50¢; 2 lb. nails, 15¢; hinges 20¢; window 75¢; total cash paid, $4.05. Then there was $4 worth of lumber, which was paid for in work, and $1.50 for hauling it over, which, together with hauling the firewood, 50¢, makes $10.05 for a place to live in and firewood enough to last all summer. After dinner we struck for Greenfield's again, and did not find anybody at home. Thinking that perhaps I might be able to get meat or potatoes from Heiser for the work I had done, I went over to see him. Two young men named Bleam were digging a well, and had got into the shale. H. could not accommodate me with the articles desired. He appeared to think I was in a hurry for the money, and told me I could have it by Saturday....

MONDAY, APRIL 16, 1877
AT THE DUGOUT, KILL CREEK, KANSAS

Settled off with Snyder. His bill was $18.12; 12½¢ per meal, and nothing for lodging or breaking sod for the ranch. That leaves me $2.20 in hand and $1.50 coming from Heiser. I moved the goods we had at Snyder's over to the ranch this morning. Had to build a chimney and fireplace before I could make dinner, and when I had it made it consisted of one dish of mush. The ranch got full of smoke, too, but I did not care much because the door and window being opposite, the place was cleared in a short time. About 4 o'clock the sky was overcast, and from then till about 7 we had a heavy thunder storm. The sky turned to a pale, bright yellow-green, and a good deal of hail fell. Some of the stones were as big as hazelnuts. I lay on the bed and heard it beat against the door until I feel asleep....

THURSDAY, APRIL 19, 1877

Maybe you think I am lonesome living all by myself, on the prairie; but I am not. Today the wind is north, but not very cold. Such a day as this I wish for a paper from home, if not a letter. Well, the mail comes in tomorrow evening, and then I may get a letter. It takes a whole week for a letter to come out here. If Stuber could photo the inside of my ranch, I don't believe that there would be as many young men without money wishing to come out here and batch it. I would not want anybody to come to call on me yet. Last night I dreamed I was at home with you, but woke up to find that my overcoat had slipped off of me. It was pretty cold, too. Families coming out here should bring no luggage but clothes and bedding and a clock, but bring all the cash they can, for then they can buy a team and go right ahead. Without a team you must depend on others and pay according. . . .

MONDAY, JUNE 18, 1877

Up bright and early, and soon after breakfast hitched up, and, after getting some things together, we started for Kill Creek. It looked as though someone was moving, for on the wagon we had a long pole, the breaking plow, axe, hatchet, monkey wrench, the halters and picket ropes, an old wash boiler full of provisions, a lot of Henry's clothes, and some bedding. We stopped in town to have the plow-lay sharpened. And then the file mysteriously disappeared. It was in its place on one of the plow handles when the plow was lifted from the wagon; but when we took hold of the plow to put it back, the file was missing. We finally got started, and arrived at my place about noon. Stopped at Bleam's on the way and bought a ham, for which I paid 10 cents per lb. It was just sweltering hot, and we hurriedly put up a tent by stretching the wagon sheet over the long pole. Had dinner and then paced off a plot of six acres. Henry went to breaking, and I talked with Pa, who had come up from Hoot's. By the time the team had made two rounds, they were covered with foam and sweat. The heat was awful, and there was very little air stirring. . . .

SUNDAY, JULY 17, 1877

Tomorrow we expect to go up to my claim and break, and when sowing time comes, I intend to have five acres put in wheat and five in rye by next spring. I hope I'll be able to stay at home most of the time. I propose to break 25 or 30 acres on the three claims to plant corn. I am much stronger than I used to be, and feel much better than when I worked in the house. I had a good sweat yesterday while I was cultivating corn. This afternoon I was at Schweitzer's and they fetched out a freezer of ice cream, and I had a big saucer full—not one of your little saloon saucers, but a regular table saucer, and there was enough in it to cool the hottest man in Kansas. This has been a "roaster," I wonder if you had such a hot day. . . .

TUESDAY, AUGUST 14, 1877
AT GSELL'S, KILL CREEK, KANSAS

Up a little before sunrise, and fixed the potatoes and corn for breakfast. We live principally on roasting ears, potatoes and bread, with now and then a mess of fried eggs. . . . We had potatoes, corn, bread and butter and coffee. About 9 o'clock the dew was pretty well dried off, and so I went over to Greenfield's to get a horse and the hay rake. I sat at the well about an hour before he came from camp meeting, and just as he drove up Pa arrived. I suppose he thought I had got lost, so he came to look for me. I wanted to throw up my part of the wood chopping and pay for the breaking he did for me, but he refused to let me off, so I'll have to chop nine cords of wood, and build my dugout, besides helping Hoot a little if he wants me —all before the 1st of September. Went to raking up the hay, and by night had it all raked and "bunched"—that is, raked into piles. Took the rake home and asked what his bill was. We had the outfit about ¾ day. He wanted to put me off by saying, "Oh, we'll fix that some time," but I told him that's not business, and he finally settled for 50 cents. . . .

MONDAY, NOVEMBER 19, 1877
AT THE DUGOUT, KILL CREEK, KANSAS

I have 2 acres of wheat out. It is coming up nicely. Also 3 acres of rye, which was put in only last week, and is not yet to be seen above the ground. Some folks say "Don't put in any rye; it don't pay to raise it." It is a surer crop than wheat, and I want something to eat if the wheat don't grow well. Rye has been known to yield 50 bushels to the acre, but if I get 20 I will be satisfied. . . .

MONDAY, DECEMBER 17, 1877

Cloudy and drizzling near all the morning. Went to work at the well soon after breakfast, but were chased into the house by a little shower. As soon as that was over, we went to work again. Dug through 5½ feet of gravel, very closely packed, which broke the points off the pick. Then got into sand, which was easier work. I was in the well, and the others at the windlass.

TUESDAY, DECEMBER 18, 1877

At the well again. Sunk it to 25 feet and struck shale. Then we quit. We'll have to go to another place to dig now. We were not very badly disappointed, because we thought we'd find plenty shale. The chance was for water, but fortune did not smile upon us. There's 3¼ days' work for nothing. . . .

SUNDAY, JANUARY 13, 1878

Went to the hole in the draw that Pa dug on Friday. It is about three feet deep. They bored down and struck water. I ran a sunflower stalk down, and the auger hole was only 4 feet deep; there were about 6 inches of water in it. The misery of the thing is that it is not on my claim.

MONDAY, JANUARY 14, 1878

Directly after Breakfast Geo. and I went to boring where Hoot had said there was water. Down twelve feet and struck shale. Would have continued boring, to see how thick the shale is, but just then Geo. Lough came for the auger, and I could not tell him he couldn't have it. Went to Hoot's and borrowed a shovel; Bub and I went to the hole in the draw (not on my claim) where Pa bored and struck water. They had dug about three feet, and I dug about four more, and then had all the water we will need for the present, though I am not yet done digging wells. I intend to dig on my place till I get water. I was a pretty specimen when I arrived on the surface. What with standing in mud and water, and the dripping from the mud bucket, and striking against the side of the well, I was coated, literally smeared, from the top of my cap to the soles of my boots, which apparently weighed a ton each. . . .

SUNDAY, FEBRUARY 24, 1878

I reckon I'll have to give a history of last week, as it was a very interesting one for me. On Monday we turned out about 5:30, and by 6 I was on the road to Osborne. The suddenness of my departure was caused by a conversation I had with Hoot in reference to having the use of his team for a couple of days to haul hay for a shed in which to put my team when I brought it from Schweitzer's. He said if I'd get the oxen I might put them behind his straw stack till I had a shelter for them, and might water them at his well until I had a well dug. So I concluded that as I could have the use of his team for only one day, I had better take up his offer and do my own hauling. I had just crossed my east line when I met August Fritsche on his way to mill. Requested him to bring my grist. He said he did not know me. Told him who I was, and he said he would bring it as far as Sam Hoot's. I could not make him understand where my dugout was. Walked to Harry Humphrey's five miles from town, and rode with him the rest of the way. Arrived in Osborne about 9:30 and went to see Watson & Gillette, who had a wagon for sale. The price was $40. That was $10 more than I had.

Then to Herzog's to see what Charley wants for his wagon. He was not home, but I got my dinner by waiting for him. He wanted $50 so that was no go. Back to W. & G.'s to see if they would not come down. But they would not. Next tried Ed Humphrey. He would sell for $30. As that was the highest figure I could go, I went to see the vehicle. Found the tongue was broken, as well as the hind bolster, and the box was not much account. I closed the bargain because I could hear of no other wagon for sale. Then went to Sears. John wanted something to read, so I took him the Phantom Ship. When I came near the house I saw Mrs. S. looking out the window and saw she did not recognize me, as I was shaved clean. Knocked at the door, and walked in and bid her "Good evening." Then she knew who I was, and we had a good laugh at her for not recognizing me at once. Had supper and then went to Schweitzer's. Talked awhile and then paid him for the oxen—$60. Turned in about 10. Next morning after breakfast Wally went out and yoked the oxen for me, and I started for town. When I got there Ed Humphrey had the wagon at the blacksmith shop, getting it repaired, and wanted to back out of the bargain. I had heard of another wagon for sale for $15 so I borrowed one of Ed's horses and rode about 4 miles from town to see the owner and the wagon but could find neither. I wanted to get a wagon offered to me for $15 or $20, so I could back Ed down on his price, but he saved me the trouble. I did not let him off very easy. Priced all the wagons I could hear or think of, but could not get a satisfactory price. At last I came across C. G. Paris and asked him whether he knew of a wagon for sale. He replied that he had one. How much? $35. Make it $30 and I'll take it. He argued about ten minutes with me, saying he'd take $30 and never ask me for the other V. Told him I did not do business on that line; that I had $30 to pay for a wagon, and I wanted a receipt in full, that I would not go in debt for even $5. Could apparently make no impression on him, so I went up town and bought a chain, and started for home without a wagon. I had not got out of town before he called me back, saying he'd take $30. So I tied the oxen, paid him and got a receipt. Then I again started for home. Got to the river, and after a little trouble succeeded in riding across on ox-back. After poking along for 2½ hours, I arrived at Paris' house. The wagon was not there, and I lost an hour getting it. Did not get home till 9:45, and found Pa and Geo. in bed. Tied the cattle to the wagon and threw them a bunch of hay, and then went in to have some supper (I had eaten nothing since breakfast) and read your letter and one from Ad. Turned in at 11. . . . Bud was down town yesterday and bought a curry comb, so now we can get the dirt out of the oxen's hides. I have something less than a dollar, and Pa has a whole dollar in cash, but we are happy anyhow. I'll have to trust to Providence to put work in my way to raise about $20 to buy a breaking plow, hoe, fork and rake, and timber for the new sod addition we intend to put to the ranch. . . .

Sunday, May 26, 1878

I have not written for a long time, and I reckon a letter will be appreciated, so I'll give you a short one. Yesterday a week, as Pa or Bub probably wrote, we began breaking. Such a time as we had, learning to get the grasshopper to go into the sod and remain there I hope never to have again. By this time the thing works all right, but the cattle skip the furrow so often that Bub has to walk alongside. But we get the sod turned. Tuesday I was out by 5, and we got the plow running by 6. Had ½ acre broken by 10:30, when we unyoked, and after having something to eat, I walked to town....

TUESDAY, JUNE 18, 1878
OSBORNE, KANSAS

Turned out about 5, and as soon as the wheat was dry enough went to cradling. Pa tied it awhile and between us we got ½ acre cut by noon. Then I started for town. It was awful hot, too. Took it easy and got to town about 6....

The threshing was done Aug. 14th, Henry Hoot taking charge of the business. The wheat yielded 28½ bu. and the rye 33 bu., which was put into straw until the old house was vacated. During September I worked in the office, getting home very late. Pa and Geo. finished the new house and cut the corn fodder. On the 28th September we moved into the new house, after having occupied the dugout for 13 months.

BONANZA FARMING IN MINNESOTA

Howard Ruede's simple account of his life revealed that a homestead on the Great Plains was no bed of roses, but for the hardy and the enterprising the rewards were great. So the pioneers came, to spread their farms westward across Kansas and Nebraska until they passed the 100th meridian, then to turn northward over the Dakotas, Wyoming, and Montana. Along this northern frontier the unique "bonanza farms" emerged. These were giant estates, numbering thousands of acres, where the principles of large-scale production were applied to agriculture during the 1870s and 1880s. C. C. Coffin, a correspondent for an eastern magazine, dredged up his most flamboyant prose to describe the bonanza farm operated by Oliver Dalrymple, who had pioneered in this type of production:[9]

Ride over these fertile acres of Dakota, and behold the working of this latest triumph of American genius. You are in a sea of wheat. On the farms managed by Oliver Dalrymple are 13,000 acres in one field. There are other farmers who cultivate from 160 to 6000 acres, The railroad train rolls through an ocean of grain. Pleasant the music of the rippling waves as the west wind sweeps over the expanse. We encounter a squadron of war chariots, not such as once swept over the Delta of the Nile in pursuit of an army of fugitive Israelites, not such as the warriors of Rome were wont to drive, with glittering knives projecting from the axles to mow a swath through the ranks of an enemy, to drench the ground with blood, to cut down the human race, as if men were noxious weeds, but chariots of peace, doing the work of human hands for the sustenance of men. There are twenty-five of them in this one brigade of the grand army of 115, under the marshalship of this Dakota farmer. A superintendent upon a superb horse, like a brigadier directing his forces, rides along the line, accompanied by his staff of two on horseback. They are fully armed and equipped, not with swords, but the implements of peace—wrenches, hammers, chisels. They are surgeons in waiting, with nuts and screws, or whatever may be needed.

This brigade of horse artillery sweeps by in echelon—in close order, reaper following reaper. There is a sound of wheels. The grain disappears an instant, then reappears; iron arms clasp it, hold it a moment in their em-

---

[9] C. C. Coffin, "Dakota Wheat Fields," *Harper's New Monthly Magazine*, LX (March, 1880), pp. 533–535.

brace, wind it with wire, then toss it disdainfully at your feet. You hear in the rattling of the wheels the mechanism saying to itself, "See how easy I can do it!"

An army of "shockers" follow the reapers, setting up the bundles to ripen before threshing. The reaping must ordinarily all be done in fifteen days, else the grain becomes too ripe. The first fields harvested, therefore, are cut before the ripening is complete. Each reaper averages about fifteen acres per day, and is drawn by three horses or mules.

The reaping ended, threshing begins. Again memory goes back to early years, to the pounding out of the grain upon the threshing-floor with the flail—the slow, tedious work of the winter days. Poets no more will rehearse the music of the flail. The picture for February in the old *Farmer's Almanac* is obsolete. September is the month for threshing, the thresher doing its 600 or 700 bushels per day, driven by a steam-engine of sixteen horse-power. Remorseless that sharp-toothed devourer, swallowing its food as fast as two men can cut the wire bands, requiring six teams to supply its demands! And what a cataract of grain pours from its spout, faster than two men can bag it!

The latest triumph of invention in this direction is a straw-burning engine, utilizing the stalks of the grain for fuel.

The cost of raising wheat per bushel is from thirty-five to forty cents; the average yield, from twenty to twenty-five bushels per acre. The nearness of these lands to Lake Superior, and the rates established by the railroad—fifteen cents per bushel from any point between Bismarck and Duluth—give the Dakota farmers a wide margin of profit.

Since the first furrow was turned in the Red River Valley, in 1870, there has been no failure of crops from drought, excessive rains, blight, mildew, rust, or other influence of climatology. The chinch-bug has not made its appearance; the grasshoppers alone have troubled the farmers, but they have disappeared, and the fields are smiling with bounty. With good tilth, the farmer may count upon a net return of from eight to ten dollars per acre per annum. The employment of capital has accomplished a beneficent end, by demonstrating that the region, instead of being incapable of settlement, is one of the fairest sections of the continent. Nor is it a wonder that the land-offices are besieged by emigrants making entries, or that the surveyors find the lands "squatted" upon before they can survey them; that hotels are crowded; that on every hand there is activity. During the months of May, June, and July, 1879, the sales of government land were nearly 700,000 acres, and the entries for the year will probably aggregate 1,500,000, taken in homestead, pre-emption, and tree claims. There are other millions of acres, as fair and fertile, yet to be occupied.

THE OKLAHOMA LAND RUSH

By the 1880s the speed with which the West was being settled brought a sense of impending doom to some homesteaders. Unless the pace slowed, all arable lands in the nation would soon be appropriated—and the pace was accelerating rather than decreasing. Free lands were running out. As panic mounted, interest focused on the last unsettled West, the Indian Territory of modern Oklahoma. Why should "savages" monopolize a golden land that could be made to blossom? This was a question that was increasingly asked during the decade, as pressure on Congress mounted to open the region to settlement under the Homestead Act. That body's first response came in 1889, when the Oklahoma District, a fertile area in the center of the territory not actually owned by any tribe, was declared a part of the public domain. This the President decreed would be opened to settlers at noon on April 22, 1889. The "boomer rush" that followed is famous in history. By the time the appointed day arrived, thousands of would-be settlers lined the borders of the district, held back by troops until the hour of noon. Then bugles sounded, and the maddest foot race in history began. A newspaper correspondent who participated left a vivid description:[10]

> The preparations for the settlement of Oklahoma had been complete, even to the slightest detail, for weeks before the opening day. The Santa Fe Railway, which runs through Oklahoma north and south, was prepared to take any number of people from its handsome station at Arkansas City, Kansas, and to deposit them in almost any part of Oklahoma as soon as the law allowed; thousands of covered wagons were gathered in camps on all sides of the new Territory waiting for the embargo to be lifted. In its picturesque aspects the rush across the border at noon on the opening day must go down in history as one of the most noteworthy events of Western civilization. At the time fixed, thousands of hungry home-seekers, who had gathered from all parts of the country, and particularly from Kansas and Missouri, were arranged in line along the border, ready to lash their horses into furious speed in the race for fertile spots in the beautiful land before them. The day was one of perfect peace. Overhead the sun shone down from a sky as fair and blue as the cloudless heights of Colorado. The whole expanse of space from zenith to horizon was spotless in its blue purity. The clear spring air, through which the rolling green billows of the promised land could be seen with unusual distinctness for many miles, was as sweet and fresh as the balmy atmosphere of June among New Hampshire's hills.
>
> As the expectant home-seekers waited with restless patience, the clear, sweet notes of a cavalry bugle rose and hung a moment upon the startled air. It was noon. The last barrier of savagery in the United States was broken down. Moved by the same impulse, each driver lashed his horses furiously; each rider dug his spurs into his willing steed, and each man on foot caught his breath hard and darted forward. A cloud of dust rose where the home-seekers had stood in line, and when it had drifted away before the gentle breeze, the horses and wagons and men were tearing across the open country like fiends. The horsemen had the best of it from the start. It was a fine race for a few minutes, but soon the riders began to spread out like a fan, and by the time they had reached the horizon they were scattered about as far as eye could see. Even the fleetest of the horsemen found upon reaching their chosen localities that men in wagons and men on foot were there before them. As it was clearly impossible for a man on foot to outrun a horseman, the inference is plain that Oklahoma had been entered hours before the appointed time. Notwithstanding the assertions of the soldiers that every boomer had been driven out of Oklahoma, the fact remains that the woods along the various streams within Oklahoma were literally full of people Sunday night. Nine-tenths of these people made settlement upon the land illegally. The other tenth would have done so had there been any desirable land left to settle upon. This action on the part of the first claim-holders will cause a great deal of land litigation in the future, as it is not to be expected that the man who ran his horse at its utmost

---

[10] "The Rush to Oklahoma," *Harper's Weekly*, XXXIII (May 18, 1889), p. 391.

speed for ten miles only to find a settler with an ox team in quiet possession of his chosen farm will tamely submit to this plain infringement of the law.

Some of the men who started from the line on foot were quite as successful in securing desirable claims as many who rode fleet horses. They had the advantage of knowing just where their land was located. One man left the line with the others, carrying on his back a tent, a blanket, some camp dishes, an axe, and provisions for two days. He ran down the railway track for six miles, and reached his claim in just sixty minutes. Upon arriving on his land he fell down under a tree, unable to speak or see. I am glad to be able to say that his claim is one of the best in Oklahoma. The rush from the line was so impetuous that by the time the first railway train arrived from the north at twenty-five minutes past twelve o'clock, only a few of the hundreds of boomers were anywhere to be seen. The journey of this first train was well-nigh as interesting as the rush of the men in wagons. The train left Arkansas City at 8.45 o'clock in the forenoon. It consisted of an empty baggage car, which was set apart for the use of the newspaper correspondents, eight passenger coaches, and the caboose of a freight train. The coaches were so densely packed with men that not another human being could get on board. So uncomfortably crowded were they that some of the younger boomers climbed to the roofs of the cars and clung perilously to the ventilators. An adventurous person secured at great risk a seat on the forward truck of the baggage car.

In this way the train was loaded to its utmost capacity. That no one was killed or injured was due as much to the careful management of the train as to the ability of the passengers to take care of themselves. Like their friends in the wagons, the boomers on the cars were exultant with joy at the thought of at last entering into possession of the promised land. At first appearances the land through which the train ran seemed to justify all the virtues that had been claimed for it. The rolling, grassy uplands, and the wooded river-bottoms, the trees in which were just bursting into the most beautiful foliage of early spring, seemed to give a close reality to the distant charm of green and purple forest growths, which rose from the trough of some long swell and went heaving away to meet the brighter hues in the far-off sky. Throughout all the landscape were clumps of trees suggesting apple orchards set in fertile meadows, and here and there were dim patches of gray and white sand that might in a less barbarous region be mistaken for farm-houses surrounded by hedges and green fields. Truly the Indians have well-named Oklahoma the "beautiful land." The landless and home-hungry people on the train might be pardoned their mental exhilaration, when the effect of this wonderfully beautiful country upon the most prosaic mind is fully considered. It was an eager and an exuberantly joyful crowd that rode slowly into Guthrie at twenty minutes past one o'clock on that perfect April afternoon. Men who had expected to lay out the town site were grievously disappointed at the first glimpse of their proposed scene of operations. The slope east of the railway at Guthrie station was dotted white with tents and sprinkled thick with men running about in all directions.

"We're done for," said a town-site speculator, in dismay. "Some one has gone in ahead of us and laid out the town."

"Never mind that," shouted another town-site speculator, "but make a rush and get what you can."

Hardly had the train slackened its speed when the impatient boomers began to leap from the cars and run up the slope. Men jumped from the roofs of the moving cars at the risk of their lives. Some were so stunned by the fall that they could not get up for some minutes. The coaches were so crowded that many men were compelled to squeeze through the windows in order to get a fair start at the head of the crowd. Almost before the train had come to a standstill the cars were emptied. In their haste and eagerness, men fell over each other in heaps, others stumbled and fell headlong, while many ran forward so blindly and impetuously that it was not until they had passed the best of the town lots that they came to a realization of their actions.

I ran with the first of the crowd to get a good point of view from which to see the rush. When I had time to look about me I found that I was standing beside a tent, near which a man was leisurely chopping holes in the sod with a new axe.

"Where did you come from, that you have already pitched your tent?" I asked.

"Oh, I was here," said he.

"How was that?"

"Why, I was a deputy United States marshal."

"Did you resign?"

"No; I'm a deputy still."

"But it is not legal for a deputy United States marshal, or any one in the employ of the government, to take up a town lot in this manner."

"That may all be, stranger; but I've got two lots here, just the same; and about fifty other deputies have got lots in the same way. In fact, the deputy-marshals laid out the town."

At intervals of fifteen minutes, other trains came from the north loaded down with home-seekers and town-site speculators. As each succeeding crowd rushed up the slope and found that government officers had taken possession of the best part of the town, indignation became hot and outspoken; yet the marshals held to their lots and refused to move. Bloodshed was prevented only by the belief of the home-seekers that the government would set the matter right.

This course of the deputy United States marshals was one of the most outrageous pieces of imposition upon honest home-seekers ever practised in the settlement of a new country. That fifty men could, through influence, get themselves appointed as deputy United States marshals for the sole purpose of taking advantage of their positions in this way is creditable neither to them nor to the man who made their appointment possible. This illegal seizure thus became the first matter of public discussion in the city of Guthrie.

When the passengers from the first train reached the spot where the deputy-marshals had ceased laying out lots, they seized the line of the embryo street and ran it eastward as far as their numbers would permit. The second train load of people took it where the first let off, and ran it entirely out of sight behind a swell of ground at least two miles from the station. The following car loads of home-seekers went north and south, so that by the time that all were in for the day a city large enough in area to hold 100,000 inhabitants had been staked off, with more or less geometrical accuracy. A few women and children were in the rush, but they had to take their chances with the rest. Disputes over the ownership of lots grew incessant, for the reason that when a man went to the river for a drink of water, or tried to get his baggage at the railway station, another man would take possession of his lot, notwithstanding the obvious presence of the first man's stakes and sometimes part of his wearing apparel. Owing to the uncertainty concerning the lines of the streets, two and sometimes more lots were staked out on the same ground, each claimant hoping that the official survey would give him the preference. Contrary to all expectations, there was no bloodshed over the disputed lots. This may be accounted for by the fact that no intoxicating liquors of any kind were allowed to be sold in Oklahoma. It is a matter of common comment among the people that the peaceful way in which Oklahoma was settled was due entirely to its compulsory prohibition. Had whiskey been plentiful in Guthrie the disputed lots might have been watered in blood, for every man went armed with some sort of deadly weapon. If there could be a more striking temperance lesson than this, I certainly should like to see it.

When Congress gives Oklahoma some sort of government the prohibition of the sale of intoxicating liquor should be the first and foremost of her laws.

It is estimated that between six and seven thousand persons reached Guthrie by train from the north the first afternoon, and that fully three thousand came in by wagon from the north and east, and by train from Purcell on the south, thus making a total population for the first day of about ten thousand. By taking thought in the matter, three-fourths of these people had provided themselves with tents and blankets, so that even on the first night they had ample shelter from the weather. The rest of them slept the first night as best they could, with only the red earth for a pillow and the starry arch of heaven for a blanket. At dawn of Tuesday the unrefreshed home-seekers and town-site speculators arose, and began anew the location of disputed claims. The tents multiplied like mushrooms in a rain that day, and by night the building of frame houses had been begun in earnest in the new streets. The buildings were by no means elaborate, yet they were as good as the average frontier structure, and they served their purpose, which was all that was required.

On that day the trains going north were filled with returning boomers, disgusted beyond expression with the dismal outlook of the new country. Their places were taken by others who came in to see the fun, and perhaps pick up a bargin in the way of town lots or commercial speculation.

The boomer rush of 1889, and others that followed as the Dawes Severalty Act was applied to the Indian Territory reservations, symbolized the end of an era in American history. Free lands were running out, just as the boomers had feared. By 1890 the director of the census could announce that the "unsettled area has been so broken into by isolated bodies of settlement that there can hardly be said to be a frontier line." Good lands remained in the West, of course; actually far more was homesteaded after 1890 than before. But psychologically the nation was asked to adjust to a new era, in which expansion was no longer possible. This realization conjured into being a number of problems that were to plague the United States during the twentieth century.

CHAPTER 28

The Twentieth-Century West: Problem and Promise

The "closing" of the frontier by the official proclamation of the Bureau of the Census had little effect on the pace of America's expansion westward. At the dawn of the twentieth century vast domains beyond the Mississippi still awaited occupation, some too arid to attract the early pioneers, some too rugged, some too isolated. As technological progress opened these areas to settlement, the national population trend continued westward; with each passing year more and more Americans forsook homes in the East to crowd into the open spaces or burgeoning cities of the Rocky Mountain country or the Pacific slope. Measured by the center of population of the nation, as plotted on a map each decade by the Bureau of the Census, the "westward tilt" of the continent was draining people toward the Pacific at a steadily accelerating pace. By the middle of the twentieth century the Far West had outstripped the claims of its most outrageous boosters. The frontier had indeed fulfilled its promise.

Yet many western problems remained to be solved. Large areas of land were still vacant or sparsely settled. In a strange and interesting way, the United States presented a paradox: it was one of the most highly developed nations of the world, and yet one of the great underdeveloped areas, even as late as 1950. While irrigation, improved roads, urban centers, and investments in recreation promised to open large areas for settlement, westerners continued to argue about Indians, land, immigrants, and migrant labor. And although middle-class Americans were already displaying tendencies toward conformity, the focus of westerners on their particular problems prevented the formation of a simple consensus.

At the heart of the problem was the question of values, which was a residue of the frontier, part of a fund of human experience that shaped American ideas about opportunity, individualism, human dignity, and even nature itself. The frontiersman was always eager for change —quick to take advantage of the products of technology and science—but jealous and selfish about his profits and about his responsibility to future generations. He frequently denied any obligation to the neighbor downstream from his farm, mine, mill, or ranch, working without regard for maintaining the balance of nature. In the same way he denied any obligation to the generations to come after him. Even the words westerners used to describe their problems and solutions were freighted with significant semantic differences, which reflected conflicting value systems.

THE INDIAN PROBLEM: A MILITARY VIEWPOINT

Perhaps the clearest illustration of this semantic problem appeared in the use of the expression humanitarianism when it was applied to the Indian. At the opening of the century, humanitarianism was either sentimental or paternalistic, but it always reflected white values, not those of the Indian. As a result, even the men who lived closest to the Indian and who should have known him best, frequently knew him scarcely at all. The old-line Indian agents, scouts, or army officers were representative of this group. Their opinion of the Indian—and their's was the view that tended to shape national Indian policy—remained virtually static. As late as 1897, Captain J. Lee Humfreville, a dedicated officer who spent twenty years in the West, presented what could be called a hard-line analysis of the Indian:[1]

The Indian has been frequently, I may say generally, represented as having been endowed with great powers of observation and extraordinary gifts of natural cunning. This is only partly true. The Indian's mental faculties were sharpened by the necessities of his existence; but, like all other savage people, his intellectual gifts were limited. From his mode of life his physical senses were highly developed. His vision was usually perfect, and his sense of hearing was phenomenally acute. . . . He depended upon his natural animal instinct more than on human judgment. Yet, granting his superiority in these and other ways, he could not compete with civilized man. There was in the Indian nature a trait of intractability not found in any other portion of the human race. So far he had shown himself incapable of even a veneer of civilization. He might be brought up in the midst of civilized surroundings and educated, but at the first opportunity he invariably relapsed into his original barbarism.

Coupled with his barbarous instincts, or rather with a part of them, was his natural inclination to cruelty. It has been said that all savage races are like children, in that they have no adequate conception of suffering or pain endured by others. They were entirely devoid of sympathy. The controlling instinct of the Indian was to kill.

The Indian could hardly be said to have possessed any moral nature. In the first place, he had no abstract ideas. He could understand nothing unless it appeared to him in the concrete. There were no words in his language to express moral ideas. Virtue, vice, generosity, hospitality, magnanimity, and all cognate words were to him unknown. He only believed what he saw or felt.

He was naturally distrustful. This was one of the impediments encountered in the work of Indian civilization. He had been for ages the slave of heredity and environment, and he suspected an enemy everywhere. Of all the savage races the Indian was the only one who never tried to imitate the white man.

Any one knowing his character would not trust him in any way. He would not do right from moral impulse, for the reason, as already observed, that his moral perceptions were limited or undeveloped. To his mind everything was right that redounded to his own interest if he could successfully perform it; and anything was wrong (or bad, as he called it) if he failed. His moral standard

---

[1] J. Lee Humfreville, *Twenty Years Among Our Hostile Indians* (New York, 1899), pp. 56–57.

was measured by the difference between success and failure.

He was the very impersonation of duplicity. He might enter the cabin of a frontiersman, or a military fort, or an Indian agency, and listen to all that was said, without giving the slightest evidence that he understood what he heard, or that he was taking notice of his surroundings. In his attitude and facial expression, he might appear as taciturn as a Sphynx, and yet understand every word that was uttered and be planning a murderous raid at the same moment.

Occasionally, it is true, the Indian evinced some commendable traits of character. But these were the exception to the rule. Doubtless there are also instances of truthfulness and fidelity on his part. But granting this, it is still an indisputable fact that the Indian, of all uncivilized people, has offered the greatest degree of opposition to the influences of civilization....

It is difficult to place the Indian intellectually. Other savage races when brought within the environment of civilization have afforded brilliant instances of individual effort, but the Indian never. There is no instance in the four hundred years of American history of an Indian who attained greatness through the channels of civilization. The few Indians who stand out prominently in our history from King Philip down to Sitting Bull, achieved greatness not by adopting the ways of the white man, but by opposing them.

In 1904, the Commissioner of Indian Affairs, W. A. Jones, expressed essentially the same idea in a different context when he observed: "It is probably true that the majority of our wild Indians have no inherited tendencies whatever toward morality or chastity, according to an enlightened standard." The implications of this kind of thinking were present as late as 1916, when the Supreme Court ruled in "United States" v. "Nice" that "Citizenship is not incompatible with tribal existence or continued guardianship, and so may be conferred without completely emancipating the Indians or placing them beyond the reach of congressional legislation adopted for their protection." Held in low esteem, with a shrinking land base on which to live and a despised culture, the Indian was entitled to humanitarian treatment but was denied dignity as a human being or an ethnic group.

A REVISED INDIAN POLICY

Fortunately for the tribes—and the national conscience—not all Americans accepted this stereotype of the Indian or the definition of humanitarianism that stemmed from it. Although sentimentalists had used the word in a different way and had been the Indian's earliest allies, a combination of education, science, and common sense gave humanitarianism a more sophisticated connotation. This found expression in a revised Indian policy, based not on the application of white values to the Indian, but on permitting him to live within his own value system. Commissioner of Indian Affairs John Collier, an Indiophile, described the revolution in Indian life which occurred between 1920 and 1940 when this enlightened humanitarianism became the basis for public policy:[2]

The situation of the Indian in our own country twenty years ago was no matter of swift external disaster, such as flood, drought, or war. The condition of the Indian in 1920 had developed cumulatively across five generations. Only by knowing how far down the Indian had been pushed and how

---

[2] From *The Changing Indian*, by Oliver LaFarge. Copyright 1942 by the University of Oklahoma Press. Pp. 5–7.

long held in suffocation, how long told that he had to die, can anyone evaluate the intensities of rebound which have gone forward in recent years.

Moving rapidly up the years from 1920, we witness first the defeat, in 1922–23, of the official attempt to disperse the Pueblos. We witness the enactment of legislation to revest the Pueblos with land. That legislation was passed in 1924. We witness the enactment, in 1926, of legislation placing executive order reservations upon a parity with treaty reservations, thus vetoing the official plan of 1923 to transfer more than half of the then Indian estates to whites. We witness, in 1926, the invoking of the help of the United States Public Health Service in an effort to check the rising death rates of the tribes. We see the Indians organizing the Council of All the New Mexico Pueblos, a still-continuing active organization, the first example of this Indian political renaissance. In 1924, expressly in recognition of their World War services, full citizenship was voted to all Indians by Congress. In 1927, for the first time, we see an action by the Department of the Interior to bring the light of social science to bear upon the Indian need and upon its Indian Bureau's operations. The monumental study by the Institute for Government Research, known as the Meriam Survey, resulted from the initiative of the then Secretary of the Interior. In 1928 the Senate moved into action, and the hearings and documents of the special committee upon Indian investigations of that body totaled thirty-six printed volumes by 1939.

With the year 1929, an intellectual revolution was in full swing within the official Indian Bureau. The schooling policies of the Indian Office were fundamentally modified starting with that year. The movement was from uniformity of curriculum to diversity, and from mere classroom activity to community schools.

In 1929, the Secretary of the Interior and the Commissioner of Indian Affairs joined in memorials to Congress, asking for legislation to re-establish the local democracy of Indians, to curtail the absolutism of the government's Indian system, to apply the concept of constitutional right to Indian economic affairs, and to settle decently and promptly the host of Indian tribal claims growing out of breached treaties and compacts of the past years.

And of inconspicuous but basic importance was an effort, beginning in 1929, to apply modern principles of personnel work in the Indian Service. That effort is not yet finished.

Public opinion could not move all at once; neither could Indian opinion, nor administrative or congressional thinking. Active, continuous attention by the chief executive was needed; and in 1933, at last, the needed assembled data and administrative trends were available to President Roosevelt. And 1933 and the ensuing years were a time of change within the government. In general, that change moved toward goals which naturally included the Indian goals of democracy and the cherishing of the land. So it was without public shock that, in 1933, by secretarial order, the sale of Indian lands was stopped. Without public shock, the Indian cultures and religions were put in possession of the full constitutional guaranties. Without public shock, the institutionalized boarding schools for Indians were cut by one-third and the children were moved to community day schools, and thousands of children never schooled before were brought into the classroom.

Then the Indian Reorganization Act was formulated. The administrators took this proposed reform legislation to the Indians in great regional meetings, and through the Indians assembled there back to all the Indian communities. For the first time in history, all Indians were drawn into a discussion of universal problems of the Indians, and these universal problems focused upon the most ancient and most central Indian institution, local democracy integrated with the land.

Congress passed the Indian Reorganization Act in 1934, and it incorporated in this act a feature new in federal legislation, the referendum. The act, as passed by the Congress and signed by the President, was by its own terms merely permissive. Every Indian tribe might adopt it or reject it by majority vote by secret ballot.

The Indian Reorganization Act, under which today 74 per cent of the Indians are living and functioning, does not contain the whole of the present Indian program. There are tribes not under the act which are realizing a creative self-determination not less than tribes that are under the act. And there are many tribes, under the act by their own choice, which have chosen to go forward with their ancient and never extinguished types of local democracy, rather than to adopt the parliamentary type of self-government.

Under governmental control, in the years prior to 1933, through overgrazing and unplanned use, even the lands still at that date owned by Indians had been damaged and in many instances had been gutted.

The year 1933 witnessed a rising Indian population upon a land base quantitatively very insufficient and qualitatively critically deteriorated. The Navajo range was two-thirds wrecked. Through the whole of the West, the Indian ranges were down as low as the average of the western range, which was more than 50 per cent down. Eroding Indian lands were threatening to shorten the life term of the great reservoirs like the Elephant Butte and Lake Mead. Eroding Indian lands had contributed to the waterlogging and the economic ruin of the middle Rio Grande Valley.

Certainly the most dramatic and nationally important phase of the Indian record across the last seven years has been the Indians' own effort at conserving their lands. No groups in the country have made voluntary sacrifices comparable to those self-imposed by tribes such as the Navajo, many of the Pueblo, the Hopi, and others which could be mentioned. These Indians have willed above all that the Indian spirit—the Indian being—should live on, and hence they have willed that their land should live on, their land being a part of their spirit.

After World War II a new Commissioner of Indian Affairs, eager to emancipate the Indian from the reservation system and the government from the responsibilities of administration, initiated a two-fold program of "termination" and "relocation." By termination he meant an end to the special relationship that had existed between the Indian and the government. Relocation called for the resettlement of the Indian in urban centers—Los Angeles and Chicago—because the Indian land base was too small to maintain a steadily growing population.

The new policy raised a sharp controversy about what was best for the tribes; this cut across party lines, divided eastern and western economic interests, and left many people confused about the issues involved. For almost a decade scholars and politicians argued the advantages and disadvantages of termination and the impact that relocation would have on the tribes. The Indians disagreed among themselves. Some were ready to enter the mainstream of American life; others were content with the paternalism of the reservation system, which they thought offered them greater opportunity for success. A shrewd group of western investors who realized that termination would revolutionize land distribution in the West denounced easterners who wanted to keep the Indians as curios in a vast ethnological museum (the reservations) and jeopardize the economic growth of the region. Others believed that the Indian still needed protection. Unfamiliar with the Indian or his unique problems, the average American could not evaluate the evidence on the success of relocation or appraise the merits of termination.

THE NEW INDIAN POLICY IS STATED

The issue has remained unresolved, although in 1961 the administration of President John F. Kennedy presented what appeared to be a compromise. The Commissioner of Indian Affairs, Philleo Nash, summarized the origin of the new policy, its goals, and its means:[3]

A "New Trail" for Indians leading to equal citizenship rights and benefits, maximum self-sufficiency and full participation in American life became the keynote for administration of the program of the Bureau of Indian Affairs of the Department of the Interior shortly after the close of the 1961 fiscal year.

This keynote was provided in a 77-page report . . . by a special Task Force on Indian Affairs . . . The report was presented shortly after the end of the fiscal year, and its major recommendations were at that time accepted and endorsed by the Secretary.

Probably the most important single recommendation was for a shift in program emphasis away from termination of Federal trust relationships toward greater development of the human and natural resources on Indian reservations.

This was coupled, however, with a recommendation that eligibility for special Federal service be withdrawn from "Indians with substantial incomes and superior educational experience, who are as competent as most non-Indians to look after their own affairs." Emphasis was also given to the beneficial nature of Federal programs—such as those under the Social Security Act and the Area Redevelopment Act—which treat Indians and non-Indians alike.

In addition, the report recommended (1) more vigorous efforts to attract industries to reservation areas, (2) an expanded program of vocational training and placement; (3) creation of a special Reservation Development Loan Fund and enlargement of the present Revolving Loan Fund, (4) establishment of a statutory Advisory Board on Indian Affairs, (5) negotiation with States and counties, and resort to the courts where necessary, to make certain that off-reservation Indians are accorded the same rights and privileges as other citizens of their areas, (6) collaboration with States and tribes to bring tribal law and order codes into conformity with those of the States and counties where reservations are located, (7) acceleration in the adjudication of cases pending before the Indian Claims Commission, and (8) more active and widespread efforts to inform the public about the status of the Indian people and the nature of their problems.

Calling attention to the complex problem of "heirship" land allotments owned by numerous Indians who either cannot be located or cannot agree on use of the property, the report advocated transferring these fractionated holdings to the tribe and permitting

---

[3] *Resources For Tomorrow: 1961. Annual Report, The Secretary of the Interior* (Washington, 1961), pp. 277–279.

the latter to compensate the owners through some system of deferred payment.

As a step toward transferring the responsibility for Indian education to local school districts, the Task Force urged renovation of present Federal school buildings, construction of new plants, and road improvements so that more Indian children can be bussed to classes. It also called for greater efforts to involve Indian parents in school planning and parent-teacher activities. As a measure to relieve over-crowding of present facilities, the report suggested that consideration be given to keeping them in use throughout the entire year. During the summer months, it added, some of these facilities could also be used for programs to help Indian youngsters make constructive use of their leisure time.

PROPOSALS FOR WESTERN IRRIGATION POLICIES

Just as Indian policy came to focus more on the goals of American society than on the control of the tribes, the land-use issue in the twentieth century was far more complex than either the pre-emption or homestead questions in the nineteenth. Popular values as well as scientific knowledge have been traditionally considered by Congress in formulating public land policy. This raised few problems so long as western ideals dominated the governmental structure, as they did through much of the nineteenth century. But at the beginning of the twentieth century, American thought and policy were dominated by the ideas of laissez-faire liberals, at a time when reformers were beginning to demand a more active role for government in men's economic affairs. J. Wesley Powell is perhaps the best example of a scientist who worked within a socio-political framework in formulating public policy regarding land. He had earned distinction as an explorer of the canyons of the West and as head of the United States Geological Survey. His work as a geographer was highly regarded; his words were frequently quoted; and his opinions were published in popular as well as scientific journals. In the following proposal for an irrigation policy, Powell demonstrated how science and social philosophy had become inseparable in formulating governmental programs:[4]

A thousand millions of money must be used; who shall furnish it? Great and many industries are to be established; who shall control them? Millions of men are to labor; who shall employ them? This is a great nation, the Government is powerful; shall it engage in this work? So dreamers may dream, and so ambition may dictate, but in the name of the men who labor I demand that the laborers shall employ themselves; that the enterprise shall be controlled by the men who have the genius to organize, and whose homes are in the lands developed, and that the money shall be furnished by the people; and I say to the Government: Hands off! Furnish the people with institutions of justice, and let them do the work for themselves. The solution to be propounded, then, is one of institutions to be organized for the establishment of justice, not of appropriations to be made and offices created by the Government.

In a group of mountains a small river has its source. A dozen or a score of creeks unite to form the trunk. The creeks higher up divide into brooks. All these streams combined form the drainage system of a hydrographic basin, a unit of country well defined in nature, for it is bounded above and on

---

[4] J. W. Powell, "Institutions for the Arid Lands," *The Century Illustrated Magazine*, XL (May, 1890), pp. 113-114.

each side by heights of land that rise as crests to part the waters. Thus hydraulic basin is segregated from hydraulic basin by nature herself, and the landmarks are practically perpetual. In such a basin of the arid region the irrigable lands lie below; not chiefly by the river's side, but on the mesas and low plains that stretch back on each side. Above these lands the pasturage hills and mountains stand, and there the forests and sources of water supply are found. Such a district of country is a commonwealth by itself. The people who live therein are interdependent in all their industries. Every man is interested in the conservation and management of the water supply, for all the waters are needed within the district. The men who control the farming below must also control the upper regions where the waters are gathered from the heavens and stored in the reservoirs. Every farm and garden in the valley below is dependent upon each fountain above.

All of the lands that lie within the basin above the farming districts are the catchment areas for all the waters poured upon the fields below. The waters that control these works all constitute one system, are dependent one upon another, and are independent of all other systems. Not a spring or a creek can be touched without affecting the interests of every man who cultivates the soil in the region. All the waters are common property until they reach the main canal, where they are to be distributed among the people. How these waters are to be caught and the common source of wealth utilized by the individual settlers interested therein is a problem for the men of the district to solve, and for them alone.

But these same people are interested in the forests that crown the heights of the hydrographic basin. If they permit the forests to be destroyed, the source of their water supply is injured and the timber values are wiped out. If the forests are to be guarded, the people directly interested should perform the task. An army of aliens set to watch the forests would need another army of aliens to watch them, and a forestry organization under the hands of the General Government would become a hotbed of corruption; for it would be impossible to fix responsibility and difficult to secure integrity of administration, because ill-defined values in great quantities are involved.

Then the pasturage is to be protected. The men who protect these lands for the water they supply to agriculture can best protect the grasses for the summer pasturage of the cattle and horses and sheep that are to be fed on their farms during the months of winter. Again, the men who create water powers by constructing dams and digging canals should be permitted to utilize these powers for themselves, or to use the income from these powers which they themselves create, for the purpose of constructing and maintaining the works necessary to their agriculture.

Thus it is that there is a body of interdependent and unified interests and values, all collected in one hydrographic basin, and all segregated by well-defined boundary lines from the rest of the world. The people in such a district have common interests, common rights, and common duties, and must necessarily work together for common purposes. Let such a people organize, under national and State laws, a great irrigation district, including an entire hydrographic basin, and let them make their own laws for the division of the waters, for the protection and use of the forests, for the protection of the pasturage on the hills, and for the use of the powers. This, then, is the proposition I make: that the entire arid region be organized into natural hydrographic districts, each one to be a commonwealth within itself for the purpose of controlling and using the great values which have been pointed out. There are some great rivers where the larger trunks would have to be divided into two or more districts, but the majority would be of the character described. Each such community should possess its own irrigation works; it would have to erect diverting dams, dig canals, and construct reservoirs; and such works would have to be maintained from year to year. The plan is to establish local self-government by hydrographic basins.

CHANGING CONCEPTS OF LAND POLICY

In the years that followed, Powell's ideas did not lose their appeal, but the quest for greater efficiency in conservation, the development of additional scientific insight, and the shock of the national depression in the 1930s produced a sharply contrasting framework for programs of land use. In 1936, President Franklin D. Roosevelt's Secretary of Agriculture, Henry A. Wallace, submitted a report on the status and future of the western range which indicated how radically changed were American ideas about control of land policy:[5]

In transmitting this report I shall resist the temptation, despite my great personal interest in the range question, to comment at length on its findings and recommendations, and instead merely emphasize three of the most important phases of the discussion.

1. The first of these is the astonishing degree to which the western range resource has been neglected, despite its magnitude and importance.

One indication of this neglect is the lack of public knowledge. The general public knows less of the range resource, and as a result has been and is less concerned about its condition and conservation than of any other of our important natural resources. This is true in spite of the fact that the range occupies about two-fifths of the total land area of the United States and three-fourths of that of the range country; that the range territory produces about 75 percent of the national output of wool and mohair, and in pounds about 55 percent of the sheep and lambs, and nearly one-third of the cattle and calves. In fact, this report represents the first attempt, although much of the range has been grazed for 50 years at least, to make an all-inclusive survey of the range resource, its original and present condition, the causes and effects of changes, the social and economic function which it does and should render to the West and to the Nation, and, finally, to outline practical solutions for at least the more important problems.

The entire history of public-land disposal under both Federal and State laws reflects this neglect. These laws have with few exceptions been framed and administered without regard to range conditions and requirements. The result is an ownership pattern so complex that satisfactory handling of the range is seriously handicapped. In this pattern is intermingled an enormous area that all of the available information indicates is submarginal for private ownership.

Further evidence of neglect is failure to regulate the use of range lands in such a way as to maintain the resource. This failure has been so general under all classes of ownership that in contrast examples of good management are decidedly conspicuous. The result is serious and practically universal

---

[5] *The Western Range.* Senate Document No. 199, 74th Congress, 2nd Session (Washington, 1936), pp. iii–vi.

range and soil depletion, which already has gone far toward the creation of a permanent desert over enormous areas. An even more serious result has been an appalling waste of the human resource. And three-fourths of the range area is still on the down grade.

The commonly accepted theory that private ownership in itself is enough of an incentive to insure the satisfactory handling of range lands has proved to be true only in the case of exceptional ranches.

State range lands have been leased without provision for the management of the resource or its perpetuation. Federal holdings are scattered among many bureaus in several departments. The national forests, which afford an example of large-scale range conservation, are administered by the Department of Agriculture. The grazing districts, which are only now being placed under administration after a half century or more of neglect, and the public domain, which is still subject to unrestricted use, fall under the Department of the Interior. These three classes of land make up the bulk of Federal holdings.

Neglect is further shown by the meager scale of research by both the Federal and State Governments. A reasonable program of research might have prevented many serious mistakes and maladjustments. Extension to carry research findings in better range practices to private owners has been practically nonexistent.

2. The second phase of the situation to which I wish to call attention is the fundamental character both of the range resource and of its use.

They have to do with land; with the production on that land of forage crops, with the utilization of the crops in livestock and, in a lesser degree, wildlife production; with the management of land and its forage cover to obtain watershed protection and the services needed primarily by agriculture for irrigation. Effectiveness in all of these things depends upon the biological and agricultural sciences. In short, they are a part, and in the West one of the most important parts of agriculture.

Furthermore, through the free play of economic forces, range livestock production— once almost wholly an independent pastoral enterprise—and cropland agriculture have become closely integrated, inseparable parts of the agricultural structure of the West. Except for specialty farms, a high percentage of the hundreds of thousands of western farm or ranch units represent widely varying combinations of range and crop agriculture. More than one-third of the feed for range livestock now comes from croplands or irrigated pastures. Problems of one part have become problems of both. Major maladjustments in either—of which there are far too many—now inevitably affect the other. No comprehensive program can be prepared for either which does not take the other definitely into account.

3. The third phase of the range situation to which I wish to call attention is a limited number of remedial measures of outstanding importance among the many that are required. The range problem as a whole has been allowed to drift for so long that its difficulties have been accentuated. It has become exceedingly broad and complex, beginning with the basic soil resource at the one extreme, and extending through a wide range of overlapping interrelated problems to human welfare at the other. No single measure offers hope of more than a partial solution.

One of the most important of the measures required is to place all range lands under management that will stop depletion and restore and thereafter maintain the resource in perpetuity, while at the same time permitting its use. This will involve many difficult operations such, for example, as drastic reductions of stock on overgrazed ranges. It will involve various forms of use such as livestock grazing, watershed services, wildlife production, etc., which should be so correlated as to obtain the maximum private and public benefits.

A second line of action involves the return to public ownership of lands so low in productivity, or so seriously devastated, or requiring such large expenditures to protect high public values, that private owners can hold them only at a loss. Closely related are a far-reaching series of adjustments in size of ownership units to make both private and public ownership feasible and effective, each in its proper sphere.

A third line of action is to put jurisdiction over publicly owned range lands on a sound basis. Unquestionably the only plan which can be defended is to concentrate responsibility for the administration of Federal lands in a single department to avoid unnecessary duplications, excessive expenditures, and fundamental differences in policies, and to obtain the highest efficiency in administration and the maximum of service to users. Since the administration of the range resource and its use is agriculture, and since the administration of federally owned ranges can and should be used as an affirmative means in the rehabilitation of western agriculture, the grazing districts and the public domain should be transferred to the Department of Agriculture.

Furthermore, the concentration of jurisdiction over federally owned range lands is a vitally important step toward the concentration in a single department of the still more inclusive functions, including aid and services to private owners of range lands, which should be exercised by the Federal Government on the entire range problem. Such a concentration is a fundamental principle of good organization if the Federal Government is to redeem its full responsibility in the restoration and care of this much-neglected resource.

The States have similar jurisdictional problems which demand attention.

A fourth measure which should be emphasized is the wide scope of research necessary to put range use for all purposes on a sound footing. Closely related is extension which will carry the information obtained to the private owner and help him constructively in its application.

With these and other recommendations of the Forest Service, I am in general accord, and I hope that in carrying them out there need not be too serious a delay, since further delay will merely serve to accentuate difficulties and increase costs.

The solution of the range problem can be made an important contribution to the conservation of our natural resources. It can be made an important contribution to the rehabilitation of western agriculture. Finally, and most important, it can be made an important contribution to social and economic security and human welfare. Public neglect is partly responsible for the aggravated character of the range problem, and this makes all the more urgent and necessary public action toward its solution.

The land question has remained unsolved. Even though Americans have accepted the idea that the federal government must play a role in the preservation and development of the nation's resources, there is sharp disagreement. Since the economic prosperity of many parts of the West depends on the exploitation of natural resources, investors and residents insist that the true meaning of conservation is the scientifically managed utilization of land and resources. They are steadfastly opposed by others who argue that conservation means withdrawing lands so that their riches can be used by later generations. This same argument exists among advocates of federally controlled recreation areas. One group of recreation enthusiasts urges the building of wilderness parks where the average citizen can enjoy the wonders of the West from the window of his automobile as he hurries from one paved campsite to another during his brief vacation; others, appalled at the thought of ruining the wilderness with roads and commercial recreation facilities, demand that the land remain untouched. The argument among competing groups has grown increasingly acrimonious, not only because of the profits to be made but also because government agencies have aligned themselves on both sides of each issue.

SOCIAL PROBLEMS OF THE NEW WEST

If the conflict between frontier tradition and the demands of a mushrooming urban-industrial nation has divided the people on the issues of Indian policy, land utilization, and recreation in the West, it has also complicated the solution of deep-seated social problems. Old-fashioned laissez-faire individualism, which was eroded away in the East during the first half of the century, found its last stronghold in the western states. This heritage was certain to cause trouble, for the corporations and wealthy individuals who controlled many of the natural resources clung most firmly to this belief, while those who worked for them held that governmental regulation was essential in the increasingly compact society of the twentieth century.

To make matters worse, a large portion of the laborers in the West in 1900 consisted of miners, lumbermen, construction day-laborers, range and ranch hands, and itinerant farm workers. Because they were seasonally unemployed, frequently members of minority groups, migratory in character, and generally unskilled, their standard of living was low and their history was a narrative of violence, abuse, and outrage. The records of the Western Federation of Miners and the Industrial Workers of the World—the IWW—are perhaps overly dramatic, but the achievements of western labor organizations tended to lag behind those of the East. Hostility toward unions, immigrants, and migratory workers seemed as compatible with the frontier experience as vigilantism and the assault on Chinese intruders in the mining camps. Until the end of the 1920s, the West was more nativistic, and more strongly anti-union, than the East.

The highly complex problems of western workers were brought into sharp focus in the 1930s, however, when both the agricultural depression and devastating dust storms upset regional equilibriums and stimulated a new westward movement of farm families. Deeply concerned about the plight of labor, especially its loss of dignity and civil rights, Wisconsin's Senator Robert La Follette headed a subcommittee of the Committee on Education and Labor in 1939 and began an investigation of conditions in the West. La Follette encountered hostility. In San Francisco a spokesman for a farm organization told him to stop giving aid and comfort to the communists and go back to Wisconsin. But California's liberal Democratic governor, Cuthbert Olson, offered to cooperate fully with the La Follette committee. Olson's testimony, although restricted in scope to conditions in California, explains the origin and history of social problems characteristic of the Far West during the previous century:[6]

At the outset, gentlemen, I should like to say that of all the grave and serious problems which the present administration has inherited from prior administrations none is,

---

[6] *Hearing Before a Subcommittee of the Committee on Education and Labor.* United States Senate Documents. 76th Congress, 2nd Session (Washington, 1940), pp. 17243–17246.

perhaps, more acute than that of migratory farm labor in this State. It is, I should like to emphasize, a problem which we have inherited or to which we have succeeded. It is in large part because of this circumstance that we welcome the co-operation and assistance of your committee in an effort to get at the roots of the problem itself; to consider not merely the social consequences of the problem but the underlying causes which have made this matter of migratory farm labor an acute social issue in California for 60 years. Farm organizations in this State as early as 1880, in their convention proceedings, recognized the gravity of the problem and the difficulties involved in its attempted solution. In fact, from 1880 to the present time, both the farm groups and various civic organizations have devoted reams of paper to resolutions acknowledging the existence of a serious problem in migratory labor; but, unfortunately, this widespread recognition of an evil condition has resulted in few concrete steps toward its solution. I am definately of the opinion that the time has now arrived—in fact, it is long overdue—when California, working in conjunction with the Federal Government, must undertake measures not only ameliorative but essentially corrective in character, and, furthermore, that it is now possible to put these measures into effect.

The problem of protecting the civil liberties of agricultural labor in California can only, I believe, be understood in light of the long history of the problem of migratory labor in California. Patterns of behavior, for example, have a tendency to survive long after the circumstances which brought them into existence have ceased to exist. For a great many years alien racial groups constituted the bulk of migratory farm workers in this State. Chinese labor, for example, was extensively used from 1870 until after the passage of the Exclusion Act in 1922; Japanese labor, in large part, took the places made vacant by the exodus of the Chinese from the fields; Mexican and Filipino labor began to be used, in large numbers, after the Japanese had ceased to be regarded as desirable farm workers. Hindus and Porto Ricans, likewise, have at various times, formed important units of the great army of migratory farm workers in this State. Serious disturbances have occurred in California in the past in connection with the employment in agriculture of these, and other, racial minority groups. From the point of view of the protection of civil liberties, the essential fact to be noted is that, for the most part, these racial groups which for 50 years or more constituted the bulk of agricultural workers, were not only aliens, and thus unable to participate in the civic life of the State, but expressly declared ineligible for citizenship. Their status as alien made them particularly vulnerable. They could not hold public office nor could they vote, and when occasion demanded it they could be threatened with deportation by the very interests who had recruited them for employment in California. Quite apart from these legal disabilities, they suffered the handicaps of all racial minorities—a lack of understanding of our institutions, a lack of familiarity with living and working standards in America, and the ever-present consciousness that they were here, so to speak, on sufferance. Since their employment opportunities were, even in periods of great prosperity, sharply limited, they were forced to accept working conditions and wage rates which at the time were admitted to be incompatible with American standards of living. Because these workers were unable to safeguard effectively their rights, employment practices arose which would never have been tolerated by American labor. Moreover, in periods of restricted economic activity, these groups incurred the active ill-will of American workmen seeking employment in agriculture. Many instances can be found in the history of this State, where serious race riots have occurred in connection with the employment of alien workers in agriculture. Agricultural labor in California has this background of being a submerged, disadvantaged, and in every sense underprivileged social class. Unfortunately, many patterns of behavior established in the long course of the employment of alien labor have survived and are operative today. It should be pointed out, moreover, that large numbers of noncitizens are still employed in California agriculture. We still employ a large amount of Mexican, Filipino, and even a small amount of Hindu field labor. The bulk of these workers are aliens and still suffer from manifold disabilities of the type I have mentioned.

Nor is this matter of legal disabilities limited to the alien groups in California agriculture. In fact, certain legal disabilities are almost inevitable so long as the bulk of agricultural labor is migratory in character. We have noted, for instance, that Dust Bowl refugees in California have been occasionally referred to, derogatorily, as "Okies" and "Arkies," and that they are regarded, in some quarters, as "aliens" in California. A migratory worker is likely to be regarded as a stranger or "alien" in the many communities in which he is forced to work during the course of a single year. Many migratory workers are not, of course, residents of the counties in which they are employed during those periods when, for example, labor disputes may occur. Thus they lack not only the security necessary to give bargaining strength, but the means of political retaliation for unfair or illegal treatment. If they are residents of any one county in California, they are seldom residents of those counties in which the denial of civil liberties is likely to occur. Strangers, in any community, particularly in rural communities, are regarded with a certain amount of provincial suspicion and potential ill-will.

Migratory workers, particularly with the large degree of turn-over that is common in agricultural employment in this State, seldom have an opportunity to make themselves generally known in any one community. One year they may work in given number of counties, and the next year they may follow an entirely different route. It is impossible to state, with any degree of accuracy, how many migratory workers are actually residents of California; nor can it be estimated what percentage have been able to comply without statutory requirements in order to vote. But it is safe to say that a very large percentage of migratory workers in California during any given period are not voters. As long as this state of affairs countinues to exist, unequal treatment at the hands of certain local law-enforcement agencies in the State is likely to occur. In the last analysis, it is largely because migratory workers are a socially disadvantaged class in California that their civil liberties have been frequently violated. For the most part, they lack the means, individually and collectively, to defend themselves against illegal practices of the type that will be revealed during the course of your investigation.

Another factor which has encouraged undue interference with the right of agricultural labor to bargain collectively in this State is the physical difficulties involved in organization. It is inherently difficult, for example, for a nondescript army of migratory workers to organize themselves into trade unions.

On many occasions, over a period of 40 years, agricultural workers have attempted to organize for purposes of collective bargaining in California. But the physical difficulties involved have been almost as influential in discouraging organization as the undue influence of employer groups. I can but mention merely a few of these difficulties: The lack of understanding among different racial groups; the low earnings resulting in inability to support or maintain an organization once effected; the difficulty of maintaining an organizational structure during the period of seasonal unemployment; and the constant influx of new workers unfamiliar with local conditions. Your own investigations have clearly indicated that workers must organize for self-protection. As long as workers are not organized in California agriculture, they are likely to be subjected to discriminatory treatment of one kind or another, and as long as the bulk of agricultural workers are migratory workers difficulties of the type I have mentioned will hinder organization.

It is quite impossible to understand the difficulties of protecting the civil liberties of agricultural workers in California apart from an understanding of the psychological tensions which make for bitterness in labor disputes in this field. Because of the nature of our agriculture, crops in this State represent an enormous investment in money, time, and effort on the part of employers. Many of these crops are, moreover, perishable in character. Certain areas of the State emphasize off-season production in which the element of timing in reaching a particular eastern market is of the greatest importance to the grower. It is quite natural, under these circumstances, that growers should regard, with great bitterness, any stoppage of work during the harvest season. Crops in this State must be harvested quickly or an entire year's investment may be lost. A great amount of the rancor and bitterness which many farm groups in this State feel toward organized labor can be traced to this constant fear of possible interruption of work during the harvest season.

Under the other hand, the miserable living and working conditions of migratory labor, the appalling low earnings available for this type of labor at present, make workers desperate. The bitterness which these conditions create among workers is just as intense as the bitterness felt by growers during a labor dispute. Fear is the element that has created the appalling bitterness, which in the past has too frequently resulted in riots, bloodshed, and murder—a fear of the loss of crops on the part of growers—fear of starvation on the part of workers. As long as this psychological tension exists—and it exists in California today—the problem of maintaining civil liberties is inherently difficult.

It is not only the growers and workers who are under the type of economic pressure that I have mentioned, for many of the townspeople in the rural areas also become involved in the same complex of forces. Many areas in the State are directly dependent upon agriculture. It is understandable, therefore, that in these areas the entire community should feel that it is directly involved in the outcome of a particular labor dispute.

The townspeople themselves become active partisans, usually on the side of the grower interests, and the entire community is divided into hostile camps. Many townspeople in the rural areas have slight sympathy for migratory labor. During the peak labor periods their hospitals are overcrowded, their schools are overrun with new pupils, and their various social agencies are burdened with the problems incident to this annual influx of nonresident workers. Having slight direct contact with the workers themselves, it is natural that they should regard them as outsiders or strangers. We have had several instances in the past, in California, where vigilante groups have been recruited in the towns. This circumstance does not make the problem of protecting civil liberties any easier in California.

One unfortunate phase of this entire problem of maintaining and protecting civil liberties in the agricultural areas is that until quite recently the workers involved had not developed competent leadership out of their own rank and file.

Sensing the desperate plight of the workers and realizing that they lacked elements of leadership, organizers have entered the rural areas unfamiliar with local conditions, and have attempted in their zeal to right in a single season the accumulated wrongs and injustices of 50 years. These ultramilitants, not even understanding the temperament of the people among whom they were working, have too often indulged in fiery oratory and have too frequently urged the adoption of methods which would be indefensible in metropolitan areas, but which, when applied in rural areas, constitute grave provocation. These hair-trigger situations which arise in the fields in California make strenuous demands upon the self-restraint and the good sense of every group involved. There is no place in such situations for firebrands, either among employers or employees. Agricultural labor in California should develop, out of its own ranks, an intelligent, competent, and, above all, a tactful and statesmanlike leadership—a leadership capable of full realization of the acute psychological tensions and economic pressures involved; a leadership that will, in the fullest and deepest sense, really represent the aims and aspirations of farm labor. This leadership must recognize that, if their cause is to be successful, they must win and maintain the confidence of the people of this State. In order that a well-informed and responsible leadership may be developed, there is a great need for workers' education in this field. The presence of irresponsible elements, who assume the functions of leadership, and who have no deep roots or ties in the rural communities, only complicates the problem of safeguarding civil liberties in California. The introduction of modern methods of dealing with industrial relations in the field of farm labor is not going to come about overnight. It is, in fact, an objective that it will take time to achieve in this State under the most favorable circumstances. The swiftness and ease with which it is achieved will largely depend upon the extent to which each group can understand the point of view of the other. What I deplore in this entire situation is the lack of mutual understanding. The use of violence is in direct relation to the lack of such understanding. Violence, in fact, is proof perfect of utter misunderstanding. This administration will not tolerate further violence in California agriculture from either side or from any elements. I take advantage of this occasion to serve notice to employers and to employees, and in particular to local law-enforcement agencies in the rural counties, that we intend to maintain not only civil liberties but the public peace in this State. We are prepared to go to any lengths, even to the point of calling out the National Guard and invoking martial law, to see to it that order is maintained and that the laws are equally and impartially enforced. I intend, moreover, to follow up such incidents as the disturbance in Madera this fall and to see to it, in this and in all other similar incidents, that the law is not enforced with an unequal hand. The sense of justice and of fair treatment of the people of this State has been exhausted and public sentiment will not tolerate a recurrence of the Salinas situation of 1936 or the Stockton cannery strike of 1937, or of Madera in 1939.

Moreover, there are certain practical considerations which make the problem of protecting the rights of agricultural workers difficult in this State. Most disputes occur, of course, during the harvest or peak labor periods, and the harvest seasons are seldom of more than a few weeks' duration. Consequently, disturbances arise quickly and are usually over in a short time. An explosion will occur, and before the State executive can ascertain whether or not the local law-enforcement agencies are performing their duties equally and impartially the strike will be over. We have discovered, therefore, that the best way to protect the civil liberties of agricultural workers is to attempt to prevent strikes from occurring—to intervene before the breach occurs.

The possibility of such effective intervention for the purpose of preventing strikes in California agriculture is limited at the present time by reason of the stand that has been consistently taken by organized farm groups in California to the effect that they are opposed to the application of the principles of collective bargaining for agricultural labor. Again and again these same groups, as you will doubtless learn during the course of your investigation, have not only actively opposed the formation of trade-unions but have publicly stated that under no circumstances would they bargain collectively with the duly designated representatives of their employees. Encouraged by the fact that there is no legal compulsion at the present time to force recognition, or collective bargaining, these same groups have carried the fight further and have unduly interfered with every attempt that has been made to bring into play the principles of collective bargaining which have long been recognized nationally as the best approach to the problem of employer-employee relations in industry. Another practical difficulty, inherent in the problem, is that a vast number of workers are involved in our agriculture during the peak periods—for example, as many perhaps as 200,000 workers—and that the areas in which they are employed extend throughout the State. A strike in cotton, by way of example, might involve as many as 35,000 workers, and it is not as simple to protect the civil rights of a group of workers of this size, employed over an area extending from Bakersfield to Merced, as it would be, say, to protect the strikers, however numerous, of a particular factory in a metropolitan community maintaining a large police department.

One difficulty involved in this problem is that representatives of the executive branch of the State government are not justified, as a matter of law, in assuming that acts of violence will occur from the mere presence, for example, of certain people in a certain place at a certain time. Generally speaking, an arrest can only be made when some overt act has been committed. We cannot establish the practice of making preventive arrests, or of taking persons into protective custody upon the mere suspicion that, unless we do so, they will commit, alone or in concert with others, some breach of the peace in the future.

Given the relation of social forces which has existed in the predominantly rural counties of the State in the past, it is not surprising to find that many counties have adopted stringent ordinances outlawing the right to engage in peaceful picketing, purporting to require permits for meetings and parades, and attempting to restrict, whether constitutionally or otherwise, those activities which have generally come to be accorded to organized labor throughout the United States.

In the absence of State legislation overriding these enactments, they remain operative even in those cases where the question of constitutionality is doubtful. The mere fact that these enactments are in effect, and can be utilized, sometimes tends to encourage employers to adopt an unreasonable and arbitrary attitude toward the demands of agricultural labor.

THE FRONTIER HERITAGE OF WESTERN CITIES

California not only served as a convenient model of western hostility toward laboring and immigrant people before 1940, but it also provided an excellent example of still another frontier heritage. In California frontier revivalism made its last stand against the encroachments of rationalism and urbanity. Appealing to newly urbanized peoples, relying on radio broadcasting, and tapping deep streams of provincialism, Southern California's revivalists during the 1920s and 1930s exercised enormous influence on public life. Systems of preaching pioneered by primitive sects along past frontiers were modernized and spread throughout the West. Among the more successful and colorful revivalists Mrs. Aimee Semple McPherson demonstrated how camp meeting style could be installed in a large city where aggregates of people, starved for emotional outlet, afraid of urban vice, and hungry for the kind of religious experiences they had known in the rural Southwest, filled a nonsectarian tabernacle, sang, and paid for the show:[7]

Take the Edendale car out of Los Angeles some Sunday afternoon toward five o'clock. Ride for a bit less than a half-hour and alight at Echo Park. Here are much shade, cool green water, pleasant grassy glades, and, beyond and above it all, looming stark, ugly, bloated, a huge gray concrete excrescence on this delightful bit of nature. It is Angelus Temple, citadel of Aimee Semple McPherson and the Four-Square Gospel.

At 6:15 the doors swing open. The Temple holds 5,300, and probably one-fourth of that number are in line at this time. Within fifteen minutes the huge auditorium with its two flaring balconies is completely filled. The interior is plain, the stained-glass windows garish, but the lighting is adequate, the opera chairs restful after your long stand in line, and the ventilation through scores of doors and transoms is satisfactory. The platform is arranged for an orchestra of fifty, and the "throne" of "Sister" McPherson on a dais just below the high organ loft, softly bathed in creamy light from overhead electrics. Behind the "throne" is a shell of flowers and greenery. The musicians, mostly young and all volunteers, come in at 6:30.

The service proper will not begin until seven, but with the entrance of the band it is seen that not a seat is vacant, and that hundreds are standing at the doors. When it is remembered that this is only a usual, unadvertised—Aimee carries no church notice in the dailies—Sunday night service, repeated fifty-two times in the year, it will be seen that here we have a phenomenon almost, if not quite, unique in American church life. We are reminded also that this is "Radio KFSG" by two microphones....

Now, at five minutes to seven, the vested choir, half a hundred strong, enters from either side. There is a moment of tension and hushed expectancy. All is in readiness. The dramatic has surely not been neglected by this superdramatist. Audience, workers, band, choir, even microphones—all are here. But the throne is still empty, bathed in its soft light. Suddenly through a door far up on the wall, opening out on her private grounds, appears Mrs. McPherson. She is clad in white, with a dark cloak thrown loosely

---

[7] Shelton Bissell, "Vaudeville at Angelus Temple," *Outlook*, vol. 149 (May 23, 1928), pp. 126–127, 158.

around her shoulders; her rich auburn hair, with its flowing permanent wave, is heaped high on her head. In her left arm she carries a bouquet of roses and lilies of the valley, artfully planned to illustrate a point in her sermon (Canticles ii. 1), a description ignorantly applied by her to Jesus; on her face is the characteristic expansive, radiant McPherson smile. She is a beautiful woman, seen from the auditorium, with the soft spotlight shining upon her. Let no man venture to deny it. And, in fact, no man will. The writer has seen screen beauties in his day, and confesses to a slight clutch of the heart as he watched her superb entrance. Assisted to her "throne," she gracefully seats herself, turns to her audience—and her microphone —and is ready to begin. . . .

It is her service, let no man forget that. Not for one moment does she drop the reins. The hand-shaking, sandwiched in between two hymns, was a clever device to create the illusion that all—sinners, saints, workers, mere spectators—are one huge happy family.

"Every one take the hand of five others all around, in front and in back," shouts the beaming Aimee.

Humming confusion with laughter and motion follow, while the five thousand stand up and stretch. The choir then sings, and sings gloriously, the composition of California's own Charles Wakefield Cadman, "The Builders." Little children file onto the stage, and they sing, too—sing so that all in the temple can hear every word, sing as I have never heard a dozen little tots sing in all my life. And the silent radio catches every note and flings it out to listening thousands. Then Aimee prays, a prayer liberally splashed with "Amens" from the crowd. A small boy, eleven years old, enlivens the occasion by playing on a guitar "made of solid silver," as "Sister" radiantly announces. Only one short encore is allowed the enraptured audience, which applauds until Aimee holds up her hand. Much is coming yet, and the time element bulks large. Mrs. McPherson carries a watch, and she never forgets to look at it. . . .

After a rather humorous song by the Male Four-Square Quartet and a piano solo ending with a tremendous crash of all the keys within reach, the platform was cleared for a wedding. The big organ boomed forth the stately chords of the "Lohengrin" march, and the wedding party was discerned crawling at a snail's pace up the long, long aisles. Attention was divided between the procession and the superb figure standing before her "throne" waiting their arrival. Two Temple workers were to be made one and sent forth to preach in a branch of the Four-Square Gospel. Being an ordained minister, "Sister" performed the ceremony, using the full Episcopal service, slipping and faltering once or twice as she read the words.

The microphone is very close here, for the grandmother of the little bride is listening in at Albuquerque, New Mexico, and after the service, which is concluded with a loud "Salute the bride" from Aimee and a shower of rice raining down from the laughing men and women in the choir, "Sister" lifts the microphone and in dulcet tones calls greetings to the listening grandmother.

Smilingly said, but the tone is that of Napoleon before battle. All settle down as the lights are lowered, and the sermon, the climax of this astonishing religious vaudeville, begins.

Aimee preaches with a beautiful white-leather Bible in her right hand. The book is open, and the leaves of her sermon are within it. She is rather closely bound to her notes, yet so deftly does she handle them that it almost seems as though she were preaching extempore. . . .

It was hopeless as a sermon, but it was

consummate preaching. She knew her audience. She knew what she was after, and she got it. She is a superb actress. Her rather harsh and unmelodious voice has yet a modulation of pitch which redeems it from utter disagreeableness. To her carefully manicured and polished finger-tips she is dramatic. In her pose, her gesture, her facial expression, her lifted eyebrows, her scintillating smile, her pathetic frown, Aimee is a perfect exponent of the art of how to say a platitude and delude her hearers into thinking that it is a brand-new truth, just minted by her. She sweeps her audience as easily as the harpist close beside her sweeps the wires in soft broken chords while she preaches. And not for one instant of time is Mrs. McPherson unmindful of that great unseen listening multitude "on the air." She moves the microphone from time to time. She rests her hand lovingly upon it. She never shifts her position one step away from it. All her climaxes are enchanced to the listening thousands throughout southern California and near-by States who regularly "tune-in" on Sunday nights. Radio KFSG is as dear to her as the five thousand and more in Angelus Temple.

At 9:25 to the dot the converts fill the platform. Just why they come is a question. But they are there, waiting for " 'Sister' to pray for them...."

At 9:30 to the second she dismisses the multitude with the benediction, inviting all "first-niters" to stay and be shown around the Temple by official guides; to see the commissary department with its store of food and clothing for the destitute to whom the Temple ministers, the carpenter shop where are made the "sets" with which Aimee frequently garnishes her evening performances and the school where more then a thousand students are taught McPhersonism and the Four-Square Gospel, to go out later as evangelists. But it is over three hours since most of those present seated themselves in the opera chairs, and three hours is longer than any church audience in America save Aimee's can be held together night after night.

The vast concourse swarms to the street. Scores of waiting electric cars take all swiftly back to the big city, swallowing up this tiny leaven of 5,500 in a garish, blatant, heedless lump of over a million souls.

What shall be said? ... A religious message utterly devoid of sound thinking, loose and insubstantial in its construction, preposterously inadequate in its social implications, but amazingly successful after five years of running, and still going strong, judging from statistics, the infallible appeal of churchmen. No American evangelist of large enough caliber to be termed National has ever sailed with such insufficient mental ballast. The power of McPhersonism resides in the personality of Mrs. McPherson. The woman is everything; the evangel nothing. There is no way to understand how a jejune and arid pulpit output has become a dynamic of literally National proportions but to hear and see the woman. To visit Angelus Temple, the home of the Four-Square Gospel, is to go on a sensuous debauch served up in the name of religion.

In 1931 the "New Republic" published an analysis on Bob Shuler, another California revivalist. Cruder than Mrs. McPherson but more cognizant of the political and economic power of the pulpit and the radio station, Shuler baited Roman Catholics, intimidated politicians, and endorsed reactionary causes in the name of patriotism and religion. In the contemporary West, Shuler more than Mrs. McPherson serves as a stereotype of the urban revivalist. The frontier preacher denounced a visible devil; the current revivalist also points out visible devils that he can bring to the bar before his congregation. But most important, the contemporary revivalist, his camp meeting counterpart, and their congregations lack formal education and share in the rural value system which has been so much a part of the frontier heritage of the nineteenth century.

Today, more powerful transmitters, which have allowed radio and television stations to blanket thousands of square miles, have only lessened the provincialism of the revivalists' appeal; the newer breed of evangelists have attracted their audiences by launching racist and anticommunist crusades. The crusaders may not have been numerous, but they were not insignificant. Many religious Americans who lived in the West were willing to tolerate even crude revivalism because they saw in it some humanizing forces. However, the same kind of argument about values affects western churches—Protestant and Catholic—as burdens other social institutions.

THE PERSISTENCE OF THE FRONTIER INFLUENCE

The western record on major issues has been no better than that of the nation as a whole. If the Mexican-American and the Oriental-American is now tolerated in the West, he is rarely welcome unless he offers necessary labor or a special skill. Unionization among these people is fought as tenaciously today as it was in the past. And the history of the Negro in the West differs little from the record in the remainder of the country, except perhaps in the Pacific Northwest.

Despite or because of its problems, however, the West has retained the image of a land of promise and opportunity for immigrants, minorities, and native whites. Midwesterners, easterners, and southerners still consider California, Arizona, Colorado, and especially Nevada as wide open. Oregon and Washington are thought of as distant lands, even though many of the airliners that carry the bulk of the nation's traffic were built in Seattle.

For many Americans the West remains a place to visit, the scene of a television horse opera, a retirement mecca, something to fly over, a vacation land, or the scene of bizarre religious cults. But the West is becoming the heartland of the United States. Centers of learning, recreation facilities and athletics, industrial units and labor, have followed the center of population westward, until the eleven western states have a financial, industrial, educational, and recreational empire of unparalleled magnitude. The West is a vital part of the nation, sharing its distinctions and contributing to its shortcomings.

To the present generation, and to the generation which preceded it, the West has been viewed through the eyes of its scholarly interpreters, especially Frederick Jackson Turner. Although the West of the twentieth century—with its new and old problems and its challenging future—will produce new interpreters of its values and goals, the history of the American frontier experience cannot be erased without a loss of something more than even national identity. As Turner observed when he appraised the influence of the frontier on American democracy:[8]

Best of all, the west gave, not only to the American, but to the unhappy and depressed of all lands, a vision of hope, and the assurance that the world held a place where were to be found high faith in man and the will and power to furnish him the opportunity to grow to the full measure of

---

[8] Frederick Jackson Turner, "Contributions of the West to American Democracy," *Atlantic Monthly*, XIC (January, 1903), p. 96.

his capacity. . . . The paths of the pioneers have widened into broad highways. The forest clearing has expanded into affluent commonwealths. Let us see to it that the ideals of the pioneer in his log cabin shall enlarge into the spiritual life of a democracy where civic power shall dominate and utilize individual achievement for the common good.